Here's a treasure trove of apologetic gems! This is an indispensable book that all Christians should keep within reach. Countless people benefited from the original version, but this updated and expanded edition makes this volume even more valuable and timely. Thank you, Josh and Sean—this classic resource has my very highest recommendation!

LEE STROBEL, bestselling author of *The Case for Christ* and professor of Christian Thought at Houston Baptist University

This book changed my life. It showed me the staggering welter of evidence for the historicity of the Bible—and convinced me that having faith in the biblical God is infinitely more rational than not having such faith. Any agnostic or atheist reluctant to become a Christian must take every precaution available to avoid this book.

ERIC METAXAS, author of *Martin Luther: The Man Who Rediscovered God and Changed the World* and host of the nationally-syndicated Eric Metaxas Show

In 1972, shortly after the accident in which I became paralyzed, I picked up a book that helped solidify my belief in God and faith in Christ. Still struggling to accept my wheelchair, I needed rock-solid evidence that there was a personal God who genuinely cared about my plight. *Evidence That Demands a Verdict* was that remarkable book, and I'm so happy that this timeless classic is now updated and being released to a whole new generation of readers! Can't recommend it enough!

JONI EARECKSON TADA, founder/CEO, Joni and Friends International Disability Center

It is not without reason that *Evidence That Demands a Verdict* has stood the test of time with readers around the world for nearly four decades. Josh McDowell has not only been a pioneer in the field of apologetics and worldviews but a friend and encourager to many, including me. I am thrilled that he has partnered with his son, Sean, to update his classic book and know it will challenge and inspire you.

RAVI ZACHARIAS, author and speaker

Significant. Timely. Life-Changing. For decades, *Evidence That Demands a Verdict* has met believers, seekers, and skeptics at the intersection of faith and fact, laying a foundation of unshakeable, time-proven truth for us to stand on through ages of skepticism, mysticism, and so-called tolerance. I am thrilled for the updated and expanded edition of this landmark resource to reach the hearts and minds of a rising generation, and I trust it will have the same impact in their lives as it did in mine. I'm grateful for Josh and Sean McDowell's relentless passion to equip and empower God's people to confidently and boldly stand for truth. You'll want to keep this book close at hand!

LOUIE GIGLIO, pastor of Passion City Church, founder of Passion Conferences, author of *Goliath Must Fall*

With over one million people impacted by this practical resource we are thrilled to see it's been updated and ready for the next million! Our hearts are united with the McDowells and their passion to see truth understood and embraced by a culture that desperately needs God's Word in their lives! May our Lord use this tool to shape his people into our Savior's image! Sanctify us in your truth O Lord!

KAY ARTHUR AND DAVID ARTHUR, founder and CEO/president of Precept Ministries International

When I was a college student full of questions about the authenticity of my faith, I used *Evidence That Demands a Verdict* as my go-to reference book. I'm grateful to Josh and Sean for this updated release for my two sons.

JIM DALY, president of Focus on the Family

Josh McDowell's *Evidence That Demands a Verdict* is now a classic of apologetics, having served to spur a renaissance of historical Christian evidences in our day. It is therefore a welcome development that this classic has now been updated in light of the recent and significant advances in biblical studies and particularly in historical Jesus studies.

WILLIAM LANE CRAIG, professor of philosophy, Talbot School of Theology; Houston Baptist University

When I was in college and needed material to discuss with skeptical friends, *Evidence That Demands a Verdict* was a key resource for me. Now it is updated and an even better repository for discussion. It remains a valuable collection of information on issues people raise to challenge the faith that not only gives the key data points but allows you to track the conversation in key resources—a real treasure.

DARRELL L. BOCK, Executive Director for Cultural Engagement, Howard G. Hendricks Center for Christian Leadership and Cultural Engagement; Senior Research Professor of New Testament Studies, Dallas Theological Seminary

My friend Josh McDowell and his son Sean have given us an updated and relevant twenty-first-century tool to encourage faith and trust in the reliability of Scripture. For those who want to understand how to defend the veracity of the Christian faith, *Evidence That Demands a Verdict* is the book for you.

DR. TONY EVANS, senior pastor of Oak Cliff Bible Fellowship and president of The Urban Alternative

When I was searching for answers to my doubt, *Evidence That Demands a Verdict* helped to keep my eyes, heart, and mind open to the truth. This new edition not only revisits the arguments from the original work, but considerably strengthens those arguments with up-to-date research from top biblical scholars. This new work is an apologetics multivitamin for the person seeking a healthy diet of truth. I was so excited to see the legacy of Josh McDowell's ministry carrying on through his son, Sean. The excellence in argumentation with the father-son author combination makes this book a true one-of-a-kind!

MARY JO SHARP, assistant professor of apologetics, Houston Baptist University; Founder of Confident Christianity Apologetics Ministry

As I think about how to help students and young adults thrive in a culture that is hostile to Christian thought, I'm most concerned about helping them access not just the best information, but the best relationships and mentorships. As your imagination is captivated by what the next decade of disciplemaking will look like, imagine the combination of the revised version of *Evidence That Demands a Verdict* combined with the power of your relationship and influence in the lives of the young people you disciple. You will be the catalyst that influences the hearts of these young life, and this remarkable resource will guide your conversation as you help shape the minds of a new generation of disciples.

MATT MARKINS, president of Awana Global Ministries

Scholars, students, and the general public will benefit greatly from this new and greatly expanded edition of *Evidence That Demands a Verdict*. One of the things I like about it is how clearly all of the relevant topics are laid out. The problems, the challenges, and grounds for skepticism are clearly and fairly expressed—there are no straw men. Josh and Sean McDowell do not dodge the issues; they tackle them head on and do so in an informed and compelling manner. *Evidence That Demands a Verdict* will serve well another generation.

CRAIG A. EVANS, PhD., D.Habil., John Bisagno Distinguished
Professor of Christian Origins, Houston Baptist University

Josh McDowell was one of the first guests to feature on my radio debate show Unbelievable? and Sean has been one of the most recent. I've been hugely impressed by both generations of Christian thinkers. In this new edition of *Evidence That Demands A Verdict*, their combined knowledge, integrity and passion for sharing the gospel has produced something truly special. *Evidence* was the book that first brought evidential apologetics to a popular audience. This updated edition, comprehensive in scope and yet immensely readable, will powerfully present the latest evidence to a new generation with a new set of questions. This book remains an essential resource for every thinking Christian who wants to give a reason for the hope that they have.

JUSTIN BRIERLEY, presenter of the *Unbelievable?*
radio show and podcast

Josh McDowell has been a heroic voice of reasonable faith for a generation. He and his son Sean now team up to answer the skeptics and cynics of today with a reason to believe.

PASTOR JACOB ARANZA, bestselling author and founder of
Our Savior's Church and Aranza Outreach

I was one of countless thousands of students who benefited greatly from the original *Evidence That Demands a Verdict*. As a college student in the 1980s, I experienced the scholarly attacks on the trustworthiness of Scripture first hand. At the time, it wasn't easy to find arguments from scholars defending the reliability of the Bible in a way that responded to serious academic attacks. The book introduced me to those scholars and convinced me that the death of God had been greatly exaggerated! That's why I'm delighted that Josh and Sean McDowell have teamed up to write this new edition of *Evidence* for a new generation. The attacks on Christianity have gotten even more intense, but Josh and Sean more than meet the attacks. They show that you don't have to choose between faith and reason. I'm confident that their book will not only help Christians fortify their own faith, but will bring many skeptics to faith in Christ.

JAY RICHARDS, PhD, assistant research professor, Busch School of
Business & Economics, The Catholic University of America

I am excited about this new edition of *Evidence That Demands a Verdict*, and honored to endorse this powerful book. Though hard to believe, this version is even better than the original and I know something about the original, because it was one of the most important books in my life—it was instrumental in my spiritual journey from skeptic to believer. Josh and Sean McDowell approach apologetics comprehensively and boldly, taking on every imaginable challenge to Christianity's truth claims, and answering every one of them thoroughly and convincingly. This father and son team represents the very best of Christian family love, and this extraordinarily important book is a glorious outworking of that love for unbelievers—because it will remove their obstacles to belief—and for believers—because it will reinforce and reinvigorate their faith like few other books on the market. God bless both Josh and Sean for this marvelous and obedient work of evangelism!

DAVID LIMBAUGH, author of seven New York Times bestsellers including *The Emmaus Code* and the #1 bestseller *Crimes Against Liberty*

I have watched for years as Christian colleges have essentially failed to teach the next generation how to defend a Biblical worldview and the orthodoxy of our faith. I am determined to not let this happen at any university under my charge. This is why we've established the Josh McDowell Institute for Christian Thought and Apologetics at Oklahoma Wesleyan University. I simply will not let my students graduate without being confronted with the *Evidence That Demands a Verdict*. I pray that all other Christian scholars and leaders would do no less.

EVERETT PIPER, PhD, president of Oklahoma Wesleyan University, home of the Josh McDowell Institute for Christian Thought and Apologetics

This book is a valuable resource for those wanting to know whether there truly is enough evidence to show that the Christian message is true. As its title suggests, it presents a case to that end, which must be considered carefully by anyone who is truly seeking an answer to the ultimate question of worldviews.

MICHAEL LICONA, associate professor of theology, Houston Baptist University

In an era where spiritual beliefs are fluid and truth is increasingly viewed as a four-letter word, *Evidence That Demands a Verdict* fills a desperate need. *Evidence* provides a logical, thorough, compelling examination of the preponderance of evidence for the truth of Christianity. With this newly updated edition of a book that was foundational in my own apologetics training as a teenager, Josh and Sean McDowell are equipping another generation for gospel conversations.
Despite our culture's current aversion to truth—or perhaps precisely because of it—it's more important than ever that Christians grasp the evidences that support their faith, so they can gently, lovingly and confidently share the Gospel with their unreached friends.

GREG STIER, founder and CEO of Dare 2 Share

EVIDENCE
THAT DEMANDS
A VERDICT

Other Josh McDowell titles available from Thomas Nelson

EVIDENCE
THAT DEMANDS
A VERDICT

LIFE-CHANGING TRUTH FOR
A SKEPTICAL WORLD

JOSH McDOWELL
AND
SEAN McDOWELL, PhD

Thomas Nelson
Since 1798

Published in Nashville, Tennessee, by Thomas Nelson. Thomas Nelson is a registered trademark of HarperCollins Christian Publishing, Inc.

Thomas Nelson titles may be purchased in bulk for educational, business, fund-raising, or sales promotional use. For information, please e-mail SpecialMarkets@ThomasNelson.com.

ISBN 978-1-401-67671-1 (eBook)

ISBN 978-1-401-67670-4 (HC)

Library of Congress Cataloging-in-Publication Data

ISBN 978-1-401-67670-4

Printed in the United States of America

19 20 21 22 23 24 25 26 27 /LSC/ 20 19 18 17 16 15 14 13 12 11 10 9 8

To Dottie, my wife of forty-six years. My inspiration, my counselor, and the greatest encourager in my life to stay true to my calling and mission. Without her patience, love, encouragement, and constructive criticism, this project could never have been completed.

Josh McDowell

This book is dedicated to the scholars who compiled the initial research that challenged my father to consider the claims of Christ. My personal thanks to John Warwick Montgomery, Wilbur M. Smith, George Eldon Ladd, Norman Geisler, Bernard Ramm, Carl Henry, F. F. Bruce, and many more. Your efforts have echoed into my life, the life of my family, and many others yet to come.

Sean McDowell

CONTENTS

FOREWORD

A mirror requires a response.

Every morning, just about every one of us stumbles into the bathroom to take a look at how much work needs to be done before we present ourselves to the outside world. In spite of the fact we've never met, I know exactly how long you stand in front of the mirror each morning. You stand there until it gets better. A lot better! Most of us would rather be late than to show up on time not looking our best. After all, nobody gets credit for looking in the mirror. We're judged by how we respond to what we see.

In 1972 Josh McDowell published a mirror for believers and skeptics; a mirror that indeed required a response, or as he so brilliantly stated it, a verdict. For over forty years, *Evidence That Demands a Verdict* has been the go-to resource for Christ followers desiring to equip themselves for the task of presenting and defending the claims of the Christian faith. Since that initial release, more than three million copies of this classic apologetics resource have been printed worldwide. More importantly, multiple millions of people all over the world have been impacted by the men and women who've read and internalized the insights and research contained in this timeless resource. And

now, Josh and his son, Dr. Sean McDowell, have partnered with over thirty graduate students and a dozen leading scholars to update and revise this fabulous resource for a new generation.

Why an update?

While the truth of the Bible doesn't change, the questions and critics do. Following the destruction of the World Trade Center and the attack on the Pentagon, the New Atheists have mounted an effective campaign against the viability of all religion. Their criticisms of Christianity have been particularly effective, especially in academic settings. If we're honest, most of us graduated high school and left home with Sunday school arguments for the reliability of the Bible and the credibility of our faith. Unfortunately, years of sermons, camps, mission trips, and personal devotions can be undermined by a single lecture in a university setting. Sunday school answers are no match for the rigors of academia. They don't fare much better under the weight of adulthood either. While a previous generation of Christians had the option to stick their heads in the sand and tune out the voices of the skeptics, Christians today don't have that luxury. The Internet has changed the game.

The voices, lectures, and arguments of the New Atheists are just a click away, and they are undermining the faith of many. So now, more than ever, we need materials designed to equip a new generation for a new generation of questions and detractors.

I'm confident this expanded and updated edition of *Evidence* will do for the modern church what the original version did for me and my contemporaries. As a parent and pastor I'm extraordinarily grateful to Josh and Sean for continuing to stand in the gap and defend our very defensible faith. After all, the foundation of our faith is not a book. It's way better than that. Our faith is in a Person. A Person who lived, died, and rose again—for which we have compelling evidence. Evidence that requires a response. A personal response. As Josh says, a verdict!

Andy Stanley

Author, Communicator, and Founder of North Point Ministries

PREFACE

Why a Massive Book about Evidence?

The story begins about forty-five years ago. After I (Josh) became a Christian, I began to speak in public forums about my spiritual journey and my extensive research into the reliability of the biblical text, as well as the evidences for the deity of Christ and his resurrection. One of my lecture series was "Christianity: Hoax or History?" People of all walks of life would come up to me and ask if they could get my research and speaking notes. You see, at that time it was very hard to find documentation of the historical evidences for the Christian faith. Students, professors, and laypeople in the church would ask, "How can we get access to what you and others are teaching on these subjects?" So it was that I began to compile my research and speaking notes to create the first edition of *Evidence That Demands a Verdict*.

Why This Revised Edition?

Since the first edition of *Evidence That Demands a Verdict* was published in 1972 and revised in 1979 and 1999, significant new discoveries have further confirmed the historical evidence for the Christian faith. For example, new archaeological finds have provided further confirmation of the credibility of both the Old and New Testaments.

Nevertheless, for the past forty years our culture has been heavily influenced by the philosophical outlook called postmodernism. People today question why evidence for the Christian faith is even necessary or important. There is a skepticism in our land and around the world that has given rise to the misguided thinking of the Jesus Seminar, or more recently, the New Atheists, to confuse and disorient people about the true identity of Jesus Christ.

To address the most current trends and examine the objections and questions that are so pervasive in our Internet world early in the twenty-first century, I am delighted that my son, Sean, agreed to direct the extensive and challenging project of revising and updating this classic book and to serve as my coauthor. Sean is a talented scholar, teacher, author, and speaker. He and his team of researchers, writers, and editors have done a terrific job in helping me to complete this massive undertaking.

It is our hope that, in providing the most up-to-date information, this fourth edition of *Evidence That Demands a Verdict* will equip Christians of the twenty-first century with confidence as they seek to understand and defend their faith. In addition, we believe that, as has happened with previous editions, many who have been confused or never exposed to the truth of Christianity will discover that Jesus Christ is who he claimed to be, that God loves them, and that he wants to welcome them into his eternal family.

Watch Your Attitude

Our motivation in using this research is to glorify and magnify Jesus Christ, not to win an argument. *Evidence* is not for proving the Word of God, but rather for providing a reasoned basis for faith. One should have a gentle and reverent spirit when using apologetics or evidences: "But sanctify Christ as Lord in your hearts, always being ready to make a defense to everyone who asks you to give an account for the hope that is in you, yet with *gentleness and reverence*" (1 Pet. 3:15 NASB, emphasis mine).

These notes, used with a caring attitude, can motivate a person to consider Jesus Christ honestly, and direct him or her back to the central and primary issue of the gospel (see 1 Cor. 15:1–4, as well as "How to Know God Personally" at the end of this book).

When I share Christ with someone who has honest doubts, I always seek first to listen. I want to hear that person's story and only then offer information to answer his or her questions. Then I turn the conversation back to the person's relationship with Christ. The presentation of evidence (apologetics) should never be used as a substitute for sharing the Word of God.

Why Copyrighted?

These notes are copyrighted, not to limit their use, but to protect against their misuse and to safeguard the rights of the authors and publishers that we have quoted and documented.

A Lifetime Investment:

We recommend the following books for your library. These are also good books to donate to your university library. (Or, a university will often purchase books for its library if you submit a request.)

Parts I and II:

Blomberg, Craig. *The Historical Reliability of the New Testament*. B&H Academic, 2016.

Bauckham, Richard. *Jesus and the Eyewitnesses*. Eerdmans, 2008.

Evans, Craig. *Fabricating Jesus*. IVP, 2006.

Licona, Michael. *The Resurrection of Jesus: A New Historiographical Approach*. IVP, 2010.

Bowman, Rob and Ed Komoszewski. *Putting Jesus in His Place*. Kregel, 2007.

Eddy, Paul Rhodes and Gregory A. Boyd. *The Jesus Legend*. Baker, 2007.

McDowell, Sean. *The Fate of the Apostles*. Routledge, 2016.

Kruger, Michael J. *The Question of Canon*. IVP, 2013.

Wright, N. T. *The Resurrection of the Son of God*, vols. 1–3. Fortress Press, 2003.

McGrew, Lydia. *Hidden in Plain View: Undesigned Coincidences in the Gospels and Acts*. DeWard, 2017.

Part III:

Kaiser, Walter C. *The Old Testament Documents: Are They Reliable?* IVP, 2001.

Hoffmeier, James K. and Dennis R. Magary. *Do Historical Matters Matter to Faith?* 2012.

Kitchen, K. A. *On the Reliability of the Old Testament*. Eerdmans, 2003.

Part IV:

Groothuis, Douglas. *Truth Decay*. IVP, 2000.

Erickson, Millard J. *Truth or Consequences*. IVP, 2001.

Keener, Craig. *Miracles*. vols. 1–2. IVP, 2012.

ACKNOWLEDGMENTS

We would like to thank the following people for their research, editing, and writing contributions for the following chapters:

A Theistic Universe . . . . Danny McDonald
The Uniqueness of the Bible . . . . Troy Peiffer & Anthony Costello
How We Got the Bible . . . . Arthur Young
Is the New Testament Historically Reliable? . . . James Johansen & Matthew Tingblad
Has the Old Testament Been Accurately
    Transmitted? . . . . Troy Peiffer & Anthony Costello
Gnostic Gospels and Other Nonbiblical Texts . . Timothy Fox
The Historical Existence of Jesus . . . . Cisco Cotto
The Lofty Claims of Jesus . . . . James Kaufman
The Trilemma—Lord, Liar, or Lunatic? . . . . Adam Kingston
Old Testament Prophecies Fulfilled in
    Jesus Christ . . . . Jonathan McLatchie
The Resurrection: Hoax or History? . . . . Shawn White
Is Christianity a Copycat Religion? . . . . Shawn White
The Deity of Jesus: An Investigation . . . . Rob Bowman & Randall Wilson
The Old Testament and Ancient Near
    Eastern Influences . . . . William Conner
Biblically Faithful Approaches to Genesis . . . . . Barrie Winn
Archaeology and the Old Testament . . . . Dr. Joseph Holden, President of Veritas
                                                    Evangelical Seminary
The Historical Adam . . . . Barrie Winn
The Historicity of the Patriarchs . . . . Aaron Bond
The Historicity of the Exodus . . . . Cisco Cotto
The Historicity of the Conquest . . . . Robert Ryals
The Historicity of the United Monarchy . . . . . . Rick Miller

We would also like to express our appreciation to the following scholars who helped provide critical feedback and editing for chapters that fell within their expertise. Our thanks to Ken Turner, Charlie Trimm, Scott Carroll, Paul Rhodes Eddy, Daniel Wallace, Michael Licona, Rob Bowman, Michael Brown, Jeff Zweerink, Casey Luskin, Timothy Pickavance, Ann Gauger, John Bloom, Fuz Rana, David Talley, Craig Blomberg, Jason Carlson, and Scott Smith.

Our thanks to Carlos Delgado for his careful and insightful edits of the entire manuscript. And we deeply appreciate Jonathan McLatchie for his extra research to find some of the most common objections raised against the last version of *Evidence* (1999) and for providing helpful responses to include in this updated version.

Many thanks to Charlie Trimm, David Talley, and Ken Turner in particular for so much work updating and expanding the chapters pertaining to the Old Testament. All three of you went far above and beyond the call of duty to help make these chapters both high quality and relevant for today.

We would like to draw special attention to the efforts and sacrifice of Don and Judy Kencke. The two of you truly put in tireless and countless hours reading, editing, and updating content throughout the entire manuscript. We truly believe God prepared you for such a time as this. And we will be forever grateful for how much energy and focus you put into making this manuscript the quality that it is. There is no way we could have done this without you.

And we would also like to offer our gratitude to Daniel Marrs, our editor from Thomas Nelson, for guiding this project from start to finish. You have truly cared about the little details and the big details, which make a project like this a success. Thanks for gently pushing back when necessary, and also for the extra effort you put into this entire project. You are truly a blessing and exactly the right person for the job.

REVISING *EVIDENCE THAT DEMANDS A VERDICT*

AN INTERVIEW WITH JOSH MCDOWELL

Although I, Sean, have had the privilege of working with my father on a variety of projects, updating *Evidence That Demands a Verdict* is perhaps the most special of all. While he has written or coauthored more than 150 books, *Evidence That Demands a Verdict* is one of his signature works.

People regularly share with me that this book helped lead them to Christ, or if they came across the book as a believer, helped them hold on to their faith during a season of doubt. And some of the most influential evangelical scholars today, such as William Lane Craig and J. P. Moreland, and leading pastors, such as Skip Heitzig, consider the book formative in their own faith journeys. While apologetics books have proliferated in recent years, in the last quarter of the twentieth century, *Evidence* was one of the few based on the historicity of the biblical accounts. For many it became their "go-to" reference book for evidence-based apologetics. *Evidence* has been truly groundbreaking and trendsetting. And this does not yet even include its

international influence! Since 1972, *Evidence* has been translated into forty-four languages and published worldwide. Millions of people from South America, Asia, Australia, Africa, the Middle East, and beyond have come to rely upon *Evidence* as one of the most important apologetics books of this generation.

No wonder I ventured into this project with both enthusiasm and trepidation! It was thrilling to be able to manage the update of such a significant project, trusting that God would use it again for a new generation, yet I also felt the weight of *getting it right*. After all, so many people all over the world consider *Evidence* an authoritative source of evidence for the reliability of the Bible, the historicity of the resurrection, and the reality that Jesus was really God in human flesh.

As I considered ways to introduce this new edition, I realized there could be no better reintroduction than an interview with my father, Josh. The revisions and expansions to this present edition remain fully grounded in Josh's own story—his reasons for writing *Evidence* in the first place and the impact the book has had on his own life and the lives of those he's ministered to over the years.

SEAN: Dad, why did you first write Evidence That Demands a Verdict?

JOSH: I wrote it as a result of a struggle. I began my college years with a lot of hurt, anger, and bitterness. I was mad at my father—your grandfather—for being an alcoholic and for destroying my family. I was also angry at Wayne Bailey, the man who worked on our farm, for sexually abusing me from ages six to thirteen. I was desperately seeking happiness and meaning in life, and simply didn't know where to find it. I was successful in school, business, sports, and even campus leadership. And even though I put on a smile and acted like I had it all together, my life seemed so empty. I desperately wanted to know truth.

And yet in the university I saw this small group of people, two professors and about eight students, whose lives were different. I wanted what they had, and so I asked them what made their lives different. One girl said, "Jesus Christ," and I laughed. Her answer struck me as the stupidest thing I had ever heard. But this group challenged me to examine the claims of Christ intellectually.

I am certainly not the smartest person in the world, but I am responsible to use my intellect to discover truth to the utmost. So I took up their challenge, and to my amazement came to the conclusion that God did manifest himself through the Scriptures and the person of Christ.

Once I came to this intellectual conviction, I began to strategize about how I could share the things I discovered with others. During the first thirteen years after becoming a Christian, I both shared my faith and continued to research the evidential basis for the Christian faith. After I would speak, people from the audience kept asking me for copies of my notes and research. That gave me the idea that I could and should publish my research to inform those who were truly seeking truth as well as to encourage followers of Christ. Eventually, I brought together a team of students from a variety of universities to work with me. They would research all day, and then I would collate their findings at night. Out of those years of work came *Evidence That Demands a Verdict*.

And yet no one wanted to publish it! I broke almost every principle of publishing, such as including lengthy quotes with full documentation. People told me that it wouldn't sell and that no one would read it. It took me nearly a year to type out the manuscript on an electric typewriter. I checked and double-checked footnotes and yet still made some mistakes. I finally published it on a Friday morning, and by that evening, it was already selling out. And it continued to sell at a feverish rate for years.

Now there are some incredible apologetics books by people such as Ravi Zacharias, Lee Strobel, Frank Turek, J. Warner Wallace, and others. But there was almost nothing like it when I first wrote *Evidence*.

SEAN: What is one of your favorite stories about the impact of Evidence?

JOSH: Probably my favorite stories come from overseas—from places like the Middle East and South Korea. One year *Evidence* was chosen by secular newspapers as the book of the year in South Korea. Honors like this are so exciting because they mean that the book is influencing lives by motivating people to dig deeper into the Scriptures.

A man walked into a Christian bookstore in an Arabic-speaking country. "I want your best book on the defense of Christianity." The bookstore manager handed him *Evidence That Demands A Verdict* in Arabic.

As the man left he exclaimed, "I'm doing my dissertation on destroying Christianity." Six months later the storeowner baptized the student who had become a believer.

SEAN: How has culture changed since you first wrote Evidence in the early 1970s?

JOSH: When I first wrote *Evidence*, there was very limited access to information. Today there is an overload of truth claims. In the 1970s people were exposed to ideas by their parents, friends, teachers in school, and then eventually professors in the university. But there wasn't the Internet, where people now have endless access to unfiltered information.

Also, when I first wrote *Evidence,* people wanted proof for their beliefs. People wanted evidence. And then it began to switch about ten to fifteen years ago. It used to be that when I made a truth claim at a university, students would say, "How do you know that's true? Give us some proof." But then students started saying, "What right do you have to make that claim? You are an intolerant bigot." Culture has gravitated away from the essence of truth to the emotion of the individual. Essentially, culture has moved from valuing substance to valuing form.

SEAN: How do you intend Evidence to be used?

JOSH: I wrote *Evidence* as a resource book for individuals and families. According to his wife, legendary Dallas Cowboys coach Tom Landry would read *Evidence* for fifteen minutes every night before bed, including the night before the Super Bowl. But he's an exception. *Evidence* is a thick book that is heavy with content. I wrote it to be a resource for individuals and families to walk through together, so they could be confident that there is a lot of evidence for Christianity and know where to find answers to common objections.

SEAN: What is your goal for this new version?

JOSH: The goal for this new version is the same as the first one: *to give people a reference book that spurs them toward truth and greater confidence in Scripture and the desire to know truth*. My hope is that *Evidence* continues to be a foundational book for pastors, teachers, parents, students, youth workers, and other Christians who want to have confidence about their own faith and be ready to give an answer for their faith.

SEAN: What role did the evidence play in your personal journey to Christ?

JOSH: My biggest objection to Christianity was that it was not true. But once I checked out the evidence firsthand, I realized that Christianity is true. Encountering the evidence was one of the biggest factors that led me to consider the claims of Christ. Through wrestling with the evidence, I learned that faith is meant to go along with evidence, not run contrary to it.

But, despite what many people think, it wasn't the evidence that brought me to Christ. What brought me to Christ was an understanding of the love of God. Jeremiah 31:3 says, "I have loved you with an everlasting love; therefore I have continued my faithfulness to you" (ESV). What brought me to Christ was the realization that if I were the only one in the world, Christ still would have died for me.

My ultimate problem wasn't intellectual—it was emotional. I had bitterness and hatred for my father because he was an alcoholic and destroyed my family. In addition, the sexual abuse I experienced for seven years by Wayne Bailey just compounded the hurt. Given my father's failures, it brought me no joy to hear that a heavenly Father supposedly loved me. Every time someone mentioned a "heavenly Father," it didn't bring joy—it brought pain. I could not decipher the difference between a heavenly Father and an earthly father because in my world and in my experience, fathers hurt people. So I wanted nothing to do with God. I never even considered the message of Christianity until I was convinced that it was true. Evidence brought me to the point of considering how the Christian message might apply to my own life. It was the evidence that first caught my attention, but it was an understanding of the love of God, as I mentioned above, that ultimately drew me to trust and follow Christ.

• • •

It truly was a joy and privilege to partner with my father, and dozens of students and scholars, on this project. God has used this book in remarkable ways over the past half century. My prayer is that God will continue to use it to ground believers with confidence in their faith and to help seekers discover how much God truly cares for them and desires for them to know him personally. I hope you find this edition faithful to the original spirit of *Evidence* but also updated for a new generation.

HE CHANGED MY LIFE

Thomas Aquinas, the thirteenth-century philosopher, wrote, "There is within every soul a thirst for happiness and meaning." I (Josh) first began to feel that thirst when I was a teenager. I wanted to be happy. I wanted my life to have meaning. I became hounded by those three basic questions that haunt every human life: *Who am I? Why am I here? Where am I going?* I wanted answers to these questions, so as a young student, I started searching for them.

Where I was brought up, everyone seemed to be into religion. Because I thought maybe I would find my answers in being religious, I started attending church—a lot. I went every time the doors opened—morning, afternoon, or evening. But I must have picked the wrong church, because I felt worse inside the church than I did outside. About the only thing I got out of my religious experience was seventy-five cents a week: I would put a quarter into the offering plate and take a dollar out so I could buy a milkshake!

I was brought up on a farm in Michigan, and most farmers are very practical. My dad, who was a farmer, taught me, "If something doesn't work, chuck it." So I chucked religion.

Then I thought that education might have the answers to my quest for meaning. So I decided to go to college. You can learn many things in college, but I didn't find the answers I was seeking. I'm sure I was by far the most unpopular student with the faculty of the first college I attended. I would buttonhole professors in their offices and badger them for answers to my questions. When they saw me coming they would turn out the lights, pull down the shades, and lock the door so they wouldn't have to talk to me. Soon I discovered that my teachers and fellow students had just as many problems, frustrations, and unanswered questions about life as I had. A few years ago I saw a student walking around with a T-shirt that read: "Don't follow me, I'm lost." That's how everyone on campus seemed to me. Education, I concluded, was not the answer!

Prestige must be the way to go, I decided. It just seemed right to find a noble cause, give yourself to it, and become well known. The people on campus with the most prestige were the student leaders. So I ran for various student offices and got elected. It was great to know everyone on campus, make important decisions, and spend the college's money doing what I wanted to do. But the thrill soon wore off, as was the case with everything else I had tried.

On Monday morning I would wake up, usually with a headache because of the way

I had spent the previous night, dreading to face another five miserable days. I endured Monday through Friday, living only for the partying nights of Friday, Saturday, and Sunday. Then on Monday the whole boring cycle would start over again. I felt frustrated, even desperate. My goal was to find my identity and purpose in life. But everything I tried left me empty and without answers.

I didn't let on that my life was meaningless: I was too proud for that. Everyone thought I was the happiest man on campus. If things were going great for me, I felt great. When things were going lousy, I felt lousy. I just didn't let it show.

I was like a boat out in the ocean, tossed back and forth by the waves. I had no rudder—no direction or control. But I couldn't find anyone who could tell me how to live any differently. I was frustrated. No, it was worse than that. There's a strong term that describes the life I was living: hell.

Around that time I noticed a small group of people—eight students and two faculty members. There was something different about them. They seemed to know who they were and where they were going in life. And they had a quality I deeply admire in people: *conviction*. There is a certain dynamic in the lives of people with deep convictions, and I enjoy being around people with that dynamic, even if their beliefs differ from mine.

It was clear to me that these people had something I didn't have. They were disgustingly happy. And their happiness didn't ride up and down with the circumstances of life; it was constant. They appeared to possess an inner source of joy, and I wondered where it came from.

But there was something else about this group that caught my attention—their attitudes and actions toward each other. They genuinely loved each other—and not only each other, but the people outside their group as well. They didn't just talk about love; they got involved in peoples' lives, helping them with their needs and problems. It was all totally foreign to me, yet I was strongly attracted to it. So I decided to make friends with them.

About two weeks later, I was sitting around a table in the student union talking with some members of this group. Soon the conversation turned to the topic of God. I was pretty skeptical and insecure about this subject, so I put on a big front. I leaned back in my chair, acting as if I couldn't care less. "Christianity, ha!" I blustered. "That's for weaklings, not intellectuals." Down deep, I really wanted what they had. But with my pride and my position on campus, I didn't want *them* to know that I wanted what they had. Then I turned to one of the girls in the group and said, "Tell me, what changed your lives? Why are you so different from all the other students and faculty?"

She looked me straight in the eye and said two words I had never expected to hear in an intelligent discussion on a university campus: "Jesus Christ."

"Jesus Christ?" I snapped. "Don't give me that kind of garbage. I'm fed up with religion and the Bible. And I'm fed up with the church."

Immediately she shot back, "Mister, I didn't say 'religion': I said 'Jesus Christ.'" She pointed out something I had never known: Christianity is not a religion. Religion is humans trying to work their way to God through good works. Christianity is God coming to men and women through Jesus Christ.

I wasn't buying it. Not for a minute. Taken aback by the girl's courage and conviction, I apologized for my attitude. "But I'm sick and tired of religion and religious people," I added. "I don't want anything to do with it."

Then my new friends issued me a challenge I couldn't believe. They challenged me, a pre-law student, to make a rigorous, intellectual examination of the claims of Jesus Christ: that he is God's Son; that he inhabited a human body and lived among real men and women; that he died on the cross for the sins of humanity; that he was buried and was resurrected three days later; and that he is still alive and can change a person's life even today.

I thought this challenge was a joke. These Christians were so dumb. How could something as flimsy as Christianity stand up to an intellectual examination? I scoffed at their challenge.

But they didn't let up. They continued to challenge me day after day, and finally they backed me into the corner. I became so irritated at their insistence that I finally accepted their challenge—just to prove them wrong. I decided to write a book that would show them that Christianity was a joke—intellectually and historically. I left college for a period of months so that I could travel throughout the United States and Europe to gather evidence in libraries and museums to prove that Christianity is a sham.

At the end of my journey in Europe, I found myself sitting in a museum library in London, England. After several hours of research studying some out-of-print books, I leaned back in my chair, rubbed my eyes, and without remembering I was in a quiet library, I spoke out loud, "It's true. It's true! It's really true!" It was about 6:30 p.m. when I left the library. As I walked along those London streets, I realized that there was no escaping the facts: the Bible is true, the resurrection of Christ really did happen, and Jesus is who he claimed to be. I did not fall on my knees and become a Christian right there, right then. But it seemed that there was a voice within

me saying, "Josh, you don't have a leg to stand on." I immediately suppressed it. But every day after that it just got louder and louder. The more I researched, the more I became aware of that same challenge. I returned to the United States and continued my research at the Harvard University and University of Michigan libraries. But I couldn't sleep at night. I would go to bed at ten o'clock and lie awake until four in the morning, trying to refute the overwhelming evidence I was accumulating that Jesus Christ is in fact God's Son.

I began to realize that I was being intellectually dishonest. My mind told me that the claims of Christ were indeed true, but my will was being pulled another direction. I had placed so much emphasis on finding the truth, but I wasn't willing to follow it once I found it. It seemed that God was challenging me with these words from the Bible in Revelation 3:20: "Here I am! I stand at the door and knock. If anyone hears my voice and opens the door, I will come in and eat with him, and he with me" (NIV). But becoming a Christian seemed so ego-shattering to me. I couldn't think of a faster way to ruin all my good times, let alone my life.

I knew I had to resolve this inner conflict because it was driving me crazy. I had always considered myself an open-minded person, so I decided to put Christ's claims to the supreme test. One night at the end of my second year of college, I became a Christian. Someone may say, "How do you know you became a Christian?" That's a fair question. Here is the simple answer: *I was there!*

I met alone with a Christian friend and prayed four things that established my relationship with God. First, I said, *"Lord Jesus, thank you for dying on the cross for me."* I realized that if I were the only person on earth, Christ still would have died for me. You may think it was the irrefutable intellectual and historical evidence that brought me to Christ. No, the evidence was only God's way of getting his foot in the door of my life. What brought me to Christ was the realization that he loved me enough to die for me.

Second, I said, *"I confess that I am a sinner."* No one had to tell me that. I knew there were things in my life that were incompatible with a holy, just, righteous God. The Bible says, "If we confess our sins, he is faithful and just and will forgive us our sins and purify us from all unrighteousness" (1 John 1:9 NIV). So I said, *"Lord, forgive me."*

Third, I said, "Right now, in the best way I know how, I open the door to my life and place my trust in you as Savior and Lord. Take over the control of my life. Change me from the inside out. Make me the type of person you created me to be."

The last thing I prayed was, "Thank you for coming into my life."

After I prayed, nothing happened. There was no bolt of lightning. If anything, I actually felt worse after I prayed—almost physically sick. I was afraid I had made an emotional decision that I would later regret intellectually. But more than that, I was afraid of what my friends would say when they found out. I really felt that they would think I had "gone off the deep end."

But over the next eighteen months my entire life was changed. One of the biggest changes occurred in how I viewed people. While studying in college, I had mapped out the next twenty-five years of my life. My goal had been to become governor of Michigan and then a United States senator. I planned to accomplish my goal by using people in order to climb the ladder of political success—I figured people were meant to be used. But after I placed my trust in Christ, my thinking changed. Instead of using others to serve me,

I now discovered that I wanted to be used to serve others. Becoming other-centered instead of self-centered was a really dramatic change in my life.

Another area that started to change was my bad temper. I used to blow my stack if somebody just looked at me wrong. I still have the scars from almost killing a man during my first year in college. My bad temper was so ingrained that I didn't consciously seek to change it. But one day, when faced with a crisis that would ordinarily have set me off, I discovered that my bad temper was gone. I'm not perfect in this area, but this change in my life has been significant and dramatic.

Perhaps the most significant change has been in the area of hatred and bitterness. I grew up filled with hatred, primarily aimed at one man whom I hated more than anyone else on the face of the earth. I despised everything this man stood for. I can remember as a young boy lying in bed at night plotting how I would kill this man without being caught by the police. This man was my father.

While I was growing up, my father was the town drunk. I hardly ever saw him sober. My friends at school would joke about my dad lying in the gutter downtown, making a fool of himself. Their jokes hurt me deeply, but I never let anyone know. I laughed along with them. I kept my pain a secret.

I would sometimes find my mother in the barn, lying in the manure behind the cows where my dad had beaten her with a hose until she couldn't get up. My hatred seethed as I vowed to myself, "When I am strong enough, I'm going to kill him." Sometimes when visitors were coming over and my dad was drunk, I would grab him around the neck, pull him out to the barn, and tie him up. After tying his hands and feet, I would loop part of the rope around his neck, hoping he would try to get away and choke himself.

Then I would park his truck behind the silo and tell everyone he had gone to a meeting, so we wouldn't be embarrassed as a family.

Two months before I graduated from high school, I walked into the house after a date to hear my mother sobbing. I ran into her room, and she sat up in bed. "Son, your father has broken my heart," she said. She put her arms around me and pulled me close. "I have lost the will to live. All I want to do is live until you graduate, then I want to die."

Two months later I graduated, and a few months later my mother died. I believe she died of a broken heart. I hated my father for that. Had I not left home a few months after the funeral to attend college, I might have killed him.

But after I made a decision to place my trust in Jesus as my Savior and Lord, the love of God inundated my life. He took my hatred for my father and turned it upside down. Five months after becoming a Christian, I found myself looking my dad right in the eye and saying, "Dad, I love you." I did not want to love that man, but I did. God's love had changed my heart.

After I transferred to Wheaton College, I was in a serious car accident, the victim of a drunk driver. I was moved home from the hospital to recover, and my father came to see me. Remarkably, he was sober that day. He seemed uneasy, pacing back and forth in my room. Then he blurted out, "How can you love a father like me?"

I said, "Dad, six months ago I hated you, I despised you. But I have put my trust in Jesus Christ, received God's forgiveness, and he has changed my life. I can't explain it all, Dad. But God has taken away my hatred for you and replaced it with love."

We talked for nearly an hour. Then he said, "Son, if God can do in my life what I've seen him do in yours, then I want to give him the opportunity." He prayed, "God, if you're really God and Jesus died on the cross to forgive me for what I've done to my family, I need you. If Jesus can do in my life what I've seen him do in the life of my son, then I want to trust him as my Savior and Lord." Hearing my dad pray this prayer from his heart was one of the greatest joys of my life.

After I trusted Christ, my life was basically changed in six to eighteen months. But my father's life changed right before my eyes. It was like someone reached down and switched on a light inside him. He touched alcohol only once after that. He got the drink only as far as his lips, and that was it—after forty years of drinking! He didn't need it anymore. Fourteen months later, he died from complications of his alcoholism. But in that fourteen-month period over a hundred people in the area around my tiny hometown committed their lives to Jesus Christ because of the change they saw in the town drunk, my dad.

But I need to tell you that as I grew up, my father was not the only person I grew to despise and deeply hate. Our hired cook and housekeeper, Wayne Bailey, was a tall thin man with a long pointed nose. He had a room upstairs in our farmhouse. To say that I grew to hate Wayne would be to put it mildly. You see, Wayne sexually abused me repeatedly, beginning when I was just six years old—until as a young teenager I became strong enough to resist. One day, when my parents were both out, Wayne from behind put his hand on my right shoulder. My body stiffened because I knew what was next. My fear and nervousness had never stopped him before. But this time I was finally ready. I spun around and slammed Wayne against the wall, grabbing his neck with my left hand and raising my right clenched fist. *"If you ever touch me again—even once—I will kill you!"* That was the day the sexual abuse stopped.

Several years later he quit his job on our farm and left for good.

But the emotional pain and deep psychological scars remained with me. Yes, I truly hated Wayne for what he had done. Forgive him? Seriously? That question is one I had to wrestle with. And I did. It wasn't until I realized afresh the enormity of what it meant that Jesus had died for me and had forgiven me that I knew that I needed to find Wayne and, as an act of obedience, forgive that man for what he had done. My pastor had told me that forgiveness doesn't mean justifying or condoning what he did, but it would begin the process of freeing me from the past, and it would offer a lost person the opportunity for redemption.

Well, I located Wayne—living in a drab house in Jackson, Michigan. Having carefully rehearsed what I would say, I told him, "Wayne, what you did to me was evil. Very evil! But I have come to know Jesus Christ as my Savior and Lord. And I have come here . . . to . . . tell you . . ." I prayed for strength and continued, "Wayne, all of us have sinned, and no one measures up to God's standard of perfection. We all need redemption, and, well, I've come here to tell you that I forgive you."

He looked at me without blinking. For a moment I wished it wasn't true, but it was true and I had to say it. "Christ died for you, Wayne, as much as he died for me." I paused and then as I turned to leave, I turned to face him one final time. "One other thing, Wayne. Don't let me ever hear of you touching a young man again. You'll regret it."

Out of obedience to God's command, I had chosen to forgive a man who had deeply hurt me. Forgiveness is an action, not an emotion. As I pulled away in my car, there was no high or low point of emotion that one might expect. Instead, I recognized a peace in my heart unlike anything I had experienced before.

You can laugh at Christianity. You can mock and ridicule it. But it works. If you trust Christ, start watching your attitudes and actions—Jesus Christ is in the business of changing lives.

Christianity is not something to be shoved down your throat or forced on you. You have your life to live and I have mine. All I can do is tell you what I have learned and experienced. After that, what you do with Christ is your decision.

Perhaps the prayer I prayed will help you: "Lord Jesus, I need you. Thank you for dying on the cross for me. Forgive me and cleanse me. Right this moment I trust you as my Savior and Lord. Make me the type of person you created me to be. In Christ's name, Amen."

Josh McDowell

INTRODUCTION

OVERVIEW

I. What Is Apologetics?

As a professor of Christian apologetics at Biola University, I (Sean) help prepare students to answer tough questions raised against the Christian faith. One day someone from outside the Biola academic community called our university to ask why we offer classes on apologizing for the faith. She thought apologetics meant teaching students to say they were sorry for their beliefs! While her question was well intentioned, she didn't grasp the nature of apologetics and its biblical role in the Christian life. Christians certainly should apologize for their faith, but not in the sense she had in mind.

Apologize . . . for What?

The word *apologetics* does not mean to say you're sorry. Instead, it refers to the defense of what you believe to be true. This book of evidence for the validity of the Christian faith is therefore a book of *apologetics*.

Theologian and apologist Clark Pinnock explains the nature of apologetics in this way:

The term apologetics derives from a Greek term, *apologia*, and was used for a defence that a person like Socrates might make of his views and actions. The apostle Peter tells every Christian to be ready to give a reason (*apologia*) for the hope that is in him (1 Pet. 3:15). Apologetics, then, is an activity of the Christian mind which attempts to show that the gospel message is true in what it affirms. An apologist is one who is prepared to defend the message against criticism and distortion, and to give evidences of its credibility. (Pinnock, A, 36)

Biblical Passages with the Word *Apologia*

The New Testament uses the Greek word *apologia*, often translated in English as "defense," eight times in the New Testament. (All passages in this list are quoted from the ESV with italics added):

1. Acts 22:1: "Brothers and fathers, hear the *defense* that I now make before you."

2. Acts 25:16: "I answered them that it was not the custom of the Romans to give up anyone before the accused met the accusers face to face and had opportunity to make his *defense* concerning the charge laid against him."

3. 1 Corinthians 9:3: "This is my *defense* to those who would examine me."

4. 2 Corinthians 7:11: "For see what earnestness this godly grief has produced in you, but also what eagerness to clear yourselves [*apologia*], what indignation, what fear, what longing, what zeal, what punishment! At every point you have proved yourselves innocent in the matter."

5. Philippians 1:7: "It is right for me to feel this way about you all, because I hold you in my heart, for you are all partakers with me of grace, both in my imprisonment and in the *defense* and confirmation of the gospel."

6. Philippians 1:16: "The latter do it out of love, knowing that I am put here for the *defense* of the gospel."

7. 1 Peter 3:15: "But in your hearts honor Christ the Lord as holy, always being prepared to make a *defense* to anyone who asks you for a reason for the hope that is in you; yet do it with gentleness and respect."

8. 2 Timothy 4:16: "At my first *defense* no one came to stand by me, but all deserted me. May it not be charged against them!"

First Peter 3:15 uses the word *defense* in a way that denotes the kind of defense one would make to a legal inquiry, asking, "Why are you a Christian?" A believer ought to give an adequate answer to this question. The command to be ready with an answer is directed toward *every* follower of Jesus—not just pastors, teachers, and leaders.

There are instances in many other passages when, even though the word *apologia* may not appear, the Bible either models or explicitly emphasizes the importance of apologetics. Consider a few: 2 Corinthians 10:5; Jude 3; Acts 2:22–24; 18:4; Titus 1:9; Job 38:1–41; Luke 24:44.

Jesus the Apologist

Except for 1 Peter 3:15, the New Testament appearances of *apologia* all come from the writing or ministry of Paul. But was Jesus an apologist? Though the New Testament does not mention Jesus using the word *apologia*, we nevertheless hold that he was, indeed, an apologist. Philosopher Douglas Groothuis has carefully studied the question of whether Jesus was a philosopher or an apologist. After giving many examples of how Jesus rationally defended the crucial claims of Christianity, Groothuis concludes:

Contrary to the views of critics, Jesus Christ was a brilliant thinker, who used logical arguments to refute His critics and establish the truth of His views. When Jesus praised the faith of children, He was encouraging humility as a virtue, not irrational religious trust or a blind leap of faith in the dark. Jesus deftly employed a variety of reasoning strategies in His debates on various topics. These include escaping the horns of a dilemma, *a fortiori* arguments, appeals to evidence, and *reductio ad absurdum* arguments. Jesus' use of persuasive arguments demonstrates that He was both a philosopher and an apologist who rationally defended His worldview in discussions with some of the best thinkers of His day. This intellectual approach does not detract from

His divine authority but enhances it. Jesus' high estimation of rationality and His own application of arguments indicates [*sic*] that Christianity is not an anti-intellectual faith. Followers of Jesus today, therefore, should emulate His intellectual zeal, using the same kinds or arguments He Himself used. Jesus' argumentative strategies have applications to four contemporary debates: the relationship between God and morality, the reliability of the New Testament, the resurrection of Jesus, and ethical relativism. (Groothuis, JPA)

Apologetics in the Old Testament

Some falsely assume that apologetics began in the New Testament era. After explaining how Jesus and Paul engaged in logical debate both to destroy faulty beliefs and to propagate the Christian faith, philosopher J. P. Moreland observes:

Jesus and Paul were continuing a style of persuasion peppered throughout the Old Testament prophets. Regularly, the prophets appealed to evidence to justify belief in the biblical God or in the divine authority of their inspired message: fulfilled prophecy, the historical fact of miracles, the inadequacy of finite pagan deities to be a cause of such a large, well-ordered universe compared to the God of the Bible, and so forth. They did not say, "God said it, that settles it, you should believe it!" They provided a rational defense for their claims. (Moreland, LYG, 132)

II. Five Reasons Apologetics Is Important Today

Reason #1: We Are All Apologists Anyway

Apologetics is not listed as a spiritual gift for teachers, preachers, or evangelists, as though only some ought to become apologists. Rather, *all* Christians are called to be ready with an answer (1 Peter 3:15; Jude 3). We all make a case for Christianity in some fashion or another—but are we doing it well? Beyond the specific Christian calling to have a ready defense for the faith, there is a sense in which everyone is already an apologist for something. The question is not *whether* we are apologists, but *what kind* of apologists we are. Christian author and social critic Os Guinness addresses this idea:

> From the shortest texts and tweets to the humblest website, to the angriest blog, to the most visited social networks, the daily communications of the wired world attest that *everyone is now in the business of relentless self-promotion—presenting themselves, explaining themselves, defending themselves, selling themselves or sharing their inner thoughts and emotions as never before in human history.* That is why it can be said that we are in the grand secular age of apologetics. The whole world has taken up apologetics without ever knowing the idea as Christians understand it. We are all apologists now, if only on behalf of "the Daily Me" or "the Tweeted Update" that we post for our virtual friends and our cyber community. The great goals of life, we are told, are to gain the widest possible public attention and to reach as many people in the world with our products—and always, our leading product is Us. (Guinness, FT, 15–16)

Reason #2: Apologetics Strengthens Believers

Many Christians claim to believe in Jesus, but only a minority can articulate good reasons for why their beliefs are true. Yet when Christians learn good evidences for the truth of the Bible, for the existence of God, or how to respond to tough challenges to the faith, they gain confidence in their beliefs. For instance, I (Sean) lead high school students

on an apologetics mission trip each year to Salt Lake City, Los Angeles, or Berkeley. To prepare for this trip, students attend weekly meetings and lengthy training sessions, and read apologetics books. Then we go meet, have conversations with, and listen to lectures from some of the best thinkers from other faiths. The vast majority of these students come back with a renewed confidence that their beliefs are not only true, but also defensible. As a result, many grow more eager and willing to share their faith.

Philosopher and apologist William Lane Craig explains how college students can gain confidence by learning apologetics:

> Typically I'll be invited onto a campus to debate some professor who has a reputation of being especially abusive to Christian students in his classes. We'll have a public debate on, say, the existence of God, or Christianity versus humanism, or some such topic. Again and again I find that while most of these men are pretty good at beating up intellectually on an eighteen-year-old in one of their classes, they can't even hold their own when it comes to going toe-to-toe with one of their peers. John Stackhouse once remarked to me that these debates are really a Westernized version of what missiologists call a "power encounter." I think that's a perceptive analysis. Christian students come away from these encounters with a renewed confidence in their faith, their heads held high, proud to be Christians, and bolder in speaking out for Christ on their campus. (Craig, RF, 21)

Reason #3: Apologetics Helps Students Hang On to Their Faith

A number of different studies track how many students leave the church during their college years, and, overall, the stats indicate that, after high school, between one-third and two-thirds of young people do leave. (Wallace, AYP) While they leave for many different kinds of reasons (moral, volitional, emotional, relational, etc.), intellectual questions are *one* important factor. Young people have genuine intellectual questions. And when these questions are not answered, many leave the church.

Both of us regularly speak at churches around the world, and frequently meet afterwards with parents who say something like, "I wish my child could have heard you a few years ago. We raised her in the faith, but now she has strayed from it. She had questions that no one could answer, and simply doesn't believe anymore." These stories are so common today, and they break our hearts. Intellectual challenges, just a click away, confront young people today more than in any other previous generation. We do, however, also frequently hear stories of how our books, articles, and videos (and those of other apologists) have helped people hold on to their faith in the face of challenges. Bottom line: *if you want to train up young people to remain strong in the Christian faith, one vital component is training in apologetics.*

Reason #4: Apologetics Helps with Evangelism

In an article about big issues facing the church, pastor Timothy Keller says the contemporary church needs a renewal of apologetics:

Christians in the West will finally be facing what missionaries around the world have faced for years: how to communicate the gospel to Muslims, Buddhists, Hindus, and adherents of various folk religions. All young church leaders should take courses in and read the texts of the other major world religions. They should also study the gospel presentations written by

missionaries engaging those religions. Loving community will be extremely important, as it always is, to reach out to neighbors of other faiths, but if they are going to come into the church, they will have many questions that church leaders today need to be able to answer. (Keller, HSC)

People naturally have questions. They always have and always will. One of the key functions of apologetics, then, is to respond to questions and clear away objections people have that hinder their trust in Christ. Apologist, author, and speaker Ravi Zacharias emphasizes the important impact of an alert response to someone's question, even in a small way: "*Do not underestimate the role you may play in clearing the obstacles in someone's spiritual journey. A seed sown here, a light shone there* may be all that is needed to move someone one step further.*" (Zacharias, AA, xvii)

In this book, we are going to take you deep. Yet our goal is that you gain knowledge not for its own sake, but for your preparation to confidently answer questions people may ask you about Christianity. If you want to share your faith effectively, you need to be ready with answers.

Professor James Beilby explains the relationship between evangelism and apologetics:

Evangelism and apologetics are closely related. Both have a common general goal: encouraging commitment to Jesus Christ. In fact, in certain theological circles, apologetics has been labeled pre-evangelism. On this understanding, apologetics clears the ground for evangelism; it makes evangelism more effective by preemptively addressing impediments to hearing the gospel. This is certainly true, but I submit that apologetics is also useful in the midst of the presentation of the gospel and after the presentation of the gospel. In other words, there is no moment in which a Christian takes off her evangelist hat and puts on her apologist hat. The relationship is more seamless than that. The difference between the two is one of focus. Evangelism is focused on presenting the gospel; apologetics is focused on defending and commending it. There is, moreover, an important difference in the audience of evangelism and apologetics. Evangelism is done only with non-Christians, but apologetics should be done with Christians and non-Christians alike. (Beilby, TACA, 32)

Reason #5: Apologetics Helps Shape Culture

Apologetics and evangelism never happen in a vacuum. In our experience, apologetics questions come from both Christians and non-Christians—*because they both live in the same cultures, and the same world influences their thinking.* Why are considerations of culture so important? Craig explains:

They're important simply because the gospel is never heard in isolation. It is always heard against the background of the cultural milieu in which one lives. A person raised in a cultural milieu in which Christianity is still seen as an intellectually viable option will display an openness to the gospel which a person who is secularized will not. For the secular person you may as well tell him to believe in fairies or leprechauns as in Jesus Christ! Or, to give a more realistic illustration, it is like our being approached on the street by a devotee of the Hare Krishna movement who invites us to believe in Krishna. Such an invitation strikes us as bizarre, freakish, even amusing. But to a person on the streets of Delhi, such an invitation would, I assume, appear quite reasonable and be serious cause for reflection. I fear that evangelicals appear almost as weird to persons

on the streets of Bonn, Stockholm, or Paris as do the devotees of Krishna. (Craig, RF, 16)

Influential theologian J. Gresham Machen perhaps said it best:

False ideas are the greatest obstacles to the reception of the Gospel. We may preach with all the fervor of a reformer and yet succeed only in winning a straggler here and there, if we permit the whole collective thought of the nation to be controlled by ideas which prevent Christianity from being regarded as anything more than a harmless delusion. (Machen, CC, 7)

Philospher and apologist Francis J. Beckwith further explains:

It is fashionable today to speak of the theological posture of Western civilization, and American intellectual culture in particular, as post-Christian. Our most important, influential and culture-shaping institutions and professions—law, medicine, education, science, media and the arts—no longer accept the presuppositions of the biblical worldview as part of their philosophical frameworks. Thus, for example, it is not unusual—in fact, it is quite common—to hear academic luminaries from different disciplines in assorted venues defend points of view that presuppose theological claims, and Christian ones in particular, are not claims of knowledge but rather religious opinions no different in nature than matters of taste. The ease by which these points of view are presented, and the absence of a call to justify them by the same standards of philosophical rigor that are required of their opposition, is testimony to how potently certain claims antithetical to the Christian worldview have shaped the ideas, opinions and policies of those who occupy the seats of culture influence in our society. (Beckwith, TEA, 16–17)

III. Christianity Is a Factual Faith

Christianity Is a Historical Faith

Christianity appeals to history. It appeals to facts of history that can be examined through the normal means of historicity. Pinnock defines these types of facts: "The facts backing the Christian claim are not a special kind of religious fact. They are the cognitive, informational facts upon which all historical, legal, and ordinary decisions are based." (Pinnock, SFYC, 6–7)

Luke, the first-century historian, demonstrates the historical nature of Christianity in his introduction to his gospel:

Inasmuch as many have undertaken to compile a narrative of the things that have been accomplished among us, just as those who from the beginning were eyewitnesses and ministers of the word have delivered them to us, it seemed good to me also, having followed all things closely for some time past, to write an orderly account for you, most excellent Theophilus, that you may have certainty concerning the things you have been taught.
— Luke 1:1–4 ESV

Among these historical, knowable events was the resurrection of Jesus Christ, an event that Luke says was validated by Jesus himself through "many proofs" over a forty-day period before numerous witnesses (Acts 1:3 ESV).

Like the Gospels, Acts records history. Concerning the genre of Acts, New Testament scholar Craig Keener observes, "Acts is history, probably apologetic history in the form of a historical monograph with a narrow focus on the expansion of the gospel message from Jerusalem to Rome. Luke's approach focuses on primary characters and their deeds and speeches, as was common in the history of his day." (Keener, AEC, 115)

We hope, then, to present the historical facts surrounding the Christian faith, and to determine whether the Christian interpretation is the most reasonable. Make no mistake—the historical facts matter for Christianity. The Christian faith is an objective faith; therefore, it must have an object that is worthy of faith. Salvation comes not from the strength of our beliefs, but from the object of our beliefs. Yes, salvation comes through faith (Eph. 2:8, 9; John 6:29), but the merit of faith depends upon the object believed (not the faith *itself*).

Let me (Josh) illustrate. Once I debated the head of the philosophy department of a Midwestern university. In answering a question, I happened to mention the importance of the resurrection. At this point, my opponent interrupted and rather sarcastically said, "Come on, McDowell, the key issue is not whether the resurrection took place or not; the key issue is this: 'Do you believe it took place?'" He was hinting at, even boldly asserting, that my *believing* was the most important thing. I retorted immediately, "Sir, it does matter whether the resurrection took place, because the value of Christian faith is not in the one believing, but in the One who is believed in, its object." I continued, "If anyone can demonstrate to me that Christ was not raised from the dead, I would not have a justifiable right to my Christian faith" (1 Cor. 15:14, 17).

The Christian must avoid the attitude, "Don't confuse me with the facts—my mind is made up!" For the Christian, the historical events reported in the Scriptures are essential. That's why Paul said, "If Christ has not been raised, then our preaching is in vain and your faith is in vain" (1 Cor. 15:14 ESV).

Christianity Is a Testable Faith

As Paul makes clear in his letter to the Corinthians, Christianity is a historical religion tied to the life, teachings, death, and resurrection of Jesus. These claims are testable, in that anyone can actually examine their validity and determine historically whether they are reliable. As noted, Paul ties the truth of the Christian faith to the historical resurrection (1 Cor. 15:14, 17). Professor of apologetics Craig Hazen considers this one of the strangest passages in all of religious literature. He says:

> I have not been able to find a passage in the Scriptures and teachings of the other great religious traditions that so tightly links the truth of an entire system of belief to a single, testable historical event. . . . This idea that the truth of Christianity is linked to the resurrection of Jesus in a testable way does set Christianity apart from the other great world religious traditions in a dramatic fashion. When you boil it down, Hinduism, Buddhism, and the like are about inner, personal experience and not about objective public knowledge. Other traditions *seem* to be about objective knowledge until you probe a little more deeply. Mormonism, for instance, seems to be about hidden gold plates, Jesus' ancient visit to the Western hemisphere, and latter-day prophets—things that could certainly, in principle, be evaluated in an objective way. However, when facing evidence contrary to these claims, the Mormon missionary, scholar, or apostle steps back and begins to talk about the special inner knowledge, a "burning in the bosom," that is the only confirmation that really counts about these unusual stories. At the end of the day, the Mormon is no different from the Buddhist in that they both rely on inner experience as their ultimate source and warrant for religious knowledge. (Hazen, CWR, 144)

IV. Clearing the Fog: Ten Misconceptions About the Christian Faith

When Sean was growing up, we lived in a small town called Julian, in the mountains outside San Diego. Sometimes the fog would get so thick that while driving we couldn't see the car directly in front of us. Though the fog made the car ahead invisible, the fog didn't change the fact that the car was still there. Fog affects visibility, but the things it hides are no less real than they are on a clear day. In a similar way, many people have "foggy" views of the Christian faith, misunderstandings we hope to clear up before we get to the evidence.

Misconception #1: "Christianity doesn't need evidence because faith is blind."

Many atheist critiques of Christianity claim that faith is blind, irrational, stupid. In his book *The God Delusion,* leading atheist Richard Dawkins asserts that faith opposes reason, and calls faith a "delusion," which he describes as "persistent false belief held in the face of strong contradictory evidence." (Dawkins, GD, 28)

A common example used to show that the Bible denigrates evidence is the story of doubting Thomas. Dawkins writes, "Thomas demanded evidence. . . . The other apostles, whose faith was so strong that they did not need evidence, are held up to us as worthy of imitation." (Dawkins, SG, 198) Was Jesus repudiating an evidence-based faith?

In *Is God Just a Human Invention?* Jonathan Morrow and I (Sean) list three problems with this claim:

> First, Jesus predicted his resurrection on multiple occasions in the presence of the disciples. Thomas should not have been

surprised at the return of Jesus. Second, Thomas heard eyewitness testimony (evidence) from the rest of the disciples and yet still refused to believe. (The vast majority of scientific knowledge we possess depends upon trusting the conclusions of other scientists, which is true for virtually all disciplines.) Third, Jesus did many miracles during his ministry as proof of his identity. In fact, right after the story of Jesus scolding Thomas, John said the miracles of Jesus were recorded "so that you may believe Jesus is the Messiah, the Son of God, and by believing you may have life in His name." (McDowell and Morrow, IGJHI, 21)

Despite what Dawkins claims, Christianity values the role of the mind, which includes the proper use of reason and argumentation. Jesus said to love God with all your heart, soul, strength, and *mind* (Mark 12:30). The Lord said to the nation of Israel, "Come now, let us reason together" (Isa. 1:18 ESV). Scripture and church history emphasize the importance of the role of the mind in discipleship and evangelism.

In the Old Testament, God showered Egypt with miracles before inviting Israel to follow him into the wilderness. Rather than asking Israel for blind allegiance, God's miracles through Moses gave them good reasons to trust him. Exodus 14:31 makes this clear: "Israel saw the great work which the LORD had done in Egypt; so the people feared the LORD, and believed the LORD and His servant Moses." Miracles preceded the call to belief, laying the foundation for a rational step of faith.

Even so, many Christians use the term "faith" to mean "blind faith" rather than biblical faith. But Christianity itself does not demand blind faith. In fact, quite the opposite: when Jesus Christ and the apostles called upon a person to exercise faith, it was not a "blind faith" but rather an *intelligent* faith. The apostle Paul said, "I *know* whom I have believed" (2 Tim. 1:12, emphasis added). Jesus specifically performed miracles to show who he was, and, as a result, many confidently placed their faith in him. During a trip to Capernaum, Jesus healed a paralytic. After forgiving the man's sins, Jesus said to the crowd, "'But that you may know that the Son of Man has power on earth to forgive sins'—He said to the paralytic, 'I say to you, arise, take up your bed and go to your house'" (Mark 2:10, 11). Jesus healed the man so people would *know* he spoke with authority from above.

Professor of philosophy David Horner explains:

> Faith and reason are friends and partners. They go together. They need each other and cannot flourish or even survive apart. Our faith should be a reasonable faith, and our reason should be a faithful reason—one that recognizes the inevitable and rationally necessary presence of trust and commitment. Trusting and committing yourself to what you have good reason to think is true and trustworthy, in those cases when doing so is appropriate or unavoidable, is the most reasonable thing you can do. (Horner, MYF, 170)

Christians are often accused of taking a "blind leap into the dark." For me (Josh), however, I found the evidence for Christianity powerful and convincing. So when I became a Christian, I hadn't leapt blindly into the dark, but stepped into the light. I placed the evidence I gathered onto the scales, and they tipped in favor of Jesus Christ as the Son of God, resurrected from the dead. Had I been exercising "blind faith," I would have rejected Jesus Christ and turned my back on all the evidence.

Of course, no one can *absolutely prove* that Jesus is the Son of God. My investigation of the evidence weighed the pros and cons. The results convinced me that Christ must be who he claimed to be, and I had to make a decision, which I did. You may be thinking, *You found what you wanted.* But this is not the case. Rather, *I confirmed through investigation what I wanted to refute.* I set out to disprove Christianity. I had biases and prejudices not for Christ but against him.

The next three objections are some of the most common ones we hear, but they also have considerable overlap. They each deal with the failure of Christians to live up to biblical ideals. For each of these, we hope you will recognize that Christians have, in fact, often fallen short of living as Christ teaches but also that Christianity itself stands or falls on its own evidential merits, regardless of how Christians may or may not live (and such is true for any other belief system too).

Misconception #2: "Christianity cannot be true because the church has committed injustices."

The world well knows the sins of the church, among them the Inquisition, witch-hunts, the Crusades, and modern-day sexual abuse. Clearly, the church has fallen short of the ideals Jesus proclaimed. Many discount the Christian message *not* because they have examined the evidence and found it wanting, but because they are personally disappointed with Christians and churches. As Keller has observed, we need to address "the behavior of Christians—individual and corporate—that has undermined the plausibility of Christianity for so many people." (Keller, RG, 52)

The fact that Christian behavior so deeply undermines the plausibility of the gospel in the minds of many people should be a wakeup call for Christians. We need to ask

ourselves some tough questions: *Have I failed to live as Jesus taught me to? How responsible am I for the negative perceptions many have of the church?* We would each do well to look at our own lives and seek God's grace and forgiveness.

If you are a non-Christian, it is important to ask yourself a few tough questions as well: Does the moral failure of Christians undermine the claim that Jesus is truly God? Have I had a negative experience with some Christians that clouds my view of the entire church? Am I really evaluating Christianity and the church fairly?

For at least two reasons, the character flaws of the church should not surprise us. First, the Bible speaks of human nature as gloriously made in God's image, but profoundly fallen in sin. Human nature is deeply flawed (Rom. 3:9–18; Mark 7:14–23). Even true Christians are capable of wretched acts. The Bible does say we are a new creation (2 Cor. 5:17), but this is only fully realized in the next life.

Second, many who claim to be Christians have not placed their faith and trust in Jesus Christ and therefore do not truly know him. Jesus taught that both believers and non-believers would be part of the institutional church, but that their true identity would not be revealed until the end (Matt. 13:24–30). He also taught that there would be people who *thought* they were acting in his name—even doing "many wonders," but they will not enter the kingdom of God (Matt. 7:21–23). Just because someone claims to be a Christian, then, does not mean he or she really is. Could it be that the church is often indicted for the actions of people who are not even Christians? This is why the standard of Scripture is so important. Ultimately, we need to compare the actions of both individuals and the corporate church with the genuine teachings of the Bible.

We ought to put the sins of the church in perspective. Philosopher John Mark Reynolds notes,

We are the people of the great cathedrals, but also of the tortures of the Inquisition. The religious fervor that would produce the American genius Jonathan Edwards would also produce the Salem Witch Trials. Sadly, most of the students in universities I meet have heard of the bad things we have done, but not the good. Secular schools have shamed us into silence. After all, if Christendom was mostly bad for the world, then decency requires withdrawing from the public square. Humility about our history is in order, but extremists in the secular community insist we feel nothing but shame. This is unnecessary, since the good of Christendom far outweighs the bad, just as good and honorable ministers outnumber the hypocrites. (Reynolds, CC, 71–72)

In his book *What If Jesus Had Never Been Born?*, pastor and evangelist D. James Kennedy provides an overview of the positive contributions Christianity has made through the centuries. (Kennedy, WIJH) Here are ten highlights:

- Hospitals, which essentially began during the Middle Ages
- Universities, which also began during the Middle Ages
- Literacy and education for the masses
- The separation of political powers
- Civil liberties
- The abolition of slavery
- Modern science
- The elevation of women
- Benevolence and charity; the Good Samaritan ethic
- High regard for human life

One of the great injustices of our day is racism. After observing that the Civil Rights movement was essentially a "religious revival," Timothy Keller notes,

When Martin Luther King, Jr., confronted racism in the white church in the South, he did not call on Southern churches to become more secular. Read his sermons and "Letter from a Birmingham Jail" and see how he argued. He invoked God's moral law and the Scripture. He called white Christians to be *more true* to their own beliefs and to realize what the Bible really teaches. He did not say, "Truth is relative and everyone is free to determine what is right or wrong for them." If everything is relative, there would have been no incentive for white people in the South to give up their power. Rather, Dr. King invoked the prophet Amos, who said, "Let justice roll down like waters, and righteousness as a mighty stream" (Amos 5:24). The greatest champion of justice in our era knew the antidote to racism was not less Christianity, but a deeper and truer Christianity. (Keller, RG, 64–65)

Misconception #3: "The hypocrisy of Christians undermines the reasonability of the Christian faith."

Christian hypocrisy has done massive damage to the Christian faith. According to Guinness, the challenge of hypocrisy is second only to the problem of suffering and evil, and is one of the main reasons people duck the challenge of the gospel. (Guinness, FT, 190) Hypocrisy is such a massive challenge, says Guinness, because Christians are called to be God's witnesses to the world (Isa. 43:10; John 3:28): "In other words, before we are asked to preach, proclaim or try to persuade people of the claims of Jesus and his Father, we are asked simply to be witnesses for him—to provide an honest and factual account of what we have seen and heard objectively, and what we ourselves have experienced ('Once I was blind, but now I can see')—and to live lives that support what we say." (FT, 188)

It is tempting for Christians to respond by pointing out the hypocrisy in other people and worldviews. For instance, the voices of tolerance and inclusiveness are often remarkably intolerant and noninclusive of people with traditional values. Such hypocrisy should be rightly pointed out. But this doesn't get Christians off the hook. After all, James said, "Be doers of the word, and not hearers only, deceiving yourselves" (James 1:22). Christians are called to a higher standard. Whether we like it or not, people will judge the truthfulness of Christianity by the lives of its adherents.

As with the charge that the church has caused injustice in the world, Christians should first look inside and see if there is any merit to this claim. *Have we been hypocritical in any way? Have our lives betrayed our principles? Have we contributed to this narrative?* Rather than blame others, we need to take an honest look inside, identify our own hypocrisy, repent of it, and then admit our shortcomings.

As for the claim itself, it is an example of a "genetic fallacy," which is a claim that is dismissed because of some perceived fault in its origin (its genesis). Guinness explains,

There is an important difference between the *source* of a truth claim and the *standard* by which it should be assessed. It is therefore wrong to reject a claim just because of the character and condition of its source. . . . The issue is always truth, and truth is not a matter of where someone is "coming from" or how oddly or shabbily they have behaved in the past before making the claim. . . . *If the Christian faith is true, it would still be true even if no one believed it, or if all who did were hypocrites; and if it is false, would still be*

false even if everyone believed it and there was no apparent hypocrisy in their behavior. (FT, 196)

If you are upset about hypocrisy in the church, then you are in good company—Jesus felt the same way. Jesus criticized the Pharisees for their religious hypocrisy, calling them blind guides, snakes, and even killers of the prophets (Matt. 23). He condemned them for not practicing what they preached. If hypocrisy troubles you, then you're on the side of Jesus.

What does hypocrisy tell us about Christianity? Scholars and teachers Clinton Arnold and Jeff Arnold explain:

When we go to church or spend time with Christians, many of us go in with the expectation that we won't find anything we don't like, including hypocrites. These people have been fixed by Jesus already, right? It doesn't take long to become disappointed if that's what we expect. But maybe this expectation is off. If you walked into a hospital, would you be surprised if you found sick people everywhere? What if some of them were *really* sick? This is much closer to how we should approach the church and Christians in general. We are not perfect; in fact, we're all still very sick. But we are getting better. It's easy to forget that we all came to the church at different points in life; many people come from broken lives that are now in the process of healing, and most of us are more sick than we realize. We should not be surprised to find people in different states of mending. It would make more sense to compare a person to how they were before they became a Christian than to compare them to perfection. The church is not a place for perfect people, it's a place for broken people slowly being made whole by Jesus. If we find ourselves surprised when we see sin in the church, we should rethink our expectations. (Arnold and Arnold, SABQ, 101–102)

Misconception #4: "The intolerance of Christians is a good reason to reject the Christian faith."

Guilty as charged. Christianity has its fair share of judgmental and intolerant people. We have no interest in covering up the misbehavior of Christians. But keep something in mind: *when Christians act in an arrogant, judgmental manner towards others, they are not following Scriptural teachings*. Pride is one of the seven deadly sins (Prov. 6:16, 17), an evil that comes from the heart (Mark 7:21–23). We apologize for judgmental Christians; remember, though, when Christians act "holier than thou," they act inconsistently with what Christianity *itself* requires. True Christians aim to be at peace with others (Heb. 12:14), build relationships with people regardless of creed, race, nationality, or sex (John 4:1–42; Luke 9:1–10), and are called to be humble and gentle (Eph. 4:2).

We must distinguish between Christians' behavior and genuine Christianity. To condemn Christianity because of the misbehavior of some Christians is another way to commit the "genetic fallacy," which is dismissing a claim because of some perceived fault in its origin.

Yes, Christians often express judgment and intolerance, failing to follow the example and teachings of Jesus. But even if Christians were kind and gracious in their attitudes, the critic might claim, wouldn't they still be intolerant for condemning the beliefs of others? Author and speaker Mark Mittelberg offers an incisive response:

What's fascinating is that the people who condemn Christians for acting as if they're right and others are wrong are, in that very action, acting as if they themselves are right and Christians are wrong. So they are at that moment doing the very thing they say is wrong. When you think about it, it's pretty silly to condemn people for thinking they are right—because aren't you simultaneously thinking *you* are right in saying they are wrong? Or, broadening the point a bit, who in their right mind *doesn't* consistently think that they are right? . . . I mean, really, do you ever think you're wrong while you're in the midst of thinking that very thought? I don't think so; I think as soon as you start to realize your thinking is wrong you change your belief and start thinking differently! Therefore, for two reasons no one should condemn Christians just for thinking they're right and others are wrong: (1) everybody else does the same thing, and (2) Christians might really be right, after all. (Mittelberg, QCH, 241)

Those who accuse Christians of being intolerant have a distorted view of what tolerance really entails. Rather than accepting all views as equally valid, true tolerance involves recognizing and respecting others when we *don't* approve of their values, beliefs, and practices. After all, we don't use the word "tolerate" for what we enjoy or approve of—such as steak or good movies. Thus, there is an intimate connection between tolerance and truth. That is, we only tolerate what we find to be false or mistaken in some capacity. If we all agreed, we would not need tolerance. Only when people genuinely disagree does tolerance become necessary. Claiming that someone is wrong for holding a different viewpoint, then, isn't itself intolerant; the attitude that accompanies the claim may, however, be intolerant. But charitably and kindly disagreeing can be an act of genuine tolerance.

This is what Jesus did. And it is how the American founders viewed tolerance as well. Groothuis explains that tolerance as understood by the founders "is a kind of patience that refuses to hate or disrespect those with

Evidence That Demands a Verdict

whom we disagree, even when disagreement concerns the things that matter most. The ideal of tolerance, in the Western classical liberal sense, is compatible with strong convictions on religious matters and with raging controversies. In fact, John Locke, one of the leading proponents of early modern tolerance, was himself a professing Christian who engaged in apologetics." (Groothuis, CA, 150)

Finally, charging Christians with intolerance assumes the existence of an objective moral standard. But if there is no God, how can there be such a standard? Ironically, as theologian and analytic philosopher Paul Copan observes, tolerance is only intelligible if God exists:

> The reality of God actually makes tolerance intelligible, because God is the source of truth and because God has made human beings in his likeness. Naturalistic secularism has no such foundation for tolerance. If tolerance is a value, it isn't obvious from nature; so if there is no God and we are just hulks of protoplasmic guck, how could tolerance be an objective value at all? Instead, if objective truth exists, as religion maintains, then we must seek and seriously discuss it despite our differing worldviews. But if objective truth doesn't exist, as secularism generally maintains, then relativism obliterates genuine differences of perspective. (Copan, TFY, 36)

Misconception #5: "There can't be just one right religion."

One of the most common questions we both receive is, "How can you say Jesus is the only way to God?" The complaint is clear: it is intolerant, exclusivist, and naïve to assume that only one religion could be correct.

Recently I (Sean) was in a conversation with a friend, and he asked how I could say that Jesus is the only way. I simply said,

"I'm not saying it. Jesus said it. Take it up with him." He certainly didn't expect that response. And I didn't mean to be rude or abrupt. My point was that Jesus was the one who first made the claim, and he has the credentials to back it up. If our claims about Jesus in this book are true, then Jesus has more credentials to speak on eternal life than anyone. He is the only virgin-born, miracle-working, sinless, resurrected Son of God! You may not *like* the idea of Jesus being the only way, but if he truly is the Son of God and said he was the only way to salvation—can you afford to ignore his claim?

It would be nice if everybody could be right, but as simple reason and basic common sense tell us, all religions cannot be true in their core beliefs. By its very nature, truth is exclusive. If 1 + 1 = 2, then it doesn't equal 3, 4, 5, and every other number. While all religions could possibly be wrong, it is not logically possible for all of them to be right when their claims differ so radically. Either they are all wrong or only one is right.

The chart "Basic Beliefs of Major Religions" shows that all religions, even by their own claims, differ from one another, having their own specific ideas of who God is (or is not) and how salvation may be attained.

Many criticize Christianity for its exclusivity, but Christians are not the only group claiming to have the truth. Notice in the chart "Basic Beliefs of Major Religions" the attitudes of each religion toward the others. Four of the five religions *claim* exclusivity. They believe that all other religions are false. Hindus often do not claim exclusivity. In fact, many are happy to say that Christianity is true. But the key is what they *mean* by it. Hindus believe all religions are true when they are subsumed within the Hindu system. In other words, Christianity is one medium by which people can experience reincarnation.

BASIC BELIEFS OF MAJOR RELIGIONS

Religion	Beliefs About God	Beliefs About Salvation	Beliefs About Other Religions
Buddhism	No God	Enlightenment	False
Hinduism	Many Gods	Reincarnation	All True*
Islam	Unitarian (Allah)	The Five Pillars	False
Judaism	Unitarian (Yahweh)	The Law	False
Christianity	Trinitarian (Father, Son, Holy Spirit)	Grace	False

* Hindus will often claim that all religions are true, but this can only be the case when other religions are subsumed within Hinduism. When taken on their own merits, all other religions are false, according to Hinduism.

But what Hindus *don't* mean is that Christianity is true on its own terms. So, like adherents of all other religions, Hindus actually believe Christianity is false, thereby joining every other religious group (including atheists and agnostics) in the belief that only their own worldview is true.

And yet, in another sense, Christianity is not exclusive at all, but is the most inclusive religion. Christ invites all unto himself. Unlike Mithraism, which apparently excluded women, or Mormonism, which formerly excluded black people from the priesthood, the message of Jesus has always been for *everyone.*

Colossians 3:11 says, "In this new life, it doesn't matter if you are a Jew or a Gentile, circumcised or uncircumcised, barbaric, uncivilized, slave, or free. Christ is all that matters, and he lives in all of us" (NLT). Christ makes no human distinctions—he died and rose again so that all people could have a personal relationship with the living God.

Christianity excludes no one who will believe, yet Christ himself offers the only way to be reconciled with God. As philosopher Stephen Davis explains, "The resurrection of Jesus, then, is God's decisive proof that Jesus is not just a great religious teacher among all the great religious teachers in history. It is God's sign that Jesus is not a religious charlatan among all the religious charlatans in the world. The resurrection is God's way of pointing to Jesus and saying that *he* is the one in whom you are to believe. *He* is your savior. *He* alone is Lord." (Davis, RI, 197)

The resurrection demonstrated the truth of what God the Father had said about Jesus at his baptism: "This is My beloved Son, in whom I am well pleased" (Matt. 3:17). If you are an honest enquirer into the truth of Christianity, the resurrection of Jesus is a great place to begin.

Misconception #6: "Christianity and science are at war."

Many believe science and religion are at war with each other. In fact, the belief that Christianity is opposed to modern science is one of the top reasons young people cite for leaving the church. (Kinnaman, YLM, 135–136)

But where did this idea come from? Is it accurate? In 1896 Cornell University president Andrew Dickson White released a book entitled *A History of the Warfare of Science with Theology in Christendom.* White is largely credited with inventing and propagating the idea that science and Christianity are adversaries in the search for truth. White cast Christians as fanatics who clung to scriptural claims that the earth was flat. But is this account true? Sociologist Rodney Stark responds,

> White's book remains influential despite the fact that modern historians of science dismiss it as nothing but a polemic—White himself admitted that he wrote the book to get even with Christian critics of his plans for Cornell . . . many of White's other accounts are as bogus as his report of the flat earth and Columbus. (Stark, FGG, 123)

Why has this warfare myth been so influential? Stark continues, "The truth concerning these matters is that the claim of an inevitable and bitter warfare between religion and science has, for more than three centuries, been the primary polemical device used in the atheist attack on faith." He concludes with the claim that "there is no inherent conflict between religion and science, but that *Christian theology was essential for the rise of science.*" (Stark, FGG, 123)

How is theology essential for science? In their book *The Soul of Science*, Nancy Pearcey and Charles Thaxton summarize the Christian assumptions that provided the backdrop for the emergence of the scientific revolution in Europe:

> Christian teachings have served as *presuppositions* for the scientific enterprise (e.g., the conviction that nature is lawful was inferred from its creation by a rational God). Second, Christian teachings have *sanctioned* science (e.g., science was justified as a means of alleviating toil and suffering). Third, Christian teachings supplied *motives* for pursuing science (e.g., to show the glory and wisdom of

the Creator). And fourth, Christianity played a role in *regulating* scientific methodology (e.g., voluntarist theology was invoked to justify an empirical approach in science). Among professional historians the image of warfare between faith and science has shattered. Replacing it is a widespread recognition of Christianity's positive contributions to modern science. (Pearcey and Thaxton, SS, 36–37)

Most scientific pioneers were theists, including prominent figures such as Nicolaus Copernicus (1473–1543), Robert Boyle (1627–1691), Isaac Newton (1642–1727), Blaise Pascal (1623–1662), Johannes Kepler (1571–1630), Louis Pasteur (1822–1895), Francis Bacon (1561–1626), and Max Planck (1858–1947). Many of these pioneers intently pursued science because of their belief in the Christian God. Bacon believed God meant for us to explore the many mysteries that filled the natural world. Kepler wrote, "The chief aim of all investigations of the external world should be to discover the rational order which has been imposed on it by God, and which he revealed to us in the language of mathematics." (quoted in Lennox, GU, 20) Newton believed his scientific discoveries offered convincing evidence for the existence and creativity of God. His favorite argument for design related to the solar system: "This most beautiful system of sun, planets, and comets could only proceed from the counsel and dominion of an intelligent and powerful being." (quoted in Pearcey and Thaxton, SS, 91)

While the theistic worldview fosters the development of science, naturalism undermines it. Since according to naturalism we humans are the product of a blind, purposeless, and unguided process, how can we trust our rational faculties? Outspoken philosopher of neuroscience Patricia Churchland agrees:

The principle chore of brains is to get the body parts where they should be in order that the organism may survive. Improvements in sensorimotor control confer an evolutionary advantage: a fancier style of representing [the world] is advantageous so long as it . . . enhances the organism's chances for survival. Truth, whatever that is, takes the hindmost. (Churchland, EAN, 548)

Notre Dame philosopher Alvin Plantinga further clarifies:

Churchland's point, clearly, is that (from a naturalist perspective) what evolution guarantees is (at most) that *we behave* in certain ways—in such ways as to promote survival, or more exactly reproductive success. The principal function or purpose, then, (the "chore" says Churchland) of our cognitive faculties is not that of producing true or verisimilitudinous (nearly true) beliefs, but instead that of contributing to survival by getting the body parts in the right place. What evolution underwrites is only (at most) that our *behavior* is reasonably adaptive to the circumstances in which our ancestors found themselves; hence it does not guarantee mostly true or verisimilitudinous beliefs. Our beliefs *might* be mostly true or verisimilitudinous; but there is no particular reason to think they *would* be: natural selection is interested, not in truth, but in appropriate behavior. (Plantinga, WCRL, 314–315)

Certainly, some Christians resist science. And, as Plantinga observes, there are some beliefs individual Christians hold that are in tension with modern science. But this is only *shallow* conflict. No real conflict between theism and science exists. As we have seen, theology provided the backdrop for the scientific revolution. The real conflict—the *deep* conflict—is between science and naturalism.

Misconception #7: "God has not provided enough evidence for rational belief."

As a college student, I (Sean) explored significant doubts I had about my faith. It bothered me that God didn't make his existence more obvious. In fact, one skeptic made me wonder, *Why doesn't God write "Jesus Saves" on the moon or "Made by God" on each cell?*

After carefully examining the evidence, however, I became convinced that God *has* made himself known (Rom. 1:18–21; 2:14, 15). Consider a few prominent arguments for the existence of God:

- *The Cosmological Argument*: Both scientific and philosophical reasons help us conclude that the universe, at some point, had a beginning. Given that something can't begin to exist without a cause, the cause must be *outside* the universe. Since matter, time, and energy simultaneously came into existence at a finite point in the past, the cause is plausibly timeless, immaterial, intelligent, powerful, and personal. Simply put, *the beginning of the universe points to a Beginner.*
- *The Fine-Tuning of the Laws of Physics*: The laws of physics that govern the universe are exquisitely fine-tuned for the emergence and sustenance of human life. The slightest changes in any number of physical constants would make our universe inhospitable. The most compelling and reliable explanation for why the universe is so precisely fine-tuned is that an Intelligent Mind made it that way. Simply put, *the fine-tuning of the universe points to a Fine-Tuner.*
- *The Design Argument from DNA*: Massive amounts of genetic information orchestrate cellular organization and

the development of living creatures, but natural forces cannot explain the origin of information (such as DNA). Yet every day we attribute the origins of information to minds. Simply put, then, *the vast amount of information contained in living organisms points to an Information Giver.*

- *The Moral Argument*: This argument reasons that since objective moral values exist, so must God. If God does not exist, then moral values are ultimately subjective and nonbinding. Yet we know objective moral values are real. Therefore, since moral values do exist, God must as well. Simply put, *the existence of moral values points to a universal Moral Lawgiver.*

Much more could be said—entire chapters and books, in fact! Ongoing debates about these arguments continue both inside and outside of academia. But after considering the scientific evidence for God, and in particular from DNA, skeptic-turned-believer Lee Strobel concluded, "The conclusion was compelling, an intelligent entity has quite literally spelled out the evidence of his existence through the four chemical letters in the genetic code. It's almost as if the Creator autographed every cell." (Strobel, CC, 244) We could not agree more. While God has not provided exhaustive knowledge of his existence, he has given *sufficient* knowledge for those with an open heart and mind.

But God is interested in much more than simply convincing us of his existence. William Lane Craig and J. P. Moreland explain:

Unsatisfied with the evidence we have, some atheists have argued that God, if he existed, would have prevented the world's unbelief by making his existence starkly apparent (say, by inscribing the label "made by God" on every atom or planting a neon cross in the heavens with the message "Jesus saves"). But why should God want to do such a thing? As Paul Moser has emphasized, on the Christian view it is actually a matter of relative indifference to God whether people believe that he exists or not. For what God is interested in is building a love relationship with us, not just getting us to believe that he exists. Even the demons believe that God exists—and tremble, for they have no saving relationship with him (James 2:19). Of course, in order to believe *in* God, we must believe *that* God exists. But there is no reason at all to think that if God were to make his existence more manifest, more people would come into a saving relationship with him. Mere showmanship will not bring a change of heart (Lk 16:30–31). It is interesting that, as the Bible describes the history of God's dealing with mankind, there has been a progressive interiorization of this interaction with an increasing emphasis on the Spirit's witness to our inner selves (Rom 8:16–17). In the Old Testament God is described as revealing himself to his people in manifest wonders: the plagues upon Egypt, the pillar of fire and smoke, and parting of the Red Sea. But did such wonders produce lasting heart-change in the people? No, Israel fell into apostasy with tiresome repetitiveness. If God were to inscribe his name on every atom or place a neon cross in the sky, people might believe that he exists; but what confidence could we have that after time they would not begin to chafe under the brazen advertisements of their Creator and even come to resent such effrontery? In fact, we have no way of knowing that in a world of free creatures in which God's existence is as obvious as the nose on your face that more people would come to love him and know his salvation than in the actual world. But then the claim that if God existed he would make his existence more evident has little or no warrant, thereby undermining the claim that the absence of such evidence is itself positive evidence that God does not exist. (Craig and Moreland, PFCW, 157–158)

If you find the evidence still wanting, perhaps consider whether you hold to non-evidential reasons for your nonbelief. Belief and unbelief often have more to do with psychology than rational argumentation. If you have a broken relationship with your father, for instance, you may find it difficult to believe in a loving, personal heavenly Father. This was certainly true for me (Josh). In fact, the idea of God as a "father" repulsed me, since my own father was an abusive alcoholic. Given the failure of my earthly father, I certainly didn't need a cosmic father telling me how to use my time, spend my money, or live my life. I didn't *want* to believe in God because it would mean radically reorienting my entire life.

Psychologist Paul Vitz has studied some of the great atheists of the past, such as Bertrand Russell, Jean Paul Sartre, Karl Marx, Camus, and Nietzsche. Remarkably, he found the vast majority had either a dead, distant, or disappointing father. He concludes, "If our own father is absent or weak or abandons us, even by dying, or is so untrustworthy as to desert us, or is so terrible as to abuse and to deceive us in various ways, it's not hard to put the same attributes on our heavenly Father and reject God." (Vitz, PA, 150)

Misconception #8: "Being a good person is enough to get to heaven."

Some time ago, I (Sean) had an in-depth discussion with a college student about the morality of hell. Even though I provided every philosophical and theological justification I could muster, he simply couldn't accept that

a loving and just God would send anyone to hell. After about an hour of conversation, it finally dawned on me. His primary problem was that he believed in the essential goodness of mankind. From his perspective, hell seemed like total overkill for basically good people who commit a few small indiscretions.

In one sense, he's right. If hell were the consequence for small missteps, it would seem remarkably unjust. C. S. Lewis has rightly observed, "When we *say* that we are bad, the 'wrath' of God seems a barbarous doctrine; as soon as we *perceive* our badness, it appears inevitable, a mere corollary from God's goodness." (Lewis, PP, 52)

The Bible has a very stark view of human nature. While human beings are the most valuable creation of a loving God, we have utterly rebelled against our Creator. We are deeply affected by sin. Theologian Wayne Grudem explains: "It is not just that some parts of us are sinful and others are pure. Rather, every part of our being is affected by sin—our intellects, our emotions and desires, our hearts (the center of our desires and decision-making processes), our goals and motives, and even our physical bodies." (Grudem, ST, 497) Thus, God doesn't send good people to hell; there is no such thing as a good person. And that includes you and me!

King David wrote, "They have all turned aside, they have together become corrupt; there is none who does good, no, not one" (Ps. 14:3). The apostle Paul wrote, "For I know that in me (that is, in my flesh) nothing good dwells" (Rom. 7:18) and, "To those who are defiled and unbelieving nothing is pure; but even their mind and conscience are defiled" (Titus 1:15). Jesus said, "What comes out of a person is what defiles him. For from within, out of the heart of man, come evil thoughts, sexual immorality, theft, murder, adultery, coveting, wickedness, deceit, sensuality, envy, slander, pride, foolishness. All these evil things come from within, and they defile a person" (Mark 7:20–23 ESV).

This depiction of human nature can be confirmed by looking at the history of humanity. Apologist Clay Jones has spent decades studying the problem of evil. He closely examined the evil perpetrated in the twentieth century by Nazis in Germany, communists in Russia, China, and Cambodia, the Japanese in World War II, and other nations including Turkey, Pakistan, Uganda, Sudan, and the United States. After immersing himself in these human tragedies, Jones concluded:

> I first began to study human evil so that no one could disqualify me for having glossed over the immense sufferings that people perpetrate on each other. I didn't want anyone to say that I had gotten God out of the problem of evil the easy way: by making evil seem less serious than it really is. But as I read about one sickening rape or torture or murder after another, something strange happened: I was struck that evil *is* human. I realized that heinous evils weren't the doings of a few deranged individuals or even of hundreds or of thousands, but were done by humankind *en masse*. I studied continent after continent, country after country, torture after torture, murder after murder and was staggered to discover that I hadn't taken Scripture seriously enough: humankind *is* desperately wicked. (Jones, CDTH, 1)

Human fallenness makes the gospel powerful: we can only appreciate the extent of the work of Christ when we understand the evil and corruption we and the world truly contain. This does not mean unbelievers cannot do some good in society—of course they can! However, sin has separated us so deeply from God that we have no power to save ourselves apart from God's grace (Eph. 2:1, 2). Paul makes it clear that "all have sinned and fall short of the glory of God" (Rom. 3:23). And this "falling short" is not merely a matter of our actions, but primarily a matter of the heart (1 John 3:15; Matt. 5:21–30).

This is why Jesus came. Although Jesus was (and is) fully God, he humbled himself to take on human flesh (Phil. 2:5–7) and experience the death that humans deserve. As a result, we can experience forgiveness for our sins and come to know God personally (John 17:1–5). Jesus explains:

> *For God so loved the world that He gave his only begotten Son, that whoever believes in Him should not perish but have everlasting life. For God did not send His Son into the world to condemn the world, but that the world through Him might be saved. He who believes in Him is not condemned; but he who does not believe is condemned already, because he has not believed in the name of the only begotten Son of God.*
> — John 3:16–18

So, is it enough to be a "good" person? It's true that many people may live outwardly good lives, but for Jesus evil is a matter of the heart. According to Jesus *no one* is good (Mark 10:18). Anyone who honestly reflects upon his life, and sincerely probes his heart, knows that this is true. Our only hope is found in Jesus Christ, the one mediator between God and man (1 Tim. 2:5).

Misconception #9: "A good God would prevent evil and suffering."

Evil and suffering become perhaps the most powerful reasons people struggle with the idea of God. Who has not at some point looked at the world and cried out, like the prophet Habakkuk, "O LORD, how long shall I cry, and You will not hear? Even cry out to You, 'Violence!' and You will not save?" (Hab. 1:2).

Evil and suffering are not merely intellectual matters to be solved, but belong to our personal experience. Evil is a matter of *both* the heart and the mind. Thus, even though this is a book of evidences, we encourage you to err on the side of being gracious and kind with others—especially those who are hurting. Sometimes arguments are unhelpful. When someone is hurting, the biblical response is to hurt with him or her (Rom. 12:15). As Christians, our ultimate response must be one of love. And yet *sometimes* love requires that we be prepared to speak the truth.

My (Josh's) father often said, "A problem well-defined is half-solved." It helps, then, first to define what we mean by *evil*. Despite what Eastern religions claim, evil is not an illusion, but neither is it a "thing." Rather, evil is a departure from the way things ought to be, a corruption of good. Just as rust cannot exist without iron, and a lie cannot exist without truth, so evil steals and corrupts from good. This means that there can be good without evil, but not evil without good. "That's why we often describe evil as negations of good things," observes apologist and speaker Frank Turek. "We say someone is *im*moral, *un*just, *un*fair, *dis*honest, etc." (Turek, SG, 117) Ironically, then, when someone raises the problem of evil, that person is assuming there is such a thing as objective good. And if there is objective good, then there must be a God.

C. S. Lewis was once an atheist who believed that evil disproved God. But upon deeper reflection, he changed his mind:

> My argument against God was that the universe seemed so cruel and unjust. But how had I got this idea of *just* and *unjust*? A man does not call a line crooked unless he has some idea of a straight line. What was I comparing the universe with when I called it unjust? (Lewis, MC, 45)

The existence of evil ends up being an argument *for* God. But if God is all-good, all-knowing, and all-powerful, wouldn't he want to end evil? Is there a contradiction in the conception of God and the reality of evil?

While critics often claim a contradiction between God and the presence of evil, thanks to Alvin Plantinga's *God, Freedom, and Evil* and the work of many other philosophers before Plantinga, professional philosophers widely regard the existence of God as not being incompatible with evil. Plantinga offers a morally sufficient reason why God may allow evil:

> A world containing creatures who are significantly free (and freely perform more good than evil actions) is more valuable, all else being equal, than a world containing no free creatures at all. Now God can create free creatures, but He can't cause or determine them to do only what is right.

My argument against God was that the universe seemed so cruel and unjust. But how had I got this idea of just and unjust? A man does not call a line crooked unless he has some idea of a straight line. What was I comparing the universe with when I called it unjust?

C. S. Lewis

For if He does so, then they aren't significantly free after all; and they do not do what is right freely. To create creatures capable of moral good, therefore, He must create creatures capable of moral evil; and He can't give these creatures the freedom to perform evil and at the same time prevent them from doing so. As it turned out, sadly enough, some of the free creatures God created went wrong in the exercise of their freedom; this is the source of moral evil. The fact that free creatures sometimes go wrong, however, counts neither against God's omnipotence nor against His goodness; for He could have forestalled the occurrence of moral evil only by removing the possibility of moral good. (Plantinga, GFE, 30)

According to Plantinga, God is not the creator of evil, nor is he morally culpable when humans misuse their freedom, any more than a car manufacturer is accountable when a drunk driver harms someone. Simply put, no logical incompatibility exists between God and the presence of evil in the world.

But doesn't evil make God *improbable*? Craig has noted that we need to consider *all* the background evidence for God, including the cosmological argument, various design arguments, the argument from mind, the moral argument, as well as all the historical evidence for the life, miracles, and resurrection of Jesus before we conclude that God's existence is improbable. "When we take into account the full scope of the evidence," says Craig, "the existence of God becomes quite probable. . . . Indeed, if [a person] includes the self-authenticating witness of the Holy Spirit as part of his total warrant, then he can rightly assert that he knows that God exists, even if he has no solution to the problem of evil." (Craig, HQRA, 90–91)

The atheist is ultimately silent in the face of evil. According to Richard Dawkins, here is what you can expect from the naturalistic account of reality:

In a universe of blind physical forces and genetic replication some people are going to get hurt, other people are going to get lucky, and you won't find any rhyme or reason in it, nor any justice. The universe we observe has precisely the properties we should expect if there is, at the bottom, no design, no purpose, no evil and no other good. Nothing but blind pitiless indifference. DNA neither knows nor cares. DNA just is. And we dance to its music. (Dawkins, ROE, 133)

But according to Christianity, God is not silent. God did not merely send an angel, prophet, or a book. In the incarnation of Jesus, *God gave himself.* God is not indifferent to our suffering. He took it on himself so we could experience salvation. Paul writes, "He who did not spare his own Son but gave him up for us all, how will he not also with him graciously give us all things?" (Rom. 8:32 ESV). At the cross, evil and sin were conquered; they await final destruction at Christ's return. Evil will not have the final word.

Misconception #10: "Biblical teaching on sex is repressive and hateful."

Let's face it; we live in a world saturated with sex. Our movies, music, novels, politics, and even advertisements are dominated by sex. Essentially, the celebrated view of sex in our culture is: *if it feels good, do it.* Anything that prevents someone from experiencing consensual sex in whatever fashion he or she desires is viewed as harmful and repressive. In *Letter to a Christian Nation*, influential atheist Sam Harris levels a common criticism against Christian sexual morality:

You [Christians] believe that your religious concerns about sex, in all their tiresome immensity, have something to do with morality. And yet, your efforts to constrain the sexual behavior of consenting adults—and even to discourage your own sons and daughters from having premarital sex—are almost never geared toward the relief of human suffering. In fact, relieving suffering seems to rank rather low on your list of priorities. Your principal concern appears to be that the creator of the universe will take offense at something people do while naked. (Harris, LCN, 25–26)

Many young Christians also see the church's sexual ethic as repressive, joyless, and controlling. (Kinnaman, YLM, 149–150) So, does God hate sex?

While Christians have certainly failed at times to teach and model the biblical view of sex, it is false to assume that God hates sex. In fact, the exact opposite is true—*God created sex and said that it was good*! Proverbs 5:18–19 says to "rejoice in the wife of your youth, a lovely deer, a graceful doe. Let her breasts fill you at all times with delight; be intoxicated always in her love" (ESV). And the Song of Solomon speaks of the power and beauty of sexual intimacy. Sex, as God designed it, is a wonderful thing. He designed it for four reasons: procreation, unity, recreation, and to glorify himself.

1. *Procreation.* Even though children don't always result, sex is a baby-making act by its very nature. In Genesis 1:28, God says, "Be fruitful and multiply and fill the earth" (ESV). It's worth noting that this is actually a *command* from God (it is also a blessing). Few complain about this command!
2. *Unity.* One of the most powerful aspects of sex is its ability to bond people together.

Genesis 2:24 says, "Therefore a man shall leave his father and his mother and hold fast to his wife, and they shall become one flesh" (ESV). In the act of sex, two people become fully united. Sex is not merely a physical act; it involves an emotional, relational, spiritual, and even transcendent connection.

3. *Recreation.* So many people think God is a cosmic killjoy when it comes to sex. But they fail to realize that God created sex to be pleasurable in the first place. God could easily have made sex boring and tedious—a mere duty, like taking out the trash or changing the oil in our car. Or he could have made humans reproduce asexually. But he made sex one of the most exhilarating of all human experiences.
4. *Glorify God.* We are to glorify God in everything we do. The apostle Paul says, "So, whether you eat or drink, or whatever you do, do all to the glory of God" (1 Cor. 10:31 ESV). When done with true love for another, in accord with God-ordained principles and boundaries, sex brings God glory.

Does God's view of sex really bring harm to people? Let us ask some simple questions: What would the world be like if everyone followed the biblical plan for sex, engaging in sexual activity in a committed, lifelong relationship with someone of the opposite sex? Would there be more suffering as Harris suggests? Or would there be less? Would we have more intact marriages, or more broken homes? Would there be more fatherless homes, or more involved fathers? Would STDs, teen pregnancies, and abortions increase or decrease?

Despite the cultural narrative that biblical guidelines bring repression and harm, medical doctors Joe McIlhaney and Freda

McKissic Bush conclude, "It appears that the most up-to-date research suggests that most humans are 'designed' to be sexually monogamous with one mate for life. This information also shows that the further individuals deviate from this behavior, the more problems they encounter, be they STDs, non-marital pregnancy, or emotional problems, including damaged ability to develop healthy connectedness with others, including future spouses." (McIlhaney and Bush, H, 129)

God doesn't hate sex. He gave it as a blessing and designed it for human flourishing. And he lovingly gave us boundaries to protect and provide for us.

V. Why Apologetics Has a Bad Name

According to Guinness, we live in a "grand age of apologetics." He says that "our age is quite simply the greatest opportunity for Christian witness since the time of Jesus and the apostles, and our response should be to seize the opportunity with bold and imaginative enterprise." (Guinness, FT, 16) Nevertheless, apologetics has often become about arguing with people rather than about truly, creatively, gently, lovingly persuading people. Thus, according to Guinness, our urgent need today "is to reunite evangelism and apologetics, to make sure that our best arguments are directed toward winning people and not just winning arguments, and to seek to do all this in a manner that is true to the gospel itself." (FT, 18)

We entirely agree. The church desperately needs an apologetics revolution that is tied to evangelism. And yet even though this need is urgent, many continue to disparage apologetics. Some criticisms come from a lack of understanding the nature, role, and importance of apologetics. Others lie at the hands of apologists themselves.

There are at least five reasons apologetics often has a bad name (adapted from S. McDowell, WAHBN):

1. *Apologists Often Overstate Their Case*: There is a huge temptation to overstate the evidence for the Bible, Intelligent Design, the resurrection of Jesus, or any other apologetics issue. We have each succumbed to this at different times. Our eagerness to convince nonbelievers, or our desire to strengthen fellow Christians, contributes to our falling prey to the temptation to state things more certainly than they are. This does not mean the evidence for Christianity is not compelling. It is. But there are smart, thoughtful people who disagree. We must acknowledge this, or we'll set up people—especially young people—for disappointment and failure.

2. *Apologists Often Do Not Speak with Gentleness, Respect, and Love*: A few years ago I (Sean) had a public debate on the question of God and morality. As part of my preparation, I watched many debates on the subject. Although I won't mention any names, a handful of Christian debaters honestly made me cringe at how they treated their opponents. One debater demeaned and personally attacked his opponent, a former Christian. We probably all have an example of some overly eager apologist who was unnecessarily argumentative rather than loving. I (Josh) have had more than 250 debates on college campuses. While I aim to win arguments, my bigger goal is to win the audience. I must show genuine love, then, toward my opponent, even while I critique his case. Of course, we must not shy away from speaking truth—but we must do it in love.

3. *Apologists Often Are Not Emotionally Healthy*: Youth expert Mark Matlock

wrote a compelling essay about apologetics and emotional development. (Matlock, AED) In it, he argues that apologetics often attracts emotionally hurt people who in turn use apologetics to hurt others. He's absolutely right. As the saying famously goes, "Hurt people hurt people." There is power in knowledge. And by gaining information, many seek the power to control and even humiliate other people. So we ask you to consider: Why (honestly) are you reading this book? Are you looking for "ammo"? Is your heart genuinely broken for non-Christians? Are you really seeking truth? Do you pray for humility and guidance in your research and conversations with both Christians and non-Christians?

4. *Apologetics Often Is Done in a Cold, Mechanical, and Rationalistic Manner*: Many think of Christian apologetics as something like the Vulcans of Star Trek, who live solely by reason—void of emotion, without passion or relationship, or even good, old-fashioned storytelling. Apologetics is often seen as a narrow discipline for lawyers and doctors. But apologetics should not be done this way. It ought to engage the mind *through the heart, imagination, and emotions.* C. S. Lewis beautifully modeled this approach with his use of fiction. I (Josh) have spoken at more than 1,200 universities worldwide. Whenever I speak on an apologetics subject, I always tell my personal story of how God transformed me from a background of hurt, anger, and abuse. People need to see the truth of Christianity, but just as importantly, they need to see how that truth can personally change their lives.

5. *Apologists Often Are Intellectually Elitist*: If you are reading this book to acquire some big words such as *evidential,*

ontological, or *bibliographical* to impress your friends, then you probably need to get a different book. Precision and clarity, while important, especially for apologists and philosophers, are not meant to make you sound smart—but for you genuinely to help people. When I (Josh) began speaking on college campuses in the 1960s, Bill Bright, founder of Campus Crusade for Christ, told me to remember K-I-S-S, which stands for "Keep It Simple, Stupid." Sometimes the "big" words apologists use detract from our effectiveness. In fact, even the word "apologetics" is unfamiliar and off-putting to many people. So while we ought to use precise words—to communicate truth clearly—let's try to focus on communicating *effectively.*

There are probably some more reasons why apologetics has a bad name in certain circles. But before we go any further, please allow us to ask you some tough questions: *Do you overstate your case? Do you speak with gentleness and love? Are you emotionally healthy? Are you coldly rational in your apologetics? Do you use sophisticated words when simple ones will do?*

For the sake of the church and wider culture, we ought to do apologetics and evangelism in the way that Jesus did—with both grace and truth.

VI. Being a Relational Apologist

The world has changed since *Evidence That Demands a Verdict* was first published in 1972. There were few popular apologetics books at that time. The kind of information you'll find in this book simply was not available to the masses, so Christians and non-Christians were often unaware of the evidence for Christianity. Today, however, we have the opposite problem. If anything, we have an overload of information. People have to determine which information is important and which information they can trust. The vast amount of information means that someone looking for something to question the truth of Christianity can always find it.

People often ask us for the "silver bullet" argument that proves Christianity. But *there's not any argument that can force anyone to believe*. Philosopher Michael J. Murray says it well:

> There are no arguments for the truth of Christianity which force the atheist or non-Christian to their intellectual knees. . . . We can't sledgehammer unbelievers into belief. At best, we can show them how the beliefs that they hold, or that they ought to hold, lead to or support the Christian view. They can continue to backtrack and readjust to avoid these conclusions. And so the best we can hope for is to show them that their worldview . . . becomes so ungainly and cumbersome in accounting for things, that it is more reasonable to give a different intellectual accounting of the world. (Murray, RH, 13–14)

So, how should Christians engage their neighbors? We commend to you four points (adapted from S. McDowell, NKA):

1. *An Apologist Must Be Gentle and Humble.* Jesus was the first Christian apologist. In John 5–8, Jesus reasoned with the religious leaders of his day, providing multiple lines of evidence that he is the Son of God. And yet, even though he is divine, Jesus willingly humbled himself for the sake of loving others (Phil. 2:5–7). We can do no less. Philosopher Dallas Willard observed,

Like Jesus, we are reaching out in love in a humble spirit with no coercion. The only way to accomplish that is to present our defense gently, as help offered in love in the manner of Jesus. But that is not all. The means of our communication needs to be gentle, because gentleness also characterizes the subject of our communication. What we are seeking to defend or explain is Jesus himself, who is a gentle, loving shepherd. If we are not gentle in how we present the good news, how will people encounter the gentle and loving Messiah we want to point to? (Willard, AG, 4)

2. *An Apologist Must Be Relational.* While labels can sometimes be helpful, depersonalizing people, by putting them into various boxes, can cause harm. If our labels cause us to ignore the unique personhood of *every* individual, we need to reexamine how we use them. We work hard to have genuine relationships with people who are atheists, Mormons, agnostics, and others who hold a variety of worldviews. Our goal is not simply to convert them, but to value them as human beings. Apologetics is not an abstract discipline, then, but an explanation offered to help people we deeply care about. If you are going to be an effective apologist today, you must build relationships with people of varying faiths, so you can speak from a heart of genuine care.

3. *An Apologist Must Be Studious.* Apologists must do their homework. We must know what we are talking about and do thorough research to back up our claims. We must critically examine our arguments and understand both sides of every issue. We encourage you to read for yourself the scholarly sources we cite. And read critical reviews of this book. Study both

sides and talk about your findings with fellow Christians and non-Christians. Apologists must do the hard work of learning a discipline and presenting the truth fairly and accurately.

4. *An Apologist Must Be a Practitioner.* Authenticity is highly prized among young people today. They want to know not only if we can make a good argument, but also whether our lives reflect the truth we proclaim. If our lives don't reflect our truth claims, what we say will fall on deaf ears. If you claim to believe in the deity of Jesus, is he really Lord in your life? If you believe in the resurrection, does it shape how you face death? How does your belief in the truth of the Bible really shape how you treat people? We must actively live the truth we proclaim.

VII. A Clear Presentation of the Gospel Is the Best Offense

My Personal Experience

For my (Josh's) philosophical apologetics course in graduate school, everyone had to write a paper on "The Best Defense of Christianity." I found myself constantly putting it off and avoided writing it, not because I didn't have the material but because I felt I was at odds with what the professor was expecting (an expectation based on the ream of my lecture notes from his class).

Finally I decided to voice my convictions. I began my paper with the sentence, "Some people say the best offense is a good defense, but I say to you that the best defense is a good offense." I proceeded by explaining that I felt the best defense of Christianity is a "clear, simple presentation of the claims of Christ and who he is, in the power of the Holy Spirit." I then wrote out "The Four Spiritual Laws" and recorded my testimony of how, on

December 19, 1959, at 8:30 p.m., during my second year at university, I placed my trust in Christ as Savior and Lord. I concluded the paper with a presentation of the evidence for the resurrection.

The professor must have agreed with my approach that the best defense of Christianity is a clear and compelling presentation of the gospel, for he gave me an A. William Tyndale was right in saying that "a ploughboy with the Bible would know more of God than the most learned ecclesiastic who ignored it." In other words, an Arkansas farm boy sharing the gospel can be more effective in the long run than a Harvard scholar with his intellectual arguments.

One precaution when using apologetics: God saves—apologetics does not. On the other hand, God often uses apologetics, or evidences, to help clear away obstacles to faith that many people erect, and also to show that faith in Christ is reasonable. The great Princeton theologian and apologist Benjamin Warfield declared:

> It certainly is not in the power of all the demonstrations in the world to make a Christian. Paul may plant and Apollos water; it is God alone who gives the increase. . . . [I]t does not in the least follow that the faith that God gives is an irrational faith, that is, a faith without grounds in right reason. . . . We believe in Christ because it is rational to believe in him, not though it be irrational. . . . We are not absurdly arguing that apologetics has in itself the power to make a man a Christian or to conquer the world to Christ. Only the Spirit of Life can communicate life to a dead soul, or can convict the world in respect of sin, and of righteousness, and of judgment. But we are arguing that faith is, in all its exercises alike, a form of conviction, and is, therefore, necessarily grounded in evidence. (Warfield, IN, 24–25)

We are not absurdly arguing that apologetics has in itself the power to make a man a Christian or to conquer the world to Christ. Only the Spirit of Life can communicate life to a dead soul, or can convict the world in respect of sin, and of righteousness, and of judgment. . . . But we are arguing that faith is, in all its exercises alike, a form of conviction, and is, therefore, necessarily grounded in evidence.

Benjamin Warfield

A Former French Atheist Becomes a Christian

Guillaume Bignon is a former French atheist who now considers himself a Christian philosopher and apologist. His story shows the importance of apologetics, but also of relationships, patience, and clearly presenting the gospel. In an interview for my blog, I (Sean) asked Guillaume what advice he has for Christians to share their faith with non-Christians. His answer is revealing:

Never assume that your hearer knows the Gospel. Between my French family and friends, and my work on Wall Street, I meet tons of people, grown ups, who have a surface level understanding of religions, but are absolutely clueless about what the Bible teaches in answer to the question "what must a sinner do to be saved?'

Somehow, I myself lived through age 25 without ever having heard that the Bible teaches sinners are saved by faith and not by works. I was stunned, and it took me a while to even process it: Heaven is for free? Given as a gift to those who would just repent of their sins and place their faith in Jesus? Amazing. So here is my tip: early on in your conversations, make sure you say something like this: "Let's set aside the arguments and reasons to think it's true. I'm not yet trying to convince you that it's a correct teaching. But let me explain to you briefly what Christianity *teaches*, what

the Christian view *is*." Go on to tell them the Gospel (of course you need to be able to do just that, so prepare yourself to explain it clearly and Biblically).

I have done this over and over again, and have surprised more than a few listeners. And how do I know they get it? Because, without fail, the first thing out of their mouth is Paul's very anticipated objection straight out of Romans: "If salvation is by faith, why not go on sinning?" Answer that too, but rest assured that *now* they get it; they get just how shocking the Gospel is, and you're prepared to discuss its merits. (Interview in McDowell, FFABC)

VIII. Conclusion

Although much more could be said, it is time to get to the evidence. We have studied the nature of apologetics, considered reasons why people often dismiss apologetics, examined why apologetics matters today, and cleared away some of the mental "fog." Now, then, we ask, "Is there compelling evidence to show that Christianity is actually true?" We believe there is. There is significant evidence to help the reasonable person conclude that God exists and has revealed himself in the person of Jesus Christ. We believe God wants us to know that we can know him personally. Read on to discover EVIDENCE THAT DEMANDS A VERDICT!

PROLOGUE: A THEISTIC UNIVERSE

OVERVIEW

I. Introduction

In the coming chapters, we will consider evidence for matters such as the reliability of the Bible, the deity of Christ, and the historical resurrection of Jesus, revealing strong historical evidence that confirms the Christian worldview. If we have the authentic words of Jesus claiming to be God, evidence that he genuinely performed miracles, and confirmation that Jesus resurrected from the grave, then Christianity is undeniably true.

But there is another way to approach our task. Rather than beginning with the historical data, we can evaluate the scientific and philosophical evidence of whether we live in a theistic or atheistic universe, and then consider what this means for the probability of the Christian worldview. If we live in an atheistic universe, then Christianity is certainly false. But if we live in a theistic universe, or if we at least have good reason to believe we do, then Christian claims become more probable. The late deist philosopher Antony Flew (who was formerly an atheist) said, "Certainly given some beliefs about God, the occurrence of the resurrection does become enormously more likely." (Habermas and Flew, DJRD, 39)

In our experience of study and dialogue with so many people who seek answers to the great questions about life's meaning—and in particular, whether they can believe in God or Christianity—we have found that resistance to the miracle claims of Jesus does not arise primarily from problems with the evidence, but from the worldview lurking *behind* consideration of the evidence—naturalism. Professor and apologist David Baggett notes:

> The presumed adequacy of naturalism is a huge driving force in the minds of those rigidly skeptical of all miracle claims. It's not necessarily an irrational position to hold; there are very intelligent atheists out there whose secular presuppositions radically differ from my own, but who strike me as fair-minded and intellectually honest. If they hold what they sincerely consider to be very principled reasons for supreme confidence in naturalism to provide all the explanations we need, it's, well, natural for them to put up great resistance against miraculous claims, or even claims likely to point in that direction.
>
> To my thinking, naturalism encounters some severe difficulties. It's challenged in explaining seemingly answered prayers and documented cases of evidentially significant near-death experiences. It fares poorly in accounting for qualia [interior awareness], consciousness, the emergence of life and the start of the universe. It lacks resources in accounting for human reason itself—if we're complicated organic machines whose every choice is caused by antecedent conditions and the physical laws of the world. I think naturalism is especially vulnerable when it comes to accounting for such realities as moral regret, moral obligations, moral rights and moral freedom, all of which makes considerably more sense from a theistic viewpoint. Naturalism certainly doesn't deserve the sort of unbridled allegiance and undying devotion that some would give it, and it certainly doesn't qualify to be what sets the terms for surrender in this debate. (Baggett, DRH, 137–138)

Needless to say, one's prior commitment to naturalism (or some other non-Christian worldview) will powerfully influence how one evaluates the evidence for the historical Jesus. Yet if we have reason to doubt naturalism, then the case for Christianity becomes more probable. New Testament scholar and philosopher of religion Gary Habermas explains,

> If it can be successfully argued that naturalism is insufficient as an explanation of the universe and that an explanation like theism, which incorporates an external intelligent source, is plausible, then it may also be rational to believe that the resurrection of Jesus was an act performed in accordance with God's attributes and will. If this is a theistic universe, then we might require even less direct evidence to affirm God's intervention in this or other historical occurrences, since miracles might follow, due to what we would know concerning the nature of the universe. (Habermas, RJFH, 53)

In this prologue, we have three goals: (1) explain the role and nature of presuppositions, (2) define naturalism, and (3) highlight six lines of evidence that undermine naturalism and point positively towards theism. Our goal in this chapter is not to *prove* the existence of God, but to show that theism is a reasonable position. In fact, we believe that, when properly understood, the universe reveals evidence of an Intelligent Mind. Naturalism simply fails to account for certain features of the universe, which by comparison, are at home in a theistic worldview. And as a result, as Flew observed, "the occurrence of the resurrection does become enormously more likely."

II. The Role of Presuppositions

This section discusses the definition of *presupposition*, followed by a short list of synonymous terms, and concludes with the nature of presuppositions.

A. A Definition of *Presupposition*

A *presupposition* is something assumed or supposed in advance. Generally, a presupposition is a basic belief—a belief that one holds as self-evident and not requiring proof for its validity. A presupposition is something that is assumed to be true and is taken for granted. Synonyms include: prejudgment, assumption of something as true, prejudice, forejudgment, preconceived opinion, fixed conclusion, preconceived notion, and premature conclusion.

B. The Nature of Presuppositions

Presuppositions serve as the glue that holds arguments together. Philosopher John Frame identifies presuppositions with *a priori* knowledge:

> *A priori* knowledge is knowledge possessed independent of experience—that knowledge which we bring to our experience in order to analyze and evaluate it. Some philosophers have tried to make the case that all our knowledge is *a posteriori*—that the mind begins as a "blank slate" (Locke) to be written out by experience. But we know some things that do not seem to be derived from experience. For example, the proposition that two times two is four—necessarily and everywhere in the universe—does not seem to be derivable from any experience. The term *presupposition* . . . captures much of the meaning that philosophers have sought to include under the label *a priori*. (Frame, CVT, 132–33)

Philosophers and apologists Steven Cowan and James Spiegel assert that,

> All truth claims which are assumed without argument are called *presuppositions*. While we could argue for each of our presuppositions . . . , every argument we used would itself make several presuppositions. In turn, we could provide arguments for those presuppositions, and so on. However, this process cannot go on forever. This shows that one cannot avoid having presuppositions. (Cowan and Spiegel, LW, 6)

No discipline operates without presuppositions guiding its study and investigation—even science, which some perceive as objective and bias-free; that is, everyone has a worldview—and worldviews inform both how we understand the world and how we answer life's ultimate questions. The beliefs comprising our worldview are intricately connected; some are basic, requiring no proof, and these are our presuppositions. Other beliefs are directly informed by presuppositions, supporting other beliefs. Every belief, then, connects to and ultimately finds its root in one or more of our presuppositions.

So we must identify our presuppositions and understand why we affirm these presuppositions as opposed to others, and we must ask whether our presuppositions are reasonable and true. After all, not everyone's presuppositions are valid; one may hold as basic a false belief. We might question beliefs due to faulty presuppositions, or note that even good presuppositions do not necessarily give rise to beliefs that are true.

Before analyzing the presuppositions of naturalism, the term *naturalism* must first be clearly defined.

III. Naturalism

The worldview of naturalism has a long and storied past. Ancient Greek philosophy—the seedbed of modern Western philosophy— witnessed influential thinkers who operated from a naturalistic perspective. Thinkers such as Democritus and Epicurus still wield significant influence for those who attempt to construct a view of the world devoid of the supernatural. Relative to its long history, however, naturalism's role as a formidable challenge to Christianity is fairly recent. As the Enlightenment emphasized human reason over divine revelation, philosophers, theologians, and scientists increasingly appealed to naturalism as a more satisfactory and sufficient explanation of the universe.

These historical and philosophical movements resulted in naturalism's omnipresence throughout Western culture. We see it whenever clergy or professors of religion explain the miracles of Jesus as "crowd psychology." We hear it whenever a PBS nature program credits nature for some remarkable wonder like the march of the penguins, rather than God. We see it when psychologists, ignoring that we are fallen beings created in the image of God, claim that we lie or cheat on our spouses because our supposed cave ancestors transmitted lying or cheating "genes" to us.

A. Defining Naturalism

Naturalism is a nuanced term, and many use it ambiguously, referring both to how we practice science and how we use it as a worldview. Such ambiguity might give the impression that the scientific endeavor itself is at odds with faith. That idea assumes that science is atheistic in its methodology and resulting knowledge. The Christian, however, need not conflate the scientific endeavor with naturalism *as a worldview*. As we saw in the introduction in the beginning of this book, the scientific revolution emerged in a culture shaped by a Christian worldview. And, in fact, some of the greatest scientific pioneers believed that design could be detected throughout nature. Philosopher Stephen Meyer explains,

As I studied the history of science, I soon discovered, however, that many of these scientists did not just assume or assert by faith that the universe had been designed; they also argued for their hypothesis based on discoveries in their disciplines. Johannes Kepler perceived intelligent design in the mathematical precision of planetary motion and the three laws he discovered that describe that motion. Other scientists perceived design in many of the structures or features of the natural world upon which the laws of nature operated. Louis Agassiz, the leading American naturalist of the nineteenth century, for whom Agassiz Chair is named at Harvard, believed that the patterns of appearance in the fossil record pointed unmistakably to design. Carl Linnaeus argued for design based upon the ease with which plants and animals fell into an orderly groups-within-groups system of classification. Robert Boyle insisted that the intricate clocklike regularity of many physical mechanisms suggested the activity of "a most intelligent and designing agent." Newton, in particular, was noteworthy in this regard . . . he made specific design arguments based upon discoveries in physics, biology, and astronomy. (Meyer, SC, 145)

As I studied the history of science, I soon discovered . . . that many of these scientists did not just assume or assert by faith that the universe had been designed; they also argued for their hypothesis based on discoveries in their disciplines.

Stephen Meyer

B. Metaphysical Naturalism

Philosophers and apologists J. P. Moreland and William Lane Craig provide a helpful definition of metaphysical naturalism:

> The term *naturalism* has many different meanings, but a standard use of the term defines it as the view that the [material] universe alone exists. Since most current forms of naturalism are physicalist in flavor, naturalism has come to mean that reality is exhausted by the spatio-temporal world of physical objects accessible in some way to the senses and embraced by our best scientific theories. (Moreland and Craig, PFCW, 184)

By the "universe," Moreland and Craig mean physical objects that are in some way accessible to the senses and scientific investigation. Thus, the universe includes individual things like rocks, atoms, rivers, flashes of lightning, and processes like osmosis.

Physicist Stephen Barr says that naturalism is the view that "nothing exists except matter, and that everything in the world must therefore be the result of the strict mathematical laws of physics and blind chance." (Barr, MPAF, 1)

Three important conclusions follow from metaphysical naturalism:

1. *No immaterial entities exist, such as souls, morals, purposes, minds, angels, and God.* Since these objects are not physical, the consistent naturalist concludes that they do not exist.
2. *Scientific investigation becomes the primary (or sole) means of gaining knowledge about the world.* According to philosopher John Cowburn, *scientism* is the view that "only scientific knowledge is valid . . . that science can explain and do everything and that nothing else can explain or do

anything: it is the belief that science and reason, or scientific and rational, are co-extensive terms." (Cowburn, *Scientism*, 14)
3. *Naturalism shapes how people live.* Philosopher Alvin Plantinga explains,

> It [naturalism] isn't clearly a religion: the term "religion" is vague, and naturalism falls into the vague area of its application. Still, naturalism plays many of the same roles as a religion. In particular, it gives answers to the great human questions: Is there such a person as God? How should we live? Can we look forward to life after death? What is our place in the universe? How are we related to other creatures? Naturalism gives answers here: there is no God, and it makes no sense to hope for life after death. As to our place in the grand scheme of things, we human beings are just another animal with a peculiar way of making a living. Naturalism isn't clearly a religion; but since it plays some of the same roles as a religion, we could properly call it a *quasi*-religion. (Plantinga, WCRL, ix–x)

C. Science vs. Metaphysical Naturalism

Metaphysical naturalism in Western culture has posed a significant challenge to Christianity. Because of its appeal to science, both Christians and non-Christians alike have often conflated the discipline of science with metaphysical naturalism. As a result, many well-meaning Christians have unnecessarily viewed science as hostile to the Christian faith. For such believers, science and the Christian faith are diametrically opposed to each other.

If viewed properly, however—that is, if science is held distinct from the worldview of metaphysical naturalism—then science can be of significant service to Christianity, explaining the many wonders of God's creation, demonstrating the orderliness of the universe, and confirming the truth of Scripture. On the other hand, metaphysical naturalism is directly opposed to Christianity because it denies the existence of the supernatural.

As a worldview, metaphysical naturalism fails to make sense of certain features of the universe. In the next section, we consider six characteristics of the world that resist a naturalistic explanation but which fit seamlessly within theism: the origin of the universe; the fine-tuning of the universe; the origin of life; consciousness; free will; and morality. We will see that these six features of the world provide good reason to believe we live in a theistic universe.

IV. Evidence for Theism

A. The Origin of the Universe

Up until the twentieth century, we had no scientific means to judge whether the universe was eternal or had a beginning. Atheists claimed the universe alone was eternal, which would have meant it was largely static and uniform. Theists countered that God is the ultimate cause of the world and that he alone is infinite and eternal. But this began to change in the early part of the twentieth century—when Einstein developed his general theory of relativity. Einstein's equations suggested that the universe was not static, but that it was either expanding or contracting. An expanding universe (measured by Hubble in 1929) coupled with general relativity strongly implies that the universe began to exist at some point in the past. After Einstein, others have discovered additional, powerful evidence that the universe had a beginning.

This has brought newfound support for an argument known as the *kalam* cosmological argument, popularized today by philosopher William Lane Craig (see Craig and Sinclair, KCA, 101–201). It has three premises:

1. Everything that begins to exist has a cause.
2. The universe began to exist.
3. Therefore, the universe has a cause.

Craig has ably defended each of these premises. As for the first premise, Craig says,

First and foremost, it's rooted in the metaphysical intuition that something cannot come into being from nothing. To suggest that things could just pop into being uncaused out of nothing is to quit doing serious metaphysics and to resort to magic. Second, if things really could come into being uncaused out of nothing, then it becomes inexplicable why just anything and everything do not come into existence uncaused from nothing. Finally, the first premise is constantly confirmed in our experience (Craig, RF, 111–112).

Critics of this argument often respond to the first premise by asking, "What caused God?" (see Dennett, BS, 242) But this misconstrues the argument. The first premise does not say that everything needs a cause, but *whatever begins to exist* has a cause. Since God did not begin to exist, he does not need a cause. This criticism also commits the category fallacy, in which things from one category are incorrectly applied to another. For instance, it would be a category mistake to ask, "What does the color red smell like?" or "How much does the musical note 'C' weigh?" Colors and smells, as well as musical notes and weight, are different categories. Similarly, it is a mistake to ask, "What caused God?" because, by definition, God is *uncaused*. God could not be caused and still be God. Asking what caused God is essentially asking a nonsense question, namely, "What caused the uncaused Creator of the universe?"

Additionally, even critics recognize that the universe beginning to exist requires something uncaused. While denying a personal, loving God, they usually argue that the "laws of physics" just exist, and given the laws of physics, the universe inevitably pops into existence. (Hawking and Mlodinow, GD, 142)

As for the second premise, Craig offers both philosophical and scientific arguments. As to scientific arguments, he points to the evidence from the second law of thermodynamics, the success of the Standard Cosmological Model (which implies an expanding universe), and the failure of other cosmological models such as the Steady State Theory and Oscillating Models. Even Vacuum Fluctuation Models, String Scenarios, and Multiverse Models don't avoid a beginning. However, a final answer to the question will require the right Quantum Gravity Model. He concludes, "The history of twentieth century cosmogony has, in one sense, been a series of failed attempts to craft acceptable non-standard models of the expanding universe in such a way as to avert the absolute beginning predicted by the Standard Model." (Craig, RF, 139)

As for the philosophical support of the second premise, Jonathan Morrow and I (Sean) put one of the arguments this way:

Imagine you went for a walk in the park and stumbled across someone proclaiming aloud, ". . . five, four, three, two, one—there, I finally finished! I just counted down from infinity!" What would be your initial thought? Would you wonder how long the person had been counting? Probably not. More likely, you would be in utter disbelief. Why? Because you know that such a task cannot be done. Just as it's impossible to count up to infinity from

the present moment, it's equally impossible to count down from . . . infinity to the present moment. Counting to infinity is impossible because there is always (at least) one more number to count. In fact, every time you count a number, you still have infinite more to go, and thus get no closer to your goal. Similarly, counting down from infinity to the present moment is equally impossible. Such a task can't even get started! Any point you pick in the past to begin, no matter how remote, would always require (at least) one more number to count before you could start there. Any beginning point would require an infinite number of previous points. Here's the bottom line: we could never get to the present moment if we had to cross an actual infinite number of moments in the past. Yet, since the present moment is real, it must have been preceded by a finite past that includes a beginning or first event. Therefore, the universe had a beginning. (McDowell and Morrow, IGJHI, 75–76)

The reality that the universe had a beginning brings us to the question of cause, the third premise. Flew puts this finding into perspective:

When I first met the big-bang theory as an atheist, it seemed to me the theory made a big difference because it suggested that the universe had a beginning and that the first sentence in Genesis ("In the beginning, God created the heavens and the earth") was related to an event in the universe. As long as the universe could be comfortably thought to be not only without end but also without beginning, it remained easy to see its existence (and its most fundamental features) as brute facts. And if there had been no reason to think the universe had a beginning, there would be no need to postulate something else that produced the whole thing. But the big-bang theory changed all that. If the universe had a beginning, it becomes entirely sensible, almost inevitable, to ask what produced this beginning. (Flew and Varghese, TIG, 136)

Even if this argument succeeds, it still does not get us all the way to the Christian God. The *kalam* argument cannot demonstrate that the Bible is reliable, that Jesus is God, or that Christianity is true; it reveals only that the universe was made and that someone made it—in short, that metaphysical naturalism does not fully account for the universe. Further, though, the *kalam* argument helps narrow the range of possible causes to a nonphysical, spaceless, timeless, changeless, and powerful being. William Lane Craig and James Sinclair conclude:

The first premise of the *kalam* cosmological argument is obviously more plausibly true than its contradictory. Similarly, in light of both philosophical argument and scientific evidence, its second premise, although more controversial, is again more plausibly true than its negation. The conclusion of the argument involves no demonstrable incoherence and, when subjected to conceptual analysis, is rich in theological implications. On the basis of the *kalam* cosmological argument, it is therefore plausible that an uncaused, personal Creator of the universe exists, who sans the universe is beginningless, changeless, immaterial, timeless, spaceless, and enormously powerful (Craig and Sinclair, KCA, 196).

To be sure, debates continue about the efficacy of the *kalam* cosmological argument. But the argument provides a significant challenge to naturalism and positive support that we live in a theistic universe. Philosopher and mathematician David Berlinski, a secular Jew, concludes:

The universe has *not* proceeded from everlasting to everlasting. The cosmological beginning may be obscure, but the universe is finite in time. This is something that until the twentieth century was not known. When it became known, it astonished the community of physicists—and everyone else. If nothing else, the facts of Big Bang cosmology indicate that one objection to the argument that Thomas Aquinas offered is empirically unfounded: Causes in nature do come to an end. If science has shown that God does not exist, it has not been by appealing to Big Bang cosmology. The hypothesis of God's existence and the facts of contemporary cosmology are *consistent*. (Berlinski, DD, 80, emphasis original)

B. A Fine-Tuned Universe

One of the most remarkable scientific findings of the twentieth century is the delicate fine-tuning of the laws that govern the universe, which enable the emergence and sustenance of intelligent life. Like the scientific confirmation of the beginning of the universe, fine-tuning poses a significant challenge to naturalism.

Scientists have been struck by how precisely the laws of physics seem to be calibrated for life. "There are many such examples of the universe's life-friendly properties," says science and nature writer Tim Folger in *Discover* magazine, "so many, in fact, that physicists can't dismiss them all as mere accidents" (Folger, SAIC). British astronomer Fred Hoyle remarked, "A commonsense interpretation of the facts suggests that a super intellect has monkeyed with physics, as well as chemistry and biology, and that there are no blind forces worth speaking about in nature." (Hoyle, quoted in Davies, AU, 118)

Let's consider some examples.

1. The Right Kind of Dimensions in Space and Time

Often, space and time are taken for granted. We live in a 3+1 universe (three large spatial dimensions + 1 time dimension), but scientists recognize that the actual number of dimensions can be fluid. They even contend that our universe contains many extremely small spatial dimensions. However, if those tiny dimensions had grown like the three large spatial ones, no life could exist. Fewer than three spatial dimensions would prohibit the complexity that life requires, but more than three would result in no stable atoms or planets. More or fewer than one time dimension would remove the predictable, reliable order to the universe that life demands. Only a 3+1 dimensional universe permits life. (Tegmark, ODS, 69–75).

2. The Right Kind of Space

The universe must expand at the proper rate in order for life's components (atoms, stars, planets, etc.) to form. The initial expansion rate, mass/energy density, and dark energy (also called the cosmological constant or space energy density) all affect the expansion rate. The gravitational attraction of the mass/energy density results in a slowing of the expansion. The dark energy causes the universe to expand more rapidly—and the larger the universe gets, the more the dark energy accelerates the expansion. The mass/energy density contributed the greatest influence earlier in the universe, but dark energy dominates today. The amount of dark energy measured by astronomers falls far below the value expected by scientists—by a factor of 10^{120}! Imagine dropping millions of planets into a very large pool of water. The expected result would be planet-sized waves. If the surface measured flat down to the atomic level, that would be 10^{16} times

smaller than expected. Not only is the dark energy miniscule compared to its expected value, only a small range of values permit a universe with atoms, planets, and stars (Lightman, AU, 14–18).

3. The Fundamental Forces of Nature

Each of the four fundamental forces of nature had to be carefully fine-tuned for life: gravity, electromagnetism, the strong nuclear force, and the weak nuclear force. In particular, the ratio of the electromagnetic force to the gravitational force must be delicately balanced to one part in 10^{40} (that is one part in 10,000,000,000,000,000,000,000, 000,000,000,000,000,000). If the ratio varied even slightly, then our universe would not have small and large stars, which are both necessary for a planet to sustain life. Large stars produced most of the elements heavier than helium. These stars burn rapidly and end with explosions that scatter the heavier elements into the galaxy for incorporation into future stars. Smaller stars (like the Sun) burn much longer, providing the stability that a life-supporting planet requires. How delicate a balance is this? Imagine covering one billion continents the size of North America with coins. Stack the coins in columns that reach to the moon. Paint one coin red and place it in one of the columns. Blindfold a friend and have her attempt to pick it out. The odds are roughly 1 in 10^{40} that she will. (Ross, CC, 117)

4. Rare Conditions on Earth

Recent scientific discoveries confirm that Earth has extremely rare conditions that allow it to support life. The vast majority of the universe is uninhabitable. Let's briefly consider a few:

- *Life must be in the right type of galaxy.* Of the three types of galaxies, only spiral galaxies with the right mass (like the Milky Way) can support life.

- *Life must be in the right location in the galaxy.* We are situated in just the right place in the Milky Way to avoid harmful radiation.
- *Life must have the right type of star.* While most stars are too large, too luminous, or too unstable to support life, our sun is just the right size and age. There is a window of time in which a sun can support complex life. It can't be too young or too old.
- *Life must have the right relationship to its host star.* If Earth were slightly closer to or farther from the sun, water would either freeze or evaporate, rendering Earth uninhabitable for complex life.
- *Life needs surrounding planets for protection.* A habitable planet must have large surrounding bodies such as Jupiter and Saturn. The early motions of Jupiter and Saturn removed most of the asteroids and comets from the solar system with two beneficial effects. First, the removal process also caused many collisions early in Earth's history. These collisions added water, ammonia and other life-essential materials to Earth. Second, the loss of comets and asteroids reduced the subsequent rate of impacts on Earth by a factor of one thousand. (Grazer, "Jupiter," 23–38)
- *Life requires the right type of moon.* If Earth did not have a moon of the right size and distance, it would be uninhabitable. The moon stabilizes the earth's tilt, preventing extreme temperatures and thus creating a stable, life-friendly environment. (Gonzalez and Richards, PP, 23)

What happens when we try to assign a probability to the fine-tuning of *all* the known constants of nature? Theoretical physicist Lee Smolin calculates a much smaller number: the probability of a universe where stars exist. "Perhaps before going further we should ask just how probable is it that a universe created by randomly choosing the parameters will contain stars. Given what we have already said, it is simple to estimate this probability. For readers who are interested, the arithmetic is in the notes. The answer, in round numbers, comes to about one chance in 10^{229}." (Smolin, LC, 45) Stated another way, if every proton in the universe represented a universe with different laws of physics, the probability calculated by Smolin means that none of those universes would contain stars!

The evidence for design is so compelling that Paul Davies, an internationally acclaimed physicist at Arizona State University, has concluded that the biofriendly nature of our universe looks like a "fix." In other words, the universe is so uniquely calibrated to support life that it seems to go beyond the reach of coincidence. He writes, "The cliché that 'life is balanced on a knife-edge' is a staggering understatement in this case: no knife in the universe could have an edge

---

The cliché that "life is balanced on a knife-edge" is a staggering understatement in this case: no knife in the universe could have an edge that fine.

Paul Davies

that fine." (Davies, CJ, 149) According to Davies, any legitimate scientific explanation must account for this overwhelming appearance of design.

5. Objections

a. Weak Anthropic Principle

Some argue that since we could not exist in a universe that was not conducive to our existence (i.e., fine-tuned), we should not be surprised that the universe is fine-tuned.

Philosopher John Leslie expands on this need for explanation in his famous "firing squad" analogy. Suppose fifty trained sharpshooters are lined up to take your life, and they all miss. You could hardly dismiss this occurrence by saying, "If they hadn't all missed me, then I shouldn't be contemplating the matter so I mustn't be surprised that they missed." (Leslie, *Universes*, 108) You should still be surprised that you are alive given the enormous unlikelihood of all the sharpshooters missing their mark. Your survival demands an explanation. And so does the fine-tuning of the laws of the universe.

b. The Multiverse Theory

Perhaps the most common naturalistic response to the fine-tuning argument is the so-called multiverse theory, or the many worlds hypothesis. According to this theory, there are many universes—perhaps infinite—and each operates according to unique laws and constants. While most universes would not sustain life, inevitably some would. Currently, the scientific community actively debates the validity of multiverse models. Although far from settled, there is scientific support for the existence of a multiverse. The key question remains though: does living in a multiverse undermine the case for God?

Distinguished philosopher Robin Collins provides multiple reasons for God's existence in the context of multiverse theory. First, we should prefer the hypothesis that naturally flows from the evidence, and for which we have independent confirmation. Collins observes, "In the case of fine-tuning, we already know that minds often produce fine-tuned devices, such as Swiss watches. Postulating God—a supermind—as the explanation of fine-tuning, therefore, is a natural extrapolation from what we already observe minds to do." (Collins, SAEG, 61)

Second, a "many universes-generator" would seemingly need to be designed as well: "It stands to reason, therefore, that if these laws were slightly different the generator probably would not be able to produce any universes that could sustain life. After all, even my bread machine has to be made just right in order to work properly, and it only produces loaves of bread, not universes!" (Collins, SAEG, 61)

Third, the multiverse theory cannot explain other features of the universe that exhibit apparent design. Collins explains:

For example, many physicists, such as Albert Einstein, have observed that the basic laws of physics exhibit an extraordinary degree of beauty, elegance, harmony, and ingenuity. Nobel prize winning physicist Steven Weinberg, for instance, devotes a whole chapter in his book *Dreams of a Final Theory* explaining how the criteria of beauty and elegance are commonly used to guide physicists in formulating the right laws. . . . Now such beauty, elegance, and ingenuity make sense if the universe was designed by God. Under the atheistic many-universes hypothesis, however, there is no reason to expect the fundamental laws to be elegant or beautiful. (Collins, SAEG, 62–63)

Astrophysicist Jeffrey Zweerink provides a fair synopsis of the present standing of the fine-tuning argument in light of the multi-verse challenge:

> Though some multiverse models appear to undermine the teleological argument, they still exhibit design and fine-tuning. Granted the design argument is more subtle and complex if a multiverse actually exists. However, as with the cosmological argument, studies of the multiverse ultimately make the teleological argument more robust. (Zweerink, WOM, 51)

C. The Origin of Life

1. The Problem of the Origin of Life

Virtually the entire scientific community agrees: the problem of life's origin is unsolved. The problem of life's beginning has become so difficult that Harvard University launched a $100 million research program to address it (Origins of Life Initiative, Harvard University, http://origins.harvard.edu/). As Harvard biologist Andy Knoll said, "The short answer is we don't really know how life originated on this planet. There have been a variety of experiments that tell us some possible roads, but we remain in substantial ignorance." (Knoll, HDLB)

How deep is the problem of explaining the origin of life? Geneticist Michael Denton explains:

> In *Evolution: A Theory in Crisis* I wrote, "Between a living cell and the most highly ordered non-biological system . . . there is a chasm as vast and absolute as it is possible to conceive." Thirty years on, the situation is entirely unchanged. Despite a vast increase in knowledge of supramolecular chemistry and of cell and molecular biology; the unexpected discovery of ribozymes; and an enormous effort, both experimental and hypothetical, devoted to providing a gradualistic function-alist account of the origin of life in terms of a long series of less complex functional repli-cating systems (e.g., the much touted "RNA world") leading from "chemistry" to the cell, no one has provided even the vaguest outlines of a feasible scenario, let alone a convincing one. A yawning gap still persists—empirical and theoretical. (Denton, ESTC, 121)

2. The Sophistication of the Cell

Life's origin is so difficult to explain because life itself is so remarkably complex and sophisticated. During the time of Darwin, scientists believed life was rather simple. And thus, there would likely emerge an explanation for how it could arise naturally. But the opposite has turned out to be true. The more we learn about the cell, the greater complexity and technological prowess we discover. In fact, nearly every feature of our own advanced technology can be found in the cell.

Biologists today describe the cell using language reminiscent of engineering and computer science. They regularly use terms such as genetic *code*, *information-processing system*, and *signal transduction*. Influential atheist Richard Dawkins writes, "Apart from differences in jargon, the pages of a molecular-biology journal might be interchanged with those of a computer-engineering journal." (Dawkins, ROE, 17)

With the discovery of the structure of DNA in 1953, scientists learned that information is basic to life. The information for organizing proteins is stored in four nucleotide bases: guanine (G), adenine (A), thymine (T), and cytosine (C). These four bases function as letters of an alphabet, creating meaningful arrangements, which is why biologists regularly refer to DNA and RNA as carriers of "information." The amount of information in the human body is outright staggering.

The human body has an average of one hundred trillion cells. In a single cell, the

DNA contains the informational equivalent of roughly eight thousand books. If the DNA from one cell were uncoiled, it would extend to about three meters in length. Thus, if the DNA in an adult human were strung together, it would stretch from Earth to the sun and back roughly seventy times! (Roberts and Whorton, HQGUC, 323)

But DNA does not just store information. In combination with other cellular systems, it also processes information. Bill Gates likens DNA to a computer program, though far more advanced than any software humans have invented. (Gates, RA, 228) This is why Davies says, "Life is more than just complex chemical reactions. The cell is also an information storing, processing and replicating system. We need to explain the origin of this information, and the way in which the information processing machinery came to exist." (quoted in Flew and Varghese, TIG, 128)

Flew, once an avowed atheist who, following the evidence, came to believe in the existence of God, clearly states the nature of the problem of the origin of life: "How can a universe of mindless matter produce beings with intrinsic ends, self-replicating capabilities, and 'coded chemistry'?" (Flew and Varghese, TIG, 124)

3. Explanations for the Origin of Life
a. Chance
What are the odds that random interactions of prebiotic soup would generate a single functional protein? Based on the work of Douglas Axe, Meyer concludes:

The calculation can be made by multiplying the three independent probabilities by one another: the probability of incorporating only peptide bonds (1 in 10^{45}), the probability of incorporating only left-handed amino acids (1 in 10^{45}), and the probability of achieving correct amino-acid sequencing (using Axe's 1 in 10^{74} estimate). Making that calculation (multiplying the separate probabilities by adding their exponents: $10^{45+45+74}$) gives a dramatic answer. The odds of getting even one functional protein of modest length (150 amino acids) by chance from prebiotic soup is no better than 1 chance in 10^{164}.... Now consider that there are only 10^{80} protons, neutrons, and electrons in the observable universe. Thus, if the odds of finding a functional protein by chance on the first attempt had been 1 in 10^{80}, we could have said that's like finding a marked particle—proton, neutron, or electron (a much smaller needle)—among all the particles in the universe (a much larger haystack). Unfortunately, the problem is much worse than that. With odds standing at 1 chance in 10^{164} of finding a functional protein among the possible 150-amino-acid compounds, the probability is 84 orders of magnitude (or powers of ten) *smaller* than the probability of finding the marked particle in the whole universe. Another way to say that is the probability of finding a functional protein by chance alone is a trillion, trillion, trillion, trillion, trillion, trillion, trillion times smaller than the odds of finding a single specified particle among all the particles in the universe. (Meyer, SC, 212)

b. Energy and Self-Organization
Could there be some self-organizational principle that causes life to emerge through laws of nature? The general problem with this approach is that energy and self-organization can generate *order*, but there is no evidence they can generate *information*. Meyer explains,

The astrophysicist Fred Hoyle had a similar way of making the same point. He famously compared the problem of getting life to arise spontaneously from its constituent parts to the problem of getting a 747 airplane to come together from a tornado swirling through a junk yard. An undifferentiated external force is simply too blunt an instrument to accomplish such a task. Energy might scatter parts around randomly. Energy might sweep parts into an orderly structure such as a vortex or funnel cloud. But energy alone will not assemble a group of parts into a highly differentiated or functionally specified system such as an airplane or cell (or into the informational sequences necessary to build one). (Meyer, SC, 257)

c. Design

Naturalistic processes are simply incapable of explaining the complex, information rich nature of the cell. But there is a third option, if someone is open to looking beyond nature itself. Biochemist Fazale Rana explains,

> Human experience consistently teaches that information emanates from intelligence. Whether written in plain or elegant scripts, messages initiate in a mind. In whatever form information takes, it's not limited to communicating ideas, needs, and desires between human minds. Information has become an integral part of modern technology. Designers and engineers routinely develop and refine information systems. Computer technologies, among many other developing innovations, fundamentally depend upon such constructs. Over the last forty years, biochemists have come to recognize that the cell's biological systems are also, at their essence, information-based. Proteins, DNA, and even oligosaccharides are information-rich molecules. By analogy, these discoveries reinforce the biochemical design argument (Rana, CD, 166).

This is not a God-of-the-gaps argument, using God as an explanation for a phenomenon presently inexplicable. While scientists certainly have an incomplete understanding of life's chemistry, the argument to design

from DNA is based upon *positive* evidence of what we do know about the abilities of intelligent agents to produce information rich systems. As with the origin of the universe, and the fine-tuning of the laws of nature, the origin of life poses a seemingly intractable problem for naturalism.

D. The Origin of Consciousness
1. The Challenge of Consciousness

The existence and reality of consciousness present one of the most pressing challenges to naturalism. As we have said, metaphysical naturalism is the view that only physical things exist. As a result, everything that exists should be describable in physical terminology, including properties such as weight, size, and location. But there are certain *subjective* aspects of the world that resist such explanation.

Analytic philosopher Paul Copan explains the challenge posed by consciousness:

> Here's the problem, though: When we consult physics textbooks to understand what matter is, *there's nothing psychological, subjective, or mental about matter.* Matter might be described as having the properties of spatial location, spatial extension, weight, texture, color, shape, size, density, mass, or atomic or chemical composition. But what will always be missing in these textbooks describing matter is *consciousness* as a characteristic or property of matter. The assumption is that matter is different than [sic] mind. We're left wondering: how could *matter* produce mind? How could nonconscious material produce consciousness? (Copan, HDYKYNW, 100, emphasis in original)

Even atheist philosopher Thomas Nagel notes how consciousness raises a problem for naturalism:

Consciousness is the most conspicuous obstacle to a comprehensive naturalism that relies only on the resources of physical science. The existence of consciousness seems to imply that the physical description of the universe, in spite of its richness and explanatory power, is only part of the truth, and that the natural order is far less austere than it would be if physics and chemistry accounted for everything. If we take this problem seriously, and follow out its implications, it threatens to unravel the entire naturalistic world picture. Yet it is very difficult to imagine a viable alternative. (Nagel, MC, 35)

2. Naturalistic Explanations for Consciousness

Naturalists have offered a variety of explanations for consciousness. We will consider three popular explanations (although there are *many* more):

a. Behaviorism

Definition: While various behaviorist explanations hope to account for consciousness, they commonly reduce mental attributes to some observable behavior.

Response: Nagel observes: "It is certainly true that mental phenomena have behavioral manifestations, which supply our main evidence for them in other creatures. Yet all these theories seem insufficient as analyses of the mental because they leave out something essential that lies beyond the externally observable grounds for attributing mental states to others, namely, the aspect of mental phenomena that is evidence from first-person, inner point of view of the conscious subject: for example, the way sugar tastes to you or the way red looks or anger feels, each of which seems to be something more than the behavioral responses and discriminatory capacities that these

experiences explain. Behaviorism leaves out the inner mental state itself." (Nagel, MC, 38)

b. Evolution

Definition: Consciousness emerges from the process of natural selection, acting upon random mutation, and offers survival advantages to species.

Response: Philosopher Colin McGinn notes, "But in the case of consciousness the Darwinian explanation does not tell us what we need to know, for the simple reason that it is unclear how matter *can* be so organized as to create a conscious being. The problem is in the raw materials. It looks as if with consciousness a new kind of reality has been injected into the universe, instead of just a recombination of the old realities. Even if minds showed no hint of design, the same old problem would exist: How can mere matter originate consciousness? How did evolution convert the water of biological tissue into the wine of consciousness?" (McGinn, MF, 13)

c. The Mind Is the Brain

Definition: This approach claims the mind is the brain. In other words, *mind* and *brain* are simply two different terms that refer to the same physical reality.

Response: Copan notes, "The fact that we can't locate, weigh, or dye thoughts—as we can physical objects—reveals the inadequacy of a view identifying the physical with the mental/soulish—or reducing the mind/soul to the physical. Brains just don't have the same properties that minds (or souls) have, and minds don't have the same properties brains do. Therefore, *the mental can't be identical with the brain—or even produced by the physical brain*." (Copan, HDYKYNW, 101, emphasis in original)

3. Worldview Implications

There are other naturalistic attempts at explaining consciousness beyond what we have explored here. Nevertheless, "The truth is," says Moreland, "that naturalism has no plausible way to explain the appearance of emergent mental properties in the cosmos." (Moreland, AC, 340) And yet this leaves naturalism in a bind, as philosopher Richard Swinburne observes: "We cannot describe the world fully if we use only terms denoting physical properties. Any world-view which denies the existence of experienced sensations of blueness or loudness or pain, does not describe how things are—that this is so stares us in the face." (Swinburne, EG, 165–166)

According to noted neuroscientist Robert Lawrence Kuhn, "Neuroscientists and many philosophers have typically planted themselves firmly on the materialist [naturalist] side. But a growing number of scientists now believe that materialism cannot wholly explain the sense of 'I am' that undergirds consciousness." (Ghose, ME) Given how intractable the problem of consciousness is for naturalism, philosopher and Brown University professor Jaegwon Kim concludes, "But if a whole system of phenomena that are prima facie not among basic physical phenomena resists physical explanation, and especially if we don't even know where or how to begin, it would be time to reexamine one's physicalist commitments." (Kim, MPW, 96)

And yet along with the origin of the universe, the fine-tuning of the universe, and the origin of life, the existence of consciousness fits naturally within the theistic worldview. If God is a supremely conscious being, and he has created us, then it makes perfect sense for human beings to be conscious agents who experience the world. God has both the power and incentive to create conscious beings.

E. The Existence of Free Will

1. Is Free Will an illusion?

The perception of free will is an unavoidable aspect of human experience. Although influenced by our environment and genes, we believe we make choices that are truly up to us. We condemn terrorists for their immoral actions because we believe they *should* have known better. And we praise individuals who personally sacrifice for the betterment of others because we realize they didn't have to be selfless. And yet if naturalism were true, our belief in free will would be baseless.

Nagel, an atheist philosopher, asserts, "There is no room for agency in a world of neural impulses, chemical reactions, and bone and muscle movements." (Nagel, VN, 111) In slight contrast, skeptic Michael Shermer believes free will is ultimately insoluble, and so we might as well just pretend we have it: "*Free will is a useful fiction.* I feel 'as if' I have free will, even though I know we live in a determined universe. This fiction is so useful that I act as if I have free will but you don't. You do the same. Since the problem may be an insoluble one, why not act as if you do have free will, gaining the emotional gratification and social benefits that go along with it?" (Shermer, SGE, 121, emphasis in original)

2. The Intuition of Free Will

Belief in free will is an intuition held by people of varying worldviews, including many atheists. Copan notes, "But if this intuition is so common, *maybe there is something to it!* According to the commonsense *principle of credulity*, we should accept the basic reliability of our everyday intuitions—whether about our freedom, the general trustworthiness of our rational faculties and sense perceptions, or our moral intuitions about the wrongness of murder, rape, and theft. The burden of proof is upon the one who would deny these obvious features of our daily lives." (Copan, HDYKYNW, 106–107, emphasis in original)

3. A Problem for Determinism: Denying Rationality

Recently I (Sean) led a group of high school students to Berkeley to interact with some skeptics, agnostics, and atheists. One evening, for a public conversation about the evidence for and against God, we met with a "free thinking" student group from Cal Berkeley. After the discussion, I met a student who said she had recently converted from believing in free will to being a determinist. I simply asked her why she changed her mind. And she effectively said, "I used to believe in free will until I really examined the evidence. I studied both the philosophy and science behind the issue and have become convinced that free will is an illusion." After a moment of reflection, I simply asked her another question: "So, you weighed the evidence on both sides of the debate and freely chose to give up belief in free will and become a determinist. Is that right?" She hesitated to respond because she saw the tension. In other words, she claimed to be a determinist (which implies that her beliefs are *not* up to her) but then offered intellectual reasons for her decision, as if she were a free agent who could rationally examine evidence and follow it where it leads. She wanted it both ways, but unfortunately, her naturalistic worldview wouldn't allow it, leaving her two options: (1) Give up naturalism and adopt a worldview that allows for free will (such as Christianity), or (2) Become a more consistent naturalist and admit that free will is an illusion and that her beliefs really weren't up to her in the way she thought they were.

Influential atheist Sam Harris, after rightly emphasizing the importance of the question of free will, also concludes that free will is an illusion. In his book *Free Will*, Harris claims we are not the conscious source of our actions and could not have behaved differently in the past from how we did. He says, "I, as the conscious witness of my experience, no more initiate events in my prefrontal cortex than I cause my heart to beat." (Harris, FW, 9) Harris explains: "The brain is a physical system, entirely beholden to the laws of nature—and there is every reason to believe that changes in its functional state and material structure entirely dictate our thoughts and actions" (Harris, FW, 11–12).

Harris rightly points out that there are three main approaches to the problem of free will: *determinism*, *libertarianism*, and *compatibilism*. He then says, "Today, the only philosophically respectable way to endorse free will is to be a compatibilist." (Harris, FW, 16) But if determinism were true, as Harris's view seems to imply, why would *any* position be philosophically respectable or unrespectable? After all, on his view, people are determined to hold their beliefs—whether compatibilist, libertarian, or determinist—by forces outside of their control. If the people who hold beliefs couldn't have believed differently, there is no need to critique or praise another's position. If his critique results merely from chemicals moving in his brain, nothing could make his chemicals more respectable than others.

Furthermore, Harris argues that giving up free will (and becoming more aware of the background causes of our feelings) allows people to have greater creative control over their lives. "Getting behind our conscious thoughts and feelings," says Harris, "can allow us to steer a more intelligent course through our lives." (Harris, FW, 47) However, clearly the idea of "steering" a more intelligent course through life seems to imply an agent view of causation—that there is a "self" beyond the physical world of cause and effect. According to naturalism, however, the belief that we can steer our lives is an illusion. All of our beliefs and behavior are *entirely* the result of forces outside our control. In one breath Harris says all our beliefs are determined, but then in another he seems to speak as if we really *should* take control over the course of our lives.

Determinists might push back and suggest that minds can be changed with the right stimuli of forces and counterforces, which are part of the larger cause-effect realm. Thus, we *feel* as if we are making free choices, but in reality, these feelings are explainable by prior physical states and interactions. This is an important objection, which comes at a high cost—the undermining of rationality. According to J. P. Moreland, rationality seems to require an agent view of the human person, which involves these four theses:

1. I must be able to deliberate, to reflect about what I am going to do. I deliberate about my behavior and not that of others, future events and not past ones, courses of action which I have not already settled. These facts of deliberation make sense only if I assumed that my actions are 'up to me' to perform or not perform.

2. I must have free will; that is, given choices *a* and *b*, I can genuinely do both. If I do *a*, I could have done otherwise. I could have chosen *b*. The past and present do not physically determine only one future. The future is open and depends, to some extent, on my free choices.

3. I am an agent. My acts are often self-caused. I am the absolute origin of my acts. My prior mental or physical states are not sufficient to determine what I will do. *I must act as an agent.*

4. Free will is incompatible with physical determinism. They cannot both be true at the same time (Moreland, STSC, 95).

Of course, this doesn't prove that free will is real and that naturalism is false. Free will may ultimately be an illusion, as determinists such as Harris suggest. But embracing determinism comes at a cost that undermines our common sense understanding of free will and rationality.

4. Conclusion

We recognize that we have only scratched the surface of the issue of free will. We have not considered many objections to the existence of free will, nor their responses. For a helpful resource that considers various attempts to explain free will using naturalistic explanations, and why these explanations fall short, see *God's Crime Scene* by J. Warner Wallace. (141–158, 250–259)

For the sake of our discussion, we simply note that the experience of free will is inexplicable for naturalists, which they themselves often admit. Consistent naturalists must either admit that free will is an illusion or hope that someday an explanation emerges. Naturalism cannot account for our deep-seated, common sense, and daily experience that we are agents who make decisions that are up to us. Theists, though, have no such problem. After all, if God is a personal, free being who can choose to act, and has created us in his image, then we have good reason to believe we genuinely experience free will.

F. The Existence of Objective Morality
1. Universal Morality

Like the issue of consciousness and free will, humans have a universal belief in right and wrong. While people do vary over specific *behaviors* they consider right or wrong, there is universal agreement on the underlying *principles* of objective morality. C. S. Lewis explains,

If anyone will take the trouble to compare the moral teaching of, say, ancient Egyptians, Babylonians, Hindus, Chinese, Greeks and Romans, what will really strike him will be how very like they are to each other and to our own. . . . I need only ask the reader to think what a totally different morality would mean. Think of a country where people were admired for running away in battle, or where a man felt proud of double-crossing all the people who had been kindest to him. You might just as well try to imagine a country where two and two made five. Men have differed as regards what people you ought to be unselfish to—whether it was only your own family, or your fellow countrymen, or everyone. But they have always agreed that you ought not put yourself first. Selfishness has never been admired.* Men have differed as to whether you should have one wife or four. But they have always agreed that you must not simply have any woman you liked. (Lewis, MC, 19)

Which worldview *best* explains the existence of objective morality? The question is not whether naturalists can be moral—or even whether they can know morality—but whether naturalism as a worldview can adequately account for the existence of objective morality.

2. Denying Objective Morality

Some naturalists may recognize the implications of their God-less worldview and claim they don't believe in objective morality.

But again, Lewis points out the inconsistency of such a view:

Whenever you find a man who says he does not believe in a real Right and Wrong, you will find the same man going back on this a moment later. He may break his promise to you, but if you try breaking one to him he will be complaining, "It's not fair" before you can say Jack Robinson. A nation may say treatises do not matter; but then, next minute, they spoil their case by saying that the particular treaty they want to break was an unfair one. But if treaties do not matter, and if there is no such thing as Right and Wrong—in other words, if there is no Law of Nature—what is the difference between a fair treaty and an unfair one? Have they not let the cat out of the bag and show that, whatever they say, they really know the Law of Nature just like anyone else? (Lewis, MC, 19–20)

3. Can Science Explain Morality?

In his book *The Moral Landscape*, Sam Harris claims science can provide a basis for objective morality. But apologist speaker and author Frank Turek notes that Harris smuggles in presuppositions his worldview cannot provide:

Science might be able to tell you *if* an action may hurt someone—like giving a man cyanide will kill him—but science can't tell you whether or not you *ought* to hurt someone. Who said it's wrong to harm people? Sam Harris? Does he have authority over the rest of humanity? Is his nature the standard of Good? To get his system to work, Sam Harris must smuggle in what he claims is an objective moral standard: "well being." As William Lane Craig pointed out in his debate with Harris, that's not the fail-safe criterion of what's right. But even if it was, what objective, unchanging, moral authority establishes it as right? . . . Only an unchanging authoritative being, who can

---

* There are some exceptions to Lewis's statement, "Selfishness has never been admired." One is Nietzsche; another is the objectivism of Ayn Rand. Both have garnered many followers. A third appears in the admiration for betrayal that Don Richardson encountered in Irian Jaya and related in his book *Peace Child*. But in defense of Lewis, we can point out that in the BBC talks that became *Mere Christianity*, he is referring to the consensus of society rather than to individual thinkers or groups within a large historic culture.

prescribe and enforce objective morality here and beyond the grave, is an adequate standard. (Turek, SG, 100)

In *The Abolition of Man*, C. S. Lewis points out that logic cannot obtain "ought" from mere descriptions of "is," that is, of the way things are. (Lewis, AOM, 12)

4. Can Evolution Explain Morality?

A few years ago, I (Sean) participated in a public debate with a skeptic about whether or not God is the best explanation for moral values (McDowell and Corbett, IGBE). My opponent appealed to evolution in his attempt to ground objective morality apart from God. But this explanation falls short. Apologists Francis J. Beckwith and Gregory Koukl explain,

Darwinists opt for an evolutionary explanation for morality without sufficient justification. To make their naturalistic explanation work, morality must reside in the genes. Good and beneficial tendencies can then be chosen by natural selection. Nature, through the mechanics of genetic chemistry, cultivates behavior we call morality. (Beckwith and Koukl, *Relativism*, 163)

Beckwith and Koukl note that this creates two problems:

First, evolution doesn't explain what it's meant to explain. It can only account for preprogrammed behavior, not moral choices. Moral choices, by their nature, are made by free agents. They are not determined by internal mechanics. Second, the Darwinist explanation reduces morality to mere descriptions of behavior. The morality

that evolution needs to account for, however, entails much more than conduct. Minimally, it involves motive and intent as well. Both are nonphysical elements that can't, even in principle, evolve in a Darwinian sense. Further, this assessment of morality, being descriptive only, ignores the most important moral question of all: Why should I be moral *tomorrow*? Evolution cannot answer that question. Morality dictates what future behavior ought to be. Darwinism can only attempt to describe why humans acted in a certain way in the past. (Beckwith and Koukl, *Relativism*, 164)

5. God Best Explains Objective Morality

The argument from objective morality to God has two simple premises and a conclusion: (1) If objective moral values exist, God must exist; (2) Objective moral values exist; (3) Therefore, God must exist. In terms of support for the first premise, we have seen that humans have a universal belief in objective morality. And as Lewis noted, those who deny objective morality will inevitably end up in contradiction. The existence of objective morality is certainly reasonable and better accounts for common human experience than its denial.*

As for the second premise, Copan notes:

Just think about it: Intrinsically valuable, thinking persons do not come from impersonal, nonconscious, unguided, valueless processes over time. A personal, self-aware, purposeful, good God provides the natural and necessary context for the existence of valuable, rights-bearing, morally responsible human persons. That is, personhood and morality are necessarily connected; moral values are rooted in personhood. Without God (a personal being), no persons—and thus no moral

---

* In The *Abolition of Man* (the publication of lectures delivered at the University of Durham), C. S. Lewis presents an extensive argument for the unreasonableness of denying moral objectivity—and for the ultimately destructive outcome for humanity if we try to base individual behavior and social polity upon that denial. (Lewis, AOM, 12, 22–24, 33, 46)

values—would exist at all: *no personhood, no moral values.* Only if God exists can moral properties be realized. (Copan, MAGE, 22, emphasis in original)

If these two premises are true, then it follows that God must exist. Even some atheists have noted the connection between God and morality. The late atheist philosopher J. L. Mackie said, "If there are objective moral values, they make the existence of a god more probable than it would have been without them. Thus we have a defensible argument from morality to the existence of a god." (Mackie, MT, 115–116) And agnostic Paul Draper noted, "A moral world is . . . very probable on theism." (quoted in Copan, MAGE, 23)

As with the origin and fine-tuning of the universe, the origin of life, the existence of consciousness, and the nature of free will, naturalism fails adequately to explain objective morality. Conversely, objective moral values provide positive support for the theistic worldview.

V. Conclusion

Naturalism permeates Western culture, claiming not only that only physical things exist but also that all phenomena can ultimately be explained by the combination of chance and natural laws. This worldview underlies much rejection of supernatural phenomena such as the deity of Christ and the resurrection.

And yet, as we have seen, naturalism cannot account for the origin of the universe, the fine-tuning of the universe, the origin of life, the existence of consciousness, the nature of free will, and objective morality. These are universal human experiences. We have argued that any worldview (such as naturalism) that cannot account for these phenomena ultimately fails to describe reality. And yet each of these phenomena also provides *positive* evidence for theism. We agree with Flew: given these features of the world, "the occurrence of the resurrection does become enormously more likely."

PART I

EVIDENCE FOR THE BIBLE

CHAPTER 1

THE UNIQUENESS OF THE BIBLE

OVERVIEW

I. Introduction

People often say to us, "Oh, you don't read the Bible, do you?" Or they say, "The Bible is just another book. You really ought to read . . ." Then they name some of their favorite books. Others have a Bible in their library, describing how it sits on the shelf next to other "greats," such as Homer's *Odyssey*, Shakespeare's *Romeo and Juliet*, or Austen's *Pride and Prejudice*. Their Bible may be dusty, not broken in, but they still recognize its historical influence, thinking of it as one of the classics. Still others make degrading comments about the Bible because they are surprised that anyone might take it seriously enough to spend time reading it. I (Josh) was once like them. I even tried to refute the Bible as God's Word to humanity. I finally concluded, however, that not accepting the Bible must result from being either biased, prejudiced, or simply unread.

Voices like those above brought up many issues with which I grappled. As a result of all my research about the Bible, I concluded that the best word to describe the Bible is the word *unique*.

This chapter focuses exclusively on the unique origin and nature of the Bible, the profound impact it has had on western civilization, and its responsibility for much of the progress of human history. This chapter will not attempt to demonstrate the validity or truth of the Bible, nor its claims to inspiration, infallibility, or inerrancy, which will be addressed in subsequent chapters.

II. Unique in Character

There are several uncommon and distinctive features of the Bible's history, composition, and content. F. F. Bruce, former Rylands Professor of Biblical Criticism and Exegesis at the University of Manchester, summarizes these characteristics:

> The Bible, at first sight, appears to be a collection of literature—mainly Jewish. If we enquire into the circumstances under which the various Biblical documents were written, we find that they were written at intervals over a space of nearly 1400 years. The writers wrote in various lands, from Italy in the west to Mesopotamia and possibly Persia in the east. The writers themselves were a heterogeneous number of people, not only separated from each other by hundreds of years and hundreds of miles but belonging to the most diverse walks of life. In their ranks we have kings, herdsmen, soldiers, legislators, fishermen, statesmen, courtiers, priests and prophets, a tentmaking rabbi and a Gentile physician, not to speak of others of whom we know nothing apart from the writings they have left us. The writings themselves belong to a great variety of literary types. They include history, law (civil, criminal, ethical, ritual, sanitary), religious poetry, didactic treatises, lyric poetry, parable and allegory, biography, personal correspondence, personal memoirs and diaries, in addition to the distinctively Biblical types of prophecy and apocalyptic. (Bruce, BP, 79)

Now let us look in more detail into some of these specific characteristics.

A. Unique in Its Time Span

While most scholars agree that all the books of the New Testament were completed by the second half of the first century AD (Kitchen, OROT, 500), there is sufficient evidence to confirm that the earliest forms of the Bible were written during the time of the Hebrew exodus out of Egypt (c. 1400–1200 BC). This means that the composition of the biblical writings, from the earliest book of the Bible to the last of the New Testament writings, spans a period of 1,300 to 1,500 years. In comparison to other literary and historical works, the Bible is exceptional in that it was written and assembled over a vast number of generations.

B. Unique in Its Geographical Production

Unlike most other literary works, the composition and transmission of the biblical books did not emerge from a homogenous community located in a single region of the ancient world. Rather, these works were written by peoples in areas as diverse as Rome in the West, Egypt in the South, and Mesopotamia in the East. This amazing geographical and ethnic diversity distinguishes the Bible's origins from that of all other books.

C. Unique in Its Authorship

The Bible is as diverse in its authorship as it is in its production over a long period of time and the multiple geographical regions in which it originated. Authored by approximately forty different people (some known, some unknown) and edited and preserved by countless scribal schools and communities, the Bible preserves for us the writings of a vast array of different personalities from widely divergent social circumstances. We discover kings surrounded by power and wealth (e.g., Solomon) on the one hand, to lower class Galilean fishermen (e.g., Peter and John) on the other. Between these two socioeconomic extremes one finds an exiled prince (Moses), military leaders (e.g., Joshua and David), trained philosophers (e.g., the authors of Job and Ecclesiastes), a tax collector (Matthew), a historian (Luke), and a zealous Pharisee (Paul). These authors recorded the stories of all kinds of people. Professor Mary Ellen Chase remarks:

> The story-tellers of the Bible . . . understood men and women of all sorts and in all conditions. There is literally no type of person whom they have neglected. All are here: the wise and the foolish, the rich and the poor, the faithful and the treacherous, the designing and the generous, the pitiful and the prosperous, the innocent and the guilty, the spendthrift and the miser, the players of practical jokes and their discomfited victims, the sorry, the tired, the old, the exasperated young, misled and impetuous girls, young men who lusted and young men who loved, friends who counted no cost for friendship, bad-mannered children and children well brought up, a little boy who had a headache in a hay-field, a little servant girl who wanted so much her master's health that she dared to give him good, if unpalatable, advice. Once one discovers such persons as these, still alive after many centuries, they become not only fascinating in themselves but typical of persons whom we know today. (Chase, BCR, 5)

D. Unique in Its Literary Genres

The Bible is also unique in that a multitude of distinct literary forms and genres can be found within its pages, as complete compositions consisting of a single genre (e.g., Song of Songs) or complete compositions imbued with multiple genres (e.g., Exodus). Gerd Theissen, professor of New Testament at the University of Heidelberg, highlights the importance of biblical genres:

> Biblical texts are of various sorts. Treatment of one sort of text provides practice in dealing with all texts of the same sort. Narrative, poetic, legal, and argumentative texts of the Bible can therefore be treated as exemplary, as well as the various biblical genres identified by that area of biblical scholarship called form criticism. In principle no single sort of text is privileged. Central themes appear in all forms: creation is recorded as *narrative*; trust is expressed in *prayer* (Psalm 23); monotheism is mandated in a *commandment* (Exod. 20:2); justification is expounded in a *disputatious letter* (Romans); theodicy—the question of God's justice—is examined in *wisdom dialogue* (Job). The Bible is not a homogenous text but a compendium of different forms and genres. Each must be appreciated on its own terms. (Theissen, BCC, 30–31)

Other ancient literary works utilize a multiplicity of literary genres, but the biblical authors use them in order to focus their audience's attention on one supreme metanarrative. Alison Jack, professor of Bible and Literature at the University of Edinburgh, illustrates the interplay between this unifying biblical motif and the multiplicity of literary forms:

> While one overarching story may be discerned, involving the central character of the one God, creator and sustainer of the earth, and his relationship with those who accept a relationship with him, and those who do not, there are many different voices behind the books of the Bible. A multitude of literary genres are found here, from long and short narratives to poetry and song, genealogies and historical accounts, biography, letters and apocalyptic writing. These voices tell different versions of the story, from a variety of perspectives. (Jack, BL, 6)

E. Unique in Its Languages

The Bible is written in three different languages (two Semitic and one Indo-European), each with a unique character and essence. Larry Walker, former professor of Old Testament and Semitic Languages at Mid-America Baptist Theological Seminary, outlines each of the biblical languages:

> Hebrew is actually one of several Canaanite dialects which included Phoenician, Ugaritic, and Moabite. Other Canaanite dialects (for example, Ammonite) existed but have left insufficient inscriptions for scholarly investigation. Such dialects were already present in the land of Canaan before its conquest by the Israelites. . . . Hebrew belongs to the Semitic family of languages; these languages were used from the Mediterranean Sea to the mountains east of the Euphrates River valley, and from Armenia (Turkey) in the north to the southern extremity of the Arabian peninsula. . . . Hebrew, like the other early Semitic languages, concentrates on observation more than reflection. That is, things that are generally observed according to their appearance as phenomena, not analyzed as to their inward being or essence. Effects are observed but not traced through a series of causes. Hebrew's vividness, conciseness, and simplicity make the language difficult to translate fully. It is amazingly concise and direct. For example, Psalm 23 contains fifty-five words; most translations require about twice that many to translate it. . . . Hebrew is a pictorial language in which the past is not merely described but verbally painted. Not just a landscape is presented but a moving panorama. The course of events is reenacted in the mind's sight. . . . Many profound theological expressions of the Old Testament are tightly bound up with Hebrew language and grammar. Even the most sacred name of God himself, "the Lord" (Jehovah or Yahweh), is directly related to the Hebrew verb "to be" (or perhaps "to cause to be"). (Walker, BL, 218–221)

Walker also explains:

> Aramaic is linguistically very close to Hebrew and similar in structure. Aramaic texts in the Bible are written in the same script as Hebrew. In contrast to Hebrew, Aramaic uses a larger vocabulary, including many loan words, and a greater variety of connectives. It also contains an elaborate system of tenses, developed through the use of participles with pronouns or with various forms of the verb "to be." Although Aramaic is less euphonious and poetical than Hebrew, it is probably superior as a vehicle of exact expression. Aramaic has perhaps the longest continuous living history of any language known. It was used during the Bible's patriarchal period and is still spoken by a few people today. Aramaic and its cognate, Syriac, evolved into many dialects in different places and periods. Characterized by simplicity, clarity, and precision, it adapted easily to the various needs of everyday life. It could serve equally well as a language for scholars, pupils, lawyers, or merchants. Some have described it as the Semitic equivalent of English. . . . Gradually, especially after the Babylonian exile, Aramaic influence pervaded the land of Palestine. Nehemiah complained that children from mixed marriages were unable to speak Hebrew (Neh. 13:24). The Jews seem to have continued using Aramaic widely during the Persian, Greek, and Roman periods. Eventually the Hebrew Scriptures were translated into Aramaic paraphrases, called Targums, some of which have been found among the Dead Sea Scrolls. . . . Aramaic served as a transition from Hebrew to Greek as the language spoken by Jews in Jesus' day. In that sense Aramaic connects Old Testament Hebrew with New Testament Greek. (Walker, BL, 228–230)

Walker continues:

The Greek language is beautiful, rich, and harmonious as an instrument of communication. It is a fitting tool both for vigorous thought and for religious devotion. During its classic period, Greek was the language of one of the world's greatest cultures. During that cultural period, language, literature, and art flourished more than war. The Greek mind was preoccupied with ideals of beauty. The Greek language reflected artistry in its philosophical dialogues, its poetry, and its stately orations. The Greek language was also characterized by strength and vigor. It was capable of variety and striking effects. Greek was a language of argument, with a vocabulary and style that could penetrate and clarify phenomena rather than simply tell stories.... The conquests of Alexander the Great encouraged the spread of Greek language and culture. Regional dialects were largely replaced by "Hellenistic" or "koine" (common) Greek. Koine Greek is a dialect preserved and known through thousands of inscriptions reflecting all aspects of daily life. The koine dialect added many vernacular expressions to Attic Greek, thus making it more cosmopolitan. Simplifying the grammar also better adapted it to a worldwide culture. ... Translation of the Hebrew Scriptures into Greek was an epochal event. The Septuagint (the earliest Greek translation of the Old Testament) later had a strong influence on Christian thought.... The New Testament epistles blend the wisdom of Hebrew and the dialectic philosophy of Greek. Sermons recorded in the New Testament combine the Hebrew prophetic message with Greek oratorical force. (Walker, BL, 230–234)

F. Unique in Its Teachings

Not only is its historical background and development unique, but the Bible's message is also unique. This is what distinguishes Christianity from all other religious and secular worldviews. Kenneth R. Samples, adjunct professor of apologetics at Biola University, and senior research scholar for Reasons to Believe, illustrates how many of the claims made by biblical Christianity fly in the face of all other worldviews:

Much of society today knows so little about the specific beliefs of classical Christianity. Therefore, many people are unaware of historic Christianity's unique perspective on God, Christ, the world, humankind, values, death, and suffering.... Historic Christianity embodies numerous beliefs that are theologically and philosophically volatile (in the best sense of the term). The Christian faith contains powerful truth-claims that have transformed the church and turned the world upside down. Christianity's initial dangerous ideas started with twelve men (Jesus' apostles) and within three hundred years came to dominate the ancient Roman world. And for more than a thousand years after that, the historic faith dominated all aspects of Western civilization.... The advance and entrenchment of secularism over the last couple hundred years make these Christian ideas fresh and explosive. Not safe, but good.... The historic Christian truth-claims presented in this book can, then, be viewed as having a renewed sense of danger. (Samples, 7T, 10)

In the following we focus on three essential (i.e., necessary or indispensable) Christian teachings, without which one would no longer be speaking of biblical Christianity.

1. The Trinity

Rooted deeply in the pages of Scripture, later formalized at councils such as Nicaea (325) and Constantinople (381), and professed in confessions such as *The Articles of Religion* (1571) and *The Westminster Confession of*

Faith (1643–1646), is the understanding of the ontology of God that can only be described as unique. Wayne Grudem, research professor of theology and biblical studies at Phoenix Seminary, gives a simple definition of the Trinity: "God eternally exists as three persons, Father, Son, and Holy Spirit, and each person is fully God, and there is one God." (Grudem, ST, 226) Another way of stating this view of God is that there is one divine nature (essence) existing as three eternal persons, the Father, Son, and Holy Spirit. While this description could increase in linguistic complexity and qualification, these simple formulations are sufficient to distinguish Trinitarian Christianity from unitarian religions (e.g., Judaism and Islam) and non-theistic religions (e.g., Buddhism). Nancy Pearcey, professor of apologetics at Houston Baptist University, captures one existential implication of this unique biblical teaching:

> The balance of unity and diversity in the Trinity gives a model for human social life, because it implies that both individuality and relationship exist within the Godhead itself. God is being-in-communion. Humans are made in the image of a God who is a tri-unity—whose very nature consists in reciprocal love and communication among the Persons of the Trinity. This model provides a solution to the age-old opposition between collectivism and individualism. Over against collectivism, the Trinity implies the dignity and uniqueness of individual persons. Over against radical individualism, the Trinity implies that relationships are not created by sheer choice but are built into the very essence of human nature. We are not atomistic individuals but are created for relationships. (Pearcey, TT, 132)

Some religious systems (e.g., fourth-century Arians, Muslims, Mormons, and Jehovah's Witnesses) have attempted throughout history to show that the Trinity is nowhere to be found in the pages of Scripture. However, careful analysis of three categories of Scripture demonstrates that this opposition is exegetically unsound and groundless. These three categories consist of Scripture that attests to: (1) God's essential oneness (i.e., monotheism); (2) the divinity of each Person (Father, Son, Holy Spirit); and (3) the simultaneous distinction of each Person.

1. *God's essential oneness (monotheism).* Both the Old Testament and New Testament confirm that there is only one God. (Throughout this chapter, Scripture quotes are taken from the NIV, unless other noted)
   - OT: Deuteronomy 6:4—"Hear, O Israel: The LORD our God, the LORD is one." (cf. Deut. 4:35, 39; 1 Kings 8:60; Isa. 43:10; 44:6; 45:5, 6, 21, 22)
   - NT: 1 Corinthians 8:6—"Yet for us there is but one God, the Father, from whom all things came and for whom we live; and there is but one Lord, Jesus Christ, through whom all things came and through whom we live." (cf. Mark 12:29; John 17:3; Rom. 3:30; 1 Tim. 2:5; James 2:19)

2. *The divinity of each person.* Both the Old Testament and New Testament confirm that the Father, Son, and Holy Spirit are each fully divine.
   - The Father: 2 Corinthians 1:2—"Grace and peace to you from God our Father and the Lord Jesus Christ." (cf. Gal. 1:1; Eph. 1:2)
   - The Son: John 1:1, 14—"In the beginning was the Word, and the Word was with God, and the Word was God. . . . The Word became flesh and made his dwelling among us. We have seen his

glory, the glory of the one and only Son, who came from the Father, full of grace and truth." (cf. Isa. 9:6; John 5:18; 8:58; 10:30; 20:28; Phil. 2:5–6; Col. 1:15; Heb. 1:3, 10; Titus 2:13; 2 Peter 1:1; Rev. 1:8; 22:12, 13, 16, 20)

- The Holy Spirit: 1 Corinthians 2:10–11— "These are the things God has revealed to us by his Spirit. The Spirit searches all things, even the deep things of God. For who knows a person's thoughts except their own spirit within them? In the same way no one knows the thoughts of God except the Spirit of God." (cf. Ps. 139:7, 8; John 3:5–7; Acts 5:3–4; 13:2; 2 Cor. 3:17–18; 1 John 3:9)

3. *The simultaneous distinction of each person.* The New Testament confirms that the persons of the Trinity are distinct. Example: Matthew 28:19—"Therefore go and make disciples of all nations, baptizing them in the name of the Father and of the Son and of the Holy Spirit." (cf. Matt. 3:16, 17; 17:5; John 14:16, 17, 26; 15:26; 16:13, 14; 17:1; Acts 10:38)

Considered in their entirety, these passages of Scripture proclaim one God, eternally existing as three distinct persons (Father, Son, and Holy Spirit), each being fully divine.

2. Incarnation and Atonement

Erwin Lutzer, senior pastor of Moody Church in Chicago, poses a provocative question to contemporary western culture: "Does Christ belong on the same shelf with Buddha, Krishna, Bahá ú lláh, and Zoroaster? Like Christ, such leaders (and others) have taught some rather lofty ethical ideas. Even if we say He stands taller than the rest, have we given Him His due? Or is He to be placed on an entirely different shelf altogether?" (Lutzer,

CAOG, 13) In answer to Lutzer's question, the Bible clearly proclaims that Jesus of Nazareth is to be placed in a separate category reserved for Him alone, that of a God-man, who enters into creation to pay the penalty for the sins we have all committed.

Grudem lays out the fundamental teaching of the incarnation as "the act of God the Son whereby he took to himself a human nature." (Grudem, ST, 543) Samples highlights this extraordinary Christian teaching:

Of all the world's religions, only Christianity proclaims that God has become embodied as a human being. Of all the founders of the world's great religious traditions, only Jesus Christ claims to be God. Only the historic Christian faith proclaims that to encounter Jesus Christ is to directly and personally encounter God himself. Indeed at the very heart of historic Christianity is a truly astounding—one may say *dangerous*—truth-claim. This central article of the Christian faith is the incarnation: *God became man in Jesus of Nazareth.* This truth is a distinctive feature of the Christian faith, for it is unique to Christianity to discover a God who not only takes the initiative in becoming flesh but also does so in order to redeem sinful human beings. (Samples, 7T, 61)

One radical, or, as Samples states, "dangerous" implication (among others) of this teaching is that God would humiliate himself by condescending to the level of humanity with all its frailties, weaknesses, and temptations. For many religions, the image of the Almighty God being born like every other human child seems so objectionable that it is blasphemous. For the Christian, however, this act of the infinite Son of God forever uniting himself to a human nature (body, soul, and spirit) is the most profound sacrificial and costly expression of divine love in history.

Throughout history, however, varying groups have taught from opposite sides of the spectrum, some rejecting the deity of Jesus (e.g., Muslims and Jehovah's Witnesses) and some rejecting his humanity (e.g., early Apollinarians and Docetists). However, a proper examination of the biblical data, once again, reveals the correct teaching that (1) Jesus is truly God and (2) Jesus is truly human.

(1) *Jesus is truly God.* As seen in the previous section, there are numerous passages of Scripture that attest to Jesus' divinity. These lead Lutzer to answer his original question when he states, "The divinity of Christ sharply divides Christianity from all of the other religions of the world. This is the great divide, the unbridgeable chasm, a gulf that extends from here to eternity." (Lutzer, CAOG, 103)

(2) *Jesus is truly human.* Luke 2:7—"And she gave birth to her firstborn, a son. She wrapped him in cloths and placed him in a manger, because there was no guest room available for them." Many other passages of Scripture clearly demonstrate Jesus' true humanity as he experienced physical limitations (Matt. 8:24; 21:18; Mark 5:30–32; Luke 22:44; John 4:6), experienced pain and death (Mark 14:33–36; Luke 17:25; 23:33; John 19:30), experienced human emotions (Matt. 26:37; Mark 3:5; 10:14; 14:32–42; Luke 7:9; 10:21; John 11:5, 35), and possessed essential human qualities (Matt. 26:12, 28; Luke 24:39; John 5:30; 11:33).

We cannot separate this unique biblical teaching of God becoming man from its ultimate purpose, the final reconciliation of man to his Creator, which was accomplished through the atonement, defined as "the work Christ did in his life and death to earn our salvation." (Grudem, ST, 568) As is shown in the New Testament writings (e.g., Rom. 3:25; 5:8; Gal. 3:13; Col. 1:13, 14; 1 Peter 1:18, 19; 1 John 2:2) the concept of God paying the price

for the sins of mankind is an indispensable truth of the Christian faith. It is this work of God that sets biblical Christianity apart from all other religious systems that are grounded in the moral actions (works) of people.

3. Faith vs. Works

C. S. Lewis once said, "The Son of God became a man to enable men to become sons of God." (Lewis, MC rev. ed., 178) While other religious systems have offered theories for how man can achieve atonement for his own wickedness, Christianity alone proclaims that God himself offers all people the salvation that they absolutely cannot achieve on their own. Craig J. Hazen, founder and director of the Biola University Master of Arts in Christian Apologetics program, states:

Christianity is unique in its offer of salvation by grace alone, a free gift from God to anyone who will receive it. In the history of religion, there have only been a couple of instances of a religious movement that considered salvation or enlightenment to be a free gift from a deity. But even in those cases (such as in *Amida* Buddhism or a certain form of *Bhakti* Hinduism), it is not a no-strings-attached kind of gift. There is still work to be done on the part of the devotees. Hence, the Christian tradition stands in a solitary spot in the spectrum of world religions when the apostle Paul writes in Ephesians 2:8–9, "For it is by grace you have been saved, through faith—and this not from yourselves, it is the gift of God—not by works, so that no one can boast." (Hazen, CWR, 146)

Samples demonstrates how a nearly identical view of humankind's salvation (based on meritorious works) arises out of dissimilar worldviews (i.e., traditional Islam and the contemporary individual spirituality of the average Westerner):

Though claiming to be heirs of the biblical tradition, Islam is not a religion of grace and redemption. Muslims believe that paradise is a just reward and hell is a rightful punishment.... It is a common Islamic belief that two angels follow each Muslim throughout life. The angel on the person's right records his or her good deeds, while the angel on the left records his or her bad deeds. A Muslim's destiny hinges on the preponderance of his actions as measured on a scale. Generally speaking, Muslims have no assurance that they will earn paradise, but this dilemma is often understood as an incentive to strive for greater submission to Allah's requirements.... In this manner, this influential world religion affirms what many religions teach: that paradise is a reward for moral goodness expressed in this life and that hell is punishment for a lack of sufficient ethical accomplishment.... Many people think God will grade on a curve and cut the virtuous among us some slack when it comes to assigning heaven and hell. Why? Because current culture says that at their core, most people are good. In other words, if their life's deeds were placed on a scale, the good would outweigh the bad. (Samples, 7T, 135–136)

Against these two worldviews (which are otherwise categorically opposed to each other, yet unified on this principle), Samples presents the teaching of biblical Christianity regarding God's grace:

Against the backdrop of a near-global consensus that God sees humankind as being basically good and, therefore, worthy of heaven stands historic Christianity's . . . revolutionary notion that . . . in the eyes of God no one is or becomes morally acceptable by his or her own merit. In fact, it is fair to say that sin (moral transgression) is a much bigger problem than most people (including many Christians) realize. But the *good news* (Gospel) is that God's grace is deeper and

Jesus Christ is a much greater Savior than most people (including Christians) realize.... Christianity at its heart is a religion not of self-help but of divine rescue. According to the Gospels, what human beings need most is not moral guidance but rather a Savior. (Samples, 7T, 136–137)

These unique Christian teachings suggest a radical departure from all other religious and secular thought. The biblical teaching about the Trinitarian nature of God clearly explains why human beings really need both (1) individual expression (each member of the Trinity is distinct and relates to humanity uniquely) and (2) relationship in community (the same three Persons exist in an eternally loving relationship with one another). The nature of the Trinity not only explains why humans long for both individuality and community, but it also provides an example for our relationships with one another. Furthermore, God affirms the intrinsic worth of every person who has ever lived by the incarnation of Jesus and his atoning sacrifice, as recorded in the Bible. Every one of us is fashioned in the "image of God" (Gen. 1:27; 9:6). Beyond this, however, the intrinsic moral worth of every human person and the divine sacrifice highlight a provocative dissimilarity between Christianity and all other religious systems. That is, a person's value is found in her very being, not in her behavior. So it follows that even those persons considered by many to be irredeemable (e.g., Osama bin Laden, Adolf Eichmann, or Kim Jong-Il) remain valuable in the eyes of God. In his uniquely narrative style, Lewis illustrates what this divine love (a love not contingent upon human behavior) would look like if ever truly applied:

I remember Christian teachers telling me long ago that I must hate a bad man's actions, but not hate the bad man: or, as they would say, hate the sin but not the sinner. For a long time I used to think this a silly, straw-splitting distinction: how could you hate what a man did and not hate the man? But years later it occurred to me that there was one man to whom I had been doing this all my life—namely myself. However much I might dislike my own cowardice or conceit or greed, I went on loving myself. There had never been the slightest difficulty about it. In fact the very reason why I hated the things was that I loved the man. Just because I loved myself, I was sorry to find that I was the sort of man who did those things. Consequently, Christianity does not want us to reduce by one atom the hatred we feel for cruelty and treachery. We ought to hate them. Not one word of what we have said about them needs to be unsaid. But it does want us to hate them in the same way in which we hate things in ourselves: being sorry that the man should have done such things, and hoping, if it is anyway possible, that somehow, sometime, somewhere he can be cured and made human again. . . . I admit that this means loving people who have nothing lovable about them. But then, has oneself anything lovable about it? You love it simply because it is yourself. God intends us to love all selves in the same way and for the same reason: but He has given us the sum ready worked out in our own case to show us how it works. We have then to go on and apply the rule to all the other selves. Perhaps it makes it easier if we remember that that is how He loves us. Not for any nice, attractive qualities we think we have, but just because we are the things called selves. For really there is nothing else in us to love. (Lewis, MC, rev. ed., 117, 120)

III. Unique in Impact

Clearly, the Bible has influenced civilization more than any other literary work in history. This section will not only provide evidence that the Bible is the most widely distributed

work ever written, but will also highlight its resilient history and demonstrate its foundational role in the advent of western civilization.

A. Unique in Its Circulation and Translation

From the first translation of the Hebrew Bible into the Greek Septuagint (LXX; see chapter 4) in the mid-third century BC, to the rise of biblical literacy with the invention of Gutenberg's printing press, to the surprising number of translations and its mass circulation, to its worldwide availability today via digital and electronic media, the Bible has registered an unparalleled history. Rodney Stark, Distinguished Professor of the Social Sciences at Baylor University, recounts one portion of this history:

> In about 1455 Johannes Gutenberg (1397–1468) printed the first Bible. It was soon followed by a flood of printed books, many of them Bibles, most of them religious. The invention of printing stimulated a very rapid expansion of literacy in Europe. Suddenly, people had something to read, and in their own language. Where once readers had numbered in the thousands, soon there were tens of thousands of readers, then hundreds of thousands. By 1500 at least 3 percent of Germans, about 400,000 people, could read. To serve this rapidly growing audience, printers opened shops in every sizable town. Soon peddlers traveled the countryside selling books and pamphlets, with the result that huge numbers of Europeans began not only to read the Bible for themselves but to read commentaries and tracts. Sales totals were incredibly high, given the size of the literate populations. (Stark, FGG, 74–75)

Today, as in the time of Gutenberg, the Bible continues to surpass all other literary works in production and circulation. While we commonly hear about books on the bestseller list, selling a few hundred thousand copies, rarely do we come across books that have sold more than a million copies. Even more rarely do we find books that have passed the ten-million mark in sales. However, the number of Bibles sold reaches into the billions, and when one considers the freely distributed copies of biblical literature, the numbers likely reach into the tens of billions. According to the United Bible Societies' 2012 statistics, in that year alone member organizations were responsible for distributing 405 million Bibles or portions thereof (of which 32.1 million were full Bibles). One interesting fact to note is that in 2012 (a year in which a record number of full Bibles was distributed), there was a dramatic increase in the distribution of Bibles or portions of the Bible in countries where persecution of Christians is widespread.

The numbers of translations of the Bible are every bit as impressive as its distribution numbers. Most books are never translated into another language. If a book is translated, it is normally published in just two or three languages at the most. Very few books are available in more than ten languages. But according to the Wycliffe Global Alliance's 2014 Scripture and Language Statistics, the Bible or portions of it have been translated into 2,883 languages! (SLS) Although this is only about 42 percent of the world's 6,901 known languages, these languages represent the primary vehicle of communication for about 80 percent (5.8 billion) of the estimated 7.26 billion people worldwide. Several languages were first committed to writing solely to transmit Scripture, including Gothic, Armenian, and Georgian. (SLS; USWPC) Perhaps more astounding was the work of the monk brothers, Cyril and Methodius, to create the Cyrillic alphabet in the ninth century AD; as a result, they extended the gospel message to the empire of the Moravians. This alphabet provided the basis for contemporary languages such as Russian, Ukrainian, Serbo-Croatian, and Bulgarian. (Geisler and Nix, GIB, 519–522)

In addition to the printed copies of biblical literature, the Internet and digital media expose even more people to the Bible. Two examples of these are directly downloadable digital texts and audio versions of every book of the Bible. One example of a digital text is YouVersion, a Bible app that has been translated into 799 languages and downloaded over 200 million times at the time of this writing. Another example: *Faith Comes by*

DISTRIBUTION OF BIBLICAL LITERATURE

Country	Rank	2011 Distribution	2012 Distribution	% Increase
Syria	4	19,000	163,105	758%
Laos	28	7,985	20,743	159%
Iraq	3	28,518	66,175	132%
Egypt	23	2,261,236	2,824,504	25%
India	21	22,790,001	27,220,467	19%
Nigeria	10	7,695,853	8,121,452	5%

Chart information adapted from WWL; SDIPH

Hearing provides audio versions of the Bible with "Bible recordings in 915 languages spoken by nearly 6 billion people. Over 334 million people in virtually every country have been reached through our wide range of programs." (SOS)

Clearly, no other book comes even close to the Bible in its distribution and translation.

B. Unique in Its Survival and Resiliency

No other written work has been so attacked, scrutinized, and persecuted as have the canonical books of the Bible. From emperors, monarchs, and dictators who tried to destroy the words of Scripture (e.g., the persecutions under Diocletian in the fourth century, Communist Russia, and Socialist China), to intellectual attempts to discredit the content of Scripture (e.g., eighteenth to nineteenth century rationalism and twenty-first-century postmodernism), the Bible has withstood all forms of opposition.

1. Through Persecution

Two examples of attempts to destroy the Bible, one ancient and one recent, demonstrate the ferocity of Christianity's opponents. Rochunga Pudaite, founder of Bibles For The World, highlights the extreme measures to which some societies will go:

Diocletian became Caesar in the year 284. For the first 19 years of his reign Christians had rest from persecution. . . . Then, under the influence of his cruel son-in-law, Diocletian issued four harsh edicts. The first called for the destruction of all places of Christian worship and the burning of all Christian books. This order also stripped Christians of all honors and civic rights. The second called for the imprisonment in chains of pastors and church officers. The third, issued on the eve of Diocletian's 20th anniversary as emperor, offered a cruel kind of amnesty. The Christian prisoners would be released if they would sacrifice to the Emperor and other Roman gods. The fourth, issued in AD 304, ordered every person in the Empire to sacrifice and make offerings to heathen gods, or suffer torture and death. Churches were destroyed all over the Empire. All Bibles and writings of the church fathers that could be found were burned in public gatherings. Christian men, women, and children were tortured, thrown to wild beasts, and burned to death. Diocletian had a monument erected at the site of one Bible burning, bearing the inscription, *Extincto nomine Christianorum*—"Extinct is the Name of Christians." . . . .

Communism came to dwarf all other foes of the Bible. Lenin and Marx both predicted that the Bible would become only a relic in a new classless, atheistic society. Adjoining countries were annexed into the Soviet Empire, religious freedom denied, missionaries banished, Bibles confiscated, and churches turned into museums or closed. Millions of citizens, including many Christians, died in Stalinistic blood purges in the 1920s and '30s. In village after village, residents were called to mass meetings and asked, "Are you with the Marxists or the believers?" Those who said "believers" were shoved into cattle cars for shipment to Siberia. . . . Millions perished in Communist countries other than the Soviet Union. Here too, Bibles were destroyed. It was a rerun of the hate-filled persecutions under the old Roman emperors, except that many, many more have died for the Christian faith and an authoritative Bible in the 20th century than in all of the bloody vendettas by the Caesars of Imperial Rome. (Pudaite and Hefley, GBEW, 47–48, 55–56)

Other examples of persecution could be cited from history to document the persistent antagonism against the Bible, yet there is no indication that the desire for or distribution of the Bible is waning (see Section III. A. above). However, the greatest current threat to the Bible is the intellectual challenge to its content and relevance.

2. Through Criticism

In spite of the intellectual skepticism that began to spread in the seventeenth century and still permeates culture today, the Bible (and its view of reality) continues to be as intellectually viable now as during the time of its composition. Bernard Ramm, former professor of religion at Baylor University, highlights the resiliency of the Bible in the face of rampant criticism:

A thousand times over, the death knell of the Bible has been sounded, the funeral procession formed, the inscription cut on the tombstone, and the committal read. But somehow the corpse never stays put. No other book has been so chopped, knived, sifted, scrutinized, and vilified. What book on philosophy or religion or psychology or *belles lettres* of classical or modern times has been subject to such a mass attack as the Bible? with such venom and skepticism? with such thoroughness and erudition? upon every chapter, line and tenet? (Ramm, PCE, 232–233)

The Bible has not only withstood these attacks from a skeptical world, but the Christian worldview that it champions has experienced a revitalization in recent years through a resurgence of scholarship in various disciplines, such as textual criticism, archaeology, anthropology, the natural sciences, and philosophy.

C. Unique in Its Impact on Western Civilization

No other book has influenced western civilization as much as the Bible. From its

historical narratives, moral teachings, and existential claims, the Bible has laid the groundwork for democratic forms of government and law, the rational exploration of the natural world, movements in both art and literature, societal morals and values. Pudaite provides a sampling of the areas that have been affected by the Bible:

Almost all of the good things of life that we take for granted bear the stamp of the Bible's influence—marriage, family, names, calendar, institutions of caring, social agencies, education, benefits from science, uplifting books, magnificent works of art and music, freedom, justice, equal rights, the work ethic, the virtues of self-reliance and self-discipline. (Pudaite and Hefley, GBEW, 114)

1. Government and Law

In the area of human governance and law, the Bible has contributed significantly to three developments that have shaped the consciousness and conscience of western civilization: (1) individual autonomy and the democratic process, (2) a separation of secular government from the religious institution, and (3) the maintaining of a system of justice. Ronald J. Sider, Distinguished Professor of Theology at Eastern University, highlights basic biblical principles that have become normative assumptions within democratic societies, showing how the biblical understanding of human nature is determinative in establishing societies that are appropriately free for the individual and that protect against totalitarian overreach:

This biblical story shapes the Christian approach to public life in profound ways. For example, persons are not merely complex machines to be programmed for the good of the state. They are immeasurably valuable beings, so loved by their Creator that he suffered the hell of Roman crucifixion for them, free beings called to shape history along with God and neighbor, immortal beings whose ultimate destiny far transcends any passing political system. Public life is important because it shapes the social context in which people respond to God's invitation to live in right relationship with both himself and neighbor. . . . Probably the best protection against political totalitarianism is the recognition that the state is not the ultimate source of value and law. If people in a society believe strongly that there exists a higher law grounded in God the Creator to which current legislation ought to conform and which citizens ought to obey even if that entails civil disobedience, totalitarianism will be held in check. . . . Decentralized decision making, even if it means a certain loss of efficiency, is in keeping with the biblical vision of persons as coshapers under God of their own history. . . . The democratic political process . . . is the political system most compatible with biblical values about the importance of the individual and the pervasiveness of sin. Genuine political democracy decentralizes political power more completely than any other form of government. As Reinhold Niebuhr never tired of pointing out, democracy is necessary precisely because people are sinful. At the same time, it is because each individual is of inestimable worth to God that every person should be free to help shape his or her political destiny. . . . The state should not promote or establish any religion or denomination. Nor is the separation of church and state merely a pragmatic necessity in a pluralistic society. Religious faith by its very nature is a free response to God. It cannot be coerced. Throughout biblical history, we see a sovereign God constantly inviting persons into free dialogue with himself. He invites obedience but is astonishingly patient with those who decline the invitation. If the history of Israel tells us anything, it discloses how much space God gives people to reject his will and still continue to enjoy the created gifts of food, health, and life. Jesus' parable of the wheat and the tares (Matt. 13:24ff.) makes it clear that God chooses to allow believers and nonbelievers to live and enjoy the world together until the end of history. Since God intends history to be the place where people have the freedom to respond or not respond to him, the state should not promote or hinder religious belief. (Sider, EVAD, 38, 41–43)

The Bible has also informed both the substance and framework of modern legal structures. Steve Jeffery, Michael Ovey, and Andrew Sach demonstrate how the biblical principle of retributive justice is still the only form of jurisprudence that is truly "just":

The principle of retribution guarantees that only *guilty* people are punished. Retribution is based on the premise that the appropriate authority should impose a punishment if, and only if, an offence has actually been committed. Retribution therefore ensures that no one is punished if he or she does not *deserve* it. Similarly, the principle of retribution also ensures a given punishment is *proportional* to its crime. It recognizes that serious crimes deserve severe punishments, whereas more trivial offences warrant milder sanctions. Finally, the principle of retribution also safeguards the principle of *equity*, for the only factors allowed to affect the severity of a punishment are those that affect the nature of the crime. Irrelevant differences such as the race, gender or social class of the offender should have no impact on sentencing. It is clear, therefore, that the principle of retribution secures those elements of a system of punishment both required by Scripture and in accord with our natural sense of right and wrong. Retribution may be combined with the elements of deterrence or correction, but by itself safeguards these biblical principles. (Jeffery et al., POT, 256)

While the quotation above explains the principle of retribution, we acknowledge that human error may fail to administer it accurately. Though space limitations do not allow us to describe the intrinsic flaws of other legal theories, we can safely say that alternative theories have often led to gross abuses.

Finally, Barbara Armacost and Peter Enns, in their close examination of the biblical prophets, describe the context within which this system of retributive justice should work:

First, biblical justice is procedural as well as substantive. It requires fair and unbiased adjudication as well as fair and principled laws. Second, justice is largely relational and has particular claims on those who are in positions of power or authority over others. Third, biblical justice requires special attention to the way laws and legal institutions treat the most vulnerable individuals in our communities. Fourth, there is a sense in which modern lawyers should see themselves as having a prophetic role in their communities, either as insiders working for justice in law and legal institutions or as outsiders who bring to light injustice and call for its eradication. (Armacost and Enns, COJ, 134–135)

2. Science and Education

In his sobering essay on how monotheism affected the shape of western civilization, Stark effectively counters many revisionist narratives that have become popular in contemporary culture. One of the biggest myths that Stark exposes is the inflated, if not totally fabricated, idea that religion (particularly Christianity) was somehow an obstacle to, rather than a catalyst for, the advent of science and the rise of higher education:

There was no "scientific revolution" that finally burst through the superstitious barriers of faith, but that the flowering of science that took place in the sixteenth century was the normal, gradual, and direct outgrowth of Scholasticism and the medieval universities. Indeed, theological assumptions unique to Christianity explain why science was born only in Christian Europe. Contrary to the received wisdom, religion and science not only were compatible; they were inseparable. . . . The reason we didn't know the truth concerning these matters is that the claim of an inevitable and bitter warfare between religion and science has, for more than three centuries, been the primary polemical device used in the atheist attack on faith. From Thomas Hobbes through Carl Sagan and Richard Dawkins, false claims about religion and science have been used as weapons in the battle to "free" the human mind from the "fetters of faith." . . . I argue not only that there is no inherent conflict between religion and science, but that *Christian theology was essential for the rise of science.* (Stark, FGG, 3, 123)

Stark summarizes the reasons for the truth of this thesis (the italicized portion above):

Christianity depicted God as a rational, responsive, dependable, and omnipotent being and the universe as his personal creation, thus having a rational, lawful, stable structure, awaiting human comprehension. . . . The rise of science was not an extension of classical learning. It was the natural outgrowth of Christian doctrine: Nature exists because it was created by God. To love and honor God, one must fully appreciate the wonders of his handiwork. Moreover, because God is perfect, his handiwork functions in accord with *immutable principles*. By the full use of our God-given powers of reason and observation, we ought to be able to discover these principles. (Stark, FGG, 157)

Both the understanding of a rational Creator of the universe and the inseparability of Christian theism from scientific truths led Sir Isaac Newton to ground his views of absolute time and space on the eternity and omnipresence of God. In his *Principia*, Newton states:

The supreme God is an eternal, infinite, and absolutely perfect being . . . , He is eternal and infinite, omnipotent and omniscient, that is, he endures from eternity to eternity, and he is present from infinity to infinity; he rules all things, and he knows all things that happen or can happen. He is not eternity and infinity, but eternal and infinite; he is not duration and space, but he endures and is present. He endures always and is present everywhere, and by existing always and everywhere he constitutes duration and space. Since each and every particle of space is *always*, and each and every indivisible moment of duration is *everywhere*, certainly the maker and lord of all things will not be *never* or *nowhere*. . . . It is agreed that the supreme God necessarily exists, and by the same necessity he is *always* and *everywhere*. (Newton, INPW, 111–112)

Finally, Stark illustrates that Christian theism provided the proper context for the flourishing of science and the humanities:

The university was a Christian invention that evolved from cathedral schools established to train monks and priests. The first two universities appeared in Paris (where both Albertus Magnus and Thomas Aquinas taught) and Bologna, in the middle of the twelfth century. Oxford and Cambridge were founded around 1200, and then came a flood of new institutions during the remainder of the thirteenth century. . . . The university was something new under the sun—an institution devoted exclusively to "higher learning." It was not a monastery or place for meditation. . . . The medieval universities were unlike Chinese academies for training Mandarins or a Zen master's school. They were not primarily concerned with imparting the received wisdom. Rather, just as is the case today, faculty gained fame and invitations to join faculties elsewhere by *innovation*. (Stark, FGG, 62–63)

3. Art, Literature, and Music

The Bible has been a fundamental source for nearly every genre of art and literature, and has provided inspiration for innumerable visionaries who have elevated the artistic endeavor to its highest form. Pudaite provides some examples of areas in which the Bible has left its mark on the arts:

Since the beginning of the Christian era, the Bible has inspired great works of art. The frescoes of the Roman catacombs reveal Biblical concepts of faith and hope. When Christianity became a legal religion in the Roman Empire, Christian art blossomed in the churches and on monuments. Through the 19th century, the greatest sculptures and paintings were based on characters or incidents in the Bible. The greatest artists—Raphael, Leonardo da Vinci, Michelangelo, Rembrandt, and others—are most remembered and appreciated for their biblical masterpieces. (Pudaite and Hefley, GBEW, 123)

T. R. Henn, former president of St. Catharine's College, Cambridge, distinguishes the Bible from all other great works of antiquity and shows the Bible's formational impact on the literature of the western world:

> As "literature" it [the Bible] is, in many ways, remote from our present consciousness. There is no single work of comparable quality and intention (still less of current availability) with which we may compare it. We may read the Koran, or the Granth Sahib, the Upanishads, the Bhagavad Gita, the Egyptian *Book of the Dead*, the Epic of Gilgamesh, the Babylonian Epic of Creation, the Law Code of Hammurabi; and these, together with various anthologies, provide some material for comparisons, throw some oblique and broken light; but little more. In its range, its unity, its diversity, its two major symphonic movements of promise and fulfilment, in its avoidance (in general) of arid and now pointless narrative or gnomic reflections that are of little relevance to the West, the Bible is unique. . . . How far, then, can the Bible be considered as literature, in any coherent sense? It is clear that it has been burned deeply into the fabric of the life and literature of the English-speaking peoples. . . . Its proverbs and its parables, its episodes sacred or profane, have been expounded in drama and poetry from the earliest written English. It has supplied the themes or framework for epic, satire, tragedy, comedy, farce, ballet; above all, its dramatic and choric potential make it specially suitable for oratorio. It has furnished allusions or depth-images to an incalculably great mass of writing. Its rhythms have been engrafted historically into much of our prose. (Henn, BAL, 21, 9–10)

Chase further emphasizes how the Bible has impacted some of history's greatest minds:

> The language of the Bible, now simple and direct in its homely vigour, now sonorous and stately in its richness, has placed its indelible stamp upon our best writers from Bacon to Lincoln and even to the present day. Without it there would be no *Paradise Lost*, no *Samson Agonistes*, no *Pilgrim's Progress*; no William Blake, or Whittier, or T. S. Eliot as we know them; no Emerson or Thoreau, no negro Spirituals, no Address at Gettysburg. Without it the words of Burke and Washington, Patrick Henry and Winston Churchill would miss alike their eloquence and their meaning. Without a knowledge of it the best of our literature remains obscure, and many of the characteristic features and qualities of our spoken language are threatened with extinction. (Chase, BCR, 9)

Pudaite illustrates how the Bible has affected some of the greatest musical composers:

> The creators of the greatest oratorios, anthems, symphonies, hymns, and other classics were inspired by the Bible. Bach's "Jesus Joy of Man's Desiring," Mendelssohn's "Elijah," Handel's "Messiah," Brahms's "Requiem," Beethoven's "Mount of Olives," and Haydn's "Creation" are some of the best known works inspired by the Bible. After hearing his magnificent work, Haydn said, "Not I, but a power from above created that." Bach often wrote I.N.J. for the Latin words meaning "In the Name of Jesus" on his manuscripts. (Pudaite and Hefley, GBEW, 123)

Influential theologian, philosopher, and author Francis Schaeffer provides even greater insight into how the Bible influenced the work of a genius like Bach:

> His music was a direct result of the Reformation culture and the biblical Christianity of the time, which was so much a part of Bach himself. There would have been no Bach had

there been no Luther. . . . It was appropriate that the last thing Bach the Christian wrote was "Before Thy Throne I Now Appear." Bach consciously related both the form and the words of his music to biblical truth. . . . This rested on the fact that the Bible gives unity to the universal and the particulars, and therefore the particulars have meaning. Expressed musically, there can be endless variety and diversity without chaos. There is variety yet resolution. (Schaeffer, HSWTL, 92)

4. Societal Norms and Values

The Bible has shaped social morality more than any other book. One glaring example where a biblically informed Christianity drastically changed a commonly held societal norm that has existed in nearly every culture throughout history is that of slavery. Stark illustrates how Christian theology, grounded in biblical principles, led fervent believers to the conclusion that slavery was morally reprehensible and therefore required organized action:

> Of all the world's religions, including the three great monotheisms, only in Christianity did the idea develop that slavery was sinful and must be abolished. Although it has been fashionable to deny it, antislavery doctrines began to appear in Christian theology soon after the decline of Rome and were accompanied by the eventual disappearance of slavery in all but the fringes of Christian Europe. When Europeans subsequently instituted slavery in the New World, they did so over strenuous papal opposition, a fact that was conveniently "lost" from history until recently. Finally, the abolition of New World slavery was initiated and achieved by Christian activists. (Stark, FGG, 291)

There are many more examples of when, where, and how the Bible has positively impacted the course of human events and thinking, but these few seem sufficient to establish the unique presence that the Bible commands in our world today.

IV. Concluding Remarks

At the time of this writing, a new museum is being constructed at a cost of nearly one billion dollars in the heart of Washington, D.C. dedicated to making accessible to the public the text, history, and legacy of the Bible. This museum will house more than forty thousand artifacts that relate to both the history told in the Bible and the history of the Bible itself. While neither this chapter nor this 430,000-square-foot museum in any way proves the claims of the Bible or certain doctrines concerning the Bible (e.g., inspiration and inerrancy), they certainly underscore the conclusion that the Bible is a central piece of humanity's shared history and that it is worthy of continued investigation, critical engagement, and appreciation. Indeed, anyone sincerely seeking truth would consider the ongoing impact of a book that, although it reached completion nearly 2,000 years ago, continues to have a range of appeal and influence that is unique.

CHAPTER 2

HOW WE GOT THE BIBLE

OVERVIEW

I. How Was the Bible Written?

As we learned in the last chapter, the Bible is unique. So how did it come into existence? Who wrote it? Who decided what writings would be included? Many have been curious about the background of the Bible, its divisions, and the material used for its production. This section will familiarize you with its construction and give you a greater appreciation for how it was compiled. In the next chapter, we will examine the evidence to determine whether the New Testament is reliable and true.

A. Materials Used

1. Writing Surfaces

a. Papyrus

The difficulty with discovering an ancient manuscript (a handwritten copy of the Scriptures) is primarily due to the perishable materials used for writing. "All . . . autographs [originals]," writes noted biblical scholar F. F. Bruce, "have been long since lost. It could not be otherwise, if they were written on papyrus, since . . . it is only in exceptional conditions that papyrus survives for any length of time." (Bruce, BP, 166) "Papyrus was the common writing material especially until the third century, for classical literature until the sixth or seventh century, and even later for some documents." (Greenlee, INTTC, 10)

The most common writing material available in biblical times was papyrus. The papyrus plant grew in the shallow lakes and rivers of Egypt and Syria. (WBE, s.v. "papyrus") Large shipments of papyrus were distributed through the Syrian port of Byblos. Scholars surmise that the Greek word for book (*biblos*) comes from the name of this port. The English word *paper* comes from the Greek word for papyrus (*papyros*). (Ewart, FATMT, 19–20)

The Cambridge History of the Bible gives an account of how papyrus was prepared for writing:

> The reeds were stripped and cut lengthwise into thin narrow slices before being beaten and pressed together into two layers set at right angles to each other. When dried the whitish surface was polished smooth with a stone or other implement. Pliny refers to several qualities of papyri, and varying thicknesses and surfaces are found before the New Kingdom period when sheets were often very thin and translucent. (Ackroyd and Evans, CHB, 30)

The oldest papyrus fragment known dates back to about 2500 BC. The earliest manuscripts were written on papyrus, and it was difficult for any to survive except in dry areas such as the sands of Egypt or in caves such as the Qumran caves where the Dead Sea Scrolls were discovered.

b. Parchment

Parchment is "writing material made from the skins of sheep, goats, or calves. Such materials are very durable. Parchment scrolls have survived from about 1500 BC." (WBE, s.v. "parchment") These skins were "shaved and scraped" in order to produce a more durable writing material. Bruce tells us that "the word 'parchment' comes from the name of the city of Pergamum in Asia Minor, for

the production of this writing material was at one time specially associated with that place." (Bruce, BP, 3–4)

c. Vellum

Vellum was "a form of fine, high-quality parchment . . . made from the skins of calves, kids, or lambs." (WBE, s.v. "parchment") Vellum was often dyed purple. Parchment is an enduring material, even including the dye, so that some of the vellum manuscripts we have today retain that ancient purple. The writing on dyed vellum was usually done with gold or silver.

d. Other Materials

Ostraca: This unglazed pottery was popular with the common people. The technical name is "potsherd." Ostraca has been found in abundance in Egypt and Palestine (Job 2:8).

Stones: Archaeologists have found common stones inscribed with an iron pen.

Clay Tablets: Engraved with a sharp instrument and then dried to create a permanent record (Jer. 17:13; Ezek. 4:1), these tablets provided the cheapest and one of the most durable kinds of writing material.

Wax Tablets: A metal stylus was used on a piece of flat wood covered with wax.

2. Writing Instruments

Chisel: An iron instrument used to engrave stones.

Metal Stylus: "A three-sided instrument with a beveled head for writing . . . was especially used to make incursions into clay and wax tablets." (Geisler and Nix, BFGU, 169)

When you come, bring . . . the books, especially the parchments.

Paul, 2 Timothy 4:13 NASB

Pen: A pointed reed "was fashioned from rushes (*Juncus maritimis*) about 6–16 inches long, the end being cut to a flat chisel-shape to enable thick or thin strokes to be made with the broad or narrow sides. The reed-pen was in use from the early first millennium in Mesopotamia, from where it may well have been adopted, while the idea of a quill pen seems to have come from the Greeks in the third century BC" (Ackroyd and Evans, CHB, 31; see also Jer. 8:8). The pen was used on vellum, parchment, and papyrus.

Ink: The ink in the ancient world was usually a compound of "charcoal, gum and water." (Bruce, BP, 5) Even better ink came from the gallnut, a nodule or blister that grows on some trees, such as oaks, when a wasp stings the tree to lay its larvae on the tree's leaves or twigs. The tree in response encases the larvae until it forms the gallnut. Some of our best dyes and inks are derived from the gallnut. (For more information about ink from gallnuts, please see the quotation from Professor Wurthwein in chapter 4, section II.B.1.)

B. Forms of Ancient Books
1. Scroll

Rolls or *scrolls* were made by gluing sheets of papyrus together or sewing sheets of parchment together with sinews from the muscles of a calf's leg and then winding the resulting long strips around a stick. Some rolls reached 144 feet long. The average scroll, however, was only about twenty to thirty-five feet. The larger the scroll, the more difficult it was to handle. It is no wonder that Callimachus, a professional cataloguer of books from ancient Alexandria's library, said "a big book is a big nuisance." (Metzger and Ehrman, TNT, 12) Though writing was usually limited to one side of a scroll, a two-sided scroll is called an "opisthograph" (Greenlee, INTTC, 10; see also Rev. 5:1).

2. Codex or Book Form

In order to make the papyrus sheets or parchments less bulky, and also to making it easier to locate and read a specific text, the sheets were assembled in leaf form and written on both sides. "The technology of the codex . . . made copying itself more efficient because pages stayed open. It is possible also that this technology hastened the formation of the canon." (Kaminsky et al., AIB, 12)

J. K. Elliot writes:

It is likely that the codex form in which the Christian scriptures circulated helped to promote the establishment of the definite, fixed canon of the 27 books we know.

When each book circulated as a separate entity, obviously there was no limit to the number of texts that could be received. When certain, approved, texts were gathered into small collections this had the effect of ostracizing and isolating texts which were not deemed suitable for inclusion. (Elliot, MCC, 106)

C. Types of Writing
1. Book-Hand Writing

According to New Testament scholar Bruce Metzger, "Literary works . . . were written in a more formal style of book-hand, which was characterized by more deliberate and carefully executed letters, each one separate from the others, somewhat like our capital letters (not *uncials,* a word that has precise meaning in Latin writing but only a derived and imprecise one in Greek)." (Metzger and Ehrman, TNT, 17) New Testament manuscripts written in this fashion, however, are called *uncials.* (Kaminsky et al., AIB, 12)

Apologists Norman Geisler and William Nix note that the "most important manuscripts of the New Testament are generally considered to be the great uncial codices that date from the fourth and following centuries." (Geisler and Nix, GIB, 391)

Probably the two oldest and most significant uncial manuscripts are Codex Vaticanus (about AD 325–350) and Codex Sinaiticus (about AD 340). Several scholars have suggested that these manuscripts may have been made by Eusebius when Constantine commissioned him to produce fifty copies of the Scriptures. (Metzger and Ehrman, TNT, 15)

2. Minuscule Writing

Minuscule writing was a cursive "script of smaller letters in a running hand . . . created for the production of books" around the beginning of the ninth century AD. (Metzger and Ehrman, TNT, 18)

3. Spaces and Vowels

The Greek manuscripts were written without any breaks between words, while the Hebrew text (also written without breaks between words) was written without vowels until sometime between the sixth and tenth centuries AD when the Masoretes added them. (Ehrman, *The Bible*, 382–383)

Both practices seem odd and confusing to most modern readers. But to the ancients, for whom Greek or Hebrew was their native tongue, these practices were normal and clearly understood. The Jews did not need to see the vowels written out. As they learned their language they became familiar with how to pronounce and interpret it.

Likewise, Greek-speaking peoples had no trouble reading their language without breaks between words. As Metzger explains: "In that language it is the rule, with very few exceptions, that native words can end only in a vowel (or a diphthong) or in one of three consonants, ν, ρ and ς. Furthermore, it should not be supposed that *scriptio continua* presented exceptional difficulties in reading, for apparently it was

customary in antiquity to read aloud, even when one was alone. Thus despite the absence of spaces between words, by pronouncing to oneself what was read, syllable by syllable, one soon became used to reading *scriptio continua*." (Metzger and Ehrman, TNT, 22–23)

D. Divisions
1. Books

See material below on "The Canon."

2. Chapters
a. Old Testament

The first divisions were made prior to the Babylonian captivity, which began in 586 BC. The Pentateuch was divided into 154 groupings, called *sedarim*, which "were designed to provide lessons sufficient to cover a three-year cycle of reading." (Geisler and Nix, GIB, 339)

During the Babylonian captivity but prior to 536 BC, the Pentateuch was "divided into fifty-four sections called *parashiyyoth*. . . . These were later subdivided into 669 sections for reference purposes. These sections were utilized for a single-year [reading] cycle." (Geisler and Nix, GIB, 339)

Around 165 BC, the Old Testament books of the Prophets were similarly sectioned for reference and ease of reading. (Geisler and Nix, GIB, 339)

Finally, "during the Reformation era the Hebrew Old Testament began to follow the Protestant chapter divisions for the most part. Some chapter divisions, however, had been placed in the margins as early as 1330." (Geisler and Nix, BFGU, 174)

b. New Testament

The Greeks first made paragraph divisions before the Council of Nicea (AD 325), perhaps as early as AD 250.

The oldest system of chapter division originated about AD 350 and appears in the margins of Codex Vaticanus. However, these sections are much smaller than our modern chapter divisions. For example, in our Bible the gospel of Matthew has twenty-eight chapters, but in Codex Vaticanus, Matthew is divided into 170 sections.

Geisler and Nix write that

it was not until the thirteenth century that those sections were changed, and then only gradually. Stephen Langton, a professor at the University of Paris and afterward Archbishop of Canterbury, divided the Bible into the modern chapter divisions (c. 1227). That was prior to the introduction of movable type in printing. Since the Wycliffe Bible (1382) followed that pattern, those basic divisions have been the virtual base upon which the Bible has been printed to this very day. (Geisler and Nix, GIB, 340–341)

3. Verses

a. Old Testament

In the Old Testament, the first verse indicators "were merely spaces between words, as the words were run together continuously through a given book. . . . After the Babylonian captivity, for the purpose of public reading and interpretation, space stops were employed, and still later additional markings were added. These 'verse' markings were not regulated, and differed from place to place. It was not until about AD 900 that the markings were standardized." (Geisler and Nix, GIB, 339)

b. New Testament

Verse markings similar to what we have in our modern Bibles did not appear in the New Testament until the middle of the sixteenth century. They actually followed the development of chapters, "apparently in an effort to further facilitate cross-references and make public reading easier. The markings first occur in the fourth edition of the Greek New Testament published by Robert Stephanus, a Parisian printer, in 1551. These verses were introduced into the English New Testament by William Whittingham of Oxford in 1557. In 1555 Stephanus introduced his verse divisions into a Latin Vulgate edition, from which they have continued to the present day." (Geisler and Nix, GIB, 341)

II. Who Decided What to Include in the Bible?

How was it decided which books would become part of the Bible? This question relates to *canonicity*. A discerning person would want to know why some books were included in the *canon* while others were excluded.

A. Meaning of the Word *Canon*

The word *canon* comes from the root word *reed* (English word *cane*, Hebrew form *ganeh*, and Greek form *kanon*). The reed was used as a measuring rod and came to mean "standard." (Ehrman, *The Bible*, 375)

The third-century church father Origen used the word "canon to denote what we call the 'rule of faith,' the standard by which we are to measure and evaluate everything that may be offered to us as an article of belief." (Bruce, BP, 86) Later the term meant a "list" or "index." (Bruce, BP, 86) As applied to Scripture, *canon* means "an officially accepted list of books." (Earle, HWGOB, 33)

The church did not *create* the canon; it did not determine which books would be called Scripture, the inspired Word of God. Instead, the church *recognized*, or *discovered*, which books had been inspired from their

A book is not the Word of God because it is accepted by the people of God.
Rather, it was accepted by the people of God because it is the Word of God.
That is, God gives the book its divine authority, not the people of God.
They merely recognize the divine authority which God gives to it.

Geisler and Nix

inception. Stated another way, "a book is not the Word of God because it is accepted by the people of God. Rather, it was accepted by the people of God because it is the Word of God. That is, God gives the book its divine authority, not the people of God. They merely recognize the divine authority which God gives to it." (Geisler and Nix, GIB, 210)

New Testament scholar Lee Martin McDonald states, "While the definition of a biblical canon has more to do with the end of a process, that is, with a fixed list of sacred Scriptures, the authority attributed to those writings was recognized much earlier." (McDonald, BC, 18)

B. Why Have a Canon?

1. Old Testament

The Old Testament canon is the treaty document that God made with Israel. The covenant is the "single most important theological structure in the Old Testament." (Walton, *Covenant*, 10) The idea of an Old Testament canon "has its roots in the covenant God made with Israel–the canon is a treaty document." (Kruger, QC, 61) New Testament scholar and expert in early Christianity Michael Kruger notes that "scholars have long observed that the concept of a treaty-covenant was not unique to the Old Testament, but was prevalent in the ancient Near Eastern world out of which this corpus of books was born. . . . In addition . . . these treaty-covenants . . . included written texts

that documented the terms of the covenant arrangement." (Kruger, QC, 59–60)

Scriptures equating the covenant and the written text:

- Exodus 24:7; 31:18; 34:1, 28
- Deuteronomy 4:13; 29:21; 30:10
- 2 Kings 23:2
- 2 Chronicles 34:30

2. New Testament

"Early Christianity and the New Testament emerged within the larger context of Judaism. To say the obvious, Jesus, Paul, and most or perhaps all of the writers of the New Testament were Jewish." (Borg, EW, 7)

Kruger states three beliefs held by Christians of the early church that would have led to the formation of the New Testament:

- Christians of the early church believed the Old Testament was unfinished.

The fact that Second Temple Jews regarded the Old Testament story as incomplete and in need of a proper conclusion has significant implications for the production of a new corpus of biblical books. If some Second Temple Jews became convinced that the story was completed in the life and ministry of Jesus of Nazareth—such as the earliest Christians did—then it is not unreasonable to think that the proper conclusion to the Old Testament might then be written. (Kruger, QC, 51–52)

The Old Testament writings themselves—from which the earliest Christians have drawn these promises—indicate that God often brings new Word-revelation after he acts to redeem his people. (Kruger, QC, 52)

When the Old Testament refers to the future eschatological age of redemption, it explicitly states that this new era will be accompanied by a new divine message. (Kruger, QC, 54; see also Deut. 18:18; Is. 11:1, 4; 2:2, 3; 61:1, 2)

- Christians of the early church believed God was ushering in a new covenant. If the Old Testament was seen as the written form of the Mosaic Covenant, then the Christians of the early church would sense the need for a written form of the fulfillment of the New Covenant mentioned in Jeremiah 31:31–34. "The covenantal context of early Christianity suggests that the emergence of a new corpus of scriptural books, after the announcement of a new covenant, could not be regarded as entirely unexpected." (Kruger, QC, 62)
- Christians of the early church believed the apostles possessed the authority of Christ.

If apostles were viewed as the mouthpiece of Christ, and it was believed that they wrote down that apostolic message in books, then those books would be received as the very words of Christ himself. Such writings would not have to wait until second-, third-or fourth-century ecclesiastical decisions to be viewed as authoritative—instead they would be viewed as authoritative from almost the very start. For this reason, a written New Testament was not something the church formally "decided" to have at some later date, but was instead the natural outworking of the early church's view of the function of the apostles. (Kruger, QC, 70)

3. Tests for Inclusion in the Canon

From the writings of biblical and church history we can discern at least five principles that guided the recognition and collection of the true divinely inspired books. Geisler and Nix present the principles as follows:

- Was the book written by a prophet of God? "If it was written by a spokesman for God, then it was the Word of God." (Geisler and Nix, GIB, 223)
- Was the writer confirmed by acts of God? Frequently miracles separated the true prophets from the false ones. "Moses was given miraculous powers to prove his call of God (Ex. 4:1–9). Elijah triumphed over the false prophets of Baal by a supernatural act (1 Kings 18). Jesus was 'attested to . . . by God with miracles and wonders and signs which God performed through Him' (Acts 2:22). . . . [A] miracle is an act of God to confirm the Word of God given through a prophet of God to the people of God. It is the sign to substantiate his sermon; the miracle to confirm his message." (Geisler and Nix, GIB, 226)
- Did the message tell the truth about God? "God cannot contradict Himself (2 Cor. 1:17, 18), nor can He utter what is false (Heb. 6:18). Hence, no book with false claims can be the Word of God." (Geisler and Nix, GIB, 226) For reasons such as these, the church fathers maintained the policy, "If in doubt, throw it out." This enhanced the "validity of their discernment of the canonical books." (Geisler and Nix, GIB, 228)
- Does it come with the power of God? "The Fathers believed the Word of God is 'living and active' (Heb. 4:12) and consequently ought to have a transforming force for edification

(2 Tim. 3:17) and evangelization (1 Pet. 1:23). If the message of a book did not effect its stated goal, if it did not have the power to change a life, then God was apparently not behind its message." (Geisler and Nix, GIB, 228) The presence of God's transforming power was a strong indication that a given book had his stamp of approval.

- Was it accepted by the people of God? "Paul said of the Thessalonians, 'We also constantly thank God that when you received from us the word of God's message, you accepted it not as the word of men, but for what it really is, the word of God' (1 Thess. 2:13). For whatever subsequent debate there may have been about a book's place in the canon, the people in the best position to know its prophetic credentials were those who knew the prophet who wrote it. Hence, despite all later debate about the canonicity of some books, the definitive evidence is that which attests to its original acceptance by the contemporary believers." (Geisler and Nix, GIB, 229) When a book was received, collected, read, and used by the people of God as the Word of God, it was regarded as canonical. This practice is seen in the Bible itself. One instance is when the apostle Peter acknowledges Paul's writings as Scripture on par with Old Testament Scripture (2 Pet. 3:16).

C. The Christian Canon (New Testament)

1. Tests for New Testament Canonicity

The basic factor for recognizing a book's canonicity for the New Testament was divine inspiration and the chief test for this was apostolicity. Geisler and Nix state, "In New Testament terminology the church was 'built upon the foundation of the apostles

and prophets' (Eph. 2:20) whom Christ had promised to guide into 'all the truth' (John 16:13) by the Holy Spirit. The church at Jerusalem was said to have continued in the 'apostles' teaching' (Acts 2:42). The term *apostolic* as used for the test of canonicity does not necessarily mean 'apostolic authorship,' or 'that which was prepared under the direction of the apostles' . . . It seems much better to agree with Louis Gaussen, B. B. Warfield, Charles Hodge, J. N. D. Kelly, and most Protestants that it is apostolic authority, or apostolic approval, that was the primary test for canonicity, and not merely apostolic authorship." (Geisler and Nix, GIB, 283)

Edward J. Young notes that the apostolic authority

which speaks forth in the New Testament is never detached from the authority of the Lord. In the Epistles there is consistent recognition that in the church there is only one absolute authority, the authority of the Lord himself. Wherever the apostles speak with authority, they do so as exercising the Lord's authority. Thus, for example, where Paul defends his authority as an apostle, he bases his claim solely and directly upon his commission by the Lord (Gal. 1 and 2); where he assumes the right to regulate the life of the church, he claims for his word the Lord's authority, even when no direct word of the Lord has been handed down (1 Cor. 14:37; cf. 1 Cor. 7:10). (Young, AOT, 113–114)

McDonald writes, "The church upheld the apostolic witness in its sacred literature as a way of grounding its faith in Jesus, represented by the apostles' teaching, and insuring that the church's tradition was not severed from its historical roots and proximity to Jesus, the primary authority of the early church." (McDonald, BC, 407) He adds,

And on the day called Sunday, all who live in cities or in the country gather together to one place, and the memoirs of the apostles or the writings of the prophets are read, as long as time permits; then, when the reader has ceased, the president verbally instructs, and exhorts to the imitation of these good things.

Justin Martyr

"If it was believed that an apostle wrote a particular book, that writing was accepted and treated as Scripture. There is no doubt that all of the books of the NT were placed in the canon because the majority believed that they were written by apostles or members of the apostolic community." (McDonald, BC, 409)

Ignatius (AD 50–115) indicated the difference between the importance of his writings and the writings of the apostles when he wrote in his letter to the Trallians, "I do not issue orders like an apostle," and "nor am I such a disciple as Paul or Peter." (Ignatius, IET, 192, 194)

Bruce states, "Those whose apostleship was recognized by fellow-Christians were acknowledged to be Christ's agents, speaking by his authority." (Bruce, CS, 119) Young observes, "The only one who speaks in the New Testament with an authority that is underived and self-authenticating is the Lord." (Stonehouse and Woolley, IW, 113–114)

2. The New Testament Canonical Books
a. Reasons for Their Collection
i) They Were Prophetic

The initial reason for collecting and preserving the inspired books was that they were prophetic. That is, since they were written by an apostle or prophet of God, they must be valuable, and if valuable, they should be preserved. This reasoning is apparent in apostolic times, by the collection and circulation of Paul's epistles (cf. 2 Peter 3:15–16; Col. 4:16). (Geisler and Nix, GIB, 277)

ii) The Needs of the Early Church

The churches needed to know which books should be read, revered, and applied to their varied and often precarious situations in a generally hostile social and religious environment. They had many problems to address and they needed assurance regarding which books would serve as their source of authority. (Geisler and Nix, GIB, 277–278)

iii) The Rise of Heretics

"When the heretic Marcion published a sharply abridged list of canonical books (c. 140), . . . the need for a complete canonical list became acute." (Geisler and Nix, BFGU, 132)

iv) The Circulation of Spurious Writings

Many churches used apocryphal books in services. "Many churches in the East (for example, Alexandria, Egypt) were reading certain books of the New Testament Apocrypha in their public services. . . . Clearly a decision needed to be made as to exactly what books were to be included in the canon." (Earle, HWGOB, 43)

v) Missions

Christianity had spread rapidly to other countries, and there was the need to translate the Bible into those other languages. . . . As early as the first half of the second century the Bible was translated into Syriac and Old Latin. But because the missionaries could not translate a Bible that did not exist, attention was necessarily drawn to the question of which books really belonged to the authoritative Christian canon. (Geisler and Nix, GIB, 278)

vi) Persecution

The edict of Diocletian (AD 303) called for the destruction of the sacred books of the Christians. Who would die for a book that was perhaps religious, but not sacred? Christians needed to know which books were truly sacred. (Geisler and Nix, GIB, 278) McDonald writes that the edict of Diocletian caused "the church to make conscious decisions about what literature it considered sacred. . . . The Christians tried to salvage as much of their sacred literature as possible by turning over to them less important texts that were not considered sacred." (McDonald, IS, 417)

b. The Canon Recognized

i) Polycarp and His Contemporaries

Polycarp (AD 115), Clement of Alexandria (about AD 200), and other early church fathers refer to the Old and New Testament books with the phrase "as it is said in these scriptures."

ii) Justin Martyr

Justin Martyr (AD 100–165) writes in his First Apology 1.67: "And on the day called Sunday, all who live in cities or in the country gather together to one place, and the memoirs of the apostles or the writings of the prophets are read, as long as time permits; then, when the reader has ceased, the president verbally instructs, and exhorts to the imitation of these good things." (Martyr, "Apology," 186) He adds in his *Dialogue* with Trypho the formula "It is written" when he quotes from

the Gospels. (Martyr, DT, 29, 151, 157, 166) Both he and Trypho must have known to what "It is written" referred and that this introduction designated that the Scripture is inspired.

iii) Irenaeus

Concerning the significance of Irenaeus (AD 180), Bruce writes:

> The importance of evidence lies in his [Irenaeus'] link with the apostolic age and in his ecumenical associations. Brought up in Asia Minor at the feet of Polycarp, the disciple of John, he became bishop of Lyons in Gaul, AD 180. His writings attest the canonical recognition of the fourfold Gospel and Acts, of Romans, 1 and 2 Corinthians, Galatians, Ephesians, Philippians, Colossians, 1 and 2 Thessalonians, 1 and 2 Timothy and Titus, of 1 Peter and 1 John and of the Revelation. In his treatise, *Against Heresies*, III, ii, 8, it is evident that by AD 180 the idea of the fourfold Gospel had become so axiomatic throughout Christendom that it could be referred to as an established fact as obvious and inevitable and natural as the four cardinal points of the compass (as we call them) or the four winds. (Bruce, BP, 100)

iv) The Muratorian Fragment

Bruce writes about the Muratorian Fragment: "An early list of new Testament Books, drawn up in the church at Rome towards the end of the second century, is called the Muratorian fragment. . . . The fragment is mutilated at the beginning, but seems to have mentioned Matthew and Mark, because it goes on to mention Luke as the 'third' Gospel; then it mentions John." (Bruce, BP, 100–101) The fragment also mentions "Acts, the Epistles of Paul, Jude, 1 and 2 John, of the General Epistles, and two Revelations, those of John and Peter (some did not want the latter to be read in the church, he says). He recommends the reading of the Shepherd of Hermas in private, and lists the Wisdom of Solomon. Missing are 1 and 2 Peter, Hebrews, 3 John, and James." (Ewert, FATMT, 126)

"Some scholars date the original text of the Muratorian Fragment near or before the end of the late second century and claim that it was written from the vicinity of Rome on the basis of internal evidence." (McDonald, BC, 371) Other scholars feel that, among other reasons, "since there are no parallels to the Muratorian Fragment until after Eusebius, the document should probably be dated some time after the mid-fourth century." (McDonald, BC, 378)

Kruger comments on the date of the fragment:

However, largely overlooked in this discussion, and many other discussions like it, is the list of books offered by Origen more than a half century earlier [than the suggested later date for the fragment] in *Hom. Jos. 7.1* (c. 249). At first glance, Origen appears to offer a complete list of NT books that is nearly the same as the 27-book canon eventually affirmed by the later church. If so, then it has the potential to challenge the suggestion that the fourth century is the first time the Church Fathers were concerned about limiting the boundaries of the NT canon. (Kruger, OL, 100)

v) Origen

In *Homiliae Josuam 7.1* (c. 249) Origen lists Matthew, Mark, Luke, and John, two epistles of Peter, James, Jude, John's epistles and Revelation, Acts, and the fourteen epistles of Paul (including Hebrews). (Kruger, OL, 108) Although some have claimed that Origen's translator, Rufinus, altered the list

to suit his own purposes, Kruger finds "there is little positive evidence that he has done so.... His translations, as a whole, remained true to Origen's sense." (Kruger, OL, 117) "The fact that *Hom. Jos.* 7.1 might just be an accurate reflection of Origen's NT finds confirmation in Origen's other (and more general) statements about the canon." (Kruger, OL, 111) Kruger finally adds, "If Origen was willing to make such a list, then we must at least consider the possibility that others may have done so prior to this time—perhaps even the author of the Muratorian fragment." (Kruger, OL, 117)

vi) Athanasius of Alexandria

Athanasius (AD 367) gave a list of New Testament books that is exactly like our present New Testament. He provided this list in a festal letter to the churches. As he put it:

Again it is not tedious to speak of the [books] of the New Testament. These are, the four gospels, according to Matthew, Mark, Luke and John. Afterwards, the Acts of the Apostles and Epistles (called Catholic), seven, viz. of James, one; of Peter, two; of John, three; after these, one of Jude. In addition, there are fourteen Epistles of Paul, written in this order. The first, to the Romans; then two to the Corinthians; after these, to the Galatians; next, to the Ephesians; then to the Philippians; then to the Colossians; after these, two to the Thessalonians, and that to the Hebrews; and again, two to Timothy; one to Titus; and lastly, that to Philemon. And besides, the Revelation of John. (Athanasius, *Letters*, 552)

vii) Jerome and Augustine

Shortly after Athanasius circulated his list, Jerome and Augustine followed suit, defining the New Testament canon of twenty-seven books. (Bruce, BP, 103)

viii) Church Councils

Bruce states that "when at last a Church Council—The Synod of Hippo in AD 393—listed the twenty-seven books of the New Testament, it did not confer upon them any authority which they did not already possess, but simply recorded their previously established canonicity. (The ruling of the Synod of Hippo was re-promulgated four years later by the Third Synod of Carthage.)" (Bruce, BP, 103–104)

Since that time there has been no serious questioning of the twenty-seven accepted books of the New Testament by Roman Catholics, Protestants, or the Eastern Orthodox Church.

c. The Canon Classified

The canonical New Testament books can be classified as follows:

- The Gospels: Matthew, Mark, Luke, John
- The History: Acts
- The Pauline Epistles: Romans, 1 Corinthians 2 Corinthians, Galatians, Ephesians, Philippians, Colossians, 1 Thessalonians, 2 Thessalonians, 1 Timothy, 2 Timothy, Hebrews, Titus, Philemon
- The General Epistles: James, 1 Peter, 2 Peter, 1 John, 2 John, 3 John, Jude
- The Prophecy: Revelation

Early manuscripts organized the books differently as well as having a different number of books. For example, Codex Sinaiticus's organization first listed the Gospels, then Paul's epistles and Hebrews, Acts, and the General Epistles, and then Revelation. Codex Vaticanus and Codex Alexandrinus both had the Gospels first and then Acts and the General Epistles followed by Paul's epistles.

In addition Codex Alexandrinus included Revelation at the end. (McDonald, BC, 451)

3. The New Testament Extracanonical Literature

a. Pseudepigrapha

Pseudepigrapha "refers to a writing that is produced by a person who is falsely claiming to be someone famous." (Ehrman, *The Bible*, 298) "During the first few centuries, numerous books of a fanciful and heretical nature arose that are neither genuine nor valuable as a whole. . . . No orthodox Father, canon, or council considered these books to be canonical and, so far as the church is concerned, they are primarily of historical value. These books indicate the heretical teaching of gnostic, docetic, and ascetic groups." (Geisler and Nix, GIB, 301)

Examples of pseudpigraphal books include (see Geisler and Nix, GIB, 302–307):

- *The Gospel of Thomas* (early second century)
- *The Gospel of the Ebionites* (second century)
- *The Gospel of Peter* (second century)
- *The Gospel of the Hebrews* (second century)
- *The Gospel of the Egyptians* (second century)
- *The Gospel of Philip* (second century)
- *The Gospel of Judas* (late second century)

b. Other Extracanonical Writings

Some early church writings had theological and historical value higher than that of the pseudepigrapha but were still not considered canonical. (Geisler and Nix, GIB, 316) Such publications included, for example, collections of Christian hymns, sermons, and apologies. (Ewert, FATMT, 118) Also, "guidelines were necessary for the believing communities to maintain the proper roles and functions of their leaders." (McDonald, IS, 424) Although "some of the Fathers and churches considered several of these books to be canonical," the testimony of the church in general disagreed with their view. (Geisler and Nix, GIB, 313) Other writings contained "much legendary material in them" and some were "strongly Gnostic in coloring." (Ewert, FATMT, 118) These were considered apocryphal.

i) Examples of Catechetical Writings (see Geisler and Nix, GIB, 313):

- Epistle of Pseudo-Barnabas (AD 70–120)
- Epistle to the Corinthians (about AD 96)
- Shepherd of Hermas (about AD 115–140)
- Didache, Teaching of the Twelve (about AD 100–120)
- Epistle of Polycarp to the Philippians (about AD 108)
- The Seven Epistles of Ignatius (about AD 100)

ii). Examples of New Testament Apocryphal Books (Geisler and Nix, GIB, 313–316):

- *The "Real" First Corinthians* (possibly alluded to in 1 Cor. 5:9; however, no such piece of literature is now extant)
- *Ancient Homily,* or the so-called *Second Epistle of Clement* (about AD 120–140)
- Apocalypse of Peter (about AD 150)
- The Acts of Paul and Thecla (AD 170)
- Epistle to the Laodiceans (probably fourth century)
- The Gospel According to the Hebrews (AD 65–100)

iii) Why They Are Not Canonical

Geisler and Nix sum up the case against the canonical status of these books:

(1) None of them enjoyed any more than a temporary or local recognition. (2) Most of them never did have anything more than a semi-canonical status, being appended to various manuscripts or mentioned in tables of contents. (3) No major canon or church council included them as inspired books of the New Testament. (4) The limited acceptance enjoyed by most of these books is attributable to the fact that they attached themselves to references in canonical books (e.g., Laodiceans to Col. 4:16), because of their alleged apostolic authorship (e.g., Acts of Paul). Once these issues were clarified, there remained little doubt that these books were not canonical. (Geisler and Nix, GIB, 317)

D. The Old Testament Canon

1. The Jamnia Theory

Many scholars have theorized that a council of rabbis that convened at Jamnia, near Jaffa, in AD 90 finally agreed upon which books would be included in the Hebrew canon and which ones would not. The problem with this theory is that the Jamnia gathering reached neither of these conclusions. The rabbis did not fix (settle upon a final list for) the canon, but rather "raised questions about the presence of certain books in the canon. Books that the council refused to admit to the canon had not been there in the first place. The primary concern of the council was the right of certain books to remain in the canon, not the acceptance of new books." (Ewert, FATMT, 71) The rabbis discussed questions surrounding Esther, Proverbs, Ecclesiastes, the Song of Songs, and Ezekiel. "It should be underscored, however, that while questions about these books were raised, there was no thought of removing them from the canon. The discussions at Jamnia dealt not so much 'with acceptance of certain writings into the Canon, but rather with their right to remain there.'" (Ewert, FATMT, 72)

H. H. Rowley writes about the Council of Jamnia: "We know of discussions that took place there amongst the Rabbis, but we know of no formal or binding decisions that were made, and it is probable that the discussions were informal, though none the less helping to crystallize and to fix more firmly the Jewish tradition." (Rowley, GOT, 170)

Prominent New Testament scholar Bart Ehrman states,

Most scholars agree that by the time of the destruction of the second Temple in 70 C.E. most Jews accepted the final three-part canon of the Torah, Nevi'im, and Kethuvim.... This was a twenty-four-book canon that came to be attested widely in Jewish writings of the time; eventually the canon was reconceptualized and renumbered so that it became the thirty-nine books of the Christian Old Testament. But they are the same books, all part of the canon of Scripture. (Ehrman, *The Bible*, 377)

Bible scholar David Ewert explains that

no human authority and no council of rabbis ever made an [Old Testament] book authoritative. These books were inspired by God and had the stamp of authority on them from the beginning. Through long usage in the Jewish community their authority was recognized, and in due time they were added to the collection of canonical books. (Ewert, FATMT, 72)

2. The Recognized Canon

The evidence clearly supports the theory that the Hebrew canon was established well before the late first century AD, more than likely as early as the fourth century BC and certainly no later than 150 BC. A major reason for this conclusion comes from the Jews themselves, who from the fourth century BC

onward were convinced that "the voice of God had ceased to speak directly." (Ewert, FATMT, 69) In other words, the prophetic voices had been stilled. No word from God meant no *new* Word of God. Without prophets, there can be no scriptural revelation.

Concerning the Intertestamental Period (approximately four hundred years between the close of the Old Testament and the events of the New Testament) Ewert observes,

In 1 Maccabees 14:41 we read of Simon who is made leader and priest "until a trustworthy prophet should rise," and earlier he speaks of the sorrow in Israel such "as there has not been since the prophets ceased to appear to them." "The prophets have fallen asleep," complains the writer of 2 Baruch (85:3). Books that were written after the prophetic period had closed were thought of as lying outside the realm of Holy Scripture. (Ewert, FATMT, 70)

The last books written and recognized as canonical were Malachi (written around 450 to 430 BC) and Chronicles (written no later than 400 BC). (Walvoord and Zuck, BKC, 1573; 589) These books appear with the rest of the Hebrew canonical books in the Greek translation of the Hebrew canon called the Septuagint (LXX), which was composed around 250 to 150 BC. (Geisler and Nix, GIB, 24)

Bruce affirms that "The books of the Hebrew Bible are traditionally twenty-four in number, arranged in three divisions." (Bruce, CS, 29) The three divisions are the Law, the Prophets, and the Writings. Here are the main categories of the Hebrew canon found in modern editions of the Jewish Old Testament.

- The Law (Torah): Genesis, Exodus, Leviticus, Numbers, Deuteronomy

- The Prophets (*Nebhim*): Joshua, Judges, Samuel, Kings (former prophets), Isaiah, Jeremiah, Ezekiel, The Twelve (latter prophets)
- The Writings (*Kethubhim* or *Hagiographa* [Greek]): Psalms, Proverbs, Job (poetical books), Song of Songs, Ruth, Lamentations, Esther, Ecclesiastes (Five Rolls [*Megilloth*]), Daniel, Ezra-Nehemiah, Chronicles (historical books)

Although the Christian church has the same Old Testament canon, the number of books differs because we divide Samuel, Kings, Chronicles, and Ezra-Nehemiah into two books each, and we make separate books out of the Minor Prophets rather than combining them into one, as the Jews do under the heading "The Twelve." (Geisler and Nix, GIB, 22–23) The church has also altered the order of books by sequencing the books in these categories: Pentateuch (Torah), History, Wisdom (some of the Writings), and Prophets.

3. Christ's Witness to the Old Testament Canon

- Luke 24:44: In the Upper Room Jesus told the disciples "that all things must needs be fulfilled, which are written in the law of Moses, and the prophets, and the psalms, concerning me" (ASV). With these words Jesus indicated "a threefold categorization of the sacred Scriptures [the Law, the Prophets, and the Writings], the third part of which is identified by its longest and presumably most important book, the Psalms." (Ehrman, *The Bible*, 377)
- John 10:31–36; Luke 24:44: Jesus disagreed with the oral traditions of the Pharisees (Mark 7, Matt. 15), but *not* with their concept of the Hebrew canon.

(Geisler and Nix, BFGU, 41) "There is no evidence whatever of any dispute between Him and the Jews as to the canonicity of any Old Testament book." (Stonehouse and Woolley, IW, 60)

- Luke 11:51 (also Matt. 23:35): "From the blood of Abel to the blood of Zechariah." With these words Jesus confirms his witness to the extent of the Old Testament canon. Abel was the first martyr recorded in Scripture (Gen. 4:8) and Zechariah the last martyr to be named in the Hebrew Old Testament order, having been stoned while prophesying to the people "in the court of the house of the LORD." (2 Chr. 24:21). Genesis was the first book in the Hebrew canon and Chronicles the last. Jesus, then, was basically saying, "from Genesis to Chronicles," or, according to our order, "from Genesis to Malachi," thereby confirming the divine authority and inspiration of the entire Hebrew canon. (Bruce, BP, 88)

New Testament scholar and author Craig A. Evans notes, "Jesus quotes or alludes to *all* of the books of the Law, *most* of the Prophets, and *some* of the Writings. Superficially, then, the 'canon' of Jesus is pretty much what it was for most religiously observant Jews of his time." (Evans, SJ, 185)

4. The Testimonies of Extrabiblical Writers
a. Dead Sea Scrolls

In the Dead Sea Scrolls document 4QMMT, "dated to c. 150 BCE," the writer states, "[. . . we have wri]tten to you so that you would understand the book of Mos[es and] the book[s of the Pro]phets and Dav[id]" indicating the three-fold division of Law, Prophets, and Writings. (Weissenberg, 4QMMT, 15, 103)

b. Ecclesiasticus

Possibly the earliest reference to a three-fold division of the Old Testament is in the prologue of the book Ecclesiasticus (about 130 BC). In the prologue the author's grandson says, "Many great teachings have been given to us through the Law and the Prophets and the others that followed them. . . . So my grandfather Jesus, who had devoted himself especially to the reading of the Law and the Prophets and the other books of our ancestors . . . ," indicating three divisions of the Hebrew canon. (Trebolle Barrera, OTOT, 129) The grandfather, named Jesus ben Sirach, had written in Hebrew. The grandson who translated the manuscript from Hebrew to Greek mentions this three-part division three times in the prologue, once as he discusses his making the translation. He encourages lovers of learning to give attention to these writings (especially that they might live according to the law with understanding and be able to help others understand). But he acknowledges that translation carries a difficulty, for words of different languages do vary: "Not only this book, but even the Law itself, the Prophecies, and the rest of the books differ not a little when read in the original." (quoted in Kaminsky et al., AIB, 249) He also "refers to Isaiah, Jeremiah, and Ezekiel, as well as 'the bones of the Twelve prophets,' testifying that these fifteen books had already come to be viewed as sacred Scripture." (Kaminsky et al., AIB, 249; see Sirach 48:20–49:10)

c. Philo

"Around the time of Christ, the Jewish philosopher Philo made a three-fold distinction in the Old Testament speaking of the '[1] laws and [2] oracles delivered through the mouth of prophets, and [3] psalms and anything else which fosters and perfects knowledge and piety' (De Vita Contemplativa 3.25)." (Geisler and Nix, BFGU, 103)

d. Josephus

The Jewish historian Josephus (end of the first century AD) also spoke about the three-fold division. And about the entire Hebrew Scriptures, he wrote:

> And how firmly we have given credit to those books of our own nation is evident by what we do; for during so many ages as have already passed, no one has been so bold as either to add anything to them or take anything from them, or to make any change in them; but it becomes natural to all Jews, immediately and from their very birth, to esteem those books to contain divine doctrines, and to persist in them, and, if occasion be, willingly to die for them. For it is no new thing for our captives, many of them in number, and frequently in time, to be seen to endure racks and deaths of all kinds upon the theatres, that they may not be obliged to say one word against our laws, and the records that contain them. (Josephus, WFJ vol. 4, 158–159)

e. The Talmud

The Talmud is an ancient "collection of rabbinical laws, law decisions and comments on the laws of Moses" (Tenney et al., ZPEB, 589) that preserves the oral tradition of the Jewish people. One compilation of the Talmud was made in Jerusalem circa AD 350–425. Another more expanded compilation of the Talmud was made in Babylonia circa AD 500. Each compilation of the Talmud is known by the name of its place of compilation—for example, the Jerusalem Talmud and the Babylonian Talmud, respectively. The Talmud helps to establish the Jewish canon by rejecting later writings, including the Christian Gospels. The Talmud rejects these later writings because they were written after the Holy Spirit ceased inspiring texts (see below) or because they judge them to be heretical works.

- *Tos. Sotah 13:2: baraita in Bab. Yoma 9b, Bab. Sotah 48b and Bab. Sanhedrin 11a* says, "With the death of Haggai, Zechariah and Malachi the latter prophets, the Holy Spirit ceased out of Israel." (R. Beckwith, OTC, 370)
- *Seder Olam Rabba 30* states, "Until then [the coming of Alexander the Great and the end of the empire of the Persians] the prophets prophesied through the Holy Spirit. From then on, 'incline thine ear and hear the words of the wise.'" (R. Beckwith, OTC, 370)
- *Tosefta Yadaim 3:5* says, "The Gospel and the books of the heretics do not make the hands unclean; the books of Ben Sira and whatever books have been written since his time are not canonical." (Pfeiffer, IOT, 63) The reference to a book making the hands unclean meant that the book was divinely inspired and therefore holy. (R. Beckwith, OTC, 278–279) Handlers of the Scriptures were required to wash their hands after touching their holy pages. "By declaring that the Scriptures made the hands unclean, the rabbis protected them from careless and irreverent treatment, since it is obvious that no one would be so apt to handle them heedlessly if he were every time obliged to wash his hands afterwards." (R. Beckwith, OTC, 280) A book that did not do this was not from God. These quotations are claiming that only the books assembled in the Hebrew canon can lay claim to being God's Word.

f. Melito, Bishop of Sardis

Melito drew up the first known list of Old Testament books from within Christian circles (about AD 170). Eusebius (*Ecclesiastical History IV. 26*) preserves Melito's comments to Onesimus:

I went to the East [Syria] . . . I accurately ascertained the books of the Old Testament, and send them to thee here below. The names are as follows: Of *Moses*, five books, *Genesis, Exodus, Leviticus, Numbers, Deuteronomy. Jesus Nave, Judges, Ruth.* Four of *Kings.* Two of *Paralipomena* [Chronicles], *Psalms of David, Proverbs of Solomon,* which is also called *Wisdom, Ecclesiastes, Song of Songs, Job.* Of prophets, *Isaiah, Jeremiah.* Of the twelve prophets, one book. *Daniel, Ezekiel, Esdras* [Ezra]. (Eusebius, EH, 164)

Bruce comments,

It is likely that Melito included Lamentations with Jeremiah, and Nehemiah with Ezra (though it is curious to find Ezra counted among the prophets). In that case, his list contains all the books of the Hebrew canon (arranged according to the Septuagint order), with the exception of Esther. Esther may not have been included in the list he received from his informants in Syria. (Bruce, BP, 91)

g. Mishnah

The threefold division of the present Jewish text (with eleven books in the Writings) is from the Mishnah (Baba Bathra tractate, fifth century AD). (Geisler and Nix, GIB, 24)

5. The New Testament Witness to the Old Testament as Sacred Scripture

- Matthew 21:42; 22:29; 26:54, 56
- Luke 24
- John 5:39; 10:35
- Acts 17:2,11; 18:28
- Romans 1:2; 4:3; 9:17; 10:11; 11:2; 15:4; 16:26
- 1 Corinthians 15:3, 4
- Galatians 3:8; 3:22; 4:30
- 1 Timothy 5:18
- 2 Timothy 3:16
- 2 Peter 1:20, 21; 3:16

"As the *Scripture* has said" (John 7:38) is all the introduction a text needed to indicate the general understanding that a saying, story, or book was the very Word of God from the prophets of God.

6. Hebrew Apocryphal Literature

The term *apocrypha* comes from the Greek word *apokruphos*, meaning "hidden or concealed." (Unger, NUBD, 85) In the fourth century AD, Jerome was the first to name this group of literature *Apocrypha*. (Unger, NUBD, 85) The Apocrypha consists of the books added to the Old Testament by the Roman Catholic Church. Protestants reject these additions as noncanonical.

a. Why Not Canonical?

Unger's Bible Dictionary, while granting that the Old Testament apocryphal books do have some value, cites four reasons for excluding them from the Hebrew canon:

1. They abound in historical and geographical inaccuracies and anachronisms.
2. They teach doctrines that are false and foster practices that are at variance with inspired Scripture.
3. They resort to literary types and display an artificiality of subject matter and styling out of keeping with inspired Scripture.
4. They lack the distinctive elements that give genuine Scripture its divine character, such as prophetic power and poetic and religious feeling. (Unger, NUBD, 85)

b. A Summary of the Apocryphal Books

In his excellent study guide *How We Got Our Bible*, Ralph Earle provides brief details of each apocryphal book. Because of its quality, accuracy, and conciseness, we present his outline here in order to give the

reader a firsthand feel of the valuable yet noncanonical nature of these books:

First Esdras (about 150 BC) tells of the restoration of the Jews to Palestine after the Babylonian exile. It draws considerably from Chronicles, Ezra, and Nehemiah. In addition, the author has added much legendary material.

The most interesting item is the Story of the Three Guardsmen. They were debating what was the strongest thing in the world. One said, "Wine"; another, "the King"; the third, "Woman and Truth." [The third, Zerubbabel, wrote, "Women are the strongest, but above all things the truth conquers." (1 Ezras/Esdras 3:12)] They put these three answers under the king's pillow. When he awoke he required the three men to defend their answers. The unanimous decision was: "Truth is greatly and supremely strong." Because Zerubbabel had given this answer he was allowed, as a reward, to rebuild the Temple at Jerusalem.

Second Esdras (AD 100–200) is a collection of three apocalyptic works containing seven visions. . . . Martin Luther was so confused by these visions that he is said to have thrown the book into the Elbe River.

Tobit (early second century BC) is a short novel. Strongly Pharisaic in tone, it emphasizes the Law, clean foods, ceremonial washings, charity, fasting, and prayer. It is clearly unscriptural in its statement that almsgiving atones for sin.

Judith (late second century BC) is also fictitious and Pharisaic. The heroine of this novel is Judith, a beautiful Jewish widow. When her city was besieged she took her maid, together with Jewish clean food, and went out to the tent of the attacking general. He was enamored of her beauty and gave her a place in his tent. Fortunately, he had imbibed too freely and sank into a drunken stupor. Judith took his sword and cut off his head. Then she and her maid left the camp, taking his head in their provision bag. It was hung on the wall of a nearby city and the leaderless Assyrian army was defeated.

Additions to Esther (about 100 BC). . . . Esther stands alone among the books of the Old Testament in having no mention of God. We are told that Esther and Mordecai fasted. No mention of prayer, however, is made. To compensate for this lack, the *Additions* have long prayers attributed to these two. Several letters supposedly written by Artaxerxes are also included.

The Wisdom of Solomon (about AD 40) was written to keep the Jews from falling into skepticism, materialism, and idolatry. As in Proverbs, Wisdom is personified. There are many noble sentiments expressed in this book.

Ecclesiasticus, or Wisdom of Sirach (about 180 BC), shows a high level of religious wisdom, somewhat like the canonical Book of Proverbs. It also contains much practical advice. For instance, on the subject of after-dinner speeches it says, "Speak concisely; say much in few words; act like a man who knows more than he says" (32:8).

In his sermons, John Wesley quotes several times from the Book of Ecclesiasticus. It is still widely used in Anglican circles.

Baruch (about 150 BC or AD 100) was reportedly written by Baruch, the scribe of Jeremiah, in 582 BC. . . . It apparently attempts to interpret the destruction of Jerusalem in either 587/586 BC or AD 70. The book urges the Jews not to revolt again and to submit to the emperor. The sixth chapter of Baruch contains the so-called "Letter of Jeremiah," with its strong warning against idolatry.

Our Book of Daniel contains twelve chapters. In the first century before Christ a thirteenth chapter was added, containing the story of *Susanna*. She was the beautiful wife of a leading Jew in Babylon falsely accused of infidelity. Because of Daniel's wisdom she was rescued. He asked each of her accusers

separately under which tree in the garden they found Susanna with a lover. When they gave different answers, they were put to death, and Susanna was saved.

Bel and the Dragon was added at about the same time and was called chapter 14 of Daniel. Its main purpose was to show the folly of idolatry. It really contains two stories. In the first, King Cyrus asked Daniel why he did not worship Bel, since that deity showed his greatness by daily consuming much flour and oil and many sheep. Daniel scattered ashes on the floor of the Temple where food had been placed that evening. In the morning Daniel showed the king the footprints of the priests and their families who had entered secretly under the table and consumed the food. The priests were slain and the temple destroyed. The story of the dragon is just as obviously legendary in character. Along with Tobit, Judith, and Susanna, these stories may be classified as Jewish fiction. They have little if any religious value.

The Song of the Three Hebrew Children follows Daniel 3:23 in the Septuagint and in the Vulgate. It describes what happened to Shadrach, Meshach, and Abednego inside the fiery furnace. Borrowing heavily from Psalm 148, it is antiphonal, like Psalm 136. The refrain "Sing praise to him and greatly exalt him forever" appears thirty-two times.

The Prayer of Manasseh was composed in Maccabean times (second century BC) or later as the supposed prayer of Manasseh, the wicked king of Judah. It was obviously suggested by the statement in 2 Chronicles 33:19: "His prayer and how God was moved by his entreaty . . . all these are written in the records of the seers" (NIV). This prayer is not found otherwise in the Bible and is likely legendary.

First Maccabees (first century BC) is perhaps the most valuable book in the Apocrypha. It describes the exploits of the three Maccabean brothers—Judas, Jonathan, and

Simon—during the Jewish revolt against the Seleucid Empire in 167–164 BC. Along with Josephus, it is our most important source for this crucial, exciting period in Jewish history.

Second Maccabees (same time) is not a sequel to 1 Maccabees. It is a parallel account, treating only the victories of Judas Maccabeus. It is generally thought to be more legendary than 1 Maccabees. (Earle, HWGOB, 39–42)

c. Historical Testimony of Their Exclusion

Geisler and Nix give ten testimonies of antiquity that argue against recognition of the Apocrypha:

1. Philo, Alexandrian Jewish philosopher (20 BC–AD 40), quoted the Old Testament prolifically, and even recognized the threefold classification, but he never quoted from the Apocrypha as inspired.
2. Josephus (AD 30–100), Jewish historian, explicitly excludes the Apocrypha, numbering the books of the Old Testament as twenty-two. Neither does he quote the apocryphal books as Scripture.
3. Jesus and the New Testament writers never once quote the Apocrypha although there are hundreds of quotes and references to almost all of the canonical books of the Old Testament.
4. The Jewish scholars of Jamnia (AD 90) did not recognize the Apocrypha.
5. No canon or council of the Christian church recognized the Apocrypha as inspired for nearly four centuries.
6. Many of the great Fathers of the early church spoke out against the Apocrypha, for example, Origen, Cyril of Jerusalem, and Athanasius.
7. Jerome (AD 340–420), the great scholar and translator of the Latin Vulgate, rejected the Apocrypha as part of the canon. Jerome said that the church reads them "for example of

life and instruction of manners," but does not "apply them to establish any doctrine." He disputed with Augustine across the Mediterranean on this point. At first Jerome refused even to translate the apocryphal books into Latin, but later he made a hurried translation of a few of them. After his death and "over his dead body" the apocryphal books were brought into his Latin Vulgate directly from the Old Latin Version.

8. Many Roman Catholic scholars through the Reformation period rejected the Apocrypha.
9. Luther and the Reformers rejected the canonicity of the Apocrypha.
10. Not until AD 1546, in a polemical action at the counter-Reformation Council of Trent (1545–63), did the apocryphal books receive full canonical status from the Roman Catholic Church. (Geisler and nix, GIB, 272–273)

III. Conclusion

After examining different issues regarding the reliability of the Bible, we agree with New Testament scholar Craig L. Blomberg's conclusion:

Ironically, what has become best known in our culture over the past generation, both inside and outside of Christian circles, is the flurry of skepticism that certain narrow segments of scholarship and pseudoscholarship have unleashed. This is ironic because in each instance *the less-quoted majority of scholars have increasingly come to recognize that the evidence is actually stronger for the trustworthiness of Scripture in each of these areas, as long as that trustworthiness is appropriately defined by the standards of antiquity* [emphasis in original]. (Blomberg, CWSBB, 213)

CHAPTER 3

IS THE NEW TESTAMENT HISTORICALLY RELIABLE?

OVERVIEW

I. Tests for the Reliability of Historical Documents Including the New Testament

In this chapter we are presenting evidence for the historical reliability of the Scripture, not its inspiration. The historical reliability of the Bible should be tested by the same criteria by which all historical documents are tested. Because the Christian faith is inextricably connected to specific events of real history, many people who are curious to evaluate what Christianity is all about find that the historical reliability of its documents makes an appropriate starting point for them in their search for truth. Donald Hagner, professor emeritus of New Testament at Fuller Theological Seminary, explains the connection between the Christian faith and real historical events with great clarity:

> True Christianity, the Christianity of the New Testament documents, is absolutely dependent on history [including its manuscript attestation]. At the heart of the New Testament faith is the assertion that "God was in Christ reconciling the world to Himself" (2 Cor. 5:19). The incarnation, death, and resurrection of Jesus Christ as a real event in time and space, i.e., as historical realities, are the indispensable foundations of the Christian faith. To my mind, then, Christianity is best defined as the recitation of, the celebration of, and the participation in God's acts in history, which as the New Testament writing emphasize have found their culmination in Jesus Christ. (Hagner, NTHHCM, 73–74)

There are specific tests that scholars, researchers, and archaeologists use to determine the authenticity of a historical document. These are the bibliographical test, the internal evidence test, and the external evidence test. Scholar Chauncey Sanders lists and explains these three basic principles of historiography in his *Introduction to Research in English Literary History*. (Sanders, IRELH, 143ff)

In this chapter we will examine the New Testament portion of the Bible to see how well it does with each test in order to determine its reliability as an accurate source for the historical events it reports.

Because the original autographs of the New Testament books have not been found, most of this chapter will examine the historicity of the early manuscript (handwritten) copies that were made from them, concentrating upon the bibliographic test.

However, to begin we will survey what is known about how those first, original writings fit into history—the likely dates at which they were written and the correspondence of their references to historical events, persons, and cultural details that historians trust as verified by external sources.

II. Dating the Four Gospels and Acts

When scholars assign dates to manuscripts, we find that those dates sometimes vary not just by a few years or even decades but even by centuries. Why is this? One major reason is the worldview and consequent presuppositions that scholars and researchers bring to their study of the writers' references to history, along with the content and language patterns of the text. To estimate the dates the manuscripts were created, all these come into play.

Conservative scholars date the writing of the New Testament earlier than do liberal scholars. We present below two lists that illustrate the differences. Then for each of the four gospels we provide additional details and sources.

The incarnation, death, and resurrection of Jesus Christ as a real event in time and space, i.e., as historical realities, are the indispensable foundations of the Christian faith. To my mind, then, Christianity is best defined as the recitation of, the celebration of, and the participation in God's acts in history, which . . . have found their culmination in Jesus Christ.

Donald Hagner

- Conservative Dating:
  - Matthew: Early 60s–80
  - Mark: Late 50s–late 60s
  - Luke: Early 60s–80s
  - John: Mid 60s–100
  - Acts: 62–64*
- Liberal Dating:
  - Matthew: 80–100
  - Mark: 70s
  - Luke: 70–110
  - John: 90–100
  - Letters attributed to Paul: 50–early second century

A. Matthew: Early 60s–80 (Liberal Dating: 80–100 AD)

The date of Matthew's writing can be deduced from this report by Irenaeus, a second-century church father, who said that Matthew composed his gospel "while Peter and Paul were preaching the Gospel and founding the church in Rome." (*Against Heresies*, III.1.1) The only time that we know of Peter and Paul together in the capital of the Roman Empire was the early to mid-60s.

There are some who reject the idea that Matthew wrote during this time. One reason is that Matthew records Jesus predicting the destruction of the temple in Jerusalem, which happened in AD 70 (Matt. 24:1, 2). They argue that Matthew must have been written after the event, because predictive prophecy like this is not possible. (They do this because they hold an antisupernatural worldview.) If it can be demonstrated that supernatural events can occur (which is one of this book's objectives), then their argument does not hold up.

Another reason for proposing a later date relates to Matthew's record of the tensions between Pharisaic Judaism and Christian Judaism. Some would argue that these tensions primarily reflect the latter half of the first century, during the war with Rome which left these two groups as the only two surviving forms of Judaism. However, this is not a strong argument as the tensions had already started in the 60s. Furthermore, Matthew also records tensions between Jesus and the Sadducees and other leaders, not just the Pharisees.

A third reason for proposing a later date for Matthew is that Matthew was most likely written after Mark, and Mark was supposedly written in the 70s or just before then. However, Mark could well have been written in the later 50s or 60s, in which case there is no problem. (Carson, NIVZSB, 1922–1923)

B. Mark: Late 50s–Late 60s (Liberal Dating: 70s)

Mark was a bilingual Hellenist—John being his Hebrew name and Mark his Greek

---

* Some conservatives are not convinced that Acts was written immediately after the events with which it ends, so they would be willing to assign a date in the 70s or 80s.

one—and relative of the wealthy Cyprian landowner Barnabas (Col 4:10; cf. Acts 4:36). John Mark's well-to-do family occupied a significant place in early Christian communities, first in Jerusalem and later in Antioch. His mother's substantial house provided a gathering point for believers in Jerusalem and was the first port of call for a recently escaped Peter (Acts 12:12–16), who when writing later from Rome described Mark as "my son" (1 Pet 5:13). Mark joined his cousin Barnabas and Paul in their early travels from Antioch (Acts 12:25; 13:2–3) and, in spite of a falling-out (Acts 13:13; 15:36–39), later worked closely with Paul (Col 4:10; Philemon 24), even being summoned to Paul's last imprisonment, also in Rome (2 Tim 4:11). (Carson, NIVZSB, 1999)

> John Mark was therefore well placed to write his Gospel. The great bulk of his oral material would have come through his regular contact with Peter, with perhaps his mother's female friends providing the information for which they are explicitly named: the events surrounding the empty tomb (15:40–16:8). Equally, some of his insights into Jesus' significance may well have come from Paul, to whom Jesus later appeared (cf. 1 Cor. 15:8). (Carson, NIVZSB, 1999)

The book of Mark is notoriously difficult to date. According to early church tradition, Mark was an associate of Peter. This is supported by the considerable amount of attention which the gospel of Mark gives to Peter, and the fact that Peter is mentioned near the beginning and the end of the narrative (Mark 1:16, 16:7) perhaps pointing back to the witness of Peter, the source of Mark's content. If this is the case, Mark would most likely have written before Peter was martyred (c. 64), or shortly thereafter. According to

Donald Hagner, "We may tentatively opt for a date of about 65, shortly after the death of Peter. This places the initial readers in a time when they would have been subject to persecution, which would make sense of that significant motif in this Gospel." (Hagner, NT, 184)

Mark may be placed earlier if we rely on much of early church tradition that states that the gospel was written while Peter was still living. Hagner mentions that Mark may have even died before Peter did. (Hagner, NT, 184)

Later in this chapter we will argue in favor of J. P. Moreland's view that Acts was written between AD 62 and 64. He believes that the gospel of Luke was written before Acts, and that Luke likely used Mark as a source for his biography, thus placing Mark even earlier.

C. Luke: Early 60s–80s (Liberal Dating: 70–110)

The gospel of Luke and the book of Acts are often referred to together as "Luke-Acts" because Luke wrote both of these accounts, probably not far apart from each other. (Hagner, NT, 246) Although the date of Luke continues to be debated, there is a general consensus that Luke wrote his gospel before Acts and after Mark.

Those who insist on a pre-AD 70 date note that Luke does not describe Paul's death (mid-60s) in Acts or show an awareness of Paul's letters. Those who argue for a date after AD 70 respond by pointing out that Luke was not writing a biography of Paul but an account of the progress of the gospel, and although Luke does not explicitly quote from Paul's letters, his writings do reflect the influence of Paul's thought. (Carson, NIVZSB, 2060)

Next we will present reasons that support a pre-70 date for the book of Acts.

D. Acts

The best estimate for the dating of Acts places the work between AD 62 and 64. J. P. Moreland lists several reasons why Acts should be given this early date (Moreland, SSC, 152–154):

- Luke shows a particular interest in the city of Jerusalem. He mentions the city about thirty times in the gospel of Luke and about sixty times in the book of Acts, which is far more than any other New Testament writer does.

- Acts reports many events that took place in Jerusalem, from the Day of Pentecost to the imprisonment of Paul. Yet Luke fails to mention one of the most important events to have ever happened in the city: the destruction of the temple in AD 70. It makes sense, then, to date the book of Acts before the temple was destroyed.

- Acts does not mention the severe persecutions of the Roman emperor Nero, which started in the mid-60s. Again, Luke would probably have recorded this dark time of Christendom had he written his book during or after those persecutions.

- Luke records the martyrdoms of Stephen and James the brother of John, but he is silent about the martyrdoms of Peter, Paul, and James. These three prominent figures in the book of Acts died between AD 61 and 67. If Luke wrote Acts after their deaths, he would probably have heard about their martyrdoms and included them in his history of the early church.

- One of the major themes in the book of Acts is the way in which the early church leaders welcomed new Gentile believers and included them in the growing communities of Christians. The leaders also specified how the Gentile Christians should relate to Jewish believers. Moreland points out that this was a very important matter before the destruction of the temple in AD 70, but much less important after the destruction. Acts also deals with other subjects that fit most naturally into the years prior to the destruction of the Temple in AD 70, such as different people groups (Jewish, Samaritan, Gentile) receiving the Holy Spirit, and the divisions between Palestinian Jews and Hellenistic Jews. Thus, we can make the case that Luke wrote before the temple's destruction, staying relevant to the issues of his time.

- Several distinctively Jewish expressions used throughout the book of Acts indicate a pre-70 Jewish-Christian audience. If the book of Acts was originally intended for the increasingly Gentile church of later decades, the author would have adjusted his vocabulary and phrasing to accommodate them. According to Moreland, "The phrases *the Son of man, the Servant of God* (applied to Jesus), *the first day of the week* (the resurrection), and *the people* (the Jews) are all phrases that readers would understand without explanation prior to 70. After 70, they would need to be explained." (Moreland, HNT, online)

- Luke does not mention the wars against the Romans, beginning in AD 66. Once again, the most logical explanation for Luke's silence about such important events in Jewish history is that he wrote Acts before they all began.

Moreland sums up:

But this means that Luke should be dated just prior to [the wars against the Romans]. Further, Matthew and Mark should be dated even earlier, perhaps from the mid-40s to mid-50s. The picture of Jesus presented in the Synoptics is one that is only twelve to twenty-nine years removed from the events themselves. And they incorporate sources which are even earlier. (Moreland, SSC, 154)

In conclusion, a very strong case can be made to date the composition of Acts in the early 60s. This in turn provides a reference point that historians can use to date the three Synoptic Gospels that preceded the book of Acts.

E. John: Mid 60s–100 (Liberal Dating: 90–100)

There is a wide possible timeframe for the date of John's writing and very little support for any specific period within the 60s–100 timeframe.

Almost any date between about AD 55 and 95 is possible. None of the arguments for a more precise date is entirely convincing. But if we must suggest a date for when John wrote the Fourth Gospel, we may very tentatively advance AD 80–85. One of many reasons for this is to allow for some time between the writing of John's Gospel and the writing of his three letters, which were probably written in the early 90s and which combat an incipient form of Gnosticism and respond in part to a Gnostic misunderstanding of the Fourth Gospel. (Carson, NIVZSB, 2140)

However, because of John's emphasis on Jesus as the divine Son of God, many liberal scholars have given John a later date, supposing that such a high view of Jesus' divinity did not form until later in history when legend took over.

As mentioned above, another plausible hypothesis is that John's gospel was written shortly before his letters, which were likely written in the 90s in response to pseudo-gnostic misinterpretations of his gospel. This estimate places John's gospel somewhere in the 80s. However, leading Bible scholar and translator Daniel Wallace dates John's gospel to the mid-60s. (Wallace, in correspondence to J. McDowell and M. J. Tingblad, June 3, 2016)

F. Conclusion Regarding the Dating of the Gospels and Acts

It can be reasonably argued that all four biographies of Jesus in the New Testament, as well as the book of Acts, were written within a few decades—and certainly within a century—of the events they describe. Even most non-Christian scholars acknowledge this and place the canonical Gospels and Acts securely within the first century. Nevertheless, even if a radically late dating were correct, we would still have records for the events surrounding the origin of Christianity that are earlier than those sometimes used to support unquestioned events in history.

III. The Bibliographical Test for the Reliability of the New Testament

The bibliographical test is an examination of the textual transmission by which documents reach us. In other words, since we do not have the original documents, how reliable are the copies we have in regard to the number of manuscripts (MSS, MS singular) and the time interval between the original and extant (currently existing) copies? (Montgomery, HC, 26) For any particular work or collection of works, the greater the number and the earlier the dating of the manuscripts, the easier it is to reconstruct a text closer to the original and identify errors or discrepancies in subsequent copies.

The importance of the sheer number of manuscripts and early patristic quotations of Scripture cannot be overstated. As with other documents of ancient literature, there are no known extant original manuscripts of the Bible. Fortunately, however, the abundance of manuscript copies makes it possible to reconstruct the original text with virtually complete accuracy. (Geisler and Nix, GIB, 386)

Peters states that "on the basis of manuscript tradition alone, the works that made up the Christians' New Testament were the most frequently copied and widely circulated books of antiquity." (Peters, HH, 50) The authenticity of the New Testament text we have today rests on a foundation of a massive amount of historical documentation.

A. The Number of Manuscripts and Their Closeness to the Original

How many manuscripts of the New Testament do we have today? It is a very large number that has not remained static—it grows even larger as new discoveries are made. Accordingly, researchers and historians are constantly revising their estimates. Without question, the New Testament boasts the best-attested manuscript transmission when compared with other ancient documents. The bibliographical test validates and confirms that the New Testament has been accurately transmitted to us through the centuries. (Jones, BTU)

It is extremely laborious to track the number of both classical and biblical manuscripts.

Many scholars base the number of New Testament manuscripts on the work of Kurt Aland and Barbara Aland of the Institute for New Testament Textual Research in Münster, Germany. Another great source for manuscript study is the Leuven Database, available online at www.trismegistos.org/ldab/. Yet another is the Center for the Study of the New Testament Manuscripts, www.csntm.org.

Four challenges face anyone hoping to estimate the number of NT manuscripts: (1) databases do not always reflect new discoveries; (2) most databases do not include the many manuscripts in private collections; (3) most databases do not include the scrolls;* and (4) most databases do not account for manuscripts that date from the Renaissance or later.

We will now list the surviving manuscripts of various languages into which the New Testament was first translated. It is important to understand that these numbers are constantly changing as new manuscript discoveries come to light. There are so many changes that by the time anything is printed the numbers may have changed drastically. That is why regularly updated online databases are so valuable in this particular field of study.

B. Counting and Dating the Early New Testament Manuscripts
1. Greek

- **Earliest MS: AD 130**

The earliest verified New Testament Greek MS is the John Rylands Papyrus of John known by the designation "P52," which New Testament scholar Bart Ehrman dates to "125–130, plus or minus twenty-five years."

---

* Scrolls were made by gluing papyrus sheets together or sewing parchment sheets together and then winding either of these onto a rod or stick—as opposed to single-sheet fragments or to a codex, which is produced by stacking sheets and carefully sewing them together along one edge. For more information on the materials and processes of manuscript preparation, see our chapter on "How We Got the Bible."

If you ever go to Manchester, England, make sure to stop at the John Rylands library, where this ancient document is being preserved. It is a great experience. As far as I (Josh) have been able to find, there is no other manuscript besides "P52" to have been officially recognized as the earliest MS of the New Testament.

However, additional manuscripts continue to be discovered on a regular basis. Many of these manuscripts are currently under review by experts; this ongoing work may well uncover a new contender for the "earliest New Testament MS."

- **Number of MSS: c. 5,856***

The current number according to the Institut für neutestamentliche Textforschung (Institute for New Testament Textual Research, hereafter the INTTR) in Münster, Germany, the official cataloger of Greek NT MSS, is c. 5,856. This includes papyri, majuscules, minuscules, and lectionaries (for more information about these manuscript types, see chapter 2). According to their tally from January 2017: minuscules = 2,937; majuscules (uncials) = 323; papyri = 131; lectionaries = 2,465 for a total of 5,856.

The official number of 5,856 requires some revision, however. One should deduct MSS that have gone missing, those that have been destroyed, and those that have been discovered to be a part of a known MS. According to Wallace, "The adjusted numbers, as of January, 2017, are now well over 5,600." (Wallace, correspondence to J. McDowell and M. J. Tingblad, January 27, 2017)

Yet one could also add to that number the many (possibly hundreds) of manuscripts in private collections that have never been published. Additionally, discoveries made in recent years have not been factored into the official count. In the words of Wallace, "The multiple new discoveries of [Greek] biblical manuscripts are like a literary tsunami." (Wallace, lecture, 2013)

2. Armenian

- Earliest MS: AD 862. A. A. S. ten Kate mentions that the oldest Armenian MS is the Gospel of Queen Mlke, dated to AD 862. (ten Kate, correspondence to J. McDowell and M. J. Tingblad, 2016; cf. Stone, AACR, 44; Adalian, HDA, 108)
- Number of MSS: 3,000+. Crowe mentions a "catalogue of scriptural holdings" which lists 207 full Bibles, 115 NTs, and 3,003 "Gospel books". That makes a total of 3,325 New Testament manuscripts. (Cowe, AVNT, 256)

3. Coptic

The Coptic language is the last stage of the written Egyptian language. It came about when the Greeks conquered Egypt and their languages merged to form Coptic. The sounds of the Egyptian language hieroglyphics were transliterated with Greek letters (not words), which makes it easy to misidentify a Coptic text as Greek.

- Earliest MS: Late third century AD (Askeland, CVNT, 209; cf. Emmel, CBE, 39)
- Number of MSS: ten Kate says there are c. 975. (correspondence to J. McDowell and M. J. Tingblad, 2016) Others estimate a larger number: "Probably at least a thousand Coptic manuscripts exist, representative of the Alexandrian text-type." (Komoszewski et al., RJ, 80)

---

* Wallace, correspondence to J. McDowell and M. J. Tingblad, January 27, 2017, with data from a prepublication draft of *Laying a Foundation: A Handbook on New Testament Textual Criticism*, Zondervan, forthcoming.

In early December 2013, I (Josh) hosted 274 scholars, apologists, and leaders from four countries for a two-day event in Dallas, Texas, to examine ancient manuscript fragments. We were thrilled to share in the discovery of a very significant papyrus: two fragments from the Sermon on the Mount. It is possible that this will be validated as the earliest papyri known of that passage from the gospel of Matthew. The preliminary examination of these fragments dates them approximately AD 350–430.

However, no one should consider this estimate to be authoritative at this time. We need to wait until the scientific analysis and publication of these findings is complete, which could take another two to four years.

Those Coptic manuscript fragments, discovered on that December weekend, are in my (Josh's) possession and are awaiting further research and publication. Here is the list of all the Coptic biblical fragments that were discovered at the event. It appears that these newly discovered Coptic manuscripts will prove to be the oldest discovered of these passages.

- Matthew 6:33 / Matthew 7:4-reverse side
- Mark 15:9
- John 14:28
- Galatians 4:17
- First John 2:21 (AD 350–430)
- Jeremiah 33:24

4. Gothic

- Earliest MS: fifth or sixth century AD. (Falluomini, GVNT, 329)
- Number of MSS: Six (Falluomini, GVNT, 329)

Bible scholars Bruce Metzger and Bart Ehrman comment, "The most nearly complete of the half-dozen extant Gothic manuscripts (all of which are fragmentary) is a deluxe copy dating from the fifth or sixth century. . . . It contains portions of all four Gospels." (Metzger and Ehrman, TNT, 115)

It is worth noting that these Gothic translations, though fragmentary, are a word-by-word translation, so they can be particularly useful. (Falluomini, GVNT, 330)

5. Ethiopian

- Earliest MS: Sixth century AD. "The oldest known Ethiopic MSS known are two Abba Garima Gospels recently dated to the sixth century." (Zuurmond, EVNT, 242)
- Number of MSS: 600+. (Zuurmond, EVNT, 242)

George Fox University professor Steve Delamarter directs the Ethiopic Manuscript Imaging Project. He summarizes the status of Ethiopian manuscripts, "Outside of Ethiopia, there are about six hundred Ethiopic manuscripts that contain the text of one or more books of the New Testament." Delamarter continues, "Within Ethiopia there are perhaps 5,000 yet to be discovered and catalogued. Among these are undoubtedly several hundred from the 17th century and earlier." (Delamarter, e-mail to J. McDowell and Clay Jones, 2011) Although most Ethiopic manuscripts have been assigned fairly recent dates, "at least one manuscript of the four Gospels dates to the tenth century and a couple of others date to the eleventh century." (Metzger, EVNT, 224–25)

6. Latin Translations

Latin translations are typically divided into Old Latin and Vulgate manuscripts. The total number of Latin MSS is 10,050+ (Wallace, correspondence to J. McDowell and M. J. Tingblad, May 5, 2016)

- Old Latin
  - Earliest MS: Fourth century AD. (Houghton, LNT, 211)
  - Number of MSS: 110. (Houghton, LNT, 209–54)

H. A. G. Houghton's carefully numbered count of 110 includes all the MSS from the Vetus Latina Register, supplements the register with a few other lists, and even adds new discoveries.

However, it should be noted that this count probably contains some overlap with the Vulgate (see next section), as some MSS contain elements of the Vulgate as well as Old Latin. VL 109 is one such example. Vetus Latina director Roger Gryson catalogues eighty-nine Old Latin manuscripts of the New Testament, dating from the fourth to the thirteenth centuries. (Metzger and Ehrman, TNT, 51)

Additionally, Old Latin MSS are counted differently from most other MSS in that a single parchment that contains, say, the gospel of Matthew and Ephesians, is counted as two manuscripts. (Gryson, AH, 9–143) Therefore, a count of fifty MSS is a more accurate apples-to-apples comparison. (Jones, BTU)

- Latin Vulgate
  - Earliest MS: Fourth century AD. (Vaganay and Amphoux, INTC, 30)
  - Number of MSS: 10,000+.

We have to be careful here, as there is no database that collects all the known MSS of the Vulgate. Many sources will mention that there are more than ten thousand. Houghton says that probably no one really knows exactly how many:

It is at least 4,000. The figure of 10,000 is still regularly bandied about, but I suspect that is because no one else has any clue either and it sounds plausible. One day I hope to get funding to make a database of as many as are known to exist. Then we might be able to come up with a better figure. Until then you can stick with over 10,000. (Houghton, correspondence to J. McDowell and M. J. Tingblad, May 12, 2016)

7. Syriac

"Syriac is the name generally given to Christian Aramaic." (Bruce, BP, 193) From its inception Christianity has been a missionary faith. "The earliest versions of the New Testament were prepared by missionaries to assist in the propagation of the Christian faith among peoples whose native tongue was Syriac, Latin, or Coptic." (Metzger, TNT, 67)

- Earliest MS: Late fourth or early fifth century AD. (P. Williams, SVNT, 145)
  - Syriac Peshitta. The basic meaning of peshitta is "simple." It was the standard version, produced between AD 300s–400s. There are more than three hundred and fifty MSS extant beginning from the fifth century. (Geisler and Nix, GIB, 317)
  - Palestinian Syriac. Most scholars date this version at about AD 400–450 (fifth century). (Metzger, TNT, 68–71)
  - Philoxenian (AD 508). Polycarp translated a new Syriac New Testament for Philoxenas, bishop of Mabug. (Greenlee, INTTC, 49)
  - Harkleian Syriac. (AD 616) by Thomas of Harkel.
- Number of MSS: 350+. Old Syriac: Two MSS. There are around sixty in the fifth and sixth centuries alone. (P. Williams, SVNT, 145–151)

One of the earliest translation of the Greek New Testament is in the Peshitta, the official Bible of the Syriac-speaking church. (Cairns, DTT, 330) The New Testament portion was probably written before AD 400, making it a significant witness to the original Greek text. (Cross and Livingstone, ODCC, 1268)

Siker estimates the MSS at more than 350. (Siker, CSCE, 316) However, Wallace states, "The surviving copies of the Syriac New Testament manuscripts number in the hundreds, perhaps thousands." (quoted in Komoszewski et al., RJ, 80) Scholar Andreas Juckel notes, "Most of the existing lists and catalogues are out of date, new acquisitions are not properly recorded, and up-to-date catalogues are delayed (e.g., Princeton Univ.; Speer Library; Moscow, St. Petersburg). There are a lot of manuscripts in private possession (USA and Canada) and in uncatalogued libraries in the Middle East (Lebanon); the catalogued ones in the Middle East (Syria, Iraq) had to be removed or split and suffered severe losses . . . so nobody is able to count." He continues, "It is possible to give an idea about the dimension only: certainly more than 1000 Syriac manuscripts including New Testament texts and written before WWI exist, but hardly more than 1500." (Juckel, conversation with M. J. Tingblad, May 18, 2016)

8. Georgian

- Earliest MS: Fifth century AD. A few fragments survive from this period. (Childers, GVNT, 295–96)
- Number of MSS: Eighty-nine. The sixty oldest ones are fragments; several later MSS are more extensive. (Vaganay and Amphoux, INTC, 41; cf. Krasovec, IB, 469)

9. Slavic

- Earliest MS: Tenth to eleventh century AD. (Vaganay and Amphoux, INTC, 44)
- Number of MSS: 4,000+.

Krasovec mentions 89 manuscript entries. (Krasovec, IB, 469) University of Indiana professor Henry Cooper writes, "The most thorough description of the manuscript holdings of a Slavic country to date, conducted in 1965 on the territory of the then Soviet Union, yielded in all about 1,500 entries dating before the fifteenth century. More than 99 percent of these manuscripts were translations (usually from Greek), and the vast majority of those were of Biblical books, especially portions of the gospels and the Psalms." (Cooper, SS, 25; see also Zukovskaja, SKSR, 177–84) Cooper adds that "a count for the fifteenth century added 3,500 more entries." (Cooper, SS, 170, n61)

On the higher end, St. Petersburg University professor Anatolij Alexeev writes that "for the first time in the history of Slavistics the number of selected Gospel manuscripts has reached the significant figure of over eleven hundred." (Alexeev, LPNL, 248) Cooper suggests that Alexeev's higher numbers "could be so, it seems to me, only if one included sixteenth-and seventeenth-century Slavonic manuscripts: manuscript production in the Slavic world continued long after the introduction of printing in Western, Central, and Southeastern Europe. In any event the later Slavonic manuscripts are of marginal value in tracing the development of the Church Slavonic Bible." (Cooper, SS, 170, n61)

10. Summary

Wallace concludes that "all told, probably between fifteen and twenty thousand texts of the ancient versions of the New Testament remain. There are no exact numbers because not all the manuscripts have been carefully catalogued." (Wallace, correspondence to J. McDowell and M. J. Tingblad, June 3, 2016)

C. The New and Old Testament Manuscript Attestations

Influential biblical scholar F. F. Bruce writes: "There is no body of ancient literature in the world which enjoys such a wealth of good textual attestation as the New Testament." (Bruce, BP, 178)

In the chart "Number of Biblical Manuscripts," the second and third columns compare both "old" and "new" dates determined for the earliest manuscript in each language. The two columns at the far right compare the "old" and "new" number of manuscripts estimated to be catalogued for that language. For each language, the data labeled "old" was tabulated in 2012. The columns labeled "new" show the data for each language as of August, 2014—with the exception of the new number of Greek manuscripts which reflects the official number as of January 2017.

This comparison reveals the change, if any, in dating and numbers of manuscripts that have occurred in that two-year interval,

NUMBER OF BIBLICAL MANUSCRIPTS

Language*	Earliest MS (old)	Earliest MS (new)	Number of MSS (old)	Number of MSS (new)
Armenian	AD 887	AD 862	2000+	2000+
Coptic	Late 3rd c. AD	Late 3rd c. AD	Around 975	Around 975
Gothic	5th or 6th c. AD	5th or 6th c. AD	6	6
Ethiopian	10th c. AD	6th c. AD	600+	600+
Total Latin Translations Old Latin Vulgate	N/A 4th c. AD 4th c. AD	N/A 4th c. AD 4th c. AD	50 10,000+	110 10,000+
Syriac	5th c. AD	Late 4th or Early 5th c. AD	350+	350+
Georgian	Late 9th c. AD	5th c. AD	43+	89
Slavic	10th c. AD	10th c. AD	4,000+	4,000+
Total Non-Greek manuscripts				18,130+
Greek	AD 130 (or earlier)	AD 130 (or earlier)	5838	5,856
TOTAL GREEK AND NON-GREEK MANUSCRIPTS				23,986
Biblical Manuscripts, Scrolls, and Translations				
New Testament Greek Manuscripts				5,856
New Testament Early Translations				18,130
Old Testament Scrolls, Codices				42,300**
TOTAL BIBLICAL MANUSCRIPT EVIDENCES				66,286

Chart adapted from Cowe, AVNT, 256.

* Many of these languages are not catalogued regularly.

** 25,000 are relatively recent, dated to the nineteenth and twentieth centuries.

through the discovery of earlier manuscripts in a particular language or by the addition of newly discovered or catalogued manuscripts. Current research continues to change these totals. And we must realize that every day, marvelous new discoveries are being made. That is why the numbers of scroll and manuscript discoveries are out-of-date as soon as you print them. We recognize how astonishingly rapid is the increase of information and even the development of new methods to recover that data from manuscripts that had been thought to be forever illegible.

D. Visualizing the Number of Biblical Manuscripts

1. The New Testament Manuscripts

How high do you think the stack of New Testament manuscripts would be? Think about this: of just the 5,800+ Greek New Testament manuscripts, there are more than 2.6 million pages. Combining both the Old and New Testament, there are more than 66,000 manuscripts and scrolls.

A stack of extant manuscripts for the average classical writer would measure about four feet high; this just cannot compare to the more than one mile of New Testament manuscripts and two-and-a-half-miles for the entire Bible. (Wallace, lecture at Discover the Evidence, Dec. 6, 2013)

2. The Old Testament Scrolls

We have added Old Testament scrolls into the mix of the total numbers of manuscripts to represent the Bible as a whole and not just the New Testament. If you do not include both the Old Testament and New Testament manuscripts and scrolls when you compare the dates and totals of biblical manuscripts with those of classical literature, then you are comparing apples to oranges. The classical works, such as the *Iliad*, are complete works and need to be compared with the Bible as a complete work, not with just a part of it. In fact, the great proliferation of New Testament manuscript discoveries has been accompanied by additional discoveries of Old Testament manuscripts (sometimes as glued papyrus scrolls or sewn parchment scrolls but also as single sheets and even as small fragments that have been recovered

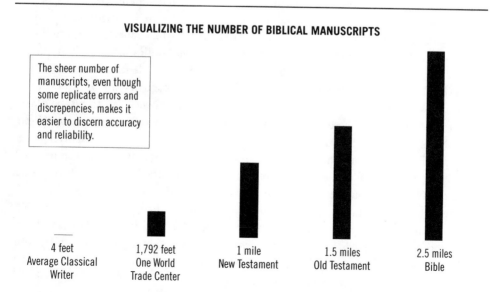

VISUALIZING THE NUMBER OF BIBLICAL MANUSCRIPTS

The sheer number of manuscripts, even though some replicate errors and discrepencies, makes it easier to discern accuracy and reliability.

| 4 feet Average Classical Writer | 1,792 feet One World Trade Center | 1 mile New Testament | 1.5 miles Old Testament | 2.5 miles Bible |

from phylacteries—the leather cases holding scripture to be tied to the hands or forehead during prayer). The Old Testament manuscripts not only enhance our awareness that many more manuscript copies are likely waiting to be found, but they help to verify the authenticity of New Testament manuscripts that quote them. Further, the scrupulous exactness that Jewish scribes devoted to their copying reinforces our awareness of the tradition in which the New Testament copyists worked—a tradition of precise care for accuracy. (We get a glimpse of that climate of reverence for the word in Acts and in the epistles, for Paul had been trained in rabbinic scholarship, and Luke's writing also shows a scholarly care for precise detail and exact language.)

In the field of Old Testament apologetics, what has been overlooked in tabulating numbers of Old Testament manuscripts is the usage of scrolls and codices. Many worn-out scrolls were carefully copied for replacement and set aside, protected but unsought, and so never entered catalogs. As seen in the chart "Number of Extant Old Testament Scrolls," the majority of extant scrolls are not in museums but in ongoing use in synagogues or seminaries, and many are in private collections. Also, codices of Hebrew texts tend to be rarer and written later than those prepared with Greek texts. I (Josh) and my wife own four complete Torah scrolls, one of which is very old and very rare. We also possess three fragments of scrolls. None of these has been recorded or registered. The numbers and dates for the Old Testament scrolls (as well as the numbers of biblical and classical manuscripts and scrolls more broadly) are constantly shifting. For example, nine small Dead Sea Scrolls have recently been rediscovered. They had been deposited in the vaults of the Israel Antiquities Authority (IAA). (NUDSSF) As said before,

it is very difficult to estimate accurately the number of extant scrolls, but Scott Carroll, director and senior research scholar at the Manuscript Research Group, suggests the following totals (correspondence to J. McDowell, November 15, 2013):

NUMBER OF EXTANT OLD TESTAMENT SCROLLS

Source	Number
The Dead Sea Scrolls	300
Green Collection	5,000
Synagogues	20,000
Museums	1,000
Private family collections	5,000
Codices	3,000
Jewish Seminaries	5,000
Individuals	3,000
TOTAL	**42,300**

3. Old Torah Scrolls, Additional Discoveries, and New Technologies

As with the New Testament manuscripts, the Old Testament manuscripts—especially in scroll form—are being found and identified with earlier dates. In 2013, a Torah scroll created headlines: "In 1889, an Italian librarian's faulty identification sentenced to archival obscurity an antique Torah scroll that has turned out to be the oldest complete such scroll in existence." (Cole, CDCW, website) "This week, University of Bologna professor Mauro Perani announced the results of carbon-14 tests authenticating the scroll's age as roughly 800 years old. . . . The scroll (a sheep-skin document, i.e., parchment) dates to between 1155 and 1225, making it the oldest complete Torah scroll on record. . . . Like all Torah scrolls, this one contains the full text of the five Books of

Moses in Hebrew and is prepared according to strict standards for use during religious services." The article continues, "What a 19th-century cataloguer had interpreted as clumsy mistakes by what he guessed was an awkward 17th-century scribe provided the very clues that led Perani to investigate further." (Cole, CDCW, website)

In April 2016, in a basement in Jerusalem, I (Josh) held in my arms a new discovery of an ancient Jewish Torah scroll carbon-dated at AD 1050. This will probably be shown to be the oldest complete Torah scroll in existence. One of the previous oldest Torah scrolls is a copy of the textual tradition called the Samaritan Torah (named for its use of a different set of letter forms and its addition of vowels, along with a focus on Mt. Gerazim). Parts of the Abisha Scroll, a Samaritan scroll in Nablus (formerly Shechem), have been dated to the twelfth to fourteenth century, although the placement of letters in a particular column names its scribe as Aaron's great-grandson. It is written in gold ink on vellum and is fragile, mended, and rarely displayed.

In 2014 an amazing total of 103 Jewish Torah scrolls, states Rabbi Slomo Koves of the Orthodox Chabad-Lubavitch community, "were discovered in the manuscript section of the Lenin State Regional Library of the western Russian city of Nizhny Novgorod." Koves said negotiations are underway with Russian officials to restore the scrolls and possibly display them in international exhibits. ("103 Torah Scrolls," online) Rabbi Koves called the find he helped make last year "of historical significance," adding that Hungary's government supports efforts to restore the scrolls. ("103 Torah Scrolls," online)

In late September, 2016, a new technology of digital scanning was employed to recover text lost when a scroll had been "reduced to charcoal in a burning synagogue 1,500 years ago." The scroll from En-Gedi had been known since 1970, but computer analysis created a 3-D "virtual unwrapping" to allow reading the text without touching it. (Hotz, ETUIBS) The recovery software offers modern applications as well as the possibility of its use to scan damaged New Testament manuscript text once thought irrecoverable.

E. Comparison with Surviving Manuscript Copies of Selected Classical Literature

The chart "Summary Chart of Selected Surviving MSS of Major Classical Works" presents our updated information for surviving classical manuscripts, with earlier dates now for the oldest copy in the case of Herodotus, Plato, and Livy, and with increased totals for several authors. These manuscript numbers raise challenging issues for skeptics because if they reject the transmissional reliability of the New Testament, then they must also consider unreliable all other manuscripts of antiquity. As celebrated scholar John Warwick Montgomery has often related: "Some years ago, when I debated philosophy professor Avrum Stroll of the University of British Columbia on this point, he responded: 'All right. I'll throw out my knowledge of the classical world.' At which the chairman of the classics department cried: 'Good Lord, Avrum, not that!'" (Montgomery, HRHD, 139)

Glenny notes, "No one questions the authenticity of the historical books of antiquity because we do not possess the original copies. Yet we have far fewer manuscripts of these works than we possess of the NT." (Glenny, PS, 96)

Wallace concludes, "If we have doubts about what the autographic NT said, those doubts would have to be multiplied a *hundredfold* for the average classical author." (Wallace, HBDSC, 29)

SUMMARY CHART OF SELECTED SURVIVING MSS OF MAJOR CLASSICAL WORKS

Work	Earliest MS (old)	Earliest MS (new)	Number of MSS (old)	Number of MSS (new)
Homer's Iliad	About 400 BC	About 415 BC	1,800+	1,900+
Herodotus—History	1st c. AD	150–50 BC	109	About 106
Sophocles' Plays	3rd c. BC	3rd c. BC	193	About 226
Plato's Tetralogies	AD 895	3rd c. BC	210	238
Caesar's Gallic Wars	9th c. AD	9th c. AD	251	251
Livy's History of Rome	Early 5th c. AD	4th c. AD	150	About 473
Tacitus's Annals	1st half: AD 850 2nd half: AD 1050	1st half: AD 850 2nd half: AD 1050	33	36
Pliny the Elder's Natural History	One 5th c. AD fragment. Others in 14th and 15th c.	5th c. AD	200	200+
Thucydides' History	3rd c. BC	3rd c. BC	96	188
Demosthenes' Speeches	Fragments from 1st c. BC	1st c. BC, possibly earlier	340	444
TOTAL				4,062+

1. A Caution When Comparing Surviving Biblical and Classical Manuscripts

One needs to be careful in comparing the survival and dating of an abundance of biblical manuscripts with classical works. Yes, we believe that God has superintended the preservation of such an abundance of biblical manuscripts. But, there are good historical reasons for the paucity of classical manuscripts. Carroll comments on the importance of caution here, lest we draw the wrong conclusions:

It is implied that an unspoken reason for the preservation of manuscripts is supernatural over against the loss of non-inspired works, but it is a bit more involved. Most classical works were in a region that could promise preservation on papyrus and were then recopied in Egypt and disseminated (not like the Christian monastic system).

These texts were systematically copied and studied at the library in Alexandria which burned partially in the first century BC, and then the texts were also systematically destroyed by Christians in the fourth century and Muslims in the seventh and eighth centuries. Christians are in part to blame for destroying around 1 million classical scrolls, and the fact that any classical texts survive in large numbers is remarkable. Centuries later, we often use the dearth of evidence [for classical works] to show the superior preservation of the Bible.

Early classical works were written primarily on papyrus, a highly perishable medium, as was the scroll format. Christians quickly transitioned to the codex [book format] and to parchment and vellum, which were much more durable and suitable for the codex and thus, these factors hastened the decline of classical works.

We also keep in mind that classical works were copied, only if by chance, by monks after the fifth century. They were left in the hands of the "enemy" so to speak to preserve and perpetuate—which they did but not as aggressively. (Carroll, correspondence to J. McDowell, October 31, 2013)

Biblical scholar, translator, and textual critic Bruce Metzger, in *The Text of the New Testament*, cogently writes of the comparison:

The works of several ancient authors are preserved to us by the thinnest possible thread of transmission. For example, the compendious history of Rome by Velleius Paterculus survived to modern times in only one incomplete manuscript, from which the *editio princeps* was made—and this lone manuscript was lost in the seventeenth century after being copied by Beatus Rhenanus at Amerbach. Even the Annals of the famous historian Tacitus is extant, so far as the first six books are concerned, in but a single manuscript, dating from the ninth century. In 1870 the only known manuscript of the Epistle to Diognetus, an early Christian composition which editors usually include in the corpus of Apostolic Fathers, perished in a fire at the municipal library in Strasbourg. In contrast with these figures, the textual critic of the New Testament is embarrassed by the wealth of his material. (Metzger and Ehrman, TNT, 34)

New Testament scholar J. Harold Greenlee writes in his *Introduction to New Testament Textual Criticism* about the time gap between the original MS (the autograph) and the extant MS (the oldest surviving copy), saying,

Since scholars accept as generally trustworthy the writings of the ancient classics even though the earliest MSS were written so long after the original writings and the number of extant MSS is in many instances so small, it is clear that the reliability of the text of the N.T. is likewise assured. (Greenlee, INTTC, 16)

2. Surviving Manuscripts of Selected Classical Writers

a. Homer—The Iliad

The epic poem *The Iliad* tells of anger and war—the final year of the Trojan War. Little is known of Homer, but the *Iliad* has been immensely important from the Classical Age, as its manuscript totals imply.

- Earliest MS: About 415 BC. The Leuven database records a direct attestation to the *Iliad* written on a piece of pottery, and dated between 420 and 410 BC, Leuven id#130496. (Bird, MHI, online)
- Number of MSS: 1900+. One of the top specialists for Homer's manuscripts is Graeme D. Bird: "Homer's *Iliad* is currently represented by more than 1,900 manuscripts (at least 1,500 of which are on papyrus, although many of these of a fragmentary nature)." (Bird, MHI, online)

It is difficult to settle on an exact number of manuscripts of Homer's work, because there are constantly new discoveries. Also, numbers used for Homer's *Iliad* do not include at least five in the Green family's collection, a number in other private collections, and twelve more manuscripts (destined for museums) that we know about. Martin L. West, senior research fellow at All Souls College, Oxford, has catalogued a total of 1,569 papyri. But, this is a papyri-only count and not a total manuscript count. (Even though "manuscript" literally means "handwritten," scholars like West sometimes use "manuscript" to refer only to non-papyri manuscripts. Papyri manuscripts they simply call "papyri.") (West, STTI, 86)

More manuscript discoveries have been made of the *Iliad* than any other classical work. And yet, the total number of MSS of the *Iliad* extant is less than 2,000. (Wallace, correspondence to J. McDowell, October 15, 2013)

b. Herodotus—Histories

Herodotus, a Greek historian from the fifth century BC, wrote of the Greco-Persian wars. A vivid storyteller, he gave attention to fascinating detail. Forty-nine papyrus fragments and about sixty non-papyrus manuscripts represent him. The oldest papyri date from the first century AD. P.Oxy 1375 (I or II), P.Oxy 1619 (end of I AD), Archiv für Papyrusforschung vol. 1, p. 471f. (I or II), British Library 1109 (Greek papyri in the British Museum III p. 57 Milne, Catalogue of the literary papyri in the British Museum no. 102) (I or II).

- Earliest MS: 150–50 BC. Many sources still say that the oldest fragments go back to the first century AD, but the Leuven Database shows one fragment dating between 150 and 50 BC. LDAB id #1119. (Priestley and Zali, BCRH, 171)
- Number of MSS: About 106. There are approximately 60 medieval and renaissance MSS. (Wilson, H, xiii)

c. Sophocles—Plays

Sophocles was one of the three great tragic playwrights of Athens, the others being Aeschylus and Euripides. Aristotle considered Sophocles' play *Oedipus the King* to be the paradigm example of tragedy and repeatedly cited it in his study of literary forms. Sophocles wrote over one hundred dramas in the fifth century BC, though few manuscripts remain.

- Earliest MS: Third century BC. LDABid #3956 has a papyrus dating

between 299–200 BC. (H. Lloyd-Jones, S, 18. See alsoTuryn, SMT, 5–9; Battezzato, RP, 102; Burian and Shapiro, CS, 189)
- Number of MSS: About 226. Lloyd-Jones estimates there are 200 medieval manuscripts and 17 earlier. (H. Lloyd-Jones, S, 18) However, the Leuven Database (as of April 29, 2016) shows that the number of manuscripts before the medieval time is now approximately 26, bringing the estimated total to 226. (P. J. Finglass, correspondence to J. McDowell and M. J. Tingblad, May 18, 2016)

d. Plato—Tetralogies

Plato has had a remarkable influence. Some have said that all philosophy is a footnote to Plato. Born in the fifth century BC, he wrote dialogues that probed the meaning of fundamental concepts such as truth, goodness, and beauty, which he argued were the highest forms of reality. His dialogue *The Republic* develops a parallel between the qualities of the best government for a city and for a person's self-government. Many of his works were compiled into groups of four called "Tetralogies." (See Brumbaugh, PM, 114–21) They provide priceless insight into Greek thought and into the Socratic method of inquiry.

- Earliest MS: Third century BC. Michael Reeve writes, "Two of his Phaedo are from the 3rd Century BC." This is confirmed on LDAB ids: 3835 and 3833. (Reeve, correspondence to J. McDowell and M. J. Tingblad, April 22, 2016) However, in December 6, 2013, I (Josh) had the privilege of organizing an event leading to the discovery of what could be a portion of a second-century-BC fragment from Plato's *Republic*. Verification of the authenticity of this fragment is currently underway.

- Number of MSS: 237. Nigel Wilson has kept an updated list of the manuscripts for Plato. In his list, 237 items belong to the tetralogies. (Wilson, LPM)

e. Caesar—Gallic Wars

Gaius Julius Caesar was a Roman general and statesman who changed the course of history in the first-century-BC wars that spread Roman authority over the Mediterranean and Europe. By defying the Roman Republic senators (who would have confined his authority to Gaul) he initiated the rise of the Roman Empire. He was a brilliant strategist and remarkably generous to those he defeated. Julius Caesar's name is recalled in our calendar: July. "From 58–50 BC Julius Caesar conquered much of Gaul and described his success in *On the Gallic War*. . . . [T]here are 251 manuscripts beginning from the ninth century (the majority are 15th century)." (V. Brown, LMCGW, 105–107)

For Caesar's *Gallic Wars* (composed between 58 and 50 BC) there are several extant MSS, but only nine or ten are in good condition. The oldest is some 900 years later than Caesar's time period.

- Earliest MS: Ninth century AD.
- Number of MSS: 261+.

f. Livy (64 or 59 BC–AD 17)—History of Rome

Livy, one of Rome's great historians, lived until the earlier years of Jesus. His history of Rome became a classic in his lifetime. It was a formidable and ambitious writing project, starting with the founding of the city and reaching the events of his own lifetime. His style influenced Roman writing for centuries.

- Earliest MS: Fourth century AD. Leuven LDAB id#: 2575, 7402
- Number of MSS: About 473. In *A Companion to Livy* by Bernard Mineo, there is a breakdown of Livy's works by groups of 10 books. (Mineo, CL, 4–17)

g. Tacitus (AD 56–c. 120)—Annals

Tacitus, whose life was shortly after Jesus, was a Roman orator, public official, and one of the great historians. He was a man of great political savvy who studied rhetoric and prose composition. His *Annals* concerned the Roman Empire from AD 14 to 68. Historian David Potter notes, "Tacitus' historical works descend in two manuscripts, one for books 1–6, another for 11–16 and the surviving portions of the history." (LTRH, 72)

- Earliest MS: 1–6 in AD 850, 11–16 in AD 1050. (Pagan, CT, 15–16; Winterbottom, T, 406–409)
- Number of MSS: 36. Reeve notes that we have only one MS for Annals 1–6, and that 7–10 are lost. For Annals 11–16, see Malloch's commentary on 11, which says we still use just one main manuscript for 11–16, and there are 34 others that postdate this manuscript. The main MS for 11–16 is also Histories 1–4, so some of those MSS may be fragments that only contain Histories. Everyone seems to treat Annals 11–16 and Histories 1–4 as a single work. So two primary manuscripts and 34 others make 36. (Malloch, AT, 9–22)

h. Pliny the Elder (AD 23/24–79)—Natural History

Pliny the Elder (Gaius Plinius Secundus) was a Roman scholar and naval commander in the first century. His monumental ency-clopedia, *Natural History,* "was regarded as a scientific authority up to the Middle Ages. From astronomy to zoology to botany to medicine, Pliny wrote with precision, even including an index. His death occurred as he tried by ship to save a friend from the eruptions of Mt. Vesuvius.

- Earliest MS: Fifth century AD. (Leuven Database id#:8912. Also 7773 and 8927, 8143—FN1)
- Number of MSS: 200+. Approxi-mately 200 manuscripts date from the fourteenth and fifteenth cen-turies. In 1942, Hilda Buttenwieser stated that she found almost seventy MSS of *Natural History* which predate the fourteenth century. (Buttenwieser, PAMA, 52–53)

i. Thucydides—History

Thucydides, a Greek historian from the fifth century BC, has been called the father of scientific history. His *History of the Pelo-ponnesian War* begins with an introduction setting out his criteria for evidence and analysis in writing history, indicating the intellectual influence of the great philoso-phers of Athens.

- Earliest MS: Third century BC. (Hammond, PW, 633)
- Number of MSS: 188. Cedopal's Mertens-Pack 3 database (similar to Leuven) has 101 MSS from Thucydides.

j. Demosthenes—Speeches

Demosthenes was an Athenian statesman and one of the greatest orators of his time, in part because he trained rigorously to over-come a speech impediment. His speeches provide valuable insight into the social, political, and economic condition of Athens in the fourth century BC.

- Earliest MS: First century BC, possibly earlier. (Sealey, DHT, 223)
- Number of MSS: 444 (Sealey, DHT, 222)

This total combines information from Sealey and from the Leuven database. Sealey writes, "Canfora (1968) recorded 258 manu-scripts of Demosthenes' speeches." (DHT, 222) He mentions that none of these has been dated earlier than the late ninth century. A Leuven Database inquiry yields 210 results for Demosthenes that predate Sealey's number. However, only 186 of those are actual manu-scripts and not quotations or summaries by other writers (258+186=444 MSS).

3. Summary

New Testament scholars and biblical lin-guistic experts Stanley E. Porter and Andrew W. Pitts observe,

When compared with other works of antiquity, the NT has far greater (numerical) and earlier documentation than any other book. Most of the available works of antiquity have only a few manuscripts that attest to their existence, and these are typically much later than their original date of composition, so that it is not uncommon for the earliest manuscript to be dated over nine hundred years after the original composition. (Porter and Pitts, FNTTC, 50)

F. Important New Testament Manuscripts

We are able to assess the importance of the following manuscripts from how much of the Bible they include and from the dates that scholars have assigned to them. Factors that help determine the age of a manuscript are:

- Materials used
- Letter size and form
- Punctuation
- Text divisions
- Ornamentation
- The color of the ink
- The texture and color of parchment (Geisler and Nix, GIB, 242–246)
- Carbon-14 dating

1. John Rylands MS (AD 130)

The John Rylands MS, which we discussed briefly earlier in this chapter, is located in the John Rylands Library of Manchester, England. Also known as "P52," it is the oldest extant fragment of the New Testament. "Because of its early date and location (Egypt), some distance from the traditional place of composition (Asia Minor), this portion of the Gospel of John tends to confirm the traditional date of the composition of the Gospel about the end of the 1st century." (Geisler and Nix, GIB, 268)

Metzger speaks of defunct criticism: "Had this little fragment been known during the middle of the past century, that school of New Testament criticism which was inspired by the brilliant Tübingen professor, Ferdinand Christian Baur, could not have argued that the Fourth Gospel was not composed until about the year 160." (Metzger and Ehrman, TNT, 39)

2. Bodmer Papyrus II (AD 150–200)

Purchased in the 1950s and 1960s from a dealer in Egypt, the Bodmer Papyrus II is located in the Bodmer Library of World Literature, and contains most of John's gospel. The most important discovery of New Testament papyri since the Chester Beatty manuscripts (see below) was the acquisition of the Bodmer Collection by the Library of World Literature at Cologny, near Geneva. P66, dating from about AD 200 or earlier, contains 104 leaves of

John 1:1—6:11; 6:35b–14:26; and fragments of forty other pages, John 14–21. (Geisler and Nix, GIB, 390) Regarding the dating of manuscripts in this collection, Metzger and Ehrman write:

Herbert Hunger, the director of the papyrological collections in the National Library at Vienna, dates [P]66 earlier, in the middle if not even in the first half of the second century....

P72, also a part of the collection, is the earliest copy of the epistle of Jude and the two epistles of Peter. P75, still another early Biblical manuscript acquired by M. Bodmer, is a single-quire codex of Luke and John.... The editors, Victor Martin and Rodolphe Kaser, date this copy between AD 175 and 225. It is thus the earliest known copy of the Gospel according to Luke and one of the earliest of the Gospel according to John. (Metzger and Ehrman, TNT, 39–40, 41)

3. The Diatessaron (c. AD 170)

This early harmony of the Gospels was produced in Syria. It has significance as an early manuscript because the remaining copies, even though they are later translations from it, bear witness to the earliest gospels. For more information, see "Tatian," in section V.A.6. of this chapter.

4. Chester Beatty Papyri (AD 200)

The manuscripts were purchased in the 1930s from a dealer in Egypt and are located in the C. Beatty Museum in Dublin. This collection contains papyrus codices, three of which contain major portions of the New Testament. (Bruce, BP, 182)

In *The Bible and Modern Scholarship*, Sir Frederic Kenyon writes, "The net result of this discovery—by far the most important since the discovery of the Sinaiticus—is, in fact, to reduce the gap between the earlier manuscripts and the traditional dates of the

New Testament books so far that it becomes negligible in any discussion of their authenticity. No other ancient book has anything like such early and plentiful testimony to its text, and no unbiased scholar would deny that the text that has come down to us is substantially sound." (A detailed listing of papyri may be seen in the Greek New Testaments published by United Bible Societies and Nestle-Aland.) (Kenyon, BMS, 20)

5. Codex Vaticanus (AD 325–350)

Located in the Vatican Library, this manuscript contains nearly all of the Bible. After a hundred years of textual criticism, many consider Vaticanus to be one of the most trustworthy manuscripts of the New Testament text.

6. Codex Sinaiticus (AD 350)

This extremely significant manuscript is located in the British Library, though the St. Catherine's Monastery and libraries in Germany and in Russia hold a few separate pages. In the Mount Sinai Monastery, celebrated biblical scholar Constantin Von Tischendorf discovered this manuscript, which contains almost all the New Testament and over half of the Old Testament, in 1859. The monastery presented it to the Russian Czar, and the Soviet Union sold it to the British government (and its people, who subscribed to share in the purchase) for 100,000 pounds on Christmas Day, 1933. For the gospel texts, its reliability is considered second only to the Codex Vaticanus. For Acts, its reliability is equal to the Codex Vaticanus, and for the epistles, its reliability is ranked first. (The Codex Alexandrinus is considered better for the book of Revelation.)

The discovery of this manuscript is a fascinating story. Metzger relates the traditional background leading to its discovery:

In 1844, when he was not yet thirty years of age, Tischendorf, a Privatdozent in the University of Leipzig, began an extensive journey through the Near East in search of Biblical manuscripts. While visiting the monastery of St. Catherine at Mount Sinai, he chanced to see some leaves of parchment in a waste-basket full of papers destined to light the oven of the monastery. On examination these proved to be part of a copy of the Septuagint version of the Old Testament, written in a nearly Greek uncial script. He retrieved from the basket no fewer than forty-three such leaves, and the monk casually remarked that two basket loads of similarly discarded leaves had already been burned up! Later, when Tischendorf was shown other portions of the same codex (containing all of Isaiah and I and II Maccabees), he warned the monks that such things were too valuable to be used to stoke their fires. The forty-three leaves which he was permitted to keep contained portions of I Chronicles, Jeremiah, Nehemiah, and Esther, and upon returning to Europe he deposited them in the university library at Leipzig, where they still remain. In 1846 he published their contents, naming them the codex Frederico-Augustanus (in honour of the King of Saxony, Frederick Augustus, the discoverer's sovereign and patron).

A second visit to the monastery by Tischendorf in 1853 produced no new manuscripts because the monks were suspicious as a result of the enthusiasm for the MS displayed during his first visit in 1844. He visited a third time in 1859, under the direction of the Czar of Russia, Alexander II. Shortly before leaving, Tischendorf gave the steward of the monastery an edition of the Septuagint that had been published by Tischendorf in Leipzig.

Thereupon the steward remarked that he too had a copy of the Septuagint, and produced from a closet in his cell a manuscript wrapped in a red cloth. There before the astonished scholar's eyes lay the treasure which he had been longing to see. Concealing his feelings, Tischendorf casually asked permission to look at it further that evening. Permission was granted, and upon retiring to his room Tischendorf stayed up all night in the joy of studying the manuscript—for, as he declared in his diary (which as a scholar he kept in Latin), *quippe dormire nefas videbatur* ("it really seemed a sacrilege to sleep!"). He soon found that the document contained much more than he had even hoped; for not only was most of the Old Testament there, but also the New Testament was intact and in excellent condition. (Metzger, TNT, 43–44)

7. Codex Alexandrinus (AD 400)

Located in the British Library, this manuscript was written in Greek in Egypt, and contains almost the entire Bible.

8. Codex Ephraemi (AD 400s)

This codex is located in the Bibliotheque Nationale, Paris. "Its 5th century origin and the evidence it supplies make it important for the text of certain portions of the New Testament." (Bruce, BP, 183) Every biblical book is represented in the manuscript except 2 Thessalonians and 2 John. "This is a fifth century document called a palimpsest. (A palimpsest is a manuscript in which the original writing has been erased and then written over.) Through the use of chemicals and painstaking effort, a scholar can read the original writing underneath the overprinted text." (Comfort, OB, 181)

9. Codex Bezae (c. AD 450)

The Codex Bezae, located in the Cambridge University Library, contains the Gospels and Acts, not only in Greek but also in Latin.

10. Codex Washingtonensis (or Freericanus) (c. AD 450)

Containing the four gospels (Greenlee, INTTC, 39), this codex is located in the Smithsonian Institution in Washington, DC.

11. Codex Claromontanus (AD 500s)

Codex Claromontanus is a bilingual collection of Pauline Epistles.

G. Patristic Quotations from the New Testament

All told, the sheer number of New Testament manuscripts and the earliness of the extant manuscripts give us great reason to believe that the New Testament accurately transmits the content of the autographs. But there's more than that. Metzger and Ehrman point out the huge number of quotations of Scripture available from the writings of the early church fathers:

> Besides textual evidence derived from New Testament Greek manuscripts and from early versions, the textual critic has available the numerous scriptural quotations included in the commentaries, sermons, and other treatises written by the early Church fathers. Indeed, so extensive are these citations that if all other sources for our knowledge of the text of the New Testament were destroyed, they would be sufficient alone for the reconstruction of practically the entire New Testament. (Metzger and Ehrman, TNT, 126; cf. Greenlee, INTTC, 54)

1. Accuracy of Manuscripts Supported by Writings of the Early Church Fathers

The patristic citations of Scripture are not primary witnesses to the text of the New Testament, but they do serve an important secondary role. They give substantial support to the existence of the twenty-seven authoritative books of the New Testament canon. It is true that their quotations were often loose (although in the case of some church fathers they were very accurate), but they do at least reproduce the substantial content of the original text. Further, their quotations are so numerous and widespread that at least an outline of the New Testament and many of its crucial details could be reconstructed from their writings if we had no manuscripts of the text itself.

2. Early Citations of the New Testament by the Church Fathers

Although quotations of Scripture among the church fathers up through the thirteenth century number well over one million, of particular significance are the quotations that date prior to (roughly) AD 325.

Porter and Pitts observe:

Quotations of the NT from early church fathers . . . play an important role in re-constructing the NT text in that they give us insight into what text types were available and in use when and where they wrote. In some cases, this makes the church fathers a more certain source than Greek manuscripts since the date and geographical location of the

church fathers are usually easy to ascertain. (Porter and Pitts, FNTTC, 69)

However, biblical scholar Joseph Angus offers these cautions concerning the early patristic writings:

- Quotes are sometimes inaccurate.
- Some copyists were prone to mistakes or made intentional alterations. (Angus, BH, 56)

Here is a selection of important early witnesses to the New Testament manuscripts among the church fathers:

a. Clement of Rome (AD 95)

Origen, in *De Principus*, II.3, calls Clement a disciple of the apostles. (Anderson, BWG, 28) Tertullian, in *Against Heresies*, chapter 23, writes that Peter appointed Clement. Irenaeus adds in his own *Against Heresies*, III.3, that Clement "had the preaching of the Apostles still echoing in his ears and their doctrine in front of his eyes." Clement quotes from the Synoptic Gospels, Acts, 1 Corinthians, Titus, Hebrews, and 1 Peter.

SCRIPTURE CITATIONS FROM SELECTED EARLY CHURCH FATHERS

Writer	Gospels	Acts	Pauline Epistles	General Epistles	Revelation	Totals
Justin Martyr	268	10	43	6	3 (266 allusions)	330
Irenaeus	1,038	194	499	23	65	1,819
Clement (Alex.)	1,107	44	1,127	207	11	2,496
Origen	9,231	349	7,778	399	165	17,992
Tertullian	3,822	502	2,609	120	205	7,258
Hippolytus	734	42	387	27	188	1,378
Eusebius	3,268	211	1,592	88	27	5,186
Grand Totals	**19,468**	**1,352**	**14,035**	**870**	**664**	**36,389**

Chart's content adapted from Geisler and Nix, FGTU, 138

b. Ignatius (AD 70–110)

Ignatius was the third bishop of Antioch (the apostle Peter is thought to have been the first there). Ignatius was martyred. He had "been a hearer" of the apostle John. (Jurgens vol. 1, 17) His seven epistles contain quotations from Matthew, John, Acts, Romans, 1 Corinthians, Galatians, Ephesians, Philippians, Colossians, 1 and 2 Thessalonians, 1 and 2 Timothy, James, and 1 Peter.

c. Polycarp (AD 70–c. 156)

Martyred at eighty-six years of age, Polycarp was bishop of Smyrna (modern-day Izmir) and a disciple of the apostle John. His second Letter to the Philippians includes allusions and paraphrases that reflect his deep assimilation of the New Testament letters and are nearly quotations from the following books: Romans, 1 and 2 Corinthians, Galatians, Colossians, 1 Timothy, Hebrews, 1 Peter, 1 and 2 John. The letter also cites Psalms, Proverbs, and Isaiah from the Old Testament.

d. Clement of Alexandria (AD 150–212)

Clement's 2,400 quotes of Scripture draw from all but three books of the New Testament.

e. Tertullian (AD 160–220)

Tertullian was a presbyter of the church in Carthage. He quotes the New Testament more than 7,000 times, of which 3,800 are from the Gospels.

f. Hippolytus (AD 170–235)

Hippolytus includes more than 1,300 quotes of Scripture.

g. Justin Martyr (AD 133)

Born into paganism, Justin studied various Greek philosophies before his conversion. He battled the heretic Marcion and later was martyred in Rome. His *Apologies* (defenses of the faith) either quote or allude to the four New Testament gospels, along with 1 Corinthians and Hebrews, and to the Old Testament books of Genesis, Deuteronomy, Isaiah, and Malachi.

h. Origen (AD 185–253/254)

This vociferous writer compiled more than six thousand works. He lists more than eighteen thousand New Testament quotes. (Geisler and Nix, GIB, 353)

i. Cyprian (d. AD 258)

A bishop of Carthage, Cyprian used approximately 740 Old Testament citations and 1,030 from the New Testament.

j. Others

Other early church fathers who quoted from the New Testament include Barnabas (c. AD 70), Hermas (c. AD 95), Tatian (c. AD 170), and Irenaeus (c. AD 170).

Geisler and Nix rightly conclude that

there were some 32,000 citations of the New Testament prior to the time of the Council of Nicea (325). These 32,000 quotations are by no means exhaustive, and they do not even include the fourth-century writers. Just adding the number of references used by one other writer, Eusebius, who flourished prior to and contemporary with the Council at Nicea, will bring the total number of citations (prior to AD 325) of the New Testament to over 36,000. (Geisler and Nix, GIB, 353–354)

To all of the above we could add the later church fathers: Augustine, Arnobius, Lactantius, Chrysostom, Jerome, Gaius Romanus, Athanasius, Ambrose of Milan, Cyril of

Alexandria, Ephraem the Syrian, Hilary of Poitiers, Gregory of Nyssa, and many others.*

H. Apocryphal Gospels

Stanley Porter and Andrew Pitts note how second-century apocryphal gospels can also help reconstruct the original text of the NT:

> A number of apocryphal Gospels (Jesus stories written in the second century and beyond) can be dated roughly with the second century and can be used in efforts to reconstruct the NT text as well, since they contain a number of canonical Gospel parallels. However, because they are not continuous text manuscripts of the NT, they must be used cautiously. (Porter and Pitts, FNTTC, 103)

I. Did the Biblical Text Become Corrupted During Transmission over Centuries?

In his popular book *Misquoting Jesus*, as well as his academic book *The Orthodox Corruption of Scripture*, Bart Ehrman argues that there are both accidental alterations in the text by scribes, but also intentional corruptions where they aimed to change the text to fit a particular doctrinal agenda. However, Porter and Pitts conclude that while

> we must allow that certain scribes may have had doctrinal agendas that impact their transmission of the text from time to time, this was the exception rather than the rule. . . . Ancient scribes generally considered it their duty to copy rather than interpret or alter the text to suit their or others' doctrinal beliefs. This is not to say doctrinal alterations did not happen from time to time, but it certainly was not part of regular scribal practice. . . . This is where Ehrman himself is inconsistent. He admits

that doctrinally motivated alteration was the exception, not the rule, but builds his entire case upon variants that are often easily explained by using . . . standard transcriptional probabilities. (Porter and Pitts, FNTTC, 119–20)

Dockery, Mathews, and Sloan have recently written, "For most of the biblical text a single reading has been transmitted. Elimination of scribal errors and intentional changes leaves only a small percentage of the text about which any questions occur." (Dockery et al., FBI, 176) They conclude: "It must be said that the amount of time between the original composition and the next surviving manuscript is far less for the New Testament than for any other work in Greek literature. . . . Although there are certainly differences in many of the New Testament manuscripts, not one fundamental doctrine of the Christian faith rests on a disputed reading." (Dockery et al., FBI, 182)

Additionally, according to textual expert Scott Carroll, "No biblical discovery has ever undermined our confidence in scripture." (Carroll, lecture, 2013) "In the last 130 years," explains Daniel Wallace, "there has not been a single manuscript discovery that has produced a new reading for the New Testament that scholars think is authentic . . . not a single manuscript that tells us a totally different story about Jesus." He continues, "In about the second century BC the rules for careful copying and textual criticism were developed heavily in Alexandria, Egypt, which became the primary scholarly city in the ancient world for book reproduction (before the New Testament was ever written). The New Testament manuscripts became benefactors of that approach." (Wallace, lecture, 2013)

---

* For more details about the accuracy of the early church fathers' quotations of Scripture, see Andrew F. Gregory and Christopher M. Tuckett, eds., *The New Testament and the Apostolic Fathers, Volume 1: The Reception of the New Testament in the Apostolic Fathers,* Oxford: Oxford University Press, 2005.

J. Results of the Bibliographic Test

Scholars representing different types of expertise and different eras agree that the text of the New Testament meets the first bibliographic test.

Even back in the late 1880s, leading biblical scholar F. J. A. Hort rightfully noted that "in the variety and fullness of the evidence on which it rests the text of the New Testament stands absolutely and unapproachably alone among ancient prose writings." (Hort and Westcott, NTOG, 561) In 1977 Greenlee stated, "The number of available MSS of the New Testament is overwhelmingly greater than those of any other work of ancient literature.... The earliest extant MSS of the NT were written much closer to the date of the original writing than is the case in almost any other piece of ancient literature." (Greenlee, INTTC, 15)

> The New Testament is the most remarkably preserved book of the ancient world. Not only do we have a great number of manuscripts but they are very close in time to the originals they represent. Some partial manuscripts of the NT are from the second century AD, and many are within four centuries of the originals. These facts are all the more amazing when they are compared with the preservation of other ancient literature. (Glenny, PS, 95)

Montgomery says that "to be skeptical of the resultant text of the New Testament books is to allow all of classical antiquity to slip into obscurity, for no documents of the ancient period are as well attested bibliographically as the New Testament." (Montgomery, HC, 29)

Metzger and Ehrman put the large number of New Testament manuscripts into perspective:

> In contrast with these figures [of other ancient works], the textual critic of the New Testament is embarrassed by a wealth of material. Furthermore, the work of many ancient authors has been preserved only in manuscripts that date from the Middle Ages (sometimes the late Middle Ages), far removed from the time at which they lived and wrote. On the contrary, the time between the composition of the books of the New Testament and the earliest extant copies is relatively brief. Instead of a lapse of a millennium or more, as is the case of not a few classical authors, several papyrus manuscripts of portions of the New Testament are extant that were copied within a century or so after the composition of the original documents. (Metzger and Ehrman, TNT, 51)

Leading Old Testament scholar Walter Kaiser reports that no time before the present has witnessed such unprecedented confirmation of "biblical events, persons, and historical settings as we have during the past century of ongoing, successful archaeological exploration." (Kaiser, ASB, ix)

Sir Frederic G. Kenyon, a British paleontologist and classical Biblical scholar, was also the director and principal librarian of the British Museum (1889–1931) and second

---

To be skeptical of the resultant text of the New Testament books is to allow all of classical antiquity to slip into obscurity, for no documents of the ancient period are as well attested bibliographically as the New Testament.

John Warwick Montgomery

---

to none in authority for issuing statements about MSS. He stated that besides number, the manuscripts of the New Testament differ from those of the classical authors. In no other case is the interval of time between the composition of the book and the date of the earliest extant manuscripts so short as in that of the New Testament. The books of the New Testament were written in the latter part of the first century; the earliest extant manuscripts (trifling scraps excepted) are of the fourth century—say from 250 to 300 years later. This may sound a considerable interval, but it is nothing compared to that which separates most of the great classical authors from their earliest manuscripts. We believe that we have in all essentials an accurate text of the seven extant plays of Sophocles; yet the earliest substantial manuscript upon which it is based was written more than 1400 years after the poet's death. (Kenyon, HTCNT, 4)

Kenyon elsewhere noted, "The interval then between the dates of original composition and the earliest extant evidence becomes so small as to be in fact negligible, and the last foundation for any doubt that the Scriptures have come down to us substantially as they were written has now been removed. Both the authenticity and the general integrity of the books of the New Testament may be regarded as finally established." (Kenyon, BA, 288) Since Kenyon wrote this, his conclusions have been verified by modern-day biblical scholarship.

IV. Internal Evidence Test for the Reliability of the New Testament

A. Benefit of the Doubt

Regarding the internal evidence test, John Warwick Montgomery reports that literary critics still follow Aristotle's dictum that "the benefit of the doubt is to be given to the document itself, not arrogated by the critic to himself." Therefore, "one must listen to the claims of the document under analysis, and not assume fraud or error unless the author disqualified himself by contradictions or known factual inaccuracies." (Montgomery, EA, 29)

Robert M. Horn amplifies this point:

Think for a moment about what needs to be demonstrated concerning a "difficulty" in order to transfer it into the category of a valid argument against doctrine. Certainly much more is required than the mere appearance of a contradiction. First, we must be certain that we have correctly understood the passage, the sense in which it uses words or numbers. Second, that we possess all available knowledge in this matter. Third, that no further light can possibly be thrown on it by advancing knowledge, textual research, archaeology, etc....

Difficulties do not constitute objections. Unsolved problems are not of necessity errors. This is not to minimize the area of difficulty; it is to see it in perspective. Difficulties are to be grappled with and problems are to drive us to seek clearer light; but until such time as we have total and final light on any issue we are in no position to affirm, "Here is a proven error, an unquestionable objection to an infallible Bible." It is common knowledge that countless "objections" have been fully resolved since this century began. (Horn, BTSI, 86–87)

B. Is the Document Free of Known Contradictions?

He was known around the seminary as the man who had learned more than thirty languages, most of them languages of Old Testament times in the Middle Eastern world. Gleason Archer, who taught for more than thirty years at the graduate seminary level in the field of biblical criticism, gives the following modest description of his qualifications to discern the meaning of difficult biblical texts:

> As an undergraduate at Harvard, I was fascinated by apologetics and biblical evidences; so I labored to obtain a knowledge of the languages and cultures that have any bearing on biblical scholarship. As a classics major in college, I received training in Latin and Greek, also in French and German. At seminary I majored in Hebrew, Aramaic, and Arabic; and in post-graduate years I became involved in Syriac and Akkadian, to the extent of teaching elective courses in each of these subjects. Earlier, during my final two years of high school, I had acquired a special interest in Middle Kingdom Egyptian studies, which was furthered as I later taught courses in this field. At the Oriental Institute in Chicago, I did specialized study in Eighteenth Dynasty historical records and also studied Coptic and Sumerian. Combined with this work in ancient languages was a full course of training at law school, after which I was admitted to the Massachusetts Bar in 1939. This gave me a thorough grounding in the field of legal evidences. (Archer, NIEBD, 11).

Archer, in the foreword to his *New International Encyclopedia of Bible Difficulties*, gives this testimony about the internal consistency of the Bible:

As I have dealt with one apparent discrepancy after another and have studied the alleged contradictions between the biblical record and the evidence of linguistics, archaeology, or science, my confidence in the trustworthiness of Scripture has been repeatedly verified and strengthened by the discovery that almost every problem in Scripture that has ever been discovered by man, from ancient times until now, has been dealt with in a completely satisfactory manner by the biblical text itself—or else by objective archaeological information. The deductions that may be validly drawn from ancient Egyptian, Sumerian, or Akkadian documents all harmonize with the biblical record; and no properly trained evangelical scholar has anything to fear from the hostile arguments and challenges of humanistic rationalists or detractors of any and every persuasion. (Archer, NIEBD, 12)

Archer concludes,

> There is a good and sufficient answer in Scripture itself to refute every charge that has ever been leveled against it. But this is only to be expected from the kind of book the Bible asserts itself to be, the inscripturation of the infallible, inerrant Word of the Living God. (Archer, NIEBD, 12)

Students of the Bible are often troubled to find statements in the Bible that appear to contradict other statements in the Bible. And,

---

As I have dealt with one apparent discrepancy after another and have studied the alleged contradictions between the biblical record and the evidence of linguistics, archaeology, or science, my confidence in the trustworthiness of Scripture has been repeatedly verified and strengthened.

Gleason Archer

---

time and again, the apparent contradictions can be resolved with a little research. For example, one of my (Josh's) associates had always wondered why the books of Matthew and Acts gave conflicting versions of the death of Judas Iscariot. Matthew relates that Judas died by hanging himself. But Acts says that Judas fell headlong in a field, and "he burst open in the middle and all his entrails gushed out" (Acts 1:18). My friend was perplexed as to how both accounts could be true. He theorized that Judas must have hanged himself off the side of a cliff, the rope gave way, and he fell headlong into the field below. It would be the only way a fall into a field could burst open a body. Sure enough, several years later on a trip to the Holy Land, my friend was shown the traditional site of Judas's death: a field at the bottom of a cliff outside Jerusalem.

C. Principles of Interpreting Ancient Literature

The allegations of error in the Bible are usually based on a failure to recognize basic principles of interpreting ancient literature. Such principles can help one discern whether there is truly an error or contradiction in the literature—in this case, the Bible. For a description of seventeen principles for resolving seeming contradictions in Scripture, see chapter 26, "Alleged Contradictions in the Old Testament."

D. The New Testament Writers Were Eyewitnesses to Events They Describe

The writers of the New Testament wrote as eyewitnesses or from firsthand information. The books of the New Testament make claims such as the following:

"Inasmuch as many have taken in hand to set in order a narrative of those things which have been fulfilled among us, just as those who from the beginning were eyewitnesses and ministers of the word delivered them to us, it seemed good to me also, having had perfect understanding of all things from the very first, to write to you an orderly account, most excellent Theophilus." — Luke 1:1–3

"For we did not follow cunningly devised fables when we made known to you the power and coming of our Lord Jesus Christ, but were eyewitnesses of His majesty." — 2 Peter 1:16

"That which we have seen and heard we declare to you, that you also may have fellowship with us; and truly our fellowship is with the Father and with His Son Jesus Christ." — 1 John 1:3

"'Men of Israel, hear these words: Jesus of Nazareth, a Man attested by God to you by miracles, wonders, and signs which God did through Him in your midst, as you yourselves also know." — Acts 2:22

"And he who has seen has testified, and his testimony is true; and he knows that he is telling the truth, so that you may believe." — John 19:35

"Now in the fifteenth year of the reign of Tiberius Caesar, Pontius Pilate being governor of Judea, Herod being tetrarch of Galilee, his brother Philip tetrarch of Iturea and the region of Trachonitis, and Lysanias tetrarch of Abilene ..." — Luke 3:1

"Now as he thus made his defense, Festus said with a loud voice, 'Paul, you are beside yourself! Much learning is driving you mad!' But he said, 'I am not mad, most noble Festus, but speak the words of truth and reason. For the king, before whom I also speak freely, knows these things; for I am convinced that none of these things escapes his attention, since this thing was not done in a corner.'" — Acts 26:24–26

E. Undesigned Coincidences

Reviving the work of Christian writers of the eighteenth and nineteenth centuries, philosopher Lydia McGrew shows that the reliability of the Gospels is supported by what is known as the argument from undesigned coincidences.

An undesigned coincidence is a notable connection between two or more accounts or texts that doesn't seem to have been planned by the person or people giving the accounts. Despite their apparent independence, the items fit together like pieces of a puzzle. (McGrew, HIPV, 12)

Such coincidences crisscross the Gospels, forming a tight web of casual interconnections best explained by the truth of the accounts.

1. Undesigned Coincidences Between the Gospel of Luke and the Other Gospels

For example, a subtle coincidence between Matthew and Luke shows that these authors had independent access to the names of Jesus' followers and even to the inner workings of Herod's household.

When Herod heard of Jesus and his miracles, the Gospels report that he was rather disconcerted and even worried that John the Baptist might have returned from death. . . . Matthew's account of Herod's perplexity contains a unique detail—that Herod was musing about Jesus' identity *to his servants*. . . . Why does Matthew specify that Herod spoke about this to his servants? Even more to the point, how could Matthew know, in the usual course of events, what Herod was saying to his servants? (McGrew, HIPV, 87–88)

The answer comes in the fact that one of Jesus' followers was Joanna, the wife of Chuza, Herod's household manager. This is noted in an entirely different context in Luke 8:1–3.

This passage is not in any way *about* Herod or about his comments concerning Jesus. Luke is merely listing those who accompanied Jesus at this point in his ministry. . . . In other words, Luke says that a follower of Jesus (or at any rate the husband of a devout follower of Jesus) was found among the important servants of Herod's household. It was therefore quite natural that information about Herod's doings and about his reaction to the stories of Jesus should come back to the community of Jesus' followers and make it into Matthew's Gospel. If Herod knew that one of his servants was connected to Jesus through his wife, it would also make sense that he would be discussing this matter with his servants and giving his own superstitious conclusions about Jesus' true identity.

The indirectness of this coincidence is particularly lovely. Only one part of the puzzle is found in each Gospel, and the connection cannot possibly be the result of design. It is beyond belief that Luke would have inserted this casual reference to Chuza in a list unconnected in any other way with Herod or with the beheading of John, in order to provide a convenient explanation for the detail about Herod's servants mentioned only in Matthew. This coincidence provides clear evidence of the independence of Matthew and Luke and confirms them both. (McGrew, HIPV, 88–89)

Undesigned coincidences occur in all parts of the Gospels, and some concern miracles. In John 18:36, Jesus tells Pilate that his kingdom is not of this world. If his kingdom were earthly, says Jesus, his servants would fight. This raises a question.

[T]he careful reader of John knows from a scene earlier in the same chapter that one of Jesus' servants, Simon Peter, *did* fight, maiming someone, to prevent Jesus from being delivered over to the Jews. Had Pilate inquired into Jesus' claim of unworldly peacefulness, wouldn't Malchus have been produced, bloody and earless, as evidence for the belligerence of Jesus' disciples and of his movement? Why (based only on John) would Jesus make this argument, knowing that such evidence could be produced against him? (McGrew, HIPV, 56)

The undesigned coincidence lies in the fact that Luke's gospel, though almost certainly written *earlier* than John's, explains John at just this point, since Luke 22:51 says that Jesus had healed the ear.

Only Luke says that Jesus healed the servant's ear, though Matthew and Mark also recount that the ear was cut off. . . . Luke supplies a unique detail within a passage that is in some respects similar to the other Synoptic Gospels. And . . . this detail is confirmed by an undesigned coincidence. If it is true that Jesus healed the servant's ear, it explains Jesus' words to Pilate, though those words are given only in John. Jesus could confidently declare that his kingdom is not of this world and even say that his servants would be fighting if his kingdom were not peaceful. If anyone tried to say that Peter cut off a servant's ear, the wounded servant himself could not be produced to show this, and an admission that Jesus healed the ear would be further evidence of Jesus' nonviolent intentions, not to mention evidence of his miraculous abilities. This undesigned coincidence thus confirms John's and Luke's separate accounts of the events of Jesus' passion and trial. (McGrew, HIPV, 56–57)

McGrew concludes,

The argument from undesigned coincidences tells us something about what the authors of these documents were like. What picture of the author of the Gospel of John emerges from what

we have seen? It is a picture of a careful recorder with a vivid and meticulous memory, someone with his own, independent, close access to the facts, someone who is not inventing, massaging, or exaggerating his data. . . . These authors have primarily a *testimonial* project rather than a literary or redactive one. They are honest witnesses giving their reports and honest historians relating witness reports—emphasizing and mentioning different details, to be sure, but ultimately aiming to tell what really happened. The providential provision of four Gospels gives us a three-dimensional view of the events. (McGrew, HIPV, 226)

2. Undesigned Coincidences Between Acts and the Epistles of Paul

Undesigned coincidences also support the reliability of the book of Acts and its authorship by the physician Luke, a close companion of Paul, as Paul notes in three of his letters (Col. 4:14; Philemon 1:24; 2 Tim. 4:11).

Luke traveled extensively with Paul on his missionary journeys, beginning with Acts 16, verses 9 and 10, where statements describing Paul's travel start to use "we" as the subject. When Paul embarked on his return to Jerusalem in Acts 20, again the pronouns "us" and "we" identify Luke's presence, including at their meeting with James and "all the elders" in Jerusalem (Acts 21:17–20). When Paul's presence in the Jerusalem temple led to a riot and his unjust arrest, the Roman military took him under escort to Caesarea where Felix retained him under custody for over two years. Acts describes in detail each of Paul's speeches at the hearings of his case in both Jerusalem and Caesarea. When Paul as a Roman citizen finally had to appeal to Caesar (Acts 26:30–32), we read, "It was decided that we should sail for Italy," and Luke again traveled with Paul on his shipwrecked voyage en route to Rome (Acts 27:1—28:31).

In Acts 18:1–5 we are told that, while Paul was in Corinth, he worked at tent-making during the week and reasoned in the synagogue on the Sabbath. But, says Acts 18:5, "when Silas and Timothy came down from Macedonia, Paul began devoting himself completely to the word, solemnly testifying to the Jews that Jesus was the Christ." (NASB)

McGrew points out,

> What these verses convey is that Paul became *particularly* dedicated to preaching after the arrival of Silas and Timothy from Macedonia. Why should this be? It is difficult to imagine a person more continuously dedicated at all times to preaching than the Apostle Paul! Why should the arrival of Timothy and Silas make any difference? . . .
>
> Prior to the arrival of Silas and Timothy, Paul works during the week at tentmaking and dedicates himself to preaching only on the Sabbath, when manual labor is forbidden to him as a Jew. After Silas and Timothy arrive, he is suddenly able to devote himself to preaching all the time and no longer has to work at his trade. What this suggests is that Silas and Timothy *brought money to Paul from Macedonia.* (McGrew, HIPV, 157–158)

This theory is confirmed in Paul's own second letter to the Corinthians: "And when I was present with you, and in need, I was a burden to no one, for what I lacked the brethren who came from Macedonia supplied" (2 Cor. 11:9).

McGrew comments,

> The delicacy of the confirmation is its greatest strength. Acts does not state that money came from Macedonia with Paul's co-workers, yet the hypothesis that it did both explains Acts and coincides perfectly with the epistles. (McGrew, HIPV, 158)

The author of Acts even seems to have known of Paul's intended travel arrangements for himself and his companions before Paul made certain trips. Acts 19:19–22 says that Paul sent Timothy and Erastus on ahead from Ephesus to Macedonia and that he himself was planning later to travel to Macedonia, then to Greece, and eventually to Jerusalem, corresponding to Paul's travel plans in 1 Corinthians 16. First Corinthians also says (1 Cor. 4:17; 16:10) that Paul had already sent Timothy to Corinth and that they were to respect him if and when he came, with the implication that the epistle itself would arrive before Timothy. The geography of the region shows how this was possible.

> Timothy . . . would have eventually traveled to Corinth in a somewhat roundabout fashion. But there is a direct sea route from Ephesus to Corinth by which Paul could have sent his epistle. . . . [W]ith a good wind, a letter could travel from Ephesus to Corinth fairly quickly. . . .
>
> This beautifully brings together the implications of both the epistle and Acts, providing strong reason to believe that Paul wrote I Corinthians from Ephesus after making these plans and sending Timothy ahead, at about Acts 19.22 when he "stayed in Asia for a while." (McGrew, HIPV, 164–165)

3. Conclusion Regarding Luke's Role as a Historian

McGrew points out what all of this means for the big picture.

> Given the minute, one might even say boring, details in Acts of Paul's life and travels corroborated by this study . . . the idea that [the author of Acts] was writing in any sense a work of fiction can be readily dismissed. The picture of that author, who is also the

author of Luke, comes shining through as exactly what Christian tradition has always held him to be—a close companion of Paul, a man who knew the apostles and had access to eyewitnesses, and a careful, conscientious historian. (McGrew, HIPV, 226)

McGrew also notes,

As the cumulative case from undesigned coincidences mounts up, it becomes increasingly difficult to deny that the author of Acts knew Paul and his travels personally and reported them reliably, though not exhaustively. The picture that emerges from these coincidences is also that of someone who had a strong drive to note and record meticulously.

The author of Acts as he emerges in these chapters would have had both the opportunity and the motivation to speak with the principal characters in the earliest chapters of Acts, such as Peter and John, and with others who had witnessed events such as Pentecost. Hence, . . . the undesigned coincidences concerning Paul, his travels, his companions, and his imprisonment support the conclusion that what Acts records about the first public teaching of the apostles, the founding of the Christian movement, and the earliest persecution of the apostles is historically trustworthy. Acts is a primary historical source showing that the disciples were willing to risk death for their public proclamation, as eyewitnesses, that Jesus of Nazareth was risen from the dead. (McGrew, HIPV, 218)

F. Summary of the Internal Evidence Test

F. F. Bruce says concerning the primary-source value of the New Testament records:

The earliest preachers of the gospel knew the value of . . . first-hand testimony, and appealed to it time and again. "We are witnesses of these things," was their constant and confident assertion. And it can have been by no means so easy as some writers seem to think to invent words and deeds of Jesus in those early years, when so many of His disciples were about, who could remember what had and had not happened.

And it was not only friendly eyewitnesses that the early preachers had to reckon with; there were others less well-disposed who were also conversant with the main facts of the ministry and death of Jesus. The disciples could not afford to risk inaccuracies (not to speak of willful manipulation of the facts), which would at once be exposed by those who would be only too glad to do so. On the contrary, one of the strong points in the original apostolic preaching is the confident appeal to the knowledge of the hearers; they not only said, "We are witnesses of these things," but also, "As you yourselves also know" (Acts 2:22). Had there been any tendency to depart from the facts in any material respect, the possible presence of hostile witnesses in the audience would have served as a further corrective. (Bruce, NTD, 33, 44–46)

But some might contend, "Come on, that's only what the writers claimed. A pseudo-author writing a century or more after the fact can claim anything."

The fact is, however, that the books of the New Testament were not written down a century or more after the events they described, but during the lifetimes of those involved in the accounts themselves. Therefore, scholars should regard the New Testament today as a competent primary source document from the first century. (Montgomery, HC, 34–35)

Further, New Testament scholar Richard Bauckham has carefully assessed the frequency of names in first-century Palestine. Among Jews of this period there were a small number of popular names and a large number of rare ones. In support of its authenticity, Bauckham notes: "The percentages [of names] for men in the New Testament thus correlate remarkably closely with those for the population in general. . . . Thus the names of Palestinian Jews in the Gospels and Acts coincide very closely with the names of the general population of Jewish Palestine in this period, but not to the names of the Jews in the Diaspora. In this light it becomes very unlikely that the names in the Gospels are late accretions to the traditions. Outside Palestine the appropriate names simply could not have been chosen." (Bauckham, JE, 73–74) Then he offers a fitting conclusion:

Onomastics (the study of names) is a significant resource for assessing the origins of Gospel traditions. The evidence . . . shows that the relative frequency of the various personal names in the Gospels corresponds well to the relative frequency in the full database of three thousand individual instances of names in the Palestinian Jewish sources of the period. This correspondence is very unlikely to have resulted from addition of names to the traditions, even within Palestinian Jewish Christianity, and could not possibly have resulted from the addition of names to the traditions outside Jewish Palestine, since the pattern of Jewish name usage in the Diaspora was very different. The usages of the Gospels also correspond closely to the variety of ways in which persons bearing the same very popular names could be distinguished in Palestinian Jewish usage. Again these features of the New Testament data would be difficult to explain as a result of random invention of names within Palestinian Jewish Christianity and impossible to explain as the result of such invention outside Jewish Palestine. All the evidence indicates the general authenticity

of the personal names in the Gospels. This underlines the plausibility of the suggestion . . . as to the significance of many of these names: *that they indicate the eyewitness sources of the individual stories in which they occur.* (Bauckham, JE, 84)

Skeptics have also doubted that the apostles could have remembered the events accurately. Bauckham has noted nine features of events that are best remembered. Overall, the Gospels fit these categories well, which increases our confidence that the traditions have been preserved reliably. (Bauckham, JE, 341–346)

- *Unique or unusual events.* The gospel stories clearly fit this category, as many of the events, such as healings and exorcisms, are unmistakably unusual.
- *Salient or consequential events.* Gospel stories often involve landmark or life changing events that would create vivid memories in people who witnessed them.
- *An event for which a person is emotionally involved.* The gospel writers were not dispassionate observers, but were personally invested and emotionally involved in the events themselves. They were deeply affected by the events.
- *Vivid imagery.* The gospel stories have little vivid imagery. Mark tends to have more than the other gospels, but it is difficult to know if this imagery is the result of Mark being close to the events or being a good storyteller.
- *Irrelevant details.* There are some irrelevant details in the Gospels, but most details have been preserved because of their significance and memorability. However, as Bauckham notes, the lack of irrelevant details is not evidence against eyewitness provenance.

- *Point of view.* People remembering events and stories often switch point of view in how they tell the story. And this occurs regularly in the Gospels. The gospel of Mark, for instance, does this to show that Mark is preserving the eyewitness testimony of Peter.
- *Dating.* People typically remember details about events, such as location, actions, time of day, emotions, and persons involved, but dates are not common. The Gospels fit this characteristic of memory, in which the recorded events only include indications of dating for specific reasons.
- *Gist and details.* The overall gist of a memory is likely to be accurate, even if details vary. We see this pattern in the Gospels (e.g., Matt 26:58, 69–75; Mark 14:54; Luke 22:54–62; John 18:15–18, 25–27).
- *Frequent rehearsal.* Stories that were told frequently were more likely to become standardized in a certain form and better remembered. As Bauckham notes, we can be sure the apostles told the stories of Jesus frequently after the events.

V. External Evidence Test for the Reliability of the New Testament

After many years of careful study, Ravi Zacharias concludes by noting not only the variety, quantity, and elapsed time between the gospel events and the manuscripts, but also the range of documents that could support or challenge the scriptures—in short, those written from an external perspective: "In real terms, the New Testament is easily the best attested ancient writing in terms of the sheer number of documents, the time span between the events and the document,

and the variety of documents available to sustain or contradict it. There is nothing in ancient manuscript evidence to match such textual availability and integrity." (Zacharias, CMLWG, 162)

"Do other historical materials confirm or deny the internal testimony provided by the documents themselves?" (Montgomery, HC, 31) In other words, what sources are there—apart from the literature under analysis—that substantiate its accuracy, reliability, and authenticity?

A. Supporting Evidence from Early Christian Writers Who Quote or Paraphrase the Bible

1. Eusebius

In his *Ecclesiastical History* III.39, Eusebius preserves writings of Papias, bishop of Hierapolis (AD c. 60–130), in which Papias reports sayings of "the Elder." There is an ongoing dialogue between scholars about whether "the Elder" is a reference to the apostle John.

The Elder used to say this also: "Mark, having been the interpreter of Peter, wrote down accurately all that he (Peter) mentioned, whether sayings or doings of Christ, not, however, in order. For he was neither a hearer nor a companion of the Lord; but afterwards, as I said, he accompanied Peter, who adapted his teachings as necessity required, not as though he were making a compilation of the sayings of the Lord. So then Mark made no mistake writing down in this way some things as he [Peter] mentioned them; for he paid attention to this one thing, not to omit anything that he had heard, not to include any false statement among them." (Eusebius, EH, III.39). Papias also comments about the gospel of Matthew: "Matthew recorded the oracles in the Hebrew (i.e., Aramaic) tongue." (Eusebius, EH, III.39)

2. Irenaeus, Bishop of Lyons

Irenaeus was a student of Polycarp, bishop of Smyrna. Polycarp had been a disciple of John the apostle. Around AD 180 Irenaeus wrote: "So firm is the ground upon which these Gospels rest, that the very heretics themselves bear witness to them, and, starting from these [documents], each one of them endeavors to establish his own particular doctrine." (AH, III.11.7)

The four gospels had become so axiomatic in the Christian world that Irenaeus could refer to the fourfold gospel as an established and recognized fact as obvious as the four cardinal points of the compass:

> For as there are four quarters of the world in which we live, and four universal winds, and as the Church is dispersed over all the earth, and the gospel is the pillar and base of the Church and the breath of life, so it is natural that it should have four pillars, breathing immortality from every quarter and kindling the life of men anew. Whence it is manifest that the Word, the architect of all things, who sits upon the cherubim and holds all things together, having been manifested to men, has given us the gospel in fourfold form, but held together by one Spirit. (Irenaeus, AH, III.11.8)

3. Clement of Rome

Clement assumed the words of Jesus were passed down faithfully. For instance, *First Clement* 13 (c. AD 95) says, "We should especially remember the words the Lord Jesus spoke when teaching about gentleness and patience. For he said, 'Show mercy, that you may be shown mercy; forgive, that it may be forgiven you. As you do, so it will be done to you; as you give, so it will be given to you, as you judge, so you will be judged, as you show kindness, so will kindness be shown to you;

the amount you dispense will be the amount you receive." (ANF, I.57–58; Scripture allusions in this passage are to Matt. 5:7; 6:14, 15; 7:1, 2, 12; Luke 6:31, 36–38)

4. Ignatius

Ignatius served as bishop of Antioch from AD 70–110. Polycarp and Irenaeus both report that Ignatius died as a martyr for his faith (Polycarp, Philippians 10.13; Irenaeus, *Against Heresies*, 5.28). According to Professor of Church History Hubertus R. Drobner, "Byzantine hagiography identified him [Ignatius] as the child whom Jesus displayed to the disciples as an example (Matt 18:2 par), whereas Jerome took him to be a disciple of the Apostle John. Both reports remain hypothetical, but there is no doubt that as far as his time and theology are concerned, Ignatius was close to the apostles." (Drobner, FC, 50)

Although some scholars question his eventual martyrdom, there is little doubt Ignatius believed the resurrection was a historical event (see Letter to the Magnesians 11) and was willing to die as a martyr so he could imitate Christ. According to Ignatius: "I am God's wheat, and I am ground by the teeth of wild beasts that I may be found pure bread [of Christ]." (Ignatius, Romans 4:1).

Ignatius gave credence to the Scripture by the way he based his faith on the accuracy of the Bible. He had ample material and witnesses to support the trustworthiness of the Scriptures.

5. Polycarp

Polycarp was a disciple of John and was martyred at eighty-six years of age for his relentless devotion to Christ and the Scriptures. Polycarp's death demonstrated his trust in the accuracy of the Scripture.

About 155, in the reign of Antoninus Pius, when a local persecution was taking place in Smyrna and several of his members had been martyred, he was singled out as the leader of the Church, and marked for martyrdom. When asked to recant and live, he is reputed to have said, "Eighty and six years have I served Him, and He hath done me no wrong. How can I speak evil of my King who saved me?" He was burned at the stake, dying a heroic martyr for his faith. (Moyer, WWWCH, 337)

6. Tatian

Tatian created the first "harmony of the Gospels," the Diatessaron. His work indicates that the four gospels were both widely known and widespread by the mid- to late second century. *Diatessaron* means "a harmony of four parts." The Greek words *dia tessaron* literally mean "through four." (Bruce, BP, 195) This synthesis of the Gospels, which selectively omitted the genealogies and some duplicates of incidents, was used in Syrian congregational reading for two centuries. The manuscript pages that remain are very helpful in analyzing the specific wording of the gospel texts. They are often older and they draw upon even older gospel manuscripts.

Eusebius, in *Ecclesiastical History* IV.29, wrote: "Their former leader Tatian composed in some way a combination and collection of the Gospels, and gave this the name of THE DIATESSARON, and this is still extant in some places."

B. Eight Different Tests for the Accuracy of the New Testament Accounts

When Lee Strobel set out to discover the truth about Christianity, he met with New Testament scholar Craig Blomberg, an expert on the biographies of Jesus. Having completed a Master of Studies in Law degree from Yale Law School, Strobel wanted to see if the biographies of Jesus stand up against scrutiny, in the same way an attorney would evaluate the story of a defendant on trial. One by one, they applied the eight different tests.

1. The Intention Test

This test evaluates whether the purported story was written with the intention of being treated as historical fact. For instance, nobody treats "The Boy who Cried Wolf" story as historical, because it fails the intention test. It was written for a lesson, not for historical purposes.

What about the story of Jesus? Are Jesus' biographies written merely for non-historical purposes, to convey wise sayings, for example? The Gospels do not leave such an impression. The introduction for the book of Luke gives a clear indication of its purpose:

Many people have set out to write accounts about the events that have been fulfilled among us. They used the eyewitness reports circulating among us from the early disciples. Having carefully investigated everything from the beginning, I also have decided to write an accurate account for you, most honorable

---

Eighty and six years have I served Him, and He hath done me no wrong. How can I speak evil of my King who saved me?

Polycarp (a disciple of John) just before being burned alive for his faith at age eighty-six

Theophilus, so you can be certain of the truth of everything you were taught. (Luke 1:1–4, NLT)

John makes a similar statement when he writes "But these are written so that you may continue to believe that Jesus is the Messiah, the Son of God, and that by believing in him you will have life by the power of his name" (John 20:31 NLT). When John penned that statement, he had just finished describing the resurrection of Jesus and several post-death appearances of Jesus. If John did not intend for the resurrection to be taken historically, why would he expect his readers to be convinced "that Jesus is the Messiah, the Son of God"?

Matthew and Mark do not contain descriptions of their intent, but a close look at their writing habits helps determine what they were intending to communicate. According to Craig Blomberg, "There's an important piece of implicit evidence that can't be overlooked. Consider the way the gospels are written—in a sober and responsible fashion, with accurate incidental details, with obvious care and exactitude. You don't find the outlandish flourishes and blatant mythologizing that you see in a lot of other ancient writing.* What does all that add up to? It seems quite apparent that the goal of the gospel writers was to attempt to record what had actually occurred." (quoted in Strobel, CFC, 50–51)

2. The Ability Test

The second test examines the ability of the authors to write down accurately the historical details of their story. Although they may have had good intentions to record history, were they capable of actually doing it? Did they know it well enough themselves?

Eyewitnesses like those who were the companions of Jesus would be the most qualified people to pass this test. Matthew was one of the twelve disciples of Jesus. Mark was an associate of Peter, a disciple of Jesus. Luke was a companion to Paul, who claimed to have personally encountered Jesus on his way to Damascus. John was also a disciple of Jesus, and one of the "inner three" of the twelve, alongside Peter.

Some have doubted that the New Testament writers were able to report accurately because there was a significant gap of years between the time of the events and the date of writing. However, it is important to understand the culture of the writers. Written material was not nearly as commonplace as it is today. During this time in the Jewish culture, communication was primarily oral. Memorization, even of entire books, was common and natural for them. So it is reasonable to suggest that the disciples of Jesus were committing to memory what they heard from Jesus, especially the teachings which ended up in their biographies. Blomberg points out that 80 to 90 percent of Jesus' words were originally in poetic form. "This doesn't mean stuff that rhymes," he cautions, "but it has meter, balanced lines, parallelism, and so forth—and this would have created a great memory help." (Strobel, CFC, 54)

3. The Character Test

The next test looks at the character of the authors of the purported history. Perhaps they intended for their story to be taken historically, but intentionally lied about certain details. Did they have malicious intent that would produce an altered version of what actually happened?

---

* Moreland summarizes his view regarding the sober and careful nature of the written accounts of these appearances: "Finally, the resurrection appearances are reported with extreme reserve. When one compares them with the reports in the apocryphal gospels (second century on), the difference is startling. In the Apocrypha, detailed explanations are given about how the resurrection took place. Gross details are added. . . . But the New Testament accounts are subdued and do not include such fanciful descriptions." (Moreland, SSC, 175)

For the gospel writers, there is no good reason to suggest that this was the case. The stories they write point toward an incredibly high standard of moral living. Are we to believe that some of the world's greatest ethical teachings came from unethical people? While possible, this hardly seems the most reasonable conclusion. Secondly, there's no reason to suggest that they had motives for material or societal gain. In fact, as I (Sean) demonstrate in *The Fate of the Apostles*, the twelve apostles, as well as Paul and James the brother of Jesus, were willing to suffer and even die for their conviction that they had seen the risen Jesus. There is no evidence any of them recanted, and we have good reason to believe that some of them died as martyrs.

Additionally, the principle of embarrassment is a criterion that looks at ancient writings to see if there are hard, embarrassing, or unfavorable details about the author(s) or with the story's purpose. If such details exist, positive conclusions can be made about the integrity of the author(s).

The principle of embarrassment can readily be applied to the Gospels' accounts. For instance: James, Jesus' own brother, is reported as being among those who thought Jesus was crazy (Mark 3:20; John 7:5). Why would a pious leader of the early church be cast in such a negative light, if not for sake of accuracy? Another example is in Mark 13:32 where, in the same breath, Jesus declares that he is the Son of God and that he does not know the time of his Second Coming. If Mark were attempting to fabricate his own story of Jesus, why would he set himself up for such a difficult theological dilemma?

Even further, why would all four gospels mention that women were the first witnesses of the empty tomb? In that time, a report from a woman was considered less reliable than that of a man, especially if it dealt with crucial matters. Also, why are the disciples of Jesus—those who became the highest authoritative figures in the early church—repeatedly shown as C students during their time with Christ (Matthew 28:17; Mark 8:14–21, 31–33; 9:31, 32; 10:35–40; John 18:25–26; 20:19)? The fact that all these hard, embarrassing, and unattractive stories exist in the Scriptures indicates that the authors were more interested in accuracy than reputability.

4. The Consistency Test

With this test we ask: "Do the stories that relate the same events agree with one another?" If the authors constantly contradict each other, there is a good reason to doubt the historicity of the events in the stories. Keep in mind that this test, like all the others, is meant to be taken from a purely historical perspective. Many Christians believe that the Bible is infallible—the true Word of God that cannot contradict itself. However, this is a different, theological perspective which is not covered in this chapter.

The consistency test allows for small discrepancies. These are minor discrepancies that are not serious enough to lead to a conclusion that the work being assessed is utterly untrustworthy. But they should be considered nonetheless.

This is possibly the most common critique of the biographies of Jesus. There are numerous examples where the Gospels appear to contradict one another.

Apparent discrepancies should be handled carefully. We need to remember that ancient expectations were often different from expectations in our current culture. For instance, sometimes the gospel writers will describe the same event but mention different characters being present. This is because they did not intend to compile a complete list. One example would be the witnesses at the empty tomb of Jesus. For more on resolving alleged contradictions in Scripture, see the appendix "Responding to the Challenges of Bart Ehrman."

Other times the gospel writers will abbreviate details with a kind of liberty that surprises readers today. For example, in Matthew a centurion speaks to Jesus (8:5). In Luke, there are two elders speaking for the centurion (7:2, 3). Luke's account is probably the more precise one here, whereas Matthew referred only to the centurion because the elders spoke as representatives for the centurion. Another example of abbreviation appears in the genealogies of Jesus, where generations are occasionally skipped.

Though the discrepancies sometimes seem problematic to the modern reader, a closer understanding of the context can help reconcile the vast majority of the differences.

Sometimes careful thinking and/or focused study of the language can help clear up discrepancies. For instance, there is a curious difference between Matthew and Luke for the location of Jesus' famous Sermon on the Mount. Luke said this happened on a level place (Luke 6:17), whereas Matthew said it happened on a mountain (Matt. 5:1). Who is correct here? Some suggest that Matthew and Luke refer to two different occasions that Jesus gave the same message. Others point out that it could have taken place on a flat part of a mountain. But setting these explanations aside, D. A. Carson points out that the word *mountain* commonly referred to hill country. Alternatively, "flat place" could also refer to a plateau in a mountainous region. (Carson, NIVZSB, 2083) There is no contradiction here. One must be careful not to assume that differences equate to contradictions. In other words, we should take care not to use "either/or" logic where "both/and" may be more appropriate.

All in all, the stories of Jesus are similar enough that they pass the consistency test, and they are different enough so that we know that the gospel writers did not conspire to fabricate accounts of events that never happened.

5. The Bias Test

The bias test considers whether the authors may have altered the text intentionally or even unintentionally due to personal bias. Did they have any reason to skew parts of the narrative?

We have already discussed in the character test that there was no reason for the gospel writers to have maliciously reported inaccurate information. Yet obviously they were devoted followers of Jesus, fully committed to him and his teachings. Could this bias have influenced the writers? Yes, but not in such a way that it disrupts the basic historical reliability of what they wrote. Matthew, Mark, Luke, and John all had different theological objectives to accomplish when writing the Gospels. So they focused on stories and details that had particular theological significance. But this doesn't necessarily affect the historicity of their narratives. In fact, their historical accuracy was probably bolstered by their love for Jesus and their commitment to his moral teachings. The next test will show this even more clearly.

6. The Cover-Up Test

Strobel explains the cover-up test: "When people testify about events they saw, they will often try to protect themselves or others by conveniently forgetting to mention details that are embarrassing or hard to explain. As a result, this raises uncertainty about the veracity of their entire testimony." (Strobel, *Case for Christ*, 62)

Yet the biographies of Jesus contain many

embarrassing details about the disciples. In Matthew 15:5–12, they took a metaphor from Jesus literally. When they didn't understand Jesus' teaching about his crucifixion, they were too embarrassed to ask for clarification (Mark 9:32). Like immature siblings, the disciples argued over who was the greatest (Mark 9:33, 34). James and John argued about who would sit in a place of honor next to Jesus, even involving their mother in the conflict (Matt. 20:20–28). When the going got rough, Peter denied knowing Jesus three times (Luke 22:54–62). He was rebuked and called "Satan" by Jesus (Mark 8:33). His lack of faith almost drowned him (Matt. 14:22–33). Peter and the other disciples were leaders of the early church when these stories were written! If indeed the gospel writers were trying to strengthen the movement of Christianity through exaggerated or untrue stories, why would they include these details? The best explanation for the inclusion of these details is that the authors were being honest and accurate.

Then there are also those teachings of Jesus that are hard to understand or seem to be out of character. When Jesus was crucified, he cried out, "My God, My God, why have You forsaken Me?" (Matt. 27:46). In John 5:19, Jesus says "the Son can do nothing by himself" (NIV). Mark 6:5 says that Jesus could not do many miracles because of the people's unbelief. In Matthew 24:36, Jesus explains that he does not know the day or the hour of his return. All of these passages seem to limit Jesus in some way. Although there are good theological explanations for these sayings, it would have been much easier for the gospel writers to have just omitted them. But they didn't. Instead, we have a report of both the good and the ugly, which is strong evidence that the authors of Jesus' biographies were not playing loose with the facts.

7. The Corroboration Test

This test aims to corroborate a story's details by using outside evidence. For instance, stories will often include names, places, dates, and events, which can be verified. If the external evidence does not agree with the details in the narrative, then the integrity of the story is called into question.

Blomberg points out that a lot of archaeological discoveries have been made within the past hundred years that help to corroborate the Gospels:

> In addition, we can learn through non-Christian sources a lot of facts about Jesus that corroborate key teachings and events in his life. And when you stop to think that ancient historians for the most part dealt only with political rulers, emperors, kings, military battles, official religious people, and major philosophical movements, it's remarkable how much we can learn about Jesus and his followers even though they fit none of these categories at the time these historians were writing. (quoted in Strobel, *Case for Christ*, 64–65)

8. The Adverse Witness Test

The final test is arguably the most difficult one to pass. What do the critics have to say? Do they admit that the stories carry truthful details? What arguments do they offer? Do they dismantle the premise? Do they sidestep the logical conclusion?

Blomberg points out that some Jewish writers claim that Jesus was a sorcerer who led Israel astray. (quoted in Strobel, *Case for Christ*, 66) This is a fascinating observation, as they could have claimed that the miracles never happened and that the stories are all legendary tales that were made up. If the enemies of Christianity needed to call Jesus a sorcerer, there is reason to believe that something miraculous did indeed happen.

C. Early Non-Christian Confirmation of New Testament History

Those who doubt the veracity of the New Testament accounts have charged or implied that the New Testament documents are unreliable since they were written by disciples of Jesus or later Christians. They sometimes claim that there is no confirmation of Jesus or New Testament events in non-Christian sources. Not only is this claim false, but, as Geisler notes,

> The objection that the writings are partisan involves a significant but false implication that witnesses cannot be reliable if they were close to the one about whom they gave testimony. This is clearly false. Survivors of the Jewish holocaust were close to the events they have described to the world. That very fact puts them in the best position to know what happened. They were there, and it happened to them. The same applies to the court testimony of someone who survived a vicious attack. It applies to the survivors of the Normandy invasion during World War II or the Tet Offensive during the Vietnam War. The New Testament witnesses should not be disqualified because they were close to the events they relate.

Geisler adds,

> Suppose there were four eyewitnesses to a murder. There was also one witness who arrived on the scene after the actual killing and saw only the victim's body. Another person heard a secondhand report of the killing. In the trial the defense attorney argues: "Other than the four eyewitnesses, this is a weak case, and the charges should be dismissed for lack of evidence." Others might think that attorney was throwing out a red herring. The judge and jury were being distracted from the strongest evidence to the weakest evidence, and the

reasoning was clearly faulty. Since the New Testament witnesses were the only eyewitness and contemporary testimonies to Jesus, it is a fallacy to misdirect attention to the non-Christian secular sources. Nonetheless, it is instructive to show what confirming evidence for Jesus can be gleaned outside the New Testament. (Geisler, BECA, 381)

The references below are discussed in greater detail in *He Walked Among Us*, a book that Bill Wilson and I (Josh) coauthored.

1. Tacitus

The first-century Roman Tacitus is considered one of the more accurate historians of the ancient world. He gives the account of the great fire of Rome, for which some blamed Emperor Nero:

> Consequently, to get rid of the report, Nero fastened the guilt and inflicted the most exquisite tortures on a class hated for their abominations, called Christians by the populace. Christus, from whom the name had its origin, suffered the extreme penalty during the reign of Tiberius at the hands of one of our procurators, Pontius Pilatus, and a most mischievous superstition, thus checked for the moment, again broke out not only in Judea, the first source of the evil, but even in Rome, where all things hideous and shameful from every part of the world find their center and become popular. (Tacitus, *Annals*, 15.44)

The "mischievous superstition" to which Tacitus refers is most likely the resurrection of Jesus.

2. Suetonius

Suetonius was chief secretary to Emperor Hadrian (who reigned from AD 117–138). He confirms the report in Acts 18:2 that

Claudius commanded all Jews (among them Priscilla and Aquila) to leave Rome in AD 49. Two references are important. First, he writes, "As the Jews were making constant disturbances at the instigation of Chrestus, he expelled them from Rome." (Suetonius, LC, 25.4) Then, speaking of the aftermath of the great fire at Rome, Suetonius reports, "Punishment was inflicted on the Christians, a body of people addicted to a novel and mischievous superstition." (Suetonius, LN, 16)

3. Josephus

Josephus (c. AD 37–c. AD 100) was a Pharisee of the priestly line and a Jewish historian, though working under Roman authority and with some care so as not to offend the Romans. In addition to his autobiography he wrote two major works, *Jewish Wars* (AD 77–78) and *Antiquities of the Jews* (c. AD 94). He also wrote a minor work, "Against Apion." He makes many statements that verify, either generally or in specific detail, the historical nature of both the Old and New Testaments of the Bible.

a. James the Brother of Jesus

Josephus refers to Jesus as the brother of James who was martyred. Referring to the high priest, Ananias, he writes: "He assembled the Sanhedrin of the judges, and brought before them the brother of Jesus, who was called Christ, whose name was James, and some others, [or some of his companions], and when he had formed an accusation against them as breakers of the law, he delivered them to be stoned." (Josephus, AJ, 20.9.1) This passage, written in AD 93, confirms the New Testament reports that Jesus was a real person in the first century, that he was identified by others as the Christ, and that he had a brother named James who died a martyr's death at the hands of the high priest, Albinus, and his Sanhedrin.

b. John the Baptist

Josephus also confirmed the existence and martyrdom of John the Baptist, the herald of Jesus. (Ant. XVIII. 5.2) Because of the manner in which this passage is written, there is no ground for suspecting Christian interpolation.

> Now, some of the Jews thought that the destruction of Herod's army came from God, and very justly, as a punishment of what he did against John, who was called the Baptist; for Herod slew him, who was a good man, and commanded the Jews to exercise virtue, both as to righteousness towards one another and piety towards God, and so to come to baptism. (Josephus, AJ, 18.5.2)

The differences between Josephus's account of John the Baptist's baptism and that of the Gospels' is that Josephus wrote that John's baptism was not for the remission of sin, while the Bible (Mark 1:4) says it was; and that John was killed for political reasons and not for his denunciation of Herod's marriage to Herodias. As Bruce points out, it is quite possible that Herod believed he could kill two birds with one stone by imprisoning John. In regard to the discrepancy over his baptism, Bruce says that the Gospels give a more probable account from the "religious-historical" point of view and that they are older than Josephus's work and, therefore, more accurate. However, the real point is that the general outline of Josephus's account confirms that of the Gospels. (Bruce, NTD, 107)

c. Jesus

For extrabiblical evidence from Josephus regarding the historical Jesus, see chapter 6.

D. Archaeology Helps to Confirm the Historicity of the Bible

For detailed archaeology examples and precautions when appealing to archaeology, see chapter 16, "Archaeology and the Old Testament."

Archaeology, a relative newcomer among the physical sciences, has provided exciting and dramatic confirmation of the Bible's accuracy. Whole books are not large enough to contain all the finds that have bolstered confidence in the historical reliability of the Bible. Presented here are some of the findings of eminent archaeologists and their opinions regarding the implications of those finds. (Remember, archaeology, as intriguing as it is, cannot "prove" the Bible. What it can do is help corroborate the historical accuracy of the Bible.)

David Graves rightly concludes that "the Bible does not need proving true, but archaeology can help shed light on the text. Therefore, the value of archaeology is not apologetic, but hermeneutic." (Graves, BA, 215–16)

Montgomery exposes a typical problem of many scholars today: "[American] Institute [of Holy Land Studies] researcher Thomas Drobena cautioned that where archaeology and the Bible seem to be in tension, the issue is almost always dating, the most shaky area in current archaeology and the one at which scientific *a priori* and circular reasoning often replace solid empirical analysis." (Montgomery, EA, 47–48)

F. F. Bruce notes: "Where Luke has been suspected of inaccuracy, and accuracy has been vindicated by some inscriptional evidence, it may be legitimate to say that archaeology has confirmed the New Testament record." (Bruce, ACNT, 331) (I [Josh] would be more comfortable saying, "archaeology is *in the process of confirming* the New Testament record.")

The Yale archaeologist Millar Burrows writes: "On the whole, however, archaeological work has unquestionably strengthened

confidence in the reliability of the Scriptural record. More than one archaeologist has found his respect for the Bible increased by the experience of excavation in Palestine." (Burrows, WMTS, 1) "On the whole such evidence as archaeology has afforded thus far, especially by providing additional and older manuscripts of the books of the Bible, strengthens our confidence in the accuracy with which the text has been transmitted through the centuries." (Burrows, WMTS, 42)

1. Journey of a Skeptical Archaeologist

Sir William Ramsay is regarded as one of the greatest archaeologists ever to have lived. He was a student in the German historical school of the mid-nineteenth century. Consequently, he believed that the book of Acts was a product of the mid-second century AD. He was firmly convinced of this belief. In his research to make a topographical study of Asia Minor, he was compelled to consider the writings of Luke. As a result, he was forced to make a complete reversal of his beliefs due to the overwhelming evidence uncovered in his research. He spoke of this when he said:

I may fairly claim to have entered on this investigation without prejudice in favour of the conclusion which I shall now seek to justify to the reader. On the contrary, I began with a mind unfavourable to it, for the ingenuity and apparent completeness of the Tubingen theory had at one time quite convinced me. It did not then lie in my line of life to investigate the subject minutely; but more recently I found myself brought into contact with the Book of Acts as an authority for the topography, antiquities and society of Asia Minor. It was gradually borne upon me that in various details the narrative showed marvelous truth. In fact, beginning with a fixed idea that the work was essentially a second century composition, and never relying on its evidence as trustworthy for first century conditions. I gradually came to find it a useful ally in some obscure and difficult investigations. (quoted in Blaiklock, LA, 36)

2. Archaeology Supports the Amazing Accuracy of Luke's Gospel

Archaeology has provided information that confirms historical detail to which Luke refers in writing the gospel bearing his name. Concerning Luke's ability as a historian, Sir William Ramsay concluded after thirty years of study that "Luke is a historian of the first rank; not merely are his statements of fact trustworthy . . . this author should be placed along with the very greatest of historians." (Ramsay, BRD, 222) He elsewhere added: "Luke's history is unsurpassed in respect of its trustworthiness." (Ramsay, SPTRC, 81)

What Ramsay had done conclusively and finally was to exclude certain possibilities. As seen in the light of archaeological evidence, the New Testament reflects the conditions of the second half of the first century AD, and does not reflect the conditions of any later date. Historically, it is of the greatest importance that this has been so effectively established. In all matters of external fact, the author of Acts is seen to have been minutely careful and accurate as only a contemporary can be.

It was at one time believed that Luke had entirely missed the boat regarding the events surrounding the birth of Jesus (Luke 2:1–3). Critics argued that there was no census, that Quirinius was not governor of Syria at that time, and that everyone did not have to return to his ancestral home. (Elder, PID, 159–160; see also Free, ABH, 285)

However, archaeological discoveries show that the Romans had a regular enrollment of taxpayers and also held censuses every fourteen years. This procedure was indeed begun under Augustus and the first took place in either 23–22 BC or in 9–8 BC. The latter would be the one to which Luke refers.

Further, we find evidence that Quirinius was governor of Syria around 7 BC. This assumption is based on an inscription found in Antioch ascribing to Quirinius this post. As a result of this finding, it is now supposed that he was governor twice—once in 7 BC and the other time in AD 6 (the date ascribed by Josephus). (Elder, PID, 160)

Last, in regard to the practices of enrollment, a papyrus found in Egypt gives directions for the conduct of a census. It reads: "Because of the approaching census it is necessary that all those residing for any cause away from their homes should at once prepare to return to their own governments in order that they may complete the family registration of the enrollment and that the tilled lands may retain those belonging to them." (Elder, PID, 159–160)

Geisler summarizes the problem and its solution:

> Several problems are involved in the statement that Augustus conducted a census of the whole empire during the reign of both Quirinius and

---

Luke is a historian of the first rank; not merely are his statements of fact trustworthy . . . this author should be placed along with the very greatest of historians. . . . Luke's history is unsurpassed in respect of its trustworthiness.

Sir William Ramsay

Herod. For one, there is no record of such a census, but we now know that regular censuses were taken in Egypt, Gaul, and Cyrene. It is quite likely that Luke's meaning is that censuses were taken throughout the empire at different times, and Augustus started this process. The present tense that Luke uses points strongly toward understanding this as a repeated event. Now Quirinius did take a census, but that was in AD 6, too late for Jesus' birth, and Herod died before Quirinius became governor.

Was Luke confused? No; in fact, he mentions Quirinius's later census in Acts 5:37. It is most likely that Luke is distinguishing this census in Herod's time from the more well-known census of Quirinius: "This census took place before Quirinius was governor of Syria." There are several New Testament parallels for this translation. (Geisler, BECA, 46–47)

3. Archaeology Supports the Reliability of the Book of Acts and the Epistles

We have been examining the historicity of Luke's gospel; his sequel is the book of Acts. The accuracy of detail that archaeology has helped to identify for Luke's writing of Acts is impressive. In Acts 16:11, the pronoun "we" begins to be used. As Paul's traveling companion (2 Tim. 4:11), Luke shared his concern for the new churches, and so we have included some of the archaeological discoveries confirming details in Paul's letters to Rome and Corinth. As historian A. N. Sherwin-White notes, "For Acts the confirmation of historicity is overwhelming. . . . Any attempt to reject its basic historicity must now appear absurd. Roman historians have long taken it for granted." (Sherwin-White, RS, 189)

Geography: Thanks to many archaeological finds, most of the ancient cities mentioned in the book of Acts have been identified. The journeys of Paul can now be accurately traced as a result of these finds. (Bruce, NTD, 95; see also Albright, RDBL, 118) Geisler reveals, "In all, Luke names thirty-two countries, fifty-four cities and nine islands without an error." (Geisler, BECA, 47)

For example, critical archaeologists initially rejected Luke's implication that Lystra and Derbe were in Lycaonia, and that Iconium was not (Acts 14:6). They based their belief on the writings of Romans such as Cicero, who indicated that Iconium was in Lycaonia. Thus, archaeologists said the book of Acts was unreliable. However, in 1910 Sir William Ramsay found a monument that showed that Iconium was a Phrygian city. Later discoveries confirm Ramsay's finding. (Free, ABH, 317)

People: Luke references Lysanias, the Tetrarch of Abilene who ruled in Syria and Palestine (Luke 3:1) at the beginning of John the Baptist's ministry in AD 27. For a time, the only Lysanias known to historians was one who was killed in 36 BC. However, an inscription found at Abila near Damascus speaks of "Freedman of Lysanias the Tetrarch," and is dated between AD 14 and 29. (Bruce, ACNT, 321)

In his epistle to the Romans, written from Corinth, Paul makes mention of the city treasurer, Erastus (Rom. 16:23). During the excavations of Corinth in 1929, a pavement was found inscribed: ERASTVS PRO:AED:S:P:STRAVIT ("Erastus, curator of public buildings, laid this pavement at his own expense"). According to Bruce, the pavement quite likely existed in the first century AD, and the donor and the man Paul mentions are probably one and the same. (Bruce, NTD, 95; see also Vos, CITB, 185)

Also found in Corinth is a fragmentary inscription believed to have borne the words *Synagogue of the Hebrews.* Conceivably it stood over the doorway of the synagogue where Paul debated (Acts 18:4–7). Another Corinthian inscription mentions the city "meat market" to which Paul refers in 1 Corinthians 10:25.

Culture: Luke writes of the riot of Ephesus, and represents a civic assembly (*ecclesia*) taking place in a theater (Acts 19:23–29). These details are supported by an inscription that speaks of silver statues of Artemis (or Diana) to be placed in the "theater during a full session of the *Ecclesia*." (Bruce, ACNT, 326) Luke also relates that a riot broke out in Jerusalem because Paul took a Gentile into the temple (Acts 21:28). Inscriptions have been found that read, in Greek and Latin, "No foreigner may enter within the barrier which surrounds the temple and enclosure. Anyone who is caught doing so will be personally responsible for his ensuing death." (Bruce, ACNT, 326)

Terminology: In some cases, Luke's usages of certain words were criticized by skeptics. For example, Luke refers to Philippi as a "district" of Macedonia (the Greek word he uses is *meris*). Hort believed Luke erred in this usage, arguing that *meris* referred to a "portion," not a "district." Archaeological excavations, however, have shown that this very word, *meris*, was used to describe the divisions of the district. (Free, ABH, 320)

Similarly, Luke was at one time charged with technically incorrect usage for referring to the Philippian rulers as *praetors*. According to critical scholars, two *duumuirs* would have ruled the town. However, as usual, Luke was right. Findings have shown that the title of *praetor* was employed by the magistrates of a Roman colony. (Free, ABH, 321) His choice of the word *proconsul* as the title for Gallio (Acts 18:12) is also correct, as evidenced by the Delphi inscription that states in part: "As Lucius Junius Gallio, my friend, and the Proconsul of Achaia." (Vos, CITB, 180; see also Graves, BA, 215–16)

Luke gives to Publius, the chief man in Malta, the title "first man of the island" (Acts 28:7). Inscriptions have been unearthed that confirm this title. (Bruce, ACNT, 325) Still another case is Luke's usage of *politarchs* to denote the civil authorities of Thessalonica (Acts 17:6). Since *politarch* is not found in the classical literature, Luke was again assumed to be wrong. However, some nineteen inscriptions that make use of the title have been found. Interestingly enough, five of these are in reference to Thessalonica. (Bruce, ACNT, 325; see also Graves, BA, 215–16) One of the inscriptions was discovered in a Roman arch at Thessalonica, and in it are found the names of six of that city's politarchs. (Bruce, ACNT, 360)

Other examples: Colin Hemer, a noted Roman historian, has catalogued numerous archaeological and historical confirmations of Luke's accuracy in his book *The Book of Acts in the Setting of Hellenistic History*. Following is a partial summary of his detailed report (Hemer, BASHH, 104–107):

- Specialized details, which would not have been widely known except to a contemporary researcher such as Luke who traveled widely. These details include exact titles of officials, identification of army units, and information about major routes.
- Details archaeologists know are accurate but can't verify as to the precise time period. Some of these are unlikely to have been known except to a writer who had visited the districts.
- Correlation of dates of known kings and governors with the chronology of the narrative.
- Facts appropriate to the date of Paul or his immediate contemporary in the church but not to a date earlier or later.

- "Undesigned coincidences" between Acts and the Pauline Epistles.
- Internal correlations within Acts.
- Off-hand geographical references that bespeak familiarity with common knowledge.
- Differences in formulation within Acts that indicate the different categories of sources he used.
- Peculiarities in the selection of detail, as in theology, that are explainable in the context of what is now known of first-century church life.
- Materials the "immediacy" of which suggests that the author was recounting a recent experience, rather than shaping or editing a text long after it had been written.
- Cultural or idiomatic items now known to be peculiar to the first-century atmosphere.

Is it any wonder that E. M. Blaiklock, professor of classics at Auckland University, concludes that "Luke is a consummate historian, to be ranked in his own right with the great writers of the Greeks"? (Blaiklock, AA, 89)

4. Important Archaeological Discoveries That Help Confirm the New Testament
a. Earliest Records of Christianity

In 1945 two ossuaries (receptacles for bones) were found in the vicinity of Jerusalem. These ossuaries exhibited graffiti that their discoverer, Eleazar L. Sukenik, claimed to be "the earliest records of Christianity." These burial receptacles were found in a tomb that was in use before AD 50. The writings read *Iesous iou* and *Iesous aloth*. Also present were four crosses. It is likely that the first is a prayer to Jesus for help, and the second, a prayer for resurrection of the person whose bones were contained in the ossuary. (Bruce, ACNT, 327–28)

b. The Pavement

For centuries there has been no record of the court where Jesus was tried by Pilate (named *Gabbatha,* or the Pavement, John 19:13). William F. Albright, in *The Archaeology of Palestine,* shows that this court was the court of the Tower of Antonia, the Roman military headquarters in Jerusalem. It was left buried when the city was rebuilt in the time of Hadrian, and was not discovered until recently. (Albright, AP, 141)

c. The Pool of Bethesda

The Pool of Bethesda, another site with no record except in the New Testament, can now be identified "with a fair measure of certainty in the northeast quarter of the old city (the area called Bezetha, or 'New Lawn') in the first century AD, where traces of it were discovered in the course of excavations near the Church of St. Anne in 1888." (Bruce, ACNT, 329; see also Graves, BA, 208)

d. The Nazareth Decree

A slab of stone was found in Nazareth in 1878, inscribed with a decree from Emperor Claudius (AD 41–54) that no graves should be disturbed or bodies extracted or moved. This type of decree is not uncommon, but the startling fact is that here "the offender [shall] be sentenced to capital punishment on [the] charge of violation of [a] sepulchre". (Hemer, BASHH, 155)

Geisler expounds upon this unusual find:

Other notices warned of a fine, but death for disturbing graves? A likely explanation is that Claudius, having heard of the Christian doctrine of resurrection and Jesus' empty tomb while investigating the riots of AD 49, decided not to let any such report surface again. This would make sense in light of the Jewish argument that the body had been stolen

(Matt. 28:11–15). This is early testimony to the strong and persistent belief that Jesus rose from the dead. (Geisler, BECA, 48)

e. Yehohanan—A Crucifixion Victim

Craig Evans explains:

The discovery in 1968 of an ossuary (ossuary no. 4 in Tomb I, at Giv'at ha-Mivtar) of a Jewish man named Yehohanan, who had obviously been crucified, provided archaeological evidence and insight into how Jesus himself may have been crucified. The ossuary and its content date to the late 20s CE, that is during the administration of Pilate, the very Roman governor who condemned Jesus to the cross. The remains of an iron spike (11.5 cm in length) are plainly seen still encrusted in the right heel bone. . . . Those who took down the body of Yehohanan apparently were unable to remove the spike, with the result that a piece of wood (from an oak tree) remained affixed to the spike. Later, the skeletal remains of the body—spike, fragment of wood, and all—were placed in the ossuary. . . . Yehohanan's leg bones were broken, but there is disagreement over how and when they were broken. (Evans, GBTER, 83–84)

f. The Pilate Inscription

In 1961 an Italian archaeologist, Antonio Frova, discovered an inscription at Caesarea Maritima on a stone slab that at the time of the discovery was being used as a section of steps leading into the Caesarea theater. The inscription in Latin contained four lines, three of which are partially readable. Roughly translated they are as follows:

Tiberium

Pontius Pilate

Prefect of Judea

The inscribed stone was probably used originally in the foundation for a Tiberium (a temple for the worship of the emperor Tiberius) and then reused later in the location of the discovery. This inscription verifies that for a time during his rulership, the title of Pontius Pilate was "prefect." Tacitus and Josephus later referred to him as "procurator." The NT calls him "governor" (Matt. 27:2), a term that incorporates both titles. This inscription is the only archaeological evidence of both Pilate's name and this title. (Dockery et al., FBI, 360)

g. The Erastus Inscription

On a slab of limestone that was a part of the pavement near the theater in Corinth, a Latin inscription was found that translates, "Erastus, in return for the *aedileship*, laid the pavement at his own expense." An *aedile* was an official who was responsible for public works and games, police, and the grain supply (all of these being connected to keeping the people contented). Erastus clearly managed city finances and had wealth of his own. In Romans 16:23 Paul (writing from Corinth) mentioned an Erastus and identified him as a city official (the ESV translates "treasurer.") It is possible this is the same person. (Dockery et al., FBI, 361)

h. New Testament Coins

Three coins mentioned in the Greek NT have been identified with reasonable assurance.

- *The "tribute penny"* (Matt. 22:17–21; Mark 12:13–17; Luke 20:20–26). The Greek word for the coin shown to Jesus in these passages is *denarius*, a small silver coin that carried the image of Caesar on one side. Its value was equal to one day's wages for an average worker in Palestine.

- *The "thirty pieces of silver"* (Matt. 26:14, 15). This amount was probably thirty silver shekels. Originally a shekel was a measure of weight equaling approximately two-fifths of an ounce. It later developed into a silver coin of about the same weight.
- *The "widow's mite"* (Mark 12:41–44; Luke 21:1–4). The passage in question reads: "two very small copper coins, worth only a few cents" (NIV). The first words translate the Greek word *lepta*, which is the smallest Greek copper coin; the second translates the Greek word *quadrans*, which is the smallest Roman copper coin. Knowing the minute monetary value of these coins brings home the point that Jesus made about the greatness of the widow's offering in comparison to the offerings of the rich: they gave larger monetary amounts but out of wealth, while she gave what she needed to live on. (Dockery et al., FBI, 362; see also Graves, BA, 218–20)

This section can be appropriately summarized by the words of this poem about the Scriptures:

Within that awful volume lies
The mystery of mysteries
Happiest they of human race
To whom God has granted grace
To read, to fear, to hope, to pray
To lift the latch, and force the way;
And better had they ne'er been born,
Who read to doubt, or read to scorn.

Sir Walter Scott

VI. Conclusion

One of the classic scholars writing about the authenticity of the New Testament was F. F. Bruce, quoted extensively throughout this chapter. He opens his study *The New Testament Documents: Are They Reliable?* with these comments:

> The Christian gospel is not primarily a code of ethics or a metaphysical system; it is first and foremost good news, and as such it was proclaimed by its earliest preachers. . . . And this good news is intimately bound up with the historical order, for it tells how for the world's redemption, God entered into history, the eternal came into time, the kingdom of heaven invaded the realm of earth, in the great events of the incarnation, crucifixion, and resurrection of Christ. . . . Christianity has its roots in history. . . . This historical once-for-allness of Christianity . . . makes the reliability of the writings which purport to record this revelation a question of first-rate importance. (Bruce, TNTD, 7–8)

As a young scholar, I (Josh) asked this question: *how can I prove that Christianity is false?* I traveled to many libraries in the US and in Europe in my search to find the answer. After trying to shatter the historicity, validity, and authenticity of the Scriptures, I (Josh) came to the conclusion that the Bible is historically trustworthy. I also discovered that if one discards the Bible as being unreliable, then one must discard almost all literature of antiquity.

One problem we constantly face is the desire on the part of many to apply one standard or test to secular literature and another to the Bible. One must apply the same test (unless guided by presuppositions that preclude historical conclusions), whether the literature under investigation is secular or religious.

Having done this, we believe that we can hold the New Testament in our hands and say, "It is trustworthy and historically reliable."

CHAPTER 4

HAVE THE OLD TESTAMENT MANUSCRIPTS BEEN TRANSMITTED RELIABLY?

OVERVIEW

I. Introduction

In the last chapter, we saw that the New Testament stands far above other ancient documents in its reliability and accuracy. This chapter discusses the transmission of the biblical books of the Old Testament, including the history and activity of early Jewish scribes, the ancient and medieval manuscripts of the Old Testament books, the ancient nonbiblical Jewish texts, and the practice and principles of Old Testament textual criticism. It concludes with a discussion of the reliability of the transmission of biblical material (both oral and written), and how, until the days of Jesus and the New

Testament writers, generations of Israelite communities viewed this material as both authoritative and binding.

II. The Methods and Principles of Jewish Scribes

This section examines the history, philosophy, and methodology of scribal traditions ranging in date from the Persian period (c. fifth to fourth century BC.) to the copying of the medieval Masoretic Text (c. ninth to twelfth century AD). When referencing the term "scribes" in this context, one should be careful to distinguish ancient Near-Eastern (ANE) scribes from later medieval copyists (working in the tradition of a monastic *scriptoria*). Emanuel Tov, professor emeritus of Bible at The Hebrew University of Jerusalem, elaborates on the role of ANE scribes:

> In antiquity, the majority of persons involved in the transmission of the biblical and other texts took more liberties than copyists of later periods ... many scribes actually took an active role in the shaping of the final form of the text, and therefore the general term "scribe" is more appropriate for them than "copyist," since it covers additional aspects of scribal activity and could easily include creative elements. (Tov, SOT, 7, 8)

One must also keep in mind the evidence for a rabbinic group of scribes (denoted by the Hebrew plural *soferim*) who specialized in the production and perpetuation of biblical texts and religious documents. These soferim seem to have solidified as an authoritative group by the time of the New Testament. Therefore, "the scribal occupation must be considered a profession, rather than an occasional activity." (Tov, SOT, 8)

A. The History of Scribal Activity

This section gives a brief outline of early scribal activity and the development of scribal functions.

1. Early Evidence of Scribal Activity

This more formal group of scribes, the soferim, known from rabbinic sources and the New Testament writings, may have originated with, or around the time of, Ezra. Tov provides a succinct history and description of the soferim:

> In rabbinic writings, from the Mishna onwards, these *soferim* are mentioned as authoritative scribes and teachers to whom a number of teachings and *halakhot* [the collective body of Jewish religious laws derived from the Written and Oral Torah] are ascribed. As a result, the *soferim* are considered to have been influential figures in Israel from the time of Ezra to the second century CE, both in rabbinic tradition and in modern scholarship . . . these persons dealt mainly with religious writings, and were possibly of priestly descent (indeed, most of the *soferim* whose genealogy is known were priests). The term *soferim* involves the combined activities of the copying of texts, especially of Scripture and other sacred documents, and an intimate knowledge of the documents, and it is often difficult to decide which nuance of the term is intended. This difficulty probably reflects the fact that most *soferim* were skilled in both aspects of their profession. (Tov, SOT, 12)

It appears that the Masorah (an apparatus of instructions for the writing and reading of the biblical text) developed during the time of Ezra and the soferim and was later preserved and continued by the Masoretes (see section III.A.1. below). In summary, Tov categorizes five scribal traditions that stand out from the time of Ezra in the fifth century BC to the end of the Masoretic era in the early twelfth century AD: (1) the scribal community at Qumran, (2) the scribes that produced the earlier paleo-Hebrew (the script of Hebrew manuscripts preceding the Aramaic square script) scrolls, (3) the school that preceded the Masoretic Text, (4) the medieval Masoretic scribal families, and (5) the medieval scribes that produced the Samaritan Pentateuch. (Tov, TC, 218)

2. The Chronology of Scribal Functions

Regarding preexilic (before 587 BC) textual transmission, several lines of evidence support scholarly conjecture regarding scribal practices prior to the time of Ezra and the soferim. Scholars have come to the following four conclusions concerning the earlier biblical texts (see Wegner, SGTC, 59–63):

- The earliest biblical texts would have been written in a paleo-Hebrew script similar to that of other Semitic languages active in Iron Age Syro-Palestine (c. 1200 to 500 BC). This early script is evidenced in the archaeological record (e.g., seal of Jeroboam, Hezekiah's tunnel inscription, and the Silver Amulets). This script was eventually replaced with the Aramaic square script sometime between the fifth and third centuries BC.
- Regarding the method of transmission, while it is likely that a *scripto continua* (continuous writing) was used, some evidence shows that spaces and markers between words were in effect (e.g., Hezekiah's tunnel inscription).
- In the earliest periods of Iron Age transmission, texts were likely written on stone, clay tablets, wood, pottery, or even metal (e.g., Silver Amulets) and

eventually replaced by scrolls made of either papyri or leather (cf. Jer. 36:2).
- Internal evidence seems to imply that these earlier texts would have been reverenced and maintained by scribes of the Levitical priestly caste.

B. The Materials and Equipment of Scribal Activity

Although we do not possess a large number of manuscripts from the ANE, scholars can ascertain with a high degree of certitude the type of equipment and materials scribes would have used in order to transmit the biblical narratives faithfully. This section will discusses the writing equipment used by scribes (e.g., ink types, pens, etc.), the materials on which the manuscripts were inscribed (e.g., papyrus, leather parchment [leather], ostraca [broken pottery], copper), and some calligraphic techniques (e.g., ruling of scrolls, word spacing, writing of the divine name).

1. Writing Equipment

Concerning the writing implements and varieties of ink employed by the scribes in the Judean Desert, Ernst Würthwein, former professor emeritus of Old Testament at Marburg University, states:

> The reed pen or *kalamos* was made from a natural reed, its point cut at an acute angle and split to permit evenly flowing lines of cursive script. To maintain this quality the reed pen had to be trimmed regularly, and for this the scribe had a special penknife (Jer. 36:23). For its protection the reed pen had a cap, just like modern fountain pens. The scribe's equipment also included a pen case . . . , usually made of wood, but luxury models were of ivory, with a compartment for pens as well as one or more shell-shaped

depressions for inks—black or a red compound of aluminum acetate, the powder for which was kept in a separate pouch. . . . In antiquity two types of ink were distinguished: the older vegetable variety and the newer metallic ink (Latin *tincta* "colored"). The vegetable ink was made of soot mixed with gum arabic, a water-soluble resin, or a vegetable oil as a binding agent for better adhesion to the writing surface. In the 3rd century BCE metallic ink was invented, called gallnut ink from its source. Gallnuts are growths or blisters formed on leaves, twigs, and buds of certain oaks attacked by gall wasps. These were dried, crushed, and boiled down with vitriol and gum arabic. The ink became permanent as it dried, and oxidation with the acids produced a jet-black color. After the introduction of gallnut, both kinds of ink, vegetable and metallic, continued to be used. Thus the use of vegetable ink has little bearing on the dating of a manuscript, whether of early or medieval provenance. In any event, the inks used at Qumran were not metallic, but vegetable and carbon. (Würthwein, TOT, 13)

2. Manuscript Materials

Regarding media of textual transmission, Tov has much to say:

The great majority of the documents from the Judean Desert were written on leather [parchment] and papyrus (the latter comprise some 14% or 131 texts of the 930 Qumran texts . . .). In addition, a large number of ostraca [broken pottery] were found, [at Masada, Murabba'at, and other Judean Desert sites] . . . Only the Copper Scrolls from cave 3 [at Qumran] were inscribed on that material. . . . Two texts were inscribed on wooden tablets. . . . The use of different materials at the various sites in the Judean Desert reflects

the differences in genre among the documents found at these locations. The great majority of the literary texts as included in the corpora found at Qumran and Masada were written on leather, while papyrus, was used for most of the documentary texts, such as letters and various administrative texts, found at Nahal Hever, Nahal Se'elim, Wadi Murabba'at, and the other sites. (Tov, SPA, 31)

Concerning papyrus specifically, Tov continues:

Papyrus probably was considered less durable than leather, and the papyri from the Judean Desert made a less professional impression (lines were less straight and no neat column structure can be observed). On the other hand, it was easier for scribes to remove letters from an inscribed papyrus than from leather. Papyrus may therefore have been preferred by certain scribes, but it was probably the availability of the writing material that determined the choice of either papyrus or leather; in the case of the biblical texts, additional factors must have played a role. (Tov, SPA, 32)

Unlike papyrus, parchment was a far more durable medium for textual transmission. Furthermore, leather was likely more readily available in Palestine, as opposed to papyrus imported from Egypt. Therefore, it is no wonder that the majority of biblical texts found at Qumran (especially those written in the paleo-Hebrew script) are inscribed on leather (some 200 scrolls) as opposed to papyrus (6 scrolls). Although it was only later rabbinic instructions that formally established the prohibition against the use of papyrus in the transmission of Scripture, it can be assumed that this custom would have been active during the Qumran period. (Tov, TC, 193–94; Tov, SPA, 32–34, 51)

3. Technical Aspects of Writing

A number of technical aspects supporting the production of ancient scrolls would have aided scribes in the transmission process, including the ruling of scrolls:

Almost all Qumran and Masada texts written on leather had ruled horizontal lines in accordance with the practice for most literary texts written on leather in Semitic languages and in Greek. Early parallels of different types allow us to assume that also the earliest biblical scrolls must have been ruled. . . . Most scribes writing on any material needed some form of graphical guide for their writing. This was provided by horizontal ruling (scoring) for the individual lines, as well as vertical ruling for the beginning and/or end of the columns. . . . The ruling was sometimes applied with the aid of guide dots/strokes, or with a grid-like device. . . . The first step in the preparation of the scrolls for writing was that of the ruling (scoring) meant to enable writing in straight lines. The so-called blind or dry-point ruling was usually performed with a pointed instrument (such instruments have not been preserved), probably a bone, which made a sharp crease in the leather, causing the leather to be easily split in two and even broken off. (Tov, SPA, 57, 58)

We see further evidence of normative scribal techniques in the arrangement of writing blocks, columns, and margins:

The idea of arranging the inscribed text in columns of more or less uniform dimension was reflected already in cuneiform clay tablets, where the text was subdivided by horizontal and vertical lines, and in ancient Egyptian papyrus scrolls. The great majority of Judean Desert texts were likewise arranged in writing blocks that cover the greater part of the surface, leaving margins on all sides of the inscribed surface. The rationale of these margins was to enable the orderly arrangement of the writing blocks in geometric shapes, even when the edges of the leather were not straight. The margins also enabled the handling of the scroll without touching the inscribed area. For this purpose the margins at the bottom were usually larger than those at the top. (Tov, SPA, 82)

Furthermore, scribes of the Judean Desert texts also employed various methods such as the insertion of dots, strokes, triangles, and single spaces in order to indicate word division, thereby increasing the overall clarity of the manuscripts. (Tov, SPA, 132–133)

Finally, another scribal technique mandated extreme care and precision in writing the name of God. This strict procedure not only highlights the care taken by the copyists in producing a highly accurate text, but also indicates the reverence in which they held the divine name. Regarding this special technique, Tov writes,

The divine names were written in a special way in many Hebrew Qumran texts:

(a) Paleo-Hebrew characters in texts written in the square script . . . .

(b) Four dots (named *Tetrapuncta* . . .)

[I]n texts written in the square script represent the Tetragrammaton in eight nonbiblical and biblical texts written in the Qumran scribal practice, as well as in four additional Qumran texts. . . . These dots and strokes were positioned level with the tops of the letters. . . . This practice undoubtedly reflects reverence for the divine name, considered so sacred that it was not to be written with regular characters lest an error be made or lest it be erased by mistake. Possibly, the dots or strokes were also meant to alert against pronouncing the divine name. (Tov, SPA, 218)

The particular materials selected, the special preparation of scrolls, and the employment of specialized techniques all point to a professional and clearly reverent scribal community.

C. The Worldview and Methodology of Jewish Scribes

This section examines how scribes approached their task of transmitting Scripture, the methodology they adopted, and the authority their final products possessed in their respective communities.

1. Scribal Approach to Scripture

What was the worldview and approach to the texts of the Hebrew Bible amongst scribal schools active in Israel between the third century BC and the sixth century AD? Scholars have concluded that we draw the majority of our information concerning scribal activity from rabbinic sources dating back to the Talmudic period (c. AD 100–500). Due to the continued presence of these rabbinic sources, the philosophy and methodology of the scribal schools designated as proto-Masoretic and Masoretic (see Tov's scribal traditions 3 and 4 above) are far more discernable than that of other scribal traditions (see Tov's scribal traditions 1, 2, and 5 above). Consider the following four observations:

- By the time of the *sopherim* (mid-third century BC), scribes were likely specialists with regard to the manuscripts they copied and the topics on which they wrote. They were well educated and well read. Additionally, religious texts could only be copied by male scribes of good standing.
- Various rabbinic rules regarding transmission procedures such as the selection of writing materials, preparation of leather, error correction, transcribing of divine names, storage and reading of scrolls, and measurements of sheets, columns, and margins all point to the reverence with which rabbinic scribes approached the biblical text.
- This reverence for Scripture was so highly regarded that it even precluded other aspects of the scribes' religious life. "The writing of Scripture and *tefillin* [small black boxes containing verses of Torah, which are bound to the head or forearm] was considered so important by the rabbis that scribes of such texts were not supposed to interrupt their work, even for the duty of prayer . . . , let alone for less significant occasions or tasks." (Tov, SPA, 11) R. Ishmael sums up this form of religiosity and meticulous care: "My son, be careful, because your work is the work of heaven; should you omit (even) one letter or add (even) one letter, the whole world would be destroyed." (quoted in Tov, SPA, 26)
- Although scribes may have known their biblical texts from memory, they were likely not allowed to copy Scripture without a *Vorlage* (the manuscript from which a scribe copied a text) in front of them. While this did not ensure a flawless transmission of the text, it did provide a structural safeguard representative of the rabbinic mind-set.

Paul D. Wegner, professor of Old Testament studies at Gateway Seminary, summarizes further safeguards and protocols that aided in the preservation and transmission of the biblical texts:

From at least the first century AD onward the proto-MT [Masoretic Text] was generally copied by well-trained, professional scribes who were meticulous in their work. Jewish writings mention that the temple employed correctors (*meggihim*) who scrutinized the scrolls to safeguard their precision. From about AD 100 to 300 a second group of scribes arose, called the Tannaim (*tannaim*), or "repeaters" (i.e., teachers), who began copying their traditions shortly after the beginning of the Christian era. Sometime during the talmudic period (100 BC to AD 400), which overlaps the periods of the Sopherim, Tannaim, and Amoraim, meticulous rules were developed to preserve the Old Testament text in synagogue scrolls:

1. Only parchments made from clean animals were allowed; these were to be joined together with thread from clean animals.
2. Each written column of the scroll was to have no fewer than forty-eight and no more than sixty lines whose breadth must consist of thirty letters.
3. The page was first to be lined, from which the letters were to be suspended.
4. The ink was to be black, prepared according to a specific recipe.
5. No word or letter was to be written from memory.
6. There was to be the space of a hair between each consonant and the space of a small consonant between each word, as well as several other spacing rules.
7. The scribe must wash himself entirely and be in full Jewish dress before beginning to copy the scroll.
8. He could not write the name Yahweh with a newly dipped brush, nor take notice of anyone, even a king, while writing this sacred name.

Later an entire tractate (a treatise) was devoted to the proper procedure for preparing a sacred scroll and included even more rules intended to assure an accurate text. (Wegner, SGTC, 7–8)

2. Communities, Their Texts, and the Authority of Scripture

Along with the rabbinical tradition of textual transmission described above, other communities of scribes produced biblical scrolls at variance with what eventually became the Masoretic Text. However, these variations that exist among different scribal communities active from the third century BC to the destruction of the Temple in AD 70 need not be of great concern. James C. VanderKam, professor of Hebrew Scriptures at the University of Notre Dame, states:

The manuscripts from the Judean wilderness provide evidence that scriptural texts were transmitted with considerable care by Jewish copyists. The differences between the Judean Desert texts and MT are indeed numerous though frequently very slight, often ones that do not affect the meaning of the text for most purposes (e.g., spelling changes, omission or addition of a conjunction). Statements in rabbinic literature describe the meticulous procedures used later in copying scriptural texts; it seems great care was also taken at an earlier time, as the Judean Desert texts suggest. The scribes were not transmitting only one form of the texts; yet, from whatever scriptural model they were copying, they presumably did the work with care according to prevailing rules of the profession. (VanderKam, DSSB, 7–8)

These other communities (e.g., Qumran scribes, the community that produced the Samaritan Pentateuch, translators of the Septuagint) would have worked simultaneously with rabbinic scribes in areas around Judea, Samaria, and, to some extent, Egypt. Eugene

C. Ulrich, professor of Hebrew Scriptures at the University of Notre Dame, describes the attitude of the Second Temple Period scribes in light of the phenomenon of pluriformity— nonidentical, yet similar, final forms of a biblical book:

> The scrolls as well as the other contemporary witnesses bountifully attest to a pluriformity— and as far as we can tell, a fully accepted pluriformity—in the text of the Scriptures. There is no noticeable indication of a widespread concern to have a single "standard text" or to move toward one. (Ulrich, QS, 86)

Regarding the question of authority in light of variants amongst the biblical traditions (e.g., MT, LXX, SP, DSS) VanderKam states:

> At the time when the communities associated with the scrolls were active, the books known today as the components of the Hebrew Bible/ Protestant Old Testament were, with one exception (Daniel), already old. Despite their age, or perhaps partly because of it, many of these books were thought by the writers to have extraordinary value for present concerns, a value so remarkable that they were believed to be authoritative in the contemporary situation—a fundamental assumption that bears repeating and whose importance can hardly be over-emphasized. (VanderKam, DSSB, 25)

While we, the authors, agree with Vander-Kam's position concerning the authority of the various traditions, we do not advocate for a late dating of Daniel. For further discussion on this issue, see chapter 25.

It is also noteworthy that while the extant manuscripts produced by these scribal communities are far removed in time from the original compositions, they still provide a type of evidence unique to ancient literary studies. VanderKam continues,

> It should be acknowledged, of course, that even the more recently accessible manuscript evidence is far removed in time from the earliest forms of the texts of scriptural books and sections, even if there is dispute aplenty about when the various compositions and sections of them were penned and arranged. If one follows those who think much of the Hebrew Bible reached its ultimate form in the Persian period, the Judean Desert manuscript finds take one back only to a point a few centuries later. That, of course, is much better than the situation confronting earlier scholars, but the chronological gap between the earliest written form(s) and the surviving manuscript evidence remains considerable. While that gap is a fact, it is also a fact that the student of the Hebrew Bible is, comparatively speaking, in a rather advantageous position. For example, the text of Plato's works, apart from some fragmentary second-third century C.E. papyri, is based on fifty-one manuscripts copied in the ninth century and later. (VanderKam, DSSB, 17)

Clearly, all the aforementioned communities of scribes esteemed the Scriptures as authoritative, perhaps even as canonical, and saw them as addressing their deepest concerns and as necessary for directing their conduct. (VanderKam, DSSB, 47–48) Finally, it seems that the communities of scribes with various worldviews and methods began to unify at the end of the first century AD. This ultimately led to a standardization of the biblical text that, albeit not intentionally orchestrated, was an inevitable result of historical circumstances. The results of the pluriformity of authoritative biblical texts produced by varying scribal communities are discussed more adequately in section V (Comparing Textual Traditions).

III. The Biblical Manuscripts

This section concentrates on extant ancient Hebrew and non-Hebrew biblical manuscripts that date from c. 650 BC. to c. AD 1100.

A. The Hebrew Sources

Among the ancient Hebrew sources, scholars are able to access the following textual witnesses (a manuscript tradition or collection that illuminates the original text): (1) the Masoretic Text (MT), (2) the Dead Sea Scrolls (DSS), (3) the Samaritan Pentateuch (SP), (4) the Nash Papyrus, and (5) the Silver Amulets.

1. The Masoretic Text (MT)

The majority of English translations of the Old Testament are derived from the ancient texts created by the Masoretes. Peter W. Flint, director of the Dead Sea Scrolls Institute at Trinity Western University, states,

The Masoretes were a group of Jewish scholars from the eighth century C.E. onward who maintained ancient traditions and developed new ones for copying the biblical text for liturgical or scholarly use. Earlier scholars who had maintained these traditions, known as scribes, had as their chief concern establishing and preserving the correct form of the biblical text. Many scholars refer to the early form of the text that the Masoretes took over as the pre-Masoretic or proto-Masoretic Text. (Flint, DSS, 36–37)

Würthwein also points out,

The Masoretes . . . sought to preserve the text of the Hebrew Scriptures as faithfully and accurately as possible, and by adding vowel signs and punctuation to establish an authoritative interpretation of the text. In this respect four integral components of the medieval MT may be distinguished: the consonant text, vocalization, organization of the text (spacing and accents), and marginal notes (Masorah parva and magna). By about the 10th century C.E. the Masoretes had achieved a textually controlled and excellent form of the text that could be called normative. . . . [T]he text of the Hebrew Scriptures had already been in circulation as a consonantal text for centuries. And studies of the early history of the text show that already in the 2nd century C.E. there was a standard form of the Masoretic consonantal text. (Würthwein, TOT, 15)

Flint outlines the three historical periods of Masoretic scribal activity:

1. The first period originated among Babylonian Jews, the Pharisees, or "temple circles," and ended with the destruction of the Temple in 70 CE or with the end of the Second Jewish Revolt (135). (The terms pre-Masoretic or proto-Masoretic are used for precursors of the MT in this period.)

2. The second period of transmission extends from the destruction of the Temple 70 CE to the eighth century, with documents that show a high degree of textual consistency. (The terms pre-Masoretic and proto-Masoretic are also used for precursors of the MT in this period.)

3. The third period extends from the eighth century until the end of the Middle Ages, and is characterized by almost complete textual unity. The complete apparatus of the Masorah (markings and marginal notes) is usually included, together with biblical quotations in the writings of medieval commentators. Since the addition of vowels and accents and the Masorah-demanded fixation of consonants, the MT became almost completely standardized. (Flint, DSS, 37)

Scholars consider the most authoritative Masoretic Text to be those manuscripts that were copied in the third historical period (c. AD 800 to 1100). Four of these codices (a codex is a manuscript in book form with pages) were produced by the Ben Asher family in Tiberias on the Sea of Galilee:

- *Codex Cairensis (C).* According to a colophon (an inscription at the end of the book that gives information concerning the scribe and the time and place of the manuscript's production), Codex Cairensis was written and vowel-pointed in AD 895 by Moses ben Asher. It contains the Former Prophets (Joshua, Judges, 1 and 2 Samuel, 1 and 2 Kings) and the Latter Prophets (Isaiah, Jeremiah, Ezekiel, and the Minor Prophets).
- *Aleppo Codex (A).* Considered to be the most authoritative copy of the MT, the consonantal text was copied by Shlomo ben Buya'a c. AD 920. Later vowel signs and notes were added by Moses ben Asher c. AD 925. Although only 294 of the original 487 pages survive, this manuscript has been used as the basis for the Hebrew University Bible Project (HUBP) in Jerusalem. (Flint, DSS, 38–39)
- *Codex Leningradensis (L).* Dated to AD 1008, Codex Leningradensis was produced in its entirety to include the consonants, vowels, and Masorah by one scribe, Samuel ben Jacob. Due to its being a complete work of the OT, Leningradensis "is used by most biblical scholars in its published edition, *Biblia Hebraica Stuttgartensia* (BHS), and now *Biblia Hebraica Quinta* (BHQ)." (Flint, DSS, 40)
- *Codex Oriental 4445 (B).* Consisting of 186 folios (folded sheets of paper yielding two book pages), Oriental 4445 contains Genesis 39:20 through Deuteronomy 1:33. Of the 186 folios 131 date to c. AD 950, while the remaining 55 folios were added c. AD 1540. (Wegner, SGTC, 158)

Other important Masoretic textual witnesses that date to the same period but are not ascribed to the Ben Asher tradition include:

- *Geniza Manuscripts.* In the 1860s, approximately 250,000 Jewish manuscript fragments were found in a *geniza* (a small storage room of a synagogue) in Cairo. These manuscripts, 15 percent of which are biblical texts in Hebrew, Aramaic, and Arabic, range in date from approximately the sixth century AD to as late as 1880. (Wegner, SGTC, 156) The majority of the biblical manuscripts are in the Masoretic tradition. (Flint, DSS, 38)
- *Leningrad (formerly Petersburg) Codex of the Prophets.* Discovered in 1839, the Leningrad Codex of the Prophets is dated to AD 916 and contains the Latter Prophets. An interesting feature of this codex is "that the Babylonian system of pointing is retained while the consonantal text, punctuation, and Masorah follow the Western tradition. Thus the Codex of the Prophets is a unique example of the Tiberian tradition beginning to replace the Babylonian tradition." (Würthwein, TOT, 43)
- *Damascus Pentateuch.* Dated to the late ninth or early tenth century AD, the Damascus Pentateuch is a consonantal text from the Tiberian school of the Masoretes that contains almost the entire Torah (Genesis 1:1–9:26 and Exodus 18:1–23a are missing). This codex was originally vowel-pointed in the Ben Naphtali tradition (another prominent scribal family from Tiberias), but later amended with accents

and vowel-points from the Ben Asher tradition. (Wegner, SGTC, 159)

- *Reuchlin Codex.* Dated to AD 1105, the Reuchlin Codex is a recension (an editorial revision) of the Ben Naphtali text.
- *Erfurt Codices.* Ranging between the twelfth and fourteenth centuries AD, the Erfurt Codices consist of three manuscripts (E1, E2, E3), all of which contain an entire OT, various Targums (Aramaic translations of Hebrew Scripture), small Masorahs (scribal notes along the outside margin of the text), and large Masorahs (textual traditions too lengthy to appear in the margin of the text and collected instead in a handbook). (Wegner, SGTC, 161)

The tradition of the MT is significant for the following reasons: (1) It provided the only textual witness to the Old Testament for more than 1,000 years (ninth century AD to 1947); (2) Its internal consistency clearly attests to the care, precision, and systematic rigor with which the Masoretic scribes copied the manuscripts (see sections II.B and II.C above); (3) The MT tradition allows the textual critic to reasonably posit a prior tradition going back to as early as AD 70; and (4) It provides the primary textual witness by which all other textual witnesses are measured (see section V below).

However, regardless of the stability of the MT, there was still one question that loomed for biblical scholars at the beginning of the twentieth century. The late classical biblical scholar Sir Frederic Kenyon surmised, "The great, indeed all-important, question which now meets us is this—Does this Hebrew text, which we call Massoretic, and which we have shown to descend from a text drawn up about AD 100, faithfully represent the Hebrew text as originally written by the authors of the Old Testament books?" (Kenyon, OB, 47)

2. The Dead Sea Scrolls (DSS)

The answer to Kenyon's question came eight years later with the discovery of the Dead Sea Scrolls at the caves of Qumran in 1947. Flint attests to the magnitude of this archaeological find:

In late 1946 or early 1947, Bedouin shepherds found several scrolls in a cave near an ancient site called Qumran, about one mile inland from the western shore of the Dead Sea, and 13 miles east of Jerusalem. This cave became known as Cave 1, which contained seven scrolls altogether, including the *Great Isaiah Scroll* and the *Rule of the Community*. By 1956, a total of 11 caves had been discovered at Qumran. These yielded various artifacts, especially pottery, but most importantly scrolls (that is, rolled manuscripts). Almost 1,050 scrolls were found in the Qumran caves in about 25,000 to 50,000 pieces.... More scrolls were discovered at other locations in the vicinity of the Dead Sea, especially at Wadi Murabba'at (about 120 scrolls in 1951–1952), Nahal Hever (over 70 scrolls in 1951–1961), and Masada (15 scrolls in 1963–1965). Thus the term *Dead Sea Scrolls* refers not only to scrolls discovered at Qumran (the main site) but also to scrolls from all sites in the vicinity of the Dead Sea.... The Dead Sea Scrolls are very ancient indeed: the earliest ones found at Qumran date from about 250 BCE or a little earlier; the latest were copied shortly before the destruction of the Qumran site by the Romans in 68 C.E. Scrolls from the other sites are somewhat later: Masada (up to 74 C.E.), Wadi Murabba'at (up to 135 C.E.), and Nahal Hever (up to 135 C.E.)....On April 11, 1948, the Dead Sea Scrolls were announced to the world by Millar Burrows, one of America's leading biblical scholars, in the *Times* of London. Soon afterward, famed archaeologist William F. Albright confirmed the antiquity of the scrolls, praising them as "the greatest archaeological find of the twentieth century." (Flint, DSS, xx, xxi)

KNOWN BIBLICAL SCROLLS

Book	Qumran	Other	Total
Deuteronomy	39	3	42
Psalms	39	3	42
Genesis	30	4	34
Exodus	30	1	31
Isaiah	22	1	23
Leviticus	22	2	24
Numbers	15	3	18
Daniel	11	0	11
12 Minor Prophets	13	2	15
Jeremiah	9	0	9
Ezekiel	6	0	6
1 and 2 Samuel	7	0	7
Job	6	0	6
Ruth	5	0	5
Song of Songs	4	0	4
Lamentations	4	0	4
Judges	5	0	5
1 and 2 Kings	5	0	5
Joshua	3	0	3
Proverbs	3	0	3
Ecclesiastes	2	0	2
Nehemiah	2	0	2
1 and 2 Chronicles	1	0	1
Ezra	1	0	1
Esther	0	0	0
(Total)	284	19	303
Adjusted Total	252	18	270
"On the Market"	48	0	48
Grand Total	300	18	318

Chart adapted from Flint, DSS, 75.

Flint developed a chart that lists the biblical scrolls (see "Known Biblical Scrolls"). He further clarifies that "the 270 total has been adjusted down from 303, since 11 scrolls from Qumran and one from Muraba'at [*sic*] preserve parts of more than one book in 33 cases. These can only be counted once." (Flint, DSS 74) Aside from biblical manuscripts, other types of manuscripts found at the Judean Desert sites include documents concerning the life of the community (e.g., *The Community Rule*), commentaries on biblical books (e.g., *Habakkuk Peshar*), works contained in the Apocrypha (e.g., *Tobit*) and Pseudepigrapha (e.g., *Assumption of Moses*), and other sectarian writings (e.g., *The War Scrolls*). A closer examination of each site highlights the richness of this historical find:

1. *Qumran.* Located on the shores of the Dead Sea, and considered by most scholars to be the dwelling of a religious sectarian community known as the Essenes (possibly meaning "doers of the Torah"), the caves at Qumran provide the majority of the manuscripts found in the Judean Desert. (See VanderKam, DSS, 101–104) Among the eleven caves at Qumran, approximately 1,050 manuscripts were discovered, all of which were written in Hebrew, Aramaic, or Greek. Roughly three hundred of those are classified as biblical manuscripts, and constitute our earliest witness to the biblical text. (Wegner, SGTC, 151–153)

   • *Cave 1.* The most outstanding of all the manuscripts, due to its near complete preservation, is the *Great Isaiah Scroll* (1QIsaᵃ), which was found in Cave 1. Fragments of other biblical works found in Cave 1 include Genesis, Exodus, Leviticus, Deuteronomy, Judges, Samuel, Ezekiel, Psalms, and Daniel. Cave 1 also yielded many nonbiblical fragments such as *Jubilees, A Lamech Apocalypse, A Testament of Levi, Words of*

Moses, various commentaries (e.g., Micah, Zephaniah, and Habakkuk), and additional psalms, liturgies, and hymns.

- *Cave 2*. Fragments from Genesis through Deuteronomy, Jeremiah, Psalms, Job, Ruth, Ben Sira, Jubilees, and others.
- *Cave 3*. Fragments of Ezekiel, Psalms, Lamentations, a commentary on Isaiah, and the so-called Copper Scroll.
- *Cave 4*. Rivaling Cave 1 in significance, Cave 4 yielded approximately 20,000 fragments representing more than 700 scrolls. Of these 700 scrolls there is wide diversity among the texts ranging from biblical, nonbiblical, and parabiblical to sectarian documents.
- *Caves 5–10*. Approximately 80 to 85 fragments containing portions of Deuteronomy, Kings, Isaiah, Amos, Psalms, Lamentations, Genesis and Exodus (in paleo-Hebrew script), Song of Songs, Daniel, Jeremiah, and other Apocryphal works.
- *Cave 11*. Fragments of approximately 31 scrolls: most notably, the *Psalms Scroll* (11QPs^a), along with the *Temple Scroll* (11QT^a), and the *Targum of Job* (11QtgJob).

2. *Wadi Murabba'at*. This series of caves, located approximately eleven miles south of Qumran, served as a refuge for Jewish rebels during the second Jewish revolt against Rome (AD 132–135). Among the 120 documents found at this location were contracts, letters signed by Simon bar Kokhba (d. AD 135), biblical scrolls (Pentateuch, Isaiah, and Minor Prophets), and a palimpsest (a manuscript whose previous writing was scraped off in order to be reused) that dates back to the seventh or eighth century BC (the original text).

3. *Nahal Hever*. Also used as a hiding place for Jewish rebels, the caves at Nahal Hever, located between Murabba'at and Masada, yielded a large number of fragments, mainly consisting of letters and legal documents from the second century AD. However, fragments of biblical scrolls were also found, including Genesis, Numbers, Deuteronomy, and Psalms (these Hebrew manuscripts date to c. AD 130 CE). Also, a near complete Greek manuscript of the Minor Prophets dated to between 50 BC and AD 50 was also discovered.

4. *Masada*. It was at this location atop Herod the Great's mountain fortress that the remains of fifteen scrolls (seven of which are biblical) were discovered between 1963 and 1965. Along with biblical fragments of Psalms 81:3 to 85:10, Leviticus, the final two chapters of Deuteronomy, an Ezekiel scroll, and a copy of Psalm 150, there were also nonbiblical scrolls of *Ben Sira*, *Jubilees*, and the *Songs of the Sabbath Sacrifice*. (Wegner, SGTC, 151–153)

The overall value of the manuscript discoveries in the Judean Desert to biblical scholarship and historical studies cannot be overstated. Tov illustrates:

Since the discovery in 1947 of Hebrew and Aramaic texts in the Judean Desert dating from approximately 250 BCE until 135 CE, our knowledge about the Scripture text has increased greatly.... It should be remembered that until the time of those discoveries no early Hebrew and Aramaic Scripture texts were known, except for the Nash papyrus of the Decalogue..., and as a result the manuscripts of 𝔐 [Masoretic Text] from the Middle Ages served as the earliest Scripture sources in the original languages. Therefore, the research before 1947 was based on Hebrew-Aramaic texts that had been copied 1200 years or more after the composition of the biblical books. At the same time, scholars also relied on manuscripts and early papyrus fragments of the ancient translations . . . , which brought them much closer to the time of the composition of the biblical books. All these, however, are translations, and the reconstruction of their Hebrew-Aramaic sources will always remain uncertain. . . . Therefore, the discovery in the Judean Desert of many Hebrew-Aramaic texts dating from two millennia ago has considerably advanced our knowledge of the early witnesses and the procedure of the copying and transmitting of texts. (Tov, TC, 17)

Adding to Tov's insight concerning textual transmission, James Alfred Loader, professor of Old Testament studies at the University of Vienna, points out the value of the Dead Sea Scrolls as the basis for intertextual studies (the way that similar or related texts influence, reflect, or differ from each other; see section V below) of the Hebrew Bible:

The Dead Sea Scrolls perhaps afford one of the best instances of the meaning of the concept of intertextuality in biblical studies. . . . This is in evidence all over the Dead Sea Scrolls and—since mainly biblical texts are concerned in this respect—biblical scholarship cannot but pay more attention to the phenomenon of intertextuality as it is exemplified in these texts. The Dead Sea Scrolls create new contexts for reading the texts of the Hebrew Bible. They do so because they are texts the origin of which was determined by a particular understanding of the pre-existing Hebrew Bible texts. . . . In

the case of the Dead Sea Scrolls, it means that they have not only originated in the context of the Hebrew Bible, but have in turn *created* contexts for the reading of the Hebrew Bible that were not there before the Dead Sea Scrolls. (Loader, CNC, 44–45)

Specifically concerning the finds at Qumran, Tov identifies four benefits that the manuscripts confer upon the biblical scholar:

- Readings not known previously help us to better understand many details in the biblical text, often pertaining to matters of substance.
- The textual variety reflected in the four groups of texts described in § 7 [Masoretic-like Texts, Pre-Samaritan Texts, Texts close to the presumed Hebrew Source of the Septuagint, Non-Aligned Texts] provides a good overview of the condition of the biblical text in the Second Temple period.
- The scrolls provide much background information on the technical aspects of the copying of biblical texts and their transmission in the Second Temple period.
- The reliability of the reconstruction of the *Vorlage* (the source text being copied) of the ancient translations, especially [the Septuagint], is supported much by the Qumran texts. (Tov, TC, 108–110)

Wegner affirms the primacy of the Masoretic tradition as attested to by all the manuscripts found at the other Judean Desert sites:

All the manuscripts found at Wadi Murabba'at are very similar to the MT (all eighteen of the additions and corrections made to the manuscripts are toward the MT) and help to confirm that during the first century AD the

MT had indeed become unified. . . . All the biblical texts [found at Nahal Hever], along with a Hebrew phylactery fragment of Exodus 13:2–10, 11–16, are dated to about AD 130 and their translations are virtually identical to the MT . . . The Masada manuscripts are written in Hebrew square script and are virtually identical to the MT (in wording as well as the divisions of the lines), except for slight differences in the Ezekiel text. (Wegner, SGTC, 150–151, 155, 153)

In addition to answering many questions concerning the textual history of the Hebrew Bible, one other area of scholarship greatly impacted by the Dead Sea Scrolls is that of New Testament studies. VanderKam states,

Despite the gulf that at times divides the religious expressions in the New Testament and in the scrolls, the latter offer much information that enriches the reading of the former. One way of putting the matter is to say that the scrolls offer backlighting on the New Testament that aids considerably in understanding parts of it. There is no need to go so far as to assert direct influence from scrolls to New Testament authors; rather, the information in some of the Qumran works allows one to interpret a series of New Testament passages in a fuller way, with a greater appreciation for them against the backdrop of their time and world. With the added knowledge about Second Temple Judaism arising from the scrolls, one's understanding of some New Testament passages can be enriched and deepened. (VanderKam, DSS, 120)

Although the Dead Sea Scrolls carry the day in terms of providing biblical scholars with a treasure trove of data concerning the transmission of Old Testament texts, there are also other Hebrew textual witnesses that deserve mention.

3. The Samaritan Pentateuch (SP)

The Samaritan Pentateuch is a version of the Hebrew Torah (the first five books of the Old Testament) that is written in a special version of an early Hebrew script that allows scholars to date the SP to as early as the Hasmonean period (third century BC). (Tov, TC, 75) While the oldest extant manuscripts of the SP date to the Middle Ages, the original SP was likely either developed by Israelites who were assimilated into the Assyrian Empire during its conquest of the Northern Kingdom in 721 BC, or by a community in the area of Samaria that developed sometime between the Persian period (538 to 332 BC) and the destruction of the Temple in Shechem in 128 BC.

As discussed in section V (Comparing Textual Traditions), while variants between the texts of the SP and the MT exist, they (1) most likely derive from the Samaritan community's shift from the Temple in Jerusalem to their own Temple on Mount Gerizim, and (2) are either orthographic (concerning letters and spelling) or stylistic in nature, which marginalizes their significance. (Würthwein, TOT, 82)

Lee Martin McDonald, professor of New Testament at Acadia Divinity College, highlights the sectarian divide between the SP and the MT:

While these two forms of the Pentateuch have much that overlaps, several textual variations may indicate two literary editions of an earlier Pentateuch. Certainly, the Samaritans considered their Pentateuch to be the authoritative form of the text. For example, the MT of Deut. 27:4–5 says that after the Jews cross the Jordan River, they are to build an altar to the Lord on Mount Ebal, but the Samaritan Pentateuch of the same passage, which may well be the earlier text, says that it is to be built on Mount

Gerizim. On the other hand, the Samaritan Pentateuch adds to the Decalogue a command to build an altar on Mount Gerizim. The Samaritans did not see themselves as a sect of Judaism, but rather as the community that interpreted the Mosaic tradition more accurately, unlike the other Jewish sects that wrongly promoted Jerusalem as the religious center of God. (McDonald, BC, 138)

The overall value of the SP cannot be denied inasmuch as it was a popular version of the Hebrew Torah in use prior to the rabbinic tradition. Furthermore, it provides the textual critic with yet another witness to the earlier forms of the Pentateuchal texts. As Wegner states, however, regarding the use of the SP, "it actually turns out to be of little value for establishing original readings of the MT because of several significant limitations: (1) it is probably a popularized revision of the text of the Old Testament; (2) no manuscripts of the SP precede the eleventh or twelfth century AD; and (3) it contains sectarian tendencies." (Wegner, SGTC, 170–171)

4. The Nash Papyrus

Until the discovery of the scrolls at Qumran, the Nash Papyrus, named after its discoverer in 1902, was the earliest textual witness to the Hebrew Bible. Dating between the second and first century BC, it contains the Decalogue (The Ten Commandments), other parts of Exodus 20 and Deuteronomy 5, and the Shema of Deuteronomy 6:4–5. (Würthwein, DSSB, 8)

5. The Silver Amulets

The Silver Amulets (c. seventh or sixth century BC) provide one final extant piece of evidence possibly attesting to the existence of an early form of the Hebrew Bible. Lawrence Schiffman, former professor of Hebrew and Judaic studies at New York University, describes the amulets:

> The priestly blessing (Numbers 6:22–27) played a major role in Jewish worship in the Temple and synagogue. Its text, inscribed in the ancient Hebrew script, was found on an amulet from the 7th–6th century BCE at Ketef Hinnom in Jerusalem. *This inscription is the earliest attestation of a text from the Torah.* Some scholars have argued that this amulet proves that the blessing preexisted the book of Numbers. In our view, the use of this passage as an amulet indicates that it was already known in its present context. (Schiffman, FTT, 25, emphasis added)

William Schniedewind, professor of biblical studies at the University of California, Los Angeles, emphasizes the importance of the amulets in the context of early Hebrew writing:

> These two amulets would not have been unique. They were not one-of-a-kind objects. We must assume that these chance finds represent a much larger phenomenon in the late monarchic period. People would use traditional texts as amulets that were worn around the neck. Although these texts were not to be read, their use speaks to the religious power that *written* texts came to have in the late Judean monarchy. (Schniedewind, HBBB, 106)

B. The Non-Hebrew Sources

This section deals almost exclusively with the Greek translation of the Hebrew Bible, known as the Septuagint (LXX), and its relationship to the Masoretic Text (MT) and Judean Desert texts (DSS). Other later Greek translations (Hexapla, Theodotion, Symmachus) are discussed briefly, but the LXX provides the most valuable non-Hebrew witness for Old Testament textual criticism.

1. The Septuagint (LXX)

After the conquest of the Middle East by Alexander the Great (c. 330 BC), Greek became the *lingua franca* extending from Egypt in the east through Palestine, all the way to the region of Persia. At some point it became the dominant language of Hellenized Jewish communities, thus prompting the translation of the Hebrew-Aramaic manuscripts into Greek. Flint gives one possible version of the origin of the LXX:

> The Septuagint was originally only the Greek translation of the Pentateuch. For most scholars, the term *Septuagint* is more wideranging and includes Greek translations of the Hebrew Bible, the additions to some books (for example, Daniel), books among the Apocrypha (for example, 1 Maccabees and Judith), and books not among the Apocrypha of the Roman Catholic Church but recognized by Orthodox churches (for example, the Prayer of Manasseh and Psalm 151). The term comes from the Latin *Septuaginta*, meaning "seventy" (hence the abbreviation LXX in Roman numerals), and is derived from a fascinating story. According to the *Letter of Aristeas* (written sometime between 150 and 100 BCE by Aristeas, a Jew from Alexandria), the Egyptian king Ptolemy II (285–247) ordered his librarian, Demetrius of Phalerum, to collect all the books in the world for his famous Library at Alexandria. Demetrius believed that this collection should include a copy of the Jewish law translated into Greek. In response to an invitation, the high priest Eleazar sent six elders from each of the twelve tribes, for a total of 72. Following their arrival in Alexandria, drafts of the translation were made, and the final version was completed in exactly 72 days. (Flint, DSS, 46)

Because scholars consider the *Letter of Aristeas* to be, for the most part, a legendary account, other theories concerning the origin of the LXX have been suggested:

> The Septuagint began to take shape in the third century BCE in response to the needs of the Alexandrian Jewish community. Initially all that was translated was a version of the Torah for worship and study. The translators may have included Palestinian scholars, and the project may even have been encouraged by the king. On the other hand, the text may have come about more informally, as an oral translation used in worship services, which later was edited and committed to writing. By the second century the books of the latter prophets, then the former, were translated as well. Some of the Writings had also been translated by the beginning of the second century BCE, whereas others were rendered into Greek only in the first century. (Schiffman, FTT, 92)

The content of the LXX differs from the Hebrew Old Testament in two respects: (1) number and order of books (issues relating to canonicity); and (2) variants within each book (an issue relating to textual criticism). The LXX contains additional books not found in the Hebrew tradition, some of which are preserved in Roman Catholic Bibles and normally referred to as the Apocrypha. These books, ranging in date from c. fourth century BC to c. first century AD, include Tobit, Judith, Additions to Esther, 1 and 2 Maccabees, The Wisdom of Solomon, Ecclesiasticus (a.k.a. Sirach, The Wisdom of Ben Sira), Baruch, and the additions to Daniel (The Prayer of Azariah and the Song of the Three Young Men, Susanna, and Bel and the Dragon). Additional books found in LXX manuscripts are maintained in some orthodox canons (e.g., Slavonic, Greek Orthodox). These books, ranging in date from c. first century BC to the late first century AD, include

The Prayer of Manasseh, Psalm 151, 1 Esdras (a.k.a. 2 Esdras), 2 Esdras (a.k.a. 3 Esdras), and 3 and 4 Maccabees. (Flint, DSS, 49–50)

The text of the LXX has been preserved in three forms: (1) ancient papyri (e.g., Chester Beatty papyri, Judean Desert fragments); (2) uncials (Greek manuscripts written in all capital letters, commonly used between the first and sixth centuries AD, e.g., Codex Sinaiticus, Codex Vaticanus, Codex Alexandrinus); and (3) medieval minuscules (Greek manuscripts written in smaller cursive script, predominantly used between the ninth and fifteenth centuries AD). Of the earliest extant fragments of the LXX, several are noteworthy.

- *Rylands Papyri.* Dating from the second century BC to the fifth century AD, this collection includes *Papyrus Greek 458* (contains Deut. 23–28), one of the oldest fragments of the Greek Bible. This collection also preserves manuscripts with portions of Genesis, Chronicles, Job, and Isaiah.
- *Chester Beatty Papyri.* Dating from the second to fourth century CE, this collection contains the remnants of eleven codices that preserve parts of Genesis, Numbers, Deuteronomy, Isaiah, Jeremiah, Ezekiel, Daniel, Esther, Sirach, 1 Enoch, and approximately fifteen New Testament books.
- *Oxyrhynchus Papyri.* Discovered in Egypt, these manuscripts, ranging in date from the first to ninth century AD, contain portions of the Pentateuch, Joshua, Judges, Ruth, Psalms, and the Prophets.
- *Freer Papyri.* Dating from the third to fifth century CE, this collection contains Deuteronomy, Joshua, the Minor Prophets, and Psalms.
- *Société Egyptienne de papyrologie.* One of the oldest of the early manuscripts,

dating to the late second or early first century BC, these fragments represent portions of three different scrolls, with texts from Genesis and Deuteronomy. One unique feature found in the Deuteronomy scroll is a space left by an initial Greek scribe allowing for a second scribe to write the Tetragrammaton in the Old Hebrew script. (Würthwein, TOT, 105)

In addition to these papyri, the earliest and most complete manuscripts of the LXX available to scholars today are Codex Vaticanus (fourth century AD), Codex Sinaiticus (late fourth to early fifth century AD), and Codex Alexandrinus (mid-fifth century AD).

Scholars also have discovered evidence of modifications made to the original translation of the LXX. These modifications to the Greek text are commonly termed *recensions*, and are defined by two characteristics: (1) they have the vocabulary of the Old Greek translations as a common base, and (2) they move the text toward a greater fidelity to the Hebrew text (i.e., proto-Masoretic Text). (Würthwein, TOT, 106) The four most identifiable recensions of the Greek Old Testament are:

- *Kaige Recension.* Previously attributed to Theodotion at the end of the second century AD, it was shown after the discovery of the Dead Sea Scrolls (cf. The Twelve Prophets scroll of Nahal Hever) that the Kaige Recension was produced much earlier (c. 50 BC to AD 50).
- *Aquila Recension.* Dated to c. AD 130, this alleged pupil of Rabbi Aquiba produced a highly literal recension toward the Masoretic Text. While this wooden literalism closely attests to the Hebrew text of the time, it made the Greek text nearly unintelligible.

- *Symmachus Recension.* A Samaritan convert named Symmachus produced a hybrid of translation and recension sometime around AD 170. This pupil of Rabbi Meir attempted to balance the Hebrew text with the Greek receptor language.
- *Theodotion Recension.* Working as late as AD 190, Theodotion expanded upon the earlier Kaige Recension, occasionally transcribing Hebrew words into the text when Greek names for specific terms were not available. (Würthwein, TOT, 108–109)

Würthwein highlights the importance of these recensions concerning the relationship between rabbinical Judaism and the early Christian Church:

It should be noted here again that the emergence of Jewish recensions developed in connection with the growing distancing of Rabbinic Judaism from the LXX. This does not mean, first, that the rabbis rejected the LXX text. They did not try to edit or to improve it, but rather looked to competing versions. In the frequent debates between Jews and Christians over the proper interpretation of certain biblical passages, when Christians appealed naturally to the current LXX text, Jews would bring out their competing translations against it. (Würthwein, TOT, 109–110)

As we have seen, the text of the LXX has experienced its own history of modification, revisions, and recensions. From the time of its original translation in the third century BC to its textual stabilization in the first and second centuries AD, various editions have naturally given rise to variants, both internal and external (in relation to MT and DSS). Würthwein gives a contemporary example of what varying editions of a base text might look like today:

Emanuel Tov's manual on textual criticism originally appeared in Hebrew in 1989, and in 1992 the author published it in English, somewhat rewritten, expanded, and improved. The German edition of 1997 by Heinz-Josef Fabry was based on the English edition in consultation with the author. Finally in 2001 a second English edition appeared, but with only a few minor revisions. Thus there are four different editions of the manual. Naturally the essential difference between this example and the OT is that the OT is a traditional literature and not a book by a single author. (Würthwein, TOT, 103)

Variants between textual witnesses (e.g., MT, LXX, SP, DSS), whether unintended errors (e.g., spelling mistakes, omission or addition of words) or intentional alterations (e.g., lexical and grammatical changes, harmonizations) are discussed further in section V below.

The historical significance of the LXX, including its various renditions, continues to be definitive in the life of the church and the realm of biblical scholarship. Raija Sollamo, professor of biblical languages at the University of Helsinki, writes,

The high prestige of the Greek Bible as an inspired translation, enjoying the same authority as the Hebrew source text, contributed to establishing the conviction that a Greek translation of the law and prophets and Psalms was not only of value for those who did not know Hebrew, but also very acceptable as the sacred text of a Greek-speaking religious community instead of the source text. (Sollamo, SSS, 501)

Concerning the value of the LXX in the process of biblical translation, Sollamo continues,

The favorable reception of the original Septuagint (Pentateuch), promoted by the Letter of Aristeas in the second century BCE, was of crucial importance as an encouraging model for all future Bible translations in whatever language. A translation, too, could be inspired and so replace the original. In the first century C.E., the Alexandrian Jewish philosopher commentator Philo was the first to attribute the translation process of the Septuagint to divine guidance. . . . Thus the Septuagint opened the door for further Bible translations. . . . The history of the Christian church came to be a history of Bible translations. . . . During the first centuries C.E. most Bible translations were made from the Septuagint, and for this reason they are designated as daughter versions, such as the *Vetus Latina* or Old Latin, the Sahidic and Bohairic Coptic, Ethiopic and Armenian translations. (Sollamo, SSS, 501, 502)

While Sollamo's comments show the value of the LXX to the first and second century Greek-speaking Jewish communities, we do not intend to suggest the inspiration of modern translations. Nor do we mean to comment on the ongoing debate amongst evangelicals regarding the inspiration of the LXX as compared to the autographs (the original documents written or dictated by the author).

Concerning the place of the LXX in the field of contemporary textual criticism, Tov states,

In the past, the value of the LXX for biblical research was viewed in different ways, with excessive stress placed either on the translators' exegesis and techniques or on the differences between their Hebrew text and MT. There certainly was (and still is) a tendency, even among critical scholars, to depreciate the value of the LXX by ascribing most of its deviations to the translators' exegesis and techniques. . . . Ever since the nineteenth century there have been scholars who, in their evaluation of the LXX,

took the middle road between recognizing Hebrew variants and the translators' exegesis. . . . The understanding and use of the LXX as a tool in biblical criticism were significantly advanced in the middle of the present century by the finds of Hebrew scrolls at Qumran. It was then recognized that many of the Hebrew readings (variants) tentatively reconstructed from the LXX did indeed exist as readings in Hebrew scrolls from Qumran. . . . These agreements between the Hebrew scrolls from Qumran and the Jewish-Greek translation of the LXX . . . enhanced the credibility of the LXX, although there inevitably continued to be a great deal of argument over matters of detail. The LXX has definitely been recognized by most biblical scholars as a tool that provides important information for the textual criticism of the Bible. (Tov, TCUS, 33, 34, 35)

Finally, Sollamo demonstrates how the use of κύριος (kyrios) in the LXX as a rendering of the Hebrew divine name יהוה (YHWH) played a crucial role in defining the authority, and indeed the identity, of Jesus Christ by the early New Testament church:

One of the most influential renderings was the regular use of the term Κύριος "the Lord" for the Hebrew proper name Yahweh, the "tetragrammaton" (four lettered name) . . . The new *terminus technicus*, Κύριος, was very suitable as a designation of a deity in the hellenistic world. . . . The title Κύριος as a surrogate for Yahweh proved very suitable for use by Christians. They ascribed the same title to the risen Christ present in the worship of the congregation. Jesus Christ probably did not receive this title through the influence of the Greek scriptures, but once it had been conferred on him, many things that those scriptures said about "the Lord" could be attributed to the new Lord, Jesus the Christ. (Sollamo, SSS, 507, 508)

2. The Hexapla

One final early non-Hebrew witness to the Old Testament is the Hexapla of Origen. Würthwein provides a concise description:

> The Hexapla of Origen is a point of intersection in the history of the text. It brought together the mainstream of the LXX tradition and engaged Jews in a discussion of the Greek text. The Alexandrian theologian, working on the church's revision between 230 and 240 C.E., arranged the biblical text in six parallel columns: (1) the Hebrew text, (2) the Hebrew text in Greek transcription, (3) the translation by Aquila, (4) the translation by Symmachus, (5) the LXX text, and (6) the translation by Theodotion. (Würthwein, TOT, 110)

Although the Hexapla does not exist in its original form, its content is known from fragments, quotations from church fathers, the Syro-Hexapla (translation of the Greek Hexapla into Syriac, in the seventh century AD by Paul from Tella), and marginal notes in Septuagint manuscripts. As to its value regarding textual criticism, in spite of internal differences likely due to varying Hebrew readings, all columns of the Hexapla, except for column 5 (LXX), reflect the MT. (Tov, TC, 146)

IV. The Nonbiblical Manuscripts

This section concentrates on extant ancient nonbiblical manuscripts that are highly valuable as resources for understanding the text of the Hebrew Bible and its interpretation. Among the ancient nonbiblical manuscripts, scholars possess the following textual witnesses: (1) the Aramaic Targums, (2) the Mishnah and the Gemara, and (3) the Midrash. Schiffman states, "These texts, orally formulated and orally transmitted and taught, set forth the basic principles of the oral law and argued for the integrity of the Torah, written and oral. These documents served as the basis for the later development of Judaism and, in the case of the Mishnah, set the agenda for all future study of Jewish law." (Schiffman, FTT, 200)

A. The Aramaic Targums

The earliest of the Aramaic Targums (Targumim) likely originated during the postexilic period when Aramaic had become the primary language in Palestine (the fourth and third century BC), roughly around the same time as the Greek translation of the Pentateuch. However, the majority of these Aramaic commentaries on the Hebrew text are dated between the second and fifth centuries AD. Tov provides a concise description of the origin and background of the Targums:

> The Targumim were created within the Jewish communities as the official companion to Hebrew Scripture in rabbinic Judaism, prepared for the learned, not for the masses. . . . These translations facilitated the introduction of some modernizations and exegesis in translation, while leaving the Hebrew text itself intact. Throughout the centuries, the Jewish Targumim retained a more special status within the Jewish communities than all other translations. The medieval commentators often quoted from them, and they were printed in full in the Rabbinic Bibles alongside the Hebrew text. Targumim were made of each of the books of the Bible (excluding Ezra, Nehemiah, and Daniel), sometimes more than one. (Tov, TC, 148)

As to the significance of the Aramaic Targums, Wegner states:

> [The Aramaic Targums] are important to textual criticism for several reasons: (1) they

may contain early traditions concerning the reading of the text; (2) they include early Jewish traditions as to the interpretation of the biblical texts; and (3) they are written in Aramaic, which is closely related to biblical Hebrew. (Wegner, SGTC, 175)

B. The Mishnah and the Gemara

Schiffman provides a clear understanding of the history and importance of the Mishnah and the Gemara to rabbinic Judaism:

The Mishnah is the basic document of Rabbinic Judaism. Compiled around 200 C.E., it is fundamentally a curriculum for the study of Jewish law, arranged topically. It contains material attributed to figures as early as the third century B.C.E. The vast bulk of the material is attributed to tannaim, sages from the latter years of the first century B.C.E. through the end of the second century C.E. The Tosefta was the earliest commentary on the Mishnah, and its compilation is therefore to be dated somewhat later. Yet many of the sayings preserved in the Tosefta are attributed to the same tannaim cited in the Mishnah. (Schiffman, FTT, 10)

Later scribes (*amoraim*), working between the third and sixth centuries AD in two locations (Babylon and Palestine), added further commentary (*gemaras*) to the Mishnah, thus resulting in what can now be called the Babylonian Talmud and the Palestinian Talmud.

C. The Midrash

In addition to the Mishnah and the Gemara, Schiffman details a third method of rabbinic exposition:

The midrashim constitute sustained interpretations of Scripture arranged according to biblical sequence. The tannaitic midrashim

preserved materials that emerged out of the discussions in the tannaitic academies but were redacted (collected and edited) in the amoraic period [c. AD 230–500]. The later amoraic expository midrashim have as their setting the synagogues of northern Palestine. The editing of some of these texts extended until the early Middle Ages. As with the Talmuds, these collections can be used for historical purposes only after the closest analysis of attributions and careful dating of materials, as well as detailed study of manuscript evidence and exegetical traditions. . . . The midrashic method is a technique of scriptural exposition. It concentrated primarily on the Torah, which was the supreme authority for the midrashic method and was studied as the basic text. Scholars and students explained how specific laws derived from biblical verses or words and how the laws were to be applied. (Schiffman, FTT, 11, 184)

This corpus of rabbinic literature, which defined Judaism after the destruction of the Temple and embodied the history of oral Torah, predominantly reflects the proto-Masoretic and later Masoretic textual traditions.

V. Comparing Textual Traditions

This section considers the nature and methodology of textual criticism, also known as "lower criticism." McDonald underscores the purpose of this process when he states:

The first responsibility of any interpreter of the Bible is to determine precisely what the author wrote. The primary goal of textual criticism is to establish the original wording of a text insofar as that is possible. Since none of the original manuscripts, or autographs, has survived antiquity, text-critical scholars evaluate a myriad of ancient manuscripts that often are remarkably different from each other, in order to determine the earliest or most original reading possible. (McDonald, BC, 356)

In his seminal work, Tov explains the necessity of this discipline as it relates to the text of the Old Testament:

The biblical text has been transmitted in many ancient and medieval sources that are known to us from modern editions in different languages: We possess fragments of leather and papyrus scrolls that are at least two thousand years old in Hebrew, Greek, and Aramaic, as well as manuscripts in Hebrew and other languages from the Middle Ages. These sources shed light on and witness to the biblical text, hence their name: "textual witnesses." All these textual witnesses differ from one another to a greater or lesser extent. Since no textual source contains what could be called *the* biblical text, a serious involvement in biblical studies necessitates the study of all sources, which necessarily involves study of the differences between them. The comparison and analysis of these textual differences thus holds a central place within textual criticism. (Tov, TC, 3)

In an earlier work, Tov lays out the task of the textual critic:

The study of the biblical text involves an investigation of its development, its copying and transmission, and of the processes which created readings and texts over the centuries. During this procedure, textual critics collect all the details in which the Hebrew and translated texts differ one from another. Some of these differences were created in the course of the textual transmission, while others derived from an earlier stage, that of

the literary growth. . . . Scholars try to isolate and evaluate the readings which were created during the textual transmission by comparing them with other textual data, especially MT. This evaluation . . . is limited to the readings created during the textual transmission (not including those created in earlier stages), and the literary growth of the book, even if those readings are included in textual witnesses. Most scholars believe that this evaluation involves a reconstruction of elements included in the original text of the Bible. (Tov, TCUS, 4)

He goes on to define the essence of a textual variant:

A *variant* is any detail in a textual source of the Hebrew Bible that differs from a specific form of MT. Thus differences in consonants and in complete words, as well as omissions, additions, and transpositions are all variants. Differences in orthography are also variants, but they are often treated as a separate category. *Retroverted variants*, that is, variants retroverted from a translation, likewise differ from MT. The term "variant" is also used for elements such as vocalization and different divisions of words and sentences which were not indicated in the scrolls used by the translators, but which necessarily are reflected in the translation. (Tov, TCUS, 124)

It is important to note at this juncture the difference between literary criticism and textual criticism. Literary criticism, as typically understood, is the study of the internal form and literary content of a written work until a final form is achieved and the transmission of that form is initiated. Textual criticism is the study of the second stage of this process, the propagation of that final literary form. This is not to imply that textual criticism issues would not arise during the period of literary development. However, this section focuses on issues that pertain to variants among the four primary witnesses mentioned above (e.g., MT, LXX, SP, DSS).

A. Methods for Determining the Best Reading

As to the methodology employed by scholars to determine the best reading of any given biblical text, there are four steps to determine the "best reading"—the most plausible original wording of the final literary form.

1. Collect the Evidence

As in any good investigation, scholars first collect all available evidence. This pool of evidence includes all of the ancient biblical sources (Hebrew and translations), as well as later medieval biblical manuscripts and contemporary scholarly compilations. A common starting place for most scholars is the MT, which has been critiqued and compiled into diplomatic editions, such as the *Biblica Hebraica Stuttgartensia* and the *Biblica Hebraica Quinta*.

2. Evaluate Internal and External Evidence

After collecting evidence from these textual witnesses, scholars use the following guidelines to determine the most plausible reading of a passage.

- Determine the reading that would most likely give rise to the other readings.
- Carefully evaluate the weight of the manuscript evidence.
- Determine if the reading is a secondary reading or a gloss (a commentary or annotation appearing alongside Scripture text).
- Determine which reading is most appropriate in its context. (Wegner, SGTC, 125)

Clearly, a certain level of subjectivity exists in each of these four guidelines. A certain amount of intuition, common sense, and skill must then play into the scholar's final judgment. Scholars use these guidelines and their own inductive reasoning to analyze the internal evidence of textual variants (i.e., intentional changes and unintentional scribal errors). While scholars debate the value of external evidence when attempting to determine the most plausible reading, these criteria may aid in making a final assessment: (1) age of the textual witness; (2) degree of geographical attestation; (3) reliability of the textual witness (traditionally scholars have weighted the MT more heavily).

3. Determine the Most Plausible Reading

Once steps 1 and 2 have been completed, a final determination can be made. Wegner summarizes the process for arriving at a conclusion:

> This evaluation process is sometimes difficult because some of the evidence may be missing. The two most important guidelines, however, are trying to determine (1) the reading that would most likely give rise to the other readings . . . and (2) the reading that is most appropriate in context. . . . Common sense, caution and logic must prevail—sometimes several readings are possible. In general the MT often contains the most reliable reading even though in some instances its readings can apparently be improved. . . . The overall thought of the passage will not usually change significantly no matter which variant is chosen. (Wegner, SGTC, 133)

4. Conjectural Emendation

One final option available to scholars, although considered highly speculative, is conjectural emendation. (See Tov, TC,

325–331) These emendations (changes) are scholarly "best-guesses" as to how the original may have read.

B. Intentional Changes and Unintentional Scribal Errors

Although it cannot be denied that unintended errors and intentional modifications have occurred to the biblical texts over time, most of these can be identified, categorized, and properly understood in their relation to the overall reliability of the transmission of the original content of Scripture.

1. Unintentional Scribal Errors

It was natural in the course of centuries of hand copying and transmitting biblical texts that unintended mistakes were made due to the fallibility of human scribes. For the most part, these mistakes are easily identified by the text critic and, therefore, do very little to obfuscate the determination of a most plausible reading of the text. Some examples are:

1. *Mistaken Letters.* The confusion of similar looking letters, such as ד (d, *dālat*) and ר (r, *rēsh*). *Example.* Genesis 10:4 mentions a people group called the "Dodanim," while the same group is called the "Rodanim" in 1 Chronicles 1:7.
2. *Homophony.* The substitution of words that sound similar. This is similar to mistaking "its" for "it's" or "there" for "their" in English.
3. *Haplography.* The omission of a letter or word, which "can easily happen when, in copying a text, one's eye skips ahead to another word or line with the same word or letter." (Wegner, SGTC, 46)
4. *Dittography.* The doubling of a letter or word (i.e. the opposite of haplography). *Example.* In Jeremiah 51:3a the verb *yidrok*

("he drew a bow") is written twice. This error was later corrected by the Masoretes by removing the second word.

Other unintended errors (e.g., metathesis, fusion, fission, *homoioteleuton*, and *homoioarkton*) are easily identified in textual transmission and bear no significant effect on the meaning of the text.

2. Intentional Changes

Manuscript evidence demonstrates a desire to preserve the biblical narratives, while at the same time attempting to make them relevant to the culture in which the scribe was living. This in no way casts doubt on the reverence that Jewish scribes had for the text, as most of these intentional changes were meant to add clarity. As Wegner states,

> The Jewish nation believed the Scriptures were a living book with continuing relevance, prompting scribes occasionally to update or expand the text to make it more readily understandable. . . . In their zealousness to preserve Scripture, scribes had a tendency to include everything in the text (e.g., glosses, marginal notes, insertions) rather than omit anything; thereby expanding the text in some places. (Wegner, SGTC, 50, 51)

Wegner lays out six categories of intentional changes made by scribes (the following information is adapted from Wegner, SGTC, 50–55):

1. *Spelling and Grammar Changes.* Archaic language tended to be updated to the language contemporary with the community and culture in order to further comprehension.
2. *Harmonization.* The modification of a passage for the purpose of bringing it in

line with a parallel passage. *Example.* In MT, Genesis 14:14 states that Abraham pursued Lot's captors as far as the city of Dan. However, according to Judges 18:29 and Joshua 19:47, the city would not have been known as Dan until much later. Hence, a scribe updated the place name in Genesis 14:14 from its older names, Laish (Judg. 18:29) and Leshem (Josh. 19:47), to the name of the same city that would have been familiar to his audience.

3. *Euphemistic Changes.* Scribes changed certain elements of the text that they considered inappropriate or offensive to the sensitivities of the culture. *Example.* A later recension of the LXX 2 Samuel 12:9 states, "Why have you despised the Lord?" The MT uses a more subtle form of the same question, "Why have you despised *the word of* the Lord?" This seems to be an attempt by the MT to lighten David's rebuking by the prophet Nathan. (Würthwein, TOT, 178–179)

4. *Theological Changes.* These occurred because God or other biblical persons were displayed in an unfavorable or irreverent manner. *Example.* Genesis 18:22 originally stated that "God remained standing before Abraham." However, the image of standing before someone had come to denote a role of servitude to that person. Therefore, the sentence structure was rearranged.

5. *Additions and Glosses.* There are many instances in which explanatory notes were inserted into the text in order to clarify words or phrases that would have been difficult to understand.

6. *Other Changes.* Typically, these would be modifications to rare words, unclear phrases, or words used in an unorthodox manner. *Example.* The MT uses the verb *hazaq* in Isaiah 39:1 to signify, "to get well, or recuperate." This seems to have been replaced with a more common word in the Qumran scroll (1QIsaᵃ), *haya*, "to live, revive, recuperate."

Despite the fact that there have been intentional modifications to the text in order to provide clarity and relevance to the community contemporary with the scribe, modern readers need not be concerned that these changes compromise the reliability or accuracy of the Bible we have today. In many cases the changes are obvious and scholars can identify the original reading with a high degree of confidence.

VI. Concluding Remarks

As to the evidence for the reliability and accuracy of the transmission of Old Testament narratives prior to our oldest extant manuscripts, our objective has been to show that: (1) oral transmission was not only primary in ANE cultures, but also reliable and authoritative; (2) evidence suggests a dramatic increase of written transmission as early as the eighth century BC; (3) archaeological evidence has confirmed to a high degree the context of even the earliest OT historical narratives; and (4) Jesus and the New Testament writers viewed the written forms of the OT as authoritative and inspired by God.

A. Oral Transmission in ANE Cultures

Embedded in the scholarship of much of contemporary biblical criticism is a reliance on false presuppositions made by nineteenth- and early twentieth-century biblical scholars who failed to account properly for the primacy and authority of orality over textuality intrinsic to the ANE cultures that they were attempting to understand. Schniedewind critiques the worldview that produced these mistaken ideas:

Such documentary theories begin with the worldview of a textual culture; that is, they begin with the worldview of modern critics, not ancient cultures. . . . Some scholars have pointed out that the oral world of early Israel hardly suits a complex documentary approach to the literature of Israel. Israel's traditions, they argue, were largely transmitted orally like the epics of Homer. . . . Widespread literacy is a relatively modern phenomenon. Ancient Israel was primarily an oral culture. . . . Orally composed literature should not be caricatured as rustic or unsophisticated. Works such as Homer's *Iliad* and *Odyssey* serve as prime examples of the power, complexity, and sophistication that oral literature can possess. Oral compositions can be complex, and written texts can be simple. Moreover, even when we begin to have written texts, the oral world leaves its mark on them. (Schniedewind, HBBB, 10, 11, 12–13)

1. Primacy of Oral Traditions

John Walton, professor of Old Testament at Wheaton College, provides a concise account of the central role oral traditions played in ancient Israel:

Returning to the hearing-dominant culture of the ancient world, it's at least clear that orality was valued over textuality in many cases. Though it seems illogical to us, the ancients considered oral texts to be adequate means of composing and communicating literature, including acts of preserving and interpreting. Even for those who had the ability to write, oral communication could be preferred. (Walton and Sandy, LWS, 95)

As to the reason for the preference of orality over textuality, Walton continues:

Textuality provided no means for relationship or discussion between teachers and students. . . . Furthermore, reading a book might lead someone to think they had learned a body of material, but for them only to repeat what was written in a book was an illusion of knowledge. . . . Orality functions particularly well in communicating powerful messages to smaller groups of people. (Walton and Sandy, LWS, 103, 92)

In light of this oral primacy, again Schniedewind writes about the inadequacy of some modern-day theories:

For example, very complex models of the composition, redaction, and editing of biblical literature into multiple layers by many different hands appear to me not only to be unreasonably subjective but also to require sophisticated concepts of textuality and quite developed Hebrew scribal schools that just cannot be warranted based on the external evidence from archaeology and inscriptions. Even if such unlikely models of multiple authors, redactors, and editors could be justified within the social, economic, and political contexts of ancient Israel, we do not have the tools to convincingly unravel the hypothetical strands. More fundamentally, however, the role of writing and social history point to much simpler models for the composition and growth of biblical literature. (Schniedewind, HBBB, 119)

2. Ability of Orators

Craig S. Keener, professor of New Testament at Asbury Theological Seminary, demonstrates the capacity of ancient Greco-Roman orators to memorize and recite large amounts of information:

Some schools were known for practicing diligent training of their memories; the Pythagoreans reportedly would not rise from bed in the mornings until they had recited their previous days' works. Difficult as it may seem to most readers today, the elder Seneca testifies that in his younger days he could repeat 2000 names in exactly the sequence in which he had just heard them, or recite up to 200 verses given to him, in reverse (Seneca *Controv.* 1. pref.2). Even if his recollections of youthful prowess are exaggerated, they testify to an emphasis on memory that far exceeds standard expectations today. Seneca also reports that another man, hearing a poem recited by its author, recited it back to the author verbatim (facetiously claiming the poem to be his own); and that the famous Hortensius listed every purchaser and price at the end of a day-long auction, his accuracy attested by the bankers (Seneca *Controv.* 1.pref.19). (Keener, GJ, 57)

In addition, Keener alludes to the higher degree of accuracy with which orators may have transmitted their narratives as compared with their scribal counterparts:

In the circles of trained storytellers and sages, memories may preserve information accurately from one generation to the next. Indeed, oral traditioning might invite less redaction than written sources would. Folklorists have shown that some communities transmit traditions faithfully, with minimal modifications; storytellers create and vary within the constraints of community tradition. Some suggest that writers were far more likely to introduce substantial changes. (Keener, GJ, 54–55)

Even today, in our highly textualized culture, we often experience the power of orally transmitted material and our own capacity accurately to retain material we have learned from oral sources. Walton illustrates this phenomenon:

People in churches today who were raised on hymns recognize immediately when even a single word has been changed, whether for updating language or gender-inclusive inclinations. . . . In a chapel service yesterday we sang a hymn that I probably had not sung or heard in decades. In the fourth verse a line was changed and it immediately caught my attention. Our ears can be very demanding about the precise transmission of treasured traditions, and that would have been even more the case in a society in which oral transmission of tradition was the norm. (Walton and Sandy, LWS, 19)

This evidence about the power and validity of oral memory and the capacity of orators in the biblical era to transmit oral material accurately establishes a trustworthy foundation upon which the biblical text was built.

3. Authority of the Spoken Word

Schniedewind shows that it was not necessarily the identity of the author of a biblical text that established its authority over a community, but the oral presentation of traditional historical narratives and religious laws:

Through such songs, stories, and proverbial sayings the traditions of the mothers and fathers were passed along to their sons and daughters. Even the Torah itself was primarily given orally to Israel—although it would come to be the *written* text above all others. The earliest account of the giving of the Ten Commandments, in Exodus 19–20, actually never even mentions writing the Commandments down. This glaring omission points to the antiquity of this account of the Sinai tradition, because it reflects a time *before books were central to Jewish culture.* . . . The fundamental orality of early Israel is reflected in the genre of many of the society's primary texts. . . . One example in biblical literature is the prophetic messenger formula, "Thus says YHWH." In the Bible, this phrase becomes a set written formula, but it has its setting in the oral delivery of messages. . . . Thus, even when we have written texts, the oral world often pervades their written expression. (Schniedewind, HBBB, 12, 13)

Having established an overall reliability of oral transmission, we can now posit a reliable transmission of biblical material from the occurrence of the events to their later textualization in written form.

B. The Bible as Text

Schniedewind convincingly counters theories from biblical minimalists who suggest the narratives of the Old Testament are late Hellenistic era inventions cut from whole cloth:

To be fair, the Bible—that is, the collection of canonized books of the Bible as we have come to know them—was produced between the fifth century BCE and the fourth century C.E. This does not mean, however, that biblical literature was first composed or written down during this period. . . . Although the fragmentary beginnings of the Bible as written literature may date back to the days of kings David and Solomon (in the tenth century BCE), the majority of the Bible was written a few centuries later, from the time of Isaiah the prophet (late eighth century BCE) until the waning days of the monarchy and the time of the prophet Jeremiah (early sixth century BCE). (Schniedewind, HBBB, 18, 19)

While Schniedewind's thesis provides good evidence for an increase in the textualization of the Torah and the authoritative

histories of Israel during the reigns of Hezekiah (715–687 BC) and Josiah (640–609 BC), he does not suggest that the stories or laws of ancient Israel were created at this time. In fact, strong evidence demonstrates that scribal writing existed long before this period, even among less advanced ANE cultures:

There were scribes in the major Canaanite cities during the second millennium BCE, even though the vast majority of people were non-literate. The use of writing and the early formation of written literature in ancient Israel depended upon the needs of the early Israelite state. Even petty Canaanite kings had royal scribes during the Late Bronze and early Iron Ages (between the fifteenth and ninth centuries BCE). Writing was not unknown in early Israel, but the level and sophistication of early Israelite literature was necessarily tied to the development of the state. (Schniedewind, HBBB, 49)

From this we can conclude plausibly that versions of the original biblical narratives existed, having been written as early as the Late Bronze and early Iron Ages. Beyond this we can juxtapose the content of each book of the Old Testament with the external archaeological evidence from those time periods. By doing so, we will be able to discover in the text details of the Late Bronze and early Iron Age cultures.

C. Archaeology and the Old Testament

At the end of his treatise on the correlation between archaeological evidence of ANE culture and the narratives and events presented in the OT books, Kenneth Kitchen, former professor emeritus of Egyptology at the University of Liverpool, concludes:

It is time to return to the questions posed at the beginning of this book: whether or not the existing Old Testament writings were composed (and their contents originated) entirely within the brief and late period of circa 400–200 BC, or whether or not their contents are pure fiction, unrelated to the world of the Near East in circa 2000–400 BC. To pursue such questions, the only practical method of inquiry was to go back to those ancient times and compare the data in the Hebrew Bible with what we have from its putative world. Merely theorizing in one's head can achieve nothing. Looking back, we do have some definite results. On the independent evidence from antiquity itself, we may safely deliver a firm "No" to both questions as posed above. Namely, the Old Testament books and their contents did *not* exclusively originate as late as 400–200 BC; and they are by no means pure fiction—in fact, there is very little proven fiction in them overall. . . . When we go back (before ca. 1000) to periods when inscriptional mentions of a then-obscure tribal community and its antecedent families (and founding family) simply cannot be expected *a priori*, then chronologically typological comparisons of the biblical and external phenomena show clearly that the Hebrew founders bear the marks of reality and of a definite period. The same applies to the Hebrew's exodus from Egypt and appearance in Canaan, with one clear mention, of course (Israel on the stela of Merenptah). The Sinai covenant (all three versions, Deuteronomy included) has to have originated within a close-set period (1400–1200) . . . The phenomena of the united monarchy fit well into what we know of the period and of ancient royal usages. The primeval protohistory embodies early popular tradition going very far back, and is set in an early format. Thus we have a consistent level of good, fact-based correlations right through from circa 2000 BC (with earlier roots) down to 400 BC. In terms of general reliability—and

much more could have been instanced than there was room for here—the Old Testament comes out remarkably well, so long as its writings and writers are treated fairly and evenhandedly, in line with independent data, open to all. (Kitchen, OROT, 499, 500)

We will present more archaeological confirmation of the Old Testament's historical accuracy in later chapters.

D. The New Testament View of the Old Testament

It is undeniable that Jesus himself, and the New Testament writers, considered the writings of the Old Testament as both inspired by God and authoritative for their respective communities.

1. Jesus' View of the Old Testament

VanderKam points to Matthew 19:3–9, which records a dispute between Jesus and the Pharisees regarding divorce, as an object lesson that demonstrates Jesus' regard for the authoritative nature of OT Scripture:

A helpful example occurs in Matt 19:3–9 (par. Mark 10:2–12), a discussion between some Pharisees and Jesus regarding a practical yet complicated issue—divorce. . . . It is evident from the ways in which the encounters are recorded that both Jesus and his opponents knew and relied upon the scriptures as determinative in disputes. . . . There is much to weigh in this passage, but the point relevant here is that both the Pharisees and Jesus assume the question they are discussing is to be answered from the scriptures—something so obvious that no one in the scene comments on it or raises a question about it. The books to which they appeal are in the Torah—Genesis and Deuteronomy—and both sides accept the authority of those books and are able to produce relevant data from them as needed. (VanderKam, DSSB, 53, 54)

Clearly, then, Jesus viewed the OT writings as authoritative because he believed they were the inspired words of God, spoken through Moses. Other passages in the Gospels indicate that Jesus believed Moses was the final authority behind the Torah, while also equally affirming the authority of the Major and Minor Prophets (e.g., Mark 7:10; 12:26; Luke 5:14; 16:29–31; 24:27, 44; John 5:45–47; 7:19, 23).

2. New Testament Authors' View of the Old Testament

It is also obvious that the Old Testament was viewed as authoritative by the New Testament authors and the early Christian Church. McDonald describes the reverence for and acceptance of the Old Testament by the New Testament authors as well as the early church fathers:

The Christians believed that the whole story of God's plans and purposes for Israel developed in the OT Scriptures had reached its completion in the life and work of Jesus. The NT writers saw continuity in what they were describing, presenting, or advocating with the ancient Jewish Scriptures. They fully accepted them as the authoritative word of God.... There can be no question that the OT Scriptures were viewed by the earliest church as an authoritative source for Christian faith and life.... Almost every point of faith, order, and morals in *1 Clement* is driven home with the aid of OT citations or quotations. For Polycarp, the Prophets were inseparable from the authority of Jesus and the apostles ... (Pol. *Phil.* 6.3, LCL). (McDonald, BC, 207, 208)

Other NT writings recognize the inspired nature and authority of the OT Law and Prophets (e.g., Mark 12:19; Luke 2:22; 20:28; John 1:17, 45; 8:5; 9:29; Acts 3:22; 6:14; 13:39; 15:1, 21; 26:22; 28:23; Romans 10:5; 1 Corinthians 9:9; 2 Corinthians 3:15; Hebrews 9:19; Revelation 15:3).

From this we can reasonably conclude that Jesus, the New Testament authors, and the early Christian Church viewed the Old Testament as inspired by God, originally written by or spoken through the prophets, and accurately transmitted through the generations to the time of Jesus Christ himself.

E. Is the Old Testament Authoritative?

Based on the evidence given, it is reasonable to conclude the following: (1) The text of the Hebrew Bible was copied with a high degree of accuracy from the time of the first century CE through the MT to our present day exemplars; (2) while numerous textual traditions existed in the Second Temple Period, this would not have been a stumbling block for the overall view of the authority of the biblical books as this pluriformity was both fully acknowledged and accepted; (3) the identifiable variants between the primary textual traditions (e.g., MT, LXX, SP, DSS) bear little significance to the core theological truths and historical accuracy contained within each text; and (4) the content of the textual witnesses of the Hebrew Bible correlate to the periods of antiquity in which they were supposedly written.

In conclusion, the words of the Chicago Statement on Biblical Inerrancy seem especially appropriate:

Since God has nowhere promised an inerrant transmission of Scripture, it is necessary to affirm that only the autographic text of the original documents was inspired and to maintain the need of textual criticism as a means of detecting any slips that may have crept into the text in the course of its transmission. The verdict of this science, however, is that the Hebrew and Greek text appear to be amazingly well preserved, so that we are amply justified in affirming, with the Westminster Confession, a singular providence of God in this matter and in declaring that the authority of Scripture is in no way jeopardized by the fact that the copies we possess are not entirely error-free.

Similarly, no translation is or can be perfect, and all translations are an additional step away from the *autographa*. Yet the verdict of linguistic science is that English-speaking Christians, at least, are exceedingly well served in these days with a host of excellent translations and have no cause for hesitating to conclude that the true Word of God is within their reach. Indeed, in view of the frequent repetition in Scripture of the main matters with which it deals and also of the Holy Spirit's constant witness to and through the Word, no serious translation of Holy Scripture will so destroy its meaning as to render it unable to make its reader "wise for salvation through faith in Christ Jesus" (2 Tim. 3:15). (quoted in Henry, GRA4, 218)

CHAPTER 5

GNOSTIC GOSPELS AND OTHER NONBIBLICAL TEXTS

OVERVIEW

I. One Christianity or Many?

Many people have speculated about how "lost" books of the Bible might radically transform the way we view Jesus and Christianity. Popular books like *The Da Vinci Code* argue that the creation of the Bible was political and that those in power purposely excluded certain books from the canon. Behind the ideas and questions in this chapter, one can discern the influence of Michel Foucault. Specifically, he says that we do not have knowledge per se—we have "power-knowledge"; that is, we have been conned by whatever authorities hold power. In other words, we have accepted a particular point of view based on what we think is reliable knowledge, but our beliefs consist of what is foisted upon us by those who hold power over public opinion. The argument of *The Da Vinci Code* about the Bible assumes that this political dynamic is the way beliefs develop and applies it to the history of Christianity.*

Is it true that there is no real orthodox Christianity, but just one type of Christianity that happened to win out over the others?

---

* Michel Foucault has been a pivotal figure behind the shift to postmodern relativism, i.e., the loss of belief in objective truth. Postmodern academic culture is pervaded by claims that so-called knowledge is really indoctrination or oppression of one sort or another. Suspicion becomes the accepted way of thinking about truth-statements, along with the assumption that researching the history of a developing idea is like researching genealogy—it will reveal a history of interacting ideas in a power struggle, and the victorious idea will be received as what everyone agrees to be the case. Pervading popular culture and fueling political correctness, Foucault's description of how cultures think asserts that our presumed truths have come to us from the winners of the struggle. Chapter 30 treats this important topic.

Could we have a drastically different Christianity today had another sect won? Are there legitimate books that should be included in the canon but were deliberately omitted?

In his book *Lost Christianities*, agnostic New Testament scholar Bart Ehrman argues the following:

> Virtually all forms of modern Christianity, whether they acknowledge it or not, go back to *one* form of Christianity that emerged as victorious from the conflicts of the second and third centuries. This one form of Christianity decided what was the "correct" Christian perspective; it decided who could exercise authority over Christian belief and practice; and it determined what forms of Christianity would be marginalized, set aside, destroyed. It also decided which books to canonize into Scripture and which books to set aside as "heretical," teaching false ideas. (Ehrman, LC, 4)

Because of the importance of this charge, we need to examine whether we ought to trust our current Bible as the source of true Christianity.

II. What Is Gnosticism?

Many of the noncanonical texts are categorized as—and were rejected for being—Gnostic. Scholars continue to debate the origins and definition of Gnosticism; many deny it ever existed as an ancient religion; instead, they say, it should be viewed as a perspective within a religion, similar to *fundamentalist* or *progressive*. Still, it is a useful category, as it enables us to distinguish between what has traditionally been held as orthodox and heretical. Broadly speaking, Gnosticism centered on knowledge (*gnosis*). A Gnostic was dedicated to searching for secret teachings and hidden wisdom, so Gnostic Christians may have focused less on Jesus as savior and more on Jesus as a teacher of wisdom. This is because a basic tenet of Gnosticism was matter-spirit dualism, meaning that matter is inherently evil—and so irredeemable. Only spirit can be redeemed. Thus, Gnostics denied a bodily resurrection; they held to a docetic view of Jesus—that, as God, Jesus did not really have a physical body but only *seemed* to be human.

III. Who Decides Orthodoxy?

Was orthodoxy established by the winners of ancient religious and political debates, as Ehrman asserts above? Esteemed historian Philip Jenkins says no:

> Far from being the alternative voices of Jesus' first followers, most of the lost gospels should rather be seen as the writings of much later dissidents who broke away from an already established orthodox church. This is not a particularly controversial statement, despite the impression that we may get from much recent writing on the historical Jesus.

Far from being the alternative voices of Jesus' first followers, most of the lost gospels should rather be seen as the writings of much later dissidents who broke away from an already established orthodox church.

Philip Jenkins

But the institutional church was by no means an oppressive latecomer, and was rather a very early manifestation of the Jesus movement. We have a good number of genuinely early documents of Christian antiquity from before 125, long before the hidden gospels were composed, and these give us a pretty consistent picture of a church which is already hierarchical and liturgical, which possesses an organized clergy, and which is very sensitive to matters of doctrinal orthodoxy. Just as the canonical gospels were in existence before their heterodox counterparts, so the orthodox church did precede the heretics, and by a comfortable margin. (Jenkins, HG, 12–13)

Michael F. Bird says:

The rejection of "other" Gospels by the proto-orthodox and orthodox churches was neither arbitrary nor merely political. The reasons for rejecting them were cogent and compelling. Among the main criticisms raised against the "other" Gospels and their authors were that (1) the "Jesus" they set forth was not recognizable as the Jesus known in other sacred writings or congruent with apostolic tradition, (2) the "other" Gospels are often esoteric, elitist, or erroneous in what they affirm about God, creation, sin, holiness, ethics, and redemption, and (3) they do not properly have origins among Jesus' earliest followers and are late and tendentious. (Bird, GL, 293)

Dating is key to determining the authenticity of extracanonical writings. New Testament scholar Craig Evans thinks "none of these extracanonical writings originated earlier than the middle of the second century" and since they are dated so late, "it is unlikely that they contain information that adds to our knowledge of Jesus." (Evans, FJ, 52) The problem is not using extrabiblical sources to

help inform our studies of the Bible but the "often uncritical acceptance of some of the extracanonical Gospels." (Evans, FJ, 54)

Aside from dating problems, Catholic scholar John P. Meier thinks none of the extracanonical gospels

offer us reliable new information or authentic sayings that are independent of the NT. What we see in these later documents is rather the reaction to or reworking of NT writings by Jewish rabbis engaged in polemics, imaginative Christians reflecting popular piety and legend, and gnostic Christians developing a mystic speculative system. (Meier, MJ, 140)

But these are the views of modern scholars. In relation to the books that did make it into the canon, how were the "lost" gospels regarded in ancient times? In an appendix to the book *The Canon Debate*, Lee McDonald provides thirty lists of New Testament collections from the second to sixth century. The *Gospel of Thomas* is the only so-called gnostic gospel that appears in any of them, and only in one. (McDonald, LCNTC, 591–597) New Testament scholar Craig Blomberg says, "There is no indication that gnostics or any other sect tried to create a rival canon or even sought inclusion of extra books in the orthodox canon." (Blomberg, CWSBB, 58) This shows that none of these "lost" gospels were ever considered to be on par with the rest of Scripture and that there was no conspiracy to exclude them.

IV. Methods of Analysis

It is important to understand the means by which scholars like the Jesus Seminar examine the Gospels, both canonical and noncanonical. They assume that because Jesus' culture was an oral one and written records were secondary, any texts must then be stripped down to their primary, oral roots. This assumption occurs because these scholars were shaped by the prevailing dogma of literary criticism in the 1960s-80s, which declared that all writing is secondary to its original oral form of communication, and that all written texts are therefore to be approached with suspicion. Accordingly, they maintained that the original teachings of Jesus must be meticulously reconstructed by sifting out from the written texts only those words that probably were those spoken by Jesus.

Evans explains that sometimes scholars are able to extract earlier sources from extant (existing) texts. For example, since Matthew and Luke contain so many similar sayings that do not appear in Mark, scholars believe they shared a common source, which they call Q. But Evans differentiates between this and what scholars such as the Jesus Seminar do when they reconstruct hypothetical texts. He says writings such as the *Gospel of Thomas* and *Gospel of Peter*

> drip with indications of lateness, yet some scholars hope to date forms of these writings to the first century. They do this by attempting to extract early, hypothetic forms of the text from the actual texts that we have. But they do this without any evidence. (Evans, FJ, 56)

New Testament scholar Ben Witherington also criticizes their methods:

> The textual scholars are dealing with actual manuscripts and are trying to reconstruct the original text from objective data. The Jesus Seminar, however, . . . must engage in

reconstruction *before* they can even consider the issues at hand. . . . There is furthermore no truly objective evidence whatsoever for supposing that *Thomas* and *Peter* are earlier documents, and/or that in almost all cases they preserve earlier traditions than does Mark. There is, however, the objective testimony of early church fathers such as Papias about the origins of Mark, however critically we must evaluate such testimonies. Such testimonies are nowhere found for *Thomas*, or *Secret Mark*, or the *Gospel of Peter*, or a variety of other documents on which Crossan and the Jesus Seminar rely so heavily. (Witherington, JQ, 78, emphasis in original)

Meier says "It is only natural for scholars—to say nothing of popularizers—to want more, to want other access roads to the historical Jesus" and that this "not always critical desire" is what leads to such a "high evaluation" of extracanonical writings. He adds, "For better or for worse, in our quest for the historical Jesus, we are largely confined to the canonical Gospels" and to include other gospels like *Peter* or *Thomas* with them "is to broaden out our pool of sources from the difficult to the incredible." (Meier, MJ, 140–141)

V. The "Lost" Gospels

Now we examine some of the most frequently cited and argued-for extracanonical writings to see why they should not be included in the canon.*

A. Gospel of Thomas

In 1945 a collection of codices written in the Coptic language was found in Egypt near

---

* For an in-depth and careful analysis of the criteria utilized by the early church for inclusion in the canon, see Michael J. Kruger, *The Question of Canon* (Downers Grove, IL: InterVarsity Press, 2013). We agree with his assessment that the canonical books were written with divine authority, were recognized and used by early Christians as Scripture, and that the church subsequently reached a consensus about these books.

Nag Hammadi. Among the discovered texts was the *Gospel of Thomas*. Upon its discovery, scholars realized three fragments of it in Greek had already been found in Oxyrhynchus, Egypt, in the 1890s, with the earliest fragment being dated to around AD 200. *Thomas* is a collection of 114 sayings mostly attributed to Jesus. It presents a very different Jesus from those in the canonical Gospels. For instance, according to saying 114, "The female element must make itself male." And sayings 2 and 3 state, "Seek until you find. The kingdom is within us." The Jesus of *Thomas* provides secret truths only to those who are qualified to learn them. Unlike the biblical Gospels, there is no narrative and no discussion of Christ's death and resurrection.

Thomas is the most hotly debated of all noncanonical gospels, with the Jesus Seminar going as far as to place it alongside Matthew, Mark, Luke, and John in their book *The Five Gospels*. Is *Thomas* truly a lost gospel?

1. The Criterion of Independence from the Synoptic Gospels

A criterion that scholars employ when assessing the value of testimony is its status as an independent witness. Those who, like the Jesus Seminar, support *The Gospel of Thomas* as a valid witness to Jesus' life therefore support its independence from the Synoptic Gospels. However, the wider community of scholars is divided as to the influence of the canonical Gospels on *Thomas*. New Testament scholar and historian of early Christianity John Dominic Crossan supports its independence. He states:

> The *Gospel of Thomas* is a completely separate and parallel stream of the Jesus tradition. It is not dependent on the inner four and they are in no way dependent on it. They are parallel traditions. (Crossan, FOG, 183)

The following are some common arguments for *Thomas*'s independence, each followed by a response to the argument.

Argument 1: Genre

Thomas is a sayings source, similar to Q, with "no trace of the narrative framework into which the sayings are often embedded in the Gospels of the canon." (Koester, ACG, 85) It is something utterly unlike the canonical gospels.

To give privileged importance to sayings rather than to narrative again reflects the intellectual climate shaping the method that theological criticism adopted from a dominant approach to literary criticism in the 1960s–80s, as noted above. New Testament expert Mark Goodacre of Duke University replies that we cannot automatically prioritize collections of sayings over narratives:

> Neither has an obviously greater antiquity, and there is no reason to imagine that the earliest Christians began with sayings collections and only later moved on to narrative books. . . . [T]he argument for *Thomas*'s antiquity based on its supposed generic similarity to Q is not strong. This comparison between a hypothetical source and an extant text only works on a sketchy level, assuming an unproven greater antiquity for sayings books over narrative books that detracts attention from more fruitful parallels in the second century. (Goodacre, TG, 14)

Argument 2: Order

If *Thomas* used the canonical gospels as a source, parallel content should also share the same order. But Crossan says they share "absolutely no traces of common order." (Crossan, FOG, 35)

Goodacre responds:

The argument from lack of common order . . . imposes an expectation derived from the sustained agreements in order among Matthew, Mark, and Luke, agreements that are unusually strong and result in part at least from their shared narrative structure. The self-consciously enigmatic nature of *Thomas*'s sayings collection precludes the likelihood of that kind of sustained logical sequence. (Goodacre, TG, 17)

In contrast to Crossan's claim that the unique order followed by *Thomas* gives evidence of its independence and thus its value, Goodacre points to its content and tone as clues to a different purpose and resulting order: Without a narrative context, the collection of sayings generates mystery, ambiguity. It doesn't make its appeal by chronological order.

Prominent New Testament scholar Simon Gathercole notes that there are in fact "several cases where adjacent sayings in *Thomas* are also juxtaposed in the Synoptics." He remarks, "A number of scholars have described *Thomas* as a 'list', sentence-collection, or anthology, in which cases one would not expect order to be as important as it clearly is in a narrative," and concludes, "the argument from lack of shared order is deeply flawed." (Gathercole, CGT, 131–132)

Argument 3: Earlier Tradition

Helmut Koester, scholar of the New Testament and early Christianity at Harvard Divinity School, argues that "in many cases a saying or parable, as it appears in the *Gospel of Thomas*, is preserved in a form that is more original than any of its canonical parallels." (Koester, ACG, 85) Koester, presuming that *Thomas* holds the record of an earlier oral tradition, considers that where a saying in *Thomas* varies from its parallel in the canonical gospels, that variance in

the wording appears because the writer of *Thomas* has used some other (and presumably earlier) source. But again, Goodacre argues that it may well differ because it comes later than the canonicals and edits them for its own purpose.

Goodacre counters:

It is in principle likely that in taking over source material, he [the author of *Thomas*] would not retain everything in the material he is using. Writers are not obliged to take over everything they find in their sources, and it is never surprising to see authors editing material to suit their needs. Indeed, one might expect the author of *Thomas* to edit source material in order to reflect his distinctive agenda, not least if the text is aiming to be enigmatic.

He continues:

We have little trouble in seeing Matthew and Luke redacting Mark without inheriting all of the tradition-historical baggage owned by the Markan text. Even a relatively short amount of time with a Gospel synopsis will provide the reader with plenty of examples of Matthew and Luke radically altering their source material . . . .

The situation is no different when it comes to sayings material. When one evangelist is working from a source, he may or may not carry over elements that illustrate that saying's tradition history.

Goodacre concludes, "It is unrealistic to expect *Thomas* to have taken over all 'the accumulated tradition-historical baggage' from the Synoptics." (Goodacre, TG, 18–19)

Argument 4: Verbatim agreement

According to this argument, *Thomas* does not have enough verbatim (word-for-word) correspondence with the Synoptics, so it must be an independent witness to the life of Jesus.

In responding, Gathercole and Goodacre both point out a false premise in the argument for independence: Has the criterion of "enough" verbatim correspondence (defined as what we see between the Synoptics) been misapplied to become a requirement for any text that might share their history or be dependent upon them? The problem is that the amount of verbatim agreement within the Synoptics can set the standard too high in assessing similarity between the Synoptics and *Thomas*. Gathercole says:

> Some scholars are impressed by the level of agreement among the Synoptics and so adopt that level as a baseline of comparison. . . . By this standard, however, a great many cases of influence in ancient literature would fail. (Gathercole, CGT, 139)

Goodacre states what the true expectation should be: "In order for *Thomas*'s familiarity with the Synoptics to be established, one only requires knowledge of the Synoptics in certain places. It does not need to be a 'consistent pattern.'" (Goodacre, TG, 46)

One of the many specific examples of verbatim agreement he provides is between Oxyrhynchus fragment P.Oxy 1.1–4 (Thomas 26), Matthew 7:5, and Luke 6:42. It is a thirteen-word agreement that he thinks "points to direct contact between the texts in question." (Goodacre, TG, 31)

2. The Argument for its Dependence on the Synoptic Gospels

Although arguments in favor of *Thomas*'s independence have been refuted, do any arguments exist to show that the author of *Thomas* was in fact familiar with the Synoptics? As noted above, *Thomas* shares some

verbatim agreement with them as well as common traditions. But this only displays mutual familiarity of content, perhaps through common sources or traditions. To prove *Thomas* is dependent on the Synoptics and therefore follows them but alters them, one must show that there are elements of *Thomas* that came directly from them, such as Matthean and Lukan redactions of Mark. However, Koester denies such dependence when he claims, "There is no evidence that Thomas knew any of the further redactions of the Markan passages by Matthew and/or Luke." (Koester, ACG, 112) Koester's claim supports the claim that Thomas has significance as a different, even a valid, account of the gospel.

But after analyzing the Greek fragments of *Thomas* and Greek versions of the Synoptics, Goodacre finds plenty of evidence that *Thomas* is dependent on them:

> The diagnostic shards . . . that are provided by the presence, in *Thomas*, of Matthean redaction . . . and Lukan redaction . . . are telling. *Thomas* has parallels to places where Matthew and Luke are clearly redacting Markan material, as well as to material that is shot through with the thought and imagery that is characteristic of the evangelists. When *Thomas* uses the Synoptics, its author does not always do so in a coherent fashion, and there is a tendency to reproduce passages with their middles missing. (Goodacre, TG, 193–194)

After a similar analysis, Gathercole concludes:

> There is in *Thomas* what one might term "significant" influence identifiable from Matthew and Luke. The influence is significant not because the redactional elements . . . which appear in *Thomas* are remarkably extensive

in any particular places, but rather because these redactional traces appear in eleven out of twenty sayings in which they might be identified. (Gathercole, CGT, 223)

He further argues "that the *Gospel of Thomas* is aware of at least one Pauline epistle." Again, this would make the author of *Thomas* dependent upon the apostolic tradition of writings that entered the canon and suggest that Thomas is put forward as an alternate view on that tradition. Gathercole thinks "The clearest sign of Pauline influence on *Thomas* is probably that of Romans 2.25–3.2 on *GTh* 53." (Gathercole, CGT, 228–229) He also speculates influence from Hebrews and the hypothetical "Two Ways" tradition. (Gathercole, CGT, 250–62 and 263–66)

Evans finds even further NT influence on *Thomas* in its "quoting or alluding to more than half of the writings of the New Testament (that is, Matthew, Mark, Luke, John, Acts, Romans, 1-2 Corinthians, Galatians, Ephesians, Colossians, 1 Thessalonians, 1 Timothy, Hebrews, 1 John, Revelation)." (Evans, FJ, 68)

If *The Gospel of Thomas* relies on an awareness of the gospels and epistles that did enter the canon, then it is not independent (with value as an equivalent or even a better record of what Jesus said), but subordinate and possibly even subversive in what it teaches. That would explain why the Jesus Seminar scholars would include it in the canon and the church fathers did not.

3. The Syrian Theory

One noteworthy theory has been raised by Nicholas Perrin, the Franklin S. Dyrness Professor of Biblical Studies at Wheaton College. While Gathercole and Goodacre argue for a Greek origin to *Thomas*, Perrin

argues that *Thomas* was written in Syria in the late second century AD. Initially, the text may appear to be a random collection of sayings with no order or structure, but when it is translated into Syrian it emerges as "a finely crafted Syriac text, completely knit together by catchwords," which are words used to connect one line or phrase to the next. (Perrin, TT, 157) Perrin believes one of the author's sources was Tatian's *Diatessaron* as it "was the first gospel record in Syriac and Tatian's was also the only Syriac gospel in existence in the second century." (Perrin, TT, 183–184) Further evidence can be seen in the similarities *Thomas* and the *Diatessaron* have in theology and "textual peculiarities," as well as their "shared sequence of sayings." (Perrin, TT, 189) Since most scholars accept that the *Diatessaron* was written around 175 AD, *Thomas* must have been composed after that. (Perrin, TT, 193)

This research into the possible Syrian origin of *Thomas* gives an interesting historical context that suggests why it shows such textual and theological distinctiveness, which again could explain why it was not accounted worthy of inclusion in the canon.

4. The Attempt to Trace Its Composition

While the extant version of *Thomas* evidently depends on the Synoptics (at least), can we find any early, independent material embedded within it? We find this question much more difficult to answer. Various theories exist about the original language and method of composition of *Thomas*. Furthermore, were the sources for *Thomas* oral, textual, or a mixture of both?

Those who argue for an early core of *Thomas* do so according to form criticism and textual reconstruction, trying to find the "purest" version of Jesus' sayings. Of course, all of this is impossible to know for certain.

All we can do is reflect upon the methodology of such critics. Goodacre states:

> The idea that *Thomas* features primitive sayings emerges from the legacy of classical form criticism of the Gospels, and it is an approach that is particularly well illustrated by the work of the Jesus Seminar. (Goodacre, TG, 145)

Goodacre criticizes the Jesus Seminar's "Rules of Oral Evidence," saying they are "form-critical assumptions that do not stand up to scrutiny," with the most problematic being "the bogus 'rule' about simplicity." He notes there is "no such rule as 'the simpler, the earlier'" and that "'simplicity' is in the eye of the beholder." He concludes:

> In classroom sessions where lecturers have an hour to explain form criticism to new students, the tendencies approach offers the chance of illustrating an observable evolutionary model of early Christian tradition. But the model is wrong, and however great the apparent utility, it needs to be abandoned. (Goodacre, TG, 149–150)

Evans lays out a similar criticism, noting that attempts to

> extract hypothetical early versions of *Thomas* from the Coptic and Greek texts that we possess today. . . . strike me as special pleading—that is, because the evidence that actually exists undermines the theory, appeals are made to hypothetical evidence more accommodating to the theory.

The problem here is that we do not know if there ever was an edition of the Gospel of Thomas substantially different from the Greek fragments of Oxyrhynchus or the later Coptic version from Nag Hammadi. Proposing an early form of *Thomas*, stripped of the embarrassing late and secondary features, is a gratuitous move. (Evans, FJ, 68)

5. The Influence of Gnosticism

Thomas claims to be a record of the "secret words" that Jesus taught, so it is not surprising to discover gnostic elements from the very beginning of the book. Evans says, "The private, esoteric orientation of the text is plainly evident. Unlike the canonical Gospels, these writings were for the spiritually elite, not common people . . . .Thomas places emphasis on knowledge and knowing." (Evans, FJ, 64–65)

Meier states, "It is clear that the overarching intention of the redactor of the *Gospel of Thomas* is a gnostic one" and it therefore cannot be relied upon as a historical record: That is not even its own purpose, for what it does is reinterpret Christianity from a later perspective than what the historical gospels give us. He finds little likelihood of its reliability:

> Since a gnostic world view of this sort was not employed to "reinterpret" Christianity in such a thorough-going way before sometime in the 2d century AD, there can be no question of the *Gospel of Thomas* as a whole, as it stands in the Coptic text, being a reliable reflection of the historical Jesus or of the earliest sources of 1st-century Christianity. . . . [I]t is somewhere in the 2d century that the composition we know as the *Gospel of Thomas* took shape as one expression of 2d-century gnostic Christianity. (Meier, MJ, 127)

6. Conclusion Regarding the Gospel of Thomas

Whether *Thomas* is a Syrian text that used Tatian's *Diatessaron* as a source or a Greek text influenced by Greek versions of the Gospels, clearly *Thomas* depends on the canonical gospels. Such dependence—as well as gnostic elements present within the text—discounts it as being an early, reliable source of information about the historical Jesus. And though some want to theorize an earlier version of *Thomas*, there is no objective evidence of such an ancient core. We must rely on the extant texts for our studies.

B. Gospel of Peter

Ancient Christian writers like Eusebius of Caesarea and Serapion, bishop of Antioch, knew of a supposed *Gospel of Peter*. In Akhmim, Egypt in the winter of 1886–1887, fragments of a gospel were found in a codex that has been attributed to Peter. In the 1970s and 80s more fragments were published, believed possibly to be portions of the *Gospel of Peter*.

1. Arguments for Its Independence

Koester thinks *Peter* is "the oldest writing under the authority of Peter himself." He says, "In a number of instances the *Gospel of Peter* contains features that can be traced back to a stage in the development of the passion narrative and the story of the empty tomb which is older than that known by the canonical gospels." (Koester, INT, 162–163) But he does think, "There are numerous features in these accounts which are obviously secondary." (Koester, ACG, 217)

Crossan goes even further, arguing that within *Peter* lies an entire tradition, the *Cross Gospel*, which is "the single known source for the Passion and Resurrection narrative." (Crossan, CTS, 404) He claims it is "earlier than and independent of the intracanonical gospels. Indeed, all four of them know of and use this source." (Crossan, FOG, 184) He proposes three stages for the development of *Peter*: (1) the *Cross Gospel*, (2) its use by the canonical gospels as the sole source of the passion narrative, and (3) the integration

of the *Cross Gospel* and details from the canonical gospels into the final *Gospel of Peter*. (Crossan, FOG, 16–30)

However, Koester finds "major problems" with Crossan's hypothesis; for example, each gospel has differing stories regarding Jesus' post-resurrection appearances. Why would each author select some details and not others? He concludes they "cannot derive from one single source. They are independent of one another. Each of the authors of the extant gospels and of their secondary endings drew these epiphany stories from their own particular tradition, not from a common source." (Koester, ACG, 219–220) But Koester still thinks *Peter*, "as a whole, is not dependent upon any of the canonical gospels." (Koester, ACG, 240)

New Testament scholar Paul Foster argues that the theory of *Peter* being "an independent and early witness to the events of the passion is incorrect." (Foster, GP, 132) After examining the parallels *Peter* has with the Gospels, he offers two conclusions:

First, the *Gospel of Peter* appears to be posterior to the canonical gospels where there are parallel passages. In those case [*sic*] where there is unparalleled material, there is little reason to suppose that this is due to anything other than the author's own creativity. Secondly, a strong case can be mounted for the literary dependence of the *Gospel of Peter* on all three of the synoptic accounts. (Foster, GP, 146)

2. Early or Late Date of Writing

Foster criticizes Crossan's early dating of *Peter*, arguing that even if it does contain a *Cross Gospel* source that does not mean *Peter* must be dated to the first century. He goes on to say, "The majority of critical scholarship, despite the challenges raised by Crossan and [others], still prefers to locate the text in the second century." Foster believes "a date of composition during the period 150–190 CE seems the most sensible suggestion." He notes that "the apparent lack of knowledge of this text in the writings of the Apostolic Fathers, Justin Martyr, or Melito of Sardis" makes it difficult to date it within the first half of the second century. (Foster, GP, 169–172)

Evans criticizes early dating of *Peter* due to ignorance of Jewish customs in the Akhmîm fragment:

> According to 8.31 and 10.38 the Jewish elders and scribes camp out in the cemetery, as part of the guard keeping watch over the tomb of Jesus. Given Jewish views of corpse impurity, not to mention fear of cemeteries at night, the author of our fragment is unbelievably ignorant. Who could write such a story only twenty years after the death of Jesus? And if someone did at such an early time, can we really believe that the Evangelist Matthew, who was surely Jewish, would make use of such a poorly informed writing? One can scarcely credit this scenario. (Evans, FJ, 83)

3. Fantastic Elements

Peter contains fantastic elements, in comparison with the other four canonical Gospel accounts of the resurrection, such as giant angels escorting Jesus from the tomb along with a cross that speaks. Evans comments:

> Can it be seriously maintained that the Akhmîm fragment's resurrection account, complete with a talking cross and angels whose heads reach heaven, constitutes the most primitive account? Is this the account that the canonical Evangelists had before them? Or isn't it more prudent to conclude that what we have here is still more evidence of the secondary, fanciful nature of this apocryphal writing? (Evans, FJ, 84)

However, Koester argues, "Even if a number of features in the *Gospel of Peter* may be due to later legendary growth of a text unprotected by canonical transmission, its basis must be an older text under the authority of Peter which was independent of the canonical gospels." (Koester, INT, 163)

4. Conclusion Regarding the Gospel of Peter

Meier directs a sharp criticism at Crossan's *Cross Gospel* theory: "Crossan has to spin a complicated and sometimes self-contradictory web as he assigns documents questionably early dates or unlikely lines of dependence." He concludes *Peter* is "a 2d-century pastiche of traditions from the canonical Gospels, recycled through the memory and lively imagination of Christians who have heard the Gospels read and preached upon many a time. It provides no special access to early independent tradition about the historical Jesus." (Meier, MJ, 116–118)

Evans concludes:

> The evidence strongly suggests that the Akhmîm Gospel fragment is a late work, not an early work, even if we attempt to find an earlier substratum, gratuitously shorn of imagined late additions. . . . we have no solid evidence that allows us with any confidence to link the extant Akhmîm Gospel fragment with a second-century text, whether the *Gospel of Peter* mentioned by Bishop Serapion or some other writings from the late second century. Given its fantastic features and coherence with late traditions, it is not advisable to make use of this Gospel fragment for Jesus research. (Evans, FJ, 85)

C. Egerton Gospel

Papyrus Egerton 2 (*Egerton Gospel*) consists of four fragments that were discovered in Egypt and delivered to scholars in 1934.

The third and fourth fragments contain only a few words total while the first two fragments contain some stories that parallel the Synoptics and John. Again, Crossan and Koester claim that it presents a very early and independent tradition.

Crossan argues, "Egerton Papyrus 2 evinces a direct relationship with both John and Mark" and that "Mark is dependent on it directly." He says it "shows a stage before the distinction of Johannine and Synoptic traditions was operative." (Crossan, FOG, 183) Koester agrees that it "may well attest an earlier stage of the development in which pre-Johannine and pre-synoptic characteristics of language still existed side by side." (Koester, ACG, 207) Thus, they both think Egerton is evidence of a tradition that existed alongside the canonical gospels. Furthermore, Koester finds it unlikely that someone would have "deliberately composed [it] by selecting sentences from three different gospel writings," and that "to uphold the hypothesis of dependence upon written gospels, one would have to assume that [it] was written from memory." (Koester, ACG, 215)

Evans offers three arguments against Crossan's and Koester's conclusions:

1. "Several times editorial improvements introduced by Matthew and Luke appear in Egerton" along with "other indications that the Egerton Papyrus is later than the canonical Gospels (for example, compare Egerton line 32 with Mk 1:40; Mt 8:2; Lk 5:12; or Egerton lines 39–41 with Mk 1:44; Mt 8:4; Lk 17:14)." (Evans, FJ, 89)
2. Countering Koester's claim that someone would not have composed Egerton by picking and choosing from the Synoptics, Evans reflects on Justin Martyr's harmony of the Synoptics and Tatian's *Diatessaron*. He asks if they, "writing in the second century, can compose their respective harmonies through the selection of sentences and phrases from this Gospel and that Gospel, why couldn't the author of the Egerton Papyrus do the same thing? Indeed, it is likely that this is the very thing he did." (Evans, FJ, 89)
3. If this gospel is as primitive as Crossan and Koester suggest, "then we must wonder why we have no other fragment or any other evidence of the existence of this extraordinarily primitive Gospel. Why don't we have other papyri, extracanonical Gospels or patristic quotations attesting this primitive pre-Synoptic, pre-Johannine unified tradition?" (Evans, FJ, 89–90)

The story of Jesus sowing seed on a river and it producing an abundance of fruit provides further evidence against the antiquity of Egerton, because of its similarity to a story contained in another extracanonical text, the *Infancy Gospel of Thomas*. Evans says it is "important to appreciate the presence of what appears to be a fanciful tale among the passages preserved by the Egerton Papyrus. The appearance of this tale, which is like those that are all too common among the later extracanonical Gospels, significantly increases the burden of proof for those who wish to argue that the Egerton traditions are primitive, even pre-Synoptic." (Evans, FJ, 91–92).]

Evans concludes, "While the hypothesis of Crossan, Koester and others remains a theoretical possibility, the evidence available at this time favors the likelihood that Papyrus Egerton 2 (or the *Egerton Gospel*) represents a second-century combination of elements from the Synoptic Gospels and the Gospel of John rather than primitive first-century material on which the canonical Gospels depended." (Evans, FJ, 92)

D. Gospel of Mary

A Coptic fragment of the *Gospel of Mary* was discovered in the late nineteenth century, with another two Greek fragments becoming known in the twentieth. There is no complete copy of *Mary*, and the three overlapping fragments comprise at most half of the gospel. It tells the story of Mary Magdalene recalling to the disciples teachings Jesus had given her. In this account, Andrew and Peter are highly skeptical as her teachings are at odds with what they have learned, which saddens her greatly. The fragmented story ends after Levi defends her and commands the disciples to continue proclaiming the gospel.

Karen L. King says that the *Gospel of Mary*

presents a radical interpretation of Jesus' teachings as a path to inner spiritual knowledge; it rejects his suffering and death as the path to eternal life; it exposes the erroneous view that Mary of Magdala was a prostitute for what it is—a piece of theological fiction; it presents the most straightforward and convincing argument in any early Christian writing for the legitimacy of women's leadership; it offers a sharp critique of illegitimate power and a utopian vision of spiritual perfection; it challenges our rather romantic views about the harmony and unanimity of the first Christians; and it asks us to rethink the basis for church authority. All written in the name of a woman. (King, GMM, 3–4)

She says scholars "assumed in advance that the *Gospel of Mary* is heretical" by comparing it anachronistically against "standard interpretations of the New Testament." She claims "its position on women's leadership is no doubt a factor in its being labeled heresy." (King, GMM, 170–171)

King notes that *Mary* was not written by Mary Magdelene but was ascribed to her "to claim apostolic authority for its teachings." (King, GMM, 184) It bears testament to the fact that "authority is vested not in a male hierarchy, but in the leadership of men and women who have attained strength of character and spiritual maturity." (King, GMM, 189)

1. The Uncertainty of Its Dating

Bock, noting *Mary*'s fragmentary nature and how little of it has been recovered, comments that its "small size makes dating difficult." (Bock, MG, 66) King dates *Mary* "to the first half of the second century" (King, GMM, 184), but Jenkins states this is "unusually early. As so often with these noncanonical works, we have no certain clues about dates, as the work is not quoted by external authorities. . . . A consensus of recent scholarship would place the writing of *Mary* not much before 180 or 200, about a hundred years later than King's figure." He continues: "One reason for suggesting a late date for *Mary* is that the work contains a kind of Gnostic mythologizing which is characteristic of the later second or early third century, and suggests the influence of Valentinus." (Jenkins, HG, 139)

2. Dependence in Part upon the Synoptic Gospels

Biblical scholar and Anglican priest C. M. Tuckett examines the parallels the *Gospel of Mary* has with the New Testament and believes that many instances show redactional elements of the gospel writings. This means the common links with the NT are "with the finished versions of the gospels, not just with the traditions which lie behind the gospels and which are common stock for many Christians." But the writer did not merely use the gospels as a source. "The author of the *Gospel of Mary* has claimed for him- or herself the right to develop the tradition far more freely and to rewrite and/ or rearrange many of the features of the story, at times quite radically." This would be consistent with a second century dating of *Mary*. Tuckett concludes:

> Given the nature of the parallels that seem to exist, and the fact that some of the parallels involve at times redactional elements on the side of the (later to become) canonical texts, it seems likely that the *Gospel of Mary* is primarily a witness to the later, developing tradition generated by these texts, and does not provide independent witness to early Jesus tradition itself. (Tuckett, GM, 73–74)

3. Were Jesus and Mary Lovers?

Some modern writings, such as *The Da Vinci Code*, speculate that Jesus and Mary were lovers. This idea is fueled in part by the *Gospel of Mary*, which says that Mary was "much loved by the Savior, as no other woman." Ehrman counters:

> It is clear that there are some who celebrate Christ's love of the woman over that of the men, but it would probably be wrong to see his love for Mary as a different in *kind* from his love of his male disciples (i.e., it's not romantic love); it is a difference instead of *degree*. (Ehrman, TFDVC, 179, emphasis in original)

He adds, "There have occasionally been historical scholars . . . who have claimed that it is likely that Jesus was married. But the vast majority of scholars of the New Testament and early Christianity have reached just the opposite conclusion."

One of his strongest reasons is that

> in *none* of our early Christian sources is there any reference to Jesus' marriage or to his wife. This is true not only of the canonical Gospels

of Matthew, Mark, Luke, and John but of all our other Gospels and all of our other early Christian writings put together. There is no allusion to Jesus as married in the writings of Paul, the Gospel of Peter, the Gospel of Philip, the Gospel of Mary, the Gospel of the Nazarenes, the Gospel of the Egyptians, the Gospel of the Ebionites—and on and on. List every ancient source we have for the historical Jesus, and in none of them is there mention of Jesus being married. (Ehrman, TFDVC, 153, emphasis in original)

E. Secret Gospel of Mark

In 1960 professor of ancient history at Columbia University Morton Smith announced to the Society of Biblical Literature that he had discovered part of a letter of Clement of Alexandria in the Mar Saba Monastery near Jerusalem while on sabbatical in 1958. It was written in Greek in eighteenth-century handwriting in the back of a 1646 edition of the letters of Ignatius. Most importantly, it quotes from a *Secret Gospel of Mark*, which contains passages that are not in the canonical Gospel of Mark. This *Secret Gospel of Mark*, quoted in Clement's letter, contains a provocative story in which Jesus raises a boy from the dead and then teaches him about the kingdom of God naked.

Some scholars believe that *Secret Mark* is the earliest version of the canonical gospel of Mark, while others are highly skeptical. Crossan criticizes the handling of *Secret Mark*:

> The authenticity of a text can only be established by the consensus of experts who have studied the original document under scientifically appropriate circumstances. Twenty-five years after the original discovery this has not happened and that casts a cloud over the entire proceedings . . . .
>
> The essential problem, then, is the lack of

several independent studies of the *original* document by experts on Greek handwriting.…

When one brings together a document neither verified nor available in its *original* rescription and a theory about Jesus as a possibly homosexual baptizer, the mixture is volatile enough for accusation and sensation .…

My own position is that independent study of the *original* manuscript is absolutely necessary for scholarly certitude. (Crossan, FOG, 100–103, emphasis in original)

But in spite of his reservations, Crossan says his "own procedure is to accept the document's authenticity as a working hypothesis." (Crossan, FOG, 103) He concludes that "canonical Mark is a very deliberate revision of Secret Mark." (Crossan, FOG, 108) Crossan's conclusion puts forward a strong claim, but research into it raises a number of questions.

Evans states that "from the start, scholars suspected that the text was a forgery and that Smith was himself the forger." He echoes Crossan's concern "that no one besides Smith has actually studied the physical document and that the paper and ink have never been subjected to the kinds of tests normally undertaken," and then laments that many scholars have still accepted the authenticity of *Secret Mark*. He states outright, "The Clementine letter and the quotations of *Secret Mark* embedded within it are a modern hoax, and Morton Smith almost certainly is the perpetrator." (Evans, FJ, 95)

In his book *The Gospel Hoax*, Stephen Carlson provides his reasoning for why *Secret Mark* is a forgery:

There are three main reasons why the manuscript is unlikely to have been penned by an eighteenth-century monk at Mar Saba. First, the execution of the script raises questions

of forgery, including unnatural hesitations in the pen strokes, the "forger's tremor," and anomalies in the shape of the letters when compared with eighteenth-century manuscripts written at Mar Saba. Second, the manuscript's provenance cannot be traced back before 1958, which means that the opportunity for a twentieth-century origin cannot be ruled out. Third, there is another, previously unnoticed manuscript at Mar Saba from the same hand, which Smith himself identified as belonging to a named twentieth-century individual. Additional samples of that individual's Greek handwriting have been obtained and are found to account for the observed anomalies. (Carlson, GH, 25)

Carlson concludes that Smith himself perpetrated the hoax, as he "meets all three criteria" of "means, motive, and opportunity." (Carlson, GH, 74)

Although *Secret Mark* has its proponents, it also has its many critics who reject it as a hoax. Therefore, as Evans says, "No research into the Gospels and the historical Jesus should take Smith's document seriously." (Evans, FJ, 97)

F. Gospel of Judas

In AD 180, Irenaeus wrote *Against Heresies* to condemn the Cainites, a group of people who worshiped the "villains" of the Bible, such as Cain, Esau, and the men of Sodom. One of the heretical texts he mentions is the *Gospel of Judas*. In 2006 it was revealed that the text itself was supposedly discovered within a codex in Egypt in the late 1970s. The writing claims to contain the secret discussions Jesus had with Judas. It elevates Judas to the level of Jesus' greatest disciple, instead of a traitor and a villain. Judas is the hero of Jesus' crucifixion, assisting Jesus in completing his mission of salvation.

Irenaeus was right in condemning *Judas* as a gnostic text because it is full of gnostic themes such as hidden knowledge and a divine light within. More specifically, it can be traced to Sethian Gnosticism—a form of Gnosticism that venerates Adam and Eve's third son, Seth, as a supposed divine incarnation—mostly because of an allusion to Barbelo, a prominent divine figure of Sethian writings. (Kasser, Meyer, and Wurst, GJ, 139–140)

Ehrman makes clear what the *Gospel of Judas* is not:

> It is not a Gospel written by Judas, or one that even claims to be. It is a Gospel *about* Judas (and, of course, Jesus). It is not a Gospel written in Judas's own time by someone who actually knew him or who had inside information concerning his inner motivations. It is not a historically accurate report about the man Judas himself. It is not as ancient as the four Gospels that made it into the New Testament. It is not even older than all of our other non-canonical Gospels. . . . The Gospel of Judas was written at least 100 or, more likely, 125 years after Judas's death by someone who did not have independent access to historical records about the events he was narrating. It is not a book, therefore, that will provide us with additional information about what actually happened in Jesus' lifetime, or even in his last days leading up to his death. (Ehrman, LGJI, 172–173, emphasis in original)

VI. Conclusion

We have examined some of the most popular extracanonical gospels and shown why they do not belong in the New Testament. They show evidence of late dating, of dependence on the Gospels, and, in the case of the *Secret Gospel of Mark*, of being an outright hoax.

This should give us confidence that there was no grand conspiracy or war of Christianities after which the victors determined the course of Christendom. Instead, the path of ortho-doxy was set very early and the sects and texts that were excluded truly were heretical.

This chapter began with a quote by the agnostic historian and Bible scholar Bart Ehrman, and it is only fitting to end with one as well, one that verifies everything we have learned so far:

> The oldest and best sources we have for knowing about the life of Jesus . . . are the four Gospels of the New Testament, Mat-thew, Mark, Luke, and John. This is not simply the view of Christian historians who have a high opinion of the New Testament and its historical worth; it is the view of all serious historians of antiquity of every kind, from committed evangelical Christians to hardcore atheists. This view is not, in other words, a biased perspective of only a few naive wishful thinkers; it is the conclusion that has been reached by every one of the hundreds (thousands, even) of scholars who work on the problem of establishing what really happened in the life of the historical Jesus, scholars who . . . have learned Greek and Hebrew, the languages of the Bible, along with other related languages such as Latin, Syriac, and Coptic, scholars who read the ancient sources in the ancient languages and know them inside and out. We may wish there were older, more reliable sources, but ultimately it is the sources found within the canon that pro-vide us with the most, and best, information. (Ehrman, TFDVC, 102–103)

Therefore, we should hold with confidence that Matthew, Mark, Luke, and John are the only true gospels and that they give us accu-rate information about the life of Jesus Christ.

PART II

EVIDENCE
FOR JESUS

CHAPTER 6

THE HISTORICAL EXISTENCE OF JESUS

OVERVIEW

I. Introduction

Before we examine the evidence for the deity of Christ, the fulfillment of prophecy, and the historical resurrection, we begin by investigating whether, in fact, a man named Jesus lived in and around Jerusalem approximately two thousand years ago. Is Jesus just a myth created solely for the benefit of those looking to start a new religious group? Theologian and self-defined atheist Robert Price believes so, continuing the work of Arthur Drews from the early twentieth century:

> The urgency for historicizing Jesus was the need of a consolidating institution for an authoritative figurehead who had appointed successors and set policy. . . . It was exactly the logic whereby competing churches fabricated legends of their founding by this or that apostle: the apostle (or Jesus) could not be much older than the organization for which he is being appropriated as founder and authority. (Price, JVP, 81)

Price believes, then, that the early church, in order to support their claim that Jesus founded Christianity, may have fabricated a Jesus who not only really lived, but lived in their day.

Conclusions such as those reached by Price are in the scholarly minority. New Testament scholar Craig Blomberg counters with the following analysis:

> An inordinate number of websites and blogs make the wholly unjustified claim that Jesus never existed. Biblical scholars and historians

143

who have investigated this issue in detail are virtually unanimous today in rejecting this view, regardless of their theological or ideological perspectives (Blomberg, JN, 439).

However, rather than simply dismiss the idea of Jesus as myth because of scholarly consensus, we want to explore for ourselves the evidence for the historicity of Jesus Christ.

II. Non-Christian Sources

In evaluating non-Christian sources for the historicity of Jesus, New Testament scholar Craig Evans says distinctions should be made when considering the quality of the sources. (Evans, JNCS, 443) We should understand that not every ancient mention of Jesus aids an investigation into whether he really lived. Similar to Evans, we discuss three categories of non-Christian sources: sources with little or no value, sources of some value, and sources of significant value.

A. Sources of Little or No Value

Just because the name "Jesus" shows up in an ancient document does not mean that it is helpful for someone trying to determine whether the founder of Christianity ever really lived. Sources that purport to discuss Jesus of Nazareth can be unhelpful for various reasons. It is to those that we turn first.

1. Rabbinic Tradition

The large collection of ancient rabbinic literature may seem promising for a study of the historical Jesus. As biblical scholar and Roman Catholic priest John P. Meier notes:

These huge collections of centuries-old traditions are treasure houses of Jewish laws, customs, homilies, legends, anecdotes, and axioms. (Meier, MJ, 94)

However, Meier expresses the challenge of looking to these documents for independent, historically reliable information about the historical Jesus:

Their primary value is as witnesses to the ongoing life of ancient and early medieval Judaism, and to ask them about Jesus of Nazareth is, in almost all cases, to ask the wrong question of a body of literature with its own valid concerns. (Meier, MJ, 94)

Biblical scholar Paul Eddy and theologian Gregory Boyd provide a concise but detailed analysis of the rabbinic literature's value to a study of whether Jesus existed. They find three considerations that lead them to conclude the rabbinic tradition is not valuable for this study:

First, the earliest rabbinic sources date from the late second to the third century and the most celebrated material even later than this. This alone raises questions about the historical value of this material. To illustrate, we possess a rabbinic account of Jesus' life (*Toledot Yeshu*) that claims, among other things, that Jesus was born out of wedlock, grew up acting disrespectful toward Jewish leaders, and mastered magical practices to gain a following. It also claims that Jesus' body was found after his death. Were this a first-or even second-century document, it might be of historical interest. However, the *Toledot Yeshu* was compiled in the fifth century. True, *Toledot Yeshu* and other Jewish literature contain traditions that predate them, but the relatively late date and clear polemical focus of *Toledot Yeshu* and other rabbinic references to Jesus render them suspect as historical sources. They tell us something about Jewish polemics against the early Christian movement, but nothing reliably about Jesus. (Eddy and Boyd, JL, 170–171)

We'll return to Eddy and Boyd in a moment, but this is a good point to bring in some other views of *Toledot Yeshu*. We begin with Craig Evans, who writes:

> [It] is nothing more than a late collection of traditions, from Christian as well as from Jewish sources. Besides the obvious anachronisms, the account is full of fictions assembled for the primary purpose of anti-Christian polemic and propaganda. The work has nothing to offer serious Jesus research. (Evans, JNCS, 450)

Theologian Robert Van Voorst adds some more specific reasons *Toledot Yeshu* is of no use to our study:

> Because of its medieval date, its lack of a fixed form, its popular orientation, and its highly polemical purpose, the *Toledot Yeshu* is most unlikely to give us any independent, reliable information about Jesus. It may contain a few older traditions from ancient Jewish polemic against Christians, but we learn nothing new or significant from it. Scholarly consensus is correct to discount it as a reliable source for the historical Jesus. (Van Voorst, JONT, 128)

Eddy and Boyd continue with their three reasons to disregard rabbinic tradition in a discussion about the historical Jesus:

> Second, in a number of instances it is not entirely clear that the rabbinic text is even talking about Jesus. For example, some have tried to argue that Ben Pandera (or Pantere), Ben Stada, and even Balaam, referred to in various rabbinic writings, are actually references to Jesus (e.g., Babylonian Talmud *Sanhedrin* 67a; *Shabbat* 104b). But there is simply no solid evidence to support these speculations.

Third, in those instances where it seems certain that an author *is* [italics theirs] referring to Jesus, there are textual indications that the material is dependent upon earlier Christian claims and/or anti-Christian propaganda. For example, Jesus is presented as being illegitimately born of a tryst between Mary and a Roman soldier named Panthera. It is significant that Panthera appears to be a play on the Greek word for virgin (*parthenos*). Hence, many scholars conclude that this story is nothing more than a contrived attack on the Christian claim that Jesus was born of a virgin.

> While the rabbinic material gives us insight into how some Jews reacted polemically against the Jesus tradition, it does not represent early, independent, or historically reliable information about Jesus. The only truly significant point about this literature is that, though it sometimes credits Jesus' power to sorcery, magic, or the devil himself, it never denies that Jesus performed miracles—let alone that Jesus existed. (Eddy and Boyd, JL, 171)

Therefore, we place rabbinic materials in the sources of little or no value category.

2. The Qur'an*

A person who has never studied Islam or read the Qur'an may be surprised to discover there are several references to Jesus contained in the book. The Qur'an presents Jesus as a miracle worker (3:49; 5:110) who brings signs (2:87, 253; possibly 5:75; 43:63; 61:6) and even speaks as an infant to establish himself as a prophet sent from God (19:29, 30). The Qur'an also affirms the virgin birth (3:45–47; 19:17–21; 21:91). In general, this could show Qur'anic agreement with the teaching of the Bible.

---

* All quotes from the Qur'an are taken from M. A. S. Abdel Haleem, *The Qur'an* (New York: Oxford University Press, 2004).

However, the Qur'an very clearly teaches that Jesus was not God, rejects the idea of God as Trinity, and denies that Jesus was crucified.

a. Jesus Was Not God

The first instance of an emphasis on the denial of Jesus' divinity includes the direct statement, "there is no god but God" (3:62), which comes right after, "In God's eyes Jesus is just like Adam: He created him from dust, said to him, 'Be', and he was" (3:59). The obvious point in these verses is Jesus was a created human being, not God.

People are warned of going "to excess in your religion" by believing Jesus was anything "more than a messenger of God" (4:171). They are reminded, "God is only one God, He is far above having a son, everything in the heavens and earth belongs to Him and He is sufficient protector" (4:171). "Those who say, 'God is the Messiah, the son of Mary,' are defying the truth" (5:17). A similar description adds, "no one will help such evildoers" (5:72). The Qur'an discusses Christians who "said, 'The Messiah is the son of God': they said this with their own mouths, repeating what earlier disbelievers had said. May God confound them! They take their rabbis, their monks, and Christ, the son of Mary, as lords beside God. But they were commanded to serve only one God; there is no god but Him" (9:30, 31).

b. Rejection of the Trinity

There are two places where the Trinity is specifically denied. "So believe in God and His messengers and do not speak of a 'Trinity'-stop [this], that is better for you" (4:171). Also, "those people who say that God is the third of three are defying [the truth]. Why do they not turn to God and ask His forgiveness, when God is most forgiving, most merciful?" (5:73, 74).

c. Denial of Jesus' Crucifixion

One of the most problematic claims about Jesus in the Qur'an is the assertion that he didn't die. The Qur'an seems to acknowledge the widespread belief that Jesus died on a cross in the way it strongly refutes that belief. The Qur'anic account states that people believed this claim (i.e., Jesus' death on a cross) because they were sealed in their unbelief by God as a penalty for breaking a pledge, rejecting God's revelations, and unjustly killing prophets (4:155). "They disbelieved and uttered a terrible slander against Mary, and said, 'We have killed the Messiah, Jesus, son of Mary, the messenger of God'" (4:156, 157). It goes on to say in no uncertain terms, "They did not kill him, nor did they crucify him, though it was made to appear like that to them. Those that disagreed about him are full of doubt, with no knowledge to follow, only supposition: they certainly did not kill him" (4:157).

d. Conclusion Regarding the Qur'an

So, which book is right, the Bible or the Qur'an? Should we weigh the Qur'anic teachings about Jesus equally with the Bible? What does the Qur'an say about the historical existence of Jesus? Consider three important observations:

- If the accounts of Jesus contained in the Qur'an are true, they would only further prove the existence of a historical Jesus. The Qur'an doesn't deny Jesus existed, just that he was God. Therefore, even someone who affirms the truth of the Qur'an must admit that it presumes the existence of an actual historical Jesus.
- The Qur'an was written and compiled much later than the New Testament accounts of Jesus' life. The definitive

text that makes up the Qur'an was compiled in about AD 653. (Watt, ISH, 48) This makes it much too late to contain any reliable independent information about Jesus.

- Since the Qur'an denies Jesus' crucifixion, which is widely affirmed to have taken place, it "raises serious questions about the historical reliability of *any* claim it makes about Jesus." (Eddy and Boyd, JL, 172)

We place the Qur'an, then, in the category of evidence that provides little or no value in an investigation into the historicity of Jesus.

B. Sources of Limited Value

1. Suetonius

Suetonius was a Roman historian and court official under the emperor Hadrian. His *Lives of the Caesars* was published around AD 120 and describes events in the lives of the first twelve Roman emperors.

In *The Deified Claudius* 25.4 he writes: "Since the Jews constantly made disturbances at the instigation of Chrestus, he expelled them from Rome." (Suetonius, 51) In Acts 18:2, Luke reports this event, which took place in AD 49.

a. Chrestus or Christus?

The Latin word for Christ is Christus, not Chrestus. Is Suetonius writing about someone other than Christ? Or did he make a spelling mistake? Some scholars argue that Suetonius is referring to an agitator in Rome who is unknown to us. Perhaps he was a Jewish radical who anticipated the kingdom to come through violence (Benko, EC, 406–418, esp. 413). There are some who believe the passage is better translated "because of the instigator Chrestus" (Van Voorst, JONT, 31). This would only enhance the possibility that

Suetonius is writing about a contemporary man. However, we have a record of the name "Chrestus" being used among Gentiles but not Jews (Van Voorst, JONT, 33). This makes it highly unlikely that Jews would be incited to the point of being kicked out of the city by someone named Chrestus.

In those days the name "Chrestus" was a popular name among the Gentiles. The most logical explanation is that Suetonius simply spelled the word with an "e" because that was the familiar and customary spelling. However, there is no general agreement among scholars as to which explanation is the correct one.

b. Nero's Fire

Suetonius also wrote about the fire that swept through Rome in AD 64 under the reign of Nero. Suetonius recounts, "Punishment was inflicted on the Christians, a class of men given to a new and mischievous superstition." (Suetonius, 110)

Therefore, we know he was at least somewhat familiar with the sect known as Christians, but he may not have been as familiar with their leader, Christus.

c. Conclusion Regarding Suetonius's Accounts

Eddy and Boyd describe the value of Suetonius:

It is very easy to surmise that Suetonius (or his source) mistakenly understood a riot that had broken out over the preaching of Christ as being instigated by Christ himself, whom, as we have suggested, he mistook to be the proper Greek name Chrestus. While certainty is impossible, at the very least we have here an early non-Christian source that confirms Luke's accuracy about the expulsion of Jews by Claudius (Eddy and Boyd, JL, 177).

2. Pliny the Younger

Pliny the Younger was Governor of Bithynia from AD 111–113. He was a prolific writer who published nine books of letters and is often credited with creating the genre of literary letter. (Van Voorst, JONT, 23) His final book, Book 10, was published after his death.

Book 10 Letter 96 is correspondence between Pliny and the Emperor Trajan. Pliny was punishing Christians who refused to renounce their faith, and he wrote to get direction from the emperor as to whether he should continue punishing in the same way or make some changes. Roman Christians who refused to recant were sent to Rome for trial. Non-Roman Christians who maintained their allegiance to Christ were executed. Letter 96 contains information Pliny gleaned from Christians who recanted their faith and began expressing allegiance to Roman gods. Pliny writes that those who deny Christ

> all venerated your image and the images of the gods as the others did, and reviled Christ. They also maintained that the sum total of their guilt or error was no more than the following. They had met regularly before dawn on a determined day, and sung antiphonally a hymn to Christ as if to a god. They also took an oath not for any crime, but to keep from theft, robbery, and adultery, not to break any promise, and not to withhold a deposit when reclaimed. (quoted in Van Voorst, JONT, 25)

The fact that lapsed Christians were encouraged to revile or curse Christ likely reflects the fact that they and Pliny believed he was a historical person. Ancient historian and New Testament scholar Paul Barnett notes that ancients would not have cursed gods. (Barnett, FHC, 61)

Furthermore, Pliny the Younger describes Christians singing to Christ "as if to a god," which suggests that Pliny thought Christ was something other than a god. (Ehrman, DJE, 52) Though it is not concrete, clearly this suggests that he believed Christ was once a man. (Van Voorst, JONT, 28)

While this letter gives us great insight into early Christian worship practices and martyrdom, it does not present us with an independent first-person account of the historical Jesus. It helps us understand, however, the significant size of early Christianity in Asia Minor in the early second century. Even so, Pliny offers us only limited evidence for considering Jesus as a historical figure. (France, EJ, 43)

3. Lucian of Samosata

A Greek satirist of the latter half of the second century, Lucian spoke scornfully of Christ and the Christians, but never assumed or argued that Christ did not really exist. His *The Death of Peregrinus* tells the story of a man who converted away from Christianity before taking his own life in AD 165. Without using Jesus' name he writes of

> that one whom they still worship today, the man in Palestine who was crucified because he brought this new form of initiation into the world (Van Voorst, JONT, 59).

Lucian says Christians consider themselves brothers the moment they stop worshiping the Greek gods and "begin worshipping that crucified sophist and living by his laws" (Van Voorst, JONT, 59).

It may be significant that Lucian uses the Greek word *anaskolopizein* (translated "crucified") instead of the common one used in the Gospels (*stauroun*). *Anaskolopizein* should be literally translated, "to impale." Eddy and Boyd believe this might show that

Lucian is not relying on Christian terminology but on independent tradition (Eddy and Boyd, JL, 178). However, this is not really definitive. Therefore, we conclude that Lucian's writings do not conclusively verify Christ's existence by documenting specific details of his life.

4. Thallus

Around AD 55, the historian Thallus wrote a three-volume account of the eastern Mediterranean world from the fall of Troy to approximately AD 50. Though most of his work has been lost, a quotation remains in *History of the World*, written by Julius Africanus around AD 220. This work by Africanus has also been lost, but a citation was included in *Chronicle*, written around AD 800 by the Byzantine historian Georgius Syncellus. (Van Voorst, JONT, 20)

Each of the Synoptic Gospels includes an account of the darkness that was visible at Jesus' crucifixion (Matt. 27:45; Mark 15:33; Luke 23:44, 45). According to Syncellus, Africanus writes: "In the third book of his history Thallus calls this darkness an eclipse of the sun—wrongly in my opinion." (Eddy and Boyd, JL, 173)

It is striking that at such an early date, Thallus already knew of the reported darkness in Jerusalem and felt it was important enough to come up with a refutation. However, he is likely responding to Christians or Christian sources. Because his account does not present independent evidence of a historical Jesus, it therefore adds only limited value to our study.

5. Celsus

Around AD 175, the thinker Celsus wrote an attack on Christianity. His *True Doctrine* has been lost, but most of it was included in Origen's *Against Celsus*, written around 250. Even though the two were written approximately seventy-five years apart, most scholars believe Origen quotes Celsus with accuracy (Van Voorst, JONT, 65).

Celsus argues against the virgin birth, alleging Jesus was conceived as the result of an affair between Mary and a Roman soldier. He presents Jesus' miracles as the result of magic or sorcery that he learned in Egypt. He says Jesus taught his followers to beg and rob. (Van Voorst, JONT, 66–67) It is likely that Celsus had access to several New Testament texts and other Christian writings. Therefore, it is unlikely he had access to any independent reports of the historical Jesus. Add to this the fact that his writing is an attack on Christianity "often resorting to caricature and lampooning," and it becomes obvious there is little of historical value to help prove Jesus' existence. (Eddy and Boyd, JL, 177)

6. Mara bar Serapion

Sometime after AD 70, Mara bar Serapion, a Syrian and probably Stoic philosopher, wrote a letter from prison to his son encouraging him to pursue wisdom. In his letter he compares Jesus to the philosophers Socrates and Pythagoras and discusses the foolishness of persecuting wise people:

What good did it do the Athenians to kill Socrates, for which deed they were punished with famine and pestilence? What did it avail the Samians to burn Pythagoras, since their country was entirely buried under sand in one moment? Or what did it avail the Jews to kill their wise king, since their kingdom was taken away from them from that time on? God justly avenged these three wise men. The Athenians died of famine, the Samians were flooded by the sea, the Jews were slaughtered and driven from their kingdom, everywhere living in the dispersion. Socrates is not dead, thanks to

Plato; nor Pythagoras, because of Hera's statue. Nor is the wise king, because of the new law which he has given. (cited in Bock, SHJ, 53)

Though Mara never uses Jesus' name, we can be certain he is referring to him because no one else at that point in history would fulfill the requirements of being known as a "wise king" who was killed by the Jews shortly before they were driven from the land. Jesus is obviously in view.

Mara certainly was not a Christian, since he puts Jesus on equal footing with Socrates and Pythagoras. Also, he has Jesus living on in his teaching rather than because he rose to life after his execution. It is interesting that a writer from outside the Roman Empire has a positive view of Christianity; however, his letter "says more about Christianity than about Christ." (Van Voorst, JONT, 57–58) Nevertheless, what he has written does provide information that is somewhat helpful as we continue our study of the historical existence of Jesus Christ.

C. Sources of Significant Value

Tacitus and Josephus, two ancient non-Christian writers, present us with information that is very valuable to our study.

1. Tacitus

Cornelius Tacitus was a Roman historian who lived approximately between AD 56 and 120. Robert Van Voorst says Tacitus "is generally considered the greatest Roman historian" and his *Annals* is his "finest work and generally acknowledged by modern historians as our best source of information about this period." (Van Voorst, JONT, 39) His *Annals* dates back to the time of Augustus through Nero. Though not all of *Annals* survives, one passage that does is key to our study.

In AD 64 there was a devastating fire for which many people believed Nero was responsible. In order to put a stop to the public outcry, Nero blamed the Christians. Tacitus explains what happened:

Therefore, to squelch the rumor, Nero created scapegoats and subjected to the most refined tortures those whom the common people called "Christians," hated for their abominable crimes. Their name comes from Christ, who, during the reign of Tiberius, had been executed by the procurator Pontius Pilate. Suppressed for the moment, the deadly superstition broke out again, not only in Judea, the land which originated this evil, but also in the city of Rome, where all sorts of horrendous and shameful practices from every part of the world converge and are fervently cultivated. (quoted in Meier, MJ, 89–90)

Paul Barnett says it is "difficult to overstate the importance of Tacitus's text for the study of Christian origins." (Barnett, FHC, 58) However, several potential objections to the authenticity and trustworthiness of this text require a response.

a. Potential Objections

(1) Could Tacitus's text be a forgery? Or, at the very least, could Christians have subsequently placed into it information locating Jesus as a historical person? This is highly unlikely. One reason is Tacitus clearly despises Christians. As explained by Barnett,

No Christian would have described his fellows in Rome as a foreign cult needing to be checked, a "disease" belonging to the "horrible and shameful things of the world" that gravitate to Rome, a people "hated for their vices," who have a "hatred of the human race" and whose terrible punishment under Nero is justified. (Barnett, FCH, 57)

If someone were altering the document, surely that forger, if a Christian, would have softened the offending rhetoric. Another feature pointing to the authenticity of this passage is the fact that it doesn't specifically mention the resurrection, something a Christian editor would have been expected to include. Finally, the text is "stylistically seamless." (Barnett, FHC, 57) There does not appear to be any evidence of another writer editing the text.

(2) Is there a challenge to the reliability of this passage by his use of the word *procurator*? One might argue against the reliability of Tacitus's account based on the fact that he refers to Pilate as "procurator" (the term used in Tacitus's day) instead of "prefect" (the title that would have been used in Pilate's time). We know from the discovery of an ancient stone that Pilate was referred to as a "prefect." (Eddy and Boyd, TJL, 180–181) Could this anachronism call into question other things that Tacitus wrote?

Tacitus is generally considered to be a reliably accurate historian. (See the final paragraph of section C1.) Beyond the general trustworthiness of Tacitus's writing, the reason for this anachronism in particular can be effectively explained, as Eddy and Boyd offer:

Regarding the ascription itself, it is entirely possible that Tacitus was intentionally anachronistic for the sake of clarity. Since "procurator" was the accepted title of Pilate's position among Tacitus's audience, he may have used the term knowing full well that the position used to be titled "prefect." But it is even more likely that we are making too much of the distinction between "procurator" and "prefect" in the ancient world, for the evidence suggest that these terms were rather fluid in the first century.

For example, though the "Pilate stone" discovered at Caesarea Maritima gives Pilate the title "prefect," both Philo (*Legat.* 38) and Josephus (*Jewish War* 2.9.2.169) refer to him as "procurator" (Greek *epitropos*), just as Tacitus does. In fact, Josephus sometimes uses the two terms interchangeably. (Eddy and Boyd, JL, 181–182)

(3) Finally, does the fact that Tacitus refers to "Christ" instead of "Jesus" show that he relies on Christian testimony instead of independent witnesses? If so, reliance upon Christian hearsay could go a long way toward discrediting him as a source of independent information about Jesus. On this question Eddy and Boyd are helpful:

No compelling case can be made that Tacitus is relying on hearsay in this passage simply because he referred to the founder of the Christian movement as "Christ" rather than by his proper name. For one thing, it is improbable that Tacitus, who elsewhere proves himself to be a reliable historian who routinely consults sources, would at this point rely solely on the hearsay of a group he himself identifies as a "pernicious superstition" and as "evil." Moreover, by the early second century, "Christ" and "Jesus" could be used interchangeably, both by Christians and non-Christians. Thus we need not suppose that Tacitus's use of the title "Christ" reflects a sole dependency on Christians as his source of information. (Eddy and Boyd, JL, 182)

Boyd and Eddy continue concerning the reliability of this passage:

In fact, three considerations lead us to conclude that, if anything, Tacitus would have been *more* motivated than usual to check out his sources on this topic.

First, the subject of the passage is an official action taken by a Roman emperor. Second, Tacitus consistently reflects an unusual fascination with, and animosity toward, "pretenders" and superstitions, particularly those connected with claims of having been raised from the dead. And third, throughout his work Tacitus is very concerned with the happenings of members of the royal court, and there is some indication that several members of the royal family had aligned themselves with this "cult."

All of this explains why Tacitus speaks so acrimoniously about the "pernicious superstition" of the Christian movement, even though he is clearly moved by the horrendous pain Nero inflicted on them. But it also suggests that, if ever Tacitus would have been concerned to check out his information, it would have been in a context such as the one we are considering. (Eddy and Boyd, JL, 183)

Van Voorst adds to the discussion concerning where Tacitus got this information about Christ:

To say where he did *not* get his information is easier than to show where he did. First, Tacitus certainly did not draw, directly or indirectly, on writings that came to form the New Testament. No literary or oral dependence can be demonstrated between his description and the Gospel accounts. The wording is too different; the only commonality is the name Pontius Pilate, and this could easily come from elsewhere. Nor did Tacitus likely draw his information from another Christian document, if his contempt for Christianity is any indication. Second, Tacitus does not seem to have drawn on general hearsay. (Van Voorst, JONT, 49)

Finally, while we are not sure where Tacitus obtained the information he used

in *Annals*, we know he had access to the *Acta Senatus*, the Roman Senate's archives of its activities. (Eddy and Boyd, JL, 184) Those Roman records could have contained reports of Jesus' crucifixion, and he could have retrieved the details from there. Or he could have learned the facts while he was proconsul in Asia. (Barnett, FHC, 59)

b. Value of Tacitus

The writings of Tacitus confirm the New Testament accounts that Jesus' crucifixion happened when Tiberius was emperor and Pilate was his appointed leader in Judea. Tacitus also confirms the spread of Christianity after Christ's death, writing, "Suppressed for the moment, the deadly superstition broke out again." While the term "superstition" may or may not be a vague reference to the resurrection, Tacitus surely points to the continued growth of Christianity in the years shortly after Jesus died as reported in the New Testament book of Acts.

Tacitus provides independent historical reporting that affirms important events recorded in the New Testament. His writings provide a source of significant value toward confirming the existence of the historical Jesus. As Eddy and Boyd write:

All these considerations suggest Tacitus is an independent—and thus important—non-Christian source about Jesus. Tacitus's report demonstrated that a mere thirty years after Jesus died (hence while many living witnesses of the founder were still alive) his followers were willing to be put to death for their faith, and in ways that were so barbaric it moved a very unsympathetic Roman historian to pity them. Thus, Tacitus's report provides solid, independent, non-Christian evidence for the life and death of Jesus, the remarkable resolve of his earliest followers, and the astounding growth of the movement he founded. (Eddy and Boyd, JL, 184)

We must observe the high esteem in which Tacitus is held as a historian. Arnaldo Momigliano, one of the foremost historiographers of the twentieth century, considered Tacitus "a writer whose reliability cannot be seriously questioned." (Momigliano, CFMH, 111–112) Historian Ronald Mellor refers to him as "the most accurate of all Roman historians." (Mellor, *Tacitus*, 40) In short, Tacitus can be trusted.

2. Josephus

Flavius Josephus was a Jewish politician, soldier, and historian who lived around AD 37–100. He is "the single most important Jewish historian of the ancient world." (Eddy and Boyd, JL, 184) *Antiquities of the Jews* was written by Josephus to explain the Jewish people and their beliefs to Romans in an effort to reduce anti-Jewish bigotry. His writing is so influential that "all discussions regarding the Pharisees, Sadducees, Essenes, and Qumran community must take Josephus into account." (Grossman, JF, 406)

Two passages in *Antiquities* are important in our investigation of the historicity of Jesus.

a. Antiquities 20.200

In *Antiquities* 20.200, Josephus writes about the death of Jesus' brother James at the instigation of the high priest Ananus,

a bold man in his temper, and very insolent; he was also of the sect of the Sadducees, who are very rigid in judging offenders, above all the rest of the Jews, as we have already observed; when, therefore, Ananus was of this disposition, he thought he had now a proper opportunity [to exercise his authority]. Festus was now dead, and Albinus was but upon

the road; so he assembled the Sanhedrin of judges, and brought before them the brother of Jesus, who was called Christ, whose name was James, and some others . . . he delivered them to be stoned. (Josephus, CW, 645)

In order to understand why this entry is important—undoubtedly one of the most significant non-Christian passages relating to the historical Jesus—we must grasp Josephus's history. He was born in Jerusalem shortly after the death of Jesus. His father was a respected high priest named Matthias, which not only places Josephus in Jerusalem right at the time the book of Acts says the new Christian church was flourishing there, but he would have been in a family that would have been acutely aware of a new religious movement that was seen as a threat to Judaism. (Licona, RJ, 235) He was in Israel until he went over to the Roman side after losing to them in battle when Rome invaded Israel in AD 66. (Barrett, FHC, 47) It is likely during these decades in Israel that Josephus heard about Christianity (and Jesus) through a vast network of contacts, and he may have even heard some of the apostles preach in person. (Licona, RJ, 237) Therefore, Josephus is not writing purely based on hearsay.

The substance of the James passage quoted above is clear. Josephus verifies that a man named James was put to death, that he was Jesus' brother, and this Jesus was called the Christ. Still, a minority of scholars argue against its authenticity, including evangelical Graham Twelftree, who claims Christians inserted this (or portions of it) into *Antiquities* after Josephus wrote it. (Twelftree, JJT, 297–301) However, good reasons support why a large majority of scholars do not question this passage's authenticity and consider it strong evidence for the historicity of Jesus. Apologist and historian Michael Licona summarizes five reasons offered by John P. Meier supporting the authenticity of the James passage:

First, it appears in all of the Greek manuscripts of *Antiquities of the Jews* 20 "without any notable variation." Second, the text provides a passing and blasé reference to James, who is here of little consequence, since Josephus is more interested in the illegal behavior of Ananus (and Jesus is even less of a subject, only inserted to identify James). Thus it fits well in the context of Ananus's removal from the office of high priest. Third, no New Testament or early Christian writer wrote of James in a matter-of-fact way as "the brother of Jesus" (*ho adelphos Iesou*), but rather—with the reverence we would expect—"the brother of the Lord" (*ho adelphos tou kyriou*) or "the brother of the Savior" (*ho adelphos tou soteros*). The words *tou legomenou Xristou* ("the one called Christ") are neutral and appear to be employed to distinguish Jesus from others in his writings by the same name.

Fourth, Josephus's account of James's execution differs significantly in its time and manner from that offered by the second-century Christian author Hegesippus and, in the third century, Clement of Alexandria. If Josephus's account was invented by a Christian, we would expect it to better reflect the Christian accounts. Fifth, Josephus's account is short and matter of fact compared to the Christian accounts by Hegesippus and Clement of Alexandria.

In short, this text gives no indication of tampering by Christians and the large majority of scholars regard the entire passage as the authentic words of Josephus. (Licona, RJ, 236–237)

In spite of the fact that Eddy and Boyd view the skeptic case against the James passage as "formidable," they draw the conclusion that the authenticity of the passage is solid. The following is a synopsis of material contained in Eddy and Boyd, *The Jesus Legend*, 185–190:

- There is little manuscript evidence for *Antiquities*. However, it is not less so than for other ancient works.
- Josephus only mentions "Christos" in connection with Jesus, even though he writes about other messianic figures. Josephus mentions twenty-one other people named Jesus. This makes it likely Josephus simply mentions that James's brother "was called Christ" in order to identify which James was killed.
- Some argue the term *legomenos* can be translated as "called" or "said to be." As it is used of Jesus in this passage and that gives it a link with the New Testament, it could mean a Christian wrote it. However, if a Christian had made a later addition they likely would have referred to Jesus as "the Christ" not "called Christ."
- Jesus is mentioned before James in the passage, which raises the question in the minds of some skeptics as to why Josephus would choose to structure the passage in this way. The structure does not elevate Jesus in a drastic way as to make him the focus of the passage. This appears to be a simple construction used by Josephus for clarity.
- This passage involves a negative view of Ananus the high priest, even though in *Jewish Wars* Josephus presents a positive view of him. Tessa Rajak finds this difference "startling." (Rajak, *Josephus*, 131) However, given the fact that we often find tension between accounts of the same event as they appear in

Jewish Wars and *Antiquities*, this is not a strong argument. Also, there is a shift between those two works in the way Josephus writes about Jewish leaders.

- The third-century theologian Origen wrote that Josephus believed the fall of Jerusalem was God's punishment of the Jews for killing James. However, no existing text of *Antiquities* contains this. Skeptics may argue against the authenticity of the *Antiquities* passage because if Christians had tampered with it by the time of Origen, then how can we trust what we currently have? However, Origen would likely not have asserted this haphazardly unless it was in other manuscripts because they were freely available in the Roman public library at the time he wrote.
- The flow of the passage would not be interrupted if the information about Jesus was removed. While this may be true, it is hardly proof of a later Christian insertion.

This helps us to understand why Barnett can say, "The authenticity of this passage is not in doubt and does not require emending." (Barnett, FHC, 52)

Josephus offers a clear non-Christian attestation of the historicity of Jesus and the New Testament assertion that James was Jesus' brother. New Testament scholar Maurice Casey offers an understatement when writing this passage is "as clear as could be." (Casey, *Jesus*, 10)

b. Antiquities 18.63

In *Antiquities* 18.63 we have a passage that is much more open to debate concerning authenticity. It is commonly referred to as the *Testimonium Flavianum*. Licona describes the challenge for scholars:

The literature on this passage is enormous. Leading Josephus scholar Louis Feldman lists eighty-seven discussions on the authenticity of this passage between 1937 and 1980. Scholars hold three general positions on this passage: (1) the entire text is authentic; (2) the entire text is a Christian interpolation; or (3) Josephus mentions Jesus in this text but it was subsequently doctored by a Christian interpolator. The first two positions have few adherents; the third enjoys a majority. (Licona, RJ, 237–238)

Here is the debated passage:

At this time there appeared Jesus, a wise man, if indeed one should call him a man. For he was a doer of startling deeds, a teacher of people who receive the truth with pleasure. And he gained a following both among many Jews and among many of Greek origin. He was the Messiah. And when Pilate, because of an accusation made by the leading men among us, condemned him to the cross, those who had loved him previously did not cease to do so. For he appeared to them on the third day, living again, just as the divine prophets had spoken of these and countless other wondrous things about him. And up until this very day the tribe of Christians, named after him, has not died out. (quoted in Meier, MJ, 60)

i) The Textual Challenge

As Licona points out:

The text leads one to believe that Josephus must have converted to Christianity. However, in the early third century, Origen claimed that Josephus was not a Christian. This creates a problem. If Origen is correct, it would be odd that a non-Christian Jew would say some of the things reported in this passage. Three parts stand out as candidates for interpolations: (1) "if indeed one should call him a man," (2) "He was the Messiah" and (3) "For he appeared to them on the third day, living again, just as the divine prophets had spoken of these and countless other wondrous things about him." (Licona, RJ, 238)

There have been several efforts by scholars to attempt to discern what is authentic in this passage and what is interpolation.

ii) Textual Options

Meier offers his take on what the authentic Josephus passage would have looked like:

At this time there appeared Jesus, a wise man. For he was a doer of startling deeds, a teacher of people who receive the truth with pleasure. And he gained a following both among many Jews and among many of Greek origin. And when Pilate, because of an accusation made by the leading men among us, condemned him to the cross, those who had loved him previously did not cease to do so. And up until this very day the tribe of Christians (named after him) has not died out. (Meier, MJ, 61)

Meier offers a number of arguments for the authenticity of this modified Josephus passage, as summarized by Licona:

First, the passage appears in every Greek and Latin manuscript of *Antiquities of the Jews* 18. It must be admitted that there are only three Greek manuscripts, the earliest of which appears to have been written in the eleventh century. However, there are numerous Latin manuscripts dating to the sixth century. It must also be noted that the passage is not mentioned by any church fathers prior to Eusebius of Caesarea in the fourth century. Second, given Josephus's later mention of "Jesus who was called Christ," some earlier reference to Jesus becomes likely, since he does not pause to explain more about Jesus.

Third, the vocabulary and grammar of Meier's modified passage "cohere well with Josephus' style and language; the same cannot be said when the text's vocabulary and grammar are compared with that of the NT . . . In fact, most of the vocabulary turns out to be characteristic of Josephus." Meier also contends that his modified *Testimonium* is a simpler move than omitting it in its entirety, which to him is "sometimes on flimsy grounds." For him, "A basic rule of method is that, all things being equal, the simplest explanation that also covers the largest amount of data is to be preferred." (Licona, RJ, 239–240)

Licona also trims the Josephus passage in an effort to discern what is authentic, but not as much as Meier. Licona's version is:

And when Pilate, because of an accusation made by the leading men among us, condemned him to the cross, those who had loved him previously did not cease to do so. For they reported that he appears to them alive. And up until this very day the tribe of Christians (named after him) has not died out. (Licona, RJ, 240)

Licona offers a defense of his less trimmed version:

It is more closely represented in all of the extant manuscripts while maintaining neutrality toward Jesus and his followers. Moreover, it provides an insight concerning *why* [italics his] the "tribe" of Christians had not died out: they were convinced that their spiritual leader had risen from the dead. (Licona, RJ, 241)

Leading scholar James Charlesworth of Princeton University offers the final amended alternative that we mention here, providing a full translation of the passage and placing items in italics that he believes are interpolations:

About this time there lives Jesus, a wise man, *if indeed one ought to call him a man*. For he was one who wrought surprising feats (and) was a teacher of such people as accept truth gladly. He won over many Jews and many of the Greeks. *He was the Messiah*. When Pilate, upon hearing him accused by men of the highest standing amongst us, had condemned him to be crucified, those who had in the first place come to love him did not give up their affection for him. *On the third day he appeared to them restored to life, for the prophets of God had prophesied these and countless other marvelous things about him*. And the tribe of the Christians, so called after him, has still to this day not (yet?) disappeared. (Charlesworth, HJ, 34)

Charlesworth sees two notable aspects of this passage:

First, there is no reason to doubt why a scribe who was a Christian would feel the need to elevate the reference and evaluation of Jesus. Perhaps these additions were first placed in the margins and subsequent scribes imagined the notes were parts of the text that should not be left out.

Second, no Christian would have written this testimony to Jesus as it is preserved. No Christian would have categorized Jesus' miracles as "surprising works," or reported that Jesus was condemned because he was "accused by the first-rate men among us." That statement implies that Jesus was rightly condemned to crucifixion. Also the final sentence implies that this "tribe" will not endure.

The reader should read the testimony [the amended alternative] two more times: once without the italicized words, observing how the statement flows with grammatical accuracy and with historical clarity, and another time stressing only the Christian additions. The intent of the Jew Josephus

and then of Christian scribes should become more obvious. (Charlesworth, HJ, 34)

c. Conclusion Regarding Josephus's Accounts

Regardless of which words a scholar chooses to classify as interpolations, the bulk of the passage is seen by many scholars as authentic to Josephus. Evans elaborates:

A number of careful, respected scholars have concluded that this passage, minus a few obvious interpolations, is authentic, demonstrating that Josephus . . . was well aware that Jesus was the founder of the Christian movement and that he had been condemned by the ruling priests and crucified by the Roman governor Pontius Pilate. The testimony of Josephus is in fact very important, even if it is not crucial. (Evans, JHW, 9)

D. Summary of Non-Christian Sources

We close this section by observing that many of these non-Christian sources were in fact hostile to Christianity. New Testament scholar Darrell Bock notes the important fact that, though they disliked and may have even wanted to get rid of Christians: "There is no evidence that those who opposed the movement attributed to him denied his existence." (Bock, HJ, 253)

We can reasonably believe, then, that most of *Antiquities* 18.63 is authentic. But even if it's not, we have substantial evidence from Tacitus and from Josephus's James passage that Jesus truly lived.

Professor Casey Elledge of Gustavus Adolphus College wraps up an analysis that includes Tacitus, Josephus, and Suetonius with a strong affirmation of the truth of the fact that Jesus was a real person:

The testimonies of ancient historians offer strong evidence against a purely mythical reading of Jesus. In contrast to those who have denied the historical existence of Jesus altogether, judging him merely to have been a mythological construct of early Christian thought, the testimonies of the ancient historians reveal how even those outside the early church regarded Jesus to have been a historical person. It remains difficult, therefore, if not impossible, to deny the historical existence of Jesus when the earliest Christian, Jewish, and pagan evidence mention him. (Elledge, JTS, 717)

Charlesworth discusses both Tacitus and Josephus: "The references to Jesus by a Roman historian and a Jewish historian disprove the absurd contention that Jesus never lived." (Charlesworth, HJ, 35)

III. Christian Sources

Skeptics may be leery of using Christian sources to prove the existence of Jesus because of the assumed bias of the documents in favor of a historical Christ. However, as Blomberg states:

It is, of course, historically prejudicial to exclude automatically all Christian evidence, as if no one who became a follower of Jesus could ever report accurately about his life and teachings, or to assume that all non-Christian evidence was necessarily more "objective." (Blomberg, JN, 439)

Therefore, we examine the Christian sources with a mind open to the possibility that they are historically reliable testimony to the historicity of Jesus.

A. NT Documents

Chapter 3 discussed the clear case for the general reliability of the New Testament documents in terms of the number and dating of their manuscripts in comparison to other ancient texts as well as the thousands of citations of them by early Christian writers. This section will address issues that specifically relate to the historicity of Jesus.

1. Gospels

As Blomberg writes, "By far the most important historical information about Jesus of Nazareth appears in the four Gospels of the New Testament." (Blomberg, JN, 441)

The authors of the four gospels present Jesus in a manner that assumes his existence. Though they want the reader to know their accounts are reliable (e.g., John 21:24), the writers are not primarily attempting to prove he existed. Instead, they are trying to convince readers that the man Jesus whom they knew is God and should be followed. As Blomberg explains:

We may affirm that the Synoptic Gospel writers would have wanted to preserve accurate history according to the standards of their day, that they had every likelihood of being able to do so, and that the overall pattern of widespread agreement on the essential contours of Jesus' life and ministry coupled with enough variation of details to demonstrate at least some independent sources and tradents on which each drew makes it very probable that they did in fact compose trustworthy historical and biographical documents. (Blomberg, JN, 456)

Leading New Testament scholar Richard Bauckham presents the Gospels as eyewitness testimony, pointing to the short distance between their writing and the people who would have seen Jesus in person:

The Gospels were written within living memory of the events they recount. Mark's Gospel was written well within the lifetime of many of the eyewitnesses, while the other three canonical

Gospels were written in the period when living eyewitnesses were becoming scarce, exactly at the point in time when their testimony would perish with them were it not put in writing. This is a highly significant fact, entailed not by unusually early datings of the Gospels but by the generally accepted ones. (Bauckham, JE, 7)

Bauckham here observes that this analysis relies upon a generally accepted early dating for the Gospels.

Many skeptical scholars question whether every story about Jesus contained in the Gospels actually took place. Robert Price argues that there is nothing analogous in our contemporary world or anywhere else to Jesus' miracles as a plausible reason for denying they happened (and, further, that Jesus existed): "Which is more likely: that a man walked on water, glowed like the sun and rose from the dead, or that someone has rewritten a bunch of well-known miracle stories?" (Price, JVP, 75) For Price, in essence, if it hasn't happened before or since, it must not have happened at all.

However, even those who do not believe in the authenticity of every story in the Gospels can still draw the conclusion that Jesus truly existed. Agnostic Bible scholar Bart Ehrman shares Price's skepticism concerning the supernatural accounts surrounding Jesus' life. However, this does not lead him to conclude that Jesus never existed. He writes specifically concerning the gospel accounts:

We are not dealing with just one Gospel that reports what Jesus said and did from sometime near the end of the first century. We have a number of surviving Gospels—I named seven—[Ehrman considers noncanonical gospels in his study] that are either completely independent of one another or independent in a large number of their traditions. These all attest to the existence of Jesus. Moreover, these independent witnesses corroborate many of the same basic sets of data—for example, that Jesus not only lived but that he was a Jewish teacher who was crucified by the Romans at the instigation of Jewish authorities in Jerusalem.... The vast network of these traditions, numerically significant, widely dispersed, and largely independent of one another, makes it almost certain that whatever one wants to say about Jesus, at the very least one must say that he existed. (Ehrman, DJE, 92–93)

Princeton scholar James Charlesworth is emphatic:

It would be foolish to continue to foster the illusion that the Gospels are merely fictional stories like the legends of Hercules and Asclepius. The theologies in the New Testament are grounded on interpretation of real historical events, especially the crucifixion of Jesus, at a particular time and place. (Charlesworth, HJBA, 694)

Beyond the manuscript evidence, Evans says archaeological evidence helps to authenticate the gospel narratives:

It would be foolish to continue to foster the illusion that the Gospels are merely fictional stories like the legends of Hercules and Asclepius. The theologies in the New Testament are grounded on interpretation of real historical events, especially the crucifixion of Jesus, at a particular time and place.

James Charlesworth

If the New Testament Gospels were nothing more than fictions and fables about a man who never lived, one must wonder how it is they possess so much verisimilitude and why they talk so much about people we know lived and about so many things we know happened. After all, the Gospels say Jesus was condemned to the cross by a Roman governor named Pontius Pilate. Not only is this man mentioned by historical sources outside the New Testament but we have found an inscribed stone on which his name appears. Indeed, we may have found the name of the Jewish high priest who condemned Jesus inscribed on a bone box. It seems these people were real—I suspect Jesus was too. (Evans, JHW, 10)

The gospel accounts alone provide ample New Testament evidence that Jesus truly existed. But there is more.

2. Paul

The apostle Paul, once a persecutor of Christians, changed dramatically into a missionary who tried to bring more people into the faith. His letters do not contain a complete picture of Jesus' life because they are occasional letters designed to address specific concerns within the churches to which he wrote. Still, clearly Paul based many arguments on the assumption that Jesus did exist. Paul's writings are important because they are the earliest Christian documents and the earliest writings we have concerning Jesus as a historical person.

a. What Paul Believed

Paul specifically affirms five things:

i) Paul believed Jesus was born.

In Galatians 4:4 Paul writes, "God sent forth His Son, born of a woman, born under the law." In Romans 1:3 Paul writes Jesus was,

"descended from David according to the flesh" (ESV). Maurice Casey believes these two passages provide evidence that Paul was making "clear Jesus' human birth." (Casey, Jesus, 174)

ii) Paul believed Jesus spoke.

In 1 Corinthians 7:10–12, Paul writes, "To the married I give this charge (not I, but the Lord): the wife should not separate from her husband (but if she does, she should remain unmarried or else be reconciled to her husband), and the husband should not divorce his wife. To the rest I say (I, not the Lord) that if any brother has a wife who is an unbeliever, and she consents to live with him, he should not divorce her" (ESV). Paul is expressing his awareness of Jesus' teaching on divorce. Casey details why this saying can't be original to Paul:

> It makes no sense as a saying of a Christian prophet. If Jesus was not responsible for the prohibition of divorce, no Christian prophet in the diaspora would have dared to invent such disruptive teaching. . . . If Paul had originated such teaching, which he was not likely to do because it was contradictory to the Jewish traditions which Paul normally drew on for his ethical teaching, he would have attributed it to himself and not to the Lord. Jesus of Nazareth, however, was an original teacher within the prophetic tradition, and this teaching fits perfectly into his efforts to foster good relationships among the Jews of first-century Galilee. (Casey, Jesus, 179)

iii) Paul believed Jesus died (e.g., 1 Cor. 15:3; 2 Cor. 4:10; Rom. 1:4; Col. 1:22; Gal. 1:1).

This is a very significant theme in Paul's writings with direct claims or allusions appearing in all of his epistles except for 2 Thessalonians and Philemon. This was not an ancillary thought in Paul's writings.

He saw it as central to the Christian faith, as Joel Green, professor of New Testament interpretation at Fuller Theological Seminary, describes:

> For Paul, the cross of Christ was critical to reflection and life, especially as the means by which God has provided for salvation and as the instrument and measure of new life in Christ. (Green, DC, 201)

First Corinthians 1:22, 23 helps us understand how unlikely it would have been for Paul to make up the story of Jesus. In particular, the crucifixion aspect of the story made missionary activity a challenge because of how it was received by Jew and Gentile alike: "Jews demand signs and Greeks seek wisdom, but we preach Christ crucified, a stumbling block to Jews and folly to Gentiles" (ESV). If Paul's account of Christ were an invention, he would not have included details that would make his missionary work that much harder.

N. T. Wright elaborates on the challenge for Gentiles:

> It flew in the face of all Hellenistic wisdom: part of the point of crucifixion was that it completely degraded the sufferer. It denied him any chance of a noble death, a considerable preoccupation among pagans. It also, in the normal run of things, denied him a proper burial as well, since the body would be eaten by birds, rats, or other carrion and any final remains dumped in a common pit. The complete helplessness of crucifixion stood in sharp contrast to the Stoic, and indeed Socratic, ideal of the person who, perhaps through committing suicide, remained in control of their own fate. (Wright, PFG, 407)

Ehrman discusses the challenge for Jews, specifically that the ancient Jewish messianic expectation was not for a crucified criminal but for a victorious ruler, thereby increasing the likelihood that Paul did not fabricate the story:

> Ancient Jews at the turn of the era held a variety of expectations of what the future messiah would be like. But all these expectations had several things in common. In all of them the messiah would be a future ruler of the people of Israel, leading a real kingdom here on earth. He would be visibly and openly known to be God's special emissary, the anointed one. And he would be high and mighty, a figure of grandeur and power.
>
> And who was Jesus? In all our early traditions he was a lower-class peasant from rural Galilee who was thought by some to be the future ruler of Israel but who instead of establishing the kingdom on earth came to be crucified. That Jesus died by crucifixion is almost universally attested in our sources, early and late. . . . The crucifixion of Jesus is the core of Paul's message and is attested abundantly in his writings as one of the—if not the—earliest things that he knew about the man.
>
> Who would make up the idea of a crucified messiah? No Jew that we know of. And who were Jesus' followers in the year immediately following his death? Jews living in Palestine. It is no wonder that Paul found their views so offensive [before his conversion (Acts 8–9)].
>
> If it is hard to imagine Jews inventing the idea of a crucified messiah, where did the idea come from? It came from historical realities. There really was a man Jesus.
>
> Since no one would have made up the idea of a crucified messiah, Jesus must really have existed, must really have raised messianic expectations, and must really have been crucified. No Jew would have invented him. (Ehrman, DJE, 162–164)

James D. G. Dunn sees the specific importance of Paul's early report of the crucifixion in 1 Corinthians 15:3:

> Where Paul recites the foundational belief which he himself had received and which was evidently taught to converts as the earliest Christian catechetical instruction: "that Christ died." The point is that Paul was probably converted about two years following the event confessed and probably received this foundational instruction at that time. In other words, in the early 30s Paul was being told about a Jesus who had died two or so years earlier. (Dunn, JR, 142–143)

The proximity to the time Jesus was reported to have died would have made it easy to prove Paul wrong if his teaching was, in fact, wrong. If Paul was looking for an easy way to get a new religion started, choosing to preach about a crucified Christ (who never existed in the first place) was not a way to do it. The only reasonable conclusion is that Paul preached about the crucifixion because he knew that Jesus truly existed and was put to death.

iv) Paul believed Jesus rose from the dead.

Paul includes specific references to Jesus' resurrection in nine of his thirteen letters (only 2 Thessalonians, 1 Timothy, Titus, and Philemon contain no explicit references). We will discuss 1 Corinthians 15 more fully in chapter 10, but we should point out here the importance of what Paul asserts in two portions of that section of the letter.

In 1 Corinthians 15:6 Paul writes, "Then he [Jesus] appeared to more than five hundred brothers at one time, most of whom are still alive, though some have fallen asleep" (ESV). Paul was stating that many who claimed to have seen the risen—and

clearly historical—Jesus were still alive. You could talk with them if you doubted whether he was real. Paul included himself in the group of people who had encounters with the risen Jesus (1 Cor. 15:8).

In 1 Corinthians 15:13, 14 Paul writes, "But if there is no resurrection of the dead, then not even Christ has been raised. And if Christ has not been raised, then our preaching is in vain and your faith is in vain" (ESV). And in 15:16, 17: "For if the dead are not raised, not even Christ has been raised. And if Christ has not been raised, your faith is futile and you are still in your sins" (ESV). Paul is clearly assuming a historical Jesus when he reassures the Corinthians that Christ's resurrection actually happened. If it were not true, then their faith would be invalid. If Jesus had never lived, then Paul couldn't assure the Corinthians he had truly died. And without a historical Jesus, Paul wouldn't have told the Corinthians it was the fact of his resurrection that formed the reason for their hope.

N. T. Wright takes a broad look at resurrection in all of Paul's writings before concluding:

> Paul's many and varied statements about future and present resurrection thus pose a historical question to which the only satisfactory answer, for him and for the historian, is his firm and sharply delineated belief in a past event, the resurrection of Jesus of Nazareth. (Wright, RSG, 374)

And Wright points out how unlikely it is that the first Christians, as a whole, decided to confess that Jesus not only rose from the dead but that the resurrection was also the destiny for his followers:

> One of the most striking features of the early Christian movement is its virtual unanimity

about the future hope. We might have expected that the first Christians would quickly have developed a spectrum of beliefs about life after death, corresponding to the spectrums we have observed in the Judaism from within which Christianity emerged and the paganism into which it went as a missionary movement: but they did not. (Wright, RSG, 209)

There was no development of that idea. It was there from the beginning in Paul and among the first Christians. What could explain this except that Paul truly believed that Jesus really existed, really was crucified unto death, and really rose from the dead?

Wright succinctly states:

They all took the resurrection of Jesus to be a solid, concrete event, leaving an empty tomb behind it, with Jesus' body being thoroughly transformed so as to leave behind forever the possibility of corruption and death (Wright, PFG, 408).

v) Paul believed there were contemporary witnesses to Jesus.

James D. G. Dunn references Galatians 1:18–20

where Paul records his first visit to Jerusalem after his conversion. If his conversion is to be reckoned about two years after Jesus' crucifixion, then his visit to Jerusalem will have to be dated no more than about five years after the crucifixion (mid-30s). On that visit he recalls that he met with "James, the Lord's brother." Later on he refers to "the brothers of the Lord" (1 Cor. 9:5).

It is a work of some desperation which denies the obvious deduction from these references, that there was a man called Jesus whose brothers were well known in the 30s to 60s. (Dunn, JR, 142–143)

We can add to that our discussion on the resurrection from 1 Corinthians 15:6–8, in which Paul tells the Corinthians that there are witnesses to Jesus' resurrection who are still alive.

b. Conclusion

We conclude the study of Paul with Barnett offering three observations in building a case for the historicity of Jesus from a broad view of Paul's writings to the Thessalonians and Corinthians:

One is that the churches in Thessalonica and Corinth came into existence as a result of Paul's proclamation to them about Jesus Christ. The second is that this proclaimed figure was exalted; he is the Christ, the Son of God the Lord. Yet, thirdly, this person, Jesus, was one about whom biographical information was known, probably though [sic] the process of the initial preaching and "handing over" of various "received traditions" to the churches, and from their questions and his answers. Jesus Christ as proclaimed—the impulse for the formation of the churches in Thessalonica and Corinth—was anchored to a historical figure, Jesus. (Barnett, JLH, 50)

Paul and the people to whom he witnessed believed in a literal, historical Jesus who lived, died, rose again, and is planning a return.

3. Other NT Writings
a. Epistles

Barnett offers analysis of the importance of the epistles of James, Hebrews, and 1 Peter for the study of the historicity of Jesus:

The letters of James, Hebrews, and 1 Peter indicate that the churches associated with these leaders also arose from the proclamation of Jesus. Again, it is a historical figure to whom they refer. (Barnett, JLH, 50)

To be sure, James makes no explicit reference to the person of the historical Jesus. There are, however, a number of ethical teachings which appear to echo the teachings of Jesus from a source which the gospel of Matthew seems to have employed. Moreover, his reference to "the wisdom . . . from above" and "the righteous man" whom the Jews killed may be oblique references to Jesus personified, as it were, as wisdom and righteousness. In short, it is clear enough that those who became attached to Jesus through proclamation about him were given instruction in the teachings of the historical Jesus. And—in all likelihood—about his person as well. (Barnett, JLH, 51)

Peter alludes to the historical Jesus, under the rubric, "the sufferings of Christ." He writes that Christ was "made manifest at the end of the times" and that he "suffered in the flesh," but that in those sufferings he did not sin by guileful, vengeful or threatening behaviour. His footprints they were to follow closely. Peter writes to those who have not seen Christ, but as one who had himself seen Christ. . . . Peter had first-hand physical knowledge of Christ. He has been a witness to the sufferings of Jesus. . . . As with other writers who make reference to Jesus, the details are selected as appropriate to the circumstances of the readers; in particular, in their faithful witness to Jesus in circumstances of hostility. Such details are given no elaboration or justification. Evidently both writer and readers knew and accepted the underlying facts about Jesus to which the references apply. (Barnett, JLH, 52–53)

No letter in the New Testament so clearly proclaims the gospel on one hand, and the reality of Jesus as a figure of history on the other, as does the letter to the Hebrews. The unknown author, who was not among the original followers of Jesus, writes as one who heard their proclamation. . . . This powerful sense of proclamation is tied to an equally strong sense of the historical Jesus. The author knows that Jesus was from the tribe of Judah, and therefore not a member of the priestly caste. He writes, "We see Jesus, who for a little while was made lower than the angels . . ." who "partook" in "flesh and blood" so as to be "like his brethren in every respect." This Jesus was "tempted in every way as we are, yet without sin," suggesting a knowledge of specific occasions of temptation faced and overcome by him. He is a compassionate heavenly high priest who "in the days of his flesh . . . offered up prayers and supplications, with loud cries and tears," and who "learned obedience through what he suffered." We sense that, although he speaks in non-specific terms, both the writer and the readers know the circumstances of Jesus' sufferings. Again, without giving details, he refers to the hostility which Jesus suffered. The author repeatedly writes of Jesus' obedience to God, expressed in his sacrificial death offered up for the salvation of others. . . . The allusions to the historical Jesus emphasize his humanity and his perseverance in the face of sufferings for the very understandable reason that his readers needed to persevere in the face of grave difficulties at that time. His very lack of detail by way of elaboration suggests that both he and they knew about the circumstances of Jesus' sufferings. In short, this remarkable document reflects both the fact of the proclamation of the gospel which had come to them and a presumed knowledge of the historical Jesus. (Barnett, JLH, 53–54)

Barnett concludes by discussing James, Hebrews, 1 Peter, and Paul's epistles:

Unless historians of the New Testament take seriously the letters in regard to both the fact of proclamation and the connection of the proclaimed figure to the historical figure of

Jesus, then the engine driving the New Testament from within—Jesus the teacher who, as risen from the dead, was proclaimed as Jesus the Lord—will remain unrecognized. Failing to discern the inner dynamic which gives the New Testament story its impulse, scholars will continue to tinker at the edges, absorbed in background studies, social and psychological analyses and various forms of textual reconstruction, missing the action in the centre which explains everything. This is the logic of history. (Barnett, JLH, 56–57)

In the letters of John, Richard Burridge and Graham Gould see the argument as one over the significance that Jesus, God himself, actually became human:

Clearly the debate here was not about what it means to call Jesus God, or Lord, or Christ, since that is taken for granted (see, for example, 1 John 4:13–15; 2 John 3, 9). Instead in these letters the question was the extent to which Jesus was human. The letters reveal a bitter argument within these churches about which group had the right ideas about Jesus—and which were wrong. John suggests in 1 John 4:2 what the test should be: "How do we know if somebody is giving a prophecy from God? By this we know the Spirit of God: every spirit which confesses that Jesus Christ has come in the flesh is of God, but every spirit which does not confess Jesus, is not of God." In other words, it is the recognition that Jesus came "as a human being among us" which is crucial. Similarly in 2 John 7, "Many deceivers have gone out who do not confess that Jesus Christ has come in the flesh. Such a person is a deceiver and an antichrist." He is referring here to a group which became known in the second century as docetics.

This idea arises from the fact that within Greek thought it was extraordinary to think

that God might actually touch physical matter. The idea of God becoming human, from a Greek philosophical point of view, was outrageous. So some people began to argue that Jesus wasn't really human. Jesus was an apparition from God who appeared to be human when he came among us. Equally, they claimed, Jesus didn't die, he just appeared to die. What these letters underline is that it is absolutely crucial that Jesus is human as well as Lord and Christ, and that Christians confess him as having come "in the flesh." (Burridge and Gould, JTN, 102–103)

On the non-Pauline New Testament epistles as a whole, Burridge and Gould conclude they "take it for granted that [Jesus] is Lord, human and divine, Son of God the Father." (Burridge and Gould, JTN, 105)

b. Revelation

On Revelation, Burridge and Gould write:

This incredibly rich picture, although in very different language from the rest of the books in the New Testament, is saying again that all our hopes, all our dreams, are made real by God in Christ, changing the world by his death, shedding his blood—and making possible the new age of life with God. (Burridge and Gould, JTN, 104–105)

c. Conclusion

The New Testament epistles and book of Revelation make no sense if they are written about a figure who never existed. The writings attempt to root the Christian faith squarely in Jesus' life, death, resurrection, and promised return. Without those things there is no reason to continue in the faith. The writers (and their readers) clearly and firmly believed that Jesus lived and died and rose again.

B. Early Christian Creeds

In a discussion of creeds, we do not mean the cherished belief statements often recited in churches such as the Apostles' Creed or the Nicene Creed. We instead refer to bits of information that would have been transmitted orally *before* the writing of the New Testament, later to be included in the New Testament. These are especially seen in Paul's writings and are "fragments enshrining cardinal beliefs present in the hymns, baptismal responses and eucharistic forms which Pauline research has brought to light." (Martin, "Creed," 190) Licona points out these oral traditions would have "played a large role in the Greco-Roman world, since only a small minority, perhaps less than 10 percent, could read and write." (Licona, RJ, 220)

1. Philippians 2:6–11

New Testament scholar and philosopher of religion Gary Habermas writes:

The earliest Christians were confident that "Jesus Christ is come in the flesh," as proclaimed in the confession found in 1 John 4:2. Seldom was Jesus' incarnation expressed more clearly than in the "pre-Pauline hymn" of Philippians 2:6ff., which speaks of both Jesus' human and divine natures. His humble life on earth is clearly contrasted with his heavenly position "in the form of God" and his later exaltation and worship. (Habermas, HJ, 144–145)

2. Second Timothy 2:8

Another ancient creed which expresses a contrast between aspects of Jesus' life is 2 Timothy 2:8. Here Jesus' birth in the lineage of David is contrasted with his resurrection from the dead, again showing the early Christians' interest in linking Jesus to history. Similarly, Romans 1:3–4 is also an ancient, pre-Pauline

creed. It juxtaposes the man Jesus "made of the seed of David according to the flesh" with the divine Jesus whose claims were vindicated by his rising from the dead. For our present purposes, we need only note the early interest in Jesus' earthly, physical connections, as he was born of a descendent of David's family. As [C. F. D.] Moule relates, it was the same human Jesus who lived, died, and was later vindicated. (Habermas, HJ, 144–145)

3. First Timothy 3:16

This creed is brief:

He was manifested in the flesh, vindicated by the Spirit, seen by angels, proclaimed among the nations, believed on in the world, taken up in glory (ESV).

Like the others, this ancient creed begins by affirming that Jesus became a human, showing how Jesus' humanity was an important aspect of Christianity from the beginning. And Habermas takes a close look at these and other "early reports of events in the life of Jesus" and notices several facts that emerge from an analysis:

We are told that Jesus was really born in human flesh (Phil. 2:6; 1 Tim. 3:16; 1 John 4:2) of the lineage and family of David (Rom. 1:3, 4; 2 Tim. 2:8). We find an implication of his baptism (Rom. 10:9) and that his word was preached, resulting in persons believing his message (1 Tim. 3:16). (Habermas, HJ, 146)

4. First Corinthians 15:3–8

Perhaps 1 Corinthians 15:3–8 contains the most important New Testament creed for the study of the historical existence of Jesus:

For I delivered to you as of first importance what I also received: that Christ died for our sins in accordance with the Scriptures, that he was buried, that he was raised on the third day in accordance with the Scriptures, and that he appeared to Cephas, then to the twelve. Then he appeared to more than five hundred brothers at one time, most of whom are still alive, though some have fallen asleep. Then he appeared to James, then to all the apostles. Last of all, as to one untimely born, he appeared also to me (ESV).

Habermas recognizes the striking and important fact: "That this confession is an early Christian, pre-Pauline creed is recognized by virtually all critical scholars across a very wide theological spectrum." (Habermas, HJ, 153)

Licona looks at the passage specifically for an examination of the claims of Jesus' resurrection, but his conclusions are valid for a broader examination of the historicity of Jesus as well:

In nearly every historical investigation of the resurrection of Jesus, 1 Corinthians 15:3–8 weighs heavily and is perhaps the most important and valuable passage for use by historians when discussing the historicity of the resurrection of Jesus. Its first valuable quality is that it is early . . . we have what seems to be tradition that predates the letter in which it appears. It is believed that Paul wrote the letter we now refer to as 1 Corinthians in AD 54 or 55. If Jesus died in AD 30, we are reading a letter that was written within twenty-five years of Jesus' death by a major church leader who knew a number of those who had walked with Jesus. If this letter contains tradition that Paul has preserved, we are even closer than twenty-five years to the events it claims to report. (Licona, RJ, 223–224)

A major reason Licona says there is widespread support for the fact that in this passage

Paul is using an ancient creed is his use of the words "delivered" and "received" in setting up his report:

Paul asserts that he is about to impart content he received from another; in other words, tradition handed down to him. Numerous Pauline passages inform us that the importance of tradition to Paul and the authority it carried cannot be overstated. Mark and Josephus report that a zeal for tradition was standard for Pharisees, a group to which Paul had belonged. (Licona, RJ, 224)

But where did Paul get the oral traditions used in 1 Corinthians 15:3–8? Habermas offers a solid explanation:

A number of scholars have arrived at the same scenario. Dating Jesus' crucifixion around AD 30, Paul's conversion would have occurred shortly afterwards, about AD 33–35. Three years after his conversion (AD 36–38) he visited Jerusalem and specifically met with Peter and James (Gal. 1:18–19). It is therefore reasoned that the gospel of the death and resurrection of Jesus would in all likelihood be the normal center of discussion, and that the presence of both Peter and James in the list of appearances (1 Cor. 15:5, 7) indicates the probability that Paul received this creed from these apostles when he visited them in Jerusalem.

A Jerusalem location would date Paul's reception of the creed at about five to seven years after the crucifixion. But we can actually proceed back two stages earlier. Since the tradition would actually have been formulated before Paul first heard it, the creed itself would be dated even earlier. Additionally, the independent beliefs themselves, which later composed the formalized creed, would then date back to the actual historical events.

Therefore, we are dealing with material that proceeds *directly* [italics his] from the events in question and this creed is thus crucial in our discussion of the death and resurrection of Jesus. (Habermas, HJ, 155–156)

And there can be no true discussion of the death and resurrection of Jesus unless he was, in fact, an actual man who walked the earth. As Habermas summarizes:

The importance of the creed in 1 Corinthians 15:3ff. can hardly be overestimated. No longer can it be charged that there is no demonstrable early, eyewitness testimony for the resurrection or for the other most important tenets of Christianity [such as the fact that Jesus truly lived], for this creed provides just such evidential data concerning the facts of the gospel, which are the very center of the Christian faith. It links the events themselves with those who actually participated in time and space. As such this creed yields strong factual basis for Christianity through the early and eyewitness reports of the death, burial, and resurrection of Jesus. (Habermas, HJ, 157)

C. Apostolic Fathers

The collection of writings from first- and second-century Christian leaders, known collectively as the Apostolic Fathers, provides significant information not only about the early church, but several of them can be traced back to the apostles, providing helpful information for this study. We examine two of them.

1. Clement of Rome

First Clement is a letter written to the church at Corinth in the late first or early second century from the church at Rome. It is widely believed Clement knew the apostles, including Peter and Paul, and may even be the

man mentioned in Philippians 4:3. (Licona, RJ, 249–250) It includes a reference to Jesus and the early church:

The Apostles received the Gospel for us from the Lord Jesus Christ; Jesus Christ was sent forth from God. So then Christ is from God, and the Apostles are from Christ. Both therefore came of the will of God in the appointed order. Having therefore received a charge, and having been fully assured through the resurrection of our Lord Jesus Christ and confirmed in the word of God with full assurance of the Holy Ghost, they went forth with the glad tidings that the kingdom of God should come. So preaching everywhere in country and town, they appointed their first-fruits, when they had proved them by the Spirit, to be bishops and deacons unto them that should believe. (quoted by Habermas, HJ, 230)

In this passage we have a description of movement from the delivery of the gospel to the apostles, to Jesus' resurrection, to the beginning of the fulfillment of the Great Commission where the apostles began missionary activity. Habermas writes:

This certification of a chain of authority from God to Jesus to the apostles to the early Christian elders is interesting not only in that it was the basis for early doctrinal proclamation and church organization. Additionally, Clement of Rome anchors this authority in the belief that Jesus was raised from the dead and in the Scripture. A miraculous event in history was thus taken as the basic sign of authority behind the preaching of the earliest Christian message. (Habermas, HJ, 230–231)

Ehrman is less sure the letter was actually written by Clement, but still sees solid value for a study of the historical Jesus:

We have an independent witness not just to the life of Jesus as a historical figure but to some of his teachings and deeds. Like all sources that mention Jesus from outside the New Testament, the author of I Clement had no doubt about his real existence and no reason to defend it. Everyone knew he existed. (Ehrman, DJE, 105)

2. Ignatius

Ignatius was the bishop of Antioch who was condemned to death in Rome in the early second century. There are several historical references to Jesus included in letters written by Ignatius including in one to the *Trallians*:

> Jesus Christ who was of the race of David, who was the Son of Mary, who was truly born and ate and drank, was truly persecuted under Pontius Pilate, was truly crucified and died in the sight of those in heaven and on earth and those under the earth; who moreover was truly raised from the dead, His Father having raised Him, who in the like fashion will so raise us also who believe on Him. (quoted in Habermas, HJ, 231)

Here we have Ignatius laying out several significant Christian doctrines, including that Jesus truly lived ("was truly born and ate and drank"), died, and rose from the dead.

In his epistle to the *Smyrneans* he writes:

> He is truly of the race of David according to the flesh, but Son of God by the Divine will and power, truly born of a virgin and baptized by John. . . .
>
> For I know and believe that He was in the flesh even after the resurrection . . . and straitway they [the apostles] touched him and they believed, being joined unto His flesh and His blood. . . . And after His resurrection He ate with them and drank with them. (quoted in Habermas, HJ, 232)

In his letter to the *Magnesians*, Ignatius attempts to sway their opinion:

> Be ye fully persuaded concerning the birth and the passion and the resurrection, which took place in the time of the governorship of Pontius Pilate; for these things were truly and certainly done by Jesus Christ our hope. (quoted by Habermas, HJ, 233)

Habermas summarizes what Ignatius is trying to do in these letters:

> Ignatius attempts to place such events firmly in the realm of history. His purpose, at least partially, is to provide an answer to the threat of Gnosticism, which often denied physical interpretations of some of these events. (Habermas, HJ, 233)

Ehrman sees Ignatius as a significant witness:

> Ignatius, then, provides us yet with another independent witness to the life of Jesus. Again, it should not be objected that he is writing too late to be of any value in our quest. He cannot be shown to have been relying on the Gospels. And he was bishop in Antioch, the city where both Peter and Paul spent considerable time in the preceding generation, as Paul himself tells us in Galatians. His views too can trace a lineage straight back to apostolic times. (Ehrman, DJE, 103–104)

3. Conclusion Regarding the Apostolic Fathers' Testimony

Clement and Ignatius not only assume a historical Jesus, but go to great lengths to affirm key facts about his life on earth. While not as important as writings from direct witnesses to the life of Jesus, they are still early, independent, and trustworthy.

IV. Archaeology

While he doesn't claim there is a "smoking gun" piece of evidence that clearly proves the existence of Jesus, James Charlesworth summarizes significant evidence that expresses the importance of archaeology for Jesus research today. Researchers now have discovered Nazareth, Cana, Bethsaida, and ancient synagogues, and there has been even more excavation of first-century Jerusalem. Charlesworth states:

> Biblical scholars ultimately no longer have the presumed luxury of avoiding data from the times and places in which the biblical records took shape and were edited. For a New Testament scholar to disavow the importance of archaeology for New Testament studies, including Jesus research, is a form of myopia. It leaves the Gospels as mere stories or relics of ancient rhetoric. Archaeological work, perhaps unintentionally, helps the biblical scholar to rethink and re-create the past. . . . The ancient world known to Jesus and his fellow Jews is beginning to appear before our eyes. (Charlesworth, HJ, 694)

Craig Evans writes concerning archaeological research:

> If archaeologists and historians could not find correlation between archaeology and the biblical text, there would be no such thing as "biblical archaeology." But of course they do find such correlation, and lots of it. (Evans, JHW, 1)

However, like Charlesworth, Evans is open about the lack of clear, direct archaeological evidence for the historical Jesus:

> Often what archaeologists uncover is not so much *proof*, but *clarification* [italics his].

The Bible may talk about a given people, a particular place or a major event, but little detail is provided. The precise meaning of the text is unclear. Then an archaeological discovery is made and we understand the story much better.

Of course, archaeology sometimes does prove things. For instance, let's consider what is called biblical minimalism, which is usually in reference to the Old Testament or Hebrew Bible. Here I have in mind especially those minimalists who have argued that David and Solomon are fictional characters, that there was no kingdom of Israel reaching back to the tenth century BCE and that if they existed, there was not the level of literacy required to record the chronicles of such persons and their deeds. Some of these minimalists think the narratives of the Hebrew Bible do not date any earlier than the fifth century BCE. As it turns out—thanks to archaeology—the minimalists are wrong on all these points. (Evans, JHW, 1)

Evans then spends the rest of his book detailing several pieces of significant archaeological evidence before concluding:

> The ideal is to have access to both artifact and text, and that is usually what we have in the study of the Mediterranean world of Jesus of Nazareth and a number of other figures; we have a number of other first- and second-century documents that provide additional information. Every major city mentioned in the Gospels and Acts has been excavated; so have several villages. We have recovered a number of amazing inscriptions, including one that mentions Pilate, the Roman authority who condemned Jesus to the cross, and another one inscribed on a burial box that may be the name of the Jewish high priest Caiaphas, who interviewed Jesus. (Evans, JHW, 141)

While no archaeological evidence clearly points us to proof that Jesus existed, significant evidence supports cities and people described in the Bible. Therefore, one should give weight to the Bible's claim that Jesus actually existed (not to mention its claims about what he did). As archaeology continues to support the Bible in other ways, it lends credence to a belief in the historical existence of Jesus Christ.

V. Concluding Remarks

Both Christian and secular scholars from a large cross section of theological schools have concluded that the evidence we have presented here provides an adequate basis to affirm with confidence that Jesus truly existed.

Maurice Casey was a non-Christian scholar who denied Jesus' virgin birth and resurrection. However, he believed Jesus actually existed. He writes that there is "abundant evidence that Jesus was a first-century Jewish prophet." (Casey, JN, 499)

As mentioned earlier, Bart Ehrman is extremely skeptical about many things affirmed by conservative Christian scholars. However, even he sees overwhelming evidence that a man named Jesus who served as the foundation of the Christian faith actually lived in ancient Israel:

> The reality is that every single author who mentions Jesus—pagan, Christian, or Jewish—was fully convinced that he at least lived. Even the enemies of the Jesus movement thought so; among their many slurs against the religion, his nonexistence is never one of them. . . . Jesus certainly existed. (Ehrman, DJE, 171–173)

Mark Allan Powell, a New Testament scholar at Trinity Lutheran Seminary, understands the widespread acceptance of the existence of the historical Jesus among scholars:

> Most historical scholars (Christian or not) find the attempt to explain away all apparent references to Jesus in Roman writings, much less New Testament epistles, to be an unconvincing tour de force that lapses into special pleading. (Powell, JFH, 254)

However, proving that Jesus existed is not the same as proving he is God, who deserves worship. It is to the subject of his divinity that we turn next.

The reality is that every single author who mentions Jesus—pagan, Christian, or Jewish—was fully convinced that he at least lived. Even the enemies of the Jesus movement thought so; among their many slurs against the religion, his nonexistence is never one of them. . . . Jesus certainly existed.

Bart Ehrman

CHAPTER 7

THE LOFTY CLAIMS OF JESUS

OVERVIEW

I. Introduction: Who Is Jesus?

Pastor Dan Kimball spent years interviewing people regarding their perceptions of Jesus Christ. In his book entitled *They Like Jesus but Not the Church: Insights from Emerging Generations*, he chronicles the positive but ill-informed perception of Jesus in modern culture: "Most people . . . understand Jesus as a peacemaker who loved others and died for what he believed in. They think of him as a rebel who fought for the poor and the oppressed and stood against religious hypocrites." (Kimball, TLJNC, 255) In short, his respondents had a markedly positive attitude toward Jesus even though most knew little

about him. Kimball acknowledged that the majority of those he surveyed had "a limited idea of who he really is." (Kimball, TLJNC, 256) Despite Jesus' renown, his identity remains a mystery to many.

No one doubts that Jesus has been one of the most influential characters of the last two millennia. Jaroslav Pelikan, Sterling Professor Emeritus of History at Yale University, writes, "Regardless of what anyone may personally think or believe about him, Jesus of Nazareth has been the dominant figure in the history of western culture for almost twenty centuries." (Pelikan, JTC, 1) Author Tim LaHaye adds, "Almost everyone who has heard of Jesus has developed an opinion about Him. That

*Regardless of what anyone may personally think or believe
about him, Jesus of Nazareth has been the dominant figure in the
history of western culture for almost twenty centuries.*

Jaroslav Pelikan

is to be expected, for He is not only the most famous person in world history, but also the most controversial." (LaHaye, WBJ, 61)

The controversy about Jesus extends to his core identity. On the one hand, adherents of Christianity believe he is the divine Son of God, the fulfillment of ancient biblical prophecies, and the promised Savior of the world. On the other hand, skeptics contend Jesus was neither divine nor claimed to be. Self-defined atheist and Jesus Seminar fellow Robert M. Price wrote an article critiquing an earlier edition of this chapter. He believes "there is zero evidence that Jesus claimed to be divine." (Price, RJMETDV, Sec. 1B) Renowned skeptic Bart Ehrman argues the concept of deity was ambiguous in Jesus' day, and any such claims (if Jesus in fact made them) are not to be taken as direct declarations of divinity (Ehrman, HJBG, 4). Ehrman believes "Jesus was not originally considered to be God in any sense at all." (Ehrman, HJBG, 44)

So which is it? Was Jesus a mere mortal— the loving, peacemaking cult hero that many today make him out to be? Or was he more than human? Did Jesus claim to be God or only an earthly agent of God? How did his followers and other contemporaries perceive him? Where does the evidence point? Fortunately, the New Testament writers invite us to examine Jesus for ourselves and to discern his significance. As Alister McGrath, Oxford professor of science and religion, writes, "The challenge posed to every succeeding generation by the New Testament witness to Jesus is

not so much, 'What did he teach?' but 'Who is he? And what is his relevance for us?'" (McGrath, UJ, 16)

The remainder of this chapter aims to address these questions by examining Jesus' claims about himself, others' perceptions of him, and relevant supporting material. We begin by reviewing self-proclamations made by Jesus during the trial that led to his death sentence.

II. Jesus' Direct Claims to Deity

A. Claims Made During Jesus' Trial Before the Sanhedrin

But He kept silent and answered nothing. Again the high priest asked Him, saying to Him, "Are You the Christ, the Son of the Blessed?" Jesus said, "I am. And you will see the Son of Man sitting at the right hand of the Power, and coming with the clouds of heaven." Then the high priest tore his clothes and said, "What further need do we have of witnesses? You have heard the blasphemy! What do you think?" And they all condemned Him to be deserving of death
— Mark 14:61–64

Jesus alluded to Daniel's vision of one "coming with the clouds of heaven" and given an everlasting kingdom over "all peoples, nations, and languages." On trial for his life, he was addressing Jewish scholars who would recognize it as an electrifying claim:

And behold, One like the Son of Man, coming with the clouds of heaven! He came to the

Ancient of Days, and they brought Him near before Him. Then to Him was given dominion and glory and a kingdom, that all peoples, nations, and languages should serve Him. His dominion is an everlasting dominion, which shall not pass away, and His kingdom the one which shall not be destroyed. — Dan. 7:13, 14

The late New York state supreme court justice William J. Gaynor assessed the arrest and trial of Jesus from a legal perspective. He concluded that, in Jesus' appearance before the Sanhedrin, blasphemy was the primary charge made against Jesus: "It is plain from each of the gospel narratives, that the alleged crime for which Jesus was tried and convicted was blasphemy. . . . It was for this that the Jews had some time before taken up stones against him as he was teaching." (Gaynor, ATJVLS, 533) Michael Bird, lecturer in theology at Ridley Melbourne College, adds that the charge of blasphemy arose from Jesus' allusion to the "Son of Man" passage in the book of Daniel. Jesus here implies "that he was going to be—or was already being—enthroned with God. . . . [H]e is placing himself within the orbit of divine sovereignty and claiming a place within the divine regency of God Almighty." (Bird, DJTHWG, 65–66)

New Testament scholar Craig Blomberg elaborates on Jesus' reference to Daniel: "In this context, 'Son of Man' means far more than a simple human being. Jesus is describing himself as the 'one like a son of man, coming with the clouds of heaven' who 'approached the Ancient of Days and was led into his presence' and given authority and power over all humanity, leading to universal worship and everlasting dominion (Daniel 7:13–14). This claim to be far more than a mere mortal is probably what elicited the verdict of blasphemy from the Jewish high court." (Blomberg, JG, 397) New Testament

scholar Darrell Bock concurs, stating, "To claim to be able to share God's glory in a Jewish context would mean pointing to an exalted status that is even more than a prophet or any typical view of the Jewish Messiah." (Bock, JAB, 92–93)

Price dismisses the idea that Jesus claimed to be divine at his trial, arguing these New Testament accounts are dubious. He writes, "One begins to suspect that the gospel writers had no real idea of what transpired at Jesus' trial and did the best they could to fill the gap from their imaginations." (Price, RJMETDV, Sec. 2B) How valid is this criticism? In fact, the depiction of Jesus' trial before the Sanhedrin is recorded in three of the Gospels, fulfilling one of Ehrman's primary criteria for authenticity. According to Ehrman, "If a story is found in several of these independent traditions [the Gospels and their source material], then it is far more likely that this story goes back to the ultimate source of the tradition, the life of Jesus itself. This is called the *criterion of independent attestation.*" (Ehrman, HJBG, 95, emphasis in original) By this standard, the account of Jesus' trial recorded in the Gospels is considered to be reliable.

We begin to see the vital importance of the interrogation during Jesus' trial. Attorney Irwin Linton sums it up when he states, "Unique among criminal trials is this one in which not the actions but the identity of the accused is the issue. The criminal charge laid against Christ, the confession or testimony . . . all are concerned with the one question of Christ's real identity and dignity." (Linton, SV, 7) To put it succinctly, Jesus professed his deity in a way the Sanhedrin clearly understood. They expressed their outrage, charged him with blasphemy, and condemned him to death.

Jesus clearly made lofty, seemingly audacious self-proclamations at his trial. Was this an isolated occurrence or indicative of a broader pattern of statements and behavior? To help address that question, we explore Jesus' other claims that ultimately led to his arrest and trial.

B. Equality with God the Father

On a number of occasions, Jesus claimed to be equal to God the Father. A selection of relevant passages is found below.

1. John 10:25–33

Jesus answered. . . . "I and the Father are one." The Jews picked up stones again to stone him. Jesus answered them, "I have shown you many good works from the Father; for which of them are you going to stone me?" The Jews answered him, "It is not for a good work that we are going to stone you but for blasphemy, because you, being a man, make yourself God" (ESV).

Just as in the account of Jesus' trial, his audience here demonstrates a full understanding of his words. There was no doubt in their minds that Jesus' claim to be one with the Father was an assertion of deity. The evangelical New Testament scholar Leon Morris writes, "The Jews could regard Jesus' word only as blasphemy, and they proceeded to take the judgment into their own hands. It was laid down in the Law that blasphemy was to be punished by stoning (Lev. 24:16)." (Morris, GAJ, 524)

2. John 5:17, 18

But Jesus answered them, "My Father has been working until now, and I have been working." Therefore the Jews sought all the more to kill Him, because He not only broke the Sabbath, but also said that God was His Father, making Himself equal with God.

In this exchange, Jesus' hearers again interpret his statement to be a declaration of parity with God. Why would they draw this conclusion merely from Jesus' reference to God as his father? The fifth-century church father Theodore of Mopsuestia explained that "he told those who were accusing him of violating the Sabbath, 'My Father is still working, and I also am working,' proving [claiming] that he had the power to work just like the Father and that he was, like the Father, immune from any rule and law. He also maintained and demonstrated his equality with God when he said that God was his Father, not in the usual way, but in a higher and more sublime way because he was born of him and was of the same nature as his Father." (Theodore of Mopsuestia, CGJ, 50)

3. John 8:57–59a

Then the Jews said to Him, "You are not yet fifty years old, and have You seen Abraham?" Jesus said to them, "Most assuredly, I say to you, before Abraham was, I AM." Then they took up stones to throw at Him.

The phrase "I AM" is broadly understood to refer to the God of the Old Testament and was so understood by Jesus' Jewish audience. (Their response indicates their instant recognition that such a statement made by a mere man would be blasphemy, deserving death.) For example, in the book of Exodus, God said to Moses, "I AM WHO I AM. . . . Thus you shall say to the children of Israel, 'I AM has sent me to you'" (Ex. 3:14). *The Tyndale Bible Dictionary* explains, "When Moses was called, he asked God to identify himself in such a way that Moses might gain acceptance from the Hebrew people. God revealed himself to Moses as the great 'I AM'" (Elwell and Comfort, TBD, 623). God uses this title as a self-reference elsewhere in the Old Testament, such as in the books of Deuteronomy and Isaiah.

In the above passage from John, Jesus' Jewish audience questions him about his claim to have known the patriarch Abraham. In response, Jesus implies his own preexistence, saying, "Most assuredly, I say to you, before Abraham was, I AM" (John 8:58). Johannine researcher Masanobu Endo writes, "This is the climactic statement of the long dialogue between the Jews and Jesus (John 8:12–59), in which Jesus' identity is hotly debated. . . . The Jews understood this saying as an assertion of the pre-existence of Jesus (John 8:57), and presumably as something related to the proclamation of deity (John 8:59)." (Endo, CC, 232–233)

As we observed in each of the prior scriptural passages examined, the reaction of Jesus' audience leaves little doubt that they understood his reference as a claim to divinity. They quickly set about to fulfill the Mosaic law for blasphemy by stoning him. Summarizing the implications of this passage, biblical scholar Raymond Brown writes, "No clearer implication of divinity is found in the Gospel tradition." (Brown, GAJ, 367)

4. John 5:22, 23

"The Father judges no one, but has given all judgment to the Son, that all may honor the Son, just as they honor the Father. Whoever does not honor the Son does not honor the Father who sent him" (ESV).

We already considered the earlier portion of this discourse in the fifth chapter of John, when Jesus portrayed himself as equal with God. In these verses, Jesus elaborates on that theme with two profound statements: First, he claims to be worthy of the same honor due God the Father. Second, he declares that God cannot be honored unless Jesus himself is also honored. Apologists Robert Bowman and Ed Komoszewski write, "In the monotheistic Jewish culture, to honor God meant to confess and live in the light of his exclusive status as the maker, sustainer, and sovereign King of all creation. . . . Linking the honor due God with the honor due anyone else in this way was unprecedented in the Jewish Scriptures. That Jesus is here claiming *divine* honor is evident from the immediate context" (Bowman and Komoszewski, PJHP, 31, emphasis in original).

5. John 14:7–9

"If you had known me, you would have known my Father also. From now on you do know him and have seen him." Philip said to him, "Lord, show us the Father, and it is enough for us." Jesus said to him, "Have I been with you so long, and you still do not know me, Philip? Whoever has seen me has seen the Father. How can you say, 'Show us the Father'?" (ESV)

Jesus here declares that to know and see him is equivalent to knowing and seeing the Father. Bowman and Komoszewski comment, "Jesus claims to be such a perfect revelation of the Father that anyone who has seen him has seen the Father. . . . What Jesus claims is astonishing. *If you want to see the Father, you cannot do any better than seeing Jesus.* Seeing Jesus the Son is as good as seeing the Father." (Bowman and Komoszewski, PJHP, 78, emphasis in original) Author and minister William Barclay adds, "To the Greeks, God was characteristically *The Invisible*; the Jews would count it as an article of faith that no one had seen God at any time. To people who thought like that, Jesus said: 'If you had known me, you would have known my Father too.' It may well be that to the ancient world this was the most staggering thing Jesus ever said." (Barclay, BL, 137–38, emphasis in original)

6. Addressing Criticism of Jesus' Claims in the Gospel of John

Skeptics commonly dismiss Jesus' statements of deity found in the gospel of John, arguing such proclamations are inventions of the gospel writer not attributable to the historical Jesus. Ehrman, for example, contends Jesus' claims to be God lack credibility because they are found only in John, "the last and most theologically loaded of the four Gospels" (Ehrman, HJBG, 86–87). He says they fail his criteria for authenticity, such as multiple attestation, dissimilarity,* and contextual credibility (Ehrman, HJBG, 125). It should be noted that Ehrman clearly acknowledges the existence of Jesus' claims to be God in the gospel of John (Ehrman, HJBG, 4–5, 86–87, 124–25, 271–72). Nevertheless, he contends their absence outside of John diminishes the gospel's credibility. He asks, "If Jesus really went around calling himself God, wouldn't the other Gospels at least mention the fact?" (Ehrman, HJBG, 87).

How should these types of concerns be addressed? Many scholars argue that Ehrman's criteria and methodologies are fundamentally flawed. Bird writes, "Approaches like Ehrman's, which begin by casting doubt on the historical value of the Gospels for reconstructing the life of Jesus, but then proceed to formulate a hypothesis about the historical Jesus anyway, are essentially creating a vacuum and then filling it with scholarly fiction. . . . Ehrman's entire approach to historical Jesus studies does not commend itself as a good way of doing history." (Bird, DJTHWG, 48–49, 51) Bird accurately notes that Ehrman's objection implies his contradictory reliance upon the historical record of the other Gospels, even while questioning the reliability of John's record. An appendix at the back of this book is dedicated to answering Ehrman's skepticism in greater detail.

Nevertheless, we have strong reasons to accept the authenticity of Jesus' claims

to deity found in the gospel of John. For example, external evidence is virtually unanimous in ascribing the gospel's authorship to the apostle John, who was an intimate eyewitness of Jesus' ministry. (Carson and Moo, INT, 1:91–104) Chapter 3 of this book more fully addresses the credibility of the gospel accounts.

Moreover, Jesus' claims to deity are by no means restricted to the gospel of John. While John's gospel bears a unique style in comparison with those of Matthew, Mark, and Luke (also known as the Synoptic Gospels), its depiction of the divine Son of God is not exclusive. We have already reviewed the account of Jesus' trial before the Sanhedrin, which is found in each of the Synoptic Gospels. In the remainder of this chapter, we examine numerous other equally profound claims by Jesus recorded outside of John.

7. Matthew 11:27

"All things have been handed over to me by my Father, and no one knows the Son except the Father, and no one knows the Father except the Son and anyone to whom the Son chooses to reveal him." (ESV)

The first part of this statement appears ordinary. When Jesus says that "no one knows the Son except the Father," he seems simply to observe about himself what many others might likewise observe: that God's knowledge of him is exceptional. However, when he continues, saying that his own knowledge of God the Father is reciprocally exceptional, he makes a remarkable claim of equality with God. Theologian Robert Reymond writes, "Jesus puts emphasis upon the exclusiveness of this mutual knowledge ('no one knows except'). But just as striking is the inference

---

* According to the criterion of dissimilarity, sayings of Jesus that appear dissimilar from what the early Christians believed and would have wanted to say about him are more likely to be authentic and attributable to the historical Jesus.

that the nature of this knowledge which Jesus claims to have lifts him above the sphere of the ordinary mortal and places him 'in a position, not of equality merely, but of absolute reciprocity and interpenetration of knowledge with the Father.'" (Reymond, NSTCF, 219) A similar account appears in Luke, reinforcing the fact that this declaration by Jesus is multiply attested outside the gospel of John.

8. Matthew 5:21–48

"You have heard that it was said to those of old. . . . But I say to you . . ."

The above statement is an excerpt from Jesus' Sermon on the Mount, where he repeatedly cites the Old Testament law, and then asserts his own authority as supreme. This was extraordinary in a Jewish culture that revered the teachings of its prophets and patriarchs as sacred. Instead of repeating the prophets by saying, "Thus saith the Lord," Jesus elevates the authority of his own words above theirs. On at least six occasions (commonly referred to as the *antitheses*), he uses the formula, "You have heard that it was said . . . but I say to you." For example, Jesus recites the commands against murder and adultery, then declares that the essence of those mandates is directed at an individual's thought life (Matt. 5:21–30), something not explicitly broached by the Mosaic Law. He later appears to undermine the Mosaic system of vows and oaths, stating, "Do not take an oath at all. . . . Let what you say be simply 'Yes' or 'No'; anything more than this comes from evil" (Matt. 5:34–37 ESV). This passage highlights Jesus' claims to authority superior to that of both Jewish tradition and the Mosaic Law.

In support of Jesus' declaration of divine authority, New Testament scholar Douglas Moo writes, "What does consistently emerge from the antitheses is Jesus' radical insistence on what *he* says as binding on his followers. He taught 'as one who had authority, and not as their teachers of the law' (Matt. 7:29 [NIV])." (Moo, LCAFLM, 350) Stephen J. Wellum, professor of Christian theology, elaborates: "The christological claim is simply staggering. Jesus understands himself to be the eschatological goal of the Old Testament . . . and thus he is the Old Testament's sole authoritative interpreter. In other words, Jesus understands himself as having the authority of God and is thus identified with him." (Wellum, DCSG, 75)

Price takes issue with this inference, arguing that Jesus' antitheses actually follow a pattern commonly found among ancient Jewish writings. He asserts, "There is nothing distinctly Christian about [the antitheses], much less anything requiring the authority of an avatar of Jehovah to establish such contrasts." (Price, RJMETDV, Sec. 7C) While antithetical statements were indeed frequent in the Jewish commentary upon the Law, intending to sift interpretations of its meanings, standing at odds with Price is Rabbi Jacob Neusner, a scholar of Talmud and rabbinic literature who has written, edited, or translated more than nine hundred books. Neusner believes the statements made by Jesus in the antitheses were uniquely bold and imply a claim of divine authority. He finds Jesus' antitheses "jarring" because his language "contrasts strikingly with Moses' language at Mount Sinai. . . . Jesus speaks not as a sage nor as a prophet." According to Neusner, "no one can encounter Matthew's Jesus without concurring that before us in the evangelist's mind is God incarnate." (Neusner, RTJ, 31)

C. Jesus Received Worship as God

1. Worship Reserved for God Only

"You shall worship the LORD your God, and Him only you shall serve" — Matthew 4:10 (cf. Luke 4:8)

The Bible issues a persistent warning against worshiping anything or anyone but God himself. The first of the Ten Commandments states, "You shall have no other gods before Me" (Ex. 20:3). The Old Testament is filled with cautions against idolatry, admonitions to those engaging in the practice, warnings of grave consequences should they persist, and detailed descriptions of those consequences as they were experienced. The New Testament similarly warns people to "flee from idolatry" (1 Cor. 10:14). In the passage referenced above, Jesus declares worship should be restricted to God alone. He taught people to worship God "in spirit and truth" (John 4:19–24).

Jesus' disciples clearly understood this message. In the book of Acts, we read of Peter's reaction to someone's attempt to worship him: "As Peter was coming in, Cornelius met him and fell down at his feet and worshiped him. But Peter lifted him up, saying, 'Stand up; I myself am also a man'" (Acts 10:25, 26). Later, we read of a similar encounter with the apostles Paul and Barnabas in Lystra: "Now when the people saw what Paul had done, they raised up their voices, saying in the Lycaonian language, 'The gods have come down to us in the likeness of men!' . . . But when the apostles Barnabas and Paul heard this, they tore their clothes and ran in among the multitude, crying out and saying, 'Men, why are you doing these things? We also are men with the same nature as you, and preach to you that you should turn from these useless things to the living God'" (Acts 14:11, 14, 15).

The New Testament makes clear that worship is equally inappropriate for elevated spiritual beings, such as angels. In the book of Revelation, the apostle John records his encounter with an angel: "And I fell at his feet to worship him. But he said to me, 'See that you do not do that! I am your fellow servant, and of your brethren who have the testimony of Jesus. Worship God!'" (Rev. 19:10).

2. Jesus Received Worship as God and Accepted It

From the above passages, we note that worship, one of the most common themes of the Bible, is suitable solely for God. Idolatry is an egregious offense. It is remarkable, then, to find that Jesus freely accepted worship. Note the following examples:

Then those who were in the boat came and worshiped Him, saying, "Truly You are the Son of God." — Matthew 14:33

Then he said, "Lord, I believe!" And he worshiped [Jesus]. — John 9:38

Jesus met them, saying, "Rejoice!" So they came up and held Him by the feet and worshiped Him. — Matthew 28:9

When one reads the full context of each of these passages, an interesting pattern develops: on no occasion did Jesus correct people for worshiping him. In contrast to his disciples and angels, Jesus readily accepted worship. Bowman and Komoszewski write, "After it is made clear in Matthew that Jesus regarded God as the only proper object of worship (*proskuneō*), it is striking that Jesus appears so frequently in the same Gospel to be the object of worship." (Bowman and Komoszewski, PJHB, 38) New Testament scholar Richard Bauckham comments that the New Testament texts "include Jesus in the unique divine identity as Jewish monotheism understood it. They do this deliberately and comprehensively by using precisely those characteristics of the divine identity on which Jewish monotheism focused in characterizing God as unique. . . . [T]hey portray him as accorded the worship which, for Jewish monotheists, is recognition of the unique divine identity" (Bauckham, JGI, 19).

3. Worship of Jesus Now and in the Future

Not only did Jesus accept worship during his first-century ministry, but the New Testament alludes to current and future worship of Jesus. For example, the book of Hebrews says, "Let all the angels of God worship [Jesus]" (Heb. 1:6). The book of Revelation likewise describes the future worship of Jesus: "And the twenty-four elders fell down and worshiped [Jesus]" (Rev. 5:14).

On this topic, McGrath concludes: "Within the Jewish context in which the first Christians operated, it was God and God alone who was to be worshipped. . . . Yet the early Christian church worshiped Christ as God—a practice which is clearly reflected even in the New Testament." (McGrath, CT, 272)

D. What Others Said
1. The Apostle Paul
a. Romans 9:5

> To them belong the patriarchs, and from their race, according to the flesh, is the Christ, who is God over all, blessed forever. Amen (ESV).

Paul concludes a discussion of the blessings and privileges given to the Jews by praising Christ as "God over all." Murray J. Harris, professor emeritus of New Testament exegesis and theology, comments on the meaning of this passage in the original Greek: "What the apostle is affirming at the end of 9:1–5 is this: As opposed to the indignity of rejection accorded him by most of his fellow Israelites, the Messiah, Jesus Christ, is in fact exalted over the whole universe, animate and inanimate, including the Jews who reject him, in that he is God by nature, eternally the object of worship." (Harris, JAG, 172)

b. Philippians 2:6–11

> Who, being in very nature God, did not consider equality with God something to be used to his own advantage; rather he made himself nothing by taking the very nature of a servant, being made in human likeness. And being found in appearance as a man, he humbled himself by becoming obedient to death—even death on a cross! Therefore God exalted him to the highest place and gave him the name that is above every name, that at the name of Jesus every knee should bow, in heaven and on earth and under the earth, and every tongue acknowledge that Jesus Christ is Lord, to the glory of God the Father (NIV).

In the beginning of this passage, the apostle Paul describes Christ as having preexisted as God before voluntarily taking on human likeness. Biblical scholar F. F. Bruce says the term "nature of God" literally means "'being already in the form of God.' Possession of the form implies participation in the essence. It seems fruitless to argue that these words do not assume the pre-existence of Christ." (Bruce, Philippians, 68) N. T. Wright similarly observes, "The idiom here used clearly assumes that the object in question—in this case equality with God—is already possessed. One cannot decide to take advantage of something one does not already have." (Wright, CC, 82)

Paul also describes Jesus as having taken on a dual nature, being both truly God and truly man. He expresses this by affirming that Jesus possessed both the "nature" (the NIV's rendering of the Greek morphē) of God (v. 6) and the "nature" (also morphē) of a human servant (v. 7). As theologian Peter Toon writes: "The contrast of the heavenly and earthly existence suggests that morphē points to a participation in God which is real, just as partaking in human life and history was real for Jesus." (Toon, OTG, 168)

Paul says that after Jesus' death, he was again exalted to the highest place, to which "every knee should bow" (v. 10). Bruce comments that this passage takes the form of a hymn reminiscent of descriptions used by God of himself in the Old Testament:

> The hymn includes echoes of Isaiah 52:13 . . . and also of Isaiah 45:23, where the one true God swears by Himself: "To me every knee shall bend, every tongue make solemn confession." But in the Christ-hymn it is this same God who decrees that every knee shall bend at Jesus' name and every tongue confess that Jesus Christ is Lord. . . . It is sometimes asked whether "the name above every name" in the Christ-hymn is "Jesus" or "Lord." It is both, because by divine decree the name "Jesus" henceforth has the value of the name "Lord" in the highest sense which that name can bear—the sense of the Hebrew Yahweh. (Bruce, JLS, 202)

Thus, Paul here confesses the deity of Christ in three ways: by his preexistent God nature, by his dual nature as both human and divine, and by ultimately equating him with the exclusive name of God (Lord, Yahweh) of the Old Testament.

c. Colossians 1:15–17

He is the image of the invisible God, the first-born of all creation. For by him all things were created, in heaven and on earth, visible and invisible, whether thrones or dominions or rulers or authorities—all things were created through him and for him. And he is before all things, and in him all things hold together. (ESV)

The apostle Paul again ascribes attributes of deity to Jesus, whom he refers to as "the image of the invisible God" (v. 15). Paul asserts that even though God the Father is unseen, his image and likeness have been conveyed through Jesus. Wheaton College scholar Christopher Beetham explains, "The phrase 'image of the invisible God' expresses the same idea as Hebrews 1:3, that the Son 'is the radiance of the glory of God and the exact imprint of his nature.'" (Beetham, KB, 30) Writer and speaker Peter Lewis adds: "What [Jesus] images he must also possess; he images God's real being precisely because he shares that real being. As the image of God, Jesus Christ is God's equivalent in the world of men (John 14:9)." (Lewis, GC, 241) The explanation that Lewis gives is so important to grasp because our modern culture has forgotten how to think of the spiritual as truly real; Jesus conveys the glory of God because he is God.

Paul then credits Jesus with a central role in creation, stating that all things were created by him, through him, and for him. Professor of theology Stephen Wellum notes that this passage is "consistent with other New Testament texts that attribute the divine work of creation to the Son, thus teaching his deity." (Wellum, DCAP, 136) Beetham adds, "Paul writes that not only is the Son the agent *through* whom God created all things, but he is also the *goal* or purpose for which they all exist. . . . Elsewhere in the New Testament, such language is reserved for God alone." (Beetham, KB, 31)

d. Colossians 2:9

For in Him dwells all the fullness of the God-head bodily.

This statement perhaps most succinctly captures the understanding of Jesus held by the apostle Paul and his contemporaries. Theologian Carl F. H. Henry, the first editor-in-chief of *Christianity Today*, comments: "The belief that gives the Christian confession its singularly unique character, that in Jesus Christ dwelt 'all the fullness of the Godhead bodily' (Col. 2:9), is an integral and definitive aspect of the New Testament teaching; it is affirmed and reiterated by the apostles who were contemporaries of Jesus." (Henry, IJN, 53)

e. Titus 2:13

> . . . waiting for our blessed hope, the appearing of the glory of our great God and Savior Jesus Christ (ESV).

Before interpreting this particular sentence in Paul's letter to Titus, it is worth recalling the widespread recognition that the Hebrew Scriptures frequently state an idea in one way and immediately echo or intensify it by a different word or set of words (parallelism). Paul, himself a highly trained Pharisee scholar, would have internalized that pattern of saying something in a double way.

In this reference to "our great God and Savior," Paul again seems clearly to declare Jesus to be God. Nevertheless, some scholars have debated the proper interpretation of the original Greek phrasing. Some understand the statement to refer to two separate persons—"the great God" and "our Savior Jesus Christ." Several older English Bibles translated the verse in this way. Others understand the two nouns *God* and *Savior* to refer to the same person, Jesus Christ. This interpretation flows from the Granville Sharp rule, which states that when two personal nouns (not proper names) are preceded by a single article and connected by "and," both nouns refer to the same person in the original Greek. Can this rule be rightly applied to the Greek construction of Titus 2:13 to underscore Paul's belief in Jesus' deity?

Daniel B. Wallace is a Greek scholar and grammarian, and the founder of the Center for the Study of New Testament Manuscripts. In his book on the Granville Sharp rule, he concludes, "The most natural way to read Titus 2:13, then, in light of its own literary style and theology, is to see 'Jesus Christ' as in apposition to 'our Great God and Savior.'" (Wallace, GSCIK, 263) In other words, the entire phrase refers to Jesus. Bowman and Komoszewski concur: "The most natural way of understanding this particular construction is that both nouns refer to the same person." (Bowman and Komoszewski, PJHP, 151) Elsewhere, Wallace writes, "There is no good reason to reject Titus 2:13 as an explicit affirmation of the deity of Christ." (Wallace, GGBB, 276) In accordance with this view, almost all contemporary versions of the New Testament are now translated as above, linking Paul's use of the word "God" with Jesus Christ. This verse thus adds to the abundance of evidence that the apostle Paul understood and declared Jesus to be God.

2. John the Baptist

> And the Holy Spirit descended on him in bodily form, like a dove; and a voice came from heaven, "You are my beloved Son; with you I am well pleased" — Luke 3:22 ESV

In John 1:29, 34, John the Baptist proclaims: "'Behold, the Lamb of God, who takes away the sin of the world! . . . I have seen and have borne witness that this is the Son of God" (ESV). Latter portions of this chapter elaborate on the uniqueness of Jesus' sonship and why John's use of the title "Son of God" in this context refers to his deity.

3. The Apostle Peter

> Simon Peter, a bondservant and apostle of Jesus Christ, to those who have obtained like precious faith with us by the righteousness of our God and Savior Jesus Christ. — 2 Peter 1:1

After dissecting this passage in the original Greek, Harris writes, "The conclusion seems inescapable that in 2 Peter 1:1 the title [our God and Savior] . . . is applied to Jesus Christ." (Harris, JAG, 238) Wallace concurs, interpreting this passage in a manner similar to that of Titus 2:13 described above. The application of the Granville Sharp rule renders this an explicit affirmation by Peter of Jesus' deity. (Wallace, GGBB, 277) Wellum elaborates on this title applied by both Paul and Peter, noting that these passages "make a similar claim even though they are written by different authors, namely, that Jesus Christ is 'our God and Savior' (tou theou hēmōn kai sōtēros). Harris notes that in the first century, the formula 'God and Savior' was a common religious expression used by both Palestinian and Diaspora Jews in reference to Yahweh, the one true God, and . . . is best explained by viewing 'God and Savior' as a title that applies to one person—Jesus Christ." (Wellum, DCSG, 146)

4. The Apostle Thomas

And Thomas answered and said to Him, "My Lord and my God!" — John 20:28

Theologian John Stott expounds on Thomas's exclamation: "John reports that on the Sunday following Easter Day, incredulous Thomas was with the other disciples in the upper room when Jesus appeared. He invited Thomas to feel His wounds, and Thomas, overwhelmed with wonder, cried out, 'My Lord and my God!' Jesus accepted the designation. He rebuked Thomas for his unbelief, not for his worship." (Stott, BC, 28–29)

5. The Writer of Hebrews

a. Hebrews 1:3

He is the radiance of the glory of God and the exact imprint of his nature, and he upholds the universe by the word of his power (ESV).

Related to the use of the phrase *exact imprint of his nature*, Bruce comments, "Just as the image and superscription on a coin exactly correspond to the device on the die, so the Son of God 'bears the very stamp of his nature' (RSV). The Greek word *charaktēr*, translated as "the exact imprint" or as "the very stamp," occurs only here in the New Testament and expresses this truth even more emphatically than *eikōn*, which is used elsewhere to denote Christ as the 'image' of God (2 Cor. 4:4; Col. 1:15)" (Bruce, EH, 48). Kathryn Tanner, Marquand Professor of Systematic Theology at Yale Divinity School, adds, "The image most properly speaking—the express or perfect image of God (following Heb. 1:3)—is the second person of the Trinity" (Tanner, CSIIG, 63).

b. Hebrews 1:7, 8

Of the angels he says, "He makes his angels winds, and his ministers a flame of fire." But of the Son he says, "Your throne, O God, is forever and ever, the scepter of uprightness is the scepter of your kingdom" (ESV).

In this case, the writer of Hebrews quotes Psalm 45 in reference to Jesus. Raymond Ortlund Jr., expert in Old Testament and Semitic languages, notes, "The author's purpose is to validate from the Old Testament the conviction that Jesus, as the Son of God, is superior to angels. . . . Psalm 45, if allowed to speak for itself, demands recognition as a prophecy of a divine-human Messiah." (Ortlund, DCOT, 46–47)

Harris elaborates on the contrast drawn by the author of Hebrews between angels and Jesus: "Over against the variability of angelic function, the author sets the stability of the Son's throne and the constancy of his rectitude. Over against the evanescence and impermanence of angelic form, the author sets the eternality and divinity of the Son's person. Whereas the angels are addressed by God, the Son may be addressed *as God.*" (Harris, JAG, 217, emphasis in original)

6. The Apostle John

a. John 1:1, 14

> In the beginning was the Word, and the Word was with God, and the Word was God. . . . And the Word became flesh and dwelt among us, and we beheld His glory, the glory as of the only begotten of the Father, full of grace and truth.

Theologian R. C. Sproul comments on John 1:1 with reference to the Word (Gk. *Logos*): "In this remarkable passage the *Logos* is both distinguished from God ('was with God') and identified with God ('was God')." (Sproul, ETCF, 109) J. Carl Laney, professor of biblical literature, says that John 1:1 affirms "the eternal existence (v. 1a), personal distinctiveness (v. 1b), and divine nature of the Logos [Word] (v. 1c)." (Laney, *John,* 37–38) Wallace elaborates on the significance of the Greek used in the phrase, "the Word was God." The phrase's composition indicates that the Word was the same essence as the God referred to in the prior phrase. Wallace writes, "The construction the evangelist chose to express this idea was the most concise way he could have stated that the Word was God and yet was distinct from the Father." (Wallace, GGBB, 269)

b. First John 5:20

> And we know that the Son of God has come and has given us understanding, so that we may know him who is true; and we are in him who is true, in his Son Jesus Christ. He is the true God and eternal life (ESV).

With the final statement, "He is the true God and eternal life," the apostle John again declares Jesus to be both the Son of God and God. Some question whether this pronouncement actually refers to Jesus or to God the Father. Wallace notes the original Greek pronoun translated *he* almost always refers to Jesus elsewhere in John's writings, and never refers to the Father. He concludes, "There are no grammatical reasons for denying that [the Greek phrase] is descriptive of Jesus Christ." (Wallace, GGBB, 327) New Testament scholar Rudolf Schnackenburg comments, "Here the full identity of Jesus with God is recognized without reserve (note the article with *theos,* God) . . . the climactic christological confession becomes visible here in all its clarity." (Schnackenburg, JE, 263) Referring to this passage, professor of New Testament Robert Yarbrough asks, "What higher commendation is possible? [Jesus] is the ultimate with respect to both who he is (God) . . . and what he confers (eternal life)." (Yarbrough, *1–3 John,* 318)

7. Skeptical Challenges to the Perception of Jesus as God

Some skeptics claim that belief in Jesus as God developed gradually and did not coalesce until long after the first century. They contend the preceding scriptural passages cannot be taken at face value as declarations of Jesus' divinity as we understand it today. Instead, there was an evolutionary process of creedal clarification that culminated in the Council of Nicea in the fourth century.

But even Ehrman concedes that belief in the deity of Christ began very early. He writes, "The idea that Jesus is God is not an invention of modern times. . . . [I]t was the view of the very earliest Christians soon after Jesus' death." (Ehrman, WJBG, 3–4) He claims, however, that the first Christians' concept of divinity was much more ambiguous than what today prevails in modern orthodoxy. The separation between mortal and heavenly beings was not distinct. Ehrman states, "The human realm was not an absolute category separated from the divine realm by an enormous and unbridgeable crevasse. On the contrary, the human and divine were two continuums that could, and did, overlap." (Ehrman, WJBG, 4) What Ehrman says about the overlapping of the human and divine aligns with many Greek (and Roman) tales of their gods, but it decidedly would not fit the Jewish high understanding of God. It is worth remembering here that the New Testament writers, aside from Paul's close companion Luke, were all Jewish, and the early Gentile church received its teaching from these Jewish writers.

In a book written with the express purpose of responding to Ehrman's claims about Jesus' deity, New Testament scholar Simon Gathercole argues the first Christians held a fully exalted view of Jesus' divinity. He notes that Ehrman believes the Synoptic Gospels consider Jesus divine, albeit in a lesser sense than the one true God of Israel. Gathercole counters that Jesus' divinity—described in the Gospels—must be understood in relation to the Jewish environment of the first century. He writes, "This divine identity cannot be seen as a lower-grade divine identity, because of the absolute distinction between God and creation presupposed in the religious environment of the earliest disciples." (Gathercole, FC, 98–99)

Robert Bowman similarly emphasizes the importance of interpreting the New Testament in its proper Jewish religious context, as opposed to a Greco-Roman context. He writes, "Ehrman's foundational premise of the fluidity of ancient concepts of the divine is certainly a major problem. Ehrman rightly finds such fluidity in Greco-Roman thought, but what he never addresses even once is the consistent, pervasive opposition to Greco-Roman notions of the divine throughout the New Testament. . . . Generalizations about 'divine humans' in antiquity are simply irrelevant to understanding the origins of a Jewish movement that regarded its crucified human founder as God." (Bowman, HJBG, Sec. Ehrman, Par. 1)

Richard Bauckham studied the relationship of early beliefs about Jesus in the context of the Jewish monotheism of the first century. He also counters Ehrman's assertions about vague Jewish conceptions of deity, writing, "When New Testament Christology is read with this Jewish theological context in mind, it becomes clear that, from the earliest post-Easter beginnings of Christology onwards, early Christians included Jesus, precisely and unambiguously, within the unique identity of the one God of Israel." (Bauckham, JGI, ix)

Bowman confirms that the biblical testimony of Jesus includes a clear concept of deity. He writes, "The Synoptic Gospels do have a Christology of divine identity in a strong sense." (Bowman, HJBG) Bowman and Komoszewski add, "The New Testament clearly teaches that Jesus is God. . . . Jesus is identified as the Lord (that is, YHWH) of the Old Testament (Rom. 10:9–13; 1 Cor. 8:6; Phil. 2:9–11; 1 Peter 3:13–15). He is the King of kings and Lord of lords (Rev. 17:14; 19:16), the divine Savior (Titus 2:13; 2 Peter 1:11), the one who says 'I am' or 'I am he' (John 8:24, 28, 58), the first and the last, the Alpha and the Omega, and the beginning and the end (Rev. 1:7–8, 17b–18; 2:8; 22:12–13)." (Bowman and Komoszewski, PJHP, 272–273) In sum, the direct claims of Jesus' eyewitnesses and others about his deity were early, clear, and unmistakable.

8. Summary of Declarations of Jesus to Be Jehovah God

The following chart identifies titles applied in Scripture to both God and Jesus, thus proving that Scripture presents Jesus as none other than Jehovah God.

JESUS IS DECLARED TO BE JEHOVAH GOD

Said of Jehovah	Mutual Title or Act	Said of Jesus
Gen. 1:1–3; Ps. 102:25; Isa. 44:24	Creator	John 1:3; Heb. 1:2—3:10
Isa. 45:15, 21, 22; 43:11	Savior	John 4:42
Deut. 32:39; 1 Sam. 2:6	Raising the Dead	John 5:28, 29; 10:27, 28
Ps. 62:12; Joel 3:12	Judge	Matt. 25:31–46; John 5:22, 23
Isa. 60:19, 20	Light	John 8:12
Ex. 3:14; Deut. 32:39; Isa. 43:10	I Am	John 8:24, 28, 58; 18:5–8
Ps. 23:1	Shepherd	John 10:11
Isa. 42:8; cf. 48:11	Glory of God	John 17:1, 5
Isa. 41:4; 44:6; 48:12	First and Last	Rev. 1:7–8,17–18; 2:8; 22:12–13
Hos. 13:14	Redeemer	Rev. 5:9
Isa. 62:5; Hos. 2:16	Bridegroom	Rev. 21:2, cf. Matt. 25:1ff.
Ps. 18:2	Rock	1 Cor. 10:4
Ex. 34:6, 7; Jer. 31:34	Forgiver of Sins	Mark 2:7, 10; Acts 5:31
Ps. 97:7; 148:2	Worshiped by Angels	Heb. 1:6
Joel 2:32; throughout O. T.	Addressed in Prayer	Acts 7:59, 60; Rom. 10:12, 13
Ps. 148:5	Creator of Angels	Col. 1:16
Isa. 45:23	Confessed as Lord (Jehovah)	Phil. 2:9–11

This chart originally appeared in Josh McDowell, *The New Evidence That Demands a Verdict* (Nashville, TN: Thomas Nelson, 1999), 148.

III. Jesus' Indirect Claims to Deity

In addition to the direct claims to deity outlined above, Jesus did and said many other things that implied his divinity. In other words, even when he did not overtly declare that he was God, his actions and words were often consistent only with his being God. Listed below are several examples of his indirect claims to deity.

A. Jesus Forgave Sins

And when Jesus saw their faith, he said to the paralytic, "Son, your sins are forgiven." Now some of the scribes were sitting there, questioning in their hearts, "Why does this man speak like that? He is blaspheming! Who can forgive sins but God alone?" — Mark 2:5–7 ESV

To the Jewish scribes steeped in the law of God, the idea that a man could forgive sins committed against God was inconceivable. Forgiveness, in that sense, was a prerogative of God alone. Stott writes, "We may forgive the injuries which others do to us; but the sins we commit against God only God himself can forgive." (Stott, BC, 29)

Some of Jesus' critics questioned whether Jesus really had the divine authority to forgive sins. He knew his audience had doubts about this, so he demonstrated his authority to them:

"Which is easier, to say to the paralytic, 'Your sins are forgiven,' or to say, 'Rise, take up your bed and walk'? But that you may know that the Son of Man has authority on earth to forgive sins"—he said to the paralytic—"I say to you, rise, pick up your bed, and go home." And he rose and immediately picked up his bed and went out before them all, so that they were all amazed and glorified God, saying, "We never saw anything like this!" — Mark 2:9–12 ESV

New Testament scholar R. T. France notes Jesus' rhetorical question to the scribes, "Which is easier to say . . . ?" and observes that "if the 'harder' of the two options can be demonstrated, the 'easier' may be assumed also to be possible.... [A] *claim* to forgive sins is undoubtedly easier to make, since it cannot be falsified by external events, whereas a claim to make a paralyzed man walk will be immediately proved false or true. . . . Jesus' demonstrable authority to cure the disabled man is evidence that he also has authority to forgive sins." (France, GM, 346, emphasis in original)

Skeptics dispute this inference, arguing that Jesus did only what a Jewish priest might do. Ehrman writes, "When Jesus forgives sins, he never says 'I forgive you,' as God might say, but 'your sins are forgiven,' which means God has forgiven the sins.... Jesus may be claiming a priestly prerogative, but not a divine one." (Ehrman, HJBG, 127) Bird counters, "Jesus was not acting like a rogue priest. He was not from the tribe of Levi anyway, and he wasn't anywhere near the temple." (Bird, DJTHWG, 58) Instead, Jesus explicitly declares that his authority to forgive sins comes from his being "the Son of Man," the divine figure in Daniel's vision (Mark 2:10; Matt. 9:6; cf. Dan. 7:13, 14). Bird concludes, "Jesus claims for himself an unmediated divine authority that, to those steeped in Jewish monotheism, looks absolutely blasphemous." (Bird, DJTHWG, 58)

B. Jesus Claimed to Be "Life"

In John 14:6 Jesus states, "I am the way, the truth, and the life." Merrill Tenney, professor of New Testament and Greek, observes, "This affirmation of Jesus is one of the greatest philosophical utterances of all time. He did not say that He knew the way, the truth and the life, nor that He taught them. He did not make Himself the exponent of a new system; He declared Himself to be the final key to all mysteries." (Tenney, *John*, 215) Jesus made a similar statement when he declared, "I am the resurrection and the life" (John 11:25). Again, he did not claim to have a path to a better life; he said that he *was* the life.

C. Jesus Has Authority

The Old Testament is clear that God is the judge over all of creation (Gen. 18:25; Pss. 50:4–6; 96:13). Yet the New Testament reveals that Jesus possesses this divine authority, fulfilling the vision of Daniel 7:13–14. Jesus, speaking of himself in the third person as the Son of Man, claims this authority. For example, in John 5:22 and 5:27 Jesus himself makes this claim even when facing the Jews' effort to kill him (John 5:18), declaring that the Father, "has given all judgment to the Son. . . . And he has given him [Jesus] authority to execute judgment, because he is the Son of Man" (ESV). Later, we hear Jesus pray, "Father, the hour has come; glorify your Son that the Son may glorify you, since you have given him authority over all flesh" (John 17:1, 2 ESV). Bird comments that Jesus "not only spoke with an unmediated divine authority, but . . . he acted in such a way as to identify himself with God's own activity in the world." (Bird, DJTHWG, 70)

At the conclusion of the gospel of Matthew, Jesus gathers a group of his disciples to a mountain in Galilee for some final words, a moment later called the "Great Commission."

He begins his directives to them with the forceful declaration, "All authority in heaven and on earth has been given to me" (Matt. 28:18). Andreas Köstenberger, senior research professor of New Testament and biblical theology, writes regarding this passage, "Jesus' authority is comprehensive (*pasa*). In fact, 'all' dominates the entire 'Great Commission' passage: Jesus has 'all authority.'" (Köstenberger and O'Brien, SEE, 103) Bowman and Komoszewski comment, "This is one way of saying that Jesus shares the seat of God's throne; his position places him over the entire universe." (Bowman and Komoszewski, PJHP, 277)

D. Jesus Pre-Existed

The New Testament makes another noteworthy claim: that Jesus consciously existed before his life on earth and was aware of it during that life. At one time, he prays, "And now, O Father, glorify Me together with Yourself, with the glory that I had with You before the world existed" (John 17:5). He also taught people, "For I have come down from heaven, not to do My own will, but the will of Him who sent Me" (John 6:38). Many similar statements are found in the Gospels and in the New Testament Epistles.*

Ehrman contests the concept of Jesus' preexistence, arguing its absence from Synoptic Gospels like Matthew and Luke. He writes, "If you read their accounts closely, you will see that they have nothing to do with the idea that Christ existed before he was conceived. In these two Gospels, Jesus comes into existence at the moment of his conception. He did not exist before." (Ehrman, HJBG, 243)

Others counter that Jesus' claims to preexistence are evident in his various "I have come" statements found in all three Synoptic Gospels. For example, Jesus declares, "I have not come to call the righteous, but sinners" (Mark 2:17; Matt. 9:13; Luke 5:32 NIV). He also said, "I did not come to bring peace but a sword" (Matt. 10:34; cf. Luke 12:51). Wellum comments, "In each of these statements. . . . Jesus understands himself to have preexisted and that his work has a transcendent quality about it, identified with the work of God." (Wellum, DCSG, 86) Gathercole adds, "He is seen as having come *from* somewhere to carry out his life's work, namely, from heaven. . . . [I]f you read Matthew and Luke carefully in the light of their Jewish background, you can see that they have everything to do with Christ existing before he was conceived, before he 'came' to embark on his earthly mission." (Gathercole, WDFCTAJ, 98)

IV. Titles of Deity

A. YHWH–Lord
1. Sacred to the Jews

Many English Bibles translate the name of God as "LORD" or "Jehovah." The word in the original Hebrew is made up of four consonants: YHWH. Many transliterate this Hebrew word as "Jehovah," but a closer phonetic rendering in English of the Hebrew consonants is probably "Yahweh." According to tradition, the Jewish people have regarded this name as unutterable, as most sacred. Toon comments, "As this Name was treated with ever more and more reverence, the Jews ceased to pronounce it during the latter part of the Old Testament period" (Toon, OTG, 96). The ancient Jewish historian Philo wrote that the name was one "which only those whose ears and tongues are purified may hear or speak in the holy place, and no

---

* Examples include the passage already examined in Philippians 2:6–11; John 3:13; 6:33, 62; 8:23; 8:58, 59; 16:28; Romans 8:3; 1 John 1:2; and Galatians 4:4.

other person, nor in any other place at all." (Philo, VM, II.114)

2. The Term Yahweh Is Applied to Jesus

Given the Jewish reverence for the name of God, it is especially striking that Jesus applied the title to himself. Wellum observes, "Repeatedly in the New Testament we have Old Testament references of Yahweh unambiguously applied to Jesus (see, e.g., Ex. 3:14 with John 8:58; Isa. 44:6 with Rev. 1:17; Ps. 102:26–27 [LXX] with Heb. 1:11, 12; Isa. 45:23 with Phil. 2:10, 11). . . . The Synoptics *implicitly* teach and announce this very same christological point as does the entire New Testament." (Wellum, DCSG, 71)

David Capes, professor of New Testament and lead scholar on the Bible translation *The Voice*, elaborates on the uniqueness and boldness of the application of the name Yahweh to Jesus: "Given the contemporary view of the divine name in Jewish life, it is amazing that Jewish-Christian exegetes in Palestine would attribute Yahweh texts to Jesus, a man recently crucified. Such a development appears to have been unprecedented in Jewish life." (Capes, OTYTPC, 167)

B. Son of God

Perhaps the best-known title ascribed to Jesus is "Son of God." It is found throughout each of the four gospels and other New Testament books. Martin Hengel, a historian of religion who focused on the Hellenistic Period of early Judaism and Christianity, notes, "More than any other title in the New Testament, the title Son of God connects the figure of Jesus with God. He is the beloved (Mark 1:11; 9:7; 12:6 par.), the only (John 1:14, 18; 3:16, 18; 1 John 4:9) and the first-born Son (Rom. 8:29; Col. 1:15, 18; Heb. 1:6; cf. Rev. 1:5). This is meant to express the fact that in Jesus, God himself comes to men." (Hengel, SG, 63)

Some skeptics argue that Jesus' claims to sonship were not unique. Citing other biblical characters referred to as God's son, such as Adam, Moses, Solomon, or the nation of Israel, they question what makes Jesus' sonship exceptional. New Testament scholar Frank Thielman says the language used to describe Jesus' sonship is unique: "Mark uses the Greek adjective *agapētos* ('only beloved') in what Greek grammarians call the 'second attributive position.' An adjective in this position receives particular stress. In both [Mark] 1:11 and 9:7, therefore, God says that Jesus is 'my son—the uniquely beloved one.'" (Thielman, TNT, 63)

Matthew describes Jesus as the Son of God—the one and only messianic son of David (Matt. 1:1, 17, 20–23; cf. Isa. 7:14). He also quotes Jesus' remarkably exclusive claim, "No one knows the Father except the Son and anyone to whom the Son chooses to reveal him" (Matt. 11:27 ESV). Ulrich Luz, Swiss theologian and professor emeritus at the University of Bern, comments, "On the basis of our text one might say that the unique

---

Given the contemporary view of the divine name in Jewish life, it is amazing that Jewish-Christian exegetes in Palestine would attribute Yahweh texts to Jesus, a man recently crucified. Such a development appears to have been unprecedented in Jewish life.

David Capes

---

aspect of the 'Son' is that he belongs to the Father. This explains why the Son of God cannot be revealed to Peter by a mortal man, but only by the Father alone (16:17). It also explains why, on the mountain of transfiguration, a heavenly voice proclaims this crucial realization a second time to the disciples." (Luz, TGM, 98–99)

John repeatedly uses the phrase "only begotten" to convey the uniqueness of Jesus' sonship. This is exemplified in John 3:16, which states, "For God so loved the world, that he gave his only Son, that whoever believes in him should not perish but have eternal life" (ESV). The first chapter of John similarly declares, "We have seen his glory, glory as of the only Son from the Father" (John 1:14 ESV). Referring to this passage, Thielman observes, "He is the Son of God, but emphatically not the Son in some way that one might also use to describe other human beings. Rather, his sonship is 'unique in kind' (*monogenes*, 1:14). Moreover, he is 'God the only Son'—somehow he is both the unique Son of God and himself God (1:18)." (Thielman, TNT, 154)

Wellum also interprets the New Testament title "Son of God" to convey Jesus' uniquely divine characteristics. He writes:

Jesus is the Son from all eternity who takes on flesh and who becomes Jesus of Nazareth (John 1:1, 14; cf. Heb. 1:1–2; Col. 1:14–17). He is described as always having been in the bosom of the Father (John 1:18; 17:5). As such, he is *the* Son of God (Luke 1:31–32; John 1:34; 1 John 5:20), God's own Son (Rom. 8:3, 32), whose sonship is prior to ours and the foundation for how we become "sons of God" (John 1:12; Rom. 8:15; Gal. 4:6), and so on. In all these ways, the New Testament stresses that Jesus' sonship is utterly unique. (Wellum, DCSG, 80)

C. Son of Man

Earlier in this chapter, we noted the implications of Jesus' "Son of Man" statement during his trial before the Sanhedrin. There, his combined reference to the Son of Man in Daniel 7 and to Psalm 110 indicates his deity. New Testament scholar Peter Stuhlmacher comments, "Jesus' sayings about the coming Son of Man therefore show that he lived in the expectation that after his earthly ministry, he would be exalted to the right hand of God according to Ps 110:1 and become the judge in the end times." (Stuhlmacher, MSG, 343)

Outlined below is a further elaboration of the three primary ways in which Jesus utilized the phrase "Son of Man."

1. Concerning His Earthly Ministry

Jesus used the term "Son of Man" when speaking of his earthly ministry, linking this exalted name to his identification with poor and lost people, his having come with godly power to bring salvation, and his taking upon himself the death that humans deserved.

Then a certain scribe came and said to Him, "Teacher, I will follow You wherever You go." And Jesus said to him, "Foxes have holes and birds of the air have nests, but the Son of Man has nowhere to lay His head." — Matthew 8:19, 20

"But that you may know that the Son of Man has power on earth to forgive sins"—then He said to the paralytic, "Arise, take up your bed, and go to your house." — Matthew 9:6

"The Son of Man came eating and drinking, and they say, 'Look at him! A glutton and a drunkard, a friend of tax collectors and sinners!' Yet wisdom is justified by her deeds." — Matthew 11:19 ESV

And Jesus said to him, "Today salvation has come to this house, since he also is a son of Abraham. For the Son of Man came to seek and to save the lost" — Luke 19:9, 10 ESV

And while He was still speaking, behold, a multitude; and he who was called Judas, one of the twelve, went before them and drew near to Jesus to kiss Him. But Jesus said to him, "Judas, are you betraying the Son of Man with a kiss?" — Luke 22:47, 48

2. When Foretelling His Passion

Jesus used the term "Son of Man" when warning his disciples of his death and connecting it with the Old Testament Scriptures.

"For as Jonah was three days and three nights in the belly of the great fish, so will the Son of Man be three days and three nights in the heart of the earth." — Matthew 12:40

Now as they were coming down from the mountain, Jesus commanded them, saying, "Tell the vision to no one until the Son of Man is risen from the dead." . . . while they were staying in Galilee, Jesus said to them, "The Son of Man is about to be betrayed into the hands of men." — Matthew 17:9, 22

"Behold, we are going up to Jerusalem, and the Son of Man will be betrayed to the chief priests and to the scribes; and they will condemn Him to death." — Matthew 20:18

3. In His Teaching Regarding His Coming Again

Jesus very appropriately uses the term "Son of Man" when he teaches about his coming again as the glorious judge of all humanity, as Daniel had prophesied.

"The Son of Man will send out His angels, and they will gather out of His kingdom all things that offend, and those who practice lawlessness." — Matthew 13:41

"For as the lightning comes from the east and flashes to the west, so also will the coming of the Son of Man be. . . . Then the sign of the Son of Man will appear in heaven, and then all the tribes of the earth will mourn, and they will see the Son of Man coming on the clouds of heaven with power and great glory." — Matthew 24:27, 30

"When the Son of Man comes in His glory, and all the angels with Him, then He will sit on the throne of His glory." — Matthew 25:31

"I tell you that He will avenge them speedily. Nevertheless, when the Son of Man comes, will He really find faith on the earth?" — Luke 18:8

"Watch therefore, and pray always that you may be counted worthy to escape all these things that will come to pass, and to stand before the Son of Man." — Luke 21:36

4. Addressing Skeptics' Arguments Regarding the "Son of Man"

Ehrman argues that Jesus actually thought the Son of Man was not himself, but another mysterious future eschatological figure whom God would use to usher in his kingdom. He claims that Jesus "talked about someone else, rather than himself, as the coming Son of Man. . . . His message is about the coming kingdom to be brought by the Son of Man. He always keeps himself out of it." (Ehrman, HJBG, 119, 121) Ehrman acknowledges that *some* New Testament passages depict Jesus as the Son of Man, but concludes those references did not come from the historical Jesus. He gives two main reasons for this conclusion. First, he argues on the basis of his criterion of dissimilarity that the sayings in which Jesus speaks as if he were the Son of Man too closely reflect the early church's view. Second, he argues that Jesus' referrals to the Son of Man in the third person show that Jesus was actually distinguishing between himself and the Son of Man. (see Ehrman, HJBG, 105–109)

But we can plainly see that the Son of Man passages listed in the sections above, in their proper context, refer to Jesus himself. Bruce writes, "All four of the evangelists regard 'the Son of man' as a self-designation of Jesus. Sometimes, indeed, a comparison of Gospels or Gospel sources indicates that on his lips it could be taken as a periphrasis for 'I.'" (Bruce, BSMS, 51) One such illustration is found in the gospel of Mark, where Jesus asks his disciples, "Who do people say that I am?" (8:27). The parallel passage in Matthew reads, "Who do people say that the Son of Man is?" (Matt. 16:13 ESV) Other passages interchange the terms in the other direction, where Matthew reads "I" and the parallel passage in Mark reads "Son of Man" (Matt. 10:32, 33; Mark 8:38). Bruce notes, "Not only in the Gospels as they stand but in the tradition behind them, 'the Son of man' was a distinctive locution of Jesus, one which he used as a self-designation" (Bruce, BSMS, 52). New Testament scholars George Ladd and Donald Hagner add, "The idea that the Son of Man might be an eschatological figure other than Jesus . . . is exceedingly difficult because there is no scrap of evidence that Jesus expected one greater than himself to come, but there is much evidence to the contrary. We maintain that the one solid critical position is the fact that in all our New Testament sources, Jesus and Jesus alone used the term 'Son of Man' to designate himself." (Ladd and Hagner, TNT, 151)

What about Ehrman's claim that Jesus' self-reference to the Son of Man fails his criterion of dissimilarity? Bruce writes:

The criteria of authenticity invoked by proponents of modern redaction criticism of the Gospels are not so conclusive as is sometimes supposed; but if one of them, the "criterion of dissimilarity," be applied to the occurrences of "the Son of man," the conclusion seems plain. . . . Here is a locution unparalleled in the Judaism of the period and one which, outside the Gospel tradition, was not current in the early church. Its claim to be recognized as an authentic *vox Christi* is thus remarkably strong. (Bruce, BSMS, 52)

In sum, Jesus referred to himself as the "Son of Man" frequently and in a wide variety of contexts. Those references depict both Jesus' humanity and his bearing the unique characteristics of God, such as his sovereign rule, forgiveness of sins, and future judgment. Ladd and Hagner conclude Jesus' use of the term Son of Man "involved implicitly more than mere messianic dignity, for it carried overtones of essential supernatural character and origin." (Ladd and Hagner, TNT, 156)

D. Abba (Father)

Theologian Michael Green writes that Jesus "asserted that He had a relationship with God which no one had ever claimed before. It comes out in the Aramaic word *Abba* which He was so fond of using, especially in prayer. . . . It is the familiar word of closest intimacy. That is why He differentiated between His own relationship with God as Father and that of other people." (Green, RW, 99–100) Nowhere in the Old Testament does this kind of familiarity with God appear. Not even King David, who wrote most of the Psalms and was known for his closeness to God, prayed in such intimate terms.

Price takes issue with this inference of intimacy from Jesus' use of the term *Father*. He argues that, by the first century AD, the term *Abba* no longer carried the connotation of "Dada or Papa." (Price, RJMETDV, Sec. 7C) While he acknowledges that Jesus' address to "'My Father' is indeed language denoting the speaker's divine status" (Price, RJMETDV, 1C), he argues these were editorial insertions of the gospel writers, and thus not to be attributed to the historical Jesus. In support, Price notes the increasing frequency of the address "Father" and "My Father" from Mark to Luke to Matthew to John, concluding, "The massive later use of this language makes the nature of it clear. . . . [I]t is theological language about Jesus only subsequently placed in his own mouth." (Price, RJMETDV, 1C)

How should we assess Price's critiques? He makes a valid point that the term *Abba* does not necessarily connote a childish address, such as *Dada* or *Papa*. But his pleading for editorial insertion of Jesus' intimate reference to the Father is a stretch. First, Price cites the increasing frequency of Jesus' personal *Father* language from gospel to gospel as a sign that the emphasis on this matter grew over time. He says each successive gospel writer exercised more editorial license by placing this language on Jesus' lips when he never actually said it. Price notes a dramatic increase in the use of the term *Father* in the material exclusive to Matthew as compared with the material exclusive to Luke. But this theory appears to assume Matthew was written after Luke. The early church fathers unanimously declared Matthew to be the first gospel written. Even if modern scholarship now holds that view in the minority, virtually no one asserts Matthew utilized Luke, and it is far from certain that Luke preceded Matthew. In any case, Price seems to work from the assumption that any theologically startling term is a subsequent editorial insertion.

More importantly, even Mark, which most critical scholars now assume to be the first gospel written, has Jesus using exceptional terms of intimacy, addressing the Father as "Abba" (see Mark 14:36). The other gospels also depict Jesus using uniquely personal terms when addressing God, and clearly the early Christians likewise learned to address God as "Abba" (see Rom. 8:15; Gal. 4:6). Joel Marcus, professor of New Testament and Christian origins at Duke, explains, "Scholars have not yet discovered a pre-Christian text in which an individual addresses God as 'abbā.'" (Marcus, *Mark 8–16*, 978) British theologian George Beasley-Murray similarly observes, "It remains the case that Jesus stands alone in his undeviating use of this mode of address in his prayers to God." (Beasley-Murray, JKG, 149) Summing up the relevant debates of modern scholarship on this topic, Máire Byrne, Milltown Lecturer in Biblical Studies and Old Testament Theology, concludes, "From the Jewish prayers many forms of address of God as Father are found, but not *abba*. Therefore, the choice of this as a form of address by Jesus is striking." (Byrne, NGJCI, 56)

The Pharisees realized the implications of the language Jesus used. As the gospel of John states, "This was why the Jews were seeking all the more to kill him, because not only was he breaking the Sabbath, but he was even calling God his own Father, making himself equal with God." (5:18 ESV)

V. Conclusion: Jesus Claimed to Be God

We began this chapter with the question, "Who is Jesus?" The New Testament consistently represents him making direct claims to deity. Jesus claimed to be equal with God the

Father and worthy of commensurate honor. He said that seeing and knowing him was the same as seeing and knowing the Father. He claimed the unique characteristics of God, such as sovereignty, judgment, divine authority, forgiveness of sins, and preexistence. These assertions—corroborated by the doctrine of Jesus' eyewitnesses (including Peter and John) and other New Testament writers—appear throughout the gospel of John and the Synoptic Gospels.

William Biederwolf, author of more than thirty books and commentaries, drew from the evidence an apt comparison: "A man who can read the New Testament and not see that Christ claims to be more than a man can look all over the sky at high noon on a cloudless day and not see the sun." (Biederwolf, RCU, 154) There should by now be no doubt Jesus claimed to be God. Still, we must ask whether those claims were true. That topic is addressed in the next chapter.

CHAPTER 8

THE TRILEMMA: LORD, LIAR, OR LUNATIC?

OVERVIEW

I. Who Is Jesus of Nazareth?

While many have asked and offered to answer the question, "Who is Jesus of Nazareth?", no one can escape the evidence that he was a historical person and that his life radically altered human history. The world-renowned historian Jaroslav Pelikan makes this clear:

> Regardless of what anyone may personally think or believe about him, Jesus of Nazareth has been the dominant figure in the history of the Western culture for almost twenty centuries. If it were possible, with some sort of supermagnet, to pull up out of that history every scrap of metal bearing at least a trace of his name, how much would be left? It is from his birth that most of the human race dates its calendars, it is by his name that millions curse and in his name that millions pray (Pelikan, JTC, 1)

Professor and apologist Craig Hazen notes that nearly every religious tradition wants to claim Jesus as its own:

> It is hard to find a major tradition or a minor movement that does not give Him [Jesus] a special place of honor and find a significant way to enfold Him into their system of beliefs. The Baha'i, the Sikhs, the Mormons, the New Age Movement, the Unitarians, Religious Science, the Jehovah's Witnesses, the Jains, the Deists, and many more find a way to put their "hand in the hand of the man from Galilee." (Hazen, CWR, 152)

A cursory glimpse at church history reveals numerous leaders who have abused the lofty ideals established by Jesus, bringing shame to his name. Often, one sect or another within recognized Christendom has propagated policies and practices completely at odds with the love of Christ. The church has at times even lagged behind the secular arena in advancing needed change. On balance, however, followers of Jesus have taken great, sacrificial steps to lift others out of the dregs of life.

Jesus of Nazareth has been transforming lives for almost two millennia, and in the process, he has rewritten the direction and outcome of human history. In fact, the teachings of Jesus have been a force for overwhelming good throughout the history of the world. In his book *What Has Christianity Ever Done for Us?* Jonathan Hill highlights some of the positive heritage of Christianity:

- Great art and literature
- Beautiful church architecture
- Mass literacy
- Great educational establishments
- The importance of history
- The philosophical basis for the context in which science could develop
- Racial equality
- The abolition of slavery

The vast impact of Jesus' life is nothing short of incredible. The key question, though, is, "Who did Jesus claim to be?"

II. Who Did Jesus Claim to Be?

What did Jesus believe about himself? How did others perceive him? *Who is Jesus of Nazareth?*

Jesus thought it was fundamentally important what others believed about him. It was not a subject that allowed for neutrality or a less-than-honest appraisal of the evidence. C. S. Lewis captured this truth in his book *Mere Christianity.* After surveying some of the evidence regarding Jesus' identity, Lewis writes:

I am trying here to prevent anyone saying the really foolish thing that people often say about Him: "I'm ready to accept Jesus as a great moral teacher, but I don't accept His claim to be God." That is the one thing we must not say. A man who was merely a man and said the sort of things Jesus said would not be a great moral teacher. He would either be a lunatic—on a level with the man who says he is a poached egg—or else he would be the Devil of Hell. You must make your choice. Either this man was, and is, the Son of God: or else a madman or something worse. You can shut Him up for a fool, you can spit at Him and kill Him as a demon; or you can fall at His feet and call Him Lord and God. But let us not come with any patronising nonsense about His being a great human teacher. He has not left that open to us. He did not intend to. (Lewis, MC, 55–56)

I am trying here to prevent anyone saying the really foolish thing that people often say about Him: 'I'm ready to accept Jesus as a great moral teacher, but I don't accept His claim to be God.' That is the one thing we must not say. A man who was merely a man and said the sort of things Jesus said would not be a great moral teacher. He would either be a lunatic—on a level with the man who says he is a poached egg—or else he would be the Devil of Hell. You must make your choice.

C. S. Lewis

Others agree that the claims Jesus made as to his identity are central to the Person that he was and is. Famed biblical scholar F. J. A. Hort points out that whatever we think about Jesus, we cannot divorce his identity from his words, which "were so completely parts and utterances of Himself, that they had no meaning as abstract statements. . . . Take away Himself as the primary (though not the ultimate) subject of every statement, and they all fall to pieces." (Hort, WTL, 207)

Kenneth Scott Latourette, the late great historian of Christianity at Yale University, echoes Hort's observation when he states: "It is not his teachings which make Jesus so remarkable, although these would be enough to give him distinction. It is a combination of the teachings with the man himself. The two cannot be separated." (Latourette, HC, 44) He adds, "It must be obvious to any

thoughtful reader of the Gospel records that Jesus regarded himself and his message as inseparable. He was a great teacher, but He was more. His teachings about the kingdom of God, about human conduct, and about God were important, but they could not be divorced from him without, from his standpoint, being vitiated." (Latourette, HC, 48)

III. Three Alternatives

Some people believe Jesus is God because they believe the Bible is the inspired Word of God, which teaches that Jesus is God. While we, too, believe the Bible is the wholly inspired Word of God, we do not think one *needs* to hold that belief in order to conclude that Jesus is God.

If, as we have seen, the New Testament books are historically accurate and

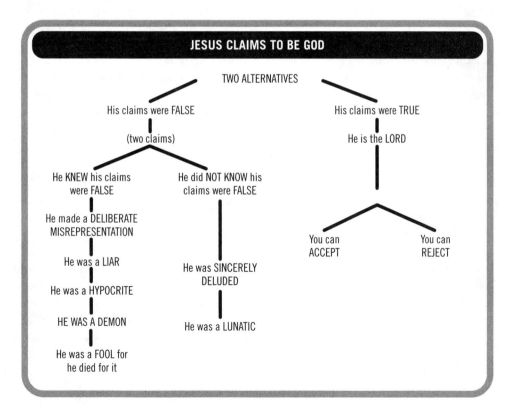

reliable—so reliable, in fact, that Jesus cannot be dismissed as a mere legend; if the gospel accounts preserve an accurate record of the things he did, the places he visited, and the words he spoke; if Jesus made firm claims to be God (see below and in chapter 7), then every person must answer the question, "Is his claim to deity true or false?" This question deserves a most serious consideration.

In the first century, when people were giving a number of answers about Jesus' identity, Jesus asked his disciples, "Who do you say that I am?" to which Peter responded, "You are the Christ, the Son of the living God" (Matt. 16:15, 16). Not everyone accepts Peter's answer, but no one should avoid Jesus' question.

As the chart makes clear, Jesus' claim to be God must be either true or false. If Jesus' claims are true, then he is the Lord, which we, "without excuse," must either accept or reject. But if Jesus' claims to be God were false, then we are left with just two options: he either knew his claims were false, or he did not know they were false. We will consider each alternative separately and the evidence for each.

C. S. Lewis is often credited with formulating the "Trilemma" argument. While Lewis certainly popularized it, the argument has earlier roots in the writings of the Scottish Christian preacher "Rabbi" John Duncan (1796–1870) and Watchman Nee, in his 1936 book *Normal Christian Faith*.* The argument reasonably concludes that the historical Jesus of the Gospels is Lord as he claimed, especially as we recognize the soundness of the texts as historical records.

A. Was He a Liar?

If Jesus knew he was not God, then he was lying. But if he was a liar, then he was also a hypocrite; he told others to be honest, whatever the cost.

More than that, he would have been a demon, because he deliberately told others to forsake their own religious beliefs and trust him for their eternal destiny. If Jesus knew his claims to be false, we would have to conclude that he was unspeakably evil. The religious leaders actually did charge Jesus with having a demon (John 8:48). But the gospel of John makes it clear Jesus was innocent of such wrongdoing (John 8:46; cf. 16:10; 1 John 3:5).

Last, if Jesus had been lying, he would also have been a fool, because his claims to deity led to his crucifixion.

But he remained silent and made no answer. Again the high priest asked him, "Are you the Christ, the Son of the Blessed?" And Jesus said, "I am, and you will see the Son of Man seated at the right hand of Power, and coming with the clouds of heaven." And the high priest tore his garments and said, "What further witnesses do we need? You have heard his blasphemy. What is your decision?" And they all condemned him as deserving death. — Mark 14:61–64 ESV

The Jews answered him, "We have a law, and according to that law he ought to die because he has made himself the Son of God." — John 19:7 ESV

But how could Jesus—as liar, con man, evil, foolish—leave us with the most profound moral instruction and the most powerful moral example in history? Could

---

* See Justin Taylor, "Is C. S. Lewis's Liar-Lord-Lunatic Argument Unsound?" February 1, 2016, http://blogs.thegospelcoalition .org/justintaylor/2016/02/01/is-c-s-lewiss-liar-lord-or-lunatic-argument-unsound/. Taylor quotes Lewis's 1950 essay, "What Are We to Make of Jesus?" In that essay Lewis points out the effect Jesus had on people—"Hatred—Terror—Adoration. There was no trace of people expressing mild disapproval." Taylor adds that Lewis's expertise as a scholar of literary history supports his recognition that the Gospels present history, not invented legends. Therefore, we confront this trilemma.

a deceiver—an imposter of monstrous proportions—teach such unselfish ethical truths and live such a morally exemplary life as Jesus did? The very notion is incredible.

John Stuart Mill, the philosopher, skeptic, and antagonist of Christianity, admitted that Jesus was a first-rate ethicist supremely worthy of our attention and emulation:

> But about the life and sayings of Jesus there is a stamp of personal originality combined with profundity of insight . . . in the very first rank of men of sublime genius of whom our species can boast. When this pre-eminent genius is combined with the qualities of probably the greatest moral reformer, and martyr to that mission, who ever existed upon earth, religion cannot be said to have made a bad choice in pitching on this man as the ideal representative and guide of humanity; nor, even now, would it be easy, even for an unbeliever, to find a better translation of the rule of virtue from the abstract into the concrete, than to endeavor so to live that Christ would approve our life. (Mill, TER, 254–255)

Even William Lecky, a noted Irish historian and a dedicated opponent of organized Christianity, noted in his *History of European Morals from Augustus to Charlemagne*:

> It was reserved for Christianity to present to the world an ideal character, which through all the changes of eighteen centuries has inspired the hearts of men with an impassioned love; has shown itself capable of acting on all ages, nations, temperaments, and conditions; has been not only the highest pattern of virtue but the strongest incentive to its practice; and has exercised so deep an influence that it may be truly said that the simple record of [Jesus'] three short years of active life has done more to regenerate and to soften mankind than all the disquisitions of philosophers, and all the exhortations of moralists. (Lecky, HEMAC, 2:8–9)

When the church historian Philip Schaff considered the evidence for Jesus' deity, especially in light of what Jesus taught and the kind of life he led, Schaff was struck by the absurdity of the explanations designed to escape the logical implications of this evidence:

> And yet this testimony, if not true, must be downright blasphemy or madness. The former hypothesis cannot stand a moment before the moral purity and dignity of Jesus, revealed in his every word and work, and acknowledged by universal consent. Self-deception in a matter so momentous, and with an intellect in all respects so clear and so sound, is equally out of the question. How could he be an enthusiast or a madman who never lost the even balance of his mind, who sailed serenely over all the troubles and persecutions, as the sun above the clouds, who always returned the wisest answer to tempting questions, who calmly and deliberately predicted his death on the cross, his resurrection on the third day, the outpouring of the holy Spirit, the founding of his Church, the destruction of Jerusalem—predictions which have been literally fulfilled? A character so original, so complete, so uniformly consistent, so perfect, so human and yet so high above all human greatness, can be neither a fraud nor a fiction. The poet, as has been well said, would in this case be greater than the hero. It would take more than a Jesus to invent a Jesus. (Schaff, HCC, 1:109)

In his work *The Person of Christ*, Schaff revisits the theory that Jesus was a deceiver, and mounts a convincing attack against it:

> The hypothesis of imposture is so revolting to moral as well as common sense, that its

mere statement is its condemnation. . . . [N]o scholar of any decency and self-respect would now dare to profess it openly. How, in the name of logic, common sense, and experience, could an impostor—that is a deceitful, selfish, depraved man—have invented, and consistently maintained from beginning to end, the purest and noblest character known in history with the most perfect air of truth and reality? How could he have conceived and successfully carried out a plan of unparalleled beneficence, moral magnitude, and sublimity, and sacrificed his own life for it, in the face of the strongest prejudices of his people and age? (Schaff, PC, 103)

The answer of course is that Jesus couldn't have.

J. Warner Wallace is a cold-case homicide detective who has been featured on *Dateline*, Fox News, and Court TV. In his book *Cold Case Christianity*, Wallace lists the three types of motives that lie at the heart of any misbehavior: (1) financial greed, (2) sexual or relational desire, and (3) pursuit of power. (Wallace, CCC, 240) Is there good reason to suspect Jesus was led to lie by any of these three motives?

- *Financial greed.* Jesus is never described as a man who possessed financial wealth. He taught his disciples to give their possessions to the needy and not to store up treasure in this life, but to store up spiritual treasure in the life to come (Luke 12:32–34). He told the rich young ruler, "If you want to be perfect, go, sell what you have and give to the poor, and you will have treasure in heaven; and come, follow Me" (Matt. 19:21). Jesus gained nothing financially from his preaching, teaching, or healing ministry.

- *Sexual or relational desire.* No evidence suggests that Jesus was motivated by lust or relationships. Many women followed Jesus (Luke 8:2, 3). By all accounts, however, he showed them the highest respect, even in ways that were countercultural at the time (See John 4:1–45: Luke 8:42–48). Jonalyn Fincher concludes:

Jesus had multiple opportunities to take advantage of women. Women longed to touch him, to serve him, to spread their perfume on his feet and support him with their money. Many men would have taken advantage of this type of female adoration. In ancient times a weakness for females was winked at as one of the particular rights of spiritual, powerful, wealthy men. But throughout his friendships with women, Jesus refused to either isolate himself from women or overindulge in romantic rendezvous. Women were not wicked distractions to him, but neither were women his lovers on his way to the cross. Instead of lewdness or asceticism we hear Jesus guiding women along the road with him. (Fincher, WJIGN, 243–244)

- *The pursuit of power.* It is utterly unreasonable to assert that Jesus lied about his identity to gain power. Rather than gaining power for himself, he modeled serving others (John 13:1–16; 15:13) and giving without expectation of return, even to the wicked and ungrateful (Luke 6:35, 36); and he taught his disciples to do the same. In a dispute over who would be greatest in the kingdom, Jesus taught his disciples that the greatest is the one who serves (Luke 22:24–27). Commentator Joel Green explains the significance of Jesus' teachings on this matter:

He does not deny, then, that some will lead, and so on; after all, he has been portrayed within the Lukan narrative as lord and king. He insists, rather, that his status as lord and king, as greatest, is expressed in the shape of his service, which is so integral to his character that it will determine the manner of his comportment with the faithful even in the eschaton (12:35–38). So also must it be the defining quality of the apostles—who, then, are to turn from their obsession with their own status to a comparable attentiveness to the needs of others. (Green, GL, 769)

Based on what we know of him through Scripture, Jesus was not motivated to lie about his identity for any reason. If Jesus was not a liar, then what are the alternatives?

B. Was He a Lunatic?

If it is inconceivable for Jesus to have been a liar, perhaps he *thought* he was God but was mistaken. After all, one might be both sincere and sincerely wrong.

We must remember, though, that for someone to think he was God, especially in a fiercely monotheistic culture—and to tell others that their eternal destiny depended on believing in him—was no slight flight of fantasy, but the thoughts of a lunatic in the fullest sense. Was Jesus such a person?

Christian philosopher Peter Kreeft presents this option and then shows why we must reject it:

A measure of your insanity is the size of the gap between what you think you are and what you really are. If I think I am the greatest philosopher in America, I am only an arrogant fool; If I think I am Napoleon, I am probably over the edge; If I think I am a butterfly, I am fully embarked from the sunny shores of sanity. But if I think I am God, I am even more insane because the gap between anything finite and the infinite God is even greater than the gap between any two finite things, even a man and a butterfly. Well, then, why not [view Jesus as a] liar or lunatic? But almost no one who has read the Gospels can honestly and seriously consider that option. The savviness, the canniness, the human wisdom, the attractiveness of Jesus emerge from the Gospels with unavoidable force to any but the most hardened and prejudiced reader. . . . Jesus has in abundance precisely those three qualities that liars and lunatics most conspicuously lack: (1) his practical wisdom, his ability to read human hearts . . . ; (2) his deep and winning love, his passionate compassion, his ability to attract people and make them feel at home and forgiven, his authority, "not as the scribes"; and above all (3) his ability to astonish, his unpredictability, his creativity. Liars and lunatics are all so dull and predictable! No one who knows both the Gospels and human beings can seriously entertain the possibility that Jesus was a liar or a lunatic, a bad man. (Kreeft, FF, 60–61)

There is more than a small difference between sincerely believing something that is wrong and believing about yourself that you are the unique, divine Son of God. The idea that Jesus was self-deceived or delusional in this regard is simply not compatible with the impression he has left on history. Even Napoleon Bonaparte is reported to have been in awe of him:

I know men, and I tell you that Jesus Christ is not a man. Superficial minds see a resemblance between Christ and the founders of empires, and the gods of other religions. That resemblance does not exist. There is between Christianity and whatever other religions the distance of infinity. . . . Everything in him astonishes me. His spirit overawes me, and his will confounds me. Between him and whoever else in the world, there is no possible term of comparison. He is truly a being by himself. His ideas and his sentiments, the truths which he announces, his manner of convincing, are not explained either by human organization or by the nature of things. . . . The nearer I approach, the more carefully I examine, everything is above me, everything remains grand—of a grandeur which overpowers. His religion is a revelation from an intelligence which certainly is not that of man. . . . One can absolutely find nowhere, but in Him alone, the imitation or the example of his life. . . . I search in vain in history to find the similar to Jesus Christ, or anything which can approach the gospel. Neither History, nor humanity, nor the ages, nor nature, offer me anything with which I am able to compare it or to explain it. Here everything is extraordinary. (Bonaparte, as quoted in Schaff, PC, 235, 238–239, 241)*

William Channing, although a nineteenth-century Unitarian and humanist, rejected the lunatic theory as a completely unsatisfactory explanation of Jesus' identity:

The charge of an extravagant, self-deluding enthusiasm is the last to be fastened on Jesus. Where can we find the traces of it in his history? Do we detect them in the calm authority of his precepts; in the mild, practical, and beneficent spirit of his religion; in the unlabored simplicity of the language with which he unfolds his high powers and the sublime truths of religion; or in the good sense, the knowledge of human nature, which he always discovers in his estimate and treatment of the different classes of men with whom

He acted? Do we discover this enthusiasm in the singular fact, that whilst he claimed power in the future world, and always turned men's minds to Heaven, he never indulged his own imagination, or stimulated that of his disciples, by giving vivid pictures, or any minute description, of that unseen state? The truth is, that, remarkable as was the character of Jesus, it was distinguished by nothing more than by calmness and self-possession. This trait pervades his other excellences. How calm was his piety! Point me, if you can, to one vehement, passionate expression of his religious feelings. Does the Lord's Prayer breathe a feverish enthusiasm? . . . His benevolence, too, though singularly earnest and deep, was composed and serene. He never lost the possession of himself in his sympathy with others; was never hurried into the impatient and rash enterprises of an enthusiastic philanthropy; but did good with the tranquility and constancy which mark the providence of God. (Channing, quoted in Schaff, PC, 107–108)

Schaff added: "Is such an intellect—clear as the sky, bracing as the mountain air, sharp and penetrating as a sword, thoroughly healthy and vigorous, always ready and always self-possessed—liable to a radical and most serious delusion concerning his own character and mission? Preposterous imagination!" (Schaff, PC, 107)

No lunatic could have been the source of such perceptive and effective psychological insight. Philosophy professor Dallas Willard addresses Jesus' insight: "Actions do not merge from nothing. They faithfully reveal what is in the heart. . . . When we hear the daily litany of evil deeds that comes to us through the media, for example, we all know well enough, if we can stand to think

---

* [17] Schaff discusses the background of this quotation from Napoleon, the precise origins of which remain undetermined, and concludes that it is probably "authentic in substance" though expanded and reworded in the telling (219–25).

of it, what kind of inner life and character produces those deeds." (Willard, DC, 144) Willard also notes, "It is precisely Jesus' grasp of the structure in the human soul that also leads him to deal primarily with the sources of wrongdoing and not the focus on actions themselves. . . . Wrong action, he well knew, is not the problem in human existence, though it is constantly taken to be so. It is only a symptom." (Willard, DC, 139)

C. S. Lewis was right. No other explanation but the Christian one will do: "The historical difficulty of giving for the life, sayings and influence of Jesus any explanation that is not harder than the Christian explanation, is very great. The discrepancy between the depth and sanity and (let me add) shrewdness of his moral teaching and the rampant megalomania which must lie behind His theological teaching unless He is indeed God, has never been satisfactorily got over. Hence the non-Christian hypotheses succeed one another with the restless fertility of bewilderment." (Lewis, *Miracles*, 109)

Jesus could have been a great teacher of ethics had his claims to divine status been wrong. However, he could never have been a moral example worthy of following had his claim to divine status been in error.

C. He Is Lord!

If Jesus of Nazareth is not a liar or a lunatic, then he must be Lord.

Simon Peter answered and said, "You are the Christ, the Son of the living God." — Matthew 16:16

[Martha] said to Him, "Yes, Lord; I believe that You are the Christ, the Son of God, who is to come into the world." — John 11:27

Thomas answered and said to Him, "My Lord and my God!" — John 20:28

The beginning of the gospel of Jesus Christ, the Son of God. — Mark, in the opening line of the New Testament book bearing his name, Mark 1:1

He is the radiance of the glory of God and the exact imprint of his nature, and he upholds the universe by the word of his power. — Hebrews 1:3 ESV

Other self-proclaimed gods and saviors have come and gone, but Jesus, standing head-and-shoulders above them all, is still here. The historian Arnold J. Toynbee spent page after page discussing the exploits of history's so-called "saviors of society"—those who tried to prevent some social calamity or cultural disintegration by heralding the past, or pointing people toward the future, or waging war or bartering for peace, or claiming wisdom or divinity. After covering such individuals for some eighty pages in the sixth volume of his magnum opus, *Study of History*, Toynbee finally comes to Jesus Christ and finds there is no comparison:

When we first set out on this quest we found ourselves moving in the midst of a mighty marching host; but, as we have pressed forward on our way, the marchers, company by company, have been falling out of the race. The first to fail were the swordsmen, the next the archaists, the next the futurists, the next the philosophers, until at length there were no more human competitors left in the running. In the last stage of all, our motley host of would-be saviours, human and divine, has dwindled to a single company of none but gods; and now the strain has been testing the staying-power of these last remaining runners, notwithstanding their superhuman strength. At the final ordeal of death, few, even of these would-be saviour-gods, have dared to put their title to the test by plunging into the icy river. And now, as we stand and gaze with our eyes fixed upon the farther shore, a single figure rises from the flood and straightway fills the whole horizon. There is the Saviour; "and the pleasure of the Lord shall prosper in his hand; he shall see of the travail of his soul and shall be satisfied. (Toynbee, SH, 278)

Who is Jesus of Nazareth? Your response must not be an idle intellectual exercise. You cannot put him on the shelf as a great moral teacher. That is not a valid option. He is either a liar, a lunatic, or the Lord. You must make a choice. "But," as the apostle John wrote, "these are written that you may believe that Jesus is the Christ, the Son of God, and that believing you may have life in His name" (John 20:31).

The evidence is in favor of Jesus as Lord. However, some people reject the clear evidence because of the moral implications involved. This moral dilemma is the true reason many people resist, not the academic dilemma. If Jesus is Lord, people are obligated to follow him or else honestly reject him and be held responsible accordingly. Therein lies the greatest challenge. There needs to be moral honesty in the consideration of Jesus as either liar, lunatic, or Lord and God.

CHAPTER 9

OLD TESTAMENT PROPHECIES FULFILLED IN JESUS CHRIST

OVERVIEW

I. Introduction

The New Testament writers establish the Messianic credentials of Jesus by referring to his resurrection and to fulfilled Messianic prophecy. The prophecies that we find in the Hebrew Old Testament differ in a significant way from those found in the Greco-Roman world. To the Greek or Roman, a prophecy was a specific prediction that anticipated a specific single fulfillment. Although the single-fulfillment form of prophecy is also found in the Hebrew Scriptures, the Hebrew understanding of prophecy was considerably broader. While an Old Testament prophecy might be fulfilled immediately or in a relatively short time frame, it may also point forward to an important long-term fulfillment.

It is important that we keep this in mind as we discuss the value of Old Testament prophecy to establish the Messianic credentials of Jesus of Nazareth. The numerous and pervasive instances in the Old Testament of description and detail that correspond to the life of Jesus are like threads in a tapestry that is gradually filled in to reveal him as the Messiah. Put another way, the Old Testament can be compared to a jigsaw puzzle. The numerous pieces remain puzzling until they are assembled enough to fill out the intended picture. In the same way, the Messianic references in the Old Testament remain puzzling until patient study begins to reveal them as a picture of the person of Jesus Christ. The New Testament is thus the decryption key for unlocking the meaning of the Old Testament Scriptures.

II. The Significance of Messianic Prophecy

A. God Is the Source of Prophecy

1. God Is True and Reliable in All He Says

"God is not man, that He should lie, nor a son of man, that He should repent. Has He said, and will He not do it? Or has He spoken, and will He not make it good?" — Num. 23:19

2. God Accomplishes All That He Says

"Remember the former things of old, for I am God, and there is no other; I am God, and there is none like Me, declaring the end from the beginning and from ancient times things that are not yet done, saying, 'My counsel shall stand, and I will do all My pleasure.'" — Isaiah 46:9, 10

3. God Announced His Messiah in Scripture and with Acts of Power

"The former things I declared of old; they went out from my mouth, and I announced them; then suddenly I did them, and they came to pass. . . . I declared them to you from of old, before they came to pass I announced them to you, lest

you should say, 'My idol did them, my carved image and my metal image commanded them'" — Isaiah 48:3, 5 ESV

Which He promised before through His prophets in the Holy Scriptures, concerning His Son Jesus Christ our Lord, who was born of the seed of David according to the flesh, and declared to be the Son of God with power according to the Spirit of holiness, by the resurrection from the dead. — Romans 1:2–4

B. Jesus, Together With the New Testament Writers, Appeals to Messianic Prophecy

1. Jesus

"Do not think that I have come to abolish the Law or the Prophets; I have not come to abolish them but to fulfill them." — Matt. 5:17 ESV

And beginning with Moses and all the Prophets, He expounded to them in all the Scriptures the things concerning Himself. — Luke 24:27

Then He said to them, "These are the words which I spoke to you while I was still with you, that all things must be fulfilled which were written in the Law of Moses and the Prophets and the Psalms concerning Me." — Luke 24:44

"You search the Scriptures because you think that in them you have eternal life; and it is they that bear witness about me, yet you refuse to come to me that you may have life. . . . For if you believed Moses, you would believe me; for he wrote of me. But if you do not believe his writings, how will you believe my words?" — John 5:39, 40, 46, 47 ESV

"This is why I speak to them in parables, because seeing they do not see, and hearing they do not hear, nor do they understand. Indeed, in their case the prophecy of Isaiah is fulfilled that says: 'You will indeed hear but never understand,

and you will indeed see but never perceive.'"
— Matthew 13:13, 14 ESV (cf. Isaiah 6:9)

Jesus said to them, "Have you never read in the Scriptures: 'The stone which the builders rejected has become the cornerstone'?"
— Matthew 21:42 (cf. Ps. 118:22)

"But all this was done that the Scriptures of the prophets might be fulfilled." — Matthew 26:56

"Then they will see the Son of Man coming in the clouds with great power and glory." — Mark 13:26 (cf. Dan. 7:13, 14)

Then He closed the book and gave it back to the attendant and sat down. And the eyes of all who were in the synagogue were fixed on Him. And He began to say to them, "Today this Scripture has been fulfilled in your hearing."
— Luke 4:20, 21

"For I tell you that this Scripture must be fulfilled in me: 'And he was numbered with the transgressors.' For what is written about me has its fulfillment." — Luke 22:37 ESV (cf. Isa. 53:12)

"But the word that is written in their Law must be fulfilled: 'They hated me without a cause.'"
— John 15:25 ESV (cf. Ps. 35:19; 69:4)

2. NT Writers Appeal to Prophecies Fulfilled in Jesus

"But those things which God foretold by the mouth of all His prophets, that the Christ would suffer, He has thus fulfilled." — Acts 3:18

"To Him all the prophets witness that, through His name, whoever believes in Him will receive remission of sins." — Acts 10:43

"Now when they had fulfilled all that was written concerning Him, they took Him

down from the tree and laid Him in a tomb."
— Acts 13:29

And Paul went in, as was his custom, and on three Sabbath days he reasoned with them from the Scriptures, explaining and proving that it was necessary for the Christ to suffer and to rise from the dead, and saying, "This Jesus, whom I proclaim to you, is the Christ." — Acts 17:2, 3 ESV

For I delivered to you as of first importance what I also received: that Christ died for our sins in accordance with the Scriptures, that he was buried, that he was raised on the third day in accordance with the Scriptures.
— 1 Corinthians 15:3, 4 ESV

. . . which He promised before through His prophets in the Holy Scriptures. — Romans 1:2

Concerning this salvation, the prophets who prophesied about the grace that was to be yours searched and inquired carefully, inquiring what person or time the Spirit of Christ in them was indicating when he predicted the sufferings of Christ and the subsequent glories. It was revealed to them that they were serving not themselves but you, in the things that have now been announced to you through those who preached the good news to you by the Holy Spirit sent from heaven, things into which angels long to look.
— 1 Peter 1:10–12 ESV

As you come to him, a living stone rejected by men but in the sight of God chosen and precious, you yourselves like living stones are being built up as a spiritual house, to be a holy priesthood, to offer spiritual sacrifices acceptable to God through Jesus Christ. For it stands in Scripture: "Behold, I am laying in Zion a stone, a cornerstone chosen and precious, and whoever believes in him will not be put to shame."
— 1 Peter 2:4–6 ESV (cf. Isa. 28:16)

And assembling all the chief priests and scribes of the people, he inquired of them where the Christ was to be born. They told him, "In Bethlehem of Judea, for so it is written by the prophet: 'And you, O Bethlehem, in the land of Judah, are by no means least among the rulers of Judah; for from you shall come a ruler who will shepherd my people Israel'" — (Matt. 2:4–6 ESV; cf. Mic. 5:2).

3. The Levitical Feasts Foreshadow the Work and Person of Christ

The Feast	The Fulfillment in Christ
Passover (April)	Death of Christ (1 Cor. 5:7)
Unleavened Bread (April)	Holy Walk (1 Cor. 5:8)
First Fruits (April)	Resurrection (1 Cor. 15:23)
Pentecost (June)	Outpouring of Spirit (Acts 1:5; 2:4)
Trumpets (September)	Israel's Regathering (Matt. 24:31)
Atonement (September)	Cleansing by Christ (Rom. 11:26)
Tabernacles (September)	Establishing the Messianic Kingdom and the Ingathering of the Nations (Zech. 13:1; 14:16–18)

4. Significance of Predictive Prophecy

The Old Testament contains numerous prophecies, types, and foreshadowings that were fulfilled in the person of Jesus of Nazareth. One such coincidence may not individually compel one to accept the Messianic credentials of Jesus. However, taken together, the numerous fulfillments of Old Testament Scripture form a tapestry, a cumulative case, for the divine inspiration of Scripture and for the Messianic credentials of Jesus.

III. Objections and Answers Regarding Predictive Prophecy

Those who object to the claim that numerous passages in the Old Testament foreshadow events in the life of Jesus advance their counterclaims by arguing that the New Testament writers purposefully shaped their material to match passages in the Old Testament, or that they stretched the meanings of obscure references, or that they took those references out of context by adopting a word or detail and inserting it into an event in the gospel. As we consider answers to these objections, it is worth remembering the account of Jesus' conversation with those who were walking to the village of Emmaus just after the resurrection, for Jesus referred to "all that the prophets have spoken" and "beginning at Moses and all the Prophets, He expounded to them in all the Scriptures the things concerning Himself." (Luke 24:25, 27)

A. Objection #1

The gospel authors deliberately crafted their biographies of Jesus so as to make Jesus appear to fulfill the Old Testament Scriptures.

Answer: There are several reasons to believe that the gospel authors reported Jesus' life and words accurately. They wrote the truth even at risk of persecution, and they did not play to what their audience might expect.

- At the time the Gospels were written, the Christian church was undergoing considerable persecution. Many Christians were martyred for their faith in excruciating and inhumane ways, such as by crucifixion, being burned alive, or being fed to wild animals. Since the gospel writers had nothing obvious to gain from inventing a new religion, and everything to lose, this suggests they recorded what actually happened and what Jesus really said.

- The Gospels, as we have them, demonstrate restraint on the part of their writers, since Jesus is conspicuously silent on many of the controversial topics that were debated in the early church, including whether Gentile Christians had to undergo circumcision, the role of women, the practice of speaking in tongues, etc. If the gospel writers had felt at liberty to make things up out of whole cloth, it seems likely that Jesus would have addressed such issues.

- It is worthy to note that, although the gospel authors evidently embrace a highly elevated Christology (e.g., Jesus is identified as Yahweh in Mark 1:2, 3), Jesus himself, in quoted speech, is remarkably cryptic about his self-identity. It seems likely that, if the gospel authors had felt themselves at liberty to make things up, Jesus would have stressed his own Messianic and divine status much more emphatically.

- The Jewish understanding of the Messianic prophecies emphasized a coming king, so that in the time of Jesus they hoped for a Messiah who would evict the Roman occupation. If the New Testament writers' motivation was to persuade people who longed for a conquering hero, they could have omitted or downplayed the crucifixion to craft a convincing presentation. But they didn't. Since instead they gave it emphasis, they wrote a truthful account, and in doing so they revealed in a far deeper way the saving role of the Messiah.

B. Objection #2

Old Testament types and foreshadowings are typically stretched and contrived, and therefore offer little evidential support for Jesus' Messianic credentials.

Answer: It is certainly true that Christians have tended to stretch some examples of Old Testament typology or look for hidden symbolism where there is probably none. In this chapter, however, we have selected only some of the clearest and most profound prophecies. It is our contention that, taken together, these biblical passages do contribute to a compelling cumulative case for Jesus as the Messiah—the Savior anticipated throughout God's revelation in the Old Testament. The close correspondence between details in the life of Jesus and various Old Testament texts can only be explained by either (1) purposeful contrivance or (2) divine orchestration. Since, as seen above, the New Testament authors wrote courageously to record real history accurately, the wealth of detailed correspondence weights the evidence toward divine orchestration as its explanation.

C. Objection #3

The gospel authors took various Old Testament texts out of context in order to prove that Jesus was the Messiah.

Answer: It is true that the authors of the New Testament applied some texts from the Old Testament to the Messiah when, in their original context, those texts do not directly apply to the Messiah. However, in many cases, when we study them more closely we discover that they may open up a wonderful insight that links both texts, revealing a multilayered meaning. The writer of Hebrews provides an example by quoting Isaiah 8:18: "Here am I and the children whom God has given Me" (Heb. 2:13). In its context in Isaiah, the statement marks Isaiah's determination to stand firmly as one who places his trust in the Lord (Isa. 8:11–18). Yet the quotation drawn from Isaiah also suits the new context in which Jesus has gathered a new people unto himself (Heb. 2:9–15). The contexts of both passages speak of the power of God—and of the Son of God—to deliver from fear.

Many New Testament writers quoted Old Testament words and set them in a new context, just as was the case when both Jewish and later Christians wrote commentaries to interpret Old Testament passages. In the early centuries of the church, different schools of thought arose concerning how this should be handled. The interpreters of the School of Alexandria were comfortable taking a word or detail out of its original context in order to illustrate and reinforce a spiritual interpretation. In contrast, the scholars in Antioch emphasized the importance of retaining the meaning of the original historical context even when reverent contemplation of the text suggested a concept that allowed additional applications.

Diodore of Tarsus (who died about AD 390) was a leader in this second school of thinking. The methodology that he described emphasizes a careful study of the original language in order to understand the historical substance and plain literal sense of the text as the foundation for understanding its deeper meaning. Theologian Christopher A. Hall tells us that Diodore's aim was to guard against the creation of meaning "out of thin air." (Hall, RSCF 160) But the method of reverent study, which "prevents a lapse into . . . interpretive freefall," does recognize that the Bible itself creates parallels between the Old and New Testaments, as when Cain and Abel "become types of Israel and the church." (Hall, 161) Similarly, Diodore saw layered meanings as he wrote his treatise on the Psalms. In the same way, Augustine of Hippo, in his *On Christian Doctrine* about rules for the interpretation of Scripture, distinguished between details that are simply things in a narrative and things that are both things in the narrative but also are signs of other things: that is, they signify a higher meaning, so as to "stimulate our appetite" for wisdom. (Augustine, OCD, I.2; II.1,6) He wrote, "The interpretation of Scripture depends on the discovery and enunciation of the meaning, and is to be undertaken in dependence upon God's aid." (Augustine, OCD, I.1)

Let us consider two examples of a passage for which the original historical context opens up to include prophetic significance. Matthew quotes Isaiah 7:14: "Behold, the virgin shall conceive and bear a son, and they shall call his name Immanuel" (Matt. 1:23, ESV). The original context of this verse refers to the invasion of Judah by its northern neighbors, Ephraim and Aram-Damascus (Syria). Through Isaiah, God informs King Ahaz that he will destroy these enemies of Judah. Isaiah directs Ahaz to ask God for a sign to confirm that the prophecy is true. Ahaz declines, stating that he will not put God to the test. Isaiah then tells Ahaz that the Lord himself will indeed give Ahaz a sign, and this sign will be the birth of a child who will be called Immanuel (meaning "God with us"). Isaiah adds that before the child has grown old enough to know the difference between right and wrong, Ephraim and Syria will be destroyed. It is clear, then, that the Immanuel child was to be born within Ahaz's own lifetime. This prophecy was fulfilled in the very next chapter (Isaiah 8), when Isaiah's wife conceived a son, who was then identified as the fulfillment of the previous chapter's prophecy. In chapter 8, verses 4 and 5, God declares the future victory of Assyria over these enemies, saying to Isaiah that "before the boy knows how to cry 'My father' or 'My mother,' the wealth of Damascus and the spoil of Samaria will be carried away" (ESV). This is the original historical context;

in a later paragraph we will consider how Matthew revealed its multilayered meaning.

Another text that might seem to be severed from its original historical context is "Out of Egypt I called My son" (Hos. 11:1), quoted in Matthew 2:15. Matthew states that Jesus' return from the flight to Egypt following the death of King Herod "was to fulfill what the Lord had spoken by the prophet." In the original context of Hosea 11:1, it is clear that the "son" called out of Egypt is in fact the nation of Israel, called out of Egyptian slavery. But Matthew revealed a multilayered prophetic meaning.

So why do the New Testament authors seem to quote certain Old Testament texts out of context in this manner? Let us remember two important things: Jewish scholars understood and interpreted their sacred Scriptures as capable of multilevel meaning. Indeed, the ancient rabbis who were writing the Midrash commentaries on Old Testament Scripture found all kinds of hidden insights in the biblical text. Early Christian scholars such as Diodore of Tarsus were familiar with this practice but carefully sought to guard against overzealous and overreaching applications. Although today we tend to interpret prophecy in terms of a single correspondence between prediction and fulfillment, interpreters in the historical tradition from the time of the church fathers believed that a prophecy could be fulfilled both initially in its original historical context and also hold a meaning that could become a type or pattern for later application. This outlook on Scripture is something like the experience of looking at a mountain range and noticing multiple peaks: the valleys between them cannot be seen. Similarly, the prophets foresaw and foretold an event clearly, simultaneously foretelling a later, additional fulfillment. The time between the two fulfillments was not

clearly seen. The apostle Peter writes about this prophetic anticipation when he discusses how the prophets sought to understand "what person or time the Spirit of Christ in them was indicating" (1 Pet. 1:10–12 ESV).

The two above examples were interpreted by Matthew to have a dual application, one in the immediate historical context of the prophecy and an additional historical fulfillment in the person of Christ. Since Jesus is understood to be the ultimate representative of Israel, or the perfect Israelite, Matthew interprets Hosea 11:1 to have a secondary application in Christ. In other words, just as the Lord God once called his "son," Israel, out of Egypt, so he now calls his Son, Jesus, out of Egypt.

In the other example, the child to be named "Immanuel," Matthew also perceives a second fulfillment for Isaiah 7:13, 14. In the first fulfillment, the child who was promised as a miraculous "sign" to King Ahaz represented the presence of God with the children of Israel ("Immanuel" literally means "God with us"). In the second fulfillment, the Word (identified as God in John 1:1–18) was made flesh in the person of Christ, and made his dwelling among us. In the person of Christ, the fullness of the divine presence was poured into a physical body. Additionally, the Immanuel prophecy was given to the house of David and not just to King Ahaz, meaning that it had greater Messianic significance. And it seems clear that Matthew was viewing Isaiah 7 in the context of Isaiah 9 and 11, some of the richest Messianic prophecies in the Bible. So, in Isaiah 7 the king in the line of David is about to be born; in Isaiah 9 he has already been born; in Isaiah 11 he is ruling and reigning on the earth.

One may now object that such typological (multiple) fulfillment offers little evidential value. For, if texts such as Isaiah 7:13, 14 and Hosea 11:1 (among others) were never interpreted as Messianic until the writing of the New Testament, then is it circular to then appeal to them as evidence of Jesus' Messianic credentials? Yet it was the actual behavior, statements, and Person of Jesus that prompted the writers to recognize in him the resonance with familiar Old Testament Scriptures. As we shall see in this chapter, many other examples, when taken cumulatively, provide very powerful support for Jesus' Messianic credentials. Not only so, but a careful study of Old Testament prophecy indicates that the Messianic hope developed gradually. Some very important promises given to Abraham and to the kings in the line of David were not fulfilled in their lifetimes. Once they were recorded in Scripture, they helped to form the larger Messianic hope and trust in God's sovereignty over history and readers of the Old Testament texts eagerly awaited the fulfillment of these promises.

IV. The Case for Jesus as the Messiah Who Fulfills Scriptural Prophecies

A. Types and Foreshadowings

In a narrative text, a detail or element can appear significant enough for a reader to feel it hints at some larger idea while remaining a real part of its own story. Centuries of biblical interpreters have followed the lead of the authors of Scripture, who quote the Old Testament to emphasize and explain a detail that they believe points to Christ. Paul does so in Galatians 4, transferring the ideas of slavery and freedom in the history of Hagar and Sarah to the freedom given through Christ. (Gal. 4:21—5:1) The authors of Scripture make these kinds of connections by recognizing a fundamental and theological unity between the element's meaning in the initial narrative and its meaning in the

life or work of Christ. The image or other element in the Old Testament is called a type; it foreshadows or prefigures what the New Testament says. In a sense, a type acts like a prophecy. Interpretation using this method must take care to be faithful to the original narrative, letting the meaning arise from the element's real function in the Old Testament. In the six categories below, we have presented side by side some examples of how the New Testament builds upon a type seen in the Old Testament and uses it to show Jesus as its fulfillment.

1. Christ Our Passover Lamb

Old Testament	New Testament
"Then Moses called for all the elders of Israel and said to them, 'Pick out and take lambs for yourselves according to your families, and kill the Passover lamb'" (Ex. 12:21).	"For indeed Christ, our Passover, was sacrificed for us" (1 Cor. 5:7).

The festival of Passover celebrates God's deliverance of the Israelite people from slavery in Egypt. In the last of the ten plagues imposed upon the stubbornness of Pharaoh, the firstborn of every household in his kingdom would die. In every Jewish slave home, the Passover lamb was sacrificed in order to spare the firstborn from the deadly plague. The lamb's blood would be smeared upon the doorposts of their houses as a mark of their faith in God. Likewise, Christ is identified in the New Testament as our Passover Lamb who was sacrificed for us (John 1:29, 36; 1 Cor. 5:7; 1 Peter 1:18, 19; Rev. 7:14; 12:11). If we apply his blood to the doorposts of our hearts, so to speak, then the Lord will "pass over" us and no judgment will fall upon us. Other historical details reinforce the validity of Jesus as the Lamb who fulfilled an Old

Testament type. The lamb was to be a "male without defect" (Ex. 12:5) which is a description given of Jesus (1 Peter 1:18, 19; Heb. 9:14). None of the lamb's bones was to be broken (Ex. 12:46). Likewise, not a bone of Jesus was broken (John 19:36).

Our sources concerning the life of Jesus tell us unanimously that Jesus was slain around the time of Passover, which further reinforces Jesus' identity as the Passover Lamb (Luke 22:1–16). For the Passover festival, the lamb was selected five days before its slaughter. Jesus entered the city of Jerusalem five days before the Passover sacrifice was slaughtered in the temple. He thus entered the city of Jerusalem on the day of lamb selection—as the ultimate Lamb of God to whom all others pointed.

2. Christ the Lord's Provision

Old Testament	New Testament
"Now it came to pass after these things that God tested Abraham, and said to him, 'Abraham!' And he said, 'Here I am.' Then He said, 'Take now your son, your only son Isaac, whom you love, and go to the land of Moriah, and offer him there as a burnt offering on one of the mountains of which I shall tell you'" (Gen. 22:1, 2).	"By faith Abraham, when he was tested, offered up Isaac, and he who had received the promises offered up his only begotten son, of whom it was said, 'In Isaac your seed shall be called,' concluding that God was able to raise him up, even from the dead, from which he also received him in a figurative sense" (Heb. 11:17–19).

God put the faith of Abraham to the ultimate test. Abraham was asked to take his son to one of the mountains in the region of Moriah and to sacrifice him there as a burnt offering. Isaac was identified as his "only son," despite the fact that he also had another (older) son called Ishmael. But Isaac was the son of the promise (Gen. 15:1–6), making

this command especially surprising. It both affected his love for his son and tested his faith in God. (Heb. 11:17) Even so, "Abraham took the wood of the burnt offering and laid it on Isaac his son" (Gen. 22:6 ESV). Thus, Isaac carried the wood for his own burnt offering. Similarly, the wood for Christ's sacrifice was laid upon his back when he was required to carry his own cross. Isaac asked his father Abraham, "My father! . . . Behold, the fire and the wood, but where is the lamb for a burnt offering?" (Gen. 22:7 ESV). Abraham replied, "God will provide for himself the lamb for a burnt offering, my son" (Gen. 22:8 ESV). At the top of the mountain, just as Abraham was about to slaughter his son, the angel of the Lord stopped him, calling his name. At Abraham's response, "Here I am," God provided the solution: The angel said, "Do not lay your hand on the boy or do anything to him, for now I know that you fear God. . . . And Abraham lifted up his eyes and looked, and behold, behind him was a ram, caught in a thicket by his horns. And Abraham went and took the ram and offered it up as a burnt offering instead of his son. So Abraham called the name of that place, 'The LORD will provide'; as it is said to this day, 'On the mount of the LORD it shall be provided'" (Gen. 22:11–14). It is worthy of our attention that the provision was made of a ram rather than a lamb. This suggests that the lamb that had been promised was still to be provided. Hence, Abraham names the mountain "The LORD will provide," saying, "On the mount of the LORD it shall be provided" (v. 14 ESV; note the future tense). As Isaac was in a sense "returned" to life, so the true Lamb of God was resurrected after his death.

Abraham's test and God's wondrous provision of the substituted ram took place on Mount Moriah. Later, Solomon built the house of the Lord (the Temple) in Jerusalem on Mount Moriah (2 Chr. 3:1). Jesus' sacrificial death in Jerusalem therefore took place on a mountain (Calvary) in the very region where Abraham prophesied: "On the mount of the LORD it shall be provided."

3. Christ Our High Priest and King

Old Testament	New Testament
"The LORD has sworn and will not change his mind, 'You are a priest forever after the order of Melchizedek'" (Ps. 110:4 ESV).	"For this Melchizedek, king of Salem, priest of the Most High God, met Abraham returning from the slaughter of the kings and blessed him, and to him Abraham apportioned a tenth part of everything. He is first, by translation of his name, king of righteousness, and then he is also king of Salem, that is, king of peace. He is without father or mother or genealogy, having neither beginning of days nor end of life, but resembling the Son of God he continues a priest forever" (Heb. 7:1–3 ESV).

The Old Testament tells very little about Melchizedek. He mysteriously shows up in Genesis 14:17–20 when he meets with Abraham who is returning from victory over a king named Chedorlaomer and the kings who joined with that king as raiders and looters. Melchizedek is a striking individual. He is one of only two in the Bible who simultaneously held the office of priest and king. His name means, "king of righteousness," and as the king of Salem, which means "peace," he is also the "king of peace." He is given no genealogy. No mention is made of his parents, nor do we read of his death. The author of Hebrews interprets this to exemplify the eternal priestly rule of our Lord Jesus Christ, who is also both priest and king

(Heb. 7:3) Further details link Melchizedek with Christ. When Melchizedek meets Abraham, he presents "bread and wine" (Gen. 14:18). This anticipates the emblems of bread and wine that Jesus spoke of when he used them at his last Passover supper, saying that they represent his body and blood, broken and shed for us for the remission of sins. (Matt. 26:26–28) Presenting a sacrifice is a priestly role, and Melchizedek is also called "priest of God Most High." (Gen. 14:18) In fact, Abraham subsequently gives "a tenth of everything" to Melchizedek, which implies Melchizedek's priestly role in receiving the tithe. The fact that Levi descended from Abraham prompts the author of Hebrews to assert that Melchizedek in receiving the tithe represents a greater priestly office than that of Levi (Heb. 7:9, 10). In the book of Hebrews, Jesus is shown as a priest whose status is far greater than the Levitical priesthood (Hebrews 7:1—8:1). As a part of that presentation the passage cites Psalm 110, which declares Christ to be a "priest forever according to the order of Melchizedek" (Ps. 110:4; Heb. 7:17) In doing so, the author of Hebrews declares the Psalm passage to be a prophecy fulfilled in Christ. He is not alone in citing this Messianic Psalm: Jesus quotes its first verse when he challenges the Pharisees to reflect on what they think about the Messiah, and Peter in his sermon at Pentecost quotes that verse as a credential for identifying Jesus as the promised Messiah (Matt. 22:41–46; Acts 2:32–36). The Psalm as a whole presents a king-priest of a very high order, acting on God's authority, and its reference to Melchizedek, a king of righteousness and peace as well as a mysterious priest, shows an Old Testament type reaching far beyond its original historical context to a fulfillment in Christ.

Now let us turn our attention to King David, who, performed some priestly functions, at one time offering sacrifices (2 Sam. 24:25) and another time wearing the priestly ephod (2 Sam. 6:14). Could it be argued that King David serves as a prototype of the Messiah, who is also a priestly king? The genealogy of Jesus traces his earthly descent from David (Matt. 1; Luke 3), making the royal line clear, yet it is intriguing to find this king exercising priestly functions. In fact, Jesus observed without criticism that David ate the dedicated bread "which is not lawful for any but the priests to eat" (Luke 6:4).

This theme of priest and king continues in the life of a man named Jehoshua or Joshua, which is equivalent to the name *Jesus.* (Zech. 3:8–11). This Joshua is a high priest whom Zechariah sees in a vision as under the care of angels and associated with two characteristically Messianic titles, "my servant" and "the Branch." So, here the Messiah is foreshadowed by a royal priest just as David had foreshadowed the Messiah as a priestly king. This is of tremendous importance, since only this dual function of the Messiah explains why many prophecies concern his suffering and many other prophecies concern his reign. A priest in the Old Testament was appointed by God to oversee the sacrifices that take away sin (Heb. 5:1, 4). But those sacrifices were temporary and required repetition; the author of Hebrews contrasts them with Jesus as a high priest who is "holy, innocent, unstained . . . perfect forever," yet who "offered up himself" to death—and that once for all (Heb. 7:23–28 ESV). In his first letter, Peter mentions both the suffering and the reign when he points out that the prophets did not understand who was meant by their prediction of "the sufferings of Christ and the glories that would follow," but they wondered about them (1 Pet. 1:10–12). As priest, Jesus suffered by allowing himself to be the sacrificed; as priest and king he "continues forever" in glory. (Heb. 7:24, 25, 28; 8:1) As author and Messianic Jew Michael L. Brown explains, "As a royal Priest, he came to make atonement for sins and offer forgiveness and reconciliation to Israel and the nations. As King, his dominion expands every day, as he rules over those who embrace him as Messiah." (Brown, AJOJ, 69)

The prophecy in Zechariah 3 is so rich and complex that it calls for attention to additional important details. In Zechariah's vision, the angel of the Lord "solemnly assured" Joshua:

"Hear now, O Joshua the high priest, you and your friends who sit before you, for they are men who are a sign: behold, I will bring my servant the Branch. For behold, on the stone that I have set before Joshua, on a single stone with seven eyes, I will engrave its inscription, declares the LORD *of hosts, and I will remove the iniquity of this land in a single day. In that day, declares the* LORD *of hosts, every one of you will invite his neighbor to come under his vine and under his fig tree." —* Zechariah 3:6, 8–10 ESV

The angel announces mysterious and powerful actions that God will take: the coming of "my servant the Branch," the placing of the engraved stone with seven eyes, the removing of iniquity "in a single day," and an invitation for neighbors to rest under a shelter. The prophet Isaiah similarly declares, "Therefore thus says the Lord GOD, 'Behold, I lay in Zion a stone for a foundation, tried stone, a precious cornerstone, a sure foundation; whoever believes will not act hastily'" (Isa. 28:16). Here a stone is "set before Joshua," and he is told of future things. The stone's seven eyes have been interpreted to refer to the divine attributes of omniscience. When Jesus was teaching in the Temple shortly before his arrest, he asked the Pharisees to recall from Psalm 118, "The stone which the builders rejected has become the chief cornerstone. This was the LORD's doing, and it is marvelous in our eyes" (Ps. 118:22, 23; Matt. 21:42). The engraved inscription on the stone set before Joshua suggests the finality of what God says and does. The removal of iniquity is a priestly role, but here it is done by God and "in a single day." The unique accomplishment of that single day reminds us of what another "Joshua," Jesus himself, would accomplish "in a single day" by his sacrificial death. Altogether, the passage in Zechariah complements the discussion of Christ as a high priest in the New Testament book of Hebrews.

In Zechariah 6:11–13, God instructs Zechariah to crown Joshua as a king:

> Take from them silver and gold, and make a crown, and set it on the head of Joshua, the son of Jehozadak, the high priest. And say to him, 'Thus says the LORD of hosts, "Behold, the man whose name is the Branch: for he shall branch out from his place, and he shall build the temple of the LORD. It is he who shall build the temple of the LORD and shall bear royal honor, and shall sit and rule on his throne. And there shall be a priest on his throne, and the counsel of peace shall be between them both."' (ESV)

This high priest, Joshua, now crowned as a king, has a role that in several ways points toward Jesus. His name means "Jehovah is Salvation," or "Jehovah Savior," like the name Jesus. He is also identified as the son of Jehozadek (meaning "Yahweh is righteous").

He is again linked to the Messianic title, "the Branch." As a priest on his throne, his role will bring peace. In chapter 3 of Zechariah, God had told him to pay attention to the promised coming of "my servant the Branch." These passages contribute to the New Testament presentation of Jesus as King and Priest.

One other ruler in the Old Testament sought to be simultaneously both a priest and a king. His name was King Uzziah. We read of his misguided attempt and its consequences in his loss of both roles in 2 Chronicles 26:16–23. "When he was strong, he grew proud, to his destruction" (v. 16 ESV). "Unfaithfully" he had attempted to burn incense to the Lord but was confronted by the chief priest Azariah and ultimately struck down with leprosy for his stubbornness in trying to usurp the role of the priest. He then "was a leper to the day of his death, and being a leper lived in a separate house . . . and Jotham his son was over the king's household, governing the people of the land" (v. 21). The passage in Chronicles ends with a reference to Isaiah (v. 22), who writes of a significant contrast between Uzziah and the true high priestly king. In Isaiah's profound vision in the temple, he sees the Lord seated on a throne, and experiences God's action to cleanse him from sin and call him as a prophet (Isa. 6:1–8). The apostle John identifies the one whom Isaiah saw as Christ himself (John 12:41). Isaiah opens the account of his temple vision, "In the year that King Uzziah died I saw the Lord sitting upon a throne, high and lifted up; and the train of his robe filled the temple" (Isa. 6:1 ESV). In other words, Isaiah begins by drawing our attention to the death of the failed high priestly king, and then introduces us to the one who would be the ultimate high priestly king.

4. The Angel of Yahweh

Old Testament	New Testament
"And the angel of the LORD appeared to him in a flame of fire from the midst of a bush. So he looked, and behold, the bush was burning with fire, but the bush was not consumed. Then Moses said, 'I will turn aside and see this great sight, why the bush does not burn.' So when the LORD saw that he turned aside to look, God called to him from the midst of the bush and said, 'Moses, Moses!' And he said, 'Here I am.' Then He said, 'Do not draw near this place. Take your sandals off your feet, for the place where you stand is holy ground'" (Ex. 3:2–5).	"No one has seen God at any time. The only begotten Son, who is in the bosom of the Father, He has declared Him" (John 1:18).

The angel of Yahweh is a character who appears throughout the Old Testament and is specifically identified as a manifestation of God himself (e.g. Ex. 23:20–33; Josh. 5:13–15; Jdg. 13:1–23). Indeed, the angel of Yahweh speaks and operates as the mouthpiece of God. On each occasion in which the angel of Yahweh appears, those to whom he appears marvel at the fact that they have beheld the face of God, and yet their life has been spared (in view of Exodus 33:20: "You cannot see my face, for man shall not see me and live" ESV). In some cases, "God" and "the angel of the LORD" are even used interchangeably. In Exodus 3, the angel of Yahweh is identified as the one who spoke to Moses from the burning bush, identifying himself as none other than God.

Numerous examples could be given. Perhaps one of the most intriguing examples is found in Judges 13, in which the angel of Yahweh appears to Manoah and his wife to announce the birth of Samson. In verses 17 and 18, Manoah asks the angel for his name and is told, "Why do you ask my name? It is beyond understanding" (NIV). "It is beyond understanding" can also be rendered, "It is wonderful." It is interesting that in Isaiah 9:6, one of the names given to the promised Messiah is "Wonderful." Also, when Manoah and his wife make an offering to the Lord, the angel of the Lord ascends in the flame. This may be an allusion to the sacrifice of Christ who, being God incarnate, was made a sacrifice unto the Father. Many students of the Bible believe that the ascension of the angel of the Lord in the flame, rising from the burnt offering on the altar, carries rich symbolic significance and almost certainly represents the coming sacrifice of Christ as an atonement for sin.

The opening to the gospel of John echoes Exodus concerning the impossibility of seeing God, but John insists that God has nevertheless manifested himself: one "who is at the Father's side, [who] has made him known." (John 1:18 ESV) Thus the gospel of John presents Christ as the One who fulfills another Old Testament type, the angel of the Lord.

5. The Bronze Serpent

Old Testament	New Testament
"Then the LORD said to Moses, 'Make a fiery serpent and set it on a pole; and it shall be that everyone who is bitten, when he looks at it, shall live.' So Moses made a bronze serpent, and put it on a pole; and so it was, if a serpent had bitten anyone, when he looked at the bronze serpent, he lived" (Num. 21:8, 9).	"And as Moses lifted up the serpent in the wilderness, even so must the Son of Man be lifted up, that whoever believes in Him should not perish but have eternal life" (John 3:14, 15).

On their journey out of slavery toward the promised land, the children of Israel reached the head of the Gulf of Akabah. The discouraged people murmured against God. As judgment upon the Israelites, God sent among them fiery serpents that carried in their fangs a lethal poison. When the Israelites urged Moses to intercede before God on their behalf, Moses was commanded to make a serpent of bronze that would be raised on a pole. Anyone who had been bitten by one of the serpents could look upon the bronze serpent and be delivered from death. This image typifies the way of salvation revealed by the New Testament. The poison represents God's judgment as a result of our sin and our rebellion against a Holy God. The serpent that was lifted up bore the image of that which brought the poison and death, just as Christ bears the nature of humanity in order to bring healing and redemption. By looking at the serpent on the pole, the bitten Israelite exercised faith. There was no work of righteousness that could have availed to save them from the death that was already working in them. In their act of faith, they experienced not merely healing, but also the gift of life.

6. The Son of Man

Old Testament	New Testament
I was watching in the night visions, and behold, One like the Son of Man, coming with the clouds of heaven! He came to the Ancient of Days, and they brought Him near before Him. Then to Him was given dominion and glory and a kingdom, that all peoples, nations, and languages should serve Him. His dominion is an everlasting dominion, which shall not pass away, and His kingdom the one which shall not be destroyed." (Dan. 7:13, 14).	"But He kept silent and answered nothing. Again the high priest asked Him, saying to Him, "Are You the Christ, the Son of the Blessed?" Jesus said, 'I am. And you will see the Son of Man sitting at the right hand of the Power, and coming with the clouds of heaven.'" (Mark 14:61, 62).

Jesus' favorite self-designation in the Gospels is the title "Son of Man." During his trial, Jesus connects this title with the image of "coming with the clouds of heaven" thus drawing our attention to the prophetic text of Daniel 7:13, 14. A typical Jewish interpretation of this text in Daniel is that the Son of Man is actually a personification of the nation of Israel. Jewish apologists draw support for this interpretation from Daniel's entire vision described in verses 13–28 of the same chapter, and in particular, in verses 18, 22, and 27, each of which mentions a plural, "the saints of the Most High." In the passage, Daniel is reassured that although his vision began with seeing four kings arise, terrifyingly strong and devouring, nevertheless the saints have hope: "'The saints of the Most High shall receive the kingdom and possess the kingdom forever, forever and ever.' . . . [In the vision, their enemies prevailed] until the Ancient of Days came, and judgment was given for the saints of the Most High, and the time came when the saints possessed the kingdom. . . . And the kingdom and the dominion and the greatness of the kingdoms under the whole heaven shall be given to the people of the saints of the Most High; his kingdom shall be an everlasting kingdom, and all dominions shall serve and obey him" (ESV). Thus these Jewish scholars read the plural from verses 18, 22, and 27 into the Son of Man references in verses 13 and 14 and say that the "son of Man" refers to the plural "saints of the most high," not the singular Messiah. They believe that this is consistent with the fact that the four beasts spoken of in Daniel 7 represent four kingdoms. Verse 17, however, tells us, "These four great beasts are four kings who shall arise out of the earth" (ESV). Each of the kingdoms, then, is represented by a king. (Historians commonly refer to a king as the country itself, for instance the king of France is called "France," and even contemporaries referred to the king of England as simply "England"). This sort of identification is also seen when Daniel states that the golden head of the statue in Nebuchadnezzar's vision is Nebuchadnezzar himself, who thereby stands for the entire kingdom of Babylon (Dan. 2:38). The assurance of the triumph of the Most High over all human rulers, however frightening, seems to be central to Daniel's vision. The role of the Son of Man is key to this triumph. The intensity of the descriptive detail is what leads many scholars to believe that a larger significance exists; indeed, Daniel was "anxious" (v. 15) and asked for "the truth concerning all this" (v. 16) and was in the end "alarmed" and pale but "kept the matter in my heart" (v. 28). The importance here of the Son of Man offers another type or foreshadowing of the Messiah, suggesting another facet for understanding his nature and mission.

The earliest exegetes (those who explain a text) of this text understood the "Son of Man" to be a Messianic reference, rather than simply a reference to the nation of Israel. John J. Collins, the Holmes Professor of Old Testament Criticism and Interpretation at Yale Divinity School, notes that "the earliest interpretations and adaptations of the 'one like a human being,' Jewish and Christian alike, assume that the phrase refers to an individual and is not a symbol for a collective entity." (Collins, *Daniel*, 306)

It also bears noting that the Greek Septuagint translation of "service" in Daniel 7:14 uses the Greek word *latreuo* when describing the service that "all people, nations, and languages" shall bring to the "Son of Man." *Latreuo* denotes the very highest form of worship and religious service, a kind that is to be given only to Yahweh. This again suggests that the "Son of Man" refers to more

than a mere human being. Moreover, it would certainly be rather odd if the text were saying that religious service was to be rendered to an entire nation rather than an individual.

An understanding of types and foreshadowings as details weighted with great significance can provide a way to interpret this passage. The Son of Man is described here as being given an everlasting dominion over all peoples and is therefore, we submit, the *head* of the saints of the Most High. Verse 27 is the final statement made in answer to Daniel's request for an explanation of his vision. It uses both the plural "saints of the Most High" and the singular "his" when it concludes in terms that parallel and echo Daniel 7:14, where the glorious, comprehensive, and indestructible kingdom is given to the Son of Man. This exaltation of the Son of Man seems to be the fundamental detail linking both Jesus' frequent use of the name (even at his trial) and the use of the name in the rest of the New Testament (e.g., Rev. 1; 11:15–18; 14:14, 15). In conclusion, we suggest that the Son of Man is another type or instance of prophetic insight identifying Jesus with deity.

B. Messianic Predictive Prophecies
1. Pre-existent and Divine

Old Testament	New Testament
"But you, Bethlehem Ephrathah, though you are little among the thousands of Judah, yet out of you shall come forth to Me the One to be Ruler in Israel, whose goings forth are from of old, from everlasting." (Mic. 5:2).	"And He is before all things, and in Him all things consist" (Col. 1:17; see also: Rev. 1:1, 2; 1:17; 2:8; 8:58; 22:13).

Bible scholar and theologian Ernst Wilhelm Hengstenberg says of Micah 5:2, "The existence of the Messiah in general, before His temporal birth at Bethlehem, is asserted; and then His eternity in contrast with all time is mentioned here" (Hengstenberg, COTCMP, 573). Here is the question: How can a future ruler have origins "from everlasting" unless he is preexistent? Some would claim that this speaks only of the Davidic origin of the Messiah, but nowhere in the Hebrew Bible is David referred to as being in the distant past, so it appears the text is speaking of more than this.

*Targum Isaiah,** an Aramaic commentary on the prophetic book, says, "The prophet saith to the house of David, A child has been born to us, a son has been given to us; and He has taken the law upon Himself to keep it, and His name has been called from of old, Wonderful counselor, Mighty God, He who lives forever, the Anointed one (or Messiah), in whose days peace shall increase upon us" (Isa. 9:6). (Stenning, TI, 32)

2. A Prophet

Old Testament	New Testament
"I will raise up for them a prophet like you from among their brothers. And I will put my words in his mouth, and he shall speak to them all that I command him" (Deut. 18:18 ESV).	"And the crowds said, 'This is the prophet Jesus, from Nazareth of Galilee'" (Matt. 21:11 ESV; see also Luke 7:16; John 4:19; 6:14; 7:40).

Aaron Judah Kligerman, an expert in messianic prophecies, says, "The use of the term 'prophet' by the Jews of Jesus' day shows not only that they expected the Messiah to be a prophet in accordance with the promise in Deuteronomy eighteen, but also that He who performed these miracles was indeed the Promised Prophet." (Kligerman, MPOT,

22–23) That is, since most of the Old Testament accounts of miracles appear in the lives of prophets and identify God's power acting through them, these Jews perceived the miracles of Jesus as evidence that identified a new prophet—after centuries without one! It had been so long that Kligerman appropriately observes that the Jews were thinking of a very great prophet—indeed, the One long promised. (Some Jews, opposing Jesus, perceived a spiritual power but declared that it came from evil or sorcery. In Luke 11:14–22, Jesus answers their objection by showing that it was not logical.)

In Deuteronomy 18:18, Moses is preparing the people for entrance into their promised land and is warning them not to follow any prophet who might lead them to worship other gods. He says that God has told him, "I will raise up for them a Prophet like you." (See also Deut. 18:15, 17.) The coming prophet was expected to be like Moses, yet caution was needed in identifying that prophet so as not to acclaim or elevate someone who would lead people away from God.

The Jewish scholar Maimonides, in a letter to the community of Yemen, denounces claims made about someone said to be a Messiah by writing: "The Messiah will be a very great Prophet, greater than all the Prophets with the exception of Moses our teacher. . . . His status will be higher than that of the Prophets and more honourable, Moses alone excepted. The Creator, blessed be He, will single him out with features wherewith He had not singled out Moses; for it is said with reference to him, 'And his delight shall be in the fear of the Lord; and he shall not judge after the sight of his eyes, neither decide after the hearing of his ears'" (Isa. 11:3). (Cohen, TM, 221)

---

* The Targums are ancient paraphrases or interpretations of the Hebrew text, at first made as oral explanations for listeners who spoke Aramaic more commonly than Hebrew. They served as translations and commentary for the listeners.

Christ compared to Moses

- He was delivered from a violent death in his infancy.
- He was willing to become redeemer of his people (Ex. 3:10).
- He worked as mediator between Yahweh and Israel (Ex. 19:16; 20:18).
- He made intercession on behalf of sinful people (Ex. 32:7–14, 33; Num. 14:11–20).
- "Sir, I perceive that You are a prophet" (John 4:19).
- "For the law was given through Moses, but grace and truth came through Jesus Christ" (John 1:17).

3. Of the Line of Jesse and the House of David

Old Testament	New Testament
"There shall come forth a shoot from the stump of Jesse, and a branch from his roots shall bear fruit. And the Spirit of the LORD shall rest upon him, the Spirit of wisdom and understanding, the Spirit of counsel and might, the Spirit of knowledge and the fear of the LORD. And his delight shall be in the fear of the LORD. He shall not judge by what his eyes see, or decide disputes by what his ears hear" (Isa. 11:1–3 ESV).	"Paul, a servant of Christ Jesus, called to be an apostle, set apart for the gospel of God, which he promised beforehand through his prophets in the holy Scriptures, concerning his Son, who was descended from David according to the flesh" (Rom. 1:1–3 ESV).

Jesse was the father of David the king (1 Sam. 16:1, 10–13; Matt. 1:6). Jewish commentators expected the Messiah to come from this genealogical line. The *Targum Isaiah* states, "And a king shall come forth from the sons of Jesse, and an Anointed One (or Messiah) from his sons shall grow up. And there shall rest upon him a spirit before the Lord, the spirit of wisdom and

understanding, the spirit of counsel and might, the spirit of knowledge, and of the fear of the Lord." (Stenning, TI, 40)

Historian and Hebrew scholar Franz Delitzsch comments,

> Out of the stump of Jesse, i.e., out of the remnant of the chosen royal family which has sunk down to the insignificance of the house from which it sprang, there comes forth a twig (*choter*), which promises to supply the place of the trunk and crown; and down below, in the roots covered with earth, and only rising a little above it, there shows itself a *netzer*, i.e., a fresh green shoot (from *natzer*, to shine or blossom). In the historical account of the fulfillment, even the ring of the words of the prophecy is noticed: the *netzer*, as first so humble and insignificant, was a poor despised Nazarene (Matt. 2:23). (Delitzsch, BCPI, 281, 282)

Jesse had at least eight sons (1 Sam. 16:10, 11). When Samuel anointed David as the king to replace Saul, the royal line of David would produce the Messiah. Scattered throughout the Talmuds are references to the Messiah as the "son of David." The Jewish philosopher-scholar Maimonides emphasized the Messiah's human heritage as a son of David. Although Maimonides did not expect the Messiah to be divine, he did describe the Messiah's knowledge of the Scriptures and a spiritual wisdom like Isaiah's prophecy. Jacob Minkin, author of *The World of Moses Maimonides*, explains: "Dismissing the mystical speculations concerning the Messiah, his origin, activity, and the marvelous superhuman powers ascribed to him, Maimonides insisted that he must be regarded as a mortal human being, differing from his fellow-men only in the fact that he will be greater, wiser, and more resplendent than they. He must be a descendant of the

House of David, and like him, occupy himself with the Study of the Torah and observance of its commandments." (Minkin, WMM, 63)

4. Judge

Old Testament	New Testament
"For the LORD is our judge; the LORD is our lawgiver; the LORD is our king; he will save us" (Isa. 33:22 ESV).	"I charge you in the presence of God and of Christ Jesus, who is to judge the living and the dead, and by his appearing and his kingdom" (2 Tim. 4:1 ESV).

Targum Isaiah on Isaiah 33:22 says, "For the Lord is our judge, who brought us out of Egypt by his might; the Lord is our teacher, who gave us the instruction of his law from Sinai; the Lord is our King, he shall deliver us, and execute a righteous vengeance for us on the armies of Gog" (Stenning, TI, 110)

Bible expositor A. R. Fausset observes: "Judge . . . Lawgiver . . . King—perfect ideal of the theocracy, to be realized under Messiah alone: the judicial, legislative, and administrative functions as King, to be exercised by Him in person (Isaiah 11:4; 32:1; James. 4:12)." (Fausset, CCEPONT, 666)

5. King

Old Testament	New Testament
"Yet I have set My King on My holy hill of Zion" (Ps. 2:6; see also Jer. 23:5; Zech. 9:9).	"And they put up over His head the accusation written against Him: THIS IS JESUS THE KING OF THE JEWS." (Matt. 27:37; see also Matt. 21:5; John 18:33–38).

Some of the leading rabbinic commentators who addressed Psalm 2 have claimed that it spoke first of David and then of the Messiah, both of whom were anointed king by God.

6. Special Presence of the Holy Spirit

Old Testament	New Testament
"The Spirit of the LORD shall rest upon Him, the Spirit of wisdom and understanding, the Spirit of counsel and might, the Spirit of knowledge and of the fear of the LORD" (Isa. 11:2).	"When He had been baptized, Jesus came up immediately from the water; and behold, the heavens were opened to Him, and He saw the Spirit of God descending like a dove and alighting upon Him. And suddenly a voice came from heaven, saying, 'This is My beloved Son, in whom I am well pleased'" (Matt. 3:16, 17; see also Matt. 12:17–21; Mark 1:10; Luke 4:15–21, 43; John 1:32).

In the *Babylonian Talmud*, the *Sanhedrin II* says, "The Messiah—as it is written, And the Spirit of the Lord shall rest upon him, the spirit of wisdom and understanding, the spirit of counsel and might, the spirit of knowledge of the fear of the Lord. And shall make him of quick understanding [wa-hariho] in the fear of the Lord. R[abbi] Alexandri said: This teaches that he loaded him with good deeds and suffering as a mill [is laden]." (Nezikin, BT, 626,627)

The *Targum Isaiah* (quoted above) also emphasizes this spiritual depth of the One who would come from Jesse.

7. Preceded by Messenger

Old Testament	New Testament
"Behold, I send My messenger, and he will prepare the way before Me" (Mal. 3:1). "A voice cries: 'in the wilderness prepare the way of the LORD; make straight in the desert a highway for our God'" (Isa. 40:3 ESV).	"The beginning of the gospel of Jesus Christ, the Son of God. As it is written in the Prophets, 'Behold, I send My messenger before Your face, who will prepare Your way before You.' The voice of one crying in the wilderness: "Prepare the way of the LORD; make his paths straight"'" (Mark 1:1–3).

According to some leading rabbinic commentators, the "LORD" spoken of here in the text is the Messiah (Isa. 40:3).

To introduce the life of Jesus, Mark begins with the explosive emergence of John the Baptist and cites both Malachi 3:1 and Isaiah 40:3 to indicate that John the Baptist is the messenger preparing the way for the Messiah (Mark 1:1–3).

8. Ministry to Begin in Galilee

Old Testament	New Testament
"But there will be no gloom for her who was in anguish. In the former time he brought into contempt the land of Zebulun and the land of Naphtali, but in the latter time he has made glorious the way of the sea, the land beyond the Jordan, Galilee of the nations" (Isa. 9:1 ESV).	"Now when he heard that John had been arrested, he withdrew into Galilee. And leaving Nazareth he went and lived in Capernaum by the sea, in the territory of Zebulun and Naphtali, so that what was spoken by the prophet Isaiah might be fulfilled.... From that time Jesus began to preach, saying, 'Repent, for the kingdom of heaven is at hand'" (Matt. 4:12–14, 17 ESV).

9. Ministry of Miracles

Old Testament	New Testament
"Then the eyes of the blind shall be opened, and the ears of the deaf unstopped; then shall the lame man leap like a deer, and the tongue of the mute sing for joy. For waters break forth in the wilderness, and streams in the desert." (Isa. 35:5, 6 ESV).	"And Jesus went throughout all the cities and villages, teaching in their synagogues and proclaiming the gospel of the kingdom and healing every disease and every affliction" (Matt. 9:35 ESV).

10. Teacher of Parables

Old Testament	New Testament
"I will open my mouth in a parable; I will utter dark sayings from of old" (Ps. 78:2).	"All these things Jesus said to the crowds in parables; indeed, he said nothing to them without a parable. This was to fulfill what was spoken by the prophet: 'I will open my mouth in parables; I will utter what has been hidden since the foundation of the world'" (Matt. 13:34, 35 ESV).

Noted New Testament scholar Craig Blomberg explains the significance of this prophecy in Matthew:

Matthew uniquely and characteristically sees Old Testament fulfillment at work, this time involving Ps 78:2. . . . This "fulfillment" is not an exegesis [explanation]of the Old Testament text but a typological application. In the original psalm, Asaph was announcing to a new generation God's mighty deeds in Israel's past. "Parable" obviously implies a quite different kind of story here. "Hidden" refers primarily to that which was not yet revealed to one group of individuals despite being well known to everyone else. But the psalmist's language also suggests that he intends to disclose patterns in the events not always recognized even by those for whom the stories were familiar. (Blomberg, *Matthew*, 221)

In this Psalm, Asaph narrates a history of the people's spiritual blindness. He names events from the exodus out of slavery onward, even to his own time, making references to Exodus, Numbers, Deuteronomy, Judges, and Joshua. He does more than simply recite this history; as Blomberg says, Asaph's language shows that he intends for these events to operate for his hearers like a parable, a story that can provoke thought and reveal truths new to people. Matthew highlights Jesus' use of parables for a similar purpose: to reach into the lives of people and call them to new truth.

11. He Was to Enter the Temple

Old Testament

"Behold, I send my messenger, and he will prepare the way before me. And the Lord whom you seek will suddenly come to his temple; and the messenger of the covenant in whom you delight, behold, he is coming, says the LORD of hosts" (Mal. 3:1 ESV).

New Testament

"And Jesus entered the temple and drove out all who sold and bought in the temple, and he overturned the tables of the money-changers and the seats of those who sold pigeons" (Matt. 21:12 ESV).

12. He Was to Enter Jerusalem on a Donkey

Old Testament

"Rejoice greatly, O daughter of Zion! Shout aloud, O daughter of Jerusalem! Behold, your king is coming to you; righteous and having salvation is he, humble and mounted on a donkey, on a colt, the foal of a donkey" (Zech. 9:9 ESV).

New Testament

"And they brought it to Jesus, and throwing their cloaks on the colt, they set Jesus on it. And as he rode along, they spread their cloaks on the road. As he was drawing near—already on the way down the Mount of Olives—the whole multitude of his disciples began to rejoice and praise God with a loud voice for all the mighty works that they had seen" (Luke 19:35–37 ESV).

13. A "Light" to the Gentiles

Old Testament

"And now the LORD says, he who formed me from the womb to be his servant, to bring Jacob back to him; and that Israel might be gathered to him—for I am honored in the eyes of the LORD, and my God has become my strength—he says: 'It is too light a thing that you should be my servant to raise up the tribes of Jacob and to bring back the preserved of Israel; I will make you as a light for the nations, that my salvation may reach to the end of the earth'" (Isa. 49:5, 6 ESV).

New Testament

"For so the Lord has commanded us, saying, 'I have made you a light for the Gentiles, that you may bring salvation to the ends of the earth.' And when the Gentiles heard this, they began rejoicing and glorifying the word of the Lord, and as many as were appointed to eternal life believed" (Acts 13:47, 48 ESV; see also Acts 26:23; 28:28).

C. The Servant Song of Isaiah

In Isaiah 52:13—53:12, there is a remarkable prophecy concerning the sufferings and mission of the Messiah. We will quote the text in full and then provide some analysis as to the identity of the servant in this amazing passage:

Behold, my servant shall act wisely; he shall be high and lifted up, and shall be exalted. As many were astonished at you—his appearance was so marred, beyond human semblance, and his form beyond that of the children of mankind—so shall he sprinkle many nations; kings shall shut their mouths because of him, for that which has not been told them they see, and that which they have not heard they understand.

Who has believed what he has heard from us? And to whom has the arm of the LORD been revealed? For he grew up before him like a young plant, and like a root out of dry ground; he had no form or majesty that we should look at him, and no beauty that we should desire him. He was despised and rejected by men, a man of sorrows, and acquainted with grief; and as one from whom men hide their faces he was despised, and we esteemed him not. Surely he has borne our griefs and carried our sorrows; yet we esteemed him stricken, smitten by God, and afflicted. But he was pierced for our transgressions; he was crushed for our iniquities; upon him was the chastisement that brought us peace, and with his wounds we are healed. All we like sheep have gone astray; we have turned—every one—to his own way; and the LORD *has laid on him the iniquity of us all. He was oppressed, and he was afflicted, yet he opened not his mouth; like a lamb that is led to the slaughter, and like a sheep that before its shearers is silent, so he opened not his mouth. By oppression and judgment he was taken away; and as for his generation, who considered that he was cut off out of the land of the living, stricken for the transgression of my people? And they made his grave with the wicked and with a rich man in his death, although he had done no violence, and there was no deceit in his mouth. Yet it was the will of the* LORD *to crush him; he has put him to grief; when his soul makes an offering for guilt, he shall see his offspring; he shall prolong his days; the will of the* LORD *shall prosper in his hand. Out of the anguish of his soul he shall see and be satisfied; by his knowledge shall the righteous one, my servant, make many to be accounted righteous, and he shall bear their iniquities. Therefore I will divide him a portion with the many, and he shall divide the spoil with the strong, because he poured out his soul to death and was numbered with the transgressors; yet he bore the sin of many, and makes intercession for the transgressors.* (ESV)

There are three main interpretations regarding the identity of the servant in this passage. One interpretation is that the passage refers to the nation of Israel as a whole. Another is that the passage refers to a righteous remnant within the nation of Israel. The third is that the text speaks prophetically of an individual to come in the future—perhaps the Messiah or some other individual.

Which of those three interpretations is the best supported? Although the national interpretation became predominant after the eleventh century AD, in previous centuries, it was just one of several interpretations. The Targum understands the text to refer to the Messiah—a warring, conquering king, while the Talmud generally takes the passage to refer to the Messiah or other individuals. The passage has even been understood to refer to Jeremiah, e.g., by Sa'adiah Gaon, an influential Rabbinic leader in the ninth century. The earliest and most authoritative traditional Jewish sources, thus, generally interpret the text to refer to an individual, and this individual was most commonly interpreted to be the Messiah. (Brown, AJOJ,III.49–57)

Reference is made to the servant of the Lord in a few different ways in Isaiah 40–51. In some cases (41:8, 9; 42:19; 43:10; 44:21; 45:4; 48:20), the title refers to national Israel. In others (49:3, 5–7; 50:10), the title refers to a righteous individual within Israel. Other cases are more ambiguous (42:1; 44:1, 2). The references to the servant as the people of Israel end with Isaiah 48:20. The references to the servant as a righteous individual who represents the nation begin in Isaiah 49 and continue until the conclusion of Isaiah 53.

The text of Isaiah 53 cannot refer to national Israel for several reasons. For one thing, the Torah promises that if Israel, as a nation, lives righteously before God, then they will be blessed and not afflicted (e.g. see Leviticus 26 and Deuteronomy 28). Second, Isaiah 52:13–15 tells us that the servant would suffer and then be highly exalted such that rulers would stand in awe of him. These verses make perfect sense in view of a Messianic interpretation, but make little sense if applied to the nation of Israel. Third, the servant is described as being totally righteous. But this is not the picture Scripture gives us of the nation of Israel. Fourthly, the suffering servant's suffering and death are said to bring us redemption and mercy. But this can hardly be applied to the sufferings of Israel, since the nations that attacked Israel were judged and punished by God. Finally, the text says in verses 8 and 9, "By oppression and judgment he was taken away; and as for his generation, who considered that he was cut off out of the land of the living, stricken for the transgression of my people? And they made his grave with the wicked and with a rich man in his death, although he had done no violence, and there was no deceit in his mouth." Who are "my people"? Surely that is a reference to Israel. That being the case, how can Israel suffer for the sins of Israel, having done no wrong herself? The reference to there being no deceit in the servant's mouth also does not comport very well with the national Israel interpretation, especially in view of Isaiah 6:5, in which the prophet says, "I am a man of unclean lips, and I dwell in the midst of a people of unclean lips.'" (Brown, AJOJ, III.49–57)

It is also worth appreciating the context for Isaiah 53, which names what the suffering servant will bring with him: peace, joy, salvation, and the rule of God. Isaiah writes:

> How beautiful upon the mountains are the feet of him who brings good news, who proclaims peace, who brings glad tidings of good things, who proclaims salvation, who says to Zion, "Your God reigns!" Your watchmen shall lift up their voices, with their voices they shall sing together; for they shall see eye to eye when the LORD brings back Zion. Break forth into joy, sing together, you waste places of Jerusalem! For the LORD has comforted His people, He has redeemed Jerusalem. The LORD has made bare His holy arm in the eyes of all the nations; and all the ends of the earth shall see the salvation of our God. — Isaiah 52:7–10

The text speaks, echoing Isaiah 40, of the Lord himself coming to Zion in order to redeem his people. The New Testament writers speak of all these blessings as coming through Christ, who is the fulfillment of these prophecies.

The first verse of Isaiah's song further speaks of the servant being "high and lifted up" and being "exalted" (Isa. 52:13), which resembles Isaiah's description of Yahweh as sitting on his throne: "I saw the Lord sitting on a throne, high and lifted up" (Isa. 6:1).

D. Prophecies Regarding the Time of Messiah's Coming

1. The Removal of the Scepter

As the patriarch Jacob blessed his sons and their descendants, he told his son Judah, "The scepter shall not depart from Judah, nor a lawgiver from between his feet, until Shiloh comes; and to Him shall be the obedience of the people" (Gen. 49:10).

The word that is translated "scepter" in this passage means a "tribal staff" or "a ruler's staff." The "tribal staff" of Judah was not to pass away before Shiloh came. For centuries Jewish and Christian commentators alike have taken the word *Shiloh* to be a name of the Messiah, for it means "peace-bringer."

The southern kingdom of Judah was deprived of its national sovereignty during the seventy-year period of the Babylonian captivity; however, it never lost its "tribal staff" or "national identity" during that time.

They still possessed their own lawgivers or judges even while in captivity (Ezra 1:5, 8).

According to this scripture and to the Jewish interpreters at that time, two signs were to take place soon at the advent of the Messiah:

- Removal of the scepter or identity of Judah
- Suppression of the judicial power

After the return from Babylon, there was no king. The Maccabean princes, who ruled for a time, were of the tribe of Levi. Herod the Great, who had no Jewish blood, succeeded the Maccabean princes and was appointed as an agent of Roman rule. Though the tribe of Judah existed, it provided no kings: the Idumean line of Herod continued to rule, under the authority of Rome.

The power of the Jewish lawgivers was also sharply restricted at the time of Christ. This restriction involved the loss of the power to pass the death sentence, and occurred after the deposition of Archelaus, the son and successor of Herod. (Josephus, AJ, XVII.13.1–5) The Roman rulers took direct rule then and removed the supreme power of the Sanhedrin in order to exercise by themselves the *jus gladii*, that is, the sovereign right over life and death sentences. All the nations subdued by the Roman Empire were similarly deprived of their ability to pronounce capital sentences.

The Sanhedrin, however, retained certain rights:

- Excommunication (John 9:22)
- Imprisonment (Acts 5:17, 18)
- Corporal punishment (Acts 16:22)

The Talmud itself admits that "a little more than forty years before the destruction of the Temple, the power of pronouncing capital sentences was taken away from the Jews." (Talmud, Jerusalem, Sanhedrin, fol. 24, recto) Rabbi Rachmon says, "When the members of the Sanhedrin found themselves deprived of their right over life and death, a general consternation took possession of them; they covered their heads with ashes, and their bodies with sackcloth, exclaiming: 'Woe unto us, for the scepter has departed from Judah, and the Messiah has not come!'" (LeMann, JBS, 28–30). Sadly, they did not recognize that their Messiah had been walking in their midst.

2. The Glory of the Lord Filling the Temple

Writing during the days of the building of the second temple sometime in the last third of the sixth century BC, Haggai prophesied in sweeping terms that the glory of the Lord would fill the temple and bring peace:

This is what the LORD Almighty says: "In a little while I will once more shake the heavens and the earth, the sea and the dry land. I will shake all nations, and what is desired by all nations will come, and I will fill this house with glory," says the LORD Almighty. "The silver is mine and the gold is mine," declares the LORD Almighty. "The glory of this present house will be greater than the glory of the former house," says the LORD Almighty. "And in this place I will grant peace,' declares the LORD Almighty.
— Haggai 2:6–9 NIV

Michael Brown notes,

The rabbis wrestled with these verses, asking, "In what way was the glory of the Second Temple greater than the glory of the First Temple?" It is true that the Persian kings helped fund the initial rebuilding of this Temple, and Herod elaborately beautified it about five hundred years later, fulfilling God's words that the silver and gold was His. Still, some rabbis realized that the "glory" of the Temple meant more than a splendid building. This is especially clear when we think of the biblical account of the dedication of the First Temple, a dedication marked by the glory of the Lord. . . . 2 Chr 5:14; 7:1–3; cf. also Exod 40:34–35, where an almost identical scene took place and the Lord filled the Tabernacle with His glory—meaning his manifest presence.

Brown then asks,

Where was this glory at the dedication of the Second Temple? It was nowhere to be seen! In fact, the rabbis noted that there were at least five important items missing from the Second Temple that were present in the First Temple: the ark with the mercy seat and cherubim; the (divine) fire (see immediately above, 2 Chr 7:1); the Shekhinah; the Holy Spirit; and the Urim and Thummim (b. Yoma 21b). It must be asked, therefore, in what way the glory of the Second Temple was greater than the glory of the First Temple. The standard answers given by the leading Rabbinic commentators were that: (1) the Second Temple stood for a longer period of time than did the First Temple, or (2) the Second Temple, as beautified by Herod, was a more splendid building. Neither of these answers, however, is satisfactory in light of the awesome presence of the glory of God that marked the dedication of the First Temple.

In addition to this, the Lord declared in Haggai 2:9 that in the Second Temple he would grant peace. However, while there were several peaceful eras during the days of that Temple, its overall history was marked by war and turmoil, much more so than the First Temple. How then was this Temple to be specially marked by "peace," and, more important,

how was its glory to surpass the glory of the First Temple? (Brown, AJOJ, I.76–77).

Brown concludes that this can only be explained by the fact that the Messiah, the Lord himself, who carried the very presence of God, came to this Temple, worked miracles there, and taught the people God's ways. The Prince of Peace visited the Temple and after his resurrection, sent his Spirit there and continued to work miracles at the Temple through his apostles. In this way, the glory of God filled the Second Temple in a way that was greater than the way he filled the First Temple (Brown, AJOJ, I.78–88).

3. Divine Visitation at the Temple Before Its Destruction

And the Lord, whom you seek, will suddenly come to His temple. — Malachi 3:1

This verse, along with four other passages (Ps.118:26; Dan. 9:26; Hag. 2:7–9; Zech. 11:13), demands that the Messiah come while the temple at Jerusalem is still standing. This is of great significance since the temple was destroyed in AD 70 and has never been rebuilt! The passage from Daniel is exact: "And after the sixty-two weeks Messiah shall be cut off, but not for Himself; and the people of the prince who is to come shall destroy the city and the sanctuary" (Dan. 9:26).

The sequence is remarkable. Chronologically:

- Messiah comes (assumed)
- Messiah cut off (dies)
- Destruction of city (Jerusalem) and sanctuary (the temple)

Titus and his army destroyed the temple and city in AD 70; therefore, either Messiah had already come or this prophecy was false.

V. Summary of Old Testament Predictions Literally Fulfilled in Christ

Floyd Hamilton, in *The Basis of Christian Faith,* writes, "Canon Liddon is authority for the statement that there are in the Old Testament 332 distinct predictions which were literally fulfilled in Christ." (Hamilton, BCF, 160) J. Barton Payne lists 191 in his *Encyclopedia of Biblical Prophecy.* (Payne, EBC, 665–670) They are listed below as an invitation to the reader for further exploration and research.

A. His First Advent

- The fact: Genesis 3:15; Deuteronomy 18:15; Psalm 89:20; Isaiah 9:6; 28:16; 32:1; 35:4; 42:6; 49:1; 55:4; Ezekiel 34:24; Daniel 2:44; Micah 4:1; Zechariah 3:8.
- The time: Genesis 49:10; Numbers 24:17; Daniel 9:24; Malachi 3:1.
- His divinity: Psalms 2:7, 11; 45:6, 7, 11; 72:8; 89:26, 27; 102:24–27; 110:1; Isaiah 9:6; 25:9; 40:10; Jeremiah 23:6; Micah 5:2; Malachi 3:1.
- Human generation: Genesis 12:3; 18:18; 21:12; 22:18; 26:4; 28:14; 49:10; 2 Samuel 7:14; Psalms 18:4–6, 50; 22:22, 23; 29:36; 89:4; 132:11; Isaiah 11:1; Jeremiah 23:5; 33:15.

B. His Forerunner

- Isaiah 40:3
- Malachi 3:1; 4:5.

C. His Nativity and Early Years

- The fact: Genesis 3:15; Isaiah 7:14; Jeremiah 31:22.
- The place: Numbers 24:17, 19; Micah 5:2.
- Adoration by Magi: Psalm 72:10, 15; Isaiah 60:3, 6.
- Descent into Egypt: Hosea 11:1.
- Massacre of innocents: Jeremiah 31:15.

D. His Mission and Office

- Mission: Genesis 12:3; 49:10; Numbers 24:19; Deuteronomy 18:18, 19; Psalm 21:1; Isaiah 59:20; Jeremiah 33:16.
- Priest like Melchizedek: Psalm 110:4.
- Prophet like Moses: Deuteronomy 18:15.
- Conversion of Gentiles: Isaiah 11:10; Deuteronomy 32:43; Psalms 18:49; 19:4; 117:1; Isaiah 42:1; 45:23; 49:6; Hosea 1:10; 2:23; Joel 2:32.
- Ministry in Galilee: Isaiah 9:1, 2.
- Miracles: Isaiah 35:5, 6; 42:7; 53:4.
- Spiritual graces: Psalm 45:7; Isaiah 11:2; 42:1; 53:9; 61:1, 2.
- Preaching: Psalms 2:7; 78:2; Isaiah 2:3; 61:1; Micah 4:2.
- Purification of the temple: Psalm 69:9.

E. His Passion

- Rejection by Jews and Gentiles: Psalms 2:1; 22:12; 41:5; 56:5; 69:8; 118:22, 23; Isaiah 6:9, 10; 8:14; 29:13; 53:1; 65:2.
- Persecution: Psalms 22:6; 35:7, 12; 56:5; 71:10; 109:2; Isaiah 49:7; 53:3.
- Triumphal entry into Jerusalem: Psalms 8:2; 118:25, 26; Zechariah 9:9.
- Betrayal by own friend: Psalms 41:9; 55:13; Zechariah 13:6.
- Betrayal for thirty pieces of silver: Zechariah 11:12.
- Betrayer's death: Psalms 55:15, 23; 109:17.
- Purchase of Potter's Field: Zechariah 11:13.
- Desertion by disciples: Zechariah 13:7.
- False accusation: Psalms 2:1, 2; 27:12; 35:11; 109:2.
- Silence under accusation: Psalm 38:13; Isaiah 53:7.
- Mocking: Psalms 22:7, 8, 16; 109:25.

- Insults, buffeting, spitting, scourging: Psalm 35:15, 21; Isaiah 50:6.
- Patience under suffering: Isaiah 53:7–9. Crucifixion: Psalm 22:14, 17.
- Offer of gall and vinegar: Psalm 69:21.
- Prayer for enemies: Psalm 109:4.
- Cries upon the cross: Psalms 22:1; 31:5.
- Death in prime of life: Psalms 89:45; 102:24.
- Death with malefactors: Isaiah 53:9, 12.
- Death attested by convulsions of nature: Amos 5:20; Zechariah 14:4–6.
- Casting lots for garments: Psalm 22:18.
- Bones not to be broken: Psalm 34:20.
- Piercing: Psalm 22:16; Zechariah 12:10; 13:6.
- Voluntary death: Psalm 40:6–8.
- Vicarious suffering: Isaiah 53:4–6, 12; Daniel 9:26.
- Burial with the rich: Isaiah 53:9.

F. His Resurrection

- Psalm 2:7
- Psalm 16:8–10
- Psalm 30:3
- Psalm 41:10
- Psalm 118:17

G. His Ascension:

- Psalm 16:11
- Psalm 24:7
- Psalm 68:18
- Psalm 110:1
- Psalm 118:19

H. His Second Advent

- Psalm 50:3–6
- Isaiah 9:6, 7; 66:18
- Daniel 7:13, 14
- Zechariah 12:10; 14:4–8.

I. His Universal, Everlasting Dominion

- 1 Chronicles 17:11–14
- Psalms 2:6–8; 8:6; 45:6, 7; 72:8; 110:1–3
- Isaiah 9:7
- Daniel 7:14

After reading through this list, someone might say: "Why, you could find some of these prophecies fulfilled in the deaths of Kennedy, Nasser, King, and other great figures." Answer: Yes, one could possibly find one or two prophecies fulfilled in the lives of other men, but could one person fulfill all of these major prophecies?

Interestingly enough, at one time a generous reward was available to anyone who could identify someone who fulfilled just half of the predictions concerning the Messiah, as listed in *Messiah in Both Testaments* by Fred John Meldau. It was the Christian Victory Publishing Company of Denver that offered that one-thousand-dollar reward. But no one was able to collect that reward, even though a lot of people could have used that extra cash.

Peter Stoner, in the book *Science Speaks*, examines the mathematical probabilities that apply to the fulfillment of these predictions. In the foreword to that book, H. Harold Hartzler, of the American Scientific Affiliation, Goshen College, writes: "The manuscript for *Science Speaks* has been carefully reviewed by a committee of the American Scientific Affiliation members and by the Executive Council of the same group and has been found, in general, to be dependable and accurate in regard to the scientific material presented. The mathematical analysis included is based upon principles of probability which are thoroughly sound and Professor Stoner has applied these principles in a proper and convincing way." (Hartzler, "F," as cited in Stoner, SS)

The following probabilities are taken from Stoner in *Science Speaks* to show that coincidence is ruled out by the science of probability. Stoner says the following by using the modern science of probability in reference to eight prophecies (all of which are listed above): the Messiah was to be born in Bethlehem. He would be preceded by a messenger. He was to enter Jerusalem on a donkey. He would be betrayed by a friend and his hands and feet pierced. His betrayer would be given thirty pieces of silver. The betrayal money would be thrown into the house of God and used to buy a potter's field. He would be silent before his accusers. His hands and feet would be pierced and he would die accounted among criminals. Stoner writes:

> We find that the chance that any man might have lived down to the present time and fulfilled all eight prophecies is 1 in 10^{17} [10 to the 17th power). That would be 1 in 100,000,000,000,000,000 (17 zeroes after the one). In order to help us comprehend this staggering probability, Stoner illustrates it by supposing that] we take 10^{17} silver dollars and lay them on the face of Texas. They will cover all of the state two feet deep. Now mark one of these silver dollars and stir the whole mass thoroughly, all over the state. Blindfold a man and tell him that he can travel as far as he wishes, but he must pick up one silver dollar and say that this is the right one. What chance would he have of getting the right one? Just the same chance that the prophets would have had of writing these eight prophecies and having them all come true in any one man, from their day to the present time, providing they wrote them according to their own wisdom.

Now these prophecies were either given by inspiration of God or the prophets just wrote

them as they thought they should be. In such a case the prophets had just one chance in 10^{17} of having them come true in any man, but they all came true in Christ. This means that the fulfillment of these eight prophecies alone proves that God inspired the writing of these prophecies to a definiteness which lacks only one chance in 10^{17} of being absolute. (Stoner, SS, 100–107)

Stoner then considers a group of forty-eight of the prophecies and reports:

> We find the chance that any one man fulfilled all 48 prophecies to be 1 in 10^{157}. This is really a large number and it represents an extremely small chance. Let us try to visualize it. The silver dollar, which we have been using, is entirely too large. We must select a smaller object. The electron is about as small an object as we know of. It is so small that it will take 2.5 times 10^{15} of them laid side by side to make a line, single file, one inch long. If we were going to count the electrons in this line one inch long, and counted 250 each minute, and if we counted day and night, it would take us 19,000,000 years to count just the one-inch line of electrons. If we had a cubic inch of these electrons and we tried to count them it would take us, counting steadily 250 each minute, 19,000,000 times 19,000,000 times 19,000,000 years or 6.9 times 10^{21} years.
>
> With this introduction, let us go back to our chance of 1 in 10^{157}. Let us suppose that we are taking this number of electrons, marking one, and thoroughly stirring it into the whole mass, then blindfolding a man and letting him try to find the right one. What chance has he of finding the right one? (Stoner, SS, 109,110)

Such is the chance of any individual fulfilling those forty-eight prophecies.

CHAPTER 10

THE RESURRECTION: HOAX OR HISTORY?

OVERVIEW

I. Introduction

This chapter discusses the resurrection of Jesus of Nazareth as a real space-time event in history. We look at the importance of a physical resurrection, its significance for the individual Christian and the church as a whole, the prophetic claims Jesus made about his death and resurrection, and why those claims are important. Then we turn our attention to the historical evidence that supports the claim that Jesus rose from the dead, setting it in its proper historical context of first-century Jerusalem life. Finally, we investigate a survey of various naturalistic theories, consider their strengths and weaknesses, and discuss why they ultimately fail under the weight of evidence supporting the resurrection.

It is important to keep in mind that three basic credentials validate Jesus' claims regarding himself: (1) The impact of his life, through his miracles and teachings, upon people throughout history; (2) fulfilled prophecy in his life; and (3) his resurrection. Other chapters in this volume address the first two credentials, but in this chapter, we take an in-depth look at the third credential. When we consider the significance of the resurrection, we see that the resurrection of Jesus and Christianity either stand together or fall together.

Here is likely the earliest resurrection narrative as recorded in Mark 16:1–8 (see also Matt. 28:1–11; Luke 24:1–12; John 20:1–18ff):

When the Sabbath was over, Mary Magdalene, Mary the mother of James, and Salome bought spices, so they could go and anoint Him. Very early in the morning, on the first day of the week, they went to the tomb at sunrise. They were saying to one another, "Who will roll away the stone from the entrance to the tomb for us?" Looking up, they observed that the stone— which was very large—had been rolled away. When they entered the tomb, they saw a young man dressed in a long white robe sitting on the right side; they were amazed and alarmed. "Don't be alarmed," he told them. "You are looking for Jesus the Nazarene, who was crucified. He has been resurrected! He is not here! See the place where they put Him. But go, tell His disciples and Peter, 'He is going ahead of you to Galilee; you will see Him there just as He told you.'" So they went out and started

running from the tomb, because trembling and astonishment overwhelmed them. And they said nothing to anyone, since they were afraid.

II. The Importance of the Physical Resurrection of Christ

For historical context it is important for us to start our study by finding out what "resurrection" meant (and did not mean) to a first-century Jewish person.

A. What Is "Resurrection"?
1. Resurrection: Its Background and Definition

In his groundbreaking historical analysis of the resurrection, leading biblical scholar and theologian N. T. Wright explains how the word *resurrection* was used and what it meant to those living in the ancient world, whether they believed in the resurrection or not.

This basic tenet of human existence and experience is accepted as axiomatic throughout the ancient world; once people have gone by the road of death, they do not return. . . . "Resurrection" was not one way of describing what death consisted of. It was a way of describing something everyone knew did not happen: the idea that death could be reversed, undone, could (as it were) work backwards. Not even in myth was it permitted. (Wright, RSG, 33)

For Wright to point out that "not even in myth was it permitted" emphasizes the uniqueness of the resurrection of Christ in an ancient world that accepted so many startling supernatural events in its stories, but did not countenance a bodily resurrection. Wright also defines what is (and is *not*) meant by "resurrection" in the ancient world:

"Resurrection" was, by definition, not the existence into which someone might (or might not) go immediately upon death; it was not a disembodied "heavenly" life; it was a further stage, out beyond all that. It was not a redescription or redefinition of death. It was death's reversal. . . . When the early Christians spoke of Jesus being raised from the dead, the natural meaning of that statement, throughout the ancient world, was the claim that something had happened to Jesus which had happened to nobody else. [see section A.1.2. below] . . . "Resurrection" (*anastasis* and its cognates) was not in use elsewhere in the ancient world as a description of nonbodily life after death. (Wright, RSG, 83–84)

Wright points out that various ancient cultures all knew what the word *resurrection* meant—even if they did not all believe that it was something that would actually happen. There was a common definition, even though there was no consensus regarding its reality.

Here there is no difference between pagans, Jews and Christians. They all understood the Greek word *anastasis* and its cognates, and the other related terms we shall meet, to mean . . . new life after a period of being dead. Pagans denied this possibility; some Jews affirmed it as a long-term future hope; virtually all Christians claimed that it had happened to Jesus and would happen to them in the future. (Wright, RSG, 31)

Bolstering his assertion, Wright explains the importance to the Greek and Roman world of "embodiment" in relation to the concept of "resurrection":

The meaning of "resurrection," both in Jewish and the non-Jewish world of late antiquity, was never that the person concerned had simply "gone to heaven," or been "exalted" in some

way which did not involve a new bodily life. Plenty of disembodied postmortem states were postulated, and there was a rich variety of terminology for denoting them, which did not include "resurrection." "Resurrection" meant embodiment; that was equally so for the pagans, who denied it, as it was for the Jews, at least some of whom hoped for it. (Wright, RSG, 694)

Before taking up the next point, we ought to stress that in no ancient culture did "resurrection" ever refer to anything other than bodily resurrection. A nonbodily resurrection would have been just as illogical as a square circle or a married bachelor.

2. Raising the Dead in Scripture: The Difference Between Resuscitation and Resurrection

In both the Old and New Testaments, a total of nine (possibly ten) individuals and one group are raised from the dead. In the Old Testament, there are three:

- Elijah raised the son of Zarephath's widow (1 Kings 17:17–24).
- Elisha raised the son of the Shunammite woman (2 Kings 4:35).
- A dead man comes back to life when his body touches Elisha's bones (2 Kings 13:21).

In the New Testament, we find the following people being raised:

- Jesus raises the widow's son at Nain (Luke 7:13–15).
- Jesus raises Jairus's daughter (Matt. 9:25; Mark 5:42; Luke 8:55).
- Jesus raises his friend Lazarus (John 11:43, 44).
- Jesus is raised from the dead (Matt. 28:5, 6; Mark 16:1–8; Luke 24:1–11; John 20:1–10).

- Peter raises Tabitha (Acts 9:36–42).
- Paul raises Eutychus (Acts 20:9–12).

A group of individuals is also raised between Jesus' death and resurrection:

- Dead saints come out of the graves (Matt. 27:52, 53).

Finally, in connection with one passage, there has been debate about whether Paul was raised from the dead:

- Paul is assumed dead after being stoned by the people (Acts 14:19, 20).

What sets apart Jesus' coming back to life from all these other miraculous events of dead people being brought back to life is the way in which Paul characterizes Jesus' resurrection:

> But now Christ has been raised from the dead, the firstfruits of those who have fallen asleep. For since death came through a man, the resurrection of the dead also comes through a man. For as in Adam all die, so also in Christ all will be made alive. But each in his own order: Christ, the firstfruits; afterward, at His coming, those who belong to Christ. — 1 Corinthians 15:20–23 HCSB

Paul says that Christ is the firstfruits of those who are resurrected. But what about those who were raised before his resurrection? What about those in the Old Testament or the ones Jesus himself raised? Wouldn't they be the firstfruits? Not according to Paul. Jesus was resurrected—never to die again. All those others who were brought back to life were raised, *but they would eventually die again*—to be raised a final time with all those who belong to Christ at his Second Coming. The quality of their resurrection was something

very different from the resurrection Jesus experienced. In addition to all this, Jesus' resurrected body had *new characteristics*, which his pre-resurrection body had not possessed. He was able to appear and disappear at will (Luke 24:31, 36, 37, 51; John 20:19, 26), and he ascended to heaven in his physical body (Acts 1:6–11). None of these other people who were raised had yet received their new resurrected bodies; they were raised in their mortal, flesh and blood bodies that they had previously died in with the expectation that they would die again. This is why their resurrections are really "resuscitations," while Jesus was resurrected in the fullest sense. The physical bodies of these others were resuscitated, but Jesus was resurrected with a body that was recognizably his own yet radically transformed.

B. The Physical Nature of the Resurrection

Having explained that resurrection really meant death's reversal by "new bodily life," Wright goes on to link the bodily resurrection of Jesus and the rise of Christianity to the empty tomb, declaring that the empty tomb is "a *necessary* condition" for the "very specific" way in which the early Christians understood it—that is, as an actual historical event.

We may insist, in fact, that whatever else had happened, if the body of Jesus of Nazareth had remained in the tomb there would have been no early Christian belief of the sort we have discovered. It will not do to suggest, for instance, that because the disciples lived in a world where resurrection was expected, this will explain why they used that language of Jesus. Many other Jewish leaders, heroes and would-be Messiahs died within the same world, but in no case did anyone suggest that they had been raised from the dead. One might imagine other kinds of early faith which could have been generated by events which did not involve an empty tomb. But the specific faith of the earliest Christians could not have been generated by a set of circumstances in which an empty tomb did not play a part. I therefore regard the empty tomb as a *necessary* [italics his] condition . . . for the rise of the very specific early Christian belief. (Wright, RSG, 695)

Apologist Norman Geisler emphasizes the importance of the resurrection of Jesus being physical in nature as a way of validating the claim that Jesus is God:

If Christ did not rise in the same physical body that was placed in the tomb, then the resurrection loses its value as an evidential proof of His claims to be God (John 8:58; 10:30). The resurrection cannot verify Jesus' claim to be God unless He was resurrected in the body in which He was crucified. That body was a literal, physical body. Unless Jesus rose in a material body, there is no way to verify His resurrection. It loses its historically persuasive value. The truth of Christianity is based on the bodily resurrection of Christ. (Geisler, BR, 36)

III. The Significance of the Resurrection

The resurrection of Jesus of Nazareth is vitally important because: (A) As the apostle Paul states so clearly, if Christ had not been raised from the dead, then nothing else matters: our resurrection, the church, or Christianity; and (B) the resurrection is the center of New Testament theology. In this section, we look at the impact of the resurrection on both these points.

A. Paul Argues If Christ Is Not Raised, Then Nothing Else Matters

Paul weaves together a tight argument in 1 Corinthians 15:12–19. Without the resurrection, all these would be lost: a foundation for faith, trust in the veracity of the apostles, redemption from sin, and hope for resurrection of our loved ones and ourselves. We would be supremely pitiable.

Now if Christ is proclaimed as raised from the dead, how can some of you say, "There is no resurrection of the dead"? But if there is no resurrection of the dead, then Christ has not been raised; and if Christ has not been raised, then our proclamation is without foundation, and so is your faith. In addition, we are found to be false witnesses about God, because we have testified about God that He raised up Christ—whom He did not raise up if in fact the dead are not raised. For if the dead are not raised, Christ has not been raised. And if Christ has not been raised, your faith is worthless; you are still in your sins. Therefore, those who have fallen asleep in Christ have also perished. If we have put our hope in Christ for this life only, we should be pitied more than anyone. (HCSB)

The importance of what Paul wrote has echoed down through history, and current

---

Unless Jesus rose in a material body, there is no way to verify His resurrection. It loses its historically persuasive value. The truth of Christianity is based on the bodily resurrection of Christ.

Norman Geisler

scholars affirm what Paul proclaimed to the church in Corinth. Philosopher Douglas Groothuis agrees:

> Of all the world's religions Christianity alone purports to be based on the resurrection of its divine founder. No other religion or worldview makes such an audacious and consequential claim. . . . The resurrection of Jesus is at the center of the Christian worldview and Christian devotion. The Gospels do not end with the death of Jesus but speak of an empty tomb, of his appearances and of a commission by the risen Jesus. (Groothuis, CA, 527–528)

Leading scholar on the topic of the resurrection Gary Habermas says, "As long as we're sure that Jesus is the son of God, who died on the cross for our sins, and was raised from the dead . . . Christianity follows." (Habermas, RJ, Lesson 1)

Another leading scholar on the resurrection, philosopher William Lane Craig, writes:

> It is quite clear that without the belief in the resurrection the Christian faith could not have come into being. The disciples would have remained crushed and defeated men. Even had they continued to remember Jesus as their believed teacher, His crucifixion would have forever silenced any hopes of His being the Messiah. The cross could have remained the sad and shameful end to His career. *The origin of Christianity therefore hinges on the belief of the early disciples that God had raised Jesus from the dead.* (Craig, SR, 128, emphasis in original)

Even skeptical scholars agree that if no resurrection occurred, then there is no Christianity, no church, no Christian. The German atheistic New Testament scholar Gerd Lüdemann writes:

> [Arguments] from fellow theologians along with further work of my own on the subject have convinced me that disproving the historicity of the resurrection of Jesus ultimately annuls the Christian heritage as error. (Lüdemann, RC, 8–9)

Pinchas Lapide is an orthodox Jew and scholar who believes in the historicity of the resurrection but does not accept Jesus as the Son of God. Instead, he believes Jesus was such a good person that God wanted to resurrect him. Even though Lapide denies the deity of Jesus, he does agree with the above scholars regarding the importance of the resurrection:

> Christianity as a historical religion of revelation is based on two fundamental events—the death of Jesus of Nazareth on the cross and his resurrection. While the first event may be considered historically certain, both according to statements of the evangelists which are basically in agreement, and also from non-Christian sources, the latter event is still controversial, cannot be conceived historically, and has led from the beginning to doubt, discord, and dissension. . . . Resurrection is by far the more important of these two pillars of the Christian faith. . . . Without the experience of the resurrection, the crucifixion of Jesus would most likely have remained without consequences and forgotten, just as were the innumerable crucifixions of pious Jews which the Romans carried out before Jesus, during the lifetime of Jesus, and up until the destruction of Jerusalem in the year 70. . . . Thus the Christian faith stands and falls not with Golgotha, the infamous "place of the skull," where thousands of Jesus' brothers were murdered cruelly by Romans mercenaries, but with the experience "on the third day" after the crucifixion, an experience which was able to defuse, to refute, and even to make meaningful this death on the cross for the community of the disciples. (Lapide, RJ, 32–34)

B. The Resurrection Is the Center of New Testament Theology*

So much of what Christians believe is connected directly to the resurrection of Jesus of Nazareth. The apostle Paul explicitly links the believers' forgiveness, salvation, and resurrection to the resurrection of Jesus. Paul indicates the comprehensive range of what God has done and will do, especially because the Greek word translated "salvation" conveys a wonderful array of meanings—rescue, deliverance, safety, defense, and wholeness.

For if the dead are not raised, Christ has not been raised. And if Christ has not been raised, your faith is worthless; you are still in your sins. Therefore, those who have fallen asleep in Christ have also perished. If we have put our hope in Christ for this life only, we should be pitied more than anyone. — 1 Corinthians 15:16–19 HCSB*

If you confess with your mouth, "Jesus is Lord," and believe in your heart that God raised Him from the dead, you will be saved. One believes with the heart, resulting in righteousness, and one confesses with the mouth, resulting in salvation. — Romans 10:9, 10

We know that the One who raised the Lord Jesus will raise us also with Jesus and present us with you. — 2 Corinthians 4:14

Since we believe that Jesus died and rose again, in the same way God will bring with Him those who have fallen asleep through Jesus. — 1 Thessalonians 4:14

Church leader, author, and clinical psychiatrist Adrian Warnock writes on the topic of Christian theology and practice as it pertains directly to the resurrection. In the course of demonstrating from the book of Acts that several Christian doctrines are based upon the resurrection, Warnock writes:

We have seen that if Jesus had not been raised, none of the following things, listed in order of their appearance in Acts, would have been possible:

- Sending of the Spirit (Acts 2:33)
- Physical healings (Acts 3:15–16)
- Conversion of sinners (Acts 3:26)
- Salvation by union with Jesus (Acts 4:11–12)
- Jesus' role as the leader of his church (Acts 5:30–31; 9)
- Forgiveness of sins (Acts 5:30–31)
- Comfort for the dying (Acts 7)
- Commissioning of the gospel messengers (Acts 9; 10:42)
- Freedom from the penalty and power of sin (Acts 13:37–39)
- Assurance that the gospel is true (Acts 17:31)
- Our own resurrection (Acts 17:31)
- Jesus' future judgment of this world (Acts 17:31) (Warnock, RC, 113–114)

IV. The Claims That Christ Would Be Raised from the Dead

A. The Significance of the Claims

Resurrection claims are significant for a number of reasons. For instance, their

---

* To read more on this topic the following books might be helpful: Ross Clifford and Philip Johnson, *The Cross Is Not Enough: Living as Witnesses to the Resurrection* (Grand Rapids, MI: Baker Books, 2012); Gary Habermas, *The Resurrection Volume I: Heart of New Testament Doctrine*, (Joplin, MO: College Press Publishing Company, 2000); Gary Habermas, *The Resurrection Volume II: Heart of the Christian Life* (Joplin, MO: College Press Publishing Company, 2000); John Frederick Jansen, *The Resurrection of Jesus Christ in New Testament Theology* (Philadelphia, PA: The Westminster Press, 1980).

* Unless otherwise indicated, all Scripture quotations in this section are from the HCSB.

prediction together with their later fulfillment gives evidence that Jesus is not a false prophet. The Old Testament had forewarned against unfulfilled claims from self-styled prophets: "When a prophet speaks in the LORD's name, and the message does not come true or is not fulfilled, that is a message the LORD has not spoken. The prophet has spoken it presumptuously. Do not be afraid of him" (Deut. 18:22).

So Jesus' prediction followed by evidence that the resurrection actually occurred strongly supports our confidence that he is who he claimed to be—God incarnate (see also chapter 7 in this book):

Then some of the scribes and Pharisees said to Him, "Teacher, we want to see a sign from You." But He answered them, "An evil and adulterous generation demands a sign, but no sign will be given to it except the sign of the prophet Jonah. For as Jonah was in the belly of the huge fish three days and three nights, so the Son of Man will be in the heart of the earth three days and three nights. The men of Nineveh will stand up at the judgment with this generation and condemn it, because they repented at Jonah's proclamation; and look—something greater than Jonah is here! The queen of the south will rise up at the judgment with this generation and condemn it, because she came from the ends of the earth to hear the wisdom of Solomon; and look—something greater than Solomon is here!"
— Matthew 12:38–42

[A]nd who has been declared to be the powerful Son of God by the resurrection from the dead according to the Spirit of holiness. — Romans 1:4

If the resurrection did not happen, then Jesus' claims to being both the Messiah and the Son of God would be false and Jesus would have been seen as a fraud and a liar. As C. S. Lewis so famously put it in his "poached egg" argument, Jesus' claim to be both the Messiah and Son of God is absolutely true or else Jesus was a liar or a lunatic. For the full argument, see chapter 8 in this book, "The Trilemma: Lord, Liar, or Lunatic?"

B. Jesus Predicts His Own Resurrection

Jesus not only predicted his resurrection but also directed the disciples to specific things they should expect or do after it happened. When the Jewish authorities demanded for a sign of his authority, he responded in terms that the disciples afterward understood as a fulfillment of an Old Testament type (see chapter 9).

From then on Jesus began to point out to His disciples that He must go to Jerusalem and suffer many things from the elders, chief priests, and scribes, be killed, and be raised the third day.
— Matthew 16:21

As they were coming down from the mountain, Jesus commanded them, "Don't tell anyone about the vision until the Son of Man is raised from the dead." — Matthew 17:9

As they were meeting in Galilee, Jesus told them, "The Son of Man is about to be betrayed into the hands of men. They will kill Him, and on the third day He will be raised up." And they were deeply distressed. — Matthew 17:22, 23

"Listen! We are going up to Jerusalem. The Son of Man will be handed over to the chief priests and scribes, and they will condemn Him to death. Then they will hand Him over to the Gentiles to be mocked, flogged, and crucified, and He will be resurrected on the third day."
— Matthew 20:18, 19

"But after I have been resurrected, I will go ahead of you to Galilee." — Matthew 26:32

They kept this word to themselves, discussing what "rising from the dead" meant. — Mark 9:10

"The Son of Man must suffer many things and be rejected by the elders, chief priests, and scribes, be killed, and be raised the third day." Then He said to them all, "If anyone wants to come with Me, he must deny himself, take up his cross daily, and follow Me. For whoever wants to save his life will lose it, but whoever loses his life because of Me will save it. What is a man benefited if he gains the whole word, yet loses or forfeits himself? For whoever is ashamed of Me and My words, the Son of Man will be ashamed of him when He comes in His glory and that of the Father and the holy angels. I tell you the truth: There are some standing here who will not taste death until they see the kingdom of God." — Luke 9:22–27

So the Jews replied to Him, "What sign of authority will You show us for doing these things?" Jesus answered, "Destroy this sanctuary, and I will raise it up in three days." Therefore the Jews said, "This sanctuary took 46 years to build, and will You raise it up in three days?" But He was speaking about the sanctuary of His body. So when He was raised from the dead, His disciples remembered that He had said this. And they believed the Scripture and the statement Jesus had made. — John 2:18–22

In his massive historical defense of the resurrection, apologist and historian Michael Licona explores four points based on biblical passages where Jesus predicts his death and his subsequent vindication via his resurrection. Here is a list of the textual references to provide biblical context for his four points:

- Mark 8:27–33
- Matthew 12:38–42
- Matthew 14:22–25
- Matthew 14:28

- Matthew 14:32–41
- Matthew 16:21–23
- Matthew 26:36–45
- Luke 9:21–22
- Luke 22:15–20
- Luke 22:29
- Luke 22:39–46
- 1 Corinthians 11:23

1. The context in which Mark 8:31 appears (Mark 8:27–33) is Jesus' rebuke of Peter who, after hearing Jesus' prediction of his impending death and resurrection, rebukes Jesus and tells him that events should not transpire in the way he has just described. There are a number of reasons for regarding this text as historical. First, we find two statements that are unlikely inventions of the early church given their embarrassing nature. Peter is reported to have rebuked [*épitimáō*] his master, Jesus. Jesus, in turn, rebukes his disciple who would become the lead apostle in the post-Easter Jerusalem Church. Both rebukes are strongly linked to Jesus' prediction of his death and resurrection, since there is no occasion for either rebuke without Jesus' prediction concerning his death and resurrection. Second, Semitic elements are present, and the parallel texts of Matthew 16:21–23 and Luke 9:22 are independent, providing multiple attestation. . . . Third, we find Jesus' use of his favorite self-designation, Son of Man, which is dissimilar to how the early Christians referred to him. Thus, the authenticity of Jesus' logion [a term used in scholarly circles to refer to a saying attributed to Jesus] in Mark 9:31 is supported by the criteria of embarrassment, multiple attestation and dissimilarity. (Licona, RJ, 284–285)

2. Many scholars have recognized that the logion of Jesus concerning his imminent death in Mark 9:31 may be quite early [i.e., circulated orally prior to the composition

of Mark's gospel] . . . Moreover, once again we find Jesus' self-designation as the Son of Man. Thus the authenticity of Jesus' logion in Mark 9:31 is supported by the criteria of early attestation and dissimilarity (Licona, RJ, 285).

3. Jesus institutes taking the bread and cup as a reminder to his disciples that his body and blood were about to be broken and poured out for them. These statements from the Last Supper are supported by primitive tradition [were orally disseminated before being recorded]. They are preserved in the pre-Pauline tradition in 1 Corinthians 11:24–25 and Luke 22:15–20. Independent tradition [another source, evident from exact detail or divergent language, therefore meeting the criterion of multiple attestation] appears in Mark 14:22–24. Pauline source material and Luke is especially apparent in the saying about the cup in 1 Corinthians 11:25 and Luke 22:20, appearing nearly word-for-word. . . . This suggests that Luke and Paul drew on a common tradition independent of Mark. That Jesus believed he would be vindicated is linked to the logia reported in Luke 22:29, where he says the Father has granted him a kingdom and when referring to his resurrection in Mark 14:28, which also seems to be implied in Mark 14:25 in light of the context. Accordingly, the authenticity of Jesus' logion of his death and vindication/resurrection uttered at the Last Supper is supported by the criteria of multiple attestation, early attestation and dissimilarity (Licona, RJ, 285–286).

4. In Jesus' prayer and discussion with his disciples in Gethsemane . . . he anticipated his impending violent death (Mk 14:32–41; Mt 26:36–45; Lk 22:39–46). Jesus' prayer contains an element that may have been embarrassing to the early Christian readers. While a number of accounts existed of Jewish martyrs who acted bravely under circumstances of extreme torture and execution, reports of Jesus' arrest and martyrdom show [the anguish and reluctance that it cost him when he faced it. Although he answered accusations firmly at his trials and even helped the high priest's servant at his arrest (Lk 22:51), in Gethsemane he admitted feeling "very sorrowful, even to death." For the gospel writers to report his repeated prayer that this "cup" could be removed might imply] a weaker and far less valiant Jesus, one that could cause embarrassment for the early Christians in contrast. . . . In addition to these embarrassing components, there appears to be independent tradition of his garden prayer in Hebrews 5:7. . . . Therefore, the authenticity of Jesus' expectation of his violent death and perhaps his vindication is supported by the criteria of embarrassment, multiple attestation and dissimilarity (Licona, RJ, 286, 290).

After probing these four passages in Mark in which Jesus predicts his death, Licona offers six general points that provide solid historical grounds for concluding that Jesus predicted his death and resurrection:

1. Some of the logia contain elements that suggest they are very early. These include pre-Pauline tradition and elements that suggest an Aramaic original.
2. The passion and resurrection predictions are multiply attested.
3. The passion and resurrection predictions fulfill the criterion of embarrassment. We observed this in the garden scene and in the portrayal of the disciples who did not understand Jesus' passion predictions or simply did not believe him (Mk 8:31–33; 9:31–32; 14:27–31; Lk 24:11, 21). Of special interest is that in the midst of these predictions the first leader of the church is portrayed in a negative light.

4. With only a few exceptions, the passion and resurrection predictions lack signs of possible theologizing by the early church. [They are presented directly, without extensive interpretation, making them more clearly a transmission of exactly what Jesus said without later additions.]

5. Jesus' passion and resurrection predictions appear together with Jesus' reference to himself as the Son of Man. Given the criterion of dissimilarity, "Son of Man" appears to have been an authentic self-designation by Jesus. [That is, the phrase "Son of Man" cannot be derived from first century Judaism or from the church that came after him, and so likely came from Jesus himself.]

6. The passion predictions fulfill the criterion of plausibility. [This criterion requires that a report fits the time and place in which it is said to arise, and also that its influence can be seen in later thinking and events.] (Licona, RJ, 290–295)

Licona summarizes:

The criteria for historicity are, of course, only blunt tools that do not produce assured results when employed mechanically. However, the plausibility and probability that a logion may have originated with Jesus may be increased in those cases when multiple criteria are present. And that is precisely what we find in our study of the predictions being observed. These six arguments strongly suggest that Jesus predicted his violent death and subsequent vindication/resurrection. (Licona, RJ, 295)

V. The Historical Approach

Because we are investigating the resurrection of Jesus as a historical event, we can approach it using historical methods and tools. Even though historical investigations

always present an incomplete picture, incompleteness does not equal inaccuracy. Licona mentions the following:

There are numerous challenges to knowing the past. Since the past is forever gone, it can neither be viewed directly nor reconstructed precisely or exhaustively. Accordingly historians cannot verify the truth of a hypothesis in an absolute sense. Our knowledge of the past comes exclusively through sources. This means that, to an extent, our only link to the past is through the eyes of someone else, a person who had his or her own opinions and agendas. (Licona, RJ, 31)

By its nature historical inquiry is always selective and limited because the historian cannot possibly mention everything. However, being selective does not mean that the historian is being untruthful or inaccurate in what is being reported. "Thus, an *incomplete* description does not necessitate the conclusion that it is an *inaccurate* description." (Licona, RJ, 33)

For an in-depth analysis of how historians approach the past, and whether or not they can investigate miraculous claims, see "Is History Knowable?" (chapter 32) and "Are Miracles Possible?" (chapter 31). For now, it is important to understand that the death, burial, and resurrection of Jesus are historical events that can be investigated using the historical method.

A. The Testimony of History and Law

Sometimes people have an aversion to believing in the resurrection because they see that the New Testament narratives do not match each other 100 percent. They conclude, therefore, that these "discrepancies" indicate that these reports of what happened are largely made-up stories. But as Groothuis points out, this is unwarranted:

Some might be troubled that the resurrection accounts in the Gospels do not seem to agree perfectly. At the extreme, Michael Martin argues that this provides strong evidence that they are fictional, not factual. But this does not follow logically. With a little patience and some careful reconstruction, the events narrated in the Gospels can be harmonized with one another. The accounts of virtually any multiply attested event of secular history display discrepancies as great or greater than those in the Gospel narratives. For example, Greek historian Polybius and the Roman historian Livy seem to disagree in their description of Hannibal's route in crossing the Alps in Italy during the second Punic War. Yet ancient historians do not question whether Hannibal made this trek. (Groothuis, CA, 561)

Groothuis continues:

Some minor differences in the telling of this story indicate authenticity, not substantial error. If each account perfectly mirrored the rest, this would likely be a sign of collusion, not accurate history told from differing (but equally truthful) perspectives. (Groothuis, CA, 562)

Retired Los Angeles Police Department cold-case detective J. Warner Wallace is a recognized authority in evaluating the testimony of eyewitnesses. As a professional expert, he has spent hundreds of hours interviewing eyewitnesses and handling eyewitness testimony. He has examined the gospel accounts and explains for us why divergent testimonies are still considered reliable, even when there are points of disagreement:

If there's one thing my experience as a detective has revealed, however, it's that witnesses often make conflicting and inconsistent statements when describing what they saw at a crime scene. They frequently disagree with one another and either fail to see something obvious or describe the same event in a number of conflicting ways. The more witnesses involved in the case, the more likely there will be points of disagreement. . . . Before I ever examined the reliability of the gospel accounts, I had a reasonable expectation about what a dependable set of eyewitness statements might look like, given my experience as a detective. . . . It turns out that my expectations of true, reliable eyewitness accounts are met . . . by the Gospels. All four accounts are written from a different perspective and contain unique details that are specific to the eyewitnesses. There are, as a result, divergent (apparently *contradictory*) recollections that can be pieced together to get a complete *picture* of what occurred. All four accounts are highly personal, utilizing the distinctive language of each witness. Mark is far more passionate and active in his choice of adjectives, for example. Several of the accounts (Mark, Matthew, and Luke) contain blocks of identical (or nearly identical) descriptions. This may be the result of common agreement at particularly important points of narrative, or (more likely) the result of later eyewitnesses saying, "The rest occurred just the way he said." Finally, the last account (John's gospel) clearly attempts to *fill in* the details that were not offered by the prior eyewitnesses. John, aware of what the earlier eyewitnesses had already written, appears to make little effort to cover the same ground. . . . I recognized that they were consistent with what I would expect to see, given my experience as a detective. (Wallace, CCC, 74–82).

This means that small discrepancies do not need to line up perfectly. We expect disagreements from witness testimony on certain points, but as long as the overall story holds together, it is more likely than not that their reports contain the core truth of the matter. All of us will recognize the minor discrepancies that detective Wallace describes among witnesses; for example, almost daily we hear divergent accounts when eyewitnesses testify to unfolding news events. Moreover, even if there were contradictions in the documents themselves, and we are in no way conceding that this is the case, such claimed contradictions would not undermine the ability to ascertain certain facts from the documents. This is because, as mentioned previously, there are other criteria employed by historians that would still allow them to distinguish facts from falsehood. So even if a document contained errors or even genuine contradictions, it would not be rendered unusable for historical investigation!

For a fuller treatment of this important topic, please refer to chapter 3 in this volume, which presents evidence for the reliability and trustworthiness of the New Testament.

B. The Testimony of the Early Church Fathers

A historical approach examines witnesses living at the time of an event or living soon enough after it to hear firsthand accounts. Having looked at the scriptural testimony to the historicity of the resurrection, we now turn to the written testimony of early church leaders.

Clement focuses upon familiar daily and seasonal experiences that show the rising of something that was once thought dead, using these parallels as reminders of what he clearly expects his "beloved" fellow believers to have confidence in—the resurrection of Jesus and therefore their own future resurrection.

Clement of Rome, in *1 Clement* (c. AD 95–96), writes:

Let us consider, beloved, how the Lord continually proves to us that there shall be a future resurrection, of which He has rendered the Lord Jesus Christ the first-fruits by raising Him from the dead. Let us contemplate, beloved, the resurrection which is at all times taking place. Day and night declare to us a resurrection. The night sinks to sleep, the day arises; the day [again] departs, and the night comes on. Let us behold the fruits [of the earth], how the sowing of grain takes place. The sower goes forth, and casts it into the ground; and the seed being thus scattered, though dry and naked when it fell upon the earth, is gradually dissolved. Then out of its dissolution the mighty power of the providence of the Lord raises it up again, and from one seed many arise and bring forth fruit. (Clement, EC, chapter XXIV)

Ignatius speaks of the resurrection as a permanent source of inner strength in his *Letter to the Smyrneans* (c. AD 107–115):

I glorify God, even Jesus Christ, who has given you such wisdom. For I have observed that you are perfected in an immoveable faith, as if you were nailed to the cross of our Lord Jesus Christ, both in the flesh and in the spirit, and are established in love through the blood of Christ, being fully persuaded with respect to our Lord, that He was truly of the seed of David according to the flesh, and the Son of God according to the will and power of God; that He was truly born of a virgin, was baptized by John, in order that all righteousness might be fulfilled by Him; and was truly, under Pontius Pilate and Herod the tetrarch, nailed [to the cross] for us in His flesh. Of this fruit we are by His divinely-blessed passion, that He might set up a standard for all ages, through His resurrection, to all His holy and faithful [followers], whether among Jews or Gentiles, in the one body of His Church. (Ignatius, EIS, chapter 1)

For I know that after His resurrection also He was still possessed of flesh, and I believe the He is so now. When, for instance, He came to those who were with Peter, He said to them, *"Lay hold, handle Me, and see that I am not an incorporeal spirit."* And immediately they touched Him, and believed, being convinced both by His flesh and spirit. For this cause they despised death, and were found its conquerors. And after his resurrection He ate and drank with them, as being possessed of flesh, although spiritually He was united to the Father. (Ignatius, EIS, chapter 3)

Polycarp, in his *Letter to the Philippians* (c. AD 110–140), encourages believers who face opposition and persecution, linking their faithfulness to their confidence in Jesus being raised from the dead:

I have greatly rejoiced with you in our Lord Jesus Christ, because you have followed the example of true love [as displayed by God], and have accompanied, as became you, those who were bound in chains, the fitting ornaments of saints, and which are indeed the diadems of the true elect of God and our Lord; and because the strong root of your faith, spoken of in days long gone by, endures even until now, and brings forth fruit to our Lord Jesus Christ, who for our sins suffered even unto death, [but] *"whom God raised from the dead, having loosed the bands of the grave." "In whom, though now you see Him not, you believe, and believing, rejoice with joy unspeakable and full of glory;"* into which joy many desire to enter, knowing that *"by grace you are saved, not of works,"* but by the will of God through Jesus Christ. (Polycarp, EPP, chapter 1)

"Wherefore, girding up your loins," "serve the Lord in fear" and truth, as those who have forsaken the vain, empty talk and error of the multitude, and "believed in Him who raised up our Lord Jesus Christ from the dead, and gave Him glory," and a throne at His right hand. To Him all things in heaven and on earth are subject. Him every spirit serves. He comes as the Judge of the living and the dead. His blood will God require of those who do not believe in Him. But He who raised Him up from the dead will raise up us also, if we do His will, and walk in his commandments, and love what He loved, keeping ourselves from all unrighteousness, covetousness, love of money, evil speaking, false witness. (Polycarp, EPP, chapter 2)

I exhort you all, therefore, to yield obedience to the word of righteousness, and to exercise all patience, such as you have seen [set] before your eyes, not only in the case of the blessed Ignatius, and Zosimus, and Rufus, but also in others among yourselves, and in Paul himself, and the rest of the apostles. [This do] in the assurance that all these have not run in vain, but in faith and righteousness, and that they are [now] in their due place in the presence of the Lord. With whom also they suffered. For they loved not this present world, but Him who died for us, and for our sakes was raised again by God from the dead. (Polycarp, EPP, chapter 9)

If we please Him in this present world, we shall receive also the future world, according as He has promised to us that He will raise us again from the dead, and that if we live worthily of Him, *"we shall also reign together with Him,"* provided only we believe. (Polycarp, EPP, chapter 5)

Justin Martyr defended the resurrection as bodily, writing an entire treatment of this topic titled *On the Resurrection* (c. AD 150–160). Here is some of what he had to say:

If He had no need of the flesh, why did He heal it? And what is most forcible of all, He raised the dead. Why? Was it not to show what the resurrection should be? How then did He raise the dead? Their souls or their bodies? Manifestly both. If the resurrection were only spiritual it was requisite that He, in raising the dead, should show the body lying apart by itself, and the soul living apart by itself. But now He did not do so, but raised the body, confirming in it the promise of life. Why did He rise in the flesh in which He suffered, unless to show the resurrection of the flesh? And wishing to confirm this, when His disciples did not know whether to believe He had truly risen the body, and were looking upon Him and doubting, He said to them, "*You have not yet faith, see that it is I;*" and He let them handle Him and showed them the prints of the nails in His hands. And when they were by every kind of proof persuaded that it was Himself, and in the body, they asked Him to eat with them, that they might thus still more accurately ascertain that He had in verity risen bodily; and He ate honey-comb and fish. And when He had thus shown them this also, that it is not impossible for flesh to ascend into heaven (as He had said that our dwelling-place is in heaven), "*He was taken up into heaven while they beheld,*" as He was in the flesh. (Martyr, OR, chapter 9)*

The resurrection is a resurrection of the flesh which died. For the spirit dies not; the soul is in the body, and without a soul it cannot live. The body, when the soul forsakes it, is not. For the body is the house of the soul. (Martyr, OR, chapter 10)

VI. The Resurrection Scene

This section examines the facts surrounding the resurrection.

A. The Pre-Resurrection Facts
1. Jesus Was Dead

The Romans were master executioners, but they were not the inventors of this exceedingly terrible method of execution.

Probably originating with the Assyrians and Babylonians, crucifixion was first used systematically by the Persians. . . . In the 4th century BC Alexander the Great adopted crucifixion and brought it to the Mediterranean shores where his successors introduced it *inter alia* to Egypt, Syria, Phoenicia and Carthage. During the Punic Wars the Romans learnt the technique and proceeded to become the principle utilisers of crucifixion for more than five centuries. (Ciliers and Retief, HPC, 938–939)

The Romans apparently learned the practice from the Carthaginians and (as with almost everything the Romans did) rapidly developed a very high degree of efficiency and skill in carrying it out. (Davis, CJ, 183)

The Romans did not invent the idea of crucifixion; however they did perfect it. (DeBoer and Maddow, ECCV, 235)

Because the Romans had a century or two to perfect this method of executing criminals and enemies, by the time of Jesus they were experts in ensuring the deaths of those they crucified. While Josephus does provide one example of someone surviving crucifixion, this is seen as the exception, not the rule:

[And] when I was sent by Titus Caesar with Cerealius, and a thousand horsemen, to a certain village called Thecoa, in order to know whether it were a place fit for a camp, as I came back, I saw many captives crucified; and remembered three of them as my former acquaintance. I

---

* We would encourage reading this treatise in its entirety because Justin Martyr provides a positive argument for the resurrection and deals with some objections along the way.

was very sorry at this in my mind, and went with tears in my eyes to Titus, and told him of them; so he immediately commanded them to be taken down, and to have the greatest care taken of them, in order to their recovery; yet two of them died under the physician's hands, while the third recovered. (Josephus, WFJ, 1:420–21)

The thing to keep in mind regarding the Josephus passage is that the three individuals removed from the cross were known to be alive at the time they were removed. They were given Rome's best medical assistance, and still two of the three died from their wounds.

However, when it comes to Jesus of Nazareth and his experience on the cross, the result is most assuredly death. Even critical scholars agree that this is the case.

Jesus' death as a consequence of crucifixion is indisputable. (Lüdemann, RC, 50)

So let's put our facts up front in order to begin our search here. What do we *know* about Jesus of Nazareth . . . ? The single most solid fact about Jesus' life is his death: he was executed by the Roman prefect Pilate, on or around Passover, in the manner Rome reserved particularly for political insurrectionists, namely, crucifixion. (Fredriksen, JNKJ, 8)

That he was crucified is as sure as anything historical can ever be, since both Josephus and Tacitus . . . agree with the Christian accounts on this basic fact. (Crossan, *Jesus*, 145)

The crucifixion of Jesus by the Romans is one of the most secure facts we have about his life. Whenever anyone writes a book about the historical Jesus, it is really (really, really) important to see if what they say about his public ministry can make sense of his death. (Ehrman, WWJK, website)

I take it absolutely for granted that Jesus was crucified under Pontius Pilate. Security about the *fact* of the crucifixion derives not

only from the unlikelihood that Christians would have invented it but also from the existence of two early and independent non-Christian witnesses to it, a Jewish one from 93–94 C.E. and a Roman one from the 110s or 120s C.E. (Crossan, HJ, 372)

Crucifixion is more than just an excruciating way to die. It also carried with it an incredibly negative stigma. It certainly would have been a poor way to start a new religion.

[For] the men of the ancient world, Greeks, Romans, barbarians and Jews, the cross was not just a matter of indifference, just any kind of death. It was an utterly offensive affair, "obscene" in the original sense of the word. (Hengel, *Crucifixion*, 22)

As to facts dealing with the death of Jesus by crucifixion, this event is recorded in all four gospel accounts:

- Matthew 27:35–50
- Mark 15:27–37
- Luke 23:33–46
- John 19:23–30

While he was already considered dead and therefore did not require having his legs broken, his side was pierced with a spear in order to confirm his death. Again, this is recorded in the Gospels:

- John 19:31–34

Moreover, the death of Jesus was confirmed by Pontius Pilate and a centurion before the body was handed over to be buried by Joseph of Arimathea:

- Matthew 17:57, 58
- Mark 15:42–45

- Luke 23:50–52
- John 19:38

2. The Tomb

a. Joseph of Arimathea's Tomb

The gospel accounts mention that Joseph of Arimathea had a rock-cut tomb, as recorded in the following passages:

- Matthew 27:57–60
- Mark 15:42–46
- Luke 23:50–53
- John 19:38–42

b. First Century Tombs and Archaeology

Archaeology has provided helpful insight into the tombs in and around first-century Jerusalem. Jodi Magness, a non-Christian archaeologist who is an expert on Jewish first-century second-temple burial practices, lists some of the important features of these rock-cut tombs. (It is likely that Joseph of Arimathea owned a rock-cut tomb.)

Scholarly and public attention has focused almost exclusively on the rock-cut tombs that surround the ancient city of Jerusalem in the late First Temple period (eighth century to 586 BCE) and the late Second Temple period (first century BCE to 70 C.E.). The following features characterize these tombs:

- The rock-cut tombs are artificially hewn, underground caves cut into the bedrock slopes around Jerusalem.
- With few exceptions, the tombs were located outside the walls of the city.
- Each tomb was used by a family over the course of several generations, as described by the biblical expression "he slept and was gathered to his fathers" (e.g., Judg 2:10; 2 Chr 34:28).
- When a member of the family died, the body was wrapped in a shroud and sometimes placed in a coffin and was then laid in the tomb as an individual inhumation, even if the bones were later collected and placed elsewhere.
- Because of the expense associated with hewing a burial cave into bedrock, only the wealthier members of Jerusalem's population—the upper classes—could afford rock-cut tombs. The lower classes apparently disposed of their dead in a manner that has left fewer traces in the archaeological record, for example, in individual trench graves or cist graves dug into the ground.
- From the earliest periods, the layout and decoration of Jerusalem's rock-cut tombs exhibited foreign cultural influences and fashions. Evidences for such influence—and indeed, for the use of rock-cut tombs—is attested only in times when Jerusalem's Jewish elite enjoyed an autonomous or semi-autonomous status, that is, in the late First Temple period and the late Second Temple period. During these periods the Jerusalem elite adopted foreign fashions that were introduced by the rulers or governing authorities. (Magness, SDOS, 145–146)

After describing the elaborate features of tombs, noting the evolution in their construction, and comparing those built during the First Temple period with those of the Second Temple period, making mention of foreign influences on the latter, Magness concludes: "Most of Jerusalem's rock-cut tombs are not display tombs but are relatively modest, with an undecorated entrance and a single burial chamber with loculi." (Magness, SDOS, 150)

Knowing how these rock-cut tombs were constructed aids in understanding what Jesus' followers experienced when they arrived at the place where he had been buried. Craig writes about the three different types of tombs discovered by archaeologists:

Archaeological discoveries have revealed three different types of rock tombs in use during Jesus' time: (1) *kokim* or tunnels perpendicular to the walls of the tomb, about six or seven feet deep, three in each of the three inner walls of the tomb, into which the body was inserted headfirst; (2) *acrosolia* or semi-circular niches 2½ feet above the floor and two to three feet deep containing either a flat shelf or a trough for the body; (3) bench tombs containing a bench that went around the three walls of the tomb on which the body could be laid. These tombs could consist of two chambers: an antechamber at the back of which was a small rectangular door about two feet high, which led to an inner chamber where the bodies were placed. The tomb was sealed with a stone slab to keep out animals. (Craig, ANTE, 186)

Craig continues, ruling out at least one of these as being the type of tomb that Joseph of Arimathea would have owned:

It is evident from the gospels' descriptions of the empty tomb that it was either of the *acrosolia* or bench type of tomb with a roll-stone for the door: In Mk. 16:5 the women see the angel seated on the right side; in Jn. 20:12 the angels are sitting at the head and the feet where the body had lain. In Mk. 16:6 the angel tells the women to "see the place where they laid him;" in Mt. 28:6 the angel invites them to "see the place where he lay." Both Lk. 24:12 and Jn. 20:5, 11 mention the necessity of stooping in order to enter or look through the low door of the tomb. Lk. 24:12 and Jn. 20:5–8 indicate that the graveclothes which had been around the body were visibly lying out. (Craig, ANTE, 187)

To Craig's point, a *kokim* style of tomb would not fit the above descriptions from the gospel narratives, but either of the other two types does fit the gospel accounts.

3. The Burial

Before looking at how Jesus was buried, it would be good to know what the burial practices were for Jews during the first century AD.

a. Historical Context for Burial Practices

The time that would lapse between death and burial was quite short. New Testament scholar Craig Evans mentions this:

First, burial took place on the day of death or, if death occurred at the end of the day or during the night, the following day . . . .We think of the story of the widow from the city of Nain: "As he approached the gate of the town, a man who had died was being carried out. He was his mother's only son and she was a widow; and with her was a large crowd from the town" (Luke 7.12). Her only son had died that day (or the evening before). Her sorrow is at its rawest when Jesus encounters her. (Evans, JHW, 114)

Magness agrees with Evans and provides further context:

Joseph of Arimathea seems to have been motivated by a concern for the observance of Jewish law. On the one hand, Deut 21:22–23 mandates burial within twenty-four hours of death, even for those guilty of the worst crimes, whose bodies were hanged after death. On the other hand, Jewish law prohibits burial on the Sabbath and festivals. Because Jesus expired on the cross on the eve of the Sabbath, he had to be buried before sundown on Friday, because waiting until after sundown on Saturday would have exceeded the twenty-four-hour time limit. (Magness, SDOS, 165)

As for preparation of the body for burial, according to the Mishna:

They prepare all that is needed for a corpse. They anoint and rinse it, on condition that they not move any limb of the corpse. (Neusner, *Mishna*)

We see this in practice with Tabitha, whose death is recorded in Acts:

In Joppa there was a disciple named Tabitha, which is translated Dorcas. She was always doing good works and acts of charity. In those days she became sick and died. After washing her, they placed her in a room upstairs.
— Acts 9:36, 37

Josephus mentions spices being part of the burial ritual in two different places:

As for his funeral, that he took care should be very magnificent, by making great preparation for a sepulchre to lay his body in, and providing a great quantity of spices, and burying many ornaments together with him, till the very women, who were in such deep sorrow, were astonished at it, and received in this way some consolation. (Josephus, WFJ, 1:665)

After this was over, they prepared for his funeral, it being Archelaus's care that the procession to his father's sepulchre should be very sumptuous. Accordingly he brought out all his ornaments to adorn the pomp of the funeral. . . . [These] were followed by five hundred of his domestics, carrying spices. (Josephus, WFJ, 1:666)

New Testament scholar Craig Keener explains why the spices were important in the burial practice:

Spices (Mk 16:1) could diminish the stench of decomposition and, in practice, pay final respects to the deceased; they were not, however, used to preserve the corpse, since the bones would be reinterred a year later. (Keener, HJG, 327)

Also, as John 11:44 and Acts 5:5, 6 indicate, the body was wrapped in burial clothes.

So how does Jesus' burial compare with what we know about these practices? These are the relevant texts:

- Matthew 27:59
- Mark 15:46a
- Luke 23:53a
- John 19:38–40

Informed by her archaeological expertise, Magness tells us that the details recorded by the biblical writers are consistent with known customs and normal practices of that time and place. (Magness, SDOS, 170)

b. Facts Surrounding Jesus' Burial

In this investigation we also look for evidence that the New Testament gives sound historical data about Jesus' burial. The circumstances surrounding it have attracted much critical discussion. One of the major voices of criticism concerning the narrative about Jesus' burial and the empty tomb is New Testament scholar Bart Ehrman, who describes himself as an agnostic-atheist. While Ehrman believes that the creedal statement from 1 Corinthians 15:3b–5a is very early, he notes that it fails to mention Joseph of Arimathea or his tomb, leading him to doubt the historicity of these elements mentioned in the Gospels. Evans sums up Ehrman's salient points on this matter:

The nonappearance of Joseph's name leads Ehrman to conclude that the "tradition that there was a specific, known person who buried Jesus appears to have been a later one." He further notes that in Paul's speech in Acts nothing is said of Jesus being buried by Joseph . . . . Ehrman also underscores the Roman practice of not allowing someone crucified to be buried, which casts further doubt on the story about Joseph of Arimathea. All of this leads Ehrman to suspect that Jesus was probably not buried, or if he was, his disciples did not know where. Accordingly, the discovery of the empty tomb is probably a later fiction and therefore the empty tomb and missing body of Jesus did not really play any role in early Christianity's understanding of Jesus' resurrection and divinity. (Evans, GBTER, 72–73)

Evans answers each of Ehrman's challenges by citing Roman policy that allowed for Jewish burials, archaeological evidence of buried crucified victims, and the reasonable plausibility that Joseph of Arimathea would have been the person to bury Jesus in a tomb.

i) Roman Policy and Jewish Tradition

Evans notes that while Ehrman can point to historical documents detailing Roman suppression of Jewish burial traditions, there are two things readers should keep in mind: (1) Ehrman fails to reference counter evidence in the historical record, and (2) Ehrman cites exceptions that prove the rule, where the rule is that Rome often allowed the Jewish people to observe their traditions as a way to keep the peace. The historical record confirms that Roman rule permitted Jewish practices. Evans writes:

> The concern, above all, is to avoid defiling the land. . . . Josephus confirms that the law of Deuteronomy 21, even during the first century CE, when Rome governed Israel, was still very much in force. Every source we have indicates that this was the practice in Israel, especially in the vicinity of Jerusalem, in peacetime . . . . Roman authority in Israel normally did permit

burial of executed criminals, and including those executed by crucifixion (as Josephus implies), but they did not during the rebellion of 66–70 CE. (Evans, GBTER, 80)

Evans then describes an important link between these Roman-permitted burials and the role of the Sanhedrin:

> There is another important point that needs to be made. The process that led to the execution of Jesus, and perhaps also the two men crucified with him, was *initiated by the Jewish Council*. According to law and custom, when the Jewish Council (or Sanhedrin) condemned someone to death, by whatever means, it fell to the council to have that person buried. . . . The Jewish Council, in concert with the aristocratic priesthood (some of whom were members of the council), was charged with protecting the purity of the sanctuary, the temple precincts, Jerusalem, and the land. . . . (These concerns with maintaining the purity of Jerusalem and the land, as well as the obligation to bury those condemned to death by the Jewish Council, are relevant for understanding the role played by Joseph of Arimathea, which we consider below.) (Evans, GBTER, 80–81)

ii) The Crucified Received Burial

Evans points out that beginning with the 1968 discovery of Yehohanan's remains, which date to approximately AD 20, archaeology has shown that individuals who were executed by crucifixion had been given proper Jewish burials. In referencing the archaeological record, Evans says:

> There are indications that suggest that many executed persons, including victims of crucifixion, were given proper burial. I refer to the discovery of dozens, perhaps more than one hundred, nails that have been received from

tombs and ossuaries, some which bear traces of human calcium. These nails, especially those with traces of calcium, were used in crucifixion and, strangely, were viewed as talismans. The presence of calcium, sometimes encircling the nail, indicates its use in crucifixion and suggests that the corpse, still pierced by the nails, was buried and sometime later (when the calcium had adhered to the nail) the nails were recovered and put to new use. (Evans, GBTER, 86)

iii) Joseph of Arimathea

For Joseph's role in burying Jesus, Evans writes:

There is nothing irregular about the Gospels' report that a member of the Sanhedrin requested permission to take down the body of Jesus and give it proper burial, in keeping with Jewish burial practices as they related to the executed. It is entirely in keeping with all that we know from the literature and from archaeology. . . . When all of the relevant evidence is considered, we should conclude that it is probable that the body of Jesus, in keeping with Jewish customs of his time, was given proper burial. (Evans, GBTER, 89)

iv) Evans's Conclusion Contra Ehrman

I conclude that the burial of the body of Jesus in a known tomb, according to Jewish law and custom, is highly probable. I think it is also probable that the tomb in which family and friends knew the body of Jesus had been placed was known to be empty. I think it is also probable that the first to discover this tomb were women, among whom Mary Magdalene was the most prominent. These conclusions make the most sense of the evidence. It was the knowledge of the tomb and the discovery that it was empty, in addition to the appearances of Jesus, that led the followers of Jesus to speak in terms of resurrection and not in other terms. (Evans GBTER, 93)

Evans's conclusion draws the most probable and likely assessment from the central evidence for the resurrection. It offers a strong counter to Ehrman. Perhaps a further question could probe one of Ehrman's key assumptions: Why does he insist that Paul necessarily must mention Joseph of Arimathea in 1 Corinthians 15:3a–5b? Ehrman is making an argument from silence, assuming that Paul's account would name the "specific known person who buried Jesus" as evidence for the known grave. However, Paul's emphasis in 1 Corinthians 15 is not on the tomb's place and the provider. Instead, Paul emphasizes the more important multiple independent appearances of Jesus. In historical study or even in eyewitness accounts of current events, an argument from silence makes a weak case. We believe that Evans's case is stronger than Ehrman's.

c. Additional Inferences Regarding the Burial of Jesus

In our book *Evidence for the Resurrection*, we list five facts and reasoned inferences for the burial of Jesus:

First, Paul confirms the burial story in 1 Corinthians 15:3–5. There is conclusive evidence that Paul drew from material predating his writing that can be traced to within three to eight years of Christ's death. Thus, the burial story can be traced back so close to the time of Christ's death that legendary development is impossible. Second, the tradition of the burial is not surrounded by adornment or embellishment. It is told in a simple and straightforward manner. Third, no conflicting tradition about the burial story exists. There are no early documents that refute the burial story as presented in the Gospels. Fourth, how could the Jewish authorities—who had tried for so long to get rid of Jesus—not pay attention to his burial? Can we believe that they simply ignored where the body was taken? Fifth, Christians inventing Joseph, a member of the court that condemned Jesus, is highly unlikely. Why would early Christians make a hero of a member of the very court that was responsible for Jesus' death? (McDowell and McDowell, ER, 173)

d. The Stone

i) Various Stone Types

What kind of stone was put at the entrance of the tomb? Traditionally we understand it to be a circular stone that was rolled in place, perhaps a stone that rolls along in a track, but square "cork" stones that were placed in front of tombs also existed and were far more common. As archaeologist Amos Kloner has written:

Of the more than 900 burial caves from the Second Temple period found in and around Jerusalem, only four are known to have used round (disk-shaped) blocking stones. . . . The handful of round blocking stones from Jerusalem in this period are large, at least 4 feet in diameter. They occur only in the more elaborate cave tombs, which had at least two rooms or, as in one case, a spacious hall. (Kloner, DRSCJT, 22–25, 28–29, 76)

In describing the other kind of blocking stone, Kloner writes:

Square or rectangular blocking stones sealed the entrance of a cave tomb much like a cork in a bottle: One end of the blocking stone fit snugly into the entrance while the other end, like the top of a cork, was somewhat larger on the outside. (Kloner, DRSCJT, 22–25, 28–29, 76)

Kloner then goes on to draw a likely inference from all this:

[In] Jesus' time, round blocking stones were extremely rare and appeared only in the tombs of the wealthiest Jews. (Kloner, DRSCJT, 22–25, 28–29, 76)

Kloner also provides an explanation for why he believes tombs with a disk-shaped stone covering the entrance served as models for how interpreters have pictured Jesus' tomb:

Both the earlier and later examples of round stones served as models for Jesus' tomb. For example, Felix-Marie Abel, the famous Dominican father who was an expert of Biblical geography, reconstructed Jesus' tomb with a round blocking stone based on two tombs he found at Abu Ghosh, outside Jerusalem. He thought the tombs dated to the Second Temple period, but it has since been shown that they are Byzantine. (Kloner, DRSCJT, 22–25, 28–29, 76)*

However, the biblical text seems to imply that the stone was round, because it was "rolled back." Consider the following narratives from Matthew, Mark, and Luke's gospels:

After the Sabbath, as the first day of the week was dawning, Mary Magdalene and the other Mary went to view the tomb. Suddenly there was a violent earthquake, because an angel of the Lord descended from heaven and approached the tomb. He rolled back the stone and was sitting on it. — Matthew 28:1, 2

---

* See endnote 7 in Kloner's article. In addition, Kloner talks about "later examples of round stones." In his article, Kloner mentions that "in later periods the situation changed, and round blocking stones became much more common. Dozens of them have been found from the late Roman to Byzantine periods (second to seventh century AD). These later round stones were much smaller than the Second Temple period stones (less than 3 feet in diameter), and they did not move on a track but simply leaned against the rock façade, making then even simpler to move."

After [Joseph of Arimathea] bought some fine linen, he took [Jesus] down and wrapped Him in the linen. Then he placed Him in a tomb cut out of the rock, and rolled a stone against the entrance to the tomb . . . . When the Sabbath was over, Mary Magdalene, Mary the mother of James, and Salome bought spices, so they could go and anoint Him. Very early in the morning, on the first day of the week, they went to the tomb at sunrise. They were saying to one another, "Who will roll away the stone from the entrance to the tomb for us?" Looking up, they observed that the stone—which was very large—had been rolled away. — Mark 15:46; 16:1–4

On the first day of the week, very early in the morning, they came to the tomb, bringing the spices they had prepared. They found the stone rolled away from the tomb. — Luke 24:1, 2

John is the only one who does not describe the stone as being "rolled":

One the first day of the week Mary Magdalene came to the tomb early, while it was still dark. She saw that the stone had been removed from the tomb. — John 20:1

Not everyone agrees with Kloner's assessment of the stone's shape. William Lane Craig believes that Joseph of Arimathea's tomb could have had a disk-shaped stone:

In a very expensive tomb, a round disc-shaped stone about a yard in diameter could be rolled down a slanted groove to cover the entrance. Although it would be easy to close the tomb, it would take several men to roll the stone back up away from the door. Only a few tombs with such disc-shaped stones have been discovered in Palestine, but they all date from Jesus' era. It is evident from the gospels' descriptions of the empty tomb that it was either of the *acrosolia*

or bench type of tomb with a roll-stone for the door. . . . Mk. 15:46; 16:3, 4; Mt. 27:60; 28:2; Lk. 24:2 indicate the stone had been rolled back from the tomb's entrance; Jn. 20:1 says it had been taken away. . . . Thus, Joseph's tomb is described as being a bench or *acrosolia* tomb; these types of tombs were scarce in Jesus' day and were reserved for persons of high rank. But such tombs were in fact used in Jerusalem during this period, as the tombs of the Sanhedria [*sic*] attest. (Craig, ANTE, 186–187)

So while Matthew, Mark, and Luke specifically mention that the stone was "rolled back," "rolled . . . against," or "rolled away," only John mentions that "the stone had been removed." Whether the stone was disk-shaped or cork-shaped (square or rectangular), it seems feasible that both could fit the description that it was rolled in place or rolled away. In either case, it would take a considerable amount of effort to move or roll the stone away and more than a single individual to do so.

ii) Average Stone Weight

Evans provides a sense of the weight of these stones: "Sealing stones weighed 200 kg [440 lbs.] or more." (Evans, JHW, 138)

Different types of stones have different densities and that affects their weight. On this topic, I (Josh) remember what happened after a lecture of mine at Georgia Tech on the resurrection of Jesus.

Two engineering professors went on a tour of Israel with other faculty members. They remembered the comments I had made about the enormity of the stone. So, being engineers, they took the type of stone used in the time of Christ and calculated the size needed in order to cover the doorway of the tomb.

Later they wrote me a letter spelling out all

their calculations in precise technical terms. They said a stone of that size would have had a minimum weight of one-and-one-half to two tons. No wonder Matthew and Mark said the stone was extremely large.

One might ask, "If the stone was that big, how did Joseph move it into position?" The answer is that he simply let gravity do it for him. It had been held in place with a wedge as it sat in a groove that sloped downward to the entrance of the tomb. When the wedge was removed, the heavy circular rock just rolled into position. Although it would be easy to roll the stone into place, it would take considerable manpower to roll it back uphill from the tomb entrance. The large stone would have provided additional security against the Jewish suspicion that the disciples of Jesus would try to steal his body. (McDowell and McDowell, ER, 176)

e. The Seal

The sealing of the stone is recorded by Matthew in his gospel: "Then they went and made the tomb secure by sealing the stone and setting the guard" (Matt. 27:66).

In our book *Evidence for the Resurrection*, we make the following observation regarding the seal:

A. T. Robertson says the stone could be sealed only in the presence of the Roman guards who were left in charge. The purpose of this procedure was to prevent anyone from tampering with the grave's contents. After the guard inspected the tomb and rolled the stone in place, a cord was stretched across the rock and fastened at either end with sealing clay. Finally, the clay packs were stamped with the official signet of the Roman government. A parallel to this is seen in the Old Testament book of Daniel: "A stone was brought and laid over the mouth of the den; and the king sealed it with his own signet ring and with the signet rings of

the nobles, so that nothing would be changed in regard to Daniel" (6:17). (McDowell and McDowell, ER, 184)

Particularly valuable here is Robertson's description of the process, purpose, and parallel to the Babylonian empire's use of a seal. His extensive commentary on the New Testament is still highly valued, though it was completed a century ago. Since that time, further research on the tomb's guard has taken place. The question of the guard's identity and source of authority will be addressed in the next section.

In his own commentary on the gospel of Matthew, Michael Wilkins also compares the situation to Daniel and points out the reason for the cord, which he notes was attached to both the stone and to the rock face from which the tomb opening was cut: Any tampering could be detected. (Wilkins, *Matthew*, 184)

Easton's Bible Dictionary explains:

The tomb was sealed by the Pharisees and chief priests for the purpose of making sure that the disciples would not come and steal the body away (ver. 63, 64). The mode of doing this was probably by stretching a cord across the stone and sealing it at both ends with sealing-clay. (Easton, "Seal")

Historian Paul Maier writes that the seal was not strong enough to keep someone out, but rather to indicate if the stone and tomb had been tampered with: "The seal was nothing more than a cord strung across the rock and fastened at each end with clay. Like any seal, its purpose was not to cement the rock but to indicate any tampering with it." (Maier, IFT, 178)

The seal was just an added precaution since a security detail was also posted to guard the tomb. Keener notes:

Sealing the stone ([Mt] 27:66) made it impossible for anyone to enter the tomb while the guards slept and then replace the stone. (Keener, GM, 696)

f. The Guard

The gospel of Matthew provides the context and narrative for the requesting and posting of a guard at the tomb where Jesus was buried:

> Now on the next day, the day after the preparation, the chief priests and the Pharisees gathered together with Pilate, and said, "Sir, we remember that when He was still alive that deceiver said, 'After three days I am to rise again.' Therefore, give orders for the grave to be made secure until the third day, otherwise His disciples may come and steal Him away and say to the people, 'He has risen from the dead,' and the last deception will be worse than the first." Pilate said to them, "You have a guard; go, make it as secure as you know how." And they went and made the grave secure, and along with the guard they set a seal on the stone. — Matthew 27:62–66 NASB

We should point out that in this passage, the Pharisees and chief priests do not believe Jesus will resurrect from the dead. Their motivation in requesting the tomb be made secure is to deter the disciples from stealing the body of Jesus and then making the claim that Jesus had resurrected.

i)Was the Guard Jewish or Roman?

Many have wondered whether the guard posted to guard the tomb was Jewish or Roman. New Testament scholar Michael Wilkins believes that it was a detachment of Roman soldiers:

> Since they had no authority to post guards around a burial site of a criminal executed by Roman authorities, the religious officials had to ask Pilate for a contingent of guards. Pilate's seemingly vague answer, "You have a guard of soldiers. . . . Go and make it as secure as you know how," has led to debate about the identity of the guards placed at the tomb. However, a contingent of Roman soldiers had earlier been assigned to the temple authorities for security, which had been used in the arrest of Jesus (cf. [Matt.] 26:47). Most likely this is the same guard troop Pilate had in mind when he told the Jewish officials, "You have a guard of soldiers." Pilate's expression signified that the Jews were now authorized to use the troops for a security detail at the tomb. The Jewish officials were not allowed to use the troops except for the purposes the Roman governor authorized. This explains why the guards will later go to the temple authorities to report Jesus' resurrection rather than to Pilate himself ([Matt.] 28:11). (Wilkins, in Howard, HACB, 188)

A. T. Robertson, noted Greek scholar, says that Pilate's response to the Jews' request is phrased in the present imperative; he adds that the Latin form *koustodia*, the term Pilate used in this passage to designate the guard he authorized, occurs as far back as the Oxyrhynchus papyrus (AD 22). (Robertson, WPNT, 239)

The great New Testament scholar Raymond Brown offers five reasons why he believes that the guard was Roman:

- The apocryphal Gospel of Peter clearly understands Pilate to offer Roman soldiers to protect the tomb.
- If the Jewish leaders had wanted to use their own Temple police, why would they request Pilate's help at all?
- Matthew's use of *koustodia* matches the picture of a Roman prefect assigning Roman troops.

- Matthew refers to the guards as "soldiers," the plural of *stratiotes*. Twenty-two of twenty-six uses of *stratiotes* in the New Testament refer to Roman soldiers. In another three references (Acts 12:4, 6, 18), *stratiotes* refers to the soldiers of King Herod Agrippa I. Never in the New Testament does the term refer to the Temple police.
- If the guards were Jewish, why would they be responsible to the governor of Rome for failing to fulfill their duties, as Matthew 28:14 implies? (Brown, DM, II.1295)

Brown provides additional arguments to support his conclusion that the guard was Roman:

Matt 27:65 has Pilate respond in direct discourse, "*Echete koustōdian.* Go, make secure as you know how." I left the first two words in Greek because of their disputed meaning. Most often they have been understood to mean: "You have a custodial guard of your own"—in other words, Pilate refuses to help and tells the chief priests and the Pharisees that they have troops of their own whom they can use to make the sepulcher secure. Numerous arguments of varied weight militate against such an interpretation wherein those who guarded the tomb would be Jewish troops mustered by Jewish authorities: . . . If the Jewish authorities had military of their own to secure the sepulchre, why did they need Pilate's help in the first place? . . . If those involved were Jewish soldiers under the control of Jewish authorities, why would they be responsible to the Roman governor for failing asleep and failing to keep watch, as 28:14 implies? Much more likely Matthew means that Pilate gave the Jewish authorities Roman soldiers to help make the sepulchre secure. (Brown, DM, vol. 2, 1295)

Keener tends to agree with Brown and Wilkins:

The chief priests would not need Pilate's approval merely to station their own guards. Using Roman guards rather than their own would leave the Jewish authorities less open to the charge of tampering with evidence. (Keener, GM, 696, note 279)

However, not everyone agrees that it must have been a Roman guard. As we point out in our book on the resurrection, where we present both sides of the argument, the Temple guards were a formidable and highly trained police force, more than capable of guarding a tomb—under normal circumstances:

If it was the Temple police that guarded Christ's tomb, that unit would not have been slouches at their job. Temple guards were responsible for protecting the courts and gates of the Temple. A unit consisted of 10 Levites who were placed on duty at strategic locations about the Temple. There were 27 such units, or a total of 270 men on duty. The guardsmen were thoroughly trained, and the military discipline of the guard was excellent. In fact, at night, if the captain approached a guard member who was asleep, he was beaten and burned with his own clothes. A member of the guard was also forbidden to sit down or to lean against anything while on duty. (McDowell and McDowell, ER, 177).

So which was it? A Roman or Jewish guard? While we believe that it was a Roman guard, the relevant point is this: whether they were Jewish or Roman, they would not have allowed the theft of the body and lived to tell the tale. The idea that they slept through a grave robbery is incredible. The idea that they participated in allowing the robbery likewise lacks credibility—failing in their task meant severe punishment. Only an actual resurrection accounts for the odd collaboration of the guards and the Jewish authorities in spreading a silly story about sleepy guards and body snatchers.

ii) The Guards' Reaction

Matthew's gospel states the guards' great fear and their effort to get help in order to account for the missing body:

Suddenly there was a violent earthquake, because an angel of the Lord descended from heaven and approached the tomb. He rolled back the stone and was sitting on it. His appearance was like lightning, and his robe was as white as snow. The guards were so shaken from fear of him that they became like dead men. . . . As they [the women] were on their way, some of the guards came into the city and reported to the chief priests everything that had happened. After the priests had assembled with the elders and agreed on a plan, they gave the soldiers a large sum of money and told them, "Say this, 'His disciples came during the night and stole Him while we were sleeping.' If this reaches the governor's ears, we will deal with him and keep you out of trouble." So they took the money and did as they were instructed. And this story has been spread among Jewish people to this day.
— Matthew 28:2–4, 11–15

The narrative of Matthew 28 is very impressive. What happened that Sunday morning was so frightening that it caused rugged soldiers to become "like dead men" (Matt. 28:4).

Whether the guards were Roman or Jewish, they found themselves in a life-threatening predicament. The next two paragraphs no doubt refer to the severity of what a Roman contingent would have faced.

Thomas Thorburn tells us that the guards who had kept the watch were in dire straits. After the stone had been rolled away and the seal broken, they were as good as court-martialed. Thorburn writes: "The soldiers cannot have alleged they were asleep, for they well knew that the penalty of sleeping upon a watch was death—always rigorously enforced." (Thorburn, RNMC, 179)

Thorburn continues: "Here the soldiers would have practically no other alternative than to trust the good offices of the priests. The body (we will suppose) was *gone*, and their negligence in *any* case would (under ordinary circumstances) be punishable by death." (Thorburn, RNMC, 181; cf. Acts 12:19)

Whoever the guards were, the story that they supposedly fell asleep and allowed the body to be stolen is unbelievable. It does not work as a fiction by early Christians intended for apologetics purposes—because it raises too many difficult questions. And yet, neither would a Roman or a Jewish guard be likely to come up with such a story—unless the resurrection had actually occurred. The most likely solution: something truly astonishing—the resurrection of Jesus—really did occur as described. The guards and Jewish authorities collaborated, each for their own reasons: the guards because they had no rational (or more believable) explanation for their failure, and the Jewish authorities because they had a vested interest in discrediting the resurrection.

iii) Objection and Response: Only One Source

Before dealing with any other questions pertaining to the guard, we must first deal with the critic's objection that Matthew is the only place that mentions the guard story, so therefore it is not historical. This objection is not entirely true as we point out in *Evidence for the Resurrection*:

Some have discounted the guard story because it only appears in one of the four Gospels: Matthew. While it is true that Mark, Luke and John do not mention the story, the apocryphal Gospel of Peter, probably written around AD 150, does mention it. It is likely that the Gospel of Peter records a tradition of the guard story that is independent of Matthew, since there are virtually no word similarities between the two accounts. Because the guard story has been transmitted through at least two different traditions, it is highly unlikely that it was a legend. (McDowell and McDowell, ER, 183).

Here is what the apocryphal Gospel of Peter says:

But the scribes and Pharisees and elders, having gathered together with one another, having heard that all the people were murmuring and beating their breasts, saying that "If at his death these very great signs happened, behold how just he was," feared (especially the elders) and came before Pilate, begging him and saying, "Give over soldiers to us in order that we may safeguard his burial place for three days, lest, having come, his disciples steal him, and the people accept that he is risen from the death, and they do us wrong." But Pilate gave over to them Petronius the centurion with soldiers to safeguard the sepulcher. And with these the elders and scribes came to the burial place. And having rolled a large stone, all who were there, together with the centurion and the soldiers, placed it against the door of the burial place. And they marked it with seven wax seals; and having pitched a tent there, they safeguarded it. (quoted in Brown, GP, website)

iv) Objection and Response: Why Did They Bother About Posting a Guard?

One objection made about posting a guard assumes that the leaders would not worry about Jesus' predictions of his resurrection and therefore would not be likely to set a guard. This objection claims that if they did set a guard, they would have been taking Jesus' predictions more seriously than his disciples did, which seems psychologically unlikely and very difficult to believe. Bible scholar John Wenham blunts this objection by pointing out that the authorities both knew and cared about his predictions:

There is certainly no reason why the Jewish authorities should not have heard talk about a resurrection on the third day. It is true that Jesus' predictions were made mainly to his followers and not to the public, though on at least one occasion in the Galilean ministry he spoke openly to some Pharisees. It is true also that, although his disciples did not grasp what he meant at the time, his words were perfectly clear and known to a good many people, including of course Judas Iscariot. In the desperate attempt to find evidence to incriminate Jesus, the chief priests had eventually picked on his alleged statement: "I will destroy this temple that is made with hands, and in three days I will build another, not made with hands." In their search for watertight evidence they must have weighed every word, and it is hardly likely that Jesus' sayings about his rising on the third day would not have come to their ears. So it is probable that they really did fear the consequences of a successful plot to simulate a resurrection. (Wenham, EE, 72–73)

v) Objection and Response: Is the Guard Apologetic Legend?

This objection typically centers on Matthew 28:15: "Their story spread widely among the Jews, and they still tell it today" (NLT). The critic's claim is that the author was writing years after the event, providing enough time to pass that this legend grew and it found its way into Matthew's narrative. William Lane Craig deals handily with this objection:

> Think about the claims and counterclaims about the Resurrection that went back and forth between the Jews and Christians in the first century. The initial Christian proclamation was, "Jesus is risen." The Jews responded, "The disciples stole the body." To this Christians said, "Ah, but the guards at the tomb would have prevented such a theft." The Jews responded, "Oh, but the guards at the tomb fell asleep." To that the Christians replied, "No, the Jews bribed the guards to say they fell asleep."
>
> Now, if there had not been any guards, the exchange would have gone like this: In response to the claim Jesus is risen, the Jews would say, "No, the disciples stole the body." Christians would reply, "But the guards would have prevented the theft." Then the Jewish response would have been, "What guards? You're crazy! There were no guards!" Yet history tells us that's not what the Jews said. This suggests the guards really were historical and that the Jews knew it, which is why they had to invent the absurd story about the guards having been asleep while the disciples took the body. (Craig, quoted in Strobel, CC, 212)

Wenham also provides an analysis of what is wrong about this objection, noting that if the story were a fiction composed for apologetic purposes, it would be

> one of the most extraordinary pieces of Christian apologetics ever written. As we have said, it bristles with improbabilities at every point: the sabbath visit to the governor, the great earthquake, the flashing angel rolling back the stone, the reporting to the chief priests, the bribe to the soldiers to tell the tale *that they were asleep on duty*—everything invites,

not belief, but incredulity. And how stupid, having introduced the useful apologetic idea of a closely guarded tomb, to give a handle to the opposition by even hinting that the guards did not do their job! It is a worthless piece of Christian apologetic at whatever date it was written, *unless it happens to be undeniably true.* (Wenham, EE, 78–79, emphasis in original)

g. The Disciples Were Scattered

Jesus' disciples end up deserting him during his arrest and remain largely in hiding during his trial, execution, and in the early days following his resurrection. In his gospel account, Matthew states it plainly:

> *At that time Jesus said to the crowds, "Have you come out with swords and clubs, as if I were a criminal, to capture Me? Every day I used to sit, teaching in the temple complex, and you didn't arrest Me. But all this has happened so that the prophetic Scriptures would be fulfilled." Then all the disciples deserted Him and ran away.*
> — Matthew 26:55, 56 (cf. Mark 14:49, 50)

Without Jesus, the disciples become dejected, losing their direction and focus. Some return to the familiarity of their past lives' work (John 21:2, 3). We also see some of them huddled away, hiding behind locked doors paralyzed by their fear (John 20:19, 26). Moreover, some of their confusion and discouragement turned into infighting and arguing with one another (Luke 24:13–17).

The inclusion of these kinds of details supports the idea that we can trust the accounts in Scripture. This is what is known as the criterion of embarrassment, which simply means that if this story had been invented, it would be less likely that they would paint themselves in such a negative light. To have done so would have required a well-coordinated conspiracy, but the details show instead that they were discouraged and bewildered, not a cohesive team. The empty tomb would then only have fueled their disorientation. They were not expecting Jesus to be resurrected. Yet when they saw him alive, they were transformed and unified.

B. The Post-Resurrection Facts

1. The Empty Tomb

First and foremost, it is important to notice that all but one of the alternate theories below (Section VII) regarding the facts of the resurrection implicitly grant the fact that the tomb was empty since they are trying to find a naturalistic explanation for Jesus' missing corpse. For instance, the claim that the disciples stole the body *assumes* that the tomb was really found empty. The only alternate theory that does not fit this profile is the Hallucination Theory, which seeks to explain the postmortem appearances, not an empty tomb.

Evidence #1: Women Were First

The first people to experience and proclaim the empty tomb were the women followers. We see in each of the Gospels:

- Matthew 28:1–10 (Mary Magdalene and the other Mary, v. 1)
- Mark 16:1–11 (Mary Magdalene, Mary the mother of James, and Salome, vv. 1, 9–10)
- Luke 24:1–10 Mary Magdalene, Joanna, Mary the mother of James, and other women, v. 10)
- John 20:1–18 (Mary Magdalene vv. 1, 2)

If one were to fabricate an empty tomb and risen Jesus in first-century Mediterranean culture, one would not cite women as eyewitnesses, given their low status as credible witnesses in the eyes of the people and the courts. It is therefore reasonable to think that what is recorded actually happened. Why would the gospel writers make up these details to support their story? They knew their culture far better than we do, and if they were making up a tale, they would not begin it with a story to cast their new religion in such a poor light. It would not be a proper way to begin their myth. Scripture's identification of women as the first witnesses of the empty tomb thus supports the historical veracity of the accounts.

Evidence #2: Multiple Attestations

The empty tomb is attested by multiple New Testament sources:

- Matthew 28:11–15
- Mark 16:1–8
- Luke 24:1–12
- John 20:11–18

Philosopher J. P. Moreland affirms this point and lists additional sources that predate the written gospel accounts, such as the preaching and sermonettes in Acts and the creedal statement of the death, burial, and resurrection:

> A variety of sources in the New Testament testify to the empty tomb: Matthew 28:11–15 (the M material special to Matthew); Mark 16:1–8; Luke 24:1–12; John 20:11–18. Apart from such explicit references to the empty tomb the speeches in Acts and 1 Corinthians 15:3–8 presuppose an empty tomb. . . . Thus, there are several different witnesses to the empty tomb, Mark 16:1–8 and 1 Corinthians 15:3–8 being the earliest. (Moreland, SSC, 160)

Evidence #3: Center of Church Preaching

Professor and author Winfried Corduan mentions the significance of the empty tomb in connection with the preaching of the early church:

If ever a fact of ancient history may count as indisputable, it should be the empty tomb. From Easter Sunday on there must have been a tomb, clearly known as the tomb of Jesus, that did not contain His body. This much is beyond dispute: Christian teaching from the very beginning promoted a living, resurrected Savior. The Jewish authorities strongly opposed this teaching and were prepared to go to any lengths in order to suppress it. Their job would have been easy if they could have invited potential converts for a quick stroll to the tomb and there produced Christ's body. That would have been the end of the Christian message. The fact that a church centering around the risen Christ could come about demonstrates that there must have been an empty tomb. (Corduan, NDAI, 222)

Moreland succinctly makes the same point:

It is highly probable . . . that the resurrection was preached in Jerusalem just a few weeks after the crucifixion. If the tomb had not been empty, such preaching could not have occurred. The body of Jesus could have been produced, and since it is likely that the location of Joseph of Arimathea's tomb was well known (he was a respected member of the Sanhedrin), it would not have been difficult to find where Jesus was buried. (Moreland, SSC, 161)

Evidence #4: Surprising Lack of Tomb Veneration

Moreland explains how the lack of veneration for the tomb provides evidence that it was empty:

In Palestine during the days of Jesus, at least fifty tombs of prophets or other holy persons served as sites of religious worship and veneration. However, there is no good evidence that such a practice was ever associated with Jesus' tomb. Since this was customary, and since Jesus was a fitting object of veneration, why were such

religious activities not conducted at his tomb? The most reasonable answer must be that Jesus' body was not in his tomb, and thus the tomb was not regarded as an appropriate site for such veneration. . . . It seems, then, the lack of veneration at the tomb of Jesus is powerful evidence that the tomb was empty. (Moreland, SSC, 161–162)

Evidence #5: Common Knowledge of the Empty Tomb

Moreland explains how the empty tomb was common knowledge in the early church:

[The] absence of explicit mention of the empty tomb in the speeches in Acts is best explained by noting that the fact of the empty tomb was not in dispute and thus it was not at issue. The main debate was over why it was empty, not whether it was empty. In Acts 2:29, Peter makes a reference to the fact that David's tomb was still with them. The implication seems to be that David was buried and remained in his tomb, but by contrast, Jesus did not remain in his tomb, as anyone listening to the speech could verify for himself. . . . This indirect reference to the empty tomb serves to underscore that no need existed for the early Christian preachers to make a major issue of the empty tomb. It was common knowledge which could be easily verified if such verification was needed. (Moreland, SSC, 163)

Evidence #6: Jewish Response Assumes an Empty Tomb

The earliest Jewish response to the resurrection assumes the tomb was found empty:

The only polemic offered by the Jews for which we have any historical evidence is the one recorded in Matthew 28:11–15. . . . This text could not have been written if, at the time of writing, there was not a Jewish counterargument to the Christian understanding of the empty tomb. But the Jewish polemic does not dispute that the tomb was empty; it gives an alternate explanation. This is a significant historical fact. . . . This is strong evidence that the tomb was in fact empty (Moreland, SSC, 163).

Moreland adds, "The presence of just one account of Jesus' burial points to the fact that it must have been known to be accurate. No other account was made which could rival the true account." (Moreland, SSC, 165)

Evidence #7: Tradition of Empty Tomb Is Very Early

Resurrection accounts appeared very early: "The pre-Markan passion narrative includes the account of the empty tomb as an essential ingredient, and since this narrative is quite early, it provides good evidence for an empty tomb." (Moreland, SSC, 163–165)

Conclusion Regarding the Empty Tomb

We heartily agree with D. H. Van Daalen's definitive assessment regarding the historicity of the empty tomb: "It is extremely difficult to object to the empty tomb on historical grounds; those who deny it do so on the basis of theological or philosophical assumptions." (Van Daalen, RR, 41)

2. The Grave Clothes

In the following narrative, John shows the significance of the grave clothes as evidence for the resurrection:

At that, Peter and the other disciple went out, heading for the tomb. The two were running together, but the other disciple outran Peter and got to the tomb first. Stooping down, he saw the linen cloths lying there, yet he did not go in. Then, following him, Simon Peter came also. He entered the tomb and saw the linen cloths lying there. The wrapping that had been on His head was not lying with the linen cloths but was folded up in a separate place by itself. The other disciple, who had reached the tomb

first, then entered the tomb, saw, and believed. For they still did not understand the Scripture that He must rise from the dead. — John 20:3–9

3. Appearances of Jesus
a. Various Appearances of Jesus

There are no fewer than twelve distinct instances where Jesus is mentioned as appearing to individuals or groups of people after his death, burial, and resurrection:

1. Mary Magdalene: John 20:11–18
2. Women leaving the tomb: Matthew 28:8–10
3. Emmaus disciples: Luke 24:13–35
4. Simon Peter: Luke 24:34 (see also 1 Corinthians 15:5)
5. Disciples without Thomas: Luke 24:36–43
6. Disciples with Thomas: John 20:24–29
7. Disciples at the Sea of Galilee (Tiberias): John 21:1, 2
8. Disciples on a mountain in Galilee: Matthew 28:16, 17
9. Disciples: Luke 24:50–52
10. 500 believers: 1 Corinthians 15:6
11. James (Jesus' half-brother): 1 Corinthians 15:7a
12. Paul (an enemy of the church): Acts 9:3–6

b. The Physical Nature of the Appearances

The disciples' claim that they encountered a physical, resurrected Jesus was not an idea they would have borrowed from anyone else; it did not arise from within their own belief system. Groothuis summarizes this point well:

[The] Second Temple Judaism of Jesus' day had no concept of disembodied resurrection. Those Jews who believed in the afterlife (unlike the Sadducees, see Mark 12:18) believed in a general resurrection of all people at the end of history. (See, for example, Jesus' dispute on the nature of the resurrected life in Matthew 22:23–33; see also Daniel 12:2.) Therefore, Jesus' resurrection differed from the prevailing view in that (1) it happened in history, not at the end of history, and (2) it happened to one individual, not to the entire human race. Given this, the early church could not have derived their idea of Jesus' singular resurrection in history from prevailing Jewish ideas. Thus if Jesus' followers (or others) had only visionary or apparitional experiences of Jesus, these would not have supported the claim that he was alive. . . . They could at best claim that Jesus' disembodied spirit was making various appearances on earth. But the New Testament nowhere makes this claim, since it emphasizes the physical resurrection of Jesus and the empty tomb. (Groothuis, CA, 547)

N. T. Wright agrees with and echoes Groothius's above statement:

[If] a first-century Jew said that someone had been "raised from the dead," the one thing they did *not* mean was that such a person had gone to a state of disembodied bliss, there either to rest forever or to wait until the great day of reembodiment. (Wright, CORJ, website)

Both Groothuis and Wright are getting at the same point. If Jesus was indeed resurrected, it then was a physical Jesus that the disciples saw and interacted with in some physical way. It was radically different from the disembodied continuation after death that appears in other ancient documents known in the Greek and Roman world that the New Testament writers (especially Paul and Luke) faced. Examples of that disembodied view of "immortality" appear in Plato, Homer, and Virgil, among others. But the New Testament insists in a bold and historically reliable way upon a resurrection that is bodily. He was not just a spirit, and the term "resurrection" is not just a figure of speech.

Norman Geisler offers a very handy chart to help analyze both the appearances and the physical nature of Jesus and his interactions with his disciples (Geisler, REF, 655)

Person or Group with Scripture Reference	Saw	Heard	Touched	Other Evidence
Mary Magdalene [John 20:10–18]	X	X	X	empty tomb
Mary with women [Matthew 28:1–10]	X	X	X	empty tomb
Peter [1 Corinthians 15:5]	X	X		empty tomb, clothes
Two disciples [Luke 24:13–35]	X	X		ate with him*
Ten disciples [Luke 24:36–49; John 20:19–23]	X	X	X**	ate food
Eleven disciples [John 20:24–31]	X	X	X**	saw wounds
Seven disciples [John 21]	X	X		ate food*
All disciples—commissioning [Matthew 28:16–20; Mark 16:14–18]	X	X		
500 brethren [1 Corinthians 15:6]	X	X		
James [1 Corinthians 15:7]	X	X		
All apostles—Ascension [Acts 1:4–8]	X	X		ate food
Paul [Acts 9:1–9; 1 Corinthians 15:8]	X	X		

* Implied
** Offered himself to be touched

For those who would discount the physical nature of Jesus' resurrected body, Licona explains the Greek language to demonstrate that in the scriptural accounts, this was not some spiritual resurrection or ethereal body the disciples encountered, but that it was in fact a physical body. Jesus appeared to his disciples in the same body that had been buried, but now it possessed some new attributes. Licona builds his case this way:

We now come to four points of contention in this passage [1 Cor. 15:42–54]. The first is Paul's statement that the body is sown *natural* (ψυχικόν) [*psuchikon*] and raised *spiritual* (πνευματικόν) [*pneumatikon*] (1 Cor 15:44). Wedderburn and the earlier Dunn to which he appeals interpret these words with the RSV and NRSV to mean *physical* and *immaterial*, although Dunn later seems to have backed away from this position. (Licona, RJ, 406)*

Some try to make a case, based on the words *natural* and *spiritual* versus *physical* and *immaterial*, that the body of Jesus could have been an immaterial body instead of a physical body. But Licona quickly deflects that with some linguistic history, demonstrating that in 846 relevant occurrences of the Greek word translated *natural*, not once does it mean "physical" or "material." Similarly, Licona found 1,131 occurrences of the word translated *spiritual*, and while there were times when it does refer to "immaterial," there are quite a number of exceptions. This survey of the language spans eleven centuries of usage from the eighth century BC through the third century AD.

Licona then turns his attention to how these words were used in the New Testament, and again he finds no support for interpreting them in a way that would imply that Jesus' "spiritual body" was immaterial or ethereal. We can conclude from Licona's analysis of these terms that these words do not deal with the *substance* of the body, but rather the *quality* of the body.

In addition, in the New Testament when Paul talks about "flesh and blood," Licona does not see this as meaning physical, or material, bodies versus nonphysical, or immaterial, bodies. "Flesh and blood" is to be understood as an idiom: "[The] term 'flesh and blood' refers to 'mortals' rather than 'physical.' Thus, even in Eph 6:12, [*pneumatikos*] probably does not mean 'ethereal.'" (Licona, RJ, 409)

Licona summarizes his research on the nature of the resurrected body this way:

A significant minority of today's commentators interpret "flesh and blood" as a synonym for "physical." However, most agree it is a figure of speech—and probably a Semitism—referring to humans as mortal beings rather than simply stating, "*The living* [in their present condition] cannot inherit the kingdom of God." . . . The expression "flesh and blood" appears five times in the New Testament (three of which are in the Pauline corpus), appears twice in the LXX and is common in the rabbinic literature, all carrying the primary sense of mortality rather than physicality. That "flesh and blood" is employed in this sense in 1 Corinthians 15 where 15:50 is undergirded by the fact that, elsewhere in 1 Corinthians 15 where the present body is described, its mortality rather than physicality is the issue. . . . If "flesh and blood" is understood with the majority of commentators as a figure of speech, interpreting Paul as claiming in 1 Corinthians 15:50 that our future bodies will be ethereal is exegetically

_____

* In order to feel the full weight of the argument that Licona puts forth, it is highly recommended that you read the entirety of his section 4.3.3.9, giving special attention to pages 400–423.

unfounded.... Moreover, since Paul strongly suggests a resurrection of our mortal bodies elsewhere (e.g., Rom 8:11, 23; 1 Cor 15:42–53; Phil 3:21), any interpretation of 1 Corinthians 15:50 that has Paul referring to an ethereal body proposes a Paul who not only contradicts Luke, but also himself. (Licona, RJ, 417–20)

i) Challenge: Were the Appearances Visions?

However, all of the arguments based on this solid evidence do not prevent some from attributing the resurrection appearances to mere visions or some form of immaterial, spiritual resurrection only. One such example is from Robert Funk, the late founder of the Jesus Seminar, who attempted to make the appearances out to be some later tradition that arose out of the Christian community:

On the basis of the aggregate evidence of these stories and reports, the Jesus Seminar agreed that: The resurrection of Jesus did not involve the resuscitation of a corpse. If the resurrection of Jesus did not involve the resuscitation of a corpse and if a christophany had developed out of an angelophany, it follows that: Belief in Jesus' resurrection did not depend on what happened to his body. Since the empty tomb story was a late development, probably created by Mark, the report that Jesus had been buried in a tomb known to the women has come under scholarly suspicion. The tendency to elaborate and enhance the burial stories* heightened that suspicion. In view of the nature of the appearances and the late emergence of stories representing the resurrection as physical and palpable, the Seminar concluded: The body of Jesus decayed as do other corpses. All the evidence, when taken together, seemed to suggest that the resurrection was not an event that happened on the first Easter Sunday; it was

not an event that could have been recorded by a video camera. The Seminar followed this trail of evidence to its conclusion, which they formulated as follows: Since the earlier strata of the New Testament contain no appearance stories, it does not seem necessary for Christian faith to believe the literal veracity of any of the later narratives. (Funk, AJ, 461–62)

In other words, he declared that the claims to physical appearances were added to the Jesus story later on and therefore do not merit belief. However, we find much more persuasive all the evidence compiled in this book for the reliable historicity of the New Testament accounts, including those of Jesus' physical resurrection.

ii) Response to the Vision Theory

Licona offers a counter to Funk and other proponents of the Jesus Seminar:

First, the appearances to Stephen and Paul are postascension appearances, which may account for why Jesus was seen in the sky or in the heavens rather than on land. Second, the same Luke who reports the appearances to Stephen and Paul is likewise very clear that he interprets the appearances to the disciples as disclosing a literal resurrection of Jesus' corpse. In Luke 24, Jesus' tomb is empty on Easter morning, and the grave clothes that had wrapped his body now contain nothing. Jesus has "flesh and bones" and eats. At his ascension in Acts, Jesus is taken up from among his disciples and is lifted up into the clouds (Acts 1:9–11). He ate and drank with his disciples before his ascension (Acts 10:39–41), and his body is said to not to have decayed as king David's did but was instead raised up (Acts 2:30–32; 13:35–37). It is

---

* In fact, the burial stories do *not* use language that elaborates and enhances them. See Moreland's description of their restraint and absence of exaggeration, cited below in point 3. (Moreland, SSC, 175)

difficult to state more clearly than Luke has done that Jesus' resurrection involved raising his corpse. Accordingly those who appeal to Acts in support of an understanding of Jesus' resurrection that did not involve his corpse must do so quite selectively, interpreting some of Luke's narratives in a manner that has him lucidly contradicting himself. Such a move is unnecessary and unattractive when Luke may be interpreted in a manner entirely consistent with himself without any forcing whatsoever. (Licona, RJ, 329–30)

Licona rightly observes how careful a writer Luke is about accurate detail: Luke declares his intention for writing about Jesus—to offer certainty for his reader, having searched, investigated, and prepared an orderly account (Lk 1:1–4). Anyone making a claim that singles out Jesus' appearances in Acts (to the disciples when he ascended, to Stephen, and to Paul near Damascus) must take into consideration this purpose and remember that Luke wrote both Acts and Luke 24 with its exactness about a physical resurrection.

iii) Evidence for the Appearances of Jesus

Moreland makes a case for the historicity of the appearances of Jesus:

Several features of the appearance narratives argue for their historicity. First, we have in 1 Corinthians 15:3–8 an early testimony by Paul himself that he saw the resurrected Christ. This is strong evidence, for Paul was obviously sincere in his testimony and he understood the resurrection of Jesus as a bodily resurrection. Second, women were the first to see the risen Christ and, given the status of women as witnesses in first-century Judaism, this fact is hard to understand if it did not really happen. Third, early, primitive phrases ("the twelve," "Cephas") are used in 1 Corinthians 15 to report the appearances. These terms show that the reports are early and are not touched up to reflect later ways of speaking. The reports of the appearances are difficult to harmonize and they are brief and sporadic. This not only shows that they are not contrived (since no attempt has been made to fit them into a coherent picture), but also is what one would expect if the reports are accurate. . . . The reports of these events bear these features because that was the way the events themselves occurred. (Moreland, SSC, 174)

Moreland summarizes his view regarding the sober and careful nature of the written accounts of these appearances:

Finally, the resurrection appearances are reported with extreme reserve. When one compares them with the reports in the apocryphal gospels (second century on), the difference is startling. In the Apocrypha, detailed explanations are given about how the resurrection took place. Gross details are added. . . . But the New Testament accounts are subdued and do not include such fanciful descriptions. (Moreland, SSC, 175)

Moreland further points out that within this context, the disciples' disbelief that Jesus would be resurrected lends credibility to the account:

In the narratives, the disciples are slow to believe. This casts the leaders of the early church in a negative, unbelieving light, and thus the picture of them in these narratives would be counterproductive to their authority and ministries. The accounts of their unbelief are most likely accurate. (Moreland, SSC, 174–75)

Professor of New Testament exegesis and theology George Eldon Ladd goes further, stating that the disciples' initial disbelief when confronted with the appearances makes the disciples psychologically sound:

> In light of these facts, the Gospel story is psychologically sound. The disciples were slow to recognize in Jesus their Messiah, for by his actions he was fulfilling none of the roles expected for the Messiah. (Ladd, IBRJ, 71–72)

Why does Ladd say this? Because the disciples did not expect the Messiah to be someone who did and said all the things that Jesus said and did. Even his teaching had surprised them. This caution or disbelief (Lk 24:11) is especially true of Jesus' death and resurrection, which was not something they had been conditioned to accept even after Jesus' repeated teaching on this point. The appearances were unexpected to the disciples precisely because they were in the right frame of mind, as Ladd observes, not because they were susceptible to seeing ghosts or hallucinations. Therefore, the appearance reports are all the more believable and likely to be historically accurate.

4. No Opposing Jewish Refutation

Another striking element of the church's resurrection narrative is the lack of alternative stories and theories contemporary to the event. Beyond the Jewish charge that the disciples stole the body, there are no other explanations for the empty tomb. In addition, the enemies of Christ were silent in other ways.

In Acts 2, Luke records Peter's sermon on the day of Pentecost. There was no refutation given by the Jews to his bold proclamation of Christ's resurrection. Why? Because the evidence of the empty tomb was there for anyone to examine. However, it was common knowledge that the grave no longer held the body of Jesus Christ.

In Acts 25, we see Paul imprisoned in Caesarea. "Seated at the judge's bench, [Festus] commanded Paul to be brought in. When he arrived, the Jews who had come down from Jerusalem stood around him and brought many serious charges that they were not able to prove" (Acts 25:6, 7).

Just what was it about Paul's gospel that so irritated the Jews? What point did they totally avoid in making their accusations? Festus, in explaining the case to King Agrippa, describes the central issue: "Instead they had some disagreements with him about their own religion and about a certain Jesus, a dead man Paul claimed to be alive" (Acts 25:19).

The Jews could not adequately explain the empty tomb. Their attempted explanation was that the disciples had stolen the body. It is therefore strange that, on the numerous occasions when the disciples were arrested and disciplined by the Jewish authorities, no follower of Jesus was ever charged with desecrating a tomb or grave robbery. That, in itself, seems highly suspicious if in fact they did steal the body. There is no record the authorities ever pressed charges for that crime.

The Jewish leaders made all kinds of personal attacks on Paul but avoided the objective evidence for the resurrection. Their arguments were reduced to subjective name-calling, and they avoided discussing the silent witness of the empty grave. As Fairbairn notes in regard to the resurrection: "[T]he silence of the Jews is as significant as the speech of the Christians." (Fairbairn, SLC, 357)

Professor Hermitage E. Day says: "The simple disproof, the effective challenging, of the fact of the Resurrection would have dealt a death-blow to Christianity. And they had every opportunity of disproof, if it were possible." (Day, OER, 34)

Theologian Wolfhart Pannenberg states:

The early Jewish polemic against the Christian message about Jesus' resurrection, traces of which have already been left in the Gospels, does not offer any suggestion that Jesus' grave had remained untouched. The Jewish polemic would have had to have every interest in the preservation of such a report. However, quite to the contrary, it shared the conviction with its Christian opponents that Jesus' grave was empty. It limited itself to explain this fact in its own way. (Pannenberg, quoted in Anderson, *Christianity*, 96)

The church was founded on the resurrection; disproving it would have destroyed the whole Christian movement. Even Paul acknowledged this in his letter to the Corinthians (1 Cor. 15:14, 17). However, instead of any such disproof, the apostles were threatened, beaten, flogged, thrown in prison, and sometimes even killed because of their faith. It would have been much simpler to have silenced them by producing Jesus' body, but this was never done.

As John R. W. Stott has well said, "What the authorities *didn't* say is as clear a pointer to the truth of the resurrection as what the apostles *did* say." (Stott, BC, 69)

5. The Ridicule of the Athenians

When Paul spoke to the Athenians about Christ, they had no answer for his claims. Instead, "when they heard about resurrection of the dead, some began to ridicule him" (Acts 17:32).

They merely laughed it off, because they could not understand how a man could rise from the dead. Though a very few people responded with interest, and some said equivocally that they would hear more another day (Acts 17:32–34), most did not even attempt to engage in serious debate on the topic. In essence, they said: "Don't confuse me, my mind is already made up."

Why did Paul encounter such unbelief in Greece, but not in Jerusalem? Because, while in Jerusalem, the fact of the empty tomb was indisputable—it was right there for people to examine, but in Athens the evidence was far enough away that it was not common knowledge. Paul's hearers had not checked the story out for themselves and rather than go to any trouble to investigate, some of them were satisfied to jest in ignorance.

Moreover, their unbelief could also be attributed, in part, to their assumptions about what it meant to be a human and what happens to a soul after one dies. Greek thought viewed the soul as the permanent thing held in the prison of its body. To escape the body was to be truly free. The resurrection would have been extremely foreign and absurd to their way of thinking, since what Paul is preaching is that after his death Jesus came back to his body.

N. T. Wright has written extensively regarding this Greek attitude, pointing out how radically hopeful is the Christian outlook and advocating that this view be taught, especially in a postmodern world that largely has accepted a naturalistic view limiting human life to the body. The clear result of such a view is our contemporary secular society's anxious preoccupation with maintaining youth and avoiding aging, while living with an unacknowledged malaise and a fear of death. Here are a couple of his observations:

Instead, the young must be taught the true philosophical view: death is not something to regret, but something to be welcomed. It is the moment when, and the means by which, the immortal soul is set free from the prison-house of the physical body. (Wright, RSG, 48)

And—this is, after all, the point for our present enquiry—neither in Plato nor in the major alternatives just mentioned do we find any suggestion that resurrection, the return to bodily life of the dead person, was either desirable or possible. (Wright, RSG, 53)

C. Established Historical Fact

The empty tomb, the silent testimony to the resurrection of Christ, is on solid historical ground. The Romans and Jews could not produce Christ's body or explain where it went. Nevertheless, they refused to believe. Even today, men and women still reject the resurrection, not because of the insufficiency of evidence, but in spite of its sufficiency.

In the preface to his book on the resurrection, the atheist German theologian Gerd Lüdemann explains the direct link between the veracity of the resurrection and the validity of the Christian faith:

My book *The Resurrection of Jesus: History, Experience, Theology* . . . has received a great deal of attention not only from the public but also within the theological guild. Indeed, it has succeeded in initiating further discussions. Its aim was to prove the nonhistoricity of the resurrection of Jesus and simultaneously to encourage Christians to change their faith accordingly by basing it entirely on the historical Jesus. Yet in the meantime, objections from fellow theologians along with further work of my own on the subject have convinced me that disproving the historicity of the resurrection of Jesus ultimately annuls the Christian heritage as error. While the 1994 book may still be consulted for secondary literature—especially from the nineteenth century—the present work

not only presents a completely revised and less technical analysis of the resurrection texts (including translations), but also spells out in detail why the result of the nonhistoricity of the resurrection of Jesus leaves little if any room for Christianity. (Lüdemann, RC, 7–8)

Theologian and preacher James Denney writes, "The empty grave is not the product of a naïve apologetic spirit, . . . it is an original, independent and unmotived part of the apostolic testimony." (Denney, JG, 145)

D. Established Psychological Fact

Professor of evangelism Paul Little asks a pertinent question:

What was it that changed a band of frightened, cowardly disciples into men of courage and conviction? What was it that changed Peter who, the night before the crucifixion, was so afraid for his own skin that three times he denied publicly that he even knew Jesus? Some fifty days later he became the roaring lion, risking his life by saying he had seen Jesus risen from the dead. It must be remembered that Peter preached his electric Pentecost sermon in Jerusalem, where all these events took place and his life was in danger. He was not in Galilee, miles away where no one could verify the facts and where his ringing statements might go unchallenged. Only the bodily resurrection of Christ could have produced this change. (Little, KWYB, 56)

Licona is also helpful here:

Historians may conclude that, subsequent to Jesus' death by crucifixion, a number of his followers had experiences in individual and group settings that convinced them Jesus had risen from the dead and had appeared to them. We may affirm with great confidence that Peter had such an experience in an individual setting, and . . . the same may be said of an adversary of the church named Paul. We may likewise affirm that there was at least one occasion when a group of Jesus' followers including "the Twelve" had such an experience. . . . I reiterate that historians may conclude that subsequent to Jesus' execution, a number of his followers had experiences, in individual and group settings, that convinced them Jesus had risen from the dead and had appeared to them in some manner. This conclusion is granted by a nearly unanimous consensus of modern scholars and may therefore be added to our "historical bedrock." (Licona, RJ, 372)

Pinchas Lapide was a New Testament scholar who was also an Orthodox Jew. Lapide believed that God resurrected Jesus from the dead, not because Jesus was the Messiah, but rather because Jesus was such a pious Jew, standing in a line of the prophets as a preparer for the Messiah-to-come, that God wanted to resurrect him. Lapide makes a very strong claim:

If the defeated and depressed group of disciples overnight could change into a victorious movement of faith, based only on autosuggestion or self-deception—without a fundamental faith experience—then this would be a much greater miracle than the resurrection itself. In a purely logical analysis, the resurrection of Jesus is "the lesser of two evils" for all those who seek a rational explanation of the worldwide consequences of that Easter faith. The true miracle is that this Jewish group of Jesus' followers came to faith, a miracle, which, like all miracles, escapes any exact description or scientific proof. Any kind of deception is excluded in any case, be it the theft of the body, trance, or the invention of a miracle. (Lapide, RJ, 126)

Religious historian Geza Vermes writes:

The opening chapter of the Acts of the Apostles takes us to the Mount of Olives, where the apostles of Jesus wave goodbye to their Master. They believe without comprehending it that he is no longer in the tomb and is on his way to the Father in heaven. It is of little importance whether this spiritual spectacle was witnessed on the third day after the crucifixion or forty days later. What matters is that within a short time the terrified small group of the original followers of Jesus, still hiding from public gaze, all at once underwent a powerful mystical experience in Jerusalem on the Feast of Weeks (Pentecost). Filled with the promised Holy Spirit, the pusillanimous men were suddenly metamorphosed into ecstatic spiritual warriors. They proclaimed openly the message of the Gospel, and the charismatic potency imparted to them by Jesus during his ministry that had enabled them to preach, heal, and expel demons burst into life again and manifested itself in word and in deed. The former terrified fugitives courageously spoke up in the presence of the authorities and healed the sick in public, at the gate of the Temple itself. (Vermes, *Resurrection*, 149–150)

N. T. Wright also lends his keen insight:

The widespread belief and practice of the early Christians is only explicable if we assume that they all believed that Jesus was bodily raised, in an Easter event something like the stories the gospels tell; the reason they believed that he was bodily raised is because the tomb was empty and, over a short period thereafter, they encountered Jesus himself, giving every appearance of being bodily alive once more. (Wright, RSG, 710)

In my book *The Fate of the Apostles*, I (Sean) remark on the courage of the disciples based on their belief in the resurrection:

It is important to grasp the significance of the earliest Christian *kerygma* for the lives of the disciples. Although they were Galileans and their lives were in danger since the arrest and death of Jesus, they stayed in Jerusalem to proclaim the resurrection. This shows their understanding and acceptance of the basic meaning of the crucified and risen savior. Otherwise, they hardly would have engaged in missionary work. If they wanted to persuade Jews in Jerusalem to believe in Jesus, it would be counterproductive to invent fictitious stories whose falsehood could easily be discovered. Thus, their preaching only makes sense if they truly believed Jesus had risen from the dead, and if the historical evidence was there to confirm it. (McDowell, FA, 23–24)

Luke also records this amazing display of courage by the apostles during their imprisonment and flogging, and despite the threat of death in Acts 5:17–42.

E. Established Sociological Fact
1. The Existence of the Christian Church

The resurrection is such a significant and momentous event that without its reality, the early Christian church could not have come into existence. Christianity was a movement begun by Jews in Jerusalem not because they were all tired of Judaism and wanted to invent something new, but because of something that they experienced. They really believed Jesus had risen. Any theory that attempts to explain away the historicity of the resurrection must provide an alternate explanation for the origin of the church. And yet the first and consistent testimony of the church is that Jesus rose from the grave.

The basic foundation for the establishment of the church was the preaching of Christ's resurrection, as is attested in Acts (1:21, 22; 2:23, 24, 31, 32; 3:14, 15, 26; 4:10; 5:30; 10:39–41; 13:29–39; 17:30, 31; 26:22, 23).

I (Sean) describe how belief in the resurrection has been at the heart of the Christian movement since the beginning:

[T]he Christian movement was a resurrection movement since its inception: that is, "to believe in Jesus" always meant "to believe that he had risen from the grave, conquering death and sin." No evidence exists that the earliest Christians considered the resurrection secondary; rather, the centrality of the resurrection in the earliest creeds, which pre-date the writing of the New Testament books (for example, Rom 1:3–4; 4:24b–25; 1 Thess 4:14; 1 Cor 15:3–7), shows just the opposite—that the resurrection, its historical reality, itself grounded faith in Jesus as Messiah. The resurrection also held a central place in the apostolic *kerygma* as represented in the sermon summaries in Acts (Acts 2:24). From the earliest records of the Christian faith to the writings of the Apostolic Fathers, it is evident the apostles had a *resurrection* faith. (McDowell, FA, 23–24)

Moreland writes that the only explanation for the Christian church's coming into being, as well as its continued existence, is the resurrection:

There never was a form of Christianity which did not emphasize the centrality of the death and resurrection of a divine Jesus. The resurrection of Jesus is the explanation the church herself gave, and it is the only adequate one. (Moreland, SSC, 181)

2. Change from Sabbath to Sunday Worship

Keeping in mind that the first and earliest Christians were Jewish, it is astonishing that they would give up worshiping on the Sabbath (Saturday) and switch to meeting and worshiping together on Sunday unless something very significant had occurred that would contribute to that shift. The best and perhaps only explanation is the resurrection of the Lord and Messiah, Jesus.

3. Change in the Meaning of Baptism

In Romans 6:1–5 and Colossians 2:12, Paul links this Christian sacrament with the resurrection in his correspondence with the church in Rome and Colossae. The Jewish practice of proselyte baptism from which the Christian practice was adapted had marked a Gentile's adoption as a Jewish convert. In the work of John the Baptist, baptism had indicated a person's intention to change—to repent (rethinking his actions and beginning a cleansed life). Moreland also points out the necessary link between baptism and the resurrection, for the Christians believed that the changed life could come about not from willpower but from identification with what Jesus had accomplished in his death and resurrection (Rom. 6:3, 4).

> The practice of baptism in the early church was probably an adaptation of proselyte baptism practiced in Judaism. The change in meaning of the act of baptism by the church points to the resurrection as a necessary precondition for such a change. (Moreland, SSC, 180)

4. Change from Passover Commemoration to Communion

The celebration of communion (also known as the Lord's Supper or the Eucharist) was first instituted by Jesus on the night of his betrayal, as he and the disciples marked the commemoration of the Passover. (Luke 22:7–22) In 1 Corinthians 11:23–26, Paul recalls that event and instructs the Corinthians regarding its ongoing practice as a commemoration of the new covenant.

Moreland writes of its tie to the resurrection:

> The first sacrament was the Eucharist. The celebration of the Eucharist was an early practice (see 1 Cor. 11) which began no later than a few years after Jesus' death. This was not a gathering to mourn at Jesus' tomb; it was a celebration. Why would people celebrate the death of one they loved? They did not celebrate his life or teachings. They celebrated his death and his continued presence with them. Such an activity made sense only on the assumption of their certainty of Jesus' resurrection from the dead. (Moreland, SSC, 180)

The Lord's Supper is a remembrance of his death, but we read in Acts 2:46 that it was a time of joy:

> *Every day they devoted themselves to meeting together in the temple complex, and broke bread from house to house. They ate their food with a joyful and humble attitude.*

And they had every reason to be joyful as theologian Michael Green explains:

> They *met* him in this sacrament. He was not dead and gone, but risen and alive. And they would celebrate this death of his, in the consciousness of his risen presence, until his longed for return at the end of history (1 Corinthians 11:26). We possess a short eucharistic prayer from the earliest Christian community, from the original Aramaic-speaking church (1 Corinthians 16:22 and *Didache*, 10). Here it is. *Maranatha!* It means, "Our Lord, come!" How that could have been the attitude of the early Christians as they met to celebrate the Lord's Supper among themselves is quite inexplicable, unless he did indeed rise from the dead on the third day. (Green, MA, 53).

5. The Phenomenon of Changing Social Structures and Beliefs

Moreland enumerates a handful of significant changes that differentiated Judaism from early Christianity:

First, there was the importance of sacrifices. While obedience to the law was slowly eroding the centrality of the sacrificial system, nevertheless the importance of sacrificing animals for various sins was a major value in first-century Judaism. Second, emphasis was placed on keeping the law. Regardless of whether one was a Sadducee or a Pharisee, respect for the law of Moses and its role in keeping people in right standing with God was a major value. Third, keeping the Sabbath was important; several laws were formulated to help define Sabbath-keeping and to maintain its prominence. Fourth, clear-cut non-Trinitarian monotheism was a defining trait of the Jew. The Shema asserts that God is one, and this doctrine was non-negotiable. Specifically, there was no belief that God could ever become a man. Fifth, the Messiah was pictured as a human figure (perhaps super-human, but not God himself), a political kind who would liberate the Jews from Gentile oppression and establish the Davidic kingdom. No conception of a crucified messiah who established a church by rising from the dead was known. (Moreland, SSC, 179)

Moreland does not just enumerate what the changes were, he also writes about the risk of the sociological impact that would have been faced by Jews who converted to Christianity, together with the surprising rapidity of these changes in contrast to the normally slow pace of sociological change. He concludes by stating the only adequate cause for such a shift:

The early church was a community of Jews who had significantly altered or given up these five major structures. What could possibly cause this to happen in so short a time? . . . Such a radical sociological shift would demand an explanation. The shift from Judaism to Christianity among the early Jewish converts is even more dramatic than the one imagined. Society did not change rapidly in those days. Jews would risk becoming social outcasts if they tampered with these five major beliefs, not to mention that they would risk the damnation of their own souls to hell. Why was such a change made in so short a time after the death of a carpenter from Nazareth—of all places—who had suffered the death of a criminal on a cross, a death expressly detested among the Jews in their belief that "cursed is he who dies on a tree"? How could such a thing take place? The resurrection offers the only rational explanation. (Moreland, SSC, 179–180)

Barry Leventhal, Distinguished Professor of Church Missions and Ministries at Southern Evangelical Seminary, offers four points regarding the radical social changes in these early Jewish converts:

First, the new believers in Christ never offered another animal sacrifice after the cross, as Christ's death was sufficient to atone for all sin (see John 19:30; Heb. 10:26–31). Second, the new believers felt free to disregard certain ceremonial aspects of the Mosaic Law, which was the key element that identified them as God's chosen people (see Acts 15:14–29; Eph. 2:11–22). Third, while the new believers remained monotheistic, they also became Trinitarian. Rather than merely believing in God as one person, they came to believe that there is one God simultaneously existing in three persons (see Matt. 28:19). Fourth, the Jewish community was expecting a political and military deliverer, not a suffering Messiah. Yet, after Christ's resurrection, the early converts understood that the Scriptures taught that the Messiah must come first and suffer for the sins of the people before entering into glory (see Luke 24:25–27, 44–48). (McDowell and McDowell, ER, 231)

6. The Phenomenon of Radically Changed Lives

The radical transformation experienced by the disciples is powerful evidence for the truth of their beliefs:

The radically changed lives of those early Christian believers are among the most telling testimonies to the fact of the resurrection. One of the most dramatic changes was their willingness to go everywhere proclaiming the message of the risen Christ. We must ask, what could have motivated such a change? Had there been visible benefits accruing to them from their efforts—such as prestige, wealth or increased social status—we might logically account for their actions. As a reward, however, for their wholehearted and total allegiance to this risen Christ, these early Christians were beaten, stoned to death, thrown to the lions, tortured, crucified and subjected to every conceivable method of stopping them from talking. Yet they were the most peaceful of men and women, who continually demonstrated love and never forced their beliefs on anyone. Rather they laid down their very lives as the ultimate proof of their complete confidence in the truth of their message. (McDowell and McDowell, ER, 232)

VII. Inadequate Alternate Theories About the Resurrection

We will now examine naturalistic theories that some have put forward in an effort to explain the various facts surrounding the resurrection via causes that do not require God or the supernatural. These theories may redefine key elements of the gospel accounts in line with their author's presuppositions. Each theory either attempts to explain the facts so as to arrive at a non-miraculous resurrection or attempts to deny the resurrection outright, by selective use of facts or by redefining them to give a misdiagnosis of the events. Winfried Corduan comments on the alternative theories to the resurrection en masse:

Non-miraculous explanations of what happened at the empty tomb have to face a cruel choice: either they have to rewrite the evidence in order to suit themselves or they have to accept the fact that they are not consistent with present evidence. The only hypothesis that fits the evidence is that Jesus was really resurrected. Could the Man who predicted His death and resurrection, only to have it come to pass exactly as He had said, be anything but God? (Corduan, NDAI, 227)

A. Apparent Death Theory

The apparent death theory posits that Jesus did not die on the cross, but only *appeared*

Non-miraculous explanations of what happened at the empty tomb have to face a cruel choice: either they have to rewrite the evidence in order to suit themselves or they have to accept the fact that they are not consistent with present evidence. The only hypothesis that fits the evidence is that Jesus was really resurrected.

Winfried Corduan

to die. Although widely criticized and even discredited, proponents of this argument illustrate the lengths, even the extremes, to which some will go in order to make a case in accord with their assumptions that preclude a miraculous resurrection.

1. Details of the Theory

According to the theory, after being removed from the cross, Jesus was placed in Joseph of Arimathea's tomb while still alive, yet unconscious. After several hours he revived in the coolness of the tomb, arose, freed himself from burial wrappings and the sealed tomb, and made his way back to his disciples to declare himself the risen Lord, the conqueror and defeater of death. This theory is very recent in historical terms, emerging in the late 1700s and evolving through the late 1800s through various liberal German theologians, including Karl Friedrich Bahrdt, Karl Venturini, Heinrich Paulus, and others. The modern version of this was popularized in the 1960s book *The Passover Plot* by Hugh Schonfield. The apparent death theory has also been been defended by Barbara Thiering, as well as T. A. Lloyd Davies and Margaret Lloyd Davies. (see Thiering, JRDSS, Lloyd Davies and Lloyd Davies, RR)

2. Response

Since 1835, no serious scholar has been willing to support the idea that Jesus merely swooned and was revived after being taken down from the cross. The apparent death theory fails to account for the known facts:

a. Crucifixion Results in Death

The evidence—both historical and medical—argues against the possibility of survival. There are at least ten reasons to be confident that Jesus did in fact die on the cross:

1. The nature of his injuries—his whipping, beating, lack of sleep, crown of thorns, and his collapse on the way to his crucifixion while carrying the cross—were so life-endangering in themselves that crucifixion would have completed the murder.

2. The nature of crucifixion virtually guarantees death from asphyxiation.

3. The piercing of Jesus' side, from which came "blood and water" (John 19:34), indicating serum separated from clotted blood, gives medical evidence that Jesus had already died.

4. Jesus said he was in the act of dying while on the cross: "Father, into your hands I commit my spirit" (Luke 23:46 ESV). John renders that he "gave up his spirit" (John 19:30).

5. The Roman soldiers, who were trained executioners, were charged to make sure that he died. Even though it was customary for soldiers to speed death by breaking the legs of the victims, they did not break his legs, for their examination determined that he was already dead (John 19:33).

6. Pilate summoned the centurion to make sure Jesus had actually died before giving the body to Joseph for burial (see Mark 15:44, 45).

7. Jesus' body was wrapped in about a hundred pounds of cloth and spices, and placed in a sealed tomb until the third day (John 19:39, 40; Matt. 27:60). If Jesus had not died from his previous torture, he would have died in the tomb from lack of food, water, and medical treatment.

8. Medical experts who have studied the circumstances surrounding the end of Jesus' life have concluded that he actually died on the cross.

9. Non-Christian historians from the first and second centuries, such as Tacitus and Josephus, recorded the death of Jesus of Nazareth (See chapter 6)

10. The earliest Christian writers after the time of Christ, such as Polycarp and Ignatius, verify his death by crucifixion on the cross as well. (McDowell and McDowell, ER, 223–224)

From a medical perspective, good scientific research has shown that the apparent death theory is way off target. In an article in the peer-reviewed *Journal of the American Medical Association*, William D. Edwards, Wesley J. Gabel and Floyd E. Hosmer write:

Jesus' death may have been hastened simply by his state of exhaustion and by the severity of the scourging, with its resultant blood loss and preshock state. The fact that he could not carry his patibulum supports this interpretation. The actual cause of Jesus' death, like that of other crucified victims, may have been multifactorial and related primarily to hypovolemic shock, exhaustion asphyxia, and perhaps acute heart failure. A fatal cardiac arrhythmia may have accounted for the apparent catastrophic terminal event. Thus, it remains unsettled whether Jesus died of cardiac rupture or of cardiorespiratory failure. However, the important feature may be not *how* he died but rather *whether* he died. Clearly, the weight of historical and medical evidence indicates that Jesus was dead before the wound to his side was inflicted and supports the traditional view that the spear, thrust between his right ribs, probably perforated not only the right lung but also the pericardium and heart and thereby ensured his death. Accordingly, interpretations based on the assumption that Jesus did not die on the cross appear to be at odds with modern medical knowledge. (Edwards, Gabel, and Hosmer, OPDJC, 1463)

Even James Tabor, who does not believe that Jesus resurrected physically, but only spiritually, agrees that Jesus died on the cross:

I think we need have no doubt that given Jesus' execution by Roman crucifixion he was truly *dead* and that his temporary place of burial was discovered to be empty shortly thereafter. (Tabor, JD, 230)

In an attempt to bolster their view, skeptics cite the historian Josephus, who describes an extremely rare case in which an individual survived crucifixion, overlooking the fact that his account describes three victims who were definitely alive when taken down, but two of whom died. (Josephus, WFJ, 1:420–21; see VI.A.1 in this chapter for a quote of Josephus's account.)

Not only is it highly unlikely that Jesus survived crucifixion, a number of other reasons give the apparent death theory considerable difficulty in accounting for certain details in the record. We list them below.

i) Escaping the Grave Linens

He would have had to free himself from his grave clothes with no assistance while in a near-death state of health. In contrast, the gospel of John tells that after the death and resurrection of Lazarus, Jesus told others who were present to release Lazarus from the linen grave clothes (John 11:1–3, 17, 43, 44).

ii) Removing the Sealed and Guarded Stone

Given his traumatized physical condition, Jesus would have had an extremely difficult, if not impossible, task of rolling the stone back from the entrance of the tomb, especially from inside the tomb, as there would be no way to obtain leverage on the stone to roll it out of the way. Evans provides an idea of the difficulty of the task, even from outside the tomb:

As the women approach the tomb, they ask: "Who will roll away the stone?" (Mark 16.3)....

In view of Jesus' status as a criminal and in view of the presence of a guard (perhaps reinforced because of the popularity of Jesus), the women knew that there would be reluctance to assist them in rolling back the stone that covered the opening of Jesus' tomb. They also knew that even their combined strength probably wouldn't be sufficient to roll it aside. Study of the skeletal remains from this period indicates that the average woman was barely 150 cm tall [4' 9"] and often weighed less than 45 kg [99 lbs.]. The average man was about 160 cm tall [5' 2"] and weighed about 60 kg [132 lbs.]. Sealing stones weighed 200 kg [440 lbs.] or more. Even round stones, which were designed to be rolled aside, would have been very difficult to move. The Markan evangelist, moreover, comments that the stone was very large (Mark 16.4b). (Evans, JHW, 137–38)

However, even if Jesus had managed to roll back the stone in his condition, could he have escaped the detection of the guards? If the apparent death theory is correct, Jesus would have been placed in the tomb while he was unconscious and would not have awoken until after he had been in the tomb for some time. This means that he would have revived after the tomb was sealed and guarded, which means that Jesus would not have known about the guards posted outside of the tomb. Even if the guards had fallen asleep, as the story goes (Matthew 28:13), would Jesus have had any reason to be quiet while rolling back the stone? It seems improbable that his attempts to escape would not have alerted the guards, and without knowledge of the guards' presence, he would have had no reason to work quietly. Whether the guards were sleepy, barely awake, or alert, in his poor physical condition, Jesus would not be likely to get away from them.

iii) Walking to Emmaus

The walk to Emmaus was seven miles. Traveling this distance while in extremely poor health seems inconceivable.

Let us describe Jesus' condition at the time he sets off on his long walk to Emmaus:

- It has been over forty-eight hours since the Passover meal concluded, which means Jesus has not had anything to eat or drink for more than two days.
- Jesus is severely dehydrated from the amount of blood and fluid loss.
- Jesus has endured beatings and scourging at the hands of the Romans.
- Jesus is exhausted from a lack of sleep and rest. (He was not allowed to sleep during his trial and he definitely did not sleep while on the cross.)
- Jesus is in a highly weakened state. After all, he was so exhausted and debilitated that he was unable to carry his own *patibulum* to the execution site. Simon of Cyrene had to be recruited to do it for him. (A cross's *patibulum* weighed approximately one hundred pounds. (Ball, CDMCJ, 81–82) This means he was unable to carry a one-hundred-pound cross beam before being crucified, but according to this theory he could manage to roll away a stone weighing not less than 440 lbs. after being crucified.)
- Jesus has suffered severe wounds beyond the beatings and the scourging. He has also been nailed to a cross— hands and feet—and has a gaping side wound after having been speared by a member of the crucifixion detail. This side wound most likely has perforated a lung and/or his heart.
- Jesus has moved a massive stone from the entrance of a sealed and guarded

tomb all by himself, which must have tired him out even more.

iv) Wounded Survivor or Risen Savior?

If Jesus had come to the disciples in the condition required by this theory, they would not have viewed him as their risen Lord or someone who had conquered death. The nineteenth-century German liberal theologian David Strauss wrote:

> It is impossible that a being who had stolen half-dead out of the sepulchre [tomb], who crept about weak and ill, wanting medical treatment, who required bandaging, strengthening and indulgence, and who still at last yielded to his sufferings, could have given to the disciples the impression that he was a Conqueror over death and the grave, the Prince of Life, an impression which lay at the bottom of their future ministry. Such a resuscitation could only have weakened the impression which he had made upon them in life and in death, at the most could only have given it an elegiac [sorrowful] voice, but could by no possibility have changed their sorry into enthusiasm, have elevated their reverence into worship. (Strauss, NLJ, 1:412)

b. No "Middle of History" Resurrections Expected

The idea of a single individual rising from the dead before the end of history was not a belief the Jews held, nor was it a concept that they would have dreamed up upon seeing Jesus walking after burial because such a concept would have been completely foreign to them. Martha states the Jewish belief in John 11:24 and implies when she says "but even now" that she has some hope of an exception for her dead brother only because Jesus has arrived and has power in prayer (John 11:22).

Author Greg Monette points this out:

There was also no Jewish belief prior to Christianity that the Messiah would rise from the dead as a sign of vindication, as Jews believe the Messiah's vindication would come through victory in battle. The idea didn't need to be invented. It may have been more convenient for Jesus to survive crucifixion, as that would have been a sign that Rome's best efforts at torture were no limit to the Messiah from Galilee named Jesus. It's extremely implausible that the early Christians would have created the idea of Jesus' resurrection if he had survived the crucifixion. (Monette, WJ, 188–89)

3. Conclusion Regarding the Apparent Death Theory

Based on what we know from scientific medical diagnosis, archaeology, and historical documentation, it is highly improbable that Jesus could have survived Roman crucifixion at the hands of trained executioners. Further, it is highly improbable that the disciples would have viewed a weak and broken Jesus as their risen Lord and conqueror of death, someone whom they would worship and follow to their own graves. Rather, they would have viewed him as a badly injured, almost dead man in desperate need of medical attention.

B. Theft Theory

The oldest of the naturalistic alternative theories, the theft theory, comes in different forms. The first form is that the disciples stole the body from the sealed and guarded tomb and then conspired to teach that Jesus had been resurrected but knowing that he had done no such thing. The second form is that grave robbers stole the body and when Jesus' followers discovered the tomb empty, they believed that Jesus rose from the dead.

1. Details of the Theory

This theory originates back to the time of the resurrection itself. It was first recorded by Matthew (28:11–15):

As they were on their way, some of the guards came into the city and reported to the chief priests everything that had happened. After the priests had assembled with the elders and agreed on a plan, they gave the soldiers a large sum of money and told them, "Say this, 'His disciples came during the night and stole Him while we were sleeping.' If this reaches the governor's ears, we will deal with him and keep you out of trouble." So they took the money and did as they were instructed. And this story has been spread among Jewish people to this day.

Matthew is not the only individual to record this early theory. It was also mentioned by Justin Martyr in the mid-second century (c. AD 165):

And though all the men of your nation knew the incidents in the life of Jonah, and though Christ said among you that He would give the sign of Jonah, exhorting you to repent of your wicked deeds at least after He rose again from the dead, and to mourn before God as did the Ninevites, in order that your nation and city might not be taken and destroyed, as they have been destroyed; yet you not only have not repented, after you learned that He rose from the dead, but, as I said before you have sent chosen and ordained men throughout all the world to proclaim that a godless and lawless heresy had sprung from one Jesus, a Galilæan deceiver, whom we crucified, but his disciples stole him by night from the tomb, where he was laid when unfastened from the cross, and now deceive men by asserting that he has risen from the dead and ascended to heaven. (Justin Martyr, DT, online)

Tertullian also describes this theory of the body being either stolen by the disciples or moved by the gardener, indicating that he is voicing the point of view of those who opposed Jesus and feared that in the event of a grave robbery, "the last deception will be worse than the first" (Matt. 27:64 NKJV).

"This," I shall say, "this is that carpenter's or hireling's son, that Sabbath-breaker, that Samaritan and devil-possessed! This is He whom you purchased from Judas! This is He whom you struck with a reed and fist, whom you contemptuously spat upon, to whom you gave gall and vinegar to drink! This is He whom His disciples secretly stole away, that it might be said He had risen again, or the gardener abstracted, that his lettuces might come to no harm from the crows of visitants!" (Tertullian, DS, online)

2. Richard Carrier's Empty Tomb Hypotheses

Nevertheless, the theory of theft recurs. Ancient historian Richard Carrier presents a strong contemporary version of it, in a view that sees the resurrection as a late invention. His interpretation derives from his naturalistic rejection of bodily resurrection, paired with assumptions about the method and purposes he sees behind the writing of Mark's gospel. The thinking that lies behind Carrier's theory surfaces when he redefines Paul's use of the term *spirit* and when he assesses Mark's use of a motif (a repeated pattern) in that gospel.

a. Theory #1: Growth of a Later Legend

Carrier believes the most plausible and probable cause of the empty tomb story being presented in the Gospels is that over time a legend grew up around it as the idea of bodily resurrection gradually won out over the earlier Christian belief of a nonbodily, spiritual resurrection. In the opening of one of his three essays regarding the empty tomb, Carrier writes:

> I argue that [Jesus] was believed to have received a new, more glorious body, one not made of flesh and blood but of the stuff of the stars, that his soul or identity left its old body on earth and was given another in heaven. So the earliest Christians would have believed Christ had *really* been raised, and raised *bodily*, even as his earthly body continued to rot in its tomb. I will also argue that the claim that his tomb was empty, and his corpse missing, arose a generation or two later. (Carrier, SBCLET, 106)

After attempting to build a case that Jesus was not bodily resurrected in the same body he was buried with, Carrier uses that as a foundation to support his claim that the empty tomb story is legendary:

> This leaves us with Mark. Even if not certain, it is a credible hypothesis that all other accounts originated with his. But where did his come from? I believe he invented it. For Mark the empty tomb was not historical, but symbolic. It *represented* the resurrection of Jesus, with a powerful symbol pregnant with meaning—not only elucidating the "core" Gospel inherited from Paul (e.g., 1 Corinthians 15:3–5, which is ambiguous as to whether Jesus rose in the flesh or spirit), but also maintaining Mark's own narrative theme of "reversal of expectation." The empty tomb was for Mark like the Exodus for Philo: educational fiction, whose true meaning was far more important than any historical claim ever could be. (Carrier, SBCLET, 156)

Carrier then provides three strands of possible origin for the empty tomb legend. The first strand is of Psalmic origins wherein Psalms 22, 23, and 24 are seen as the death, burial, and resurrection of Jesus respectively, in that there are literary parallels where Psalm 22 is day 1, Psalm 23 is day 2, and Psalm 24 is day 3. The second strand is identified as having Orphic origins. After showing several parallels between Mark's gospel and the Orphic doctrines, he concludes: "Thus, Mark's empty tomb story mimics the secret salvation narratives of the Orphic mysteries, substituting Jewish-Messianic eschatology for the pagan elements." (Carrier, SBCLET, 163)

The final strand Carrier gives for possible origin is something he calls the "Reversal of Expectation" motif. (Carrier, SBCLET, 163) This is the idea that what the reader is expecting to happen in the narrative is suddenly reversed by the author in order to surprise and confound the audience. As Carrier states:

> The parables of Jesus are also full of the reversal of expectation theme, and Mark appears to agree with the program of concealing the truth behind parables. And so, the empty tomb is probably *itself* a parable, which accordingly employs reversal of expectation as its theme. The tomb *has* to be empty, in order to confound the expectations of the reader, just as a foreign Simon *must* carry the cross, a Sanhedrist *must* bury the body, and women (not men) *must* be the first to hear the Good News. . . . Just as reversal of expectation lies at the heart of the teachings of Jesus—indeed, of the very Gospel itself—so it is quite natural for Mark to structure his narrative around such a theme. This program leads him to "create" thematic events that thwart the reader's expectation, and an empty tomb is exactly the sort of thing an author would invent to serve that aim. After all, it begs credulity to suppose that so many convenient reversals of expectation actually happened. It is more credible to suppose that at least some of them are narrative inventions. And one such invention could easily be the

empty tomb. And as we saw above, an empty tomb would have made a tremendously powerful parabolic symbol, rich with meaning (Carrier, SBCLET, 164–65).

Carrier concludes this portion of his essay in this way:

What I have presented so far is an articulation of my theory as to the origins of the empty tomb story, first as a metaphor in Mark, then as an inspiring element in the development of a Christian heresy that took the empty tomb as literal, using it to bolster their own doctrine of a resurrection of the flesh. That this heresy became the eventual orthodoxy is simply an accident of history and politics. (Carrier, SBCLET, 167)

b. Response to Carrier's Legend Theory

Carrier's theory rests on his assumptions and redefinitions that impel him to consider the empty tomb as a late invention; from this, he attempts to muster up three possible explanations for the origin of this fabrication. There are problems with each.

First, the idea that the empty tomb is a late invention layered over the Christian system one or two generations later completely ignores the evidence that the church, from its inception, preached the risen Jesus, which only made sense with an empty tomb, as its core message.

Second, this teaching occurred in the very place where the death, burial, and resurrection took place: Jerusalem.

Third, the teaching began a mere fifty days after Jesus' death, burial, and resurrection.

Finally, to disprove any of the claims being made by the apostles, one merely needed to produce the body from the tomb, which was well known to several different groups of people: (1) the women, (2) the male disciples,

(3) Joseph of Arimathea, who was part of the Sanhedrin, the Jewish leaders who requested the guard and sealing of the tomb, (5) the Roman guards, and (6) Pilate, who allowed the Jewish leaders to post the guard. (Would Pilate do such a thing without also possibly knowing the location?) As we also demonstrate in chapters 3 and 6 the legendary theory is at odds with the historical evidence.

c. Theory #2: Theft

While Carrier believes the legend theory to be the most probable, he also puts forth the theft theory:

Elsewhere I have argued that the original Christians probably did not believe Jesus was literally resurrected from the grave, but that this belief arose as a consequence of the legendary development of an empty tomb story. I think that this is the best account of the facts as we have them. But there are still other accounts that remain at least as good as the supernatural alternative. So even if the empty tomb story is not a legend, it is not necessary to conclude that only a genuine resurrection would explain it. One prominent natural explanation is theft of the body. (Carrier, PT, 349)

Carrier's main purpose here is to disprove a statement that noted Christian apologist William Lane Craig makes regarding the alleged theft of Jesus' body. Carrier thinks that Craig's reasoning is without merit and offers six counter proposals as to why it is more likely that the body was stolen instead of being supernaturally resurrected. Without delving into all the detail that Carrier provides, he essentially says that the theft could have been the result of grave robbers intent on using the body for magical incantations, or it could have been an overzealous follower (one of the seventy) who was "willing to engage in such a pious deceit." (Carrier, PT, 352) Carrier concludes his six points by saying,

> There is simply nothing improbable in an empty tomb being the result of a theft, which then is linked with, or even inspires (by leaving the suggestion of an ascension or escape in people's minds), independent reports of appearances, especially appearances of a visionary kind, such as that which converted Paul. (Carrier, PT, 354)

However, Carrier is not quite done, as he anticipates a rejoinder of there being a guard present to watch over the tomb. Carrier responds:

> But more importantly, the fact that the guard was not even placed until sometime Saturday (Matt. 27:62–65) means the whole night and part of the morning would still have been available for the unguarded body to be stolen. For in the account given, the Jews were evidently satisfied by the fact the stone appeared unmoved (or they could not legally move it): for no one is said to have checked to see if the tomb was already empty—the closed tomb simply had a seal and guard placed on it (Matt. 27:66). So even if the story of guards is *true* it does little to argue against the possibility of theft. . . . Likewise, Matthew has no problem showing the guards taking bribes to lie (28:12–15), so it is hardly incredible that they might take bribes to allow the theft—or indeed, taking both bribes and being twice the richer for it. (Carrier, PT, 358)

d. Response to Carrier's Theft Theory

The theft theory and its problems find their response below. In regard to Carrier's objections about the account given the guarding of the tomb in Matthew, please read section VI.A.3. earlier in this chapter as the historicity is handled there.

e. Theory #3: Buried in a Criminal's Graveyard

In another essay, Carrier presents a different naturalistic explanation for the empty tomb:

> Was Christianity begun by a mistake? It is a distinct possibility. The surviving evidence, legal and historical, suggests the body of Jesus was not formally buried Friday night when it was placed in a tomb by Joseph of Arimathea, that instead it had to have been placed Saturday night in a special public graveyard reserved for convicts. On this theory the women who visited the tomb Sunday morning mistook its vacancy. That, in conjunction with other factors (like reinterpretations of scripture and things Jesus said, the dreams and visions of leading disciples, and the desire to seize an opportunity to advance a moral cause of Jesus), led to a belief that Jesus had risen from the grave (probably, originally, by direct ascension to heaven, as I argued in a previous chapter). And so Christianity began. (Carrier, BJLJL, 369)

For a response to this theory, please see section VI.A.3. for both the historical context of first-century burial practices and for particular questions about Roman burial of a convict (even of one crucified) and the role of the Jewish Sanhedrin in such a case.

2. Response to the Theft Theory in General

We have already quoted Justin Martyr (second century) and Tertullian (late second and early third century) as early church fathers who responded to the theory of theft. In the fourth century, John Chrysostom found many problems with this theory:

> How did they steal Him? O most foolish of all men! . . . For how, I ask, did the disciples steal Him, men poor and unlearned, and not

venturing so much as to show themselves? What? Was not a seal put upon it? What? Was there not so many watchmen, and soldiers, and Jews stationed round it? What? Did not those men suspect this very thing, and take thought, and break their rest, and continue anxious about it? And wherefore moreover did they steal it? That they might feign the doctrine of the resurrection? And how should it enter their minds to feign such a thing, men who were well content to be hidden and to live? And how could they remove the stone that was made sure? How could they have escaped the observation of so many? Nay, though they had despised death, they would not have attempted without purpose, and fruitlessly to venture in defiance of so many who were on the watch. And that moreover they were timorous, what they had done before showed clearly, at least, when they saw Him seized, all rushed away from Him. If then at that time they did not dare so much as to stand their ground when they saw Him alive, how when He was dead could they but have feared such a number of soldiers? What? Was it to burst open a door? Was it that one should escape notice? A great stone lay upon it, needing many hands to move it. (Chrysostom, HGSM, online)

The theory that the disciples (or someone else) stole the body fails for a number of reasons:

a. The Problem of Conspiracy by the Disciples

The theory that Jesus' disciples stole the body rests on the assumption that the disciples deliberately conspired with one another to steal the body and then make up a false story that Jesus had risen from the dead. But conspiracies tend to fall apart because someone breaks down under pressure and betrays his coconspirators. This did not happen with the disciples. If they had conspired to invent the resurrection, they would have spent their entire lives preaching a story that they knew to be untrue as their central message, building an entire movement around it, even under the threat of torture and death. Gary Habermas and Michael Licona describe what the disciples did and enumerate their reasons why this theory fails:

> The data we have strongly suggest that this was not what happened. First . . . the disciples of Jesus claimed to have seen the risen Jesus because they really believed that they had seen him. Shortly after Jesus' crucifixion, their lives were radically transformed to the point that they were willing to endure imprisonment, sufferings, and even martyrdom. This indicates that their claim of seeing the risen Jesus was the result of a strong and sincere belief they truly had seen him. In all the political scandals that occurred over recent generations, one or more of the guilty party was often willing to tell the truth rather than face a lengthy prison term. The disciples of Jesus, on the other hand, boldly proclaimed the risen Christ in the face of severe persecution and death. They faced dungeons, torture, and brutal executions— not the white collar prisons that hold today's corrupt politicians. . . . Second, a mere story propagated by the disciples would not have convinced Paul, who was an enemy of the church. . . . Instead of rejecting the claims of Jesus' resurrection as fraud, Paul was convinced by what he described as the risen Jesus appearing to him. Third, it is doubtful that fraud [theft] on the part of the disciples would have convinced James who, even though he may have heard of Jesus' miracles, had rejected him prior to his resurrection. . . . Like Paul, James appears to have been convinced by what he believed was an appearance of the risen Jesus to himself. (Habermas and Licona, CRJ, 93–95)

b. The Problem of Unknown Thieves

The theory that someone other than the disciples stole the body faces the same issues surrounding the notion of the disciples' conspiracy. Habermas and Licona respond to this version of the theory as well, pointing out that the accounts show men and women who thought just as carefully as we would: It was not the emptiness of the tomb but the appearances of Jesus that convinced them.

First, an empty tomb by itself would not have convinced the church persecutor Paul. Instead, he would have suspected foul play. . . . Second, an empty tomb by itself would not have convinced the skeptic James who, like Paul, appears to have been convinced by an appearance of the risen Jesus to him. [1 Cor 15:7] Third, the empty tomb did not appear to lead any of Jesus' followers except John to believe that he had risen from the dead. Indeed, the gospel of John reports that Mary Magdalene immediately jumped to the conclusion that someone had stolen the body upon discovering the empty tomb. Her first thought was not that Jesus had risen. The gospels further report that Peter, upon seeing the empty tomb, was unconvinced as well. Thomas was unconvinced by reports of an empty tomb and reports of appearances by the risen Jesus to the others. It was the appearances that led to the disciples' belief that Jesus had risen from the dead. Fourth, *even if true*, Fraud 2 [someone else stole the body] could only call into question the cause of the empty tomb, not the Resurrection itself. . . . The empty tomb convinced no one. Rather, it was the appearances that brought about belief in friends and foe alike. (Habermas and Licona, CRJ, 95–97)

c. The Problem of the Disciples' Lack of Courage

The disciples were scared and in hiding and would not have wanted to take on a sealed and guarded tomb, since they were probably afraid of suffering the same fate that Jesus had suffered: crucifixion. Remember that the disciples ran away during his arrest, as predicted by Jesus:

Then Jesus said to them, "Tonight all of you will run away because of Me, for it is written: I will strike the shepherd, and the sheep of the flock will be scattered." — Matthew 26:31

At that time Jesus said to the crowds, "Have you come out with swords and clubs, as if I were a criminal, to capture Me? Every day I used to sit, teaching in the temple complex, and you didn't arrest Me. But all this has happened so that the prophetic Scriptures would be fulfilled." Then all the disciples deserted Him and ran away. — Matthew 26:55, 56

But even someone like Peter, though he tried to summon up the courage to follow, ended up distancing himself through his words and behavior, again according to Jesus' prediction about him:

"Lord," Simon Peter said to Him, "where are You going?" Jesus answered, "Where I am going you cannot follow Me now, but you will follow later." "Lord," Peter asked, "why can't I follow You now? I will lay down my life for You!" Jesus replied, "Will you lay down your life for Me? I assure you: A rooster will not crow until you have denied Me three times." — John 13:36–38

Meanwhile, Simon Peter was following Jesus, as was another disciple. That disciple was an acquaintance of the high priest; so he went with Jesus into the high priest's courtyard. But Peter remained standing outside by the door. So the other disciple, the one known to the high priest, went out and spoke to the girl who was

the doorkeeper and brought Peter in. Then the slave girl who was the doorkeeper said to Peter, "You aren't one of this man's disciples too, are you?" "I am not!" he said. Now the slaves and the temple police had made a charcoal fire, because it was cold. They were standing there warming themselves, and Peter was standing with them, warming himself. . . . Now Simon Peter was standing and warming himself. They said to him, "You aren't one of His disciples too, are you?" He denied it and said, "I am not!" One of the high priest's slaves, a relative of the man whose ear Peter had cut off, said, "Didn't I see you with Him in the garden?" Peter then denied it again. Immediately a rooster crowed.
— John 18:15–18, 25–27

These were not the actions of a group of followers bent on standing up to soldiers guarding a tomb. As Matthew reminds us, the tomb was guarded (Matthew 27:62–66).

Licona comments, "Today, skeptics simply deny the historicity of Matthew's story about the guards, asserting Matthew invented it, since he is the only one to mention it." (Licona, email correspondence to Sean McDowell)

Craig acknowledges the skepticism leveled against Matthew's guard story but insists that although it deals with the earliest of many later theories of theft, its apologetic purpose does not make it unhistorical (even those with an agenda can speak or write truth):

Matthew's account has been nearly universally rejected as an apologetic legend, though the reasons for this assessment are of unequal worth. For example, the fact that the story is an apologetic answering the allegations that the disciples stole the body does not therefore necessarily mean that it is unhistorical. (Craig, ANTE, 211)

d. Resurrection Not Expected by Either Gentiles or Jews

As noted earlier, resurrection was not the first thing the disciples concluded when discovering the tomb empty. They immediately jumped to naturalistic conclusions, just as any modern person would. Consider their various responses:

- Someone moved the body (John 20:2).
- The gardener moved the body (John 20:13–15).
- The women were accused of speaking nonsense, and the men did not believe them (Luke 24:1–11).
- The body was stolen (Matt. 28:11–15).

It was not until after they saw him that they started to understand he had been resurrected. Wright points out that no one at the time expected a resurrected Messiah: "No second-Temple Jewish texts speak of the Messiah being raised from the dead. Nobody would have thought of saying, 'I believe that so-and-so really was the Messiah; therefore he must have been raised from the dead.'" (Wright, RSG, 25) Wright further notes that the Christian belief in the resurrection is a dramatic change, occurring in response to an event that changed the disciples' thinking. "The early Christian worldview [regarding the resurrection of the Messiah Jesus Christ within history] is . . . best understood as a startling, fresh mutation within second-Temple Judaism." (Wright, RSG, 28)

Neither Gentiles nor Jews expected a bodily resurrection of the Messiah. It was an entirely new concept. Their new belief must have been caused by a dramatic event.

3. Conclusion Regarding the Theft Theory

The idea that the disciples would somehow summon the courage to come out of hiding, confront an armed guard, steal the body of their leader, concoct a story of a resurrection, and then base an entire movement on his resurrection and celebrate him as a risen Lord, conqueror of death, is extremely farfetched.

Ironically, this theory has one surprise benefit: the Jewish leaders tacitly acknowledged that the tomb was both known and was empty. Otherwise, why make up a story? Church father John Chrysostom of Antioch calls attention to relevant detail and offers logical inference that provides an apt conclusion to our argument against the theft theory:

> And what mean also the napkins that were stuck on with the myrrh; for Peter saw these lying. For if they had been disposed to steal, they would not have stolen the body naked, not because of dishonoring it only, but in order not to delay and lose time in stripping it, and not to give them that were so disposed opportunity to awake and seize them. Especially when it was myrrh, a drug that adheres so to the body, and cleaves to the clothes, whence it was not easy to take the clothes off the body, but they that did this needed much time, so that from this again, the tale of the theft is improbable. (Chrysostom, HGSM, website)

C. Hallucination Theory
1. Hallucination Definition

Defining a hallucination can be difficult, but in their seminal work on the topic, neuroscientist André Aleman and pyschopathologist Frank Larøi offer what they consider a good working definition:

> A hallucination can be defined as a conscious sensory experience that occurs in the absence of corresponding external stimulation of the relevant sensory organ and has a sufficient sense of reality to resemble a veridical perception. In addition, the subject does not feel

he or she has direct and voluntary control over the experience. (Aleman and Larøi, *Hallucinations*, 23)

By "veridical perception," Aleman and Larøi mean "the accurate perception of what is real." (Aleman and Larøi, *Hallucinations*, 15)

Aleman and Larøi continue analyzing the various types of hallucinations that a person could experience, summarizing that "hallucinations may occur in a number of different modalities (auditory, visual, tactile, olfactory, etc.) and, more rarely, in multiple modalities at the same time." (Aleman and Larøi, *Hallucinations*, 46)

2. Details of the Theory
a. Michael Goulder: Hallucination Theory

Biblical scholar Michael Goulder claims that Peter experienced what he has termed "conversion-visions," hallucinations brought on not by the will or rational thinking, but by some kind of crisis with one's self-image and identity. Given that Peter was already prone to visions (Mark 9:2–7; Acts 10:9–16), Goulder says Peter might also have experienced false perceptions of a risen Jesus. Having concluded that Peter's vision was psychologically caused, Goulder then turns our attention to Paul and claims that somewhere along the way Paul began to entertain doubts regarding his hostile views towards Christians and their movement while simultaneously experiencing a growing distaste for his own Judaism. Goulder cites Galatians 5:1 and Romans 8:15 as support for his views about Paul. Then, Paul succumbed to those thoughts and converted to Christianity after those thoughts caused him to have a hallucination of Jesus.

Goulder further believes that the visions are what best explains the early conversions of the first disciples because he also believes that there were two competing camps within the early Christian church. One camp held to a spiritual resurrection and the other a physical resurrection:

> Belief in Jesus' resurrection does not rest on a fraud. Peter and Paul and the others had genuine conversions which they experienced as visions; in the circumstances of the time, when there was a widespread belief that the Kingdom of God was coming, and that the dead would be raised, these were quite naturally interpreted as evidence that Jesus had risen from the dead. At first people accepted this without much question; but from the 50s and for perhaps a century, two theories were competing in this Church. The Paulines, Mark, Luke and John, elaborated the traditions of the appearances with an empty tomb story, and the details of touching and seeing. But it is now obvious that these were interpretative additions to counter the spiritual theory; [sic] and that neither the eating and touching stories nor the empty tomb story have any basis in the most primitive tradition. So there was no resurrection of Jesus. Psychological explanations are available for the early, appearance traditions; and known intra-ecclesial controversies about the nature of the resurrection explain the Gospel additions. (Goulder, BFV, 58)

Goulder's interpretation denying the resurrection is shaped by his belief that Christian theology was formed through a gradual development that involved "interpretive additions" to what "Peter and Paul and the others . . . experienced as visions." He believes that what we call evidence for the empty tomb and for a physical resurrection were part of these later, invented additions.

b. Gerd Lüdemann: Vision Theory

German atheist and New Testament theologian, Gerd Lüdemann, one of the leading proponents of the hallucination theory, remarked during a debate against Craig:

> At the heart of the Christian religion lies a vision described in Greek by Paul as ōphthē— "he was seen." And Paul himself, who claims to have witnessed an appearance, asserted repeatedly, "I have seen the Lord." So Paul is the main source of the thesis that a vision is the origin of the belief in the resurrection. . . . When we talk about visions, we must include [within that definition] something we experience every night when we dream. That's our subconscious way of dealing with reality. A vision of that sort was at the heart of the Christian religion; and that vision, reinforced by enthusiasm, was contagious and led to many more visions, until we have an "appearance" to more than five hundred people. (Copan and Tacelli, JR, 45)

Lüdemann subtly undermines the very notion of a vision by redefining it as a type of dream, an experience we know to be untrustworthy. In another place, Lüdemann explains Peter's encounter with the risen Jesus as a mixture of reaction to Jesus' sudden death, intense feelings of guilt at his abandoning and denying Jesus, his dependency upon Jesus since he left his livelihood and banked everything on Jesus, and his wish that Jesus were still alive and leading the group:

> Here normal reality controls can break down when the unconscious is unable to bear the loss of a beloved person and creates artificial fulfillments for itself. Judged in this way, however, Peter's vision would be delusion or wishful thinking. Indeed, his vision is an example of unsuccessful mourning, because it abruptly cuts off the very process of mourning, substituting fantasy for unromantic reality. . . . By a bold if unconscious leap Peter entered

the world of his wishes. As a result he "saw" Jesus and thus made it possible for the other disciples to "see" Jesus as well. And if that was not enough, a few years later another Jew, Paul—later missionary to the Gentiles—"saw" Jesus, too, although he had never met him personally. The consequences of this vision have in large measure directed the course of Western civilization for almost two thousand years. (Lüdemann, RC, 165–166)

Essentially, Lüdemann believes Peter was so grief-stricken, guilt-ridden, and dependent upon his relationship with Jesus that he "saw" him and then spread this vision to the other disciples, which resulted in all of them believing that they "saw" Jesus, thus thinking he had risen from the dead. Later on, Paul, in persecuting the Christians, experienced deep psychological tension (as Goulder described above, for Lüdemann is in agreement with him on the source of Paul's vision) that eventually led him to a crisis that precipitated a break with his former outlook, followed by an acceptance of Jesus as the risen Messiah, which further caused him to join up with Peter's group and begin spreading the gospel message to the Gentiles.

3. Response
a. Hallucinations and the Science Behind Them

While arguably the most widely held naturalistic theory for the resurrection, the hallucination theory lacks the most evidential support for its case—more than any of the other theories. Summarizing William Paley, Craig provides five reasons why hallucinations are a poor explanation:

Paley answers the allegations that the resurrection appearances were the result of "religious enthusiasm" (that is, were hallucinations) by arguing that the theory fails on several counts.

First, not just one person but many saw Christ appear. Second, they saw him not individually but together. Third, they saw him appear not just once, but several times. Fourth, they not only saw him, but touched him, conversed with him, and ate with him. Fifth and decisively, the religious enthusiasm hypothesis fails to explain the non-production of the body. It would have been impossible for Jesus' disciples to have believed in their master's resurrection if his corpse still lay in the tomb. But it is equally incredible to suppose that the disciples could have stolen the body and perpetrated a hoax. (Craig, RF, 338)

b. Group Hallucinations Lack Scientific Support

It should be noted that scientific hallucination studies lack data on group hallucination phenomena. Why? Licona reminds us that a hallucination is an internal mental event and observes how unlikely it would be, given the lack of a shared external stimulus, for multiple people to experience the same hallucination. He compares the unlikely group hallucination with the unlikelihood of sharing an identical dream:

Since hallucinations are mental events with no external referent, one cannot share in the hallucination of another. In this sense, hallucinations are similar to dreams. Accordingly I could not awaken my wife in the middle of the night and tell her I am having a dream that I am in Hawaii and then have her return to sleep and join me in my dream where we would enjoy a free vacation. We may both return to sleep and experience dreams of being in Hawaii in which the two of us are present. But it is highly unlikely that we will dream the same dream and have the same conversations in both dreams. (Licona, RJ, 484)

To lend some weight to what he has written regarding group hallucinations, Licona includes some private correspondence from a licensed clinical psychologist who studies this topic and has responded to Licona's inquiries regarding group hallucinations:

> Gary A. Sibcy is a licensed clinical psychologist with a Ph.D. in the subject and has a great interest in whether hallucinations can be shared by groups. He writes, "I have surveyed the professional literature (peer-reviewed journal articles and books) written by psychologists, psychiatrists, and other relevant healthcare professionals during the past two decades and have yet to find a single documented case of a group hallucination, that is, an event for which more than one person purportedly shared in a visual or other sensory perception where there was clearly no external referent." (Licona, RJ, 484)

Not satisfied with just that one opinion, Licona also e-mailed Aleman and Larøi asking the same question:

> After reading the book by Aleman and Larøi, I emailed the authors asking why they did not touch on the issue of collective or group hallucinations. Larøi replied that they had "wished to mention collective hallucinations" in their book but that there is "very little (scientific) documentation on this topic." (Licona, RJ, 484–485)

c. Hallucinations and the Disciples

The question of individual hallucinations remains, and Licona reports that studies of hallucination show that their likelihood increases with factors such as age or grief. Yet very few hallucinations possess the critical visual component that is reported in the New Testament. In terms of which populations, or groups of people, that hallucinations are most likely to affect, Licona summarizes the data from hallucination studies:

> Approximately 15 percent of the general population will experience one or more hallucinations during their lifetime. Females are more likely to experience a hallucination than males. Some personalities are more hallucination-prone than others. And the older one grows, the more likely he or she is to experience a hallucination. Thus it should be of no surprise to learn that senior adults who are grieving the loss of a loved one are among those most likely to experience a hallucination: roughly 50 percent. Yet only 14 percent of these (or seven percent of all bereaved senior adults surveyed) are visual in nature. (Licona, RJ, 483–484)

In short, individual hallucinations are real, and people can experience them. However, group hallucinations are something entirely different, and there appears to be no recorded scientific evidence to support the idea that people experience group hallucinations, much less that the disciples and Jesus' other followers did so in this case. Licona highlights this deficiency nicely:

> Although grief, life-threatening stress and fatigue can contribute to an emotional state where a hallucination may result, the reality of such a proposal [for the case of the disciples] is initially problematic since each of the Twelve were males who probably belonged to various age groups and almost certainly possessed different personality types. Far more punishing to such a proposal, however, is the requirement of mind-boggling coincidences. Despite the fact that hallucinations are experienced by roughly 15 percent of the general population and a much larger 50 percent of recently bereaved senior adults (only 14 percent of which are visual in nature), an incredible 100 percent of the Twelve would have experienced a hallucination of the risen Jesus (rather than something else such as guards), simultaneously, in the same

mode (visual) and perhaps in multiple modes. It would be an understatement to claim that such a proposal has only a meager possibility of reflecting what actually occurred. Embracing it would require an extraordinary amount of faith. (Licona, RJ, 484–485)

Philosophers Peter Kreeft and Ronald Tacelli offer thirteen reasons why the hallucination theory cannot be considered a reliable or reasonable naturalistic explanation for the resurrection.

1. There were too many witnesses. Hallucinations are private, individual, subjective. Christ appeared to Mary Magdalene, to the disciples minus Thomas, to the disciples including Thomas, to the two disciples at Emmaus, to the fishermen on the shore, to James . . . , and even to five hundred people at once (1 Cor 15:3–8). Even three different witnesses are enough for a kind of psychological trigonometry; over five hundred is about as public as you can wish. And Paul says in this passage (v. 6) that most of the five hundred are still alive, inviting any reader to check the truth of the story by questioning the eyewitnesses—he could never have done this and gotten away with it, given the power, resources and numbers of his enemies, if it were not true.

2. The witnesses were qualified. They were simple, honest, moral people who had firsthand knowledge of the facts.

3. The five hundred saw Christ together, at the same time and place. This is even more remarkable than five hundred private "hallucinations" at different times and places of the same Jesus. Five hundred separate Elvis sightings may be dismissed, but if five hundred simple fishermen in Maine saw, touched and talked with him at once, in the same town, that would be a different matter.

4. Hallucinations usually last a few seconds or minutes; rarely hours. This one hung around for forty days (Acts 1:3).

5. Hallucinations usually happen only once, except to the insane. This one returned many times, to ordinary people (Jn 20:19–21:14; Acts 1:3).

6. Hallucinations come from within, from what we already know, at least unconsciously. This one said and did surprising and unexpected things (Act 1:4, 9)—like a real person and unlike a dream.

7. Not only did the disciples not expect this, they didn't even believe it at first—neither Peter, nor the women, nor Thomas, nor the eleven. They thought he was a ghost; he had to eat something to prove he was not (Lk 24:36–43).

8. Hallucinations do not eat. The resurrected Christ did, on at least two occasions (Lk 24:42–43; Jn 21:1–14).

9. The disciples touched him (Mt 28:9; Lk 24:39; Jn 20:27).

10. They also spoke with him, and he spoke back. Figments of your imagination do not hold profound, extended conversations with you, unless you have the kind of mental disorder that isolates you. But this "hallucination" conversed with at least eleven people at once, for forty days (Acts 1:3).

11. The apostles could not have believed in the "hallucination" if Jesus' corpse had still been in the tomb. This is a very simple and telling point; for if it was a hallucination, where was the corpse? They would have checked for it; if it was there, they could not have believed.

12. If the apostles had hallucinated and then spread their hallucinogenic story, the Jews would have stopped it by producing the body—unless the disciples had stolen it, in which case we are back with the conspiracy theory and all its difficulties.

13. A hallucination would explain only the post-resurrection appearances; it would not explain the empty tomb, the rolled-away stone, or the inability to produce the corpse. No theory can explain all these data except a real resurrection. (Kreeft and Tacelli, HCA, 186–88)

4. Conclusion Regarding the Hallucination Theory

In short, one or two individuals might have had a hallucination. But when it comes to group hallucinations, things become quite problematic. First, as we have just seen, no scientific data exists to support such a claim. Second, the chances of individuals having identical subjective, internal dreamlike experiences called hallucinations where they share the same experience is beyond unlikely.

It seems far more reasonable and plausible that the disciples had real-life experiences with the risen Jesus. There was an external referent (the physical body and person of Jesus) to which they could all attribute a shared experience rather than flimsy subjective hallucinations lacking any such community event. Moreover, those best in a position to have charged the disciples with hallucinations and seeing ghosts would have been the high priests, but instead they accused the disciples with theft of the body. This indicates that the high priests must have investigated and found the body to be missing and knew that claiming the disciples hallucinated would not have fit the facts.

D. Wrong Tomb Theory

The wrong tomb theory holds that those who went to the tomb Sunday morning to pay their respects to Jesus went to the wrong tomb, and when they found it empty, they mistook this for Jesus' resurrection.

1. Details of the Theory

Professor Kirsopp Lake, one of the initiators of this theory, surmises that the women did not know where Jesus was buried and mistakenly went to the wrong tomb. As a result of arriving at an empty tomb, they were convinced that Jesus had resurrected.

2. Response

Habermas and Licona list six major problems with the wrong tomb theory that ultimately cause it to fail:

1. Even if the disciples went to the wrong tomb, this does not account for their belief that they had *seen* the risen Jesus.
2. The testimony of the Gospels is that the empty tomb convinced no one but John. Mary concluded that the gardener stole the body. The disciples did not believe upon seeing the empty tomb, but rather were confused.
3. The church persecutor Paul converted based on the appearance of the risen Jesus, not on an empty tomb. Paul would have assumed that someone had stolen the body or that the wrong tomb was visited.
4. The skeptic James would not have been convinced merely by an empty tomb. Like Paul, James was convinced by an appearance.
5. No sources support the wrong tomb theory. If the women and disciples had gone to the wrong tomb, all that the Roman and Jewish authorities would have had to do would have been to go to the right tomb, exhume the body, publicly display it, and clear up the misunderstanding. Yet, not a single critic is recorded to have even thought of this explanation for the Resurrection during the first few centuries of Christianity.
6. The evidence suggests that the tomb's location was known, because a well-known

man, Joseph of Arimathea, buried Jesus in his own tomb. If the burial by Joseph was an invention, then we might expect ancient critics to state that Joseph denied this version of the story. Or the critics could have denied the existence of Joseph if he had been a fictitious character. (Habermas and Licona, CRJ, 97–98)

Geza Vermes, a skeptical scholar who considers the resurrection to be an apparition, nevertheless highlights some of the inadequacies of the wrong tomb theory:

Matthew, Mark, and Luke firmly stress that the Galilean women knew where Jesus was buried. While all the cowardly male disciples kept out of sight, the two Marys (Mk and Mt) or the Galilean women (Lk) watched the burial party led by Joseph of Arimathea (Mk 15:47; Mt 27:61; Lk 23:55). Bearing in mind the attitude of male superiority adopted by the apostles on hearing the report of female witnesses about the empty tomb (Lk 24:11), it strikes as most likely that they suspected that Mary Magdalene and her friends had gone to the wrong tomb. If the rock cavity into which the corpse of Jesus was hurriedly laid was freshly prepared to house someone else's remains, no doubt it was in a location reserved for burials with similar tombs surrounding it. In the semidarkness of dawn mistake was easy. A present-day reader would wonder why Peter and his colleagues, who considered the women untrustworthy, did not consult Joseph of Arimathea, who was apparently the owner of the tomb (Mt 27:60). Presumably the answer is that, in the logic of the Gospel narrative, the apparitions of Jesus soon rendered such an inquiry superfluous. The theory of mistaken identity of the tomb, while not inconceivable, certainly does not impose itself. (Vermes, *Resurrection*, 144)

3. Conclusion Regarding the Wrong Tomb Theory

The wrong tomb theory simply fails to account for the known evidence. In fact, it ignores nearly all the available evidence. And it constructs the theory entirely according to a preconceived notion. Moreover, this theory fails to provide any solid explanation for how or why Paul or James would have come to believe in Jesus as the Messiah. It also fails to explain how the idea of the resurrection became central to the apostles' early preaching and teaching and such a core doctrine in the early Christian church and faith.

E. Family Tomb Theory

The family tomb theory, also known as the Talpiot tomb theory, became a media sensation with the release in 2007 of a book and a documentary film presenting it. This theory claims that Jesus was reburied in the family tomb at Talpiot, five kilometers south of Jerusalem, after spending the Sabbath buried in Joseph of Arimathea's tomb.

1. Details of the Theory
a. Brief History of the Talpiot Tomb

The Talpiot tomb is claimed to be the family tomb of Jesus of Nazareth. It is further claimed to be his final resting space after a rushed burial on the day of his death, done in order not to violate the Sabbath by handling and burying a corpse after the Sabbath began at sundown. According to this view, Joseph of Arimathea's tomb was temporary, and Jesus' body was moved prior to the women coming to Joseph's tomb to complete the burial process. We are not told who moved the body for reburial.

How did the Talpiot tomb come to be linked with Jesus of Nazareth and his family, and why is it thought to have been Jesus' final resting place? Charles Quarles, professor of

New Testament and Greek and the Division of Christian Studies Chair at Louisiana College, details the beginning of the media feeding frenzy:

On February 25, 2007, a newswire announced a press conference to be held in New York City at 11:00 AM on February 26 in which bone boxes believed to have belonged to Jesus of Nazareth and Mary Magdalene would be dramatically unveiled. The press release advertised a documentary titled *The Lost Tomb of Jesus* that would air on Sunday, March 4, on the Discovery Channel. The documentary was produced by James Cameron, the award-winning director of the film *Titanic*, and was directed by Simcha Jacobovici, the popular host of the History Channel's *Naked Archaeologist*. The release also contained a brief mention of a book written by Jacobovici and Charles Pellegrino titled *The Jesus Family Tomb*. . . . The next day reporters from all over the world flocked to the main branch of the New York Public Library for the conference. Perhaps inspired by the Academy Awards from the night before, Oscar-winning filmmaker James Cameron and Emmy award-winning director Simcha Jacobovici put on a show that would make P. T. Barnum green with envy. Cameron began the session with an announcement of the remarkable discovery after which security guards lifted crushed black velvet sheets to unveil two ossuaries that dazzled viewers as they reflected the brilliant lights of the television cameras. (Quarles, BHRS, 1)

Quarles summarizes the argument made for the significance of the Talpiot tomb:

James Tabor, chair of the Department of Religious Studies at the University of North Carolina in Charlotte . . . and Charles

Pellegrino . . . joined Cameron and Jacobovici in explaining the significance of the ossuaries. They argued that the original archaeological team that had excavated the tomb in Talpiot where the ten ossuaries were found dismissed the significance of the ossuary with the inscription "Jesus, son of Joseph" because of the popularity of the names Joseph and Jesus in Palestine in the ossuary period. The mistake of the original team was that they failed to consider the names in the other ossuary inscriptions in the group which were associated with Jesus in the New Testament Gospels. The ossuaries purportedly bear such inscriptions as "Jesus, son of Joseph," "Judah, son of Jesus," "Matthew," "Mary the master," "Mary," and "Jose [or Joseh]" (a diminutive form of Joseph). Jacobovici argued that "Mary the master" was Mary Magdalene, the wife of Jesus, and that this point was confirmed by DNA analysis. "Jose" was a brother of Jesus mentioned in the Gospel of Mark. "Mary" was the mother of Jesus. The investigators also claimed that a new method called "patina fingerprinting" demonstrated that the controversial James ossuary bearing the inscription "James, son of Joseph, brother of Jesus" was stolen from the Talpiot tomb. Tabor compared the likelihood of finding the names George, John, Paul, and Ringo in closely connected tombs in Liverpool. Just as the pool of names in the Liverpool tomb would suggest that the men buried there were Beatles, the pool of names from the Talpiot tomb strongly suggested that this was the family tomb of Jesus. (Quarles, BHRS, 2)

It is important to note that the Talpiot tomb had originally been excavated in 1980, twenty-seven years prior to this media announcement, and was fairly well known in the academic literature, so these ossuaries were not new to archaeologists.

b. The Names on the Talpiot Tomb Ossuaries (Claimed as the Family of Jesus)

Evans summarizes the history of the tomb's discovery, looting, contents, and claims that it should be regarded as the final resting place of Jesus of Nazareth and his family:

> The tomb was uncovered by a construction crew in 1980 and before Amos Kloner and his team could excavate it properly it was looted and vandalized. In the tomb were ten ossuaries (or bone boxes), six with inscriptions. Some seventeen skeletons were in the ossuaries and another eighteen or so were lying on niches (or shelves) or scattered about on the floor. Many of the bones were broken or crushed into powder. Coins, pottery, and other artifacts were apparently stolen by looters. Among the inscriptions on the ossuaries, we find the following names:
>
> - Jesus(?), son of Joseph [The inscription is only partially legible. It has been interpreted as "Yeshua bar Yehosef."]
> - Mariamne Mara
> - Maria
> - Matia
> - Judah, son of Jesus
> - Joseh [or Jose]

Jacobovici and Cameron think most, if not all, of these names belong to people in the New Testament. *Jesus* (or Yeshua) refers to Jesus of Nazareth. *Mariamne Mara* refers to Mary Magdalene, *Mara* refers to Mary the mother of Jesus, *Matia* refers to Matthew, *Joseh* refers to Jesus' brother Joses, and *Judah, son of Jesus* (who may not be mentioned in the New Testament)—some suggest—may be the "disciple whom Jesus loved," mentioned in the Gospel of John. They also wonder if the James Ossuary, which is of uncertain provenance, originally came from the Talpiot Tomb. The James Ossuary has an inscription, which reads: "James, son of Joseph, brother of Jesus." If the James Ossuary is added to the other ossuaries of the Talpiot Tomb, then the statistical chances that it is indeed the family tomb of Jesus are increased. So go the claims and the argument. (Evans, TJF, website)

From these various ossuaries with inscriptions, James Tabor concludes that it is "possible-to-likely" that the Talpiot tomb is that of the Jesus of Nazareth family. But if the supposition is correct that the James Ossuary was also in the Talpiot Tomb, then Tabor thinks this would make the identification "close to certain." (Habermas, STT, 18–19)

c. Summary of the Investigation's Further Proposed Evidence

With regard to the DNA sample testing that was conducted, the following claim was given in the film:

> Steven Cox, a forensic scientist, collected samples of residue from the Jesus and Mariamne ossuaries for testing by the Thunder Bay Paleo-DNA lab. The narrator explained: "If these bone samples truly do belong to Mary Magdalene and Jesus of Nazareth, we would expect the tests to show that they are not genetically related. We would expect to find DNA representing two individuals with no familial ties. And that would be an extremely rare discovery in a family tomb unless the individuals were husband and wife." Unfortunately, the lab could not recover nuclear DNA from the samples. It was, however, able to recover, amplify, clone, and sequence the mitochondrial DNA. Comparisons of the Jesus and Mariamne DNA sequences highlighted several polymorphisms or variations between the sequences that demonstrated conclusively that this Jesus

and Mariamne were not maternally related and were "most likely husband and wife." (Quarles, BHRS, 14)

With regard to the "patina fingerprinting" analysis, we get the following claim:

The researchers submitted the James ossuary and Mariamne ossuary to a test that they called "patina fingerprinting." They analyzed the chemical composition of the patina for the two ossuaries and compared these to random samples. Of the ossuaries analyzed, the Mariamne ossuary and the James ossuary had the most similar patina. Pelegrino [sic] exclaimed, "The signature is the same! It matches!" (Quarles, BHRS, 15)

The following claims are made about the James Ossuary:

The researchers claimed that the highly debated James ossuary, which bears an inscription reading, "James, son of Joseph, brother of Jesus," is indeed authentic and is in fact a missing ossuary from the Talpiot tomb. The researchers claimed that only 9 of the 10 ossuaries of Talpiot were actually delivered to the Rockefeller Museum. Tabor claimed to have compared the dimensions of the James ossuary and the missing but catalogued tenth ossuary and stated: "The dimensions of the ossuary are the same!" He admitted that the Israel Antiquities Authority ruled that the original inscription was "James, son of Joseph" and that the words "brother of Jesus" were a later forgery. But he suggested that the evidence supported the claim that the James ossuary was from the Tomb of the Ten Ossuaries. He stated, "We are speculating but the time is right, the name is right, and that I think would make it fairly clear that this is the Jesus family." (Quarles, BHRS, 14–15)

With regard to the one ossuary from the Talpiot tomb that had the inscription "Judah, son of Jesus," the film makes the following claim:

Finally, the film discussed ossuary 80.501. The inscription on the ossuary reads, "Judah, son of Jesus." Based on the assumption that Jesus was married to Mary Magdalene, the narrator claimed: "The NT doesn't say that Jesus had a son. But perhaps in this instance, archaeology forces us to throw a different light on the NT." The silence of the New Testament regarding the existence of a son of Jesus could be easily explained. Since Jesus died a criminal's death, had claimed to be a king, and his son would be born of this royal bloodline, Judas's existence would have been kept a secret for his own protection from the Roman authorities. The book and the film both speculate: "Perhaps the unnamed Beloved Disciple referred to in the Book of John is actually the son of Jesus who remains unnamed in the text to conceal the child's lineage." Although John 19:6 has been traditionally interpreted as Jesus' words to Mary his mother and the apostle John, the film suggested that Jesus was actually addressing Mary Magdalene and Judas and cryptically urging Mary to protect their son. On the other hand, the narrator admitted that the presence of a son in the tomb might preclude the tomb from belonging to Jesus of Nazareth. (Quarles, BHRS, 15–16)

d. James Tabor's Overall Conclusion

The argument for the Talpiot tomb belonging to Jesus and his family states that because six of the ten ossuaries have names like those in the New Testament, then they must refer to Jesus of Nazareth and his family members. But does this have to be the case? It is worth noting that James Tabor has a naturalistic bias against any supernatural event as the cause for the empty tomb, and thus is predisposed to particular conclusions about the Talpiot tomb. He clearly states his assumptions:

> Women do not get pregnant without a male—ever. So Jesus had a human father, whether we can identify him or not. Dead bodies don't rise—not if one is clinically dead—as Jesus surely was after Roman crucifixion and three days in a tomb. So if the tomb was empty the historical conclusion is simple—Jesus' body was moved by someone and likely reburied in another location. (Tabor, JD, 233–234)

2. Response
a. Problems with New Claims About the Talpiot Tomb

Evans disagrees with the conclusions of Tabor, Jacobovici, and Cameron, and he explains why:

> There are several problems with this radical and new interpretation of the Talpiot Tomb. *First*, the name *Jesus* in the "Jesus(?), son of Joseph" inscription is far from certain. Some experts think it is actually a different name.... They are unsure of the reading. If the first name is not Yeshua (or Jesus), then the new theory collapses.... *Secondly*, almost no one agrees that the name *Mariamne* refers to Mary Magdalene, or that *Mara* means "Lady" or "Master," as though it were a title of honor. It is, rather, an abbreviation of Martha, which is attested in other inscriptions.... *Thirdly*, the reading *Joseh*, said to agree with the name of Jesus' brother given in Mark 6:3; 15:40, 47 is also problematic. The spelling probably should be vocalized *Josah*. If so, we have yet another inconsistency with attempts to identify these names with the known names of members of Jesus' family. *Fourthly*, the James Ossuary was in circulation in the 1970s, before the

Talpiot Tomb was discovered. It is therefore highly unlikely that it was originally from this tomb. .... *Fifthly*, the DNA taken from bone fragments in the "Jesus(?), son of Joseph" ossuary and the "Mariamne" ossuary proves very little. Tests show that the man and the woman were not related by blood (and therefore were not brother and sister). It is not warranted to infer from this they must have been married. .... *Sixthly*, the names, "Jesus," "Mary," "Judah," and "Joseph" were very common among Jews of the New Testament era. The presence of these names—even in one multi-generation tomb—means very little. .... And finally, there are no Christian markings or inscriptions in the Talpiot Tomb. Moreover, there is no indication that this tomb was ever venerated or visited by pilgrims. .... Absence of such evidence argues against identifying the Talpiot Tomb as the Tomb of the Family of Jesus. It might also be added that surely Jesus' family and followers ... would not inscribe Jesus' ossuary simply as "Jesus, son of Joseph." We would expect "Messiah" or the Aramaic "Lord," or "Son of God." (Evans, TJF, website)

Evans is not alone in his opposition to the theory. Over a dozen prominent and responsible scholars who participated in the Princeton Theological Seminary Symposium held in Jerusalem in 2008 to discuss the Talpiot Tomb have protested that their contributions to the conference were misrepresented by Jacobovici and Cameron. Evans mentions this authoritative consensus in his own evaluation of the theory:

> All of these factors taken together make the theory proposed by Jacobovici and Cameron very doubtful. For these reasons and others, recognized historians and archaeologists do not think that the Talpiot Tomb is the Tomb

of the Family of Jesus and that Jesus himself was buried there. In my view, it is a most unlikely theory and will not be embraced by competent archaeologists and scholars. (Evans, TJF, website)

In spite of widespread scholarly caution and dismissal of the theory, however, a great many people have been influenced by this media sensation. So we include below some further specific responses to the key issues: the names, the DNA testing, the patina fingerprinting, the James ossuary, contradictions with known burial practices of poor families, and the selective editing used in the film.

i) The Names on the Ossuaries Are Common Family Names

Much of this debate centers on the ossuaries and the names inscribed on them. In regard to the names found on the ossuaries, Quarles writes:

Amos Kloner, Frank Moore Cross, and David Mevorah, curator of the Israel Museum, insisted that the names of Talpiot are all common names. Mevorah adamantly insisted, "We find that these names are in many other places. So suggesting that this tomb was the tomb of the family of Jesus is a far-fetched suggestion. You need to be very careful with that." (Quarles, BHRS, 11)

ii) The DNA Evidence Argument Is Based on a Questionable Assumption

When it comes to the film's claims about the DNA being able to identify Jesus and Mariamne as husband and wife, Quarles brings up the following counterpoint:

This claim involves a huge assumption. The DNA evidence is consistent with a number of other possible family relationships. For example, Mariamne could have been a half sister, sister-in-law, cousin, or aunt from the father's side, rather than the wife of Jesus of the ossuary. (Quarles, BHRS, 14)

iii) The Patina Fingerprinting Analysis Is Not Conclusive

In response to the "patina fingerprinting" analysis that was conducted:

[Ted] Koppel read another statement by Robert Genna, director of the Suffolk County Crime Laboratory, which had conducted the tests on the patina of the Mariamne ossuary and James ossuary that were used to claim that the two ossuaries originated in the same tomb. The statement included a serious disclaimer: The elemental composition of some of the samples we tested from the ossuaries are consistent with each other. But I would never say that they're a match. . . . No scientist would ever say definitely that one ossuary came from the same tomb as another. . . . We didn't do enough sampling to see if in fact there were other tombs that had similar elemental compositions. . . . The only samples that we can positively say are a "match" from a single source are fingerprints and DNA. (Quarles, BHRS, 17–18)

iv) The James Ossuary Is Not from the Talpiot Tomb

Beyond what Evans says, Quarles points out the professional competence that stands behind Kloner's denial that the James ossuary belongs to the tomb, as opposed to Tabor's inclusion of it:

Amos Kloner was quoted as insisting that the tenth ossuary . . . could not be the James ossuary, which bore a clear inscription. Tabor suggested that Kloner missed the inscription.

[Jonathan] Reed denied that an archaeologist of Kloner's competence would have overlooked the inscription. (Quarles, BHRS, 18)

v) The Tomb Contradicts the Gospel Accounts and the Burial Practices of the Poor

Quarles refers to Jodi Magness, the non-Christian archaeologist whom we cited in our earlier discussion of first-century rock-cut tombs:

Magness argued that if Jesus' body were given a second burial by His disciples, as Jacobovici claimed, the disciples would have dug a rectangular trench in the earth, placed Jesus' enshrouded body in the grave, and then marked the grave with a crude headstone. Magness insisted that ossuaries were associated only with rock-cut tombs, never with trench graves. Thus, one would not expect to find an ossuary of Jesus of Nazareth even if one dismissed the Gospel claims of Jesus' resurrection. Magness also argued that since Jesus' family had no known connections to Jerusalem, His body would likely have been buried in Galilee along with other family members rather than in Jerusalem. (Quarles, BHRS, 7–8)

Magness, writes:

The identification of the Talpiyot tomb as the tomb of Jesus and his family contradicts the canonical Gospel accounts of the death and burial of Jesus and the earliest Christian traditions about Jesus. This claim is also inconsistent with all of the available information—historical and archaeological—about how Jews in the time of Jesus buried their dead, and specifically the evidence we have about poor, non-Judean families like that of Jesus. It is a sensationalistic claim without any scientific basis or support. (Magness, HTJBD, website)

vi) The Film Editing Is Selective

In responding to the overall slant of the film, Quarles points out the protests of the experts:

[Ted] Koppel observed that several of the experts who were interviewed in the program felt that their comments had been mishandled and that some were angered by the film. Koppel read a statement by Carney Matheson of the Lakehead University Paleo-DNA Laboratory in which he denied that the DNA evidence proved that the persons in the Jesus and Mariamne ossuaries were husband and wife as Jacobovici had claimed and noted that several other family relationships were possible. (Quarles, BHRS, 17)

William Dever, professor of Near Eastern Archaeology at the University of Arizona, who had retired in 2002, also commented on the slight-of-hand editing done by the film team:

It's a very clever film. I think it will be persuasive to millions of people. . . . I noticed that many of the experts are quoted out of context. I can assure you that Frank Cross, who was my own teacher and who read the inscriptions for you and confirmed your reading, does not agree with you, and I noticed that he was carefully edited out just when he finished the reading, which was convenient for you. (Dever, quoted in Quarles, BHRS, 17)

Jonathan Reed, a professor of religion at the University of La Verne and coauthor of *Excavating Jesus: Beneath the Stones, Behind the Texts*, made the following strongly worded comment regarding the film:

It's what I call "archaeoporn." It's very exciting, it's titillating. You want to watch it. But deep down you know it's wrong. . . . It's not the kind of thing that a long-lasting relationship is made up of and that's the relationship between science, archaeology, and the Bible. (quoted in Quarles, BHRS, 16–17)

William Dever also provided his thoughts on the entire matter:

I think I'm open minded. I'm certainly not trying to defend the Christian tradition. I'm not a believer. As I've said to the press, I've no dog in this fight. I'm trying to be a good scholar and an honest historian and stick with the facts and not go beyond them. One of the problems that I have with this whole project is that it puts archaeology in a rather bad light. . . . For me it represents the worst kind of biblical archaeology even if its [sic] antibiblical because it seems to me that the conclusions are already drawn in the beginning. . . . I think that the argument goes far beyond any reasonable interpretation. (quoted in Quarles, BHRS, 16)

Quarles is convinced this is not Jesus' family tomb, and he sums up the case of the Talpiot tomb by calling for a patient examination of all the evidence:

If its claim were convincing, *The Jesus Family Tomb* could constitute the death certificate of Christianity. But it won't. Jacobovici and Pellegrino are simply not qualified coroners. They are more like little children who scream "Mommy is dead!" because they see her lying down with her eyes closed even though she is really only napping. The arguments of Jacobovici and Pellegrino are filled with similar leaps in logic that bypass important evidence that a qualified coroner would never overlook. A close examination of all the evidence will lead those concerned by the children's screams to end the panicked 911 call abruptly: "Sorry. False alarm. The Christian faith is alive and well after all." (Quarles, BHRS, ix)

b. Conclusion

All of this taken together ultimately paints a rather bleak picture for the Talpiot tomb hypothesis. It seems to be nothing more than a media and book-selling blitz that sets aside real, honest scholarship in order to garner television ratings, and book and video sales. Scholars across the ideological spectrum have denounced the Talpiot tomb theory, seeing it for what it is: style over substance.

F. Conclusion Regarding Naturalistic Explanations for the Empty Tomb

Clearly, naturalistic explanations fail in multiple ways. First, they rarely account for all the facts. Second, they are largely speculative, either lacking evidential support or relying on support of inferior quality and of a late date, that is, so long after the events that error becomes likely. These theories are usually put forward by those who hold an antisupernatural worldview. Given the failure of naturalism to explain the facts of the resurrection, the best explanation, given all the facts, is that the resurrection of Jesus happened just as the historical record indicates.

William Lane Craig sums it up well:

We have seen that multiple lines of historical evidence indicate that Jesus' tomb was found empty on a Sunday morning by a group of his women followers. Furthermore, no convincing natural explanation is available to account for this fact. This alone might prompt us to believe that the resurrection of Jesus is the best explanation. (Craig, RF, 377)

VIII. Conclusion: He Is Risen; He Is Risen Indeed!

We believe that the resurrection is true, and the accounts of it have provided adequate evidence to certify it as a real event. The importance of the resurrection to the faith of the believer and the life of the church cannot be overstated. The apostle Paul suspends the entire weight of Christianity on the single thread of the historical resurrection of Jesus of Nazareth:

> *If Christ has not been raised, then our preaching is vain, your faith also is vain. . . . If Christ has not been raised, your faith is worthless; you are still in your sins. . . . If we have hoped in Christ in this life only, we are of all men most to be pitied.* — 1 Corinthians 15:14, 17, 19 NASB

Paul is clear: to lose the resurrection is to lose Christianity. As the resurrection goes, so goes Christianity. This is what makes this subject not just interesting but vitally important. Even the skeptics do not go so far as to deny the effects of the resurrection (the existence of the church and of the new first-century meanings of baptism and communion as central sacramental rites). When they contest the recorded facts describing the burial and the empty tomb; or the narratives of the radically changed lives of the disciples after seeing the risen Jesus; or the immediate and amazing conversions of more than 3,000 on the Day of Pentecost, of James, of Paul, and others named throughout the New Testament; their conclusions and claims spring from prior underlying assumptions. What the skeptics ultimately have an issue with is the supernatural component and the theological implications of the resurrection.

Both the skeptic and the Christian believe that dead people do not come back to life via natural means. This is why the skeptic must spend time coming up with alternate theories to explain the effects and the facts of the resurrection. On the other hand, the Christian is able to point to a supernatural event as the clear and only viable explanation for the fact and effects of the resurrection: God raised Jesus from the dead. This is why a Christian burial service used for centuries and in many places around the globe can speak of the "sure and certain hope of the resurrection to eternal life through our Lord Jesus Christ." (*The Book of Common Prayer*, 485, 501, bcponline.org)

While a single alternate theory might be capable of explaining just one piece of evidence, none of the alternate theories can account for all the evidence. This is what leads Habermas and Licona to list four reasons why simply stitching various alternate theories together fails to give the skeptic what he or she wants: a purely naturalistic explanation of the effects and facts:

> At least four major problems beset all combination theories. First, combinations of theories generally lead to higher *improbability*, not a more probable solution. If a combination theory is to be true, all of its subtheories must be true. If one is not, then the theory fails to account adequately for all the data. If one subtheory fails, the combination fails. . . . Second, while combination theories do a better job of accounting for more of the data, many of the problems that are present when considered individually remain when considered together. . . . Third, it ends up sounding *ad hoc*. Even if there were no remaining problems, five component theories must be employed in order to account for the data. . . . So it appears that the theory was contrived to make everything fit. . . . Fourth, even if no problems remained and no signs of

an *ad hoc* component were present, the mere stating of an opposing theory does nothing to prove that this is what really happened. The burden lies on the shoulders of the one with the opposing theory to demonstrate that this is not only possible but that each component is a probable explanation of the facts. (Habermas and Licona, CRJ, 120–121)

Employing careful historical analysis and probability theory, philosopher Richard Swinburne concludes, "It is indeed very probable that Jesus was God Incarnate who rose from the dead." (Swinburne, RGI, 215)

In closing, William Lane Craig helpfully reminds us that "the Christian faith is based on the *event* of the resurrection. It is not based on the *evidence* for the resurrection." (Craig, SR, 7) Given all we that we know about the resurrection as a historical event, we must conclude with all those across the centuries who placed their confidence in the resurrected Christ and found their lives transformed: Christ is risen! He is risen indeed!

CHAPTER 11

IS CHRISTIANITY A COPYCAT RELIGION?

OVERVIEW

I. Introduction

As a young man growing up in a Christian home, I (Sean) had little reason to question the teachings of my parents. Christianity made sense, and I knew my parents loved me and wanted the best for me. But when I entered college, I encountered new and challenging people and ideas. One idea, which completely caught me off guard, was the idea that Christianity was borrowed from ancient pagan mystery religions. In other words, Christianity was nothing more than a patchwork of pagan and mystery religions stitched together to create a copycat religion.

This objection was one factor that spun me into a mild faith crisis. Now I can look back and see the frivolity of this objection, but at the time it was quite unsettling. And I was certainly not alone in wondering whether Christianity is really true. This same idea and ideas like it have been popularized in movies such as *Zeitgeist, The Da Vinci Code,* and *Religulous.* In fact, *Religulous* states it this way:

Written in 1280 BC, the Egyptian Book of the Dead describes a god, Horus. Horus is the son of the god Osiris born to a virgin mother. He was baptized in a river by Anup the Baptizer who was later beheaded. Like Jesus, Horus was tempted while alone in the desert, healed the sick, the blind, cast out demons, and walked on water. He raised Asar from the dead. "Asar" translates to "Lazarus." Oh yeah, he also had 12 disciples. Yes, Horus was crucified first and after 3 days, two women announced Horus the savior of humanity had been resurrected.*

While it is tempting to write off these works as inconsequential, the ideas they peddle continue to have sweeping influence. The cover of Dan Brown's book claims it has sold more than eighty million copies. Copycat arguments appear frequently on the Internet. We regularly receive questions about this objection from both students and adults. Although the "mythicist" position is almost entirely rejected in academic circles, it continues to have an influence on the wider public and warrants a response.

II. Background: Religious Plagiarism?

The regions surrounding the Mediterranean world gave birth to several mystery religions and cults. In broad terms, these religions can be divided into two groups: (1) state or civil religions, which achieved a certain level of cult status, and (2) private, or individualistic, religions. Philosopher Ronald Nash provides a quick sketch of the mystery religions:

Out of Greece came the cults of Demeter and Dionysus, as well as their later developments, the Eleusinian and Orphic mystery religions. Asia Minor (more specifically, the region known as Phrygia) gave birth to the cult of Cybele and Attis. The cult of Isis and Osiris (later Serapis) originated in Egypt, while Syria and Palestine saw the rise of the cult of Adonis. Finally, Persia (Iran) was a leading early locale for the cult of Mithras. (Nash, GG, 106)

Because these religions were practiced during the formative years of Christianity, questions arose: Did early Christians copy or borrow certain rituals and key concepts from these pagan religions and weave them into Christianity in order to make their religion more appealing to potential converts? Did Christianity plagiarize these mystery religions? Are there any aspects genuinely unique to Christianity? An exploration of these questions became a factor in the conversions to Christianity of two major figures of the twentieth century, T. S. Eliot and C. S. Lewis.

The charge that Christianity plagiarized from surrounding pagan religions came to the fore in the late nineteenth century and became prominent in academic circles at the turn of the twentieth century. In 1890 Sir James G. Fraser, a cultural anthropologist, first published *The Golden Bough*, a study of the similarities among ancient religions (especially Eastern Mediterranean examples) that worshiped a mythical god who died each year at harvest along with the vegetation and then revived with the new planting of the next agricultural cycle. Ceremonies were meant to hurry and celebrate his reviving and return. According to Fraser, among some

---

* *Religulous*, Larry Charles, Santa Monica: Lionsgate, 2008. The text is superimposed over the film roughly between 53–57 minutes into the film. Also, to help reinforce the text, The Bangles' "Walk Like an Egyptian" is playing in the background at this point in the film.

of these pagan groups, a "fisher-king" was thought of as the incarnation of the god, so he also would decline in vitality. King, god, and the land all needed reviving. Fraser's book raised an outcry, for it included Christianity among the dying-and-rising-god religions. Yet Fraser expanded the book in later editions (1900 and then 1906–15, when it had grown to twelve volumes), which suggests the general interest in the book and its impact upon the academic community. The publication dates reflect the new century's confidence (in concert with Fraser) that science would eclipse religion, providing wonderful new inventions for comfort and mobility and entertainment. The thought was that cultural interests could eclipse Christianity. Jessie Weston popularized Fraser's study of the patterns shared by these religions with her argument that the tales of King Arthur and the Grail were the link between ancient pagan rituals and Christian teaching about the role of Christ and communion. (She declared in *From Ritual to Romance* that the Grail—the cup used by Christ at the Last Supper—had its origins in fertility symbols from these ancient religions.) So Christianity came to be viewed as a weak copycat religion to people delighted by the new century's inventions and global empires. World War I rocked that confidence, and the poet T. S. Eliot describes the bleak aftermath of the war in *The Waste Land*, a poem that weaves together the postwar jazz and city gossip with layers of history and echoes of these ancient myths (such as the cult of Adonis, but also adding in some Buddhist and Hindu tales). Further, he includes many fragmentary quotations from the Old and New Testaments as well as imagery that alludes to events described in Scripture, such as the exodus and Jesus' arrest in Gethsemane. Eliot was asking what a person might believe—and he presented the situation so vividly that students at Oxford University are said to have declaimed on the street memorized passages of the poem soon after it was published. Five years later, Eliot was baptized as a Christian. Since that fascination a century ago, the idea that Christianity has plagiarized from surrounding pagan religions has been largely rejected by the academic community, but it still hangs around as a vague idea in popular culture.

Nash observes:

> During a period of time running roughly from about 1890–1940, scholars often alleged that primitive Christianity had been heavily influenced by Platonism, Stoicism, the pagan mystery religions, or other movements in the Hellenistic world. Largely as a result of a series of scholarly books and articles written in rebuttal, allegations of early Christianity's dependence on its Hellenistic environment began to appear much less frequently in the publications of Bible scholars and classical authors. Today most Bible scholars regard the question as a dead issue. (Nash, GG, 1)

III. Nature and Features of Mystery Religions

We have limited information about the mystery religions, partly because of a vow of secrecy imposed upon the initiates. Their beliefs and practices also varied from place to place and from time to time. What follows is an overview of what is known about those mythologies. We highlight three key features of the mystery religions and then contrast them with Christianity, demonstrating enormous worldview differences between the two.

A. Cyclical View of Time

Mystery religions were based on a cyclical view of time. Nash notes,

Central to the mysteries was their use of the annual vegetation cycle, in which life renewed each spring and dies each fall. Followers of the mystery cults found deep symbolic significance in the natural process of growth, death, decay, and rebirth. (Nash, GG, 113)

The mystery deities were tightly bound up in and correlated to the annual vegetation cycle, so this was a repetitive, yearly process. Leading biblical scholar and theologian N. T. Wright observes, "These multifarious and sophisticated cults enacted the god's death and resurrection as a *metaphor*, whose concrete referent was the cycle of seed-time and harvest, of human reproduction and fertility." (Wright, RSG, 80)

B. Secret Ceremonies

The inner workings of the mystery religions are not well documented and available in the public domain. Both the rites they participated in and the knowledge they passed to their initiates were closely guarded, accessible only to those who were accepted into the group. Outsiders had little to no knowledge of what transpired. According to Nash,

[Each] mystery religion made important use of secret ceremonies, often in connection with an initiation rite. The mystery rites tied the initiates together at the same time they separated them from outsiders. . . . Whatever place particular mysteries allowed knowledge to have in their cult, it was a secret, or esoteric, knowledge, attainable only by the initiated and never revealed to those outside the circle of the religion. While several cults did stress the role of knowledge (*gnosis*) in achieving redemption, the term referred not so much to the cognizance of a set of truths as to a "higher knowledge" associated with their secret ceremonies. (Nash, GG, 113)

Samuel Angus, former professor of New Testament and church history at St. Andrews College, University of Sydney, notes that every mystery religion "imparted a 'secret,' a special knowledge of the life of the deity and the means of union with that deity. There was a sacred tradition of ritual and cult usages expounded by hierophants [interpreters] and handed down by a succession of priests or teachers." (Angus, MR, 53)

C. Doctrine Minimized

Mystery religions did not place a high premium on intellect, truth, or doctrinal soundness. They were less concerned about having correct teaching (orthodoxy) and intellectual rigor than about feeding and exciting the emotions of their initiates and followers. According to Angus,

Thus the Mysteries, with the exception of the Hermetic theology and Orphism, were never conspicuously doctrinal or dogmatic: they were weak intellectually and theologically. (Angus, MR, 61)

Angus also observes, "Speaking generally, the Mysteries made their appeal not to the intellect, but through eye, ear, and imagination to the emotions." (Angus, MR, 59)
Nash concurs:

The mysteries had little if any use for doctrine or correct belief. They were primarily concerned with the emotional state of their followers. . . . The mysteries used many different means to affect the emotions and imaginations of their followers in order to quicken their union with the god: processions, fasting, a play, acts of purification, blazing lights, and esoteric liturgies. (Nash, GG, 114)

Once the followers achieved union with their god through trumped-up emotions, two other goals became the focus of the mystery religions: salvation (or redemption) and immortality.

> The immediate goal of the initiates was a mystical experience that led them to feel that they had achieved union with their god. But beyond this quest for a mystical union were two more ultimate goals: some kind of redemption, or salvation, and immortality. The initiation ceremony was supposed to end the alienation of the *mystes* (initiate) from his god, making possible communion with the deity and eventual triumph over death. (Nash, GG, 114)

Angus goes a little more in depth on this point:

> A Mystery-Religion was a religion of Redemption which professed to remove estrangement between man and God, to procure forgiveness of sins, to furnish mediation. Means of purification and formulae of access to God, and acclamations of confidence and victory were part of the apparatus of every Mystery.... These redemption-religions thus promised salvation and provided the worshiper with a patron deity in life and death. This salvation consisted in release from the tyranny of Fate, alleviation from the burdens and limitations of existence, comfort in the sorrows of man's lot, a real identification with his god guaranteeing *palingenesia* (rebirth), and hope beyond. (Angus, MR, 50, 52)

Angus's analysis of the salvation offered in these religions makes clear their appeal to people who were otherwise helpless before an implacable Fate and the erratic will of often capricious gods. Angus's analysis also identifies something that T. S. Eliot recognized as a truth evident in tragic drama but missing in various religions—the horrifying realization of objective morality, that is, of the tragic flaw of sin in human life and the need for the conclusive work of a redeemer. (Both the New Testament and Aristotle in his writing about the Greek tragedies use the same Greek word for sin and error: *hamartia*.)*

IV. Contrast with Christianity

The mystery religions promoted a cyclical view of time, held secret ceremonies, and placed little emphasis on doctrine. In sharp contrast, Christianity is a historically based religion, with public proclamations; it places emphasis on true belief and biblically virtuous behavior. We will now consider each of these points in turn.

A. Historically Based

None of the other so-called resurrected gods of the mystery religions is a genuine historical figure. In contrast, Jesus is depicted in the Bible as a real historical person. The gospel accounts contain many anchors that hold in place, so to speak, vessels full of evidential treasures for anyone to examine, especially for those who wonder about the truth of Christianity.

Ed Komoszewski, James Sawyer, and Daniel Wallace observe,

> What makes Christianity unique among world religions is that it is grounded in history. More specifically, the Christian faith rests on the

---

* Cleo McNelly Kearns writes in *T. S. Eliot and Indic Traditions* about Eliot's response to his doctoral studies in Eastern religions (for which Eliot learned to read Sanskrit): "Eliot's fundamental objection to Indic religion was what he saw as its failure to understand the fundamental reality of human sin." (Kearns, TSEIT, 138) This lack of hope seems to be the reason that Hindu thought, like the mystery religions, perceives time as an endlessly repeated cycle. V. S. Naipaul has suggested in *The Wounded Civilization* that this frame of thought lies behind much of the suffering in India. In contrast, the New Testament book of Hebrews proclaims the finality of Christ's sacrifice as the answer to repeated cycles of sacrifice (Heb. 7:26–28).

person of Jesus Christ as a real, historical man. The notion that God became man in space-time history, that he lived among us, that he died on a Roman cross and rose from the dead is the core of the Christian proclamation. Indeed, one implication of the Incarnation—of God becoming man—is that the Incarnation invites us and even requires us to examine its historical credibility. The Gospels go to great lengths to speak to the where, who, and when of Jesus' ministry. They practically beg the reader to check out the data, to see if these things are so. (Komoszewski, Sawyer, and Wallace, RJ, 220)

For instance, consider a few passages that clearly indicate the historical nature of the biblical account:

> Now in the fifteenth year of the reign of Tiberius Caesar, Pontius Pilate being governor of Judea, Herod being tetrarch of Galilee, his brother Philip tetrarch of Iturea and the region of Trachonitis, and Lysanias tetrarch of Abilene, while Annas and Caiaphas were high priests, the word of God came to John the son of Zacharias in the wilderness. And he went into all the region around the Jordan, preaching a baptism of repentance for the remission of sins. — Luke 3:1–3

> And if Christ is not risen, then our preaching is empty and your faith is also empty. Yes, and we are found false witnesses of God, because we have testified of God that He raised up Christ, whom He did not raise up—if in fact the dead do not rise. For if the dead do not rise, then

> Christ is not risen. And if Christ is not risen, your faith is futile; you are still in your sins! — 1 Corinthians 15:14–17

B. Public Proclamation

While the early Christians were known for certain "insider" rituals like baptism, the Eucharist, and prayers, these were not practiced solely in secret but were performed and proclaimed in public. (In the early church, inquirers were welcome to attend the preaching portion of the service as learners, but they did not take part in the communion (Eucharist or Lord's Supper) until after their baptism.) This public proclamation of Christianity is made clear in several passages of Scripture.

> Men of Israel, hear these words: Jesus of Nazareth, a man attested to you by God with mighty works and wonders and signs that God did through him in your midst, as you yourselves know—this Jesus, delivered up according to the definite plan and foreknowledge of God, you crucified and killed by the hands of lawless men. God raised him up, loosing the pangs of death, because it was not possible for him to be held by it. — Acts 2:22–24 ESV

> So everyone who acknowledges me before men, I also will acknowledge before my Father who is in heaven, but whoever denies me before men, I also will deny before my Father who is in heaven. — Matthew 10:32, 33 ESV

The Christian faith rests on the person of Jesus Christ as a real, historical man. . . . Indeed, one implication of the Incarnation—of God becoming man—is that the Incarnation invites us and even requires us to examine its historical credibility.

Komoszewski, Sawyer, and Wallace

For we did not follow cunningly devised fables when we made known to you the power and coming of our Lord Jesus Christ, but were eye-witnesses of His majesty. — 2 Peter 1:16

Christianity was a very public religion, and oftentimes its being a public religion got its adherents into serious trouble. For instance, the apostles were threatened, beaten, and put in prison for *publicly* proclaiming the gospel (see Acts 4:1–3; 5:17–42).

C. Doctrine Matters

As we have seen, the mystery religions emphasized emotional experiences rather than doctrine. In contrast, the Christian Scriptures place a high importance on teaching and believing. These are examples from both the Old and New Testaments:

Therefore you shall lay up these words of mine in your heart and in your soul, and bind them as a sign on your hand, and they shall be as frontlets between your eyes. You shall teach them to your children, speaking of them when you sit in your house, when you walk by the way, when you lie down, and when you rise up. And you shall write them on the door-posts of your house and on your gates, that your days and the days of your children may be multiplied in the land of which the LORD swore to your fathers to give them, like the days of the heavens above the earth. For if you carefully keep all these commandments which I command you to do—to love the LORD your God, to walk in all His ways, and to hold fast to Him—then the LORD will drive out all these nations from before you, and you will dispossess greater and mightier nations than yourselves. — Deuteronomy 11:18–23

And Jesus came and spoke to them, saying, "All authority has been given to Me in heaven and on earth. Go therefore and make disciples of all the nations, baptizing them in the name of the Father and of the Son and of the Holy Spirit, teaching them to observe all things that I have commanded you; and lo, I am with you always, even to the end of the age." — Matthew 28:18–20

He must hold firm to the trustworthy word as taught, so that he may be able to give instruction in sound doctrine and also to rebuke those who contradict it. — Titus 1:9 ESV

V. Five Reasons the Mystery Religions Did Not Influence Christianity

A. Reason #1: True to its Jewish roots, Christianity did not accept other gods.
1. Jews were committed to an exclusive faith.

Unlike the Gentiles of that era, Jews refused to blend their religion with other religions (syncretism). Mystery religions were *inclusive*, but Judaism and Christianity were *exclusive*. Generally speaking, Jews intensely resisted pagan ideas. In his *Antiquity of the Jews*, first-century Jewish historian Josephus relays the following story of the Romans attempting to enforce Roman standards on the Jews and their response to Pilate and his troops:

But now Pilate, the procurator of Judea, removed the army from Cesarea to Jerusalem, to take their winter quarters there, in order to abolish the Jewish laws. So he introduced Caesar's effigies, which were upon the ensigns, and brought them into the city; whereas our law forbids us the very making of images; on which account the former procurators were wont to make their entry into the city with such ensigns as had not those ornaments. Pilate was the first who brought those images to Jerusalem, and set them up there; which was done without the knowledge of the people, because it was done in the nighttime; but as soon as they knew it, they came in multitudes to Cesarea, and interceded with Pilate many days, that he would remove the images; and when he would not grant their requests, because it would tend to the injury of Caesar, while yet they persevered in their request, on the sixth day he ordered his soldiers to have their weapons privately, while he came and sat upon his judgment seat, which seat was so prepared in the open place of the city, that it concealed the army that lay ready to oppress them; and when the Jews petitioned him again, he gave a signal to the soldiers to encompass them round, and threatened that their punishment should be no less than immediate death, unless they would leave off disturbing him, and go their ways home. But they threw themselves upon the ground, and laid their necks bare, and said they would take their death very willingly, rather than the wisdom of their laws should be transgressed; upon which Pilate was deeply affected with their firm resolution to keep their laws inviolable, and presently commanded the images to be carried back from Jerusalem to Cesarea. (Josephus, WFJ, 18:55–59)

Komoszewski, Sawyer, and Wallace observe:

The first-century Jewish mind-set loathed syncretism. Unlike the Gentiles of this era, Jews refused to blend their religion with other religions. Gentile religions were not exclusive; one could be a follower of several different gods at one time. But Judaism was strictly monotheistic, as was Christianity. As the gospel spread beyond the borders of Israel, the apostles not only found themselves introducing people to the strange idea of a man risen from the dead; they also came face-to-face with a polytheistic culture. But they made no accommodation on this front. (Komoszewski, Sawyer, and Wallace, RJ, 233)

2. Paul maintained and taught devotion to the one true God both before and after his dramatic conversion.

Paul had been trained as an orthodox Jew. He held steadfastly to orthodox beliefs about the one true God and would have been unwilling to compromise them for pagan mythology no matter the cost.

Circumcised on the eighth day, of the people of Israel, of the tribe of Benjamin, a Hebrew of Hebrews; as to the law, a Pharisee; as to zeal, a persecutor of the church; as to righteousness under the law, blameless. But whatever gain I had, I counted as loss for the sake of Christ.
— Philippians 3:5–7 ESV

And I was advancing in Judaism beyond many of my own age among my people, so extremely zealous was I for the traditions of my fathers.
— Galatians 1:14 ESV

Significantly, Paul in these passages and in his defense when on trial describes his strict training by the Pharisees—but explains that he was transformed only when and because he realized that the risen Christ was indeed the promised Messiah (Phil. 3:8–10; Gal. 1:15, 22, 23; Acts 24:14, 15; 26:5–23).

B. Reason #2: The differences between Christianity and mystery religions are greater than the similarities.

In *The Jesus Legend*, Paul Rhodes Eddy and Gregory A. Boyd write:

[As] soon as we become critical of reading parallels into the evidence, we discover that the differences between Christianity and the mystery religions are far more pronounced than any similarities. While there are certainly parallel *terms* used in early Christianity and the mystery religions, there is little evidence for parallel *concepts*. For example, as we have noted, both Christianity and the mystery religions spoke of salvation—as do many religions throughout history. But what early Christians meant by this term had little in common with what devotees of mystery religions meant by it. To site just one difference, there was in the mystery religions nothing similar to Paul's idea that disciples participate in the death and resurrection of their Savior and are adopted as God's children by placing their trust in him. (Boyd and Eddy, JL, 142)

For instance, theologian and New Testament scholar J. Gresham Machen describes the myth of Cybele and Attis:

The myth of Cybele is narrated in various forms. According to the most characteristic form, the youthful Attis, beloved by Cybele, is struck with madness by the jealous goddess, deprives himself of his virility, dies through his own mad act, and is mourned by the goddess. The myth contains no account of a resurrection; all that Cybele is able to obtain is that the body of Attis should be preserved, that his hair should continue to grow, and that his little finger should move. (Machen, OPR, 227–228)

Osiris is another figure often considered a "dying and rising god." In reality, the earliest accounts have him leading a life beyond the tomb that nearly replicates earthly life. He actually rules over the land of the dead and will never again be among the living. And perhaps most significantly, Egyptians did not believe in bodily resurrection. (Yamauchi, LDA, 22, 27)

It is quite a stretch to conclude that Christians could have borrowed from this tradition in formulating their first doctrines of Jesus.

C. Reason #3: Parallels comparing the two prove nothing.

What if we told you about a British ocean liner that was about eight hundred feet long, weighed more than sixty thousand tons, and could carry about three thousand passengers? The ship had a top cruising speed of twenty-four knots, had three propellers, and about twenty lifeboats. What if I told you that this ocean liner hit an iceberg on its maiden voyage in the month of April, tearing an opening in the starboard side, forward portion of the ship, sinking it along with about two thousand passengers? Would you recognize the event from history? You might say, "Hey, that's the *Titanic!*" Well, believe it or not, you would be wrong. It's the *Titan*, a fictional ship described in Morgan Robertson's 1898 book called *The Wreck of the Titan: or Futility*. This book was written fourteen years before the disaster took place, and several years before construction began on the *Titanic!* (Robertson, WT, website)

Here is the point: just as the fictional account of the *Titan* does not undermine the reality of the sinking of the *Titanic*, fictional accounts of dying and rising gods would not undermine the historical reality of the life, death, and resurrection of Jesus. The presence of parallels alone proves nothing about borrowing or the historicity of Jesus.

D. Reason #4: Mystery religions seem to be influenced by Christianity, not the other way around.

Eddy and Boyd tackle the "parallel" claim by investigating the dating:

A second obstacle to any attempt to understand first-century Christianity in light of ancient Greco-Roman mystery religions is that virtually all of our evidence for these religions comes from the second to fourth centuries. . . . Trying to explain a first-century religious movement by appealing to evidence for a "parallel" phenomenon a century or more later is questionable, to say the least. True, it is not unreasonable to assume that there were first-century precursors to the mystery cults of the second century and beyond. But this is an argument from silence, and in any case we are left with nothing conclusive about these precursor movements. Hence, any argument that Christianity was influenced by, let alone modeled after, these precursors must be judged as unwarranted speculation grounded in anachronism. (Boyd and Eddy, JL, 139–140)

Nash tells us about a ritual called the "taurobolium," Christian rituals likely influenced the cult of Cybele, one of the mystery religions. During this ritual,

> initiates would stand or recline in a pit as a bull was slaughtered on a platform above them. The initiate would then be bathed in the warm blood of the dying animal. The taurobolium has been alleged to be a source for Christian language about being washed in the blood of the lamb (Rev. 7:14) or sprinkled with the blood of Jesus (1 Peter 1:2). (Nash, GG, 143)

Could this pagan ritual have influenced the biblical writers? The core problem is the dating of the ritual, which first appeared in the West in the second century *after* the emergence of Christian teaching. Nash continues: "All of the extant evidence points to a chronology that makes it impossible for the taurobolium to have influenced first-century Christianity. Moreover, the evidence supports the hypothesis that the later changes in the blood bath reflect a Christian influence. It is clear, then, that the New Testament emphasis on the shedding of blood should not be traced to any pagan source. The New Testament

teaching should be viewed in the context of its Old Testament background—the Passover and temple sacrifices." (Nash, GG, 146)

Fielding the question of who might have influenced whom, Eddy and Boyd conclude:

> The crucial point here is that if there was any line of influence, it would seem more reasonable to argue that it was from Christianity to the mystery religions rather than the other way around. (Boyd and Eddy, JL, 140)

Finally, T. N. D. Mettinger, a senior Swedish scholar and professor at Lund University, wrote in *The Riddle of Resurrection* that there is near universal consensus that there were no dying and rising gods that predated Christianity (although he personally believes there may have been some exceptions):

> There is, as far as I am aware, no *prima facie* evidence that the death and resurrection of Jesus is a mythological construct, drawing on the myths and rites of the dying and rising gods of the surrounding world. While studied with profit against the background of Jewish resurrection belief, the faith in the death and resurrection of Jesus retains its unique character in the history of religions. The riddle remains. (Mettinger, RR, 221)

E. Reason #5: The death of Jesus is unique.

The death of Jesus is strikingly different from the deaths of various gods of the mystery religions. (see Nash, GG, 160–161)

1. The deaths of pagan gods were not sacrificial.

According to Christianity, Jesus' death was sacrificial. His death literally substituted his righteousness for the sins of each individual who has put his or her faith in Jesus. He takes on their sin and shields them from punishment so that they will not have to bear it (see John 10:11; 15:13; 1 John 3:16).

With regard to the mystery religions, Nash writes: "None of the so-called savior-gods died for someone else. The notion of the Son of God dying in place of His creatures is unique to Christianity." (Nash, GG, 160)

2. Jesus died for the sins of everyone.

Jesus did far more than just die on behalf of his friends. He specifically died *for* the sins of his immediate friends and followers and all those who would believe in him in the future (see Rom. 3:23–26; 1 Cor. 15:3; 2 Cor. 5:14, 15, 17–19, 21; Gal. 1:3, 4). Nash provides the contrast: "Only Jesus died for sin. It is never claimed that any of the pagan deities died for sin." (Nash, GG, 160)

3. Jesus died only once.

The deaths of the mystery religion gods were cyclical in nature, but Jesus is never represented in Scripture as dying, rising, dying, rising, *ad infinitum, ad nauseam*; that is, the nauseous recoil comes from a despair that there is no hope of escaping the repetition of the yearly cycle in which vegetation dies, kings decline and die, and people live toward death. The biblical pattern is that Jesus died once for all and came to give life abundant (see Heb. 7:27; 9:25–28; 10:10–14; John 10:10).

However, the "mystery gods were vegetation deities whose repeated death and resuscitation depicted the annual cycle of nature." (Nash, GG, 161)

4. Jesus' death was a historical event.

The death of Jesus was not some made-up tale told by his followers in order to start a new religious movement. His death is grounded in history, supported by strong historical evidence (see Acts 2:22, 23; 1 Cor. 15:14, 17; 2 Peter 1:16). Chapter 10 of *Evidence* examines this understanding.

Nash's following statement supports this point:

> Jesus' death was an actual event in history. The death of the god described in the pagan cults is a mythical drama with no historical ties; its continued rehearsal celebrates the recurring death and rebirth of nature. The incontestable fact that the early church believed that its proclamation of Jesus' death and resurrection was grounded upon what actually happened in history makes absurd any attempt to derive this belief from the mythical, nonhistorical stories of pagan cults. (Nash, GG, 161)

5. Jesus' death was voluntary.

Jesus makes it plain that he would lay down his life at a time of his own choosing (John 12:20–33). Although the gospel accounts tell us that the religious leaders attempted to arrest Jesus and kill him, Jesus always slipped away from them and thwarted their plans because it was not yet the right time (see John 7:30; 10:17, 18; 19:10, 11). But when he knew the time had come, he quietly submitted to being arrested in the garden of Gethsemane (John 13:1; Luke 22:47–53).

Nash comments: "Unlike the mystery gods, Jesus died voluntarily. Nothing like the voluntary death of Jesus can be found in the mystery cults." (Nash, GG, 161)

Machen contrasts the death of Jesus with the "dying and rising" mystery gods:

> One difference, of course, is perfectly obvious and is indeed generally recognized—the Pauline Christ* is represented as dying voluntarily, and dying for the sake of men. He "loves me,"

---

* That is, the way Paul describes Christ in his epistles preserved in the New Testament.

says Paul, "and gave himself for me." There is absolutely nothing like that conception in the case of the pagan religions. Osiris, Adonis, and Attis were overtaken by their fate; Jesus gave His life freely away. The difference is stupendous; it involves the very heart of the religion of Paul. (Machen, OPR, 315)

6. Jesus' death ended in victory, not defeat.

The historical record regarding Jesus does not end on a bloody cross or in a rock cut tomb. It ends with an empty tomb on an early Sunday morning and his ascension. The resurrection provides hope and the promise of eternal life. The end is triumph, not tragedy (see 1 Cor. 15:54, 55).

Contrasting Christ's death and resurrection with the mystery religions and their dying gods, Nash writes:

And finally, Jesus' death was not a defeat but a triumph. Christianity stands entirely apart from the pagan mysteries in that its report of Jesus' death is a message of triumph. Even as Jesus was experiencing the pain and humiliation of the cross, He was the victor. The New Testament's mood of exultation contrasts sharply with that of the mystery religions, whose followers wept and mourned for the terrible fate that overtook their gods. (Nash, GG, 161)

VI. Conclusion: Myth Becomes Fact

The resurrection of Jesus, as we have seen, was a unique event in world history. There is no compelling reason to think the first Christians borrowed concepts from the mystery religions to concoct the Christian faith.

Nevertheless, there are vague hints of gods who visit humankind, die, and rise to bring them to victory. Humphrey Carpenter, in *The Inklings*, relates this vital conversation about the vague hints in these old religions, despite their errors:

On Saturday night, September 19, 1931, in Oxford, England, J. R. R. Tolkien and C. S. Lewis went walking with a friend (Hugo Dyson) and discussed these myths when "a sudden rush of wind" prompted Tolkien to remark that the trees and the stars revealed how people once imagined a world that was alive, "myth-woven." Lewis, not yet a Christian but no longer an atheist, responded that myths are lies, powerfully written and crucial to the history of language and literature, but not for believing. Tolkien argued that even when humans lie, our human thoughts and imaginations must reflect something of our Creator—that the myth-making storyteller is "fulfilling God's purpose, and reflecting a splintered fragment of the true light." That led to a conversation on Christianity. Lewis knew well the mythical emphasis on sacrifice and blood, and "indeed he had examined the historicity of the gospels" enough to be "*nearly* certain that it really happened" and to recognize that the New Testament centered on words such as "sacrifice" and "the blood of the Lamb." But, he wondered, "What was the point of it all? How could the death and resurrection of Christ" have 'saved the world'?" Tolkien's response was that the old pagan stories of a dying god provided a clue: They were in fact "God . . . using the images of their 'mythopoeia' [story-making] to express fragments of his eternal truth." But with Christianity, "the enormous difference [was] that the poet who invented it was God Himself, and the images he used were real men and actual history. . . . Here is a *real* Dying God, with a precise location in history and definite historical consequences. The old myth has become a fact." Within two weeks, Lewis wrote, "I have just passed on from believing in God to definitely believing in Christ—in Christianity. . . . My long night talk with Dyson and Tolkien has a good deal to do with it." (Carpenter, TI, 42–45, emphasis in original)

Despite the enormous difference between these pagan mystery religions and the New Testament, C. S. Lewis makes an important observation:

We should, therefore, expect to find in the imagination of the great Pagan teachers and myth makers some glimpse of that theme which we believe to be the very plot of the whole cosmic story—the theme of incarnation, death, and rebirth. And the differences between the Pagan Christs (Balder, Osiris, etc.) and the Christ Himself is much what we should expect to find. The Pagan stories are all about someone dying and rising, either every year, or else nobody knows where and nobody knows when. The Christian story is about a historical personage, whose execution can be dated pretty accurately, under a named Roman magistrate, and with whom the society that He founded is in a continuous relation down to the present day. It is not the difference between falsehood and truth. It is the difference between a real event on the one hand and dim dreams or premonitions of that same event on the other. (Lewis, ITP, 128–129)

CHAPTER 12

THE DEITY OF JESUS: AN INVESTIGATION

OVERVIEW

I. Introduction: Considering the Hypothesis That Jesus Was God

Was the man Jesus really God come in the flesh as a human being? In chapters 6 through 11 we have already seen the evidence supporting the following set of conclusions, which combine to form the argument for such a comprehensive understanding of who he was and is:

- Jesus was a real human being (chapter 6).
- Jesus claimed to be the unique, eternal Son, one with the Father, and thus to be fully God (chapters 7 and 8).
- Jesus' claims, and the life that supported them, were anticipated prophetically in the Old Testament (chapter 9).
- Jesus' claims to deity were validated historically by his resurrection from the dead, marking both Christ himself and the Christian religion as utterly unique (chapters 10 and 11).

In this chapter, we build upon the case for the deity of Jesus Christ by thinking about the subject a little differently. This is the sort of question that can have only two answers—yes or no. Therefore, it allows us to conduct a thought experiment in which we compare two views of Jesus: that he was no more than a man (even if a very great one), and that he was God the Son come as a man. We test these views to see which one of them has the stronger claim to be true. An idea or belief to be tested to see how likely it is to be true is called a *hypothesis*. We commonly test different hypotheses by investigating how well each hypothesis explains all of the available evidence.

This method of testing competing explanations is used all the time in science, history, and even in the courtroom. Suppose,

for example, the police find a man dead in his apartment from a gunshot wound to the head, with the gun still in his right hand. This evidence may seem to support the hypothesis that the man committed suicide. However, investigators soon discover that the man was left-handed; that there were almost no fingerprints on the gun, even though the dead man was not wearing gloves; and that a large sum of cash that he had withdrawn from the bank earlier in the day was nowhere to be found. After reviewing all of the available evidence, the detective investigating the case concludes that the man was most probably murdered. Someone who did not want to accept this conclusion might be able to come up with creative ways of explaining the evidence (for example, that the man killed himself but went out of his way to make it appear that he had been murdered), but murder would still be a far more reasonable explanation than suicide.

Philosopher of history C. Behan McCullagh calls this form of reasoning "arguments to the best explanation." He discusses in some detail how such arguments work in historical studies. They determine whether one hypothesis or explanation better accounts for all the facts. "In particular, if the scope and strength of an explanation are very great, so that it explains a large number and variety of facts, many more than any competing explanation, then it is likely to be true." (McCullagh, JHD, 26) This is the kind of argument we use in this chapter.

We should acknowledge that if Jesus really was God come in the flesh, such a fact would be most unusual. If Christianity is true, then God has become a man and entered human history. If Jesus was God incarnate, we should therefore be cautious about making assumptions about what he should or should not have done. For example, one might imagine that if God were to become a man, he would appear suddenly in a glorious human form like Hercules or Apollo, immediately announce himself as God, and establish a worldwide kingdom with himself enthroned in a magnificent palace. The New Testament flatly rejects such ideas, even implicitly contrasting Jesus with Caesar, as New Testament scholar James Edwards explains:

> The disarming intrusion of God into the world in the birth of Jesus stands in sharp contrast to the imperial ambitions of Caesar Augustus. God does not break into the world in a world leader, Führer, or cosmic hero—all of which Caesar epitomized. God penetrates the defensive armor of the world by sending his Son as a child, not to the well-connected and established, but to shepherds who live on the precarious margins of society. (Edwards, GAL, 66)

Similarly, some skeptics argue that if God became a man in the ancient world, he should have taught modern science and introduced modern medicine and technologies. All such claims assume a position of knowing what God should do if he came to earth as a human.

On the other hand, we also ought to refrain from simply asserting that if God were to become a man he would necessarily have done it just in the way we read in the New Testament. To put the matter in this way would assume dogmatically that Christianity is true. And even if Christianity is true, it does not follow that God had no choice about how he would become human or what he would do once he was a man.

In short, to reach a reasoned conclusion about whether Jesus was and is God, we should avoid making assumptions either for or against the Christian belief. Instead, we should consider with an open mind the evidence for what Jesus actually said and did, asking whether that evidence is best explained on the hypothesis that he was no more than a man or the hypothesis that he was God incarnate.

What sorts of evidence need to be considered? Presumably, anyone who was God would have been *different* from other people in specific ways. At the very least, if we are to have good reasons to believe that Jesus was God, we would need to see *some* differences in his life that distinguish him from other people, and these differences would support the conclusion. Without prejudging what those differences should be, we can propose four categories to analyze: (1) how Jesus' earthly human life began; (2) what kind of a person Jesus was (his character); (3) what Jesus did (his actions); and (4) how Jesus' earthly life ended.

These are the categories we would want to consider with regard to *anyone* who claimed to be God. As it turns out, we have good evidence in each of these categories to support the conclusion that Jesus was God. This hypothesis accounts for all of the evidence about Jesus more completely than the hypothesis that he was no more than a man. In the rest of this chapter, we review this evidence.

If Jesus were not God incarnate, his birth would be normal, his character would exhibit a mixture of strengths and weaknesses such as we find in ourselves and others, his actions would have purely natural explanations, and death would conclude his life. But none of these conditions apply to Jesus' life. We propose that research into the evidence supports the hypothesis that Jesus was God and explains:

- The uniqueness of Jesus' entrance into human history
- The matchlessness of Jesus' perfect, sinless life
- The wonder of Jesus' miracles
- The ultimate victory of Jesus' conquest of death

II. The Uniqueness of His Entrance into Human History

The Apostles' Creed, an early creed of the Christian faith, affirms that Jesus Christ "was conceived by the Holy Spirit, born of the virgin Mary." If this belief is true, it would mean that Jesus' entrance into human history was indeed unique. But is it true?

In the nature of the case, the virginal conception* of Jesus in the womb of his mother is not the sort of event that can be "proved" historically. We cannot make the same kind of historical argument for the virgin birth that we have made, for example, for the resurrection. In the case of the resurrection, there were numerous eyewitnesses that saw him die and that later also saw him come back from the dead. In the case of the virgin birth, on the other hand, no eyewitnesses other than Mary can attest to how she became pregnant. That Jesus was born and was a real human being can be proved. However, if Jesus was conceived by the Holy Spirit, that event was a private, unseen occurrence.

Although we cannot prove that Jesus was miraculously conceived by the Holy Spirit, there are several good reasons to think it really happened.

A. The Virgin Birth of Jesus Is Plausible If God Exists

Whether one finds the virginal conception and birth of Jesus to be plausible depends largely on one's view of the existence of God. If there is a God who created the universe and also created life on this earth, he certainly would have no trouble at all making a new human life begin within the womb of a young woman without her coming into sexual contact with a man. If no such God exists, then the whole issue is a nonstarter. For someone such as the late Christopher Hitchens, one of the prominent "new atheists" who began aggressively criticizing belief in God in the early years of the twenty-first century, it is a simple matter of biological impossibility: "In any case, parthenogenesis is not possible for human mammals." (Hitchens, GING, 114).

In one sense, of course, Hitchens is correct: humans, like other mammals, are normally incapable of parthenogenesis (a word that derives from Greek words meaning "virgin" and "birth"). However, this normative observation in no way proves that God could not cause a woman to conceive a child in her womb without the involvement of a human father.

The point may be illustrated from an article by two scientists in India published in 2013 in the peer-reviewed science periodical *Advances in Bioscience and Biotechnology*. The authors define parthenogenesis as "a form of asexual reproduction found in females, where growth and development of embryos occurs without fertilization by a male." They note that scientists generally agree that "parthenogenesis is not a form of natural reproduction in mammals." (Kharche and Birade, PAMO, 170) Note their use of the word *natural* here: their point is that parthenogenesis in mammals does not occur *naturally*, not that it is impossible. They go on immediately to discuss "induced parthenogenesis" as an increasingly important process in contemporary biotechnology with roots in experiments done as far back as the 1930s. By "induced"

---

* Scholars often point out that more precisely one should speak of the virginal *conception* of Jesus rather than the virgin *birth*, since the latter expression has often been understood to mean that Mary's hymen miraculously remained intact after giving birth to Jesus. However, the more conventional sense of the term *virgin birth* is simply that Mary had no sexual intercourse at any time prior to her giving birth to Jesus. With this understanding in mind, we use the two terms more or less interchangeably.

they mean that human scientists can artificially manipulate conditions in experiments on mammals to cause them to reproduce by parthenogenesis. This is something that scientists are actively pursuing:

> There has since been abundant confirmation of the possibility of inducing parthenogenetic development in mammals by experimental procedures but none of the embryos so formed has survived beyond the embryonic period. (Kharche and Birade, PAMO, 170)

However, in 2004, scientists "used parthenogenesis successfully to create a fatherless mouse at Tokyo University of Agriculture" in Japan. (Kharche and Birade, PAMO, 171) The authors conclude:

> Since the birth of Fatherless mouse (Kaguya) the first viable parthenogenetic mammal in 2004 in Japan, significant advances have been made in the field of parthenogenetic research in order to understand the molecular processes involved during genomic imprinting process which is the main (perhaps the only) barrier to parthenogenetic development in mammals, in which the individual contains no paternal genetic material. (Kharche and Birade, PAMO, 177)

The point here is *not* that the birth of Jesus might have been an instance of "parthenogenesis" in a biologically natural way. These scientific advances show that what could not have occurred spontaneously through natural processes might be possible with the intelligent intervention of someone with sufficient knowledge and power to "induce" conception. Of course, no human being had such knowledge or power in the ancient world, but God has always had those resources.

In short, one cannot criticize the virginal conception of Jesus because it is not something that happens naturally in mammals. People in the ancient world knew that human conception naturally required sexual intercourse with a man, and for that reason viewed Jesus' conception by Mary as a miracle, as C. S. Lewis pointed out years ago:

> Such people seem to have an idea that belief in miracles arose at a period when men were so ignorant of the course of nature that they did not perceive a miracle to be contrary to it. A moment's thought shows this to be nonsense: and the story of the Virgin Birth is a particularly striking example. When St Joseph discovered that his fiancée was going to have a baby, he not unnaturally decided to repudiate her. Why? Because he knew just as well as any modern gynaecologist that in the ordinary course of nature women do not have babies unless they have lain with men. No doubt the modern gynaecologist knows several things about birth and begetting which St Joseph did not know. But those things do not concern the main point—that a virgin birth is contrary to the course of nature. And Joseph obviously knew *that*. (Lewis, *Miracles*, 73–74, italics original)

Even scientists seem confused on this point, implying that Christians claim Jesus was born through an unusual but ultimately natural process of parthenogenesis, when in fact they claim a divine intervention that reconfigured the normal course of events. For example, in 2015 two scientists at the University of Lausanne in Switzerland published an article in *Current Biology* on the possible implications of parthenogenesis. The authors chose to begin by commenting on the virgin birth of Christ, even though that was not the subject of their article:

The first account of parthenogenesis in the literature is the prophecy of Jesus Christ's birth in Isaiah 7:14: "Therefore the Lord himself will give you a sign: The virgin will conceive and give birth to a son, and will call him Immanuel." This reference to parthenogenesis is unusual in two ways: first, it is the only account of "natural parthenogenesis" in a mammal. Mammals are believed to be completely unable to reproduce via parthenogenesis because of a number of developmental and genetic restraints. Second, while the "Blessed Virgin Mary" might have been able to conceive a daughter via parthenogenesis, the conception of a son is highly unlikely. As male sex in humans is determined by genes on the Y chromosome, Mary, as a woman, could not have transmitted any Y chromosomes to her offspring. (van der Kooi and Schwander, "Parthenogenesis," R659)

The authors are quite right that if a woman did have a child by "natural parthenogenesis" it could not be a boy, but Christianity does not claim Jesus was conceived by natural parthenogenesis! Rather, it claims that the Holy Spirit miraculously caused Mary to conceive without her having sexual relations.

Skeptics commonly assume that affirming the virgin birth of Christ as "miraculous" means believing that the "laws of nature" have been "broken" or "violated" in some way, but this misunderstands the nature of a miracle. As C. S. Lewis explained so memorably, miracles do not break natural laws but rather introduce new events into the natural realm:

If God annihilates or creates or deflects a unity of matter He has created a new situation at that point. Immediately all Nature domiciles this new situation, makes it at home in her realm, adapts all other events to it. It finds itself conforming to all the laws. If God creates a miraculous spermatozoon in the body of a virgin, it does not proceed to break any laws. The laws at once take over. Nature is ready. Pregnancy follows, according to all the normal laws, and nine months later a child is born. (Lewis, *Miracles*, 94)

It is therefore atheism, not science, driving Gerd Lüdemann, an atheist New Testament scholar, to say:

A firm line must be drawn. The statement that Jesus was engendered by the Spirit and born of a virgin is a falsification of the historical facts. At all events he had a human father. From that it follows, *first*, that any interpretation which fails to take a clear stand here is to be branded a lie. (Lüdemann, VB, 140)

The assertion that "at all events he had a human father" begs the question; it assumes that the virgin birth of Christ is impossible because it is *naturally* impossible. This categorical decision to beg the question is made prior to testing the evidence—in fact, ruling the evidence out of court before the case is ever considered.

Darrell Bock, New Testament professor at Dallas Theological Seminary and author of more than thirty books, explains that how one views the accounts of Jesus' birth depends to a great extent on what one thinks about God:

The issue of historicity in these accounts is a judgment that reflects the worldview of the interpreter. . . . Many interpreters do speak of a core of historicity in these accounts, but they tend to demur at different points. Nonetheless, one's judgment about historicity, especially in view of the presence of angels and a miraculous birth, depends more on how one sees

God's activity in the world than on the data of the text. (Bock, *Luke 1:1–9:50*, 71–72)

As New Testament professors Andreas Köstenberger and Alexander Stewart point out, much of the criticism of the gospel accounts of Jesus' birth proceeds from hostile assumptions:

The only reason to doubt the possibility of the miracle itself would be a prior commitment to philosophical naturalism, that is, the belief that the material world is all that exists and that there is no such thing as God or supernatural intervention. From this perspective, miracles just don't happen. This worldview assumes that science can explain everything, but such an approach demands more from science than it can produce. If one, however, acknowledges the existence of a God powerful enough to create all that exists, there remains no reason to doubt that such a God could intervene in history in this supernatural kind of way. This is indeed the God who is presupposed on every page of the Bible and who has been worshiped and served by human beings from the creation of the world. Could a God who spoke the universe with its countless galaxies into existence be unable to cause a virgin to conceive? (Köstenberger and Stewart, FDJ, 52–53)

William Lane Craig, a Christian philosopher and New Testament scholar, has acknowledged that at one time he found the virgin birth too difficult to believe:

In my own case, the virgin birth was a stumbling block to my coming to faith—I simply could not believe such a thing. But when I reflected on the fact that God had created the entire universe, it occurred to me that it wouldn't be too difficult for him to create the genetic material necessary for the virgin birth!

Once the non-Christian understands who God is, then the problem of miracles should cease to be a problem for him. (Craig, RF, 281)

If you are unsure about such matters as God's existence and whether he performs miracles, it may be helpful to consider whether a long-familiar worldview makes it difficult for you to keep an open mind with regard to the evidence for the supernatural in the life of Jesus Christ.

B. The Idea That Jesus Was Born of a Virgin Originated Very Early

Skeptics commonly assert that the story of Jesus being born of a virgin must have arisen as a legend or myth. There are several problems with this skeptical claim, one of which is that the story arose very early within Christianity and was contradicted by no one in the first century.

1. Matthew and Luke were written within the lifetimes of some eyewitnesses.

The New Testament contains two accounts of the miraculous conception of Jesus by the Holy Spirit, found in the opening chapters of the gospels of Matthew and Luke. The precise dates of these gospels are matters of considerable debate among scholars, due largely to disagreements about their possible literary relationships to each other and to the gospel of Mark. However, virtually everyone agrees that all three of these gospels (called the Synoptic Gospels because of the similarity in their overall content) were written sometime between AD 50 and 90, less than a century after Jesus was born and less than sixty years after his death (in AD 30 or 33). That is not very much time for a legend or myth to arise and take such detailed forms as we find in Matthew and Luke.

We have good reasons to think that at least

one of these gospels was written much earlier than the decade of the 80s. The gospel of Luke is the first of a two-volume work on the origins of Christianity. The gospel, which is part one, focuses on Jesus from his conception and birth through his death, resurrection, and ascension. The book of Acts, which is part two, is an account of the first thirty years or so of the Christian church from the ascension of Jesus to Paul's house arrest in Rome (c. 60–62). (Alexander, CP, 102–123) This means that AD 62 is the earliest that Acts could have been completed, but it also at least suggests that it was finished not long after that date, likely sometime in the 60s. Darrell Bock gives several reasons to favor dating Acts in the 60s:

> Reasons for this date include the following: (1) the picture in Acts that Rome, knowing little about the movement, is still deciding where Christianity fits; (2) failure to note the death of either James (AD 62) or Paul (c. late 60s); (3) the silence about Jerusalem's destruction, even in settings where it could have been mentioned editorially (e.g., Acts 6–7 [the Stephen account], 21–23 [Paul's arrest in Jerusalem]); and (4) the amount of uncertainty expressed about internal Gentile-Jewish relations, especially table fellowship, which fits a setting parallel to the Pauline letters that deal with similar tensions (Romans, Galatians, 1 Corinthians 8–10, Ephesians). (Bock, TLA, 40)

If Acts was written in the 60s, then the gospel of Luke, which was written earlier than Acts, must also have been written no later than the 60s. This would mean that Luke's account of Jesus' conception and birth was written no more than about thirty years after Jesus' death. In any case, neither Matthew nor Luke was written in the second century. Whether we date these gospels to the 60s or the 80s, viewing such writings about Jesus as mythology, considering how close in time they were to their subject, is probably incorrect, as prolific New Testament scholar Craig Keener explains:

> While foundation stories about the distant, legendary past were inevitably mythical, schools tended to preserve information about more recent founders, a more appropriate comparison for first-century Gospels about the recent figure Jesus. (Keener, HJG, 83)

2. The accounts in Matthew and Luke give independent testimonies to the virgin birth.

Whatever the precise dates of the gospels of Matthew and Luke, a comparison of their accounts of Jesus' conception and birth demonstrates that neither gospel writer invented the story. That is, the basic storyline was already in place sometime before either gospel was written. We know this because their two accounts differ so greatly and yet share many striking similarities. It is the combination of these similarities and differences that is important here.

First, consider the differences. Matthew begins with a genealogy tracing Jesus' ancestry from Abraham to Joseph. He then narrates Joseph being told by an angel in a dream to take Mary as his wife. Matthew reports that Mary gave birth to a son in Bethlehem and then was visited by Magi who had seen his star in the east. After the Magi left, Joseph took Mary and Jesus to Egypt to escape Herod's slaughter, returning to Nazareth after Herod's death.

Luke's account is more than twice as long as Matthew's and is very different. It begins with an angel's announcement to Zechariah that his barren, elderly wife Elizabeth will have a child, followed by that angel's announcement to the young virgin Mary that she will have a child despite not having consummated her marriage. Luke then narrates Mary's visit to see Elizabeth and John's birth. Next, he tells about Joseph taking Mary to Bethlehem, where she gave birth to Jesus, and about the shepherds coming to see the child. They then went to Jerusalem, where Jesus was circumcised, and where a prophet named Simeon and a prophetess named Anna recognized the child as the Messiah. The family went home to Nazareth but returned to Jerusalem every Passover; when Jesus was twelve, he stayed behind while his parents left, talking to the teachers in the temple. After his account of John's baptism of Jesus when they were both adults, Luke gives a very different genealogy, tracing Jesus' ancestry backward from Joseph to Adam (see the table "Differences Between Matthew's and Luke's Infancy Narratives").

As one can see by comparing these outlines of the two narratives, they do not have a single passage or unit of material in common. The differences are especially noteworthy because elsewhere the gospels of Matthew and Luke do have a considerable amount of material in common. For example, both give very similar (though not identical) accounts of Jesus' baptism by John (Matt. 3:1–17; Luke 3:3–9, 15–17, 21, 22) and of Jesus' three temptations by the devil after fasting in the wilderness for forty days (Matt. 4:1–11; Luke 4:1–13).

The complete lack of parallel units of material in the infancy narratives makes it all but certain that neither gospel writer drew on the other's narrative in composing his own. As one somewhat skeptical scholar puts it: "The opinion favored by most scholars is that the two infancy accounts are independent of each other." (Robinson, MNS, 111)*

At this point, one might suppose that Matthew and Luke independently made up their stories. However, besides considering the differences between the two accounts, we must also consider their similarities. Biblical scholars, including some who are skeptical about the virgin birth or at least

---

DIFFERENCES BETWEEN MATTHEW'S AND LUKE'S INFANCY NARRATIVES

Matthew 1–2	Luke 1–2
Genealogy of forty-two generations from Abraham to Joseph (1:1–17)	Gabriel told Zechariah and Mary that they would each have a son (1:5–38)
Mary found with child; Joseph told by angel in a dream to take her as his wife (1:18–25)	Mary visited Elizabeth and returned home, after which Elizabeth had her son John (1:39–80)
Magi visited the child in Bethlehem after first speaking with Herod (2:1–12)	Joseph took Mary to Bethlehem, where Jesus was born and visited by shepherds (2:1–20)
Joseph, warned in a dream, took Mary and Jesus to Egypt (2:13–15)	Jesus was circumcised and seen by Simeon and Anna; later they went home to Nazareth (2:21–40)
Herod had male babies in Bethlehem two years and younger killed (2:16–18)	When Jesus was twelve, he stayed behind in Jerusalem talking in the temple (2:41–52)
After Herod died, Joseph took his family back to Israel, and they lived in Nazareth (2:19–23)	Genealogy of about seventy generations from Joseph back to Adam (3:23–38)

---

* Robinson, a British biblical scholar, is inclined to be skeptical about the historicity of the accounts "except perhaps in respect of the details that they share" (p. 112).

about some elements of the infancy narratives, have identified a long list of these similarities*:

- Mary was Jesus' mother (Matt. 1:16, 18; 2:11; Luke 2:5–7, 16, 34).
- Joseph and Mary were betrothed but not married when Mary became pregnant (Matt. 1:18; Luke 1:27–38; 2:5).
- Mary was a virgin, i.e., she had not had sexual relations with Joseph or any other man when she conceived Jesus (Matt. 1:23–25; Luke 1:27, 34).
- An angel announced the birth of the child (Matt. 1:20, 24; Luke 1:26, 30, 34–38; 2:9–13).
- An angel explained that the child was conceived by the Holy Spirit (Matt. 1:20; Luke 1:35).
- An angel stated that the child was to be named Jesus (Matt. 1:21; Luke 1:31).
- An angel declared that Jesus would save his people (Matt. 1:21) or be their Savior (Luke 2:11).
- Jesus was descended from David (Matt. 1:1, 17; Luke 1:32, 69; 3:31; see also Mark 10:47, 48).
- Joseph was a descendant of David (Matt. 1:16, 20; Luke 2:4, 16).
- Jesus was to rule as the Davidic king of the Jews (Matt. 2:2; Luke 1:32, 33).
- Jesus was the Christ (Matt. 1:17; 2:4; Luke 2:11).
- Jesus was born during the reign of Herod the Great (Matt. 2:1, 3, 7, 12–22; Luke 1:5).
- Jesus was born in Bethlehem (Matt. 2:1; Luke 2:4–7).

- Visitors went to see Jesus in Bethlehem (Matt. 2:11; Luke 2:15, 16).
- The birth of Jesus was the occasion of great "joy" for the visitors (Matt. 2:10; Luke 2:10).
- Jesus was born after Joseph and Mary began living together (Matt. 1:25; Luke 2:5–7).
- Joseph and Mary raised Jesus as their son (Matt. 1:16; 2:13–23; 13:55; Luke 2:16, 33, 48; see also Mark 6:3; John 1:45; 6:42).
- Jesus grew up in Nazareth (Matt. 2:23; Luke 1:26; 2:39, 51; see also Mark 1:9, 24; John 1:45, 46).

The number and specificity of these similarities demonstrate that they go back to a common origin. Yet they cannot both originate from a common earlier story or narrative (written or oral) because if they did, they would have at least some narrative material in common. This means that the two accounts derive from different sources that happened to include many of the same ideas, even if presented very differently. As New Testament scholar Michael Bird states in the *Routledge Encyclopedia of the Historical Jesus*, "The differences between Matthew and Luke in the birth narratives are so sharp that they probably wrote their accounts independently from one another and used different sources." (Bird, BJ, 72)

Those different sources, of course, must have obtained their information earlier than either Matthew or Luke. Thus, we can now state confidently that the basic storyline that

---

* For examples of lists similar to this one, see Joseph A. Fitzmyer, *The Gospel According to Luke I-IX*, Anchor Bible 28 (New York: Doubleday, 1981), 307; Raymond E. Brown, *The Birth of the Messiah: A Commentary on the Infancy Narratives in Matthew and Luke*, rev. ed. (Garden City, NY: Doubleday, 1993), 34–35; Jane Schaberg, *The Illegitimacy of Jesus: A Feminist Theological Interpretation of the Infancy Narratives* (Sheffield: Sheffield Academic Press, 1995), 79–80; Edwin D. Freed, *The Stories of Jesus' Birth: A Critical Introduction* (Sheffield, UK: Sheffield Academic Press; St. Louis, MO: Chalice Press, 2001), 57–59; Patricia M. McDonald, "Resemblances between Matthew 1–2 and Luke 1–2," in *New Perspectives on the Nativity*, ed. Jeremy Corley (London: T&T Clark, 2009), 200–201. None of these scholars takes a conservative view of Scripture.

the two gospels have in common originated earlier than either of the gospels. In short, *the idea that Jesus was conceived of a virgin predated both Matthew and Luke.* Moreover, this idea was understood in the context of a number of specific details about how this came about: that his mother Mary became pregnant with Jesus when she was betrothed to Joseph but had not yet begun living with him as his wife; that Joseph took Mary as his wife despite not being her child's biological father; that Jesus was born in Bethlehem but raised in Nazareth; and so forth. Mark Roberts, a popular author, pastor, and gospel scholar, explains the implications this way:

> Contrary to what is sometimes stated by hyper-critical scholars, *you can tell the whole Christmas story with all the key facts by using only what is common to both Matthew and Luke.* This means that we have two, relatively early, independent accounts of the birth of Jesus that confirm each other's reliability. They agree on the major characters, the major timing, the major places, and the major miracles of the Christmas story. Both accounts were written within about fifty years of Jesus' death, maybe quite a bit less. And both, it is most likely, utilized older sources, written and oral, in their writing. Thus we have good reason to believe that Matthew and Luke were telling the story of what really happened in

the birth of Jesus, at least in the main flow of their narratives. It's therefore highly unlikely that either gospel writer made up the main elements of the story, even if you believe that they were creative about the details. (Roberts, BJ, website, emphasis in original)

What were those different sources from which Matthew and Luke drew their infancy narratives? The authors don't tell us outright, but in comparing the differences in the accounts we find a telltale clue. Leaving aside the genealogies, Matthew's infancy narrative (Matt. 1:18–2:23) mentions Joseph by name six times and Mary only three times, whereas Luke mentions Joseph by name three times and Mary *twelve* times. (In addition, both Matthew and Luke refer to Mary simply as Jesus' "mother" four times.) If we read the two narratives with these contrasting numbers in view, we can see that *Matthew's account is told from Joseph's point of view, whereas Luke's account is told from Mary's point of view.* This is why Matthew tells about the angel appearing in Joseph's dreams and about Joseph taking the family to Egypt and then to Nazareth, while Luke tells about Mary's relatives Elizabeth and Zechariah, about Mary's experience of seeing the angel Gabriel, and about events in Jesus' childhood that made a strong impression on Mary (Jesus' circumcision and his temple visit at age twelve).

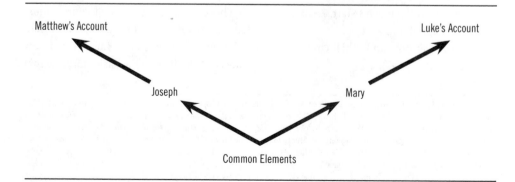

Matthew's Account   Luke's Account

Joseph   Mary

Common Elements

Now we can explain to a great extent both the similarities and the differences between the two accounts.

The simplest explanation for the similarities and the differences between Matthew's and Luke's accounts is that Matthew's account derived from Joseph and Luke's derived from Mary. This explanation doesn't require that Matthew and Luke spoke with Joseph and Mary directly. Joseph is generally thought to have died before Jesus began his public ministry. Presumably his story was passed on to his sons, including James, the Lord's half-brother, whom Matthew would have known personally when both of them were apostles and leaders in the early Jerusalem church (Acts 1:13; 12:17; 15:13; 21:18; 1 Cor. 15:7; Gal. 1:19; 2:9, 12). Depending on when one dates Luke's gospel, Luke may have heard Mary's story from Mary herself or perhaps from the apostle John or one of the women who had known Mary (see John 19:25–27). Or, her story may have been passed down as an oral tradition that Luke received secondhand. British New Testament scholar Richard Bauckham has argued that much of the material in Luke's gospel that is not found in the others likely stemmed from the testimonies of such women as Joanna and Susanna (see Luke 8:3; 24:10) (Bauckham, GW, 186–194), both of whom no doubt knew Mary.

Many scholars today believe that the gospel writers exercised some measure of creativity in their narratives, particularly in the infancy narratives. How much creativity is attributed to the authors varies from one scholar's estimation to the next. For our purposes here, we should not let this question, which has some legitimacy from the standpoint of a literary and historical analysis of the Gospels as ancient texts, distract us from the evidence that the gospel writers were not simply making up stories about Jesus. As we have seen, Matthew and Luke, despite working entirely independently from each other and not being dependent on the same source, agree on an amazing number of very specific facts about the events surrounding the birth of Jesus. We have also seen that these agreements point to Joseph and Mary as the ultimate sources of the information reported. In short, where the two accounts agree, we are on solid ground in concluding that the accounts are factually based.

3. The lack of references to the virgin birth in the rest of the New Testament is not a problem.

A common objection to the virgin birth comes from the fact that, in the New Testament, only Matthew and Luke mention it. Robert Miller, of the Jesus Seminar, states, "The New Testament writings of Mark, John, and Paul show no hint whatsoever that these authors believed in the virgin birth." (Miller, BD, 252) Even *Newsweek* magazine has raised this objection: "If the virginal conception were a historical fact, however, it is somewhat odd that there is no memory of it recorded in the Gospel accounts of Jesus' ministry or in the Acts of the Apostles or in the rest of the New Testament." (Meacham, BJ, website)

This objection, though, is nothing more than an argument from silence. From Paul's silence on the virgin birth, nothing follows other than the conclusion that he did not mention it. Paul makes no mention in his epistles of Galilee or Nazareth, never mentions Joseph or Mary by name,* and in general says very little about events in Jesus' life. The reason for his "silence" on such matters is simply that they were not germane to the issues that prompted the writing of his

---

* The Mary mentioned in Romans 16:2 is clearly not the mother of Jesus but another woman with the same name. Mary was the most common name among Jewish women in the first century.

epistles to churches and church leaders. He was writing epistles, not giving biographical stories about Jesus, and his epistles generally were written in response to questions the churches were asking, false doctrines that needed to be refuted, and other such challenges.

Bock offers the following brief comment on the matter:

> The absence of details about Jesus' birth and origins in the NT corresponds with the general absence in the NT of material about the life of Jesus outside the Gospels. The only omission that is surprising is Mark's, but he ignores Jesus' childhood entirely, so his omission may be explained simply as literary choice. (Bock, *Luke 1:1–9:50*, 104)

Although Mark does not mention the virgin birth of Christ, his narrative at one point implicitly reflects the fact that it was known in Jesus' home town of Nazareth that Joseph was not Jesus' biological father:

> *He went away from there and came to his hometown, and his disciples followed him. And on the Sabbath he began to teach in the synagogue, and many who heard him were astonished, saying, "Where did this man get these things? What is the wisdom given to him? How are such mighty works done by his hands? Is not this the carpenter, the son of Mary and brother of James and Joses and Judas and Simon? And are not his sisters here with us?" And they took offense at him.*
> — Mark 6:1–3 ESV

As various scholars have pointed out, the reference to Jesus as "the son of Mary" rather than "the son of Joseph" is surprising, since the conventional practice in Jesus' culture was to identify a man by his father's name. Moreover, this was not merely a naming

convention, but reflected the cultural values of that society, as New Testament scholar Ben Witherington explains:

> In Jesus' world, people were important because of who they were related to, or even where they came from, not so much because of who they were in themselves. Take for example Peter, or to use his Jewish name, Simon bar Jonah (cf. Mt 16:17). He is identified and singled out by whose son he is. . . . In such a society paternity or even communal origin was often thought to determine one's destiny. (Witherington, JQ, 35)

The reference to Jesus as the "son of Mary" by the people of Nazareth appears to be a slight, an expression of disdain. Gerd Lüdemann, an atheist New Testament scholar, has observed, "The phrase 'son of Mary' remains all the more unusual since a Jewish male would normally be associated with the name of his father." There were some exceptions, including if the man's father had children by more than one wife or if the father was Gentile while the woman was Jewish—but not simply because the father had died. (Lüdemann, VB, 51) The most relevant exception was that "illegitimate sons were not named after their father but after their mother," as in the case of Jephthah, the son of a harlot (Judg. 11:1). (Lüdemann, VB, 52) Lüdemann gives additional reasons for thinking this was the point of the expression "son of Mary," including the fact that in context the phrase was being used by people in Jesus' hometown who were critical of or even hostile to Jesus. (Lüdemann, VB, 54)

Lüdemann, consistent with his atheist assumptions, concludes that "the Christians developed the notion of the conception of Jesus and the virgin birth" as a later "reaction to the report, meant as a slander but historically correct, that Jesus was conceived or born outside wedlock. . . . It has a historical foundation in the fact that Jesus really did have another father than Joseph and was in fact fathered before Mary's marriage, presumably through rape." (Lüdemann, VB, 60, 138) Many if not most of the leading critics of the virgin birth today agree that Joseph was not Jesus' biological father, preferring to agree with Christianity's early critics that Jesus was illegitimate.*

In the nature of the case, one cannot prove absolutely that Jesus was not conceived by natural means out of wedlock. Nor should Christians react to this suggestion in a way that might be understood as agreeing with demeaning attitudes toward "illegitimate" children (or their mothers, for that matter). Hypothetically, there is no reason why God could not choose, for example, to call a man as a prophet, teacher, or leader who was the product of rape or other sexual activity outside of marriage. However, the claim that the story of the virgin birth was a late bit of propaganda designed to cover up Jesus' illegitimacy is not likely:

- The story that Jesus was born of a virgin arose very early, as we have shown, and the Gospels' sources for their accounts of Jesus' conception and birth likely go back to Joseph and Mary themselves.
- Inventing a fiction of a virgin birth would simply not have been a plausible way to cover up an illegitimate birth. If coming up with a cover story had been the intention of the gospel writers or their sources, and if they had felt at liberty to make up a story, it would have been more plausible had they simply asserted that Joseph was the real father.

With regard to the gospel of John, two points should be made. First,

John omits many events and teachings included in the other Gospels (e.g., Jesus' baptism, the Sermon on the Mount, the institution of the new covenant, etc.), likely not because he didn't believe they happened historically, but because he assumes his readers already knew the basic gospel story and key events in Jesus' life from the other, earlier Gospels. (Köstenberger, review of Lincoln, BV, online)

Second, John indicates he was aware of Jesus' virgin birth and assumed his readers were also aware of it. He does so in the central part of the "prologue" to his gospel:

But to all who did receive him, who believed in his name, he gave the right to become children of God, who were born, not of blood nor of the will of the flesh nor of the will of man, but of God. And the Word became flesh and dwelt among us. — John 1:12–14 ESV

Sir Edwyn Hoskyns, dean of Corpus Christi College, Cambridge, explains that John's train of thought in this passage implies an awareness of the virgin birth:

The Evangelist did not write simply *The Word became flesh*, as though he were beginning a new topic. He wrote *And the Word became flesh*. That is to say, he links v. 14 closely to v. 13. . . . To the Evangelist the thought of the regeneration of the believers at once suggests the thought of the Son of God who for their salvation became flesh and was born. . . . The question arises whether the language does not presuppose the Virgin Birth. (Hoskyns, FG, 164)

---

* Most notably Jane Schaberg, *Illegitimacy of Jesus* (cited earlier), whose work has been foundational for the views of several scholars since.

John's description of the birth of believers as God's children emphasizes that their birth is not a physical birth. In the course of making that negative point in three ways, John finishes by denying that their new birth is "of the will of man." The word *man* here is not the generic Greek word *anthropos*, which means human being or humanity, but rather *anēr*, which means specifically a male human being or husband. The text is so easily understood as alluding to the virgin birth that several of the early church fathers actually quoted John 1:13 as affirming it outright, as saying "who was born" (meaning Jesus) rather than "who were born" (meaning believers in Jesus). (May, VBFG, 59–64)* Although that particular nuance does not appear to be supported, John 1:13 does reflect John's acceptance of the virgin birth.**

C. The Story of Jesus' Virgin Birth Did Not Derive from Pagan Myths

Skeptics commonly claim that the virgin birth is derived from ancient pagan myths about noble human figures being the offspring of the gods with mortal women. Critics who draw parallels between such stories and the infancy narratives of Matthew and Luke often couch their descriptions of these pagan myths in language that deliberately imitates Christian language. The following statement by Marina Warner, a British novelist and literature scholar, is an excellent example:

The historical fact remains that the virgin birth of heroes and sages was a widespread formula in the hellenistic world: Pythagoras, Plato, Alexander were all believed to be born of woman by the power of a holy spirit. (Warner, AAHS, 36)

Notwithstanding such rhetorically clever statements, the pagan myths actually do not have anything to do with virgin births. Bart Ehrman, a famous agnostic-atheist New Testament scholar, makes the point as emphatically as anyone:

In none of the stories of the divine humans born from the union of a god and a mortal is the mortal a virgin. This is one of the ways that the Christian stories of Jesus differ from those of other divine humans in the ancient world. It is true that (the Jewish) God is the one who makes Jesus' mother Mary pregnant through the Holy Spirit (see Luke 1:35). But the monotheistic Christians had far too an exalted view of God to think that he could have temporarily become human to play out his sexual fantasies. The gods of the Greeks and Romans may have done such things, but the God of Israel was above it all. (Ehrman, HJBG, 24)

The more specific the skeptics' own descriptions of the supposed virgin-birth myths of ancient pagan cultures, the more clearly one can see that no useful comparison exists between those myths and the biblical accounts of the virginal conception and birth of Jesus. Consider, for example, the litany of supposed virgin birth myths offered by Hitchens:

---

* May argues this might have been the original reading, even though it is not found in any of the Greek manuscripts. In the same volume, McKeever, "Born of God," 131, concludes that the Greek manuscript evidence must be regarded as conclusive. He takes the view, explained above, that John was alluding to the virgin birth in describing the spiritual birth of believers.

** There is another possible allusion to the virgin birth in John's first epistle: "We know that everyone who has been born of God does not keep on sinning, but he who was born of God protects him, and the evil one does not touch him" (1 John 5:18 ESV). The allusion depends on the manuscripts that read "protects/keeps him [*auton*]" (followed by most modern translations) rather than those that read "protects/keeps himself [*heauton*]" (as followed in the KJV and NKJV).

The Greek demigod Perseus was born when the god Jupiter visited the virgin Danaë as a shower of gold and got her with child. The god Buddha was born through an opening in his mother's flank. Catlicus the serpent-skirted caught a little ball of feathers from the sky and hid it in her bosom, and the Aztec god Huitzi-lopochtli was thus conceived. The virgin Nana took a pomegranate from the tree watered by the blood of the slain Agdestris, and laid it in her bosom, and gave birth to the god Attis. The virgin daughter of a Mongol king awoke one night and found herself bathed in a great light, which caused her to give birth to Genghis Khan. Krishna was born of the virgin Devaka. Horus was born of the virgin Isis. Mercury was born of the virgin Maia. Romulus was born of the virgin Rhea Sylvia. (Hitchens, GING, 23)

Several of these examples are obviously so far afield as to be completely irrelevant to the question of the origin of the gospel infancy narratives. There is no realistic chance of any substantial contact by Christians in the Mediterranean world with myths about Krishna or the Buddha within the first fifty years or so of Christianity. The Aztecs, of course, lived on the other side of the world in Central America, and did not emerge as a culture for several hundred years after Jesus was born. Coatlicue, whom Hitchens called "Catlicus," was not a mortal woman, but an earth goddess figure in late pre-Columbian Aztec mythology. (Read and González, MM, 150–152; Koch, ACMMC, 32–35)* Adducing Genghis Khan is just absurd, since he lived twelve centuries after Jesus!

Christian scholar Ronald Huggins has documented that Hitchens's review of these supposed virgin birth stories was plagiarized from a book by an early twentieth-century British secularist named Chapman Cohen, down to several misspellings of the pagan deities ("Catlicus" should be "Coatlicue," "Agdestris" should be "Agdistis," and "Devaka" should be "Devaki"). (Huggins, CHP, website) The spelling errors are inconsequential in and of themselves but betray the lack of any informed understanding of the facts. As Huggins explains in another article, for example, Krishna was hardly born of a virgin:

Krishna was the 8th son of Vasudeva and Devaki. The name of their first son was Kirtiman. The BP [Bhagavata Purana] credits the pregnancy to "mental transmission" through the mind of Vasudeva into the womb of Devaki. That detail is from a late source (c. 950 AD), does not really represent a virgin birth, since Devaki was not a virgin, and is not present in the earlier accounts of Krishna's birth in the H [Harivamsha] (c. 450 AD) and VP [Vishnu Purana] (c. 400–500 AD). (Huggins, KC, online)

It is instructive to place these dates in some perspective. The traditional period to which Hindus date Krishna is roughly 3100 BC, which means the earliest written accounts appeared about 3,500 years later and the one that is misrepresented as claiming a virgin birth for him was produced about four thousand years later! By contrast, the four gospels of the New Testament were written no more than sixty-five years after Jesus'

---

* Like other authors whose knowledge of Christian theology is less than competent, Koch refers to Coatlicue's pregnancy as an "immaculate conception," no doubt trying to help readers connect the myth with something familiar to them. (The Spanish writers who published the Aztec and Mayan myths after their conquest of Central America did the same thing, often making those myths sound somewhat more akin to Christianity than they were.) However, the term *immaculate conception* refers to the Catholic belief that Mary was conceived in her mother's womb without sin, a different idea than the virginal conception of Jesus in Mary's womb (moreover, the idea of the immaculate conception is not found in the Bible).

death—a blink of an eye when it comes to the development of actual mythology.

What about stories of men whose fathers were gods and whose mothers were mortals in the Greco-Roman culture in which the Gospels were written? As Ehrman (quoted earlier) notes, these stories are not about virgin births at all. The gods of Greco-Roman mythology were thought of as anthropomorphic beings capable by nature of coming into physical contact with humans and engaging in sexual activity with them. Where such stories avoided describing the gods as coming in explicit human form to impregnate women, the conception is still presented as the consequence of some physical phenomena. The point may be illustrated with the stories of the conceptions of Alexander and Caesar Augustus. First the story of Alexander's conception as told by the Roman writer Plutarch:

> As for the lineage of Alexander, on his father's side he was a descendant of Heracles through Caranus, and on his mother's side a descendant of Aeacus through Neoptolemus; this is accepted without any question. And we are told that Philip, after being initiated into the mysteries of Samothrace at the same time with Olympias, he himself being still a youth and she an orphan child, fell in love with her and betrothed himself to her at once with the consent of her brother, Arymbas. Well, then, the night before that on which the marriage was consummated, the bride dreamed that there was a peal of thunder and that a thunder-bolt fell upon her womb, and that thereby much fire was kindled, which broke into flames that travelled all about, and then was extinguished. At a later time, too, after the marriage, Philip dreamed that he was putting a seal upon his wife's womb; and the device of the seal, as he thought, was the figure of a lion. The other seers, now, were led by the

vision to suspect that Philip needed to put a closer watch upon his marriage relations; but Aristander of Telmessus said that the woman was pregnant, since no seal was put upon what was empty, and pregnant of a son whose nature would be bold and lion-like. Moreover, a serpent was once seen lying stretched out by the side of Olympias as she slept, and we are told that this, more than anything else, dulled the ardour of Philip's attentions to his wife, so that he no longer came often to sleep by her side, either because he feared that some spells and enchantments might be practised upon him by her, or because he shrank for her embraces in the conviction that she was the partner of a superior being. (Plutarch, LA, 7:226–227)

A thunderbolt that fell on the mother's womb and a snake that slithered next to her body—these visually fantastical details are hardly comparable in any serious way to the gospel reports of Jesus being conceived in the womb of Mary by the Holy Spirit. Further, Plutarch's work (dated somewhere between AD 75 and 115) was written well over four centuries after Alexander was born in 356 BC.

Here is the story of the conception of Augustus as told by the Roman biographer Suetonius:

> I have read the following story in the books of Asclepias of Mendes entitled *Theologumena*. When Atia had come in the middle of the night to the solemn service of Apollo, she had her litter set down in the temple and fell asleep, while the rest of the matrons also slept. On a sudden a serpent glided up to her and shortly went away. When she awoke, she purified herself, as if after the embraces of her husband, and at once there appeared on her body a mark in colours like a serpent, and she could never get rid of it; so that presently she ceased ever to go to the public baths. In the tenth month after

that Augustus was born and was therefore regarded as the son of Apollo. Atia too, before she gave him birth, dreamed that her vitals were borne up to the stars and spread over the whole extent of land and sea, while Octavius dreamed that the sun rose from Atia's womb. (Suetonius, LA, 1:266–267)

Here again, as in the case of Alexander, the god's impregnation of a woman is represented by the image of a snake coming beside her while she slept. Suetonius wrote this story about 180 years after Augustus was born (*at least* twice as long a period as between Jesus' birth and the accounts in Matthew and Luke). As UCLA professor of classics Robert Gurval points out, we know virtually nothing about Suetonius's source Asclepias. The story may have originated during Augustus's lifetime during his rise to power in Rome, but, if so, as Roman poetic propaganda designed to exalt Augustus as a figure comparable to Alexander the Great, about whom (as we saw previously) a similar story had been told. (Gurval, AA, 100–102)

Granted, it is possible to see in Luke's account an implicit contrast between Caesar Augustus (mentioned in Luke 2:1 shortly before the birth of Jesus in Luke 2:6–7) and Jesus Christ, who was born during the reign of Augustus. One might plausibly understand Luke to be suggesting that it is Jesus, born in humble conditions in Bethlehem, who is the real ruler of the world, and not Augustus, enthroned in regal splendor and military power in Rome. But this interpretation at most would inform our understanding of Luke's presentation of the significance of the virgin birth; it would not in any way explain the origin of the story that Jesus was born of a virgin. As we saw earlier, Matthew's account is in no way dependent on Luke's; the two accounts arose independently and drew on different sources.

We conclude, then, that the gospel accounts of Jesus' virgin birth did not derive from pagan myths, nor are they comparable to them as myths.

D. The Story of Jesus' Virgin Birth Was Not Invented to Make Jesus Fulfill Prophecy

If the origin of the biblical accounts of Jesus' virgin birth cannot be traced to pagan myths, those who doubt or reject these accounts must explain their origin in a different way. The usual alternative explanation is that the story was invented to present Jesus as the "fulfillment" of the Hebrew Scriptures. A typical statement of this theory comes from Sam Harris, another of the influential "new atheists":

It is often said that it is reasonable to believe that the Bible is the word of God because many of the events recounted in the New Testament confirm Old Testament prophecy. But ask yourself, how difficult would it have been for the gospel writers to tell the story of Jesus' life so as to make it conform to Old Testament prophecy? Wouldn't it have been within the power of any mortal to write a book that confirms the predictions of a previous book? In fact, we know on the basis of textual evidence that this is what the Gospel writers did.

The writers of Luke and Matthew, for instance, declare that Mary conceived as a virgin, relying upon the Greek rendering of Isaiah 7:14. The Hebrew text of Isaiah uses the word 'almâ, however, which simply means "young woman," without any implications of virginity. It seems all but certain that the dogma of the virgin birth, and much of the Christian world's resulting anxiety about sex, was a product of a mistranslation from the Hebrew. (Harris, LCN, 57–58)

Harris's claim here is that the gospel writers knew only the Greek translation of the Old

Testament (commonly called the Septuagint) and therefore did not know that the Greek text of Isaiah 7:14 had mistranslated the Hebrew. On the basis of this mistranslation, then, they came up with the idea that Jesus' mother, in order to fulfill the prediction of Isaiah 7:14, needed to be a virgin—and so simply made it up. The two Swiss scientists quoted earlier in this chapter draw exactly the same conclusion:

> As it turns out, even the most famous speculation about parthenogenesis, Jesus Christ's birth, owes its existence not to a miracle but to a human error during the translation of Isaiah 7:14 from Hebrew to Greek: The Hebrew word *almah* can refer to a young woman of marriageable age, whether married or not. The "young woman" became a "virgin" in the gospel according to Matthew, where *almah* was translated as the Greek *parthenos*. (van der Kooi and Schwander, "Parthenogenesis," R661)

Matthew's citation of Isaiah 7:14 (Matt. 1:22–23) has attracted more controversy and debate than almost any other element in the gospel infancy accounts.* Two issues need to be kept distinct: whether Christian reading of Isaiah 7:14 in any way prompted the idea of the virgin birth of Christ, and whether Matthew's use of Isaiah 7:14 involved a mistranslation or misinterpretation of that verse. We address each issue in turn.

We can easily and summarily dismiss that the Greek translation of Isaiah 7:14 somehow precipitated or was a catalyst for the idea that Jesus was born of a virgin. This theory simply does not explain Luke's telling of Jesus' virgin birth independent of Matthew's, or Matthew's source, as we saw previously. In order to make this idea that the concept of the virgin birth

of Jesus originated in Matthew on the basis of a supposed mistranslation of Isaiah 7:14, the Jewish biblical scholar Geza Vermes is forced to deny that Luke also reported a virgin birth. (Vermes, *Nativity*, 59–72) However, this claim depends on a very strained interpretation of Luke and misses the fact that Luke alludes to Isaiah 7:14 without actually quoting it:

> Behold, the virgin shall have in [her] womb and she shall give birth to a son, and you shall name him Emmanuel. — Isaiah 7:14 (LXX)

> To a virgin . . . . "And behold, you shall conceive in [your] womb and you shall give birth to a son, and you shall name him Jesus." — Luke 1:27, 31**

The allusion to Isaiah 7:14 in Luke alongside the quotation of Isaiah 7:14 in Matthew reveals that Isaiah 7:14 was connected by Christians to Jesus' birth well before the gospels of Matthew and Luke were written. Again, the two gospels drew on different sources, which we have shown probably go back to Mary and Joseph, so the origin of this connection of the story to Isaiah 7:14 must have come very early. In fact, it arose while the Christian movement was still predominantly Jewish and was being led by Jesus' original Galilean disciples, including Jesus' half-brother James. This means that belief in the virgin birth of Christ could not have arisen by Greek-speaking Christians reading Isaiah 7:14 in the Greek Septuagint translation and being ignorant of what the Hebrew text said.

The claim that the Septuagint mistranslated Isaiah 7:14 has been confidently (even dogmatically) stated so many times that it may seem obvious, but the assertion reflects a rather elementary mistake in how one views

---

* The one exception is Luke's reference to the census (Luke 2:1–5), which many critics regard as an error.

** The two verses have been translated here very literally from the Greek in order to reflect their similar wordings.

translation. It assumes that the translator is supposed to assign a single verbal equivalent in his language to each word of the original text and use that equivalent expression everywhere the word occurs regardless of context. Eugene Nida, a leading expert on translation theory in biblical scholarship in the twentieth century, years ago explained why such an approach to translation is actually amateurish:

> Some Bible students have attempted to translate in what they feel is a consistent manner by always rendering the same Hebrew or Greek word by the same English word, and similarly for many types of grammatical constructions. This type of translation, which has been called "concordant," makes an immediate appeal to those uninformed about the problems and principles of linguistic usage. But no two languages correspond throughout in their words or grammatical usages, and such a literal type of translation actually distorts the facts of a language rather than reveals them. (Nida, BT, 11–12)

Most English versions of the Bible, even those commonly regarded as more "literal," do not rigidly follow a "word for word" approach to translation. Why, then, would we expect the ancient Septuagint to do so?

The usual dictionary or lexical definition in English for the Hebrew word *'almāh* is "young woman," but this definition is quite ambiguous and even potentially misleading. We might think of a woman in her late 20s and married with two children as "a young woman," but it is very unlikely that an ancient Hebrew would have used the word *'almāh* to refer to such a woman. The word occurs in only six other places in the Old Testament and does not seem anywhere to be used of a married woman (Gen. 24:43; Ex. 2:8; Ps. 68:25; Prov. 30:19; Song 1:3; 6:8). The limited number of occurrences and their varying contexts complicates the task of settling on a precise definition:

- In Genesis, Rebekah is described as the *'almāh* whom God brought to Abraham's servant to become Isaac's bride (Gen. 24:43). She is a virgin, as the text elsewhere makes clear (24:16). This is the one other place that the Septuagint translates *'almāh* with the Greek word *parthenos* ("virgin").
- The infant Moses' older sister (Miriam) is called an *'almāh*; she is implicitly still an unmarried girl (probably a young teen) but her virginal condition and unmarried status are not of any apparent relevance (Ex. 2:8).
- Psalm 68:25 uses the plural form *'ālāmôt* in reference to girls playing tambourines in a procession along with the male musicians and singers. The text does not seem to provide any clear indication of the marital status of these "young women."*
- Proverbs 30:19 speaks of the wondrous and mysterious nature of "the way of a man with a maid [*'almāh*]." This poetic statement is perhaps the most ambiguous of all the occurrences of *'almāh*, and its meaning continues to be debated. However, it does not sound like it refers to a husband's relationship with his wife.
- In the Song of Solomon (1:3; 6:8), the *'ālāmôt* are girls that attend the king

---

* Richard Niessen, "The Virginity of the *'almāh* in Isaiah 7:14," *Bibliotheca Sacra* 137 (1980): 138, infers that since these girls were expected to be chaste (a reasonable supposition), they were necessarily virgins (which does not follow, since young married girls could still be considered chaste).

but are distinguished from his "queens" (i.e., considered to be his wives) and his "concubines" (i.e., slave women with whom he might have sex). Although they were probably part of the king's harem, evidently they had not yet become his sexual partners.* In any case, they are not married women.

From these occurrences of the word, we may draw the following conclusions: (1) in most of these occurrences the girls are clearly unmarried virgins; (2) in no case are the girls clearly married or not virgins, though in one or two places they might be. Thus, even though the word 'almāh does not have "virgin" as its fixed definition (as if it were a technical term always denoting a virginal female), the word usually referred to girls who were in fact virgins, and in some contexts "virgin" might be an appropriate translation.

If "virgin" is a potentially legitimate translation of 'almāh in Isaiah 7:14, this does not necessarily mean that Matthew's interpretation of Isaiah 7:14 is correct. We still need to consider the meaning of the verse in its context. Many critics also find fault with Matthew in this regard.

Sam Harris, whom we quoted earlier, assumed that Matthew intended to claim that Isaiah was directly predicting that the Messiah would be conceived and born of a virgin. If this were so, it would open Matthew up to criticism, since the historical context of Isaiah 7:14 was concerned with the immediate situation in the eighth century BC with Ahaz, the king in Jerusalem. Ahaz's kingdom was threatened by an alliance of Syria's king Rezin with the northern kingdom of Israel, which was separated from the southern kingdom of Judah where Ahaz reigned (Isaiah 7:1–3). In response to Ahaz's fear, Isaiah gave him the word of the Lord that their alliance against his kingdom would fail: "It shall not stand, and it shall not come to pass. For the head of Syria is Damascus, and the head of Damascus is Rezin. And within sixty-five years Ephraim will be shattered from being a people" (Isa. 7:7, 8 ESV).

Isaiah invited Ahaz to ask God for a sign that this promise would be kept. When Ahaz refused to ask for a sign (feigning humility), Isaiah announced the sign that God would give:

> Therefore the Lord himself will give you a sign. Behold, the virgin shall conceive and bear a son, and shall call his name Immanuel. He shall eat curds and honey when he knows how to refuse the evil and choose the good. For before the boy knows how to refuse the evil and choose the good, the land whose two kings you dread will be deserted. — Isaiah 7:14–16 ESV

In context, the "son" whom the virgin will bear is "the boy" who will not have reached the maturity to be accountable for right and wrong by the time the land of those two kings would be deserted. In short, this "son" is in the immediate context a boy that was born in the late eighth century, sometime after Isaiah gave the prophecy (735 BC) but before the Assyrians had conquered both Syria (732 BC) and Israel (722 BC). Presumably the boy's mother was at the time of Isaiah's prophecy a young teenage girl, perhaps not yet married or newly married, who would soon become pregnant with her first child.

If Isaiah's prophecy was literally fulfilled in the eighth century BC, how can Matthew say that Jesus' birth "fulfilled" that same

---

* Agreeing with Niessen, "Virginity," 141, and against John Walton, "'alûmîm," in *New International Dictionary of Old Testament Theology & Exegesis*, ed. Willem A. VanGemeren (Grand Rapids: Zondervan, 1997), 3:417. Walton thinks that what distinguished these girls from the concubines was that they had not yet borne children.

prophecy? The reason is that the immediate fulfillment in Isaiah's day did not resolve in a final way the larger issue addressed in the book of Isaiah, which was the realization of God's promise of an eternal kingdom to the "house of David" (Isa. 7:2, 13). That promise, Isaiah went on to prophesy, would be ultimately realized in a future son of David:

> For to us a child is born, to us a son is given; and the government shall be upon his shoulder, and his name shall be called Wonderful Counselor, Mighty God, Everlasting Father, Prince of Peace. Of the increase of his government and of peace there will be no end, on the throne of David and over his kingdom, to establish it and to uphold it with justice and with righteousness from this time forth and forevermore. The zeal of the LORD of hosts will do this. — Isaiah 9:6, 7 ESV

In this prophecy, the child is to rule "on the throne of David" forever, something that of course did not happen with anyone living in the eighth century BC. Isaiah expands on this announcement in Isaiah 11:1–10, where he prophesies that "a shoot from the stump of Jesse" (11:1), that is, a descendant of David's father Jesse, will come forth in the future after the Davidic kingdom has seemingly come to an end. The imagery of a "shoot" emerging from the stump of a royal tree, when used in reference to a human being, is a metaphor for the birth of a new king. This latter-day Davidic king's rule will bring righteousness (11:3–5) and peace (11:6–9), just as Isaiah 9:7 had also announced.

Because of the thematic connections between Isaiah 7 and Isaiah 9 and 11 (the birth of a son and the preservation of the Davidic kingdom), we can reasonably understand the prophecy in Isaiah 7 as anticipating a great fulfillment about which Isaiah expands in Isaiah 9 and 11. Matthew, then, applies the language of Isaiah 7:14 to the birth of Jesus to Mary, who in that greater fulfillment was a virgin not only before she became pregnant but throughout her pregnancy.

Several contemporary biblical scholars agree with this line of interpretation. Craig Blomberg, for example, in the excellent academic reference work *Commentary on the New Testament Use of the Old Testament*, explains:

> Matthew recognized that Isaiah's son fulfilled the dimension of the prophecy that required a child to be born in the immediate future. But the larger, eschatological context, especially of 9:1–7, depicted a son, never clearly distinguished from Isaiah's, who would be a divine, messianic king. (Blomberg, "Matthew," 5)

Köstenberger and Stewart have drawn the same conclusion:

> The prophecy makes complete sense in its original historical context, but other factors within the context—the name Immanuel and the description of the child in Isaiah 9:6–7—also point forward in time to the birth of another child. (Köstenberger and Stewart, FDJ, 58)

R. T. France, in one of the best commentaries on the gospel of Matthew, explains the point very helpfully:

> These last two prophecies [Isaiah 9:6–7 and 11:1–5] would have been recognized then, as they still are today, as messianic prophecies, and it seems likely that Isaiah's thought has moved progressively from the virgin's child, "God with us," to whom the land of Judah belongs, to these fuller expressions of the Davidic hope. If then Isa 7:14 is taken as the opening of what will be the developing theme

of a wonder child throughout Isa 7–11, it can with good reason be suggested that it points beyond the immediate political crisis of the eighth century BC, not only in Matthew's typological scheme but also in Isaiah's intention. (France, GM, 57)

It turns out, then, that Matthew did not misinterpret Isaiah 7:14. When Matthew referred to events in Jesus' life as having "fulfilled" Old Testament prophecy, he generally did not mean that the Old Testament author had given direct and explicit predictions that certain things would happen in the life of Jesus. Generally speaking, what Matthew meant was that Jesus was the fulfillment or complete realization of God's promises to the people of God in the Old Testament, the one in whom all of the hopes and expectations that Israel had from God were coming true. Matthew made this point not by taking isolated statements out of their context but by placing them in their broader context. It is really those who claim that Isaiah 7:14 has no significance beyond the eighth century BC who are ignoring its context in the progressively developed revelations of the coming Messiah in Isaiah 7–11.

E. Conclusion: That Jesus Was Born of a Virgin Is Well Supported by the Evidence

We have not attempted to prove that Jesus was born of a virgin. However, the evidence we have surveyed shows that a good case can be made that the virgin birth is the best explanation of the available evidence, provided one accepts the existence of God or is at least open to the possibility of his existence. We have made three important points to support this conclusion.

First, the idea that Jesus was born of a virgin originated extremely early in Christianity. It is attested in two independent

documents, written some twenty-five to fifty-five years after Jesus' death, that drew on completely different sources of information yet agree on a large number of very specific facts concerning the circumstances of Jesus' birth. Moreover, we found that those different sources probably stemmed from the testimonies of Joseph (reflected in Matthew) and Mary (reflected in Luke). In short, the story of the virgin birth probably dates from a time no later than the first generation of the Christian movement and appears to have derived ultimately from eyewitness testimonies, as Luke himself explicitly claimed (Luke 1:1–4). This finding rules out viewing the virgin birth as a later Hellenistic myth or pious legend that would have developed over time as the church became increasingly Gentile.

Second, we found that the gospel accounts of Jesus' birth owe nothing to ancient pagan myths of gods impregnating mortal women. In those stories, the gods are anthropomorphic beings, the women are not virgins, and the accounts are with rare exceptions about legendary figures who lived hundreds or even thousands of years earlier, if they were real persons at all. The Gospels reflect an entirely different cultural and religious perspective.

Third, we showed that the idea of Jesus having been born of a virgin was not a pious fiction created to present Jesus as fulfilling an Old Testament prediction about the Messiah. Rather, the belief that Jesus was born of a virgin led believers within the first generation or so of the Christian movement to see his unprecedented entrance into the world as part of the larger story of his fulfilling the Messianic expectations of Israel. Matthew's quotation of Isaiah 7:14 was not a mistranslation and was not used in a way that misinterpreted the meaning of Isaiah 7:14 in its original context.

If the idea that Jesus was born of a virgin

did not originate with paganism and was not invented to manufacture fulfillment of the Jewish Scriptures, then what was the origin of this remarkable idea? The best explanation is that the idea originated from the testimony of Jesus' own family, several members of which were leaders in the early church. As Darrell Bock has argued, "No adequate explanation for the origin of the concept, outside the event itself, has been posited." (Bock, *Luke 1:1–9:50*, 121) Even if the evidence stops short of being definitive proof, we are on solid ground in concluding that Jesus truly was born of a virgin.

Admittedly, for those who are skeptical about God's existence or the supernatural, the conclusion that the virgin birth actually happened seems intolerable. But such a skeptical stance, to be consistent, must also reject the other evidence for the supernatural in the life of Jesus Christ. As atheist New Testament scholar Gerd Lüdemann, who is indeed doggedly consistent in this regard, points out, "The miraculous birth of Jesus and his miraculous resurrection from the tomb are simply two sides of one and the same coin." (Lüdemann, VB, xiii) If Jesus rose from the dead—and as we have seen, there is impressive, strong evidence that he did—then the idea that he entered into human life in a miraculous way becomes eminently plausible.

That Jesus Christ was born of a virgin is a dramatic sign that he is indeed Immanuel, "God with us" (Matt. 1:22, 23). Christian theologians have debated the question of whether it was strictly necessary that Jesus be born of a virgin in order for God the Son to become incarnate as a human being. We need not settle that question here. What is clear is that the virgin birth marks Jesus as unique among the human race. It is one of several truths about Jesus that is best explained as a revelation of his deity.

III. The Matchlessness of His Perfect, Sinless Life

If the holy, morally perfect God were to become incarnate as a human being, one would reasonably expect that he would live a good and righteous life. There are solid reasons to think that Jesus Christ did fit this description.

That Jesus Christ lived such a perfect life is the consistent testimony of the New Testament. Given that all of the New Testament books were composed less than seventy years after Jesus' death, it is actually somewhat surprising to discover how often they describe Jesus' sinless, perfect life. Such descriptions can be found in all four gospels, in reports of speeches by early Christian leaders in the book of Acts, in epistles written by four different authors, and in the book of Revelation (Matt. 4:1–11; 27:4, 19, 23, 24; Mark 1:12, 13, 24; Luke 4:1–13, 34; 23:14, 15, 41, 47; John 5:19; 7:18; 8:46; Acts 3:14; 7:52; 22:14; 2 Cor. 5:21; Heb. 1:9; 4:15; 7:26; 1 Peter 1:19; 2:21, 22; 3:18; 1 John 2:1, 2, 20; 3:5; Rev. 3:7).

As New Testament scholar George H. Guthrie has noted, "It was a widely disseminated tradition in earliest Christianity that Jesus was sinless . . . a claim made all the more pointed by the fact that many of the church's leaders were drawn from Jesus' family members or closest associates." (Guthrie, *2 Corinthians*, 313)

A. The Apostolic Writings Give Multiple Independent Witnesses to Jesus' Sinlessness

Four of the New Testament authors—Paul, Peter, John, and the author of Hebrews—explicitly affirm that Jesus Christ was sinless. The earliest of these statements comes from Paul, in an epistle written about AD 56, little more than twenty years after Jesus' death and resurrection: "For our sake he made him to be sin who knew no sin, so that in him we might become the righteousness of God" (2 Cor. 5:21 ESV).

Paul's statement here means that Jesus never was personally a sinner, but for our sake God punished Jesus for our sin as though Jesus had been the guilty party. New Testament scholar Murray J. Harris comments, "Although Christ was aware of the reality of sin and observed sin in others (cf. Heb. 12:3), he himself, Paul affirms, never had any personal involvement in sin. . . . Neither outwardly in act nor inwardly in attitude did Christ sin, and at no time was his conscience stained with sin." (Harris, SEC, 450)

Three other New Testament authors make the same point in somewhat different ways and do not appear to be simply parroting Paul's phrasing:

> For to this you have been called, because Christ also suffered for you, leaving you an example, so that you might follow in his steps. He committed no sin, neither was deceit found in his mouth.
> — 1 Peter 2:21, 22 ESV

> For we do not have a High Priest who cannot sympathize with our weaknesses, but one who in every respect has been tempted as we are, yet without sin. — Hebrews 4:15 ESV

> And you know that He was manifested to take away our sins, and in Him there is no sin.
> — 1 John 3:5

In short, the consistent testimony of first-century Christians to the character of Jesus was that he was without sin, perfect in holiness and righteousness. There are no dissenting statements from Christians in the first century (or in the second century, for that matter). As G. C. Berkouwer,

a twentieth-century theologian at the Free University of Amsterdam, notes, "Ancient heretics, however divergent they were in Christology, did not attack the sinlessness of Christ." (Berkouwer, PC, 240) It seems to have been generally understood from the beginning of the Christian movement that its founder, Jesus Christ, was a morally and spiritually perfect human being. Granted, zealous followers sometimes have an excessively high opinion of their master, but that does not seem to have been the case here.

B. Jesus Implicitly Claimed to Be Sinless While Remaining Humble

Jesus' followers viewed him as sinless— but did Jesus view himself in that way? Just as Jesus did not proclaim himself to be God in a direct and imperial fashion, he did not speak directly about his own sinlessness or perfection. This is perfectly understandable if Jesus was, as the New Testament represents him to have been, the divine Son come in humility (Phil. 2:6, 7) in order to redeem us from *our* sin.

In a kind of sideways fashion, much of what Jesus said assumed or presupposed his own lack of sin. This is perhaps most noticeable with regard to the issue of forgiveness. Jesus forgave other people's sins (Matt. 9:2–6; Mark 2:5–10; Luke 5:20–24; 7:47–49) and taught his followers to forgive others and to pray for God's forgiveness for their own sins (Matt. 6:12–15; 18:21–35; Mark 11:25; Luke 6:37; 11:4; 17:3, 4). Yet Jesus never said anything about needing forgiveness himself, a surprising omission since good spiritual teachers typically use themselves as object lessons or at least model for their disciples what they are teaching them. As the famous historian Kenneth Scott Latourette remarked:

It is highly significant that in one as sensitive morally as was Jesus and who taught His followers to ask for the forgiveness of their sins there is no hint of any need of forgiveness for Himself, no asking of pardon, either from those about Him or of God. (Latourette, HC, 47)

Drew University theologian Thomas Oden has written one of the best expositions and defenses of the sinlessness of Christ in his textbook on systematic theology. (Oden, WL, 254–260) He explains why Jesus' lack of any apparent guilt over his own sin is quite revealing:

Those who have walked the furthest on the way to holiness are those likely to be most keenly aware of their own guilt. St. Teresa of Avila, for example, understood most acutely how distant she was from the full possibility of life in Christ, but it was not because she was living distantly from that life but so near to it. . . . This was not morbid preoccupation with guilt but simply the expression of a daily life lived so near to God that she was more painfully aware of each small increment of distance from God than others might have known in a lifetime. Yet Jesus, whose closeness to God could hardly be questioned, showed no evidences of such guilt or remorse or distance but rather sustained the closest filial relation. (Oden, WL, 259)

The gospel of John reports moments when Jesus indirectly attests to his knowing himself to be without sin:

So Jesus said to them, "Truly, truly, I say to you, the Son can do nothing of his own accord, but only what he sees the Father doing. For whatever the Father does, that the Son does likewise" — John 5:19 ESV

"And he who sent me [the Father] is with me. He has not left me alone, for I always do the things that are pleasing to him. . . . Which one of you convicts me of sin? If I tell the truth, why do you not believe me?" — John 8:29, 46 ESV

Jesus' question, "Which one of you convicts me of sin?" invites us to consider what others, including both his friends and his critics, actually said about Jesus.

C. Jesus' Contemporaries Attested in Different Ways to His Sinlessness

1. Jesus was known as "the Holy One of God."

In the New Testament, a surprising variety of sources refer to Jesus as "the Holy One of God." An example is the affirmation of Peter: "Lord, to whom shall we go? You have the words of eternal life. Also we have come to believe and know that You are the Christ, the Son of the living God." (John 6:68, 69).

It may seem easy for skeptics to dismiss this statement attributed to Peter during Jesus' public ministry as a later fiction originating in the early church or invented by the gospel writer, but that is unlikely. The early church used a variety of titles for Jesus—Messiah or Christ, Son of God, Lord, and so on—but rarely used the title "the Holy One." For example, this title never appears in the epistles of Paul, Peter, James, or the book of Hebrews.

Although it might not seem too surprising that Peter would refer to Jesus as the Holy One, Mark and Luke both record an incident in which "an unclean spirit," that is, a demon, identified Jesus with the same title:

Now there was a man in their synagogue with an unclean spirit. And he cried out, saying, "Let us alone! What have we to do with You, Jesus of Nazareth? Did You come to destroy us? I know who You are—the Holy One of God!" — Mark 1:23, 24 (cf. Luke 4:33, 34)

Whereas the demon was an "unclean" spirit, it recognized Jesus as the very opposite, "the Holy One of God"—and the demon didn't like Jesus! Evidently Jesus radiated a holiness, a purity, to which the demons were sensitive and against which they reacted with anger or fear. After Jesus' resurrection, the early church leaders used this title a few times for Jesus (Acts 2:27; 13:35; 1 John 2:20; Rev. 3:7). They also referred to him as "the Righteous One" (Acts 7:52; 22:14) and "the Holy and Righteous One" (Acts 3:14). All of these statements in Acts were made in a context of mostly Jewish hearers or readers, perhaps because it would have been more immediately meaningful to them.

2. Jesus' critics and enemies were unable to find any fault with his character.

In some passages in the Gospels, speakers refer to Jesus' goodness in a specific context, especially his having been innocent of any wrongdoing justifying his execution. We should not rush past these statements, however, because they were not made by believers. Judas Iscariot, Herod Antipas, Pontius Pilate, Pilate's wife, and the centurion in charge at Jesus' crucifixion all declared that Jesus was innocent of any wrongdoing (Matt. 27:3, 4, 19, 23, 24; Luke 23:14, 15, 40, 41, 47). As Oden comments, "This is a remarkable confluence of testimony among precisely those who had conspired in bringing his life to a bloody end." (Oden, WL, 257)

This is not to suggest that everyone in Jesus' day acknowledged Jesus' goodness. The Gospels report that certain Jewish critics, especially among the Pharisees and other leaders, actively sought to find fault with him. As Oden points out, "They were constantly trying to trap him in his own words (Mark 12:13). They watched him, surveilled him constantly, looking for some slight misstep (Mark 3:2)." (Oden, WL, 256) So then, what faults did they claim to have exposed after all that effort? The list is highly illuminating:

- He broke the Sabbath by doing work on it (Matt. 12:1–14; Mark 2:24; 3:1–6; Luke 6:1–9; 13:14–16; 14:1–5; John 5:16–18; 9:14, 16)
- He was a friend of tax collectors, sinners, especially by eating and drinking with them (Matt. 9:10, 11; 11:19; Mark 2:16; Luke 7:34, 39; 15:1, 2; 19:7)
- He deceived and misled the people (Matt. 27:63; Luke 23:2)
- He claimed to be the king of the Jews in rebellion against Caesar (Matt. 27:11, 37; Mark 15:2, 26; Luke 23:2, 38; John 19:12, 19–21)
- He taught the people that they should refuse to pay taxes to Caesar (Luke 23:2)
- He threatened to destroy the Jerusalem temple (Matt. 26:61; Mark 14:58; 15:29)
- He was in league with Beelzebul, i.e., the Devil, enabling him to cast out demons (Matt. 9:34; 12:24; Mark 3:22; Luke 11:15)
- He committed blasphemy by forgiving sins (Matt. 9:3; Mark 2:7; Luke 5:21; see also Luke 7:49)
- He committed blasphemy by claiming to be the Son of God or equal with God (Matt. 26:63–66; Mark 14:61–64; John 5:18; 10:31–33; 19:7)

Some of these criticisms, ironically, now can be seen from our later point of view to reflect very well on Jesus. That he did not let legalistic judgments about what was "work" keep him from doing good on the Sabbath is for most people today a point in Jesus' favor.

Similarly, the fact that Jesus befriended those whom the self-righteous avoided with disdain is for almost all modern readers quite admirable behavior, whereas in his day some, perhaps many, Jews were scandalized by it. They were especially offended by his eating and drinking with the wrong sorts of people (Matt. 11:19).

Tom Holmén, a New Testament scholar in Finland, has pointed out, "There is in scholarship a virtual consensus about the fact that Jesus accepted the company of sinners and the like." (Holmén, "Sinners," 575) These "sinners" were people whom Jews in that culture generally regarded as immoral or as ungodly in their lifestyle. Jesus was not endorsing their sinful conduct, but was befriending them to free them from it. Because they were humbly admitting their need for forgiveness and mercy from God, Jesus warned the Jewish leaders that "tax collectors and the prostitutes go into the kingdom of God before you" (Matt. 21:31, 32 ESV).

The tax collectors were not Roman governmental officials but Jewish "middlemen" who collected the taxes on behalf of the Romans. They were "men who made their money by charging more than what they had to pass on to their imperial overlords." (Blomberg, CH, 23–24) For both political and economic reasons, then, most Jews despised tax collectors as greedy collaborators with their conquerors.

Jesus' practice of seeking out such tax collectors and sinners and even eating with them was contrary to the prevailing Jewish understanding that the path to holiness before God was to avoid being contaminated by sinful people. Jesus instead sought to "contaminate" the sinners with his holiness in order to welcome them into the kingdom of God. Craig Keener comments:

Scripture was already clear that one should not have fellowship with sinners (Ps 1:1; 119:63; Prov 13:20; 14:7; 28:7), though the point in each instance was to warn against being influenced by sinners. Jewish tradition developed this warning against improper association with the wicked. Jesus' behavior thus thoroughly violated his contemporaries' understanding of holiness. Yet had the Pharisees valued his objective more than his method they should not have been annoyed. In Jesus' case the influence was going one way—from Jesus to the sinners (Mk 2:15, 17; Lk 15:1; cf. Ps 25:8). (Keener, HJG, 212)

Several of the criticisms leveled at Jesus were claims by the Jewish authorities in Jerusalem that Jesus was a threat to the peace and stability of Roman occupation. This is obviously the case with regard to the accusations that Jesus claimed to be "the King of the Jews" and that he had supposedly forbidden people to pay taxes to Caesar (both claims that the authorities asserted were attempts to mislead the Jewish people). According to the Gospels, the first of these accusations was a half-truth and the second was false: Jesus made no claim to be an earthly king of Israel as a political rival to Caesar (e.g., John 6:15) and if anything told those who questioned him that they should give Caesar's coin back to him in the tax (Matt. 22:17–21; Mark 12:14–17; Luke 20:22–25).

The harshest criticism against Jesus was that he was guilty of blasphemy. All four gospels report that this accusation was made on different occasions both in Galilee and in Jerusalem. The basis for the accusation was that Jesus claimed prerogatives that belonged to God alone (Matt. 9:2, 3; Mark 2:5–7; Luke 5:20, 21; John 5:17, 18). This objection should not be brushed aside lightly. If Jesus went around claiming to forgive people's sins, to be the Lord of the Sabbath, to be the one who would judge the world at the end of history, and the like, his opponents' censure of these claims made some sense. A verdict must be reached at this point: either this man really was the divine Son and rightfully exercised prerogatives of deity, or he indeed made blasphemous claims about himself.

It is interesting to see how Jesus answered the charge. As proof that he had the divine authority to act as God would, he pointed to the fact that he did certain things that only God could do. These divine works, which we call miracles, demonstrated that his claims to the prerogatives of God were neither idle nor blasphemous. For example, when challenged about his forgiving a man's sins, Jesus asked:

> "Which is easier, to say, 'Your sins are forgiven you,' or to say, 'Rise up and walk'? But that you may know that the Son of Man has power on earth to forgive sins"—He said to the man who was paralyzed, "I say to you, arise, take up your bed, and go to your house." Immediately he rose up before them, took up what he had been lying on, and departed to his own house, glorifying God.
> — Luke 5:23–25

But did Jesus really perform such miracles? We consider this question next.

IV. The Wonder of His Miracles

The miracles of Jesus Christ are an essential part of his story and an essential part of the Christian faith. Removing the miracles from Christianity is not an option. As C. S. Lewis put it:

> All the essentials of Hinduism would, I think, remain unimpaired if you subtracted the miraculous, and the same is almost true of Mohammedanism. But you cannot do that

with Christianity. It is precisely the story of a great Miracle. A naturalistic Christianity leaves out all that is specifically Christian. (Lewis, *Miracles*, 108)

It turns out that the evidence that Jesus performed miracles is quite strong—so strong, in fact, that skeptical scholars generally admit he did so without conceding that they were literally supernatural.

A. Jesus' Miracles Are Generally Conceded by Modern Skeptical Scholars

In the nineteenth and twentieth centuries, many historians, philosophers, and even theologians were skeptical of miracles in general and of Jesus' miracles in particular. Such skepticism has not entirely disappeared—atheists remain adamant that belief in miracles is irrational—but scholarly skepticism has become surprisingly muted in recent years. With regard to Jesus, scholars often assent to his healing people in ways that seemed miraculous. Indeed, even scholars who vocally reject miracles have had to admit that Jesus did things that people in his day understood as miracles.

Consider the example of Rudolf Bultmann, a famous German New Testament scholar of the first half of the twentieth century who dismissed "the spirit and wonder world of the New Testament." (Bultmann, NTM, 4) After asserting that most of the miracle accounts in the Gospels are legendary, Bultmann immediately admitted that Jesus performed what everyone took to be miracles:

> But there can be no doubt that Jesus did the kind of deeds which were miracles to his mind and to the minds of his contemporaries, that is, deeds which were attributed to a supernatural, divine cause; undoubtedly he healed the sick and cast out demons. (Bultmann, JW, 173)

Thus even when strict critical standards have been applied to the miracle stories, a demonstrably historical nucleus remains. Jesus performed healings which astonished his contemporaries.

Joachim Jeremias

The same conclusion was reached by an influential German New Testament scholar in the second half of the twentieth century, Joachim Jeremias. After paring away every miraculous element that skeptical assumptions could dismiss or call into question, Jeremias found that a substantial core of historical miracles of healing could not be eliminated. He therefore drew the following conclusion:

> Thus even when strict critical standards have been applied to the miracle stories, a demonstrably historical nucleus remains. Jesus performed healings which astonished his contemporaries. (Jeremias, NTT, 92)

At the end of the twentieth century, New Testament scholar Barry Blackburn could describe this view as the near unanimous position of biblical scholars:

> That Jesus acted as an exorcist and healer can easily be described as the consensus of the modern period. . . . Scholars almost unanimously agree that this Galilean performed both cures and exorcisms, the success of which led both to a devoted following and opponents who charged him with sorcery. (Blackburn, MJ, 362, 392)*

The situation reversing the nineteenth century dominance of skepticism toward accounts of Jesus' miracles has remained basically unchanged in the twenty-first century. As Craig Keener points out in his magisterial two-volume study of miracles, "There is a general consensus among scholars of early Christianity that Jesus was a miracle worker. . . . Most scholars today working on the subject thus accept the claim that Jesus was a healer and exorcist." (Keener, MCNTA, 19, 23)

The reason contemporary scholarship has swung in the direction of acknowledging that Jesus performed miracles is simple: *the evidence is overwhelming*. As scholars have applied their critical methodologies to the Gospels, even in a rather skeptical fashion of accepting as factual only what those methods can show most likely must have happened, they have found that there is no escaping that Jesus performed marvelous feats of healing. The statement by Jeremias quoted above illustrates the point: by "strict critical standards" he meant the application of what we could call a "when in doubt throw it out" method. Yet at the end of the weeding process the fact remains that Jesus healed people in ways that his contemporaries could only explain supernaturally.

B. Jesus' Miracles Were Conceded by the Jews in the First Century and Beyond

One of the reasons scholars acknowledge that Jesus performed works that appeared to be miracles is that Jews who did not accept Jesus as the Messiah conceded the point in his own day and for centuries afterward.

---

* See also Jostein Ådna, "The Encounter of Jesus with the Gerasene Demoniac," in *Authenticating the Activities of Jesus*, eds. Bruce Chilton and Craig A. Evans (Leiden: Brill, 2002), 279–302.

1. Jesus' Jewish critics admitted miracles but attributed them to the Devil.

The ancient opponents of Jesus and of early Christianity never denied that Jesus had performed miracles; instead, when they offered any opinion about them, they characterized them as sorcery or as the work of the Devil. We can see this in the Gospels themselves, where they report the scribes as offering this explanation: "And the scribes who came down from Jerusalem were saying, 'He is possessed by Beelzebul,' and 'by the prince of demons he casts out the demons.'" (Mark 3:22 ESV; see also Matt. 9:34; 10:25; 12:24; Luke 11:15)

It is highly unlikely that the gospel writers, or their Christian sources, would volunteer to nonbelievers this way of explaining away Jesus' miracles. We may therefore consider it certain that first-century Jewish critics of Christianity were claiming that Jesus performed miracles by the power of the Devil. The way the criticism is articulated is important here. The scribes referred to the Devil as "Beelzebul" and "the prince of demons," expressions used by first-century Jews and that would not likely be familiar to most Gentile Christians. *Beelzebul* was an alternate form of the name *Baal-zebub*, which appears in the Bible only in 2 Kings 1:2–16 as the name of a Philistine deity.* Almost certainly, this criticism was being made in Jesus' day, as the Gospels report. One reason this is most likely is that Mark and Luke were written mainly for Gentile readers, yet they both include the reference to the Devil as Beelzebul. This tells us that this specific criticism came to the Gospels in that form and predated both gospels.

2. Josephus described Jesus as "a worker of amazing deeds."

Toward the end of the first century, the Jewish historian Josephus described Jesus as "a worker of amazing deeds" (Josephus, AJ, 18.3.3 §63) in the midst of a passage controversial for its clear reflection of a Christian perspective (and no one thinks Josephus was a Christian). For example, the passage states about Jesus, "He was the Messiah," and affirms the resurrection of Jesus as a fact. Some skeptics still argue that the entire passage was added by a later Christian writer. However, as theologian Robert Van Voorst observes, "The majority of scholars today prefer a middle position between accepting the entire passage as authentic or rejecting the entire passage as inauthentic." These scholars generally maintain that one can eliminate the obvious Christian elements as later additions (called *interpolations*) and what remains is a religiously "neutral" description of Jesus as an historical person. (Van Voorst, SENT, 605)

One of the statements about Jesus in the passage that scholars are generally in agreement was written by Josephus is the description of Jesus as "a worker of amazing deeds [*paradoxōn ergōn*]." If this had been a Christian interpolation, one would have expected the language to be stock Christian terminology for miracles. The three terms most commonly used in the New Testament for miracles are *dunamis* ("deed of power," "mighty work"), *teras* ("wonder"), and *sēmeion* ("sign"). All three of these words occur together in Acts 2:22, where the apostle Peter says that God performed "mighty works and wonders and signs" through Jesus. The word *paradoxos* (from which our word *paradox* originates) is used in reference to

---

* The KJV's rendition, following the Latin Vulgate, uses the form *Beelzebub*, a compromise between the form found in the Old Testament and the form found in the Greek text of the Gospels.

a miracle only once in the New Testament, when the people in Galilee commented about Jesus' miraculous healings, "We have seen amazing things [*paradoxa*] today!" (Luke 5:26 NLT). On the other hand, as Josephus scholar Steve Mason has pointed out, Josephus used the precise expression "amazing deeds" (*paradoxōn ergōn*) in two other places in the same book (*Antiquities of the Jews* 9.182; 12.63). (Mason, JNT, 233)

All in all, then, the evidence shows that Josephus did make reference to Jesus as someone who was known as a miracle worker, while using "carefully neutral" language that stopped short of endorsing Jesus' miracles as divine in origin. (Van Voorst, JONT, 104) Josephus, although Jewish, wrote primarily for Roman readers after the fall of Jerusalem in AD 70; considering his Roman audience, for whom Jesus' religious activities were not as contentious an issue as they were for Jews, he did not need to criticize Jesus' miracles or take a stand as to whether they were demonic or holy.

3. Jews after the first century conceded Jesus' miracles but attributed them to sorcery.

Various Jewish sources over the next several centuries referred to Jesus' miracles. The best known of these sources is the Babylonian Talmud, which stated that Jesus was guilty of "sorcery" (*b. Sanh.* 43a). The Babylonian Talmud was compiled from about the third to the fifth centuries (probably achieving final form somewhat later) and includes rabbinical traditions going back to the time of Jesus and earlier.

Not everything the Talmud says about Jesus is historically reliable. For example, the same passage says something no historian thinks actually took place: that a herald or crier announced for forty days that Jesus was to be executed before the sentence was carried out. This means that we need to be cautious about basing strong claims on the Talmud's brief references to Jesus. Nevertheless, where it agrees with earlier sources, it may be regarded as adding confirmation or support to what those earlier sources say.

Obviously, the Talmud's statement that Jesus was guilty of sorcery did not come from Christians. Instead these writers were reporting how the Jewish rabbis who rejected Jesus as the Messiah viewed his miraculous works. This makes their statement an independent testimony to the fact that Jesus was well known in Jewish history as a miracle worker. Graham Twelftree comments:

> Although this material does not give us contemporary evidence of Jesus being a miracle worker, it does give us (importantly) independent and indirect evidence in that it shows that Jesus was (or at least had come to be) remembered as a sorcerer-healer. . . . Though the rabbinic material is late, it is valuable in that it does not appear to be dependent on Christian traditions. (Twelftree, JMW, 254–255)

The evidence from the Gospels, Josephus, and the Talmud all support the conclusion that Jesus performed healings that appeared to be miraculous. The Jews who did not believe in him did not dispute this. What they disputed was the source of Jesus' miraculous power.

C. Jesus' Miracles Are Attested in the Gospels and All of Their Sources

Because of their careful study of the Gospels themselves, biblical scholars, even rather skeptical ones, have conceded that Jesus performed works appearing to be miracles. As they have attempted to "drill down" beneath the surface of the Gospels to find the earliest sources of information about Jesus, they have been unable to find any evidence of a Jesus who did not perform miracles.

Although scholars disagree about the origins of the Gospels, almost all agree that the gospel writers drew on various sources—oral, written, or both. Luke refers to earlier writings about Jesus and to the existence of eyewitnesses whose testimonies preserved memories of what Jesus had said and done (Luke 1:1–4). By comparing the Gospels with one another, scholars can make reasonable inferences about the sources underlying the Gospels, taking careful note of what materials they have in common and what materials are unique to each book. The more independent sources of information support the same claims about what Jesus said and did, the more difficult it becomes to undermine the trustworthiness of the testimony of the gospel writers. Scholars call this principle *multiple attestation*. It doesn't mean that events and details found only in one source are necessarily suspect; rather, it means that if those events and details are discovered in multiple independent sources, they become difficult to discount, even on skeptical grounds.

Applying this line of reasoning, scholars have found impressive multiple attestation for the reports that Jesus performed both healings and exorcisms. Each gospel contains miracle reports that are unique to that gospel, such as the casting out of a demon from a mute man (Matt. 9:32–34), the healing of a blind man by touching him a second time (Mark 7:31–37), the raising of the widow's son in Nain (Luke 7:11–17), and Jesus healing a man who had been born blind (John 9:1–39). The healing of the centurion's boy is found only in Matthew (8:5–13) and Luke (7:1–10); the healing of the Gentile woman's daughter is found only in Matthew (15:21–28) and Mark (7:24–30); and the casting out of the unclean spirit in the synagogue is found only in Mark (1:21–28) and Luke (4:31–37). Matthew, Mark, and Luke share some nine different miracles of Jesus, such as the raising of the synagogue official's daughter and the healing of the woman with a blood flow (Matt. 9:18–26; Mark 5:21–43; Luke 8:40–56). One miracle of Jesus, the feeding of the five thousand, is found in all four gospels (Matt. 14:13–21; Mark 6:33–44; Luke 9:12–17; John 6:1–15). So pervasive are miracle accounts in all of the different parts of the Gospels that it is clear that *all* of the sources on which the Gospels drew included such accounts.

Scholars of varying theological points of view agree on this point. Keener comments:

> So central are miracle reports to the Gospels that one could remove them only if one regarded the Gospels as preserving barely any genuine information about Jesus. . . . Very few critics would deny the presence of any miracles in the earliest material about Jesus. (Keener, MCNTA, 23–24)

Not only are miracle accounts found in every layer of the gospel narratives, references to miracles are found in an impressive variety of contexts. The variety of contexts alters the picture, for if the only context were simply reports of his performance, that limitation of form would lead some to surmise that the gospel writers merely set down legendary narratives to elevate the reputation of their teacher. Instead, the variety of literary forms in the Gospels transcends any limitation to miracle tales. As it turns out, references to Jesus' miracles are found in virtually every literary form or context of the Gospels. Twelftree lists some of these forms:

> The witness of various literary forms in the Gospels also gives support to the view that Jesus performed miracles. There are biographical sayings, parables, a dispute story, sayings of instructions and commissionings, as well

as the stories of exorcism, healing, raising the dead and so-called nature miracles. (Twelftree, JMW, 256)

This collection of multiple independent sources and multiple literary forms or contexts all referring to Jesus performing miracles constitutes a strong "one-two punch" against the notion that the idea of Jesus as a miracle worker originated as legend or myth in the early church. All this proves that Jesus was known as a miracle worker during his time on earth. As John P. Meier, a Catholic scholar whose approach is deliberately somewhat skeptical, concludes:

> In short, multiple sources intertwine with multiple forms to give abundant testimony that the historical Jesus performed deeds deemed by himself and others to be miracles. . . . For hardly any other type of Gospel material enjoys greater multiple attestation than do Jesus' miracles. (Meier, MJ, 622)

D. The Early Church Had No Motive to Invent the Idea That Jesus Was a Miracle Worker

The fact that the Gospels and their sources all spoke of Jesus as performing miracles might be dismissed as evidence if we had reason to suspect that the early church would have felt it necessary to invent the miracle stories in order to "sell" Jesus to the Jews as a prophet or Messiah, or to Gentiles as a redeemer. As it turns out, we have good evidence that they had no such motive.

1. Stories of miracle workers were rare during the time of Jesus.

Most people in the ancient Mediterranean world seem to have believed in the possibility of miraculous events, but stories of such occurrences were surprisingly uncommon. The modern assumption that ancient people were superstitious folk who easily believed in miracles is something of a half-truth at best. While it is true that ancient people did explain natural phenomena (especially in the heavenly bodies and in the forces of nature) as in some way to be the activity of the gods, that doesn't mean they uncritically accepted claims about supposed miracle workers. Gospel scholar Graham Stanton explains why belief in Jesus as a miracle worker cannot be chalked up to the credulousness of people in the first century:

> In antiquity miracles were not accepted without question. Graeco-Roman writers were often reluctant to ascribe miraculous events to the gods, and offered alternative explanations. Some writers were openly sceptical about miracles (e.g. Epicurus; Lucretius; Lucian). So it is a mistake to write off the miracles of Jesus as the result of the naivety and gullibility of people in the ancient world. (Stanton, GJ, 235)

Indeed, during the era in which Jesus lived few persons claimed to be miracle workers, as historian A. E. Harvey explains:

> If we take the period of four hundred years stretching from two hundred years before to two hundred years after the birth of Christ, the number of miracles recorded which are remotely comparable with those of Jesus is astonishingly small. On the pagan side, there is little to report apart from the records of cures at healing shrines, which were certainly quite frequent, but are a rather different phenomenon from cures performed by an individual healer. Indeed it is significant that later Christian fathers, when seeking miracle workers with whom to compare or contrast Jesus, had to have recourse to remote and by now almost legendary figures of the past such as Pythagoras or Empedocles. (Harvey, JCH, 103)

2. The stories of Apollonius of Tyana date from almost two centuries after Jesus and cannot be taken seriously as history.

The usual example of a first-century miracle worker cited today by those who are skeptical of Jesus' miracles is Apollonius of Tyana. Apollonius was a first-century AD Greek philosopher from Asia Minor (modern-day Turkey) who advocated a form of Pythagoreanism. The frequency with which this particular individual is cited as disproving the uniqueness of Jesus as a miracle worker is itself a testament to the fact that Jesus was at the very least quite unusual in this regard. Apollonius's reputation as a miracle worker is logically irrelevant to the question of whether Jesus was a miracle worker; the evidence for each must be assessed on its own merit.

There are at least three reasons why historians are justified in rejecting the accounts of Apollonius's miracles while accepting the accounts of Jesus' miracles. First, the documentary evidence supporting Apollonius's miracles is pitifully weak. We have essentially just one source for the stories of Apollonius's miracles: the Greek author Philostratus. But we have multiple sources for the life of Jesus and his miracles, including the four gospels and additional sources outside the New Testament that confirm that Jesus was a miracle worker. As we have explained, the Gospels provide multiple, independent sources of information about Jesus' miracles. The Gospels were written between AD 55 and 95, roughly 25 to 65 years after Jesus' death; Philostratus's book was written around AD 220, some 125 to 140 years or more after Apollonius's death and nearly 200 years after Jesus' ministry. Since it was written 125 years or more after the last of the four gospels was written, any similarities between the two figures are possibly the result of Philostratus

basing his characterization of Apollonius on Jesus. Bird explains:

> In the case of the similarities between the gospel accounts of Jesus and Philostratus's biography of Apollonius of Tyana, written at least a hundred years after the Gospels, it seems clear to me that Philostratus's biography has been written as a polemical parody of the Gospels, a type of refutation by imitation. Apollonius could be held up as a pagan antitype to Jesus. If so, there were occasions when pagans modeled stories from Christian sources rather than vice-versa. (Bird, OGAM, 26)

Second, Philostratus's book is not a biography of Apollonius, but more like an ancient novel loosely based on the historical figure of Apollonius. Keener draws important contrasts between Philostratus and the Gospels:

> The Gospels are ancient biography, with the strongest parallels in those sources; Philostratus, by contrast, employs at least many novelistic elements, especially in exotic locations.... Likewise, Babylonian and Indian kings implausibly discuss Greek philosophy with Apollonius. Such novelistic features are not surprising in this work, however; Philostratus, like the writers of the apocryphal gospels, wrote in the heyday of Greek novels. (Keener, MCNTA, 55–56)

Keener's reference to the apocryphal gospels specifically applies to some of the literature of the gnostic sects and others in the second and third centuries that told fanciful stories about Jesus performing miracles for show (which is never the case in the New Testament gospels). Philostratus's stories about Apollonius fit the same general pattern.

Philostratus's portrait suits a late second-or third-century setting (i.e., Apollonius's); his accounts of Apollonius even resemble reports from Christian gospels, though especially of the "apocryphal" variety. This is very possibly deliberate; by the fourth century, pagan writers explicitly used Apollonius as an alternative to Jesus, claiming that the pagan world offered its own healers. (Keener, MCNTA, 54)

This assessment of Philostratus's book as fiction is not the opinion of one or even a few critics. One of the leading scholars on Apollonius of Tyana, the Finnish scholar Erkki Koskenniemi, explains that for the past century most historians who have studied Philostratus have concluded that his book about Apollonius is largely fiction. It has been generally agreed that the "religious climate" to which it belongs is that of the third century rather than the first:

Consequently, few scholars today venture any statement on the historical Apollonius, while the Philostratean image of Apollonius is currently a concrete object of study. This change of venue from the first to the third century ushers in the judgment that the traditions on Apollonius reflect not the religious environment of the period in which the NT was written but that of the apocryphal Gospels and Acts. (Koskenniemi, AT, 461)

Third, the reported miracles of Apollonius lack credibility not because they are supernatural but because they are silly, as New Testament scholar Craig Evans explains:

The miracle stories attributed to Apollonius offer a few general parallels to the miracle stories of the Gospels, but they are not impressive. We encounter elements of gimmickry and trickery on the part of

Apollonius, such as removing and replacing his foot in leg irons while in prison (*Vit. Ap.* 7.38). We find other bizarre elements, such as scaring off an evil spirit by writing a threatening letter (*Vit. Ap.* 3.38) or by making tripods walk and performing other telekinetic acts (*Vit. Ap.* 3.17; cf. Eusebius, *Against the Life of Apollonius of Tyana* 18). There are some interesting parallels to be sure, but Apollonius comes across more as a wizard (of which he is frequently accused)…. The closest parallels to the miracles of Jesus are not found in Greco-Roman stories, but are found in biblical literature (esp. Elijah and Elisha) and in rabbinic traditions. (Evans, JHC, 249250)

We should understand that not all "miracle" stories are equally plausible. Chasing away an evil spirit by writing it a letter is clearly less plausible than casting out a demon by command, in the power of God. Making a lame man walk is miraculous in a way that is meaningful and profound; making a tripod walk just isn't. Christians who believe in the miracles of Jesus are not being inconsistent if they reject comparatively absurd miracle stories, just as they are not being inconsistent by accepting the idea of God, the Creator of all life, miraculously causing Mary to conceive in her womb while rejecting the story of Apollo coming in the form of a snake to sire Augustus.

3. No reliable accounts exist of other Jewish miracle workers in the time of Jesus.

Miraculous or supernatural acts have been reported throughout history, but with rare exceptions these miracles appear to have been isolated incidents. In this sense, supernatural events likely did occur in the first century apart from the direct involvement of Jesus Christ. What made Jesus so unusual was his well-deserved reputation as a remarkably successful miracle worker.

For example, there are references to Jews during the same general period as Jesus who performed exorcisms; Jesus himself even mentioned them (Matt. 12:27; Luke 11:19). None of these Jewish exorcists, however, seems to have gained widespread recognition (or notoriety, depending on one's point of view) for their work as Jesus did. So impressive was Jesus' work in casting out demons that some Jewish exorcists even tried to cast out evil spirits using the name of Jesus, an attempt that did not end well (Acts 19:13–16). Twelftree adds: "Jewish healers took up Jesus' name into their incantational repertoire. This is plainly evident in that the rabbis prohibited healing by Jesus' name." (Twelftree, JE, 139) Evans wryly observes, "Evidently, some rabbis believed it was better to die than to be healed in the name of Jesus." (Evans, FJ, 157)

Although some Jews in the general time period of the New Testament did seek miracles of exorcism and healing, few (other than Jesus) attained enough success to be remembered by name. Two men are commonly named as exceptions: Honi the Circle-Drawer, of Judea, and Hanina Ben Dosa, of Galilee.

Honi (called Onias in Greek), a first-century-BC rabbi, is known for one miracle, a rainstorm that came in answer to his prayer. The evidence for this miracle is credible in that it appears in two sources (history and theological commentary): it is reported in Josephus's *Jewish Antiquities* (14.19–28) and is discussed somewhat more elaborately in the Mishnah (*Taanit* 3.8), a compilation of Jewish traditions written down in the third century but originating earlier. Of course, one miracle does not a miracle worker make. Essentially, this is likely a true story of a miraculous answer to prayer. It should not be denigrated in the least, but at the same time Honi is not in the same category as Jesus.

The case of Hanina is a bit more difficult. Jewish traditions do refer to him as someone in whose life a lot of miracles took place. Unfortunately, the information available about Hanina is of debatable reliability. The accounts of his miracles generally come from the Talmud, written down several centuries after he lived—whenever that was. Scholars differ among themselves as to when Hanina lived, with some dating him to the first century BC (and thus a contemporary of Honi) and others to the first century AD (living perhaps at or somewhat after the time of Jesus).

Eric Eve, in his academic monograph putting Jesus' miracles in their Jewish context, points out that the miracles associated with Hanina are largely characterized as answers to prayer:

> Hanina is portrayed as a poor, pious rabbi, living at home with his wife and daughter, occasionally called upon to help in cases of accident, fever and venomous reptiles, and occasionally assisted by bizarre divine interventions. (Eve, JCJM, 285)

One of Hanina's miracles, in which a rabbi's son is healed at a distance, sounds a lot like Jesus' healing of the centurion's boy (Matt. 8:5–13; Luke 7:2–10). Even in this story as it appears in the Talmud, however, the miracle is in no sense credited to Hanina, but is viewed simply as an answer to prayer. When he prays for the rabbi's son and announces that he will be healed, he explicitly denies that he is even a prophet:

> I am no prophet, neither am I a prophet's son, but this is how I am blessed: if my prayer is

fluent in my mouth, I know that the sick man is favoured; if not, I know that the disease is fatal. (Berakoth 34b, quoted in Vermes, JHJC, 7)

Eve points out the key difference between Hanina and Jesus in this regard:

Whereas Jesus heals at a distance, Hanina merely prays at a distance. . . . Hanina, on the other hand, apparently has no idea whether his prayer will prove efficacious until he prays it. This story does *not* therefore portray Hanina as a miraculously gifted healer, but rather as someone who is especially proficient in prayer. (Eve, JCJM, 289)

4. The Jews did not assume that a prophet or the Messiah would perform miracles.

A skeptic might suppose that even if miracle workers were rare in the New Testament era, the early Christians might have invented stories of Jesus performing miracles to buttress their claim that he was a prophet or the Messiah. In response, scholars have noted that Jews in that period did not assume that such figures would perform miracles. For example, as Keener has observed, in contrast to the consensus in the ancient world that Jesus was a miracle worker, there was "unanimous silence in Christian, Jewish, and even Mandean tradition concerning any miracles of respected prophetic figures like John the Baptist." (Keener, MCNTA, 25; cf. Twelftree, JMW, 247) (The Mandeans held John in especially high regard.) The Bible specifically comments on the fact that John did not perform miracles (John 11:41). Miracles also do not seem to have been a customary element in Jewish expectations about the Messiah:

We lack substantial contemporary evidence that Jewish people expected a miracle-working

Messiah. . . . Rather than Christology causing miracle claims to be invented, claims already circulating about Jesus' miracles, once combined with other claims about Jesus, undoubtedly contributed to apologetic for a higher Christology. (Keener, MCNTA, 27)

E. Jesus' Miracles Revealed Him to Be *More* Than a Teacher or Prophet

Clearly, essentially everyone in the ancient world at all familiar with Jesus regarded him as a miracle worker. We have seen that Jesus' critics among his own Jewish people during his lifetime and afterward conceded his miracles but denied that God was their source. All of Jesus' followers agreed that Jesus performed miracles by the power of God. Thus, the only question his contemporaries had was how to explain his amazing deeds. Stanton puts it this way:

In Jesus' own lifetime follower and foe alike accepted that Jesus had unusual healing powers. The question was not, "Did Jesus perform miracles?" for that was taken for granted. What was in dispute was on whose authority and with whose power Jesus performed unusual deeds. (Stanton, GJ, 235)

The fact that Jesus performed a variety of miracles, especially exorcisms and healings, means that many popular modern theories about Jesus are out of touch with the historical reality attested by the evidence described above. Notions of Jesus as a teacher of morals or a critic of the establishment are exposed as obvious attempts to modernize Jesus. Meier criticizes "the perennial desire to make Jesus seem 'reasonable' or 'rational' to post-Enlightenment 'modern man,' who looks suspiciously like a professor in a Religious Studies Department at some American university." (Meier, MJ, 837)

In sum, the statement that Jesus acted as and was viewed as an exorcist and healer during his public ministry has as much historical corroboration as almost any other statement we can make about the Jesus of history.... Any historian who seeks to portray the historical Jesus without giving due weight to his fame as a miracle-worker is not delineating this strange and complex Jew, but rather a domesticated Jesus reminiscent of the bland moralist created by Thomas Jefferson. (Meier, MJ, 970)

If we are to understand who Jesus is, then, we need to understand the significance of his miracles. One thing they were not: as mentioned before, Jesus never performed miracles to show off; he was not seeking to gain anything for himself. Ancient historian and New Testament scholar Paul Barnett puts us on the right track:

The miracles of Jesus were always within the bounds of nature and not "contrary" to nature's patterns, that is, freakish or bizarre like the "signs" and "portents" that the Jews sought. His miracles were restrained, done for the good of those in need and not as spectacles in the manner of magicians. They served to point to Jesus as at one with the Creator in achieving his beneficent, end-time purposes on earth. In the miracles of Jesus the kingdom of God was present among them as the Son of Man went about doing good. (Barnett, FHC, 240)

Barnett's reference to the kingdom of God brings up what is widely understood now in gospel scholarship as the central point of the miracles performed by Jesus. Jesus' miracles were intimately bound up with his message that the kingdom of God was at hand and that in a sense it had arrived in his own person. When he began his ministry, his message was summed up by the announcement of the kingdom: "The time is fulfilled, and the kingdom of God is at hand. Repent, and believe in the gospel" (Mark 1:15).

This "gospel" or good news was the message that God was exercising his kingly rule in the fallen, sinful world in a new way. Miracles were an essential part of this message: "And he went throughout all Galilee, teaching in their synagogues and proclaiming the gospel of the kingdom and healing every disease and every affliction among the people" (Matt. 4:23 ESV; see also 9:35).

Among the miracles that were integral signs of the kingdom of God were exorcisms. Jesus himself connected the two explicitly: "But if I cast out demons by the Spirit of God, surely the kingdom of God has come upon you" (Matt. 12:28; see Luke 11:20).

Twelftree, in his important monograph on the exorcisms of Jesus, explains that Jesus' connection of exorcism with the kingdom of God was a completely new claim:

In the casting out of demons, the mission of Jesus itself was taking place, being actualized or fulfilled. In short, *in themselves the exorcisms of Jesus are the kingdom of God in operation*. It is this conclusion and this dimension to Jesus' exorcisms, more than anything else, which sets him out over against his background and environment. Even if every other aspect of Jesus' technique may have had at least a faint echo in other material, it is this indivisibility of miracle and message which reveals the exorcisms of Jesus to be especially unique. Jesus' exorcisms were not simply "healings" but were the coming of the kingdom of God. (Twelftree, JE, 170–171, emphasis in original)

The significance of exorcisms in relation to the kingdom of God is that in exorcism the demons who control the demoniacs in an especially overt way are thrown out; their influence is brought to a decisive end. Jesus understood his work of casting out demons as the first campaign in his offensive against Satan. In the Jewish (especially Pharisaic) theology of the time, there was a general understanding that God would defeat Satan in two stages. As Twelftree explains, in the first stage, "Satan would be bound so that, in the end, he could be finally destroyed. It seems that Jesus saw his, and the exorcisms of his disciples, as the first stage of the defeat of Satan." (Twelftree, JE, 228)

In this context of the "invasion" or "landing" of the kingdom of God in the world oppressed by the rule of the Devil, Jesus' miracles—his exorcisms, healings, and other works of supernatural power—were unique. His performance of these miracles contrasts even with the miracles that took place through the apostles, as Robert Bowman and Ed Komoszewski point out in their book on the deity of Christ:

> The Gospels rarely record Jesus uttering any sort of prayer before performing a miracle, and the exceptions are prayers of thanks or blessing, not prayers asking God to effect a miracle (Matt. 14:19; 15:36; Mark 6:41; 8:6; Luke 9:16; John 6:11; 11:42, 43). . . . By way of contrast, the book of Acts reports both Peter and Paul praying prior to performing miracles of healing (Acts 9:40; 28:8). . . . Jesus also never invokes anyone else's name when performing a miracle. One might have expected him to pronounce healings "in the name of my Father" or with some similar locution, but he never does. The apostles, on the other hand, healed in Jesus' name. (Bowman and Komoszewski, PJHP, 199–200)

The best explanation for the unique manner in which Jesus performed miracles is that he understood them to be expressions of the power of God in him (Luke 5:17). Jesus' miracles revealed the kingdom of God because Jesus *was* the King himself.

V. The Ultimate Victory of His Conquest of Death

Although Jesus performed many miracles during his ministry in Galilee and Judea, his miracle for which we have the best historical evidence is his own resurrection from the dead. That crowning miracle is so important that we have devoted a full chapter to the evidence supporting it. Even so, here we consider how Jesus' resurrection relates to the other facts about Jesus we have discussed in this chapter.

A. The Miracle-Working Jesus Could Have Escaped from Being Crucified

Suppose we assume for the moment that had Jesus lived long enough, he would eventually have died of old age. Even if one makes that assumption, it should be clear now that Jesus could have avoided the horrible death of crucifixion. Remember, this was a man who had astounded people throughout the region with his miracles. However one explains those miracles, it should be obvious that an accomplished miracle worker could have easily persuaded the authorities to let him live.

Even Jesus' enemies admitted this point in a backhanded way. While Jesus hung on the cross, some of the chief priests and scribes mocked Jesus by saying to one another, "He saved others; Himself He cannot save" (Mark 15:31). Their taunt implicitly acknowledged that Jesus was known to have miraculously saved others from death. Even if one supposes that it would have been too difficult for Jesus to get down from the cross—a supposition the Gospels do not support—surely Jesus could have saved himself from being crucified in the first place. All he would have needed to do would be to perform some miracle for the benefit of the Jewish or Roman authorities.

Jesus did not use miraculous power to escape from the cross because the cross was the reason he had come in the first place. This was a point to which he had alluded many times, sometimes adding that he could escape death if he so chose:

> "For even the Son of Man did not come to be served, but to serve, and to give His life a ransom for many" — Mark 10:45

> "Or do you think that I cannot now pray to My Father, and He will provide Me with more than twelve legions of angels? How then could the Scriptures be fulfilled, that it must happen thus?" — Matthew 26:53, 54

> "For this reason the Father loves me, because I lay down my life that I may take it up again. No one takes it from me, but I lay it down of my own accord. I have authority to lay it down, and I have authority to take it up again. This charge I have received from my Father." — John 10:17, 18 ESV

Despite his ability to perform wondrous miracles, that Jesus allowed himself to be captured, tried, and executed speaks volumes about how he viewed himself and his mission. He clearly viewed the death to which he submitted to be of central importance to the coming of the kingdom of God. The Christian doctrine that Jesus died on the cross to redeem us from our sins is not a later myth intended to rationalize the tragic reality that a beloved rabbi had gotten himself caught in the cogs of the Roman machine. It is the explanation, found in the teachings of Jesus himself, for why he allowed himself to be crucified.

The resurrection of Jesus confirms that Jesus had indeed chosen to accept crucifixion for God's purpose. It also supports the gospel accounts that Jesus performed miracles, a point made by resurrection scholar Michael Licona:

Historical confirmation of Jesus' resurrection renders greater plausibility to the reports of Jesus' miracles. For if Jesus was raised, one would be hard-pressed to regard healing a man born blind as too fantastic for belief. (Licona, NSPHJR, 125)

B. Jesus' Resurrection Vindicated His Innocence and His Divine Mission

Jesus' death by crucifixion must have appeared to his disciples, in the dark hours that followed, to call into question everything they had believed about him. Crucifixion was not an honorable death. Far from it: crucifixion was designed to be the most shameful way to die. The victim was typically stripped naked and exposed near a public thoroughfare. He would suffer in agony for hours, finding it increasingly difficult to breathe.

Historical confirmation of Jesus' resurrection renders greater plausibility to the reports of Jesus' miracles. For if Jesus was raised, one would be hard-pressed to regard healing a man born blind as too fantastic for belief.

Michael Licona

There was also the statement in the Law of Moses that "he who is hanged is accursed of God" (Deut. 21:23), or as the Greek Septuagint put it, "every one that is hanged on a tree is cursed of God" (Deut. 21:23 LXX). No wonder the two disciples on the road to Emmaus spoke of their faith in Jesus in the past tense: "But we *were hoping* that it was He who was going to redeem Israel" (Luke 24:21, emphasis added). Jesus' claims must all have seemed discredited by his ignominious death. The Sanhedrin—the Jewish council led by the chief priest—had apparently been right in viewing Jesus as a blasphemer.

The resurrection of Jesus changed all that. As pastor and New Testament scholar William Kynes puts it: "God has overturned the verdict of the court." (Kynes, CS, 182) Australian theologian Graham Cole comments: "Jesus' vindication was his resurrection. The world's verdict about him was proved wrong. He was no blasphemer, no fraudulent claimant to royal dignity." (Cole, HWGL, 165)

Catholic scholar Frank Matera explains well how Jesus' resurrection vindicated Jesus:

Does Jesus have the God-given authority to teach, preach, and heal in the service of the kingdom of God, or has he usurped what properly belongs to God? Jesus' death upon the cross seems to belie his ministry, but by raising Jesus from the dead, God vindicates and confirms Jesus' God-given authority. (Matera, NTC, 246)

In the first Christian sermon, the apostle Peter affirmed that Jesus was "a man attested to you by God with mighty works and wonders and signs that God did through him in your midst, as you yourselves know" (Acts 2:22 ESV). Despite the clear testimony of the miracles, the Jewish authorities had handed him over to the Romans to be crucified. But "God raised him up" (2:24). Jesus' resurrection vindicated him as God's "Holy One" (2:27) and revealed him to be "both Lord and Christ" (2:36).

The same idea is expressed by the apostle Paul in his epistle to the Romans. The gospel is the message of God "concerning his Son, who was descended from David according to the flesh and was declared to be the Son of God in power according to the Spirit of holiness by his resurrection from the dead, Jesus Christ our Lord" (Rom. 1:3, 4 ESV). Acclaimed biblical scholar and theologian N. T. Wright comments on this passage:

Jesus' resurrection was the divine *vindication* of him as Messiah, 'son of God' in that sense, the representative of Israel and thence of the world. . . . The resurrection demonstrates that the cross was not just another messy liquidation of a would-be but misguided Messiah; it was the saving act of God. (Wright, RSJ, 248)

C. Jesus' Resurrection Renders Credible His Virgin Birth

Earlier we showed that the virgin birth of Jesus Christ, while not something that can be proved historically (since there was only one human witness, Mary herself), was not a later legend or myth but was part of the earliest Christian traditions about Jesus, probably originating from Jesus' family members. This evidence is perhaps not enough by itself to convince a skeptic—even an open-minded one—that the virgin birth is historical fact. However, the virgin birth does not stand on its own without some context. It is part of the early church's testimony to someone that we know performed amazing miracles during his mortal lifetime and rose from the dead to immortality. In the context of Jesus' miraculous ministry and especially his miraculous resurrection, his virgin birth looks far more credible than it would otherwise.

We are not arguing that the virgin birth is as central to the Christian message as the resurrection, or that if you believe in the resurrection, then you must automatically also believe in the virgin birth. Rather, the point is that the resurrection shows that the entire story of Jesus in the Gospels, including his birth to a virgin, is consistent with what the resurrection reveals about Jesus. The two make eminent sense together. Thomas Torrance, a renowned theologian at the University of Edinburgh, explains:

> We must not start out with a minimized conception of God such that a miracle like the Virgin Birth of Jesus is automatically excluded from sane consideration. We are to think of it as we must think of all the other miracles and particularly as we do the miracle of the resurrection of our Lord at the end of his earthly life: the Virgin Birth of Jesus and the Resurrection of Jesus complement one another. (Torrance, DJC, 116)

In the virgin birth, the Son of God comes down from heaven, humbling himself to take our frail form, and eventually suffers the ultimate humiliation in the Crucifixion. In the resurrection, the Son of God comes up from the grave, ascends to heaven, and is glorified and exalted, raising our frail form to glorious immortality with him. As C. S. Lewis famously put it, "In the Christian story God descends to reascend." (Lewis, *Miracles*, 179)

VI. Conclusion:
The Hypothesis Confirmed

For the sake of simplicity, consider two rival hypotheses:

- Jesus was a good teacher, perhaps something of a prophet, who ran afoul of the political authorities and was executed. As the years passed following his death, legends developed about Jesus performing miracles and rising from the dead, even being born of a virgin. These legendary elements eventually led to the belief that Jesus was God incarnate. In short, the early church invented claims of deity for Jesus and the stories that supported those claims.

- Jesus was a teacher but an extraordinary one, performing miracles that astounded the people. He also made divine claims for himself in connection with these miracles that the Jewish authorities considered blasphemous. They had him arrested and handed over to the Roman authorities, who crucified him as a potential threat to order. He then rose from the dead, appeared to his followers, and ascended to heaven. The community of believers that he left behind, which included members of his family, preserved their recollections of the things that Jesus had said and done. His family passed on to others their own stories, including that Jesus' mother Mary was a virgin when he was born. As the early church reflected on what they knew about Jesus, they understood that he was the divine Son of God who had come down from heaven. In short, the early church accepted Jesus' claims to deity in light of the evidence that supported those claims, especially his resurrection.

Which of these two hypotheses about Jesus is best supported by the evidence? Let's review the evidence surveyed in this chapter, but in reverse order, beginning with the resurrection.

1. As we have just explained in the preceding section, the resurrection of Jesus is historical fact for which strong evidence has been marshaled. It vindicates Jesus' claims to be the divine Messiah and establishes the credibility of the gospel accounts of Jesus as a supernatural figure.

2. Examining the Gospels even in a fairly critical fashion, biblical scholars now widely agree that Jesus performed exorcisms and healings that were understood by everyone in his society as miraculous or supernatural.

3. We also found that Jesus was an honorable, innocent man who was ahead of his time in his moral vision; the criticisms that people made against him at the time were either false accusations or faulted him for challenging their limited cultural attitudes in ways that we can see today were admirable.

4. Finally, the accounts in Matthew and Luke of Jesus' conception and birth of the Virgin Mary provide independent testimonies to that fact, probably stemming from Joseph and Mary themselves. They are not plausibly explained as imitating pagan stories of gods impregnating mortal women or as fictions composed to present Jesus as the fulfillment of Old Testament prophecy. The best explanation for these accounts is that they go back to the experience of Mary herself. In the light of Jesus' miracles and resurrection, the virgin birth is certainly consistent with everything else we know about Jesus.

On the basis of these findings, the hypothesis that Jesus really was the divine Son of God come in the flesh does a far better job of explaining the evidence than the hypothesis that he was a good teacher whom the early church divinized after his tragic death. Christian philosopher Kenneth Samples nicely sums up the matter:

> Jesus' credentials as the divine Messiah are indeed formidable—matchless personal character, incalculable influence upon history, fulfillment of prophecy, power to perform miracles, extraordinary wisdom, bodily resurrection, and so forth. Alternatives that deny his true deity offer no adequate explanation for these credentials. (Samples, WD, 118)

Jesus' credentials as the divine Messiah are indeed formidable—matchless personal character, incalculable influence upon history, fulfillment of prophecy, power to perform miracles, extraordinary wisdom, bodily resurrection, and so forth. Alternatives that deny his true deity offer no adequate explanation for these credentials.

Kenneth Samples

CHAPTER 13

THE MARTYRDOM OF THE APOSTLES

OVERVIEW

I. The Argument

The willingness of the apostles to suffer and die for their faith is one of the most commonly cited arguments for the resurrection. However, scholars debate both the historicity of the apostles' martyrdoms and the apologetic significance of their martyrdoms. What is the evidence they actually died as martyrs? And to what extent does their martyrdom count as evidence for the resurrection? In this chapter, we will explore answers to these questions. Much of this chapter relies upon my (Sean's) academic book *The Fate of the Apostles: Examining the Martyrdom Accounts of the Closest Followers of Jesus.*

A. Carefully Stating the Argument

Here is how the argument can be carefully stated:

The apostles spent between one and a half and three years with Jesus during his public ministry, expecting him to proclaim his kingdom on earth. Although disillusioned at his untimely death, they became the first witnesses of the risen Jesus and they endured persecution; many subsequently experienced martyrdom, signing their testimony, so to speak, in their own blood. The strength of their conviction, marked by their willingness to die, indicates that they did not fabricate these claims; rather, without exception, they actually believed Jesus to have risen from the dead. While in and of themselves these facts prove neither the truth of the resurrection in particular nor Christianity as a whole, they do demonstrate the apostles' sincerity of belief, lending credibility to their claims about the veracity of the resurrection, which is fundamental to the case for Christianity. In other words, *their willingness to face persecution and martyrdom indicates more than any other conceivable course their sincere conviction that, after rising from the dead, Jesus indeed appeared to them.* (McDowell, FOTA, 2).

B. Scholars Cite the Argument

Scholars often point to the willingness of the apostles to suffer and die as evidence for their sincere belief that Jesus had risen from the grave.

New Testament scholar E. P. Sanders argues that "many of the people in these lists [of eyewitnesses] were to spend the rest of their lives proclaiming that they had seen the risen Lord, and several of them would die for their cause." (Sanders, THFOJ, 279–280).

Apologist and historian Michael Licona notes:

> After Jesus' death, the disciples endured persecution, and a number of them experienced martyrdom. The strength of their conviction indicates that they were not just claiming Jesus had appeared to them after rising from the dead. They really believed it. They willingly endangered themselves by publicly proclaiming the risen Christ. (Licona, TRJ, 366).

New Testament scholar Keener argues:

> The disciples' testimony was not fabricated. Ancients also recognized that the willingness of people to die for their convictions verified at least the sincerity of their motives, arguing against fabrication. People of course die regularly for values that are false; they do not, however, ordinarily die voluntarily for what they believe is false. Intentional deception by the disciples is thus implausible. (Keener, THJOTG, 342).

C. Clarifying the Argument

In her book *The Myth of Persecution*, University of Notre Dame professor Candida Moss claims Christians "like to think of their martyrs as unique. The fact that early Christians were willing to die for their beliefs has been seen as a sign of the inherent truth of the Christian message. . . . Christianity is true, it is said, because only Christians have martyrs." (Moss, TMOP, 17, 81).

There are two problems with her formulation of the argument:

> First, as I demonstrate, there *are* many martyrs outside Christianity; I don't claim that *only* Christians have martyrs, but that *the apostles died uniquely for the belief that they had*

The disciples' testimony was not fabricated. Ancients also recognized that the willingness of people to die for their convictions verified at least the sincerity of their motives, arguing against fabrication. People of course die regularly for values that are false; they do not, however, ordinarily die voluntarily for what they believe is false.

Craig S. Keener

---

actually seen the risen Christ, which demonstrates the sincerity of their convictions. The deaths of others for their religious causes in no way undermine the evidential significance of the fate of the apostles. Second, the apostles' willingness to die for their beliefs does not demonstrate "the inherent truth of the Christian message," but that the apostles *really believed* that Jesus had risen from the grave. The apostles could have been mistaken, but their willingness to die as martyrs establishes their unmistakable sincerity. The apostles were not liars; rather, they believed they had seen the risen Jesus, they were willing to die by this claim, and many actually did die for it. (McDowell, FOTA, 3)

II. Evidence for the Historicity of the Apostles' Suffering and Martyrdom

Were the first Christians actually persecuted for their faith?

Persecution against the first Christians provides a helpful setting for evaluating the likelihood of the martyrdoms of individual apostles. Even though persecution was sporadic and local, there is evidence that the public proclamation of the faith could be costly. John the Baptist was imprisoned and beheaded (Matt. 14:1–11). Jesus was crucified. Stephen was stoned to death after his witness before the Sanhedrin (Acts 6–8). And Herod Agrippa killed James the brother of John (Acts 12:12), which led to the departure of the rest of the Twelve from Jerusalem. The first statewide persecution of Christians was under Nero (AD 64), as reported by Tacitus (*Annals* 15.44:2–5) and Suetonius (*Nero* 16.2). The apostles publicly proclaimed the resurrection of a crucified criminal with full awareness of what their actions might cost them.

The apostles should not have been surprised that they faced persecution. Jesus taught that his followers would suffer for the sake of righteousness, and be killed as Israel had killed the prophets, for their proclamation of the name of Jesus before men (Matt. 5:10, 11, 43, 44; 21:33–40; 22:6; 23:30, 31, 34, 37; 24:9; Mark 12:1–11; Luke 6:22–23; 11:47–50; 13:34; 20:9–18; 21:12–13, 17.) Suffering was a central theme in the life and teachings of Paul. And as I discuss at length in *The Fate of the Apostles*, the expectation of suffering and persecution is a central theme through the New Testament, Old Testament, and pre-Christian Jewish literature such as 2 Maccabees. There was an anticipation during the first century AD that prophets would suffer and die at the hands of their own people as well as secular authorities. (McDowell, DARD, 14).

Suffering is also a central theme throughout the first epistle of Peter, especially in chapters 2 through 4, where he gives specific advice for facing testing and trials. The letter opens with his emphasis upon the believers' living hope through the resurrection of Jesus Christ from the dead," which frames his vibrant encouragement to them (1 Peter 1:1–3). His emphasis upon the joy that the scattered believers may surely experience—even if they face grief and many types of testing—gives additional evidence for how he understood the consequences of belief in the resurrection.

There is good reason to believe the first Christians, including the apostles, suffered for their faith. But what is the evidence the apostles actually died as martyrs?

A. General Claims for the Martyrdom of the Apostles

1. Polycarp, Letter to the Philippians

Therefore I urge all of you to obey the word of righteousness and to practice all endurance, which you also observed with your own eyes not only in the most fortunate Ignatius,

Zosimus, and Rufus, but also in others who lived among you, and in Paul himself and the other apostles. You should be convinced that none of them acted in vain, but in faith and righteousness, and that they are in the place they deserved, with the Lord, with whom they also suffered. For they did not love the present age; they loved the one who died for us and who was raised by God for our sakes. (quoted in Ehrman, TAF, 345)

2. Fourth Century Syrian Father Aphrahat, *Demonstration XXI: Of Persecution*

Great and excellent is the martyrdom of Jesus. He surpassed in affliction and in confession all who were before or after. And after Him was the faithful martyr Stephen whom the Jews stoned. Simon (Peter) also and Paul were perfect martyrs. And James and John walked in the footsteps of their Master Christ. Also (others) of the apostles hereafter in diverse places confessed and proved true martyrs. (Schaff & Wace, NAPF, 2:401)

3. Value of these passages

Noted skeptic and New Testament scholar Bart Ehrman notes, "Polycarp shows that he knows that like Paul and the other apostles, Ignatius had already been martyred for his faith." (Ehrman, TAF, 327).

These two passages certainly don't prove the apostles died as martyrs. In fact, most of the apostles are not even named. And it is not clear exactly what Polycarp means by "apostle," since he includes Paul, who was not one of the Twelve. And Aphrahat seems to indicate that John was martyred along with his brother James, which does raise questions about the reliability and source of the tradition. But these two references do provide (somewhat) early evidence for a tradition that the apostles were in fact martyred. (McDowell, DARD, 14).

B. Evidence for Individual Apostles

In this section we will analyze the likelihood of the martyrdom of each of the apostles using the following probability scale: *strong historical probability, moderate historical probability,* and *inconclusive historical record.*

1. Claims That Have Strong Historical Probability
a. Peter

The traditional view is that Peter was crucified in Rome during the reign of Nero between AD 64 and 67. The earliest evidence for the martyrdom of Peter comes from John 21:18, 19, which was written no later than thirty years after Peter's death and possibly before AD 70. Most commentators agree that this passage predicts the martyrdom of Peter. Ehrman concludes, "It is clear that Peter is being told that he will be executed (he won't die of natural causes) and that this will be the death of a martyr." (Ehrman, PPMM, 84). Other early evidence for Peter's martyrdom can be found in writings such as Clement of Rome (*1 Clement* 5:1–4), Ignatius (*Letter to the Smyrneans* 3:1–2), *The Apocalypse of Peter, The Ascension of Isaiah, The Acts of Peter, The Apocryphon of James,* Dionysius of Corinth (Eusebius, *Ecclesiastical History* 2.25.4), *Muratorian Canon,* and Tertullian (*Scorpiace* 15, *The Prescription Against Heresies* 36). The early, consistent, and unanimous testimony is that Peter died as a martyr.

b. Paul

The traditional view is that Paul was beheaded in Rome during the reign of Nero between AD 64 and 67. Scripture does not directly state his martyrdom, but there are hints in both Acts and 2 Timothy 4:6–8 that Paul knew his death was pending. The first extrabiblical evidence is found in *1 Clement* 5:5–7 (c. AD 95–96) in which Paul is described as suffering greatly for his faith and then being "set free from this world and transported up to the holy place, having become the greatest example of endurance." While details regarding the manner of his fate are lacking, the immediate context strongly implies that Clement was referring to the martyrdom of Paul. Other early evidences for the martyrdom of Paul can be found in Ignatius (*Letter to the Ephesians* 12:2), Polycarp (*Letter to the Philippians* 9:1–2), Dionysius of Corinth (Eusebius, *Ecclesiastical History* 2.25.4), Irenaeus (*Against Heresies* 3.1.1), *The Acts of Paul*, and Tertullian (*Scorpiace* 15:5–6). The early, consistent, and unanimous testimony is that Paul died as a martyr.

c. James, the Son of Zebedee

There are only a few apocryphal accounts surrounding James, the son of Zebedee. The *Acts of Saint James in India* reports a tradition that he went to India along with Peter. *The Apostolic History of Abdias* (sixth and seventh centuries) tells a story of James and his interaction with two pagan magicians who eventually confess Christ. The most likely reason apocryphal accounts about James are rare is because his martyrdom in Judea (AD 44) was so firmly entrenched in the early church and limited the trajectory of such stories. His martyrdom is first recorded in Acts 12:1, 2. The brevity of the account may be unexpected, but it does serve to strengthen its reliability. No legendary details creep into the narrative. In fact, quite the opposite is true. The account reads like an official execution. There is no good reason to doubt Luke's version of the fate of James, the son of Zebedee.

d. James, the Brother of Jesus

The earliest evidence for the death of James comes from Josephus in his *Antiquities* 20.197–203 (c. AD 93/94). Unlike the *Testimonium Flavianum* (*Antiquities of the Jews* 18.3.3), this passage is largely undisputed by scholars. It allows the dating of James's execution to AD 62, since Josephus places his death between the terms of two Roman procurators, Festus and Albinus. According to this account, the high priest Ananus had James stoned to death. The death of James is also reported by Hegesippus (Eusebius, *Ecclesiastical History* 2.23.8–18), Clement of Alexandria (*Hypotyposes* Book 7), *The First Apocalypse of James* (gnostic text), and the Pseudo-Clementines (*Recognitions* 1:66–1.71). The case for the martyrdom of James is strengthened by the fact that there are Christian (Hegesippus, Clement of Alexandria), Jewish (Josephus), and gnostic (*First Apocalypse of James*) sources that affirm its occurrence within a century and a half of the event, which suggests an early, widespread, and consistent tradition regarding the fate of James.

2. Claims That Have Moderate Historical Probability

a. Thomas

The traditional story is that Thomas traveled to India where he was speared to death. Although some Western scholars are skeptical, the Eastern Church has consistently held that Thomas ministered in India and died there as a martyr. There are records of travel from the Middle East into India during the first century, so there is no reason to doubt Thomas *could* have made the journey. Additional evidence comes from the *Acts of Thomas* (c. AD 200–220), which records the traditional story of his fate. Many write off this account as entirely fictional, but the mere fact that it contains historical figures, such as Thomas, Gondophares, Gad, and *possibly* even Habban and Xanthippe, Mazdai, and also the city of Andrapolis, indicates that it is not entirely divorced from a historical memory. While there is not any written history in India prior to the arrival of the

Portuguese in the sixteenth century, there certainly was a sense of history passed down orally through poems, songs, customs, and celebrations of the people. The St. Thomas Christians, for instance, are utterly convinced that their heritage, including the introduction of the Syriac or Chaldaic (East Syriac) languages, traces back to the apostle Thomas himself. The community has preserved many antiquities that testify to their traditions.

b. Andrew

The earliest written record of the martyrdom of Andrew comes from the *Acts of Andrew* (c. AD 150–210). This text concludes with Andrew speaking directly to the cross of his crucifixion, as if it were a living person, and then demanding the executioners kill him. Many later written accounts of Andrew's death exist, but they all appear to have originated with the *Acts of Andrew*. As a whole, the *Acts of Andrew* received a mixed reception in the early church—ranging from condemnation (Pope Innocent I) to adaptation and use for popular piety (Gregory of Tours). The *Acts of Andrew* is part of the first wave of Apocryphal Acts, including the *Acts of Peter, Paul, Thomas,* and *John*. While these contain legendary accretion, they also preserved the most likely fate for their respective apostle, including a natural death for John. Although the writers of the various Apocryphal Acts took creative license, they were bound by a known tradition. The same may also be true for the *Acts of Andrew*. Hippolytus's *On the Twelve* (c. third century) may possibly preserve an independent tradition of his fate when it describes Andrew as "crucified, suspended on an olive tree, at Patrae." But we cannot be sure. The *Acts of Andrew* clearly contains legendary embellishment, but there is some indication it may have been connected to a reliable tradition about the fate of Andrew.

3. Claims with an Inconclusive Historical Record

It is difficult to know for sure what happened to the remaining apostles (excluding John).* The evidence is late and filled with legendary accretion. The claim that Bartholomew was skinned alive, for instance, doesn't show up until about AD 500. And there are varying accounts that he died by drowning, beating, and crucifixion. Does that make each of these false? Not necessarily. But it makes it difficult to have much historical confidence in his actual fate. And the same is true with the other "minor" apostles. While there are no early accounts that any of the apostles recanted, we simply don't know how many of them were killed because of their testimony about Christ.

C. Conclusion Regarding the Historical Record

We have strong historical evidence that at least some of the apostles were martyred for their faith in the risen Christ, and significant, persistent traditions attest to their conviction that Jesus literally rose from the dead and appeared to them. We turn now to the apologetic significance of the apostles' martyrdom.

III. Common Objections to the Apologetic Value of the Apostles' Martyrdoms

A. Others Have Died for Their Beliefs
1. Objection

One of the most common responses to the deaths of the apostles is the claim that others have died for their beliefs. For instance, on September 11, 2001, nineteen radical Muslims hijacked four planes and, killing themselves

---

* While we believe John died a natural death, there are leading conservative scholars who believe he died as a martyr. For instance, see Ben Witherington, "The Martyrdom of the Zebedee Brothers," in *Biblical Archaeological Review* 33 (May/June): 26. For an in-depth analysis of the martyrdom of John, see Sean McDowell, *The Fate of the Apostles*, 135–156.

in the process, attacked and killed thousands of people. Is this evidence, then, for the truth of Islam?

2. Response

This objection misses a key difference between the deaths of the apostles and modern martyrs.* Modern martyrs die for what they sincerely believe is true, but their knowledge comes secondhand from others. For instance, Muslim terrorists who attacked the Twin Towers on 9/11 were not eyewitnesses of any miracles by Mohammed. In fact, they were not eyewitnesses of *any* events of the life of Mohammed. Rather, they lived over thirteen centuries later. No doubt the Muslim radicals acted out of sincere belief, but their convictions were received secondhand at best from others. They did not know Mohammed personally, see him fulfill any prophecy, or witness him doing any miracles such as walking on water, healing the blind, or rising from the dead. There is a massive difference between willingly dying for the sake of the religious ideas accepted from the testimony of others (Muslim radicals) and willingly dying for the proclamation of a faith based upon one's own eyewitness account (apostles). The deaths of the nineteen terrorists provide no more evidence for the truth of Islam than my death would provide for the truth of Christianity. My martyrdom would show I really believed it, but nothing more.

In contrast to the beliefs of Buddhist monks and Muslim radicals and any other modern martyrs, including Christians, the beliefs of the apostles was [sic] not received secondhand, but from personal experience with the risen Jesus

(Acts 1:21, 22; 1 Cor. 15:5–8). They proclaimed what they had seen and heard with their own eyes and ears, not stories received from others (Acts 1:3; 2:22–24). Peter not only claims that he was an eyewitness but that the events took place in public and that his audience had full knowledge of them. The events were not done secretly in a corner. Buddhist monks and Muslim terrorists are certainly willing to suffer and die for a faith they received secondhand, but the apostles were willing to suffer and die for what they had seen with their own eyes.

If Jesus had not risen from the grave and appeared to his apostles, they alone would have known the falsity of his claims [that he would be resurrected]. In other words, if the resurrection did not happen, the apostles would have willingly suffered and died for something they knew was false. While people die for what they believe is true, it is a stretch to think *all* the apostles were willing to suffer and die for a claim they *knew* was false. The suffering and deaths of the apostles testify to the sincerity of their beliefs that they had seen the risen Jesus." (McDowell, FOTA, 260).

B. They Were Not Given the Opportunity to Recant

1. Objection

Moss believes the lack of official records of the apostles being given the opportunity to recant and live undermines the validity of their testimony. This is the missing element, she claims, required to make the argument they died *for* Christ (Moss, TMOP, 137).

2. Response

She [Moss] is right that there is not a record of the apostles being offered the opportunity

---

* We hesitate even to use the term "martyr" to refer to Muslim terrorists (or *any* terrorists, for that matter). Christian martyrs accept suffering and death at the hands of others, whereas Muslim terrorists intentionally take the lives of others. Islamic terrorists expect their suffering to be brief—an instant annihilation, in some cases. And they expect to cause even further injury and suffering to those who do not actually die immediately.

to recant, but they ministered in potentially caustic environments with full awareness of the possible consequences for their actions (See Acts 4; 5; 6:8—8:3, and 12:1–5). The fact that their founding leader was a crucified criminal of the Roman Empire also certainly plays a part of their collective consciousness. Jesus even warned his disciples that the world would hate and even persecute them, as it did him (John 15:18–25). Every time the apostles proclaimed the name of Christ, then, they knowingly risked suffering and death. Even so, they continued to teach and preach the risen Jesus. Given their active proclamation of Christ, and their full awareness of the cost of such proclamation, if some of the apostles died for their faith, they qualify under the traditional definition of martyr. (McDowell, FOTA, 8).

IV. Conclusion

The willingness of the apostles to suffer and die for their faith does not *prove* the resurrection is true. For the larger resurrection argument, see chapter 10. But it does show the depth of the apostles' convictions. They were not liars. They did not invent the resurrection stories. As Blaise Pascal once said, "I only believe histories whose witnesses are ready to be put to death." (Pascal, *Pensees*, 249) The apostles proclaimed the risen Jesus to skeptical and antagonistic audiences with full knowledge they would likely suffer and die for their beliefs. All the apostles suffered and were "ready to be put to death," and we have good reason to believe some of them actually faced execution. There is no evidence they ever waivered. Their convictions were not based on secondhand testimony, but personal experience with the risen Jesus, whom they truly believed was the risen Messiah, banking their lives on it. It is difficult to imagine what more a group of ancient witnesses could have done to show greater depth of sincerity and commitment to the truth.

PART III

EVIDENCE FOR THE OLD TESTAMENT

CHAPTER 14

THE OLD TESTAMENT AND ANCIENT NEAR EASTERN INFLUENCES

OVERVIEW

I. Introduction

The similarities between ancient Near East (ANE) texts and the Old Testament (OT) are striking because the flow of the narratives often mirror one another. Did the biblical writers simply copy from ANE sources? Do these commonalities undermine the reliability of the OT accounts? It would be dishonest to say that these resemblances are unimportant, and they cannot be considered mere coincidence. We must ask ourselves,

"What is the relationship of these stories to one another, and how do we accurately account for the similarities?"

The fields of study surrounding the ANE and the OT are very complex. They include, for instance, the study of historical records of empires and events; languages (linguistics and devices of language such as metaphor or idiom); comparative literature (literary genres such as narrative, law, proverb, letter, or poetry); and archaeological investigation. This chapter makes inquiries into the relationship between ANE literature, beliefs, and practices, and the OT, including a history of ANE studies and an introductory discussion of the range of approaches to this scholarship and the methodologies used to understand the relationship of the OT to the ANE. Finally, this chapter compares examples of the various literary genres, creation accounts, origins of deity, flood accounts, and a selection of religious and cultural beliefs of the ANE with corresponding examples from the OT.

II. History of Ancient Near Eastern Studies

Studies surrounding the ANE have their roots in the late eighteenth century. Despite their seemingly recent inception, these studies have greatly expanded our knowledge of history. The fields of study surrounding the ANE are rife with opportunity and are becoming increasingly specialized. The contributions of each field enhance our understanding of the ANE.

A. The Early Years: 1798–1900

Before the late eighteenth and early nineteenth centuries we had little knowledge of the ANE and the world of OT Israel in general. Discoveries made in quite recent history (as compared with the millennia between modernity and the events themselves) have brought about an interesting dynamic in our current understanding of the OT and in the recent history of interpretation. The viewpoints emanating from modern scholarship, especially those from recent archaeological discoveries, often differ from the traditional understandings of earlier church fathers, who were influenced by Greek philosophy and Western concepts.

1. Discoveries in Egypt

During Napoleon's invasion of Egypt in 1798, he commissioned an expeditionary group to survey Egypt's ancient monuments. The discoveries they recorded and published in the early nineteenth century were paramount in propelling Western civilization into an era of discovery regarding ANE civilization. (Currid, AG, 13) Napoleon's expedition uncovered the Valley of Kings, an important moment in Egyptian archaeology because it unearthed the royal tombs of the eighteenth–twentieth dynasties. This proved to be especially interesting because the time frame of these dynasties was also known as the New Kingdom Period that ranged from 1550–1070 BC and included the time frame in which many scholars believe the Hebrew exodus out of Egypt took place. (Currid, AG, 13)

John Currid, the Carl McMurray Professor of Old Testament at the Reformed Seminary, points out the extreme importance of this famous discovery:

The most significant find of the Napoleonic excursion was the Rosetta Stone (1799). It proved to be invaluable because it was the key to unlocking ancient Egyptian hieroglyphics, a picture script unutilized for over fourteen hundred years. Dating to the time of King Ptolemy V (204–180 BC), the Rosetta Stone is inscribed in three scripts: demotic [an ancient Egyptian script used between the Late Egyptian and Coptic languages and first used by the Greek historian Herodotus], Greek, and hieroglyphs. The Greek proved to be a translation of the ancient Egyptian language on the stone. The linguistic study of the of the Rosetta Stone by the English physician Thomas Young (1819) and the Frenchman Jean-Francois Champollion (1822) "marked the beginning of the scientific reading of hieroglyphs and the first step toward formulation of a system of ancient Egyptian grammar, the basis of modern Egyptology." [Andrews, RS, 619–20] Thus the first true archeological find in the Near East was one of the greatest and most critical discoveries in the history of the discipline! (Currid, DALB, 18–20)

The ability to decipher hieroglyphs of ancient Egypt turned out to be the key that scholars had needed to open up the door to a much better understanding of Egypt's highly civilized culture of previous centuries. It also provided verification of certain OT biblical accounts, including the invasion of Israel in the tenth century BC, as recorded in 1 Kings 14:25, 26 and 2 Chronicles 12:2–4. (Currid, AG, 15)

2. Discoveries in Mesopotamia

The early-to mid-nineteenth century also brought us abundant and fresh sources of archaeological data from the ancient Mesopotamian region, as highlighted by Israel Finkelstein and Neil Asher Silberman in their book *The Bible Unearthed*:

Beginning in the 1840s, scholarly representatives of England, France, and eventually the United States and Germany uncovered the cities, vast places, and cuneiform archives of the empires of Assyria and Babylonia. For the first time since the biblical period, the main monuments and cities of those powerful Eastern empires were uncovered. Places like Nineveh and Babylon, previously known primarily from the Bible, were now seen to be the capitals of powerful and aggressive empires whose artists and scribes thoroughly documented the military campaigns and political events of their time. Thus references to a number of important biblical kings were identified in Mesopotamian cuneiform archives—the Israelite kings Omri, Ahab, and

Jehu and the Judahite kings Hezekiah and Manasseh, among others. These outside references allowed scholars to see biblical history in a wider perspective, and to synchronize the reigns of the biblical monarchs with the more complete dating systems of the ancient Near East. Slowly the connections were made, and the regnal dates of the Israelite and Judahite kings, Assyrian and Babylonian rulers, and Egyptian pharaohs were set in order, giving quite precise dates for the first time. (Finkelstein and Silberman, BU, 18)

The discoveries within ancient Mesopotamia turned out to be even more relevant to the history of the OT than those that were being found in Egypt, bearing as they did upon a longer and closer association between ANE and OT cultures. (Finkelstein and Silberman, BU, 18)

3. Origins of the Old Testament Questioned

As creation and flood accounts of other cultures surfaced in the late nineteenth century, ANE scholars questioned whether the Hebrew writers of the OT hadn't simply borrowed myths from other cultures and stripped them of their pagan elements and tailored those myths to fit their own beliefs. Scholars often concluded that the OT had a purely human origin, i.e., was solely and entirely the result of human activity, lacking any divine influence. (Walton, ANETOT, 16) The more that ANE texts with a correspondence to the OT were discovered or translated, the more did critical scholars propose that the OT borrowed from other ANE sources, and the more the chasm widened between the view of an OT with only human origins and the view of an OT with claims of divine inspiration. Friedrich Delitzsch, noted Assyriologist of the early twentieth century, went so far as to say that "the OT was no book of Christian religion and should be excluded from Christian theology." (Walton, ANETOT, 17)

He explained further:

> How great the similarity between all things in Babel and Bible! Here as well as there the fondness for rendering speech and thought vivid by symbolical actions (I cite here merely the scapegoat which is chased away into the desert); here as well as there the same world of constant wonders and signs, of perpetual revelations of the divinity, particularly through dreams, the same naive conceptions of the divinity! As in Babel the gods eat and drink and even retire to rest, so Yahweh goes walking in Paradise in the cool of the evening, or takes delight in the smell of Noah's sacrifice. And just as in the OT Yahweh speaks to Moses and Aaron and to all the prophets, so also in Babel the gods speak to men, either directly or through the mouth of their priests and divinely inspired prophets and prophetesses. (Delitzsch, BB, 91–92)

Delitzsch wasn't the only one who had his doubts about the origins of the Bible. A growing number of nineteenth-century scholars charged the OT writers with plagiarism of other ANE texts. (Currid, AG, 17) In fact, many scholars still see remnants of ANE mythology hidden in the Old Testament today. However, nearly a century later, scholars are able to understand that, according to biblical scholar John Walton, "Delitzsch's lectures were not motivated solely by a sense of scientific objectivity." (Walton, ANETOT, 17) In fact, questions have been raised about Delitzsch's motivation—he was known as a scholar with an anti-Semitic and an anti-Christian bias, which may have influenced the haste and even naiveté of the conclusions we find in his two lectures on *Babel and Bible*. (Currid, AG, 17)

B. The Later Years: 1900–Today

The early twentieth century brought with it a continued flood of discoveries, including thousands of inscriptions and tablets from the Hittite city of Bagazkoy and the royal Hittite archives, allowing historians to gain insights into ancient Hittite history and culture that are still being pieced together today.

Beginning around 1900, major advances in the linguistic studies of ANE texts and the greatly increasing amount of information make it nearly impossible for any scholar to keep abreast of all of the discoveries. No longer do some historians solely focus on OT biblical history. Instead they choose to specialize upon a precise topic, while drawing upon a wide range of sources from individual cultures and languages.

1. Critical Scholarship:

Some contemporary scholars claim that the question of the relationship of the OT and ANE civilizations has become less relevant. A high level of cynicism and suspicion is evident on the more skeptical side of modern scholarship when dealing with the OT. One such example of this suspicion can be seen in Thomas Thompson's comments on the OT:

> We have seen that the biblical chronologies are not grounded on historical memory, but are rather based on a very late theological schema that presupposes a very historical world-view. Those efforts to use the biblical narratives for a reconstruction of the history of the Near East, in a manner comparable to the use of the archives at Mari and similar finds, can justly be dismissed as fundamental [flawed in a fundamental way]. (Thompson, HPN, 315)

Thompson here seems to take the stance of many who follow the higher criticism (arising in the nineteenth century) that critiques the formation of the Bible. The assumption is that writers of the Bible had no direct memory of the historical events they recorded. They are said to have set down a tradition and to impose the worldview of their own time as they wrote about much earlier times.

Currid argues that these scholars hold that the history of Israel in the OT is "nothing more than a Judaic *Iliad*, *Odyssey*, or even *Winnie-the-Pooh*." (Currid, AEOT, 172–173)

2. Balanced Perspective

Thompson's statement, however, is not characteristic of the majority of scholars today. In fact, many critical scholars still see historical value extending back to David/Solomon. Walton suggests that challenges to Thompson's view have come from "competent Assyriologists and Egyptologists such as K. A. Kitchen, D. J. Wiseman, A. R. Millard, K. L. Younger, and J. Hoffmeier, who not only refute some of the charges leveled by skeptics, but also provide evidence of the Bible's reliability through their cultural and comparative studies." (Walton, ANETOT, 36) Walton elaborates:

> Scholars engaged in this work use their research to challenge the conclusions of critical scholarship and in the process to authenticate the biblical text. Such studies intend to exonerate the Old Testament and defend against spurious attacks on its integrity. (Walton, ANETOT, 36)

Archaeological evidence relating to the OT is highlighted in much greater depth in many other chapters of this book. This chapter's focus is the substance of the texts.

III. The Old Testament and Ancient Near Eastern Scholarship

This section concentrates on the varying perspectives within the field of OT and ancient Near Eastern scholarship, examining how these perspectives shape scholars' interpretations of what biblical authors write. In particular, the section examines the ways that biblical authors take well-known expressions and motifs from the ANE milieu and apply them to the person and work of Yahweh within the OT while avoiding giving credence to the other gods of the ancient world.

A. A Continuum of Viewpoints*

There is a continuum of viewpoints as to how the OT relates to the ANE. On one side of this continuum are those who assert or imply that the narratives and beliefs chronicled in the OT are mere adaptations and retellings of the myths of other ANE cultures. Critical Old Testament scholars in this camp readily deny the existence of stark contrasts between the OT and other texts of the ANE, claiming that a closer relationship exists between them than the evidence might reveal.

On the other side of this spectrum are OT scholars who, with strong and often unreasonable presuppositions of their own, generally dismiss any similarities between the OT Israelites to the ancient Near Eastern civilizations. Many of these scholars oppose any study that looks at the full context and setting of the text in relation to its meaning. These individuals feel that comparative studies of these texts pose a potential threat to the doctrine of inspiration. (Walton, ANETOT, 36)

---

* For further study into the various viewpoints that make up this continuum see John H. Walton, *Ancient Near Eastern Thought and the Old Testament: Introducing the Conceptual World of the Hebrew Bible* (Grand Rapids, MI: Baker Academic, 2006); John D. Currid, *Against the Gods: The Polemical Theology of the OT* (Wheaton, IL: Crossway, 2013); John N. Oswalt, *The Bible among the Myths: Unique Revelation or Just Ancient Literature?* (Grand Rapids, MI: Zondervan, 2009); Bruce K. Waltke and Charles Yu, *An OT Theology: An Exegetical, Canonical, and Thematic Approach* (Grand Rapids, MI: Zondervan, 2007).

Walton highlights the differences in these two camps: "Critical scholars [those who view the OT as a mere myth and latecomer in world literature] considered their opponents to be naïve traditionalists. Confessional scholars [those seeking to fit Assyriology into their theological presuppositions] considered their opponents to be godless heretics." (Walton, ANETOT, 36)

Between these two extremes, then, much is at stake—for both camps. On the one hand, for critical scholars to accept the uniqueness of the OT is to risk accepting its divine inspiration and giving up one's naturalistic presuppositions; on the other hand, for confessional scholars to deny similarities between OT and other ANE texts risks misunderstanding the OT's historical relationship to the surrounding cultures that no doubt influenced the composition of the OT. Both of these extremes fail to interpret properly the evidence that has accumulated over the last two hundred years relating to the OT and the ANE. Cultural and comparative studies continue to illuminate the evidence and aid in painting a more accurate picture of the past that points to the historicity of the Old Testament, the uniqueness of Scripture, the divine influence of the text, and the lack of original contradictions. (All of these topics are covered in much greater detail throughout various chapters of this book.)

B. The Evangelical Scholar

Somewhere in the center of this continuum we find a number of OT scholars honestly searching to discern the true meaning, context, and relationship of the various ANE and OT texts. Recognizing both similarities and differences between these texts, conservative evangelical scholars' conclusions sometimes differ, but they all share some core commitments:

1. High View of Scripture

Evangelical OT scholars remain unanimous in their high view of Scripture, even though extensive debate concerning the nature and extent of inerrancy continues. John Walton and D. Brent Sandy characterize a high view of Scripture in this way:

Fundamentally, we believe that the Bible deserves the highest possible honor as the richest, deepest, most powerful book ever written—there are simply no contenders. It is a literary masterpiece, a magnum opus, a stellar performance. But there's more to the story. The ultimate importance of the Bible lies elsewhere: it is the inspired revelation of Almighty God, a heavenly treasure in a world of impoverished ideas, a sparkling mountain stream in the driest of deserts. Our point, however, is not to worship the Bible; we worship the God of the Bible. (Walton and Sandy, LWS, 11–12)

2. Polemical Theology (Definition and Potential Use)

Polemical theology, as defined by Currid, "is the use by biblical writers of the thought forms and stories that were common in ancient Near Eastern culture, while filling them with radically new meaning." (Currid, AG, 25)

This angle of study seeks to protect orthodox theology by interpreting the biblical writers' use of ANE forms and details in order to refute polytheism. Therefore these scholars underline the distinctions between the worldviews of the ANE and that of the OT, especially within the OT texts and concepts that exhibit the greatest similarities with those of the ANE.

Currid explains what polemic theology reveals to us about the Old Testament, although we believe it is also used in historical scholarship as well:

Fundamentally, we believe that the Bible deserves the highest possible honor as the richest, deepest, most powerful book ever written — there are simply no contenders. It is a literary masterpiece, a magnum opus, a stellar performance. But there's more to the story. The ultimate importance of the Bible lies elsewhere: it is the inspired revelation of Almighty God.

Walton and Sandy

The primary purpose of polemical theology is to demonstrate emphatically and graphically the distinctions between the worldview of the Hebrews and the beliefs and practices of the rest of the ancient Near East. It helps to show that Hebrew thought is not a mere mouthpiece of other ancient Near Eastern cultures. . . . The purpose of polemical theology is to demonstrate the essential distinctions between Hebrew thought and ancient Near Eastern beliefs and practices. (Currid, AG, 25–26)

3. The Use of Polemics (An Example)

Polemical theology rejects any encroachment of false gods into orthodox belief; there is an absolute intolerance of polytheism. Accordingly, polemical theology emphasizes the monotheistic nature of the OT; however, not all scholars who accept the monotheism of the OT feel that polemics are the sole avenue to demonstrate this.

Many scholars agree that the Biblical writers, while using elements of ANE beliefs and practices, do so to highlight divergence in thought and narrative and therefore they demonstrate Scripture's uniqueness. While some scholars, like Walton, do not hold as strongly to polemical theology, Currid argues "that many of the parallels between ancient Near Eastern literature and the Old Testament, from creation accounts to flood stories, may be properly and fully understood only through the right use of polemical theology." (Currid, AG, 31)

For example, several times within Exodus (3:19, 20; 6:1; 13:3, 14–16; 15:6, 12, 16; 32:11) as well as Deuteronomy (3:24; 6:21; 9:26; 26:8), there are references to Yahweh's deliverance of his people with an outstretched arm or a mighty (strong) hand. Similarly, within the texts of ancient Egypt, we see a consistent description of Pharaoh's power over his enemies being characterized by a "strong hand" and "strong arm." (Currid, AG, 26) K. A. Kitchen concludes that there "appears to be here a deliberately adopted Egyptianism in Hebrew, as riposte to the ubiquitous pose of Pharaoh smiting his enemies and being endlessly entitled 'Lord of the strong arm' (*neb khopesh*)." (Kitchen, OROT, 254)

Currid uses the same anti-Pharaoh example to illustrate how the OT authors deliberately borrowed concepts and expressions from other ANE cultures: "The biblical writers employ such borrowing for the purpose of taunting. The Hebrew authors use polemic to call into question the power of Pharaoh, and to underscore the true might of Yahweh!" (Currid, AG, 27)

4. A Caution Regarding Polemics

The OT is full of theological polemics; however, like any other device, if you make polemics an undue focus of OT scholarship, you may miss out on the rest that the text has to offer. D. A. Carson states that "while polemical theology is just about unavoidable in theory and should not, as a matter of faithfulness, be skirted, one worries about those who make it their specialism." (Carson, "Editorial," 156)

In addition, Walton makes these observations regarding the improper use of polemics by the untrained individual:

> As was early evident in the field of biblical archaeology, many who would take upon themselves the mantle of apologist have not had the scholarly training to give them discernment for their task. Misinterpreted data, out-of-date or disproven arguments, haphazardly selected factoids, and neglect of information that would negate their point all characterize the special pleading that is too often obvious in this approach. Though lacking credibility, these polemical approaches can gain a wide following among a sometimes gullible public. This is not to label such writers as charlatans. They are zealots with a mission that in and of itself may be admirable. It is just that they are insufficiently schooled in the methods that would allow them to use properly the tools that they are exploiting. Of course, not all apologists are lacking scholarly credentials, nor does the apologist's task necessarily involve special pleading or distortion of the data. (Walton, ANETOT, 37)

Walton's correct description of the dangers for those in the field of biblical archaeology apply to any untrained scholars who hold on tightly to strong presuppositions that elevate theological polemics to a supreme status above all other approaches. The warning, in fact, expands to apply in any case where an apologist's commitment to polemics outruns other considerations. This runs the risk of improperly discerning the cultural, historical and geographical context of the Old Testament.

C. Textual Synthesis

Those who recognize a greater synthesis between the OT and the texts of the ANE do not deny the importance of theological polemics, but instead focus heavily on the comparative studies of the texts in order to understand whether a particular motif, passage, or narrative within the OT suggests a polemic or perhaps a simple element of commonality. That is not to say that either those who suggest a greater level of polemical theology or those who see a greater synthesis between the texts operate with a faulty hermeneutic but that there are differences in some of their conclusions.

Walton points out that a scholar can identify and understand some degree of synthesis or commonality by attention to elements of both the cultural content and the literary form of the texts: "The range of this understanding can include behavior and belief within the culture, or the ways in which a culture is represented in art or literature. Within the literary category, areas for research include the larger issue of literary genre, the analysis of specific traditions and texts, and the use of individual metaphors, idioms, and words." (Walton, ANETOT, 37)

Comparisons of the OT with ANE texts reveal many similarities. However, rather than simply listing the similarities, comparative research allows us to "classify nuances of relationship more precisely." (Walton, ANETOT, 26) While one may be tempted to write off the OT's unique status as God's Word because of these similarities, Walton provides some reasoning as to why that should not be the case, especially when comparing texts written in the same genres:

> Occasionally comparisons within genres (such as law, story, or poem) reveal very close similarities between the biblical and ancient Near

Eastern literatures on the level of content. Such similarities do not negate the individuality of either. Even if the Hebrew Bible had the very same law or the very same proverb that was found in the ancient Near East, we may find uniqueness in how that law or proverb was understood, or how it was nuanced by the literary context in which it was incorporated. At other times the Israelite version may not be noticeably different from the ancient Near Eastern example at any level. (Walton, ANE-TOT, 23)

1. An Example: Cosmos Temple

Walton describes a striking example of textual synthesis between the OT and ANE, in that both think of and describe the cosmos as a temple:

> In Isaiah 66:1 the Lord indicates: "Heaven is my throne and the earth is my footstool, where is the house you will build for me, where will my resting place be?" This is not like the claim in Jeremiah 10, where the human crafts-manship of the idols invalidates their role. God is not suggesting that a human temple is somehow sacrilegious and incompatible with his transcendence. But he is referring to the inadequacy of a human-made temple as being considered the true temple (cf. 1 Kings 8:27). It is only a micro-scale representation of the cosmic temple. Psalm 78:69 communicates a similar idea when it indicates that the temple was built on the model of the cosmos. Ideas like these are also found in literature from Mesopotamia that compares temples to the heavens and the earth and gives them a cosmic location and function. It is evident, then, that Israel and their neighbors shared an ideology that understood the cosmos in temple terms and viewed the temple as a model of the cosmos or as the cosmic temple." (Walton, ANETOT, 127)

2. A Caution Regarding Textual Synthesis

Scholars who subscribe to at least some level of textual synthesis understand that these instances are not a denial of the fundamental differences between the OT and other ANE texts. However, without proper grounding in the hermeneutical process the temptation can be to latch onto a particular standpoint and stretch the evidence.

For example, some scholars attempt to read common ANE creation conflict into the OT creation account, specifically into the Genesis 1:2: "The earth was without form, and void; and darkness was on the face of the deep. And the Spirit of God was hovering over the face of the waters." Some scholars argue the word *tehom* ("deep") directly relates to the goddess Tiamat found in the Enuma Elish. (In that Babylonian creation account, the god Marduk combats her, kills her, and creates the universe from her body, afterward creating humans from the blood of another god.) In speaking of the Genesis account and its relation to the Enuma Elish, Christine Hayes states,

> The similarities here [Genesis] are imme-diately apparent. Our story opens with a temporal clause and a wind that sweeps over the chaotic water or deep (like the wind of Marduk released against the chaotic waters of Tiamat). The Hebrew word for "deep" is *Tehom*, the Hebrew equivalent of Tiamat. In fact, a better translation of verse 2 might read "darkness was on the face of the Deep," without a definite article and capitalized almost as if deep were a proper name. (Hayes, IB, 38)

In response to the suggestion that the goddess Tiamat is directly equivalent to the "deep" (*tehom*) in Genesis 1:2, John Bloom and C. John Collins state:

Many have come to acknowledge that the supposed parallel between Babylonian Tiamat and Hebrew *tehom* ("the deep") is very unlikely. The linguistic details show that there is no way that Hebrew *tehom* can be a borrowing from Akkadian Tiamat; likewise, "without form and void" (Gen. 1:2) is a phrase, not for "unruly and disorderly chaos," but for "an unproductive and uninhabited place." Further, nothing in Genesis 1 can be reasonably said to imply any kind of struggle on God's part: Psalm 33:9 ("for he spoke, and it came to be; he commanded, and it stood firm") is an excellent summary of the creation story. (Bloom and Collins, CAANER, 20–24)

The danger in taking textual synthesis too far is to run the risk of de-historicizing or even mythicizing the Old Testament. The task for scholarship that would both honor the Old Testament as the unique revelation of God and also recognize the similarities with ANE texts has been faced in a similar way even before the ANE discoveries of the past two centuries. Augustine (354–430), who was deeply trained in the Greek and Roman scholarship of his day, asked (rhetorically) in *On Christian Doctrine* how to proceed in scriptural interpretation. He addressed topics that touch on those in Greco-Roman texts, and he encouraged biblical interpreters toward a cultural awareness that recognizes both the insights and the erroneous polytheistic views in texts that arose amidst polytheism. He pointed out, "Let every good and true Christian understand that wherever truth may be found, it belongs to his Master; and while he recognizes and acknowledges the truth, even in their religious literature, let him reject the figments of superstition. . . ." (II.18) Augustine ends the chapter by quoting Romans 1:21–23, underlining his understanding that wherever a glimpse of truth appears, God has sovereignly permitted its presence, and it bears witness to him.

3. Scholarly Middle Ground

It is not easy to find middle ground between those who would hold to a greater level of polemical theology and those who propose a greater synthesis of the texts between the OT and ANE. However, scholars at both ends of the spectrum recognize the importance of this middle ground. For example, Currid, who relies heavily on polemical theology, offers a very honest assessment:

[The relationship between the writings of the Old Testament and other ancient Near Eastern literature] is a difficult, complicated, and much-debated topic in the field of biblical studies today. To be frank, there is little consensus regarding exactly how the two relate to each other. There are extremes, to be sure: on the one hand, some believe that ancient Near Eastern studies have little to contribute to our understanding of the Old Testament and, in fact, constitute a danger to Scripture. On the other hand, there are some who would say that the Old Testament is not unique but it is merely another expression of ancient Near Eastern literature that is grounded in myth, legend, and folklore. Surely the truth lies somewhere between the two extremes. It is certainly undeniable that the historical, geographical, and cultural context of the Bible is the ancient Near East, and study of the era has much to add to our understanding of the Old Testament. But it is also true that the Old Testament worldview is unique in the ancient Near East, and this is immediately confirmed by its all-pervasive monotheism. It simply does not swallow ancient Near Eastern thought hook, line, and sinker. And so, the question for modern minds in this regard is, what precisely is the relationship of the OT to ancient Near Eastern literature? (Currid, AG, 9)

Walton proposes a greater synthesis between the OT and ANE. Recognizing the spectrum of scholarship relating to the similarities and differences between ANE and OT texts, he suggests that students undertake background and comparative study with four goals in mind to help us understand the OT better.

- Students may study the history of the ancient Near East as a means of recovering knowledge of the events that shaped the lives of people in the ancient world.
- Students may study archaeology as a means of recovering the lifestyle reflected in the material culture of the ancient world.
- Students may study the literature of the ancient Near East as a means of penetrating the heart and soul of the people who inhabited the ancient world that Israel shared.
- Students may study the languages of the ancient Near East as a means of gaining additional insight into the semantics, lexicography, idioms, and metaphors used in Hebrew. (Walton, ANETOT, 27–28)

Understanding the various subtleties that make up either end of the spectrum can assist in helping us to find the scholarly middle ground and perhaps the proper understanding of the relationship of the texts.

IV. Comparison Studies of the ANE and Old Testament

We will now compare the various literary genres, creation accounts, flood accounts, religious and cultural beliefs, and practices of the ANE and the OT in order to understand

more clearly the influences the ANE may have had on the OT.

A. Literary Genres*
1. Importance of Literary Genre

In order to understand context and intent, we ought to evaluate the literary genre of OT and ANE texts we study. Interestingly, while genre (such as prose, poetry, law, etc.) was evaluated before the discovery of the various ANE texts, it was never considered important until the similarities between the ANE and OT started becoming more apparent. (Halton et al., GHFN, 173) Charles Halton points out this shift in scholarship:

> The study of genre came to the fore after the discovery of ancient Near Eastern texts that bear a remarkable similarity to the Bible. In the nineteenth century, the scholarly world was abuzz over newly discovered Babylonian creation accounts, Assyrian prophecies, and Sumerian king lists. Almost immediately, people began making comparisons between these texts and the themes and forms of Sacred Scripture. Yet, before these discussions could develop too far, another conversation had to take place. (Halton et al., GHFN, 173)

What was needed was a conversation yielding a more complex understanding of genre, including the acknowledgment that a single text may include multiple genres and that ancient texts may be written in forms unfamiliar to us.

2. Comparing and Contrasting Genre

In order to bring about meaningful results by comparing ANE to OT literature, we need

---

* For a more in-depth study of literary genres see D. Brent Sandy and Ronald L. Giese, *Cracking Old Testament Codes: A Guide to Interpreting Literary Genres of the Old Testament* (Nashville, TN: Broadman & Holman, 1995); John H. Walton, *Ancient Israelite Literature in Its Cultural Context: A Survey of Parallels between Biblical and Ancient Near Eastern Texts* (Grand Rapids, MI: Regency Reference Library, 1989); Victor Harold Matthews and Don C. Benjamin, *Old Testament Parallels: Laws and Stories from the Ancient Near East* (New York: Paulist, 1991).

to compare like genres. If the genres are not the same, similarities and differences within the texts tell us very little. Even though comparisons don't lose all meaning between different genres, such comparisons do not carry the same weight of those comparisons made in similar genres. (Halton et al., GHFN, 173)

3. Scholarly Debate About Genre

As in many fields of study, the study of genre is not without its disagreements and varying opinions. Some scholars, like Herman Gunkel, whom some consider to be the formative voice on genre study, have "a very rigid conception of genre." (Halton et al., GHFN, 173) On the basis of that strict definition, Gunkel concludes that every text is comprised of only one genre and there can be no simultaneous multiplicity of genres for any given text. (Halton et al., GHFN, 173) However, many scholars now believe that multiple genres can be present in a single text simultaneously, making an accurate analysis of the texts that much more difficult. James Hoffmeier highlights two potential dangers in conducting genre analysis as it relates to the book of Genesis:

One of the dangers of doing genre analysis of a large piece of ancient literature—be it in the Hebrew Bible, or Mesopotamian or Egyptian literature—is in imposing a single literary category on a work that is quite complex and made up of a variety of types of literature. Then too, one mistake of modern scholarship is to press onto ancient literature modern literary categories that did not exist in the ancient world. (Hoffmeier, GHT, 25)

However, the challenges of genre study should not hinder us from recognizing its importance. Old Testament scholar Ronald Geise observes:

Unfortunately, many who study the Bible are unaware of genre as a critical step in interpretation. . . . [But] in the last two decades the context of literary forms has begun to be discussed in the scholarly literature. Even with this beginning, little has been written for a more general audience, and that is especially unfortunate. Ignorance of this level of context leads to some of the worst mistakes of interpretation. On the other hand, familiarity with this context provides a window through which we can greatly increase our understanding of what the biblical authors were trying to say. (Sandy and Geise, COTC, 167)

Clearly, differences in our understanding of genre influence how we view the relation of OT text to those of the ANE. Nonetheless, genre, though often ignored completely, is actually the level of context to which an interpreter should give the most attention.

B. Creation Accounts

Most ANE cultures provide a cosmogony, which is a story about the origin of the universe. We will now examine the ANE creation accounts from Mesopotamia and Egypt and seek to understand how the cosmogony of the Old Testament, specifically Genesis 1 and 2, parallels them, differs from them, or employs their form and detail to offer polemic.

1. Mesopotamian Creation Accounts*

Unlike the biblical account of creation, the Mesopotamian accounts have been shown to

---

* For more resources on Mesopotamian creation accounts see John Walton, *The Lost World of Genesis One* (Downers Grove, IL: IVP Academic, 2009); Johnny V. Miller and John M. Soden, *In the Beginning . . . We Misunderstood* (Grand Rapids, MI: Kregel Publications, 2012).

PARALLELS BETWEEN ENUMA ELISH AND THE BIBLICAL CREATION ACCOUNT

Enuma Elish	Genesis
Divine spirit and cosmic matter are coexistent and coeternal	Divine spirit creates cosmic matter and exists independently of it
Primeval chaos; Tiamat enveloped in darkness	The earth is desolate and waste, with darkness covering the deep (*tehom*)
Light emanating from the gods	Light created
The creation of the firmament	The creation of the firmament
The creation of dry land	The creation of dry land
The creation of the luminaries	The creation of the luminaries
The creation of man	The creation of man
The gods rest and celebrate	God rests and sanctifies the seventh day

Adapted from Currid, AG, 37.

exhibit a greater abundance of sources and variations. Out of this abundance the story of the Enuma Elish is most often compared to the OT creation account. (Gordon and Rendsburg, BANE, 42)

Most scholars believe the Enuma Elish—often referred to as the Babylonian creation account—was written near the end of the second millennium BC. Walton offers a basic summary:

> One of the best known of the ancient texts, *Enuma Elish* gets its title from the first words of the text, often translated "When on high." This text, dated to the end of the second millennium BC, is a hymn commemorating the elevation of Marduk to the head of the pantheon. It includes some of the most detailed information about divine conflict and about cosmology available from ancient Mesopotamia. The first tablet opens with a cosmogony/theogony and introduces Tiamat in conflict with the gods and the slaying of Apsu, interwoven with the account of Marduk's birth.

The conflict escalates in tablet two as Tiamat and the rebels threaten the gods. Marduk is finally selected as the champion of the gods with the understanding that if he wins he will be elevated to the head of the pantheon. All the negotiations and preparations come to a climax in tablet four as Marduk defeats Tiamat and lays out the cosmos using Tiamat's corpse. Establishing the functions of the cosmos continues into tablet six and concludes with the creation of people from the blood of Tiamat's partner, Kingu, and the building of Babylon and a temple for Marduk. Tablet seven draws the piece to a conclusion as the fifty names of Marduk are proclaimed to name his attributes, delineate his jurisdiction, and identify his prerogatives. (Walton, ANETOT, 46–47)

2. Egyptian Creation Accounts*

Traditionally, the ancient Egyptian creation accounts have not been treated with the same attention and scrutiny as the Babylonian account of Enuma Elish; however, modern

---

* For more resources on Egyptian cosmogony see James Hoffmeier, *Israel in Egypt: The Evidence for the Authenticity of the Exodus Tradition*, (New York: Oxford UP, 1997); Miller and Soden, *In the Beginning . . . We Misunderstood.*

scholars have begun to turn their attention to these accounts and their relationship to the OT. Currid provides a brief summary background on the various Egyptian creation accounts:

> There are a variety of accounts of how Re created the other gods who are personified in the various parts of creation. One account pictures him squatting on a primeval hillock, pondering and inventing names for various parts of his own body. As he named each part, a new god sprang into existence. Another legend portrays Re as violently expelling other gods from his own body, possibly by sneezing or spitting. A third myth describes him creating the gods Shu and Tefnut by an act of masturbation. These gods in turn gave birth to other gods. Re, however, is not the only god portrayed as creator in ancient Egypt. For example, the Memphite Theology depicts Ptah as a potter creating the universe. In another text, the "Great Hymn to Khnum," the god Khnum is pictured as forming everything—man, gods, land animals, fish, and birds—on his potter's wheel. (Currid, AG, 38–39)

Because ancient Egypt produced multiple creation accounts, we need to take pieces from each individual story to understand their overall depiction of creation. When we put these various pieces of the Egyptian creation stories

PARALLELS BETWEEN EGYPTIAN AND BIBLICAL CREATION ACCOUNTS

Egyptian Sources	Genesis 1:1—2:3
Watery, unlimited, darkness, imperceptibility	The Spirit of God was hovering over the face of the waters (1:2)
Atum (or Ptah) speaks creation into existence	God creates by divine command (1:3, 6, 9, 11, 14, 15, 20, 24)
Light created before the sun is in place	Light created before the sun is in place
The gods create by separating the waters to create an atmosphere	God creates by separating the waters to create an atmosphere (1:6, 7)
Initially in creation, the first little hillock of land (primordial mound) rises out of the water	God creates by separating the land from the waters (1:9)
Creation of vegetation	God creates plants (1:11, 12)
The sun rises on the first day	God creates the sun (day four) after the light (day one) (1:14–18)
The gods create plants, fish, birds, and animal life	God creates fish, birds, and animal life (1:20–25)
The gods create man in their image, formed out of clay	God creates mankind in his image (1:26–28)
Ptah rests after completing his work of creation (Memphite Theology)	After completing creation, God rests (2:1–3)
Out of unlimited, imperceptible, dark waters, the god creates himself (including light), atmosphere, land, and luminaries in the heavens (the sun rises), followed by plants, creatures, and man; then he rests	Out of desolate, empty, dark waters, God creates light, atmosphere, land, plants, the luminaries in the heavens, creatures, and man; then he rests (1:2—2:3)
The creator god claims sovereign rule of state	God as creator claims sovereignty over all creation and so all nations (1:2—2:3)

Adapted from Miller and Soden, IB, 78.

together and place them next to the Genesis account, as seen in the chart "Parallels Between Egyptian and Biblical Creation Accounts," the similarities are remarkable. Biblical scholars Johnny Miller and John Soden provide further insight about the Egyptian texts themselves: "These documents represent a mixture of times and theologies (covering more than two millennia), many of them in tension with one another, a situation that did not seem to bother the Egyptians." (Miller and Soden, IB, 78)

a. Accounting for Similarities

Scholars do not completely agree on how to account for the similarities between the creation accounts of the ANE and the OT. In fact, many scholars presuppose a theological polemic while others see a greater potential for borrowing by the OT authors. Regardless of where a scholar comes down on this issue, there are indeed similarities, and we must honestly assess how we should accurately account for them. Historian and archaeologist Wilfred Lambert makes a strong point in relation to the similarities:

Parallels to Genesis can indeed be sought and found there [Mesopotamia], but they can also be sought and found among the Canaanites, the ancient Egyptians, the Hurrians, the Hittites and the early Greeks. When the parallels have been found, the question of dependence,* if any, has to be approached with an open mind. (Lambert, NLBBG)

In addressing the nature of Egyptian influence on OT writers, Hoffmeier observes, "There are extremely few cases where direct borrowing of an Egyptian literary work (or for that matter any other near eastern literature) can be demonstrated. . . . Most of the influences from Egypt come by way of diffusion of ideas and motifs, often by artistic objects." (Hoffmeier, STG, 41)

Miller and Soden offer their own conclusion in accounting for the similarities of Egyptian and OT accounts:

Put all the parallels between the creation accounts together, and we can see remarkable similarity. In considering the correspondences between the two sets of creation accounts, "the magnitude of parallels cannot be mere chance. We dare not call this situation a freak of antiquity." [Currid, AEOT, 72] There is clearly a correlation between Egyptian material and the biblical account. We would expect this if Israel did indeed have a history in Egypt as the Old Testament claims. Understanding the biblical allusions to Egyptian mythology greatly enhances our understanding of the biblical text, including its theological perspective, and the worldview that Moses portrays with his account. The biblical similarities with and allusions to Egyptian creation accounts, however, ultimately serve to highlight the theological differences between Moses and the Egyptians. Genesis 1 challenges the theological suppositions Israel had learned in Egypt and would subsequently face with new neighbors. (Miller and Soden, IB, 95)

In relating the creation account in Genesis to that in the Enuma Elish, Hoffmeier points out: "In the past several decades a number of Assyriologists who have studied the Babylonian creation story have rejected any possible connection [reliance] between Genesis and Enuma Elish." (Hoffmeier, STG, 40) While this assessment by Hoffmeier directly calls out the Enuma Elish, there are scholars who would extend his comments to cover other ANE accounts.

Assyriologist and biblical scholar Alexander Heidel proposes a helpful analogy to understand how we can accurately account for the similarities of the text:

---

* Dependence as noted here refers to the thought that the OT relies on and borrows directly from ANE sources.

Since the OT was intended also for the gentile world, it is but natural that the biblical authors availed themselves of figures of speech and imagery with which also Israel's neighbors were familiar, or which were at least easily understandable to them. It may be added, however, that identical phraseology does not necessarily imply identical theology. (Heidel, BG, 140)

b. Conclusion

The similarities between Mesopotamian, Egyptian, and OT creation accounts are certainly significant. Yet the differences are arguably even more profound. The depth and dignity of the OT is unparalleled when compared with any other creation account from the ANE. (Heidel, BG, 140)

3. A Comparison of Pre-Creation Conditions

In both the Egyptian and Mesopotamian creation accounts, we observe that creation originated from a preexistent cosmic matter, often viewed as primordial water that existed prior to the gods themselves. (Currid, AG, 41) As it relates to the OT account, some scholars propose that the Genesis narrative, like those of the ANE, also contains pre-creation conditions and does not imply creation *ex nihilo* ("out of nothing"). While this is a point of contention within OT scholarship, a majority of evangelical scholars propose that Genesis 1:1 differs from ANE accounts precisely in its implication of creation *ex nihilo*.

Walton, in assessing the opening verses of Genesis and the translation of the word *bârâ'* ("create"), concludes that an accurate translation does not imply creation *ex nihilo*. He does, however, believe that his interpretation of Genesis 1:1 does not change the doctrine of *ex nihilo* as taught by Scripture:

If we conclude that Genesis 1 is not an account of material origins, we are not thereby suggest-

ing that God is not responsible for material origins. I firmly believe that God *is* fully responsible for material origins, and that, in fact, material origins do involve at some point creation out of nothing. (Walton, LWGO, 42)

Some evangelical OT scholars share Walton's view on the use of *bârâ'*; however, it is not a majority opinion. Many other scholars, including Walter Kaiser, Collins, and Currid submit that even though the verb *bârâ'* does not automatically require the assumption that the creating is out of nothing, its use in Genesis 1:1 does in fact imply exactly that. Collins states:

The sentence of Genesis 1:1 taken as a whole does in fact imply creation from nothing. "The heavens and the earth" likely refers to "everything in the material universe." And "in the beginning" tells us what time the author is speaking of. Hence, if God created everything at the beginning, then "before the beginning"–whatever that might mean–there was nothing. Therefore Genesis 1:1 clearly *implies*, though it does not explicitly *state*, that God created from nothing and that the material universe has an absolute beginning. (Collins, LLTC, 55, emphasis in original)

Similarly, in their study of creation *ex nihilo*, apologists William Lane Craig and Paul Copan conclude that several reinforcing features within Genesis 1:1 make it reasonable to accept an "implicit understanding of creation *ex nihilo*":

These features include (1) the uniqueness of the Genesis creation account in comparison to other ANE epics, (2) the literary elegance and the structural and grammatical necessity of the absolute sense in Genesis 1:1, (3) the uniqueness of *bârâ'*, and (4) the creation of God by his word alone. Hence, we see emerging a strong cumulative case for creation *ex nihilo*. In light of the entire fabric of Genesis 1, creation out of nothing is the only proper inference to draw. No other conclusion can be properly secured. (Copan and Craig, CON, 59–60)

4. A Comparison of Creative Works

The methods by which the gods carried out creative acts, particularly in Mesopotamian traditions, often involved some sort of sexual procreation, unlike creation by spoken word as seen in the OT. However, within some Egyptian creation accounts, particularly in Memphite Theology, we see the god Ptah using spoken word as a means of creating. (Walton, GBTCL) Bloom and Collins observe that "this method of creation is certainly in line with the God of the Bible commanding, 'Let there be,' and is a step above the standard sexual procreation method of creation found elsewhere." (Bloom and Collins, CAANER, 20–24) They do not, however, understand this to point to a borrowing on the part of the Israelites in developing their own creation account. After all, the god Ptah, in Egyptian creation accounts, was self-created by a separating of the preexistent primordial waters as opposed to the uncreated God of the OT.

A lack of borrowing, however, does not negate the importance of this similarity in the two texts. Instead, this similarity helps to highlight how central proclamations were in both Israelite and Egyptian texts. Walton states, "Just as the gods of the ancient world set destinies in the cosmos by decree, so Yahweh established order and function by his spoken word." (Walton, NIVAC, 126) These ANE accounts all differed from the account we receive in Genesis 1, where a sovereign, omnipotent, incomparable, and uncreated God creates through spoken word.

5. A Comparison of the Creation of Mankind

Regarding the creation of mankind, Currid points out that "God gave mankind privileged status over the created order," while in the Enuma Elish and other Mesopotamian myths, man is created in order to do the bidding of the gods. (Currid, AG, 42) Old Testament scholar John Oswalt comments on the creation of mankind:

> To be sure, humanity is created last in the Babylonian account [Enuma Elish], as in the Bible. But here the similarity stops. In the Babylonian account humanity is an afterthought, brought into being from a combination of dust and the blood of one of the chaos monsters in order to provide the gods with food and adulation. In the Bible, humanity is created last because it is the apex of all that has gone before and because humans are to be given lordship over all the creation. (Oswalt, BAM, 70)

To illustrate the reason behind man's creation by the gods, Alan Millard uses the Sumerian example of the creation of mankind by Enki and the mother-goddess:

> The gods were tired of the work they had to do, tilling the ground and digging canals to grow the crops for their food. Enki had the idea of making a clay figure that the mother-goddess would bring to birth. This was done, resulting in man. Ever since, man has had to work the ground in order to grow food for the gods and himself. (Millard, EHWR, 61)

Walton highlights the status of mankind within the biblical account:

> The order imposed through the creation narrative in Genesis 1 sees people, rather than the gods, as the keystone in definition of order. The biblical text repeatedly offers the formula "it was good" to describe the successful setting of each piece in its ordered place. The functions described are designed for the benefit of

humans.... This functional nuance of "good" in the biblical text is confirmed by a comparison of what is not good–that is, it is not good for man to be alone (2:18). (Walton, ANET, 187)

The OT not only differs from its ANE counterparts in the status of mankind in creation but also in its portrayal of the human progenitors of the race, as Walton points out:

> The ancient Near East texts typically speak of human origins in collective terms (polygenesis). There is no indication of an original human pair that became progenitors of the entire human race (monogenesis). This is one of the distinctives of the Genesis account. (Walton, ANET, 187)

This distinctive emphasizes the value of persons, reinforcing the biblical theme of God's love for his creatures; instead of the ANE collective anonymity, the OT presents a complementary pair, male and female, in a relationship of individual persons.

6. A Comparison of the Creator

Without a doubt the biggest difference between the OT and ANE literature is the nature of the creator. Currid compares God and the deities of the ANE as they directly relate to creation:

> The creation account of Genesis . . . presents God as all-powerful, incomparable, and sovereign. He owes nothing to the agency of another. In addition, creation did not occur as the result of a contest or a struggle between gods, as it did in Mesopotamian myths. In the Enuma Elish myth, creation was a mere consequence of a war aimed at determining

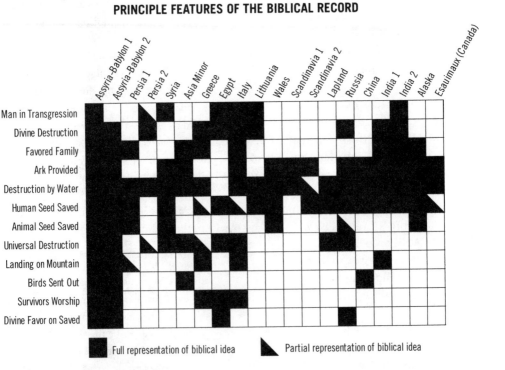

PRINCIPLE FEATURES OF THE BIBLICAL RECORD

■ Full representation of biblical idea   ◣ Partial representation of biblical idea who would be the main god. In Genesis 1–2, this is a question not even asked or worthy of consideration because there exists only one God, and he is all powerful. (Currid, AG, 41)

7. A Final Thought on Cosmogony

In highlighting the difference of the OT from the cosmogony of the ancient Near East, Christine Hayes, the Robert F. and Patricia Ross Weis Professor of Religious Studies at Yale University, states that the first chapter of Genesis

reflects the view that there is one supreme god who is creator and sovereign of the world. He simply exists. He appears to be incorporeal, and the realm of nature is subservient to him. He has no life story (mythology), and his will is absolute. This god creates through the simple expression of his will. "Elohim said, 'let there be light' and there was light" (Gen 1:3).

The deity expresses his will, and it comes to be—so different from ancient Near Eastern cosmogonies in which creation is always a form of procreation, the combination of male and female principles. (Hayes, IB, 34)

C. Flood Accounts

This section compares the OT story of the Flood with the various flood accounts of the ANE.

1. Similarities in the Flood Accounts

Numerous accounts of flood stories exist within the ancient Near East and throughout the rest of the world. Anyone who makes an effort to study these texts finds parallels in the details, structure, and flow of these stories, as seen in the chart "A Comparison of the Epic of Gilgamesh and the OT." (adapted from Nelson, DST, Fig. 38)

PRINCIPLE FEATURES OF THE BIBLICAL RECORD (CONTINUED)

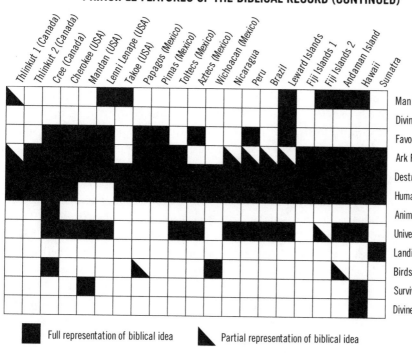

Columns: Thlinkut 1 (Canada), Thlinkut 2 (Canada), Cree (Canada), Cherokee (USA), Mandan (USA), Lenni Lenape (USA), Takoe (USA), Papagos (Mexico), Pimas (Mexico), Toltecs (Mexico), Aztecs (Mexico), Wichoacan (Mexico), Nicaragua, Peru, Brazil, Leward Islands, Fiji Islands 1, Fiji Islands 2, Andaman Island, Hawaii, Sumatra

Rows: Man in Transgression, Divine Destruction, Favored Family, Ark Provided, Destruction by Water, Human Seed Saved, Animal Seed Saved, Universal Destruction, Landing on Mountain, Birds Sent Out, Survivors Worship, Divine Favor on Saved

Full representation of biblical idea Partial representation of biblical idea

A COMPARISON OF THE EPIC OF GILGAMESH AND THE OT

Epic of Gilgamesh	Genesis
Divine warning of doom (lines 20–26)	Divine warning of doom (6:12, 13)
Command to build ship (lines 24–31)	Command to build ark (6:14–16)
Hero constructs ship (lines 54–76)	Noah builds ark (6:22)
Utnapishtim loads ark, including his relations and animals (lines 80–85)	Noah loads ark, including his family and animals (7:1–5)
The gods send torrential rains (lines 90–128)	Yahweh sends torrential rains (6:17; 7:1–12)
The flood destroys humanity (line 133)	The Flood destroys humanity (7:21, 22)
The flood subsides (lines 129–132)	The Flood abates (8:1–3)
The ship lands on Mount Nisir (lines 140–144)	The ark settles on Mount Ararat (8:4)
Utnapishtim sends forth birds (lines 146–154)	Noah sends forth birds (8:6–12)
Sacrifice to the gods (lines 155–161)	Sacrifice to Yahweh (8:20–22)
Deities bless hero (line 194)	Yahweh blesses Noah (9:1)

Adapted from Currid, AG, 55.

This chart shows that the Epic of Gilgamesh holds one of the largest numbers of flood details that are the same or similar to those in the Genesis account.

George Smith, who discovered the Epic of Gilgamesh tablets in 1872, says this: "On reviewing the evidence it is apparent that the events of the flood narrated in the Bible and the Inscription are the same, and occur in the same order." (Smith, TSBA, 232) The similarities of the texts are also observed by Currid:

Not only are many of the details parallel, but the structure and flow of the stories are the same. Such overwhelming similitude cannot be explained as a result of mere chance or simultaneous invention. . . . How do we account for the many similarities between the biblical narrative of the flood and the other ancient Near Eastern stories? Clearly there is a relationship, but the question is one of defining the nature of that connection. (Currid, AG, 55)

2. Do These Similarities Suggest a Common Source?

There are three general positions OT scholars adopt to explain the similarities in flood accounts.

a. Common Origin

As noted by Peter Enns in his book *Inspiration and Incarnation*, it seems entirely possible that the flood stories may simply have a common origin:

As with Enuma Elish, one should not conclude that the biblical account is directly dependent on these flood stories. Still, the obvious similarities between them indicate a connection on some level. Perhaps one borrowed from the other; or perhaps all of the stories have older precursors. The second option is quite possible, since, as mentioned above, there exists a Sumerian flood story that is considered older than either the Akkadian or biblical versions. (Enns, II, 29)

b. Separate Accounts from a Common Event

Currid proposes that the biblical account of the Flood is perhaps a completely separate tradition that originates from the same historically known flood of the ANE. A common origin does not necessarily infer that one source has built off of another but instead each account has delivered a completely different version of a common account. He writes:

If the biblical stories are true, one would be surprised not to find some reference to these truths in extrabiblical literature. And indeed in ancient Near Eastern myth we do see some kernels of historical truth. However, pagan authors vulgarized or bastardized those truths–they distorted fact by dressing it up with polytheism, magic, violence, and paganism. Fact became myth. From this angle the common references would appear to support rather than deny the historicity of the biblical story. (Currid, AEOT, 32)

Some, including Currid, who take a more polemic approach, go so far as to say that the biblical story is designed to mock those of the ANE while at the same time providing the true flood account.

3. Reasons for the Flood
a. Ancient Near East Reasons

The flood stories of the ANE are polytheistic and involve deities who closely reflect human characteristics. In the Epic of Atrahasis the flood is a result of humans disturbing the sleep of the gods. In the Sumerian flood story of Ziusudra, an assembly of the gods decide they want to end the kingship of men. In the epic of Gilgamesh the gods argue about the purpose of the flood and their action seems arbitrary.

In highlighting the reason for the flood as understood within the Atrahasis Epic, historian Norman Cohn explains the lack of forethought of the gods and petty reasoning:

The author of the Atrahasis Epic clearly thinks well of mankind, poorly of almost all the gods. This is not a story about sin and its consequences. . . . The offence of human beings is simply that they multiply and, as a result, make too much noise for the gods' comfort. That such a slight and unwitting offence evokes such a lethal response is clue to the shortcomings of the gods: they are tyrants—and stupid tyrants at that. (Cohn, NF, 6)

b. Old Testament Reasons

Just like the biblical creation account, the biblical flood narrative is strictly monotheistic. The sovereign God of the Bible controls everything relating to the flood events and neither answers to, nor cowers before, any other deity. (Currid, AG, 57) We see in Genesis 6:5–7 that the reason for the Flood is man's wickedness and sin:

The LORD saw that the wickedness of man was great in the earth, and that every intent of the thoughts of his heart was only evil continually. And the LORD was sorry that He had made man on the earth, and He was grieved in His heart. So the LORD said, "I will destroy man whom I have created from the face of the earth, both man and beast, creeping thing and birds of the air, for I am sorry that I have made them."

Old Testament professor Kenneth Mathews notes, "Genesis . . . repeatedly attributes the flood to the wickedness of man and explains that the corruption of the earth has merited the response of a moral God. There is no flood story comparable to the moral stature of Genesis." (Mathews, NAC, 101)

Heidel concludes:

> In the biblical story . . . the flood is sent by the one omnipotent God, who is just in all his dealings with the children of men, who punishes the impenitent sinner, even if it means the destruction of the world, but who saves the just with his powerful hand and in his own way. In Genesis the deluge is clearly and unmistakably a moral judgment, a forceful illustration of divine justice meting out stern punishment to a "faithless and perverse generation" but delivering the righteous. (Heidel, GEOTP, 268)

4. A Comparison of the Deities Responsible for the Flood

Cohn exposes the frailty of the gods and their seeming regret with regard to the flood in the Epic of Gilgamesh:

> Everything was turned to blackness, the mountains disappeared under water, the people were all drowned. The pounding storm, the raging flood were like a war. The gods themselves were terrified, crouching and cowering like dogs, and struggling to escape from the earth to the sky. Deprived of the offerings of food and drink on which they depended, they mourned the destruction of mankind; with burning lips and parched throats they sat, humbly weeping and sobbing. And the mother-goddess reproached herself bitterly for having consented to the catastrophe that had destroyed her people. (Cohn, NF, 5)

Hoffmeier, writing of the gods responsible for the floods in the Mesopotamian texts, describes an almost comical nature or foolishness of the gods:

> At every turn in the Mesopotamian flood tradition(s), one can imagine the biblical authors having a good laugh as they read or heard these stories. While Israelites believed that their God, Yahweh, neither slumbers nor sleeps (Ps 121:4), the Babylonian gods in the flood tradition suffered from insomnia because of human noise! The bickering and intrigue among the pantheon must have struck the Hebrew writer and his audience as odd. Then too, the fact that the gods were frightened by the very deluge they had ordained makes them look impotent and foolish, compared with the portrayal of the Hebrew God who controlled his creation, bringing the flood as planned, and then causing a mighty wind (or his spirit, *ruah*) to push back the waters so that the land would dry out (Gen 8:1). Like various Mesopotamian flood heroes, Noah made an offering after disembarking and "the LORD smelled the pleasing aroma" (Gen 8:21), but there is no comical depiction of God being hungry and thirsty, craving human sustenance and buzzing around the offering like a famished fly! (Hoffmeier, GHT, 53)

Hoffmeier concludes that the "different presentations of deity in the Hebrew and Mesopotamian traditions could not be more striking. Genesis seems aware of the Babylonian versions, and while agreeing that there was a flood, and ark, and a survivor, the theological perspective is radically different and is consciously aimed at refuting the Babylonian worldview." (Halton et al., GHFN, 757)

5. A Comparison of the Flood Heroes

There seems to be an important difference between Noah and other ANE heroes, as Currid explains:

> Noah was chosen by Yahweh to construct an ark for survival because he "found favor in the eyes of the Lord" (Gen. 6:8). Noah was delivered because of his righteousness and God's grace. Atrahasis and the other pagan heroes

of the flood saved themselves because of their bravery and human wisdom. (Currid, AG, 58)

The consequences of the flood within Mesopotamian narratives include the flood survivor's immortality. This is contrary to the Genesis account that highlights Noah's mortality and dismisses any notion of a divine nature or immortality within him. (Matthews, NAC, 101)

6. A Narrative Comparison of the Flood

In comparing the biblical account of the Flood against the Mesopotamian accounts, renowned Old Testament scholar Bruce Waltke highlights the ways in which the biblical account stands apart from the others:

> The biblical narrative . . . stands apart in significant ways, both in wisdom and in theology. For example, the dimensions of Noah's ark are those of modern ships, but the Babylonian ship, though pitched within and without, is an unstable cube. Noah sensibly first releases the raven, which braves the storm, can feed on carrion, and can remain in flight much longer than the dove. He then releases the gentle, timid, and low-flying dove. The hero in the Babylonian parallel, however, sends in sequence a dove, a sparrow, and then a raven. The most radical difference in the two accounts is the Bible's investing the story with a covenant concept. In the Mesopotamian accounts, overpopulation or humanity's noise interrupts the sleep of the gods and provokes their wrath, and the hero's wisdom and bravery saves him. In the Bible, humanity's wickedness arouses God's anger, and Noah's righteousness, not his wisdom and bravery, motivates God to save him. The biblical narrative is calculated to place all wisdom on God and promote human trust and obedience to him. In the Mesopotamian account, the gods gather around the

sacrifice like flies because they are hungry; in the biblical account, Noah's sacrifice assuages God's heart with regard to sin. (Waltke and Yu, OTT, 291)

Specifically highlighting the difference in sacrifice motif, Mathews states:

> First, the Mesopotamian accounts are crude polytheistic tales that depict selfish, deceptive deities embroiled in a dispute. The pagan ideology of the stories is seen, for instance, in the postdiluvian sacrifice by Utnapishtim that serves as food for the hungry deities who have gone without animal offerings during the flood: "The gods smelled the sweet savor / The gods crowded like flies about the sacrificer." (Mathews, NAC, 101)

7. A Covenant Polemic

Explaining the unique covenant concept found in the biblical account, Currid expands on Waltke's above comparison:

> One of the unique aspects of the Noahic flood narrative is the Lord's establishment of a covenant with Noah. As a physical sign of the reality of the covenantal relationship, Yahweh places the rainbow in the sky ("my bow in the cloud"; Gen. 9:12–13). The bow is like a billboard for all to see that God has made an enduring covenant with all living creatures. (Currid, AG, 63)

Some believe the rainbow, symbolizing a covenant between God and mankind, is a conscious polemic against pagan mythology that often used the "bow" to symbolize battle between gods, or between gods and humans. (Currid, AG, 63)

Other scholars, including Herbert Wolf, understand the covenant rainbow in a slightly different light. Wolf states:

The Noahic covenant was an everlasting covenant made with Noah and his descendants. God promised that never again would He destroy the world with a flood (Gen. 9:8–11). As a sign of the covenant, God designated the rainbow as a reminder of His binding promise. Since the word for "rainbow" also means a "war bow" (*qešet*), it has been suggested that a bow pointed toward the heavens constitutes a self-maledictory oath. Von Rad argues that the rainbow was a sign that God had laid aside His war bow; the judgment was over. (Wolf, IOTP, 42)

8. A Comparison of Genre

As we have seen, the style of writing in the ANE is important to understanding the literary goal. Genesis 6–9, which encompasses the flood story, is written in the form of historical narrative, and according to Currid, clearly bears the markings of that genre:

> A most important grammatical marker in biblical Hebrew is a device called a *vav-consecutive-plus-imperfect*. Often simply translated as "and it was," the device is the way in which a Hebrew writer presents events in a historical sequence. It appears commonly throughout Hebrew narrative but rarely in other genres such as poetry. In Genesis 6:5–22, that device appears at least a dozen times. Also, in Hebrew narrative the writers often employ a word that serves as a sign of the coming direct object—it is the word *'et* (Hebrew את). It almost never occurs in poetry, but it is a clear, distinctive marker of historical prose. The sign of the direct object appears at least fifteen times in Genesis 6:5–22. . . . [And] the style of writing used in the cosmological texts in the ANE is best described as "mythic narrative." (Currid, AG, 58)

Currid concludes: "The Genesis writer is a radical monotheist. His presentation of the flood account not only relays the event in a historical manner; it also contains harsh and radical rebukes of the pagan myths." (Currid, AG, 61)

9. A Final Thought on the Flood

The similarities between the OT and ANE flood accounts suggest a common origin, but the differences prove to be decisive:

> The available evidence proves nothing beyond the point that there is a genetic relationship between Genesis and the Babylonian versions. The skeleton is the same in both cases, but the flesh and blood and, above all, the animating spirit are different. It is here that we meet the most far-reaching divergencies [*sic*] between the Hebrew and the Mesopotamian stories. (Heidel, GEOTP, 268)

D. Origins of the Gods

A theogony is an origin story or genealogy for a god or gods. In the various theogonies of the ANE, individual gods always had a beginning (no matter how supreme they were).

1. Ancient Near Eastern Theogony vs. the Old Testament

While theogonies differed between people groups in the ANE, each people group was clear that the gods were in fact created. Walton helps us understand the various accounts of how the gods of the ANE came into being:

> The mythology of both Mesopotamia and Egypt makes clear that the gods had origins. They exist in familial relationships and there are generations of gods. When the texts speak of theogony (origins of the gods) they include a number of elements in the presentation. In Egyptian literature it is most common to think of the earliest gods coming into being through bodily fluids (the creator god spitting, sneezing, sweating, or masturbating),

while the later deities are simply born to a previous generation of deity. In the *Memphite Theology* the gods are brought into being by Atum separating them from himself. One way that creation was expressed was by "the mouth which pronounced the name of everything." Typically the first gods created are primordial cosmic gods. Since the forces of nature are expressions and manifestations of the attributes of deities, cosmogony and theogony become intertwined as the natural world comes into being along with the gods who embody the various elements of the cosmos. (Walton, ANETOT, 87–88)

In comparison we can see that the OT does not contain a view of theogony at all:

The most obvious difference is seen in the absence of any theogony in Israel. The biblical text offers no indication that Israel considered Yahweh as having an origin, and there are no other gods to bring into existence either by pro-creation or separation. (Walton, ANETOT, 91)

2. A Stark Contrast

This lack of theogony highlights an obvious difference between the OT and other ancient texts, and understanding the gravity of this difference allows us to see the foundation on which each culture derived its worldview. Hayes points out the stark contrast of what this means for the God of the OT in comparison to the gods of ANE myth:

The absence of theogony and mythology means the absence of a metadivine or primordial realm from which the biblical god emerges. It also means the absence of the idea that this god is immanent in nature, natural substances, or phenomena. Therefore, the biblical god's powers and knowledge are not limited by the existence of any superior power or substance. Nature is not divine. The created world is not divine. It is not the physical manifestation of various deities. There is no intrinsic, material connection between the deity and creation. The line of demarcation is clear. (Hayes, IB, 34)

3. The Gods of the Ancient Near East vs. the God of the Old Testament*

a. Gods of the ANE

In order to assess accurately the relationship between the ANE and Old Testament, we need to understand how these cultures characterized the deities that they worshiped.

The characteristics of ANE deities reveal their close commonalities with humanity:

i) Immorality:

Regarding the behavior of the ANE gods, Oswalt notes,

The gods are untrustworthy, seeking their own ends rather than caring for their worshipers' ends. They are constantly fighting among each other, often over the most petty matters. They are fearful, especially of death, but they can do nothing lasting about their fears, for each of them, like the stars in their orbits, are fixed to a certain fate. They are limited, both in knowledge and in power. (Oswalt, BAM, 58–59)

Walton expands upon the human characteristics of these deities:

What attributes did Yahweh not have that other deities possessed? This list would include

---

* For a deeper understanding of the characteristics of ANE gods and their relationship to humanity, see Daniel Block, *The Gods of the Nations: Studies in Ancient Near Eastern National Theology* (Jackson, MS: Evangelical Theological Society, 1988); John H. Walton, *Ancient Near Eastern Thought and the Old Testament: Introducing the Conceptual World of the Hebrew Bible* (Grand Rapids, MI: Baker Academic, 2006).

those attributes that assumed a polytheistic system or human foibles, such as craftiness, lust, deception, sexuality, and a host of others. Many more items would be included on this list . . . because the baser qualities came with the fact that the deities of the ANE were perceived in human terms. (Walton, ANET, 110)

Quite often the characteristics attributed to a deity find their way into human society. Known as *imitatio dei*, this doctrine highlighted the belief that man can and should be godlike in his conduct. Thus, if the god was told to do certain things, then the people were given license to do those same things. This, of course, often led to heinous acts on the part of the worshipers, particularly among those who worshiped the Canaanite god Baal:

Although we have only Canaanite deities involved in incest and bestiality, there can be no doubt that Canaanite people engaged in these acts as well. . . . In Canaanite society, if one had the power, one exercised it, first by coveting and then by putting these thoughts into action. (Gordon and Rendsburg, BANE, 159)

Gordon and Rendsburg also give examples of transvestism, ritual prostitution, and incest in addition to bestiality and covetousness. Though we cannot know what percentage of the Canaanites would have partaken in these actions of the gods, we can be sure that many did because of the noble manner in which they were portrayed. (Gordon and Rendsburg, BANE, 159–161)

ii) Petulance

Unlike the God of the Old Testament, the gods of the ANE were very easily offended and the response to such offenses often led to an increase in giving, temple remodeling,

treaties with neighboring peoples, etc. (Walton, ANETOT, 138) Such whims often resulted in rituals designed to appease the gods. One such ritual was the "substitute king ritual." Markham Geller, in *Ancient Babylonian Medicine*, summarizes this ritual:

A Substitute King was appointed after an eclipse or unfavorable omen considered to be dangerous to the reigning king, and the ritual provided for the king to step down from his throne for a period of time (of up to six months) in favor of his substitute, who was later executed, thereby fulfilling the ominous prediction. (Geller, ABM, 188)

iii) Natural Characteristics

In speaking of the Sumerian gods in particular, Millard shows how natural forces often characterized the gods:

The gods of the Sumerians were the powers of nature as revealed in the world. So the sun-god was the sun and the power within it. Just as human activities are limited, so were the gods each restricted to their own sphere. The myths show the gods acting their own positions. They fight to hold their place against evil powers that want to break down their ordered way of life, they quarrel over their areas of influence, they engage in trickery and show every kind of human emotion and vice. (Millard, EHWR, 61)

b. The God of the OT (Yahweh)

In the Old Testament, Yahweh is not characterized with inherent human traits, or those of nature, including sexuality. (Oswalt, BAM, 71) He also does not contain any traits that would be considered evil or negative. Of course this results in far fewer characteristics than those of the gods of ANE because Yahweh's traits are primarily limited to those consistent with a monotheistic worldview, interiority, moral character, and formal relationships. (Walton, ANETOT, 110)

In describing the difference between the OT's Yahweh and the gods of the ancient Near East, Gordon and Rendsburg explain that "Yahweh was never a specialized phenomenon of nature, such as the sun. Yahweh is represented in the patriarchal narratives as being the supreme God, Who created heaven and earth (Genesis 14:22). As His name indicates, He is, the One Who 'Calls into Being' or the Creator." (Gordon and Rendsburg, BANE, 85–86)

Daniel Block echoes:

On the one hand, insofar as the gods of the nations outside Israel tolerated the worship of other divinities, even by their own people, their absolute status as national deities was diminished. On the other hand, in Israel Yahweh's position was to be unchallenged; his intolerance of rivals was total, particularly in the minds of orthodox Yahwists. However, the fact that he welcomed the worship of persons from outside the national group served as an additional limiting factor to his national deity status. While Yahweh had established a special covenant relationship with Israel, his true devotees proclaimed him simultaneously to be the universal God. (Block, GN, 74)

E. Nature of Humanity in the ANE vs. Old Testament

1. Humanity in the ANE

The role of humanity within the ANE can be seen clearly expressed within the art, history, and culture of recovered ANE artifacts, but our greatest understanding again comes from the numerous myths of the various cultures of the ANE.

Addressing the Mesopotamian view of humanity in particular, Alan Wiggermann recounts their understanding of the status of humanity:

According to the myths, the great gods, organizing the world after the separation of heaven and earth, had the lesser gods dig rivers and canals and build their houses. The lesser gods rebelled, went on strike, and demanded to be relieved of their burden. The great gods consented to the creation of a substitute, man, to carry out these tasks but also had one of the rebels killed to show their displeasure and discourage future rebels. . . . Thus the burden of the lesser gods was transferred to human beings. (Wiggerman, CANE, 1859)

This subservient motif was used often within the ANE to understand the proper place of man in relation to the gods. The same motif was used to also explain death, justify the actions of the governing body, and set up a system by which society would operate.

When humanity multiplied, death was decreed as its fate in order to keep the population in check, and "kingship was lowered from heaven" in order to coordinate his efforts. The ruler organized his subjects in a state whose only purpose was to provide the gods with whatever they desired and thus justify the continuation of human existence. (Wiggerman, CANE, 1859–60)

The relationship between humanity and the gods of the ANE hinged upon how humanity fulfilled the needs of the gods. Regular care and maintenance was demanded of both the local temple deities and the family god(s). Block summarizes the tasks necessary for taking care of the gods:

In the ancient world all formal and public worship revolved around the image. It marked the deity's presence and was the center of any ceremony involving the divine. The image would be awakened in the morning, washed, clothed, given two sumptuous meals each day (while music was played in its presence), and put to bed at night. Thus, worship involved primarily caring for the needs of the god through his image, thereby ensuring the continued presence of the deity in the image. (Block, IAKLI, 311)

Humanity relied upon the gods' satisfaction, while the gods relied upon humanity for a life of leisure. This caused humanity anxiety—for no one knew whether his service warranted reward or long life. If humanity failed in serving the gods in a satisfactory manner, they were punished with adversity, disease, and even an early death. (Wiggerman, CANE, 1861)

Social rejection of an individual was commonplace if one was a victim of any sort of misfortune—for misfortune was understood to be a result of being out of favor with the gods.

2. Humanity in the Old Testament
a. The Image of God

The OT shows a very different perspective on the role and importance of humanity. Unlike the myths, customs, and rituals of the ANE, which promote a very low view of humanity, the OT posits a very high view. This divergence from common ANE thought places man at the pinnacle of creation, made in the "image of God" with freedom and a sense of personhood. (Walton, ANETOT, 69) Being made in the image of God as opposed to the gods being made in the image of man brought great significance to the existence of humanity, as Oswalt points out:

Part of the significance of "the image of God" in humans relates to the significance of personality that is found in the Old Testament. Whatever else the Bible tells us about God, it shows us a full-orbed Person who is capable of interacting with his creation on any number

of different levels. . . . This is a Person who laughs and cries, who roars and croons, who loves and hates, who is frustrated and triumphant, who shows us that personality is not something accidental, to be downplayed as we seek the great commonalities of existence, but something at the very heart of existence itself. (Oswalt, BAM, 70)

Genesis 1:26–28 highlights man being made in the image of God and soon after being put into a position of responsibility over creation:

Then God said, "Let us make man in our image, after our likeness. And let them have dominion over the fish of the sea and over the birds of the heavens and over the livestock and over all the earth and over every creeping thing that creeps on the earth." So God created man in his own image, in the image of God he created him; male and female he created them. And God blessed them. And God said to them, "Be fruitful and multiply and fill the earth and subdue it, and have dominion over the fish of the sea and over the birds of the heavens and over every living thing that moves on the earth." (ESV)

b. Implications of the Image of God

The OT's view of humanity being in the image and likeness of God has profound implications for our responsibility to and treatment of other people. The reason we are to love our neighbor as ourselves (Lev. 19:18) and to care for widows and orphans (James 1:27) is because every human being has dignity and value as an image-bearer of God.

Of course, being made in God's image also functions as a polemic of sorts. While the ANE kings and rulers were generally considered closer to the status of the gods and often gods themselves, the OT removes the distinction between rulers and the common man. While kings held an important position within the structure of society, they were still mere men sharing the same likeness as the lowest servants.

F. Monotheism vs. Polytheism

At the most foundational level of the ANE and OT texts, we observe the greatest distinction between the worldviews: monotheism. (Oswalt, BAM, 64)

1. The Focus on Monotheism in the Old Testament*

There are only three major world religions that posit a singular God: Judaism, Christianity, and Islam. Interestingly enough, all three of these monotheistic religions were derived from the OT, which maintains the only consistently monotheistic view of God in the ANE. Regarding the Israelites' unique worldview, Oswalt states:

> Only once in the history of the world has a culture contrived to attain and maintain the idea of the absolute unity of deity. On every side of it peoples far more brilliant than Israel were maintaining with vehemence the multiplicity of deity. Israel alone insisted on the oneness of God, even in the end to the death if necessary. (Oswalt, BAM, 64)

There are many OT passages that reference monotheism, including:

Hear, O Israel: The LORD our God, the LORD is one! — Deuteronomy 6:4

Do we not all have one father? Has not one God created us? — Malachi 2:10 NASB

I am God, and there is no other. — Isaiah 45:22

Cohn claims that the biggest difference of all between Yahweh and other ANE gods is that "Yahweh is no mere chief of the gods, he is the one and only god." (Cohn, NF, 16)

2. Old Testament Monotheism was a Unique Worldview in the Ancient Near East

The teachings and literature of the ANE cultures run contrary to the OT teachings of monotheism. While at times dabbling in monotheistic ideas, these cultures never fully embraced monotheism, and so they reverted to polytheistic philosophies. All of the ancient Near Eastern cultures believed in a multitude of divine beings, and not one of these gods maintained a position of sovereignty over the rest.

Paul Copan highlights the uniqueness of the monotheistic view of the Old Testament:

> The Jews introduced a robust monotheism. Rather than being just one god in a pantheon of others or just a regional deity, Yahweh was/ is the only deity who matters. Indeed, he is the only one who exists. Along with this, the Jews introduced a new way to experience reality. There is a divine being who regularly, personally engages humans, whose choices really make a difference. (Copan, IGMM, 217)

3. Old Testament Polemics Against Polytheism:

Oftentimes people point to passages in the OT that may imply the existence of other gods (Num. 21:29; Deut. 4:19; Judg. 16:23–24; etc.). These verses and many like them seem to call into question the belief that the people of Israel were purely monotheistic from the

---

* For more information on the differing views on monotheism in the Old Testament, see Daniel Block, *Israel: Ancient Kingdom or Late Invention?* (Nashville, TN: B & H Academic Group, 2008); John H. Walton, *Ancient Near Eastern Thought and the Old Testament: Introducing the Conceptual World of the Hebrew Bible* (Grand Rapids, MI: Baker Academic, 2006); John H. Walton, Victor H. Matthews, and Mark W. Chavalas, *The IVP Bible Background Commentary: Old Testament* (Downers Grove, IL: Intervarsity Press, 2000).

start. However, it is always important to examine further evidence.*

Polytheistic practices were, in fact, not representative of the Israelite religion of the Old Testament; rather, the OT would call out such practices as foolishness. However, this does not automatically assume that the Israelite people always lived according to the teachings of the OT.

Some OT scholars believe Exodus 20:3 shows this polemic in the first of the Ten Commandments: "You shall have no other gods before Me." Alternatively, other scholars believe this verse shows that the OT promotes henotheism—worship of one God even though others may exist. It is important to note that even though the author of Exodus was speaking against the worship of other gods that does not mean he actually believed them to exist. Even though the author of Exodus did not have a robust Trinitarian view of God, he likely took the same approach as Paul in 1 Corinthians 8:4–6:

> *Therefore concerning the eating of things offered to idols, we know that an idol is nothing in the world, and that there is no other God but one. For even if there are so-called gods, whether in heaven or on earth (as there are many gods and many lords), yet for us there is one God, the Father, of whom are all things, and we for Him; and one Lord Jesus Christ, through whom are all things, and through whom we live.***

On the other hand, even if the author did believe other lower gods to exist, this does not necessarily detract from the monotheistic thrust of the OT.

Though often hotly debated in terms of its translation and intent, Deuteronomy 6:4 lays a strong claim to the fact that there is only one God. This does not show an inconsistency between the passages or a contradiction, but instead serves as an instance of polemical theology in order that the people of Israel would understand there is only one God. To worship another is nonsensical.

G. Images
1. Images in the Ancient Near East

Among all of the cultures of the ancient Near East, the various gods were represented by images and caricatures of the natural world in which they manifested their presence. In an effort to curb any sort of confusion on the matter of images (idols), it is important to point out that these images were not believed to be the actual deity but a vessel in which they could manifest their presence. As explained by Walton:

> The deity's presence was marked by the image of the deity. . . . [I]n this way the image mediated the worship from the people to the deity. . . . [W]e can conclude that the material image was animated by the divine essence. Therefore it did not simply represent the deity, but it manifested its presence. We should not conclude, however, that the image was the deity. The deity was the reality that was embodied in the image. (Walton, ANETOT, 114–116)

Because it was believed the gods manifested these images, great care was taken to make sure they were comfortable. Millard

---

* For a study on polytheism and the OT in greater depth, see Miller and Soden, *In the Beginning . . . We Misunderstood*; John Oswalt, *The Bible among the Myths: Unique Revelation or Just Ancient Literature?* (Grand Rapids, MI: Zondervan, 2009); Walton, Matthews, and Chavalas, *The IVP Bible Background Commentary: Old Testament*.

** Regarding the identity of "so-called gods" in this discussion of idolatry, Paul clarifies in 1 Corinthians 10:19, 20, "What am I saying then? That an idol is anything, or what is offered to idols is anything? Rather, that the things which the Gentiles sacrifice they sacrifice to demons and not to God, and I do not want you to have fellowship with demons."

highlights the attentiveness required to look after a temple image. He states that "each day the statue had to be washed, dressed, and fed. The clothes and food were supplied by the worshipers as offerings, or drawn from the wealth of the temple." (Millard, EHWR, 60)

2. The Old Testament's Polemic on Images

One of the greatest polemics of the OT addresses the use of images in the worship and manifestation of gods. The OT maintains an iconoclasm, which views the use of religious images as heretical.

Much like its position of monotheism, the OT is paramount to understanding the foundations of iconoclasm. Three great world religions maintain the monotheistic worldview of the OT; all have also needed to define a strong position on iconoclasm. Judaism has maintained it most consistently, and Islam has maintained it with great rigor (especially in sacred places, but in some eras and places easing its restrictions for secular art). Christianity has known extended periods when icons became a great internal controversy, with the theology of the Incarnation influencing many Christians to accept icons as prompts to prayerful aspiration toward a holy life, unlike the ANE view of them as divinely animated. As Oswalt points out, "there is only one culture in the world where iconoclasm originated and was then maintained as a consistent principle." (Oswalt, BAM, 65) That vigor is clear in the OT polemic against placing trust in them: they were to be seen as man-made, empty of spiritual power.

Scripture openly mocks the ANE practices surrounding images. Isaiah 46:5–7 states:

To whom will you liken me and make me equal, and compare me, that we may be alike? Those who lavish gold from the purse, and weigh out silver in the scales, hire a goldsmith, and he

makes it into a god; then they fall down and worship! They lift it to their shoulders, they carry it, they set it in its place, and it stands there; it cannot move from its place. If one cries to it, it does not answer or save him from his trouble. (ESV)

Walton delineates the polemic used by the OT prophets to castigate the images and idols of its neighboring cultures:

They criticize the idea that true deity could in any way be present in a humanly made image. They do not treat as credible the disclaimers of the craftsmen who ritually and symbolically return the image to the divine realm after its manufacture is complete. The rituals seek to accomplish just that, and the actual discussions found in Assyrian texts show that the Assyrians wrestled with these same issues. While the Mesopotamians attempt to resolve the problems cultically and thus justify the continued use of the image, the prophets see the obstacles as impassable and ridicule the attempts as they flaunt the superiority of Yahweh. (Walton, ANETOT, 116–17)

Oswalt adds:

On every side of Israel opulent religious practices centering on images were taking place. Yet Israel's prophets represent the worship of idols as perhaps the most basic departure from Israel's ancient faith. They act as though the denial of idolatry was at the very heart of Israel's understanding of reality. (Oswalt, BAM, 65)

V. Concluding Remarks

Though we have only scratched the surface of a comparative study of the ANE texts and the OT, we have seen that the surface similarities between these texts are small compared to the radical worldview differences. These differences, however, do not justify abandoning all similarities, as recognizing similarities can help elucidate proper understanding of the Old Testament. The similarities in literary style or cultural imagery do not invalidate the truth claims of the OT but instead show a commonality within humanity that is evidenced in the literature of today. As Heidel suggests:

> The sacred writers took over figures of speech derived from foreign literature . . . just as certain of the classical writers of the Christian Era patterned some of their finest literary productions after Greek and Roman masterpieces. Since the Old Testament was intended also for the gentile world, it is but natural that the biblical authors availed themselves of figures of speech and imagery with which also Israel's neighbors were familiar, or which were at least easily understandable to them. (Heidel, BG, 138)

Despite the claim by many critical scholars that the OT is merely a retelling of ancient myths plagiarized from other cultures and adjusted to fit the Hebrew worldview, it is far more likely that *the OT is a unique text among ANE accounts.*

CHAPTER 15

BIBLICALLY FAITHFUL APPROACHES TO GENESIS

OVERVIEW

I. Introduction

Genesis 1 inspires some of the most heated, sensitive—and yet important—controversies within the whole Christian church today. Our understanding of Genesis 1 has implications for how we understand the rest of Scripture, modern science, and the nature of the gospel itself. Young Christians indicate that the supposed conflict between Christianity and science is one of the main reasons many of them leave the church. (Kinnaman, YLM, 131–148) It is critical, then, that Christians think through the proper interpretation of Genesis 1 and what implications this has for the intersection of faith and science.

Because of space limitations and the larger focus of this book, this chapter is limited to an inerrantist view of Scripture. By "inerrant" we mean the "position . . . that the Bible is without error in everything that it affirms." (Geisler and Nix, GIB, 156) This position is articulated more fully in the Chicago Statement on Scripture (1978). (Geisler and Nix, GIB, 180–185) Our goal in this chapter is not to settle the matter. Many scientific, philosophical, and theological issues related to this topic go beyond the scope of this chapter (and book). Rather, we hope to portray various

403

responsible approaches for inerrantist Christians in terms of how they interpret Genesis 1. Unlike the historical resurrection, the interpretation of Genesis 1 is a subject over which Bible-believing Christians can have disagreements. Because of space limitations, and the centrality of the first chapter in Genesis to the overall biblical narrative, we limit our discussion to Genesis 1:1—2:4.

A. Genesis 1: Unique Account of Origins

Among the oldest known copies of Genesis is a fragment of a Dead Sea scroll containing the description of the first three days of creation. (LLDSS) This would have been copied from older scrolls, with the original document commonly attributed to Moses. While there is disagreement over the extent of Moses' authorship of Genesis, there is general agreement among conservative biblical scholars that he was the primary source behind it.

As archaeologists have discovered other ancient Near East (ANE) texts, scholars have shown great interest in comparing and contrasting them with the Genesis text. A range of views exist concerning how these other ANE sources influenced the Old Testament (see chapter 14). Many Old Testament scholars see a stark contrast between other ANE accounts of creation and the Genesis account. An example is the Babylonian *Epic of Creation* (*Enuma Elish*): the god Marduk kills the goddess Tiamat, creates the universe from her body, (Dalley, MM, 254–255) and then creates humans from the blood of another god, Qingu. (Dalley, MM, 260–261) Old Testament scholar Kenneth J. Turner notes the following contrasts between Genesis 1 and other ANE creation accounts:

> Monotheism versus polytheism (including the sun, moon, and sea as creations rather than

gods); the agency of the divine word versus a divine power struggle (e.g., Marduk and Tiamat); structure and order versus chaos and accident; God as nongendered versus ANE gods who are gendered (male or female) and sexually active; humanity as divine images versus slaves of the gods; God's rest versus perpetual restlessness of the ANE gods. (Turner, TG, 191–192)

The uniqueness of Genesis 1 among the ANE creation accounts is primarily theological: Yahweh is vastly different from the other gods. Indeed, Genesis 1 has been characterized as a polemic against the beliefs of Israel's pagan neighbors. (Currid, AG)

B. What Guidelines Should We Follow in Interpreting Genesis 1?

1. Respect the Hebrew Text

Genesis was written in Hebrew, and a responsible interpretation requires a good understanding of the Hebrew text. Since most of us rely on Hebrew scholars to translate the text, we ought to select translations that both faithfully convey the message of the original text and show where the Hebrew is not so simple or obvious. In addition, the use of commentaries that shed light on the nuances of the Hebrew text, for example, the meaning of words, genre, verb tenses, literary devices, and the culture of the day, can be of considerable help in understanding the original meaning of a passage.

2. Recognize the Unique Literary Genre of Genesis 1

The books of the Bible, and even passages within books, are written in a variety of literary genres. Examples are historical narrative (e.g., the books of Samuel and Kings), prophecy (e.g., Isaiah) and letters (e.g., Romans). A responsible interpretation of a passage requires the recognition of its literary genre.

However, Genesis 1 may not fit neatly into any of the genres recognized in the rest of Scripture. Old Testament scholar C. John Collins, after describing four possible ways of interpreting Genesis, argues that "the author was talking about what he thought were actual events, using rhetorical and literary techniques to shape the readers' attitudes toward these events." (Collins, DAERE, 16) This approach recognizes both the historical nature of the account, indicating that it is referring to real events in the past, as well as some measure of metaphorical language. The perspective of Collins is often considered a moderate view. However, it is important to recognize that even his view is debatable. Some argue that Genesis 1 is entirely (or *almost* entirely) metaphorical while others do not find any metaphorical language at all.

3. Respect the Coherence and Inerrancy of Scripture

There are many examples in Scripture where different perspectives are provided for specific events. For example, the creation of humans as described in Genesis 1 is somewhat different from the account in Genesis 2. Such differences are not contradictions, but instead give us a more complete understanding. Theologian and philosopher John Frame notes, "Similarly confused is the notion that accounts of the same event are contradictory unless they have exactly the same emphasis and perspective. . . . God gave us four Gospel documents that together give us a fuller picture of Jesus than any one of them could have. They are supplementary, not contradictory. The Bible contains no error, but many

different perspectives on the truth." (Frame, DWG, 195) Along with apologist Norman Geisler and the Chicago Statement on Scripture, we place confidence "in everything that it [the Bible] affirms," while recognizing these complex aspects of interpretation.

C. Diversity of Christian Interpretations

As far as we know, never in church history have we reached a universal consensus on how to interpret Genesis 1. Christians have differed over (1) the genre of Genesis; (2) how to interpret the "days" of creation; (3) the purpose of the early chapters in Genesis; and (4) other relevant interpretive factors. Theologians intending to take a responsible approach to Scripture have drawn different conclusions. We will first summarize the main interpretations that emerged from the early church fathers, and then consider the main interpretations within conservative Protestant churches today.

D. Unity of Truth

Christians have always believed that God reveals himself in two books: the book of Scripture and the book of nature. This conviction is rooted in the testimony of Scripture (Psalm 19:1–4, 7, 8) and has been affirmed by historic Christian creeds.* Thus, properly understanding the natural world requires the accurate integration of both of these books of God's revelation. We believe that both books are true when properly interpreted and integrated. We interpret the book of nature through the physical sciences, and the book of Scripture through the discipline of theology. If we find apparent contradictions between

---

* "We know him by two means; first, by the creation, preservation and government of the universe; which is before our eyes as a most elegant book, wherein all creatures, great and small, are as so many characters leading us to contemplate the invisible things of God, namely His power and divinity, as the apostle Paul says, Rom. 1:20. All which things are sufficient to convince men, and leave them without excuse. Secondly, he makes himself more clearly fully known to us by his holy and divine Word, that is to say, as far as is necessary for us to know in this life, to his glory and our salvation." Creeds of Christendom, *The Belgic Confession (1561)*, http://www.creeds.net/belgic/.

the two books, we must go back and reevaluate our science and/or our hermeneutics.

Several interpretations of Genesis 1 will be presented in this chapter. While they are not all mutually exclusive, it is important to remember that they cannot all be true. Perhaps even none of them is correct. But certainly two interpretations cannot both be correct unless those two are not mutually exclusive. Ultimately, our desire is that the body of Christ recognizes that well-meaning Christians can hold differing interpretations of Genesis 1 and still remain within orthodoxy.

II. Patristic Interpretations of Genesis 1

A study of the early church fathers' writings reveals more than one interpretation of Genesis 1. It is difficult to align the views of some of these fathers with modern interpretations, and some are cited in support of more than one modern interpretation. (see Hagopian, GD, 47–48, 68–69, 99–102) This section will review three different patristic interpretations presented in the approximate chronological order of their earliest proponents.

A. Epoch Day View

Irenaeus (c. AD 120/140–200/203), in writing about the sixth day of creation, suggested that this day could have been a thousand-year epoch. In commenting on God's warning to Adam in Genesis 2:17 ("But of the tree of the knowledge of good and evil you shall not eat, for in the day that you eat of it you shall surely die"), Irenaeus wrote: "Thus, then, in the day that they did eat, in the same did they die, and became death's debtors, since it was one day of the creation . . . he [Adam] did not overstep the thousand years, but died within them, thus

bearing out the sentence of his sin." (ANF, I.551) Irenaeus concluded that based on the scriptural teaching that for God one day is as a thousand years (Ps. 90:4; 2 Peter 3:8) and the fact that Adam lived for 930 years before dying (Gen. 5:5), the sixth day of creation was a thousand-year epoch. Justin Martyr (c. AD 100–165) also suggested this in his *Dialogue with Trypho*. (ANF, I.239–40) Although it is not clear what they believed concerning the length of the other creation days, it is clear that they recognized that *yôm*, the Hebrew word used for "day" in Genesis 1, could be interpreted as an epoch or age.

B. Allegorical/Figurative Day View

Several early church fathers recognized a challenge in understanding the nature of the creation days: the sun, moon, and stars were not created until day four, so the first three days could not have been normal calendar days in terms of the earth's movement in relation to those celestial bodies. Clement of Alexandria (c. AD 150–215) thought that the creation week communicated the order of creation. Concerning its timing he stated: "And how could creation take place in time, seeing time was born along with things which exist." (ANF, II.513) Origen of Alexandria (c. AD 185–254) apparently did not think the creation days were to be taken as calendar days. He wrote: "And with regard to the creation . . . we have treated to the best of our ability in our notes on Genesis, as well as in the foregoing pages, when we found fault with those who, taking the words in their *apparent* signification, said that the time of six days was occupied in the creation of the world." (ANF, VI.601, emphasis in original) Augustine of Hippo (AD 354–430), in his book *The City of God*, wrote: "As for these 'days', it is difficult, perhaps impossible to think—let alone to explain in words—what they mean." (Augustine, CG, 196) In his commentary *The Literal Meaning of Genesis* he argued that a creation day was not a typical calendar day: "Even if it is a physical day of goodness knows what kind of light quite beyond our ken, or (as we have been arguing) a spiritual day in the harmonious unity of the angels' mutual companionship, [it] is certainly not such as the one we are familiar with here." (Augustine, LMG, 278) Concerning the duration of the creation week, Augustine believed "that God made all things together simultaneously." (Augustine, LMG, 279)

C. 24-Hour View

Many church fathers held the twenty-four-hour view of the creation days. Professor of theology James Mook refers to them as "literalists," meaning they "specified that the six days of creation were each 24 hours long." (Mortenson and Ury, CGG, 29) He cites as examples Lactantius (c. AD 250–325), Victorinus (d. AD 304), Ephrem the Syrian (c. AD 306–373), Basil of Caesarea (c. AD 329–379), and Ambrose of Milan (c. AD 338–397). (Mortenson and Ury, CGG, 29–32, 35) An interesting emphasis in Basil's *Hexaemeron* is the contrast he made between the Genesis account and the Greek concepts of his day; for example, the belief that the universe was eternal and governed by chance. Concerning the age of the earth, he wrote: "You may know the epoch when the formation of this world began, if, ascending into the past, you endeavour to discover the first day." (NPNF, II.55) This suggests that determining the age would not be straightforward, which was clearly less important to him than the need to refute pagan concepts of the universe being eternal.

III. Modern Interpretations of Genesis 1

Toward the end of the eighteenth century, two developments provided an impetus for more thinking and debate over the interpretation of Genesis 1: the perceived indications of an ancient earth provided by the new discipline of geology, and archaeological discoveries of ANE civilizations and their records. As a result, over the following two centuries additional interpretations of Genesis 1 have been proposed. We have grouped these modern interpretations under two broad categories: concordist and nonconcordist.* The rationale for these categories is that they reflect two distinct presuppositions underlying modern interpretations. Concordism is "the supposition that the biblical and nonbiblical data on a given topic can and should be harmonized." (Turner and Eisenback, DVC) On the other hand, non-concordism does not try to harmonize the biblical text with science because it doesn't believe the intent of the biblical writer was to address modern science.

A. Concordist Interpretations

These interpretations are driven by what some believe are remarkable agreements between the biblical text and modern science. Astronomer Robert Jastrow, for instance, has said such instances of concordance are significant: "Astronomers now find they have painted themselves into a corner because they have proven, by their own methods, that the world began abruptly in an act of creation. . . . That there are what I or anyone would call supernatural forces at work is now, I think, a scientifically proven fact." (Durbin, SCBTF, 15, 18)

Zoologist Andrew Parker, professor at the Natural History Museum in London, was

---

* This approach has been adopted by others; for example, Deborah B. Haarsma and Loren D. Haarsma, *Origins: A Reformed Look at Creation, Design & Evolution* (Grand Rapids, MI: Faith Alive Christian Resources, 2007).

so struck with the agreement between the sequence of events in Genesis 1 and the modern scientific understanding of these events that he wrote *The Genesis Enigma*, in which he describes this agreement and concludes:

> Here, then, is the Genesis Enigma: The opening page of Genesis is scientifically accurate but was written long before the science was known. How did the writer of this page come to write this creation account? . . . I must admit, rather nervously as a scientist averse to entertaining such an idea, that the evidence that the writer of the opening page of the Bible was divinely inspired is strong. I have never before encountered such powerful, impartial evidence to suggest that the Bible is the product of divine inspiration. (Parker, GE, 219, emphasis in original)

These are strong words coming from a scientist who does not profess to be a believer.

Concordist interpretations fall into two categories based on views concerning the age of the earth. "Old Earth" interpretations accept the mainstream scientific dating of 4.5 billion years. "Young Earth" interpretations claim that the earth is 6,000–10,000 years old, based on the creation days of Genesis being literal 24-hour calendar days and using the Genesis genealogies to estimate the date of the creation week. The lower age assumes no gaps in the Genesis genealogies. Other Young Earth interpretations allow for gaps in the genealogies, but would only extend the age of the earth by a few thousand years. The Young Earth views, rather than harmonizing with mainstream science, believe that mainstream science has incorrectly concluded that the earth is ancient and that the scientific evidence needs to be reconsidered.

1. Old-Earth Creationism (OEC)

OEC holds the belief that the universe is ancient, and when Scripture is properly understood, it matches up with the mainstream scientific conclusions. So, OEC accepts standard scientific dating for the age of the universe. This does not mean, however, that OEC necessarily embraces some form of evolution. An ancient earth is necessary for evolution, but not sufficient. In other words, evolution requires an old earth, but just because the earth is old does not mean evolution is true. Just because someone believes in OEC doesn't mean they believe in neo-Darwinian evolution, although many in fact do. The different views within OEC are an attempt to reconcile the mainstream scientific position of an ancient earth with Scripture.

a. Gap View

This interpretation, popularized by the Scofield Reference Bible (Scofield, SRB, 3–4), holds that Genesis 1:1 describes the creation of a perfect universe and the earth, and that

---

The opening page of Genesis is scientifically accurate but was written long before the science was known. How did the writer of this page come to write this creation account? . . . I must admit, rather nervously as a scientist averse to entertaining such an idea, that the evidence that the writer of the opening page of the Bible was divinely inspired is strong.

Andrew Parker

this was followed by an undefined period of rebellion (or "gap") during which Satan was cast down to earth, destroying it and leaving it in the condition described in Genesis 1:2. This view posits that the "gap" between these two verses could have lasted millions of years, providing concordance with the mainstream scientific view of an old earth. This view has grown out of favor with scholars in recent times because the grammatical construction of Genesis 1:2 makes the position's required translation, "and the earth *became*," difficult to justify. (Collins, G1–4, 128)

b. Day-Age View*

Proponents of this view maintain that the days of creation are long but finite periods of time: "ages." They note that the Hebrew word for day, *yôm*, has different meanings depending on the context in which it is used. One of those meanings is a long but finite time period (Gen. 2:4). Day-Age proponents make several arguments in favor of this definition for the days of creation, including:

- The amount of activity in the sixth day implies the passage of more time than a calendar day.
- Adam's response to seeing Eve: "this *at last* is . . ." (Gen. 2:23 ESV, emphasis added) suggests a long time had elapsed between the time Adam began his work of naming the animals and the creation of Eve. (These two arguments assume that the events of Genesis 2 occurred in the sixth day.)
- The absence of an end to the seventh day implies that we are still in this day, the day of God's rest from creation.

Day-Age proponents appeal to the "two-book" principle discussed earlier in their acceptance of mainstream scientific dating to estimate the length of the creation days.

c. Intermittent Day View

Newman, Phillips, and Eckelmann developed a modification of the Day-Age interpretation that maintains "that the creation events described in Genesis took place over a long period of time, are subdivided into six parts, and each part is introduced by a literal day." (Newman, Phillips, and Eckelmann, GOOE, 1435–1436) This theory provides harmony between the interpretation of *yôm* as a literal calendar day and today's mainstream scientific view that the events described in Genesis 1 must have occurred over long periods of time.

d. Days of Divine Fiat View

Physicist Alan Hayward argues for a theory that "suggests that Genesis does not intend us to take the six days of creation as the days on which God did the actual work. Instead, they could be the days in which God issued his creative commands, or 'fiats' as they are usually called." (Hayward, CE, 167) He notes that the narrative of Genesis 1 is punctuated with parenthetical statements describing the outworking of the fiats, which were uttered on "six (presumably literal and consecutive) days" (Hayward, CE, 170), whereas the actual time taken for the outworking of creation can be estimated by modern scientific methods.

2. Young-Earth Creationism (YEC)
a. 24-Hour View**

Proponents of this view claim that the

---

* For a good description of this view, see Hugh Ross, *A Matter of Days: Resolving a Creation Controversy,* 2nd ed. (Covina, CA: Reasons to Believe, 2015).

** A good reference is: Terry Mortenson and Thane H. Ury, eds., *Coming to Grips with Genesis: Biblical Authority and the Age of the Earth* (Green Forest, AR: Master Books, 2008).

most natural reading of Genesis 1 is to interpret the Hebrew word for day, *yôm*, as a literal calendar day, or twenty-four-hour day. They point out that the fourth commandment—"Six days you shall labor and do all your work" (Ex. 20:9)—is accompanied with an explanation of God's creative work over six days, followed by a Sabbath day. "God gave no modifiers or extenuating qualifiers in the text to indicate anything other than a normal day." (Hagopian, GD, 36) Young-Earth Creationists make several arguments in favor of their understanding of Genesis 1, including:

- "Evening came and then morning" seems to indicate a literal day (Gen. 1:13 HCSB).
- Sabbath rest (Ex. 20:11) seems to imply six literal days of work during the creation week.
- The sun was created on day four, but there was life on day 3 (Gen. 1:11–13). Life cannot exist for long periods without sunlight, and so the days were not long ages.
- If the earth were old, then there would have been death and decay before sin. And yet the Bible says death is an enemy (1 Cor. 15:54). How could there be death and decay in God's original "good" creation?

Implicit in this view is a young age for the earth and universe. YEC is not opposed to scientific inquiry, but argues that mainstream science has been biased towards an ancient earth and universe by naturalistic presuppositions. Instead, YEC insists that the biblical record of six twenty-four-hour creation days must be the lens through which all scientific evidence is viewed.

i) Harmonizing a Young Earth with the Geologic Record

Efforts to harmonize the geologic record with the book of Genesis go back several centuries. Many early geologists attempted to use the Flood to explain the geologic record, including William Buckland (1784–1856), who held the first faculty position in geology at Oxford University. (Lindberg and Numbers, WSCM, 139–40) While Buckland and other geologists eventually decided that the Flood could not explain all features of the geologic record, flood geology was revived by the writings of Seventh Day Adventist George McCready Price (1870–1963). An even wider interest in flood geology was sparked by the publication of *The Genesis Flood* by theologian John Whitcomb and engineer Henry Morris, who developed the case that the worldwide flood of Genesis chapters 6 through 8 can explain the earth's geological and fossil data. (Whitcomb and Morris, GF) While most serious YECs do not follow all of the Whitcomb/Morris explanations, the global flood as an explanation of geological data is still important to YEC models. An example is the model of paleontologist Kurt Wise, who suggests a possible mechanism for the Flood from the theory of plate tectonics. (Wise, FFT, 179–209)

ii) Harmonizing a Young Universe with Distant Starlight

YEC generally holds that the whole universe is as young as the earth. Different approaches have been taken to explain a young universe in light of the mainstream scientific view that some starlight has been traveling for billions of years. Astronomer Danny Faulkner has summarized the merits of seven different approaches and proposed an eighth. (Faulkner, PNSLTTP) One of the approaches he discusses is based on a model using general relativistic effects to get light to reach the earth very quickly. This is the approach proposed by physicist D. Russell Humphreys (Humphreys, ST) and has some similarities with the theory proposed by physicist Gerald Schroeder, who reconciles the six calendar days of creation with a fifteen-billion-year old universe using time dilation in an expanding universe. (Schroeder, SG)

iii) Questioning the Dating Techniques and Results of Mainstream Science

YECs have questioned the reliability and assumptions of many popular dating techniques used by the mainstream scientific community that seem to support an ancient universe and earth. YEC argues there is much counterevidence pointing to a young earth. (see Wise, FFT, 58–71)

b. Mature Creation View

This view agrees with the calendar-day interpretation that the creation days are normal twenty-four-hour days. However, this view is not so much concerned with countering the mainstream views in geology and astronomy of an ancient earth and universe; rather, it attempts to harmonize these views with the biblical record of six twenty-four-hour days. To do this, proponents of this view hold that God created the universe and all that is in it with the appearance of age. While some contend that this would amount to deception, geologist Kurt Wise disagrees with this charge, citing several examples from Scripture where Jesus performed miracles that "created an apparent but non-existent history." (Wise, FFT, 59) These include the creation of fish and bread when feeding the five thousand and four thousand, and the creation of wine from water at the wedding in Cana.

B. Nonconcordist Interpretations

The principle motivating nonconcordist interpretations is to understand both authorial intent and how the original ANE audience would have interpreted the text, bearing in mind that the worldview of the original audience was very different from modern worldviews. Nonconcordist interpretations are generally not concerned with finding harmony between the Bible and current scientific theories of origins.

1. Framework View*

In this interpretation the seven-day account of creation is considered to be a figurative framework describing real history. There are many variations of this interpretation; some accept some degree of chronology. The framework consists of two parallel triads: days one through three and days four through six, followed by a Sabbath day. The first triad addresses the creation of three "kingdoms": light on day one; sky and surface water on day two; seas, dry land, and vegetation on day three. The second triad addresses the "kings" who rule the kingdoms: luminaries on day four; sea and winged creatures on day five; land animals and humans on day six. There are other examples in Genesis 1 and 2 of this nonsequential feature, temporal recapitulation: the twofold account of the creation of man (Gen. 1:26–28 and Gen. 2:7, 21–25) and the twofold account of Adam's placement in Eden (Gen. 2:8, 15). The sabbatical symbolism in the creation week is also used elsewhere in Scripture; for example, the seventy weeks of Daniel and Matthew's genealogy of Christ.

This view maintains there are two "registers" of creation: the upper (invisible) and the lower (visible). There are several analogies

---

* This is described and defended by Lee Irons with Meredith Kline, "The Framework View," in *The Genesis Debate*, 217–303.

between the two registers; for example the creation week belongs to the upper, while there is a lower-level parallel in the earthly week. "The complete seven-day framework is a metaphorical appropriation of lower-register language denoting an upper-register temporal reality." (Hagopian, GD, 247)

Regarding concordist interpretations, Lee Irons and Meredith Kline comment, "While we agree that concord between the Bible and science is achievable in principle, the engine driving the interpretive train should not be the experimental testability of a particular interpretation, but rather, how well it *exegetically* harmonizes with the whole Bible." (in Hagopian, GD, 182)

2. Analogical Days View

C. John Collins developed this interpretation using a literary-theological method that focuses on details of the Hebrew text and the literary devices used by the author and applies contemporary discourse analysis to determine authorial intent. (Collins, G1–4, 1–32; see also Collins, RG1–2G, 73–92) He describes this view as "the analogical days position": namely, the days are God's workdays, their length is neither specified nor important, and not everything in the account needs to be taken as historically sequential." (Collins, G1–4, 124) Collins notes that this view has historical precursors (Collins, G1–4, 124); for example, Herman Bavinck and William Shedd. (Shedd, DT, 366–379) He writes: "Genesis 1:1 describes the initial creation of all things, some unspecified time before the first day begins in 1:3," and "it is possible that parts of the days overlap and that events on a particular day may be grouped for logical rather than chronological reasons." (Collins, G1–4, 129)

Collins concludes "that Genesis 1:1–2:3 is not a scientific account. . . . I would claim

that it lays the foundation for all good science and philosophy, by telling us that the world came from a good and wise Creator." (Collins, G1–4, 266)

3. Functional Cosmic Temple View

Old Testament scholar John Walton presents this interpretation in *The Lost World of Genesis One* and in the more scholarly *Genesis 1 as Ancient Cosmology*. He argues that the use of the verb *bārā'* in describing God's creative activity refers to the creation of function rather than material. The days of creation are considered sequential calendar days, but are "not given as the period of time over which the material cosmos came into existence, but the period of time devoted to the inauguration of the functions of the cosmic temple, and perhaps also its annual reenactment." (Walton, LWGO, 92) The key functions necessary for life were created during the first three days: the basis for time on day one (periods of light); the basis for weather on day two (water cycle); and the basis for food on day three (land and vegetation). The functionaries associated with these functions were created on the next three days: celestial functionaries on day four; sea and winged creatures on day five; and land animals and humans on day six. Walton argues from an ANE perspective that divine rest is in a temple, and that the seventh day, the day of rest, represents God taking up his dwelling in the functioning cosmic temple. "Though all of the functions are anthropocentric, meeting the needs of humanity, the cosmic temple is theocentric, with God's presence serving as the defining element of existence." (Walton, LWGO, 85) The central feature of this interpretation is functional ontology rather than material ontology. Walton specifically denies scientific concordism, writing: "We gain nothing by bringing God's revelation into accordance with today's science." (Walton, LWGO, 17)

4. Historical Creationism View

In his book *Genesis Unbound* Old Testament scholar John Sailhamer presents an interpretation of Genesis that he terms historical creationism. He contends "that this view of the Genesis creation account can be traced back to a way of reading Genesis 1 and 2 that flourished before the rise of science and its use in biblical interpretation." (Sailhamer, GU, 49) Central to this view is a proper translation of the Hebrew word 'ereṣ (typically translated "earth" or "land"), which first appears in Genesis 1:1 as part of the phrase "heavens and earth." Sailhamer argues that this phrase is a merism (a figure of speech used to denote something with a phrase including several of its traits) expressing the concept of the entire universe. When 'ereṣ is used alone, as in the rest of Genesis 1, it should be translated "land." Sailhamer makes the case that in the context of the Pentateuch this should be understood as the land where Eden was located, and that this is the same as the land promised to Abraham. Thus, Genesis 1:1 refers to the creation of the universe and all that is in it, while Genesis 1:2 through 2:4 describes God's work of preparing the land that would eventually be promised to Abraham and his descendants. Concerning the overall Genesis account, Sailhamer writes: "The biblical location of 'the land' with respect to the city of Babylon 'in the east' indicates that throughout these narratives the author has in mind the promised land." (Sailhamer, GU, 57)

In summary, historical creationism maintains "that God created the universe during an indeterminate period of time before the actual reckoning of a sequence of time began. In Genesis 1, the period which follows 'the beginning' is a single, seven-day week, which itself is followed by a vast history of

humanity, leading ultimately to Abraham and the people of Israel." (Sailhamer, GU, 44)

5. Days of Revelation View

P. J. Wiseman has argued that the Genesis 1 creation account "is a series of statements to man about what God had done in the ages past. It is a record of the six days occupied by God in revealing to man the story of creation." (Wiseman, CRSD, 40). The days are not to be understood, in this view, as a list of time periods in which God accomplished the acts of creation.

IV. Hallmarks of Faithful Interpretations

The various interpretations of Genesis 1 described in this chapter adhere in general to the guidelines of faithful interpretation described in this chapter's introduction, specifically respecting the Hebrew text and the coherence and inerrancy of Scripture. The Presbyterian Church in America commissioned a study of several interpretations of the creation account, including all of the views discussed in this chapter except the functional cosmic temple interpretation (which was published after the study was conducted). We agree with this study's second recommendation that concluded: "Such diversity as covered in this report is acceptable as long as the full historicity of the creation account is accepted." (PCA Historical Center, http://www.pcahistory.org/creation/report.html) The authors of the study recognize that Bible-believing Christians will disagree on how Genesis 1 is to be interpreted, in particular as it relates to the age of the earth. This is not an essential issue that should divide Christians. As stated earlier, properly understanding creation requires an accurate integration of the book of Scripture and the book of nature.

CHAPTER 16

ARCHAEOLOGY AND THE OLD TESTAMENT

OVERVIEW

I. Definition

Biblical archaeology is defined as the investigation of ancient material cultures with a view to illuminating the cultural milieus of biblical narratives.

II. Understanding the Relationship Between Archaeology and the Bible

A. Archaeology Is a "Soft Science"

By its nature archaeology is a "soft" science employing "harder" sciences in its analysis—disciplines such as chemistry, physics, geology, zoology, and botany; still, conclusions drawn on the basis of mostly mute artifacts and related data are, by nature, *interpretations*. Rarely do analyses of archaeological data support a single interpretation or conclusion. Ideally, there is an attempt to sift carefully through data sets and logically weigh evidences for or against a range of possible interpretations.

But this does *not* always happen as it should. Occasionally, the preconceptions and biases of researchers complicate the process. Conventional wisdom, even one's worldview, can slant an interpretation in a particular direction. On the one hand, then, those tending toward an antibiblical bias adopt interpretations of archaeological data that "disprove" the Bible. On the other hand, scholars who favor the historical credibility of Scripture most often reach conclusions that support the Bible's claims. Yet both anti- and pro-Bible scholars are drawing from a range of reasonable interpretations. In the final analysis, we seek an *objective interpretation* that best corresponds to, and adequately explains, the material data discovered in any given excavation. After all, truth is that which corresponds to reality.

B. Is Biblical Archaeology Dead?

A significant volume of material deriving from ancient Near Eastern (ANE) studies and archaeology intersects with the study of the Hebrew Scriptures. As interpreted by scholars, some of it tends to corroborate elements of biblical history, while some of it does not. This notwithstanding, one thing is certain: the euphoric sentiment—"The Bible is confirmed by every turn of the spade"—formerly attributed to mid-twentieth century scholars (like Nelson Glueck, William F. Albright, Millar Burrows, G. Ernest Wright, Merrill Unger, Joseph Free, and Mitchell Dahood) is no longer held by the vast majority of the archaeological community. In most archaeological circles, biblical archaeology itself is considered loathsome and to be avoided if at all possible. The "death" of biblical archaeology is commonly celebrated.

A very effective illustration of the differences between the outmoded mid-twentieth-century biblical archaeology and the early twenty-first-century world of ANE archaeology can be found by comparing the "Archaeology and Biblical Criticism" chapter

in previous editions of this book with the one in this newly revised and updated version. While some things remain the same, such as hard artifacts like Sennacherib's prism, which describes the invasion of Israel and the siege of Jerusalem by Assyrian forces, other things must change in light of more recent research, such as the former interpretations by Giovanni Pettinato of the Ebla tablets. In the 1970s Pettinato believed that the Ebla tablets contained the names of various biblical cities and personal names, which, if true, would lend support to the early chapters of Genesis. It is now widely recognized that Pettinato misunderstood the texts. By the year 2000 the majority of his original conclusion had been rejected. The Ebla tablets' connection to the Bible was a false alarm.

So many advancements in archaeological science have been made in the past twenty-five years—and the pace has accelerated since 1999—that invoking the views and conclusions of past scholars in support of the biblical text is highly suspect. From a Christian apologetics perspective, then, making a case for the historical credibility of the Bible must now focus on more recent methodologies, data, and discoveries, being careful to utilize pre-1999 material *only after meticulous re-analysis* in the light of more advanced technologies and current knowledge.

C. Errors of Nineteenth-and Twentieth-Century Archaeology

This chapter offers the most recent scholarship, emphasizing the proper relationship between archaeology and biblical studies. Twenty-first-century biblical scholars, including biblical archaeologists and apologists, must avoid the errors of the nineteenth and twentieth centuries; biblical archaeology of the past, however—that of Albright, Wright, Free, and their contemporaries—was not entirely without merit. Far from it. There remain many valid viewpoints and discoveries that corroborate the biblical text in remarkable ways. Even so, clarifying the proper relationship between biblical text and archaeological science begins by shifting away from words such as *prove* and *proof*, in favor of terms like *consistent with*, *corroborate*, and *commensurate with*. Both biblical and archaeological scholarship must go where the evidence leads. When archaeology elucidates a biblical passage, it does so because the world of the Bible is the same world that produced the material excavated by the archaeologist. The reverse can also happen when a biblical text provides a historical framework for an archaeological find. This is a relationship that should be encouraged, not discouraged.

D. The New Face of Archaeology

While the most influential ANE archaeologists are not people of faith who regard the Hebrew Scriptures—the Torah in particular—as worthwhile history, and while the focus of ANE archaeology no longer aims to "prove" the historicity of biblical narratives, the new archaeological era, with its ever-emerging technologies and more advanced research paradigms, is still poised to illuminate the biblical text as never before—*and is already doing so.*

Responsible archaeology uses every available resource to gain insight into the past. For example, sites such as Sodom, Heshbon, Aroer, Dibon, Nebo, Bethany beyond Jordan, Jerusalem, Hazor, Megiddo, Lachish, Gath, and many others, are principally identified because they appear in biblical narratives with enough embedded geographical data to aid in locating them.

E. Correct Methodology

Rigorous scholarship can either confirm links between biblical locations and archaeological sites or deny them. But bias should not force us to avoid evidence. We must instead establish clear principles, methods, and criteria, and then follow the evidence wherever it leads. This is the strict method of good science, and biblical archaeology must adhere to it.

It is not intellectually appropriate to categorically ignore the Bible as a valuable source when formulating a historical framework or a parameter for identifying geographical sites. The Bible remains one of the best extant historical and geographical sources from the ancient Near East. That is why certain archaeological excavations receive more attention than others. This is perfectly reasonable.

In all archaeological endeavors, the fair goal is objectivity. Indeed, sites with no clear biblical connection are also important for determining the history of the region. Archaeological importance should never be equated solely with its potential value to corroborate the biblical account.

F. Fact and Faith: Wrestling with Objectivity vs. Subjectivity in Biblical Archaeology

Why is it critical to address the Bible's historical authenticity? Part of the answer is that an evidence-based apologetic for the Bible's historicity inherits the discipline's own history described above: scholars have been in strong disagreement over interpreting the sometimes limited data and have at times rejected conclusions that formerly were celebrated. The degree of confidence in the potential value of discoveries has varied. Therefore, from an evidential apologetic angle, this question insists upon careful attention to the preconceptions and methods that enter into the research: any defense of biblical credibility in the historical arena must offer evidence that a reasonable mind would accept as a plausible demonstration of the facts in the case. Apologetics sifts the factual evidence. It does not operate in blind faith. In reality, faith is best understood as being built upon fact that is understood to have adequate grounds for its acceptance. Establishing whether the interpretation of a fact is reasonable is precisely the task of archaeology. Anselm's famous motto, "faith seeking understanding," applies in this search for historical evidence, just as it does in philosophical argument.

III. Supernatural History in the ANE (Ancient Near East)

A. History and the Divine

The historian might say, "How can we wrap our history-writing around an act of God?" Secular historians and archaeologists alike—not to mention a majority of philosophers and scientists—avoid mixing divine causalities into their work. But even when people of faith write history, they have ways of stroking readers' skepticism by weaving in threads of rationalism, suggesting, for example, that "miracles" like the fleeing Israelites crossing the Red Sea (or "Reed Sea" as some scholars suggest) involved a convergence of natural phenomena. (One professor said to me [Josh] that the Red Sea was only twelve inches deep. I was facetious in my response: "Oh, so the entire Egyptian army drowned in twelve inches of water?") Merely mentioning that God could have used wind and simple physics to "part" the water introduces a comfort-level for accepting what is, by all definitions, a miracle. But if God does exist, then would he not have a fundamental power and freedom to intervene in the processes of the nature that he created?

B. Logic and Reason

The tendency of historians to avoid the "supernatural" is understandable. Certainly, logic and reason *should* prevail when writing about the past. But one must exercise care in what passes for logic and reason. For example, if God exists and *is* the Creator of all, and *is* actively involved in his universe, then it would make no sense to write him out of his own story. In formulating histories involving the ancient Near East, all too often, scholars who deny the supernatural can be illogical and unreasonable in their exclusion of biblical material not only by dismissing the divine element, but also by denying historicity to people and events—even certain cities, towns, and geographical locations—found in biblical texts. For example, not only do many disallow Moses' interface with Yahweh, but they also reject the existence of Moses himself, a rather strange *modus operandi* when one considers just how ANE history is composed in general.

Steven Collins, an archaeologist and director of eleven excavation seasons at Tall

---

[The] categorical dismissal of the historical character of the biblical narratives is, from an historiographical perspective, sheer nonsense. Such anti-biblical bias is clearly exposed when we realize how our understanding of history is pieced together from extant ancient Near Eastern records.

Steven Collins

---

el-Hammam/Sodom in Jordan, speaks to the point: "This kind of categorical dismissal of the historical character of the biblical narratives is, from an historiographical perspective, sheer nonsense. Such anti-biblical bias is clearly exposed when we realize how our understanding of history is pieced together from extant ancient Near Eastern records." (Collins, DFLCA, 214–215)

Renowned Egyptologist, ANE scholar, and professor emeritus at the University of Liverpool, Kenneth A. Kitchen speaks to the same issue:

> [Assyrian] campaign reports contain a large amount of good firsthand information. Yet at intervals the Assyrian kings also attribute this or that success to the overwhelming splendor of their god Assur, or of this terrible weapon. In his campaign against Hezekiah of Judah and allies in 701, Sennacherib did just this, "trusting in Assur my lord." That he did so has no bearing whatsoever on the historicity of his main account, successively conquering Phoenicia . . . then Joppa and Ekron, and Lachish. (Kitchen, AOOT, 48)

The approach that Kitchen uses in response to Sennacherib's reference to "Assur my lord"—an attitude of reserve regarding an artifact's or a document's stated supernatural orientation, combined with a careful analysis of the event it reports—is what we would like to see when archaeologists deal with biblical material.

Collins adds:

> [Often] when historians and archaeologists approach biblical stories, key characters— Abraham, Joseph, Moses, Joshua—and the accomplishments attributed to them are called fictional, non-historical, or mythical simply because of their relationship to Yahweh. (Collins, DFLCA, 215)

C. Antisupernatural Bias and Its Effects

By impugning the historical integrity of the Bible, liberal scholars are compelled by their antisupernatural biases to assign late Iron Age (post c. 1000 BC) dates for the origin of biblical stories. In doing so they frequently multiply their errors. One good example of this— though there are scores of them—is the use of *selective comparisons*. This happens when pieces of biblical narrative are purposefully laid alongside cultural contexts considerably later in date than the timeframe demanded by reasonable biblical chronologies. Egyptologist James K. Hoffmeier observes the inherent weakness of J. Van Seters's comparison of the Israelite crossing of the Jordan River during flood stage with the much later Neo-Assyrian (c. eighth century BC) accounts of Sargon II and Ashurbanipal's crossing of the Tigris and Euphrates during the spring high-water season. (Hoffmeier, IE, 40)

Hoffmeier counters:

> Van Seters's treatment of this matter fails on two points. First, the spring of the year was the traditional time for kings to go to war in Israel (cf. 2 Sam. 11:2) as well as in Mesopotamia. . . . Spring is also when the rivers, the Jordan as well as the Tigris and Euphrates, are at their highest levels because of melting snow from the mountains to the north. Secondly, the seemingly miraculous crossing of raging rivers by a king is well attested in earlier Near Eastern sources [such as] Hattusili I (ca. 1650 BC) [and] Sargon the Great (ca. 2371–2316 BC). Consequently, there is no basis for Van Seters's assertion. The river crossing in Joshua 3 by Israel's forces accurately reflects the seasonal realities of military life in the Near East throughout the three millennia BC. (Hoffmeier, IE, 40)

One must recognize that presuppositions and biases exist in the scholarly world. Not infrequently, these predilections create blind spots and gaps in research and publication that are often difficult to identify. Because the anti-Bible bias is so strong in current academia, an adherence to facts and reasonably interpreted data is critical. One also has to be able to allow for changes in thought when better methods and new data point in a different direction. On balance, the twenty-first-century world of archaeology demonstrates the historical authenticity of the biblical record in ways never imagined in the "Albrightian old days." (Albright lived from 1891 to 1971.) We have excellent reasons to trust the historical quality of the Old Testament. While God will not turn up on the blade of a trowel, Albright's conception of history provides a framework of *true narrative representation* that must not be ignored in the composition of ancient history. (Oller and Collins, LTNR, online; Collins and Oller, IBTNR, online)

The historicity of the Bible does not need to be propped up by false "evidence." Proper, scientific archaeology is consistent with biblical history, and the archaeological pendulum *is* swinging back toward confirmation of the historical authenticity of the Bible. Christian apologists and Bible students are well advised to keep up with the pace of discovery in the *legitimate* archaeological arena.

IV. Biblical Archaeology After Its Heyday in 1885–1985

A. A New Day for Biblical Archaeology

It is a new day for biblical archaeology, one in which the Bible does not get a pass simply because it is fashionable or self-serving to do so. It is an environment in which every link between the Bible and archaeology is rigorously scrutinized and challenged. But within scientific disciplines, as well as in biblical apologetics, this is how it should be.

Joseph Holden and Norman Geisler of Veritas Evangelical Seminary recognize the importance of a proper scientific foundation for biblical archaeology:

> Archaeology . . . has its limitations. Although it deals with artifacts, features, measurements, and tangible data, archaeology also involves many interpretive judgments and probabilities. Any interpretations and conclusions must be considered in light of human fallibility and the sparse nature of the data itself. . . . [T]his is compounded by the fact that only a small amount of the evidence has survived and can be either isolated or disconnected from its in-situ environment. Floods, fires, warfare, natural deterioration, burial, temperature, political climate and time, have all collaborated to make the discovery of biblical artifacts difficult. Therefore, archaeology cannot be classified as an "exact" science; but neither can any empirical science for that matter. Despite its limitations, archaeology is governed by generally accepted principles and methods as a forensic science and is a valuable tool in uncovering the past. Therefore, archaeology has become an indispensable discipline in the historian's tool belt to unearth data supporting the historical reliability of the Bible beyond a reasonable doubt. (Holden and Geisler, PHAB, 200–201)

B. A Pendulum Swing in Archaeology

The new order in biblical archaeology offers a wealth of solid data from the ancient Near East, supported by better logic, critical thinking, superior methods, more rigorous scholarship, and an active opposition mounting challenges all along the way. Iron sharpens iron.

Holden and Geisler recognize the benefits of this swing of the archaeological pendulum back in favor of Christian apologetics:

In the twenty-first century, the previous century's debate over the historical reliability of the Bible has taken on a new face and has gained fresh momentum in light of recent discoveries unearthed through archaeological excavation of the Holy Land. Many of these findings relate either directly or indirectly to the people, places, events, customs, and beliefs recorded in the Bible. As a result, the assertion by critical scholars that the Bible's historical descriptions are a product of human invention can no longer be maintained without facing strong counterarguments. (Holden and Geisler, PHAB, 15)

V. Twenty-First-Century Resurgence of Biblical Archaeology

A. The Present and Future of Biblical Archaeology

Conservative scholars today have taken up the challenge to reinterpret old data and introduce new data from across the spectrum of ancient Near Eastern studies. This includes archaeology corroborating the historical authenticity of Old Testament narratives. This material is even demonstrating the historical character of the Genesis patriarchal narratives, as we describe in chapter 18.

The crux of the matter is data interpretation and this question: Is there reasonable correspondence and/or consistency between the biblical text and the archaeological data?

K. A. Kitchen emphasizes that the two *are* compatible:

The Sinai covenant (all three versions, Deuteronomy included) has to have originated within a close-set period (1400–1200)—likewise other features. The phenomena of the united monarchy fit well into what we know of the period and of ancient royal usages. The primeval protohistory embodies early popular tradition going very far back, and is set in an early format. Thus we have a consistent level of good, fact-based correlations right through from circa 2000 BC (with earlier roots) down to 400 BC. In terms of general reliability . . . the Old Testament comes out remarkably well, so long as its writings and writers are treated fairly and evenhandedly, in line with independent data, open to all. (Kitchen, AOOT, 500)

B. A Dialogical Approach

An examination of Collins's *dialogical approach* to archaeology and the Bible is most helpful:

I have observed that scholars on both extremes of what I often call the *Bible believe-o-meter* [italics his] have adopted structurally similar, but opposite, approaches. Minimalists, to the extent possible, do not allow the Bible to intersect with their archaeology. Maximalists (those who accept the biblical account even if no archaeological data exists) as far as possible,

---

In terms of general reliability . . . the Old Testament comes out remarkably well, so long as its writings and writers are treated fairly and evenhandedly, in line with independent data, open to all.

K. A. Kitchen

---

throw out archaeological conclusions that challenge "traditional" interpretations of biblical texts, allowing only data that harmonize with their textual preconceptions. . . . If both "sides" are willing to admit that no scholars are infallible or in possession of *all* the facts, then we can view points of correspondence (or lack thereof) between text *and* tell with better objectivity. . . . In short, we need to *talk*! And we need to do so without thinking that we, individually, must come away with a victory for our own point of view. Has archaeology gone too far in throwing out the Bible? Yes! But have some scholars gone too far in throwing out archaeology? Yes! (Collins, HAGO, online)

Collins's solution is to

approach the subject of the Bible and archaeology dialogically. . . . First, each "side" must give up the idea that those on the opposite end are "fringe lunatics." We may never agree completely, but at the very least we need to understand and respect how others arrived at their positions. Archaeologists on the minimalist side should recognize the worldviews and biases that permeate their thinking. Archaeologists on the maximalist side should do the same. . . .

Second, a pragmatic suggestion for archaeological purposes: maximalists—lay aside categorical rejection of the Bible at the level of history and geography; minimalists—disconnect biblical history and geography from theology. Both sides need to think scientifically in terms of observation, degrees of correspondence between biblical and ancient Near Eastern history, and the incorporation of new or better evidence. . . .

Third, think geographically. Is anyone actually going to deny the importance of biblical texts in terms of geography? My long-running dialogue with the late Anson Rainey taught me a lot about this process. He was always willing to concede points when they were valid and he could not reasonably overturn them. Although we were miles apart on the subject of biblical historicity, we were on the same page when it came to the fact that ancient writers—regardless of their culture of origin—did not create fictitious geographies! Whether their stories were fact or fiction, they were layered over real-world landscapes. To ignore biblical geography would be nonsensical. Biblical texts are, at the geographical level, the product of ancient observers who lived on that terrain. They deserve our respect and careful attention.

Fourth, be open to cause-and-effect relationships between biblical and ancient history when reasonable observations from numerous data sets—including the biblical text—converge. When levels of correspondence rise to statistically meaningful levels, do not ignore them merely because they contradict previously accepted ideas. . . .

Fifth, let both archaeology and the biblical text participate in the dialogue. Both have something to say. (Collins, HAGO, online)

C. The Resurgence of Biblical Archaeology

Speaking of modern developments in biblical archaeology, Collins notes,

It is hard to understand how any scholar—regardless of "pet" theories about textual origins—could toss the Bible out of the repertoire of archaeological tools. Seriously?—eliminate an ancient text full of geographical and historical clues from the archaeological process? Because of what? Because Yahweh enacted a covenant with Abraham? Because Moses had face-to-face conversations with Yahweh? Because the Israelites told stories that cast a less-than-flattering light on their (often enemy) neighbors? Really? On *this* basis we shall finally eliminate most everything we know about the ancient Near East. Archaeology cut loose from religiously-loaded texts? Good luck with that!" (Collins, HAGO, online)

One of the leaders of this resurgence of respect for the Bible as an archaeologically significant source is Kenneth A. Kitchen, whom we quoted earlier in this chapter. His propensity for logic and heavy documentation demonstrate convincingly that Abraham, Isaac, and Jacob authentically belong to the Middle Bronze Age (c. 1950–1540 BC) and could not have originated in the imaginations of late Iron Age Judahite priests as the proponents of OT higher criticism maintain. Kitchen further confirms that cultural elements found in the stories of Moses and Joshua match those of the late Bronze Age. We discuss the evidence for the existence of the patriarchs, the exodus, the conquest, and other key OT events and figures in chapters to come.

For now, it seems fitting to end this chapter with a quote from Kitchen, who aptly sums up how the resurgence in ancient Near Eastern archaeology coincides with Old Testament history:

The theories current in Old Testament studies, however brilliantly conceived and elaborated, were mainly established in a vacuum with little or no reference to the Ancient Near East, and initially too often in accordance with *a priori* philosophical and literary principles. It is solely because the data from the Ancient Near East coincide so much better with the existing observable structure of Old Testament history, literature and religion than with the theoretical reconstructions, that we are compelled—as happens in Ancient Oriental studies—to question or even to abandon such theories regardless of their popularity. Facts, not votes, determine the truth. (Kitchen, AOOT, 172)

CHAPTER 17

THE HISTORICAL ADAM

OVERVIEW

I. Introduction

The overarching theme running through all sixty-six books of the Bible is the story of God's creative work, of humanity's rebellion against God, and of God's work to redeem fallen humanity. Adam is a central figure in the Genesis account of creation and of humanity's rebellion, and the church has historically viewed him as a real person. This view has come under criticism in recent years. This criticism raises questions about the interpretation of the biblical narrative concerning Adam and of Christian doctrines that depend on this narrative.

A. The Debate Over Adam

While doubts about Adam's historicity are hardly surprising in a secular society that largely rejects the authority of the Bible, it has surprised some to see debate about this issue occur among Bible-believing Christians. The

423

debate is captured in the book *Four Views on the Historical Adam*, where the following four positions are presented and defended: (Barrett and Caneday, FVHA)

1. No Historical Adam: Theistic Evolution / Evolutionary Creation (TE/EC)* View

Professor of science and religion Denis Lamoureux argues that Adam never existed, but his story remains "a vital, but *incidental*, ancient vessel that transports *inerrant* spiritual truths: only humans are created in the Image of God, only humans have fallen into sin, and our Creator judges us for our sinfulness." (in Barrett and Caneday, FVHA, 37, emphasis in original)

2. A Historical Adam: Archetypal Creation View

Professor of Old Testament John Walton asserts that

> Adam and Eve are historical figures–real people in a real past. Nevertheless I am persuaded that the biblical text is more interested in them as archetypal figures who represent all of humanity. . . . If this is true, Adam and Eve also may or may not be the first humans or the parents of the entire human race. Such an archetypal focus is theologically viable and is well-represented in the ancient Near East. (in Barrett and Caneday, FVHA, 89)

3. A Historical Adam: Old-Earth Creation (OEC) View

Professor of Old Testament C. John Collins argues "that the best way to account for the biblical presentation of human life is to understand that Adam and Eve were both real persons at the headwaters of humankind."

In other words, he believes Adam and Eve really existed and that the Fall was both *moral* and *historical*. If there originally were more human beings than Adam and Eve, claims Collins, then they were a single tribe of closely related members. Nevertheless, Adam and Eve were historical figures. As far as how we should interpret Scripture, Collins says "that the nature of the biblical material should keep us from being too literalistic in our reading of Adam and Eve, leaving room for an Earth that is not young, but that the biblical material along with good critical thinking provides certain freedoms and limitations for connecting the Bible's creation account to a scientific and historical account of human origins." (in Barrett and Caneday, FVHA, 143)

4. A Historical Adam: Young-Earth Creation (YEC) View

Professor of Old Testament William Barrick states,

> Adam's historicity is foundational to a number of biblical doctrines and is related to the inspiration and inerrancy of Scripture. . . . The biblical account represents Adam as a single individual rather than an archetype or the product of biological evolution, and a number of New Testament texts rely on Adam's historicity. (in Barrett and Caneday, FVHA, 197)

Three questions are at the heart of this debate:

1. Was Adam a historical person?
2. Was Adam the first human and, with Eve, father of all humanity?

---

* This view is described as Evolutionary Creation in the book, but it represents what has typically been referred to as Theistic Evolution. We refer to it as the TE/EC view.

This is not to imply that these are the only available options regarding the historical Adam. We recognize that there are others. Not all who affirm the Archetypal view, for instance, believe in Adam's historicity and some embrace evolution. And there are some Old Earth Creationists who strictly reject the existence of any other early humans besides Adam and Eve. We are simply adopting the positions from *Four Views on the Historical Adam* for the sake of convenience.

3. Was Adam created via an evolutionary process or was he a *de novo* creation (created as a new, fully formed being)?

In this chapter we examine answers to these questions from Scripture and from the book of nature. In regard to the various interpretations of these two books, we note key distinctions distinguishing among the four views of Adam outlined above.

B. The Theological Significance of Historical Adam

The name "Adam" is from the Hebrew 'ādām, a word that can mean "humanity" (male and female collectively, as for example in Genesis 1:27 and Genesis 5:2); "man" (for example in Genesis 2:7); or a proper name (for example in Genesis 5:1a). When used with the definite article it is never a proper name; without the definite article it can be "Adam" or "humanity." (Barrett and Caneday, FVHA, 91) The creation of 'ādām in Genesis 1:26, 27 describes the creation of humanity in general, while the accounts in Genesis 2:7 and 2:21, 22 refer to the creation of two individuals: a man and a woman. These individuals are subsequently identified as Adam and Eve (Gen. 2:20; 3:20). Theologians from Patristic to modern times have recognized the importance of Adam to Christian doctrine, in particular the doctrines of man, sin, and salvation. (VanDoodewaard, QHA)

1. The Doctrine of Man

The creation of humanity described in Genesis 1:26, 27 emphasizes the unique status of humans as God's image-bearers. Theologians have interpreted the "image of God" in different ways. According to one view, humans resemble God in some way;

according to another, humans are God's representatives on earth; a third view holds that humans, like God, are relational beings. John Collins has argued that these three views are not mutually exclusive, and notes five characteristics of God taken from the creation account evident in humans: displaying intelligence, using language, appreciating aesthetic and moral goodness, relating, and following a cycle of work and rest. (Collins, G1–4, 61–67) Some of these characteristics are important criteria for identifying the evidence of human behavior in the archaeological record (see section III.C.2 in this chapter).

Humanity's shared status as image-bearers of God acts as the basis for two hallmarks of the Christian doctrine of man: the *equality* and the *value* of all human beings. For instance, the historical understanding that Adam and Eve are the parents of all humanity, implied in Adam's naming his wife "the mother of all living" (Gen. 3:20), means that all humans are members of the same family, emphasizing the equality of all humans. The YEC and most OEC* views of Adam and Eve hold to the historical understanding, and the Archetypal view leaves it as a possibility. The TE/EC view is "that God ordained and sustained a teleological process of evolution that led ultimately to the creation of humanity, who bear His Image." (Lamoureux, EV, 284) While TE/EC ultimately rejects the atheistic view of man's origin as a chance event, that view does believe that God used Darwinian evolutionary processes to create humanity—processes that appear to be blind and undirected. Even some atheists question the ability of naturalistic evolution to account for mankind's origin. (Nagel, MC)

---

* This is the view of the OEC model proposed by Reasons to Believe (RTB), as described in Hugh Ross, *More Than a Theory: Revealing a Testable Model for Creation* (Grand Rapids, MI: Baker, 2009).

2. The Doctrine of Sin

Theologian Wayne Grudem has defined sin as "any failure to conform to the moral law of God in act, attitude, or nature." (Grudem, ST, 490) Genesis 3 describes the events leading up to the first sin: Adam and Eve chose to disobey God's command not to eat fruit from the tree of the knowledge of good and evil, resulting in God's curse on them and on the ground, and their expulsion from the garden of Eden. Their alienation from God was followed by alienation between humans, as epitomized by Cain's murder of Abel (Gen. 4:1–16) and the murderous behavior of Cain's descendants (Gen. 4:23, 24). This alienation, reflected in the universally shared sense of loss and yearning for justice and a better world, has characterized human experience and history since Adam's sin. This led G. K. Chesterton to observe: "original sin . . . is the only part of Christian theology which can really be proved." (Chesterton, Orthodoxy, 28) Grudem uses the phrase "inherited sin" rather than "original sin" to make clear the biblical teaching that all humans inherit sin from Adam. There are two aspects of this inheritance. First, because Adam represented all of humanity in Eden, all humans are counted guilty with him. Second, all humans inherit a sinful nature from Adam. This sinful nature is manifest in our thoughts, actions, and relationships. When discussing divorce, Jesus described one of sin's effects as "hardness of heart" (Matt. 19:8 ESV). The reality of our shared sinful nature was highlighted dramatically in the trial of Adolf Eichmann, a chief architect of the Holocaust. After recognizing that Eichmann appeared to be a normal person—and that all of us have the potential to be just as evil—an Auschwitz survivor collapsed when testifying against him. (Colson, TT, website)

Because of Adam's central role in the first sin, the historicity of Adam is important to the doctrine of sin. The inheritance of Adam's guilt and sinful nature has been the position of Christians for centuries. (Madueme and Reeves, AFOS, 85–324) The YEC, OEC, and Archetypal views of Adam agree with this position, although there are different explanations for how this nature is passed from generation to generation.

The TE/EC view, which generally denies a historical Adam, states: "original sin was manifested mysteriously and gradually over countless many generations during the evolutionary processes leading to men and women." (Lamoureux, EC, 292) TE/EC physicist Karl Giberson comments, "In the conclusion to Saving the Original Sinner I argue that a deep and meaningful concept of sin as an intrinsic part of human nature is a natural implication of our evolutionary origins. If we understand sin as a 'pathological selfishness' (which I think captures it nicely), we can easily see how it was produced by natural selection." (Wilson, SOS, website) Giberson maintains that humans did not willfully rebel against God but rather we acquired our sinful tendencies through evolution, leading him to call Darwinism an "acid" that destroys belief in "the fall, 'Christ as second Adam,' [and] the origins of sin." (Giberson, SD, 10)

The view, then, that human moral sense reflects the image of God, with that image having been marred as a consequence of Adam's historical act of disobedience, is the view the church has largely held since the beginning, and the one we find to be the most compelling account of the biblical record.

3. The Doctrine of Salvation

In explaining the doctrine of salvation, the apostle Paul identified Adam as the man responsible for sin entering the world.

He then identified Jesus as the "last Adam" (1 Cor. 15:45), who bore the penalty of the first Adam's sin and made possible the forgiveness of sins, as well as the eternal life lost as a result of Adam's sin (Rom. 5:12–21; 1 Cor. 15:20–22, 44–49). In writing that sin entered the world through one man, and that the consequences of this sin have been borne by one man, it seems clear that Paul, in making a supremely important theological statement, was referring to persons he considered to be historical. However, while all Christians recognize that Jesus was historical, the TE/EC view generally denies the historical Adam. A TE/EC explanation for this is explored in II.E below.

II. The Evidence from the Bible and Jewish Texts for Adam and His Family

A. The Genesis Record

The man whose creation is described in Genesis 2:7 is identified as "Adam" several times in Genesis chapters 2 through 5. The creation of humanity described in Genesis 1:26, 27 does not use this proper name, and theologians differ on the relationship between these two creation accounts. John Collins argues that the traditional interpretation (Genesis 2 elaborates the creation of humanity described in Genesis 1) is supported by the fact that Jesus in Matthew 19:3–9 combines Genesis 1:27 with Genesis 2:24 in his teaching on marriage. (Barrett and Caneday, FVHA, 127) The YEC and OEC views follow the traditional interpretation, understanding that Genesis 2 teaches the *de novo* creation of Adam and Eve as deliberate, miraculous acts. While some interpret the description of these miracles literally, others argue that God could have used an evolved hominin as the

basis for the creation of Adam. Theologian John Stott comments on this as follows:

> Adam, then, was a special creation of God, whether God formed him literally "from the dust of the ground" and then "breathed into his nostrils the breath of life" [Gen. 2:7 NIV], or whether this is the biblical way of saying that he was created out of an already existing hominid. The vital truth we cannot surrender is that, though our bodies are related to the primates, we ourselves in our fundamental identity are related to God. (Stott, RGGN, 164*)

In presenting the TE/EC interpretation of Genesis 1 and 2, Denis Lamoureux makes the case that the two accounts come from two different sources and are complementary. (Lamoureux, EC, 198–202) While agreeing that Genesis 2 describes *de novo* creation, he does not consider it to be a historical event. In fact, he questions the historicity of the first eleven chapters of Genesis, writing: "Real history in the Bible begins roughly around Genesis 12 with Abraham." (Barrett and Caneday, FVHA, 44)

In presenting the Archetypal view, John Walton proposes a third interpretation: "The second account is not detailing the sixth day, but identifying a sequel scenario, that is, recounting events that potentially and arguably could have occurred long after the first account. . . . Adam and Eve would not necessarily be envisioned as the first human beings, but would be elect individuals drawn out of the human population and given a particular representative role in sacred space." (Barrett and Caneday, FVHA, 109) Biologist Denis Alexander has suggested an evolutionary model incorporating the

---

* See also Alister McGrath's excellent article, "Augustine's Origin of Species," *Christianity Today* (May, 2009): 39–41.

archetype concept: "God in his grace chose a couple of Neolithic farmers in the Near East . . . or maybe a community of farmers, to whom he chose to reveal himself in a special way. . . . [T]his first couple, or community, have been termed *Homo divinus* . . . corresponding to the Adam and Eve of the Genesis account. . . . [Adam] is therefore viewed as the federal head of the whole of humanity alive at that time." (Alexander, CE, 290) Under this view, Adam and Eve were not specially created by God and were not the progenitors of the human race.

Genesis 3 gives the sad account of Adam and Eve's disobedience and of God's pronouncement of the consequences of their disobedience. The interpretation of these events by the different views of Adam was discussed under I.B.2.

Genesis 4 describes the birth of Adam and Eve's sons Cain, Abel, and Seth, and of Abel's murder by his brother Cain. This chapter also describes some of Cain and Seth's immediate descendants. John Walton discusses an issue that has raised questions for centuries: the apparent reference to other humans living at the same time as Adam and Eve. He notes, "From Genesis 4:14, 17 we could reasonably deduce that there are other people around—in fact, that may be the easiest reading." (Barrett and Caneday, FVHA, 94) The traditional interpretation is that these people are other descendants of Adam and Eve, but this is not stated explicitly in Scripture. Walton suggests that they are not Adamites.

Collins has reviewed a few proposals to account for non-Adamites present at the time of Genesis 4. (Collins, DAERE, 124–131) These include the "Neolithic farmer" model of Denis Alexander mentioned earlier, as well as the thinking of Old Testament scholar Derek Kidner and of C. S. Lewis. In discussing these possible scenarios Collins notes that any account including "polygenesis" (humans other than Adam and Eve at the beginning of mankind) must "envision these humans as a single tribe. Adam would then be the chieftain of this tribe (preferably produced before the others), and Eve would be his wife. This tribe 'fell' under the leadership of Adam and Eve. This follows from the notion of solidarity in a representative." (Collins, DAERE, 121)

Genesis 5 gives the genealogy of Adam's descendants through Seth and notes that he had other children. There is also a comment that Seth was "a son in [Adam's] own likeness, after his image" (Gen. 5:3). This echoes the words used in Genesis 5:1 to describe God's creation of Adam in his own likeness and implies that the image of God in Adam, though marred by sin, was passed on to his descendants.

B. Biblical Genealogies

Adam is included in three biblical genealogies:

- Adam's family tree through Seth (Gen. 5:1; also mentioned in Jude 1:14)
- The family tree of David and Israel (1 Chr. 1:1)
- The family tree of Jesus (Luke 3:38)

Adam's inclusion in the family trees of David and Jesus, both of whom are clearly portrayed as historical figures, provides strong evidence that the biblical authors believed in a historical Adam. Yet, in defending his position of no historical Adam, Lamoureux argues that biblical genealogies were written to provide theological truth, not a twenty-first-century understanding of genealogy. (Lamoureux, EC, 206–14) However, he does not make a convincing case against the historicity of people included in these genealogies.

C. Second Temple Literature

The Second Temple period refers to the time between the rebuilding of the temple after the Babylonian exile (c. 516 BC) and the destruction of the temple by the Romans in AD 70. A study of literature from this period provides insight into the cognitive environment of the New Testament writers. In presenting a review of this literature, John Collins focused on the Apocrypha and the writings of the Jewish historian Josephus (37–c. 100 AD) as being within the mainstream of Jewish thought. (Madueme and Reeves, AFOS, 27–31) Josephus calls Adam "the first man, made from the earth." (in Madueme and Reeves, AFOS, 30) References to Adam in the Apocrypha describe him as a real person, for example: "Thou madest Adam and gavest him Eve his wife as a helper and support. From them the race of mankind has sprung. Thou didst say, 'It is not good that the man should be alone; let us make a helper for him like himself'" (Tobit 8:6 RSV). Collins concludes: "In the period that bridges the Old Testament and the New, the Jewish authors most representative of the mainstream consistently treat Adam and Eve as actual people, at the head of the human race." (in Madueme and Reeves, AFOS, 31)

D. Teachings of Jesus

In response to a question from the Pharisees about divorce, Jesus cites the marriage union of the man and woman in Genesis 2:24 (Matt. 19:3–12; Mark 10:2–12). In his warnings to the Pharisees, he mentions Adam and Eve's son "righteous Abel" (Matt. 23:35). These passages seem to imply that Jesus thought of Adam and Eve and their family as real people. Denis Lamoureux,

who denies a historical Adam, explains that Jesus "accommodated by using ancient science in His teaching." (Barrett and Caneday, FVHA, 61) Lamoureux also cites history as an accommodation used by Paul. However, it is difficult to see how the hermeneutical assumption of accommodation is consistent with Lamoureux's use of *inerrancy* to describe spiritual truths carried by a "vital, though *incidental*" individual, precisely because the New Testament *is* making theological claims based on the historicity of Adam himself. (Barrett and Caneday, FVHA, 37)

E. Teachings of Paul

Paul's descriptions of Adam's sin in the passages from Romans 5 and 1 Corinthians 15 cited in section I.B.3 seem to demonstrate he believed Adam was the historical father of all humanity. Old Testament scholar Tremper Longman expresses a dissenting view from this traditional understanding. He cites New Testament scholar James Dunn to argue that Paul's analogy of Jesus as the last Adam "does not require that Jesus, an indisputably historical figure, be compared with a historical figure.... As Dunn points out, such literary-historical analogies are known from the time of Paul." (Charles, RG, 124)

Denis Lamoureux admits that the passages from Romans 5 and 1 Corinthians 15 are a challenge to the TE/EC view of historical Adam. In response, he argues that in this and other passages Paul communicated inerrant theological truth through the incidental (and erroneous) ancient history and science of his day. (Lamoureux, EC, 324–331)

In other passages, Paul mentions Eve's participation in Adam's sin and refers to both Adam and Eve as historical people when giving pastoral instructions to Timothy. Alluding to Genesis 2:21, 22 where Eve is made from Adam's side, Paul endorses the special creation of Eve, saying she was created "from man" (1 Cor. 11:8, 9 NIV; 1 Tim. 2:13, 14). This language would seem to preclude an evolutionary view of Eve's origins. When he addressed the Greek philosophers in Athens, Paul taught that God had "made from one man every nation of mankind to live on all the face of the earth." (Acts 17:26 ESV)

F. Other Biblical References to Adam and His Family

Other references to Adam and his family in Scripture are often used to indicate that the biblical authors believed they were real people. Some examples are listed below.

- Isaiah may have been referring to Adam when writing: "Your first father sinned" (Isa. 43:27).
- Hosea, in preaching about Israel, declared: "But like Adam they transgressed the covenant" (Hos. 6:7 ESV). There is disagreement over whether this refers to the historical Adam, human beings in general, or a location. (Madueme and Reeves, AFOS, 26)
- Job, in proclaiming his own righteousness, contrasted himself with Adam, who "covered [his] transgressions" (Job 31:33 NASB). There is disagreement over the interpretation of this text as well. (Madueme and Reeves, AFOS, 27)
- In the New Testament Abel is cited as an example of faith in contrast with Cain (Heb. 11:4), who is cited as a murderer (1 John 3:12).

G. Conclusions

The evidence from the Old Testament, from Second Temple literature, and from the New Testament seems to indicate firmly that the biblical authors viewed Adam as a real person.

In addition to affirming the historical Adam, the scriptural evidence seems to support the traditional view that Adam and Eve were the first humans, specially created by God, and that the entire human race descended from their offspring. However, John Walton has argued from Genesis that there may have been other humans present at the time of Adam and Eve. He argues that Adam and Eve were archetypes who represent all of humanity, not necessarily specially created by God, and may or may not have been the biological parents of all humanity. For a possible resolution to this uncertainty, we will now explore evidence from the book of nature and search for an answer to the question of whether Adam and Eve were *de novo* creations.

III. The Evidence from Science for Adam and His Family

A. Genetic Evidence

One of the more popular genres on American television is the crime drama. Through this medium of entertainment, the use of DNA evidence for identifying criminals has become a technique familiar to most people. While DNA profiling to resolve criminal cases, paternity suits, etc., is done using sections of DNA, the sequencing of the full human genome by the Human Genome Project* provides much more than a genetic "fingerprint." It provides the full sequence of the 3.2 billion base pairs ("letters" making up the genetic code) in human DNA, opening the door for molecular anthropology, the search for links between ancient and modern human populations around the world.

---

* The Human Genome Project was announced by President Clinton in June 2000, with the first draft published in 2001 and the project completed in 2003. (National Human Genome Research Institute, AAHGP, website)

These links are established by determining differences in sequences between individuals. These differences are attributed to mutations that have taken place over time. Genetic information that has been uncovered in the past few decades has shed considerable light on human origins. Primate genomes that have been sequenced include those of the chimpanzee (2005), macaque (2007), orangutan (2011), gorilla (2012), bonobo (2012), and gibbon (2014). (Seven Bridges, GGRNI, website) Evolutionary biologists compare the human genome with those of the primates to build evolutionary relationships. Skeptics of Darwinism maintain that genetic similarities between humans and other species are better understood as the result of common design rather than common ancestry. We examine this evidence below.

1. Genetic Diversity

One technique for studying human ancestry is to compare the base-pair sequences of a specified segment of DNA between individuals from different people groups. Such comparisons show that:

Human beings display much less genetic diversity than any other species. For example, several recent studies report a much more extensive genetic diversity for chimpanzees, bonobos, gorillas, and orangutans than for people. . . . The human similarity is observed worldwide, regardless of race or ethnicity. The limited geographical range of the great ape species, contrasted to the widespread geographical distribution and extensive biological variation of humans, makes this observation impressive. . . . Molecular anthropologists pose what they sometimes call the "Garden of Eden hypothesis" to explain the limited genetic diversity. This model maintains that humanity had a recent origin in a single location and

the original population size must have been quite small. . . . Molecular anthropologists observe the greatest genetic diversity among African populations and conclude that these groups must be the oldest. (Rana and Ross, WWA, 63–64)

Comparisons using much longer data sequences from the Human Genome Project confirm the "very limited genetic diversity among human populations," as well as the conclusion "that the African population groups are the oldest." (Rana and Ross, WWA, 65)

2. Mitochondrial Eve

One of the most widely used techniques in molecular anthropology is the study of DNA taken from cell mitochondria, the organelles where energy-storing molecules are produced. Since mitochondrial DNA (mtDNA) is inherited only from our mothers, molecular anthropologists can use it to trace humanity's maternal line. A landmark study carried out on samples of mtDNA from 147 people from five geographic populations was reported in 1987. (Cann, Stoneking, and Wilson, MDHE, 31–36) The study's authors concluded that all of the mtDNA stemmed from one woman who lived in Africa roughly 200,000 years ago. Additional studies conducted over subsequent years confirmed the conclusion that humanity can trace its maternal lineage back to a single ancestral mtDNA sequence: one woman in a single location (probably east Africa). The science community named her "mitochondrial Eve." The "mitochondrial Eve" hypothesis does not necessarily mean that this hypothetical mother was the first human or the only human alive in her time. Rather, from an evolutionary view, it means that her mitochondrial DNA is the only lineage not to become extinct and is now ubiquitous throughout the entire human race. Nonetheless, this viewpoint is compatible with the view that there was an original mother and father who were the first parents of the entire human race. One of the original study's authors clarified: "She wasn't the literal mother of us all, just the female from whom all our mitochondrial DNA derives." (Stringer and McKie, AE, 124) The evidence from mtDNA led to the "Out of Africa" model of human origins, in which all humans share a common African ancestor. While there was resistance to this model of human origins by those who held to the "Multiregional" model (in which humans evolved from different hominin populations around the world), the "Out of Africa" model has since gained widespread acceptance. (Gibbons, OAL, 1272–1273; Hedges, HE, 652–563)

3. Y-Chromosomal Adam

Most of the DNA in the human cell is in our chromosomes. Humans have twenty-three pairs of chromosomes, with one pair being the sex chromosomes. Males have one X and one Y sex chromosome, while females have two X chromosomes. Since Y-chromosomal DNA passes from father to son, molecular anthropologists study it to trace humanity's paternal line. One of the advantages of Y-chromosomal data compared with mtDNA is a longer DNA sequence, providing more opportunity to detect mutations. A number of studies carried out on Y-chromosomal DNA from men representing different races and regions of the world have been reported in the literature. (Hammer, ARCA, 376–378) The consensus of these studies is that humanity can trace its paternal lineage to a single man in a single location in Africa, "the same time and place where mitchondrial [sic] Eve lived." (Gibbons, YCSTAWA, 804–805) The

science community has named him "Y-chromosomal Adam." Like "mitochondrial Eve," the "Y-Chromosomal Adam" hypothesis does not necessarily mean that this hypothetical father was the first human or the only human alive in his time. Rather, it means that his Y-chromosomal lineage is the only example of such a lineage not to become extinct and is now ubiquitous throughout the entire human race. Nonetheless, this viewpoint is compatible with the view that there was an original mother and father who were the first parents of the entire human race.

4. Genetic Evidence for the First Humans

The findings of molecular anthropology outlined above point to the recent origin of humanity (within the last 200,000 years) from a single location (probably east Africa), with a single ancestral mtDNA sequence, "mitochondrial Eve," and a single ancestral paternal DNA sequence, "Y-chromosomal Adam." While the evidence of a single female ancestral sequence and a single male ancestral sequence seems to be consistent with the biblical account of Adam and Eve as the parents of all humanity, evolutionary biologists do not think that there was an original pair. Instead, they believe that humans evolved from an earlier hominin population composed of thousands of individuals. As a result of a postulated population collapse, humans passed through a "genetic bottleneck," with the ancestral sequences being from one of the females and one of the males. Evolutionary biologists use a variety of mathematical models based upon population genetics to estimate the size of the genetic bottleneck. The resulting estimates are dependent on a number of factors; a 2014 study noted a range in the literature of "1,000–10,000" for the archaic population size. (Elhassan et al., EGDDMH, e97674) Denis Alexander cites three studies with a range of 9,000–12,500 for the "founder population that was the ancestor of all modern humans." (Alexander, CE, 265)

Biologists Dennis Venema and Darrel Falk, writing from a Christian perspective, reviewed the findings of three different methods of genetic analysis to estimate the size of the human genetic bottleneck; all three methods concluded that the original population size was "several thousand." (Venema and Falk, DGPSPC, website) Venema and Falk believe that all humanity is descended from a small ancestral population but reject the claim that humanity is descended from an original pair. One possible way to harmonize this with Scripture is to accept the possibility discussed in II.A that other humans were present at the time of Adam and Eve, as argued by the Archetypal view. The TE/EC view generally follows mainstream science, while denying a historical Adam.

The population genetics models that claim humans descend from a population of thousands of individuals rather than an initial pair are based upon a number of assumptions. The standard and often unstated assumptions behind these models include:

- That common descent really occurred and there was no time where God specially or instantaneously created humans (whether two humans or many) with a wide range of genetic diversity.
- That random processes are the only causes of genetic change over time (i.e., that there is a constant rate at which mutations accumulate over time). Possible other factors like hotspot mutations, differential selection, or intelligent design, could undermine this key assumption. Even under a Darwinian view, if natural selection acted strongly upon certain alleles over the course of evolution, then that could also challenge this assumption.
- That there was random breeding between individuals in the population.
- That there was no migration in or out of the population.
- That there was a relatively constant population size.

Each of these assumptions of this model is simply that—an assumption. But if any of the assumptions are not valid, the model fails.

Indeed, while evolutionary biologists believe that humanity has descended from an archaic population size of several thousand, some scientists disagree that the biblical claim of an ancestral pair has been disproved by genetics. Biologist Ann Gauger, for example, made a detailed critique of evolutionary biologist Francisco Ayala's challenge to the concept of an original human pair using the genetic variation in one of the human leukocyte antigen (HLA) genes, the highly variable DRB1 gene. (Ayala, ME, 1930–1936) His analysis led him to conclude that the minimum size of the initial ancestral human population was four thousand, with a long-term average effective population of one hundred thousand. Gauger showed that the outcome of his analysis is very sensitive to the assumptions made, (Gauger, SAE, 105–122) and concluded: "Adam and Eve have not been disproven by science, and those who claim otherwise are misrepresenting the scientific evidence." (Gauger, SAE, 121) She has noted that a follow-up study using sequence data from the entire DRB1 gene found only four versions of the gene at the time of our assumed last common ancestor with chimpanzees. (von Salomé, Gyllensten, and Bergström, (FSA, 261–271) Since an ancestral pair can carry four versions of one gene, she contends the data suggest the possibility of an ancestral pair. (Gauger, private communication) Gauger is on a team developing a population genetics model based on the assumption of an ancestral pair with created diversity. This team argues that such a model seems to explain modern genetic diversity as well as, if not better than, models based on the assumption of common descent. (Hössjer et al., GM, online)

Biochemist Fazale Rana also disagrees that genetics disproves the biblical claim of an ancestral pair; with astronomer Hugh Ross, Rana has given several reasons to question the mainstream consensus: (Rana and Ross, WWA, 77–80, 349–353)

- There is evidence that the models used to estimate the original population size do not agree with experimental observation. They cite three field studies with large mammals (sheep, horses, and whales) to make the point that when an original population size was known, the genetic diversity after several generations was greater than predicted by the models. The sheep study had an ideal scenario: two sheep introduced on a remote island and the population studied for 46 years. (Kaeuffer et al., UHIMPFSPI, 527–533) Dennis Venema has provided a counter-argument to the sheep study. (Venema, WLCMSH, website)
- There are questions as to whether the fundamental assumptions in the models are correct. They cite several papers questioning these assumptions, including one showing "that variation in the rate of mutation rather than in population size is the main explanation for variations in mtDNA

diversity observed among bird species." (Ellegren, IGDRHLP, 41)
- Evidence from conservation biology challenges the concept of recovery from a population collapse. They cite examples of fieldwork and theoretical work to make this point.

The YEC and some OEC views agree with the arguments challenging the mainstream consensus and see the evidence of "mitochondrial Eve" and "Y-chromosomal Adam" as consistent with the biblical view of an ancestral pair. They think that evolutionary models are based upon assumptions—assumptions that would likely not hold true under a naturalistic scenario of human origins, and certainly would not hold true if humans were specially created by God.

5. Genetic Evidence and Human Origins

Most evolutionary scientists maintain that the human genome is full of nonfunctional "junk" DNA that we share with other mammals, such as apes and mice. They argue that this shared, nonfunctional DNA can only be explained if the "junk" arose when random mutations blindly produced useless genetic mutations in an organism that became the common ancestor of many modern species, passing its "junk DNA" on to its descendants. Francis Collins, NIH director and formerly head of the Human Genome Project, promotes this view when he argues that human DNA provides strong evidence that we share common ancestry with other mammals:

Even more compelling evidence for a common ancestor comes from the study of what are known as ancient repetitive elements (AREs). These arise from "jumping genes," which are capable of copying and inserting themselves in various other locations in the genome, usually without any functional consequences. Mammalian genomes are littered with such AREs, with roughly 45 percent of the human genome made up of such genetic flotsam and jetsam.... Of course, some might argue that these are actually functional elements placed there by the Creator for a good reason, and our discounting of them as "junk DNA" just betrays our current level of ignorance. (Collins, LG, 135–136)

The caveat that Collins expressed turns out to have been prescient. Six years after the publication of *The Language of God*, the ENCODE project published their findings to date, stating their "data enabled [them] to assign biochemical functions for 80% of the genome, in particular outside of the well-studied protein-coding regions." (ENCODE, IEDEHG, 57–74) While these findings have been controversial and have not shaken the basic evolutionary paradigm,* in January 2015 Francis Collins revealed just how far the consensus has moved. At a healthcare conference in San Francisco, Collins was asked about junk DNA. He said, "We don't use that term anymore.... It was pretty much a case of hubris to imagine that we could dispense with any part of the genome—as if we knew enough to say it wasn't functional." He concluded that most of what had been considered junk DNA "turns out to be doing stuff." (Zimmer, IMODG, website) The growing consensus in molecular biology is that non-coding DNA is not junk, severely undercutting junk-based arguments for human-ape common ancestry.

Even though the term "junk DNA" is falling out of favor, the presence in the human genome of "pseudogenes," genes that appear to have lost their function, is considered by evolutionary biologists to be strong evidence for common descent. Denis Alexander considers them to be "valuable genetic fossils for tracking our own evolutionary history." (Alexander, CE, 244) Evolutionary biologists compare the location of these "fossils" in the human genome with their location in the genomes of our purported ancestors to develop this history. In response, Darwin skeptics point out that many pseudogenes are already known to exhibit evidence of function. (Luskin, FC, 86–92; Luskin and Gage, RFC, 216–235) The ENCODE project reported that more than eight hundred pseudogenes in the human genome show evidence of function. (ENCODE, IEDEHG, 58) Another scientific paper observes that "pseudogene regulation is widespread in eukaryotes." (Wen et al., PANPA, 27–32) We are just beginning to develop biochemical techniques for studying the functions of pseudogenes, and evolutionary assumptions that pseudogenes are "junk" may be hindering our ability to discover their true functions. (Wen et al., PANPA, 27–32) As one paper in *Annual Review of Genetics* notes, "pseudogenes that have been suitably investigated often exhibit functional roles." (Balakirev and Ayala, PATJFD, 123–51) Gauger points out that the similarity in DNA sequences between species leads one to expect functionality and that we are likely to continue to discover functions in pseudogenes. (Gauger,

---

* ENCODE's results showing that the vast majority of our genome is functional are experimentally derived, whereas criticisms of the project typically stem from mere theoretical considerations derived from an evolutionary paradigm. For a review of why arguments against ENCODE fail, see: Casey Luskin's series of articles: "The ENCODE Embroilment: Part I: Why Are Biologists Lashing Out Against Empirically Verified Research Results?," *Salvo Magazine* (Issue 31, Winter, 2014); "The ENCODE Embroilment, Part II: Denying Data Won't Change the Emerging Facts of Biology," *Salvo Magazine* (Issue 32, Spring, 2015); "The ENCODE Embroilment, Part III: Evolution Proves Our Genome Is Junky ... Which Proves Evolution ... ," *Salvo Magazine* (Issue 33, Summer, 2015); and "The ENCODE Embroilment, Part IV: Rewriting History Won't Erase Bad Evolutionary Predictions," *Salvo Magazine* (Issue 34, Fall, 2015).

private communication) If pseudogenes are in fact functional, they might point to common design rather than common descent.

Another line of evidence for human evolution comes from a particular comparison of the human and chimpanzee genomes: human chromosome 2 is very similar to a proposed fusion of chimpanzee chromosomes 2A and 2B. Evolutionary biologists argue that this fusion event is strong evidence for a shared ancestry for humans and chimps. In response, Rana and Ross point out "while it is not unusual for chromosomes to fuse, they will almost never fuse with intact chromosomes because of telomeres. These structures, in addition to providing stability, are designed to *prevent* chromosomes from undergoing fusion with chromosome fragments. . . . [They suggest that] the unlikely nature of these events could be taken as evidence for the Creator's role in engineering or designing the fusion." (Rana and Ross, WWA, 355–56) Moreover, the supposed fusion site is greatly lacking in repetitive DNA that should have been present if two chromosomes were fused end-to-end. (Fan et al., GSEACFS, 1651–22) But even if the fusion is real, because it is found only in our human lineage, at most this "fusion evidence" can only show that a fusion event took place somewhere along the human line; it cannot determine whether our lineage leads back to a common ancestor shared with apes. (Gauger, Axe, and Luskin, SHO, 92–99)

6. Where and When Did the First Humans Live?

As described earlier, molecular anthropologists have found the greatest human genetic diversity to be among African populations, leading them to conclude that humanity originated in Africa, most likely east Africa. (Elhassen et al., EGDDMH, e97674) They continue to use DNA from different populations to determine how humanity populated the earth. National Geographic's Genographic Project, launched in 2005, invites the public to participate in this study by contributing DNA for analysis. The project website includes a map of human migration routes based on DNA evidence. (National Geographic, HS, website) This evidence is consistent with the biblical account of humanity originating at one location, although the biblical account suggests a Middle Eastern location. However, as discussed in III.C.1, the Bab el Mandeb strait and much of the Red Sea were dry near the end of the last ice age, facilitating human migration from the Middle East to east Africa (for instance following banishment from the garden of Eden) and vice-versa. Hence, genetic evidence pointing to an east African location for human origins is not inconsistent with a Middle Eastern location for Eden.

Using estimates of mutation rates, molecular anthropologists can turn differences in DNA sequences into "molecular clocks." Rana and Ross have reviewed the results of recent studies carried out to estimate independently the "molecular clock" ages of Y-chromosomal Adam and mitochondrial Eve. (Rana and Ross, WWA, 265–67) Scientists have calibrated the mtDNA "clock" using DNA from human remains that were dated using carbon-14 methods. The validity of this calibration was demonstrated with mtDNA recovered from a human femur estimated to be 45,000±2,000 years old by carbon-14 dating. Molecular clock dating of the mtDNA yielded an age of 49,000±17,000 years. (Qiaomei Fu et al., GS, 445–449) While the error bar on the molecular clock age is significant, the agreement is nevertheless impressive. The current estimates for Adam are based on larger portions of the Y chromosome than in earlier studies, as well as the use of rare Y chromosome variants. A study published in 2013 concluded that the "time to the most recent common ancestor" of the Y-chromosome was 120,000–156,000 years, and to that of mtDNA was 99,000–148,000 years. (Poznik et al., SYCRDT, 562–65) Proponents of the YEC and OEC views of Adam see this independent determination of comparable ages through the maternal and paternal DNA lines as consistent with the traditional biblical account of an ancestral pair, although YEC would consider these ages to be overestimated.

B. Paleontological Evidence

Most of us have seen the standard *March of Progress* diagram depicting a sequence of primates beginning with a hunchbacked ape and ending with an upright-walking modern human. This iconic diagram summarizes the message that humans evolved. While this is accepted by the TE/EC view of Adam (and some proponents of the Archetypal view), the OEC and YEC views believe that God intervened supernaturally in some manner in Adam's origin. All views must address the paleontological evidence for the first humans.

Paleoanthropologists have been attempting to construct an evolutionary history for humans since Darwin's time. As recently as 1981, John Reader (author of *Missing Links*) wrote: "The entire hominid collection known today would barely cover a billiard table." (Reader, WHZ, 802) However, that collection has grown significantly since 1981. While each new find is encouraging to proponents of evolution, the relationships between hominin fossils are not always clear and paleoanthropologists continue to revise their thinking on the postulated pathway to humans. But evolutionary pathways are unclear. A 2015 review of human evolution by two leading paleoanthropologists admitted "[t]he dearth of unambiguous evidence for ancestor-descendant lineages," and states:

"the evolutionary sequence for the majority of hominin lineages is unknown. Most hominin taxa, particularly early hominins, have no obvious ancestors, and in most cases ancestor-descendant sequences (fossil time series) cannot be reliably constructed." (Serrelli and Gontier, MEIE, 365)

There are several reviews of the paleontological data from a Christian perspective. Lamoureux provides a TE/EC view (Lamoureux, EC, 432–442); Alexander provides an evolutionary/Archetypal view (Alexander, CE, 252–262); Rana and Ross provide an OEC view, including a focus on the most recent finds (Rana and Ross, WWA, 31–43; 143–158; 277–289); Marvin Lubenow provides a YEC view. (Lubenow, BC) William Stone summarizes the scientific consensus in 2011 regarding the hominin species. (Madueme and Reeves, AFOS, 56–60)

The traditional evolutionary view is that *Homo habilis* evolved from one of the species in the *Australopithecus* genus. This genus includes the "gracile" forms *africanus* and *afarensis* (which includes the famous "Lucy") and the "robust" forms, sometimes classified as a separate genus, *Paranthropus*. The *Homo* genus also includes different forms, such as *Homo erectus*, the Neanderthals, and modern humans that are classified as *Homo sapiens sapiens*. However, a number of paleoanthropologists dispute that "*Homo*" *habilis* could serve as such a link, with many arguing that it does not even belong in the genus *Homo* due to its australopith-like traits and noting that unambiguous *Homo* remains from about two million years ago predate *habilis* in the fossil record. (Spoor et al. INE; Wood and Collard, HG; Gibbons, WWHH; Berger et al. HN; Spoor et al., IEH; Hartwig-Scherer and Martin, WLMH)

The oldest fossil remains of what appear to be anatomically modern humans are claimed to be those found in the Kibish Formation in the lower Omo valley, in southern Ethiopia. (McDougall, Brown, and Fleagle, SPAMHKE, 733–36) The ^{40}Ar/^{39}Ar dating of a layer below the fossil find gave an older age limit of 198,000±14,000 years; dating of a layer above the find gave a younger age limit of 104,000±7,000 years. Both the location of these fossils, as well as the date range of strata above and below the fossil find, are reasonably consistent with the conclusions of molecular anthropology regarding the location and estimated age of the earliest humans. Other ancient fossil remains of anatomically modern humans have been reported in Africa and the Middle East. The estimated age of these remains range from 70,000 to 130,000 years. (Rana and Ross, WWA, 275) Caution must be exercised in the interpretation of ancient human fossils, as the appearance of anatomical similarity to modern humans is not necessarily indicative of modern human behavior (discussed in III.C.2).

After reviewing the paleoanthropological evidence of the *Australopithecus* and *Homo* genera, Stone concludes that the discontinuity between the two suggests that it is the dividing line between nonhumans and humans, and proposes to place Adam at the root of the genus *Homo*. (Madueme and Reeves, AFOS, 63–81) Indeed, a number of paleoanthropologists have admitted a distinct gap in the fossil record between humanlike members of our genus *Homo* and apelike species such as the australopithecines. (Gauger, Axe, and Luskin, SHO, 45–83) As the great evolutionary biologist Ernst Mayr stated: "The earliest fossils of *Homo* . . . are separated from *Australopithecus* by a large, unbridged gap." (Mayr, WMBU, 198) Likewise, three Harvard paleoanthropologists admitted, "we lack many details about exactly how, when, and where the transition

occurred from *Australopithecus* to *Homo*." (Shea and Lieberman, TP, 1) This poses a severe challenge to the standard evolutionary view, generally endorsed by the TE/EC camp, that humans evolved from the apelike australopithecines.

Proponents of the OEC and YEC views point to the discontinuities in the hominin/human fossil record as evidence of God's miraculous intervention in Adam's origin. Most OEC views put this at the root of *Homo sapiens*, since it is closest to the origin of modern human physical capability, as well as the use of symbolism and appreciation of aesthetic goodness. The YEC view rejects the mainstream ages given for the fossil record in general.

C. Archaeological Evidence
1. The Garden of Eden

As noted in chapter 16, there are currently no archaeological data for the garden of Eden. However, scholars have attempted to deduce its location from the evidence in the biblical account, which names four rivers associated with the river flowing through Eden (Gen. 2:10–14). Two of those rivers, the Tigris and the Euphrates, are presumed to be the same as those known to us today, as is the location of the country (Assyria) identified with the Tigris. The identity of the other two is less certain. One, the Pishon, is said to wind through the land of Havilah, where there is gold, aromatic resin, and onyx. The other is the Gihon, said to flow around the land of Cush. Many different locations for these rivers and of Eden have been proposed. Astronomer Hugh Ross has made a suggestion informed by satellite imagery:

> The details here point in the direction of the Hejaz, a mountainous region in the west central part of Saudi Arabia. This 6,000-foot range

contains the only known source of workable gold in the region. The land of Cush has long been identified with Ethiopia and the Horn of Africa. Given that the Bab el Mandeb strait and much of the Red Sea were dry near the end of the last ice age (between 20,000 and 7,000 BC), Cush would have included the mountains in Arabia's southwestern corner. . . . Satellite imagery reveals the dry beds of two major rivers that once flowed from west-central and southwestern Arabia into the Persian Gulf region. (Ross, NG, 97–8)

Ross notes that the one location where these two rivers could come together with the Tigris and Euphrates is in the Persian Gulf region. (Ross, NG, 99) Archaeological finds on the northern coast of the Arabian Peninsula and on islands in the Persian Gulf, notably the island of al-Bahrain, are associated with the ancient kingdom of Dilmun. (Britannica, s.v. "Dilmun") Interestingly, ANE literature refers to the land of Dilmun as an ancient paradise reminiscent of Eden. (Arnold and Beyer, RANE, 15–19)

2. Earliest Evidence of Modern Human Behavior

As mentioned in I.B.1, aspects of the image of God in humans include displaying intelligence, using language, and appreciating aesthetic goodness. Archaeological evidence of such behavior appears to have arisen suddenly. Anthropologist Christopher Stringer has written about this sudden appearance:

For millennia upon millennia, [*Homo sapiens*] had been churning out the same forms of stone utensils. . . . But about 40,000 years ago, a perceptible shift in our handiwork took place. Throughout the Old World, tool kits leapt in sophistication with the appearance of Upper Paleolithic style implements. Signs of

the use of ropes, bone spear points, fishhooks, and harpoons emerge, along with the sudden manifestations of sculptures, paintings, and musical instruments. . . . We also find evidence of the first long-distance exchange of stones and beads. Objects made of mammal bones and ivory, antlers, marine and freshwater shells, fossil coral, limestone, schist, steatite, jet, lignite, hematite, and pyrite were manufactured. Materials were chosen with extraordinary care: some originated hundreds of miles from their point of manufacture. . . . It is an extraordinary catalogue of achievements that seem to have come about virtually from nowhere–though obviously they did have a source. The Question is: What was it? (Stringer and McKie, AE, 195–96)

While Stringer evaluates the evidence within an evolutionary paradigm, the sudden appearance is consistent with the OEC and YEC views that God intervened supernaturally in the origin of humanity. The recent discovery of ancient cave paintings in Indonesia dated to 40,000 years ago adds to the list of evidence. The announcement states: "The discovery of 40,000-year-old cave paintings at opposite ends of the globe suggests that the ability to create representational art had its origins further back in time in Africa, before modern humans spread across the rest of the world." (Ghosh, CPCIAOA, website)

In surveying the most recent finds, Rana and Ross note that archaeologists have discovered evidence in Africa of modern human behavior older than 40,000 years. (Rana and Ross, WWA, 271–76) Nevertheless, the "sociocultural big bang" of 40,000 years ago fits well with the sudden appearance of modern humans. Quite a few archaeologists have acknowledged a sudden "explosion" of modern humanlike behavior in the archaeological record around this time. (White, PA;

11, 231; Mellars, NMHC, Nowell, FPA) This is consistent with an OEC viewpoint.

3. Earliest Evidence of Human Civilization

The traditional "cradle of civilization" is in Mesopotamia, where, according to standard dating, the Neolithic Revolution began around twelve thousand years ago. One feature of this revolution was organized agricultural activity, including farming and animal domestication. While the timing of this revolution is significantly more recent than the evidence of modern human behavior discussed above, recent discoveries have revealed earlier dates for agricultural activity. This includes evidence of "small-scale trial cultivation" twenty-three thousand years ago on the shore of the Sea of Galilee (Snir et al., OCPWLNF, website), and grain processing more than thirty-two thousand years ago in Italy. (Lippi et al., MFPPGP, 12075–80) These discoveries place the development of organized agriculture before the Neolithic Revolution and closer to the earliest evidence for modern human behavior.

IV. Literary and Linguistic Evidence for Adam and His Family

Evolutionary biologists have faced great difficulty in trying to explain the origin of human language in evolutionary terms. A 2014 paper coauthored by leading evolutionary paleoanthropologists admits that we have "essentially no explanation of how and why our linguistic computations and representations evolved" and "the origins and evolution of our linguistic capacity remain as mysterious as ever" since "studies of nonhuman animals provide virtually no relevant parallels to human linguistic communication, and none to the underlying biological capacity." (Hauser et al., MLE, 1) Under a biblical view, however, one would expect humans to have a distinct form of communication not seen among lower animals.

A biblical view also makes it reasonable to expect that stories concerning our ancient ancestors would persist in cultures around the world. These stories would have been preserved as oral traditions until systems of writing were developed.

A. Cuneiform Tablets

The Sumerian civilization in southern Mesopotamia (c. 3500–2000 BC) is credited with developing the world's first written language. The oldest written Sumerian records date to 3100 BC. (Britannica, s.v. "Languages of the World: Language Isolates") The system of writing used was a pictographic type of cuneiform, which gradually changed to conventionalized linear drawings. These were pressed into soft clay tablets with the edge of a stylus, giving it a characteristic wedge-shaped appearance. Cuneiform was adopted for use in other languages, for example Akkadian and Babylonian. (Britannica, s.v. "cuneiform writing") Archaeologists have uncovered thousands of cuneiform tablets in the Middle East. Many of these have been studied and translated by scholars around the world, enabling them to gain great insight into ANE beliefs about origins. Collins has described how three texts from ancient Mesopotamia demonstrate some parallels with Genesis 1–11. (Collins, DAERE, 137–160)

B. Chinese Characters

There is written evidence for the first humans from a civilization far from Mesopotamia: ancient China. Modern Chinese can trace its roots to inscriptions that have been found on oracle bones dating back to the second millennium BC. (Thong, FOF, 46) Chinese has remained a pictograph-based language since that time, although the characters have changed over the centuries. The characters used today have been grouped into six categories. (Thong, FOF, 47) As described for example by Chan Kei Thong, two of these categories are pictographs and ideographs. (Thong, FOF, 51–52) Pictographs depict objects while ideographs convey abstract ideas and are composed of two or more pictographs. A study of ideographs reveals some of the stories that inspired the ancient people who developed them. Thong demonstrates how several ideographs show clear consistency with the Genesis account of Adam and Eve and their disobedience in the garden of Eden. The three examples listed below are formed using these pictographs: 口 (mouth), 木 (tree) and 女 (female).

The symbol 束 (*shu*), meaning "to restrain," is represented by a mouth superimposed over a tree. This correlates to the first restraint placed on Adam, namely the prohibition from eating of the tree of the knowledge of good and evil. (Thong, FOF, 56–57)

The symbol 婪 (*lan*) meaning "to covet," is represented by two trees on top with a female on the bottom. The use of two trees correlates with the two key trees in the garden of Eden: the tree of knowledge of good and evil, and the tree of life. The female correlates with Eve, the first human to covet something forbidden (fruit from the tree of the knowledge of good and evil). Thong notes: "The composition of this character is even more interesting when one recalls that in ancient China, women had no place in society. . . . Yet, the ancient Chinese chose to use the character for 'woman' rather than the one for 'man'. . . . This shows that the ancient Chinese had some knowledge of the story of the first act of disobedience against God." (Thong, FOF, 58)

Finally, the symbol 喪, meaning "death," shows that death is associated with two mouths eating from a tree. This correlates with Adam and Eve's disobedience, for which they suffered the promised consequence of death. (Thong, FOF, 61)

The fact that these three characters have ancient forms demonstrates that they were formulated long before the first Christian missionaries visited China, generally considered to be Nestorians in AD 635. (Neill, HCM, 95) While Thong has acknowledged that Chinese calligraphy scholars do not necessarily agree with his interpretations, he argues that one of the artifacts from the San Xing Dui civilization discovered near Chengdu, Sichuan Province, a bronze tree dated to 1600 BC, supports his view that the ancient Chinese had some knowledge of the events from the garden of Eden. The tree includes fruit, knives protruding from the branches as if to guard the fruit, a feminine hand reaching to the tree, and a serpent. (Thong, private communication)

V. Conclusions

The straightforward way of reading the Bible is that Adam was a historical person. It also seems clear that Scripture teaches that all humanity descended from Adam and Eve, although some believe they were archetypes and not necessarily the biological parents of all humans.

Within the last thirty years scientific evidence for Adam has emerged from the study of human genetics. The once-dominant multiregional model of human origins has been replaced with a model of humans spreading around the world from a small founding population in one location, possibly east Africa. The identification of single ancestral maternal and paternal DNA sequences, while not proof of an ancestral pair, is evidence one would expect from the biblical account of origins. What's more, data from the DRB1 gene suggest the possibility of an ancestral pair.

Paleontology and archaeology reveal at least three discontinuities in human history: the abrupt appearance of the genus *Homo* about two million years ago, the appearance of anatomically modern humans at around 130,000 BC, and the appearance of physical capability underwriting modern human behavior at around 40,000 BC. Physicist John Bloom argues that the two recent, abrupt discontinuities are evidence against a smooth, naturalistic transition and for the special creation of humanity. (Bloom, OHO, 181–203)

Finally, Scripture, the book of nature (including genetic, paleontological, and archaeological evidence), and linguistic evidence join together to present a cumulative case for the historicity of Adam.

CHAPTER 18

THE HISTORICITY
OF THE PATRIARCHS

OVERVIEW

TIMELINE

Early Bronze Age	Middle Bronze Age	Late Bronze Age	Iron Age I	Iron Age II
3000–2100 BC	2100–1550 BC	1550–1200 BC	1200–650 BC	650–150 BC

I. Introduction: The Problem of the Patriarchs

Many current Old Testament scholars would say that the stories regarding the patriarchs found in Genesis do not record accurate history. They reach this conclusion in part because up to this point no direct archaeological or extrabiblical evidence has been discovered to prove absolutely that the patriarchs, such as Abraham, Isaac, or Jacob, actually existed. Yet even without the walled settlements that usually draw the attention of archaeology, the biblical record of the patriarchs' nomadic life can be confidently investigated and compared with what is known of customs and artifacts from their historical era.

A. The Problem of the Patriarchs Explained

Influential scholar Thomas Thompson writes, "On the basis of what we know of Palestinian history of the second millennium BC, and of what we understand about the formation of the literary traditions of Genesis, it must be concluded that any such historicity as is commonly spoken of in both scholarly and popular works about the patriarchs of Genesis is hardly possible and totally improbable." (Thompson, HPN, 328)

Similarly, John Van Seters states, "The conclusions to this study regarding the Abrahamic tradition lie in two principal areas: the dating of the tradition and the nature of its literary development . . . there is no unambiguous evidence that points to a great antiquity for this tradition." (Van Seters, AHT, 309)

However, Kenneth A. Kitchen, professor emeritus at the University of Liverpool, draws upon his extensive research into the history, archaeology, and literature of Egypt and of the eastern Mediterranean to declare that the patriarchs were not a glorified later "mirage." He writes, "It should be clear, finally, that the main features of the patriarchal narratives either fit specifically into the first half of the second millennium or are consistent with such a dating." (Kitchen, OROT, 372)

B. Changing Views on the Historicity of the Patriarchs

Christians in general believe the historicity of Abraham based on the teachings of Jesus (John 8:31–59) and Paul (Rom. 4; Gal. 4:21–31), both of whom built the strength of their arguments in large measure by appealing to Abraham as a person of historical significance. Currently, however, conservative scholars who conclude that the Bible records accurate history are in the minority. (Moore and Kelle, BHIP, 38) But the current consensus against the historicity of the patriarchs is a relatively new development. While evangelical scholars are now a small minority in the archaeological community, their views regarding the historicity of the patriarchs were once considered mainstream.

1. The Maximalist Viewpoint

The "maximalist" viewpoint captures the conservative perspective, affirming that a biblical history of Israel corresponds with the real history of Israel. (Block, IAKLI, 12) In the middle of the twentieth century, a majority of historians believed that recent archaeological discoveries, such as the Mari Archives, provided data that supported the general claims of the biblical stories. These discoveries would place the patriarchs approximately in the middle of the Bronze Age period (2000–1500 BC).

The most influential maximalist scholar of the last century is William F. Albright. He writes in *The Archaeology of Palestine and the Bible*: "Discovery after discovery has established the accuracy of innumerable details, and has brought increased recognition of the value of the Bible as a source of history." (Albright, APB, 128)

Again Albright writes in *The Archaeology and Religion of Israel*: "There can be no doubt that archeology has confirmed the substantial historicity of the Old Testament tradition." (Albright, ARI, 176)

2. The Minimalist Viewpoint

The "minimalist" viewpoint gained popularity in the 1970s with Thomas Thompson's *The Historicity of the Patriarchal Narratives* and John Van Seters's *Abraham in History and Tradition*. These two books dramatically changed the interpretation of the patriarchal narratives and Israel's past. (Moore and Kelle, BHIP, 19)

Thompson starts his book by noting that

"Nearly all accept the general claim that the historicity of the biblical traditions about the patriarchs has been substantiated by the archaeological and historical research of the last half-century." (Thompson, HPN, 1) He goes on to argue against these claims, and his book has had a significant impact on scholarly perspectives of Abraham's existence.

Van Seters attempted to reassess the sources for the patriarchal traditions from the early second millennium by arguing that they fit more naturally into a first millennium setting. (Moore and Kelle, BHIP, 19) He concludes, "Thus far the conclusion reached is that the tradition as it stands reflects only a rather late date of composition and gives no hint by its content of any great antiquity in terms of biblical history." (Van Seters, AHT, 122)

II. Investigating the Patriarchal Narratives

A. Developing a Historical Framework

Because of both the lack of direct historical evidence outside of the Bible and literary questions raised within the text itself, most scholars no longer accept the historicity of the Genesis narratives. In order to make a reasonable argument for the historicity of the patriarchs, then, both challenges need to be addressed, making it necessary to investigate the cultural environment in which these details are located to interpret the stories more carefully.

B. The Ancient World of the Patriarchs

The patriarchal stories are set in three regions of the ancient Near East: Mesopotamia (Ur), Canaan, and Egypt. Understanding these ancient cultures allows for examination of the details in order to analyze the reliability of the Genesis narratives.

1. Mesopotamia

Abraham was called to be the father of the chosen nation while living with his father, Terah, in Ur (Gen. 11:27–32). Ur was a "famous Sumerian city located by the Euphrates River about 150 miles northwest of the present coast of the Persian Gulf in modern Iraq." (Merrill, KP, 41–42)

Leading Old Testament scholar Eugene Merrill reports, "Sargon (2340–2284 BCE) had created the Semite-dominated Akkadian Empire at Agade, nearly two hundred miles northwest of Ur, Abram was almost certainly bi-lingual, commanding both the Sumerian and Akkadian languages." (Merrill, KP, 42)

Merrill also reports the cultural and religious significance of Ur:

The principal deity worshipped at Ur was the Sumerian moon god Nannar, known in Akkadian by the name Sin. It is certain that Abram and his family were faithful devotees of Sin and his coterie of fellow deities, for Joshua 24:2 speaks of them as having served other gods beyond the river. . . . Moreover, some scholars identify the name Terah as a form of the Hebrew word *yārēaḥ* ("moon"), so that his very name may testify to his religious orientation. (Merrill, KP, 43*)

Historian and ANE specialist Amelie Kuhrt notes that within Mesopotamian culture, "they lived and worked in family groups. Nowhere, in this case, are the workers landless, propertyless, kinless 'serfs' or 'helots.'" (Kuhrt, ANE, 62) This fits well with the patriarchal family accounts in Genesis.

---

* Merrill is assuming Abram was an idolater. Joshua 24:2 says Terah "served other gods," but leaves Abram's status prior to his calling unknown.

Merrill explains a possible migration of Abraham and his family during this time when he writes, "perhaps the political and cultural upheavals caused by the Guti conquest played some role." (Merrill, KP, 45)

2. Canaan

Kitchen quotes Oppenheim's observation that, "there seem to have been very few periods in the history of the region when . . . (as in the Old Babylonian period) . . . a private person could move around freely." (Kitchen, OROT, 316)

Merrill writes,

Abram would have become conversant in the Amorite Semitic dialects spoken there and would have imbibed the more nomadic lifestyle that he encountered later in Canaan. By this time the Amorites not only occupied the major cities of northwest Mesopotamia but also had begun to expand, primarily for commercial reasons, to the southeast and southwest. (Merrill, KP, 45)

Kitchen describes the movement of pastoralists—who were sheep or cattle farmers of Western Asiatic or Semitic lineage—during this time: "From Larsa in the east to Amurru in the west, the wanderings of segments of the Mare-Yamina cover all but the extremities of the journeyings of Terah and Abraham from Ur to Canaan." (Kitchen, OROT, 317)

Kitchen concludes,

In later times (late second/early first millennium), the general movement of steppe tribes into agricultural areas tended to be more or less from north(west) to south(east) so far as Mesopotamia was concerned . . . but in the second millennium this northwest to southwest drift is not the sole current of movement,

despite erroneous claims to the contrary. (Kitchen, OROT, 317)

Van Seters believed that Abraham's move from Harran to Palestine is problematic because there was, "no sociological or historical reason to suggest that nomads migrated from Harran to Palestine." (Van Seters, AHT, 24)

To respond directly to Van Seters's objection, Kitchen quotes Jean Robert Kupper from his work, *Nomades*, in which Kupper concludes, "It is in this constant flux and reflux of people on the move that one may fittingly situate the migration of Abraham, going back up from Ur to Harran, his true homeland." (Kitchen, OROT, 317)

3. Egypt

Kitchen reports that the nineteenth Egyptian dynasty built a new residence in the area of Pi-Rameses that was only used until 1130 BC. He concludes "that visits by an Abraham or a Jacob to a pharaoh in the East Delta palace are only feasible in Egyptian terms within circa 1970–1540, if they are not turned into contemporaries of Moses." (Kitchen, OROT, 319)

James K. Hoffmeier notes that the pharaohs of the early second millennium period also built a series of forts to limit and control Asiatic visitors from Canaan. "It has been well known for decades, however, that there were Semites in the delta starting after the collapse of the Old Kingdom (c. 2190) and reaching a zenith during the Hyksos or Second Intermediate Period (c. 1700–1550 BC) and on into the New Kingdom (1550–1069 BC)." (Hoffmeier, IE, 22–23)

4. Conclusion Regarding the Patriarchs' Cultural Setting

This brief overview reveals that these ancient cultures' political, economic, social, and religious characteristics are reflected in Scripture. This backdrop is necessary for the biblical narratives to be understood and properly placed in a specific setting and time period.

III. The Evidence for the Patriarchs

The following are the key questions for us as we investigate the historical evidence for the existence of the patriarchs: What are the proposed time frames for the patriarchs? What is this based on? Why is this important for Bible-believing Christians?

The authors of *A Biblical History of Israel* write:

> Passages outside the book of Genesis, however, appear to allow us to situate the patriarchs in real time—at least if we believe that the whole Bible gives accurate, though perhaps at times approximate, chronological indicators—and suggest that Abraham was born in the middle of the twenty-second century BC. The evidence is as follows: 1 Kings 6:1 states that Solomon began the temple construction 480 years after the Israelites left Egypt. This year is Solomon's fourth year as king, and if we follow Thiele, that date would be 966 BC. A straight reading of this passage places the exodus in the middle of the fifteenth century. Furthermore, Exodus, 12:40 asserts that the children of God sojourned in Egypt 430 years. Finally, we may arrive at the length of time from Abraham's birth to Jacob's descent into Egypt by adding the 100 years of Genesis 21:5 (the age of Abraham when Isaac was born) to the 60 years of Genesis 25:26 (the age of Isaac when Jacob was born) to the 130 years of Genesis 47:9 (the age of Jacob when he first arrived in Egypt) to reach a period of 290 years. So beginning with 966 BC, a number of scholars add the 480 of 1 Kings 6:1 to the 430 years of

the Egyptian sojourn to the 290 years of the Patriarchal period to end up with a birth date for Abraham in 2166 BC, which then leads to a date of 2091 BC for his arrival in Palestine (cf. Gen. 12:4). (Provan, Long, and Longman, BHI, Loc. 2951)

The authors go on to say that this formula is not as neat as it first appears because there are some textual variations and the numbers appear to be rounded. However, the dating provided from the Hebrew text does provide a solid biblical foundation to begin to assess the patriarchal narratives in relation to a specific time period's sociological and cultural features. As Ian Provan, V. Phillips Long, and Tremper Longman state, much of the debate depends on whether "we believe that the whole Bible gives accurate, though perhaps at times approximate, chronological indicators."

Can we give a specific date for the life of Abraham beyond a shadow of a doubt? The answer is no. Can we have confidence from the overlapping story developed from biblical texts, sociological indicators, and ancient Near Eastern evidences that Abraham likely lived near the end of the 3rd century BC? The answer would have to be that it is not only possible, but probable.

After raising some challenges to the dating theory outlined above, Provan, Long, and Longman write,

> In sum many earlier arguments trying to show that patriarchal customs were peculiarly related to the time period of the second millennium have been effectively disputes. This notion, however, far from demonstrates that the patriarchal narratives overall are at odds with the picture of the period as we know it from ancient Near Eastern sources, even if we must take account for a certain degree of

anachronism in the presentation. (Provan, Long, and Longman, BHI, Loc 3072)

This research and historical analysis provides a reasonable basis to believe that the Abraham recorded in Genesis lived in the twenty-second century BC. Because of the lack of explicit, direct archaeological evidence for Abraham and the other patriarchs, the debate revolves around whether the features of the biblical narrative accurately reflect the archaeological evidence regarding the customs and conditions of the time periods during which the patriarchs purportedly lived. We can demonstrate that the biblical narratives display an extraordinary level of accuracy in relation to archaeological evidence as presented below. This provides good evidence that the patriarchs of Genesis were real people in history, not the figments of a later writer's imagination.

A. Nomadic and Settled Civilizations

1. The Challenge

Van Seters argues the accounts of the patriarchs cannot be credible because their narratives record nomadic lifestyles in the same place as settled agricultural communities. (Van Seters, AHT, 38) His solution is that the stories of the patriarchs more effectively belong to the first millennium rather than in the late third or early second millennium setting.

Van Seters writes:

> There is nothing in the presentation of the "nomadic" patriarchs which is inappropriate to the portrayal of nomadic life in the period of the late Judean monarchy or exilic periods, but much that speaks against the choice of an earlier period. (Van Seters, AHT, 38)

2. The Mari Archives

The discovery of the Mari Archives revealed the existence of a unique commu-

nity of Amorites, the Binu Yamina tribal coalition. These archives contain nearly twenty-five thousand documents discovered in the ancient city of Mari (modern-day Tell Hariri, on the present day border of Syria and Iraq). In particular, the Mari documents have detailed how a powerful king named Zimri-Lim simultaneously ruled over both an Amorite tribal state (the Sim'alites) and an urban empire. The tribal culture shares proximity in space, language, and chronology with ancient Israel. Because of these similarities, cultural features may have been transmitted, borrowed, or influenced between the Amorite Mari Tribes and early Israel. (Arnold, GN, 40)

Biblical scholar and Assyriologist Daniel Fleming writes,

> Because Zimri-Lim maintained both his identity as a tribal king and active ties with the mobile pastoralist component of his tribal people, the letters from his administration must be treated as a secure source of information regarding both tribal organization and pastoralist subsistence during this period. Zimri-Lim even created a new administration for the Mari kingdom with two entirely separate hierarchies, one for districts defined by their settled populations and ruled by governors called *sapitums*, and the other for his own Binu Sim'al tribespeople who could be ruled from the back country without registration by towns. (Fleming, GHT, 204)

3. Conclusion Regarding Nomadic and Settled Civilizations

It seems entirely plausible for the patriarchal background to be rooted in northern Syria communal origins. The existence of both pastoral and settled communities seems to have occurred in the very area from where Abraham is said to have migrated.

Fleming concludes by describing Zimri-Lim as "a king who retains his tribal and pastoralist connections at the same time as he embraces the achievements of urban civilization." (Fleming, GHT, 204)

B. Laws and Covenant Customs

1. Slave Prices

John Collins challenges rejecting the patriarchal stories on the basis of discrepancies within the text. One specific example is whether it was the Ishmaelites (Gen. 39:1) or Midianites (Gen. 37:36) who sold Joseph into Egypt. Collins writes, "This argument would not apply to the contradiction as to whether he was sold by the Midianites or Ishmaelites. It may be that the Midianites are introduced secondarily by an editor who wanted to excuse the brothers of the charge of selling Joseph into slavery, which was a crime liable to the death penalty according to Deut. 24:7." (Collins, IHB, 103) The confusion over the names of the buyers could be solved in a number of ways. What is not challenged is the recorded price of twenty shekels of silver for this transaction, which is a significant time-marker in dating the events within these stories.

The price of slaves inflated over time and there is historically credible information about slave prices at any given time in history. The price recorded for the sale of a slave would be a way of fixing the patriarchal stories to a specific era in time, just as one could use prices for gasoline or a gallon of milk to fix it to a recent time period.

All of the prices mentioned match the going rate at a specific place and time. Records of slave prices derived from law codes throughout the ancient Near East corroborate the prices recorded in Genesis, Exodus, and 2 Kings—from the time of Joseph until the divided Kingdom. (Kitchen, OROT, 344–45)

- Genesis 37:27, 28: Joseph is sold by his brothers for twenty shekels of silver.
- The Code of Hammurabi (1760 BC) sets the price at twenty shekels in sections 116, 214, and 252. (Roth, LCMAM, 71–143) This dating fits within the Middle Bronze period.
- Slave prices increased from ten to 120 shekels over a two-thousand-year period. (Kitchen, OROT, 344–45)
- According to Exodus 21:32, thirty shekels was a standard price, but Leviticus 27:3–7 gives a scale of from three to fifty shekels according to age and sex, with a provision for an appeal to the priest in case of uncertainty (Lev. 27:8). Twenty shekels is the price set for a young man (Lev. 27:5), and this corresponds with the sum paid for Joseph (Gen. 37:28).
- Later recorded data in 2 Maccabees 8:11 fixes the average slave price as ninety for a talent, that is, forty shekels each. The ransom of an entire talent for a single man (1 Kings 20:39) means that unusual value (far more than that of a slave) was set on this particular captive. (Kitchen, OROT, 344–45)

The parallel evidence of treaty structure and slave prices show that details of the patriarchal narratives fit within an earlier time frame than the first millennium. These details are important because had these stories originated at a later date, many of these particulars would have been impossible to replicate consistently. Kitchen concludes,

Thus our biblical figures in each case closely correspond to the relevant averages for their periods: 20 shekels for Joseph in the early second millennium, 30 shekels under Moses in the later second millennium, 50 shekels for

Assyria under Menahem in the eighth century. (Kitchen, OROT, 344–45)

2. Covenant Forms

Excavations at Mari and Tell Leilan, in northern Syria, have unearthed many tablets that contain a specific type of covenant protocol unique to the early second millennium BC. (Kitchen, OROT, 323)

a. Objections

Van Seters argues that the Abrahamic narratives were shaped much later, during the time of exile, to give the Israelites a sense of identity. If Van Seters is correct, the credibility of the patriarchal narratives decreases because the origin of the stories, or at the very least their purpose, comes into question. In light of these claims, and in order to explain the similarities in covenant forms between the earlier covenants given to Abraham and the later covenant structure in the exile, Van Seters asserts that the similarities should be explained as follows:

The promises to the fathers, when viewed in terms of the history of their form and in a comparison with both the pre-exilic theology of Deuteronomy and the concerns of the exilic prophets, can best be understood as a response to the needs of the late exilic period. The whole orientation is similar to that of Deutero-Isaiah, and it was at this time that the Abrahamic tradition was taken up and given its present basic shape as the fundamental unifying identity for the people of Israel, on the threshold of restoration. (Van Seters, AHT, 278)

Van Seters's references to the period of exile reflect his belief that the patriarchal covenants (including God's promises) employ a form that matches the concerns, hopes, and outlook of the later chapters in Isaiah. For our discussion of the challenge his thinking poses regarding the composition of the Pentateuch and the prophets, please see chapters 23 and 24.

b. Response

Kitchen reports that covenants discovered at Mari and Tell Leilan dating from 2000–1500 BC contain five elements: (Kitchen, OROT, 323)

1. Witnesses (a deity)
2. Oath
3. Stipulations
4. Ceremony
5. Curse

This format mirrors Genesis 21:23–31; 26:29–31; and 31:51–54. (Kitchen, OROT, 323)

- They contain the same five elements.
- They are in roughly the same order.

Taking the biblical data at face value, the format of the treaties found in northern Syria situates the Genesis covenants in the Middle Bronze Age, and not in a later period. This is especially evident when the structure of second millennium treaties, discussed above, is compared with later Assyrian treaties from the first millennium. (Kitchen and Lawrence, TLCANE, 69–250)

3. Sister/Wife Laws Reflected from Nuzi Tablets

Observations regarding cultural parallels to the patriarchal stories supports a common argument used by maximalists for locating the existence of the patriarchs in a certain era. A common example is when Abraham pretends that his wife is his sister in order to be safe in a foreign land (Gen. 12:13; 20:2). It has been proposed that these patriarchal accounts can be correlated to Hurrian marriage customs, found in the Nuzi texts, in which a wife was also adopted by her husband as a sister to gain superior status. (Van Seters, AHT, 71)

a. Objections

Van Seters summarizes the difficulties scholars have with applying the Nuzi texts so directly to the patriarchal situations:

> First, some parallels have been proposed between the Biblical story and the Nuzi texts; these were based on a serious misunderstanding of the cuneiform sources. . . . Secondly, some parallel customs are common to both the second and first millennia BC and so are completely indecisive for the dating of the traditions. Thirdly, there may be some elements of the story, such as the remarks of Laban's daughters, that actually seem to reflect more closely the situation expressed in the texts of the mid-first millennium BC. (Van Seters, AHT, 84–5)

b. Response

In response to these criticisms Eugene Merrill says,

> The most reasonable position is that the Nuzi tablets reflect customs that were not initiated there but had already been prevalent for centuries. Indeed customs similar to those at Nuzi are attested from many earlier sites, and these continue to be helpful in understanding the patriarchal way of life. (Merrill, KP, 56)

Merrill concludes: "There is nothing . . . that necessitates a date later than that

required by biblical considerations, nor do these incidents appear as unique events without contemporary analogues." (Merrill, KP, 56)

C. Western Semitic Name Types
1. Significance of Name Types

Thompson says, "The discussion about names similar to those of the patriarchs which would have been found in extrabiblical sources is the most important single issue in the debate over historicity." (Thompson, HPN, 17) Further, Thompson goes on to make the argument that, "the name Abram is a West Semitic name of quite common sort, and can be expected to appear wherever we find names from West Semitic peoples. . . . [T]he name is not to be dated to any specific period." (Thompson, HPN, 35–6)

The names of people and places also serve a parallel line of evidence. Just as you can identify the era or cultural setting of a picture from the style or shape of an automobile, or the style of clothing that is worn, names are usually a dead giveaway of something belonging to a specific era. (Kaiser, OTD, 87–88) The names and spellings of the patriarchal characters also best reflect a certain geographical area and specific time.

2. A Review of Name Types in the Patriarchal Narratives

Abraham's relatives, such as his great-grandfather Serug, his grandfather Nahor, and his father Terah, all have names that have been confirmed in documents and reports as coming from the Euphrates-Habur region of Upper Mesopotamia from the time period of the early second millennium. (Kitchen, OROT, 341–2)

Kitchen writes, "One important fact to notice is that these names are above all personal names, the kinds used by individuals; they are not tribal or clan names, despite misguided attempts by some Biblicists to have it so." (Kitchen, OROT, 341–2)

Patriarchal names with i/y prefixes, such as Yitzchak, Ya'akov, Yoseph, and Yishmael, all belong to the Northwest Semitic language group of the Amorite population of the early second millennium BC and are common in the Mari archives dating from this same time period. (Kitchen, OROT, 341–2)

Ancient historian and Assyriologist I. J. Gelb conducted a survey of more than six thousand ancient Amorite names throughout history. The results showed that these i/y names in the early second-millennium account for about 55 percent of all the names structured with this Semitic pattern. (Kitchen, OROT, 342)

Kitchen continues,

In the Late Bronze Age up to 500 years later, at Ugarit, only 30 and 25 percent of the initial i/y names are of this type in the alphabetic and syllabic texts respectively—a colossal drop by half, of 55%! In the Iron Age it gets worse. . . . [There] are only 12% of all the known i/y names—less than half of the previous figures! (Kitchen, OROT, 342)

The evidence indicates that the popularity and consistency of the patriarchal name type and structure fit most comfortably in the early second millennium BC, rather than at a later time period where minimalist scholars would attempt to place these traditions.

D. Archaeology
1. Fort of Abraham

Currently the only possible nonbiblical written reference to Abraham is found in Egyptian records. Kitchen writes, "No external, firsthand source of Moses' time or earlier explicitly mentions Abraham, Isaac, Jacob or the latter's sons. The only suggested extrabiblical mention of Abraham is in the topographical list of Shoshenq I, Shishak of Egypt in 925, giving what may be read as 'The enclosure of Abram,' which is fairly widely accepted." (Kitchen, OROT, 313)

Responding to this finding, Thompson says, "It is possible that this inscription contains the name Abram as a place name, but this cannot be said with complete confidence. The existence of such a place name in tenth century Palestine could be important for biblical interpretation." (Thompson, HPN, 34–35)

The significance of this name can be seen in the following possibility, as Roland Hendel reveals: "When a government builds fortifications, it is natural to name them for illustrious or national heroes. Abram (Abraham) of biblical fame surely fits the bill." (Block, IAKLI, 89)

It is significant that a building referred to in Egyptian records at this time is linked to the name of the Patriarch. While not a concrete conclusion, this marker supports the plausibility for a historical and biblical Abraham.

2. Haran

Haran (also spelled Harran) is an ancient city in northern Syria that has no direct interest to biblical writers outside of Genesis. Within Genesis, it is a significant location for the patriarchs: Genesis 12:5 defines Haran as Abraham's point of departure for the promised land and as Jacob's destination when he flees to his mother's family. (Gen. 27:43; 28:10; 29:14). Yet controversy exists over the likelihood of the city's association with the patriarchs. Van Seters assigns the writing of the patriarchal stories to the neo-Babylonian period (626–539 BC) and dates references to

Ur and Haran to that later period. Fleming observes that a writer of the patriarchal accounts, if working during the monotheistic Jewish monarchy, would be unlikely to associate the patriarchs with Haran because of its pagan gods, but Fleming does note other reasons (tribal and linguistic) for the link to Haran.

a. Van Seter's Position

Van Seter's thesis in *Abraham in History and Tradition* is that the Israelite tradition of the patriarchs better fits in the first millennium BC. Van Seters summarizes his argument in saying, "The reference to Ur of the Chaldees and its association with Harran and a route to the West reflect the political circumstances of the Neo-Babylonian period. The place names in Palestine are those which have a special place in the history of the monarchy." (Van Seters, AHT, 121)

b. Fleming's Position

However, Fleming provides several answers to objections raised in regard to associating Abraham with Haran:

- Haran had a longstanding tradition of worshiping the moon god. This would make the city an unlikely choice for Abraham's home, as Israel's religious emphasis in the first millennium was monotheistic. (Fleming, GHT, 216)
- Mari documents describe a sacrifice to the moon god in the temple at Haran: "Asdi-takim and the kings of Zalmaqum, with the chiefs and elders of the Yaminites, have slain the ass together in the Sin temple of Harran." (Fleming, GHT, 216)
- Remarkably, Haran was the cultic center for the Binu Yamina coalition mentioned earlier.

- Fleming argues, "It appears, then, that both the existence of a tribe named Benjamin and the attachment of Israel's ancestor to Harran are not simply ancient Amorite, but are specifically features of the Yaminite tribal people who are known from the second millennium texts in Mari." (Fleming, GHT, 219)
- Fleming also notes, "The Genesis tribal split and Amorite tribal pair share a remarkably similar set of assumptions. Both traditions use the language of right and left hands, a pair defined by the human body, for tribal pastoralists who are allotting pasturelands." (Fleming, GHT, 222) This language of the left and right is similar to the language used by Abraham and Lot in dividing the pastureland (Gen. 13:7–12).

Fleming's conclusion regarding Haran is that "without a compelling political or population link to Haran, for which we have no evidence, an ideology of ethnic identification with this far-northern town makes no sense." (Fleming, GHT, 216) Yet some of the information he provides seems to offer ethnic and linguistic evidence for a link with Haran.

c. Summary

- The pastoral descriptions of Abraham and his family reflect an origin that is possibly rooted in northern Syrian (Amorite) ancestry. The relationship between the name Binu Yamina and the specific Israelite tribe of Benjamin is an intriguing connection.
- The fact that the wandering outback tribes of the Binu Yamina were referred to as the *ibrum*, which has a possible

relation to the name Hebrew as applied to Abraham, is significant. (Fleming, GHT, 228)

- The division of grazing land using the terms *left* and *right hand* along with the Harran origin tradition, is significant.

Taken together, the evidence seems to point to the reality of a person, conceivably Abraham, who had Binu Yamina tribal connections in his ancestral background.

Fleming argues,

My selection of comparative evidence from Mari is limited and depends especially on the presence of Harran and Benjamin in the biblical tradition, joined to the new realization that Mari's Binu Yamina were a huge tribal coalition whose range brought some of them remarkably close to Palestine, even in the early second millennium. I argue that these two names would not appear in the ancestor traditions of Genesis unless some component of the Israelite population had roots among the Yaminite tribal peoples of Syria. (Fleming, GHT, 227)

3. Ancient Cities in Abraham's Journey

Thompson asserts that archaeological efforts to discover the sites reported in the Genesis accounts have not proved conclusive. He says,

Returning to the question of the historical background of the patriarchal narratives: it can be seen that the methods used by those who have sought the background in the early part of the Second Millennium are wholly inadequate to dealing with a period from which the historical materials are so limited and so chronologically and geographically scattered. (Thompson, HPN, 320)

a. Beersheba

Van Seters reports a lack of settlement in Beersheba before the Iron Age (1200–650 BC), an observation that agrees with Thompson's caution about the scarcity of archaeological material dating from the early Second Millennium: "Recent archaeological excavation at Beersheba reveals that there was no settlement before the Iron Age." (Van Seters, AHT, 111)

Merrill gives several alternative explanations for the lack of Bronze-Age archaeological evidence at the sites reported to have been inhabited by the patriarchs:

Archaeological evidence suggests that Beersheba was not founded until well after the Middle Bronze period, and so it is likely that Abraham and his family did not occupy the area in a permanent way but only as a pilgrimage shrine and campsite in their seasonal migrations." (Merrill, KP, 59)

b. Shechem

Regarding Shechem, Merrill writes,

Most scholars agree that Shechem was founded at about this time (ca. 1910 BC), but it is unlikely that it bore his name in Jacob's day. Without a doubt it was named for the son of Hamor (33:19), the head of the clan that lived in the area, but his name would almost certainly not have been given within the lifetime of Shechem himself. Moreover, it is possible that the clause, "Jacob . . . arrived safely (in peace) at the city of Shechem" (33:18) should be understood as "Jacob arrived at Shalem, that is, at the city of Shechem." This would mean that the city of Jacob's time was called Shalem and later renamed Shechem in honor of the young man of the biblical story. (Merrill, KP, 63)

c. Sodom and Gomorrah

The miraculous destruction of Sodom and Gomorrah is often given as evidence against the reliability of the Genesis narratives. Thomas Thompson again questions the patriarchal stories when he says, "Not only was the settlement of the Transjordan not abandoned any time during the Bronze Age, but there is no evidence that the EB IV/MB I sites were destroyed at a single time." (Thompson, HPN, 320)

Merrill reports that the Ebla inscriptions likely mention Sodom and Gomorrah. Since those documents are no later than 2500 BC, it means that these two cities were not destroyed before that point in time. Merrill also points out, "excavations at Bab edh-Dhra' and other sites on and near the el-Lisan Peninsula at the southeast end of the Dead Sea have revealed the remains of at least five ancient urban complexes, the latest of which is apparently earlier than 2000 BC." (Merrill, KP, 57)

Merrill concludes, "It is impossible to be dogmatic on this main point in light of the absence of extrabiblical literary attestation from these sites, but clearly the patriarchal history does seem to have more corroboration on this point than ever before." (Merrill, KP, 57)

4. Joseph in Egypt

Israel Finkelstein and Neil Silberman write, "One thing is certain. The basic situation described in the Exodus saga—the phenomenon of immigrants coming down to Egypt from Canaan and settling in the eastern border regions of the delta—is abundantly verified in the archaeological finds and historical texts." (Finkelstein and Silberman, BU, 52–53)

Finkelstein and Silberman conclude by asking two key questions: First, who were these Semitic immigrants? And second, how does the date of their sojourn in Egypt square with biblical chronology? The second question is to be answered in a succeeding chapter. However, the first question is relevant to the investigation into the reliability of the patriarchal narratives. (Finkelstein and Silberman, BU, 52–53)

James K. Hoffmeier states that we shouldn't be surprised at the lack of evidence for immigrating pastoralists in Egypt, given the situation. He says,

> One normally does not expect pastoralists to leave much evidence of their presence, other than burials, given the short duration of their visits and movements. And presently, archaeologists and anthropologists are unable to distinguish the various ethnicities of pastoral groups from the Semitic world when they leave their traces in Egypt. This means that Hebrews, Shasu, or "Amu" cannot be differentiated archaeologically. (Hoffmeier, EWN, 54)

Old Testament scholar Bill Arnold concludes,

> Although many Egyptian elements in the Joseph narrative may be denied or contested in their individual particulars, the cumulative weight of the evidence affirms that the picture portrayed in the Joseph narrative is "compatible with what is known from Egyptian history," and that the body of evidence suggests that the main points of the Joseph narrative are plausible. (Arnold, GN, 44)

E. Alleged Anachronisms in the Patriarchal Narratives

In their discussion of alleged anachronisms in the Genesis narratives, Finkelstein and Silberman state, "So the combination of camels, Arabian goods, Philistines . . . as well as other places and nations mentioned in the patriarchal stories in Genesis are highly significant. All the clues point to a time of composition many centuries after the time in which the Bible reports the lives of the patriarchs took place. These and other anachronisms suggest an intensive period of writing the patriarchal narratives in the eighth and seventh centuries BCE." (Finkelstein and Silberman, BU, 38)

1. Camels

Finkelstein and Silberman present the supposed challenge posed by the presence of camels in the Genesis narratives:

We know through archaeological research that camels were not domesticated as beasts of burden earlier than the late second millennium and were not widely used in that capacity in the ancient Near East until well after 1000 BCE. And an even more telling detail—the camel caravan carrying "gum, balm, and myrrh," in the Joseph story reveals an obvious familiarity with the main products of the lucrative Arabian trade that flourished under the supervision of the Assyrian empire in the eighth-seventh centuries BCE (Finkelstein and Silberman, BU, 37)

Kitchen responds that there is remarkably little presence of camels in the patriarchal narratives. They are listed as the last and least of both Abraham and Jacob's possessions (Gen. 12:16; 30:43; 32:7, 15) and were used solely for long-distance, desert travelling to Haran and back (Gen. 24:10-64; 31:17, 34). It is also recorded that the Midianites used them for their desert

travels. After the exodus camels are mentioned among Pharaoh's transport animals (Ex. 9:3) and on the list of creatures not to be eaten (Lev. 11:4; Deut. 14:7). Kitchen also adds that several archaeological references to camels from the early second millennium exist, from Egypt, through Canaan, to as far as northern Syria. (Kitchen, OROT, 338–339)

Kitchen concludes, "The camel was for long a *marginal* beast in most of the historic ancient Near East (including Egypt), but it was *not* wholly unknown or anachronistic before or during 2000–1100." (Kitchen, OROT, 338–339)

2. Philistines

A second problem raised with the early dating of the Genesis text is the existence of the Philistines in the land. Finkelstein and Silberman write,

Then there is the issue of the Philistines. We hear of them in connection with Isaac's encounter with "Abimelech, king of the Philistines," at the city of Gerar (Genesis 26:1). The Philistines, a group of migrants from the Aegean or eastern Mediterranean, had not established their settlements along the coastal plain of Canaan until sometime after 1200 BCE (Finklestein and Silberman, BU, 37)

Merrill recognizes these issues when he says,

Of greater historical interest and difficulty is the identification of Abimelech as a Philistine (Gen. 21:32, 34; cf. 26:1). It is generally assumed that this identification is anachronistic at best because the Philistines, as part of the Sea Peoples migration, did not enter and subdue lower coastal Canaan until 1200 BC or later.

Moreover, the name Abimelech is Semitic and not Philistine. (Merrill, KP, 58)

And yet, "The problem of the presence of the Philistines in Canaan nearly a millennium before the arrival of the Sea Peoples is . . . perplexing but not insoluble." (Merrill, KP, 58) He goes on to provide possible solutions: "The name Abimelech means 'my father is king' and could well be a title rather than a personal name." He also notes that "different rulers of the same place did in fact have the same name."

Merrill concludes,

The later arrival of the Sea Peoples could have augmented the Philistines already living in the land. This hypothesis, in addition to supporting the historicity of the patriarchal encounters with early Philistines, also accounts for Israel's decision not to take the way of the sea en route to Canaan from Egypt though it was shorter (Exodus 13:17), for it would have meant certain and disastrous opposition from the Philistines. (Merrill, KP, 58–59)

Kitchen also suggests that the term *Philistine* could have been an editorial update where "some earlier and obsolete term would have been replaced" with a newer, more familiar term. (Kitchen, OROT, 340)

IV. Conclusion

Biblical theologian John Goldingay concludes:

All of this points to the conclusion that Israel's ancestors known to us in the Genesis accounts were real individuals, living during a period of time only imprecisely understood but likely in the Bronze Age, and at some distance from the authors of the Biblical texts. The extrabiblical evidence does not demand the historicity of Abraham, Isaac and Jacob, but it certainly allows it in accord with the biblical data. Israel understood these accounts to be fundamentally factual, and with that factuality the patriarchal narratives have sense but not reference. (Goldingay, PSH, 29)

Theologian Victor P. Hamilton, acknowledging the historicity of Abraham, summarizes the situation thus:

There are no references to Abraham, Isaac, or Jacob in any other inscriptions that are contemporary with any writing of the Old Testament. Names like those of the patriarchs do appear in cuneiform literature, but nobody suggests that any of these are the patriarchs themselves. Thus our knowledge of Abraham and his family is limited to the Old Testament. Of course, this limitation in itself does not cast

---

All of this points to the conclusion that Israel's ancestors known to us in the Genesis accounts were real individuals, living during a period of time only imprecisely understood but likely in the Bronze Age, and at some distance from the authors of the Biblical texts. The extrabiblical evidence does not demand the historicity of Abraham, Isaac and Jacob, but it certainly allows it in accord with the biblical data.

John Goldingjay

a cloud of doubt over Abraham's existence. (Hamilton, BG, 60)

Old Testament scholar and archaeological expert Kenneth Kitchen concludes:

We are compelled, once and for all, to throw out Wellhausen's bold claim that the Patriarchs were merely a glorified mirage of/from the Hebrew monarchy period. For such a view there is not a particle of supporting factual evidence, and the whole of the foregoing indicative background material is solidly against it. It should be clear, finally, that the main features of the patriarchal narratives either fit specifically into the first half of the second millennium or are consistent with such a dating. (Kitchen, OROT, 372)

CHAPTER 19

THE HISTORICITY OF THE EXODUS

OVERVIEW

I. Introduction

A. The Importance of the Exodus

No doubt the exodus of the Israelites from Egypt is one of the most important historical events for both the Jewish and Christian faiths. That central experience of rescue for the helpless out of a desperate condition has been recognized as a key example of God's love in making salvation (wholeness, healing, and restoration) available. Theology is connected to these historical events. The Old Testament testifies to God saving his people from the oppression of the Egyptian Pharaoh. The Bible says God did this as an act of mercy toward his people:

> *"I have surely seen the affliction of My people who are in Egypt, and have heard their cry because of their taskmasters, for I know their sorrows. So I have come down to deliver them out of the hand of the Egyptians, and to bring them up from that land to a good and large land, to a land flowing with milk and honey."* — Exodus 3:7, 8

The saving power of God as shown in the event of the exodus is woven throughout the Bible and ancient Israelite beliefs and practices. And it is presented as historical fact. James Hoffmeier stresses the importance of the ancient acceptance of the fact of the exodus:

The priests, prophets, psalmists, people of Israel, and foreigners believed these events occurred, and consequently they celebrated festivals, sang songs, dated events, and observed laws that assumed that Yahweh's salvation from Egypt was authentic. (Hoffmeier, TTH, 133)

Old Testament scholar and biblical theologian Eugene Merrill explains the pre-Christian importance of the exodus to ancient Jews and draws a connection to Jesus:

The exodus is the most significant historical and theological event of the Old Testament because it marks God's mightiest act in behalf of his people, one that brought them from slavery to freedom, from fragmentation to solidarity, from a people of promise (the Hebrews) to a nation of fulfillment (Israel). To the exodus the book of Genesis provides an introduction and justification, and from the exodus flows all subsequent Old Testament revelation, a record that serves the exodus as inspired commentary and detailed exposition. In the final analysis, the exodus became a type of the exodus achieved by Jesus Christ for people of faith; thus it is a meaningful event for the church as well as for Israel. (Merrill, KP, 73–74)

As Merrill observes, the exodus and Jesus Christ's provision of salvation are connected as *type* and *fulfillment*, and both are real events that reveal theology. Although modern critics (especially since the nineteenth century) have suggested that biblical stories merely present comforting symbolic ideas, believers for over 1500 years linked history and theological insight. Christopher Hall shares the declaration of Diodore of Tarsus (fourth century), that our understanding of Scripture *never sets aside its historical starting point*. (Hall, RS, 158–163) Similarly, Augustine in *On Christian Doctrine* emphasizes the layered truth of Scripture, counseling believers to study both the Old Testament words themselves (because they name real things) and also the *meanings* that the Old Testament words reveal. (OCD, Books I–II) In the early 1300s, Dante wrote to his patron to explain how *The Divine Comedy* presented the work of God in Christ. He cites Psalm 114:1, 2, which connects the historical exodus with the theological understanding of God's holy presence among his people. Dante states that the exodus (the "departure from Egypt") is the historical record of saving rescue, which allows us to understand "our redemption wrought by Christ . . . from the grief and misery of sin to the state of grace," and teaches us to hope in "the liberty of eternal glory." (Dante, LCG, 121–22)

B. Questioning the Exodus

Throughout most of Jewish and Christian history, the exodus as a literal event has not been questioned. However, in contemporary scholarship, especially among archaeologists whose theology tends toward liberalism, the historicity of the exodus has been doubted or even disbelieved entirely. Israel Finkelstein and Neil Silberman believe archaeology has disproven the possibility that the exodus events happened as they are relayed in the Old Testament:

Unfortunately for those seeking a historical Exodus, they [the sites mentioned in the exodus narrative] were unoccupied precisely at the time they reportedly played a role in the events of the wandering of the children of Israel in the wilderness. (Finkelstein and Silberman, BU, 64)

The saga of Israel's Exodus from Egypt is neither historical truth nor literary fiction . . . to pin this biblical image down to a single date is to betray the story's deepest meaning. Passover proves to be not a single event but a continuing experience of national resistance against the powers that be. (Finkelstein and Silberman, BU, 70–71)

William Ward charitably suggests the writers of the exodus narrative actually believed what they wrote, even if it wasn't fully true:

There is no Egyptian evidence that offers direct testimony to the Exodus as described in the Old Testament. There are hints here and there to indicate that something like an exodus could have happened, though on a vastly smaller scale, but there is not a word in a text or an archaeological artifact that lends credence to the biblical narrative as it now stands. Egypt remains silent, as it always has. From the Egyptian viewpoint, the Old Testament narrative records a series of earthshaking episodes that never happened. . . . They believed that a sea was rolled back, that the sun stopped in the heavens one day, that cities fell before the trumpet's blast. This is the way history was written in those days; you recorded what you believed had happened, not necessarily what you could prove had happened. (Ward, SC, 105, 111)

Volkmar Fritz adds quite bluntly: "The biblical story of a long stay in Egypt is fiction." (Fritz, Israelites, 192)

C. Standard of Evidence

We discover that often a different standard of evidence is applied to the Bible as opposed to other ancient manuscripts. Leading archaeologist and Old Testament scholar James K. Hoffmeier explains the double standard:

The reason is straightforward: there is a general skepticism toward the Bible as a reliable source for history. If it were not still Scripture to Jews and Christians, the Bible probably would not be treated in such a condescending and dismissive manner. Because of this hermeneutic of suspicion, the Bible is not treated as a historical source unless there is external corroborating archaeological or historical (textual) evidence. In the case of the Israelite sojourn and exodus, no direct, clearly identifiable support has come to light in Egypt. (Hoffmeier, EWN, 48)

In this chapter we present and evaluate the latest evidence for the historicity of the exodus. At the outset we must say the extrabiblical evidence is far from overwhelming. We have no smoking gun providing clear, solid evidence that Israel lived in Egypt and Moses led the Hebrews out of the country. Biblical theologian John Sailhamer acknowledges the lack of clear Egyptian evidence while downplaying its significance:

No Egyptian records describe the Exodus. One would not expect such an account. The primary purpose of Egyptian records at that period was to cast pharaoh in a positive light, and the events of the biblical narratives would do anything but that. (Sailhamer, BA, 50)

While this lack of clear evidence doesn't mean it didn't happen, the available evidence deserves an honest appraisal. Hoffmeier explains the challenge of archaeological data:

> As a field archaeologist myself, I am keenly aware of how little has actually survived from the ancient past, owing to natural forces, such as moisture in many forms, deflation, and earthquakes, as well as human impact in the form of later occupation (in ancient times), reusing earlier building materials, human destruction (war and burning), and modern development (urban and agricultural). Realistic expectations about what archaeology can and cannot do for biblical studies must always be kept in mind. (Hoffmeier, TTH, 101)

It is not academic backpedaling for a Christian to manage expectations about what may or may not be discovered from the time of the exodus. The lack of an unambiguous extrabiblical reference does not rule out the fact, or at least plausibility, of the exodus as an historical event. Therefore, in this chapter we attempt to show the Old Testament exodus story is plausible, even if seemingly improbable.

II. The Historical Nature of the Biblical Account

First we consider the biblical account of the exodus. Why should we pay attention to this evidence when so many are quick to ignore it? Why should we not focus solely on extrabiblical evidence? We do not overlook it because the biblical account presents us with very valuable evidence for our study, and responsible investigation begins with openness to all potentially significant details.

A. Old Testament

A more thorough treatment of the trustworthiness of the Old Testament in general appears in chapter 4. However, we should discuss a few main points here. At the very least, the Bible presents the exodus as a historical event.

First, a straightforward reading of the details in the book of Exodus leads a reader to recognize the text is being presented as an authentically historical account, not mythology. The narrative tells us of specific people (e.g., Moses and Aaron, including their genealogy in 6:14–27), places (e.g., Egypt, Goshen, Pithom, Raamses, Midian, and the Nile), and events (e.g., the plagues, Israelite slavery).

Second, the exodus is treated as historical throughout the Old Testament. We should note that the Bible is not a single source. It is actually multiple sources, all maintaining the authenticity of the exodus tradition. Any historian knows the likelihood of the authenticity of an event increases as independent sources that verify it are discovered. As Hoffmeier notes:

> In addition to the testimony in the Pentateuch (all five books place the Hebrews in Egypt or refer back to the sojourn respectively), aspects and details of the exodus and wilderness stories

---

No Egyptian records describe the Exodus. One would not expect such an account. The primary purpose of Egyptian records at that period was to cast pharaoh in a positive light, and the events of the biblical narratives would do anything but that.

John Sailhamer

---

are used in a multiplicity of ways in the books of Joshua, Judges, 1-2 Samuel, 1-2 Kings, Psalms, and in the Prophets . . . often simple, passing allusions are given, indicating that the audience needed no further elaboration. With this overwhelming evidence within the Bible regarding the Egyptian sojourn, exodus, and wilderness episodes, evidence coming from a variety of types of literature and used in a host of different ways, it is methodologically inadvisable, at best, to treat the Bible as a single witness to history, requiring corroboration before the Egypt-Sinai reports can be taken as authentic. (Hoffmeier, EWN, 48–49)

To summarize, the Old Testament contains many independent sources that all present the exodus as historical.

Finally, Yahweh is known and presented as trustworthy specifically because he brought his people up out of Egypt. This theme appears in Exodus, Leviticus, Numbers, Deuteronomy, Judges, 1 and 2 Samuel, 1 and 2 Kings, 1 and 2 Chronicles, Nehemiah, Psalms, Jeremiah, Ezekiel, Daniel, Hosea, Amos, and Micah. The Passover is not only instituted as a national and perpetual celebration, but participants are told to tell their children it is celebrated because "of what the LORD did for me when I came up from Egypt" (Ex. 13:8). And celebrating it properly was so important that someone who did it wrong was to be "cut off from Israel" (Ex. 12:15, 19).

None of this supports the idea that the biblical presentation of the exodus should be understood as a myth in the sense of imagined fable or invented folklore.

B. New Testament

In chapter 3 we make the case for the reliability of the New Testament in general. Here, we simply list examples of how the New Testament presents the exodus as a literal event.

- Stephen's sermon in Acts 7 clearly recounts the fact that Israel was literally led out of the wilderness.
- Acts 13:17 describes a sermon Paul gave in Antioch in which he declares God "exalted the people when they dwelt as strangers in the land of Egypt, and with an uplifted arm He brought them out of it."
- The writer of Hebrews encourages readers not to rebel like those in the wilderness in Hebrews 3:16: "For who, having heard, rebelled? Indeed, was it not all who came out of Egypt, led by Moses?"
- Jude 5 attributes divinity to Jesus by giving him credit as the one "who saved the people out of the land of Egypt."
- Jesus authenticated the exodus tradition by placing such a high value on the trustworthiness of the Law and the Prophets for their prophetic witness of him (John 5:45–47; Luke 24:27).

The exodus account appears throughout the Bible. The history of Israel is dated from the Passover, just as the United States is dated from the Declaration of Independence.

III. Moses

Any Moses other than the one described in the Pentateuch (the first five books of the Bible) is a modern invention and can be given any set of characteristics the researcher or filmmaker imagines (or wishes) Moses to have. For example, the 2014 film *Exodus: Gods and Kings* stars Christian Bale as Moses. In the film, Moses is portrayed as an Egyptian military general who is eloquent (unlike the biblical description of Moses as "slow of speech and slow of tongue" [Ex. 4:10]). In the 1998 DreamWorks animated film *The Prince of Egypt*, Moses is not reunited with his mother, and as an adult he accidentally kills the Egyptian, instead of murdering him. If there was no historical Moses, then these modern works would challenge nothing. Artists would be simply taking a mythical character and making him their own.

However, if there was no historical Moses then we would most likely have no historical exodus, so the stakes are high. The challenge in proving there was a historical Moses is that we have no extrabiblical evidence clearly proving he existed. Therefore, our task is to show that it is plausible that the Moses portrayed in the Pentateuch could have lived in that historical context. Rather than imagining a hypothetical Moses, we shall deal with the text itself and see if Moses, as he is presented in the Pentateuch, is plausible.

A. Moses' Birth

Exodus describes Moses as a descendant of the people who came into Egypt with Jacob/Israel (i.e., he was an Israelite). Although he grew up in Pharaoh's court, Moses' own Hebrew mother raised him. Therefore, we can reasonably assume he would have been made familiar with Israel's arrival in Egypt and its subsequent history. We can also assume he would have been taught Hebrew by his birth mother/nanny.

1. Was the Birth Narrative Copied?
a. Similarities

Some familiar with Moses' birth story claim it is copied from the ancient Akkadian "Legend of Sargon." (Hoffmeier, IE, 136–137; see also Provan et al., BHI, 177–178; Bauer, HAW, 235–236; Cohen, OEMNS, 9–10) If this is true, it might support the case against the historicity of Moses. To be sure, there are similarities:

Sargon, the mighty king, king of Agade,
am I.

My mother was a changeling, my father I
knew not.
The brother(s) of my father loved the hills.
My city is Azupiranu, which is situated on
the banks of the Euphrates.
My changeling mother conceived me, in
secret she bore me.
She set me in a basket of rushes, with
bitumen she sealed my lid.
She cast me into the river which rose not
(over) me,
The river bore me up and carried me to
Akki, the drawer of water.
Akki, the drawer of water lifted me out as he
dipped his e[w]er.
Akki, the drawer of water, [took me] as his
son (and) reared me.
(Pritchard, ANE, 85–86)

Sargon's mother puts him in a basket and places him in the water where he is saved. And someone other than his mother adopts him as a son. These similarities are clear.

b. Differences

However, there are also significant differences. There are many ancient texts that feature the "exposed child" motif, where a "child is placed in a small vessel, set upon waters, then rescued." (Studevent-Hickman and Morgan, OAPT, 23) With respect to the "exposed child" motif, Moses and Sargon fall into different and distinct categories. (Hoffmeier, IE, 136–138) Sargon was abandoned because of embarrassment; Moses was not abandoned. Rather, to prevent certain execution, he was purposefully placed where someone could find and rescue him.

Many scholars highlight the distinctly Hebrew and Egyptian linguistic patterns in the Exodus account, which counter the theory that the story was borrowed from the Akkadian account:

It seems that the Egyptian setting of the story is itself responsible for the Egyptian pericope. Furthermore, it seems unlikely that a scribe during the late Judean monarchy or the exilic period (or later) would have been familiar with these Egyptian terms. (Hoffmeier, IE, 136–40)

And even within the "exposed child" motif, there is a significant difference between Moses' birth account and the others (including the Sargon account), as Charlie Trimm notes:

The birth narrative of Moses and his failure to act as an effective military hero is a broken form of the exposed infant form. The narrator employed the genre not to glorify Moses, but to reverse the story and show how Moses was not to become a military leader or a king. (Trimm, YFT, 188)

c. Common Motif

Hoffmeier acknowledges there are many ancient accounts of children set adrift in water, but he believes it may be because of an actual practice of commending problem births to providence:

In the end, the reason for the multitude of stories from across the Near East and Mediterranean of casting a child into the waters is that it may reflect the ancient practice of committing an unwanted child, or one needing protection, into the hands of providence. A modern parallel would be leaving a baby on the steps of an orphanage or at the door of a church. (Hoffmeier, IE, 138)

Provan, Long, and Longman agree:

In both cultures, the idea behind the basket on the water is the commission of the child into the care of the deity who controls the waters (in the case of Exodus, Yahweh himself)—the

ancient equivalent to the modern practice of leaving an unwanted child on the threshold of a house or hospital. (Provan et al., BHI, 177–178)

d. Conclusion

Despite the similarity of the accounts, there is no strong evidence that Moses' birth narrative is borrowed.

2. Archaeological Evidence

There are burial baskets on display in the Cairo Museum that date to the Bronze Age. (Freund, DTB, 58) These would perhaps be similar to what Moses' mother would have used to place him in the Nile River.

B. His Life at Court

According to Exodus, Moses was raised in the royal court as the Pharaoh's daughter's son. It was common practice from at least Thutmose III (1457–1425 BC) to raise foreign children in the Pharaoh's court. (Hoffmeier, IE, 142) The royal court raised children of conquered and allied countries to serve the royal court. Such children were steeped in Egyptian language, culture, religion, and loyalty. (Kitchen, OROT, 297) Whether they remained serving the court or returned to their own country, they would be more Egyptian than not. There is evidence of sons of Syro-Canaanite kings in the Pharaoh's courts and a semitically named vizier titled "child of the nursery." (Hoffmeier, IE, 143) Children of the nursery received a formal education in the language and writing of Egypt. An extant letter from the thirteenth century thanks Pharaoh for sending foreigners to be taught and trained to serve the harem. (Kitchen, OROT, 297) It was common for Semites, Hurrians, and others of foreign birth to serve as cupbearers, foremen, scribes, generals, etc. (Kitchen, OROT, 297) Moses would simply "be one among many." (Kitchen, OROT, 297)

According to Exodus, Moses was so Egyptianized that when he fled from Pharaoh he was mistaken for an Egyptian: "They said, 'An Egyptian delivered us from the hand of the shepherds, and he also drew enough water for us and watered the flock.'" (Ex. 2:19)

The overall portrait of a foreign child taken to court by a princess, raised, educated, and otherwise prepared to serve the Pharaoh is "consistent with the emerging information." (Hoffmeier, IE, 143)

C. Moses as Antihero

If the story of Moses is fiction, then he is presented in an unusual way. Instead of presenting him solely as an ethical, strong leader, the book of Exodus portrays a cowardly murderer with a speech impediment.

1. The Fleeing Felon

The Pentateuch describes Moses' flight to Midian to prevent reprisal by the Pharaoh for murdering an Egyptian. There are similarities in Moses' account and numerous accounts of political figures fleeing one jurisdiction to another. (Hoffmeier, IE, 144) However, Moses was a fugitive, not a political refugee. Exodus does not record his requesting asylum or divulging why he came to Midian. The Pentateuch admits its central figure was a murderer. It neither aggrandizes nor justifies Moses' actions. Instead, it indicates Moses knew the act was wrong and attempted to cover it up: "He looked this way and that way, and when he saw no one, he killed the Egyptian and hid him in the sand" (Ex. 2:12).

2. Hesitation

Thereafter, Moses served his wife's father as a shepherd until Yahweh appeared to him. One of the most interesting aspects of the burning bush account is Moses' response. He does not act the hero and say, "Here I am; send me." Instead, thirteen times he says, "Oh, my Lord, please send someone else." (e.g., Ex. 4:13 ESV). It is not until "the anger of the LORD was kindled against Moses" that Moses acquiesces (Ex. 4:14).

Though not necessarily a reflection of his cowardice, it's important to note the account does not tell us that Moses leads the Hebrews out of Egypt by his bravery or strength; instead, it is Yahweh who does it. (Trimm, "YFT," 188–189)

3. Speech Impediment

One of the reasons Moses gives when asking God to send someone else is his apparent speech impediment:

> *But Moses said to the LORD, "O my Lord, I am not eloquent, neither before nor since You have spoken to Your servant; but I am slow of speech and of tongue." — Exodus 4:10*

This does not appear to be something that would be included unless it was true.

4. Significance of Moses as Antihero

Moses does not exhibit characteristics of the typically invented hero. The initial portrait of Moses is as the son of a slave, an adopted child, a person with anger management issues, a murderer, and an outlaw with a speech impediment. Normally,

> declarations against interest are regarded as having a high degree of credibility because of the presumption that people do not make up lies in order to hurt themselves; they lie to help themselves. (Gordon-Reed, TJSH, 217)

Whether these first chapters of Exodus are biography or autobiography—or even legend—they certainly do not herald his future as prophet, priest, and leader.

D. Naming Conventions

Much has been written about the name Moses. Some strongly contend it is Hebrew, others that it is Egyptian. (Hoffmeier, IE, 140–142) If it is associated with the Hebrew verb "to draw out," it has a Hebrew etymology. If the Egyptian princess gave her adopted Semitic child a name using the Egyptian verb meaning "to give birth," associated with many well-known Egyptian names, including Thutmose and Rameses, the name is clearly Egyptian. The biblical text indicates a Hebrew folk etymology associated with an Egyptian name. (Provan et al., BHI, 178) Thus, Hebrew, Egyptian, Egyptian with Hebrew connotation; all are consistent with the Pentateuchal account. (Hoffmeier, IE, 140–142; Kitchen, OROT, 296–297)

E. Conclusion Regarding Moses' Historicity

We see nothing in the indirect evidence that rules out the plausibility of a historical Moses, specifically as he is presented in the Pentateuch. As Kenneth Kitchen writes:

> As for the role of a Moses, there is no factual evidence to exclude such a person at this period, or his having played the roles implied in Exodus to Deuteronomy. A large amount of inconclusive discussion by biblical scholars in almost two hundred years has established next to nothing with any surety. (Kitchen, OROT, 299)

As for the plausibility that we have a reliable record of Moses' life contained in the Pentateuch, Provan, Long, and Longman continue:

> It is not unreasonable, then, to think that written tradition, as well as oral tradition, could have existed in the time of Moses and could have been transmitted to subsequent

generations from that time as the primary "Israel tradition" that we find reflected in the Pentateuch. (Provan et al., BHI, 80)

Additionally, according to Baruch Halpern, "The story of Moses growing up in the court mirrors the practice of Egyptian kings raising the children of their Semitic vassals as hostages in the court." (Halpern, EE, 104) In other words, it is possible and consistent with what modern scholarship knows concerning scribal traditions of ancient Egypt for the Moses described in the Pentateuch to record what it says he recorded.

IV. Archaeological and Textual Evidence

As stated at the beginning of this chapter, no single piece of extrabiblical evidence serves as a smoking gun proving the exodus happened. The lack of any specific evidence is one of the main reasons cited by skeptical scholars for disbelief in the historicity of the exodus. Baruch Halpern bluntly states:

> The actual evidence concerning the Exodus resembles the evidence for the unicorn. We have replicas, even cuddly reproductions, but we never seem to lay our hands on the real thing. (Halpern, EE, 91)

However, significant evidence points to the plausibility of the exodus as the historical event that is detailed in the Old Testament.

A. Loanwords

A loanword is a word that has been borrowed from another language. If it can be shown that there are a significant number of Egyptian loanwords in the exodus and wilderness accounts, especially when compared with the rest of the Hebrew Old Testament and other ancient Northwest Semitic texts, then that would provide evidence for the authenticity of the texts that make up those accounts.

Benjamin Noonan has noted there are twenty-seven different Egyptian loanwords in the exodus and wilderness narratives (i.e., Exodus-Numbers), compared with just fifty-one in the rest of the Hebrew Old Testament. Noonan has also analyzed several Northwest Semitic languages and texts and concludes they "generally lack Egyptian terminology, demonstrating that the high proportions of Egyptian loanwords in the exodus and wilderness narratives are atypical of Northwest Semitic and almost certainly due to a particular historical circumstance that gave rise to the borrowing of so many Egyptian words." (Noonan, EL, 61–62) In addition, Noonan's analysis shows at least some of the loanwords in the exodus and wilderness accounts are borrowed from the Late Bronze Age. Noonan sees a simple and logical explanation for this data:

> Just as one concludes that the sudden increase of French loanwords in the English language ca. AD 1050–1400 reflects some particular circumstance in history, so one should conclude that a high concentration of Egyptian loanwords in the exodus and wilderness traditions reflects some particular historical circumstance. Given the observation that at least some of the Egyptian loanwords in the exodus and wilderness narratives were borrowed during the Late Bronze Age, it is likely that the events of these narratives took place during the Late Bronze Age, just as one would expect if they represent authentic history. (Noonan, EL, 66–67)

B. Israel in Egypt

As was stated earlier, we should not expect to find historical (literary or archaeological) proof for Israel living in Egypt; environmental factors make preservation of ancient written materials from the Nile Delta unlikely. Additionally, Egyptians might never have written about the Hebrews. Richard Freund has studied ancient Egypt for many years and has become convinced

> that they [Egyptians], like the Stalinist regime of the former Soviet Union, were concerned with controlling the information flow, had an overarching perspective on their cumulative history, and were indeed experts on public relations. I cannot imagine that they would have advertised in their written or pictorial history their need to enslave anyone to create the marvelous institutions of Egypt. In addition, as with many other peoples in antiquity, the recorded history of the Egyptians was the history of elite indigenous Egyptians, excluding any "foreigners/peoples" that may have populated Egypt in any particular period. (Freund, DTB, 56)

Since we do not anticipate finding direct evidence of the Hebrews in Egypt, Hoffmeier describes what we can expect to find:

> No serious archaeologist thinks that direct archaeological evidence will be found that can verify the historicity of Abraham, Isaac, and Jacob, or that the latter and his clan moved to Egypt. The question, rather, is, Does evidence exist from Egyptian sources to demonstrate that Egypt was a place where pastoralists [sheep or cattle farmers] come for refuge from droughts to preserve their flocks and livelihood? Could it be that the portrayal of the Hebrews emigrating to Egypt is reflective of a broader pattern? Here the data from Egypt make it very clear that pastoralists from the southern Levant, Transjordan, and Sinai regularly came to Egypt under such circumstances. (Hoffmeier, EWN, 50)

There are two categories of evidence for pastoralists in Egypt: textual and archaeological.

1. Textual Evidence

Hoffmeier details three clear references to pastoralists (specifically sheep or cattle farmers of Western Asiatic or Semitic lineage) being present in Egypt:

a. The Wisdom of Merikare

The Wisdom of Merikare from the First Intermediate Period (c. 2181–c. 2055 BC) features King Meryibre Khety lamenting "the presence of troublesome 'Asiatics.'" (Hoffmeier, EWN, 52) It says:

Now speaking about these foreigners, As for the miserable Asiatic, wretched is the place where he is; Lacking in water.... Food causes his feet to roam about. (Hoffmeier, IE, 55)

b. The Prophecies of Neferti

The "Prophecies of Neferti," written approximately 1990–1960 BC, is written "to criticize the current government of the realm on the one hand, and to legitimize the monarchy of Amenemhet I on the other." (Shupak, PN, 106–107)

He was concerned about what was happening in the land, calling to mind the state of the east with the Asiatics traveling in their strength upsetting those who were harvesting and grabbing the taxes (assigned) for the time of ploughing. All good things have passed away, the land is burdened with misfortune because of those looking for food, Asiatics roaming the land. Foes have arisen in the east, Asiatics have descended into Egypt. The Asiatics will fall to his slaughter. One will build the Walls of the Ruler to prevent Asiatics from descending to Egypt. They will beg for water

in the customary manner, in order to let their herds drink. (Shupak, PN, 107–110)

c. The Story of Sinuhe

The Story of Sinuhe, written sometime in the mid-twentieth century BC, narrates how an Egyptian court official named Sinuhe flees Egypt for political reasons. (Arnold and Beyer, RANE, 77)

Then I made my way northward. I reached the Walls of the Ruler, which were made to repel the Asiatics and to crush the Sand-farers. I crouched in a bush for fear of being seen by the guard on duty upon the wall. (Lichtheim, AEL, 224)

d. Beni Hasan

The famous Beni Hasan scene and inscriptions offer a report of thirty-seven Asiatics brought to Egypt for commercial reasons. (Hoffmeier, IE, 61) They are brought to Egypt by Abi-sha, "an obviously Semitic name." (Muhlestein, LTE, 205)

e. Summary of Textual Evidence

Not only do these texts reflect the very real presence of Semites in Egypt but also that they posed a problem in the land. Pastoralists (sometimes with permission and other times without it) were regularly trying to enter Egypt to graze and water sheep. (Hoffmeier, EWN, 53)

2. Archaeological Evidence

A surprising amount of archaeological evidence for pastoralists in Egypt has been uncovered. Biblical scholar Carol Meyers describes how clear and widely accepted it is:

Information about intermittent movements by Asiatics into Egypt is plentiful for nearly all periods of Egyptian history, from the fourth millennium onward. However, in the second half of the second millennium BCE, when Egypt exercised hegemonic control of Syria-Palestine, substantial numbers of people from western Asia found themselves in Egypt. Many were brought there as slaves, captured by Egypt's frequent military expeditions into the southern Levant and beyond. (Meyers, ENCBC, 8)

a. The Memphis and Karnak Stelae

Among the proofs for significant Semitic movement to Egypt is the Memphis and Karnak Stelae of Amenhotep II, which describes many of the king's athletic and military achievements, including carrying more than 100,000 Asiatics back to Egypt, though the numbers may be hyperbolic. (Hoffmeier, MKSA, 22)

b. Pottery and Weapons

Hoffmeier gives some more specific archaeological evidence that helps to confirm what is found in the textual evidence:

> In the Wadi Tumilat, the sites of Tell el-Maskhuta and Tel el-Retabeh have yielded signs of Middle Bronze Age Syro-Canaanite presence, including burials with pottery and weapons from the Levant. In the east Nile Delta, Tell el-Yehudiyeh was the first site to yield the presence of settling Asiatics. Nineteenth-century excavations conducted by Edouard Naville and then Flinders Petrie produced what appears to have been a Middle Bronze era defense system. Syro-Canaanite remains from the Second Intermediate period have been discovered at other Nile Delta sites such as Inshas, Tell Farasha, and Tell el-Kebir, but the most important site is Tell el-Dab'a. This latter site has been investigated by Manfred Bietak of the University of Vienna regularly since 1966, and it is the long-sought capital of

the Hyksos, Avaris, mentioned in Josephus's quotation of Manetho (Ag. Ap. 1.78). Avaris was a major urban center, with Levantine-type tombs, pottery, and architecture. (Hoffmeier, EWN, 54)

The Hyksos were a Semitic people who entered Egypt around 1750 BC and established significant political and military power based in Avaris. The Hyksos were expelled from Egypt in c. 1570 BC, though their reign shows there were Semitic people in Egypt for many years. Though there is no clear archaeological link, the Hebrews could have been living alongside or under the rule of the Hyksos. Walter Kaiser attempts to make a connection and says the Hebrews could have been left behind when the Hyksos were expelled because, as objects of Hyksos oppression, they would have been seen as a separate people. (Kaiser, HI, 79–82)

c. Ancient Script

In 1999 writing was discovered in Egypt that is likely the earliest known piece of alphabetic writing:

> Carved in the cliffs of soft stone, the writing, in a Semitic script with Egyptian influences, has been dated to somewhere between 1900 and 1800 BC, two or three centuries earlier than previously recognized uses of a nascent alphabet. The first experiments with alphabet thus appeared to be the work of Semitic people living deep in Egypt, not in their homelands in the Syria-Palestine region, as had been thought. (Wilford, FEDAEE, website)

Scholars who affirm the historicity of the exodus generally fall into one of two camps regarding when the exodus actually happened: early (fifteenth century BC) or late (thirteenth century BC). We discuss this in more detail later in the chapter, but we must note here that this ancient script reflects the fact that Semitic people were living in Egypt long before either the late or early dates for the exodus.

d. Raamses

The Bible mentions several Egyptian cities in its exodus narratives in Exodus and Numbers. Many of these cities have been discovered with a high degree of confidence by archaeologists, and there is evidence of Asiatics living in at least one of them, Raamses. Those who hold to the late date for the exodus see this as highly significant.

Exodus 1:11 says Raamses (or Rameses) was a city that the Israelites helped to build while slaves in Egypt, and Exodus 12:37 and Numbers 33:5 say this was the first city the Hebrews left during the exodus. After much archaeological back and forth, "widely accepted today is the belief that Rameses is located at Qantir (Tell el-Dab'a), about seventeen miles southwest of Tanis. Excavations of the site in the last twenty-five years have confirmed that identification." (Currid, AEOT, 127)

William Hallo and William Simpson conclude:

> The non-Egyptian pottery and grave goods are identical to those of the Middle Bronze Age in Palestine. Archaeologically it is as if the site were actually in Palestine. (Hallo and Simpson, ANE, 251)

Hoffmeier concurs:

> The domestic and religious architecture, burial traditions, ceramics, and bronzes all show strong connections to the Levant [lands in and around the Eastern Mediterranean], although there was increased Egyptianization of the pottery as time went on. (Hoffmeier, IE, 63)

e. Summary of Archaeological Evidence

While this archaeological evidence shows that pastoralists lived in Egypt, that doesn't mean we can clearly tell which were Hebrew and which were not—or even if any of them were Hebrew at all. There were many different nomadic populations, and sorting them out may be impossible. (Hawkins, HIBP, 73–74)

However, our goal has been to show that Israelites living in Egypt is plausible, and we have found that these inscriptions and details from archaeological digs show people *like* those described in the book of Exodus did in fact live in Egypt.

C. The Plagues

Exodus 7–12 details the ten plagues Yahweh brought upon Egypt that resulted in the exodus of the Hebrews from the land. These plagues involved animals, pests, and natural wonders. Is the story, as detailed in Exodus, reliable? Modern scholars have sought to explain the account of the plagues in a variety of ways.

1. Literary Creation

Some, including John Van Seters, believe the plague accounts are the "literary creation" of a later author:

> Consequently, there is no mystery about the form and history of the plagues tradition. The Yahwist created it by expanding the very general statements in Deuteronomy about God's judgments upon Egypt in order to construct a prophetic narrative in which the judgments were a series of curses separately invoked and enacted until the final judgment led to the people's release. In other words, the plagues narrative is a literary creation by the Yahwist that made use of the varied traditions of Hebrew prophecy, both the legends and the classical prophets, as well as the common Near

Eastern and biblical curse tradition. There is no primary and secondary material, no ancient oral tradition behind the text. The plagues narrative did not exist as a specific tradition before the Yahwist's work and is, therefore, no older than the exilic period. (Van Seters, PE, 38)

For a response to this claim by Van Seters, please see chapter 4 on the transmission of the Old Testament and chapter 23 on the composition of the Pentateuch.

2. Natural Causes

Other scholars believe a naturalistic phenomenon might have been behind the plagues. While not discounting a supernatural cause, Hoffmeier believes what is known about Egypt makes it reasonable to conclude that God could have timed the occurrence of natural disasters to cause at least some of the plagues:

Some have theorized that the first plague—in which the Nile turns blood red—is associated with the presence of microscopic flagellates in the water that account for the colour. This phenomenon is associated with the annual inundation of the Nile that begins in August, crests in September and ends in October. These microbes consume large amounts of oxygen from the water which results in fish dying and causes a rank smell, rendering the water undrinkable as described in the Bible (Exodus 7:21). If indeed a contaminated annual flood marked the beginning of the plagues, which would have begun in the period of August to October, and since the Passover is observed in the period March-April (that is, seven to nine months later), the ninth plague—three days of darkness—might have been caused by a severe dust storm or *khamsin*. Such dust storms can still blanket Egypt for

days at a time during the months of March and April. They even darken the sun, and fine dust covers everything. This scenario for the ninth plague certainly fits the description that it was "a darkness to be felt" (Exodus 10:21). By using the forces of nature against Egypt, the God of Israel demonstrated his superiority over the gods of Egypt and over Pharaoh, who was responsible for maintaining cosmic order in the land. (Hoffmeier, AB, 54)

Some parallels have been found between the Exodus account of the plagues and the ancient Ipuwer Papyrus. (Rohl, EMH, 150–152) There are two compelling parallels worth mentioning.

Parallel #1. The Exodus account of Moses pouring water from the Nile on the ground and the river turning to blood (Ex. 4:9; 7:20, 21) compared to Ipuwer: "Behold, Egypt has fallen to the pouring water. And he who poured water on the ground seizes the mighty in misery. The river is blood! As you drink of it you lose your humanity and thirst for water."

Parallel #2. The Exodus account of darkness covering the land (Ex. 10:22) compared to Ipuwer: "Those who had shelter are now in the dark of the storm. The whole of the delta cannot be seen."

The Ipuwer Papyrus is widely believed to have been written long before the early or late dates for the exodus, likely between 2134–2040 BC. (Bunson, AI, 13) Therefore, most Egyptologists do not believe it describes the historical exodus. However, even scholars skeptical of both the exodus account and the relevance of the Ipuwer Papyrus to it admit similarities in the descriptions. (Enmarch, RMEP, 173–175) Times of significant plagues were not completely unknown in ancient Egypt. With this background information, it makes sense that at least some of the plagues could have been of the kind described in Exodus.

3. Death of the Firstborn

Coming from the perspective of an early date for the exodus, John Sailhamer believes there is a clue that the deaths of a large number of men in Egypt happened during the reign of Amenhotep II (Amenophis II):

> In the reign of Amenophis II, Thutmosis' successor, however, Egyptian military power seems to have suffered a considerable setback. This pharaoh launched only two military campaigns in his life. During his reign, Egypt's borders receded from the Euphrates River to well within the confines of the land of Canaan. The significance of such a drastic reversal of military power may well have been the effect of the events of the Exodus, particularly the loss of a large portion of the Egyptian strike force in the waters of the Red Sea. Another possible indication of the events of the Exodus can be seen in a curious inscription set up in front of the famous Sphinx. In the inscription, Thutmosis IV, the son and successor of Amenophis II, tells of a promise made to him by the Sphinx. In a dream as a young man, the Sphinx promised to give the kingship to Thutmosis IV, suggesting that Thutmosis IV did not have a natural claim to the throne; he had to appeal to a divine promise. Perhaps Thutmosis IV was not the heir apparent because of the death of an elder brother. If that were the case, it would accord well with the biblical account of the death of the firstborn son of the pharaoh of the Exodus. (Sailhamer, BA, 50–51)

D. The Exodus

Even if we are able to show it is plausible that Israelites lived in Egypt and several disasters happened, a further question about the exodus of the Hebrews is this: Do the details of the Israelite departure from Egypt, such as the sheer number of people leaving at once and the route that they follow, point to a possible event?

1. Number

The sheer number of people reported in the biblical account may make it seem impossible for such a massive migration to have occurred. Indeed, there is a solid argument to be made after examining archaeological and ancient textual evidence that the large numbers used in many places in the Bible (including the exodus account) are merely hyperbole. (Fouts, DHILNOT, 377–387) If these large numbers are hyperbolic, designed merely to reinforce the dramatic scope of the amazing actions of God, then this mass migration could have happened. Our understanding would then be that the biblical account presents a historical event while at the same time for emphasis it uses a literary device for the large number. Here is another example using this dramatic hyperbole: when the Israelites sing that as news of the exodus spreads, "all the inhabitants of Canaan have melted away . . . they are still as stone," their description dramatizes the fear of those who might become a threat to them. (Ex. 15:15, 16) With this interpretation, then, there is still a reasonable basis to believe the Hebrews did migrate en masse out of Egypt.

However, there are some who take the large numbers in the exodus account at face value, believing that such a massive exodus is not impossible. Richard Freund sees plausibility for the biblical exodus because of his research of modern migrations:

> If we uncritically look at the sheer numbers, 603,550 men plus their wives and children, this would be millions of people leaving in a single event. What makes it so difficult for scholars

and casual readers is the fact that this number of exiles would represent a large percentage of the entire Egyptian population of the time. It just seems too large to be possible. Of course, today we look at the nearly twelve million Mexicans who have come in small bands and waves over the border of the United States, many illegally, and see that the number while large is not unprecedented. In the most recent conflicts in the Middle East in the past half century, millions of refugees moved from one part of the Middle East to another in waves. In the 1980s to 1990s millions of Russian Jews left the former Soviet Union in what was described as an "Exodus." Yet even in modern Egyptian history, it is now accepted that the Hyksos, the rulers of Egypt for almost two centuries in antiquity, made a mass Exodus from Egypt, although there is little scientific evidence to support this Exodus. So why is the Hyksos Exodus more palatable than the Israelite Exodus? I think it is because there are no Hyksos to use this event in the modern period but the Israelite event may be viewed as having modern implications. (Freund, DTB, 53)

These recent and contemporary mass migrations add credibility to the numbers recorded in Exodus. In addition, Freund's final sentence in which he compares the possible agenda that may exist for modern historians in regard to Israelites—because people of that name continue to complicate modern politics, while the Hyksos do not exist as a contemporary rival—reminds us yet again that underlying presuppositions silently shape many arguments.

2. Route

Archaeologists almost universally believe a city discovered at Qantir is ancient Pi-Ramesses. (Hoffmeier, EWN, 61) This ancient royal residence would correspond to the biblical Rameses. If so, then this would mean Israel began the exodus from this city. From here, the most natural route seems like it would have been to head north via an already established road to Canaan:

> If one were traveling out of the northeast Nile Delta from the area of Pi-Ramesses and Avaris, that would be the route to take to get to Canaan. The road actually began at this point in the Nile Delta. Known as the "Way/s of Horus" in Egyptian texts, this route has long been called the "military highway" that stretched across north Sinai to Gaza, the entryway to Canaan. (Hoffmeier, EWN, 65)

But Israel did not take this most obvious route. Exodus 13:17 says, "When Pharaoh let the people go, God did not lead them by way of the land of the Philistines, although that was near" (ESV). Hoffmeier connects "the way of the land of the Philistines" with this northern route. (Hoffmeier, EWN, 65) Instead, Exodus 12:37 and Numbers 33:5 say the Hebrews left Rameses and camped at Succoth. Most archaeologists believe ancient Succoth has been located at Tell el-Maskhuta, southeast of Qantir or at least in the general area around it. (Kitchen, OROT, 258–259; Hoffmeier, IE, 120; Currid, AEOT, 130)

The reason God led Israel southeast instead of by the expected northern route is explained in Exodus 13:17: "For God said, 'Lest the people change their minds when they see war and return to Egypt'" (ESV). Archaeological discoveries have shown fortifications that lead researchers to conclude that following the northern road to Canaan would have indeed subjected Israel to war, which confirms the Exodus account of why they avoided it. (Hoffmeier, EWN, 65–69)

V. Dating the Exodus

A. The Challenge

Some scholars who believe the exodus tradition is authentic argue for a fifteenth century BC date (or "early date"). Others, who also believe the exodus really happened, argue for a thirteenth century BC date (or "late date"). While both camps believe the exodus actually happened, their methodologies differ, resulting in two different conclusions about when it happened. The time gap is significant, yet each camp has solid evidence upon which to base its conclusion. However, as we will see, this is an intramural debate that has limited impact on the most important aspect of our study.

B. The Case for an Early Date

In 1 Kings 6:1 we read, "In the four hundred and eightieth year after the people of Israel came out of the land of Egypt, in the fourth year of Solomon's reign over Israel, in the month of Ziv, which is the second month, he began to build the house of the LORD" (ESV). Merrill writes:

> The exodus occurred 480 years before the laying of the foundations of Solomon's temple. Solomon undertook the project in his fourth year, 966 BC, and so the exodus, according to normal hermeneutics and the objective appropriation of the chronological data of the narrative, took place in 1446. (Merrill, KP, 74)

Provan, Long, and Longman provide an additional biblical reference, which appears to provide support for the early date:

> This date seems to be generally supported by the reference in Judges 11:26 to the three hundred years before the time of Jephthah that the Israelites controlled the Transjordan

region now (in Jephthah's time) disputed by the Ammonites, and the dating is unproblematic in respect of other details of biblical chronology. (Provan et al., BHI, 183)

Kaiser sees Judges 11:26 as evidence that corroborates the information in 1 Kings 6:1:

> Thus, the case for the early date is not so weak as it has often been made out to be. It has some very strong claims to be considered as fully legitimate as any of its contenders have enjoyed in the past. (Kaiser, HI, 109)

An archaeological find supporting an early date is the Merneptah Stele, discovered in 1896 by Flinders Petrie. This monument details victories of the Egyptian Pharaoh Merneptah over forces in Libya and Canaan and includes the phrase, "Israel is laid waste." The Merneptah Stele is dated approximately 1210 BC. Ralph Hawkins explains the challenge for harmonizing the stele with the late date:

> This new data appeared to require that Israel had already been settled there [Canaan] by the end of the thirteenth century BCE Placing Israel in Canaan this early in the reign of Merneptah raised obstacles for his having been the pharaoh of the exodus. Israel obviously could not have left Egypt in the first year of Merneptah's reign, wandered in the wilderness for forty years, and then appeared in Canaan as a settled ethnic group in his fifth year. The radical reduction of the duration of the wilderness wandering that this would require presented an insurmountable obstacle for evangelicals. (Hawkins, HIBP, 49)

The 1446 date appears to be the result of a straightforward reading of the biblical text with some math thrown in. However, even Merrill, who holds to the early date, acknowledges:

> But for a variety of reasons this date is almost universally rejected in favor of a date sometime in the thirteenth century, generally about 1260. (Merrill, KP, 83)

C. The Case for a Late Date

Why the widespread rejection of the early date? First, the biblical evidence. Exodus 1:11 reads, "Therefore they set taskmasters over them to afflict them with their burdens. And they built for Pharaoh supply cities, Pithom and Raamses."

Hoffmeier explains the significance of this passage for the dating of the exodus:

> It is generally accepted that this Hebrew name is the writing for the Egyptian royal name Ramesses. Only Ramesses II (1279–1213 BC) built a city in the north-east Delta that he named after himself. Pi-Ramesses means "house or domain of Ramesses." For some, the reference to the city in Exodus 1:11 points to the reign of Ramesses as the period of the exodus and the forty-year sojourn in Sinai. (Hoffmeier, AB, 50)

Kitchen concludes confidently: "Thus, the occurrence of Raamses is an early (thirteenth/twelfth century) marker in the exodus tradition, and that fact must be accepted." (Kitchen, OROT, 256)

Other scholars see weaknesses in the conclusion. Kaiser writes:

> If the name Rameses is an allusion to Pharaoh Rameses II of the later nineteenth dynasty, who reigned from 1290–1224 BC (or 1279–1213), then Israel could not have left Egypt in the fifteenth century (1440 BC). However, it must be acknowledged that the name Rameses appears

in the Joseph story in Genesis 47:11 to describe the region in the Nile Delta where Jacob and his sons settled. No one dates the settlement of this area by Jacob and his sons to the thirteenth century BC, therefore Rameses is either a name being used retrospectively (just as later and better known names are applied to locales that originally bore other names, e.g. we often refer to regions in America by their present state names in discussing events that took place when Native Americans were the only inhabitants), or the name Rameses has a prior history to the pharaohs of the nineteenth dynasty. If either theory is true for Genesis 47:11, then it could also be true for Exodus 1:11. (Kaiser, OTD, 114)

The naming of the store city of Raamses is widely accepted as solid evidence by those who hold to a late date. How, then should the 1 Kings reference to "the four hundred and eightieth year," pointing toward an early date, be understood?

In order to harmonize the conflict between the findings of the Merneptah Stele and dating of the building of Pi-Ramesses with a literal reading of the biblical text, some scholars began reexamining the biblical material to see whether it required an early reading. John Bright sees the 480 figure of 1 Kings 6:1 as referring to generations, not literal years:

> Since, however, forty is a well-known round number, often for a generation (as the forty years of wilderness wandering), it is likely that this four hundred and eighty years is itself a round number for twelve generations. Actually, a generation (from birth of father to birth of son) is likely to be nearer twenty-five years, which would give us some three hundred years rather than four hundred and eighty, and a date for the exodus in the mid-thirteenth century. (Bright, HI, 123)

Hawkins argues scholars have not uniformly concluded that 480 years is even what the Bible actually presents:

> A literal reading of the numbers could produce a duration of 515 years from the exodus to the beginning of construction on the temple; D. I. Block reaches an aggregate total of 593 years; and [James] Hoffmeier tabulates 633 years. There was apparently confusion about the duration from the exodus to the beginning of construction on Solomon's temple in the ancient world as well. The LXX [the Septuagint, the ancient Greek Old Testament] records 440 years instead of 480 (1 Kgs 6:1). Josephus [the ancient Jewish historian] gives two different numbers for the period. In his *Antiquities* he reports the duration as covering 592 years, and in *Against Apion* he recounts it as 612 years. Surely the authors of the LXX were concerned to give the "scriptural" length of the period from the exodus to the founding of the temple! And surely Josephus did not want to be regarded as unreliable in his reporting. (Hawkins, HIBP, 51)

Hawkins does not eliminate the possibility of the 480-year span (which is necessary for the early date), but attempts to show it's not totally unambiguous.

As to the reference in Judges 11:26, where Jephthah gives a boastful challenge to the Ammonite king by summarizing his people's history in Canaan, Kitchen colorfully but confidently dismisses this verse as not attempting to present historical truth:

> Brave fellow that he was, Jephthah was a roughneck, an outcast. . . . What we have is nothing more than the report of a brave but ignorant man's bold bluster in favor of his people, not a mathematically precise chronological datum. So it can offer us no practical help. (Kitchen, OROT, 209)

In addition to the biblical evidence, archaeological evidence points to the late date. The Amarna letters were discovered in 1887 around two hundred miles south of Cairo. The site was the capital of Egypt during the reign of Pharaoh Amenophis IV in the fourteenth century BC. The collection consists of letters from Canaanite leaders to the Egyptian Pharaoh. It is important to note that in more than three hundred letters from several different leaders there is no clear mention of Israel. (Hawkins, HIBP, 67–70) Though this is an argument from silence, it is not unreasonable to assume if Israel was a significant presence in Canaan in the 1300s that some of these leaders would have mentioned them.

D. Conclusion Regarding the Date of the Exodus

Hoffmeier expresses the importance of remembering not to be preoccupied "with *when* the exodus occurred while the real issue being debated is *whether* it happened at all!" (Hoffmeier, WIBDE, 226) The arguments presented above show a conservative evangelical can certainly hold to either an early or late date. However, we must effectively show critics why we believe that there was a historical exodus regardless of when it happened. Without its central meaning—an account in real history of God's loving awareness of his people and his saving action on their behalf—much of the Bible also comes under attack.

VI. Concluding Remarks

As stated at the beginning of this chapter, we have not proven concretely that Moses existed, that Israel lived in Egypt, or that this group of Hebrews fled from Pharaoh. We have shown, however, that the historicity of the biblical narrative is plausible. It is likely a man such as Moses existed, a people such as Israel lived in Egypt, and these people left Egypt via the route detailed in the Bible.

In fact, even without the extrabiblical evidence there is enough contained in the Bible to make the story believable. John Bright notes the biblical data alone should be enough to clearly establish the presence of Israel in Egypt:

> Although there is no direct witness in Egyptian records to Israel's presence in Egypt, the Biblical tradition *a priori* demands belief: it is not the sort of tradition any people would invent! Here is no heroic epic of migration, but the recollection of shameful servitude from which only the power of God brought deliverance. (Bright, HI, 121)

Provan, Long, and Longman believe this is one reason why we can believe the biblical account has been transmitted accurately:

> Indeed, a clear indication of this retention is that the biblical tradition has as one of its central emphases—and though unflattering, it governs both Israelite religion and ethics— that Israel was in the beginning a slave people in Egypt. This does not look like the kind of tradition that a people invents about itself. (Provan et al., BHI, 80)

If it didn't happen, why tell such a humiliating story? "Nobody else in Near Eastern antiquity descended to that kind of tale of community beginnings." (Kitchen, OROT, 254) Baruch Halpern states:

> There is something behind the Israelite tradition . . . and this is true of the peasant revolt school or the conquest theory, and even the so-called archaeological approach to the conquest—the problem is that you wind up

with Israel with an Exodus tradition, a tradition of having been in bondage in Egypt. (Halpern, EE, 115)

Even critical scholar William Dever concedes, "I do think . . . that behind the literary tradition there must indeed be some sort of genuine historical memory; but it is unfortunately not accessible either to the text scholar or to the archaeologist." (Dever, HTCI, 31) In addition, scholar Anthony Frendo insists:

> Israel must have somehow (at least partially) come from outside Canaan in view of the multiple texts in the Old Testament which point in this direction. Why should the Old Testament authors have made this up? Should we not try harder to understand our texts in connection with the results of good archaeology, rather than superficially to dismiss the former? (Frendo, BB, 42)

Moreover, if the exodus happened, someone like Moses had to lead it. Kitchen, one of the world's leading Egyptologists, says plainly:

> In short, to explain what exists in our Hebrew texts, we need a Hebrew leader who had had an experience of life at the Egyptian court . . . including knowledge of treaty type documents and their format as well as of traditional Semitic legal social usage more familiar to his own folk. In other words, somebody distressingly like that old "hero" of biblical tradition, Moses, is badly needed to make sense of the situation as we have it. Or somebody in his position of the same or another name. (Kitchen, OROT, 295)

Finally, we conclude our discussion in agreement with Alan Millard of the University of Liverpool:

The history of religions, literary criticism and other forms of study applied to the Hebrew books has led to a variety of hypotheses about the story. On one view, a small group escaped from Egypt and joined related tribes in Canaan or a separate group (the Kenites), who worshipped Yahweh at Sinai, introduced their religion to tribes in Canaan and "converted" them; or, a variety of folk-stories have been woven together, with little or no historical basis; or there was no Exodus and the whole is a pious fiction. Lacking any trace of Joseph, Moses, or Israelites in Egypt, many have concluded they were never there. Yet no pharaoh would boast of the loss of his labour force on a monument, and administrative records on papyrus, leather or wooden tablets which might have registered such events would perish rapidly in the Delta's damp soil. It is equally unlikely that a camping crowd would leave recognizable remains from a semi-nomadic life in the Sinai Wilderness and in Transjordan. The absence of evidence is not, therefore, evidence of absence! (Millard, *Exodus*, 112)

CHAPTER 20

THE HISTORICITY OF THE CONQUEST

OVERVIEW

I. Introduction

The biblical accounts in Joshua and Judges tell the story of how, after the exodus from Egypt, the Israelites came to possess the promised land of Canaan. Naturally, much of modern archaeology in the area has focused on finding biblical sites and confirming Bible narratives, as the Bible is the primary source of information about this area during the Late Bronze Age (c. 1550–1200 BC).

A. Early Scholarship

Early scholars excavating the Holy Land in the late nineteenth and early twentieth century AD found what they believed was strong support for a number of biblical sites. In the 1930s and 1940s, archeological surveys led by William F. Albright, the early pioneer of biblical archaeology, confirmed a number of sites with evidence of destruction dating to the thirteenth century BC, leading him to write, "The progress of excavation and of philological interpretation of inscriptions has made it absolutely certain, in the writer's judgement, that the principal phase of the Conquest must be dated in the second half of the thirteenth century." (Albright, BPAE, 27)

B. Later Scholarship

Later studies with more advanced research and dating techniques have called some of these earlier conclusions into question. Excavations have found more modest populations and fewer sites of epic destruction than expected. These findings have led some scholars—who expected to find a heavily populated Canaan and areas of widespread destruction during this era—to question the historical accuracy of biblical conquest accounts and the rise of Israel as a people.

This skeptical view is explained by Canaanite scholar and professor of Jewish history at Tel Aviv University, Nadav Na'aman, who concluded that the biblical account is not supported by "the new archaeological surveys and excavations, which indicate that the hill country was sparsely inhabited in the Late Bronze Age and that no military power prevented pastoral groups from penetrating it and settling in its large uninhabited areas." Na'aman goes on to state, "It is commonly accepted today that the majority of the conquest stories in the Book of Joshua are devoid of historical reality." (Na'aman, CCBJH, 347)

C. The Emergence of Israel

Yet it is clear that during this period, a unified Israel did in fact emerge. "That Israel did eventually exist as a community of some sort in Palestine is taken for granted by most historians of ancient Israel. Furthermore, most historians believe that the meaningful genesis of this community in Palestine took place in the Late Bronze and Early Iron Ages (ca. 1200)." (Moore and Kelle, BHIP, 96)

Tracing the history of Israel has a number of complications. As Lawson Stone, professor of the Old Testament at Asbury Theological Seminary, states, "A comprehensive proposal would need to explain not only how an ethnic group calling itself 'Israel' came to claim possession of Canaan and evolve into a monarchic state that would last for centuries but also how it ultimately produced the Hebrew Scriptures and birthed three world religions." (Stone, EIIAC, 131) While no comprehensive theory currently explains all the data and nuances, an analysis of the major theories, along with a review of the available information at hand, can begin to fill in some of the picture of how Israel developed.

As we shall discover by examining the evidence, Israel emerged as a people who occupied the land of Canaan during this period, laying the societal groundwork conducive to the subsequent development of a ruling monarchy. In this chapter we explore how the biblical account of this process aligns with modern archaeological research and what that archaeological research shows us about the development of the people of Israel.

II. Challenges in Determining the Historicity of Joshua and Judges

A. Writing Did Not Emerge in Israel Until the Tenth Century BC

The study of Canaan during the Late Bronze Age is complicated by the lack of written records. The Egyptians kept written records prior to and during this period; however, their influence in this area was declining, and little is reported. Writings have been discovered from the Canaanite city-states in this region from the Middle Bronze Age (a period prior to the conquest, c. 1500) such as the Amarna letters from the fourteenth century BC. (Moore and Kelle,

BHIP, 110) However, with the urban decline of the area and movement to a more pastoral society, the art of writing was lost in this area during the Late Bronze and Early Iron Ages. This leads Na'aman to conclude that the development of Israel and the conquest of Canaan occurred in pre-history:

> It was only in the eighth-seventh centuries BCE that Israel entered into the realm of history, when literacy spread in the kingdom of Israel and Judah and the earliest works of the history of Israel were composed. The "Conquest Period" should be included in the prehistory of Israel; the immense problems involved with the historical investigation of the conquest narratives are the direct result of this literary situation. (Na'aman, CCBJH, 329)

Ralph K. Hawkins, associate professor of religious studies at Averett University with a PhD in Near Eastern archaeology, describes as a dark age these late Bronze and early Iron Ages when population, urban centers, and Egyptian influence all went into decline:

> By the time that historical data begins to become available again, in about the tenth century BCE, the Eastern Mediterranean world had undergone a great deal of change. . . . The inhabitants of the region differed from those who had inhabited it two hundred to three hundred years earlier, and the two periods are separated by a Dark Age, making it difficult to determine how the transition occurred. (Hawkins, HIBP, 84)

While the lack of written records is problematic, it is not unusual. Na'aman concludes,

> The line between prehistory and history is demarcated by the availability of written sources, not by the actual settlement process.

There are many peoples who settled in their countries for hundreds of years and established states and institutions, but left no records, so that their history is entirely obscure. (Na'aman, CCBJH, 329)

Scholars commonly affirm that the events of the conquest and formation of Israel would have occurred sometime in the Late Bronze Age/Early Iron Age between 1450 and 1100 BC. However, this history was preserved through oral tradition until the story was put into written form a few hundred years later. This gap between the conquest events and the development of written histories has led to some skepticism of the biblical account, and Na'aman believes "we must treat it with caution and may question the historical reliability of many of its details." (Na'aman, CCBJH, 330)

In the absence of an extrabiblical written history, the historical accuracy of Bible as it relates to the conquest of Canaan and development of the Israelite people must be pieced together from the Bible itself, a small sample of external writings, and archaeological evidence. We examine each of these streams of evidence, keeping in mind the comments of Alan R. Millard, professor of Hebrew and ancient Semitic languages at the University of Liverpool: "Two principal sources of information are available for exploring the early history of Israel: the written records and the archaeological remains. Each is subject to interpretation, and each has yielded many different interpretations." (Millard, WIRC, 158)

B. The Primary Purpose of the Biblical Accounts

Some of the controversy surrounding the accuracy of the biblical accounts can be attributed to their interpretation or, often, misinterpretation. It is best to start with an understanding of what the Bible specifically says and how we perceive its message through our modern-day expectations. Stories of the conquest fire up the imagination. It isn't difficult to imagine a massive conquering army marching through Holy Land, leaving Canaanite destruction in its wake. But a more thorough reading shows that "the biblical texts themselves reveal a more complex account of Israel's arrival in Canaan than usually is admitted. It shows that the standard picture often is a caricature." (Stone, EIIAC, 135)

So what was the purpose of these early accounts of Israel? While historical in nature, the primary purpose of Joshua and Judges was not to capture a dispassionate record of events similar to a modern-day history book. The modern use of textbooks and reference works may lead us to expect that any record of historical events necessarily was written primarily to document precise facts, sequences, or causes. But this assumption about the writing of history arose only in the nineteenth century and may misdirect our attention or mislead us to the wrong conclusions. As Hawkins, states, "Joshua is historical in nature; however, it utilizes its historical material *primarily for the purpose of preaching*, not for writing an exhaustive, secular history that explains Israel's appearance in the land of Canaan, with all its sociological, domestic, economic, and agricultural details." (Hawkins, HIBP, 23) Hawkins continues,

The author of the book of Joshua is not trying to write a comprehensive, secular history of the process by which Israel entered into the land. He does not discuss what kinds of villages they

established when they entered the land, how they ordered their domestic lives, what kinds of pottery they used, what sort of house structure they used, or any of these other kinds of details. These are the kinds of facts, however, for which historians and archaeologists are searching in the gaps, and their absence from the book of Joshua suggests that the historiographer's interests were other than producing a scientific-historical reconstruction of the appearance of Israel in Canaan. (Hawkins, HIBP, 21)

Hawkins concludes that in Joshua, "activities are religious in nature, not military. Battles are recounted in the book of Joshua, but compared to the overall mass of religious events recorded, they are few in number." (Hawkins, HIBP, 22) In fact, the book of Joshua only describes three cities as having been burned: Jericho, Ai, and Hazor. (Hawkins, HIBP, 34) This undermines the position of skeptics who claim that the lack of archaeological evidence for widespread destruction detracts from the credibility of the biblical accounts.

C. Late Bronze Age/Early Iron Age Overview of Canaan

In the Old Testament, the land of Canaan is also referred to as the promised land: "In general, the geographical term denotes the traditional boundaries of the promised land, from a line between the southern tip of the Dead Sea to the 'Brook of Egypt' (i.e., the Wadi al 'Arish) to as far north as the city of Dan. . . . As named in the Bible, the occupants of 'Cannaan' [sic] are diverse, including Amorites, Perizzites, Hivites, Jebusites, and, of course, Canaanites." (Stone, EIIAC, 128)*

The period of Israel's emergence from 1500–1200 BC was marked by great upheaval

---

* The term "Canaanites" can refer to a particular people group, as well as to the collective population of Canaan prior to and during the conquest.

in the entire Mediterranean region, which historians have termed "the catastrophe" or "the great collapse." (Stone, EIIAC, 139) Na'aman found "indications that the transition from Middle Bronze Age III to Late Bronze Age II was marked by a drastic decline in the population." (Na'aman, CCBJH, 331)

While scholars propose a number of potential elements explaining the collapse, historians nevertheless agree that famine played a prominent role. "The Mesopotamian documents indicate that an enormous population displacement was taking place as a result of the destruction of the urban culture in vast areas of Hither Asia." (Na'aman, CCBJH, 335) According to Na'aman,

> Famine played an important role in the large-scale migrations of late thirteenth-twelfth centuries BCE. Documents from Hattusha, Ugarit, and Egypt indicate severe food shortage in the closing decades of the Hittite empire, culminating in a disastrous famine. . . . Further evidence of drought and severe famine in the eleventh century appears in Assyrian and Babylonian sources. . . . Remarkable in these documents is the concentration of natural catastrophes that caused severe food shortages, obliging pastoral groups to obtain food supplies by raids on the settled areas. (Na'aman, CCBJH, 340–341)

Hawkins sums up the region-wide impact of this turmoil:

> The great states lost much of their power and some disappeared completely. The level of economic activity sharply declined. As a result, culture declined, and there is little in the way of building remains, art or even texts to illuminate this period. There was minimal urbanization during this period, and many people either lived in villages or migrated with their herds. New arrivals gained political power, including the Libyans in Egypt, Arameans in Syria and Mesopotamia, Persians in western Iran, Philistines and Israelites in Palestine, and others. (Hawkins, HIBP, 84)

In the midst of these changes, the Israelites emerged as a people. Many of the large urban centers we visualize from traditional interpretations of the Bible were more likely groups of nomads and less fortified cities. As respected archaeologist Kathleen Kenyon reports, "There is no firm evidence of urban occupation [around Edom, Moab, and Ammon] until about the ninth century BC and an even later date might eventually emerge." (Kenyon, BRA, 33)

Na'aman sees this lack of population as evidence against the biblical accounts. (Na'aman, CCBJH, 348) However, as Kenyon points out, "The Exodus group under Moses was therefore not diverted by urban-based kingdoms; but they could equally well have been blocked by a strong tribal-nomadic group. The archaeological evidence for towns in Transjordan is therefore irrelevant." (Kenyon, BRA, 33)

While we want to look for historical clues in the places, activities, and events of the Bible, extra care must be taken not to fill in the gaps with modern prejudices or expansive assumptions. For example, sites like Jericho and Ai were referred to as cities. However, in that era, a city could have been a large settlement, a smaller outpost, or even a tent village or military encampment. When a city was referred to as great, it could have meant strategic importance or military presence, not necessarily size. (Hawkins, HIBP, 110–111) It is important therefore not to set expectations based upon our current perceptions, but attempt to understand what the writer was trying to say.

D. The Earliest Origins of Israel

The first extrabiblical reference to Israel is the Merneptah Stele, an Egyptian monument that speaks of battle victories. The inscription is a "victory hymn, which describes Pharaoh Merneptah's conquests, including the first historical reference to Israel." In the Merneptah Stele, Israel is included among a list of peoples who were conquered around 1210 BC. (Moore and Kelle, BHIP, 110)

"Most readers infer from this that in Merneptah's perception, Israel is present in Canaan, identifiable as a 'people,' not associated with urban centers and not in sufficient control of the land, or at least not in control long enough to have rated a geographic determinative." (Stone, EIIAC, 142) Interestingly, in addition to listing them among the conquests, Pharaoh made a point to add that "their seed is not," indicating that the Israelites were annihilated. "Thus among all the peoples and towns of Canaan, Merneptah felt it necessary to affirm that he had totally annihilated one particular people group, the one named, 'Israel.' One can only speculate why the pharaoh felt compelled to report publically, in this monumental inscription, that he had annihilated Israel." (Stone, EIIAC, 142)

There are two other potential references to Israel that appear in Egypt during this period. One is from a fragmentary inscription from a column base from the period of Ramses II. According to Stone, the fragment

features captive lists in which Ashkelon and Canaan are followed by a broken name-ring which can plausibly be restored as "Israel" once the archaizing spelling tendencies of such inscriptions is accounted for. Lastly, notice should be taken of two captive lists found on column bases at the Soleb temple of Amenhotep III (1390–1352) and a copy at

the Amarah West temple of Ramesses II. Both identify one captive group as "Yhw'" (in) the land of the Shasu. While the name "Yhw'" might be a place name, it represents exactly the way the Hebrew divine name would appear in hieroglyphic. (Stone, EIIAC, 142–143)

Stone concludes, "If these connections stand, then allusions to Israel or Yahweh may be pushed back at least to the time of Ramesses II if not much earlier, to the pre-Amarna period," prior to 1350 BC. (Stone, EIIAC, 143)

Clearly, during the Late Bronze Age and Early Iron age, the land of Canaan underwent a fundamental change with the decline of urban centers and shift to a more pastoral society. Against this backdrop, we look at three different theories of how the Israelites came to possess the promised land.

III. Theories of the Israelite Settlement in Canaan

A. Conquest Theory

1. History of the Conquest Theory

The traditional view of the conquest is of Joshua and a large Israelite army marching through and conquering Canaan in a single campaign, leaving a large swath of destruction in its wake. "The Conquest Model is built on the idea that the settlement of the Israelite tribes in the land of Canaan was a process that was undertaken primarily through violent warfare. It has conventionally been thought of as following the biblical account most closely." (Hawkins, HIBP, 30)

This was the prevalent model through much of the twentieth century and was strongly supported by Albright. His theory essentially followed the biblical story of the Pentateuch and Joshua, which he believed was based on underlying history. After having left Egypt in an exodus event, the Israelites migrated through the desert and ultimately invaded Canaan from the east. Albright believed that the invading Israelites were ethnically and religiously distinct from the indigenous populations of Canaan. (Hawkins, HIBP, 30)

This theory has been questioned more recently as archaeological excavations have failed to find large settlements throughout certain areas of Canaan during the proposed conquest periods. Sites traditionally identified at Jericho and Ai have posed problems because little hard evidence has been found that these sites were occupied during the time of the conquest.

This absence of conclusive archaeological evidence has led some scholars to conjecture that much of the conquest story is myth. Na'aman proposes instead that "the author borrowed the military outlines from concrete events that had taken place in the history of Israel." (Na'aman, CCBJH, 348)

2. Actual Level of Destruction Defined

In his book *Who Were the Early Israelites and Where Did They Come From?*, William Dever, professor emeritus of Near Eastern archaeology and anthropology at the University of Arizona in Tucson, points to thirty-one different sites west of the Jordan River that were called out in the book of Joshua, their proposed locations, and the current archaeological findings at those sites. Based upon his analysis of the lack of population and destruction, he concludes that "we now must confront many 'ugly facts that kill the elegant theories' regarding Israelite settlement in Canaan west of the Jordan River." (Dever, WWEI, 54–57)

But have we interpreted Joshua correctly? The conquest model implies a large invasion force marching through the land destroying cities in its wake. But a careful reading of Joshua actually points to a more modest military campaign. "Indeed, Joshua does claim that cities were taken and kings killed, but only three cities—Jericho, Ai, and Hazor—are specifically claimed to have been burned. Charts listing 'destruction layers' suffer from the same kind of simplistic reading of the data that undermined the Conquest Theory." (Hawkins, HIBP, 34) So, an archaeologist looking for many sites of massive destruction would be sorely disappointed. In fact, it would make sense to avoid the wholesale destruction of most cities, "because an incoming people could make use of existing buildings for themselves, just as the Israelites would take advantage of the produce of Canaan once they had crossed the Jordan." (Millard, WIRC, 161)

That doesn't mean the Israelites could necessarily have taken the land without some military action, however. Many scholars hold that the early Israelites were involved in warfare, even if there is dispute about the extent and location of the campaigns. As Megan Bishop Moore and Brad E. Kelle state in their book *Biblical History and Israel's Past*, "A variety of scholars, conservative and mainstream, hold on to the possibility that early Israel was involved in military action, and that part of its identity was formed by joint warfare. The archaeological evidence discussed here is part of the basis for these assumptions, but the biblical memory of Israel as a military entity early on seems to be equally compelling to scholars." (Moore and Kelle, BHIP, 129) It is also important to note that "the first extrabiblical record of Israel, the Merneptah Stela, also is a war text." (Moore and Kelle, BHIP, 129)

Stone points out,

Despite current scholarly prejudice against "conquest" models, it is difficult to imagine any people group establishing a claim over Canaan, the scene of constant military clashes for the entire LBA [Late Bronze Age], without any acts of warfare against the urban centers that controlled Canaan on behalf of Egypt. How could a group's putative annihilation merit notice in the inscription of an Egyptian Pharaoh, Merneptah, if this group posed no formidable threat? In fact, urban destruction wrought by unforeseen "barbarian" groups conspicuously characterizes the end of the LBA throughout the eastern Mediterranean. (Stone, EIIAC, 158)

Stone goes on to argue that extrabiblical sources describe these Late Bronze Age clashes in rather stylized, heroic terms:

The rhetoric of extreme destruction and annihilation of all life likely reflects the fixed idioms of ancient military jargon. K. Lawson Younger Jr., both in a monograph and in a focused study, has pointed out the pervasive use of a very stilted and stereotypical military language that should not be pressed in all its literal detail. In essence, any decisive victory finds expression in the most extreme language of annihilation, even if followed almost immediately by statements of the tributes to be levied on the (presumed dead!) population. . . . Most of the urban centers destroyed in the LBA seemed to have been abandoned before their final capture and destruction. To make archaeological traces of near-apocalyptic destruction the standard for demonstrating the historicity of the Joshua narratives is to misunderstand the texts from their literary, theological, and historical perspectives. (Stone, EIIAC, 159–160)

The massive population decline and disrepair of the cities would have made the Israelites' military campaigns much easier. As Na'aman points out,

The almost total lack of new fortification projects in Late Bronze Canaan was the direct result of the shortage of human resources. We may recall that nomads were liable for public works, at least in return for food and salary. Thus, the lack of fortification works supports the claim of a drastic reduction in the overall population of Canaan—including the nomadic sector—during the Late Bronze Age. (Na'aman, CCBJH, 332)

Instead of conquest and annihilation, Joshua's campaigns seem to have served a more strategic military and security function.

Conquest is not a term used in the biblical narrative, but rather is of modern manufacture. If the objective of the military action was to kill the city rulers, thus breaking up Egypt's administration of Canaan and possibly preventing reprisals from those cities at Egypt's behest, then it is impressive that most of the cities engaged form two "belts," one to the south and one to the north of the main area of Israelite settlement, in which no fighting is reported.

The battles reported in Joshua could be seen as two campaigns aimed primarily at neutralizing the ability of the city rulers to act against the new settlers. Certainly the book of Joshua reports the opposition to Israelite presence (cf. 5:1; 9:1; 10:1–5; 11:1–5; 19). The two campaigns in effect created a ring of fire, or firewall, protecting the new hill-country settlements. With the destruction of Jericho and Ai, and with the alliance with Gibeon, these campaigns gave Israel control over important segments of the highway network in Canaan. (Stone, EIIAC, 162–163)

3. Purpose of the Military Stories in Joshua

It is also important to understand that the primary purpose of including these military campaigns in the Bible was not to laud Israelite military might, but to show God's faithfulness. "David Merling has recently made the case that the few accounts of military victories in the book of Joshua have a special function, which is to serve as 'confirmation events.' These events testify to what God could and would do if Israel were faithful to the covenant and if they carried through with the conquest of Canaan." (Hawkins, HIBP, 22)

When reviewing the archaeological evidence, it is also important to remember that the conquest of Canaan was only partially complete. Several biblical references including Joshua 13:1 and Judges 2:2, 3 make it clear that many lands remained unconquered, and foreign peoples remained.

Clearly, some warfare would have been required to take strategic areas of Canaan, but, outside of a few specific examples, this warfare would not have necessitated the widespread destruction that would leave a significant archaeological footprint. So the conquest model, while containing elements of truth both biblically and archaeologically, ultimately fails as a complete theory because of its absolute reliance on the military element in the establishment of Israel. The ultimate process was much more complex, as we see in the two other theories.

B. Peaceful Infiltration Model

1. History of the Peaceful Integration Model

The second theory of Israel's development doesn't involve military conflict, but points to the migration and settlement of nomadic tribes in Canaan. This model is summarized by Professor William Dever, distinguished professor of Near Eastern archaeology at Lycoming College in Pennsylvania:

In the 1920s and 1930s leading German biblical scholars such as Albrecht Alt and Martin Noth put forward what soon became known as the "peaceful infiltration" model.

It comprised two elements. The first was the biblical tradition of Israel's ancestors as mobile, tent-dwelling shepherds, as recalled vividly in the Genesis narratives. The second was modern ethnographic studies of the sedentarization of Middle Eastern pastoral nomads, which documented that for millennia tribal peoples in this part of the world had migrated over long distances, but that many had eventually settled down to become peasant farmers or townspeople.

According to the peaceful infiltration model, those who settled the highlands of Canaan, or western Palestine, in the 13th–12th centuries BC had originally been nomadic tribespeople of the semi-arid regions of Transjordan. Crossing the Jordan River on their annual trek in search of pasture and water, some of them had stayed on longer and longer each season in the cooler, well-watered, fertile hill country. Eventually they settled there and emerged in the light of written history as the biblical "Israelites." (Dever, WWEI, 50)

As Alt states,

The outward details of the immigration of the Israelites into Palestine were completely different; this was no single movement completed in a relatively short time. . . . It was in fact a series of movements by single tribes and bands which may well have lasted for several centuries; and in the majority of cases they did not proceed by force of arms, so that although the accounts of individual military victories over older towns may well be correct, they insulated themselves into thinly populated or even totally unpopulated districts where there was no chance of serious opposition. (Alt, EOTHR, 175)

This pattern of invasion led to what Alt described as an "incomplete settlement" that led to "several groups, whose lands were separated from one another by chains of non-Israelite townships." (Alt, EOTHR, 175) Alt's theory extends to the time beyond the book of Joshua and describes the type of behavior we would expect during the time of Judges.

Alt further hypothesized that a second stage of settlement occurred late in the Iron Age I, in which the Israelites undertook military action in order to expand their territory. In this stage, which corresponds with the descriptions in the book of Judges, individual tribes waged battles over the land. As the settlements increased in number, occasional battles broke out between the new Israelites and the Canaanites. As the cities declined and the Egyptian empire lost its grip on Canaan, the Israelite settlers gradually became the dominant force in the land. (Hawkins, HIBP, 37)

2. Archaeological Evidence for External Settlers

Archaeology continues to find new settlements from this era, supporting the likely influx of new populations, lending support to the theory that the Israelites came from outside Canaan and providing substantiation to portions of the peaceful infiltration model. The renowned historical geographer Anson Rainey writes,

> Everyone agrees that there is an amazing proliferation of small village sites in the hill country areas during this period. One of the most recent analyses and summaries (Stager 1998) notes that in the twelfth-eleventh centuries BCE there were approximately 600 more sites than in the preceding, thirteenth, century, over 300 of those new sites in the hill country.... [A]reas that had been largely unsettled in the Late Bronze Age ... were now filled with small, usually un-walled, sites in the Iron Age I." (Rainey, WCITL, 46)

There are, however, a number of drawbacks to the peaceful infiltration model. As Hawkins notes, "the Peaceful Infiltration Model was based on nineteenth-century concepts of nomadism that are now known to be wrong. ... Ethnographic studies have revealed that nomadism was not some kind of intermediate stage in evolutionary development at all." (Hawkins, HIBP, 40) Dever concurs: "We now know that Bedouin typically are not 'land-hungry hordes,' they do not usually 'infiltrate' or settle of their own initiative." (Dever, WWEI, 52)

The vast difference between this theory and the biblical accounts poses another issue according to Hawkins:

> The Peaceful Infiltration Theory fails to explain why the Hebrews composed the stories of the exodus-conquest if their origins were the result of a peaceful, evolutionary process. If the Israelites entered the land in a gradual process that occurred peacefully over several centuries, why does the Hebrew Bible tell such a different story of the origins of Israel? (Hawkins, HIBP, 40)

It is important to note, however, that the Bible points to some level of peaceful infiltration; according to the biblical account, the conquest of Canaan and the driving out of the existing Canaanites was never completed. For example, the Lord said to Joshua, "You are now very old, and there are still very large areas of land to be taken over" (Josh. 13:1b NIV). Also, at the time of Joshua's death, an angel of the Lord spoke to the Israelites about disobeying God's command; God had told them "You shall not make a covenant with the people of this land, but you shall break down their altars. Yet you have disobeyed me" (Judg. 2:2 NIV). These statements are in harmony with archaeological evidence that at least some of the people who came into the land settled peacefully among the native Canaanite population, which was likely absorbed into Israel. This inclusion of the native Canaanites in Israelite culture is highlighted in several biblical stories recounted by Stone:

> The book of Joshua surprisingly includes a number of stories implying that many in Israel derived from Canaan. The programmatic position of the Rahab story at the beginning of the Joshua narrative and the way the terminology used in her confession of faith (Josh 2:9–11) reappears, with a different outcome, in the reports of how the kings of Canaan were conspiring against Israel (cf. 5:1; 9:1–3; 10:1–5; 11:1–5)—all this highlights the thematic importance of Rahab's inclusion in Israel. Later biblical tradition names her in genealogical lists and identifies her as an ancestor of David and, ultimately, of Jesus. The story of the Gibeonite deception clearly describes the entry of an indigenous Canaanite group into the ranks of Israel (Josh. 9). "Foreigners" or "sojourners," along with "native-born" Israelites, made up Israel in the ceremony at Gerizim and Ebal and thus indicate not just presence but also some status in the covenant community. Inclusion in a ritual community implies a degree of social acceptance.
>
> By the same token, the final speech at Shechem in Joshua 24 contrasts with Joshua's "Well Done, Mission Accomplished" speech in Joshua 23 by challenging the hearers to enter into covenant with Yahweh—to serve Yahweh—and warning them to put away foreign gods from their midst. Given the severity with which any deviation from the

covenant was punished in the book, the only persons who might be in possession of non-Israelite cultic images would be elements of the Canaanite population who have affiliated with Israel but have not been fully assimilated or identified as "Israel."

> The book of Joshua thus begins with the assimilation of a Canaanite prostitute and ends with a mass "Ellis Island" type of swearing-in ceremony in which many non-Israelites enter the covenant. (Stone, EIIAC, 156)

3. Assimilation of Canaanites into Israel

According to the biblical stories, some assimilation of the indigenous Canaanite population did occur. Therefore, archaeological evidence for some elements of the peaceful infiltration theory lends credence to the biblical accounts. It is also historically plausible that this process would have occurred over a number of centuries as laid out in the book of Judges. Na'aman points to the evidence of a slow decline in the Canaanite urban culture as damaging to the credibility of the Bible. "Late Bronze Urban culture was gradually destroyed in a process that lasted for more than a century." (Na'aman, CCBJH, 321) However, this objection appears to come from a misinterpretation of the Joshua narrative. An incomplete conquest combined with gradual encroachment from sparsely populated areas into urban areas characterized by ongoing skirmishes as outlined in the book of Judges, is very similar to the scenario that Na'aman lays out.

Na'aman also states that archaeological surveys show that the lack of population rendered large-scale military action unnecessary. He goes on to conclude, "The Iron Age I settlement process in the hill country is hardly illuminated by the biblical conquest tradition." (Na'aman, CCBJH, 348) While the book of Joshua does include several strategic military battles that would have been necessary to secure the land, it does not expressly state that all land had to be taken by conquest. Just as with news reports today, the writer likely would have reported the spectacular battles that confirmed God's deliverance instead of focusing on the mundane elements of settling sparsely inhabited areas. In fact, it is logical that many would settle in predominantly uninhabited areas when available and able to sustain their way of life. And in fact, some of the tribes did (Num. 32; Josh. 13).

Hawkins confirms the gradual process of Israel's ascendancy: "As the cities declined and the Egyptian empire lost its grip on Canaan, the Israelite settlers gradually become the dominant force in the land." (Hawkins, HIBP, 37) As the Israelite population continued to grow, they naturally started coming into conflict with other peoples and would band together under the judges for protection until they ultimately developed the monarchy.

C. Social Revolution (Peasant Revolt) Model

The social revolution theory postulates that the Israelites came from Canaanites who rejected their Canaanite society and moved out of the cities to form counter-communities. George Mendenhall, who compared the cultures and concluded that the Israel society and its rules must have been formed as a rejection to the Canaanite culture, set this theory forth:

Early Israelite tradition everywhere presupposes Canaanite culture as a contrast, or as the origin of certain features. The very insistence of early Israelite law upon a single norm or procedure to be binding upon every person, the amazingly tender concern for the slave which in effect made slavery a voluntary status, and for the non-citizen, presupposes a violent rejection of the highly stratified

society of Late Bronze Canaan. . . . It can be summed up in the observation that Canaan is consistently presented as the polar opposite to that which early Yahwism represented. This is best understood under the assumption that the earliest Israelites actually had been under the domination of the Canaanite cities, and had successfully withdrawn. (Mendenhall, HCP, 76–77)

Scholars have articulated a number of criticisms of the social revolution model. Ralph Hawkins points out, "It has been argued that the Social Revolution Model goes too far beyond the evidence, particularly in the application of Marxist ideology to the emergence of early Israel." (Hawkins, HIBP, 42) Hawkins also points out that "there is no archeological evidence that a 'peasant revolt' occurred." (Hawkins, HIBP, 42) His biggest criticism of the model, however, is based on its wide variance from biblical accounts. He contends that

The Social Revolution Model fails to offer a sufficient explanation for why the Hebrew Bible gives an account at such variance with the reconstruction of the theory. . . . If an element of the Canaanite society had either peacefully withdrawn from the cities or violently revolted against their Canaanite overlords, would not this group have also felt that their experience was one of salvation brought about by Yahweh? Why would it not have been included in the biblical account? (Hawkins, HIPB, 42–43)

The social revolution model is also not supported by recent demographic studies. Lawrence Stager, professor of the archaeology of Israel at Harvard University, states, "This extraordinary increase in population in the Iron [Age] I cannot be explained only by natural population growth of the few Late

Bronze Age city-states in this region: there must have been a major influx of people into the highlands in the twelfth and eleventh centuries BCE." (Stager, FI, 134)

Finally, the social revolution model does not account for the religious development of the Israelite society. As Millard notes, "the worship of Israel's God was hardly a new phenomenon in the ninth century, its earlier history should be investigated. Those who see the roots of Israel in a 'peasants' revolt' are forced to suggest some movement of people who brought the new beliefs into the land." (Millard, WIRC, 165)

D. Summary of Settlement Theories

Most experts now agree that a Canaanite social revolution does not provide a satisfying primary portrait of the rise of Israel. Even so, some disenfranchised Canaanites could have ultimately joined the Hebrew nation. However, given the population trends and other causes for the decline of the regional urban populations, this theory has largely been dismissed.

One important point to note is that all three theories rely heavily on religion as the cause for the rise of Israel. "All three models [conquest, peasant revolt, and peaceful infiltration] involved religion in their explanation for Israel, and thus posited explanations for Israel that can be called ideological." (Moore and Kelle, BHIP, 126) While there may be differences of opinion as to the actual mechanics of the rise of Israel, it is difficult to dispute one of the primary reasons was for the worship of God.

The rise of the Israelite nation was complex and likely influenced by several factors. It is inconceivable that Israel emerged without some armed conflict, so elements of the conquest model are important in understanding how they came to possess the land.

Demographic studies and analyses of religious influence clearly indicate that the core of the Israelite nation likely came from outside Canaan. However, it is also clear both from biblical accounts and archaeological evidence that some Canaanites were adopted into Israel.

IV. Development of the Israelite Culture

A. Material Differences

Much has been made of the lack of physical differences in the sites from the period of Canaanite occupation compared to the time when Israel was emerging. For example, Moore and Kelle point out that "Escapees from Egypt would presumably bring pottery-making and other material culture traditions from there, but no Egyptian influence was seen on the Iron Age village pottery, house forms, or other artifacts." (Moore and Kelle, BHIP, 118) Writing in 2008, Millard notes, "This perspective is reflected in a current display in the British Museum, which qualifies Israelites in parentheses as 'pastoral Canaanites'. In this way an opinion currently propagated with great vigor receives wide publicity." (Millard, WIRC, 162)

A closer look indicates that dramatic differences should not be expected. As Stone explains,

The ancestors of the Israelite nation lived in Canaan for centuries prior to the Egyptian sojourn. Indeed, New Kingdom Egypt deported a great many farmers and tradesmen from Canaan to Egypt, and to the Egyptians no significant difference between Canaanites and the ancestors of Israel would be discernible. They would speak the same language, share the same physical features, and likely share much material culture. Moreover, as practitioners of mixed agriculture and pastoralism, many cultural affinities would link the Israelites and Canaanite peasantry. So in Israelite settlements we should not expect to see the kind of distinct material culture that characterizes the early Philistine sites. (Stone, EIIAC, 155)

If the Israelites had left Egypt with only what they could carry, they would have needed to use the tools and homes found in the area after the exodus. Millard points out that the biblical account is indeed compatible with the archaeological evidence for little change in material culture:

> The biblical texts make it plain that the Israelites did not have a distinctive material culture of their own. . . . Israel was expected to occupy Canaan, destroying the previous inhabitants and the religious items they used in worship of the gods. Otherwise, she was to take over their homes and all their equipment. . . . Evidence for Israelites living in Canaanite towns, with a late Bronze Age culture continued, would not be visible in the material remains. This distinction between the Israelites and the Canaanites and other nations was to lie in their behavior and attitudes to God and to other people, rather than in their houses, their tableware, their dress, or their language. (Millard, WIRC, 167–168)

Millard also observes:

> How might the archaeological record indicate the presence of Israelites as occupants of existing towns or new settlements in this period? Archaeologists have located the sites of scores of small villages across the central hill country of the Promised Land, notably in the areas of Ephraim and Manasseh, but also further south. Many of these were new settlements in the twelfth and eleventh centuries BC, and many of them existed for only a short time. (Millard, WIRC, 161)

B. Religious Differences

As one would expect, the development of the Israelite nation displayed more changes in religious culture than in material culture. These changes are congruent with the major theories of the conquest of Canaan, which cite religion as the underlying basis for the formation of Israel as a people.

Several key markers can be found in the transitioning religious practices, starting with the abrupt abandonment of the earlier worship sites. As Na'aman finds, "The fact that all Late Bronze Age I outdoor temples on both sides of the Jordan disappeared in Late Bronze Age II (Tell Kittan, Tell el-Hayyat, Shiloh and possibly Tel Mevorakh) is remarkable." (Na'aman, CCBJH, 332) Millard reaches a similar conclusion: "One change that appears to be very significant is the abandonment of the shrines in the towns of the Late Bronze Age. Scholars cannot identify a single site in which worship continued from the Late Bronze Age well into the Iron Age." (Millard, WIRC, 166) Millard further notes how the dramatically abrupt abandonment of shrines in this era supports the entry of the Israelites:

> An end to the sanctity of a place surely signals a major change in the beliefs of the populace. Remarkably, during the Iron Age in Palestine, the range of sacred places that had existed in the previous era ceased. If the Canaanites actually moved from the towns into the hill country villages, would they have abandoned the worship of the divinities to which they had been attached when they lived in their cities? This seems unlikely. . . . [I]t is hard to suppose that a new faith would have been accepted almost universally in those villages and at the same time. The cessation of worship at the Late Bronze Age sites, the absence of clear cultic installations in the hill villages, and the

rise of the worship of the God of Israel may be pointers to the entry into Canaan of large numbers of a new population, the Israelites. (Millard, WIRC, 167)

Another interesting marker for the transition from Canaanite culture to the Israelites relates to the Jewish prohibition of pork. Archaeology has found that these new settlers into Canaan did not raise pigs, in keeping with the Jewish law. According to Rainey,

One striking aspect has emerged from the analysis of animal bones in the Early Iron Age. The hill country people did not have pigs. In contrast, the Philistines at Ekron did have pigs, and pig bones are also typical of the older Canaanite sites in the coastal plain areas. . . . It cannot be argued that the hill country areas were unsuitable for raising pigs since quite the opposite is true. If the new settlers of the Iron Age I had come from the lowlands, where pigs were domesticated and utilized, why did they not continue that tradition? (Rainey, WCITL, 48)

C. Conclusions Regarding Israelite Culture

The Israelites came from the same region, shared the same lifestyle, and likely lived among the Canaanites prior to the enslavement in Egypt. It is therefore reasonable to assume that the material culture they left behind would not vary significantly from that of the Canaanites living in the area. Archaeological remains do, however, point to the changing religious practices that occurred as the Israelites settled in the area. The unprecedented abandonment of Canaanite religious sites and the rise of practices consistent with biblical law strongly suggest the influx of a large number of Israelites who came to dominate the region.

V. Key Sites and Current Findings

Next we consider the archaeological evidence surrounding the destruction claims in the book of Joshua. There are several challenges when conducting surveys of the Late Bronze Age sites in this area. First, the lack of written records means that the dates and locations of many sites must be determined by secondary methods, such as Egyptian records, biblical descriptions, pottery shards, dated Egyptian scarabs, and even local tradition. There can be disagreement over which excavation matches which biblical city. Second, as Albright points out, site names can migrate or refer to a large area: "It is quite true that names are much less motile than traditions, yet names of countries and districts often make remarkable shifts (e.g., Syria) and names of towns and villages are frequently displaced over a considerable local area (e.g., Jericho)." (Albright, ICCLA, 14) Third, erosion, development, and treasure seekers have taken a toll on many sites over the thousands of intervening years. Finally, we have to recognize that any site or evidence not found is an argument from silence, capable of yielding only provisional conclusions until methods are discovered that can adequately assess all past activities in the area.

While modern archaeology techniques and more extensive excavations are improving our ability to date sites, it is still common for the occupation dates around sites to be revised a number of times as new items are uncovered and more is learned about items found at a site. In any endeavor where "you don't know what you don't know," conclusions should always be treated as the best theory from the most educated minds, based upon the available evidence. They should always carry the caveat that new theories, different minds, and additional evidence may later call a currently accepted theory into question.

A. Jericho

1. Excavation History and Strategic Importance

Of the stories of the Israelite's settlement of the Holy Land, none is more dramatic than the battle at Jericho. The primary account, provided in Joshua 6, tells how God delivered the city into the Israelite's hands. Jericho was closed tight, but God would tear down the walls if the Israelites followed his instructions. This story emphasizes God's leadership of Israel and demonstrates the blessings they would receive for obedience.

The battle is described in Joshua 6:20. "So the people shouted, and the trumpets were blown. As soon as the people heard the sound of the trumpet, the people shouted a great shout, and the wall fell down flat, so that the people went up into the city, every man straight before him, and they captured the city" (ESV). Verse 24 describes how the Israelites ultimately razed the city: "They burned the city with fire, and everything in it. Only the silver and gold, and the vessels of bronze and of iron, they put into the treasury of the house of the LORD" (ESV).

From a geographic perspective, it is logical that the Israelites would have needed to make the capture of Jericho a priority. According to Bryant Wood, Jericho was certainly of strategic importance during this time. Its abundant water supply, favorable climate, and geographic location made it a key site in ancient Canaan. Anyone who wished to conquer the central hill country from the east, as the Bible describes Joshua and the Israelites doing, would first need to secure Jericho. (Wood, DICJ, 1–2)

The ruins of Jericho are generally believed to be a large mound at the oasis of Tell es-Sultan. Multiple settlements have been at Tell es-Sultan, and the dating of the occupations and destructions has been revised with each subsequent excavation. The first excavation

of this site started with a sounding in 1867 (Kenyon, BRA, 33) and "the first scientific excavations at Tel es-Sultan were carried out from 1907–1909 and again in 1911 under the direction of Ernst Sellin and Carl Watzinger." (Hawkins, HIBP, 92) Watzinger's original dating of the site was consistent with the biblical story, however he "later revised his views and concluded the outer revetment had been destroyed in about 1600 BCE and the walls dated to the third millennium BCE" (Hawkins, HIBP, 92)

The next excavation was conducted from 1930–1936 by John Garstang. He proposed a date of 1250–1200 BC for the fall of Jericho and end of main City IV (the city supposedly destroyed by Joshua) to the mid-fourteenth century. This led him to the conclusion that "the destruction of the Fourth City corresponds in all material particulars with the Biblical narrative of the Fall of Jericho before the Israelites under Joshua." (quoted in Hawkins, HIBP, 93)

This finding was challenged by the most famous and influential excavation of Jericho, conducted by Dame Kathleen Kenyon from 1952–1958. Most of the currently accepted dating is based upon her research. By the time she started digging in the 1950s, excavation techniques had improved considerably. (Kenyon, BRA, 33)

Kenyon's excavation "showed that there were no less than seventeen buildings and rebuildings of the city wall during the eight hundred years or so of the Early Bronze Age." (Hawkins HBIP, 93) Kenyon recounts the subsequent settlements up until the sixteenth century:

[The walled town] was succeeded by a camping settlement and then an unwalled village of the EB-MB period that represents the incursion of the semi-nomadic Amorites. . . . A walled town was re-established in the succeeding Middle Bronze Age, probably c. 1900 BC. . . . In the eighteenth century a new system of fortification was introduced in which a great artificial bank was piled up, for the most part on the crest of the pre-existing mound. . . . These Middle Bronze Age defences lasted from the eighteenth century to about the middle of the sixteenth century. (Kenyon, BRA, 36–38)

2. Dating the Occupation and Destruction of Jericho

Kenyon's early dating of the destruction at Jericho does not match dates traditionally given for the exodus and conquest. However, she does note that the Middle Bronze Age walls

could have survived sufficiently to be repaired for use in the Late Bronze Age towns, but since so much of the Middle Bronze Age defences have disappeared, it is absolutely certain that nothing at all of walls of the later town, to the period of which the entry into Palestine must belong, can survive. Archaeology will thus never be able to provide visual evidence of the walls that fell down in front of the attacking Israelites. (Kenyon, BRA, 38)

In addition to the dating of the destruction, there is a question as to whether the site was even occupied during the Late Bronze Age. Kenyon believes that the best opportunity to date occupation at the site comes from the burial tombs originally excavated by Professor Garstang in the 1930s. A few of these Middle Bronze Age tombs were opened and reused in the Late Bronze Age; however, the dating of the Mycenaean vessels found in the tombs led Kenyon to state that, while dating cannot be precisely made, they cannot be dated any later than 1300 BC. (Kenyon, BRA, 40)

Kenyon did conclude that the excavations had "produced enough evidence that there was a Late Bronze Age town and to give some slight evidence of the date at which it was destroyed." (Kenyon, BRA, 38) From one small area at the edge of the destroyed remains of the Middle Bronze occupation, Kenyon discovered

the stone foundations of a single wall. This wall was so close to the modern surface that only about a square metre of the contemporary floor survived, with elsewhere the modern surface cutting down into it. The one juglet surviving on its surface, lying by a small clay oven, and a limited amount of Late Bronze Age pottery beneath the floor, suggests that the building is late fourteenth century in date. A Late Bronze Age occupation of the site is thus proved, but the excavations within the town provide little detail. (Kenyon, BRA, 38–39)

According to Hawkins, "She admitted the possibility however, that 'a yet later Late Bronze Age town may have been even more completely washed away than that which so meagerly survives.'" Kenyon stressed repeatedly in numerous publications the extensive damage that erosion had done at Tell es-Sultan." (Hawkins, HIBP, 94)

3. New Analysis of Archaeological Data

Kenyon's raw data and final report, however, were not published until after her death. Wood explains:

Kenyon died in 1978 without living to see the final publication of her excavation of the tell. Her conclusions were reported only in a popular book published the year before she completed her fieldwork, in a series of preliminary reports and in scattered articles. The detailed evidence, however, was never supplied. (Wood, DICJ, 7)

The raw data became available in 1982–83, and analysis has raised some questions about her dating methods. "Some 30 years after her excavation of the site—indeed, 12 years after Kenyon's death—the detailed evidence has now become available in the final report. So it is time for a new look." (Wood, DICJ, 1–2) After his review and analysis of Kenyon's research, Wood concluded that Kenyon based her dating on the absence of popular imported pottery from the Later Bronze Age, which may have led to incorrect conclusions:

> To understand how Kenyon reached her conclusion, we must piece together scattered statements in various writings. When we do this, it becomes clear that Kenyon based her opinion almost exclusively on the absence of pottery imported from Cyprus and common to the Late Bronze I period (c. 1550–1400 BCE). This imported Cypriote ware had been previously found mainly in some Megiddo tomb groups, and Kenyon used this pottery to construct her ceramic typology for the Late Bronze I period. Although she also mentions certain local pottery types used in this period, it is obvious she paid little attention to these common domestic forms since they appear regularly in the final phases of City IV. (Wood, DICJ, 7)

Wood goes on to explain the challenges posed by this type of analysis.

> Dating habitation levels at Jericho on the absence of exotic imported wares—which were found primarily in tombs in large urban centers—is methodologically unsound and, indeed, unacceptable. . . . A careful examination of the Jericho excavation reports as a whole, moreover, makes it clear that both Garstang and Kenyon dug in a poor quarter of the city where they found only humble domestic dwellings. . . . Why then would anyone

expect to find exotic imported ceramics in this type of cultural milieu? To make matters worse, Kenyon based her conclusions on a very limited excavation area—two 26-foot by 26-foot squares. An argument from silence is always problematic, but Kenyon's argument is especially poorly founded. She based her dating on the fact that she failed to find expensive, imported pottery in a small excavation area in an impoverished part of a city located far from major trade routes! (Wood, DICJ, 8)

When comparing Kenyon's expectations with some of the pottery Garstang found in the 1930s, examples of likely Late Bronze Age pottery appear. It just was not recognized during Kenyon's time and was not located in the area of her excavations. Wood explains:

> Ironically, Garstang found a considerable quantity of pottery decorated with red and black paint which appears to be imported Cypriot bichrome ware, the type of pottery Kenyon was looking for and did not find! Cypriot bichrome ware is one of the major diagnostic indicators for occupation in the Late Bronze I period. At the time of Garstang's excavation, the significance of this type of pottery was not recognized, so it was simply published along with all the other decorated pottery without being singled out for special notice. . . . As fate would have it, Kenyon, who well knew the link of such ware to the Late Bronze Age, conducted her dig too far north of the eroded runoff to find any bichrome ware. Had she dug further south, or had she been aware of Garstang's finds, the debate over the date of Jericho's fall could have taken a very different course: Kenyon might have dated Jericho's demise to about 1400 BCE, (as Garstang did) and not to about 1550 BCE, the end of the Middle Bronze Age. (Wood, DICJ, 10–11)

Wood believes the destruction of the site should be dated to the Late Bronze Age. In addition to the pottery evidence, Egyptian scarabs found at the site point to the fact that the cemetery at Jericho was used up until the end of the Late Bronze Age:

> Scarabs are small Egyptian amulets shaped like a beetle with an inscription (sometimes the name of a pharaoh) on the bottom. In his excavation of the cemetery northwest of the city, Garstang recovered a continuous series of Egyptian scarabs extending from the 18th century BCE (the XIIIth Dynasty) to the early 14th century BCE (the XVIIIth Dynasty). The XVI-IIth Dynasty scarabs include four royal-name scarabs—one of Hatshepsut (c. 1503–1483 BCE), one of Tuthmosis III (c. 1504–1450 BCE) and two of Amenhotep III (c. 1386–1349 BCE)—as well as a seal of Tuthmosis III. The continuous nature of the scarab series suggests that the cemetery was in active use up to the end of the Late Bronze I period. (Wood, DICJ, 11–12)

In addition to signs of occupation during the Late Bronze Age, there are other archeological finds at the site that parallel the biblical narrative. David Graves, assistant professor at Liberty University, points out,

> The siege of Jericho was short, as the grain stored in the city was not consumed. . . . [C]harred grain indicate [sic] they did not have time to consume the grain and reveals a short siege as described in the biblical narrative. Contrary to what was customary, the grain was not plundered to feed their armies, or taken by the citizens, but in accordance to God's command Joshua was to burn the grain (Josh 6:1, 17–18). This discovery is unique in archaeology, given the high value of grain in ancient culture. It would be like taking a bank and burning the money. (Graves, BA, 152)

Finally, Wood notes that the carbon dating on charcoal from the site has produced mixed results, showing dates from 1600 BC to 1347 BC: "C14 dates are consistently 100–150 years earlier than historical dates." (Wood, C14DJ, website) So, the carbon dating could potentially support claims of occupation and destruction during the Late Bronze Age.

4. Jericho as a Military Outpost

Another possible solution is that Jericho could have been a military outpost or fort. In this case, it is unlikely that significant archaeological remains of the occupation would be discovered. Stone points out that it is highly unlikely the area would have been completed deserted for hundreds of years. "Given the strategically vital nature of the site, with its spring and ready control of important highways and the Jordan River crossing, the idea that Tell-es-Sultan sat uninhabited for centuries after 1550 BCE is almost inconceivable." (Stone, EIIAC, 144)

Richard Hess, professor of Old Testament and Semitic languages at Denver Seminary, believes based on linguistic evidence from Scripture that at the time of the conquest Jericho was most likely a fort. (Hess, JABJ, 35) He also points out that Tell el-Sultan and the biblical Jericho were likely small sites. "The biblical picture suggests that Jericho was small enough that the Israelites could march around it seven times in one day and then have sufficient energy to fight a battle against it." (Hess, JABJ, 35) Based upon troop sizes mentioned in the Amarna letters from the Late Bronze Age, "It would not seem preposterous if the number of men defending Jericho was 100 or fewer." (Hess, JABJ, 41–42)

Hess also points out that aside from Rahab and her family, no other nonmilitary personnel are mentioned. "The text refers to Rahab with her family. She is involved with the inn. However, no other noncombatants are singled out. . . . All of this coincides with the portrait of a small and militarized center." (Hess, JABJ, 36) So how does this interpretation match the reference in Joshua 6:21, where they "destroyed with the sword every living thing in the city—men and women, young and old, cattle, sheep, and donkeys" (NCV)? Hess explains this reference is literally translated as "from man (and) unto woman," and from other references "appears to be stereotypical for describing all the inhabitants of a town or region, without predisposing the reader to assume anything further about their ages or even their genders. It is synonymous with 'all, everyone.'" (Hess, JABJ, 39)

5. Conclusion

The most recent analysis of archaeological data points to a Late Bronze Age occupation and destruction of this site. Pottery and burial artifacts support a destruction of the city around 1400 BC. Evidence hints at habitation of the site throughout the Late Bronze Age into the mid-1200s; however, extensive erosion at the site over the past three thousand years has made finding significant archaeological evidence of this habitation impossible.

B. Ai

After the destruction of Jericho, the Bible tells us that Joshua's army moved on to Ai. After a failed campaign against the city, attributed to disobedience from the Israelites, the Lord instructed Joshua to take the city. In keeping with the Lord's commands, "Joshua burned Ai and made it forever a heap of ruins, as it is to this day" (Josh. 8:28 ESV).

While the site at Jericho shows signs of habitation and destruction during the Late Bronze Age, et-Tell, the site generally associated with Ai, does not. The most recent excavations of this site, conducted by Joseph Calloway from 1964–1970, found no archaeological record of habitation of the site between 2400 and 1230 BC, which encompasses the most likely timeframes for the Israelite invasion. (Graves, BA, 153) This excavation has led Calloway to conclude that "Ai is simply an embarrassment to every view of the conquest that takes the biblical and archeological evidence seriously." (Calloway, NECA, 312) Kenyon concurs that "on the whole, the probability is that there is no historicity in the story of the attack on 'Ai.'" (Kenyon, BRA, 41)

A number of different locations had been suggested for Ai (Wood, SJA, 207–209). But the excavations and writings of William Albright convinced the scientific community that ancient Ai was located at the modern-day site of et-Tell:

> Albright's 1924 article, for all intents and purposes, set the identification of et-Tell as Ai in concrete. His basis was that it is the only Canaanite ruin in the vicinity meeting the topographic requirements of being east of Beitin (Gen 12:8, 13:3; Josh 7:2, 8:9) and in the vicinity of Beitin (Josh 8:17, 12:9). Most scholars have accepted the identification as certain, to the extent that if one wishes to look up et-Tell in an archaeological dictionary or encyclopedia, one must look under "Ai." (Wood, SJA, 209)

Since et-Tell does not fit the requirements of a city inhabited during the period of the conquest, two alternative explanations have been explored in recent years. Some scholars believe the site at et-Tell may be misidentified with Ai, while others propose that Ai of the Late Bronze Age may have been represented by a less permanent settlement or a military encampment.

Two alternate sites have been proposed

for Ai. David Livingston has excavated the site at Khirbet Nisya, which he proposes is a more viable alternative, while Bryant Wood and Scott Stripling have proposed the site at Khirbet el-Maqatir as a better match.

The chart below shows the geographical and archaeological comparisons of et-Tell and Khirbet el-Maqatir and how they align with the biblical references in Joshua. It is important to note that identification of Ai depends in part on the identification and location of

the city of Bethel. Albright identifies Bethel as the site at Beitin, while Wood and Stripling identify Beitin as the city of Beth-aven, with Bethel actually located at el-Bira. Based upon their analysis, Wood and Stripling point out that Khirbet el-Maqatir is a much better match for the biblical description of Ai.

In addition to being a good match geographically, archeological evidence at Khirbet el-Maqatir also supports the possibility that this is the site of the city of Ai.

Biblical Reference	et-Tell	Khirbet el-Maqatir
	William Albright proposed et-Tell in 1924 and it is the currently accepted site for Ai.	Bryant Wood and Scott Stripling proposed this alternative in 2008.
Adjacent to Beth-aven (Josh. 7:2)	Several nearby sites have been proposed as Beth-aven, but none has Late Bronze Age occupation.	Site is 1.5 km from Beitin/Beth-aven and separated by a narrow valley. The sites are visible to each other.
East of Bethel (Josh. 7:2)	The site is 2.4 km southeast of Beitin/Bethel and 5 km northeast of el-Bira.	Site is 3.5 km northeast of el-Bira/Bethel.
An ambush site between Bethel and Ai (Josh. 8:9, 12)	There is a small hill 0.7 km northwest of et-Tell that could hide a small force, but would still be visible from Beitin/Bethel.	The Wadi Sheban Valley is a very deep valley running between the sites and could easily hide a large ambush force.
A militarily significant hill north of Ai (Josh. 8:11)	The hill to the northwest could provide a command post for the attack.	Jebel Abu Ammar is 1.5 km north and the highest hill in the region, providing a strategic view of the surrounding area.
A shallow valley north of Ai (Josh. 8:13, 14)	The valley Wadi el-Gayeh to the north is deep and narrow and does not match the biblical description or purpose.	Here the valley Wadi Gayeh is shallow and easily visible from the site.
Smaller than Gibeon (Josh. 10:2)	At 27 acres, et-Tell is more than twice the size of Gibeon.	The fortress from the conquest period is approximately three acres in size.
Occupation at the time of the conquest	Unoccupied during the conquest time period	Abundant amounts of pottery from the fifteenth century BC have been found at the site.
Fortified at the time of the conquest (Josh. 7:5; 8:29)	Unoccupied during the conquest time period	A small Late Bronze Age fortress with 4m thick walls has been uncovered at the site.
Gate on the north side of the site (Josh. 8:11)	No construction during the conquest time period	The gate of the Late Bronze Age fortress is on the north side.
Destroyed by fire at the time of the conquest (Josh. 8:19, 28)	Unoccupied during the conquest time period	Evidence of destruction by fire at the site including ash, refired pottery, burned building stones, and calcined bedrock.
Left in ruins after 1400 BCE (Josh. 8:28)	Unoccupied during the conquest time period	While parts of the site were robbed out to build later structures, some of the fortress ruins remain today.

Evidence shows that Khirbet el-Maqatir was occupied during the Late Bronze Age (c. 1500–1400 BC), as revealed by the discovery of pottery and a rare Egyptian scarab from that period. (Graves, BA, 155) Using a statistical analysis approach, Peter Briggs of Trinity Southwest University analyzed the three sites and concluded, "Only Kh. el-Maqatir satisfies all fourteen parameters of the critical screen, thus providing conclusive evidence that the conquest of Ai narrative is a True Narrative Representative and that Kh. el-Maqatir is the site of the fortress of Ai conquered by Joshua." (Briggs, TFCAN, 1) In addition, Briggs reports finds at the site including Late Bronze Age pottery "suited to a small military outpost, including large, commercial-grade pithoi for the storage of grains, water and olive oil, and common ware for cooking and table service." (Briggs, TFCAN, 28)

This evidence for Ai being located at Khirbet el-Maqatir is compelling. However, even if Ai should be located at et-Tell, Richard Hawkins proposes that there could have been a less permanent settlement:

> Could it be that et-Tell is the correct location of biblical Ai, that its current occupants lived among the ruins of the Middle Bronze Age city, and that they experienced a sort of scaled-down conquest? . . . [T]hen it could cohere with a thirteenth century BCE Israelite emergence with a scaled-down level of military engagement. (Hawkins, HIBP, 111)

C. Hazor

The destruction of Hazor during the conquest period by the Israelites is generally accepted. John Monson, associate professor of Old Testament and Semitic languages at Trinity International University, describes the destruction: "Hazor's archaeological excavations have yielded Late Bronze Age

finds that correlate with the book of Joshua very well. The site has destruction layers that fit both the early and late dates of the exodus/conquest." (Monson, EJ, 436) Monson also notes that Hebrew University professor Amnon Ben-Tor, who has been excavating Hazor since the 1990s, "contends that the Israelites were most likely the people who ransacked this large city." (Monson, EJ, 436)

D. Greek Texts Supporting Israel's Military Campaign

Anthony J. Frendo in *Palestine Exploration Quarterly* has called attention to Greek texts that explicitly attest to the tradition that early Israel emerged on the basis of military operations led by Joshua son of Nun. These texts in the form of two inscribed columns provide extrabiblical attestation to the belief that the emergence of Israel had a military component. According to Frendo, this proof is

> provided by Procopius of Caesarea, a Greek historian of the sixth century A.D. . . . who was an assessor and counsellor of Belisarius, the great general of the eastern emperor Justinian. . . . In his eight-volume work, *Histories of the Wars of Justinian,* Procopius refers to the Canaanites who had built a fortress at Tigress in Numidia; more interestingly he mentions the fact that they had left two columns inscribed in the Phoenician language wherein they claimed that they had fled from Joshua the son of Nun. In Book IV: X: 21–22 of this historical work Procopius writes (289): They [the Canaanites of the Old Testament] also built a fortress in Numidia, where now is the city called Tigisis. In that place are two columns made of white stone near by the great spring, having Phoenician letters cut in them which say in the Phoenician tongue: "We are they who fled from before the face of Joshua, the robber, son of Nun." (Frendo, TLPI, 38)

Frendo notes that Procopius was "basically a reliable historian" and it was "virtually certain that Procopius did see the two above-mentioned inscribed columns." This firsthand reference by a noted historian provides strong attestation to an Israelite military campaign led by Joshua. (Frendo, TLPI, 37)

VI. Conclusion

When we put the archeological and sociological findings in context with what the Bible actually claims, we start to see a fuller picture of how Israel came to possess the promised land, in which they afterwards developed a monarchy—a picture that can be harmonized with the findings in the area. This scenario is summed up well by James Hoffmeier, professor of Old Testament and ancient Near Eastern history and archaeology at Trinity International University:

> When Joshua is viewed as a piece of Near Eastern military writing, and its literary character is properly understood, the idea of a group of tribes coming to Canaan, using some military force, partially taking a number of cities and areas over a period of some years, destroying (burning) just three cities, and coexisting alongside the Canaanites and other ethnic groups for a period of time before the beginnings of a monarchy, does not require blind faith. (Hoffmeier, IE, 43)

CHAPTER 21

THE HISTORICITY OF THE UNITED MONARCHY

OVERVIEW

I. Introduction

This chapter focuses on the period known as the United Monarchy (approximately 1050–930 BC), when a single monarch ruled all the tribes of Israel—first under Saul, then under David, and finally, under Solomon. Because the history of the United Monarchy involves David and the special relationship God established with him, this topic has special religious significance for Christians. For it was with David that God established a covenant in which he promised a descendant who would sit on David's throne forever. That descendant was Christ, and it is through Christ that God brought the new covenant.

Whether or not one accepts the religious aspect of the biblical story, the reigns of Saul, David, and Solomon have long been accepted as historical. Consequently, when archaeologists went to the Holy Land to look for ancient cities and civilizations, they used the Bible as a guide. This initially proved very successful in locating many ancient sites and validating the biblical narrative.

However, in the 1970s skeptics known as

"minimalists" maintained that only a small core of biblical stories were true, claiming that problems with previous archaeological evidence called for alternative explanations. Just as it seemed that this challenge could be met by continued archaeological examination, a new set of skeptics arose in the 1990s, led by Israel Finkelstein, who explained the archaeological finds by shifting the accepted dates of those finds forward a century. While this shift appears relatively minor, its advocates are well aware that it undercuts the biblical story. Instead of the story of the glory of the United Monarchy, it "puts the spotlight on [the] Northern Kingdom of the Omride Dynasty as the real first prosperous state of early Israel." (Finkelstein, LCU, 39)

Still other minimalists contend that there is no historical truth to the Bible at all, claiming that the Deuteronomic (sixth century BC) writers invented the history of the United Monarchy for political reasons. They assert that "we do not have evidence for the existence of kings named Saul, David or Solomon; nor do we have evidence for any temple at Jerusalem in this early period." (Thompson, MP, 164)

This chapter addresses the evidence for the existence of the United Monarchy. Traditional dating places the reign of David in the tenth century before Christ. Even though the remains of civilizations of that ancient time are limited, we have a surprising wealth of evidence. However, outside of Scripture, we find only fragments of the overall picture. While we would be glad for an excavation to come upon a throne with an inscription stating, "King David ruled from here," that is unrealistic. Instead, we have many individual pieces of evidence which, when taken together, present a very compelling picture.

II. The Cumulative Case for the United Monarchy

Many scholars and historians believe that the United Monarchy began around 1050 BC with the reign of Saul, who ruled Israel for forty-two years (1 Sam. 13:1; cf. Acts 13:21).* David and Solomon each reigned forty years (2 Sam. 5:4; 1 Kings 11:42). After Solomon's death, the kingdom began a period of divided rule when Jeroboam rebelled against the rule of Rehoboam, son of Solomon. The period of the United Monarchy, then, occurred roughly between 1050 and 930 BC. The Bible tells us it was a time of great prosperity, with major construction occurring during David's rule and increasing dramatically with Solomon. We build our case by considering evidence that supports the biblical account.

First, we provide background evidence to show that, prior to the time of the United Monarchy, a substantial civilization existed in the land of Israel—i.e., a foundational civilization matching the biblical story of the time of the judges—which dispels critics' contention that the area was a sparsely populated agrarian society without the necessary infrastructure for the establishment of a kingdom.

We then provide direct archeological evidence for the existence of the United Monarchy, which links to the biblical story, as well as indirect evidence of a robust economic environment that supports the accounts found in Scripture.

Finally, we show a great deal of evidence from the period immediately following the United Monarchy that corroborates the existence of the Davidic line of kings. We consider other evidence that demonstrates the existence of an organizational structure

---

* The length of Saul's reign is unknown. Translators conjecture 42 years, though the correct reading of the Hebrew is uncertain.

best explained by a strong central government from the time of the United Monarchy.

The evidence shows a flourishing Israelite culture, the building blocks for the Israelite kingdom. The United Monarchy unified the Israelite peoples and provided a period of great construction and commerce. With the division of the kingdom, the two remaining kingdoms looked back to the United Monarchy as a source of legitimacy and heritage.

We provide an early documentary view into the history of Israel. Each piece of evidence supports the biblical account, and the strength of the remaining story increases. We also must make sure we don't overly rely upon any one archaeological find. As Nadav Na'aman, professor of Jewish history at Tel Aviv University, puts it,

Like the written sources, the results of the archaeological excavations are open to different, sometimes even contradictory, interpretations. The archaeological literature is replete with controversies on an endless number of issues, including stratigraphy and pottery typology, the function of the excavated buildings and artifacts, settlement hierarchy, population estimate, among many others. (Na'aman, DARDS, 167)

Moreover, all the evidence must be taken in context. When we do this, we find that our research unveils an overall picture that supports the historicity of the United Monarchy.

III. The Evidence for Israel Prior to the United Monarchy

The Bible tells us that the period of the United Monarchy was preceded by a multicentury period of rule by judges, lasting from the death of Joshua until Saul was made king; the period of the judges was marked by repeated conflicts in which Israel was led by judges raised up by God.*

Outside the Bible, the best evidence for the existence of a strong civilization in the land of Israel during the time of the book of Judges comes from two archaeological finds in Egypt. The Amarna tablets provide details of the cultural environment just prior to the arrival of the Israelites, and the Merneptah Stele provides evidence of a confederation of peoples, already known as Israel, capable of resisting an external army.

A. The Amarna Tablets

While critics contend that the land of Israel was a sparsely populated, agrarian area that could not have been home for a kingdom such as described in the Bible, archaeological evidence presents a different picture.

In the late 1800s, at the site of the capital of the Pharaoh Akhenaten, a large number of clay tablets were found that document correspondence between the Egyptian royal court and representatives in foreign cities of Canaan. This correspondence is best known as the Amarna tablets because el-Amarna is the modern name for the site where they were discovered.

The picture presented in the tablets of the population of Canaan was of thriving kingdoms centered in Jerusalem and Shechem. Indeed, the Amarna letters include seven long letters from the king of Jerusalem, which contain descriptions of visits with Egyptian officials, the sending of a tribute caravan back to Egypt, and complaints about territorial conflicts with adjacent kings. The "picture

---

* There is debate regarding the exact length of the time of judges. First Kings 6:1 mentions the "four hundred and eightieth year after the Israelites came out of Egypt, in the fourth year of Solomon's reign" (NIV). If you remove Saul and David's reign, and the time in the wilderness and Joshua's conquest, you arrive at approximately 350 years.

arising from these letters suggests a kingdom of substantial strength, with Jerusalem as its capital city, enjoying a solid economy and dominating a territory that spread east of the foot of the central mountain range." (Na'aman, TVT, 54) This picture contrasts with the archaeological evidence, which shows a much more sparsely populated, moribund society. The difference between the archaeological evidence and extant documentation can be explained several ways. First, ancient cities that have a long period of continuous occupation are a challenge for archaeologists. Archaeological evidence may be damaged or destroyed when decaying structures are renovated or removed. Additionally, this area presents a problem because the bedrock is found at a relatively shallow depth. This inhibits the accumulation of debris and contributes to mixing of artifacts between the built-up strata. A truer picture of the area is derived when one can validate the archaeological data with available documentary evidence.

Not only do the Amarna letters provide background information for the population of the area the Israelites would soon occupy, but the letters also show the difficulty of overreliance on archaeological evidence, especially in difficult environments. While the Amarna letters let us correct the archaeology from the Middle Bronze Age, we lack the "corrective of a contemporaneous archive for the period of the United Monarchy." (Na'aman, TVT, 52)

As noted by Na'aman, "the picture we get from the Amarna letters—of two rulers of city-states (Jerusalem and Shechem) who wielded considerable influence over developments throughout the country—has little support in the archaeological findings." We need to keep this in mind as we consider the rest of the evidence. The skepticism for the

United Monarchy is fueled by the sparsity of archaeological evidence. Yet if we apply that skepticism to the period documented by the Amarna letters, the same scarcity of evidence would mean "we would never have suspected that Egypt dominated all of Canaan in the time of the 18th Dynasty." (Na'aman, TVT, 52)

B. The Merneptah Stele

Egyptian pharaohs regularly documented their wars at the temple in Thebes. In about 1210 BC, the Pharaoh Merneptah erected a stele documenting his victory over foes in the land of Canaan. Discovered in the late 1800s, this stele, now widely known as the Merneptah Stele, provides the first external mention of Israel. Leading Near Eastern archaeologist, William G. Dever, notes,

> All scholars would agree that the date is fixed within a margin of less than five years by astronomical reckoning; that the reading "Israel" is certain; that "Israel" is followed by the Egyptian plural gentilic or determinative sign for "peoples," rather than a kingdom, city-state, or the like, and must therefore designate some ethnic group; and that this entity, whatever it is, was distinct in the minds of the Egyptians from Canaanites, Hurrians, Shasu-bedouin, or other groups in Canaan well known to Egyptian intelligence and mentioned in this and other Egyptian texts. (Dever, WDBWK, 1408)

We see, then, that during the time of the judges a people distinct from the other peoples of the Canaanite region were capable of putting up an army to fight the Egyptians.

Additionally, in the structure of the inscriptions on the stele and how they reference other encounters, scholars are able to infer that "Israel was a significant socioethnic entity that needed to be reckoned with. Certainly Israel was no less significant than

Ashkelon and Gezer, two of the more important city-states in Palestine at the time." (Hasel, IMS, 56)

IV. Direct Archaeological Evidence for the United Monarchy

Archaeology has produced several types of direct evidence for the United Monarchy. The first type comes from structures and inscriptions that represent tangible physical confirmation of the existence of the government or structures. Another type of evidence shows that activity was occurring that can be reasonably linked to the existence of the prosperity attributed to the United Monarchy. Finally, evidence of thriving culture and commerce arising in adjacent territories can support the increase of activity in united Israel.

A. Excavations in Jerusalem

In the initial stages of the United Monarchy, Saul ruled from his capital of Gibeah (1 Sam. 15:34). Subsequently, David ruled at Hebron for his first seven years, then transferred his capital to Jerusalem (2 Sam. 5:5).

Therefore, it would be reasonable to expect to discover the most evidence for the United Monarchy in Jerusalem. However, significant problems exist with archaeological findings in Jerusalem, particularly a sparsity of findings corresponding to the time period of the United Monarchy. In fact, much of the skeptical criticism of the biblical history of the United Monarchy arises from the lack of evidence found in Jerusalem. Critics assert that, as David's capital city and the subject of much of the Davidic story, Jerusalem should contain much more archaeological evidence of an advanced settlement. They contend the Jerusalem of the tenth century BC was either not settled or a very small village of no significance—hardly the setting described in

the Bible or the one that we see described in the Amarna letters.

Yet when we investigate more closely, we do not find this critique convincing. In fact, there has indeed been a great deal of evidence uncovered, much of it recently, that demonstrates a significant settlement in Jerusalem. However, much of this evidence is dismissed by skeptics, who discount the reports from Scripture and label as unscientific those who advocate for their use in reconstructing the period. When evaluating archaeological evidence that seems to support the Bible. they demonstrate their own bias by assuming that the biblical stories are fiction.

Moreover, when we note the sparsity of archaeological evidence within Jerusalem, we should take into account specific difficulties unique to this city (a problem that is inherent to cities continuously occupied in antiquity):

First, the area of Jerusalem's public buildings is under the Temple Mount and cannot be examined. The most important area for investigation, and the one to which the biblical histories of David and Solomon mainly refer, remains terra incognita. Second, there is an uninterrupted continuity of settlement in the Ophel Hill from the tenth to the early sixth century BCE. As is well known, conquest, destruction and desolation leave distinct marks that archaeologists can easily expose; uninterrupted continuity of settlement, on the other hand, leaves only a few remains of the earlier building activity. No wonder, then, that the remains of the tenth-ninth-centuries city was discovered mainly in fills or building fragments and that the city destroyed in 587/586 is the best known. Third, the old city of Jerusalem, built on terraces and bedrock, was settled for thousands of years, each new city erecting its foundations on bedrock and destroying what was underneath. The old buildings were utterly destroyed by later building activity, their stones robbed and reused. (Na'aman, CALDJ, 3)

This difficulty is most acute when dealing with the search for the Solomonic temple. Critics argue that there has been no evidence found of that temple. While this is true, if it were to be found, it would most likely be beneath the current Temple Mount, where no archaeological excavation is allowed. As with all critical assessments, we cannot require more evidence than can reasonably be expected to be found. Some level of common sense must be used in analyzing the situation. Archaeologist Amihai Mazar notes the most practical observation about the lack of archaeological evidence from the Solomonic temple:

> The temple and palace that Solomon supposedly built should be found, if anywhere, below the present Temple Mount, where no excavations are possible. If the biblical account is taken as reliable, Solomon's Jerusalem would be a city of twelve hectares with monumental buildings and a temple. Should Solomon be removed from history, who then would have been responsible for the construction of the Jerusalem Temple? There is no doubt that such a temple stood on the Temple mount prior to the Babylonian conquest of the city, but we lack any textual hint for an alternative to Solomon as the builder. (Mazar, SDS, 127–128)

1. The Palace of King David in Jerusalem

Eilat Mazar, perhaps the most experienced modern archaeologist in Jerusalem, has been participating in or leading excavations there for the last thirty years. Excavations have uncovered a great deal of evidence that suggests the location of the royal palace in Jerusalem. These include several stone structures, inscriptions, and pottery.

a. The Large Stone Structure

In February 2005, new excavations by Eilat Mazar were begun at the summit just south of the Temple Mount. The digging quickly uncovered remnants of a massive stone structure whose walls were dated to the time of the United Monarchy. Mazar has suggested that this find is linked to the remnants of David's royal palace. Critics have charged that her dating was incorrect and that the walls were actually from different periods. However, since then she has uncovered numerous local pottery shards that can be dated to about 1000 BC, supporting her initial hypothesis. With the report of this additional evidence, other archaeologists are increasingly supporting her conclusions. For instance, Avraham Faust, professor of archaeology at Bar-Ilan University asserts,

> The results of Eilat Mazar's second season have resolved, in my view, the issue of the date of the structure in an almost final manner. As we shall presently see, it is clearly an Iron Age structure (i.e., from the Biblical period, not the Hellenistic period); or, in case not all of the walls belong to the same building, there was at least a large early Iron Age structure here. Although it is possible that some of the walls do not belong to this building, most of them do. It is immaterial if some of them do not. (Faust, DEMFDP, 47)

Several subsequent excavations supported Mazar's findings. First was the discovery of an imported clay juglet from Cyprus. She was able to date this vessel to the "tenth-ninth centuries BCE (Iron Age IIa), providing a nice confirmation of our dating of the local pottery to the same date." (Mazar, DIFKDP, 25)

Further excavation in the structure uncovered a *bulla*, a seal for official correspondence. On this bulla, archaeologists were able to discern the name "Yehuchal," which would correspond with the royal minister Jehukal from the preexilic court of King Zedekiah. (Mazar, DIFKDP; cf. Jer. 37:3) Though we can't be certain that the bulla refers to the same person mentioned in Scripture, paleographic dating places it in the appropriate timeframe. (Mykytiuk, CUIBP, 89) This discovery adds credence to the determination that this was a part of the royal palace in Jerusalem and that the Davidic royal palace continued to be used by the Davidic royal line until its destruction by Nebuchadnezzar.

b. The Stepped Stone Structure

Adjacent to the Large Stone Structure is a steep, terraced stone structure that has been known since early twentieth-century excavations. While many explanations for the structure have been postulated, the excavations of Mazar provide a link to the United Monarchy. It was established that Stepped Stone Structure was actually integral to the Large Stone Structure and acted as a retainer for it. (Mazar, DM, 164) It was most probably constructed "between the twelfth and ninth centuries BCE. It is thus legitimate to conclude that the building was either constructed or continued to be in use during the tenth century, the alleged time of David and Solomon." (Mazar, DM, 126)

Regardless of the purpose ascribed to this structure, when taken together with the Large Stone Structure, we now have evidence of a magnitude of construction that is far beyond any comparable building project anywhere in ancient Israel until the early ninth century BC. That evidence alone can be considered "a clear indication that Jerusalem was much more than a small village; in fact it contained the largest-known structure of the time in the region and thus could easily serve as a power base for a central authority." (Mazar, DM, 126–127)

2. Signs of Advanced Culture

In an advanced ancient culture with a centralized government, there should be other evidence of activities that arise as stability increases and commerce occurs. Indeed, we find just such evidence in analyzing settlement patterns, literacy, and commerce in Jerusalem.

a. The Center of Political Activity: A Statistical Inference

The indications that Jerusalem was the center of the kingdom of the United Monarchy go beyond simple archaeological finds. Avi Opher did an extensive study of 334 dated settlements of the highlands of Judea. He used a statistical analysis tool known as "rank size analysis" to compare occurrences of pottery shards found across the dated period, in relation to the size of the settlements excavated in the Judean Highlands. This tool revealed relationships between sites, and by mapping them he was able to see which site was dominant in a region and "should be therefore the capital." (Opher, MPJH, 24) For the highlands of Judah, the first time a site clearly indicated a capital ranking was "in Iron Age 2a–around 1000 BCE." (Opher, MPJH, 24) Furthermore, Jerusalem evidently continued to exert influence after this period. From his analysis, Opher was able to conclude that "the socio-economic and political structure of Judah at that period is that of a well-integrated unit, most probably a kingdom, most probably subject to the site of Jerusalem." (Opher, MPJH, 27)

b. Fish Bones and Other Signs of Commerce

Excavations near the spring located in ancient Jerusalem resulted in the discovery of a rock-cut pool that had been part of the ancient water system and then abandoned. It was later filled over in the late eighth century to allow construction of a house upon the fill. The debris used for the fill seems to have been from scrap that was adjacent to the area, found to be about three meters deep and comprising about 250 cubic meters.

Sorting of the material in the fill occurred in 2005 and 2006, and the results are very revealing of the activities in Jerusalem. While the fill occurred in the late eighth century, the debris was older, and in fact the "pottery found here seems to belong to the early eighth century and perhaps even to the late ninth century." (Reich, Shukron, and Lernau, RDCDJ, 156) Thus we get a good picture of the period just adjacent to the United Monarchy.

The debris included "approximately ten seals and scarabs (some broken and thus cancelled) and fragments of over 170 clay bullae," none bearing markings in a local language. (Reich, Shukron, and Lernau, RDCDJ, 156) Instead, those that were marked bore signs from Egypt or Samaria or Phoenicia.

Additionally, a significant quantity of fish remains were found among the debris. From the almost eight thousand identifiable skeletal fish parts, more than 90 percent were from saltwater fish. (Reich, Shukron, and Lernau, RDCDJ, 158) In reviewing these findings, Na'aman concludes:

> This accidental find makes it possible to re-evaluate the society, economy and culture of Jerusalem in the ninth century BCE. The importation of a large amount of fish from the Mediterranean and the Nile testifies that a network of commerce with the coast of Philistia was already developed at that time. The papyrus imprints on the bullae indicate extensive writing, though it may have been

used only by the royal palace and the elite. The many different designs on the bullae, each representing the seal's owner, show that seals were used by many court officials and private citizens. The absence of writing on the seal impressions shows that the fashion of inscribing the owner's name on a seal was introduced later, in the second half of the eighth century BCE. The sealed artifacts must have been commercial commodities, or taxes, brought to the court from the surrounding districts. (Na'aman, DARDS, 170)

We can thus deduce that Jerusalem experienced a period of great, far-reaching commerce. Combining all the evidence from Jerusalem leads Na'aman to conclude "that Jerusalem must have been a governing center of a kingdom in the tenth century BCE." (Na'aman, CALDS, 14)

B. General Building Activity in the United Monarchy

A period of United Monarchy as described in Scripture would have resulted in great prosperity and growth for the kingdom of Israel and the surrounding region. The building activities, commerce, security, and stability that extended out from the central government would have positively affected the region. We see evidence of the United Monarchy reflected in finds as diverse as mining activities, the production of honey, and increasing literacy.

1. Mining Activity in the Jordan Rift Valley

Most early archaeological work in the Near East affirmed that the copper mining activity found in the Jordan rift valley confirmed the Solomonic activity of the United Monarchy. This view changed in the 1960s as new archaeological theory contended that mining evidenced in the southern areas occurred much earlier than the United Monarchy period, while the works in the mines of the northern area appeared to have occurred during a much later period. Much of this new dating was based on pottery found within the mine area. However, several more recent studies using more accurate radiocarbon dating have challenged this assumption and reestablished the timeline for the operation of these mines concurrent with the period of the United Monarchy.

a. Faynan Mines

The Faynan mines in the northern rift valley were the first of the rift valley mines to be dated through the large scale use of radiocarbon dating. The study found that there was "unambiguous 14C AMS dating evidence presented here for industrial-scale metal production at KEN during the 10th and 9th c. BCE." (Levy et al., HPRD, 16465) This new dating reestablished the traditional timeline, and showed that assumption of "large-scale 7th c. BCE copper production in Faynan is no longer tenable." (Levy, HPRD, 16465)

b. Timna Mines

New evidence for the United Monarchy has also been found at the Timna mines. There the new minimalist view had asserted that the date of operation of these mines was significantly before the United Monarchy. Based on pottery dating, minimalists asserted that the Timna mines must have been an operation under Egyptian oversight. An initial small set of radiocarbon samples seemed to confirm their assumptions.

However, following Faynan, recent and more precise radiocarbon dating that leveraged a large twenty-one-sample set has caused rethinking of the minimalist view. Results from this large scale sample reset the dating of Timna back to "the same time frame represented in Faynan" (Ben-Yosef et al., NCFIA, 31–32), that is, to the traditional time of the United Monarchy.

Archaeologists posit a couple of reasons that the results from pottery and small scale samples were erroneous. First, they conjecture that the radiocarbon samples "were obtained from charcoal samples and were probably biased by the 'old wood effect,' which, as demonstrated above, can render the age up to 160 years older than the actual smelting operation." (Ben-Yosef et al., NCFIA, 63–64) They then explain the variance from the pottery fragment dating was due to the fact that there was intermixing of the layers in the excavations and the "pottery identification and stratigraphic discernment of the Arabah Expedition were confused." (Ben-Yosef et al., NCFIA, 63–64)

Significantly, in reviewing the overall mining operations of the Jordan rift valley, archaeologists have concluded that there was a "social unity between the two regions during the Iron Age; i.e., the same social groups inhabited both regions and operated the copper extraction systems simultaneously and under the same general production system and organization management." (Ben-Yosef et al., NCFIA, 63–64)

Though the archaeologists have avoided reaching conclusions from the dating and organizational studies, it should be obvious that a large-scale and regionally defined mining operation supports a well-defined social structure. That this was in the period of the United Monarchy is hardly coincidental. This fits neatly into our cumulative case for the United Monarchy.

2. Beehives at Tel Rehov

Large-scale commerce occurs when there is a strong regional government and is absent when commerce is more localized and large production would outpace available demand. The discovery, then, of a massive production of honey at Tel Rehov adds to our cumulative case.

A large scale apiary (bee farm) is a complex undertaking to support, as is distributing the vast amount of honey generated. At Tel Rehov, the beehives discovered are estimated to have supported at least one million bees. (Mazar and Panitz-Cohen, IILH, 210) Archaeologists have concluded that:

> Based on the ceramic evidence and C14 dates, the apiary at Tel Rehov was in use during the latter part of the United Monarchy and/or during the initial period of the Northern Kingdom of Israel, prior to the Omride Dynasty. The organized establishment and efficient operation of the Rehov apiary, as well as its related cultic practices, indicate that there had been a robust central authority that was able to conduct such a specialized industry and to force the populace to tolerate a huge number of bees in the center of their town. (Mazar and Panitz, IILH, 218)

3. Signs of Literacy

Literacy is considered a hallmark of an advanced ancient civilization. Critics have long claimed that literacy in Israel at the time of the United Monarchy was virtually nonexistent. Without literacy it is very difficult to establish and develop an advanced civilization. Further, without written documentation, biblical history would have been maintained only in oral tales, distorted over time, and not written down until the postexilic period. So the discovery of meaningful literacy near the time of the United Monarchy would provide significant weight to the biblical account and our cumulative case.

In the last several decades a number of inscriptions from the period of the United

Monarchy have been found. The rate of discovery of new texts occurs so frequently that between an accounting published in 2009 that "half a dozen Judahite texts from tenth century BCE are now known" (Becking, DBIE, 20) and the 2014 release of a study on the Tel Rehov inscriptions, the list related by archaeologists grew to "13 tenth century inscriptions, and 12 ninth century ones." (Mazar and Ahituv, ITRTC, 57–58)

In addition to the growth in the number of known inscriptions, there are several other rebuttals to the skeptic's claim that Israel lacked literacy and was not an advanced nation at the time of the United Monarchy. First, when comparing the number of known inscriptions from the disputed tenth century BC to the ninth century when "all agree that states run by royal dynasties existed in both Judah and Israel," there is no large discrepancy. The number of inscriptions from the uncontroversial period is "also small and, in fact, is no larger than the number of inscriptions dating to the tenth century BCE. Thus, the quantitative aspect of literacy cannot serve as a reliable criterion for determining whether or not there was a state in Israel during the tenth century BCE." (Mazar and Ahituv, ITRTC, 63)

Additionally, when we analyze the writing, we see that much of it is dedicated not to the formal areas of temple or royal writing, but to everyday tasks such as accounting for commerce or marking up imported goods. While temple or royal scribal activity might be very limited, from this everyday routine writing, "It can be surmised that there was a larger body of writing on perishable materials such as papyri that have not been preserved." (Mazar and Ahituv, ITRTC, 63)

In the following sections we explore additional evidence of literacy in Israel during the United Monarchy period.

a. Tel Zayit

In July 2005, archaeologists discovered an inscription on the side of an ancient building in Tel Zayit. Because of its "well-defined archaeological context," (Tappy et al., AMTC, 5) archaeologists concluded that the "writing must date no later than the mid tenth century BCE" (Tappy et al., AMTC, 22)

b. Tel Rehov

A cache of storage jars at the Tel Rehov excavation revealed a number of inscriptions with references to the name Nimshi, a name also recorded in the Bible for the clan or father of King Jehu (1 Kings 19:16 NIV). As we see elsewhere, the frequency of names used in a given culture can be linked to certain time periods. Therefore, while it is nearly impossible to establish that it is a biblical person who is named in the inscriptions, we can often make a probable link because of the evidence. Archaeologists have speculated that the link at least establishes the "central role of the Nimshi clan as an elite one at Tel Rehov and the Beth Shean Valley," which would appear to be where "Jehu came from." (Mazar and Ahituv, ITRTC, 64)

c. Jerusalem

The lack of writing from the time of a united kingdom fosters much of the skepticism about Jerusalem being the center of such a kingdom. Increasingly, however, inscriptions are being found outside of Jerusalem (including inscriptions with foreign writing that were obviously imported into the area), but very few provide evidence of literacy in the city. So it was of great importance when in 2012 a new inscription on pottery shards was discovered during excavations in Jerusalem at the Ophel (the part of the eastern hill that is located between the city and the Temple Mount). This inscription has been dated

to the second half of the tenth century BC, which makes it the oldest Hebrew inscription found in Jerusalem by several centuries. (Galil, OHIJ, 21–22) The inscription is limited, but seems to refer to a container of wine.

C. Khirbet Qeiyafa

In 2007, excavations started at Khirbet Qeiyafa overlooking the Elah valley. The remains of this massive fortress are located in a desolate area twenty miles southwest of Jerusalem, above what would have been the main route between Philistia on the coastal plain and Jerusalem. Ideally positioned as the best meeting place for forces from the mountainous areas to confront those coming up from the plains, tradition identifies this as the site of the battle between David and Goliath.

There are several reasons for linking this site to the United Monarchy. First, the city appears to have had only one Iron Age occupation period before it was suddenly destroyed. So artifacts from the city can be dated rather closely to that destruction period. Radiometric dating of those artifacts with a series of separate tests indicates that the destruction of the city occurred between 1006 and 970 BC. (Garfinkel et al., IIKQ, 222)

Second, the city layout of Khirbet Qeiyafa reveals casemate walls at the back of a perimeter of dwellings. This is the oldest example of this Iron Age II design, which is also used in four other cities of that period—cities that are located within the kingdom of Judah.

Additionally, excavations have revealed two gates for the city, which is a unique feature of cities of that era, even very large cities. This has led archaeologists to link Khirbet Qeiyafa to the biblical city of Sha'arayim (Shaaraim), which means "two gates" in Hebrew. (Garfinkel and Ganor, KQ, 3) That city is linked to David two of the three times it is mentioned in the Bible (1 Sam. 17:52; 1 Chron. 4:31).

Further, in July 2008 an ostracon (broken pottery with an ink inscription) was discovered that is dated approximately to the period of Iron Age IIA. Analysts assert that the language of the ostracon is an early form of Hebrew and confirms the existence of writing just prior to the period of the United Monarchy. The inscription also shows a Jewish character, as its reconstruction seems to address themes that "suggest that some of the same concerns expressed in the Torah were already present in Israelite society of the eleventh or tenth century BCE." (Hawkins and Buchanan, KQI, 234)

Two other inscriptions were also found, one of which has recently been deciphered and contains the personal name 'Ešbaʿal. This name is the same as Eshbaʿal Ben Shaul, (or Ish-Bosheth son of Saul) who ruled over part of Israel at the same time as David (2 Sam. 2–4). Analysis links it not only to the biblical story but also to the period itself. As archaeologist Yosef Garfinkel writes, the "name 'Ešbaʿal is recorded for one biblical king and likely three other biblical individuals, all from the 10th century BCE. In the following centuries, however, the personal name Ešbaʿal or any other personal name with the element Baʿal disappears from the biblical text." (Garfinkel et al., IIKQ, 230)

One final piece of evidence for the site being occupied by an early Jewish settlement consists not of what was found, but what was missing. While many bones of food animals were found at the site, few pig bones were found. Though this is not conclusive evidence that this was a Jewish settlement, the scarcity of pig, a staple of the Philistine population, does contribute to the cumulative case.

Not only does the archaeological evidence from Khirbet Qeiyafa support the biblical narrative of the United Monarchy, but the location only makes sense if there was a well-organized civilization in the highlands with the capability and need to defend itself from the occupants of the coastal plains. Assessing this evidence, Garfinkel concludes, "These are the animal bones, these are the radiocarbon dating, this is the inscription, these are the fortifications, and then you have the biblical tradition. And what do you know—they just happen to fit nicely with each other." (Garfinkel, as quoted in Zimmerman, DDSE, website)

D. Solomon's Building Activity

The Bible describes some major building activities of Solomon outside of Jerusalem, specifically mentioning construction at Hazor, Megiddo, Gezer, Lower Beth Horon, Baalath, and Tamar (1 Kings 9:15–18). In fact, it describes the Pharaoh conquering Gezer and giving it to his daughter, who was Solomon's wife.

Consequently, we should expect to find archaeological evidence of this construction activity as excavation is completed at the sites of these cities. Yet the archaeological studies conducted at the sites have provided some contradictory evidence.

Early excavations in the 1950s and 1960s seemed to provide substantial evidence for linking Hazor, Megiddo, and Gezer to the time of Solomon. Each had the same distinctive gate and wall construction and seemed to be constructed at the same time. Archaeologist Yigael Yadin noted that the parallel features that so closely match the biblical story "could hardly be a coincidence." (Dever, WDBWK, 1540) Additionally, Gezer had a destruction layer dated by pottery to the tenth century BC. This closely matched the destruction by Pharaoh Shishak, which then allowed placement of the construction zone to "fall within the ca. 970–930 date that the biblical accounts would give for Solomon's reign." (Dever, WDBWK, 1553)

A first challenge, posed by minimalists in the 1970s and 1980s, asserted that the evidence was tainted by the archaeologists' desire to align evidence with the biblical record. Lead archaeologist William Dever has responded by asking how the historical record of the Bible is not only ignored, but treated as a poison pill. He asks why "the biblical texts are always approached with postmodernism's typical 'hermeneutics of suspicion,' but the nonbiblical texts are taken at face value? It seems to be that the Bible is automatically held guilty unless proven innocent." (Dever, WDBWK, 1517)

Indeed, Dever asserts that the present evidence at the sites still shows destruction clearly linked to the Pharaoh's campaign, which can be dated based on Egyptian sources and pottery shards that are unique to that period. Yet, minimalists simply pass over the evidence of the tie between the Shishak raid and the destruction layers, saying it still doesn't "prove the existence of a 'state' of Israel or Judah." (Dever, WDBWK, 1577)

As the minimalist challenge faded, a new challenge in the 1990s arose in the "low chronology" of Israel Finkelstein. He acknowledges most of the archaeological evidence, but instead of using the Shishak raid of 925 BC to anchor the chronology, Finkelstein uses similarities between the building style of palaces from Samaria and Megiddo. He contends the Samarian palace can be securely dated to the ninth century BC by extrabiblical texts in Assyrian records, and so the strata at Megiddo and subsequently similar layers at sites throughout northern Israel must be moved forward. His dating would "bring the date of 11th-century BCE assemblages to the early-to-mid 10th century, and 10th

century BCE assemblages to the early 9th century, with the late Iron I/early Iron IIA transition fixed in the late 10th century BCE." (Finkelstein, LCU, 39)

If, like Finkelstein, one discounts the Bible as historical, then dating the evidence of Solomonic activities becomes a choice of whether you choose to link the archaeological strata to the raid from Shishak attested by Egyptian texts or the building of the Samarian palace attested by Assyrian records. However, while skeptics might find bias in those who see the Bible as adding historical weight, they are hardly neutral themselves. This can be seen in Finkelstein's summary of an update to his chronology in which he insinuates that those who disagree with his conclusions are only doing so because of a desire to see the biblical story prevail. He contends:

> The only disadvantage of the Low Chronology— at least for some—is that it pulls the carpet from under the biblical image of a great Solomonic United Monarchy and puts the spotlight on the Northern Kingdom of the Omride Dynasty as the real first prosperous state of early Israel. Here is the dilemma: How can one diminish the stature of the "good guys" and let the "bad guys" prevail? (Finkelstein, LCU, 39)

Conversely, if we just treat the biblical text as another historical text on par with textual evidence from other ancient sources, without privilege or denigration, we can more fairly evaluate the evidence. The archaeological data from the gates and building activity at Hazor, Megiddo, and Gezer, as well as the remarkably close correlation of physical to textual evidence, supports an interpretation that is "most likely to represent the physical realities" that we see in the story of the United Monarchy. (Kitchen, OROT, 150) Thus, we gain additional strong evidence for our cumulative case.

V. Evidence for the United Monarchy from Postmonarchy Discoveries

Postmonarchial activities that corroborate the existence of the Davidic line of kings and the biblical story provide evidence for the United Monarchy. First, recent discoveries reference the house of David as continuing to rule Judah from the period soon after the United Monarchy. Second, evidence supports the historicity of the battles recorded in the biblical text that pertain to the remnant of the monarchy era, which includes another possible reference to the house of David. This provides indirect evidence for the United Monarchy; and when one sees many points of evidence in a story being supported by outside information, one can have more confidence in the overall story.

A. The Tel Dan Stele

At an archaeological excavation at the ruins of the ancient city of Dan, a stone monument or stele was discovered, and it contains the first extrabiblical reference to the "house of David." The stele consisted of three separate pieces, the first found in 1993 and the remaining two in 1994. The inscription found on the monument celebrates the victory in approximately 800 BC of the king of an Aram-Damascus army over a combined army of the two Jewish states of the divided kingdom. The stele claims that in his victory over the army, he killed the king of Israel, and the king of the line of David.* (Athas, TDI, 281)

This stele documents the existence of a royal line of David within two hundred years

of his reign and within one hundred and fifty years of the end of Solomon's reign. It establishes a direct reference to David that is much nearer his time than any previous references and "shows that David was not a late fiction." (McKenzie, KD, 13)

This evidence has convinced even a proponent of the "low chronological" view such as Israel Finkelstein that the "mention of the 'House of David' in the Tel Dan inscription from the ninth century BCE leaves no doubt that David and Solomon were historical figures." (Finkelstein, KSGA, 114) Dever notes that the authenticity of the inscription is supported by most of the "world's leading epigraphers" who say that in their opinion, the inscription is authentic and the most likely reading is that the inscription "means exactly what it says." (Dever, WDBWK, 1518)

B. The Mesha Stele

The Mesha Stele, originally discovered in 1868 and dated to about 850 BC, contains another reference to the kingdom of Israel. The inscription on this stele, which was destroyed in a battle over ownership, exists now only in a paper facsimile. Its inscription describes how the king of Moab, Mesha, broke from Israel after being under its control for many years. This Mesha seems most likely to be the same King Mesha of Moab that rebelled against Israel after the death of Ahab (2 Kings 3).

In addition to this well-accepted reading of the Mesha Stele inscription, it may also contain a direct reference to the Davidic kingdom. Philologist Andre Lemaire, who has spent many years studying the inscription, announced in 1994 that he found in line thirty-one of the inscription the "only possible restoration is bt[d]wd, the "House of David." (Lemaire, HDRMI, 36)

---

* Some argument exists about exactly which kings were referred to in the inscription. For instance, in an extensive study of the Stele, George Athas concludes that the king of Israel was Jehoahaz ben-Jehu and the king of Judah was Joash ben-Ahaziah.

Critics who argue against the stele's link to the biblical story say the battle described on the stele does not mention an alliance of Judah and Israel, so it does not match the biblical story of the revolt of Mesha. Lemaire notes the discrepancy is very understandable if the battle went as poorly for the Moabites as the Bible described. Additionally, Lemaire suggests that the stele could merely be describing a different battle in a longer Moabic war for freedom from subjugation. (Lemaire, MSOD, 141)

C. The Shoshenq Relief

Solomon's successor was his son Rehoboam. According to the biblical story, God had led the prophet Ahijah to announce the division of the United Monarchy to Jeroboam, who fled to Egypt to await his opportunity to return (1 Kings 11:29). With the ascension of Rehoboam, Jeroboam returned and led the breakoff of the northern tribes to form the kingdom of Israel. Rehoboam was left leading Judah from his capital in Jerusalem.

The Bible describes how in the fifth year of his reign he was attacked by "Shishak king of Egypt" (1 Kings 14:25 NIV), the Pharaoh under whom Jeroboam found refuge during his Egyptian exile. We find external evidence for this attack carved among the reliefs in the temple of Amun in Karnak. Here we find that the Pharaoh Shoshenq I (Shishak) documents a campaign against cities in Palestine. Egyptian pharaohs commonly documented cities they conquered in their campaigns. So while the list does not explicitly name Jerusalem or Rehoboam, it does show a series of cities conquered on both sides of the newly divided Jewish kingdoms. K. A. Kitchen notes that this "shows that Shoshenq I chose not only to cow and loot Rehoboam of Judah, but also to bring his former protégé Jeroboam of Israel to heel." (Kitchen, OROT,

34) With this extrabiblical documentation, we now possess supporting evidence of the biblical account within a decade of the death of Solomon.

Critics attack this link primarily by showing that the biblical story seems to indicate that Egyptian forces attacked Jerusalem and carried away the Solomonic temple and palace treasures (1 Kings 14:25–27). However, Jerusalem is not shown anywhere in the list of conquered cities. There are several explanations for the absence. First, the list at Karnak is fragmentary and Jerusalem very well could be on the portion of the relief that is damaged. Second, Rehoboam could have submitted and the items listed as being seized could have been the result of tribute paid to turn aside the Egyptian army from actually conquering the city. Third, the political situation with the Divided Monarchy was very complex. Jeroboam had sought and received refuge from Shishak in Egypt while waiting for his opportunity to contend for the throne (1 Kings 11:40). Likely, he had made some assurances to Shishak about submitting to him if he attained his kingdom. If he had not paid any tribute after ascension, it would go far in explaining Shishak's expedition against Palestine and may have influenced how the expedition was documented at Karnak. It is also possible that Shishak was there on Jeroboam's invitation to help in his battle against Rehoboam, and the attack on Jerusalem was considered more of a raid than a conquest. Regardless of the reasons, this critical inscription provides solid evidence for the biblical description of the reign of Rehoboam and "the historian can only recognize that 1 Kgs 14:26 indicates that Shoshenq entered and plundered Jerusalem." (Lemaire, TLSJ, 175)

More speculatively, Kitchen has recently suggested that a reference to David appears on the relief at Karnak. In row 8, which discusses southern Judah, symbol numbers 105 and 106 reference "'highland of d-wt'." (Kitchen, PMD, 40) Possible interpretations for the "d-wt" include Dawit (David), Dot, or Dod. Since Dot does not have any associated references, the likely interpretations are Dod, which critics speculate was an ancient deity, or David. While the speculation for the god Dod is popular with historians,

> there is not one scintilla of respectable, explicit evidence for his/her/its existence anywhere in the biblical and ancient Near Eastern world. No ancient king ever calls himself "beloved of Dod'; no temple of Dod has ever been found, and clearly identified as such by first-hand inscriptions. We have no hymns to Dod, no offering-lists for Dod, no published rituals in any ancient language for Dod, no statues of Dod, no altars, vessels, nor any other ritual piece or votive object dedicated to Dod as a clear deity. (Kitchen, PMD, 41)

On the other hand, the surrounding text does mention dynastic rulers of the locations that are referenced. "Many scholars of varying background are happy enough to read numbers 71 + 72 as 'the field/terrain of Abram'." (Kitchen, PMD, 42) Considering the evidence, Kitchen's identification of another reference to David seems plausible, even likely.

VI. Summary

Skeptics spend a great deal of energy attacking the historicity of the United Monarchy by disputing individual pieces of the evidence we have provided. However, when we examine all the evidence, we are left with a solid, cumulative case for the biblical story.

While critics contend that the agrarian nature and the population of Israel in the time of the judges would not support a monarchy, we do have archaeological and documentary evidence consistent with the biblical story. With the rise of the monarchy, we see evidence of the building activity along with evidence supporting commerce and prosperity. And as the divided kingdom continued to build we see evidence that not only supports the biblical story of that time, but points back to the founding Davidic monarchy.

While critics primarily treat the Bible with skepticism, we have no reason to believe it should not at least have the same evidentiary status as other ancient texts. Even though it is a religious text, the Bible provides detailed historical information that can be verified.* As that information is supported by external evidence, the validity of the Bible as a very valuable historical record is strengthened and confirmed.

Against every attack we can confidently defend each argument of the case we have built, while understanding that the cumulative case is our greatest strength.

---

* For additional information, see Cyrus Gordon's article, "Homer and Bible: The Origin and Character of East Mediterranean Literature," *Hebrew Union College Annual* 26 (1955): 43–108.

CHAPTER 22

THE HISTORICITY OF THE DIVIDED MONARCHY AND EXILIC PERIOD

OVERVIEW

I. Introduction

This chapter focuses on the time of Israel's history called the Divided Monarchy. After Solomon's death, the north (commonly called Israel) split off from the south (Judah); the two kingdoms never reunited. This chapter considers the evidence for the period through the fall of the north to Assyria in 722 BC, the final fall of Jerusalem to Babylon in 586 BC, and the return from exile under Persia. While the United Monarchy is not well represented in extrabiblical sources, Israel and Judah in the Divided Monarchy era appear frequently in the records of other nations, especially during the latter part of the period.

II. Current Objections to the Biblical Narrative

However, in spite of these records, many scholars doubt the historicity of the biblical account of the Divided Monarchy. We will explore two prominent objections to the traditional dating of the historical records of the divided kingdom and exile.

A. Finkelstein's "Low Chronology"

Based on his interpretation of archaeological evidence, influential scholar Israel Finkelstein has proposed a new chronological scheme for the Divided Monarchy. (Finkelstein and Silberman, BU) He acknowledges that David and Solomon existed and were sovereign over their people, but he takes the view that "we still have no hard archaeological evidence—despite the unparalleled biblical descriptions of its grandeur—that Jerusalem was anything more than a modest highland village in the time of David, Solomon, and Rehoboam." (Finkelstein and Silberman, BU, 158) Finkelstein dates much of what has been traditionally ascribed to the early kingdoms of Israel and Judah, such as the six-chambered gates at Megiddo, Hazor, and Gezer, to the later dynasty of the Omrides. Based on that premise, he argues, Solomon could not have built the cities, walls, reservoirs, and other projects with which he has traditionally been credited. Likewise, he argues that the conquests of David do not appear to be confirmed by archaeology, as Canaanite culture continued in the archaeological record without any apparent change.

Finkelstein's views are also partly based on a rejection of the possibility of true prophecy. A central example of this "theologizing" of history by later revisionists can be found in how Finkelstein understands the alleged prophecy in 1 Kings 13 regarding the rise of Josiah some three hundred years later:

> It is something like reading a history of slavery written in seventeenth century colonial America in which there is a passage predicting the birth of Martin Luther King. . . . The precision of the earlier prophecy of the "man of God" gives away the era when it was written. . . . The inescapable fact is that the books of Kings are as much a passionate religious argument—written in the seventh century BCE—as they are works of history. (Finkelstein and Silberman, BU, 165–166)

Under the pressure of the above assumptions, Finkelstein reconfigures his understanding of the Divided Monarchy's timeline and characteristics, resulting in a rejection of much of the historical detail in Scripture regarding the earlier United Monarchy. In sum, while Finkelstein agrees that David and Solomon were historical characters, he contends the biblical account of them is not historically accurate. Instead, much of the grand archaeological material formerly assigned to them should be associated with later kings of the Divided Monarchy.

B. Minimalism

Secondly, "minimalist" scholars assert that not only is the history of the Bible inaccurate, but that much of it was constructed many hundreds of years later in order to create a sort of national identity for a hitherto scattered and nomadic set of tribal groups. (Davies, SAI) Like Finkelstein, minimalists doubt that David and Solomon ruled kingdoms as the Bible describes. They also doubt that most of the events of the Divided Monarchy happened as described in the Old Testament. Biblical scholar and archaeologist Philip R. Davies argues that the Hasmonean dynasty (beginning in the second century BC)

> must be seen as the nearest that Judah ever approached to the ideal enshrined in its literature: a monarchic state stretching over most of Palestine, and defeating its neighbors, the erstwhile Ammonites, Moabites and Edomites, as well as inflicting revenge, finally, on the erstwhile kingdom of Israel by destroying the Samaritan sanctuary. (Davies, SAI, 149)

While minimalists usually recognize that extrabiblical records refer to the kingdoms of Israel and Judah, they see these kingdoms as very different from those recorded in the Old Testament.

III. Hebrew Records of the Divided Kingdom and Exilic Period

As most scholars today agree, "Hebrew royal monuments are yet to be found; their absence is due to the hazards of survival and discovery." (Millard, IAHLI, 261) The region of ancient Canaan was repeatedly ravaged and traded between the world powers of Egypt, Assyria, Babylon, and Persia. Nevertheless, it was rebuilt in the interim of relative peace between these conquests, but always at the price of its history. This was common practice at the time. Finkelstein writes, "At Dan, the victory stele* of Hazael was apparently smashed and the fragments reused in later construction. . . . At Bethsaida, the stele bearing the Aramean-style deity was likewise intentionally upended and laid upside down." (Finkelstein and Silberman, BU, 207) Still, a few scraps of archaeological evidence have survived, though not nearly as many as we would like.

Israelite kings enjoy little record outside of the Bible. As Kitchen says, "The famous seal of 'Shema servant (= minister of state) of Jeroboam' is almost universally recognized to belong to the reign of Jeroboam II of Israel." (Kitchen, OROT, 19) Finkelstein echoes this sentiment: "The design of the lion on the seal is typical of the eighth century BCE, so it cannot be ascribed to Jeroboam, who ruled earlier." (Finkelstein and Silberman, BU, 209) Another seal, which reads, "Abdi, servant of Hoshea," mentions the second king of the "house of Israel," the final family ruling Israel. (Kitchen, OROT, 19)

Some evidence for Judah's kings is also available but, like Israel, it consists mostly of small fragments and seals. Various artifacts, apparently belonging to servants of

"Hezekiah, (son of) Ahaz, King of Judah," give evidence for that king's rule and family. The majority of finds, especially for those of Josiah, "are without certainty and do not rank as firm evidence." (Kitchen, OROT, 19–20)

Since we possess only a few extrabiblical Hebrew inscriptions, nearly all of the historical data we have from the Hebrew perspective can be found within Kings and Chronicles, biblical books. Therefore, we turn to these documents, not to assume their veracity but to compare the Bible's claims with outside historical and archaeological evidence. The biblical record of dynastic rulers that followed the split of the united kingdom under Solomon is extensive. The records of both the kingdoms of Israel and Judah list around forty total rulers. Because many of these rulers enjoy little to no extrabiblical attestation, it is not necessary to explore the reigns of all of them. Rather, we will content ourselves to look at the "big picture" of dynastic families, including the lineages of Rehoboam and Jeroboam, Omri, Hezekiah, Josiah, and Jehoiakim/Jehoiachin. We reference these as they tie in with the evidence from foreign powers in conflict with Israel and Judah at the time, since neither Israel nor Judah operated in a vacuum.

As Kitchen points out:

Thus we find in Kings a very remarkably preserved royal chronology, mainly very accurate in fine detail, that agrees very closely with the dates given by Mesopotamian and other sources. Such a legacy would, most logically, derive from then-existing archives (such as the "book(s) of the annals of the kings of Judah" and "of Israel" mentioned in Kings), besides archives of administrative, legal, or other documents. It cannot well be the free

---

* A stele is a large stone or wooden slab erected by ancient Near Eastern rulers to commemorate important events or mark out national borders.

Thus we find in Kings a very remarkably preserved royal chronology,
mainly very accurate in fine detail, that agrees very closely with
the dates given by Mesopotamian and other sources.

K. A. Kitchen

creation of some much later writer's imagination that just happens (miraculously!) to coincide almost throughout with the data then persevered only in documents buried inaccessibly in the ruin mounds of Assyrian cities long since abandoned and largely lost to view. (Kitchen, OROT, 29–32)

Millard echoes this sentiment when he says that since much of the historical record is independently attested, "they cannot be dismissed as inventions." (Millard, IAHLI, 267) Additionally, Millard points out that ascribing victory in battle and other major accomplishments to a deity were commonplace throughout the ancient Near East. If the historical credibility of the Aramean, Assyrian, Egyptian, and Babylonian records can be considered more or less intact despite frequent praise to deities, then why should the Hebrew record be treated differently?

A. Tenth and Ninth Centuries*

1. Shishak, Pharaoh of Egypt

Almost immediately after the division of Israel and Judah, foreign powers, sensing weakness and hoping for expansion and profit, invaded both kingdoms. In the fifth year of Rehoboam, the Bible reports that Shishak, king of Egypt, invaded Jerusalem (1 Kings 14:25; 2 Chron. 12:2). As Finkelstein and Silberman put it, "The pharaoh

Shishak, founder of the Twenty-second Dynasty (known as Sheshonq in Egyptian inscriptions), launched an aggressive raid northward. This Egyptian invasion is mentioned in the Bible . . . in a passage that offers the earliest correlation between external historical records and the biblical text." (Finkelstein and Silberman, BU, 161) External historical records document Shishak's Egyptian invasion at the beginning of Rehoboam's independent rule over Judah. (Greenwood, LTNCI, 290–291) The key is that at least two separate Egyptian records confirm the biblical account—one discovered in Egypt and one in the Canaanite city of Megiddo. Finkelstein describes the Egyptian source as "a triumphal inscription commissioned by Sheshonq for the walls of the great temple of Karnak in Upper Egypt." (Finkelstein and Silberman, BU, 161) The Canaanite source is a victory stele bearing the name of Shishak, which lists "the once-great Canaanite cities of Rehov, Beth-shean, Taanach, and Megiddo . . . as targets of the Egyptian forces." (Finkelstein and Silberman, BU, 161)

2. Mesha, King of Moab

Mesha, the king of the Moabites, ruled simultaneously with the Omride dynasty in general and Ahab in particular. Mesha was a ruler "whose principal wealth was in

---

* For a survey of the historical issues during this time period, see Kyle Greenwood, "Late Tenth-and Ninth-Century Issues: Ahab Underplayed? Jehoshaphat Overplayed?," in *Ancient Israel's History: An Introduction to Issues and Sources*, ed. Bill T. Arnold and Richard S. Hess (Grand Rapids: Baker, 2014), 286–318.

sheep" (Kitchen, OROT, 13), something one of the surviving Hebrew accounts also mentions (2 Kings 3:4). According to the Bible, Omri achieved leverage over the people of Moab—something his son, Ahab, continued to wield when he ascended to power. Second Kings 3:4, 5 states that Mesha paid significant tribute to the king of Israel, which ended upon Ahab's death. Mesha, eager to throw off his vassal status to Israel, rebelled at the earliest opportunity (2 Kings 3:5). Significant external record of Mesha and his relationship to Israel comes from Mesha himself. In 1868 archaeologists uncovered a fragmentary stele in southern Jordan. The site of the discovery was, more specifically, "the site of biblical Dibon, the capital of the kingdom of Moab." (Finkelstein and Silberman, BU, 177) The inscription includes the following account of Mesha's interaction with Omri and Ahab:

> Omri was the king of Israel, and he oppressed Moab for many days, for Kemosh was angry with his land. And his son succeeded him, and he said—he too—"I will oppress Moab." In my days did he say [so], but I looked down on him and on his house, and Israel has gone to ruin, yes, it has gone to ruin for ever [sic]! And Omri had taken possession of the whole la[n]d of Medeba, and he lived there (in) his days and half the days of his son, forty years, but Kemosh [resto]red it in my days. (Smelik, WAI, 33)

Finkelstein continues: "Though Mesha barely disguises his contempt for Omri and his son Ahab, we nonetheless learn from his triumphal inscription that the kingdom of Israel reached far east and south of its earlier heartland in the central hill country." (Finkelstein and Silberman, BU, 177) For historians, the Mesha Stele also gives us "the first nonbiblical description of the Omrides ever found," serving to confirm the historical existence of Omri, Ahab, and their relationship to one another. (Finkelstein and Silberman, BU, 177) While how exactly the event recorded on the stele fits with the biblical account of Israelite-Moabite relations is debated (in particular, whether the stele recounts the same event as 2 Kings 3), this particular discovery helps to confirm the biblical account from the perspective of an enemy of Israel.

3. Hazael, King of Aram-Damascus

The Aramean king Hazael is one of the more interesting foreign rulers mentioned in the Hebrew records, not in small part due to his being anointed as king of Aram by the Hebrew prophet Elijah (1 Kings 19:15). Hazael's forces later became a nearly constant military harassment to the Hebrew kingdoms, and to Israel in particular (2 Kings 8:28, 29; 9:14, 15; 10:32; 12:17, 18; 13:3, 22; 2 Chron. 22:5, 6). Historically verifiable connections between Hazael and the kings of Israel and Judah are widely accepted by scholars today. In similar fashion to the Mesha Stele, inscriptions attributed to Hazael of Aram-Damascus corroborate the biblical account. Finkelstein, discussing the inscription discovered in 1993 at Tel Dan, writes:

> Although the name of the monarch who erected it was not found on the fragments that have so far been recovered, there is little doubt, from the overall context, that this was the mighty Hazael, king of Aram-Damascus. . . . From the inscription, it seems that Hazael captured the city of Dan and erected a triumphal stele there around 835 BCE. The inscription records the words of the victorious Hazael in his angry accusation that "the king of I[s]rael entered previously in my father's land." Since this inscription apparently mentioned the

name of Ahab's son and successor, Jehoram, the implication is clear. (Finkelstein and Silberman, BU, 178; for the text see Millard, TDS, 162)

4. Shalmaneser III, King of Assyria

Shalmaneser III ruled Assyria from 859–824 BC. (For his inscriptions, see "Shalmaneser III," translated by K. Lawson Younger, in Hallo and Younger, CS, 2.113:261–71; Grayson, AREFM, 5–179.) His "black obelisk" names two Israelite rulers. Next to a relief of Jehu bowing to Shalmaneser the inscription reads, "I received tribute from Jehu (Iaua) of the house of Omri (Ḥumrî): silver, gold, a gold bowl, a gold tureen, gold vessels, gold pails, tin, the staffs of the king's hand, (and) spears." (Grayson, AREFM, 149) Finkelstein comments that "the fact that Jehu is named 'son of Omri'—in essence son of the family he is reported to have exterminated—implies only that he ruled a vassal kingdom whose capital city was founded by Omri." (Finkelstein and Silberman, BU, 206)

Another relic of Shalmaneser's reign, the Monolith Inscription, was discovered by an English explorer in the mid-1800s. In it, Shalmaneser claims victory over the anti-Assyrian forces he fought, among them listing "2,000 chariots (and) 10,000 troops of Ahab (Aḫabbu) the Israelite (Sir'alāia)." (Grayson, AREFM, 23) As Finkelstein goes on to point out, this is "the earliest nonbiblical evidence of a king of Israel," and "Thus we learn from three ancient inscriptions [the Mesha Stele, Dan Stele, and Monolith Inscription] (ironically from three of Israel's bitterest enemies) information that dramatically supplements and supports the biblical account." (Finkelstein and Silberman, BU,

178–179) However, the stele also illustrates potential difficulties in correlating biblical and extrabiblical sources. The Aramean king according to Shalmaneser III is Hadadezer, but according to the biblical account his name is Ben-Hadad. Rather than speculating that a story that happened later has been moved to this time period, some propose it is more likely that Ben-Hadad was a throne name for Hadadezer (as it is apparently used in Amos 1:4 as a throne name for Hazael). (Greenwood, LTNCI, 308–9)

5. Idolatry of the Israelites

The Old Testament frequently proclaims the idolatry of the Israelites throughout their history. Evidence of this has been found in a variety of sources outside of the Bible. For example, several texts associating YHWH with Asherah (a Canaanite goddess) have been found, showing syncretistic Israelite worship. (e.g., "Kuntillet 'Ajrud," translated by P. Kyle McCarter in Context of Scripture 2.47:171–73) The idolatry of Jeroboam has also found archaeological proof through the archaeological excavations at Dan. When the Israelites left Judah, Jeroboam placed two golden calves at either end of his territory: Dan in the north and Bethel in the south (1 Kings 12:28, 29). A sanctuary has been found at Dan that dates to his time period, indicating the place where the golden calf would have been placed. (Kitchen, OROT, 54)

B. Eighth Century*
1. Tiglath-Pileser, King of Assyria

This Assyrian king Tiglath-Pileser, who reigned from 745–727 BC, is mentioned briefly by his alias, Pul, as having successfully

---

* For more on the historical events of this time period, see Sandra Richter, "Eighth-Century Issues: The World of Jeroboam II, the Fall of Samaria, and the Reign of Hezekiah," in *Ancient Israel's History: An Introduction to Issues and Sources*, ed. Bill T. Arnold and Richard S. Hess (Grand Rapids: Baker, 2014), 319–49.

made Israel into an Assyrian vassal state (2 Kings 15:19). Biblical support for his being the same person may be found in 1 Chronicles 5:26, where the exact same formulaic structure is used of both names. As Kitchen points out, he "is the earliest Assyrian king named in Kings and Chronicles, and the third ruler of his name." (Kitchen, OROT, 15) The shorthand "Pul" has also been found outside the biblical accounts in a Babylonian king list. ("Babylonian King Lists" in Hallo and Younger, CS, 1.134:462; "The Babylonian King List A" in Pritchard, ANET, 272) Like the other Assyrian emperors, Tiglath-Pileser is depicted as an opportunistic ruler who capitalized on the relative weakness of the surrounding region to expand his borders and influence (2 Kings 15:29; 16:7–18).

A relief, recovered from the time of Tiglath-Pileser, mentions the expansion of his empire into Israelite territory. Finkelstein gives us the translation: "The land of Bit-Humria [i.e., the House of Omri], all of whose cities I leveled to the ground in my former campaigns. . . . I plundered its livestock, and I spared only isolated Samaria." (Finkelstein and Silberman, BU, 215)

2. Rezin, King of Aram

Rezin king of Syria continued the Aramean pattern of attempted conquest against Judah, this time with help from Pekah of Israel. However, according to the Hebrew records, he was repeatedly unsuccessful (2 Kings 15:37; 16:5, 9; Isa. 7:1). This may have been due, in part, to larger problems for Aram. According to Kitchen, "Rezin was the last Aramean ruler at Damascus, suppressed by Tiglath-pileser III in 732 (2 Kings 16:9)." (Kitchen, OROT, 14; cf. Tadmor and Yamada, RITP, 58–59) After the death of Rezin, the Assyrian Empire's influence over the region continued to grow.

3. Shalmaneser V and Sargon II, Kings of Assyria

Shalmaneser V's superior forces held Israel as a tributary state—a fragile balance with which the Israelite king Hoshea later meddled, to his own peril. Attempting to strike a secret anti-Assyrian accord with Egypt, Hoshea sent messages and tribute to So, pharaoh of the Egyptians. His plan was discovered and reported to Shalmaneser V, who, the Bible says, quickly descended upon Israel and laid siege to it (2 Kings 18:9–12).

Shortly after his conquest of Samaria, Shalmaneser V died and was replaced by Sargon II. (see "Sargon II," translated by K. Lawson Younger, Jr. in Hallo, CS, 2.118: 293–300) Sargon is absent from the records of Kings and Chronicles, but he is mentioned briefly by Isaiah in reference to the coming captivity of Israel by the Assyrian forces (Isaiah 20:1–6). As part of his attempt to establish his rule, Sargon II claimed that he, rather than his predecessor, conquered Samaria. Sargon boasts,

> I counted as spoil 27,280 people, together with their chariots, and gods, in which they trusted. I formed a unit with 200 of [their] chariots for my royal force. I settled the rest of them in the midst of Assyria. I repopulated Samerina [Samaria] more than before. I brought into it people from countries conquered by my hands. I appointed my eunuch as governor over them. And I counted them as Assyrians. (see "Nimrud Prisms D & E," translated by K. Lawson Younger in Hallo and Younger, CS, 2.118D:295–296)

However, most scholars think that Sargon II claimed a victory that properly belonged to Shalmaneser V. The biblical ascription of the conquest to Shalmaneser V is supported by a Babylonian text, which reads that Shalmaneser V "ravaged Samaria." (Grayson, ABC, 73) As Kitchen explains,

> Following Shalmaneser V's very brief reign, which ended before any account of his last year could be monumentalized, Sargon II replaced him in a coup d'etat, and subsequently claimed the capture of Samaria for himself. . . . To the biblical writers, it was of no importance which Assyrian king reduced Samaria—only the event and its significance for them (seen as a judgment) actually mattered. (Kitchen, OROT, 39)

4. Sennacherib, King of Assyria

Shortly after the fall of Israel, and during the reign of Hezekiah, Judah became the target of the next king of Assyria—Sargon's son, Sennacherib (2 Kings 18:13). (For Sennacherib's inscriptions, see Grayson and Novotny, RIS, parts 1 and 2.) As Finkelstein describes it, "after the death of Sargon in 705 BCE, when the ability of the empire to control its faraway territories looked questionable, Judah entered an anti-Assyrian coalition, which was backed by Egypt (2 Kings 18:21; 19:9). . . . Four years later, in 701 BCE, the new Assyrian king, Sennacherib, came to Judah with a formidable army." (Finkelstein and Silberman, BU, 251)

Sennacherib describes his conquest of Hezekiah in the following quotation. Although he does not refer to the loss of troops at the hands of an angel as recorded in the Bible (2 Kings 19:35), his limited victory is the closest an Assyrian king can come to an admission of defeat. (The fact that he does not remove Hezekiah from power as he normally would treat a rebellious ruler seems significant evidence for his tacit acknowledgment of a less-than-final victory.)

> As for him (Hezekiah), I confined him inside the city of Jerusalem, his royal city, like a

bird in a cage. I set up blockades against him and made him dread exiting his city gate. I detached from his land the cities of his that I had plundered and I gave (them) to Mitiniti, the king of the city Ashdod, and Padî, the king of the city Ekron, (and) Ṣilli-Bēl, the king of the land Gaza, (and thereby) made his land smaller. To the former tribute, their annual giving, I added the payment (of) gifts (in recognition) of my overlordship and imposed (it) upon them. (Grayson and Novotny, RIS, 65)

The archaeology of Jerusalem has revealed many connections to Hezekiah. The most impressive is the Siloam Tunnel, dug by Hezekiah to bring water inside the city during a siege (2 Kings 20:20). An important inscription was found inside the tunnel that was apparently made by the workers who constructed the tunnel. Written in Hebrew, it describes the day that the two teams (working from either end of the tunnel) reached each other and opened the complete tunnel. (Younger, STI, 145–146) Monumental walls were also built at this time to help defend the city; the bottom portion of these walls can still be seen in Jerusalem today. (Richter, ECI, 342–349)

An inscription that also relates to this period was discovered in the village of Silwan (across the Kidron Valley from Jersualem), from an ancient Judean cave. Though the reading was damaged by Byzantine monks who later lived in the cave, the inscription most likely belonged to Shebna, who is mentioned in Isaiah 22:15–25. (see "The Royal Steward Inscription" in Hallo and Younger, CS, 2.54:180)

C. Seventh and Sixth Centuries
1. Nebuchadnezzar, King of Babylon

While Egyptian and Assyrian influence waned, Babylon rose to prominence over the ancient Near East, conquering and forcing Judah into servitude (2 Kings 24:1). Jehoiakim rebelled against his new Babylonian masters, but he died and left his son, Jehoiachin, to face Nebuchadnezzar. The Bible states that, unlike his father, Jehoiachin would not receive help or protection from the Egyptians; the Babylonians already had a stranglehold on any potential Egyptian interference (2 Kings 24:6, 7). Nebuchadnezzar laid siege to Jerusalem and eventually conquered it, taking many prominent Judeans into Babylonian captivity, including King Jehoiachin (2 Kings 24:10–16).

Nebuchadnezzar then placed Jehoiachin's uncle, Zedekiah, in power. After nine years, Zedekiah incited rebellion against the Babylonians, which was met with a prolonged siege and ultimately the destruction of the city (2 Kings 25:1–21). Nebuchadnezzar's lineage would continue for some forty years through Nabonidus and Belshazzar until the rise of the Persian Empire (Cyrus) in 539 BC.

The archaeological findings from the land of Israel and Judah are consistent with the assertion in 2 Kings 24 that not everyone was taken captive. Kitchen states, "The idea that the Babylonians carried *everybody* from both Jerusalem and Judah off to Babylon is true neither archaeologically nor to the biblical text itself." (Kitchen, OROT, 67) However, records have been recovered that show captives were definitely taken. As Kitchen writes, "From a vaulted building closely adjoining the royal palace proper came a series of cuneiform tablets dated to the tenth to thirty-fifth years of Nebuchadnezzar II (595–570), being 'ration tablets' for people kept or employed in Babylon and its palace. Among the beneficiaries in receipt of oil were 'Jehoiachin king of Judah' . . . and 'the 5 sons of the king of Judah in the care of (their

guardian?) Qenaiah." (Kitchen, OROT, 68; see also "Nebuchadnezzar II" in ANET, 308)

A Babylonian text also records the defeat of Judah at the hands of Nebuchadnezzar:

The seventh year: In the month Kislev the king of Akkad mustered his army and marched to Hattu. He encamped against the city of Judah and on the second day of the month Adar he captured the city (and) seized (its) king. A king of his own choice he appointed in the city (and) taking the vast tribute he brought it into Babylon. (Grayson, ABC, 102)

2. Cyrus, King of Persia

Beyond the books of Kings and Chronicles, the postexilic rulers mentioned in Scripture consist exclusively of Babylonian and Medo-Persian regents. Cyrus is mentioned at the very end of 2 Chronicles, briefly in the book of Isaiah, and throughout the exilic book of Ezra as having decreed the return of the Jewish people to their homeland to rebuild the temple in Jerusalem and restart worship (2 Chron. 36:22; Isa. 44:28—5:1; Ezra 1:1–4).

Kitchen summarizes the archaeological landscape: "For all its vastness, and its immense impact in ancient history, we possess only very uneven original and allied sources for the Persian Empire." (Kitchen, OROT, 72) For Cyrus, the best external support we have to date comes not from firsthand sources, but from the *Histories* of Herodotus. A well-known inscription from Cyrus records his version of his conquest of Babylon. Though it does not mention the Jews, his treatment of the Babylonians is similar to that of the Jews, as he treats them kindly, seeks to honor their god, and rescues them from hardship. (see "Cyrus Cylinder," trans. by Mordechai Cogan in *Context of Scripture* 2.124:314–16)

IV. Conclusions and Final Thoughts

We have looked at how the Bible portrays the periods of the Divided Kingdom and the exile. We have also reviewed related archaeological and historical evidence of the period's foreign rulers that are mentioned in the Bible. We have seen the best and most widely accepted evidence from Hebrew, Canaanite, Egyptian, Assyrian, and Babylonian perspectives, and, based on the evidence, we can conclude that the separate kingdoms of Israel and Judah did exist as described in the biblical text.

When the Bible mentions foreign rulers and campaigns, its account does not contradict the records we have from external sources. For some of the particular rulers and periods in the history of these kingdoms, the biblical narrative is the only source we have. Nevertheless, when sources external to the Bible do refer to Israelite and Judahite rulers and events, they do not contradict the biblical account in either chronology or outcome—bearing in mind the exception that nearly all ancient kings glorified themselves, as when Sennacherib conveniently omitted the failure of his siege against Hezekiah or when others claimed for themselves the victories and accomplishments of their vassals and/or predecessors.

The biblical account is written from a distinctly theological perspective, but this is neither unique to the Hebrew historical record nor uncommon among contemporary kingdoms and cultures of the time.

What explanation best accounts for these facts? A significant number of the kings, events, and campaigns recorded in the Bible are independently attested by external (non-Hebrew) sources. Many of these sources would have been unavailable to Hebrew writers a few hundred years later. It is therefore *highly implausible* that the history of the divided kingdoms and exilic periods portrayed in the biblical narrative were the fabrications of later writers. Given the evidence, the most plausible and defensible position is that the narrative in the Bible may be relied upon as a historically accurate account of the events that occurred during this time period.

CHAPTER 23

THE COMPOSITION
OF THE PENTATEUCH

OVERVIEW

I. Importance of the Pentateuch

The Pentateuch is a core text for three world religions. It claims to be God's revelation, disclosing humanity's origins, meaning, purpose, and destiny. This was the traditional view for centuries, and it remains widespread, despite the critical challenges that it has sustained in modernity. Questions of authorship and composition are critical in Pentateuchal scholarship and are especially important for Christian apologists who aim to defend the Scriptures.

This chapter describes the nature and importance of the Pentateuch by surveying a range of relevant data, including medieval Jewish scholarship, critical scholarship, and theologically conservative scholarship since the seventeenth century. We conclude by affirming the plausibility of the traditional view because it best accounts for the majority of relevant data.

A. What Is the Pentateuch?

The term "Pentateuch," a transliteration of a Greek term for "five-volume work," is used to denote the first five Old Testament books: Genesis, Exodus, Leviticus, Numbers, and Deuteronomy. Origen, a third-century church father, was the first to give the name Pentateuch to these five books of Moses. (Harrison, IOT, 496) Jesus frequently refers to these works as Moses' teachings, which was the default term for naming them in first-century Judea. The Pentateuch, a fundamentally important section of Jewish Scriptures (which also includes the Prophets and the Writings), is referred to as "teaching, instruction" or, in Hebrew, Torah.

Referencing a 160-page Pentateuchal bibliography, Jonathan Huddleston claims more has been written on the Pentateuch than on the rest of the entire Hebrew Bible combined. (Huddleston, RSP; Sparks, PAB) The Pentateuch is the foundation of the Christian Bible and the Jewish Scriptures. Bible scholars, commentators, and others see "echoes" of the Pentateuch throughout the Old Testament (Sailhamer, MP, 14–16) Jesus declared Moses' writings included references to himself (Luke 24:27). According to Robert Alter, Professor of Hebrew and Comparative Literature at the University of California, Berkeley, some Jewish traditions claim the world's existence depends on it. (Alter, FBM,

112–114) Indeed, the God revealed in the Pentateuch lays claim to all of creation, from "the heavens and the earth" (Gen. 1:1), to the song Moses writes at the end: "Give ear, O heavens . . . and let the earth hear. . . . For I will proclaim the name of the LORD; ascribe greatness to our God!" (Deut. 32:1, 3).

Both Jews and Christians believe that the Pentateuch, which has profoundly affected billions of people, is a revelation of the one true God and portrays the human condition accurately. As detailed in other parts of this book, plausible evidence exists to believe Jesus rose from the dead. But why did he rise from the dead? The Pentateuch holds the answer. Without the Pentateuch, the New Testament is a nonsensical ending to a story without a beginning. For example, in the wilderness, the people's rebellion brought punishment in the form of serpents entering the camp, and when they repented, God directed Moses to place a bronze serpent high upon a pole. Anyone injured, "when he sees it, shall live" (Num. 21:7–9). Later, Jesus told Nicodemus that what Moses was told to do provided the pattern that he himself, the Son of Man, would fulfill, "that whoever believes in him may have eternal life" (John 3:15). In another example, Genesis 3 explains humanity's fall into error and rebellion, together with God's statement to the serpent about Eve's offspring, "he shall bruise your head, and you shall bruise his heel" (Gen. 3:15). Beyond commonplace human confrontations with snakes, something more important is predicted: the crucifixion fulfills the injury to the heel—but victory over the serpent requires resurrection afterward, "bruising his head" in a final way.

B. Why Question the Composition of the Pentateuch?

For Jewish and Christian sacred writings, authorship and authority have always had a significant bearing on the recognition of inspiration, that is, the acknowledgment of divine revelation and consequent canonization. (Beckwith, CHBOT, 100–102; Bruce, CS, 28–42) Regarding the Pentateuch's authorship and authority, we must ask two questions: (1) "Was Moses its author?" (2) "Are these texts a unitary work such as we might expect from a single author, or are they the outcome of a longer process of composition to which a number of authors contributed?" With regard to the first question, if we have reason to believe Moses existed and possessed suitable skills, abilities, and access to record the events of the Pentateuch, we have strong reasons to take its claims seriously. Conversely, if Moses did not exist, or was a minor historical figure, or was unable to record the events and sayings found in Scripture, the Pentateuch may be merely an interesting artifact of the ancient Near East (ANE). ANE is generally defined as the region that today corresponds with southern Turkey, Armenia, Iran, Iraq, Saudi Arabia, northeast Egypt, Israel, Jordan, Lebanon, Syria, and Cyprus. In section II we will examine evidence for the Pentateuch's authorship by Moses, and in section III we will examine theories and evidence concerning its composition.

II. Traditional Authorship, Authority, and Influence

Technically, the Pentateuch is anonymous. However, it records YHWH commanding Moses to preserve received revelation. Further, there is intrabiblical testimony in the Old Testament of Mosaic involvement in Pentateuchal composition. In addition, Jesus and his apostles acknowledge a significant connection between Moses and the Torah. (Longman and Dillard, IOT, 41) Jewish historian Josephus and Jewish philosopher Philo,

writing in the first century AD, attest to a long tradition of Mosaic authorship. (Josephus, WJ, 115–116; Philo, WP, 3, 492, 495, 517) For most of the Pentateuch's existence, scholars, theologians, historians, and laypeople have thought the great Hebrew prophet composed its contents during the Israelite desert sojourn. (Finkelstein and Silberman, BU, 233–234) Defending Mosaic authorship, seventeenth/eighteenth-century Dutch theologian Hermann Witsius said the evidence was, "of such a kind, that there will be no difficulty in deciding the question of the authorship of the Pentateuch." (Witsius, WMAP, 6)

A. Evidence from the Pentateuch

Testimony to Moses' involvement in authoring the Pentateuch begins in Exodus (unless otherwise indicated, all Scripture quotations in this chapter are taken from the ESV):

1. Exodus 17:14

Then the LORD said to Moses, "Write this as a memorial in a book and recite it in the ears of Joshua, that I will utterly blot out the memory of Amalek from under heaven."

Notably, regardless of the historicity of the battle, there is no longer a people group independently known as Amalekites, whereas a people known as Israelites continues to this day.

2. Exodus 24:4

And Moses wrote down all the words of the LORD.

3. Exodus 24:7

Then he took the Book of the Covenant and read it in the hearing of the people.

(This sentence builds on Ex. 24:4 and emphasizes a written memorial record.)

4. Exodus 34:27

And the LORD said to Moses, "Write these words, for in accordance with these words I have made a covenant with you and with Israel."

5. Numbers 33:2

Moses wrote down their starting places, stage by stage, by command of the LORD, and these are their stages according to their starting places.

Importantly, respected scholar John Currid, in a defense of the exodus's historicity, notes: "Numbers 33 is an original and true account of the Hebrews' wilderness journey." He demonstrates the accounts' similarity with ANE military itineraries, and contends that nothing within the text should cause doubt either to the authenticity of the itinerary or the claim of authorship. (Currid, AEOT, 121–123)

6. Deuteronomy 31:24–26

When Moses had finished writing the words of this law in a book to the very end, Moses commanded the Levites who carried the ark of the covenant of the LORD, "Take this Book of the Law and put it by the side of the ark of the covenant of the LORD your God, that it may be there for a witness against you."

B. Evidence from the Rest of the Old Testament

Testimony to Moses' role in lawgiving is woven throughout the Old Testament.

1. Joshua 1:7, 8 and 23:6

"Only be strong and very courageous, being careful to do according to all the law that Moses my servant commanded you. This Book of the Law shall not depart from your mouth, but you shall meditate on it day and night, so that you may be careful to do all that is written in it."

This command to Joshua is something he passed forward to Israel's leaders when he became old, saying to them, "Therefore be very strong to keep and to do all that is written in the Book of the Law of Moses, turning aside from it neither to the right hand nor to the left" (Josh. 23:6). To generations of Jews and Christians it makes sense that something as important as the Law YHWH gave to Moses would be written down so it could be read to, for, and by the generation to which it was given, and passed on to future generations.*

2. First Kings 2:3

King David giving final instructions to his son, Solomon, says

"Keep the charge of the LORD your God, walking in his ways and keeping his statutes, his commandments, his rules, and his testimonies, as it is written in the Law of Moses, that you may prosper in all that you do and wherever you turn."

3. Second Chronicles 17:9

And they taught in Judah, having the Book of the Law of the LORD with them. They went about through all the cities of Judah and taught among the people.

This is a brief account of teaching of the Law that occurred during Jehoshaphat's reign.

4. Second Chronicles 23:18

And Jehoiada posted watchmen for the house of the LORD under the direction of the Levitical priests and the Levites whom David had organized to be in charge of the house of the LORD, to offer burnt offerings to the LORD, as it is written in the Law of Moses, with rejoicing and with singing, according to the order of David.

---

* For a study of the reliable transmission of the OT, see chapter 4, "Has the Old Testament Been Transmitted Reliably?"

This is an account of one of several revivals that occurred in the kingdom of Judah before final destruction by Babylon.

5. Second Chronicles 25:4

> But he did not put their children to death, according to what is written in the Law, in the Book of Moses, where the LORD commanded, "Fathers shall not die because of their children, nor children die because of their fathers, but each one shall die for his own sin."

This details why Amaziah did not kill the children of the men who assassinated his father, King Joash.

6. Daniel 9:11, 13

As Daniel laments Israel's exile, he refers to Moses' written law,

> All Israel has transgressed your law and turned aside. . . . And the curse and oath that are written in the Law of Moses the servant of God have been poured out upon us, because we have sinned against him. . . . As it is written in the Law of Moses, all this calamity has come upon us.

7. Ezra 3:2

> Then arose Jeshua the son of Jozadak, with his fellow priests, and Zerubbabel the son of Shealtiel with his kinsmen, and they built the altar of the God of Israel, to offer burnt offerings on it, as it is written in the Law of Moses the man of God.

This is from the account of returned exiles as they rebuild Jerusalem.

8. Ezra 6:18

> And they set the priests in their divisions and the Levites in their divisions, for the service of God at Jerusalem, as it is written in the Book of Moses.

This also comes from the account of returned exiles as they rebuild Jerusalem. The description complies with instructions in Numbers 3 and 8.

9. Nehemiah 1:8, 9

> Remember the word that you commanded your servant Moses, saying, "If you are unfaithful, I will scatter you among the peoples, but if you return to me and keep my commandments and do them, though your outcasts are in the uttermost parts of heaven, from there I will gather them and bring them to the place that I have chosen, to make my name dwell there."

This is a prayer of Nehemiah in which he quotes parts of the Pentateuch (Lev. 26:33; 39–42; Deut. 4:25–31; 9:29; 12:5; 28:64; 30:2–4) after hearing of the plight of the returned exiles in Jerusalem.

10. Psalm 105:26

Hebrew poetry and hymnody speak frequently and loudly both of Moses and of the Law. An example of the Psalms' attestation to Moses:

> He sent Moses, his servant, and Aaron, whom he had chosen.

Although this does not attest to his writings, it speaks of how essential his existence was for the role he and his brother played in the exodus.

11. Psalm 78:5–7

> He established a testimony in Jacob and appointed a law in Israel, which he commanded our fathers to teach to their children, that the next generation might know them, the children yet unborn, and arise and tell them to their children, so that they should set their hope in God and not forget the works of God, but keep his commandments.

This psalm attests to Israel's tradition of remembering and passing on God's laws and works. It does not attest to writing by Moses per se. Nevertheless, even critical scholars admit many psalms attest to Pentateuchal traditions:

It can be said that most of the historical summaries demonstrate the special status of the Pentateuchal narrative (often focusing on the Moses story). . . . I think it has been demonstrated that allusions to "history" in the Psalms indeed belong to current Pentateuchal research. (Römer, EPBE, 487–488)

12. Malachi 4:4

"Remember the law of my servant Moses, the statutes and rules that I commanded him at Horeb for all Israel."

These final words from the last of the prophets close out the Old Testament, with verses 5 and 6 pointing toward the coming of "Elijah the prophet" as the forerunner to "the great and awesome day of the Lord," who will restore hearts. Placing a reference to Moses and the law in this position emphasizes once more the centrality of "all" the law (statutes and rules) given to Moses. In the ongoing revelation of the New Testament, Jesus will identify John the Baptist as the promised "Elijah" (Matt. 11:14; 17:10–12).

C. Evidence from the New Testament

The New Testament also speaks of Moses' significant involvement in the Pentateuch's composition.

1. Jesus Spoke of Mosaic Authority

A plurality of Jesus' Scripture quotations comes from books traditionally attributed to Moses: eleven from Deuteronomy, eight from Exodus, three each from Leviticus and Genesis, and one from Numbers. (Moyise, JS, 4)

"For if you believed Moses, you would believe me; for he wrote of me." — John 5:46

In other words, Jesus specifically states Moses wrote at least portions of the Jewish Scriptures.

And beginning with Moses and all the Prophets, he interpreted to them in all the Scriptures the things concerning himself. — Luke 24:27

After his resurrection Jesus gives an additional authority to these books of the Old Testament Scripture when he teaches the two who walk with him to Emmaus how these writings point to himself and are fulfilled in him. Luke, narrating this, credits Moses with involvement in writing the Scriptures.

Jesus taught from the Pentateuch, saying,

"And as for the dead being raised, have you not read in the book of Moses, in the passage about the bush, how God spoke to him, saying, 'I am the God of Abraham, and the God of Isaac, and the God of Jacob'?" — Mark 12:26

2. Paul Spoke of Moses' Authorship

For Moses writes about the righteousness that is based on the law, that the person who does the commandments shall live by them. — Romans 10:5

Yes, to this day whenever Moses is read a veil lies over their hearts. — 2 Corinthians 3:15

In the synagogue worship service, the Torah would be read, and an explanation of the reading often would be given from a place called "Moses' seat," such as the one in old synagogue ruins in Sardis. Reading the Pentateuch was culturally referred to as "reading Moses." Again, Paul's use of this wording could be simply naming the

Pentateuch, but it does indicate thinking of Moses as the author.

3. Peter Spoke of Moses' Authority

Moses said, "The Lord God will raise up for you a prophet like me from your brothers. You shall listen to him in whatever he tells you." — Acts 3:22

4. The Sadducees Spoke of Moses' Authorship

"Teacher, Moses wrote for us that if a man's brother dies and leaves a wife, but leaves no child, the man must take the widow and raise up offspring for his brother." — Mark 12:19

5. James Spoke of Moses' Influence

"For from ancient generations Moses has had in every city those who proclaim him, for he is read every Sabbath in the synagogues." — Acts 15:21

D. What Does This Prove?
1. The Importance of Moses

Old Testament and New Testament references to Moses demonstrate why both Jews and Christians regard him as the main author of the Pentateuch. The book itself clearly and consistently testifies to Mosaic authorship, authority, and influence. Granted, none of this *proves* Moses was involved in Pentateuchal authorship. Nevertheless, as Rolf Knierim demonstrates, it does show his importance:

Exodus-Deuteronomy without the person of Moses would not exist. In fact, this work is not only framed by the narrations of Moses' birth and death; throughout it is pervaded by and based upon the central importance of Moses. . . . Moses' work and Yahweh's work, indeed Israel itself, would not exist without the person of Moses. . . . [C]reation, human history and the patriarchal period cannot be properly understood if not seen in the light of the life and work of Moses. (Knierim, TOTT, 376–379)

Much of the Pentateuch reads as his biography or perhaps autobiography. Some commentators say the Pentateuch is not about Israel's beginnings; rather, it is about Moses' life, which is central to Israel's beginnings. Moreover, with two exceptions—Genesis 9:4–7 and 17:10–14—Moses mediates all Pentateuchal law. (Hagedorn, TPTFC, 56) Importantly, life stories demonstrating and recalling the public importance of an individual's lifework, such as Moses' life story in the Pentateuch, are common in the Mediterranean world, including in Egyptian and Hittite cultures during the time Moses is supposed to have lived and written.

2. Historical Consciousness of the Jews

Moses' overwhelming presence in the Pentateuch is even more important if "Ezra, or some other divinely-inspired writer" did a final edit. (Witsius, WMAP, 19) It was not some exilic or postexilic hero they wrote about. It was Moses. They did not attribute the Law to Josiah or David or Solomon, nor to the Persians or Babylonians. Not even the Patriarchs were worthy of attribution. They attributed it specifically and distinctly to Moses. The obvious question is, "Where did he come from if not history?" This is an especially pertinent question for the Jews, who were (and are) a historical people. Gerhard Maier observes:

Like no other people in the Near East or perhaps in the entire history of the world, Israel was nurtured in the understanding of history. To inquire into the understanding of history and in particular into the relation between truth and reality is thus not a question inappropriate to the Old Testament texts but an inquiry that emerges directly from and is most consistent with the Old Testament itself. (Maier, TRHU, 7:206)

Americans have figures such as Paul Bunyan, Daniel Boone, Pecos Bill, and Kit Carson. All have legendary aspects; nevertheless, we know who is real and who is not. Only cultural arrogance credits postexilic Jews with less historical intelligence.

To the question, "Aren't Moses' miracles suggestive of Paul Bunyan and Pecos Bill?" the answer is no. The incredible acts assigned to Paul Bunyan and Pecos Bill enhance their own stature and prowess, whereas Moses' miracles are not his at all—they are YHWH's. Tellingly, although the Psalms frequently speak of Moses' role in the exodus, the Psalms directly attribute the miracles to YHWH. Furthermore, the Pentateuch records that YHWH prevented Moses from leading the Israelites into the promised land because of Moses' sins of disbelief and perhaps pride. Moses is not incredible. What is incredible is that someone else would invent a story of a hero who worked such miracles and within that story would include Israelites who rebelled against that hero. (Examples even greater than their periodic grumbling complaints occur in Exodus 32, when they constructed a golden calf, and in Deuteronomy 1, when they refused to enter the promised land at Moses' direction.)

3. Embarrassing Facts About Moses

Dying alone at the brink of the glorious end to a forty-year quest is a nontraditional end for a leader of Moses' stature. He also had a nontraditional beginning in his birth story. Although valid comparisons exist to the Akkadian "Legend of Sargon," there are critical differences. Sargon was abandoned as an infant because of embarrassment; Moses was not abandoned. Instead, to prevent certain execution it is most likely that the baby Moses was purposefully placed where someone would find him. Furthermore, scholars highlight the distinctly Hebrew and Egyptian linguistic patterns in the Moses account: "It seems that the Egyptian setting of the story is itself responsible for the Egyptian pericope. . . . [I]t seems unlikely that a scribe during the late Judean monarchy or the exilic period (or later) would have been familiar with these Egyptian terms." (Hoffmeier, AIS, 136–140)

Additionally, if the account followed traditional lines, Moses would have returned to his people as a military leader to liberate them forcibly from Egypt. However, his initial attempts at leadership failed so badly he was forced to flee. The Pentateuch describes Moses' flight to Midian to prevent reprisal by the Pharaoh for murdering an Egyptian, admitting its central figure is a murderer and fugitive. It neither aggrandizes nor justifies Moses' actions. Instead, it indicates Moses knew the act was wrong and attempted to cover it up: "He looked this way and that, and seeing no one, he struck down the Egyptian

Like no other people in the Near East or perhaps in the entire history of the world, Israel was nurtured in the understanding of history. To inquire into the understanding of history and in particular into the relation between truth and reality is thus not a question inappropriate to the Old Testament texts but an inquiry that emerges directly from and is most consistent with the Old Testament itself.

Gerhard Maier

and hid him in the sand" (Ex. 2:12). Moses' entire life up to the time of his flight from Egypt is a broken form of the exposed infant story, purposefully done by the narrator to clearly indicate Moses was to be neither general nor king. (Trimm, YFT, 188–189)

Thereafter, Moses serves his wife's father as a shepherd until YHWH appears. A curious aspect of the burning bush account is Moses' response. He does not act the hero saying, "Here I am, send me." Instead, thirteen times he requests God send someone else (e.g., Ex. 4:13). It is not until God gets angry with Moses that he acquiesces (Ex. 4:14).

The initial portrait of Moses describes him as the son of a slave, adopted child, a person with anger management issues, a murderer, and an outlaw. Normally, "Declarations against interest are regarded as having a high degree of credibility because of the presumption that people do not make up lies in order to hurt themselves; they lie to help themselves." (Gordon-Reed, TJSH, 217)

4. The Origin of Israel

Finally, the reality of the exodus has a significant bearing on Moses' existence, importance, and likelihood to record its major events. The exodus is the major event of the Old Testament. Virtually all scholars, whether or not they believe it actually happened, would concur with A. C. Hagedorn that it seems "to address the origin of Israel." (Hagedorn, TPTFC, 57) Israel's history begins at Passover and the exodus, just as the United States dates its beginnings from the Declaration of Independence and the Revolutionary War. Israel's origins detail less-than-auspicious beginnings as escaped slaves, less-than-reverent gratitude to YHWH for that deliverance, and at the first opportunity to enter the promised land, less-than-exemplary courage. If it did not

happen, why tell such a humiliating story? Kenneth Kitchen notes, "Nobody else in Near Eastern antiquity descended to that kind of tale of community beginnings." (Kitchen, OROT, 245)

Baruch Halpern states,

There is something behind the Israelite tradition . . . and this is true of the peasant revolt school or the conquest theory, and even the so-called archaeological approach to the conquest—the problem is that you wind up with Israel with an Exodus tradition, a tradition of having been in bondage in Egypt. (Halpern, EE, 1804–1806)

William Dever observes, "I do think . . . that behind the literary tradition there must indeed be some sort of genuine historical memory; but it is unfortunately not accessible either to the text scholar or to the archaeologist." (Dever, HTCI, 485–488)

Moreover, if the exodus happened, someone like Moses had to lead it. Kitchen says:

In short, to explain what exists in our Hebrew texts, we need a Hebrew leader who had had experience of life at the Egyptian court . . . including knowledge of treaty type documents and their format, as well as of traditional Semitic legal/social usage more familiar to his own folk. In other words, somebody distressingly like that old "hero" of biblical tradition, Moses, is badly needed . . . to make any sense of the situation as we have it. (Kitchen, OROT, 295)

Whether the first chapters of Exodus are biography or autobiography—or even legend—they certainly do not herald Moses' future as prophet, priest, and leader. Rather, "he is a kind of anti-hero: someone who does not easily serve in the native tradition as a role model, someone who cannot really be emulated." (Machinist, MM, website) He cannot be emulated because he is *sui generis*. Who would *invent* such a hero as the founder of a nation?

III. Development of Modern Pentateuchal Studies

Until the eighteenth century AD, Mosaic authorship of the Pentateuch was largely unchallenged. However, anomalies did not go unnoticed. For example, could Moses have described his own death in Deuteronomy 34? Philo of Alexandria claimed that Moses received and recorded this by prophecy prior to his death. However, most scholars consider that an addendum by a later editor.

It is a common belief that Pentateuchal criticism began during the Enlightenment. However, esteemed scholar of Judaic studies Frederick Greenspahn contends modern biblical scholarship is merely the next chapter of what began with medieval Jewish scholarship. For example, Benedict Spinoza, considered the father of modern Pentateuchal studies, admitted to deriving some of his insights from the twelfth century Jewish scholar, Abraham Ibn Ezra. (Greenspahn, BSMM, 245–259) Enlightenment philosophers such as Spinoza and Hobbes credited fifth century BC scribe/priest Ezra for the Pentateuch's final edit. (Arnold, HPC, 622; Rogerson, HCAB, website) Roman Catholic writers such as Du Maes and Pereira echoed that view.

Spinoza requires special mention. Although not the first critic of Mosaic authorship, his criticism was frank and voluminous. Julius Wellhausen, arguably the most influential and significant Old Testament scholar of the late nineteenth and early twentieth centuries, acknowledged his debt to Spinoza in his famous *Prolegomena to the History of Ancient Israel*. (Wellhausen, PHAI) Born into a respected family in Amsterdam's seventeenth-century Jewish community, Spinoza not only dismissed Mosaic authorship, he rejected the Torah as YHWH's revelation and also Israel's special place in that revelation. In his focus on reason, he echoed Descartes, who set out to defend God and revelation on a solid foundation of something he logically could not doubt—I think, therefore I am, therefore I was made, and by Someone (also a person) greater than my person: God.

Spinoza, however, promoted and articulated the position that human reason and rationality reign supreme. Spinoza discarded the authority of tradition and replaced it with the principles and ideals of the Enlightenment. Meaning only comes through understanding the historical context of the author, audience, and events surrounding both reception and canonization of the text. To Spinoza, interpreting Scripture as YHWH's revelation is not faith—it is superstition. In other words, the Scriptures are not a divine work; they are manifestly human and are only understandable in that context. Such historical and/or literary reconstruction of a text became a cornerstone of critical scholarship. (Gignilliant, BHOTC, 15–17, 25, 30–36)

Spinoza's and similar positions notwithstanding, men such as Witsius did not leave those doubts unanswered. Witsius's small dissertation responding to Spinoza, Hobbes, and fellow Dutch theologian, Le Clerc, so effectively answered their skepticism that Le Clerc withdrew his doubts and thereafter echoed Witsius's view of Mosaic authorship.

A. The Origin of the Documentary Hypothesis

In 1753 a French physician, Jean Astruc, published *Conjectures sur la Genese (Conjectures on Genesis)*, a nascent documentary hypothesis. All documentary hypotheses postulate the author(s) of the Pentateuch used written (but no longer extant) source documents to compose the final version. Astruc believed Moses composed Genesis from two sources or "memories." He based this on the use of different names for God in Genesis. He labeled all citations with YHWH as one source and all with Elohim as another. He dismissed apparent inconsistencies and contradictions as scribal errors. He hypothesized that except for those passages that specifically highlighted Moses' interaction with YHWH, the Pentateuch was Moses passing along history, not necessarily revelation. (Acosta, CS, 257–258)

Throughout the eighteenth and into the mid-nineteenth century, men such as Eichorn, Ilgen, Geddes, Vater, de Witte, Reuss, Hupfeld, Kuenen, and Graf followed Astruc's lead. They expanded his "conjectures" and developed an early documentary hypothesis questioning Mosaic authorship.

Initially, research focused on Genesis; however, a *fragmentary hypothesis* that included the entire Pentateuch soon developed. Its name came from the notion that although a single editor may have compiled it, sources comprising the Pentateuch were fragments so varied and small they did not attain the status of documents. At the other end of the spectrum was the *supplementary hypothesis*. It claimed a single basic document comprised the first *six* books of the Bible (Hexateuch). Nonetheless, this basic document was significantly supplemented and edited on its way to a final edition.

Since the nineteenth century, many scholars insist on expanding the Pentateuch to include everything up to Kings or reducing it by removing either Genesis or Deuteronomy. They claim such a collection makes more sense than the standard five-volume Pentateuch. However, longstanding Jewish and Samaritan Pentateuchal traditions treat the five books as "separate sections of a self-contained corpus," that is, as a single story from "in the beginning" to the death of Moses. The reason for this tradition is threefold: the Pentateuch is what Moses could have written, concludes with his biography, and "ends the narrative begun in Genesis 1:1." (Knoppers, PT; Nihan, EPT; Block, GD) Regardless of these scholars' redefinitions of the proper number of biblical books to be considered as part of the Pentateuch, the "new Documentary Hypothesis" entered the arena as a robust articulation of the multiple source theory of the Pentateuch.

B. Prolegomena to the History of Ancient Israel

Wellhausen opened his famous *Prolegomena to the History of Ancient Israel,* a study of the first six books of the Bible, with the following proposition:

> In the following pages it is proposed to discuss the place in history of the "law of Moses;" more precisely, the question to be considered is whether that law is the starting-point for the history of ancient Israel, or not rather for that of Judaism, i.e., of the religious communion which survived the destruction of the nation by the Assyrians and Chaldeans. (Wellhausen, PHAI, 2–3)

In other words, is the Pentateuch a historical account of the beginnings of the Israelite people and nation, or is it a fiction written during the Babylonian and Persian periods to explain Judah's origins?

1. Is There a Source Behind the Pentateuch?

Wellhausen sought the "Ur-document," or original first source behind the Pentateuch. He thought that would shed light on Israel's original faith and provide insight into Israel's move from its preexilic faith to the faith of Judaism. (Sailhamer, MP, 141) To discover the Ur-document, he used a historical criticism technique called source criticism. It attempts to find indicators in extant texts to identify and reconstruct earlier lost writings that contributed to the final document. (Carr, SC, 1)

Focusing on the Pentateuch but including Joshua, he employed this technique to shift the traditional perspective of the Bible as a history of Israel and the revealed Word of God, to the Bible as a record of and instrument for the rise of religio-politico Judaism. Wellhausen was instrumental in propagating the theory that divided Jewish religion and history into three periods. The first division was pre-seventh century BC, during which there was much similarity with the Canaanite culture. (Clines, P, 580) The second division was from the seventh century to the Babylonian exile (c. 586 BC) during which Josiah enacted his 622 BC reforms. (Clines, P, 580) Finally, the last division was postexile, the time postulated by Wellhausen for the composition of Exodus, Leviticus, and Numbers. (Rogerson, AOHOTS, 20–21)

Interestingly, even though significant archaeological advances were being made as Wellhausen focused on discovering the sources of the Pentateuch, he largely chose not to include such evidence in his analysis. Peter Machinist, Professor of Hebrew and other Oriental Languages at Harvard Divinity School, suggests this was because Wellhausen considered understanding the "compositional development" of the Old Testament based on the "internal analysis" of ancient Israel and Judah's culture so important and required so much work that he consciously choose to not fully incorporate extrabiblical evidences. (Machinist, RNT, 518–522)

2. The Documentary Hypothesis

According to Wellhausen and his classic formulation of the documentary hypothesis, the Pentateuch is composed of four distinct sources. The oldest, c. 840 BC, is the Jahwist (Yahwist) or simply "J." J sources are characterized as those that use Yahweh or YHWH for God. Similarly, "E" sources (Elohist) use a form of El for God and date to roughly 700 BC. According to this view, "D" sources (Deuteronomic) date just before Josiah's reforms, approximately 623 BC. Finally, the Priestly or "P" source, bears a postexilic date of 500–450 BC.

Throughout the *Prolegomena* Wellhausen answered affirmatively the question (quoted above) with which he began his introduction: for him, the Pentateuch was a propagandistic document that supported the needs of the ruling and priestly classes, particularly in the postexilic community of Judah. Wellhausen advanced the concept that the stories of the patriarchs were largely mythology, and he detailed his belief that King Josiah, motivated by political aspirations, wrote Deuteronomy. Furthermore, Wellhausen claimed Ezra and Nehemiah designed the Pentateuch's final form to support their plan to introduce it as the law of the land in postexilic Judah under the imprimatur of the Persian king, Artaxerxes.

Interestingly, Wellhausen and other European scholars of the time tended toward anti-Semitism. (Silberman, WJ,

75–82) Because of this anti-Semitism, Jewish scholars have shied away from higher critical studies until recently. (MST, website) In fact, the tendency toward anti-Semitism was so strong during Wellhausen's time, that scholars without such bias struggled professionally, particularly in Germany at least until the end of WWII. Wellhausen claimed,

> The Jews had no historical life, and therefore painted the old time according to their ideas, and framed the time to come according to their wishes. They stood in no living relation with either the past or the future; the present was not with them a bridge from the one to the other; they did not think of bestirring themselves with a view to the kingdom of God. They had no national and historical existence, and made no preparations to procure such a thing for themselves. (Wellhausen, PHAI, 503)

For a refutation of Wellhausen's claims, please compare section II.D.2. "Historical Consciousness of the Jews" in this chapter, and especially Gerhard Maier's declaration that the Jews were and are a historical people.

3. The Denial of the Existence of the Israelites

This marked the beginning of an interesting phenomenon in modern Pentateuchal studies. Some scholars all but deny the existence of a separate people, the Israelites. (Knoppers, VS, 19–44) While many accept the reality of ancient Israel, they declare the Old Testament, including the Pentateuch, almost useless to discover Israel's history. (Provan, Long, and Longman, BHI, 258ff)

However, Walter Kaiser, Distinguished Professor Emeritus of Old Testament and Old Testament Ethics and president emeritus of Gordon-Conwell Theological Seminary, informs us that it is through the Old Testament that Sargon, king of Assyria, was known, and only through the Old Testament were Balaam, Ahab, and Hezekiah spoken of until archaeology independently discovered remains of their existence . . . and supported the historical veracity of the Old Testament, including the Pentateuch. (Kaiser, OTD, 99–102)

It is important to note that none of the documents to which Wellhausen, his predecessors, or successors refer has ever been found to exist. (Whybray, IP, 135) Though frequently discussed as if available for study in a museum, archive, or library, they remain simply a hypothesis: "No one has ever seen any such documents . . . or any allusions to them in any ancient literature." (Kaiser, OTD, 17)

C. Source Criticism

Source criticism—an approach or method for investigating a text in order to determine what sources went into its composition—comprises four stages: (1) deciding to investigate a text; (2) analysis of the text; (3) development of a model in which to place the analyzed data; and (4) arranging and dating the sources relative to one another and absolutely referenced (assigned to a definite date or range of dates by reference) to the known date of external sources. The most critical stage is textual analysis (2). Typically, source critics attempt to identify four or five types of indicators or criteria.

1. Divine Names

Advocates of the documentary hypothesis claim one source preferred Yahweh (J), another Elohim (E); hence, at least two sources. Since Astruc, the number of apparently identified sources for each preference has grown significantly beyond two.

2. Literary Style and Vocabulary

Stylistic and vocabulary differences are often assumed to indicate separate authors. For example, the first account of creation in Genesis is more formal than the second. Source critics attribute that to separate sources.

3. Anachronisms, Discontinuities, Contradictions, and Inconsistencies

Assuming a single author would not contradict him- or herself, source critics propose multiple sources to account for apparent contradictions. Differing accounts of creation are critical examples of this indicator. Likewise, unusual time differences between an event and the recording of the event could signify multiple sources. The standard example for the Pentateuch is that of Moses supposedly recording his own death.

4. Doublets or Duplicative Narratives— Two Accounts of the Same Event

Genesis is again the prime example. Supporters of source criticism see at least two sources in the two accounts of creation in Genesis 1:1—2:3 and immediately thereafter in 2:4–25. A more challenging example is the city of Luz, renamed Bethel twice by Jacob. (Baden, CP, 16–19)

Advocates of the documentary hypothesis and source criticism argue that the more of these criteria are present in a single account, the stronger the case for multiple sources. According to Old Testament scholar G. I. Davies, duplicative accounts, inconsistencies, and contradictions are most useful for detecting separate sources. (Davies, IP, website) Such criteria are frequently used to argue against an account's historicity.

IV. Challenges to the Documentary Hypothesis

A. Arguments Against the Documentary Hypothesis

All documents referenced are hypothetical. They are, as Astruc appropriately described, *conjectures.* All that exists is the current form of the Pentateuch.* As a result, the documentary hypothesis was modified, supplemented, praised, and disparaged from inception. That should be expected. "One good question can give rise to several layers of answers, can inspire decades-long searches for solutions, can generate whole new fields of inquiry, and can prompt changes in entrenched thinking." (Firestein, IHIDS, 11) Wellhausen's hypothesis certainly did that; his tenets used to identify and date the hypothesized sources have been significantly challenged.

Although now several decades old, an analysis by Umberto Cassuto, a Jewish scholar from the first half of the twentieth century, summarizes arguments against the documentary hypothesis. (Cassuto, DH) His arguments remain apropos, capturing many of the scholarly challenges to the documentary hypothesis.

1. Divine Names

Cassuto provides reasons other than authorship differences for the use of divine names in the Pentateuch and the rest of the Old Testament. Instead, context and intention determined naming conventions.

> It [the Torah] selected the name YHWH when the text reflects the Israelite conception of God, which is embodied in the portrayal of YHWH and finds expression in the attributes

---

* Variations are Masoretic, Samaritan, Dead Sea Scrolls texts, Targums, Peshitta, The Three, and Septuagint. "Most of the Pentateuch is the same in the main witnesses ... there are also some substantial areas of differences." See Williams, TC; Wolters, TOT.

traditionally ascribed to Him by Israel, particularly in His ethical character; it preferred the name Elohim when the passage implies the abstract idea of the Deity prevalent in the international circles of "wise men." (Cassuto, DH, 31)

Along with many conservative and critical scholars, Duane Garrett concludes, "It is true that Cassuto exploits this distinction too rigorously and goes beyond what the text intends at some points, but the distinction is valid." (Garrett, RG, 16) In other words, Wellhausen's original assertions have been tempered considerably. Scholars today generally agree with Cassuto that the primary reason for name distinction within the Pentateuch is usage rather than varying authors. (Schwartz, DRSC, 78:3–16)

2. Literary Style and Vocabulary

Cassuto argued cogently that established rules of Hebrew grammar adequately explain language and style variations. (Cassuto, DH, 54)

> We must not rely upon the differences in language in order to determine the origin of the sections, which we shall subsequently use to decide the linguistic characteristics of the sources, for in that case we shall indeed fall into the snare of reasoning in a circle . . . nor [should we] consider words and forms mechanically, as though they were divorced from their context and the latter could have no bearing on their use. (Cassuto, DH, 44)

Jean-Louis Ska agrees with Cassuto: "Hebrew grammar and stylistics" can account for at least some phenomena typically attributed to multiple sources. (Ska, LI, 78: 109–122) Like modern authors, ancient authors often changed style according to

topic, character, or some other reason. Style and vocabulary vary throughout the Pentateuch. Unfortunately, there are no agreed upon parameters for consistently distinguishing between a single author's natural variation and variation caused by different authors. Therefore, it is challenging to consistently determine the cause and meaning of observed variation.

3. Anachronism, Discontinuity, Contradictions, and Inconsistency

Cassuto goes to great lengths to demonstrate that many alleged instances of contradictions and inconsistencies are not real issues at all. For example, there are differences throughout the Pentateuch regarding the naming of a child—sometimes it comes from the father and other times it comes from the mother. Many critical scholars attribute this to different and contradictory sources.

Cassuto, however, claims that in the Pentateuch most children receive their name because of a specific event prior to or at birth involving either the father or mother. When the father is involved, he names the child, and when the mother is involved, she names the child. Furthermore, the documentary hypothesis does not solve remaining issues. Cassuto is adamant that "an editor who does his work conscientiously is obliged to avoid inconsistencies not less than the author, possibly even more so." (Cassuto, DH, 55–68; cf. Garrett, RG, 23–27) Furthermore, some scholars have noted the lack of complete consistency among modern authors as well. (Whybray, IP, 16, 23)

4. Doublets or Duplicative Narratives

Employing the scientific convention of Ockham's razor, Brodie suggests it is often "easier and more coherent to account for the two-part design by saying that the entire present text was planned as two-part." (Brodie, GAD, 32–35) In other words, many of the doublets exist not because of multiple authors but because of authorial design. Briggs echoes the contention that doublets and duplicative narratives are intentional, claiming they enhance and reinforce the truth and importance of the item duplicated. (Briggs, TFROTC, 95–112)

Similarly, Cassuto preceded Briggs's contention by several decades. Referencing the Torah itself, he notes, "And the doubling of Pharaoh's dream means that the thing is fixed by God, and God will shortly bring it about" (Gen. 41:32). In other words, Cassuto claims doublets and duplicative narratives are frequently used deliberately to emphasize specific concepts, theological or otherwise. (Cassuto, DH, 69–82) Significantly, many interpreters have noticed that biblical poetry typically employs this device of stating something in two or even three ways in the same verse—deliberately emphasizing or extending the thought. Duplicate narratives could well be the same design on a larger scale.

B. Current Status of the Documentary Hypothesis

Critics of Wellhausen and source criticism note that while the multiple-source-hypothesis places accountability for inconsistences with the editors and redactors, it does not *explain* them unless one assumes the editors were careless, indifferent, or stupid. A common response to source critics who point to such textual inconsistencies as evidence for multiple authors is this: editors of the ancient world operated with different assumptions from modern editors, who tend to assume that facts have an either/or status. In contrast, ancient editors purposefully incorporated all or at least many of the

witnesses available to them. (Brettler, CRT, website) Potential reasons for such inclusiveness are editorial respect for the sources; that is, multiple sources each had such stature that the editor was unable or unwilling to choose between them, and somewhat related, the editor considered "the sources they preserved as valid. . . . [T]hey preserved what they had received . . . leaving the rest to future readers." (Tigay, DHEM, 125–126)

Regardless of the exact reasons for "inconsistencies," viable alternative explanations exist that do not require multiple authors. Even when accepted, multiple sources do not necessarily discount the veracity and historicity of the accounts. The Pentateuch admits to use of sources, even by Moses. Commenting on the reference in Numbers 21:14 to *The Book of the Wars of the Lord*, Sailhamer says, "The manner of its citation in Numbers reflects a surprisingly modern historiography, including an awareness of written sources." (Sailhamer, MP, 258–259)

Although Wellhausen's views dominated twentieth-century Old Testament thought, alternative methods and perspectives on ways to study and assess the Pentateuch have proliferated, including the concept that there should be no "theoretical focus." (Schmid, HESADH, 78:30)

Gordon Wenham has said, "Much of the argument is convoluted and depends on assumptions that are not universally shared." (Wenham, PST, 3) Likewise, Whybray states, "It must be admitted that as far as assured results are concerned we are no nearer to certainty than when the critical study of the Pentateuch began." (Whybray, IP, 12) Rendtorff bluntly comments, "I believe the traditional Documentary Hypothesis has come to an end." (Rendtorff, PC, 44–46) A leading advocate of Wellhausen, Nicholson concedes, "Those who adhere to the

Documentary Theory are very much on the defensive.... [T]oday it is in sharp decline—some would say in a state of advanced *rigor mortis*—and new solutions are being argued and urged in its place." (Nicholson, TUA, 96) Finally, some scholars are so bold as to say the documentary hypothesis "as a starting point for continued research, is dead. ... [T]he arguments that support it have been effectively demolished by scholars from many different theological perspectives and areas of expertise." (Garrett, RG, 11)

V. Pentateuchal Research Since Wellhausen

The Skeptics Dictionary states, "We know from experience that more often than not the theory that requires more complicated machinations is wrong." (Carroll, OR, website) In other words, the simpler the theory is, the more likely it is to be correct. The model that remains the simplest explanation for the Pentateuch's composition is the traditional Jewish and Christian model: Moses as the original author used some sources (as mentioned above in the reference to *The Book of the Wars of the Lord* in Numbers 21:14), and later editor(s) updated the text to ensure it was understandable to contemporary readers ("maintenance changes").

Nevertheless, alternative models proliferate. Additional forms of historical criticism, such as tradition criticism, have been brought to bear. Yet others argue for a unified Pentateuch. Dating of the final documents has tended to move later and later. The theory of an E source has largely been rejected, though not universally. Biblical scholars' toolkits now include literary and canonical criticism. Interestingly, researchers studying the same evidence frequently develop contradictory conclusions because of their different methods. Hans-Georg Gadamer's masterful *Truth and Method* explains how an interpreter's method affects the resulting conclusion: those who interpret a text differ in their "fore-meanings," or what they expect to find, so that their method shapes what they find. "It is the tyranny of hidden prejudices that makes us deaf to what speaks to us in tradition.... All understanding inevitably involves some prejudice." (Gadamer, TM, 270)

The Enlightenment prejudice, however (along with critical schools since the Enlightenment) insists on a "fundamental prejudice ... against prejudice itself, which denies tradition its power." (Gadamer, TM, 270) The result is a "critique ... primarily directed against Christianity—i.e., the Bible." (Gadamer, TM, 272) He goes on to call upon interpreters to "remain open to the meaning of the other person or text." If a person fails to hear what the other person is really saying, he "will not be able to fit what he has misunderstood into the range of his own various expectations of meaning." (Gadamer, TM, 269) Thus, the same textual evidence may lead researchers to different conclusions.

Those who adhere to the Documentary Theory are very much on the defensive. . . . [T]oday it is in sharp decline—some would say in a state of advanced rigor mortis—and new solutions are being argued and urged in its place.

Ernest Nicholson

A. The Challenge of Interpretation

1. Same Data, Different Methods, Different Interpretations

As we have seen above, scholars using different methods reach very different conclusions even when the same data is the source of their study and research. In fact, Damian Wynn-Williams compares the complexity of critical Pentateuchal study, in which scholarly methodology shapes conclusions, to that of quantum mechanics. (Wynn-Williams, SP, 252)

2. Same Data, Different Assumptions, Different Interpretations

Many scholars and individuals discount the supernatural accounts of God's intervention reported in the Bible. It is understandable that this presupposition will shape how they interpret a text.

Jeffrey Tigay illustrates how different assumptions concerning God's interaction with humanity lead to different interpretations. Conservative and critical scholars acknowledge the Old Testament's account of preexilic polytheistic practices. Critical scholars believe cultural monotheism was not possible at that stage of Israel's development. Denying the validity of the Old Testament, they reject the idea of a radical shift from polytheism to monotheism. Conservative scholars, however, following the biblical text, accept that the practice of polytheism had been and continued to be officially banned, and that monotheism was to be the norm, not the exception. (Tigay, IR, 157–158) According to the biblical text, polytheism continued not because monotheism had not yet developed, but rather because of humanity's innate sinfulness and consequent rebelliousness. That sinful impulse in the case of the Israelites who turned to idols includes the attractiveness of what is readily visible and perceived

to be good, or the prevention of something feared—appeals that echo what Eve found appealing in the temptation account of Genesis 3. Tigay goes on to say that if our knowledge of Israelite religious practices were based solely on *extrabiblical* witnesses, there would be little to indicate polytheism existed within ancient Israel. The onomastic and epigraphic evidences attest to monotheism as the norm. The Bible itself highlights the *deviation* from the norm—as well as the reasons for the deviation.

This illustrates two common characteristics of critical scholarship. First, it frequently opposes the biblical text on the basis of presuppositions. Second, it chooses which parts of the text to accept and which to discard. Conversely, conservative scholarship attempts to make sense of the whole enterprise of interpretation in a coherent and consistent manner.

The investigator's philosophy generates the approach to interpretation, both in the scientific methods and the model used. As demonstrated, the model employed to assess the data puts constraints around possible interpretations. It may ipso facto prevent identification of the most correct interpretation because the model *a priori* excludes particular options. (Long, "Introduction" to Long, et al. WOTH, 8–12; Kofoed, EHM, 23–40)

B. Multiplication of Sources

Critical scholarship contends that the work of various redactors or editors subdivided, combined, expanded, and condensed each main category of sources. Wellhausen postulated that the composition of the Pentateuch involved so many sources that his own work was only the beginning of understanding the Pentateuch. Since Wellhausen's time, the alleged J and E sources have morphed or subdivided to the point where they are now referred to as J and E schools. Theoretical P sources also multiplied, and so we have new hypothetical sources, such as lay (L), nomadic (N), Kenite (K), Southern (S), etc. (Stern, RTBSC, 183) In biblical studies in general and Pentateuchal studies in particular, proliferation of potential sources without consistent and agreed to criteria is a hallmark feature that continues today. Old Testament professor David Talley notes, "There is a huge amount of fragmentation and creativity in OT scholarship. It is almost anything goes because divine inspiration is not accepted. However, the whole debate has even been questioned by the postulation of a unity behind the sources." (Talley, personal email correspondence with the authors) Furthermore, Blenkinsopp points out,

> The problem inherent in these procedures is fairly obvious. If the demand for absolute consistency is pressed, the sources tend to collapse and disintegrate into a multiplicity of components or strands. . . . If, on the other hand, variations and inconsistencies are admitted within one and the same composition, a situation entirely normal in literary works ancient and modern, it would be a short step to questioning the need for distinct sources or documents identified by features peculiar to each. (Blenkinsopp, PIFFBN, 14)

To illustrate the dangers inherent to historical criticism, Clines subjected A. A. Milne's Winnie the Pooh stories to the methodology to which scholars subject the Bible. He footnoted his satire with actual academic references. (Clines, NDPS, 830–839) He established that because Milne's name is only mentioned once and not within the text itself, his authorship and even existence is questionable. Clines concluded the various names for the main character (Pooh, Pooh Bear, Winnie the Pooh, etc.) decisively indicate "interweaving of a number of sources." (Clines, NDPS, 830) He deduced that Winnie the Pooh also went by the name Sanders (Pooh's home has "Mr. Sanders" above the door), but for reasons unknown, that tradition was purposefully and rigorously expunged. Doublets were clearly present, as when Pooh got stuck in Rabbit's hole. The text contains traditions of Pooh attempting to back out and attempting to go forward. A later redactor purposely conflated this by having Pooh exclaim, "I can't do either. Oh help and bother." (Clines, NDPS, 832) He goes on to identify J, E, P, and D sources resident within the various parts of the Pooh corpus. The J, Genius, sources speak of Pooh's wisdom while the E, Egghead, sources portray him as an idiot. Both differ from the D, Dopey, sources that describe Pooh's difficulties brought on by his own stupidity, and the P source that "has little of significance . . . beyond editorial matter." (Cline, NDPS, 833) Clines notes in passing that J as the siglum for Genius is in keeping with "the classical documentary theory" in which "J never stands for words beginning with J (cf. J for Yahwist)." (Clines, NDPS, 833) Continuing to interpret Pooh using traditional methods of biblical criticism, he proclaims Honey as the god worshiped by Winnie the Pooh and consort of the dying and rising vegetation god Christopher Robin; he describes various cultic traditions represented by Pooh and Piglet and finally declares the accounts of Pooh as "cultic wisdom literature in the epico-mythological form." (Clines, NDPS, 839) For those familiar with critical biblical scholarship and Winnie the Pooh, Clines's interpretation ranges from mildly humorous to slightly sad. Conceivably, it may upset some.

Obviously, it is possible to account

for many alleged discrepancies without resorting to multiple sources. Even so, the Pentateuch itself attests to the use of sources in its composition. Sources per se really have little bearing on initial authorship, authority, or veracity. As Alter says, "The Torah exhibits seams, fissures, and inner tensions that cannot be ignored, but it has also been artfully assembled through the ancient editorial process to cohere strongly as the foundational text of Israelite life and the cornerstone of the biblical canon." (Alter, FBM, 232–234)

C. Unified Source

For most of its history, critical biblical scholarship parsed the Old Testament and the Pentateuch in particular into various sources, exemplified by the documentary hypothesis. However, a volume of scholarly work published by the Society for Biblical Literature in 2011 documents the trend toward reading it as a unified whole. (Dozeman, Römer, and Schmid, PHE) The introduction to that work states, "It is no longer possible to interpret these bodies of literature as though they were separate and independent literary works. . . . [T]raditional divisions may be supported to some extent by further research, but there may also emerge a clear need to abandon at least some of these assumptions to gain a plausible image of the literary growth of Genesis–Kings." (Dozeman, Römer, and Schmid, PHE, 1–2, 8)

The impetus for this comes from at least two directions. One is that the current form of the Pentateuch is all that is available for study. Second, a unitary reading simply makes sense. Sailhamer observes,

This is not meant to imply that OT scholars have come over to the other side and now accept Mosaic authorship. That is not the case. What appears to have happened in many cases is an acceptance of the idea that the Pentateuch, when viewed as the product of an intelligent design, has a certain unity and message as a whole. (Sailhamer, MP, 355)

Many literary critics today are viewing the Pentateuch holistically, not as an amalgamation of hypothetical sources gathered over centuries. When they view the Pentateuch as a work of literary art, this results in an appreciation for the Pentateuch as a complex but unified work. In addition we are reading many arguments against the documentary hypothesis, such as explaining doublets not as indicators of sources but as literary techniques. (Longman, LAOTS, 97–100)

Similarly, canonical criticism focuses on the final form of the Old Testament, including the Pentateuch. Blenkinsopp notes, "The basic point seems to be that the appropriate object of theological reflection is the biblical text in its final form rather than hypothetically reconstructed earlier stages of formation." (Blenkinsopp, PIFFBN, 28) As is the case with literary criticism, most individuals do not reject the use of some forms of biblical criticism. Instead, they reject the extreme conclusions based on assumptions that any variation is the trace of a different author's hand. They contend that the theological implications of the Pentateuch's final form are more important than or at least must be balanced against individual sources or traditions used in its formation.

A principal advocate of the unitary approach is Whybray, who arrived at this position because of the advances made in Pentateuchal understanding by literary critics and because of the weaknesses of the various source-critical methodologies. He argues that the first edition of the Pentateuch is the last edition of the Pentateuch. Although he does not deny that the "author, redactor, or editor" used sources, he sees it more along the lines of the earlier fragmentary hypothesis. He argues the composer of the Pentateuch used an enormous amount of material that included folk tales and recent writings "radically reworking the material . . . with substantial additions of his own invention," to create a "literary masterpiece." Whybray further suggests that the composer may have intended this to be a way of providing a sense of a uniform understanding for Israelites to understand their origins in the angst of the postexilic reconstruction of their national identity. (Whybray, MP, 232–242)

D. Dating

The date at which a text was composed is important for properly understanding it. Unfortunately, scholars have never agreed on the dates for any of the sources or traditions supposedly behind the Pentateuch.

Dating the various written sources that stand behind the Pentateuch, as well as the stories passed along by memory, gives important context for their authority and meaning. Both conservative and critical scholars tend to agree the Pentateuch in its final form could not have existed prior to the sixth century BC. (Alexander, AP, 64–72; see also Whybray, MP, 235) For example, Sailhamer states the phrase in Deuteronomy 34:10, "And there has not arisen a prophet since in Israel like Moses" (ESV), could not have been written until "after the last prophet, Malachi." (Sailhamer, MP, 24) However, some scholars, variously known as revisionists or minimalists, argue for a Hellenistic date of 300 BC or later. Conversely, many scholars, both conservative and critical, agree many of the narratives recorded in the Pentateuch have an ancient lineage. Nicholson concludes: "Attempts to limit the creation of such a

literature to a largely scribal activity carried out in the interests of political propaganda or for the purpose of legitimizing a newly founded state of the Persian period or later are in the face of overwhelming evidence to the contrary." (Nicholson, CRLOT, 19) In short, even if the books came into final form relatively late, this would not necessarily undermine their authority or inerrancy.

E. Rejection of E

By the early 1930s, scholars began questioning the validity of E. (Whybray, MP, 35) By the late 1980s, many scholars believed distinguishing between J and E on style alone was inadequate. Eventually, most scholars concluded that E did not actually exist or at least could not be effectively separated from other sources. Dozeman sums up the current status: "Thus scholars debate whether there ever was an independent E source." (Dozeman, CE, 36)

Nevertheless, while admitting that the Elohist's existence is frequently denied, R. K. Gnuse claims significant evidence exists to argue for an Elohist source, i.e., a source separate from J, P, or D. Contending that the Elohist was preexilic and was responsible for laying the "seedbed" for radical postexilic monotheism, he provides a set of distinct characteristics. Claiming these characteristics generally occur together and provide the overall personality of the chosen accounts, he lists attributes such as the traditional use of Elohim, the fear of God, a distant God, as well as moral sensitivity and tests placed before individuals and the people as a whole to elicit obedience. Although he concedes the use of Elohim alone is insufficient to isolate an Elohist source, he nevertheless argues there is a unique and consistent "vocabulary" distinct enough to isolate Elohist texts. (Gnuse, "Elohist," 59–69)

F. Tradition Criticism

"Traditio-historical criticism," "tradition criticism," and "tradition history" are all terms used to describe the critical methodology that attempts to identify folk traditions behind Pentateuchal narratives. This approach claims that the Pentateuch is not a single narrative, but was composed from multiple narratives throughout Israel's history that were eventually combined into what is now the Pentateuch. The relative chronology of preliterary stages is sought in an attempt to understand the entire path from origins to extant version. The search for the overall preliterary sociocultural context that produced the oral tradition's basis for the written text is an important aspect of tradition criticism. Advocates contend this enables discovery of the original meaning. They assume texts develop over a long period based on oral traditions. Those who finally recorded those traditions merely reshaped established customs, rituals, and behaviors. Tradition criticism is not concerned merely with the composition of the Pentateuch but also with the history of Israelite traditions (not the history of Israel) and with the overall development of its religion. (see Whybray, MP, 135; Garrett, THC, 865)

In recent years, scholars have focused on whether the patriarchal and exodus accounts have separate origins, and if so, when the integration occurred. Konrad Schmid contends biblical evidence, particularly the Psalms, presupposes independent original sources for Genesis and Exodus. Further, he argues that the absence in Genesis of any reference of a "detour to Egypt" as well as no mention of a several-hundred-year waiting period before promise fulfillment points toward independent narratives. (Schmid, GEAT, 190–192; however, see Gen. 15:13–16) This leads him to surmise history is not the basis of Israel's theology; rather, it is the "continuing interpretation of narrative traditions." (Trimm, personal correspondence, January 2016) Interestingly, although there is significant disagreement about *how* and *when* integration of the patriarchal and exodus narratives occurred, most agree on their original separation. (Carr, WIRIP, 159–180)

Nevertheless, tradition criticism is based entirely on hypothesis. (Rendtorff, PC, 36) Just as no source documents referred to in any documentary hypothesis exist, there are no records of the preliterary stage of Pentateuchal development. Kitchen emphasizes that only guesswork exists. Even pseudo-epigraphal and apocryphal writings discovered at Qumran lack evidence of these hypothetical sources. (Kitchen, OROT, 492–494) Therefore, Kaiser contends that emphasis should be on extant documents and epigraphic evidence from other ancient Near East sources, rather than on the *hypothetical* sources. (Kaiser, OTD, 17)

VI. Arguments for Mosaic Authorship and Authority

A. The Complexity of Discovering and Understanding Pentateuchal Evidence

Assessing the positive evidence for Mosaic authorship is not an easy task. Among the challenges is the complexity of studying documents that could be as recent as approximately 200–300 BC to as ancient as mid second millennium BC. Furthermore, the Pentateuch interacts with and contains cultural traditions from Egypt, Assyria, Babylon, Canaan, Asia Minor, the Arabian Peninsula, and northern Africa. Its history involves invasion and conquest, destruction and rebuilding, abandonment and resettlement. Some material disintegrates naturally and other material is destroyed by human activity. Even now, war is destroying evidence of the region's history, including perhaps evidence of the Pentateuch's composition. Important material from the time of the Pentateuch may be forever beyond our reach.

B. Christian Response to Biblical Criticism

Few biblical scholars would disagree with Wenham's assessment of a reader's first adventure into the Pentateuch: "[They] will soon be surprised, puzzled and sometimes shocked. . . . [I]ts ideas often seem utterly alien. . . . Its approach to chronology, history, ethics and God challenge the modern world view at so many points that readers may be tempted to stop reading very quickly. But this would be a great mistake." (Wenham, EOT, xiii) Furthermore, Klingbeil notes: "A large portion of the Pentateuch can be described as historical writing, that is, texts that describe events in the past in a context involving human beings and their interconnection with other human beings and with Yahweh, the covenant God of the OT account." (Klingbeil, HC, 404)

If both previous statements are accurate and if contradictions, inconsistencies, and other elements that do not appear coherent from our contemporary understanding of history (and even of God's character) exist within the Pentateuch, can it really be God's Word? This is the question of critical scholarship. Critical explanations for these phenomena point to multiple authors or redactors as responsible for the seemingly variant data. However, the methods used by critical scholarship change frequently, and succeeding generations have developed their own perspectives on why Moses could not have authored the Pentateuch.

In contrast, conservative scholars evaluate the same evidence and conclude that, when properly interpreted and analyzed,

the traditional understanding of the Pentateuch stands strongest among the various contenders.

Consider an example: There are a few facts that convince most scholars that there are some "post-Mosaic elements" in the Pentateuch: the introduction of Deuteronomy, the past tense description of Israel's conquest in Deuteronomy 2:21, Moses' obituary in Deuteronomy 34:5–10, the reference to *The Book of the Wars of the Lord* in Numbers 21:14, and the scroll of the generations of Adam in Genesis 5:1. Consequently, it is unwise to argue that Moses wrote every single word of the extant Pentateuch; nevertheless, post-Mosaic elements don't diminish the text's witness to significant Mosaic authorship in a way that is faithful to the scriptural passages above.

1. A Classical Response

Decrying the "developmental hypothesis" set forth by critical scholarship, influential Old Testament scholar R. K. Harrison called for a "correct methodology grounded firmly upon an assured foundation of knowledge concerning the manifold facets of ancient Near Eastern life . . . setting the Biblical writings in proper historical and cultural perspective." (Harrison, IOT, 497–532)

Furthermore, while he did not completely eschew comparative studies, Harrison argued that differences were more critical and important than similarities. He emphasized the high literacy rate in the ANE and noted that oral and written records frequently circulated simultaneously. Echoing traditional perspectives, and perhaps literary and canonical criticism, he called for Pentateuchal studies to recognize the inherent unity of the Pentateuch. Interestingly, he warned against both dismissing Moses as a historical figure and building him up as a superman that wrote every word of the Pentateuch.

Using that methodology and a contemporary understanding of biblical and extrabiblical research, Harrison concluded that Moses' role was preeminent, and that the Pentateuch could have been largely in its present form by the late Joshua period. But he allowed for significant linguistic updating, addition, removal, and other forms of alterations in keeping with the literary habits and customs of the ANE. With that background of academic understanding, he still considers the Pentateuch to be divine revelation. (Harrison, IOT, 499–541)

2. Scripture Trumps Non-Scripture

Most Christians believe the Bible is God's revelation to humanity. The present authors certainly do. Given its track record of accuracy and reliability, we believe the Bible should get the benefit of the doubt when faced with difficult challenges.

Some scholars only consider and evaluate biblical material that has external corroboration. However, William Barrick considers this an evidential fallacy. Additionally, he notes that an antisupernatural bias often controls the conclusions certain scholars allow. From his perspective, however, since the Bible is the inerrant Word of God, areas that challenge human understanding merely highlight the ignorance of the interpreter, not the incoherence of the text. (Barrick, EF, 15–27)

Barrick uses the biblical phrase, "Ur of the Chaldeans," as a case study for demonstrating these principles. (Barrick, UC, 7–18) Admitting that it is currently impossible to prove either biblical or nonbiblical veracity, he offers a solution supported by "linguistic, genealogical, and historical evidence." (Barrick, UC, 7)

Many biblical scholars contend that the phrase "Ur of the Chaldeans," in Genesis 11:28–31 is either an anachronism or post-Mosaic textual update. The reason given for such conclusions is that Assyrian records do not mention Chaldeans until significantly later than the purported time of Moses. Noting that it is prudent to be skeptical of Assyrian records and noting that the Bible consistently mentions the Chaldeans in connection with the patriarchs, Barrick offers an argument he believes plausibly accords with the biblical text. (Barrick, UC, 10) He offers linguistic support for the claim that Abraham was from Ur of the Chaldeans through an understanding of a phonetic shift that occurred between 1500–600 BC. Additionally, he contends there was more than adequate time for the Chaldeans to move from their homelands into the region of Ur prior to the time of Moses and even of Abraham. Finally, using the example of the discovery of Hittites, he argues that a simple *lack* of archaeological evidence is a poor excuse for discounting biblical testimony. (Barrick, UC, 17) As Anthony Frendo so aptly states, "Indeed, when archaeological evidence is not to be found in support of a claim made by the biblical text, it certainly does not follow that the text is necessarily false." (Frendo, BB, 42) Barrick notes that the doctrine of biblical inerrancy requires faith in future resolution of biblical problems rather than resorting to "anachronism or textual updating." (Barrick, UC, 18)

3. Mosaic Authorship and Inerrancy

For some Christians, Mosaic authorship is unnecessary, perhaps even irrelevant. These individuals, at the opposite end of the spectrum from Barrick, take seriously the Christian belief that the Bible is God's Word, yet they allow for human fallibility in transmission. Peter Enns claims,

The Bible is the book of God for the people of God. It reveals and conceals, is clear yet complex, open to all but impossible to master. Its message clearly reflects the cultural settings of the authors. . . . It tells of God's acts but also reports some events that either may or may not have happened or have been significantly reshaped and transformed by centuries of tradition. It presents us with portraits of God . . . that at times comfort and confirm our faith while at other times challenge and stretch our faith to the breaking point. This is the Bible we have, the Bible God gave us. (Enns, IHD, 83)

While conceding that historical critical scholars have made unwarranted claims and demonstrated unjustified confidence, Enns claims biblical inerrancy is only a theory and such charges can and "should be leveled, against any ideologically driven approach to biblical interpretation." (Enns, IHD, 90) He goes on to state that few biblical scholars of any persuasion would deny the advancements in Old Testament studies resulting from critical scholarship.

Therefore, Enns is unconvinced that inerrancy can be effectively nuanced to describe the Bible as it exists today; that is, Enns believes the very concept of inerrancy "sells God short." (Enns, IHD, 84) Inerrancy, he says, assumes God must communicate to modern man the way modern man wants God to communicate, rather than the way God chooses to communicate. Giving primacy to extrabiblical evidence and using God's call to exterminate the Canaanites in Deuteronomy as a case study, he claims the current lack of archaeological evidence demonstrates the falsity of the biblical record.* Nevertheless, he does not see this as an insurmountable problem concerning the overall divine nature of Scripture: "What should be brought explicitly to the forefront here is the manner in which God speaks truth, namely, *through the idioms, attitudes, assumptions, and general worldviews of the ancient authors.*" (Enns, IHD, 87, emphasis in original) Recalling C. S. Lewis's caution, he urges Christians not to view the Bible as a reference book on history, but as a way to understand and educate themselves in God's overall message. Instead of focusing on how God expressed himself in a variety of historical and cultural periods, Enns claims a better starting point for the discussion of Christianity generally and the usefulness and genuineness of the Bible specifically is the reality of God's incarnation in the form of Jesus.

Kenton Sparks shares many of Enns's perspectives concerning the role of inerrancy and the value of biblical criticism. While he does warn of unwarranted claims of biblical critics, he supports many of the standard critical conclusions and warns of wholesale rejection of its benefits. (Sparks, GWHW) Beginning with his overall premise—that humans as fallible beings do not *need* an inerrant Bible—he argues that humans might not even understand an inerrant perspective. Describing temporal change in biblical interpretation based on changing hermeneutics contemporaneous with the larger interpretive community, he suggests that God in his infinite wisdom spoke to humans through an "adequate" rather than inerrant means, enabling humans to comprehend his revelation, regardless of time, place, language, etc. Sparks encapsulates this overall perspective of the reality and veracity of the Bible by declaring,

---

* For a more thorough study of the archeological record regarding the conquest of Canaan and the period of the judges that Enns selects as his case study, read chapter 19.

To the extent that the Bible is properly interpreted as a canonical document, and in light of the Christian tradition and created order, it offers us the wholly adequate Word of God. But it does not offer, and in fact warns that we cannot and should not have, perfect, God-like knowledge. . . . [T]hat the critics have discovered human errors in Scripture should not be a surprise . . . once we admit that the Bible, as divine discourse, is accommodated to various human viewpoints and contexts, we will listen with more care to all that it says. (Sparks, GWHW, 54–55, 358)

4. Authorship and Authority

One of the difficulties we as modern readers have assimilating the Bible to our habitual notions of literary expression is the stubborn resistance it offers to our readerly or critical need for an informing authorial presence. . . . Western literature is . . . framed by the conspicuous personalities of its major authors. . . . What are we to do with a set of ancient narratives that aspire to speak out of the void in an authoritative voice that masks authorial presence? (Alter, WBL, 153–154)

With those words, Alter summarizes a significant area of study and debate; that is, how modern historians and others should begin to address ANE texts. John Walton and D. Brent Sandy claim that Moses (when properly understood), will be recognized primarily as the authority for the Pentateuch rather than its author. Although he probably had scribal training, given his stature during the exodus period, it is more likely that subordinate scribes were recording his sermons, prayers, and other words, some during his lifetime and some after his death.

Maintaining that anachronistic misconceptions are the major challenges to current tradition criticism, Walton and Sandy call for a new model to understand literary production principles in the ANE. Concurring with the conclusions of historical criticism, they acknowledge the lateness of the Pentateuch as a whole and that Moses is not strictly the author of the Pentateuch as it exists today. In this model, Moses is decidedly the *authority* from which the Pentateuch emanated, in keeping with typical ANE literary methodology and what the Pentateuch itself claims. Although the specifics of this cannot be determined, and although the process was likely long and complex, Pentateuchal authority is unaffected. In their view, Moses as the authority figure either generated or caused to be generated the initial documents, and he did so with God's imprimatur. Likewise, the revisions were made with the cognizance of the original tradition and again with the imprimatur of God. Walton and Sandy contend that at least some of the plausibility of their model comes via the institution of the temple, which played a major role "throughout the ancient world as traditions were maintained and transmitted." (Walton and Sandy, LWS, 61–66)

Much of their model revolves around the concept of authority versus authorship. In other words, the written words may not have been written by Moses himself, or even while Moses was alive; however, the meaning, theology, and even history portrayed adequately reflect what Moses did say, pray, or sing. Similarly, a journalist's report about a president's speech may not have been authored by the president, but can accurately reflect the president's meaning and intent. Perhaps better comparisons are the president's spokesperson, whose assignment is to represent accurately the president's entire perspective on an issue, and the president's official biographer, whose job it is to reflect accurately the president's life even if the biographer rarely quotes the president. Likewise, Walton and Sandy claim, "Authority is identifiable in the beliefs of a community of faith . . . that God's communications through authoritative figures and traditions have been captured and preserved." (Walton and Sandy, LWS, 68) Specifically regarding the Pentateuch, this places Moses in the role of senior archivist of the traditions contained in Genesis, ensuring the recording and transmission of those traditions, although final compilation may not have occurred for centuries.

Furthermore, Walton and Sandy contend Exodus and Numbers are typical of writings produced during the Late Bronze Age, such as documents found at Ugarit. Again, although compilation may not have occurred for quite some time, the authority clearly stems from Moses. He is more closely identified with these documents (than with the Genesis documents) because they were initially generated in connection with the wilderness experience. Concerning Deuteronomy, Walton and Sandy claim there are no reasons to doubt Moses' authorship of the oral tradition or some of the written records. However, it is both possible and expected that revisions and updating occurred throughout its history right up until compilation of the final version.

Although they concur somewhat with Sparks, declaring there is a great deal of accommodation by God within the Bible, Walton and Sandy strongly deny that God's accommodation includes errors of meaning in the text. They dismiss contentions that the Bible, including the Pentateuch, contains forgeries, pseudepigraphy, or false attribution. They further dismiss that narrative portrayals of people and events (which constitute significant portions of the Pentateuch) that purport to record the real past are anything other than historically true records of those events.

Similarly, Christopher Ansberry and Jerry Hwang claim that although historical-critical scholarship may be correct in concluding that the final form of Deuteronomy is postexilic and may have been constantly updated to ensure intelligibility for contemporaneous audiences, it need not undermine Deuteronomy's Mosaic "authorship" or its authority as God's Word. They urge all scholars to change significantly the way authorship and authority are viewed. Historical criticism is not a threat if Deuteronomy is viewed with the understanding that the ANE "authors" were more concerned with properly maintaining the "codified oral and written materials" that contained the traditions of a culture than with the intricacies of intellectual property rights. They argue that even if Deuteronomy were written in post-exilic Judah, it would contain a faithful transmission of the Mosaic tradition. From this perspective, historical criticism provides the Christian community with an enhanced ability "to grasp the human, literary and historical means by which God worked." (Ansberry and Hwang, NCBE, 74–94)

5. Inspired Author, Authority, Compiler, and Editor

Richard Averback claims:

The trick for conservative evangelical scholars . . . is to be willing and able to follow the text wherever it takes us, even if we have trouble fitting it into what we have been taught or currently believe based on our current level of understanding. We need to know the difference between what we believe to be true and what we can actually show to be so under intellectually honest "critical" examination, properly understood. (Averback, PCPT, 3741–3744)

Along these lines, Daniel Block argues for the necessity of abandoning "tight mechanical theories" of inspiration, without going as far as Enns or Sparks. Rather, Averback and Block argue that the Pentateuch was composed through a centuries-long process that involved multiple authors and editors, all working under God's specific guidance.

Using Deuteronomy as a test case, Block contends that the biblical understanding of inspiration covers a "broad range of communicative activities," from guiding Moses' original thoughts, to Moses' oral communication of those thoughts, to the initial written recording of the oral communication, to all the collation and editing necessary up to final recognition of canonization. That Deuteronomy is technically anonymous should not cause undue concern. First, ascription of authorship in the ANE is uncommon. ANE authors were ostensibly more concerned with the message they delivered than marketing themselves. Perhaps most importantly, the Deuteronomic claim that it is the "Book of Moses" does not demand that he personally wrote the text. In sympathy with Walton and Sandy's arguments concerning authority, Block claims there is no reason to doubt Mosaic authority behind the entire Pentateuch, not simply Deuteronomy. Deuteronomy is unequivocal about Moses' role both in speaking God's Word and in personally recording some of it. Those who recorded that which Moses did not specifically author were nonetheless recording an inspired word from YHWH and were not undermining its Mosaic roots. Block claims the narrator of Deuteronomy was an inspired "prophet like Moses," who wrote an inspired narrative of Moses' life including the inspired speeches, songs, and prayers. (Block, RVM, 386–408)

This position is in concert with Michael Grisanti, professor of Old Testament at The Master's Seminary. He proposes that inspiration includes everything necessary to make a biblical document understandable to successive generations up to its recognition of final canonization.

Grisanti uses examples of biblical books such as Psalms and Proverbs that were composed over a long period to demonstrate that because canonization is obviously not "punctiliar," inspiration must also be a process, and perhaps even a very long process. Additionally, in Genesis he cites examples where the "updating of the onomastic entries [relating to the origin of proper names] indicates the antiquity of the source document and was done to make the text intelligible to the reader." In doing this, he acknowledges the work of critical scholarship yet does not diminish either Mosaic authority or God's superintendence. He goes through several examples that both critical scholarship and a plain reading of the text use to indicate that "the original form of a biblical book was not transmitted absolutely unchanged." He terms these "maintenance changes" performed by a "prophetic figure . . . to make a given text more intelligible to a later generation of readers." (Grisanti, IIOTC, 582–588) Additionally, using the example of changes to the English language and claiming analogous changes in Hebrew, he suggests we should expect revisions to the Pentateuch consistent with the semantic development of the Hebrew language.

Grisanti surveys several conservative scholars who concur with this broader understanding of inspiration and inerrancy. He concludes by saying any changes to a book prior to the final canonical form are inspired editorial updates performed by a prophetic figure. (Grisanti, IIOTC, 592–598) This is interestingly close to Witsius's statement five hundred years ago:

In expressing these views, I am not to be understood . . . that there is extant in the Pentateuch nothing which did not proceed from the pen of Moses himself. I readily agree with those who believe that in some places, some word or sentence, more in harmony (with the knowledge) of later times, was added or modified by Ezra, or some other *divinely-inspired writer*, during the process of collecting the sacred writings. (Witsius, WMAP, 19, emphasis added)

VII. Conclusion

In an article highlighting biblical inconsistencies and contradictions, Donald Morgan says,

Some . . . may be resolvable on certain interpretations—after all, almost any problem can be eliminated with suitable rationalizations—but it is the reader's obligation to test this possibility and to decide whether it really makes appropriate sense to do this. (Morgan, BI, website)

As we have seen, presuppositions greatly influence the analyses and conclusions of scholars who study both the biblical and extrabiblical evidence for the Pentateuch and seek to explain apparent difficulties that have been identified in the first five books of the Bible. If there is a naturalistic or minimalistic bias, then little can be done to convince someone that a biblical claim (especially a miracle) is justified. Nevertheless, if we consider the case that can be made for the reliability of the Old Testament by scholars such as Kitchen, Provan, Block, etc., we can see that it holds up remarkably well when treated similarly to other data from the same time and environment.

While the existence of Moses cannot be proven with mathematical certainty, there is good evidence for his existence and his authorship of the Pentateuch from such sources as the Old Testament, the New Testament, extrabiblical writers like Josephus and Philo, the reasoning about the plausibility of the narrative, and the necessity of a figure like Moses to account for the exodus tradition. Although critical scholarship has brought some needed corrections, it has failed to overturn the traditional view about the source and traditions of the Pentateuch. Proof of that failure includes the ongoing attempts to develop new and novel ways to account for the Pentateuch by means other than those it claims for itself.

CHAPTER 24

THE COMPOSITION OF THE BOOK OF ISAIAH

OVERVIEW

I. Introduction

In this chapter we examine the history of critical scholarship relating to the book of Isaiah and the theologically conservative responses to those critiques. The book of Isaiah has undergone sustained critiques since the mid-nineteenth century concerning its origin, historical accuracy, and prophetic content. In evaluating both the evidences presented by critical scholars and the more conservative responses, we must be careful not to overstate our case for the unity and accuracy of the book as significant evidence that would provide a concrete case for the conservative position has not yet been discovered. Similarly, much evidence that would support the cases put forward by critical scholars has not yet been found.

Our intention is to prove the feasibility of our position rather than to prove our case unequivocally.

Much of the historical debate concerning Isaiah hinged upon the validity of predictive prophecy as an indicator of the divine inspiration of Scripture. Accordingly, much of the debate centered around whether or not two or more authors had written the descriptions of the Babylonians and Cyrus the Great (which appear starting at chapter 40 and continue through the end of the book) at the time of those events or if Isaiah had written predictively centuries earlier. The conservative scholars who defended the single authorship of the book did so with the understanding that to split the book into multiple parts, written by different authors over the course of centuries, was to deny that God could supernaturally intend a future event and reveal it centuries in advance, thus implicitly denying the possibility of the supernatural.

It should be noted that while the question of multiple authors is still debated today for this same reason, there has been a general shift among many conservative scholars to a more moderate view of the issue. This is due primarily to the recognition that it is possible to affirm the divine inspiration of Scripture and to also affirm that God could use multiple authors over an extended period of time. Indeed, the Christian defense of the unity of Scripture rests upon this same premise in that God intended many authors over a period of thousands of years to write a unified whole that has been canonized as Scripture. Thus we set forth in this chapter the arguments against and for the single authorship of the book of Isaiah, intending to demonstrate that it is still plausible to affirm the unity of the work and the possibility of predictive prophecy while also realizing that should the book have multiple authors this in no way invalidates God's divine agency in Scripture as a whole.

II. Summary of Critical Approaches to Isaiah

In this section we examine the reasons critical scholars see Isaiah as being compiled either by multiple authors or a redactor over a period of centuries. Old Testament scholar Christopher R. Seitz gives a brief explanation of what motivated scholars starting in the mid-nineteenth century to begin deconstructing many of the Old Testament prophetic books. He states,

In the 19th century, much of what passed as critical readings of the Old Testament focused on questions of (what was called)

"authenticity." That is, using some tool of literary analysis, combined with historical judgments, the interpreter sought to pare away what was secondary and tertiary and get at what could be traced to the individual prophetic agent himself. This was done in the name of a high doctrine of inspiration, it could be argued, or at least one whose theological warrants was reasonably clear: get to the man and you will get to the divine word and you will get to the divine. (Seitz, PH, 159)

Because, along with the Pentateuch, Isaiah was such an integral part of the Old Testament, it became a battleground between critical scholars and those defending more conservative positions of authorship and historical reliability.

Critical scholars inquired into the actual date of composition for Isaiah, and a theory emerged that what we have as the completed book of Isaiah was not the product of the eighth-century BC prophet Isaiah ben Amoz (meaning the son of Amoz) of Jerusalem. Marvin A. Sweeney, professor of Hebrew Bible at Claremont School of Theology, summarizes the critical position:

There are convincing indicators, however, that not all of the material in the book comes from Isaiah ben Amoz. Much of the book presupposes the Babylonian conquest and deportation of Judah which took place in 587 BCE, as well as the coming restoration of the Temple in Jerusalem in the latter part of the sixth century. In two instances, the book refers explicitly to Cyrus, king of Persia, whose decree in 538 BCE initiated the Judean restoration two centuries after the lifetime of Isaiah ben Amoz. Other passages presuppose that the Temple is already rebuilt.

Most scholars view the Book of Isaiah as an anthology of writings from several different prophets, spanning many centuries. Thus, the words of Isaiah ben Amoz appear only in chapters 1–39. A second, unnamed prophet, Deutero-Isaiah or Second Isaiah, wrote chapters 40–55 near the end of the Babylonian exile in the mid-sixth century. A third prophet or group of prophets, Trito-Isaiah or Third Isaiah, wrote chapters 56–66 during the Judean restoration in the late sixth and fifth centuries. (Sweeney, RPT, 20)

Many critical scholars consider the work done by the nineteenth century German and English critics to be definitive statements regarding the origin of Isaiah. Old Testament scholar Joseph Blenkinsopp articulates the opinion of many other critical scholars: "Since the late eighteenth century it has been generally accepted that Isaiah 40–66 cannot have been by the Isaiah of the Assyrian period to whom the entire work is attributed." (Blenkinsopp, SLTI, 403) Old Testament professor Brevard S. Childs states a similar opinion when he says that "by the end of the nineteenth century the force of the historical critical arguments against a unified authorship appeared to have convinced the great majority of Old Testament scholars." (Childs, IOTAS, 317)

Accordingly, to understand the critical position we turn to one of these early scholars to see what arguments were being presented contra the more traditional, conservative position. Hebrew scholar Samuel R. Driver wrote one of the most comprehensive early English language monographs outlining the difficulties perceived within the book of Isaiah. His arguments encapsulate the lines of evidence that led critical scholars to believe Isaiah had been compiled over the course of several centuries by at least two authors. He gives three primary lines of evidence to support this view.

First, he notes that there are allusions within the prophecies of Isaiah 40–66 that would indicate that these chapters were written to a different audience than would be expected if the author were truly Isaiah ben Amoz writing in the eighth century BC. He argues that the primary evidence for a later date of authorship is "*internal evidence supplied by the prophecy itself respecting the period at which it was written.*" (Driver, IHLT, 185, emphasis in original) He continues,

The reader . . . will not need to be reminded how numerous are the allusions to the ruined and deserted condition of Jerusalem . . . to the sufferings which the Jews had experienced, or are experiencing at the hands of the Chaldeans . . . to the prospects of return which, as the prophet speaks, is imminent. . . . The desolation of Jerusalem is even described as of long standing, or "ancient" (lviii. 12; lxi. 4). Those whom the prophet addresses, and whom . . . he addresses in *person,* are not the men of Jerusalem, contemporaries of Ahaz or Hezekiah, or even of Manasseh; they are the exiles in Babylonia. (Driver, IHLT, 185)

Furthermore, any chance of Isaiah ben Amoz having received a predictive prophecy of future events is rejected because "the prophet is, in the first instance, *the teacher of his own generation*; hence it is a fundamental principle of prophecy that the historical situation of the prophet should be the basis of his prediction." (Driver, IHLT, 126, emphasis in original) We should point out that Driver has in fact redefined the term prophet to exclude prediction, and he has claimed that his new definition is a fundamental principle of prophecy.

There is *no* analogy for the case of a prophet, transported in spirit to a future age, and predicting *from that standpoint*, a future remoter still. In the prophecy before us [Isaiah 40–66], there is no *prediction* of exile; the exile is not announced as something yet future, it is *pre-supposed*. Had Isaiah been the author, he would, according to analogy, have predicted, *both* the exile *and* the restoration. He would have represented *both*, as Jeremiah and Ezekiel do, as lying equally in the future. (Driver, IHLT, 186, emphasis in original)

A key piece of evidence in this argument was the repeated mention of Cyrus as the deliverer of Israel in Isaiah 44:28 and 45:1 as well as direct references to Babylonian deities and an expected repatriation of Judah. Gary V. Smith argues, "[Isaiah] 41:2–3, 25 present the initial work of Cyrus as already completed (implying a date after 550 BC). Therefore, the text is arguing that the Israelite audience can trust God's word about the future work of Cyrus in 44:24—45:7 because God's earlier words about Cyrus have already been fulfilled." (Smith, *Isaiah 40–55*, 703) Robert H. Pfeiffer, the late Chairman of the Department of Semitic Languages and History, and Curator of the Semitic Museum, Harvard University elaborates further on how the dating for these passages dictates that they must have been written after 586 BC.

It is evident that Is. 40–48 was written after the destruction of Jerusalem in 586 BC. Judah's capital and other cities have been destroyed and depopulated (44:26, 28; cf. 49:8, 19; 51:3). Israel has been deported from its land and scattered to the four winds (41:8 f.; 42:22; 43:5 f.; 45:13; cf. 49:5 f., 19–21; 52:9).

It is obvious from all this that the tragedy of 586 is some years in the past and that the Second Isaiah is addressing the exiles in Babylonia. He is convinced that the sufferings of the Jews are at an end and that Cyrus (44:28;

45:1) will deliver them from exile. Cyrus king of Anzan deposed his sovereign Astyages of Media about 550, conquered Lydia in 546 and Babylon in 538. Before 546, the Second Isaiah could not have regarded Cyrus as the restorer of the fortunes of the Jews. For it is clear that Cyrus had initiated his great conquests (41:2f.; 45:1–4; 46:11, 48:14f.) and is on his way toward Babylon (41:25; 43:14). But since the conquest of Babylon is still in the future (47, 48:14), most critics have concluded that the Second Isaiah wrote Is. 40–48 between 546 and 539, either at one time or . . . in successive years during period 546–539. (Pfeiffer, IOT, 456)

Furthermore, the two primary sections of Isaiah (from here on First Isaiah and Deutero-Isaiah) are said to be marked by a drastically different prophetic tone and focus in content. Sweeney provides a summary of the supposed differences between the two sections.

The first thirty-five chapters contain prophecies of punishment as well as prophecies of comfort which will be realized after the punishment has taken place. The common elements uniting this material are that the punishing agent will be the Assyrian empire, and that the punishment is yet to come.

Chapters 40–66 present a different picture. The punishment has already taken place and it is now time for restoration. However, the agent of God's punishment is not the Assyrians but the Babylonians. They have fulfilled their role, and now they are cast aside so the restoration may take place. (Sweeney, RPT, 22)

Some perceive this shift in message—often denoted within First Isaiah as the "Book of Judgment" and within Deutero-Isaiah as the "Book of Comfort"—as evidence that the author of Deutero-Isaiah indeed wrote much later in time than Isaiah ben Amoz. Old Testament scholar Ronald E. Clements explains that this shift in tone is the result of a change in the way in which Israel is perceived in the eyes of God in these prophecies and is indicative of two different timeframes for composition. The "Book of Comfort" is

> another group of passages in chs. 40–55, which are usually reckoned as the work of "Second Isaiah", where a conscious allusion back to the language of Isaiah of Jerusalem appears intended. This concerns the varied expressions which are employed to affirm *the divine election of Israel*; to stress that Yahweh really has chosen it, in spite of all appearances to the contrary, and to make plain that God has not rejected it . . . .
>
> Can there be any real doubt here, in view of the clear nature of the original language in Isaiah affirming that God has rejected his people, that this highly distinctive aspect of the teaching of Deutero-Isaiah has arisen in conscious awareness that the opposite had earlier been affirmed? The later prophecy is making unmistakably plain that the time of rejection is now past and that a new age is about to dawn in which the closeness of Yahweh's relationship to his people will be especially evident. (Clements, BTH, 105–106)

Critical scholars have argued to extend a further separation between Isaiah 40–55 and Isaiah 56–66, claiming that the latter section was written by an author now referred to as Trito-Isaiah. Critical scholars make this division because of another shift in the message of Isaiah. Isaiah 40–55 is concerned with "the Servant," while the focus in Isaiah 56–66 is "the servants of Yahweh." Blenkinsopp assigns this particular division of Isaiah not to an individual author but to a group of disciples that were attempting to mimic the style of Deutero-Isaiah. He notes that the message and content of Trito-Isaiah is

> in several respects closely related to Isaiah 40–55, especially the latter part of it (chapters 49–55). One of these connecting strands links disciples with the prophetic figures designated "the Servant" who speaks and is spoken of in the last three of Duhm's "Servant Songs." It seems likely that these disciples formed a prophetic-eschatological group within the postexilic community under a leader whose voice is heard proclaiming his mission in the Spirit (Isa. 59:21; 61:1–4). (Blenkinsopp, HPI, 216)

Biblical studies professor Kenton L. Sparks provides two additional lines of evidence for this division, but he is willing to admit that the evidences for this division are not as strong as that for separating Deutero-Isaiah from First Isaiah.

> The case for the existence of Trito-Isaiah is perhaps not so strong as the case for Deutero-Isaiah. Scholars date the last part of Isaiah to the postexilic period for two primary reasons. First, while Deutero-Isaiah describes Israel as innocent and redeemed (40:1–2), Trito-Isaiah depicts Israel as guilty and idolatrous. . . . This contrast suggests a very different context for the two parts of Isaiah. Second, this last section of Isaiah talks frequently about the rebuilding of Jerusalem and the restoration of the temple and its ritual cult (56:1–8; 58:12; 60–62). All of these features suit a postexilic context, when a community of Jews was busy attempting to reconstitute itself in the land of Palestine. (Sparks, GWHW, 108)

Returning to Driver's work we find that his second line of evidence for different authors in Isaiah is the marked contrast in language between Isaiah 1–39 and 40–66. He argues:

> Different authors may approximate—as witness Jeremiah and Deuteronomy—in the use of similar phraseology; but difference of style is a common, if not a universal distinction, which obtains between different authors. Especially do differences of style sometimes show themselves in types of expressions, or, as they may be termed, mannerisms, affected by particular authors, which are employed by them without deliberation, and which betray themselves unconsciously. (Driver, IHLT, 193)

Differences of language between chapters 1–39 and 40–66 convince Driver that there were at least two distinct authors. Comparing these two sections he states of chapters 40–66, "Terms and expressions which, in the former series of prophecies [1–39], Isaiah uses, and uses repeatedly, are absent. . . . [C]onversely, new terms and expressions appear in chaps. xl–lxvi, which are without parallel in the first part of the book." (Driver, IHLT, 193)

Driver provides an extensive list of the differences between the two sections but finds the greatest indication of a difference in authors in the phrase "in that day." He remarks on the distinct lack of usage of this phrase in Isaiah 40–66 as an indication of different authorship by comparing it to the writing of Mark in the New Testament.

> *In that day* is a form of expression into which Isaiah as naturally and readily falls, in his description of the future, as St. Mark falls into in the use of *straightway* in his descriptions of the past. It is as difficult to believe that, had he been the author of a prophecy as long as chapters xl.–lxvi., and dealing even more with the future than the prophecies in Part I [chapters 1–39], would have been content to

use this expression but once—and that once by no means in his usual manner—as it is to believe that had St. Mark written, as St. Luke wrote, a sequel to his Gospel, the word *straightway* would have been found in it but once only. (Driver, IHLT, 196, emphasis in original)

Finally, Driver's third line of evidence is the difference in the theological focus of each section in Isaiah. Between First Isaiah and Deutero-Isaiah, he finds a conception of God that cannot be reconciled in any other way than believing that the later author has expanded upon the much simpler theology of Isaiah ben Amoz. He elaborates on these differences by noting,

> Isaiah depicts the majesty of Jehovah; the author of chaps. xl.–lxvi. His *infinity*. This is a real difference. It would be difficult to establish from Isaiah—not the greatness merely, but—the *infinitude* of the Divine attributes: the author of chaps. xl.–lxvi. exhausts the Hebrew language in the endeavor, if possible, to represent it. . . . [T]he truth is, the prophet of the exile *moves in a different region of thought* from Isaiah. . . . [E]ven where there is a point of contact between the two parts of the book or where the same terms are employed, the ideas attached to them have, in chaps. xl.–lxvi., a wider and fuller import. But this is exactly what would be expected from a later writer expanding and developing, in virtue of the fuller measure of inspiration vouchsafed to him, elements due, perhaps, originally to a predecessor. (Driver, IHLT, 206–207, emphasis in original)

Clements does not take up Driver's argument for drastically different theologies between the two sections, but he does recognize that Deutero-Isaiah is more theologically developed than First Isaiah. This development occurs through the extension of prophetic material found in First Isaiah to cover new aspects within Deutero-Isaiah. His argument concerning this development is not that it was accomplished by a single later author, but that a series of redactions by a later editor allowed for the creation of a more developed theology in the later sections of the book. (Clements, BTH, 101–111) He states,

> The distinctive connections that are observable in the formation of the book of Isaiah, where one prophetic saying provides a basis for the development of further sayings related to it, appears as a distinctively prophetic feature. It related to the very nature of prophecy itself, in which particular words and images could be regarded as fraught with special power and significance. So they could be re-applied, re-interpreted and even re-cast altogether. (Clements, BTH, 110)

III. Responses to Critical Scholarship

Evangelical scholars were not willing to let the positions of critical scholars go unchallenged.

Biblical scholar Oswald T. Allis provides an extensive defense of the unity of Isaiah that encapsulates the classic key arguments given by evangelical scholars. His argument can be broken down into three lines of evidence pointing to single authorship.

First, Allis argues that the "most obvious reason for regarding Isaiah as the author of the book which for centuries has borne his name is the heading: 'The vision of Isaiah the son of Amoz'" because it follows in the tradition of the other fifteen books that comprise the "Latter Prophets." (Allis, UI, 39) If the book of Isaiah begins with this heading but does not contain the actual words of the prophet Isaiah, it would be an anomaly among the prophetic books. Allis argues that for this to be the case would mean

that a collection of anonymous prophecies nearly half as long as the collection known as "The Twelve" had been included among the writing prophets. Obadiah, Joel, Nahum, Habakkuk are tiny books as compared with Isa. 40–66. But not one of them is anonymous. The names "Obadiah," or "Joel, the son of Pethuel" may mean little to us. But at least their names are given. A "great Unknown," as the author of this group of chapters, or several such Unknowns, would be an anomaly. (Allis, UI, 39–40)

Second, Allis points out that within the manuscript evidence no indication exists that there was ever a break in the text of Isaiah between chapters 39 and 40. The Isaiah Scroll discovered at Qumran provides evidence of continuity within the book as Isaiah 40:1 continues "the very last line of the column which contains 38:9—39:8." (Allis, UI, 40) Allis states that this continuity of text indicates "the scribe was not conscious of the alleged fact that an important change in situation, involving an entire change of authorship begins with chapter 40." (Allis, UI, 40)

Biblical scholar Kenneth A. Kitchen has added to this argument by noting that a break does occur within the Isaiah Scroll, but, given critical arguments, not where one would expect. He points out that the scribe's break in the scroll occurs between 33:24 and 34:1, which is "very close to the midpoint of the entire book as he had it, and as we have it." (Kitchen, OROT, 378) This break causes the book neatly to parallel itself in a number of ways as the division "has chronological significance; 1–33 comes under Uzziah to Ahaz, while 34–66 comes under the time of Hezekiah. . . . Each half corresponds well to the other in order and subject of topics covered; each is in seven parts." (Kitchen,

A TWOFOLD STRUCTURE OF ISAIAH

Part 1	Part 2
A. 1–5 Judgment and restoration	A. 34–35 Desolation and restoration
B. 6–8 Biographical/historical and oracles	B. 36–39 Historical/biographical accounts
C. 9–12 Words of blessing and judgment	C. 40–45 Words of blessing and judgment
D. 13–23 Oracles on foreign nations (and one on Jerusalem)	D. 46–48 Oracles on foreign nations (and on Babylon)
E. 24–27 Destruction, restoration, deliverance	E. 49–55 Restoration, destruction, deliverance
F. 28–31 Social and ethical justice	F. 56–59 Social and ethical justice
G. 32–33 Restoration of the nation	G. 60–66 Restoration of the nation

Adapted from Kitchen, OROT, 379.

OROT, 379; see chart "A Twofold Structure of Isaiah")

Allis's final argument is that the historical record found within the New Testament gives no indication or acknowledgment of multiple authors within Isaiah:

Isaiah is quoted *by name* about twenty times, which is more often than all the other "writing prophets" taken together. Furthermore, in those books where he is so quoted most frequently, citations are made from both parts of the book. Matthew quotes Isaiah by name six times, three times from the first part and three from the second. Paul in Romans quotes Isaiah five times by name, and from both parts of the book. . . . Such evidence indicates with sufficient clearness that none of the New Testament writers "dreamt" that the name Isaiah was of doubtful or ambiguous meaning. (Allis, UI, 42, emphasis in original)

Taken together, Allis's evidences cannot be easily dismissed. For any nonbiblical text an ascription, manuscript evidence, and book citation would likely be considered as significant evidence in favor of there being one author. If so, shouldn't the same apply to Isaiah?

A. The Consequences of Dividing Isaiah

Allis's arguments did not, however, prevent critical scholars and even some conservative scholars from rejecting them as incompatible with evidence provided by higher criticism. Seitz comments on the traditional view of Isaiah: "Once critical judgment was able to operate with principles external to the literature itself, defense of the older view began to look strained, idiosyncratic, and suspiciously defensive." (Seitz, OI, 17)

Sparks believes, regarding higher criticism, that "the critical consensus on the Bible is essentially correct and reasonably justified." (Sparks, GWHW, 76) This blanket acceptance of higher criticism leads Sparks to conclude:

Evangelical arguments against biblical criticism vary widely in quality, ranging from simple and unsophisticated critiques that seem to hang in epistemological thin air, to more complex and nuanced critiques that should be taken more seriously. Nevertheless, in the end, I do not believe that any of these arguments resolve the essential conflict between biblical criticism and traditional readings of Scripture. So, while there is much to be valued in these conservative theological critiques of biblical criticism, one of my primary purposes ... is to demonstrate that these traditional responses do not adequately resolve the theological difficulties presented by biblical criticism. (Sparks, GWHW, 134)

Seitz echoes Sparks' statement by stating, "It appears that with the Book of Isaiah, we have at last found one of those cases where 'the assured results of critical scholarship' are in fact assured." (Seitz, OI, 14)

The end result of the critical understanding of Isaiah destroyed the message of the book as it had been held for close to two thousand years. Historian and archaeologist Charles C. Torrey recognized this as early as 1928 in his efforts to unify the last half of the book of Isaiah under a single author. Torrey begins his work by citing the theory of three separate authors of Isaiah as leading to a greater fragmentation of the book itself into isolated sections that had no relationship to each other.

Instead of a comprehensive unit, the best scholarship of the present day offers us here only an incomprehensible scrap-heap. The necessity of making the division into "Deutero-Isaiah" (chapters 40–55) and "Trito-Isaiah" (56–66), with all that it involves, would of itself be a sufficiently great misfortune. That it is not possible to take this step without going still farther, the recent history of exegesis has clearly shown. The subsequent dissection of "III Isaiah" is a certainty, while that of the curtailed II Isaiah is not likely to be long delayed. We have here a good example of that which has happened not a few times in the history of literary criticism, where scholars have felt obligated to pare down a writing to make it fit a mistaken theory. The paring process, begun with a penknife, is continued with a hatchet, until the book has been chopped into hopeless chunks. (Torrey, SI, 13)

Childs echoes Torrey's assessment in reviewing the effects of critical scholarship in recent years. He writes,

The critical study of Isaiah has brought with it a whole set of new problems which have grown in size rather than diminished over the years. First of all, critical scholarship has atomized the book Isaiah into a myriad of fragments, sources, and redactions which were written by different authors at a variety of historical moments. To speak of the message of the book as a whole has been seriously called into question.... [C]ritical exegesis now rests upon a very hypothetical and tentative basis of historical reconstructions. Since it is no longer possible to determine precisely the historical background of large sections of Isaiah, hypotheses increase along with the disagreement among experts. Finally, the more the book of Isaiah has come into historical focus and been anchored to its original setting, the more difficult it has become to move from the ancient world into a contemporary religious appropriation of the message. (Childs, IOTAS, 324)

This fragmentation of meaning is evidenced in the continued splitting of Isaiah into smaller and smaller sections, accommodating perceived differences in historical background and authorship. Bible professor Elizabeth Achtemeier provides a summary of the extent of this division in relation to First Isaiah as an individual section of the whole book.

The book divides itself very easily into sections. Chapters 1–12 are oracles against Judah and Jerusalem, ending with a doxology in Chapter 12. Chapters 13–23 are made up of oracles, some of them non-Isaianic (chaps. 13–14, maybe 23), against various enemies of

Israel. . . . Chapters 24–27 have been called apocalyptic and assigned a postexilic date, and while the section probably does not come from Isaiah and has apocalyptic elements in it, it is not a unity, consisting variously of apocalyptic judgments, salvation oracles, laments, and judgment oracles. . . . With chapter 28, the genuine oracles of judgment against Judah are taken up again and run through chapter 33. Chapters 34–35 have often been attributed to Second Isaiah, and perhaps the most we can say is that they are from the Isaiah school. Chapters 36–39 form a historical appendix largely paralleling portions of 2 Kings 18:3, 17–20:19, with some omissions and additions. With chapter 40, Second Isaiah begins. (Achtemeier, IJ, 25–26)

Achtemeier seems to be assuming that a different genre means a different author. But why adopt this assumption? If we consider modern authors, such as T. S. Eliot, Dante, Charles Williams, and C. S. Lewis, we can see that it is common for writers to employ a variety of genres.

B. Contemporary Views on the Unity of Isaiah

Recognizing that the continued fragmentation of the book of Isaiah would render its message trivial, recent critical scholars have moved to see Isaiah as a unified literary whole achieved through a process of redaction and editing—not as compiled sections of text added as addenda to the original writings of Isaiah. This had been posited initially in respect to Deutero-Isaiah and Trito-Isaiah as the means by which Isaiah was created. Rather, the book as a whole had to have an internal unity placed upon it either by a later single editor or by a group of disciples that compiled the work.

Clements finds that such redactors "may more truly be regarded as the 'authors' of the books of prophecy than even the prophet himself" (Clements, WIBMS, 151) This mindset focuses the study of a given book not on the original historical intent of the passages, but upon what the redactor intended to convey to his audience. Clements continues that "it is reasonable to assume that it was such redactors who looked for a greater level of ideological consistency in the prophet's words than would have been the case among an open-air audience. Differences needed to be explained, even when full consistency was never expected." (Clements, WIBMS, 151)

Accordingly, critical scholars have placed an emphasis on finding the literary whole of the book of Isaiah while still recognizing that it had several periods of composition. Clements comments:

What has consistently provided the backbone of the conventional critical understanding of the book of Isaiah is that the apportionment of material among the pre-587, exilic, and early postexilic periods accords reasonably well with the major classes of editorial referencing that the book contains. What is different in the new criticism, though often more implicit in the earlier critical studies than is usually recognized, is that these three categories of material are interwoven in a highly intricate way. They cannot simply be found in wholly separate "blocks" within the book. . . . The consequence is that an awareness of the book's wholeness as a literary creation is important if we are not to be misled into premature and unwarranted assumptions about how it was put together. (Clements, WIBMS, 152)

Critical scholars have thus turned to a diachronic reading of the book of Isaiah that seeks to "correlate shifts in theological emphasis and linguistic usage with changes in historic context by positing redactional processes." (McInnes, MRURI, 68) Jim McInnes comments at length on how this type of reading of Isaiah effects interpretation and study of the book.

> Those scholars with a diachronic interest trace the unifying themes in Isaiah back through the editorial stages of the book's development in order to give an account of their current placement and function. They look for points of distinction and difference to determine the development of Isaiah. They tell us to pay attention to the many layers of composition in a book that addresses Israel at different points in its history, and therefore must also have been composed in a complicated historical process of writing, reinterpretation and redaction over at least two centuries. . . . Unlike the older source-critical approaches, much recent diachronic scholarship denies the existence of independent sources for First, Second and Third Isaiah. Instead it maintains that later writing is dependent upon, and stimulated by, earlier prophecy, faithfully reinterpreting its central message for a new generation. (McInnes, MRURI, 69)

Critical scholars have attempted to find these layers of redaction by positing an Isaianic school that worked to transmit and reinterpret prophecies faithfully within the ever-changing historical situations of Israel. Evidence of this group is believed to be found in Isaiah 8:16 in which Isaiah commands a group to "seal the teaching among my disciples" (ESV). Religious studies scholar Charles D. Isbell posits that Isaiah formed this group of prophetic disciples to ensure that there were witnesses who would later be able to testify to the veracity of his prophetic utterances. He states, "Who better to preserve

into the future and certify the dating and the veracity of the words of Isaiah than a group of the prophet's own students, doubtless members of an intergenerational guild that would outlast any single individual and thus would presumably be around long after the death of both king and prophet." (Isbell, LBI, 100)

Other critical scholars have pointed out that adopting this approach does not address how Isaiah is a unified whole, because the argument itself is circular. Clements points out this inherent flaw in the argument by noting of this theoretical Isaianic school:

> Their existence over a period of at least two centuries is postulated without any clear identification of where, or how, such a group maintained itself. The argument in fact rapidly becomes completely circular in that the existence of such a group is attested from the book, the structure of which is assumed to be illuminated by the identification of such disciples. The value of such a hypothesis, therefore, becomes gravely vitiated in the absence of any clear indication of what constituted membership of such a body of prophetic disciples. We have no information to confirm that such a circle actually existed, and to postulate their existence for such a long period of time after the original prophet's death renders the concept of "disciple" virtually meaningless. (Clements, UBI, 119)

Conservative scholar Richard L. Schultz also comments on recent attempts to find redactional unity within Isaiah.

> This type of redactional analysis is, of course, based on a number of presuppositions about Old Testament prophets and prophecy that cannot be proved, or disproved: (1) that a prophet/editor would not use the same concept or theme in more than one way (e.g., both

literally and figuratively); (2) that a prophet would not reuse, allude to, or elaborate upon his own (earlier) oracles (i.e., that any such action must be the work of another); and (3) that a prophet would not proclaim anything that was not clearly relevant and perspicuous for his contemporaries (i.e., that any such texts must be dated to a later date when they would be pertinent and clear). Furthermore, since the prophets are uniformly presented in the Bible as divine spokespersons, one is, in effect, presupposing what God could or would communicate to a particular prophet in a particular era. (Schultz, IICS, 256)

C. Recent Evidences of Single Authorship

Recent conservative scholarship has worked to demonstrate the faulty assumptions underlying many of the ideas that drove critics such as Driver and Torrey to assume only a later author could have written particular sections of Isaiah. Several scholars point to the structure and content of passages assigned to later authors as having a message pertinent to those who would have lived at the time of Isaiah ben Amoz. We consider three of these arguments in brief.

As noted above, many of the critical assumptions about the division of Isaiah rest upon perceived content in chapters 40–66 that is believed could not have been written in a preexilic setting. Biblical scholar Gary V. Smith has recently examined seven particular passages within Isaiah 40–55 that he believes point to a preexilic audience rather than an exilic or postexilic audience. The passages and the relevant points concerning the intended audience are summarized in the chart "Analysis of the Intended Audience in Isaiah 40–55." (Smith, *Isaiah 40–55*, 705–712)

ANALYSIS OF THE INTENDED AUDIENCE IN ISAIAH 40–55

Passage	Content	Reason for Preexilic Audience
Isaiah 41:8–16	Declaration of God's protection from those who wage war on Israel	There are no references to any nation making war on Israel in any of the exilic books: Jeremiah, Ezekiel, Daniel; best reference would be Nebuchadnezzar attacking Jerusalem prior to the exile.
Isaiah 42:22–25	Reference to Israelites being kept hidden away in caves and pits from their enemies and God causing a great victory	No evidence of this occurring during the exile; fits well into the events of the Assyrian attack upon Jerusalem in 701 BC.
Isaiah 43:3	God promises to use Egypt, Seba, and Cush as a ransom to redeem his people	Does not fit the evidence of Cyrus's conquests; matches the Assyrian attacks under Sennacherib against these countries prior to the exile.
Isaiah 43:14	A violent overthrow of Babylon	Does not match the peaceful conquest by Cyrus of Babylon; does match the destruction of Babylon by Sennacherib in 689 BC.
Isaiah 43:28	The coming destruction of the temple	Verse uses future tense verbs to speak of the destruction of the temple; indicates the verse was written prior to the exile.
Isaiah 46–47	The fall of Babylon and her gods	Cyrus did not overthrow Babylon and her false gods when he conquered it; Babylon was overthrown and her idols destroyed under Sennacherib's conquest in 689 BC.
Isaiah 52:3–5	Oppression by Egypt and Assyria mentioned, but no oppression by Babylon	Does not match the events of the exile with Israel being subjugated to Babylon; does match the events of Sennacherib's invasion in 701 BC.

Smith comments on these and other passages:

> Some of these texts include enough historical hints (war, future destruction of the temple) to demonstrate that pre-exilic setting is not just possible, but a likely understanding of the audience's setting in Isaiah 40–55. It is also interesting that a couple places suggest a location in Judah.... For example, (a) the repeated reference to Palestinian trees rather than Babylonian trees (Isa. 41:19); (b) the statement that the location of Ur was "at the far ends of the earth" (Isa. 41:9) and not just next door, suggesting that the Israelites were not a few miles away from Babylon; and (c) the repeated condemnation of making and worshiping idols which was a pre-exilic problem in Judah, but not a problem for the exiles in Babylon. (Smith, *Isaiah 40–55*, 712)

Old Testament scholar Eric Ortlund has addressed the charge that Isaiah 1–39 evidences insertions by a later redactor. He specifically addresses charges that "passages making up these chapters [Isa. 11; 30; 2] were written centuries apart, later passages being inserted in order to fill out putative gaps in the prophetic message of those chapters."

(Ortlund, RCLSI, 211) He finds that proposed interpolations by later redactors can more easily be attributed to the author purposefully placing imagery and events out of the expected order as a literary technique. Such reversed chronologies are used to highlight particular aspects of God's salvation or coming kingdom. (See chart below, which was formulated from information appearing in Ortlund, RCLSI, 211–221)

Ortlund contends that these passages do not evidence a later redaction. Rather, they are intentionally reversed for "both literary and theological reasons" to have "the effect of highlighting divine mercy." (Ortlund, RCLSI, 222–223) Further, such an approach to these texts "posits a relatively simple prehistory to the text . . . and a more complex literary relationship between the passages making up these chapters," rather than a more complex, and less evidenced, redactional history. (Ortlund, RCLSI, 223)

Finally, Kitchen has drawn attention to prophetic traditions in the ancient Near East in Mari and Assyria to demonstrate that prophecies in religious contexts were recorded early and accurately so as to be later verified. Within these areas "an accurate, independent, and permanent record of

Passage	Out of Order Chronology Supposing Later Redactor	Literary Reason for Earlier Author to Place Out of Order
Isaiah 11:1–9, 11–16	Peace occurs *before* Israel is restored to the promised land by the actions of the root of Jesse judging the nations.	Imagery of the root of Jesse is juxtaposed closely against the trees (nations) felled by YHWH in punishment in Isaiah 10:33–34.
Isaiah 30:1–17, 18–26, 27–33	Judgment is declared against Israel; Israel is presented as being in proper relationship to God/creation is renewed; Assyria is judged and destroyed. (Restoration occurs after an enemy's destruction, not before.)	Restoration is placed in the midst of judgment to highlight YHWH's gracious intervention for his people.
Isaiah 2:1–5, 6–22	Mount Zion is exalted as a beacon to draw in the nations for worship of YHWH; Israel is then condemned for its idolatry and YHWH's destruction of idols is promised.	Passage implies that the nations will come to Zion to worship but will only do so after they are humbled and their idols destroyed.

prophecies was needed, to stand as lasting witness for when possible fulfillment might occur or be required to be checked." (Kitchen, OROT, 393) In reviewing prophetic records from Mari and Assyria, Kitchen concludes that this demand for accurate recording of prophecy prohibited any sort of later redaction or prophetic school. He writes:

> Thus, throughout the centuries, across the biblical world, the firsthand external evidence shows clearly and conclusively that the record of prophecies among contemporaries and their transmission down through time was *not* left to the memories of bystanders or the memory-conditioned oral transmission—and modification—by imaginary "disciples" of a prophet or their equally imaginary successors for centuries before someone took the remnants at a late date to weave them into books out of whole new cloth, having little or nothing to do with a reputed prophet of dim antiquity whose very name and existence might thus be doubted. For the mass of highly ingenious guesswork and scholarly imagination along these lines, poured out of the presses for over a century now, and never more than in recent decades, there is not one respectable scintilla of solid, firsthand evidence. Not one. (Kitchen, OROT, 392, emphasis in original)

IV. Conclusion

We believe that the internal and external evidence points to a plausible conclusion that the whole of the book of Isaiah was in fact authored by Isaiah ben Amoz. We use the word "plausible" because at this point not enough evidence has been discovered to reach a verdict beyond a reasonable doubt. This should in no way raise doubts about God's agency in superintending the creation of an inspired, authoritative message throughout the book as a whole, even if that message was written by more than one person.

Early defenders of a single author for the book were concerned that evidence of multiple sources—and some with quite late dates at that—could lead to undermining confidence in the divine inspiration not only of Isaiah, but of the whole body of Scripture. Yet there is convincing evidence to affirm God's authoritative revelation in Scripture and also affirm his inspiration of multiple authors over many centuries. Indeed, those same evidences that demonstrate that the Bible is a unified whole are just as applicable to the book of Isaiah, even if it could be shown that the book had multiple authors. We believe that God has divinely superintended and delivered his authoritative message to the world. And that includes the book of Isaiah.

CHAPTER 25

THE HISTORICITY OF DANIEL

OVERVIEW

I. Introduction to the Book of Daniel

In this chapter we examine the historical issues that have made Daniel a focus of critical scholars since the nineteenth century. Due primarily to the extremely accurate predictive prophecies contained within Daniel's last six chapters, scholars consider it a key book in the discussion of the validity of the Old Testament. Much like the book of Isaiah, the responses of conservative scholars to these problems do not always equate to certain proofs. Therefore, when evaluating and presenting this evidence, it must be done with the recognition that potential solutions are just that—potential.

II. The Date of Authorship

The book of Daniel's date of authorship comes to the forefront primarily in relation to its highly accurate prophecies in chapters 7–12. These prophecies have led critical scholars to date the book of Daniel much later than the book itself attests. Summarizing the issue, Old Testament scholar Tremper Longman III says the problem arises because "the first six chapters, while presenting themselves as historical narrative, are surrounded by issues of historical accuracy, while the second six chapters, which are prophecy, are uncannily accurate and precise through the second century BC." (Longman, *Daniel*, 22)

An example of these uncannily accurate predictions is found in Daniel 11:45, which predicts the death of Antiochus IV Epiphanes as occurring in Palestine during a failed attempt to capture Jerusalem. Antiochus did not die in Palestine but in a failed attempt to conquer Persia in 164 BC. For critical scholars this discrepancy indicates that Daniel must have been written after the events described in Daniel 10–11 but prior to the death of Antiochus in 164 BC. Therefore, as Hebrew professor Andrew E. Steinmann notes, critics since Porphyry, who wrote in the third century, have contended that

> Daniel was written as if it was predictive prophecy, but [it] was actually written during the first half of the second century BC after the supposed events that it prophesied concerning Antiochus IV Epiphanes. . . . The prophecies that attempted to prophesy events later than in the reign of Antiochus (11:40–45) were inaccurate, demonstrating that there is no divinely revealed predictive prophecy, and also betraying the author's real identity: a Jew in Palestine about the year 165 BC. (Steinmann, *Daniel*, 3)

Since according to critical scholars Daniel cannot be prophecy in any traditional sense, they attempt to explain what type of literature Daniel is. The general consensus has been that Daniel was composed as two discrete books that editors fused together. The first book, consisting of Daniel 1–6, contains a series of court tales concerning an archetypal hero. Biblical scholar Ernest Lucas provides an overview of the customary form of court tales in the ancient Near East.

> The tales of court conflict are structured as follows. 1. The heroes are in a state of prosperity. 2. The heroes are endangered, usually because of a conspiracy. 3. The heroes are condemned to death or prison. 4. The heroes are released, for various reasons. 5. The heroes are restored to positions of honour and, in some cases, promoted. (Lucas, AOTC, 26)

The author of these tales, according to one argument, intended to "edify the readers as well as entertain them." (Lucas, AOTC, 26) In the presentation of Daniel as the hero of the stories in Daniel 1–6, biblical scholar C. L. Seow finds evidence that they were written as legendary accounts. The chief line of supporting evidence he finds is that "the prophets of the Old Testament are typically introduced by their father's name, profession, or place of origin, but Daniel is simply called 'Daniel,' without other personal details about him, as if the original reader would have known who he was." (Seow, *Daniel*, 3) Readers would have an understanding of Daniel functioning as a stock character of ancient wisdom literature. Seow points to both biblical and nonbiblical examples of the character Daniel as evidence of this.

> The book of Ezekiel, a work from the early sixth century BCE, mentions a Daniel, along with Noah and Job, as persons of exemplary righteousness (Ezek. 14:14, 20). Daniel was apparently also known to the audience of Ezekiel as a paragon of wisdom, for the arrogant prince of Tyre reportedly believed himself "wiser than Daniel" (Ezek. 28:3). . . . A Daniel, however, is known from a story from the ancient city of Ugarit . . . about a man from long ago who trusted his gods and was apparently known for his righteousness and wisdom. The Daniel of Canaanite lore worshiped a god named El (hence the name Daniel, etymologically explained as "My judge is El"). (Seow, *Daniel*, 3–4)

This view claims that to this collection of tales focusing on a legendary hero, editors appended a second book comprising Daniel 7–12. This second book recorded a series of apocalyptic visions declaring God's judgment upon Antiochus IV Epiphanes for his desecration of the temple.

While the preceding hypotheses have been generally accepted by critical scholars, Lucas notes two distinct problems with their assumptions:

It has often been argued that the visions of the second century were linked with the stories because this linkage would have enhanced the authority and acceptability of the visions. It is not clear that this would be the case. First . . . the stories would have been "entertaining anecdotes about another place and time," and it is hard to see that this would have enhanced the authority of the visions. Secondly, simply on the basis of stories, it is not obvious that Daniel would have been a sufficient hero figure to have given prestige to the visions. (Lucas, AOTC, 313)*

However, based upon perceived historical difficulties and a supposed division within the book, critical scholars have continued to advocate for a dating of around 165 BC. It is to these perceived difficulties that we now turn in order to demonstrate that they in no way prohibit a date of composition in the sixth century BC, which is the traditional dating for the book of Daniel.

III. Answering Challenges to Daniel's Historicity

A. Daniel 1:1

Critical scholars believe the first verse of Daniel contains one of the most glaring historical errors, since it recounts that during the third year of the reign of King Jehoiakim Jerusalem was besieged by Nebuchadnezzar.

Seow gives three reasons this statement mitigates against the historical accuracy of Daniel:

1. According to other passages in the Bible, Nebuchadnezzar did not officially begin to reign until the fourth year of Jehoiakim's reign.
2. Although Babylonian records indicate that Nebuchadnezzar led a number of expeditions into Palestine when he was a crown prince, no attack on Jerusalem is mentioned.
3. All sources indicate a siege of Jerusalem in 597 BCE, during the reign not of Jehoiakim but of Jehoiachin and then, again, in 586 BCE, long after Jehoiakim had died. (Seow, *Daniel*, 21)

Rebuttals to this argument have followed one of two distinct paths. Tremper Longman III explains that the first means of harmonizing the passage has been to recognize Daniel 1:1 as historically accurate by seeing it as being anticipatory:

Daniel 1:1 may well refer to Nebuchadnezzar as king in an anticipatory sense. After all, it is soon after Daniel's report of a siege of Jerusalem that Nabopolassar's death would bring Nebuchadnezzar to the throne. No one doubts, based on Babylonian records themselves, Nebuchadnezzar's presence as crown prince

---

* A conservative reading of Daniel 1–6 might instead notice that these chapters emphasize Daniel's resolute moral integrity and keen mental heroism. Furthermore, each story points with praise to God's revelation of himself—metaphysically, epistemologically, ethically! Receptive humility becomes the proper human response, even for foreign kings, to the discovery of God's existence, his truth, and his eternal and just rule over history. In *Mimesis: The Representation of Reality in Western Literature,* Erich Auerbach compares the way Homeric and biblical heroes are presented. Writing about Abraham's offering up of Isaac, Auerbach declares that "overwhelming suspense is present," and it serves to "indicate thoughts which are unexpressed." That is how the text directs and concentrates the reader's attention, not to entertain but to serve a truth claim—to present "the only real world" and to give "due place within its frame" to the history of all mankind. . . . The Scripture stories do not, like Homer's, court our favor, they do not flatter us that they may please and enchant us—they seek to subject us, and if we refuse to be subjected we are rebels." (Auerbach, M, 11, 14–15) Virginia Stem Owens quotes Auerbach and adds a succinct summary: She defends the reticence of biblical writers who leave some things unsaid, producing "the gaps which, Auerbach says, 'are intended to overcome our reality.' . . . Instead of explaining the biblical world in our terms, we must 'fit our own life into its world' and allow ourselves 'to be elements in its structure of universal history.' The gaps are meant to swallow us." (Owens, CJ, 48)

and field commander of the Babylonian armies against Egypt in the area of Syria-Palestine in the years before 605 BC. (Longman, *Daniel*, 43–44)

The second method of harmonization has been to understand that Daniel 1:1 can be accounted for due to two distinct methods of dating that were used in the ancient Near East. Longman again explains how the dates of Nebuchadnezzar's siege and the reign of Jehoiakim can be reconciled in this way:

> We can also harmonize the data by reminding ourselves . . . that there were two systems of dating current in the ancient Near Eastern world, both of which can be found in the Old Testament. The above passage may be harmonized by assuming that Jeremiah utilized the Judaean method of chronological reckoning which counts the first year of a king's reign as the first year, and that Daniel used the Babylonian system, which counts the first year as an "accession year." (Longman, *Daniel*, 44)

Lucas provides some additional detail to demonstrate how accounting for these two different dating systems resolves the supposed contradiction.

> According to the Babylonian method of reckoning regnal years, in his second year the king would have ruled for part of one year (his accession year), a full year (year 1 of his reign) and part of another year (year 2). By Hebrew usage, which reckoned part of a year as a whole year, three years could be said to have elapsed (cf. 2 Kings 18:9–10, where a siege that lasted between one and two calendar years, from the fourth to the sixth years of Hezekiah's reign, is said to have taken three years). (Lucas, AOTC, 62)

Lucas also addresses the claim that the author of Daniel conflated 2 Kings 24:1 and 2 Chronicles 36:6 to create Daniel 1:1.

> It is often suggested that Dan. 1:1–2 is based purely on 2 Chr. 36:6–7 combined with 2 Kgs. 24:1, with the author of Daniel assuming that Jehoiakim's three years of servitude to Nebuchadnezzar were the first three years of his reign . . . after which he rebelled and was punished as stated in 2 Chronicles. This seems unlikely, since Dan. 2:1 has Daniel and his friends in Babylon in Nebuchadnezzar's second year. Moreover, the author of the book in its final form (who was probably responsible for these verses) was clearly acquainted with Jer. 25 (Dan. 9:2), in the first verse of which Nebuchadnezzar's first year is equated with Jehoiakim's fourth. It seems more likely that the author Dan. 1:1–2 knew a version of the same tradition as that used by the Chronicler, which included the dating. (Lucas, AOTC, 52)

B. The Language of Daniel

Because Daniel was written in both Hebrew and Aramaic, and because both Greek and Persian words appear in the manuscripts, linguistic issues have also sustained the debate regarding the historicity of Daniel. We consider each debate in turn.

First, let us look at the division of Daniel based upon it being written in both Hebrew and Aramaic. Daniel 1:1–2:4a is written in Hebrew but transitions suddenly to Aramaic in 2:4b. The text continues in Aramaic through 7:28 and then returns suddenly to Hebrew for the remainder of the book. Critical scholars have generally seen these sudden shifts in language as evidence of a later redaction of the book. C. L. Seow, for instance, believes the shift in language is evidence of a second-century-BC redaction by a Jewish sect that intended to use the court tales of Daniel 1–6 to preserve Jewish national identity. Key to his argument is that the Aramaic of Daniel 2:4b–7:28 does not appear to be consistent with sixth century Aramaic. He contends:

> In general, the Aramaic of this portion of Daniel appears to be typologically more advanced than the Aramaic of the sixth and fifth centuries and possibly even of the Aramaic of the Samaria Papyri from the first half of the fourth century, but the Aramaic is more conservative than the dialects dating from 200 BCE onward.
>
> The existence of a collection comprising the Aramaic portions of the book seems likely, with Daniel 7 being the latest component added to the collection. . . . From [chapter 8] on out, the visions are much more directly concerned not with the exploits of individual Jews in the dispersion, as in chapters 1–6, but with the survival of the Jewish people and their faith in the face of the greatest threat to confront them since the destruction of Jerusalem in the sixth century.
>
> This threat of a loss of national identity may account for the linguistic shift from Aramaic, still the language of international relations in those days, to the rejuvenated national language of the Jewish people. The author of the Hebrew composition in 8:1–12:4, thus, added the new materials to the earlier Aramaic anthology (2:4b–7:28). In addition, a Hebrew introduction (1:1–2:4a) has been put at the beginning. Finally, to this whole work, a postscript (12:5–13) was later added (probably some time in the spring of 163 BCE) to update the final revelation in 10:1–12:4. (Seow, *Daniel*, 8–9)

In a similar vein, Old Testament scholar John E. Goldingay argues that the division of the book into Aramaic and Hebrew potentially indicates that multiple authors wrote Daniel over an extended period. He supposes the Aramaic tales "concern life at court in the dispersion and speak directly to Jews with leadership positions there," whereas the Hebrew visions "presuppose a quite different audience, in second-century BC Jerusalem." (Goldingay, WBC, 328) When taken together, both sections

> manifest a generally consistent viewpoint, though this need not suggest common authorship. . . . Diversity of authorship might be one of the reasons for diversity of language; perhaps Hebrew writing authors added chaps. 8, 9, and 10–12 to the Aramaic chiasm. . . . Although in their period one might have expected an introduction that was less friendly to foreign powers . . . they may also have been responsible for chap. 1. (Goldingay, WBC, 327)

Conservative responses to these arguments have either attempted to demonstrate that the division of language does not correspond necessarily to a division in dates of authorship, or that the division of language aims to highlight certain aspects of the text. Ernest Lucas points out that the forms of Aramaic and Hebrew do not necessarily point to dates in the fourth and second centuries that critical scholars argue for. He points out that "the Aramaic used in Daniel is the Official Aramaic that was used from about 700 to 200 BC"; furthermore, he argues, comparative studies of papyri are based on "the implicit assumption that linguistic developments would have occurred uniformly throughout this area." (Lucas, AOTC, 307) Additionally, the Hebrew sections have "more in common with the Late Biblical Hebrew of Ezra, Nehemiah and Chronicles than it does with the exilic Hebrew of Ezekiel." (Lucas, AOTC, 307) This does not, however, automatically presuppose a late date for the Hebrew sections. The Hebrew of the second century

BC would be closest to that of the Qumran community, and "there are clear differences between this and the Hebrew of Daniel; for instance at Qumran there is a much greater use of pseudo-cohortative forms and vowel letters." (Lucas, AOTC, 307) When these two characteristics are taken together, he argues, "the character of the Hebrew and Aramaic could support a date in the fifth or fourth century for the extant written form of the book, but does not demand a second-century date." (Lucas, AOTC, 308)

Lucas's conclusion is not a recent one. Kitchen notes:

> The word-order of the Aramaic of Daniel (and Ezra) places it squarely in full blooded Imperial Aramaic—and in striking contrast with *real* Palestinian post-Imperial Aramaic of the second and first centuries BC as illustrated by the Dead Sea Scrolls.
>
> If proper allowance be made for attested scribal usage in the Biblical Near East (including orthographical and morphological change, both official and unofficial), then there is nothing to decide the date of composition of the Aramaic of Daniel *on the grounds of Aramaic* anywhere between the late sixth and

the second century BC. Some points hint at an early (especially pre-300), not late, date. . . . The date of the book of Daniel, in short, cannot be decided upon linguistic grounds alone. (Kitchen, AD, 78–79, emphasis in original)

Steinmann provides a similar analysis of the Hebrew portions of Daniel:

> Given our fragmentary state of knowledge about the history of linguistic developments in Biblical Hebrew, use of linguistic evidence to argue for a late date of Daniel's Hebrew is unwarranted since the linguistic evidence is, at best, mixed. The most that can be said is that Daniel's Hebrew is much more like the Hebrew of other acknowledged exilic books of the OT than like the Hebrew of the Qumran documents, making Daniel unlikely to be a composition from the Hellenistic era as higher critics contend. (Steinmann, CC, 8)

Steinmann also addresses the second response to the critical evaluation of Daniel's language split. He argues that the structure of the language division results in two interlocking chiasms (see chart below taken from Steinmann, CC, 22):

Chiastic Structure	Genre	Language
Introduction 1: Prologue 1:1–21	Narrative	Hebrew
A Nebuchadnezzar dreams of four kingdoms and the kingdom of God (2:1–49)	Narrative	Aramaic
B Nebuchadnezzar sees God's servants rescued (3:1–30).	Narrative	Aramaic
C Nebuchadnezzar is judged (3:31–4:34 [ET 4:1–37]).	Narrative	Aramaic
C' Belshazzar is judged (5:1–6:1 [ET 5:1–31]).	Narrative	Aramaic
B' Darius sees Daniel rescued (6:2–29 [ET6:1–28]).	Narrative	Aramaic
A' Introduction 2: Daniel has a vision of four kingdoms and the kingdom of God (7:1–28).	Vision	Aramaic
D Details on the post-Babylonian kingdoms (8:1–27)	Vision	Hebrew
E Jerusalem restored (9:1–27)	Vision	Hebrew
D' More details on the post-Babylonian kingdoms (10:1–12:13)	Vision	Hebrew

A Hebrew introduction followed by an Aramaic chiasm interlocked with an Aramaic introduction and a Hebrew chiasm. Instead of indicating some long process of accumulation and redaction of narrative tales and visions, the Hebrew and Aramaic languages of the sections were carefully chosen to serve as a way to unite two different genres (narrative and vision) in one book. Therefore, the dual languages and two genres of the book are not a problem stemming from the book's redactional history, but a deliberate result of its careful composition. (Steinmann, CC, 23)

We now turn our attention to the issue of Persian and Greek loanwords in the text of Daniel. Critical scholarship relies heavily in this area on S. R. Driver's analysis of the book of Daniel. Driver is often quoted for his statement, "The verdict of the language of Daniel is thus clear. The *Persian* words presuppose a period after the Persian Empire had been well established: the Greek words *demand*, the Hebrew *supports*, and the Aramaic *permits*, a date *after the conquest of Palestine by Alexander the Great* (332 BC)." (Driver, ILOT, 508, emphasis in original)

Driver found within the text of Daniel at least fifteen Persian loanwords that he believes would have been foreign to both Israelite and Babylonian speech during the period just after the exile:

Some of these describe offices or institutions not found elsewhere, or only in Ezr. Neh. Est. [Ezra, Nehemiah, and Esther]; others . . . are used exactly as in the later Aramaic, and are of a kind that would not be borrowed by one people from another unless intercourse between them had subsisted for a considerable time. The argument is confirmed by the testimony of the Inscriptions. The numerous contract-tablets which have come down to

us from the age of Nebuchadnezzar and his successors, and which represent the everyday language of commercial life, shows no traces of Persian influence: and if the language of Babylonia was uninfluenced by Persia, that of Israel would be far less likely to be so influenced. (Driver, ILOT, 501)

In addition to the Persian loanwords, three words are clearly of Greek origin. These occur in Daniel 3:5, 7, 10, and 15, in the lists of musical instruments that are to be played when homage is to be given to Nebuchadnezzar's statue. Driver finds it unlikely that these three words describing musical instruments could have made their way into a text that was supposedly written at the time that Daniel 1:1 sets as the timeframe for the work.

Anyone who has studied Greek history knows what the condition of the Greek world was in that century and is aware that the arts and inventions of civilized life streamed then into Greece from the East, not from Greece eastwards. . . . These words, it may be confidently affirmed, could not have been used in the Book of Daniel unless it had been written *after the dissemination of Greek influences in Asia through the conquests of Alexander the Great*. (Driver, ILOT, 502, emphasis in original)

As with the supposed problem with the dual languages, critics who claim that Persian and Greek words demand a late composition date overstate their case. In analyzing the Aramaic of Daniel, Kitchen came to the conclusion that the Persian words of Daniel point toward an earlier date rather than a later one.

The Persian words in Daniel are specifically *Old Persian* words. The recognized divisions of Persian language-history within Iranian are: Old down to c. 300 BC, Middle observable during c. 300 BC to AD 900, and New from AD 900 to the present. Now, the fact that the Iranian element in Daniel is from *Old* Persian and not middle indicates that the Aramaic of Daniel is in this respect pre-Hellenistic, drew on no Persian from after the fall of that empire—and not on any Middle Persian words and forms that might have penetrated Aramaic in Arsacid times (c. 250 BC, ff.). (Kitchen, AD, 43–44, emphasis in original)

Steinmann adds that Daniel's audience may initially have been those Jews of the diaspora who were living and serving in Babylon under the new Persian imperial administration. "They would have readily understood such Persian words, which had recently become current in their environment. Therefore, the presence of Persian words in Daniel does not present an argument for a date of composition later than 560 BC." (Steinmann, CC, 10)

Recent discoveries of Babylonian texts have also eliminated much of the supposed problem created by demonstrating that there was Greek influence within the region of Babylonia during the time of Nebuchadnezzar. Alan R. Millard, professor of Hebrew and Ancient Semitic languages, points out,

The Greek words in chapter 3, which are all names of musical instruments, became more acceptable in a sixth-century setting with the publication of lists of rations issued to people kept in the palace of Nebuchadnezzar. Beside Jehoiachin, king of Judah, there were other people from the Levant and Anatolia, including Greeks. A few further attestations of Greeks living, even owning property in Babylonia have been traced in legal texts. (Millard, DB, 278–279)

The documentary evidence shows how Greek words might have worked themselves into the vocabulary of someone living during the period of the Babylonian Empire and the early Persian Empire. After reviewing these lines of evidence, Steinmann concludes:

Neither the Persian nor the Greek loanwords offer any proof that Daniel is a late composition. Of themselves, they also do not provide any conclusive evidence that the book is an early Persian composition. The same is true of the other linguistic evidence, both Hebrew and Aramaic. The best that can be said about the linguistic evidence is that it suggests that Daniel was not written before about 560 BC and not later than 300 BC. (Steinmann, CC, 10)

C. Nebuchadnezzar's Madness

In 1956 J. T. Milik published a text that had been discovered at Qumran. Labeled as 4QPrNab, it has come to be known commonly as the Prayer of Nabonidus because it recounts a prayer by King Nabonidus when he was stricken with a disease. The translation of the text is as follows (with reconstructed portions of missing text indicated by brackets):

1 The Words of the prayer that King Nabonidus of [Baby]lon, [the great] king prayed [when he was smitten]

2 with a serious skin disease by a decree of G[o]d in Teman: ["I, Nabonidus by a serious disease]

3 was smitten for seven years and wh[en] G[od turned his face to me, I was healed]

4 and my sin was forgiven by him. A diviner, A Judean fr[om the exiles came to me and said,]

5 'Write a declaration to give honor and exalt[ation] to the name of G[od Most High.' So I wrote as follows:]

6 'I was smitten with a ser[ious] skin
   disease in Teman [by a decree of God
   Most High.]

7 For seven years I had bee[n] praying
   [before] the gods of silver and gold,
   [bronze, iron,]

8 wood, stone clay because [I had thou]ght
   that [they were] gods."

                    (Steinmann, CC, 216)

Since its publication, critical scholars have believed this to be evidence that the account in Daniel 4 of the madness of Nebuchadnezzar is a conflation by a later scribe of Nebuchadnezzar and Nabonidus. The Late Old Testament professor Norman W. Porteous admits,

> Indeed there is no record of Nebuchadnezzar's having had leave of absence from his royal duties on account of insanity. The possibility has to be considered that the account of the dream of Nebuchadnezzar is actually a reminiscence of what was told of Nabonidus, the last Babylonian king, especially of his strange retirement to the oasis of Teima at a critical time in his empire's fortunes. (Porteous, DC, 70)

Matthias Henze, professor of Hebrew Bible and Early Judaism, is willing to admit that the assumed correlation between "the legend of Nebuchadnezzar's madness and the Nabonidus material is merely hypothetical." (Henze, MKN, 64) However, he recognizes that for many scholars, "Nabonidus' sojourning at Teima is held to provide the key to unlock the riddle of Nebuchadnezzar's enigmatic exile in the biblical narrative: the biblical account was modeled on a concrete historical incident." (Henze, MKN, 64)

Both Henze and Steinmann see a number of direct parallels between the two texts. First, both are first-person accounts by the king recounting an illness. Second, both suffer under the effects of the illness for seven years. Third, both are ministered to by a Jewish diviner who states that they should give praise to God. (Steinmann, CC, 217; Henze, MN, 65–66)

However, both scholars agree that while there are striking parallels, the disagreements between the two texts are just as striking. Henze notes that within the text, "The three most prominent elements shared by both stories are the Babylonian monarch, the Jewish seer, and the affliction suffered by the protagonist. In none of these cases do the two texts agree." (Henze, MKN, 66) These, along with other smaller differences in the details, lead Henze to suggest "that at times scholars have seen dependencies where there are parallels, and parallels where there are lacunae." (Henze, MKN, 68) His ultimate conclusion is that "discrepancies between the Prayer of Nabonidus and the tale of Nebuchadnezzar's madness are significant enough to exclude the possibility of direct literary relationship. Neither text has served as the *Vorlage* [template] of the other." (Henze, MKN, 68)

Steinmann differs from Henze; he believes a correlation exists between the texts, but one in which the Prayer of Nabonidus was derived from the earlier text of Daniel 4. After examining a series of textual similarities, he provides the following analysis of the text to support his argument:

> 4QPrNab ar contains only about seventy words, some of them only partially preserved. If one excludes fragment 4, whose preserved lines are all too short to enable sound conclusions, only fifty-six words remain. Of those, the fourteen discussed above (comprising twenty-five of the total intelligible text) have striking parallels with similar wordings and

thematic employment in Daniel 2–5. I find it almost impossible to deny that one text must depend on another. While the narrative of the Prayer of Nabonidus is most closely parallel to the account of Daniel 4, the prayer appears to draw on language from a total of four chapters in Daniel. This is strong evidence that the prayer is dependent on Daniel—indeed, that its author actively borrowed from Daniel. (Steinmann, *Daniel*, 225)

Thus, while there may be some correlation between the Prayer of Nabonidus and the account of Nebuchadnezzar's madness in Daniel 4, that correlation is not strong enough to warrant the claim that Daniel was written in imitation of the Prayer of Nabonidus.

D. Belshazzar

Within the stream of historical criticism of the book of Daniel, one of the consistent objections to the historicity of the book centers on the existence of the king Belshazzar. Initially no description of him as a real person outside of the biblical text had been discovered. This led to the charge that the author of Daniel had no clear conception of the line of kings in Babylon after Nebuchadnezzar because he had not actually written during that period. This charge was repudiated in the mid-nineteenth century with the discovery of cuneiform inscriptions that explicitly mention Belshazzar as the vice-regent of Babylon under his father, Nabonidus. Lucas provides a brief summary of this controversy and its resolution:

For many centuries "King Belshazzar" of Babylon was known only from the references to him in the book of Daniel and one in Baruch 1:11, which is clearly dependent on Daniel in its reference to "Nebuchadnezzar and his son Belshazzar." He is not mentioned in any extant classical sources. There seemed no place for him among the kings of Babylon, since Nabonidus was known to be the king at the time Babylon fell to Cyrus. This led to some doubt as to his existence as a historical person. In 1854 some inscribed, barrel-shaped cylinders were found at the corners of the temple of the moon-god Sin in Ur. They recorded the repair work Nabonidus had done on the temple, and ended with a prayer for Bēl-šarra-usur, son and heir of the king (see Gadd 1929: 34–36). Since then, a considerable number of references to him have come to light in cuneiform sources. (Lucas, AOTC, 206)

In light of this, more recent discussions of Belshazzar have revolved not around his existence but the statement in Daniel 5:2 that Nebuchadnezzar is Belshazzar's father. Driver considers this to be erroneous data and therefore one of the key evidences that Daniel was written much later than the book claims. In brief he states, "Belshazzar is represented as *king* of Babylon; and Nebuchadnezzar is spoken of throughout [chapter] 5 (v. 2, 11, 13, 18, 22) as his *father*. In point of fact Nabonidus (Nabu-nahid) was the last king of Babylon; he was a usurper not related to Nebuchadnezzar, and one *Belsharuzur* is mentioned as his son." (Driver, ILOT, 498, emphasis in original)

While Driver allows the possibility that Nabonidus may have married into Nebuchadnezzar's family to strengthen his position as king, he maintains that "the terms of [chapter] 5, however, produce certainly the impression that, in the view of the writer, Belshazzar was actually [Nebuchadnezzar's] son. The historical presuppositions of Dan. 5 are inconsistent with the evidence of the contemporary monuments." (Driver, ILOT, 499)

This argument, while favored in the early part of the twentieth century, has not maintained its credibility among critical scholars today. C. L. Seow articulates the position currently held by the majority of critical and conservative scholars:

> Belshazzar could not have been the literal son of Nebuchadnezzar. One should keep in mind that in the Semitic languages "father" is not limited to that of a biological or even adoptive parent. The term may be used simply of an ancestor or a progenitor. So Jabal is called the "father" of all those who live in tents and have livestock, and Jubal is regarded as the "father" of all those who play musical instruments (Gen. 4:20–21). . . . By the same token, the term "son" is used of a descendant, a successor, or simply a member of a group or class. . . . From the point of view of the narrator of Daniel 5, who is reflecting on the beginning and end of the Chaldean dynasty, Nebuchadnezzar was in some sense the father and Belshazzar was his son. And that father-son language is, in fact, reiterated through the chapter (Dan. 5:2, 11, 13, 18, 22). Perhaps to the narrator, Nebuchadnezzar and Belshazzar both belonged to the same family of arrogant Chaldean oppressors. (Seow, Daniel, 77)

E. Darius the Mede

The identity of Darius the Mede presents itself as one of the more puzzling aspects of the book of Daniel, challenging both critical and conservative scholars. In particular, scholars have struggled to identify who Darius the Mede is because, outside of Daniel 6, no record exists that names any such person who ruled in Babylon after the fall of the Babylonian Empire to the Persians until Darius I in 522 BC, a full seventeen years after the events of Daniel 6.

Scholar William H. Shea describes the scope of the problem for conservative scholars:

The standard-historical-critical view of the book of Daniel makes the book a pseudepigraph composed in Judea in the second century BC. Cited in support of this view is the idea that the author was not well acquainted with Babylonian and Persian history of the sixth century BC, the setting in which the book itself was placed. A prominent feature of this theory is that the author supposed that there was a separate Median kingdom between the rule of the Babylonians and the Persians. Evidence for this comes in particular from the figure of Darius the Mede who is taken as ruler over the independent Median kingdom. Since no such kingdom is known—and hence no such ruler, either—the book of Daniel is seen as lacking historicity, a product of a late and geographically-removed author. (Shea, DMHP, 235)

Lester R. Grabbe, historian of ancient Judaism, has written one of the more influential papers in recent scholarship from a critical perspective on the personage of Darius the Mede. "For some time now, the consensus of scholarship has been that 'Darius the Mede' is a composite character, created by the author of Daniel from a few historical remembrances set in a theologically structured framework." (Grabbe, ALGDM, 198)

Grabbe believes that it is neither necessary nor probable that the author of Daniel created the person of Darius the Mede through a misunderstanding or false knowledge of actual historic persons. Rather,

> all the characteristics of Darius the Mede are either those important for the schematic representation required by the Book of Daniel or those which are only the inherited clichés of folk tradition about the Persians. Darius the Mede could have been created by a person with only commonplace and

trivial knowledge of things Persian plus an acquaintance with the OT prophetic literature. (Grabbe, ALGDM, 213)

Conservative scholars have responded to this challenge by presenting three different historic persons who, to varying degrees, match what is known from Daniel about Darius the Mede. These three persons are Cyrus's general Gubaru (or Gobryas), Gubaru of the Nabonidus Chronicle, and Cyrus himself. We consider each person in turn.

Shea provides perhaps the most comprehensive argument in recent scholarship that Darius the Mede is another name for Cyrus's general Gubaru. Shea's argument relies heavily upon the usage of titles as applied to Persian kings in Babylonian contracts and court documents. The assigning of titles to kings in the Neo-Babylonian and Persian Empires went through a series of developments: "(1) for Neo-Babylonian kings, 'king of Babylon'; (2) for early Persian kings, 'king of Babylon, king of Lands'; and (3) for later Persian kings 'king of Lands.'" (Shea, DM, 236) Shea finds this pattern to be consistent through all extant records except for one notable exception: "it is clear from the contract tablet evidence that Cyrus *did not* take up the title 'King of Babylon' during his accession year and most of his first year of rule there." (Shea, DM, 236, emphasis in original)

Shea believes that the most likely explanation is that someone else held this title for a period of close to one year and ruled in place of Cyrus in Babylon as a co-regent or viceroy. He identifies Cyrus's general Gubaru as the person who held this position based upon his reading of the Nabonidus Chronicle. Scholars have generally understood the Nabonidus Chronicle to record the city of Babylon being captured by Gubaru, followed by Gubaru's

death a few weeks later. Shea, however, believes that grammatical markers within the Chronicle point to a later date than has been previously assumed. These grammatical markers would place Gubaru's death not a few weeks after the capture of Babylon but more than a year later. (Shea, DM, 240–245) Shea finds in this period enough time for Gubaru to serve as king of Babylon, coinciding with the events recorded in Daniel 6.

While Shea's argument is well presented, it has been rejected by both critical and conservative scholars in light of new evidence identifying who was king in Babylon during the first year of Cyrus's reign. Two tablets, *Cyrus* 16 (BM 75405) and *CT* 57, #345 (BM 55923), give direct evidence that the king of Babylon during the first year of Cyrus's reign was Cambyses, Cyrus's son. Grabbe correctly notes, "Once it is recognized that Gubaru did not reign and that 'unknown king' is actually Cambyses, Shea's argument simply evaporates." (Grabbe, ALGDM, 204)

The second possible person that matches to Darius the Mede is the governor Gubaru, who is distinct from Cyrus's general Gubaru. John C. Whitcomb proposed the governor Gubaru as a possible fit for the person of Darius the Mede based upon a series of cuneiform tablets that listed him as a high ranking government official in the Persian court. Whitcomb believes that the general Gubaru died just three weeks after capturing the city of Babylon and that the Gubaru

who is mentioned in cuneiform documents dated in the fourth, sixth, seventh, and eighth years of Cyrus (535, 533, 532, and 531 BC), and in the accession year and second, third, fourth, and fifth years of Cambyses (530, 528, 526, and 525 BC) is the same person as the *Gubaru* of the Nabonidus Chronicle, Column III, Line 20, who is spoken of as the governor of Cyrus that appointed governors in Babylon on the 3rd of Marcheswan (October 29, 539 BC). (Whitcomb, DM, 21, emphasis in original)

Identifying Gubaru as governor of Babylon on October 29, 539 BC would locate his rule over Babylon well within the bounds that Daniel 6 delineates for the rule of Darius the Mede. This leads Whitcomb to assert, "We believe that this identification is the only one that satisfactorily harmonizes the various lines of evidence which are found in the book of Daniel and in the contemporary cuneiform records." (Whitcomb, DM, 24)

However, several flaws in Whitcomb's argument arise from his interpretation of titles and cuneiform characters within the tablets he references. For example, the timeline he proposes for Gubaru to be governor of Babylon does not match the dates provided by the texts that he references. As Grabbe notes,

In pointing to the governor of Babylon and Ebir-nari in various texts down to (possibly) the beginning of Darius' reign, he is evidently unaware that this Gubaru did not take office until Cyrus' *4th year*, long after the alleged activities of the Darius the Mede of Daniel. (Grabbe, ALGDM, 206, emphasis added)

The third, and perhaps simplest, explanation is that Darius the Mede is none other than Cyrus himself. D. J. Wiseman proposed this position, and it has been adapted by other scholars in intervening years. Wiseman's proposal rests upon an alternate translation of the *waw* conjunction in Daniel 6:28 as being exegetical rather than copulative. This translation would render Daniel 6:28 as "So this Daniel prospered in the reign of Darius, *that is*, in the reign of Cyrus the Persian" rather than "in the reign of Darius and the

reign of Cyrus the Persian." Whitcomb provides evidence that this construction is within the realm of possibility based upon other instances within the Old Testament, the key case being that of 1 Chronicles 5:26 in which "the God of Israel stirred up the spirit of Pul king of Assyria, that is, Tiglath-Pileser king of Assyria."

Wiseman augments his argument with several additional lines of evidence that point to Darius being Cyrus. First, Cyrus may very well have been referred to as a Mede by the Babylonians since "by 550 BC Cyrus had taken over Media and joined it to the 'Persian' federation." (Wiseman, SHPBD, 13) Additionally, "when Nabonidus in 546 BC declared that the 'King of the Medes' welcomed his proposed return from exile he could at this time refer to no other than to Cyrus." (Wiseman, SHPBD, 13) Second, Daniel 5:31 says Darius was about sixty-two years of age, which matches Cyrus's age when he conquered Babylon in 539–538 BC. Third, while Cyrus was the son of Cambyses, the reference in Daniel 9:1 to Cyrus being the "son of Ahasuerus" may actually refer "to his Median grandfather, since 'Ahasuerus' could be a Hebrew rendition of the Median name (translated into English as) Astyages. Alternately, 'Ahasuerus' may be an ancient Achaemenid royal title bestowed on one of Cyrus' ancestors." (Steinmann, CC, 294)

Lucas believes that Wiseman's argument is not definitive, but it is entirely possible since "the *waw explicativum* is well attested in Hebrew, Aramaic, Ugaritic, and Akkadian" and there is evidence that "Cyaxares (whom [Xenophon] equates with the 'king of the Medes' mentioned in Nabonidus' Harran inscriptions) gave Cyrus the crown of Media and also his daughter in marriage." (Lucas, AOTC, 136)

IV. Conclusion

Our survey of the critical claims about the historicity of the book of Daniel offers a brief series of possible solutions to the major objections made by critical scholars. In some cases, the best possible solutions are not concrete proofs that guarantee the validity of conservative, evangelical thought. However, understanding that the claims of critical scholarship are not as concrete or as uniform as critical scholars present them should do much to encourage Christians that the purported problems are neither insurmountable nor unanswerable. We can present a case that there is indeed evidence that Daniel is rooted firmly within the historical milieu during which it presents itself as having been written.

CHAPTER 26

ALLEGED CONTRADICTIONS IN THE OLD TESTAMENT

OVERVIEW

I. Introduction

In this chapter, we explore the claim that the Old Testament contradicts itself. We define what is meant by a contradiction, consider some common mistakes made by critics, offer responses to ten alleged contradictions, and provide concluding remarks.

Since we believe that the Bible is God's Word and are therefore committed to the inerrancy of Scripture, we believe that alleged contradictions are not real, and that the Bible truly does harmonize when properly understood. There are times, however, when we do not have all the facts to harmonize seemingly contradictory passages. What then? We recognize there are a few difficult passages of this nature and yet believe that there are good, overriding reasons to hold that if all the facts were to come to light, the alleged contradictions would disappear. As shown below, this approach has served inerrantists well. There are many examples of alleged contradictions being overturned when relevant discoveries come to light.

II. History of Harmonizing Alleged Contradictions in the Bible

Augustine of Hippo advises, "If we are perplexed by an apparent contradiction in Scripture, it is not allowable to say, *The author of this book is mistaken*; but either the manuscript is faulty, or the translation is wrong, or you have not understood." (Augustine, RFM, 180) History bears witness to Augustine's advice as a great many harmonization attempts span the last two millennia. The following sample of historical documentation demonstrates not only the church's awareness and transparent ownership of alleged discrepancies, but also its unceasing quest for accurate interpretations.

It should be noted, however, that few, if any, extant medieval works concerning this subject have been discovered, and that the methods invoked by the early church fathers and medieval scholars to resolve apparent discrepancies generally differ from the methods employed by modern evangelicals. (Kaiser et al., HSB, 32) For example, Michael Graves, professor of Old Testament at Wheaton College, observes:

Many ancient interpreters [such as Philo, Origen, and Augustine] believed that Scripture conveys symbolic meanings through texts that are not factually correct. . . . In some instances, [others, such as Tertullian and John Chrysostom,] were willing to concede minor discrepancies in Scripture without feeling the need to harmonize them. . . . Interpreters who made much of allegorical interpretation were sometimes willing to acknowledge certain kinds of flaws at the literal level while affirming the truth of the text's spiritual meaning. There were also Church Fathers who tried to resolve problems in Scripture working with the literal sense. (Graves, IIS, 88–92)

We, on the other hand, believe that Scripture certainly conveys propositional truths, and symbolic truths at times, through texts that *are* factually correct. It is true that not every statement in the Bible is presented to us in propositional form. Apologists Norman Geisler and William Roach explain this more fully: "Certainly, there are questions, commands, prayers, exclamations, and confessions that are not propositional in form. . . . Though not all truth claims in the Bible are in propositional form (many are in stories and parables), nonetheless all truth in the Bible is propositionalizable." (Geisler and Roach, DI, 141–142) Therefore, we affirm the literal, historical-grammatical approach to interpretation and reject the allegorical approach to interpretation. (Geisler, ST, 415–428)

The following are some of the dates, authors, and works of those dealing with difficulties and alleged contradictions in the Bible.

If we are perplexed by an apparent contradiction in Scripture, it is not allowable to say, The author of this book is mistaken; but either the manuscript is faulty, or the translation is wrong, or you have not understood.

Augustine of Hippo

When	Who	What
4th century	Eusebius of Caesarea	*Ecclesiastical History*
5th century	Augustine of Hippo	*Harmony of the Gospels*
1527–1st ed. 1582–16th ed.	Andreas Althamer	*Conciliationes Locorum Scripturae, qui specie tenus inter se pugnare videntur, Centuriae duae*
1662	Joannes Thaddaeus, Thomas Man	*The Reconciler of the Bible Inlarged [sic]*
1791	Oliver St. John Cooper	*Four Hundred Texts of Holy Scripture with their corresponding passages explained*
1843	Samuel Davidson	*Sacred Hermeneutics, Developed and Applied*
1874	John W. Haley	*An Examination of the Alleged Discrepancies of the Bible**
1950	George W. DeHoff	*Alleged Bible Contradictions*
1952	Martin Ralph De Haan	*508 Answers to Bible Questions*
1965	J. Carter Swaim	*Answers to Your Questions About the Bible*
1972	F. F. Bruce	*Answers to Questions*
1979	Robert H. Mounce	*Answers to Questions About the Bible*
1980	Paul R. Van Gorder	*Since You Asked*
1982	Gleason L. Archer	*Encyclopedia of Bible Difficulties*
1987	David C. Downing	*What You Know Might Not Be So: 220 Misinterpretations of Bible Texts Explained*
1992	Norman L. Geisler, Thomas Howe	*The Big Book of Bible Difficulties: Clear and Concise Answers from Genesis to Revelation*
1996	Walter C. Kaiser Jr., Peter H. Davids, F. F. Bruce, Manfred T. Brauch	*Hard Sayings of the Bible*
2001	Gleason L. Archer	*Encyclopedia of Bible Difficulties (updated)*
2013	Josh McDowell, Sean McDowell	*The Bible Handbook of Difficult Verses: A Complete Guide to Answering Tough Questions*
2016	Michael R. Licona	*Why Are There Differences in the Gospels?*

* Haley's treatise cites forty-two works from the Reformation or post-Reformation era that are not listed here. (Kaiser et al., HSB, 32)

III. Approaching Contradictions

A. What Is a Contradiction?

Logically speaking, a contradiction arises when two or more statements affirm and deny a truth-claim at the same time and in the same way. For example, the statement, "The Old Testament does contain contradictions," and its negation, "The Old Testament does not contain contradictions," are logically contradictory because one affirms and the other denies the claim that the Old Testament contains contradictions. Clearly both statements cannot be true. But the key question is not necessarily what the Bible *says*, but what it *means*.

The Old Testament is composed of thirty-nine smaller books that are written by a variety of authors, at different times, with different styles, and in different genres. The poetry of Psalms, for instance, should be read differently than the historical narrative of Joshua, the laws in Leviticus, or individual proverbs. When we consider alleged contradictions, then, we ought to remember that inerrantists claim *the Bible is authoritative and without error in what it actually teaches and all that it intends to affirm.* So we recognize the rich diversity of genres in which God has chosen to reveal himself. The Bible is much more than a series of propositions. And yet, Scripture does contain propositions (both implicit and explicit) that need to be examined for their consistency.

Example #1: Did God Create Plants or Humans First?

Genesis 1:12, 26 says that man was created *after* the plants. But Genesis 2:5, 7 says, "When no bush of the field was yet in the land and no small plant of the field had yet sprung up. . . . then the LORD God formed the man of dust from the ground and breathed into his nostrils the breath of life, and the man became a living creature" (ESV). Which is it? OT scholars offer several resolutions to this apparent contradiction. Here is a common one: although there appears to be a contradiction, the context reveals that the tension is only surface deep. The first chapter of Genesis is giving a macro view of the seven days of creation, while Genesis 2 focuses specifically on the creation of man on day six. So, the mention of plants in Genesis 1 is a reference to the plants over the face of the earth. But in Genesis 2, the "bush of the field" refers to the plants specifically in the garden of Eden

that Adam and Eve were to cultivate. There were no cultivated plants because there were not yet people to cultivate them.

While there is a surface difference between how Genesis 1 and 2 report the creation chronology of humans and plants, there is not a genuine contradiction. It is important to remember that a difference is not identical to a contradiction. A difference arises when things are not recorded in the same way and so only seem to be at odds. But in a contradiction, there is no possible way to reconcile competing claims. Let us consider one more example.

Example #2: Did Saul Commit Suicide or Was He Murdered?

First Samuel 31:1–4 reports King Saul asking his armor-bearer to kill him, but the armor-bearer refused, and so Saul fell on his own sword and committed suicide. However, in 2 Samuel 1:10, a young man reports to King David that he personally killed King Saul upon his request. Both cannot be true, right? There is certainly a difference in how the books report the death of Saul, but there is not a genuine contradiction. Again, Old Testament scholars offer various solutions. Here is one common one (which is even accepted by many critical scholars): the author of 1 Samuel reported the death of Saul by suicide. However, the author of 2 Samuel recorded the words of a young man who *claimed* to have killed King Saul. It is very likely that this young man thought that David would be thrilled at his actions, and so he invented a story that was not true. As with the example in Genesis, the accounts in 1 and 2 Samuel can be harmonized when properly understood.

B. The Bible Contains Alleged, Not Authentic, Contradictions

As mentioned in the introduction, we believe the Bible is without error. Certainly, some passages appear contradictory, but we have compelling, independent reasons to believe that in light of all the information, the Bible reveals itself to be inerrant. We do not aim in this chapter to resolve all contradictions, but to give a few examples and show in principle how they can be resolved. In the introduction to the book *Hard Sayings of the Bible*, Walter Kaiser provides a healthy and helpful perspective for approaching this task:

> Any observant Bible reader who compares statements of the Old Testament with those of the New Testament, statements of different writers within either Testament, or even at times different passages within the same book will notice that there are apparent discrepancies. These statements, taken at face value, seem to contradict one another.
>
> The Christian church has held over the centuries that there is an essential unity of the Holy Scriptures, that they form a divine library that is consistent and unified in its approach and teaching. Alas, however, as the scope of lay readership and the depth of scholarship have increased, an ever-increasing supply of alleged discrepancies and hard sayings has demanded attention.
>
> Why are there so many discrepancies and difficulties? There are a great number of sources to which we can trace them: errors of copyists in the manuscripts that have been handed down to us; the practice of using multiple names for the same person or place; the practice of using different methods for calculating official years, lengths of regencies and events; the special scope and purpose of individual authors, which sometimes led them to arrange their material topically rather than chronologically; and differences in the position from which an event or object was described and employed by the various writers.
>
> All of these factors, and more, have had a

profound influence on the material. Of course, to those who participated in the events and times these factors were less of a barrier than they are to us. Our distance from the time and culture exacerbates the difficulty. (Kaiser et al., HSB, 17–18)

C. Unexpected Benefits of Examining Alleged Contradictions

Given that the Bible is such a large and diverse book, inevitably many apparent contradictions arise. Examining these claims can be unsettling for Christians. Kaiser adds to the analysis presented above by providing a valuable perspective as to how Christians can thoughtfully assess alleged contradictions and examine these claims carefully and patiently:

> Why should we contemplate hard sayings at all? The obvious answer is that scores of serious readers want to understand the difficult issues in Scripture. Besides this, by wrestling with Scripture, we can sharpen our attention to the details in all of our Lord's Word. Thus the more intently and patiently we examine the text, the more handsome the dividends to our spiritual growth. . . .
>
> Disagreements within Scripture also supply strong incidental proof that there was no collusion among the sacred writers. The variations, instead, go a long way toward establishing the credibility of both the writers and their texts.
>
> These hard sayings also may be viewed as a test of our commitment to Christ. Difficult passages can be handy excuses for begging off and following the Savior no longer. Our Lord spoke in parables for just this reason: so that some who thought they saw, perceived and heard would actually miss seeing, perceiving and hearing (Mk 4:12). Indeed, the apparent harshness and obscurity of some of our Lord's sayings rid him of followers who were unwilling to be taught or were halfhearted in their

*Why should we contemplate hard sayings at all? . . . [B]y wrestling
with Scripture, we can sharpen our attention to the details in all of our
Lord's Word. Thus the more intently and patiently we examine the text,
the more handsome the dividends to our spiritual growth.*

Walter Kaiser

search (Jn 6:66). They were not willing to look beyond the surface of the issues. . . . For those [presently] who seek an occasion to cavil at difficulties, the opportunity is hereby offered in these hard sayings.

There is nothing wrong or unspiritual, of course, about doubting—so long as one continues to search for a resolution. But there are some who, as John W. Haley put it so well, "cherish a cavilling spirit, who are bent upon misapprehending the truth, and urging captious and frivolous objections [and who] find in the inspired volume difficulties and disagreements which would seem to have been designed as stumbling-stones for those which "stumble at the word, being disobedient: whereunto also they were appointed" [1 Pet 2:8]. Upon the wilful votaries of error God sends "strong delusion, that they should believe a lie" [2 Thess 2:11], that they might work out their own condemnation and ruin."

That is strong medicine for our more urbane and tame ways of disagreeing with objectors today; nevertheless, the matters Haley's quote raises are highly relevant to the discussion of hard sayings. (Kaiser et al., HSB, 16–17)

D. Common Mistakes Critics Commit When Alleging Contradictions

Alleged contradictions come in various kinds and forms, so we must get below the surface to see what assumptions guide the critique. In *The Big Book of Bible Difficulties*, philosophers Norman Geisler and Thomas Howe identify seventeen prevalent mistakes Bible critics commit when alleging biblical contradictions. We are presenting them below for the benefit of those who may not have access to the book. While many of the examples they provide are from the New Testament, the principles apply to the Old Testament as well.

1. *Assuming That the Unexplained Is Not Explainable*: No informed person would claim to be able to fully explain all Bible difficulties. However, it is a mistake for the critic to assume, therefore, that what has not yet been explained never will be explained. When a scientist comes upon an anomaly in nature, he does not give up further scientific exploration. Rather, he uses the unexplained as a motivation to find an explanation. . . . Likewise, the Christian scholar approaches the Bible with the same presumption that what is thus far unexplained is not therefore unexplainable. He or she does not assume that discrepancies are contradictions. And, when he encounters something for which he has no explanation, he simply continues to do research, believing that one will eventually be found.

2. *Presuming the Bible Guilty until Proven Innocent*: Many critics assume the Bible is wrong until something proves it right. However, like an American citizen charged with an offense, the Bible should

be presumed "innocent" until it is proven guilty. This is not asking anything special for the Bible, it is the way we approach all human communications. If we did not, life would not be possible. For example, if we assumed road signs and traffic signals were not telling the truth, then we would probably be dead before we could prove they were telling the truth. Likewise, if we assume food labels are wrong until proven right, we would have to open up all cans and packages before buying. . . . The Bible, like any other book, should be presumed to be telling us what the authors said and heard.

3. *Confusing Our Fallible Interpretations with God's Infallible Revelation*: Jesus affirmed that the "Scripture cannot be broken" (John 10:35). . . . But, while the Bible is infallible, human interpretations are not. The Bible cannot be mistaken, but we can be mistaken about the Bible. The meaning of the Bible does not change, but our understanding of its meaning does. . . . And even though God's Word is perfect (Ps. 19:7), as long as imperfect human beings exist, there will be misinterpretations of God's Word and false views about His world.

4. *Failing to Understand the Context of the Passage*: Perhaps the most common mistake of critics is to take a text out of its proper context. As the adage goes, "A text out of context is a pretext." One can prove anything from the Bible by this mistaken procedure. The Bible says "there is no God" (Ps. 14:1). Of course, the context is that "The fool has said in his heart, 'There is no God'" (Ps. 14:1) . . . Failure to note that meaning is determined by context is perhaps the chief sin of those who find fault with the Bible. . . .

5. *Neglecting to Interpret Difficult Passages in the Light of Clear Ones*: Some passages of Scripture are hard to understand.

Sometimes the difficulty is due to their obscurity. At other times, the difficulty is because passages appear to be teaching something contrary to what some other part of Scripture is clearly teaching. For example, James appears to be saying salvation is by works (James 2:14–26), whereas Paul taught clearly that it was by grace (Rom. 4:5; Titus 3:5–7; Eph. 2:8–9). In this case, James should *not* be construed so as to contradict Paul. Paul is speaking about justification *before God* (which is by faith alone), whereas James is referring to justification *before men* (who cannot see our faith, but only our works).

6. *Basing a Teaching on an Obscure Passage*: Some passages in the Bible are difficult because their meanings are obscure. This is usually because a key word in the text is used only once (or rarely), and so it is difficult to know what the author is saying, unless it can be inferred from the context. . . . At other times, the words may be clear but the meaning is not evident because we are not sure to what they refer. . . . When we are not sure, then several things should be kept in mind. First, we should not build a doctrine on an obscure passage. The rule of thumb in Bible interpretation is "the main things are the plain things, and the plain things are the main things." This is called the perspicuity (clearness) of Scripture. If something is important, it will be clearly taught in Scripture and probably in more than one place. Second, when a given passage is not clear, we should never conclude that it means something that is opposed to another plain teaching of Scripture. God does not make mistakes in His Word; we make mistakes in trying to understand it.

7. *Forgetting That the Bible Is a Human Book with Human Characteristics*: With the exception of small sections, like the Ten

Commandments which were "written with the finger of God" (Ex. 31:18), the Bible was not verbally dictated. The writers were not secretaries of the Holy Spirit. They were human composers employing their own literary styles and idiosyncrasies. These human authors sometimes used *human sources* for their material (Josh. 10:13; Acts 17:28; 1 Cor. 15:33; Titus 1:12). In fact, every book of the Bible is the composition of a *human writer*—about forty of them in all. The Bible also manifests different *human literary styles . . . human perspectives . . . human thought patterns . . . human emotions . . .* [and] *human interests. . . .* But like Christ, the Bible is completely human, yet without error. Forgetting the humanity of Scripture can lead to falsely impugning its integrity by expecting a level of expression higher than that which is customary to a human document.

8. *Assuming That a Partial Report Is a False Report*: Critics often jump to the conclusion that a partial report is false. However, this is not so. If it were, most of what has ever been said would be false, since seldom does time or space permit an absolutely complete report. Occasionally the Bible expresses the same thing in different ways, or at least from different viewpoints, at different times. Hence, inspiration does not exclude a diversity of expression. The four Gospels relate the same story in different ways to different groups of people, and sometimes even quote the same saying with different words.

9. *Demanding That NT Citations of the OT Always Be Exact Quotations*: Critics often point to variations in the NT's use of the OT Scriptures as a proof of error. However, they forget that every *citation* need not be an exact *quotation*. It was then (and still is today) a perfectly acceptable literary style

to give the *essence* of a statement without using precisely the *same words*. The same *meaning* can be conveyed without using the same *verbal expressions*. Variations in the NT citations of the OT fall into different categories. Sometimes they vary because there is a change of speaker. . . . At other times, writers cite only part of the OT text. . . . Sometimes the NT paraphrases or summarizes the OT text. . . . Others blend two texts into one. . . . Occasionally a general truth is mentioned, without citing a specific text. . . . There are also instances where the NT applies a text in a different way than the OT did. . . . In no case, however, does the NT misinterpret or misapply the OT, nor draw some implication from it that is not validly drawn from it.

10. *Assuming That Divergent Accounts Are False Ones*: Just because two or more accounts of the same event differ, it does not mean they are mutually exclusive. For example, Matthew (28:5) says there was one angel at the tomb after the resurrection, whereas John informs us there were two (20:12). But, these are not contradictory reports. In fact, there is an infallible mathematical rule that easily explains this problem: wherever there are two, there is always one—it never fails! Matthew did not say there was *only* one angel. One has to add the word "only" to Matthew's account to make it contradict John's.

11. *Presuming That the Bible Approves of All It Records*: It is a mistake to assume that everything contained in the Bible is commended by the Bible. The whole Bible is true (John 17:17), but it records some *lies*, for example, Satan's (Gen. 3:4; cf. John 8:44) and Rahab's (Josh. 2:4). Inspiration encompasses the Bible fully and completely in the sense that it records accurately and truthfully even the lies and errors of sinful

beings. The truth of Scripture is found in what the Bible *reveals*, not in everything it *records*.

12. *Forgetting That the Bible Uses Nontechnical, Everyday Language*: To be true, something does not have to use scholarly, technical, or so-called "scientific" language. The Bible is written for the common person of every generation, and it therefore uses common, everyday language. The use of observational, nonscientific language is not *unscientific*, it is merely *prescientific*. The Scriptures were written in *ancient* times by ancient standards, and it would be anachronistic to superimpose *modern* scientific standards upon them. However, it is no more unscientific to speak of the sun "standing still" (Joshua 10:12) than to refer to the sun "rising" (Joshua 1:16) [*sic*: see Joshua 1:15]. Contemporary meteorologists still speak daily of the time of "sunrise" and "sunset."

13. *Assuming That Round Numbers Are False*: Another mistake sometimes made by Bible critics is claiming that round numbers are false. This is not so. Round numbers are just that—round numbers. Like most ordinary speech, the Bible uses round numbers (1 Chron. 19:18; 21:5). For example, it refers to the diameter as being about one third of the circumference of something. It may be imprecise from the standpoint of a contemporary technological society to speak of 3.14159265 . . . as the number three, but it is not incorrect for an ancient, nontechnological people. Three and fourteen hundredths can be rounded off to three. That is sufficient for a "Sea of cast metal" (2 Chron. 4:2, NIV) in an ancient Hebrew temple, even though it would not suffice for a computer in a modern rocket. But one should not expect scientific precision in a prescientific age.

14. *Neglecting to Note That the Bible Uses Different Literary Devices*: An inspired book need not be composed in one, and only one, literary style. Human beings wrote every book in the Bible, and human language is not limited to one mode of expression. So, there is no reason to suppose that only one style or literary genre was used in a divinely inspired Book. The Bible reveals a number of literary devices. Several whole books are written in *poetic* style (e.g., Job, Psalms, Proverbs). The synoptic Gospels are filled with *parables*. In Galatians 4, Paul utilizes an *allegory*. The NT abounds with *metaphors* (e.g., 2 Cor. 3:2–3; James 3:6) and *similes* (cf. Matt. 20:1; James 1:6); *hyperboles* may also be found (e.g., Col. 1:23; John 21:25; 2 Cor. 3:2), and possibly even *poetic figures* (Job 41:1). Jesus employed *satire* (Matt. 19:24 with 23:24), and *figures of speech* are common throughout the Bible. It is not a mistake for a biblical writer to use a figure of speech, but it is a mistake for a reader to take a figure of speech literally. . . . We must be careful in our reading of figures of speech in Scripture.

15. *Forgetting That Only the Original Text, Not Every Copy of Scripture, Is Without Error*: When critics do come upon a genuine mistake in a manuscript copy, they make another fatal error—they assume it was in the original inspired text of Scripture. They forget that God only uttered the original text of Scripture, not the copies. Therefore, only the original text is without error. Inspiration does not guarantee that every copy of the original is without error. Therefore, we are to expect that minor errors are to be found in manuscript copies. . . . Several things should be observed about these copyist errors. First of all, they are errors in the copies, not the originals. No one has ever found an original manuscript

with an error in it. Second, they are minor errors (often in names or numbers) which do not affect any doctrine of the Christian faith. Third, these copyist errors are relatively few in number. . . . Fourth, usually by the context, or by another Scripture, we know which one is in error. . . . Finally, even though there is a copyist error, the entire message can still come through. In such a case, the validity of the message is not changed. . . . So, for all practical purposes, the Bible in our hand, imperfect though the manuscripts are, conveys the complete truth of the original Word of God.

16. *Confusing General Statements with Universal Ones*: Critics often jump to the conclusion that unqualified statements admit of no exceptions. They seize upon verses that offer general truths and then point with glee to obvious exceptions. In so doing, they forget that such statements are only intended to be generalizations. The Book of Proverbs is a good example of such an issue. Proverbial sayings by their very nature offer only general guidance, not universal assurance. They are rules for life, but rules that admit of exceptions. Proverbs 16:7 is a case in point. It affirms that "when a man's ways please the Lord, He makes even his enemies to be at peace with him." This obviously was not intended to be a universal truth. Paul was pleasing to the Lord and his enemies stoned him (Acts 14:19). Jesus was pleasing the Lord, and His enemies crucified Him! Nonetheless, it is a general truth that one who acts in a way pleasing to God can minimize his enemies' antagonism.

17. *Forgetting That Later Revelation Supersedes Previous Revelation*: Sometimes critics of Scripture forget the principle of progressive revelation. God does not reveal everything at once, nor does He always lay down the same conditions for every period of time. Therefore, some of His later revelation will supersede His former statements. Bible critics sometimes confuse a *change* of revelation with a *mistake*. The mistake, however, is that of the critic. For example . . . when God created the human race, He commanded that they eat only fruit and vegetables (Gen. 1:29). But later, when conditions changed after the flood, God commanded that they also eat meat (Gen. 9:3). This change from herbivorous to omnivorous status is progressive revelation, but is not a contradiction. (Geisler and Howe, BBBD, 15–26)

IV. Scholarly Diagnoses of Ten Alleged Contradictions in the Old Testament

Attempting to address the alleged contradictions in the Old Testament is a daunting task. Entire books have been written to address specific claims, and scholars continue to discuss and debate them in academic literature. It is also important to see how differently people can interpret the meaning of the alleged contradictions. Bart Ehrman believes contradictions undermine the reliability of the Bible in its entirety. (Ehrman, JI) On the other hand, some professing evangelicals accept biblical contradictions. For instance, in his popular-level book, *The Bible Tells Me So*, Peter Enns says, "The biblical writers often disagree, expressing diverse and contradictory points of view about God and what it means to be faithful to him." (Enns, BTMS, 25)

We differ from both Ehrman and Enns. While we recognize the difficulty in the task at hand, we believe that the Bible is the inspired and inerrant Word of God. Some of the alleged contradictions are easy to resolve. Others are quite difficult. But we believe that plausible explanations are available for those willing to probe deeply enough.

In the following section we take a look at some popular alleged contradictions in the Old Testament. Quite obviously, however, we have not yet scratched the surface of a number of important issues. We do not have the space to provide the various possible resolutions or to enter into the nuances of the scholarly debate surrounding each. We aim simply to introduce ten alleged contradictions that we have encountered in our studies and ministries, and to provide reasonable solutions. We hope you gain the confidence that alleged contradictions in the Old Testament are not nearly as problematic for the Christian faith as many critics claim.

A. Genesis 6:3 with Genesis 11:10–32
1. Alleged Contradiction

Genesis 6:3 states, "Then the LORD said, 'My Spirit will not contend with humans forever, for they are mortal; their days will be a hundred and twenty years'" (NIV). This seems to indicate that human longevity will not exceed 120 years, yet each of Noah's posterity listed in Genesis 11:10–32, lived longer than 120 years.

2. Scholarly Diagnosis

In *The Book of Genesis*, Victor P. Hamilton provides some helpful perspective:

> Is this an age limit, or is it a period of grace prior to the Flood (i.e., [Noah's remaining] days shall be 120 years)? The first alternative faces the difficulty that most of the people in the rest of Genesis lived well beyond 120 years. It is possible to interpret the longer life spans of the patriarchs as a mitigation or suspension of the divine penalty, just as an earlier announced divine penalty ("on the day you eat of it you shall surely die") was not immediately implemented.

> But the (imminent) withdrawal of the divine Spirit as a means of lowering the life span of humanity does not make a great deal of sense. Rather, it seems to presage some event that is about to occur. Accordingly, we prefer to see in this phrase a reference to a period of time that prefaces the Flood's beginning. It is parallel to Jon. 4:5, "Yet forty days, and Nineveh shall be overthrown." God's hand of judgment is put on hold. (Hamilton, BGC, 269)

B. Genesis 6:19, 20 with Genesis 7:2, 3
1. Alleged Contradiction

According to Genesis 6:19, 20, God instructed Noah to gather two of every kind of animal into the ark, but in Genesis 7:2, 3, God required seven pairs of all clean animals and seven pairs of birds.

2. Scholarly Diagnosis

Kaiser explains,

> The truth is that there is no inherent incompatibility between the two texts as they presently stand. Genesis 7:2–3 is just more precise than 6:19–20 on the question of the types and numbers of animals and birds that would board the ark.

> Noah's first instruction was to admit pairs of all kinds of creatures on the ark to preserve their lives (Gen 6:19–20). That was the basic formula. Then he was given more specific instructions about admitting seven pairs of each of the clean animals and seven pairs of each kind of bird. The purpose of this measure was to become clear only after the flood. Birds would be needed to reconnoiter the earth (Gen 8:7–12), and the clean animals and birds would be offered in sacrifice to the Lord (Gen 8:20). If Noah had taken only one pair of each and then offered each of these pairs in sacrifice, these species would have become completely extinct.

The simplest and most adequate explanation is that chapter 6 of Genesis contains general summary directions—take two of each. After Noah had understood these general instructions, God spoke more specifically about the role the clean beasts and birds were to play. (Kaiser et al., HSB, 112)

C. Genesis 17:1 with Exodus 6:3

1. Alleged Contradiction

Genesis 17:1 says, "When Abram was ninety-nine years old, the LORD appeared to him and said, 'I am God Almighty; walk before me faithfully and be blameless'" (NIV). In this passage, God conspicuously identified his name to Abram, but Exodus 6:3 indicates that he did not make himself known to the patriarchs.

2. Scholarly Diagnosis

In his tome *On the Reliability of the Old Testament*, K. A. Kitchen provides one possible response, that in Exodus, the words permit reading the grammar as a question—in fact, a rhetorical question that implies its own answer:

[T]he final narrator in Genesis commonly speaks of the deity of the patriarchs as YHWH (proper name) or as Elohim ("God"). Both terms also occur in words ostensibly spoken by the patriarchs and their contemporaries. Often Exod. 6:3 is understood to signify the opposite; namely, that the name YHWH was unknown to the patriarchs. If that were so, then it is very strange that it should ever have been introduced at all into the text of Genesis; the supposed contradiction would have been just as obvious to the ancients as to any modern reader of these books. However, there is very good reason to translate Exod. 6:3 understanding a rhetorical negative that implies a positive, as "I appeared to Abraham, Isaac and Jacob as El-Shaddai ("God Almighty')—and

by my name YHWH did I not declare myself to them?"

This would find support from two angles. First, the "name" or character of a deity in the ancient Near East was by no means a rigidly fixed entity right from the beginning and forever after; more came to be known about, or attributed to, deities as time passed. Second, YHWH served as the proper name of the "God of the fathers," precisely as with other deities in the early second millennium, and (as with these) was not used all the time.... [F]or his part, YHWH revealed himself to Moses in new roles for the Israelites, not known by the patriarchs even if his name was....

And now the second angle of support for reading Exod. 6:3 as a rhetorical negative.... From Exod. 6:2–3 we would learn . . . that YHWH was known to the patriarchs both as El-Shaddai ("God Almighty" in many English versions) and as YHWH; the former is an epithet, just as are "God of Abraham," "God of Isaac," "God of Jacob," the latter being his proper name. This is no different to other examples in the biblical world.... El-Shaddai also appears to be of ancient format and origin. (Kitchen, OROT, 329–330)

D. Genesis 25:1 with 1 Chronicles 1:32

1. Alleged Contradiction

Keturah is Abraham's wife in Genesis 25:1, but she is his concubine in 1 Chronicles 1:32.

2. Scholarly Diagnosis

One option to resolve this apparent dilemma is to understand that there were various levels of marriage in the culture of this time. So, "concubine" is a lower-level form of marriage than "wife." Hamilton provides another way to resolve this tension:

This is the only passage in Genesis that mentions *Keturah*. Here she is called Abraham's *wife*, but in 1 Chr. 1:32 she is identified as "Abraham's concubine." This coidentification is comparable with Bilhah, who is called both Jacob's concubine (35:22) and Jacob's wife (30:4). By contrast, Zilpah is identified as Jacob's wife (30:9) but never as his concubine. If "by concubines" in 25:6 is a reference to Hagar and Keturah . . . then again both Hagar (16:3) and Keturah (25:1) are called "wife" in one place but "concubine" in another (25:6).

The emphasis on Keturah's status as wife would suggest that Abraham married her after the death of Sarah. If the emphasis is on her status as concubine then one would think that Abraham married her while Sarah was still living, as he did with Hagar. In that case one would have to understand *married* in this verse as a pluperfect—"had married." (Hamilton, BGC18–50, 164–165)

E. Numbers 22:20 with Numbers 22:21, 22
1. Alleged Contradiction

In Numbers 22:20, God granted Balaam conditional permission to travel, but according to the following two verses, Balaam's decision to travel kindled God's indignation.

2. Scholarly Diagnosis

In his commentary *The Book of Numbers*, Timothy R. Ashley rejoins,

The most common question about this verse is the motive for God's anger with Balaam. At the very least it seems capricious for God to tell Balaam to go on his way in v. 20 and then to become angry with Balaam because he was going in v. 22. The question is whether the [Hebrew] particle [that was used] (usually translated "because, since" in this verse) should not have another of its well-attested meanings, viz., "when" or even "as" with the participle. This construction is somewhat rare, but not unknown in Biblical Hebrew. If one

translates temporally, as above, then God no longer becomes angry with Balaam on the grounds of his going (since God had given him permission to go in v. 20), but *as he was going*, i.e., somewhere on the journey for an unspecified reason. This view admittedly sidesteps the issue of the motive for God's wrath, but, if the translation proposed is correct, so does the text itself. (Ashley, BN, 454–455)

F. Deuteronomy 15:4 with Deuteronomy 15:7, 11
1. Alleged Contradiction

Deuteronomy 15:4 states that no poor would be amongst Israel, but verse 7 of the same chapter prescribes for Israel instructions should a brother become poor and verse 11 instructs that the poor will always reside in the land. Will there be poor in the land or not?

2. Scholarly Diagnosis

Old Testament scholar Eugene Merrill explains that the key issue is a matter of the ideal for the land (v. 4) and the reality of how the land will *actually* be (v. 11):

This seems to be the best understanding of v. 4 [that poverty ought not to exist in the rich land the Lord would give them] rather than the idea that there would absolutely not be any poor among them. Complete absence of poverty is squarely contradicted by v. 11, which avers that "there will always be poor people in the land." The tension between the two statements is indicative of the gulf that exists between the ideal and actual, what could be the case were God's purposes carried out and what inevitably occurs when they are not. This is the import of v. 5, which plainly states that full compliance with covenant requirements was the precondition to Israel's prosperity in the land. When this was achieved, not only would Israel be blessed but, in line with the ancient patriarchal promises, they would be the means of blessing the whole world and having dominion over the nations (v. 6; cf. Gen 12:2–3; 17:4–6; 26:3–4). They would be the lender to whom all others would be in debt (cf. Deut 28:12–13). (Merrill, *Deuteronomy*, 244)

G. Deuteronomy 24:16 with 2 Samuel 12:14–19

1. Alleged Contradiction

According to Deuteronomy 24:16, children were not to be put to death for their father's sins, but in 2 Samuel 12:14–19, the Lord afflicted David's son on the basis of David's sin.

2. Scholarly Diagnosis

Geisler and Howe respond:

First, the passage in Deuteronomy is a precept laid down by which the legal system of Israel would function once they were established in the land. It was not the right of the human courts to exact capital punishment from the children of guilty parents if the children were not personally guilty of the crime. However, that which restricts the power of human courts does not restrict the right or authority of God.

Second, the Scripture does not indicate that David's child was being punished for David's sin. Rather, the Bible indicates that the death of the child was David's punishment (2 Sam. 12:14). If it is thought that allowing the child to die was an unjust way to punish David, it must be remembered that David trusted in the righteousness of God when he said in faith, "I shall go to him, but he shall not return to me" (2 Sam. 12:23). David trusted that God had taken his child to heaven and that he would be with the child when he died. God always acts according to His righteousness, and the restrictions of such precepts as this

are designed to prevent men from perverting justice. (Geisler and Howe, BBBD, 129–130)

H. Psalm 51:16, 17 and Hosea 6:6 with Psalm 51:19

1. Alleged Contradiction

Both Psalm 51:16, 17 and Hosea 6:6 assert that God does not delight in sacrifices, but Psalm 51:19 maintains that God derives pleasure from them.

2. Scholarly Diagnosis

Nancy deClaissé-Walford, in the commentary *The Book of Psalms*, expounds:

In these verses of Psalm 51, the psalmist reflects on the nature of *sacrifice*. Sacrifices are not offered by humanity to appease God. Sacrifices are necessary because humanity needs symbols, acts with which to come before God to restore right relationships. But the symbol is not the sole element of the sacrificial system. Proper sacrifice requires proper attitude; in the case of the singer in Psalm 51, the attitude is *a spirit being broken* and *a heart being broken and crushed*. The word translated *broken* is from [a particular] Hebrew root . . . and includes the ideas of "contrite, sorry, and humble."

In Leviticus 1–7, God gives to the people of Israel instructions concerning the sacrificial system. An important element of that system is outlined in Lev. 6:2–7. The text tells us that if a person defrauds, robs, or swears falsely against a neighbor, the first thing that person must do upon realizing what they have done is to restore that which was taken to its rightful owner, along with an additional 20 percent of its value. Then, and only then, must the person go to the priest and present a guilt offering. Verses 16–17 of Psalm 51 are not a polemic against the sacrificial system. They are a polemic against sacrifice of material goods without sacrifice of spirit and heart. In the same way that sin cannot be forgiven without a *broken spirit and heart*, so proper sacrifice cannot be offered without a proper attitude. (deClaissé-Walford et al., BP, 457)

I. Proverbs 26:4 with Proverbs 26:5

1. Alleged Contradiction

Proverbs 26:4 advises one not to answer a fool, yet the following verse advises otherwise.

2. Scholarly Diagnosis

In his commentary *The Book of Proverbs: Chapters 15–31*, Old Testament scholar Bruce Waltke retorts,

[T]he wise son/disciple needs to give the fool a verbal answer. . . . The apparent contradiction between their admonitions, "do not answer a fool" versus "answer a fool," is resolved by clarifying the ambiguous [Hebrew] preposition ([translated as] "according to") in light of the negative consequence to be avoided [in the second half of each verse] . . . The son's answer must distinguish between what is unfitting (v. 4) and fitting (v. 5). It is unfitting to meet the fool's insult with insult (2 Pet. 3:9). Should the disciple reply vindictively, harshly, and/or with lies—the way fools talk—he too—"yes, even you"—would come under the fool's condemnation. Rather, without lowering himself to the fool's level in a debate, but by overcoming evil with good (25:21–22), the wise must show the fool's folly for what it is. The wise do not silently accept and tolerate the folly and thereby confirm fools in it. Both proverbs are absolutes and applicable at the same time, contrary to the opinion of many commentators, who think they are relative to the situation. To be sure, there is a time to be silent and a time to speak (Eccl. 4:5), but one must always, not in only certain situations, answer a fool to destabilize him, but,

always, not sometimes, without becoming like him.

The rationale for the admonition not to answer a fool according to his folly (v. 4a) is to avoid the negative consequence of becoming like the fool (v. 4b). . . . [The wise person] should stand in contrast to the fool.

The rationale for answering a fool according to his folly (v. 5a) is to avoid the negative consequence that the fool arrogantly replaces the LORD's heavenly wisdom with his own (v. 5b). . . . The wise person must expose the fool's distortions to serve his own interests at the expense of the community and must not silently accept it and thereby contribute to establishing his topsy-turvy world against the rule of God. An answer that is in agreement with the LORD's wisdom puts the fool's topsy-turvy world rightside up and and [sic] so is fitting. Granted the discomfort and even danger of such association, someone has to speak up for wisdom. (Waltke, BPC, 348–350)

J. Amos 4:4 with the Old Testament

1. Alleged Contradiction

In Amos 4:4, the prophet tells the northern kingdom to multiply transgression, but over and over, in multiple contexts, the Old Testament clearly forbids deliberate transgression.

2. Scholarly Diagnosis

After explicating Amos 4:1–3, Karl Möller, in his book *A Prophet in Debate*, elaborates on the prophet's awareness of the people's sinful duplicity in the way they worship, which makes the seeming command actually ironic.

Without any transition or introduction, Amos then goes on to invite the people to come to Bethel and Gilgal. Both—the former being Israel's national sanctuary or the king's sanctuary, as the priest Amaziah preferred to call it (Amos 7:13)—were important cult centres. Imitating a priestly invitation to worship, Amos sarcastically calls the Israelites not to come to these places and worship, but to come and sin. Thus, whereas the purposes of such a pilgrimage should have been, and in the eyes of the prophet's audience would have been, thanksgiving and the fulfilment of vows, Amos equates the Israelites' cultic performances with the war crimes condemned in Amos 1–2. . . .

The sinfulness of the worship is underlined by the ironic command to multiply their sins . . . as well as by the use of another heptad, in this instance consisting of seven imperatives, which, again ironically, calls on the people to outperform the law's cultic requirements. Mocking their attitude, especially their reliance on outward gestures, Amos asks the Israelites to offer sacrifices every morning instead of once a year and give their tithes every three days rather than once in three years. By the same token, he calls on his audience to offer thank offerings along with freewill offerings but what is missing, rather conspicuously, is any mention of sin offerings or indeed anything related to the issues of sin and repentance. What Amos does stress, referring to "*your* offerings", "*your* tithes", and so on, is the people's egotism, which is at the heart of their remarkable display of religious zeal. . . .

The transition from the initial oracle in 4:1–3 to the present one may seem somewhat abrupt, given the lack of connectives . . . as well as the change of topic. Yet, the combination of social issues (vv. 1–3) with religious or cultic ones (vv. 4–5) is a recurrent feature in the book of Amos. . . . From a rhetorical point of view, it should also be noted that the present arrangement results in an interesting ironic effect, as the people are said to display an impressive religious drive that goes far beyond the requirements of the law while at the same time disobeying the heart of the law by exploiting and abusing the poor. . . . Punctilious as they were in their observance of cultic requirements they believed that they would not have to face Yahweh's punitive intervention. Amos responds to this with heavy irony, inviting the people to come and revel in a "gala barbecue" consisting in a multitude of offerings and sacrifices, only to condemn their religious zeal, quite brutally . . . as something akin to the horrible war crimes committed by Israel's enemies. (Möller, PD, 262–264, 266–267)

Hence, no contradiction exists.

V. Concluding Remarks

Though critics commonly assert that the Old Testament contains authentic contradictions, many Bible scholars have provided plausible harmonizations over the centuries. Alleged contradictions often arise from mistakes in interpretation, ignoring genre or literary devices, or through a host of other faulty assumptions. Some alleged contradictions require further research, and others have been satisfactorily resolved. But given the track record of scholarship in this area, we have good reason to believe that if all the facts were known, all alleged discrepancies would disappear.

Because human knowledge is limited and history is messy, we should expect to face puzzling issues, since we don't have God's all-knowing gaze. There is good reason to believe the Bible is true, and so we give it every benefit of the doubt. Given how many supposed contradictions have been resolved in light of recent discoveries, Christians can have confidence that the Bible is *authoritative and without error in what it actually teaches and all that it intends to affirm.*

PART IV

EVIDENCE
FOR TRUTH

CHAPTER 27

THE NATURE OF TRUTH

OVERVIEW

I. Does Truth Matter?

The study of truth might seem dull and unimportant. As we live our everyday lives, defining truth doesn't often rank very high on the list of our priorities. In fact, this may seem to be a subject reserved for ivory tower academic types. "Why do we need to worry about truth anyway?" it could be asked. However, there are at least three reasons we should worry about truth and its implications.

A. Truth Is the Most Important Pursuit

When all is said and done, there is no pursuit more worthy than following the truth, wherever it may lead. In fact, even though we don't think about truth a lot, our actions show we know that finding truth is extremely important. Noted author, speaker, and apologist Ravi Zacharias explains it this way:

In the childhood years, wonder can be attained by dabbling in the world of fantasy. That is both the glory and the fragility of childhood. But as the years pass, wonder is eroded in the face of reality and in the recognition that life may not be lived in a fairy-tale world. A displacement is brought about by the ever-increasing demand of the mind, not just for the fantastic, but for the true. The search for truth

Aristotle was right when he opined that all philosophy begins with wonder; but the journey, I suggest, can only progress through truth.

Ravi Zacharias

then becomes all-pervasive, encompassing implications for the essence and destiny of life itself. Even if not overtly admitted, the search for truth is nevertheless hauntingly present, propelled by the need for incontrovertible answers to four inescapable questions, those dealing with origin, meaning, morality, and destiny. No thinking person can avoid this search, and it can only end when one is convinced that the answers espoused are truth. Aristotle was right when he opined that all philosophy begins with wonder; but the journey, I suggest, can only progress through truth. (Zacharias, CMLWG, 93)

Once we arrive at a certain time in our lives, discerning and finding the truth becomes the inevitable focus. Humanity's search for answers can only be found in the truth. It must be grounded in reality.

B. Truth Matters to Us in Personal and Practical Ways

Not only do we intuitively search for truth, but many everyday actions depend on using and realizing the truth. In his book *Truth Considered and Applied: Examining Postmodernism, History, and Christian Faith*, Stewart E. Kelly lists five ways truth matters practically. He writes that (1) truth matters for daily life; (2) the pursuit of truth is correlated with happiness; (3) science is a truth-seeking enterprise; (4) knowledge is a veritistic enterprise; and (5) truth is intrinsically valuable. (Kelly, TCA, 262–267) Of particular relevance:

Our jobs require us to perform, hopefully successfully, a number of tasks. If the boss wants to know whether you've sent the package to Boston, talked to a client in California, and read over the relevant memo in preparation for a meeting later in the day, your chances of being promoted and/or appreciated are greatly enhanced if you bring it about that all of these states of affairs actually obtain. In other words, it matters to the boss, the company, and to your continuing at the job that, by the end of the day, it is *true* that all three of these things have happened. (Kelly, TCA, 262–263)

He continues:

Our medical situations require a grasp of the truth. Suppose we are not feeling well, we go to the doctor, and the doctor recommends that we begin a course of antibiotics. You ask if there are any alternatives and the doctor suggests that you could take a placebo for the ten days instead of (e.g.) amoxicillin. Amoxicillin has a proven track record of truly responding to some kinds of infections, while placebos (e.g. a sugar pill) are of little value here. . . . It is not merely the doctor's opinion or the opinion of the medical establishment but rather such a proposition is true because it picks out an actually obtaining state of affairs. In other words, the truth of the proposition somehow corresponds with the objectively real world (in this case, our physical bodies). Modern medicine is committed to the idea that some medicines truly work (and can be verified through careful research), while others are of less or no value. (Kelly, TCA, 263)

Kelly further explains that "the pursuit of happiness, like many other human activities, is enhanced by *veritistic* or truth-seeking beliefs and practices" before also showing that the realm of science, and even the pursuit of knowledge itself, requires assuming truth to be a real thing. (Kelly, TCA, 264–265) Regarding knowledge, he explains, "Knowledge . . . requires that the belief in question be true if it is to be marked off from lucky beliefs and guesses." (Kelly, TCA, 265) Finally, Kelly reminds us that we seek truth because we intuitively know that truth is valuable. It is worth quoting him at length again:

> As Lynch argues, "We want more than illusion [however nice it may be]. We want the truth, warts and all." Convenient fictions are nevertheless fictions, and most people want more than that. This point is nicely illustrated in the popular movie *The Matrix*. Here the main character is given a set of choices, each involving a particular pill. Pill 1 will give him a life of perfect illusion. He will not even remember that he ever chose such a pill. But if he chooses pill 2, then he will find out about both his life and reality, "a truth he is warned will be unpleasant. He chooses, unsurprisingly to the audience, the truth." Pill 2 is the better option because, in part, humans are truth seekers. But another key reason is that knowing the truth is *ceteris paribus*, an intrinsically good state of affairs. (Kelly, TCA, 267)

We innately know that to live in reality, to live a life in truth, is better than to be fooled or to fool ourselves forever. Truth is a worthy goal for its own sake.

Recently, I (Josh) had just finished my opening address at the National Apologetics Conference in Charlotte, NC. A student approached me as I was leaving.

"Dr. McDowell, why does truth even matter?" I thought for a moment and replied, "Do you want the truthful answer or the false answer?" Then I smiled slightly, turned, and walked away. Glancing back at the young man, I could see his bewilderment. I don't think he got it.

C. Truth Matters in Evangelism and Cultural Engagement

Not only do we need truth to function in the mundane and more commonplace events in our lives, but if we as Christians hope to serve our God well, we need to use the truth well. In order to spread the gospel to all nations truth must be something we are intimately acquainted with. Again Zacharias is helpful here:

> Indeed, the first and most vital task of apologetics is to clarify truth-claims. [Walter] Martin identified this as "scaling the language barrier." When asked to define a word such as truth, however, many Christians freeze, for they have seldom paused to consider what it means even as they themselves quote Jesus as "the way, the truth and the life." This easy mistake is a costly one. (Zacharias, CTC, 339)

If those of us who are Christians hope to represent Christ well and share the gospel with friends, neighbors, and family, we must commit to explaining the truth. We need a firm grasp on the existence and knowability of the truth. Not only this, but a culture's attack on truth ultimately affects the culture itself. Zacharias traces our culture's descent into a fascination with violence and sexual license to a "willful suppression of truth that results in an assault upon the sacred in the pursuit of the profane." (Zacharias, CMLWG, 100) He continues:

These two truths—that humanity is made in God's image and that the body is the temple of God—are two of the cardinal teachings of Scripture. What else will entertainment do when it gets profane but attack the two principal teachings of human essence? Violence defaces the image of God, and sensuality profanes the temple of God. The image of God and the temple of God have both been violated and replaced with the gods and idols of our time. Thus, when former Vice President Dan Quayle reprimanded Hollywood for what it was doing, he was angrily castigated because he touched the idols of our age. And even though *Atlantic Monthly* ran the cover story "Dan Quayle Was Right" some months later, what difference does that confession make if nobody really cares what is true anymore? The loss of truth, like the loss of wonder, filters down into our day-to-day lives and takes its toll upon society. (Zacharias, CMLWG, 100)

We must be willing to stand up for truth, or we may find our efforts to share the gospel and engage our culture falling on deaf ears.

II. What Is Truth?

A. Preliminary Concerns

In order to define and discuss truth well, one word we need to explain here is *metaphysics*. Traditionally, metaphysics has referred to the philosophical study of existence—that is, the study of reality itself. Metaphysics answers questions such as, "What really exists?" and "What is its nature?"

Another important term is *epistemology*, or the study of knowing things. *The Oxford Dictionary of Philosophy* defines epistemology as "the theory of knowledge," or how we came to know what we know. Do we know, for example, that our senses are not fooling us in terms of what they tell us is the reality around us? We turn first to what truth is and then to how we know it.

In this chapter, we focus on the metaphysics of truth, concerning ourselves with the nature and reality of truth itself. Although this has implications for the epistemology (or *knowability* of truth), we leave that until later.

B. Truth Corresponds with Reality
1. Defining Truth

By far the most believed theory about the nature of truth is called the *correspondence theory of truth*. This view has been around for a very long time and has withstood many challenges. It states that truth is that which corresponds to its referent (that to which it refers). Metaphysical truth is that which corresponds with reality or reflects reality. By *correspondence* we mean agreement with something—in this case, a thought or statement about reality agrees with reality. By *reality* we mean that which is, or exists. (Whether or not we can know that they correspond is discussed more fully in the next chapter, "The Knowability of Truth.") Influential philosopher and apologist J. P. Moreland summarizes the correspondence theory of truth:

> In its simplest form, the correspondence theory of truth is the view that a claim—technically, a proposition—is true just in case it corresponds to reality; that is, a proposition is true when what it asserts to be the case is the case. (Moreland, PT, 113–114)

2. Aristotle and Truth

The Greek philosopher Aristotle summarizes the difference between *true* and *false*: "To say of what is that it is not, or of what is not that it is, is false, while to say of what is

In its simplest form, the correspondence theory of truth is the view that a claim — technically, a proposition — is true just in case it corresponds to reality; that is, a proposition is true when what it asserts to be the case is the case.

J. P. Moreland

that it is, and of what is not that it is not, is true; so that he who says of anything that it is, or that it is not, will say either what is true or what is false; but neither what is nor what is not is said to be or not to be." (Aristotle, *Metaphysics*, 4.7.)

Aristotle argues that truth relies on the actual existence of the thing which a thought or statement is about:

> The fact of the being of a man carries with it the truth of the proposition that he is, and the implication is reciprocal: For if a man is, the proposition wherein we allege that he is is true, and conversely, if the proposition wherein we allege that he is is true, then he is. The true proposition, however, is in no way the cause of the being of the man, but the fact of the man's being does seem somehow to be the cause of the truth of the proposition, for the truth or falsity of the proposition depends on the fact of the man's being or not being. (Aristotle, *Categories*, 20.12.14)

Aristotle also suggests that a statement or belief can change from true to false only if that to which it refers actually changes:

> But statements and opinions themselves remain unaltered in all respects: it is by the alteration in the facts of the case that the contrary quality comes to be theirs. The statement "he is sitting" remains unaltered, but it is at one time true, at another false, according to circumstances. What has been said of statements applies also to opinions. Thus, in respect of the manner in which the thing takes place, it is the peculiar mark of substance that it should be capable of admitting contrary qualities; for it is by itself changing that it does so.
>
> If, then, a man should make this exception and contend that statements and opinions are capable of admitting contrary qualities, his contention is unsound. For statements and opinions are said to have this capacity, not because they themselves undergo modification, but because this modification occurs in the case of something else. The truth or falsity of a statement depends on facts, and not on any power on the part of the statement itself of admitting contrary qualities. In short, there is nothing which can alter the nature of statements and opinions. As, then, no change takes place in themselves, these cannot be said to be capable of admitting contrary qualities. (Aristotle, *Categories*, 8–9:5)

3. Christian Thinkers and Truth

Thomas Aquinas asserts that "truth is defined by the conformity of intellect and thing; and hence to know this conformity is to know truth." (Aquinas, ST, Q. 16, Art. 2)

More recently, theologian and analytic philosopher Paul Copan has defined truth especially clearly:

> That's what truth is—a belief, description, or story that matches the way things truly are. Compare it to a socket wrench (belief, statement, story) that fits onto or corresponds

to a bolt (reality); the connecting relationship between them is truth. (Copan, TYNM, 19)

Elsewhere he adds:

We can't escape the view of truth as corresponding to or mirroring the way things really are. The better our views approximate reality, the more accurate or true they are. If I say, "There's a computer screen in front of me," it's true because there is, in fact, a computer screen in front of me. Truth is like the fit of a socket wrench: the *socket attachment* represents our *belief*, and the *bolt* to be (un)tightened represents *reality*. When a belief "fits" or corresponds to reality, then it's true. When it doesn't fit, it's not. (Copan, HDYK, 39, emphasis in original)

4. Non-Christian Thinkers and Truth

Even Bertrand Russell, an outspoken atheist, held to a version of the correspondence theory. We cite Russell here to show that the correspondence theory of truth is not a uniquely Christian or even Greek concept of truth; it is a human concept that is both commonsensical and defensible. Russell distinguishes two facts about beliefs:

Although truth and falsehood are properties of beliefs, yet they are in a sense extrinsic properties, for the condition of the truth of a belief is something not involving beliefs, or (in general) any mind at all, but only the *objects* of the belief. A mind, which believes, believes truly when there is a corresponding complex not involving the mind, but only its objects. This correspondence ensures truth, and its absence entails falsehood. Hence we account simultaneously for the two facts that beliefs (a) depend on minds for their existence, (b) do not depend on minds for their truth. (Russell, PP, 129)

When Russell says beliefs do not depend on minds for their truth, he means that the truth is determined by something in reality, not by what we think. In another work, Russell argues that there is a world of objective facts independent of our minds:

The first truism to which I wish to draw your attention—and I hope you will agree with me that these things that I call truisms are so obvious that it is almost laughable to mention them—is that the world contains facts, which are what they are whatever we may choose to think about them, and that there are also beliefs, which have reference to facts, and by reference to facts are either true or false. (Russell, RM, 101)

G. E. Moore, another non-Christian thinker, believes similarly. He defines true and false belief:

"To say that this belief is true is to say that there is in the Universe a fact to which it corresponds; and that to say that it is false is to say that there is not in the Universe any fact to which it corresponds." (Moore, SMPP, 277)

Moore states again:

When the belief is true, it certainly does correspond to a fact; and when it corresponds to a fact it certainly is true. And similarly when it is false, it certainly does not correspond to any fact; and when it does not correspond to any fact, then certainly it is false. (Moore, SMPP, 279)

Moore suggests that truth is a property that can be common to any belief that corresponds to the facts:

We have said that to say it is true is merely to say that it does correspond to a fact; and obviously this is a property which may be common to it and other beliefs. The shopman's belief, for instance, that the parcel we ordered this morning has been sent off, may have the property of corresponding to a fact [i.e., that the parcel was actually shipped], just as well as [a] belief that I have gone away may have it. And the same is true of the property which we have now identified with the falsehood of the belief. The property which we have identified with its falsehood is merely that of not corresponding to any fact [the parcel was not sent off]. (Moore, SMPP, 277)

5. The Correspondence Idea of Truth Is Intuitive

When we make sentences or statements, we are trying to match up our words with the reality of the external world around us. This is our common sense notion of how communication works in regards to truth. John Searle, in his book *The Construction of Social Reality*, defends this idea:

In general, statements are attempts to describe how things are in the world, which exists independently of the statement. The statement will be true or false depending on whether things in the world really are the way the statement says they are. Truth, in short, is a matter of accuracy of a certain sort of linguistic representation. So, for example, the statement that hydrogen atoms have one electron, or that the earth is ninety-three million miles from the sun, or that my dog is now in the kitchen are true or false depending on whether or not things in the hydrogen atom, solar system, and domestic canine line of business, respectively, really are the way these statements say they are. (Searle, CSR, 200)

Unless we are given a tremendous amount of evidence to the contrary, the correspondence theory of truth is preferable to other theories. Our common sense view of truth as matching to the way things really are needs a lot to dethrone it. As Stewart Kelly observes:

The Correspondence Theory accords well with our basic intuitions about truth and reality. When we say, "The cat is on the mat," we know it is true because there is a corresponding state of affairs (the cat being on the mat). We also know the claim would be false if there was a catless mat here. As such, it is an eminently congenial view. Default positions "are the views we hold prereflectively so that any departure from them requires a conscious effort and a convincing argument." (Kelly, TCA, 268)

C. Truth Is Logical

Logic presupposes that truth is real. All thought and knowledge require logic, and logic assumes both the existence of a reality "out there" and ways to describe that reality. Put another way, to use logic assumes the correspondence theory of truth. This is how "first principles" work. First principles are truths that cannot be denied. They are self-evident. Norman Geisler and Ronald Brooks explain this more fully:

First principles, which are the starting point of all truth and the foundation of all thought, are these kinds of statements (ones that cannot be denied without affirming their truth).

Logic applied to reality is a key example. Now all logic can be reduced to one single axiom—the law of noncontradiction. This law says that no two opposite statements can both be true at the same time in the same sense. Logicians usually simplify that to A is not non-A. If we try to deny that, we get, "Two contradictory statements can be true," or "A is not [not non-A]." Both of these statements have a problem. They assume what they are trying to deny. In the first, it still assumes that there can be truth without the law of noncontradiction. But if opposites can be true then there is no difference between true and false, so this statement cannot be true, as it claims to be. . . . The law of noncontradiction cannot be denied because any denial assumes that opposites cannot be true, and that is exactly what is being denied. . . .

But the statement, "Logic applies to reality," is also undeniable. To say that logic does not apply to reality, you have to make a logical statement about it. But if it takes a logical statement to deny logic, then your actions defeat the purpose of your words. Either way, logic must apply to reality. And if logic applies to reality, then we can use it to test truth claims about reality. (Brooks and Geisler, WSA, 270)

So to use logic assumes the existence of truth about facts in the real world.

D. Two Ways to Think about Truth: Subjective and Objective
1. Subjective Claims

Some claims do change from person to person, or are based on the circumstance. These are *subjective* claims having mostly to do with one's personal preferences or desires. The reason they are called subjective is because the beliefs of the *subject* are the determining factor in whether the claims are true or not. In other words, if the subject believes something, then it is true for him/her:

Knowing truth helps us to make right moral decisions. But not all decisions in life deal

with morality. Most choices we make, in fact, are not moral choices at all. Should we go bowling tonight, or should we go to the movies? Do I prefer Chocolate-Peanut-Butter-Cup or Cookies-and-Cream ice cream? Should I wear my green shirt or my black shirt? These are personal choices relative to the individual. The way one would answer these questions would be considered subjective truths. The phrase "Chocolate ice cream is the best flavor" may be true for you but not for me. These types of truths are based on preference or feeling and can easily change. (McDowell, *Ethix*, 28–29)

2. Objective Truths

Subjective claims apply to things like preferences, but *objective* truth deals with the real, mind-independent world. Objective truths are true no matter what we prefer or believe. They do not change because of our thoughts or whims. They are mind-independent and depend on the *object* itself. Here is how I (Sean) put it in my book *Ethix*:

Objective truths, as opposed to subjective preferences, are based on the external world. They are related to the world independently of how we think or feel. For example, the sentences "1 + 2 = 3," "George Washington was the first president of the United States," and "Sacramento is the capital of California" are all objective truths, that is, they are accurate statements even if we don't believe them. (McDowell, *Ethix*, 29)

We have seen that truth is defined as correspondence to reality. This means that truth is objective. We may have subjective preferences, but the external world is not affected by our beliefs, desires, or preferences. The facts of the matter do not change because of our disagreements either.

3. Problems for Relativism

Those who argue that all truth is subjective are espousing a form of relativism. Relativism creeps into our vocabulary in statements like, "Well, that's true for you, but not for me." Unfortunately for those who do hold to relativism, the idea of relativism is fraught with a number of problems. Let's consider two of the main problems.

a. Relativism Is Self-Defeating

Kelly observes that attempts to deny truth are hopeless before they even begin:

> There is such a thing as truth. If there were, hypothetically speaking, no such thing as truth, then would it be true that there is no truth? How could a veritistically challenged person commend their view to us if it weren't true? (Kelly, TCA, 298)

Zacharias clarifies the implications:

> Truth by definition is exclusive. If truth were all-inclusive, nothing would be false. And if nothing were false, what would be the meaning of true? Moreover, if nothing were false, would it be true to say that everything is false? It quickly becomes evident that the denial of truth as an absolute either ends up denying itself or else in effect not making any truthful assertion about truth. (Zacharias, CTC, 339–340)

This puts relativists between a rock and a hard place. Either they need to deny objective truth fully (even their own position) for consistency's sake, or they need to embrace that which they are denying. Copan explains:

> To be consistent, the relativist must say, "Nothing is objectively true—including my own position. So you're free to accept my view

or reject it." Normally, when the relativist says, "Everything is relative," he expects his hearers to believe his statement and embrace his view of reality. And he expects his statement to pertain to all statements except his own. (Copan, TYNM, 27)

Norman Geisler puts it especially poignantly:

> The only way the relativist can avoid the painful dilemma of relativism is to admit that there are at least some absolute truths. As noted, most relativists believe that relativism is absolutely true and that everyone should be a relativist. Therein lies the self-destructive nature of relativism. The relativist stands on the pinnacle of an absolute truth and wants to relativize everything else. (Geisler, BEA, 744)

The self-defeating nature of relativism and subjectivism soon becomes clear: the very nature of these claims contradicts the claims themselves. That is, one cannot hold to relativism and insist that others do so as well.

b. Relativism Leads to Absurd Logical Outcomes

The logical outcomes that naturally follow from such a view taking a relative or subjective view of truth is that subjectivism leads to some very hard conclusions.

i) Relativism and Subjectivism Leave No Room for Morality, Ethics, or Human Value

Subjectivism makes it impossible to argue for any sort of binding morality or ethics. In fact, relativism undermines even the value of humanity. Gregory Koukl explains:

> When truth dies, all of its subspecies, such as ethics, perish with it. If truth can't be known, then the concept of moral truth becomes incoherent. Ethics become relative, right and

wrong matters of individual opinion. This may seem a moral liberty, but it ultimately rings hollow . . . .

The death of truth in our society has created a moral decay in which "every debate ends with the barroom question 'says who?'" When we abandon the idea that one set of laws applies to every human being, all that remains is subjective, personal opinion. (Beckwith and Koukl, RFFP, 20)

He continues, "If there is no truth, nothing has transcendent value, including human beings. The death of morality reduces people to the status of mere creatures. When persons are viewed as things, they begin to be treated as things." (Beckwith and Koukl, RFFP, 22) In other words, if there is no such thing as truth, there can't be such a thing as moral or ethical truth. If this is the case, then all moral and ethical value are rendered as meaningless opinion. What's more, the relativist is usually arguing that we should accept the absolute truth of relativism for moral or ethical reasons. While holding to a view that cannot handle truth, they proclaim relativism with moral urgency.

ii) If Relativism or Subjectivism Were True, the World Would Contain Contradictory States of Affairs

The nature of relativism, if true, leads to contradictory instances in the world. Once it is found that there is no truth, we cannot defend against the notion of two complete opposites occurring or obtaining. Norman Geisler is helpful here:

If relativism were true, the world would be full of contradictory conditions. For if something is true for me but false for you, then opposite conditions exist. For if I say "There is milk in the refrigerator" and you say "There is not

any milk in the refrigerator"—and we both are right, then there must both be and not be milk in the refrigerator at the same time and in the same sense. But that is impossible. So, if truth were relative, then an impossible would be actual. (Geisler, BEA, 744)

E. Why Do People Still Deny Objective Truth?

Often, people deny objective truth because there is some truth in the claims that relativists make. That is, our perspectives do change the way we view events, and sometimes what some see as true has been influenced mightily by outside forces or the group in power. However, the presence of an element of truth to the reasons behind relativism doesn't mean relativism itself is true. Philosopher Douglas Groothuis explains that the claims that lead people to question objective truth do "contain some truthful insights. For instance, social and personal power relationships do tend to define what people take to be true and false; they do not, however, determine what is true or false with respect to objective reality." (Groothuis, TD, 31) In other words, we may not see the truth correctly, but this does not diminish the actual reality "out there."

Copan explains that one reason people believe relativism is that, "on the surface, relativism sounds relaxed and easygoing. Only when we think through its implications and apply them rigorously to life do we see the pitfalls of being so 'accommodating.'" (Copan, TYNM, 26) He explains further:

Truth's elusiveness in some areas of life is a major reason people believe something can be "true for you, but not for me." Looking around, the relativist comes to one firm conclusion: Too many people genuinely disagree about too many things for us to know truth. Significant—almost irreconcilable—differences in vital dimensions like religion, morality, politics, and philosophy can make it seem rash or even arrogant to say one perspective is true or mostly true and others are partially or totally wrong.

Supposedly, then, the sensible conclusion to draw is that relativism *must* be true. Somehow, people move from what is the case (the descriptive) to what they think *should* be the case (the prescriptive); from recognizing disagreement to lobbying for all things being equal. But concluding that relativism must be right is hardly the right move. (Copan, TYNM, 32, emphasis in original)

As we have seen, relativism poses numerous problems. No matter how attractive it may seem to adopt a relativist point of view, it is untenable to believe in relativism. This is why Kelly says, "In most philosophical circles, relativism concerning truth is still the kiss of death (to be avoided at all costs)." (Kelly, TCA, 282)

III. Mistaken Theories of Truth

Some people object to the correspondence theory of truth. For one reason or another they do not agree that truth is agreement with reality. As a result there have been a number of alternatives proposed. Some of these views are worth considering and understanding, though ultimately they are unsatisfactory.

A. A Fatal Consideration

Although we will look at some other theories of truth and identify problems with each view, it is helpful to realize that every other view of truth besides the correspondence view suffers from a fatal flaw. All of these views presuppose or use the correspondence idea of truth to argue for their own view of truth. Geisler explains:

All noncorrespondence views of truth imply correspondence, even as they attempt to deny it. The claim: "Truth does not correspond with what is" implies that this view corresponds to reality. Then the noncorrespondence view cannot express itself without using a correspondence frame of reference. (Geisler, BEA, 742)

B. Coherence View

The coherence view of truth is probably the second most believed theory of truth.

1. Defining the Coherence View

The coherence theory of truth holds that something is true if it coheres internally. Another way of putting this is that something is true if it fits together or does not contradict itself.

Kelly puts it this way:

Rather than understanding truth as a matter of correspondence between a truth bearer (e.g., a proposition) and a "slice of reality" (e.g., a state of affairs), the coherence theorist sees truth as a matter of a given belief cohering, meshing, fitting, or being logically consistent with our already established beliefs. A belief is thus seen as one of many parts of a large (epistemic) puzzle, a puzzle governed by meta-rules such as logical consistency and the like. So, for example, any belief that fails to cohere or mesh will be rejected as "false," while beliefs that mesh well will be regarded as "true." (Kelly, TCA, 274–275)

Hunter Mead, in *Types and Problems of Philosophy*, describes the "already established beliefs" of Kelly's definition in slightly different words, saying that "a statement or proposition is true if it harmonizes with other established truths or with our knowledge as a whole." (Mead, TAPOP, 155) His example is how we are taught to reason using Euclid's geometry, from axioms to a final declaration of proof. When he adds "other established truths," he implies a trust in something larger than our own beliefs. Perhaps this is how we actually engage a new idea—testing both its internal coherence and its coherence with a framework that others established but that we have also come to trust. Yet the limits of a coherence theory are clear: Euclid's geometry is a closed system.

Geisler explains, "Some thinkers have suggested that truth is what is internally consistent; it is coherent and self-consistent." (Geisler, BEA, 741) This definition of truth does have some merit. Something that is true should be consistent with other truths. However, instead of being the definition of truth, this is really only a helpful test to discern what is true.

2. Problems with the Coherence View

As stated above, when someone argues that the coherence theory of truth is true as opposed to the correspondence theory, they assume the correspondence theory of truth in order to argue for coherence. This is one problem; however, there are more.

One of the biggest problems for the coherence theory is that, if true, contradictions would be possible because the option of choosing between two theories by reference to something external to either of them has been excluded. For example, the atheist worldview could be coherent or internally consistent and therefore regarded as true on the correspondence theory of truth. However, a theistic worldview could also be coherent and regarded as true as well. Kelly is helpful here:

The Coherence Theory of Truth allows for contradictory beliefs to be justified. Any theory of truth that allows both the propositions P and not P to be true is seriously flawed. And given that the coherence theory does just this, it is seriously flawed. (Kelly, TCA, 277)

To modify Kelly's example a little, suppose that:

[P] Abraham Lincoln was the US president in 1862,

while

[not P] Abraham Lincoln was not the US president in 1862.

Kelly continues:

Suppose that (P) is viewed as true because it coheres with Sara's belief set, while not P is viewed as true because it coheres with Sam's belief set. Is this a genuine possibility on the coherence theory of truth? If coherence simply amounts to logical consistency, then the answer is a definite yes. (Kelly, TCA, 277)

However, there are some sophisticated theorists who argue coherence is more than just agreement within its own system. Does this escape the force of the objection? Kelly argues no:

Blanshard might claim that a maximally comprehensive set of beliefs will greatly limit how many patently false beliefs will be accepted as "true" (meshing with the maximal set). Questions would remain whether any one person possesses such a maximal set. Furthermore, how successfully would a person be in the building of such a set without allowing such patently false beliefs to be part of the maximal set? Weeding out the patently false seems to presuppose a large and stable set of already accepted ("true") beliefs, but the acquisition of the already accepted also seems to presuppose a large and stable set. Under such conditions it is far from clear how the coherence theorist could ever get their project off the ground without allowing either a preexisting notion of truth (e.g., correspondence) so as to avoid a regress, or lack the large and stable set needed to preclude patently false beliefs. (Kelly, TCA, 277)

In other words, coherentists must assume or accept correspondence or leave themselves open to seeing contradictions as true.

C. Pragmatist View

The pragmatist view of truth attracts many people.

1. Defining the Pragmatist View

The pragmatist theory of truth states that truth is what works. This appeals to many people because we need the things we believe and do to work every day. Here is how Copan puts it:

> The pragmatist says that *truth is what's useful.* If it *"works," brings good results, helps us to cope, or contributes to human well-being,* then it's true. For the pragmatist, true beliefs are those that encourage actions with desirable results and benefit human beings. (Copan, HDYK, 32, emphasis in original)

As with the coherence theory, the pragmatic theory is attractive because it does hold some truth. Things that are true must work in some way. Thus, it seems that the pragmatic view of truth is also a good test to help discern what is true, but it is not a definition of truth itself.

2. Problems with the Pragmatist View

Again, arguments for the pragmatist view of truth presuppose the correspondence theory of truth. But there are some other problems as well. One problem comes to light when one asks, "Works for whom?" We quickly realize that one person may say something works for him, but another person might say the opposite works for her, so we would still need to ask, "Who is right? Which view is true?" Kelly captures this problem poignantly by quoting F. C. S. Schiller's observation that "there are as many pragmatisms as pragmatists." (Kelly, TCA, 279) Pragmatism does not get us any closer to truth when people assert differing preferences about what they want to work. Copan explains further:

> We'd have to consider contradictory points of view true if they prove to be useful for opposing "peer groups," but this is obviously problematic. What if an abortionist believes he's helping "unexpectedly expecting" women to uphold their "right" to "control their own bodies" and their "freedom of choice"? And what if the abortionist claims he finds the work of killing unborn babies satisfying and useful for the upward mobility of women in society? Well, pragmatism bumps up against the "problem of the other side": What about volunteers at a pro-life counseling center who are richly rewarded and gratified by counseling women considering abortion to keep their babies in the face of challenging circumstances—or to give them up for adoption? These volunteers are also aware of post abortion trauma and the psychological (and physiological) havoc that abortion wreaks on women; so they show concern for the well-being of the mother as well . . . .
>
> So to say "whatever works for you" leads to a deep conflict. Both cannot be true, however well they may "work" for each party. But pragmatism would lead to this kind of incoherence. (Copan, HDYK, 35–36)

This problem, as well as others, makes it untenable to hold to the pragmatic view of truth as a definition of truth. Whether something "works" may help us decide or know if something is true, but it cannot be the sole component of the definition of truth itself.

And the test itself as to whether something "works" rests on assessing whether the view corresponds with the facts in the case, such as the consequences of thinking it is true. So the correspondence theory inevitably comes into play.

IV. The Biblical View of Truth

In recent years, some scholars have taken to defending the biblical idea of truth. These scholars noticed a need to explain how the Bible views truth. They found that although the Bible does not explicitly articulate the correspondence theory of truth, it implicitly assumes the correspondence principle throughout its pages. One example that directly employs the test of correspondence applies it in determining whether a prophet has truly spoken from God: "If the word does not come to pass or come true, that is a word that the Lord has not spoken; the prophet has spoken it presumptuously" (Deut. 18:22, esv). The test of correspondence has settled the question. Another example occurs when Pharisees and lawyers challenge Jesus for telling a man that his sins are forgiven. Jesus' response employs a double use of the correspondence theory. He invites them to reason about which is easier, to declare something that is invisible or something visible. Then, prefacing his action by telling the Pharisees why he is undertaking the action—"that you may know that the Son of Man has authority on earth to forgive sins,"—he directs the man to "rise, pick up your bed and go home." (Luke 5:20–26, esv) The correspondence between hearing Jesus' words and seeing the walking man was a clear test of the truth of what Jesus said. In other words, while the Bible is not a philosophical treatise on truth, the correspondence theory of truth underlies many of its claims.

A. Compatible with the Correspondence View

The Bible, then, sees truth as matching with reality. This means that the Bible's view of truth is completely compatible with the correspondence theory of truth we encountered above. Geisler and Brooks say:

> The Scriptures use the correspondence view of truth quite a bit. The ninth commandment certainly presupposes it. "You shall not bear false witness against your neighbor" (Ex. 20:16) implies that the truth or falsity of a statement can be tested by whether it checks out with the facts. When Satan said, "You shall not surely die," it is called a lie because it does not correspond to what God actually said. (Brooks and Geisler, WSA, 262)

In his book *Truth Decay: Defending Christianity Against the Challenges of Postmodernism*, Douglas Groothuis devotes a whole chapter to describing the biblical idea of truth. It is worth engaging a few quotes from this chapter:

> To cite just one book of the New Testament, the Gospel of John employs *aletheia* ("truth") and related words very frequently in a variety of settings. . . . John's understanding of truth presupposes a correspondence view of truth, but it also builds on this foundation theologically by adding specific content concerning the manifestation of truth in Jesus Christ (Jn 7:28; 8:16). (Groothuis, TD, 62)

> Both the Hebrew Scriptures and the New Testament draw a clear contrast between truth and error. John warns of distinguishing the "Spirit of truth and the spirit of falsehood" (1 Jn 4:6). Paul says that those who deny the reality of the God behind creation "suppress the truth by their wickedness" (Rom 1:18). Before Pilate, Jesus divided the field into truth and error: "For this reason I was born, and for this I came into the world, to testify to the

truth. Everyone on the side of truth listens to me" (Jn 18:37). Pilate took the side of falsehood. (Groothuis, TD, 63)

The Bible does not present truth as a cultural creation of the ancient Jews or the early Christians. They received truth from the God who speaks truth to his creatures, and they were expected by this God to conform themselves to this truth. (Groothuis, TD, 64)

Groothuis goes on to list eight distinctives of the biblical view of truth: (Groothuis, TD, 65–81)

1. Truth is revealed by God.
2. Objective truth exists and is knowable.
3. Christian truth is absolute in nature.
4. Truth is universal.
5. The truth of God is eternally engaging and momentous, not trendy or superficial.
6. Truth is exclusive, specific, and antithetical.
7. Truth, Christianly understood, is systematic and unified.
8. Christian truth is an end, not a means to any other end.

Kelly agrees with Groothuis. He explains that the biblical view of truth fits with the correspondence view of truth, but is also much richer:

Christians should also recognize that faithful Christianity concerns more than propositional truth. . . . Christian scholars have long pointed out that at the linguistic level the "truth" word group in the Bible covers a wide range of meanings. It may mean "faithful" or "trustworthy" or "reliable," as well as "conforming to reality" or "propositionally veridical [coinciding with reality]." . . .

A fully biblical view of truth would go beyond the propositional nature of truth, but it would never be less than that. The English word *true* "comes from the same etymological root as 'trust' and 'trustworthy,' and all these from the Indo-European root '*deru*' for 'tree,' suggesting uprightness and reliability generally." (Kelly, TCA, 313–314)

B. Ultimately Revealed in a Person

Jesus claims to be *the* truth. This claim has huge implications for our study on truth, since it suggests that it is impossible to know truth fully apart from a relationship with Jesus Christ as Savior and Lord. After commenting on how culture denies the truths of humanity being made in the image of God and that the body is a temple for the Lord, Zacharias shows how this works:

The Christian message is unique and brings a clue to help us break loose from this asphyxiating context. Just as wonder was found in a person, so the Scriptures claim and prove that truth is fully embodied in a person, the person of Jesus Christ. It is not merely that He has the answers to life's question as much as that He is the answer. Once again we find the truth

---

The Bible does not present truth as a cultural creation of the ancient Jews or the early Christians. They received truth from the God who speaks truth to his creatures, and they were expected by this God to conform themselves to this truth.

Douglas Groothuis

---

not merely in abstraction or creedal affirmations, but in knowing Him. When the apostle Thomas asked Jesus to show him the way to God, Jesus answered, "*I am the way and the truth and the life. No one comes to the Father except through me*" (John 14:6). (Zacharias, CMLWG, 100–101; emphasis in original)

He continues:

To restate, Jesus' absolute claim that He is the way, the truth, and the life means categorically that anything that contradicts what He says is by definition false. I challenge you to have the courage to study His claims and His teaching, and you will find a message that beautifully unfolds, encompassing the breadth of human need and the depth of human intellect. It is the beauty of Jesus' life that children can understand Him, and yet, the staunchest of skeptics such as Paul can ultimately bend that knee and call Him Lord. (Zacharias, CMLWG, 101)

This shows the ultimate answer to the ultimate pursuit. We have seen that truth is the most important endeavor we could ever undertake. Here we see that Jesus is the goal and fruition of all that searching.

CHAPTER 28

THE KNOWABILITY OF TRUTH

OVERVIEW

I. Introduction

A. We Can Know Truth

Having defined truth as the correspondence of our thoughts or statements to objective reality, we also must offer evidence that it is possible to *know* if they correspond—that is, whether we can actually *know* truth.

The field of philosophy that deals with *how we know* is called epistemology. Essentially, epistemology is the study of knowledge. For instance, the question, "Is there evidence for the existence of God?" is an epistemological question that deals with whether we *know* God exists or not. By contrast, the question, "Does God exist?" is a metaphysical question about whether or not God actually exists. There is a big difference between the existence of God and our *knowledge* of his existence. Epistemology deals with the latter issue.

In this chapter, our goal is not to explain fully how we know things. Rather, we aim to highlight something that we all intuitively know—*that we do in fact know certain things about reality*. Those who deny this obvious truth end up mired in contradiction. We do

621

not, then, conduct an exhaustive investigation of any specific way in which we know reality; rather we flesh out the reality that we do know truth.

This is an important distinction, because some contemporary philosophers deny that we can know reality, and ultimately truth; they make the mistake of attempting to construct epistemological systems to explain *how* we know reality without first acknowledging the fact that we *do* in fact know reality. After they begin within the mind and find that they cannot construct a bridge to reality, they then declare that we cannot know reality. It is like drawing a faulty road map *before* looking at the roads, then declaring that we cannot know how to get from Chicago to New York!

In this chapter, we consider specific instances where it is very clear that we do have knowledge. If it is true that in the following cases we do have knowledge, then it must be the case that we can in fact know truth.

B. The Problem of the Criterion

One of the most important debates in epistemology is known as "the problem of the criterion." The issue involves what we know and how we know it. In other words: *What do we know and what is our criterion for knowledge?*

There are three primary ways to resolve these questions. First, the skeptic either questions or denies that we have knowledge. For a response to skepticism, see chapter 30. The second response is called "methodism," which holds that we must first have a criterion before we can evaluate any knowledge claim. In other words, we begin with a criterion and then find claims that meet the chosen criterion. The problem with this claim, however, is that it leads to an infinite regress. For if each knowledge claim requires a criterion, then

that criterion would need a further criterion, and so on, ad infinitum. The third response is called "particularism." Philosopher J. P. Moreland explains:

> According to particularists, we start by knowing specific, clear items of knowledge: for example, that I had eggs for breakfast this morning; that there is a tree before me or, perhaps, that I seem to see a tree; that 7 + 5 = 12; that mercy is a virtue; and so on. I can know some things directly and simply without needing criteria for how I know them and without having to know *how* or even *that* I know them. We know many things without being able to prove that we do or without fully understanding them. We simply identify clear instances of knowing without having to possess or apply any criteria for knowledge. We may reflect on these instances and go on to develop criteria for knowledge consistent with them and use these criteria to make judgments in borderline cases of knowledge, but the criteria are justified by their congruence with specific instances of knowledge, and not the other way around. (Moreland, LYG, 140)

How does this work in practice? Moreland explains:

> I may start with moral knowledge (murder is wrong) and legal knowledge (taxes are to be paid by April 15) and go on to formulate criteria for when something is moral or legal. I could then use these criteria for judging borderline cases (intentionally driving on the wrong side of the street, for example). In general, we start with clear instances of knowledge, formulate criteria based on those clear instances, and extend our knowledge by using those criteria in borderline, unclear cases. (Moreland, LYG, 140–141)

In other words, humans operate by assuming that they have knowledge in some realms. We all do it. Even the skeptic who claims we cannot have knowledge assumes he knows we cannot have knowledge. Believing we really do have knowledge is inevitable. In this chapter, we do not develop an entire system for *how* we know things. Rather, we point out, and build upon, the fact that we really do know things.

II. The Knowability of Truth

A. First Principles of Logic

First principles are fundamental principles that we use in the demonstration of further principles. They provide the basis for all the conclusions drawn in any area of knowledge, whether in science or philosophy. Aristotle noted how evidence relies on first principles. He observed that "demonstration must depend on what is prior and more familiar." (Aristotle, *Posterior Analytics*, 1.3) "For it is impossible that there should be demonstration of absolutely everything; there would be an infinite regress, so that there would still be no demonstration." (Aristotle, *Metaphysics*, 4.4)

Thomas Aquinas clarifies what the term *principle* means. "Anything whence something proceeds in any way we call a principle." (Aquinas, ST, 173) A *first* principle, Aquinas says, "does not signify priority [in time], but origin." (Aquinas, ST, 173)

James B. Sullivan defines first principles as "the most general judgments conceivable and the most evident, *which presuppose no others in the same order for their proof, and are implicit in every judgement.*" (Sullivan, EFPT, 33)

Apologist Norman Geisler states that a first principle is

the ultimate starting point from which all conclusions may be drawn in a given area of

knowledge or reality. First principles are necessary constituents of all knowledge, but they do not supply any content of knowledge.... There are as many first principles as there are orders of knowledge and reality.... Since a first principle is that from which everything else in its order follows, first principles of knowledge are those basic premises from which all else follows in the realm of knowing. (Geisler, TA, 72–73)

A first principle is taken as a starting point, like a given in mathematics. It is the point of departure.

L. M. Regis states: "A first principle is, therefore, a first among firsts." He continues, "The expression *first principles* must therefore be understood to mean a group of judgments by which the intellect observes the existence of necessary bonds between several primary concepts, bonds that oblige it to identify them in affirmation or to separate them by negation." (Regis, *Epistemology*, 378)

B. The Need for First Principles

But do we need first principles? And if so, why? Aquinas states that there must be a beginning point of demonstration: "If there were an infinite regress in demonstrations, demonstration would be impossible, because the conclusion of any demonstration is made certain by reducing it to the first principle of demonstration." (Gardeil, IPSTA, 256)

Philosopher George Mavrodes argues that first principles are more basic than argumentation. He concludes that "if there is any knowledge at all then there must be some source of knowledge other than argumentation." (Mavrodes, BG, 49)

C. How Do We Know First Principles?
1. First Principles Are Self-Evident

By "self-evident" we mean truths that are not proven from anything else. They show themselves to be true. First principles, then, do not need to be deduced from other principles, and they become the basis of all knowledge. As Robert Audi says, "They are presumably called *self-evident* because they are thought to be evidently true taken by themselves, with no need of supporting evidence." (Audi, ECI, 104) They can play a role in demonstration, but they do not themselves require a demonstration. Audi goes on to say of self-evident truths, "Indeed, they are often considered *obvious* in themselves, roughly in the sense that simply upon attentively coming to understand them, one normally sees their truth and thereby knows them." (Audi, ECI, 104, emphasis in original) Aquinas says further that our intellect "cannot be in error with respect to those statements that are known as soon as the meaning of the terms is known, as with first principles, from which we proceed to conclusions whose scientific certitude has the infallibility of truth." (Aquinas, AR, 202)

Scott MacDonald comments that immediate propositions depend on reality. They are the factual basis of all inference, and it is impossible to be mistaken about them:

Which propositions are immediate, then, depends solely on what real natures there are and what relations hold among them, that is, on the basic structure of the world, and not on the psychology or belief-structure of any given epistemic subject. . . . Non-inferential justification, then, consists in one's being directly aware of the immediate facts that ground a proposition's necessary truth. When one sees that a proposition expresses an immediate fact of this sort, one cannot doubt its truth (since one cannot conceive of its being false) or be mistaken in holding it. (MacDonald, TK, 170–171)

MacDonald's point is that self-evident propositions are not filtered through any belief system, but rather they are simply true in virtue of "the basic structure of the world."

2. First Principles Are Derived from Reality

Now that we have a better understanding of what first principles are, we can look at whether we have any reason, apart from the assertion that they are self-evident, to think that we in fact know these first principles.

Aquinas states that the first thing we apprehend is being: "A certain order is to be found in those things that are apprehended universally. For that which, before aught else, falls under apprehension, is *being*, the notion of which is included in all things whatsoever a man apprehends." (Aquinas, ST, Q. 94, Art. 2)

Mortimer Adler points out that it is the mind that conforms to reality, not reality to the mind:

Underlying [the correspondence] definition of truth and falsity are two assumptions that Aristotle and Aquinas made, which, in my judgment, are philosophically defensible and tenable. The first is that there exists a reality that is independent of the human mind, to which the mind can either conform or fail to conform. In other words, what we think does not create or in any way affect what we are thinking about. It is what it is, whether we think about it or not and regardless of what we think about it. The second assumption is that this independent reality is completely determinate. This is Aristotle's metaphysical principle of contradiction. Nothing can both be and not be at the same time. Anything which does exist cannot both have and not have a certain attribute at one and the same time. (Adler, TR, 133)

As we see below, other first principles are reducible to the law of noncontradiction.

3. First Principles Are Undeniable

By saying that first principles are undeniable, we are not giving a positive evidence for first principles but negative evidence that first principles *cannot* be consistently denied. John Duns Scotus notes that Avicenna suggested, "Those who deny a first principle should be beaten or exposed to fire until they concede that to burn and not to burn, or to be beaten and not to be beaten, are not identical." (Scotus, PW, 9) While this is a bit extreme, it does make the point that first principles are undeniable.

More significantly, one must use first principles in any attempt to reject them. To this point, Geisler states,

First principles are undeniable or reducible to the undeniable. They are either self-evident or reducible to the self-evident. And self-evident principles are either true by their nature or undeniable because the predicate is reducible to the subject. That the predicate is reducible to the subject means that one cannot deny the principle without using it. For example the principle of noncontradiction cannot be denied without using it in the very denial. (Geisler, BECA, 250)

Philosopher Ronald Nash admits that no direct proof can be offered for the law of noncontradiction. But he notes that there are indirect arguments that can be put forward by highlighting the logical consequences that follow from its denial. Nash makes three points:

1. If the law of noncontradiction is denied, then significant thinking is impossible.

2. If the law of noncontradiction is denied, then significant human conduct is impossible.

3. If the law of noncontradiction is denied, then significant communication is impossible.

According to Nash, if denial of the law of noncontradiction leads to such absurdities, then there is no good reason to reject it, and we have indirect proof for its truth. (Nash, LUQ, 196)

Adler explains that common sense finds noncontradiction an undeniable attribute of reality:

Common sense would not hesitate for a moment to assert that at a given time a particular thing either exists or does not exist, that a certain event either occurred or did not occur, that something being considered either does or does not have a certain characteristic or attribute. Far from being an outrageous, not to say erroneous, assumption about the reality to which our beliefs or opinions may or may not correspond, this view of reality seems undeniable to common sense. (Adler, SGI, 36)

Any attempt, then, to disprove first principles ultimately fails, due to the nature of first principles. Because of the key role they play in demonstration and proofs, one cannot construct a demonstration or proof against first principles, because one would ultimately be using what he is trying to rid himself of.

4. First Principles Have Indemonstrability

We are not claiming indemonstrability (a proposition not subject to proof) is an evidence for first principles; rather we are only saying that indemonstrability is in fact true of first principles. Remember that there

Truths called self-evident provide the most obvious examples of knowledge in the strong sense of that term. They are called self-evident because our affirmation of them does not depend on evidence marshaled in support of them nor upon reasoning designed to show that they are conclusions validly reached by inference. We recognize their truth immediately or directly.

Mortimer Adler

is no other evidence for first principles except themselves—they are self-evident. They are our basis for all *other* demonstration and argumentation.

Aristotle states what *indemonstrable* means:

> But *we* say that neither is all understanding demonstrative, but in the case of the immediates it is non-demonstrable—and that this is necessary is evident; for if it is necessary to understand the things which are prior and on which the demonstration depends, and it comes to a stop at some time, it is necessary for these immediates to be non-demonstrable. (Aristotle, *Posterior Analytics* 1.3, emphasis in original)

Aquinas illustrates the futility of an infinite regress of demonstrations:

> Suppose that someone who has a demonstration [for a given conclusion] syllogizes on the basis of demonstrable (or mediate) premises. That person either possesses a demonstration for these premises or he does not. If he does not, then he does not have *scientia* with respect to the premises, and so does not have *scientia* with respect to the conclusion that he holds on account of the premise either. But if he possesses a demonstration for the premises, he will arrive at some premises that are immediate and indemonstrable, since

in the case of demonstrations one cannot go on ad infinitum. . . . And so it must be that demonstration proceeds from immediate premises either directly or indirectly through other mediating [propositions]. (quoted in MacDonald, TK, 168)

Alasdair MacIntyre states clearly: "Argument *to* first principles cannot be demonstrative, for demonstration is *from* first principles." (MacIntyre, FPFE, 35) Mortimer Adler argues that there is no evidence for a self-evident truth other than itself:

> Truths called self-evident provide the most obvious examples of knowledge in the strong sense of that term. They are called self-evident because our affirmation of them does not depend on evidence marshaled in support of them nor upon reasoning designed to show that they are conclusions validly reached by inference. We recognize their truth immediately or directly from our understanding of what they assert. We are convinced—convinced, not persuaded—of their truth because we find it impossible to think the opposite of what they assert. We are in no sense free to think the opposite. (Adler, SGI, 52)

D. Examples of First Principles

We now look at some specific examples of first principles.

1. Identity (B Is B)

Many philosophers consider identity the most simple of all relations. Simply put, identity is the relation that everything has to itself. I am identical to myself, the chair you are sitting in is identical to itself, and for any other object we could think of, no matter how little we may know about it, we can know for certain that it is identical to itself. From an understanding of what identity means, logicians and philosophers alike have been able to derive certain first principles relating to identity.

We consider four key aspects of identity: the law of the indiscernibility of identicals, the reflexivity of identity, the symmetry of identity, and the transitivity of identity.

a. The Laws of the Indiscernibility of Identicals

This law is well known to philosophers and is relatively uncontroversial. The authors of the book *Language, Proof, and Logic* summarize this principle, saying that "if we can prove, from whatever our premises happen to be, that b = c, then we know that anything that is true of b is also true of c. After all, b *is* c." (Barker-Plummer, Barwise, and Etchemendy, LPL, 49) To put it more simply, we can take C. Anthony Anderson's phrasing: "For any *x* and *y*, if *x* is identical with *y*, then whatever is true of *x* is true of *y* and vice versa." (Anderson, IEL, 55)

But what does this actually mean? Well, let's take the example of Mark Twain and Samuel Clemens. Mark Twain was a famous author of books such as *The Adventures of Huckleberry Finn*. Yet as many people know, his given name was Samuel Clemens, not Mark Twain. There are two names for the same person. If Samuel Clemens was born in 1835, you automatically know that the same is true for Mark Twain. How were you able to do that? Whether you realized it or not,

you used the law of identity known as the indiscernibility of identicals. Although there are two distinct names, you knew that both "Mark Twain" and "Samuel Clemens" refer to the same person. Therefore, if something is true of one of them (e.g., birth year), you automatically know that it applies to the other.

This deduction may seem like common sense, but it is crucial for making important distinctions about truth. If two things are identical, then they share all properties in common. To show, then, that two referents are not identical, we merely need to show *one* difference between them. For instance, some claim the brain and mind are identical, that the mind *is* the brain. But to disprove this claim, we need only to demonstrate one property that is true of the mind that is not true of the brain, or vice versa. And this is easy to do. The brain has mass, color, extension in space, and a particular odor. But the mind has none of these properties. The mind is immaterial and has ideas *about* things (which is not true for physical things). Therefore "mind" and "brain" are not identical.

b. The Reflexivity of Identity

The reflexivity of identity is another important aspect of identity. Anderson sums up this idea well when he says that "pretty clearly everything is identical with itself." (Anderson, IEL, 55) As we described in the beginning of this section, this is just what identity means. Identity is the relation of things to themselves. The atmosphere stands in the "above" relation to the ground; elephants stand in the "bigger than" relation to ants; and everything whatsoever stands in the "identity" relation to itself. Barker-Plummer and colleagues say that one can validly infer that something is identical to itself "from whatever premises are at hand, or from no premises at all." (Barker-Plummer et al., LPL, 50) This means that if Person A were to state that something is identical to itself and Person B demanded that Person A provide a proof for this statement, Person A would be under no obligation to provide such a proof. This is partially because no such proof exists other than to refer back to what identity actually means. To say something is identical to itself is just to express what identity means, and rejection of a statement such as a = a tells us more about the person's misunderstanding of the concept of identity than it tells us about the properties of "a."

c. The Symmetry of Identity

The symmetry of identity is the property of identity that "allows us to conclude b = a from a = b." (Barker-Plummer, Barwise, and Etchemendy, LPL, 50) Anderson summarizes this principle saying that "if one thing is identical with a second, then the second is identical with the first." (Anderson, IEL, 55) All this principle is saying is that identity is a two-way street. If you are identical with something, that something is identical with you. Take, for example, Peter Parker and Spider-Man. If Spider-Man is Peter Parker, then it follows that Peter Parker is Spider-Man. The order of the names is irrelevant. It would make no sense to say that Spider-Man is the very same thing as Peter Parker, but that Peter Parker is not in fact the very same thing as Spider-Man. In saying that the first is the second, we are affirming the fact that the second is the first.

d. The Transitivity of Identity

The last essential property of identity in our discussion is the transitivity of identity. Anderson puts the idea this way: "If one thing is identical with another and the second with a third, then the first is identical with the third." (Anderson, IEL, 55) It might be easiest

to think about this property of identity in a case where a single person has three or more titles or roles. If the mayor of a small town is also the judge, and the judge of that small town is also the jailer, then we know that the mayor of that small town is also the jailer. How do we know this? Simple: because there is only one person that we are talking about. The mayor and the judge are identical, meaning there is only one person; that is to say, the mayor and the judge are the very same thing. Additionally, we know that the judge and the jailer are identical, meaning that, again, there is only one person we are talking about. But there is an overlap in these two cases. The judge is the *very same thing* as both the mayor and the jailer. We can deduce that the mayor and the jailer are in fact identical, because they are one in the same person.

2. Law of Noncontradiction (B Is Not Non-B)
a. Definition

Aquinas provides a helpful definition of the law of noncontradiction: "The first indemonstrable principle is that *the same thing cannot be affirmed and denied at the same time,* which is based on the notion of *being* and *not-being*: and on this principle all others are based." (Aquinas, ST Q. 94, Art. 2, emphasis in original)

Plato's definition in *The Republic* adds a quality that people often quote, that a thing cannot be true at the same time *and in the same way*: "It is clear that one thing cannot act in opposite ways or be in opposite states at the same time and in the same part of itself in relation to the same other things." (Plato, R, 436b)

b. Foundational

Aristotle considered the law of noncontradiction to be foundational for all other knowledge:

The most certain principle of all is that regarding which it is impossible to be mistaken; for such a principle must be both the best known . . . and non-hypothetical. . . . This, then, is the most certain of all principles, since it answers to the definition given above. For it is impossible for anyone to believe the same thing to be and not to be. . . . This is naturally the starting-point even for all the other axioms. (Aristotle, *Metaphysics* 4.3)

c. The Nature of the Law of Noncontradiction

Adler notes that the law of noncontradiction deals with both metaphysics (being) and epistemology (knowing):

Among the first principles of Greek logic is the rule governing the truth and falsity of incompatible propositions: either that both cannot be true, though both may be false, or that one must be true and the other must be false. Underlying this rule is an ontological [metaphysical] axiom—a truth about reality—that the Greeks thought was self-evident; namely, that nothing can both be and not be at the same time. (Adler, TR, 70–71)

d. The Law of Noncontradiction Is Self-Evidently True

And as with the other first principles, the law of noncontradiction is self-evident. Adler explains:

The law of [non] contradiction, as a statement about reality, says what is immediately obvious to common sense. A thing—whatever it may be—cannot both exist and not exist at the same time. It either exists or it does not exist, but not both at once. A thing cannot have a certain attribute and not have that attribute at the same time. The apple in my hand that I am looking at cannot, at this instance, be both red in color and not red in color.

This is so very obvious that Aristotle calls the law of [non] contradiction self-evident. Its self-evidence, for him, means its undeniability. It is impossible to think that the apple is both red and not red at the same time. (Adler, AE, 140)

3. Law of Excluded Middle (Either B or Non-B)
a. Definition

Geisler provides a helpful definition: "Since being and nonbeing are opposites (i.e., contradictory), and opposites cannot be the same, nothing can hide in the 'cracks' between being and nonbeing. The only choices are being and nonbeing." (Geisler, BECA, 251)

b. Example

Consider the abortion debate. Scott Klusendorf, perhaps the most articulate spokesperson for the pro-life position in America, is often asked to debate pro-abortion advocates at universities and other public settings. He often begins his argument in this manner: "We should allow abortions in all nine months of pregnancy as is currently legally allowed in the United States." At this point, all the pro-lifers who thought Scott was on their side are confused until he says the magic word *if*. "Abortion should only be legal *if* it can be demonstrated that the unborn are not members of the human family." According to the law of excluded middle, the unborn is either a human person or not a human person—there is no middle ground. There are significant moral implications that flow from whether or not the unborn is a human person. Clarifying whether the unborn is a human person of equal worth and due dignity, in turn, clarifies the entire debate. And the law of excluded middle helps us know that there are only two options— either the unborn *is* a human person or it is *not* a human person. (Klusendorf, CL, 23–25)

4. Tautologies

The word *tautology* is a very technical term that is used in logic. (It differs from the more familiar use of the word for the unnecessary restatement of an idea with additional words but no new content—a rhetorical tautology.) Gerald Runkle tells us that in the study of logic, "a *tautology* is a sentence which cannot possibly be false. The structure of the sentence itself guarantees its truth." (Runkle, GT, 94) To see the truth of a tautology, "all we need understand is the syntax of the sentence. Our confidence is based not on a factual investigation of the world but on analysis of language." (Runkle, GT, 94–95) Richard Jeffery expands on this saying that "the sentences [A or not-A] and [B or not-B] are *logical truths* or *tautologies* since they are true in every case concerning the truth and falsity of sentence letters." (Jeffery, FL, 30) In his statement, "[A or not-A]" is called a sentence because logic uses a formula to present a statement; the "sentence letters" A or B could be replaced by any other letter. What he is saying is that (as in algebra) we can plug anything we like into A or B and evaluate it, in this case, with confidence that the sentence (that is, the expression marked within the square brackets) is true, because *either A or not-A* is true. Jeffery reminds us that "to know that either of them is true, we need not know which case is actual." (Jeffery, FL, 30) In other words, to know that the proposition "A or not-A" is true, we do not need to know specifically which of the two choices *is* true; instead we only need to know (by the law of noncontradiction) that *one* of the two must be true.

E. The Mind Is Predisposed to Truth

Aristotle states that the mind is predisposed to truth: "Truth is the intellect's good and the term of its natural ordination; and

just as things without knowledge are moved toward their end without knowing it, so sometimes does the human intellect tend toward truth although it does not perceive its nature." (Aristotle, *Physics*, 10.5)

Aquinas observes that the mind has a natural appetite for truth. He explains what he means by this: "The *natural appetite* is that inclination which each thing has, of its own nature, for something; wherefore by its natural appetite each power desires something suitable to itself." (Aquinas, ST, Q. 78, Art. 1) Adler clarifies that we do not have certainty about all truth, only about self-evident truths:

> The human mind has a grasp on the truth to whatever extent the judgments it makes agree with or conform to reality—to the way things are or are not. To say this does not involve us in claiming that the human mind has a firm, final, and incorrigible grasp on any truth, though I personally think that there is a relatively small number of self-evident truths on which our grasp is firm, final, and incorrigible. However that may be, we must acknowledge that truth is *in principle* attainable, even though we may never in fact actually attain it. (Adler, TR, 116–117, emphasis in original)

III. Responding to Objections

A. First Principles Are Only a Western Way of Thinking

Alan Watts was an Anglican priest who became a Buddhist. After attempting to blend Christianity and Buddhism, he eventually concluded that they are irreconcilable. In offering justification for his conversion, he argued that reality is not governed or bound by logic. Ultimately he concluded that reality is nonrational. Theologian and analytic philosopher Paul Copan comments on the contradictory means of his justification:

Watts dismissed the rationality of Christianity . . . as useless "Western logic." But there's a catch: to reject Christianity, *Watts used the very logic he denied as valid.* He knew that Christianity and Buddhism were incompatible, and he assumed that he had a yardstick to judge Christianity as being wrong. Yet as he *chose* "Eastern logic" (the absorbent "both/and" kind) rather than "Western logic" (the "either/or" kind), he had to use the "either/or" method in his selection. Put baldly, he had to *use* "Western" (or Aristotelian) logic in order to reject "Western" logic. (Copan, TYNM, 29, emphasis in original)

Speaker, author, and apologist Ravi Zacharias tells the following story that further illuminates the futility of this line of argument:

As the professor waxed eloquent and expounded on the law of noncontradiction, he eventually drew his conclusion: "This [either/or logic] is a Western way of looking at reality. . . . The real problem is that you are seeing that contradiction as a Westerner when you should be approaching it as an Easterner. The both/and is the Eastern way of viewing reality." After he had belabored these two ideas of either/or and both/and for some time . . . I finally asked if I could interrupt his unpunctuated train of thought and raise one question. . . . I said, "Sir, are you telling me

that when I am studying Hinduism I *either* use the both/and system of logic *or* nothing else?" There was pin-drop silence for what seemed an eternity. I repeated my question: "Are you telling me that when I am studying Hinduism I *either* use the both/and logic *or* nothing else? Have I got that right?" He threw his head back and said, "The either/or does seem to emerge, doesn't it?" "Indeed, it does emerge," I said. "And as a matter of fact, even in India we look both ways before we cross the street—it is either the bus or me, not both of us." Do you see the mistake he was making? He was using the either/or logic in order to prove the both/and. The more you try to hammer the law of noncontradiction, the more it hammers you. (Zacharias, CMLWG, 128–129, emphasis in original)

B. Logical Laws Don't Apply to Reality

Nash answers:

The law of noncontradiction is not simply a law of thought. It is a law of thought because it is first a law of being. Nor is the law something someone can take or leave. The denial of the law of noncontradiction leads to absurdity. It is impossible meaningfully to deny the laws of logic. If the law of noncontradiction is denied, then nothing has meaning. If the laws of logic do not first mean what they say, nothing else can have meaning, including the denial of the laws. (Nash, WC, 84)

The law of noncontradiction is not simply a law of thought. It is a law of thought because it is first a law of being. Nor is the law something someone can take or leave. The denial of the law of noncontradiction leads to absurdity. It is impossible meaningfully to deny the laws of logic. If the law of noncontradiction is denied, then nothing has meaning.

Ronald Nash

Rudolph G. Bandas concurs:

If the notion of being does not possess onto-logical value, the principle of contradiction would be a law of logic but not necessarily of reality. This supposition, however, is even subjectively unthinkable: The idea of being is absolutely simple and nothing can correspond to it only partially. Whatever conforms to it is being; whatever does not, is nonbeing. Our intelligence and act of knowing, then, are essentially intentional and relative to being. If this relation is denied, everything becomes unintelligible. (Bandas, CPTP, 65)

Nash explains the absurdity of the claim that logic does not apply to reality:

There is no quicker way to become swallowed up in nonsense than to deny the distinction between B and non-B. I once heard a young man who was called into his local office of the Internal Revenue Service for an audit. The reason for his trouble was his failure over several years to file a tax return. When asked by the IRS agent why he had failed to file, the youth replied that in college he had learned that the law of noncontradiction is an optional, nonnecessary principle. Once he had learned that there is no difference between B and non-B, it was only a matter of time before he realized that no difference exists between filing a tax return and not filing a tax return. "That's very interesting," said the tax agent. "I've never heard that one before. Since you believe that no difference exists between B and non-B, I'm sure you also believe that there is no difference between being in jail and not being in jail." (Nash, LUQ, 195)

C. Defending the Law of Contradiction Is Circular

Norman Geisler notes:

This objection confuses the issue. For the law of noncontradiction is not used as the *basis* of the indirect proof of its validity; it is simply used in the *process* of defending its validity. Take, for example, the statement "I cannot speak a word in English." This statement is self-destructive, since it does what it says it cannot do. It uses English to deny that it can use English. So it disproves itself. The indirect proof for the law of noncontradiction is similar. We cannot deny the law of noncontradiction without using it in the very sentence that denies it. For the sentence that denies noncontradiction is offered as a noncontradictory sentence. If it is not, then it makes no sense. In like manner, if I say "I can utter a word in English," it is obvious that I uttered a word in English in the process of doing so. But there is nothing self-defeating about using English to say I can use English. There is only something self-defeating about using English to deny I can use English. Like-wise, there is nothing wrong with using the principle of noncontradiction to defend the principle of noncontradiction. There is only something wrong about using the principle of noncontradiction to deny that principle. (Geisler, TA, 79)

D. There Is No Truth That Corresponds to Reality

Zacharias points out the self-defeating nature of this truth statement: "For anyone to take seriously the statement that there is no truth that corresponds to reality defeats the statement itself by implying that it is not reflective of reality. If a statement is not reflective of reality, why take it seriously? Truth as a category must exist even while one is denying its existence and must also afford the possibility of being known." (Zacharias, CMLWG, 125)

Geisler explains that

even the intentionalist theory depends on the correspondence theory view. The intentionalist theory [is a pragmatic theory that] claims something is true if the accomplishments correspond to the intentions. Without correspondence of intentions and accomplished facts there is no truth. (Geisler, WIBT, 38, emphasis in original)

E. If All Argumentation Needs a Basis, Then What About First Principles?

The claim is not that every statement needs a basis. Rather, as Geisler notes, "once one arrives at the self-evident, it need not be evident in terms of anything else." (Geisler, BECA, 260) This is a crucial point to remember when discussing this issue with those who demand evidence for first principles: *there is no evidence for first principles other than themselves—they simply are self-evident.*

F. Not Everyone Sees These Principles As Self-Evident

This may be true. However,

simply because some things are not evident to everyone does not mean they are not self-evident in themselves. The reason a self-evident truth may not be evident to someone could be because the person has not analyzed it carefully. But their failure in no way invalidates the self-evident nature of the first principles. (Geisler, BECA, 260)

IV Conclusion

All thinking, including thinking about knowledge, must begin with something. Even Descartes's famous effort to exclude everything he could possibly doubt left him with the unassailable starting point that he was in fact thinking. That need to take certain first principles as a point of departure for

a working hypothesis (while acknowledging the assumptions that are being made) underwrites both modern science and good business management.

In this chapter we have explored the parallel role of initial, intuitive truths for epistemology. We ask whether and how we can know what we know. A key term, "the hermeneutical circle," describes our efforts to interpret (that is, our hermeneutics) as a process that operates in a circular fashion. Whether we aim to interpret a text or the world, we make a beginning and then examine the information—and when we are stumped, we circle back to check our starting point. Without a conscious beginning point, we are left with agnosticism or an interrogation of regress back into an abyss of ignorance.

If this sounds abstract, perhaps the following example may help. A twelve-year-old boy repeated to his nine-year-old sister what he was being taught—in a middle-school class, no less—that you can't know truth, you just know what you think. They argued, but neither would budge. What cleared the air was this counsel: In a way, yes, you do *start* from the position of what you think, but you *need to and can choose* your place to start, just as, for instance, you choose where to jump onto a moving merry-go-round. But once there, knowing you've chosen that initial point, you start testing what you see—and if you were wrong, you can jump off. That is, you can be self-critical about your first principles but you must use them to think at all, and from that beginning, you can test and know truth. Mortimer Adler describes that process of starting with self-evident truth and testing our growing understanding this way:

I will be using the term "knowledge" to cover the necessary and self-evident truths we know with certitude and also the opinions we are able to assert on the basis of sufficient evidence and reasons to outweigh any contrary opinions. I will be using it to cover things about which we can say both that we know them and also that we believe them, because some measure of doubt remains about them. (Adler, TPM, 90)

Hans-Georg Gadamer, in *Truth and Method*, describes this circular process as it is used in reading, although he says that it is "a procedure that we in fact exercise whenever we understand anything." (Gadamer, TM, 267) We begin with an initial meaning, which we project upon the matter at hand. We come to the text expecting it to have something to tell us but knowing (1) that other possibilities of meaning exist and (2) that we have necessarily brought some assumptions to our engagement with it. We will be brought up short (or taken aback) when our expectations do not fit what the text seems to say to us. The situation is rather like a conversation: both we and the text's author (or first readers) have questions in mind, questions that hover behind what we may at first think is the meaning of what we read, hear, or see. Those questions, rising from our situatedness in a time and place (like the twelve-year-old above) create a horizon around each party to the conversation. With awareness, the two horizons may come to overlap in a community of meaning. (Gadamer, TM, 265–270) Starting from first principles, we may extend our knowledge to receive the new. The hermeneutical circle applies to both life and reading, and in both we may become aware of our presuppositions, know our starting point, and proceed with the confidence that we can—and do in fact—know truth.

CHAPTER 29

ANSWERING POSTMODERNISM

OVERVIEW

I. What Is Postmodernism?

Though contemporary culture is largely pervaded by postmodern philosophy, many find it difficult to describe exactly what postmodernism is. Postmodern thought is often seen as being connected to the idea that truth is relative—in other words, that truth can be seen as variable according to whoever relates to it. Maybe you have heard someone say, "Well, that's your truth," or, "There is no such thing as absolute truth." Or you may have heard that truth is really dependent upon such things as culture, education, gender, race, etc. In one way or another such statements may refer to a particular aspect of postmodern thought, but they are of little help in understanding the concept itself.

The term *postmodern* has actually been in use for quite some time. In Arnold Toynbee's twelve-volume *A Study of History* (1934–61), he coined the term *postmodernism* to describe what he saw as the beginning of a new historical epoch of "mass" culture that after about 1875 would signal the decline of Western civilization's confidence in its own capitalistic culture. The word has also been used in connection with the arts, theater, and architecture since the 1930s. (Grenz, PP, 16) However, Jean-Francois Lyotard may rightfully be credited with placing the word *postmodern* into the philosophical lexicon with his influential work *The Postmodern Condition: A Report on Knowledge,* published in 1979. (Lyotard and Bennington, PC, xxiii)

Lyotard offers a Spartan definition of postmodernism: "An incredulity toward Metanarratives." (Lyotard and Bennington, PC, xxiv) This definition, while concise, is not itself illuminating until its terms are understood. *The Oxford Dictionary of Philosophy* defines it this way: "In its poststructuralist aspects it includes a denial of any fixed meaning, or any correspondence between language and the world, or any fixed reality or truth or fact to be the object of enquiry." (Blackburn, ODP, 284) While giving us more to consider, this definition also needs expansion because it defines postmodernism only in negative terms.

Richard Tarnas, a cultural historian, provides a more robust introduction to the concept of postmodernism:

> What is called postmodern varies considerably according to context, but in its most general and widespread form, the postmodern mind may be viewed as an open-ended, indeterminate set of attitudes that has been shaped by a great diversity of intellectual and cultural currents; these range from pragmatism, existentialism, Marxism, and psychoanalysis to feminism, hermeneutics, deconstruction, and postempiricist philosophy of science, to cite only a few of the more prominent. . . . There is an appreciation of the plasticity and constant change of reality and knowledge, a stress on the priority of concrete experience over fixed abstract principles, and a conviction that no single *a priori* thought system should govern belief or investigation. It is recognized that human knowledge is subjectively determined by a multitude of factors; that objective essences, or things-in-themselves, are neither accessible nor positable. (Tarnas, PWM, 395–396)

Even though this longer explanation seems more comprehensible than the previous, more abbreviated versions, it appears that the more one says about postmodernism, the more difficult it becomes to put a finger on exactly what it entails. Given the intrinsically broad and diffuse nature of postmodern thought, an in-depth study of postmodernism would be well beyond the scope of this work. So, we will attempt only to illumine the basic concepts of postmodernism by looking at some of its most influential thinkers. In so doing, we consider a range of thinking often referred to as being postmodern.

A. Rejection of All Metanarratives

Not only did Lyotard's *Postmodern Condition* establish the word *postmodern* in the philosophical lexicon, it also articulated a central tenet of postmodern thought: "incredulity toward Metanarratives." As we have seen, for Lyotard, this simple expression captured the essence of that which he considered postmodern. But his definition raises two questions: What is a Metanarrative, and why would one want to express incredulity toward them?

Walter Truett Anderson describes a Metanarrative "as a story big enough and meaningful enough to pull together philosophy and research and politics and art, relate them to one another, and—above all—give them a unifying sense of direction. Lyotard cited as examples the Christian religious story of God's will being worked out on Earth, the Marxist political story of class conflict and revolution, and the Enlightenment's intellectual story of rational progress." (Anderson, TAT, 4) Lyotard adds that narratives "determine criteria of competence and/or illustrate how they are to be applied. They thus define what has the right to be said and done in the culture in question." (Lyotard and Bennington, PC, 23)

Postmodern thinkers view Metanarratives as meaningless. To understand why, it is helpful to consider them from the perspective of Lyotard, whose view of Metanarrative was largely informed by Ludwig Wittgenstein's notion of language games. Lyotard explains, "What he [Wittgenstein] means by this term [language-game] is that each of the various categories of utterance can be defined in terms of rules specifying their properties and the uses to which they can be put—in exactly the same way as the game of chess is defined by a set of rules determining the properties of each of the pieces, in other words, the proper way to move them." (Lyotard and Bennington, PC, 10)

Wittgenstein observes that "there are countless kinds [of sentences]: countless different kinds of use of what we call 'symbols,' 'words,' 'sentences.' And this multiplicity is not something fixed, given once for all; but new types of language, new language-games, as we may say, come into existence, and others become obsolete and get forgotten." He describes a "multiplicity of language-games," such as "giving orders, and obeying them . . . describing the appearance of an object . . . reporting an event . . . solving a problem in practical arithmetic . . . asking, thanking, cursing, greeting, praying." (Wittgenstein, PI, 11–12)

Lyotard notes not only the unavoidable nature of language-games, but also the uniqueness of each game. He states "that even an infinitesimal modification of one rule alters the nature of the game" and "every utterance should be thought of as a 'move' in a game." (Lyotard and Bennington, PC, 10) Thus, though there exists a vast array of individual games, the authority of any particular game is limited by its unique nature. Or, stated differently, the rules of each game apply only to itself. Lyotard declares

that "the 'moves' judged to be 'good' in one cannot be of the same type as those judged 'good' in another, unless it happens that way by chance." (Lyotard and Bennington, PC, 26) This is analogous to there being no universal sense of English, only particular instances of the English language, such as those written and spoken in Britain in the time of Jane Austen.

As Stanley Grenz observes, "Postmodern thinkers have given up the search for universal, ultimate truth because they are convinced that there is nothing more to find than a host of conflicting interpretations or an infinity of linguistically created worlds." (Grenz, PP, 163) According to Grenz, postmodern thinkers do not deny the existence of truth but rather assert that our linguistic blinders prevent us from knowing what that truth is. Pauline Marie Rosenau sums up the posture of postmodernism toward overarching narratives:

> Post-modernism challenges global, all-encompassing world views, be they political, religious, or social. It reduces Marxism, Christianity, Fascism, Stalinism, capitalism, liberal democracy, secular humanism, feminism, Islam, and modern science, to the same order and dismisses them all as logocentric [Derrida's term that is an adjective used to describe systems of thought that claim legitimacy by reference to external, universally truthful propositions], totalizing Metanarratives that anticipate all questions and provide predetermined answers. All such systems of thought rest on assumptions no more or no less certain than those of witchcraft, astrology, or primitive cults. The postmodern goal is not to formulate an alternative set of assumptions but to register the impossibility of establishing any such underpinning for knowledge. (Rosenau, PMSS, 6)

Simply put, from this view a Metanarrative is not just a big story, but one told from a distinctly modern standpoint—a view that presupposes our ability to access and directly perceive universal, ahistorical truths without consideration of our own intrinsically limited perspective.

B. Rejection of Truth
1. The Tenets of Modernism

Postmodernism sets itself up in contrast to modernism. To understand postmodern thought, then, we must understand what constitutes modern thought. An in-depth understanding would require exploring issues more nuanced and complex than we can cover in a short chapter. Fortunately, Millard Erickson provides a helpful list that allows us to survey several of the more salient features of modernism:

- Naturalism. Reality is believed to be restricted to the observable system of nature. Its immanent laws [what David Hume called the "general laws" of nature, operating without any intervention by a transcendent God] are the cause of all that occurs.
- Humanism. The human is the highest reality and value, the end for which all of reality exists rather than the means to the service of some higher being.
- The scientific method. Knowledge is good and can be attained by humans. The method best suited for this enterprise is the scientific method, which came to fruition during this period [of modernity]. Observation and experimentation are the sources from which our knowledge of truth is built up.
- Reductionism. From being considered the best means for gaining knowledge, the scientific method came increasingly to be considered the only method, so that various disciplines sought to attain the objectivity and precision of the natural sciences. Humans in some cases were regarded as nothing but highly developed animals.
- Progress. Because knowledge is good, humanly attainable, and growing, we are progressively overcoming the problems that have beset the human race.
- Nature. Rather than being fixed and static, nature came to be thought of as dynamic, growing, and developing. Thus it was able to produce the changes in life forms through immanent processes of evolution, rather than requiring explanation in terms of a creator and designer.
- Certainty. Because knowledge was seen as objective, it could attain certainty. This required foundationalism, the belief that it is possible to base knowledge on some sort of absolute first principles.
- Determinism. There was a belief that what happened in the universe followed from fixed causes. Thus, the scientific method could discover these laws of regularity that controlled the universe. Not only physical occurrences but human behavior were believed to be under this etiological control.
- Individualism. The ideal of the knower was the solitary individual, carefully protecting his or her objectivity by weighing all options. Truth being objective, individuals can discover it by their own efforts. They can free themselves from the conditioning particularities of their own time and place and know reality as it is in itself.
- Anti-authoritarianism. The human was considered the final and most complete measure of truth. Any externally imposed authority, whether that of the group or of a supernatural being, must be subjected to scrutiny and criticism by human reason. (Erickson, PF, 16–17)

Postmodern thought essentially rejects, undermines, and calls into question these modern ideas.

2. The Influence of Immanuel Kant

Along with René Descartes, Immanuel Kant is commonly acknowledged as one of the founders of modern thought. Ironically, Kant may also have sown the seeds for the rejection of modernism. As Tarnas notes, Kant is credited with articulating the view that "the human mind can claim no direct mirrorlike knowledge of the objective world." (Tarnas, PWM, 417) Paul Guyer and Allen W. Wood tell of Kant asserting, "The 'laws of intuitive cognition,' or the laws of the representation of things by means of the senses, characterize how things necessarily *appear* to us, but not how they actually are in themselves." (Kant, CPR, 36) Thus, Kant notes that our sensibility and intellect present us with two different accounts of objects. (Kant, CPR, 36)

Kant not only speaks of differences between how things appear and how things are in themselves, but he also introduces a fundamental change of orientation. He states, "Up to now it has been assumed that all our cognition must conform to the objects. . . . [L]et us once try whether we do not get farther with the problems of metaphysics by assuming that the objects must conform to our cognition." He continues, "This would be just like the first thoughts of Copernicus, who, when he did not make good progress in the explanation of the celestial motions if he assumed that the entire celestial host revolves around the observer, tried to see if he might not have greater success if he made the observer revolve and left the stars at rest." (Kant, CPR, 110)

Tarnas notes, "Kant's penetrating critique had effectively pulled the rug out from under the human mind's pretensions to certain knowledge of things in themselves, eliminating in principle any human cognition of the ground of the world." (Tarnas, PWM, 351)

C. Truth Does Not Correspond to Reality
1. Truth As Illusion

There are differing perspectives within postmodernism as to the perceived disconnect between truth and reality. One view, articulated by Nietzsche, maintains that truth is an illusion, declaring,

What then is truth? A mobile army of metaphors, metonymies, and anthropomorphisms—in short, a sum of human relations, which have been enhanced, transposed, and embellished poetically and rhetorically, and which after long use seem firm, canonical, and obligatory to a people: truths are illusions about which one has forgotten that this is what they are; metaphors which are worn out and without sensuous power; coins which have lost their pictures and now matter only as metal, no longer as coins. (Nietzsche, PN, 46–47)

2. Truth As Relative

Another perspective is that truth is distinctly relative in nature. As Tarnas declares, "The mind is not the passive reflector of an external world and its intrinsic order, but is active and creative in the process of perception and cognition. Reality [truth] is in some sense constructed by the mind, not simply perceived by it, and many such constructions are possible, none necessarily sovereign." (Tarnas, PWM, 396) He concludes by stating, "The nature of truth and reality . . . is radically ambiguous." (Tarnas, PWM, 397)

3. Truth As Pragmatic

Richard Rorty, a philosopher who taught at Princeton University, the University of Virginia, and Stanford University, articulates a third perspective, that of the pragmatist: "Pragmatists tell us, it is the vocabulary of practise rather than of theory, of action rather than contemplation, in which one can say something useful about truth." (Rorty, CP, 162) The pragmatist "drops the notion of truth as correspondence with reality altogether, and says that modern science does not enable us to cope because it corresponds, it just plain enables us to cope." (Rorty, CP, xvii) Rorty elsewhere asserts "that truth is made rather than found. What is true about this claim is just that languages are made rather than found, and that truth is a property of linguistic entities, of sentences." (Rorty, CIS, 7)

Although Rorty sees truth as being "made rather than found," he is not a relativist, declaring, "The pragmatist does not have a theory of truth, much less a relativistic one. As a partisan of solidarity, his account of the value of cooperative human inquiry has only an ethical base, not an epistemological or metaphysical one. Not having any epistemology, *a fortiori* he does not have a relativistic one." (Rorty, ORT, 24) He observes that "several hundred years of effort have failed to make interesting sense of the notion of 'correspondence' (either of thoughts to things or of words to things)," and that "there is no interesting work to be done" with regard to defining terms like *good* or *true*. (Rorty, CP, xvii, xiv)

4. Concluding Thoughts About Truth

Grenz offers a perspective which summarizes the general tenor of these thoughts: "Postmodern thinkers no longer find this grand realist ideal [that truth ultimately corresponds to reality] tenable. . . . They argue that we do not simply encounter a world that is 'out there' but rather that we construct the world using concepts we bring to it. They

contend that we have no fixed vantage point beyond our own structuring of the world from which to gain a purely objective view of whatever reality might be out there." (Grenz, PP, 41)

D. Truth Cannot Be Perceived— Epistemic Isolation

Postmodernism offers a number of arguments as to why truth cannot be apprehended. Among them are the views that reality is inaccessible, that justifying belief entails an unbridgeable, infinite regress, and that the entire notion of epistemological justification should be rejected. (See section II.B for a brief description of epistemic justification.)

1. Truth Is Inaccessible

Regarding truth's inaccessibility, Tarnas explains: "It is recognized that human knowledge is subjectively determined by a multitude of factors; that objective essences, or things-in-them-selves, are neither accessible nor positable; and that the value of all truths and assumptions must be continually subjected to direct testing. The critical search for truth is constrained to be tolerant of ambiguity and pluralism, and its outcome will necessarily be knowledge that is relative and fallible rather than absolute or certain." (Tarnas, PWM, 395–396)

2. Truth Needs a Starting Point

Anthony Quinton speaks to a different problem—that of identifying a solid starting point for justified belief. He states, "If any beliefs are to be justified at all . . . there must be some terminal beliefs that do not owe their . . . credibility to others." (Quinton, NT, 119)

Laurence BonJour expands on this thought: "Empirical knowledge is threatened with an infinite and apparently vicious regress of epistemic justification. Each belief is justified only if an epistemically prior belief is justified, and that epistemically prior belief is justified only if a still prior belief is justified, and so on, with the apparent result, so long as each new justification is inferential in character, that justification can never be completed, indeed can never even really get started—and hence that there is no empirical justification and no empirical knowledge." (BonJour, SEK, 19)

Rorty moves in a completely different direction, viewing epistemology in terms of rules and advancing a negative view of the entire epistemic enterprise: "The tendency of normal epistemologically centered philosophy [is] to block the road by putting itself forward as the final commensurating vocabulary for all *possible* rational discourse." (Rorty, PMN, 387, italics in original) He states, "By 'commensurable' I mean able to be brought under a set of rules which will tell us how rational agreement can be reached on what would settle the issue on every point where statements seem to conflict." (Rorty, PMN, 316)

3. Everything Is Interpretation

Rorty describes the role of epistemology as "that of the cultural overseer who knows everyone's common ground—the Platonic philosopher-king who knows what everybody else is really doing whether *they* know it or not, because he knows about the ultimate context (the Forms, the Mind, Language) within which they are doing it." (Rorty, PMN, 317–318) Rorty's caricature and rejection of epistemology's role seems implicitly connected to the idea that no one can ever lay claim to an unmediated, neutral viewpoint and thus, know what the truth really is. Such a view is often connected to the idea that *everything is interpretation*, a perspective

most famously articulated by Jacques Derrida, the French philosopher often considered the founder of deconstruction. James K. A. Smith notes the "*radical* way" in which Derrida emphasizes the all-encompassing scope of interpretation, observing, "He means that there is no reality that is not always already interpreted." (Smith, WAP, 224, emphasis in original) According to Derrida, language is the mediating lens through which interpretation takes place. (Smith, WAP, 225) This view is central to the concept of textual deconstruction.

E. Truth Cannot Be Communicated in Text—Textual Deconstruction
1. We Think Only in "Signs"

Jacques Derrida declares, "A text is not a text unless it hides from the first comer, from the first glance, the law of its composition and the rules of its game. A text remains, moreover, forever imperceptible. Its law and its rules are not, however, harbored in the inaccessibility of a secret; it is simply that they can never be hooked, in the present, into anything that could rigorously be called a perception." (Derrida, *Dissemination*, 69) Derrida frequently spoke of texts as having mere "traces" of what might have been said. A reader who pursued the trace would not come to truth, only to an *aporia*, an impasse.

Derrida often speaks of language in terms of signs, where meaning does not reside in the word (signifier) itself, but rather is found in its relation to other words. Signs, after all, direct attention to things other than themselves. As Rorty explains Derrida's view, "Words have meaning only because of contrast-effects with other words. 'Red' means what it does only by contrast with 'blue', 'green', etc. . . . No word can acquire meaning in the way in which philosophers from Aristotle to Bertrand Russell have hoped it might—by being the unmediated expression of something non-linguistic." (Rorty, DT, 172–173) Derrida makes the scope of his view evident when he asserts, "From the moment that there is meaning there are nothing but signs. We *think only in signs*." (Derrida, OG, 50, emphasis in original)

2. The Impossibility of Interpretation

Expanding on Derrida's second thought, Richard Macksey observes,

> If, as Derrida puts it, linguistic signs refer themselves only to other linguistic signs, if the linguistic reference of words is words, if texts refer to nothing but other texts, then, in Foucault's words, "If interpretation can never accomplish itself, it is simply because there is nothing to interpret." There is nothing to interpret for each sign is in itself not the thing that offers itself to interpretation but interpretation to other signs.... Interpretation does not shed light on a matter that asks to be interpreted, that offers itself passively to interpretation, but it can only seize violently an interpretation that is already there, one which it must overturn, overthrow, shatter with the blows of a hammer. (Macksey, SC, 96)

Rejecting modernity's belief in the objective certainty of knowledge (recall Erickson's list earlier in this chapter), Frank Lentricchia, literary critic and professor at Duke University, also sees violence intrinsic to interpretation. He asserts that interpreting text is not connected to passively encountering a firm representation of the world, but is rather characterized by "a violence of mastery and substitution." (Lentricchia, ANC, 179)

Michel Foucault, another central postmodern thinker, was a French philosopher who could be regarded as a "founder of discourse," just as he said that Freud and Marx had been—that is, someone who has produced "the possibilities and the rules for the formation of other texts [an entire new conversation on a subject]." (Foucault, FR, 113–114) Foucault adds that "interpretation can never be completed, [and] this is quite simply because there is nothing to interpret. There is nothing absolutely primary to interpret, for after all everything is already interpretation, each sign is in itself not the thing that offers itself to interpretation but an interpretation of other signs." (Foucault, EWF, 275)

Rosenau summarizes by declaring, "There is no single meaning for any text, for any political, social, economic event. An infinite number of interpretations of any scenario is possible." (Rosenau, PMSS, 41) Later she observes, "Language produces and reproduces its own world without reference to reality . . . it is impossible to say anything definite because language is purely an artificial sign system and cannot assure truth." (Rosenau, PMSS, 79)

F. Rejection of Foundational Knowledge

Philosophers have traditionally sought to identify the first principles that can provide a foundation for reasoning, as described in chapter 28. According to foundationalism, says *The Stanford Encyclopedia of Philosophy*, "Our justified beliefs are structured like a building: they are divided into a foundation and a superstructure, the latter resting upon the former. Beliefs belonging to the foundation are *basic*. Beliefs belonging to the superstructure are *nonbasic* and receive justification from the justified beliefs in the foundation." (Steup, Epistomology)

However, postmodernism rejects such a view. As Tarnas observes, "The postmodern paradigm is by its nature fundamentally subversive of all paradigms, for at its core is the awareness of reality as being at once multiple, local, and temporal, and without demonstrable foundation." (Tarnas, PWM, 401)

In an earlier work, BonJour questions the feasibility of foundational knowledge. Though he makes reference to the infinite regress explored earlier, his primary concern is whether the "basic" beliefs that are necessary for foundational knowledge are even possible.

> The fundamental concept . . . of empirical foundationalism generally, is the concept of a basic empirical belief. It is by appeal to basic beliefs that the threat of an infinite regress is to be avoided and empirical knowledge given a secure foundation. But a new problem now arises: how can there be any empirical beliefs which are thus basic? For although this has often been overlooked, the very idea of an epistemically basic empirical belief is more than a little paradoxical. On what basis is such a belief supposed to be justified, once any appeal to further empirical premises is ruled out? . . . How can a contingent, empirical belief impart epistemic "motion" to other empirical beliefs unless it is itself in "motion"? (Or, even more paradoxically, how can such a belief epistemically "move" itself?) Where does the noninferential justification for basic empirical beliefs come from? (BonJour, SEK, 30)

Richard Fumerton restates the foundationalist's problem:

> It is crucial that the foundationalist discover a kind of *truth* that can be known without inference. But there can be no bearers of truth value without judgment and judgment involves the application of concepts. But to apply a concept is to make a judgment about class membership, and to make a judgment about class membership always involves relating the thing about which the judgment is made to other paradigm members of the class. (Fumerton, FTEJ, website)

Rorty offers one postmodern alternative to foundationalism: "If we are not to have a doctrine of 'knowledge by acquaintance' which will give us a foundation, and if we do not simply deny that there is such a thing as justification, then we will claim with Sellars that 'science is rational not because it has a foundation, but because it is a self-correcting enterprise which can put *any* claim in jeopardy, though not *all* at once.'" (Rorty, PMN, 180–181)

Tarnas summarizes the larger point, declaring, "There is no empirical 'fact' that is not already theory-laden, and there is no logical argument or formal principle that is *a priori* certain. All human understanding is interpretation, and no interpretation is final." (Tarnas, PWM, 396–397) Rorty reflects this idea when he declares that the postmodern philosopher can only "decry the very notion of having a view, while avoiding having a view about having views." (Rorty, PMN, 371)

II. Answering Postmodernism

A. Background

Providing a satisfactory response to postmodernism is not a straightforward affair, for it is a theoretical stance of great variety. Recall Richard Tarnas's description of postmodernism:

> What is called postmodern varies considerably according to context, but in its most general and widespread form, the postmodern mind may be viewed as an open-ended, indeterminate set of attitudes that has been shaped by a great diversity of intellectual and cultural

currents; these range from pragmatism, existentialism, Marxism, and psychoanalysis to feminism, hermeneutics, deconstruction, and postempiricist philosophy of science, to cite only a few of the more prominent. (Tarnas, PWM, 395)

The adjectival flavor of this sentence is reminiscent of Winston Churchill's famous description of Soviet foreign policy preceding World War II, which he characterized as "a riddle wrapped in a mystery inside an enigma." Similarly, it seems likely that any attempt to provide a point-for-point response to a system of thought so varied, general, open-ended, indeterminate, diverse, and wide-ranging would itself be destined to yield a result so thin and vague as to be of little use. Therefore, while we offer responses to the specific expressions of postmodern thought described earlier, we present them peripherally. We hope primarily to be directed toward identifying and critiquing the underlying forces that might be said to animate postmodernism, considering postmodernism's self-contradictory nature and, briefly, the ramifications of viewing story as truth.

1. The Heart of Postmodern Thought

At first blush, what most seems to define postmodern philosophy is a rejection of the notion of truth. Recall some of the characterizations concerning truth cited earlier. To Nietzsche truth was an "illusion" (Nietzsche, OTL, 47), to Tarnas something "radically ambiguous" (Tarnas, PWM, 397) and inaccessible (Tarnas, PWM, 396), and to Rorty, a thing "made rather than found." (Rorty, CIS, 7) Although these statements explicitly state truth as their subject, is truth the *actual* target of their skepticism?

To answer this question we must take a closer look "under the hood" of the examples of postmodern thought in section I of this chapter. Consider Rosenau's observation of the postmodern goal to "register the impossibility of establishing any . . . underpinning for knowledge" (Rosenau, PMSS, 6), Rorty's plain admission of "not having any epistemology" (Rorty, ORT, 24), and BonJour's claim that "empirical knowledge is threatened with an infinite and apparently vicious regress of epistemic justification." (BonJour, SEK, 19) Here we see that, generally speaking, the real object of postmodern skepticism and doubt is not the existence of truth itself but rather *our ability to perceive* truth. To evaluate this skepticism we must make a brief excursion into the philosophical realm of epistemic justification.

2. What Is It to Know Something?

This is an epistemological question. Epistemology is "the theory of knowledge. Its central questions include the origin of knowledge; the place of experience in generating knowledge, and the place of reason in doing so." (Blackburn, ODP, 118) Richard Feldman concisely articulates the traditional definition of knowledge as "*justified true belief.*" (Feldman, *Epistemology*, 23, italics in original) With specific regard to our discussion of postmodernism, we are most concerned with just one of these components: that of epistemic *justification*. Feldman defines justification as one having "extremely good reasons for their beliefs." (Feldman, *Epistemology*, 15)

René Descartes offers perhaps the earliest and most serious study of epistemic justification. His interest was connected to a personal observation:

> There is no novelty to me in the reflection that, from my earliest years, I have accepted many false opinions as true, and that what I have

concluded from such badly assured premises could not but be highly doubtful and uncertain. (Descartes, DMM, 75)

BonJour describes how Descartes engaged in a "process of systematic doubt," whereby he rigorously attempted to *justify* his beliefs and discover what he truly knew. (BonJour, ECP, 11) He began "to tentatively reject any view or opinion or principle that is not 'completely certain and indubitable,' any for which he can find 'some reason for doubt.'" (BonJour, ECP, 10) It is critical to pay attention to Descartes's objective. He is engaging in the systematic application of doubt to accomplish the modernist goal of establishing what he knows *for certain*. He is *not* seeking to demonstrate that such knowledge is unobtainable (the goal of postmodernists more than two hundred years later). To accomplish his goal, Descartes constructed a thought experiment using his famous "evil genius" hypothesis: (BonJour, ECP, 10)

> I will therefore suppose that, not a true God, who is very good and who is the supreme source of truth, but a certain evil spirit, not less clever and deceitful than powerful, has bent all his efforts to deceiving me. I will suppose that the sky, the air, the earth, colors, shapes, sounds, and all other objective things [that we see] are nothing but illusions and dreams that he has used to trick my credulity. I will consider myself as having no hands, no eyes, no flesh, no blood, nor any senses, yet falsely believing that I have all these things. (Descartes, DMM, 80)

In the end Descartes recognized that "there is at least one thing that cannot be doubted on this basis, something about which even the evil genius cannot deceive him, namely, his own existence. . . . [T]hough he

does not use exactly this wording . . . the gist of this argument is captured in the famous Latin formula 'Cogito ergo sum,' 'I think, therefore I am.'" (BonJour, ECP, 11)

As BonJour observes, "The view that has been ascribed as standard to Descartes is that only beliefs that are *infallible*, beliefs that are *guaranteed* to be true, can really count as knowledge." (BonJour, ECP, 21) Given these extremely high standards, one does not need to be an advocate of postmodernism to rightly reject Descartes's brand of foundationalism as unrealistic.

B. Discerning Truth Does Not Require Infallible Perception
1. Descartes and Certain Truth

As observed by BonJour, for Descartes beliefs must be "infallible" and "guaranteed to be true" to be counted as knowledge. Thus, he notes that the Cartesian concept of knowledge possesses a "very strong version of the belief or acceptance requirement—one that many or probably most of the things that we seem ordinarily to regard as instances of knowledge . . . would not satisfy." (BonJour, ECP, 27) Under Descartes's strict view, knowledge of causal facts (plants will die without water), facts about our personal past (our memories), and facts of personal awareness (there is music playing) are not considered legitimate instances of knowledge. (BonJour, ECP, 2–3)

We do not need postmodernism to reject Descartes's unyielding standards of justification or to acknowledge our inability to access infallible truth. As Feldman observes, "No one is ever absolutely certain of anything about the external world." (Feldman, *Epistemology*, 117) Similarly, atheist philosopher Thomas Nagel notes that, "it is perfectly possible that the truth is beyond our reach, in virtue of our intrinsic cognitive

It is perfectly possible that the truth is beyond our reach, in virtue of our intrinsic cognitive limitations, and not merely beyond our grasp in humanity's present stage of intellectual development. But I believe that we cannot know this, and that it makes sense to go on seeking a systematic understanding of how we and other living things fit into the world.

Thomas Nagel

limitations, and not merely beyond our grasp in humanity's present stage of intellectual development. But I believe that we cannot know this, and that it makes sense to go on seeking a systematic understanding of how we and other living things fit into the world." (Nagel, MC, 128) Virtually everyone—both postmodernists and their opponents—agree that our access to truth is often flawed. The relevant issue is whether or not our beliefs *really* require infallibility or pristine vantage points to rightly count as knowledge.

2. Knowledge Without Certainty

Fallibilism acknowledges the inevitable errors and limits of our knowledge (their fallibility). Nevertheless, fallibilism asserts that we have good reasons for living our lives under the assumption that we possess knowledge, and that "it is not necessary that beliefs be certain, or grounded on certainty." (Blackburn, ODP, 130) Not only are these reasons quite practical, they reflect how we actually live our lives. For example, as Nagel observed above, we should not be paralyzed by our limited access to truth. In reality, as Feldman notes, this outlook is demonstrated by postmodernists themselves, for "in living their lives, they are likely to do all sorts of things that suggest that they think they know things. For example, they will enter into conversations with others. Doing so seems to presuppose that they think they know that

there are other people present and that they know what those other people are saying. For another example, they will get out of the way of oncoming trucks, suggesting that they know that walking in front of a moving truck is dangerous." (Feldman, *Epistemology*, 120)

According to fallibilism, we have no reason to jettison the kinds of knowledge we so clearly seem to possess. It explores standards of epistemic justification that are more compatible with both our experience and common sense. Feldman observes, "We are absolutely certain of very few propositions. But, according to fallibilists, this is not a problem because knowledge does not require absolute certainty. For example, when there is a table in front of you, the lighting is good, your visual system is working properly, and you believe as a result of your visual impression and your background information that there is a table in front of you, then you can have knowledge that there is a table there. While there is, from your perspective, some remote chance of error, there is no reason at all to think that you are making an error, and excellent reason to think that you are not making an error. If your belief is true, then you do have knowledge." (Feldman, *Epistemology*, 122)

3. Justification Comes in Degrees

Roderick Chisholm shows us that though justification for our beliefs may not be *infallible*, it nonetheless exists in various degrees. For example, he observes that "It is, at best, only probable for you that you will be alive a year from now; and it is, at best, only probable for you that you will be alive six months from now. But you are *more justified* in believing that you will be alive six months from now than in believing that you will be alive a year from now. In this case, we may say, of two propositions each of which is merely probable for you, that one of them is *more probable* for you than the other." (Chisholm, TK, 10) Chisholm continues, "To say that a proposition is probable for us, in this fundamental sense, is to say simply that we are more justified in believing that proposition than in believing its negation." (Chisholm, TK, 10)

4. Perspective Does Not Undermine Knowledge

John Searle comments on the postmodern criticism that our individual perspectives disqualify us from true knowledge, observing that from the postmodern perspective, "somehow or other, knowing reality directly as it is in itself requires that it be known from no point of view. This is an unjustified assumption to make. For example, I directly see the chair in front of me, but of course, I see it from a point of view. I know it directly from a perspective. Insofar as it is even intelligible to talk of knowing 'reality directly as it is in itself,' I know it directly as it is in itself when I know that there is a chair over there because I see it. That is to say, perspectivism, so defined, is not inconsistent with either realism or the doctrine of epistemic objectivity that says we have direct perceptual access to the real world." (Searle, MLS, 21)

J. P. Moreland also asserts our ability to be acquainted with reality, even though one's perspective impacts one's awareness. He recasts the idea of those "social, cultural, linguistic, spatiotemporal, and tradition-bound factors that characterize most of us" as our *situatedness*. (Moreland, TARD, 309) Moreland views our situatedness within the context of *attentive influence*, "according to which situatedness may influence and even distort knowledge by acquaintance or propositional knowledge of an object, but direct access is still possible and available for subsequent adjustment." (Moreland, TARD, 310) He describes how "over time, people fall into ruts and adopt ways of seeing things according to which certain features are noticed and others are neglected." (Moreland, TARD, 311) He continues,

> I am not claiming this is a good or bad thing. I am simply noting that it happens. I suggest that situatedness functions as a set of habit forming [*sic*] background beliefs and concepts that direct our acts of noticing or failing to notice various features of reality. Depending on various factors, such situatedness may yield accurate or inaccurate experiences and beliefs. It is not that we cannot see reality itself. In fact, through effort we can look at things from a different perspective and further confirm or disconfirm our previous viewpoint. Habit-forming beliefs do not stand between a person and reality as do glasses. Rather, they habitualize ways of seeing and thinking which, through effort, can be changed or retained, hopefully on the basis of comparing them with reality itself. (Moreland, TARD, 311)

C. Perceptual Experience Provides a Basis for Foundational Knowledge
1. Embracing Foundationalism

What of postmodernism's criticism concerning foundational knowledge, and specifically, basic beliefs? The question remains, "On what basis is such a belief supposed to be justified, once any appeal to further empirical premises is ruled out?" (BonJour, SEK, 30)

Though quoted earlier as one who offered influential opposition to foundationalist theory, Laurence BonJour has since changed his mind and come to embrace foundationalism, declaring:

> I myself have played a role in these developments, offering some of the arguments against foundationalism. . . . But having labored long in the intriguing but ultimately barren labyrinths of coherentism, I have come to the conviction that the recent anti-foundationalist trend is a serious mistake, one that is taking epistemological inquiry in largely the wrong direction and giving undeserved credibility to those who would reject epistemology altogether. (BonJour, FEW, 229–230)

BonJour offers a glimpse at the reason he changed his mind: "Foundationalists such as C. I. Lewis and Richard Fumerton, among many others, have spoken at this point of 'immediate apprehension of' or 'direct acquaintance with' the relevant experiential content. Contrary to my own earlier arguments, I now believe that there is a way to understand such formulations that leads to a defensible view." (BonJour, FEW, 230–231) Generally speaking, BonJour's argument is based upon the view that "basic or foundational beliefs are justified by appeal to experience." (BonJour, FEW, 230) More specifically, he points to the "built-in" awareness of content that is an unavoidable part of the most basic beliefs connected to our experiences. (BonJour, FEW, 232) He declares, "as far as I can see, such a non-apperceptive, constituent awareness of content is strictly infallible in pretty much the way that foundationalist views have traditionally claimed, but which most have long since abandoned." (BonJour, FEW, 232)

For example, Bonjour describes the experience of sitting at his desk, noting that such an awareness of sensory content is in no need of justification and is indeed infallible in the sense that there is no sort of mistake that is even relevant to it: since it is this awareness of sensory content that gives my experiential state the specific content that it has and thus constitutes it as the specific experiential state that it is, there is no logical room for this awareness to be mistaken about the content in question. And thus such an awareness of sensory content is also apparently available to justify foundational beliefs. (BonJour, FEW, 233–234)

2. Perception Leads Us to Basic Beliefs

Though based on different philosophical principles, Chisholm and Bertrand Russell also affirmed that perception has the capacity to lead us to basic belief. In effect, they could be said to share a view that these perceptions should be considered innocent until proven guilty. Chisholm states, "Our perceptual principles are instances of the more general truth: 'It is reasonable to trust the senses until one has positive reason for distrusting them.'" (Chisholm, TK, 23) Seeking to pursue a view more "interesting" than skepticism, Russell chose to develop "the opposite hypothesis, according to which beliefs caused by perception are to be accepted unless there are positive grounds for rejecting them." (Russell, IMT, 133)

3. We Can Access the World

Edmund Husserl articulated a robust theory concerning our ability directly to access the world as it is. This access need not take place in a single moment, but rather may take place over a period of time. In considering Husserl's viewpoint, R. Scott Smith notes,

"For Husserl, there is a progression of evidence available for *verifying* that an object given in conscious awareness is indeed as it is thought to be. That is, a mental representation of any object has built into it a method for 'coming closer' epistemically to the object—to see, or come to know it better." (Smith, SMK, 298)

Moreland notes, "As Scott Smith has pointed out, from children to average folk to specialists in a field, we all regularly experience what Edmund Husserl called fulfillment structures in which we (1) compare our concepts and thoughts to things in themselves via direct access and (2) thereby adjust—verify, disconfirm, clarify—the former. . . . Indeed, people count on this success in living their lives, and those whose views deny such fulfillment structures will sooner or later conduct their lives, theorizing, and so forth as though they are available, whatever they say." (Moreland, TARD, 310; see also Smith, PFTT, 359–361)

D. Postmodernism Is Self-Refuting

Perhaps the most common criticism of postmodern thought is that, to the degree it advocates a skeptical view, it unavoidably contradicts its own tenets. Feldman offers this simple illustration:

It is surely true that skeptics cannot consistently claim to know that no one knows anything about the external world. Compare:
I know that no one knows anything.
There is no way that [this principle] could be true. For if it were true, then, given what it says, I do know something, namely that no one knows anything. But if I knew that, then the proposition [above] says I know would be false, because I would know something. (Feldman, *Epistemology*, 120)

Speaking to the postmodernist reaction to this criticism, Rosenau observes, "Although warning of modernity's inconsistencies, they reject being held to consistency norms themselves. They openly deny that they need make any special effort to avoid self-contradiction; this hardly seems fair." She continues, "Postmodernists contend that anything they say or write is itself only a local narrative, relevant only for its own constituency. But very few post-modernists entirely relinquish the truth claims of what they write, and this also makes for self-contradiction." (Rosenau, PMSS, 177)

However, if these claims are in fact confined to the scope of local narrative, then they are merely claims that reside and apply to that local narrative. On what basis should this particular narrative have authority over other narratives that happen to see truth differently? This is why Alvin Goldman noted, "Indeed, if one examines the debunkings of truth on the grounds that truth claims merely cloak a drive for domination, almost all of these debunkings themselves depend on truth claims!" (Goldman, KSW, 35)

In *The Last Word*, Nagel speaks forcefully against those who interpret disagreements of belief as due to "different frames of reference, forms of thought or practice, or forms of life,

---

Post-modernists contend that anything they say or write is itself only a local narrative, relevant only for its own constituency. But very few post-modernists entirely relinquish the truth claims of what they write, and this also makes for self-contradiction.

Pauline Rosenau

---

between which there is no objective way of judging but only a contest for power." (Nagel, LW, 4) In contrast to this perspective—which he labels "subjective"—he offers a clear argument that human reason is a means by which we have "access to universally valid methods of objective thought." (Nagel, LW, 4) In pointing out the absurdity of the subjective view, Nagel gives this plain assessment:

> To put it schematically, the claim "Everything is subjective" must be nonsense, for it would itself have to be either subjective or objective. But it can't be objective, since in that case it would be false if true. And it can't be subjective, because then it would not rule out any objective claim, including the claim that it is objectively false. There may be some subjectivists, perhaps styling themselves as pragmatists, who present subjectivism as applying even to itself. But then it does not call for a reply, since it is just a report of what the subjectivist finds it agreeable to say. If he also invites us to join him we need not offer any reason for declining, since he has offered us no reason to accept.
>
> Objections of this kind are as old as the hills, but they seem to require constant repetition. Hilary Putnam once remarked perceptively on "the appeal which all incoherent ideas seem to have." In spite of his perennial flirtation with subjectivism, Putnam himself has restated very forcefully the case for the incoherence of relativism. It is usually a good strategy to ask whether a general claim about truth or meaning applies to itself. Many theories, like logical positivism, can be eliminated immediately by this test. The familiar point that relativism is self-refuting remains valid in spite of its familiarity: We cannot criticize some of our own claims of reason without employing reason at some other point to formulate and support those criticisms. (Nagel, LW, 15)

E. Story Cannot Serve as Truth

R. Douglas Geivett puts the preceding discussion into perspective by offering these observations characterizing the relationship between a narrative (oriented toward storytelling), and an account (oriented toward explanation):

> An account purports to assist us in getting our bearings within the world. We seek an account when we desire to find our place in the world by taking its measure, adopting accurate beliefs about it, and acting in accordance with those beliefs—often on the supposition that our flourishing is at stake.
>
> A narrative, on the other hand, is associated with the idea of story. The power of a particular story or narrative may depend on our capacity to suspend belief (or disbelief). A narrative is compelling if it represents a world, or part of a world, in a way that supports imaginative entrance into that world, irrespective of how things actually are. This effect of story may require the suspension of conviction about how things stand within the actual world. We become denizens of a world of make-believe. And making believe is not the same as believing. We make believe when we play a role as if we believed. Thus, the world of make-believe must at least be believe-able. (Geivett, IGS, 38–39)
>
> Since beliefs are action-guiding, we want our beliefs to be true so that our action is responsible and effective. For example, if we desire to cross safely to the other side of a busy street, we want to have the true belief that the traffic has died down enough to proceed safely across the street. (Geivett, IGS, 45)

What the postmodernist offers is not an alternative theory of justification, but a substitute for any theory of justification. For a theory of justification is inherently concerned with specifying the conditions that indicate the likely truth of a belief. For the postmodernist, this is a hopeless task. Inquiry is not about fixing our beliefs in accordance with truth-conducive grounds. Arguably, it's not about fixing belief at all. For there is no concern about what to believe without concern for truth. And there is little point to being concerned about believing what's true if there's nothing one can do to improve one's stock of beliefs or one's chances of acquiring true beliefs. No wonder narrative has replaced explanatory account as the focus of postmodern reflection. The propositional ordering of our lives is inescapable. Narratives at least provide a framework for such ordering. But for the postmodernist, such ordering is doxastically vacuous. (Geivett, IGS, 50)

III. Conclusion

It does in fact seem inescapable that our lives are propositionally ordered (i.e., we live according to various beliefs about the world, such as "that car is getting closer" or "this skillet is hot"). As Alan Sokal declares, "There *is* a real world; its properties are *not* merely social constructions; facts and evidence *do* matter. What sane person would contend otherwise? And yet, much contemporary academic theorizing consists precisely of attempts to blur these obvious truths." (Sokal, PECS, website)

More sobering still is the fact that our beliefs are drained of all significance once their connection to a meaningful notion of truth has been severed. Francis Bacon observed, "After the human mind has once despaired of finding truth, everything becomes very much feebler, and the result is that they turn men aside to agreeable discussions and discourses, and a kind of ambling around things, rather than sustain them in the severe path of inquiry." (Bacon, NO, 56) In conclusion, the antifoundationalism of postmodernism is not only untenable as a philosophical system, but ultimately incompatible with Christian faith for which belief is fundamentally oriented toward historical and theological truths.

CHAPTER 30

ANSWERING SKEPTICISM

OVERVIEW

I. Introduction

A few years ago, I (Sean) took a group of high school students on an apologetics mission trip to Berkeley, California, to interact with skeptics, atheists, and people of various faiths. My friend Brett Kunkle, an apologist, youth worker, and author, planned and led our trip. We invited a "free thinking" student group to make presentations to our students. An agnostic student gave a forty-five-minute talk about how we should be skeptical of truth claims and not accept them on authority.

During the Q&A time, Brett asked a penetrating question: "If we are supposed to be skeptical of truth claims, should we be skeptical of your truth claims about being skeptical?" What a great question! By asking this question, Brett was pointing out the self-refuting nature of the student's presentation. The student wanted us to be skeptical of all truth claims, but to make an exception for his own truth claim. This, of course, is entirely inconsistent. Our point here is simple: many people who claim to be skeptics simply are not skeptical enough. There is some merit to certain kinds of skepticism, but as this story illustrates, it can also be self-refuting.

In this chapter, we define skepticism, look at its origins and history, consider several different types of skepticism, and present three key responses to its claims.

Philosophical skepticism "refers to the position that, with respect to a particular class of beliefs, those beliefs cannot be instances of knowledge." (Blaauw and Pritchard, *Epistemology A–Z*, 138) Generally, if a view or theory casts doubt on what would normally be considered a category of knowledge, it is regarded as skeptical; therefore, the key to discerning whether or not a view is truly skeptical lies in noticing how difficult it is to alleviate the doubt that the skeptic expresses. (Pritchard, CS, website)

II. History of Skepticism

A. Ancient Schools

When we consider an idea, we ought also to consider the history of that idea. In ancient Greece, two schools of skeptical thought arose. Some pre-Socratic philosophers occasionally sounded skeptical, but for the most part, Plato's Academy did not advance skepticism until after the death of Aristotle. These teachings began with Arcesilaus. (Vogt, AS, website)

A second school of skeptical thought was Pyrrhonian Skepticism, named after its founder Pyrrho of Ellis (365–275 BC), whose teachings were later collected by Sextus Empiricus. Pyrrho encouraged his followers to argue for both sides of any debate, because any conclusion is impossible. (Cicero, ND, 60) In essence, he taught that any belief is neither true nor false.

Essentially, the difference between Academic skeptics and Pyrrhonian skeptics is this: the Academics thought reaching certainty was not very likely, but they did not completely dismiss the possibility. Pyrrhonian skeptics refused to make a judgment as to whether or not certainty is possible and also refused to come to a conclusion on any other argument. (Thorsrud, AGS, website)

B. Medieval Period

The medieval period began with the long shadow of Augustine of Hippo (AD 354–430), who had studied classical philosophy and rhetoric, becoming a teacher of rhetoric in Carthage and in Milan. His book *Against the Skeptics* convincingly argued against the validity of skepticism. Some medieval thinkers interacted with skepticism, but it was not until the mid-1600s that skepticism once again flourished as a possible philosophical option, when ancient skeptical writings were rediscovered and gained popularity.

C. Enlightenment Period

Skepticism experienced a revival around the time of René Descartes (1641), when the writings of Sextus Empiricus were discovered and published in Latin, causing the embrace of Pyrrho's philosophy. After Descartes (whose views we consider below in more detail), Pierre Bayle (1697) "undermined all of man's intellectual efforts and left an incoherent shambles as the legacy of the new philosophy and the new science." (Popkin, HRP, 35) After Bayle's attempt to push philosophers towards fideism (the belief that knowledge is only attained by faith and that reason is useless), David Hume, one of the most influential skeptics in history, argued that "all our ideas are nothing but copies of our impressions, or, in other words, that it is impossible for us to *think* of any thing, which we have not antecedently *felt*." (Hume, ECHU, 3) We discuss Hume's philosophy below; significantly, he went one step beyond

Bayle's belief that one must first have faith rather than reason to attain knowledge.

D. Contemporary Views

Currently, some philosophers still argue for skepticism. However, we should note a distinction between groups such as the Skeptics Society and those who advocate philosophical skepticism. The Skeptics Society advances scientific empiricism (the view that all the sciences are unified) and emphasizes experimentation as the means of gaining knowledge; but the Society does not advance a philosophical argument regarding the possibility of knowledge or justification. As we demonstrate below, pure scientific empiricism could be classified as a type of skepticism, but it is not the only form of skepticism.

III. Categories of Skepticism

Skepticism can be divided and subdivided in numerous ways as we seek to define and understand it more fully. It's helpful to think of the following definitions in six categories, two dealing with scope (breadth) and four dealing with depth.

A. Scope of Skepticism
1. Global Skepticism

This type of skepticism "holds that no one knows anything at all. It is universal in scope." (Feldman, *Epistemology*, 109) Global skepticism applies to all knowledge, including the possibility of a mind-independent world (both material and immaterial reality), religious truths, eyewitness testimony, and any other instance of knowledge. Nothing is knowable.

2. Local Skepticism

This type of skepticism "denies knowledge in certain areas or topics." (Feldman, *Epistemology*, 109) "More specifically, local skeptics can direct their skepticism at certain alleged objects, faculties or subject matters of knowledge." (Moreland and Craig, PFCW, 95) Local skepticism, however, is not the same as the experience one has when doubting in a normal, everyday occurrence. In normal circumstances, the person doubting thinks it's possible to remove the doubt.

For example, suppose you are at a friend's house and he points to his dog, saying, "Look, I have a poodle." You respond, "No, that's a Chihuahua." You then search the Internet for images of poodles and Chihuahuas to determine whose knowledge is correct. If this evidence is inconclusive, you could even ask a dog breeder, who confirms the dog is a poodle. From a skeptical approach, however, none of this evidence would be enough to prove what breed the dog is; thus, the specific doubt is never removable.

The difficulty of finding any convincing evidence to sway even a local skeptic in the case of the poodle, however, does indicate a problem in the stance a skeptic takes toward potential evidence. Noted philosophers and apologists J. P. Moreland and William Lane Craig make a helpful point regarding local skepticism, stating that "it is hard to sustain local skepticism because the considerations that drive it in some specific domain are hard to limit solely to that domain. Skeptical considerations have a tendency to spill out into other areas." (Moreland and Craig, PFCW, 96) In other words, local skepticism can easily turn into global skepticism.

B. Depth of Skepticism
1. Knowledge Skepticism

Knowledge skepticism states that it is not possible for people to have knowledge. Moreland and Craig explain this strain of skepticism: "One could deny knowledge on the grounds that there is no such thing as truth (and since knowledge includes justified *true* belief, there is no knowledge) or on the grounds that the standards for knowledge are so high (e.g., knowledge requires absolute certainty) that they are never met." (Moreland and Craig, PFCW, 94–95, emphasis in original)

2. Justification Skepticism

Justification skepticism is similar to knowledge skepticism but is aimed at the justification of knowledge rather than at the possibility of knowledge. In the study of philosophy, *justification* refers to the evidence one possesses for belief. This type of skepticism can accept the fact that there is knowledge while at the same time doubting the existence of evidence for that knowledge, because justification is not part of knowledge. (Moreland and Craig, PFCW, 94–95)

3. Pyrrhonian Skepticism

Pyrrhonian skepticism refrains from making judgments. It claims that no "conflicting accounts [*sic*] takes precedence over any other as being more convincing. Suspension of judgment is a standstill of the intellect, owing to which we neither reject nor posit anything. Tranquility is freedom from disturbance or calmness of soul." (Empiricus, OS, I.iv) Pyrrhonian skeptics also believed they effectively withheld beliefs regarding a mind-independent reality: "[Skeptics] say what is apparent to themselves and report their own feelings without holding opinions, affirming nothing about external objects." (Empiricus, OS, I.vii)

4. Iterative Skepticism

In iterative skepticism, the skeptic continuously asks how one knows any assertion given by an opponent without ever giving an argument himself. This type of skeptic is not at all interested in acquiring knowledge or a

method to gauge truth claims. Moreland and Craig point out that this is a "verbal game and should be treated as such." (Moreland and Craig, PFCW, 93)

IV. Examples of Skepticism

Throughout history, many philosophers have been skeptics. Studying all of them is beyond the scope of this chapter, but we can examine two of them here—one from history (David Hume) and the other from contemporary philosophy (Peter Unger).

A. David Hume

David Hume (1711–1776), a Scottish philosopher, applied scientific empiricism to human reason. He doubted that the world was created and doubted that the natural world was understandable by human reason. He is significant in the history of philosophy because he was the first great philosopher to question these foundational beliefs in so profound a way that Western philosophers who immediately followed him had to respond to his challenge, which they did either by purposing to rebuild confidence in reason (the rationalist approach) or by analyzing how to restore confidence in knowledge of the natural world (the empirical approach). In essence, Hume believed "human reason is fundamentally similar to that of the other animals, founded on instinct rather than quasi-divine insight into things." (Hume, ECHU, ix)

1. All Knowledge Is Obtained Via the Senses or Relations of Ideas

Hume explains two different kinds of reasoning:

All the objects of human reason or enquiry may naturally be divided into two kinds, to wit, *Relations of Ideas*, and *Matters of Fact*. Of the first kind are the sciences of Geometry, Algebra, and Arithmetic; and in short, every affirmation, which is either intuitively or demonstratively certain.... Matters of fact ... are not ascertained in the same manner; nor is our evidence of their truth, however great, of a like nature with the foregoing. The contrary of every matter of fact is still possible.... *That the sun will not rise to-morrow* is no less intelligible a proposition, and implies no more contradiction, than the affirmation, *that it will rise*. (Hume, ECHU, 4.1.1–2, italics in original)

In other words, for Hume, relations of ideas are necessarily true. It is this type of reasoning that allows for a logical argument known as a syllogism, which, when it follows certain rules, leads to a true conclusion. For example:

All men are mortal.

Billy is a man.

Therefore, Billy is mortal.

If the first two sentences are true, then the conclusion must be true. Another example of this reasoning is when a sentence carries in the definitions of its words the truth of the statement. The statement can't be false. For example, "All squares have four sides." This sentence is necessarily true, because the definition of a square is a geometrical shape with four sides of the same length and four right angles. Both of these are examples of what Hume would have called a relation of ideas. In the discipline of logic, this is defined as deductive reasoning.

Matters of fact, on the other hand, could be false or true. The conclusion can be arrived at by observation and relying on our senses. But nothing about this type of reasoning leads to certainty. An example of this type of reasoning is, "If you throw a rock, it will fall to the ground." We arrive at this after throwing a rock numerous times. In a logic textbook, this type of reasoning is defined as inductive reasoning. For Hume, it is not clear that we are justified in thinking this. We do not know whether the future will vary from what we have seen even a thousand times. Matters of fact, for Hume, are not *necessarily* true.

This understanding of knowledge caused Hume to believe that strict philosophical reasoning would cause the individual to fall into complete Pyrrhonian skepticism, since most general knowledge is not gained by deductive reasoning. And, as we discuss below, Hume thought our understanding of cause and effect is unable to give conclusions that we can be certain about. Yet in the end, natural instinct is too strong to allow anyone to maintain certain skeptical positions for very long.

2. Causation Is Illusory

Causality is a condition or situation that brings about a certain effect. It deals with the relationship between a cause and its effect. Hume summarizes why he thinks a particular cause cannot be inferred with absolute certainty from an effect:

In a word, then, every effect is a distinct event from its cause. It could not, therefore, be discovered in the cause, and the first invention or conception of it, *a priori*, must be entirely arbitrary. And even after it is suggested, the conjunction of it with the cause must appear equally arbitrary; since there are always many other effects, which, to reason, must seem fully as consistent and natural. In vain, therefore, should we pretend to determine any single event, or infer any cause or effect, without the assistance of observation and experience. (Hume, ECHU, 4.1.11)

Hume undermined inductive reasoning, stating that it is not possible to predict how the future will be affected by the present; cause-and-effect reasoning should be given up.

According to Hume, we cannot infer any connection between a cause and its effect apart from our own experience. Thinking about a particular object does not allow us to know the effect that object could cause. For example, while you are thinking about throwing a rock over a cliff, you cannot know the rock will fall, even if you have seen a rock thrown over a cliff before. Thought also cannot demonstrate for us the absolute connection between a cause and any given effect (such as gravity acting on the rock once it leaves your hand). Hume states categorically, "All inferences from experience, therefore, are effects of custom, not of reasoning." (Hume, ECHU 5.1.5) For Hume, "Custom is that principle, by which this correspondence [our perception of events as being causally related] has been effected; so necessary to the subsistence of our species, and the regulation of our conduct, in every circumstance and occurrence of human life." (Hume, ECHU 5.2.55).

Hume concludes that, because we cannot know the cause of a rock falling, neither can we know the cause of the world:

> While we cannot give a satisfactory reason, why we believe, after a thousand experiments, that a stone will fall, or fire burn; can we ever satisfy ourselves concerning any determinations we may form with regard to the origin of the worlds, and the situation of nature, from, and to eternity? . . . It seems to me, that the only object of the abstract sciences of demonstration is quantity and number, and that all attempts to extend this more perfect species of knowledge beyond these bounds are mere sophistry and illusion. (Hume, ECHU 12.3.25, 27).

For Hume, we cannot predict a future effect, since no law says that the future always resembles the past. Our belief in causal relationships is therefore habituated into us, rather than being based on reason: "Since nothing is ever really present to the mind, besides its own perceptions, 'tis not only impossible, that any habit shou'd ever be acquir'd otherwise than by the regular succession of these perceptions, but also that any habit shou'd ever exceed that degree of regularity." (Hume, THN, 141) Thus, when we see an apparent instance of cause and effect, we are merely noticing two events happening at similar times. Hume believes we should hold very loosely to the knowledge we claim regarding any type of causal relationship.

Peter Millican notes that in the end, Hume's skepticism "does not aspire to certainty, limits our scientific ambitions, and restricts them to subjects within the scope of our experience." (Millican, Introduction to ECHU, xxx)

B. Peter Unger

Peter Unger is a contemporary philosopher and could be classified as a global knowledge skeptic; occasionally, he sounds similar to a Pyrrhonian skeptic. He merely refrains from taking the last additional step of stating that we should refrain from judgment.

1. Philosophical Relativity

Unger argues for "philosophical relativity," which means that "for certain traditional problems, perhaps there really is no objective answer, neither positive nor negative, neither 'commonsensical' nor 'skeptical.'" (Unger, PR, 4) In other words,

> A certain set of assumptions yields one answer, another set another; whatever facts pertain to

the problem fail to decide between the one set and the other.

Where such a situation exists, if it ever really does, we may say that there is *philosophical relativity*. One position on a philosophical problem is to be preferred only *relative to* assumptions involved in arriving at its answer to the problem; an opposed position is to be preferred only relative to alternative assumptions; there is nothing to determine the choice between the diverse assumptions and, hence, between the opposed positions. (Unger, PR, 5)

Unger goes on to discuss philosophical relativism in relation to the field of semantics. Because people use words differently, one person's understanding of a particular word will affect that person's understanding of another word. For Unger, this leads to the conclusion that we cannot get to objective knowledge. (Unger, PR, 5–6)

2. Ignorance: Our Lack of Knowledge

Unger writes, "What we are arguing for, no matter what the argument is called, is the thesis that no one ever knows anything to be so." (Unger, ICS, 93) Unger argues for this conclusion by way of a logical syllogism:

1. If someone *knows* something to be so, then it is all right for the person to be absolutely *certain*. . . .
2. It is never all right for anyone to be absolutely *certain* that anything is so.
3. Therefore,
4. Nobody ever *knows* that anything is so. (Unger, ICS, 95, emphasis in original)

In other words, knowledge and certainty are so closely connected, they are almost synonymous. Unger inverts Descartes's claim (which we consider below) that certainty is required for one to have knowledge, saying

rather that knowledge is required prior to certainty.

Unger goes on to say, "If I *know*, then no new experience can possibly do anything to *clarify* any further for me whether the thing is so; the only significant effect it might have is to make it somewhat *less clear* to me." (Unger, ICS, 147, emphasis in original) He also asserts that anyone who accepts his argument does so because he/she is a speaker of English. He concludes,

[W]e have made, I think, quite a convincing case for the idea that ignorance is absolutely universal. And because we have grounded our case in the absolute justifying power which our language requires of knowing, we have been able to extend our treatment of absolute terms to give an analytic basis for our argument. The argument, then, is seen to turn on connections which are both normative and analytic. And this explains why our ignorance is, not only universal or complete, but, in the strictest sense, absolutely inevitable and necessary. (Unger, ICS, 148)

As you can see, Unger's views are similar to the Pyrrhonist of ancient Greece. The only difference is that Unger argues forcefully for his own view, rather than refraining from judgment, as a Pyrrhonist would.

V. A Failed Attempt to Answer Skepticism: René Descartes

Often, René Descartes is thought of as a skeptic, but that is to misunderstand his arguments. Descartes was reacting against Michel de Montaigne, a skeptic who was popular at the time Descartes was writing. De Montaigne stated, "Every human presupposition and pronouncement has as much authority as every other." (de Montaigne,

ARS, 102) In the introduction to one of his major works, *Meditations on First Philosophy*, Descartes states, "I must once for all seriously undertake to rid myself of all the opinions which I had formerly accepted, and commence to build anew from the foundation, if I wanted to establish any firm and permanent structure." (Descartes, MFP, 45)

A. Absolute Certainty

Descartes believed that absolute certainty was required before one could obtain knowledge: "I ought no less carefully to withhold my assent from matters which are not entirely certain and indubitable." (Descartes, MFP, 46) As we saw earlier through Unger, it is this need for certainty that allows skeptical attacks on knowledge itself.

B. Descartes's Arguments for Skepticism

Descartes gave three arguments for skepticism, aiming to interact with the strongest version of skepticism possible. He then attempted to refute the arguments he devised for skepticism. After giving these counterarguments, Descartes believed that he had succeeded in achieving certainty. In essence, he believed he had discovered knowledge through skepticism itself. (Popkin, HRP, 11)

Descartes's arguments were:

- The dream argument: "There are no certain indications by which we may clearly distinguish wakefulness from sleep." (Descartes, MFP, 47)
- The deceiving God argument: "How do I know that He has not brought it to pass that there is no earth, no heaven, no extended body, no magnitude, no place." (Descartes, MFP, 48)
- The evil demon argument: "Suppose... some evil genius not less powerful than deceitful, has employed his whole

energies in deceiving me; I shall consider . . . [I have] no hands, no eyes, no flesh, no blood, nor any senses." (Descartes, MFP, 49)

These three arguments Descartes went on to refute, stating, "Thought is an attribute that belongs to me; it alone cannot be separated from me. I am, I exist, that is certain." (Descartes, MFP, 52–53) For Descartes, the act of thinking could not be doubted, for doubting itself was in fact thinking; his thoughts proved that he existed, and consequently, he could build to other truths he believed to be certain.

However, his refutations of those arguments he gave in favor of skepticism were not satisfactory. Descartes failed adequately to answer skepticism because his certainty requirement undermined his rebuttals. Today, philosophers still interact with his evil demon argument, which can be seen in the "brain in a vat" argument. (Putnam, BV, 27–42) For an illustration of this argument, just think back to the 1990s blockbuster film *The Matrix*, in which humans live in a virtual world devised by the hostile artificial intelligence they created.

VI. Responses to Skepticism

A. "I Have a Hand" and the Moore Shift

G. E. Moore, a well-respected Cambridge philosopher, used two arguments to rebut skepticism: one defending the existence of the external world, and the other circumventing the conclusion of a skeptical argument by changing the argument. In essence, there is no way to *prove* the external world's existence, which the skeptic questions; but Moore gives what he calls "conclusive evidence" to believe in the external world. (Moore, PEW, 149) Here is an adaptation of his argument for the external world based on his hands' existence (based on Moore, PEW, 146–147):

> Here is one hand.
> Here is another.
> Two external objects exist.
> An external world exists.

For Moore, the alternate claim that his hands don't exist offers less evidence than that his hands do exist: "How absurd it would be to suggest that I did not know it, but only believed it, and that perhaps it was not the case!" (Moore, PEW, 146) When he considers whether he can prove that which he knows, Moore states that it is perfectly legitimate to know something without being able to prove it. If someone is unhappy with him for claiming knowledge without proof, they "have no good reason for their dissatisfaction." (Moore, PEW, 150)

Within the world of philosophy, this response of Moore's highlights a split when it comes to the criterion of having knowledge itself. This split is between two schools of thought: *particularists* and *methodists*. This concept is handled in more depth in our chapter in this book on "The Knowability of Truth," but suffice it to say here that particularists think it important first to answer the question, "What do I know?" Methodists first answer the question, "How do I know?" (Chisholm, FK, 61–76) This has been a debate within philosophy for millennia, and has never been satisfactorily answered to the extent that all involved come to a consensus. This debate has resurfaced numerous times. Usually, those involved in the debate lose interest over time; eventually, however, the debate is revived at a later date. In Moore's example regarding the two hands above, he takes the particularist stance by

offering an instance in which we do have knowledge of the external world. In other words, he *begins* with an example of knowledge to rebut the skeptic who denies the external world.

In a second argument, known as the "Moore Shift," Moore reverses the order of a skeptical syllogism to rebut skepticism. The skeptic claims that if skepticism is true, we cannot know of the external world.

Moore flips the order, using a pencil as evidence for the external world. He states, "This is a pencil," and goes on to state that in his judgment, this proposition is more likely to him than the skeptic's argument. (Moore, FFS, 226) In syllogism form, the skeptical argument is on the left, and Moore's argument is on the right.

If P, then Q	If P, then Q
P	Not Q
Therefore Q	Therefore, not P

P stands for the skeptical argument, and Q for the consequent nonexistence of the pencil.

Is it, in fact, as certain that all [the skeptic's] assumptions are true, as that I *do* know that this is a pencil and that you are conscious? I cannot help answering: It seems to me *more* certain that I *do* know that this is a pencil and that you are conscious, than that any single one of these . . . assumptions is true. . . . And how on earth is it to be decided which of the two things it is *rational* to be most certain of? (Moore, FFS, 226, emphasis in original)

Moore levels the playing field between skeptical arguments and common sense knowledge. In the end, it is actually more reasonable to disbelieve the skeptic's argument, since skepticism leads us to disbelieve in an external world.

B. Gratuitous Explainers

A contemporary philosopher, Paul Moser, answered Descartes's evil demon argument:

My current experience of an apparent white piece of paper is better explained by the . . . proposition that there is a white piece of paper here than by the proposition that a Cartesian demon is stimulating my brain in a certain way. Even if these competing propositions answer the same why-questions about my subjective contents [what I see], only the Cartesian proposition posits a gratuitous item in answering those questions. A Cartesian demon, I'm glad to report, is *not* represented in my experience by means of any of its own features, whereas a white piece of paper is. (Moser, TRS, 133)

Moser is advocating for the ability to look at a white piece of paper and notice within our conscious experience different aspects about that paper. It is possible to describe this paper either accurately or inaccurately regarding our experience of it (i.e., say it's yellow when we are experiencing it as white). Skeptics don't allow for this type of description. To summarize the key point of Moser's argument, the simplest explanation is usually the correct one, and in the evil demon argument, more explanations are given than are needed.

It's not entirely necessary to have a defense of one's understanding of the world, for "the typical four-year-old is able to have various justified beliefs about her favorite toys, for example, but she is quite innocent of actual premises in support of such beliefs." (Moser, TRS, 138)

In the end, a skeptical argument, such as Descartes's evaluation of whether perception is manipulated into illusion by some malign agency, is not needed to explain our perception of the external world's existence. What appears to be true (that an external world exists with which I interact) is simpler than the explanation that an evil demon or mad scientist is deceiving me; therefore, it is a better explanation.

C. Skepticism Is Self-Refuting

Augustine argues against a type of skepticism that requires certainty: "I don't know whether we should talk to those who don't know [that] . . . they are alive at present—or rather, they claim not to know what they cannot fail to know. For nobody is allowed not to know that he is alive, seeing that he can't even fail to know something if he isn't alive! Failing to know, as well as knowing, are features of the living. But clearly by not assenting that they are alive, they seem to guard themselves against error, even though by being in error they are proven to be alive, since the one who is not alive cannot be in error." (Augustine, AAT, 162)

A position is self-defeating if, when it is true, it proves itself false.* For example, the sentence, "No sentence has five words," refutes itself, since it is a sentence, and it has five words. Similarly, "to say that it is impossible to have knowledge is itself a knowledge claim, and thus this position is self-defeating." (Dew and Forman, HDWK, 158) Thus, the skeptic refutes the skeptical claim by stating that knowledge isn't possible.

To avoid the contradiction of using a knowledge claim to refute knowledge, some skeptics go the way of Pyrrhonism and refrain from making any knowledge claims at all. However, as Mortimer Adler points out, this does not help, as demonstrated by the

---

* I (Sean) have a blog post that lists some of the most common self-defeating statements. See Sean McDowell, "Self-Refuting Statements You Must Know" http://seanmcdowell.org/blog/self-refuting-statements-you-must-know.

logical law of non-contradiction: "This principle [non-contradiction] provides a complete refutation of the skeptic who declares that no statement is either true or false. For if the skeptic's declaration is true, then there is at least one statement which is true rather than false. And if it is false, then there may be many statements which are either true or false. And if it is neither true nor false, then why should we pay any attention to what the skeptic says?" (Adler, TR, 133–134)

Hence, in order to refute skepticism quite soundly, one only needs to allow the argument to reach the logical conclusion: its positive declaration is its own negation.

VII. Conclusion

All versions of skepticism have a similar goal: calling knowledge into question. Note that this intellectual goal is not the same thing as biblical discernment, which is "the ability to judge wisely and objectively." (Dillon, "Discernment," 122) The skeptic's views are not what the Bible intends when it commands us to practice discernment; rather, discernment is the fruit of spiritual discipline, which is developed through prayer, study, and practice by the mature Christian. Discernment is the action by which a believer notices what is good or evil (Heb. 5:14).

While it is true that being skeptical of certain things is often warranted, skepticism as a method or attitude negatively impacts Christianity, which is based on thoughtful examination of what can be said (as Luke proposed in writing to Theophilus, Luke 1:1–4) and the choice of trust in Christ. Jesus told a crowd who wondered about his learning, "Anyone who chooses to do the will of God will find out whether my teaching comes from God or whether I speak on my own" (John 7:17, NIV). Jesus also focused on the mind in his response to another crowd: "Then they said to him, 'What must we do, to be doing the works of God?' Jesus answered them, 'This is the work of God, that you believe in him whom he has sent'" (John 6:28, 29, ESV). (Significantly, the original Greek term for "believe" carries the meaning of placing one's trust in the reliability of what is believed—in this case, belief in a person.) The biblical outlook honors the human mind, even though it has fallen into great error; the Bible encourages the sincere search for wisdom and the validity of trusting in what can be perceived in the external world. If the existence of the external world is uncertain, the apostles could not have known that Christ was crucified, buried, and rose from the dead. (Nicholas of Autrecourt, NA, 14) If, as Moore and others have demonstrated, all things are equal between skepticism and other theories of knowledge, then the Christian is justified in rejecting skepticism.

In summary, Moore and others open the possibility of pursuing a particular goal of rationality: to believe as many truths as possible and to disbelieve as many falsehoods as possible. If this is one's goal, skepticism cannot be embraced.

CHAPTER 31

ARE MIRACLES POSSIBLE?

OVERVIEW

I. Introduction

Years ago I (Sean) was speaking with a physics PhD student who considered himself an atheist. He asked me, "How can you believe in miracles like the resurrection of Jesus? Hasn't science shown that when people die, they stay dead?" I simply responded by saying, "You're right, science has shown that under normal conditions dead people stay dead. But the Christian claim is that Jesus rose supernaturally, that is, that God has acted in history by raising Jesus from the dead. If there really is a God who created the world and designed its laws, then the natural norm of dead people staying dead can't restrict God from supernaturally raising his Son."

Here's the simple point: if God exists, then miracles are *possible*. As C. S. Lewis wrote, "But if we admit God, must we admit Miracle? Indeed, indeed, you have no security against it. That is the bargain. Theology says to you in effect, 'Admit God and with Him the risk of a few miracles, and I in return will ratify your faith in uniformity as regards the overwhelming majority of events.'" (Lewis, *Miracles*, 109)

Some skeptics want to dismiss the possibility of miracles unless God's existence can first be proven. But this is backwards. It is not up to the theist to prove God's existence, for if God even *possibly* exists, then miracles are possible. To reject miracle claims outright, the skeptic needs to prove that God does not exist. But the nonexistence of God has never been shown. Yet, since the mid-nineteenth century and ever more frequently, God's nonexistence has simply been assumed to be the case. In fact, there are powerful reasons to believe God does exist. (For more information, turn to the prologue to this book, "A Theistic Universe.")

Philosopher and apologist William Lane Craig remembers that the evidence for God's existence shaped how he viewed miracles on his journey to faith:

> In my own case, the virgin birth was a stumbling block to my coming to faith—I simply could not believe such a thing. But when I reflected on the fact that God had created the entire universe, it occurred to me that it would not be too difficult for Him to make a woman become pregnant. Once the non-Christian understands who God is, then the problem of miracles should cease to be a problem for him. (Craig, AI, 125)

II. Defining the Term *Miracle*

What is meant by the term *miracle*? T. H. Huxley, who coined the term "agnostic" to define his own principle of suspending judgment about statements for which he had no evidence to give them certainty, states:

> The first step in this, as in all other discussions, is to come to a clear understanding as to the meaning of the terms employed. Argumentation about whether miracles are possible and, if possible, credible, is mere beating the air until the arguers have agreed what they mean by the word "miracle." (Huxley, WTHH, 153)

Defining a miracle can be a difficult task. If the scope of the definition is too narrow, one can risk excluding what might actually be the occurrence of a miracle. Or, if the scope of the definition is too broad, then anything could be considered a miracle. For example, people often use the word *miracle* in a generalized or figurative way without meaning that a literal miracle has occurred. In a figurative sense, someone might be speaking of the low probability of an event, "It was a miracle he survived the car crash." Or, addressing a natural phenomenon, someone might say, "It is a miracle that birds can seemingly escape gravity." Someone might even say, "It is a miracle I made it through the day." However, when the term *miracle* is taken in a literal sense, we speak of special acts of God in the world.

But if we admit God, must we admit Miracle? Indeed, indeed, you have no security against it. That is the bargain. Theology says to you in effect, "Admit God and with Him the risk of a few miracles, and I in return will ratify your faith in uniformity as regards the overwhelming majority of events."

C. S. Lewis

David Hume wrote in the eighteenth century, in an era called the "Enlightenment" by thinkers such as Immanuel Kant who declared that people had until then largely lived as if they were underage thinkers to be mentally shaped by authority and tradition. Shaking off his own Scots Calvinist upbringing, Hume wrote the classic analysis that ruled out any speculation that supernatural intervention in the world would produce a miracle. His definition of a miracle argues that the laws of nature operate inexorably—and modern definitions typically also refer to the laws of nature. Hume defines a miracle as a violation of the laws of nature.

In a definition similar to Hume's, famous atheist turned theist Antony Flew states that to most people, a miracle is "a term that has been variously understood, but is most commonly taken to mean an act that manifests divine power through the suspension or alteration of the normal working laws of nature." (Flew, DP, 234)

However, philosopher Tim McGrew reminds us that the idea and definition of a miracle existed long before the modern concept of a natural law and that intervention (or the "productive power" that enables miracles) could be reframed in a more positive way.

Bringing the concept of natural laws into the definition of "miracle" is . . . problematic, and for a variety of reasons many writers have found it untenable. First, the concept of a miracle predates any modern concept of a natural law by many centuries. While this does not necessarily preclude Hume's concept, it does raise the question of what concept or concepts earlier thinkers had in mind and of why the Humean concept should be thought preferable. One benefit of defining miracles in terms of violations of natural law is that this definition entails that a miracle is beyond the productive power of nature. But if that is the key idea, then it is hard to see why we should not simply use that as the definition and leave out the problematic talk of laws.

Second, it becomes difficult to say in some cases just which natural laws are being violated by the event in question. That dead men stay dead is a widely observed fact, but it is not, in the ordinary scientific use of the term, a law of nature that dead men stay dead. (McGrew, "Miracles," website)

Since there are serious questions regarding the definition provided by Hume, one might opt for a different definition, one that focuses on the connection to the event in question. Philosopher and apologist Francis Beckwith states a miracle is: "*A divine intervention that occurs contrary to the regular course of nature within a significant historical-religious context.*" (Beckwith, TMMM, 221, italics in original)

Beckwith continues:

First, a divine intervention refers to the action of a nonnatural agent. Second, that which occurs contrary to the regular course of nature refers to an event that overrides scientific laws, that cannot reasonably be accounted for either by the actions of natural agents (e.g. human beings, extraterrestrials) or by nature left to its own devices. Third, a significant historical-religious context refers to the purpose attached to the miracle because of when, where, and to (or for) whom the miracle occurs. That is, the historical-religious context of the event typically grounds the event's existential and teleological significance, and may serve as the basis by which to infer agent causation. (Beckwith, TMMM, 221)

If an event occurs that fits this definition and the characteristic criteria mentioned below in section III, it seems reasonable to conclude that a miracle has occurred. Beckwith's definition—by shifting to "a significant historico-religious context" and the "connection" (or application) to an event—in fact *sets up an alternate arena* rather than staying with the one Hume has set up. The fundamental factor that separates the definitions, however, surely is the power of their authors' specific presuppositions about law and nature and the active or inactive role of a God who is personal—Hume's presuppositions exclude the supernatural, as opposed to those of the person who believe that God is and that he personally acts upon the nature he has created; in other words, miracles can be expected.

III. The Nature and Characteristics of a Miracle

To qualify as a miracle, an event must possess certain characteristics. The characteristics that follow are not exhaustive, but they seem to provide a good lens for recognizing and distinguishing a miracle from a non-miraculous event. Richard L. Purtill notes five characteristics of a miracle. "A miracle is an event (1) brought about by the power of God that is (2) a temporary (3) exception (4) to the ordinary course of nature (5) for the purpose of showing that God has acted in history." (Purtill, DM, 72) We consider these characteristics and highlight additional traits next to define a miracle from the perspective of one who agrees with Purtill.

A. Miracles Are Supernatural Events

By definition miracles are supernatural events, and not events produced by finite power. *There is some agent external to the world who brings about* the event we call a miracle. In Beckwith's definition above, he names angels as nonnatural agents. But the word "agent" can mean either independent agency or the dependent agency of one acting on another's authorization. While angels do operate within a supernatural realm that transcends human powers, still, within their different order, in a Judeo-Christian understanding they are creatures, finite agents, whose power comes from God. In the traditional Medieval and Renaissance "great chain of being" that seems an echo of Psalm 8:5, they are not deity but created beings and in some sense "natural." Their powers of movement, appearance, speech, or other action come from their obedience to God. They don't work the miracles; God does. As the theologian and philosopher Thomas Aquinas says:

> When any finite power produces the proper effect to which it is determined, this is not a miracle, though it may be a matter of wonder for some person who does not understand that power. For example, it may seem astonishing to ignorant people that a magnet attracts iron or that some little fish might hold back a ship. But the potency of every creature is limited to some definite effect or to certain effects. So, whatever is done by the power of any creature cannot be called a miracle properly, even though it may be astonishing to one who does not comprehend the power of this creature. But what is done by divine power, which, being infinite, is incomprehensible in itself, is truly miraculous. (Aquinas, SCG, 3.102.3)

If a miracle attempt is not successful, then it is not a miracle. No one would call a failed attempt to raise someone from the dead a miracle because no actual supernatural event took place. Norman Geisler states, from a worldview anchored in a Creator who remains passionately watchful over his creation:

Indeed, the Bible records that God is always successful in His efforts. Diseases always vanish at His command, demons always flee at His order, nature is always open to His intervention. This is an important characteristic of the fingerprint of God which bears repeating. The supernatural acts of God in the Bible were and are always successful. That is, God always accomplished what He intended to accomplish. If He desired to heal someone, they were completely healed. There are no exceptions. (Geisler, SW, 28–29)

B. Miracles Are Immediate

Another characteristic of miracles is that they are always immediate. Geisler notes:

With specific regard to the healing ministry of Jesus, the results were always immediate. There were no instances of gradual improvement over a few days. Jesus commanded the invalid to "Arise, take up your pallet and walk," and "immediately the man became well" (John 5:8 NASB). In Peter's ministry in Acts 3 we see God healing a lame man instantly at Peter's hand. "Peter said, 'I do not possess silver and gold, but what I do have I give to you: In the name of Jesus Christ the Nazarene—walk!' And seizing him by the right hand, he raised him up; and immediately his feet and ankles were strengthened" (Acts 3:6–7 NASB). There was no lapse of time over which the man gradually improved. The restoration of this man's health was instantaneous and complete. (Geisler, SW, 29)

C. Miracles Are Rare Events

Miracles are rare events. C. S. Lewis writes in *Miracles: A Preliminary Study*, "A miracle is by definition an exception. How can the discovery of a rule tell you whether, granted a sufficient cause, the rule could be suspended?" (*Miracles*, 47) In the epilogue to that book, he adds,

You are probably quite right in thinking that you will never see a miracle done. . . . God does not shake miracles into Nature at random as if from a pepper-caster. They come on great occasions; they are found at the great ganglions of history—not of political or social history, but of that spiritual history which cannot be fully known by men. If your own life does not happen to be near one of those great ganglions, how should you expect to see one? . . . Miracles and martyrdoms tend to bunch about the same areas of history—areas we naturally have no wish to frequent. (Lewis, *Miracles*, 173–74)

Because miracles are indeed rare and connected to God's high oversight of history, then we would be presumptuous to expect predictability or demand a miracle. If miracles were frequent, they would seem predictable. If they were predictable, then what is to distinguish a miracle from the normative course of nature? New Testament scholar Craig Keener notes the sobering fact that not everyone who seeks healing receives it. "Affirming the reality of miracles also does not give us the right to ignore the fact that miracles very often do not happen. Tragically and disappointingly, large numbers of people who seek supernatural (or natural) healing are not healed." (Keener, MCNTA, 603)

Even in the Bible there are time periods in which miraculous events are rare. Until God prepared Moses to lead the exodus, there is no record of a miraculous event during Israel's four hundred years of slavery in Egypt. In 1 Samuel 3:1 it is specifically noted that even visions and messages from the Lord were rare at the time.

D. Miracles Are Unpredictable

Keener notes that miracles are unpredictable because a person cannot always predict the activity of an intelligent agent. God is under no compulsion to perform a miracle, so if God brings about a miracle, it is due to his initiative and will. Since God is a free agent, there is no conclusive formula that allows us to determine when, or where, a miracle will occur. Keener explains that if someone makes the hypothesis that a particular event may be a miracle, the hearers will normally be more inclined to trust that judgment in a case in which the speaker had accurately predicted it beforehand. Yet even so, some hearers would claim it was coincidence. Keener points out that some academic disciplines (such as history and the social sciences) generally cannot make precise predictions either, since they involve the study of persons who are not always predictable. Rather than believing miraculous accounts are "coincidence," Keener says:

> I prefer a different hypothesis: a personal God ready and able to heal, but one who often allows created nature to take its own course and who is not manipulated by formulas, as perhaps impersonal or merely psychological force could be. Although miracles are consistent with the character of the biblical God, we cannot always predict a personal deity's future actions, especially when our knowledge about the factors involved in those actions are [sic] limited. If miracles happened with absolute regularity, we would view them as part of the course of nature; their occurrence beyond providence in nature allows them to function more specifically as signs revealing God's activity and character. (Keener, MCNTA, 740–741)

Among the important distinctions of Keener's hypothesis is the emphasis upon a personal God: the god of Enlightenment deism was imagined as impersonal, one who establishes a working machine but does not relate to it in any personal way.

E. Miracles Cannot Be Tested by Scientific Means

Miracles cannot be tested by the means used in scientific inquiry. J. Harold Ellens reasons, "It is obvious that miracles cannot be investigated by the usual scientific methods since we cannot control the variables and perform experiments." (Ellens, BMPP, 266) However, just because miracles cannot be tested via scientific inquiry, one should not conclude that miracles cannot be investigated in any manner. Keener explains we must utilize the proper methodology: "Miracles must be investigated by means of the appropriate methodology, one suited for individual events. Miracles are distinct acts in history (on theistic premises, actions of an intelligent agent) and thus no more subject to experimentation than other historical events like Napoleon's defeat at Waterloo." (Keener, MCNTA, 608)

F. Miracles Always Promote Good and Glorify God Alone

Norman Geisler and Ronald Brooks explain that a miracle will always promote good, and never promote evil: "Morally, because God is good, miracles only produce and/or promote good." (Geisler and Brooks, WSA, 88) In addition, since God is good, they glorify him, as he is deserving all of the credit and glory for the miracle. "A miracle is never merely for show: Miracles are never performed for entertainment, but have the distinct purpose of glorifying God and directing men to Him." (Geisler and Brooks, WSA, 89)

G. Miracles Are More Than Astonishing

Miracles are not merely astonishing acts; such a definition is too broad. A magician can perform astonishing acts, through sleight of hand or through manipulating perception. Pharaoh's magicians and others encountered by the apostles in Acts also astonished people—but within limits that they admitted (see Acts 8; 16; and 19). However, a magician's tactics can be reduced to merely natural means. These acts, though capable of producing wonder in the minds of the audience, are purely natural events. A miracle is a supernatural event, is rare, and demonstrates divine power. Therefore, a miracle is much more than an astonishing event. C. S. Lewis remarks on that blinding power: "If the ultimate Fact is not an abstraction but the living God, opaque by the very fullness of His blinding actuality, then He might do things. He might work miracles." (*Miracles*, 98)

H. Miracles Are Not Contradictions

Finally, miracles are not contradictions. God could not cause a square circle to appear in the sky because square circles are a logical contradiction. Note there is nothing logically contradictory about some events that are considered physically impossible. For example, it is physically impossible for a man to walk on water; however, there is nothing self-contradictory about this idea and thus God *can* bring it about. Peter Kreeft and Ronald Tacelli explain, "A man walking through a wall is a miracle. A man both walking and not walking through a wall at the same time and in the same respect is a contradiction. God can perform miracles but not contradictions—not because his power is limited, but because contradictions are meaningless." (Kreeft and Tacelli, HCA, 109)

IV. The Purpose of Miracles

A. Miracles Can Confirm a *Message* from God

E. J. Carnell argues miracles are the only confirmation of a reference point that stands outside the system of natural law and establishes that law in being, subject to its Creator's will:

> Miracles are a sign and a seal of the veracity [truthfulness] of special revelation, revelation which assures us exactly how God has elected to dispose of His universe. In this revelation we read that He Who made us, and Who can also destroy us, has graciously chosen to keep the universe regular according to the covenant which He made with Noah and his seed forever. If the scientist rejects miracles to keep his mechanical order, he loses his right to that mechanical order, for, without miracles to guarantee revelation, he can claim no external reference point; and without an external reference point to serve as a fulcrum, the scientist is closed up to the shifting sand of history. (Carnell, ICA, 258)

Carnell concludes,

> In such a case, then, how can the scientist appeal to the changeless conviction "that the universe is mechanical," when from flux and change only flux and change can come? The scientist simply exchanges what he thinks is a "whim of deity" for what is actually a "whim of time and space." Why the latter guarantees perseverance of a mechanical world, when the former seemingly is impotent so to do, is not easy to see. (Carnell, ICA, 258)

B. Miracles Can Confirm a *Messenger* of God

Another purpose of miraculous "signs," as Norman Geisler notes, is

> to provide divine confirmation of a prophet of God. The religious ruler Nicodemus said of Jesus: "We know that you are a teacher who has come from God. For no one could perform

the miraculous signs you are doing if God were not with him" (John 3:2). Many people followed him because they saw the signs he performed on those who were sick (John 6:2). When some rejected Jesus, even though he had cured a blind man, others said, "How can a sinner do such miraculous signs?" (John 9:16). The apostles were confident in proclaiming, "Jesus the Nazarene was a man accredited by God to you by miracles, wonders, and signs, which God did among you through him, as you yourselves know" (Acts 2:22). For his credentials to the Corinthians, the apostle Paul claimed that the signs of a true apostle were performed among them (2 Cor. 12:12). He and Barnabas recounted to the apostles "the miraculous signs and wonders God had done among the Gentiles through them" (Acts 15:12). (Geisler, MMM, 98)

R. C. Sproul, John Gerstner, and Arthur Lindsley argue that a miracle is the only unquestionable confirmation God could have used:

Now if God would certify His messengers to us—as we have shown He would do if He intends to send them at all—He would give them credentials that only He could give. Thus, we would know indubitably that they are to be received as the messengers of God. What would God give His messengers that all could see could come only from God? Since the power of miracle belongs to God alone, miracles are a suitable and fitting vehicle of attestation. (Sproul, Gerstner, and Lindsley, CA, 144)

V. Objections Raised Against Miracles

We now consider a variety of objections that have been raised against miracles. Some argue that miracles are not possible. Others conclude miracles cannot truly happen because they are not scientific, in that they lack predictive value and are not replicable—that is, they cannot be tested by the methods of scientific experimentation. Some plead ignorance, taking an agnostic position like that defined and popularized by T. H. Huxley in the nineteenth century, determining to remain uncommitted to any conclusion and anticipate that natural explanations will eventually arise for all miracle claims. Others concede that miracles are possible but suggest they cannot be accepted as credible evidence in historical accounts or empirical study. We consider each of these objections along with possible responses to their arguments.

A. Hume's Objection

While Hume's arguments are certainly the most significant challenge to the possibility of miracles, and they have been the signal influence upon a climate of thought that cuts off any supernatural intervention into the normal course of events, they are not insurmountable. In fact, Hume's arguments against miracles are not only rejected by Christian scholars, they are also rejected by non-Christian scholars like John Earman, professor of the history and philosophy of science at the University of Pittsburgh, and author of *Hume's Abject Failure*. Though it does not seem that the best definition of a miracle should incorporate reference to a violation of the laws of nature, this does not answer the question as to whether or not particular events called miracles are, in fact, a violation of these laws. However, as many have noted, miracles are not violations of nature, especially in the form that Hume proposes. It is important to note that Hume does not deny that miracles are *metaphysically* impossible—meaning there is nothing strictly impossible about the occurrence of a miracle. Rather, Hume objects that one cannot have epistemic warrant for *knowing* a miracle occurred. He makes this objection so stringently because he trusts in the uniformity of the laws of nature: the operations that they carry out are what they have always done and will continue doing. They have, in his view, been "wound up" when they were made and have been left to run on their own, uniformly, whether we like the results or not. Accordingly, Hume challenges the identification of a miracle, not its occurrence:

> A miracle is a violation of the laws of nature; and as a firm and unalterable experience has established these laws, the proof against a miracle, from the very nature of the fact, is as entire as any argument from experience can possibly be imagined. . . . Nothing is esteemed a miracle, if it ever happened in the common course of nature. It is no miracle that a man, seemingly in good health, should die on a sudden: because such a kind of death, though more unusual than any other, has yet been frequently observed to happen. But it is a miracle, that a dead man should come to life; because that has never been observed in any age or country. There must, therefore, be a uniform experience against every miraculous event, otherwise the event would not merit that appellation. And as a uniform experience amounts to a proof, there is here a direct and full proof, from the nature of the fact, against the existence of any miracle; nor can such a proof be destroyed, or the miracle rendered credible, but by an opposite proof, which is superior. (Hume, ECHU, 144–146, 148)

1. Miracles as Violations of Nature

Hume's argument is rather clever, as Hume builds upon the confidence in natural order that had underwritten many of the early scientists' boldness to undertake experimentation (and Hume himself had shocked his readers by arguing that even cause and effect are ultimately only a connection that we imagine—because our sense experience comes to us in a series of separate sensations that only become "cause and effect" due to our describing them that way). Having undermined a science that relies on natural order, as philosopher Ronald Nash explains, Hume springs the trap:

> First, Hume cleverly manipulates the theist into admitting that he (the theist) must believe in a natural order since without such an order, there cannot be any way of recognizing exceptions to the order. Then, Hume hammers the theist with the obvious fact that the probability for the theist's alleged violations of natural laws must always be much less than the probability that the exception has not occurred. (Nash, FR, 230)

a. Are Miracles Interruptions in Nature?

According to C. Stephen Evans, the description of miracles as a "break" or "interruption" with respect to natural law incorrectly presumes God's absence from creation prior to his miraculous activity. But God is constantly present in his creation as the sustaining, necessary Being. Hence, whereas miracles entail special acts of God, nature is still held in being by the normal activity of God. Evans explains:

> It is, however, somewhat incorrect to call such special actions "breaks" or "interruptions" in the natural order. Such terminology implies that God is not normally present in the natural order; but if God exists at all, then he must be regarded as responsible for the whole of that natural order. The contrast, then, is not between "nature" and very unusual divine "interventions" into nature, but between God's

normal activity in upholding the natural order and some special activity on God's part. Thus, when God does a miracle, he does not suddenly enter a created order from which he is normally absent. Rather, he acts in a special way in a natural order which he continually upholds and in which he is constantly present. (Evans, WB, 88)

b. Are Laws of Nature Inviolable?

Another question worth asking is whether or not it is appropriate to categorize the laws of nature as inviolable. Keener observes this is often included as an assumption in the way natural laws are defined. "Most natural laws by definition assume a closed system; they make normal predictions but do not claim to account for influences outside the system in question." (Keener, MCNTA, 129)

We cannot reason from the nature of science that God is unable to act uniquely in the world. As Templeton laureate John Polkinghorne notes, "Science simply tells us that these events are against normal expectation. We knew this at the start. Science cannot exclude the possibility that, on particular occasions, God does particular, unprecedented things. After all, God is the ordainer of the laws of nature, not someone who is subject to them." (Polkinghorne, QCC, 100)

Hume defined a system that failed to recognize the significance of God acting as a volitional agent, because he did not think of God as personal. But Keener explains the larger perspective of what a personal agent can do without destruction of the predominant operations, "The action of agency (whether divine or human) need not violate the laws of nature; in most cases it merely changes the initial and boundary conditions on which the laws of nature operate." (Keener, MCNTA, 182) Furthermore, it is important to note the difference between a human and

a divine perspective. "Miracles might *appear* contrary to nature, Augustine concedes, but they do not appear so for God; 'For him "nature" is what he does.'" (Keener, MCNTA, 130, emphasis in original)

Keener explains by noting that even within scientific inquiry we observe unusual behavior under unusual conditions.

At different levels or on different conditions, the laws may be subject to higher or more complex principles. Thus these laws "behave in extreme ways in unusual contexts (for example, superconductivity or black holes)." Principles applicable to some kinds of matter under some conditions may need to be adjusted under significantly higher temperatures, density, and so forth, so that even voluminous observations limited to one setting need not predict phenomena for all conditions; by the same token, we should not expect norms of nature to predict conditions if an active intelligence beyond the universe would choose to act in distinctive ways in it. One therefore need not speak of apparent anomalies in terms of violations of a rigid, deterministic system. In fact, the violation concept of a miracle is not feasible on any of the three major theories of natural law prevailing today, rendering Hume's primary philosophic argument untenable. In a different cosmological framework plausible today, Hume's very argument works against him. (Keener, MCNTA, 136)

c. Do Regularities Determine What We Can Expect to Observe?

Many have argued the laws of nature can be utilized to place boundaries on what kind of observations we should expect to make as we examine the world around us. Others have argued against this assumption of uniformity by reexamining the concept of a law of nature. Stewart E. Kelly explains:

Such laws were indispensable for the Newtonian world order, but such a view was eclipsed a long time ago. Now there are regularities and order found in nature, [sic] they simply don't give us adequate reason for seeing these regularities as prescriptive. (Kelly, MMM, 55–56)

Should we be surprised to discover that nature is never surprised when something out of the ordinary occurs? Here is how C. S. Lewis answers in his landmark book on miracles:

If events ever come from beyond Nature altogether, she will be no more incommoded by them. Be sure she will rush to the point where she is invaded, as the defensive forces rush to a cut in our finger, and there hasten to accommodate the newcomer.... The divine art of miracle is not an art of suspending the pattern to which events conform but of feeding new events into that pattern. It does not violate the law's proviso, "If A, then B": it says, "But this time instead of A, A2," and Nature, speaking through all her laws, replies, "Then B2" and naturalizes the immigrant, as she well knows how. She is an accomplished hostess. (Lewis, *Miracles*, 60)

Terrence L. Nichols also criticizes the idea that the laws of nature can prescriptively describe what we can or cannot expect to occur:

Yet, if the hallmark of empirical science is impartial openness to evidence, such a way of proceeding [that is, pre-emptively excluding supernatural interventions] can hardly be called scientific. If scientific laws are held to be not only descriptive but also prescriptive, telling us what can and cannot occur in nature, then we have to dismiss all evidence that cannot be explained by present scientific theory. For example, recent experimental evidence, which has established that widely separated "entangled particles" interact nonlocally (or else communicate at faster-than light speeds), would have to be rejected because it is inexplicable according to current scientific theory. (Nichols, MST, 704–705)

It is important to clarify that we are not denying that nature is an ordered system full of regularities. Peter Kreeft and Ronald Tacelli note that theism assumes a system of natural law: "The concept of miracles presupposes, rather than sets aside, the idea that nature is a self-contained system of natural causes. Unless there are regularities, there can be no exceptions to them." (Kreeft and Tacelli, HCA, 109)

d. Do Hume's Argumentative Methods Lead to His Conclusion?

Hume was mistaken in his use of inductive principles. Stanley Jaki observes, "[Hume] failed to come to grips with the fact that on the basis of the bare inductionism he advocated one could never establish the existence of [immutable laws of nature]. An inductionism severed from metaphysics could not yield that completeness which was meant by universally and permanently valid laws." (Beckwith, DHAAM, 38).

Hume's argument depends heavily on his definition of a miracle. As Keener writes: "Thus, on the usual reading of Hume, he manages to define away any possibility of a miracle occurring, by defining 'miracle' as a violation of natural law, yet defining 'natural law' as principles that cannot be violated." (Keener, MCNTA, 134) Yet there are good reasons for rejecting Hume's definition.

It is important to note, the theist does not deny the uniformity of nature; nor does she deny that there is natural order. In fact, the identification of a miracle presupposes uniformity in nature. Rather, the presupposition scientists take today is called *methodological naturalism*. Essentially, methodological naturalism entails that supernatural causes should be excluded *a priori* in scientific inquiry. However, this view is essentially flawed. Take for example a theistic worldview, which also presupposes order in nature and that most causes have natural explanations. However, if one takes this approach, but allows for the world to be an open system—a system where the intervention of a divine being is possible—then it does not take away from the proficiency of scientific inquiry. Rather, adding the possibility of miracles does not take away from the efficiency of the scientific method, miracles just add to the scope of possible explanations that explain certain events and features in nature. (personal correspondence with Blake Giunta, founder of BeliefMap.org)

2. Hume's Rejection of Testimony

Having discussed Hume's definition of miracles as violations of natural law, we now consider Hume's rejection of eyewitness accounts of miracles. Those who haven't experienced or witnessed a miracle firsthand must rely on the testimony of others in their consideration of the evidence for miracles. Hume set very high standards for an individual to meet before that person's testimony of a miracle could be considered credible. Some argue these standards are impossible to meet. "Hume's position demands 'overwhelming evidence' before accepting the validity of a miracle. Yet Hume deliberately sets the standard of 'overwhelming' as virtually impossible, rejecting virtually any historical or present testimony." (Keener, MCNTA, 647) Keener continues:

Hume also argued, apparently based on his first argument against miracles, that eyewitness testimony can never be sufficiently persuasive to overcome the uniform experience against miracles. If this argument against testimony is understood as it usually is, it likewise constitutes a circular argument, since whether human experience is uniformly against miracles is precisely the question under debate. Given abundant and sometimes well-attested claims of miracles today, Hume's argument on this point should appear even less persuasive in a twenty-first-century multicultural context than it appeared in his own day. (Keener, MCNTA, 169)

The question remains: Is human experience uniformly against the occurrence of miracles? This part of Hume's objection introduces another aspect of the subject—not our assessment of miracles' possibility when we consider our direct empirical observation of an event, but instead, our assessment of the reports or accounts (written or spoken) made by other people. Keener, a leading authority on this topic, has authored a two-volume study defending the credibility of miracle reports in both historical and modern-day human experience. His research clearly demonstrates it is inappropriate to presume that miracle claims are incredibly rare. On the contrary, hundreds of millions of people, ranging across a multitude of cultural perspectives, adamantly testify they have experienced a miracle firsthand. The precision of Keener's work is respected among leading authorities in a variety of academic disciplines. A case can be made that Western intellectuals who dismiss his research out of hand have fallen prey to an ethnocentric prejudice.*

---

* These millions of reports do not undermine our claim that miracles are relatively rare occurrences. For all the millions of reports, these events remain exceptions to everyday experience, far outweighed by the uncounted trillions upon trillions of instances when everything proceeds according to the normal laws of nature.

Many healing claims involve blindness, inability to walk, and even raisings from death; other claims involve sudden changes in nature after prayers. Despite some debatable instances, some other cases are fairly clearly extraordinary. It seems to me that to dispute that such phenomena have sometimes occurred is not really possible for open-minded people. (Keener, MCNTA, 599)

Following this conclusion, Keener explores a variety of possible explanations for such phenomena. He makes a strong case suggesting the best explanation for some miracle claims is divine activity. This study serves as further support for our argument that Hume's universal rejection of testimony regarding miracles is inappropriate and strongly contradicted by the present evidence.

Mark Larson argues that a testimony's credibility is primarily grounded in the character of the person giving the testimony along with the nature of that testimony. "The proper way to assess testimonial evidence is to ascertain the sincerity of the witnesses and the causes of their convictions. The testimony of a witness should be received and believed if the witness is sincere and if the facts to which he testifies are indeed the only possible explanation for his testimony." (Larson, TCO, 89)

In fact, a significant portion of our general knowledge relies on the testimony of others' experiences. J. S. Lawton summarizes George Campbell's *Dissertation on Miracles* when he explains, "Hume was contrasting experience and testimony as distinct sources of knowledge, the former being greatly superior to the latter. But, says Campbell, children give unlimited assent to testimony long before they have experience to act for themselves: how then can the acceptance of testimony be grounded in experience?" (Lawton, MR, 56).

Furthermore, Hume sets impossibly high standards for what it means to give a credible testimony (see chapter 32, V.A.1.a). Gary G. Colwell asks a few pertinent questions:

Has any event, let alone a miracle, ever had such attestation as Hume requires? Can we think of any ancient historical event whose chronicler can pass the test which Hume wants to use on persons who recount miracle stories? Can we not doubt any chronicler's motives, as well as his education, his sincerity and his reputation—not to mention his possible habit of writing at 3 a.m. with a bottle of spirits at his side? Phrases like "of such unquestioned good sense" and "of such undoubted integrity" contrive impossible situations; for as soon as one begins to question a man he ceases from being a man of unquestioned good sense, no matter how far above reproach he has previously been known to be. (Colwell, MH, 10)

Today we have far more miracle claims to consider than Hume did in his day. However, Keener notes that "already in Hume's day, it was clear to some that he failed to take into adequate account that the confluence of multiple, independent, and reliable witnesses increases the probability of a testimony's accuracy." (Keener, MCNTA, 152–153)

a. Does Religious Diversity Discredit Miracle Claims?

Hume observed some miracle claims *must* be false because they independently support incompatible religions. The decision to dismiss all miracle claims based on this observation about competing religious contexts is faulty. Robert Larmer observes, "If in fact the evidence for miracles in a certain religion is very strong and the evidence for miracles in other religions is very weak, there exists no reason for seriously questioning the strongly evidenced claims." (Larmer, WIW, 108) Moreover, Craig Keener notes,

> Most important, Hume's counting the testimonies of different religions against one another is poor logic in any case; no court would throw out two testimonies on the allegation that one is false. Some could be true and others false; but the recognition that some miracle claims may be (and in fact are) false does nothing to damage the possibility that some other miracle claims may prove true. (Keener, MCNTA, 197)

This kind of reasoning would lead us to dismiss almost everything we know to be true: "It is a logical fallacy to reject stronger claims simply because weaker ones exist; on such grounds one could dispute most kinds of truth claims, since they usually have false or weaker competitors." (Keener, MCNTA, 197) Keener continues:

> While frauds exist and are probably common, one cannot extrapolate from a number of fraudulent claims to the conclusion that all miracle claims are fraudulent. Extrapolating from some claims being false to all claims being false involves a common logical fallacy: generalizing based on specific cases, hence illegitimate transference, that is, guilt by association. This approach lumps all supernatural claims together as a single group, then evaluates the entire group based on some claims." (Keener, MCNTA, 615)

Hasty generalizations often overlook alternate possible explanations. If a religious context is accepted as presenting an opening for acknowledging a supernatural event (as, perhaps, with Beckwith's definition), then particular interpretations given by one religion with fraudulent claims would not limit a supernatural God by falsifying the interpretations and claims of another context.

b. Why Are We Automatically Suspicious of Supernatural Claims?

Keener points out that automatic suspicion of supernatural claims may be rooted in a specific cultural context and intellectual era:

> We typically ground our critique of supernatural phenomena in a modern Western worldview that we do not question, and then use those untested assumptions to posit an authoritative Metanarrative or construal of reality. As children of the Western Enlightenment, many Western biblical scholars reject all reports of supernatural activity out of hand without critically examining the philosophic prejudices that we ourselves bring to the table. . . . It was the radical Enlightenment, however, that introduced thoroughgoing suspicion of all supernatural claims. While many scholars continue to operate with this radical Enlightenment paradigm, its dogmatism, perhaps inherited from an earlier era of religious disputes, fares poorly when evaluated from the perspectives and claims of many other cultures or a post-Enlightenment critique. The radical Enlightenment perspective on miracles has its own cultural and historical context that is not even the context of current Western scientific discovery. (Keener, MCNTA, 102, 106)

Keener also suggests a flaw in the outlook that dismisses miracle claims without a solid argument for the presuppositions that led to this dismissal. "It seems to me that such disdain for vast numbers of claims (apparently hundreds of millions of them) from other cultures, purely on the basis of unproved presuppositions inherited from the radical wing of the Enlightenment, risks the charge of ethnocentric elitism." (Keener, MCNTA, 762)

c. Is Indirect Evidence Valuable?

Moreover, Hume overlooks the importance of indirect evidence in support of miracles. As Nash argues:

Hume was wrong when he suggested that miracles are supported only by direct evidence cited in the testimony of people who claim to have witnessed them. There can also be important indirect evidence for miracles. Even if some person (Jones, let us say) did not observe some alleged miracle (thus making him dependent on the testimony of others who did), Jones may still be able to see abiding effects of the miracle. Suppose the miracle in question concerns the healing of a person who has been blind for years. Jones may be dependent on the testimony of others that they saw the healing occur, but perhaps Jones is now able to discern for himself that the formerly blind person can now see. The situation is analogous to that of someone who hears the testimony that a tornado has ravaged his city. Since he was not an eyewitness to the storm, he is dependent on the testimony of eyewitnesses who were there. But when this person arrives on the scene and sees the incredible devastation—cars on top of houses, other houses blown apart, trees uprooted—all this functions as indirect evidence to confirm the eyewitness testimony of others. In this way, certain effects of a miracle that exist after the event can serve as indirect evidence that the event happened. (Nash, FR, 233)

British Philosopher C. D. Broad appealed to indirect evidence to support the cornerstone miracle of the Christian faith—the resurrection of Christ:

We have testimony to the effect that the disciples were exceedingly depressed at the time of the Crucifixion; that they had extremely little faith in the future; and that, after a certain time, this depression disappeared, and they believed that they had evidence that their Master had risen from the dead. Now none of these alleged facts is in the least odd or improbable, and we have therefore little ground for not accepting them on the testimony offered us. But having done this, we are faced with the problem of accounting for the facts which we have accepted. What caused the disciples to believe, contrary to their previous conviction, and in spite of their feeling of depression, that Christ had risen from the dead? Clearly, one explanation is that he actually had arisen. And this explanation accounts for the facts so well that we may at least say that the indirect evidence for the miracle is far and away stronger than the direct evidence. (Broad, HTCM, 91–92)

3. Additional Reasons to Reject Hume's Argument

a. Hume's Arguments Are Circular

Beyond the responses listed above, Hume's argument against miracles contains serious logical flaws. Hume's notion of uniform experience either begs the question or is guilty of special pleading—that is, either Hume assumes the truth of his conclusion in order to arrive at his conclusion, or Hume applies rules and standards that he does not apply to his own view, without any explanation of why his own view does not fall victim to the same standards.

Further, Lewis exposes the circular character of Hume's use of "uniform experience" in the following passage:

Now of course we must agree with Hume that if there is absolutely "uniform experience" against miracles, if in other words they have never happened, why then they never have. Unfortunately, we know the experience against them to be uniform only if we know that all the reports of them are false. And we can know all the reports to be false only if we know miracles have never occurred. In fact, we are arguing in a circle. (Lewis, *Miracles*, 102)

Hume's argument merely restates the conclusion as part of his argument. In this way, Hume is presenting his own worldview concerning whether or not supernatural activity is to be expected. He is not presenting a solid *argument* for this conclusion. Charles Talbert observes, "Worldviews are highly resistant to disconfirmation. The materialistic worldview, represented by Lüdemann [the German New Testament scholar], dictates that the world was and is ruled by iron physical laws that not even God could or can bend." (Talbert, RLAMM, 215–216)

b. Hume Assumes the Probability of a Miracle Is Zero

Michael P. Levine explains the flaw in assuming that because a miracle is unprecedented, its probability must be zero. If this were true, based on probability, we should believe any other explanation with a non-zero probability before we believe a miracle has occurred, even if miracles are logically possible. The question becomes, is it appropriate to assign a probability of zero to a miracle's occurrence?

By treating a miracle as an event in the normal course of events as Hume must do if probability is to be applicable to determining whether to believe a miracle occurred, Hume assures that its probability rating will be zero. A miracle is infinitely improbable because it is totally unprecedented. The only way one can obtain an infinite improbability is to make the kind of implicit *a priori* assumption about the uniformity of nature that Hume makes. Assuming we

do not presuppose the principle that entails the concept of miracle as a violation of the laws of nature is incoherent (i.e. that a miracle cannot occur), the probability of a unique event is not zero as Hume would have it. Rather, it cannot be determined. (Levine, HPM, 34)

Again, the problem originates in the presuppositions made by definition before considering any particular account of a miracle. Keener observes we do not have all the information we need to rule out miracles based on the uniformity of nature. "We could reason from nature's uniformity only if we knew all the causal conditions present and could exclude intelligent (and in this case extranatural) causes. Probability estimates for rolls of dice will be skewed if the dice are loaded and if one allows for the possibility of distinctive divine action in some circumstances, one cannot rule out miracles in those circumstances." (Keener, MCNTA, 183)

c. Hume Confuses Evidence with Probability

Beckwith notes Hume's failure to make an appropriate distinction between evidence and probability:

Hume has failed to realize that the wise and intelligent person bases his or her convictions on *evidence,* not on Humean "probability." That is, an event's occurrence may be very improbable in terms of past experience and observation, but current observation and testimony may lead one to believe that the evidence for the event is good. In this way, Hume confuses evidence with probability. (Beckwith, DHAAM, 38).

d. Hume Is Inconsistent

Another challenge Hume faces in defending his argument against miracles is the fact that it seems inconsistent with his arguments elsewhere in support of ethics and ordinary life. For Hume, miracles cannot be claimed as causes: in fact, he argued that no causation at all is provable. He said we observe events and infer what they mean, but what we experience is actually only a succession of disconnected sensations. We have no proof they will repeat that succession. In this sense, he was radically skeptical. Keener explains:

> Hume's usual empiricism was so radical that it allowed only disconnected experiences, not determinations of causation, which are interpretive. The past sequence of events arouses expectation of their continuation, but cannot justify our expectations. For example, far from endorsing nature's uniformity, Hume argued that one might presume that the sun would rise the next day out of habit, but one could not be certain about it. He critiqued conventional notions of causality, treating laws as "merely observed uniformities" and, against earlier rationalists, denying them any metaphysical role. Thus some argue that Hume himself could not support the notion of inviolable laws (as opposed to mere habits of interpretation); if taken to its logical conclusion, the epistemological rigor in his miracles essay would have undercut even Newton's physics. (Keener, MCNTA, 136–137)

Despite his bleak conclusions about what a mind could know, Hume met death with tranquility, and he discussed with James Boswell, Samuel Johnson's biographer, matters of economics and philosophy and his own writing on history: Hume did not live according to the extreme skeptical conclusions of his essays. (Smith, DH, 78)

e. Hume Has a Defective View of Probability

Moreover, Hume confuses the probability of historical events with the way in which scientists employ probability to formulate scientific law. Nash explains:

> Finally, critics of Hume have complained that his argument is based on a defective view of probability. For one thing, Hume treats the probability of events in history like miracles in the same way he treats the probability of the recurring events that give rise to the formulation of scientific laws. In the case of scientific laws, probability is tied to the frequency of occurrence; the more times scientists observe similar occurrences under similar conditions, the greater the probability that their formulation of a law is correct. But historical events including miracles are different; the events of history are unique and nonrepeatable. Therefore, treating historical events including miracles with the same notion of probability the scientist uses in formulating his laws ignore a fundamental difference between the two subject matters. (Nash, FR, 234)

The task of assigning probabilities to the nature of an explanation is complicated and deeply influenced by the assigner's presuppositions. According to Keener:

> For most Western observers, the interpreter's assumptions determine *how* improbable natural explanations must be before supernatural explanations will be considered. Some rule out all evidence that they could explain by some other means, no matter how improbable the other explanations are, because they presuppose that supernatural explanations are always more improbable than even the weakest natural ones. In this case, they do not merely assign the burden of proof wholly to supernaturalists, despite antisupernaturalism being the minority position historically and globally. They also demand a standard of evidence impossible for any person to meet,

because evidence that contradicts one's position can virtually always be explained away. (Keener, MCNTA, 601)

B. Spinoza's Objection

Benedict de Spinoza argues that miracles are metaphysically self-contradictory. As one of the characteristics of a miracle is that it is not contradictory (see section III.H. above), this could be a serious objection to the possibility of miracles. Spinoza actually goes beyond the critique of miracles by Hume, but Spinoza's criticism against the possibility of miracles suffers from the same shortcoming of fallacious reasoning. We will identify those flaws, as seen from the perspective of one who accepts the concept of a personal God who not only created the cosmos but has the power and will to intervene in it.

1. Spinoza's Pantheistic View Of God

Van der Loos explains, "For Spinoza God, substance, and nature are identical concepts. God as the natura naturans, the first cause of all things, acts in accordance with strict laws. The universal laws of nature are eternal dispensations of God, embracing eternal truth and necessity. This system leaves no room for miracles." (van der Loos, MJ, 11) Moreover, Ernst and Marie-Luise Keller state that "For [Spinoza] non-natural or supernatural miracles are 'a mere absurdity.' If they really existed they would do away with all certainty in human affairs." (Keller, MID, 33–34).

Further, Spinoza claims that miracles would be a contradiction, not in the occurrence of miracles with the natural world, but with the very nature of God. Spinoza writes, "Nature cannot be contravened, but . . . she preserves a fixed and immutable order. . . . If anyone asserted that God acts in contravention to the laws of nature, he, *ipso*

facto, would be compelled to assert that God acted against His own nature—an evident absurdity." (Spinoza, TPT, 48)

2. Refuting Spinoza's Objection

Spinoza's objection is rather strange. It appears to apply only to his rational pantheistic view of God, not to the personal concept Christians hold. The biblical concept of God does not declare that God is identical to nature; thus, the laws of nature are not part of God's nature. If God interacts with, supervenes, violates, or disrupts the laws of nature, it does not follow by this view that God is violating his own nature; he is merely interacting with his creation in an unexpected or unusual manner. Keener writes:

> As Polkinghorne and others have responded, why should God choose to be limited to one way of working? Granted that God would be free to work through the apparent randomness of nature (and human lives) to achieve long-range purposes, is there any reason why God could not sometimes work differently, to communicate something special by making it distinct from the broader general revelation? Such a supposition requires no inconsistency in God's character, only multiple means of achieving divine ends, just as humans can perform physical work either directly or through verbal communication that elicits a physical response. (Keener, MCNTA, 181–182)

It is worth noting that even humans interact with nature in a complex way. Keener argues:

> Intelligent actors may not "disrupt" the "regularity" of nature but their existence operates on a level of complexity quite different from most of the vaster cosmos of which they are a

Why should God choose to be limited to one way of working? Granted that God would be free to work through the apparent randomness of nature (and human lives) to achieve long-range purposes, is there any reason why God could not sometimes work differently, to communicate something special by making it distinct from the broader general revelation? Such a supposition requires no inconsistency in God's character, only multiple means of achieving divine ends.

Craig S. Keener

part. How much more should this be true of a putative divine actor not subject to a cosmos that this actor originated? Those who, with Scripture and/or creed ("maker of heaven and earth"), affirm a Creator would hardly be impressed with any demand that this God be subject to patterns of nature that this God initiated. (Keener, MCNTA, 184)

3. Spinoza "Begs the Question"

In addition, Norman Geisler argues that Spinoza's argument begs the question:

Spinoza's Euclidean (deductive) rationalism suffers from an acute case of *petitio principii* (begging the question). For, as David Hume notes, anything validly deducible from premises must have already been present in those premises from the beginning. But if the antisupernatural is already presupposed in Spinoza's rationalistic premises, then it is no surprise to discover him attacking the miracles of the Bible.

Geisler adds, "What Spinoza needed to do, but did not, was to provide some sound argument for his rationalistic presuppositions." Spinoza "spins them out in the thin air of rational speculation, but they are never firmly attached to the firm ground of empirical observation." (Geisler, MMM, 18, 21)

4. Proper View of God's Interaction with the World

Contrary to Spinoza, influential philosopher Richard Swinburne argues for a normative understanding of the biblical conception of God's nature—a concept that entails the expectation of God to act in nature. In contrast to the deist or pantheist, if the theist believes that God will act in nature, then there is great credence given to the belief in favor of the possibility of miracles.

If there is no God, then the laws of nature are the ultimate determinants of what happens. But if there is a God, then whether and for how long and under what circumstances laws of nature operate depend on God. Any evidence that there is a God, and, in particular, evidence that there is a God of a kind who might be expected to intervene occasionally in the natural order will be evidence leading us to expect occasional violations of laws of nature. And any evidence that God might be expected to intervene in a certain way will be evidence supporting historical evidence that he has done so. (Swinburne, ER, 198)

C. The Objection That Miracles Are Impossible

Even with reasonable responses to Hume's and Spinoza's objections available, the question of whether or not miracles are possible continues to arise, and, as explained at the opening to this chapter, it has become almost the default view of a great many people in the Western world as the twenty-first century opens. For the theist, miracles are possible if God exists. However, a number of thinkers still argue against the possibility of miracles based on a variety of antisupernatural presuppositions.* Craig Keener summarizes Keith Ward's argument (Ward, MT, 137–138): "An atheist has reason to presuppose miracles impossible on the premise of atheism, but they are not *logically* impossible; the degree of probability assigned to miracles depends on one's prior assumptions." (Keener, MCNTA, 139)

1. Supposing the Impossible

The question then becomes, is it reasonable to rule out divine activity as a starting point? Keener gives reasons for concluding that the answer to this question is no.

Is it really intellectually necessary to dismiss as possible the explanation that large numbers of actual observers believe far more consistent with the most relevant evidence—namely, the explanation of divine activity? The majority of those who assume as necessary Hume's argument or antitheism are not themselves professional philosophers. They seem to simply take for granted that philosophy has excluded the possibility of miracles, when in fact, contrary to the belief of some outside academic philosophy, theism remains an acceptable subject of discussion in that discipline. (Keener, MCNTA, 740)

2. Miracles Are Possible

Even Hume did not accept that miracles are *logically* impossible. The person whose presuppositions propose that miracles are logically impossible goes even further than did Hume, the best-known critic of miracles. The modern critic of miracles who asserts the illogicality of affirming what he does not know is true would seem to be following in the wake of Thomas Henry Huxley, who declared that belief in the supernatural aspects of the Gospels would be "that which the candid simplicity of a Sunday scholar once defined it to be. 'Faith,' said this unconscious plagiarist of Tertullian, 'is the power of saying you believe things which are incredible.'" (Huxley, AAC, 1452) Those who believe miracles are not logically possible have no justification for the belief except their refusal to commit to anything for which they do not yet see the proof. Huxley in fact declared that agnosticism was not

a creed of any kind, except insofar as it expresses absolute faith in the validity of a principle . . . that it is wrong for a man to say that he is certain of the objective truth of any proposition unless he can produce evidence which logically justifies that certainty . . . yet that the application of that principle results in the denial of, or the suspension of judgment concerning, a number of propositions respecting which our contemporary ecclesiastical "gnostics" profess entire certainty. (Huxley, AAC, 1450)

Huxley and those who withhold judgment to remain neutral are actually basing their own beliefs on unsupported assumptions—that is, their "absolute faith" in the validity of the principle that judgment should be deferred for topics about which they have no certain knowledge and that they see as

---

* For further discussion on how presuppositions affect the position a person takes about knowledge, see these other chapters in this book: "The Nature of Truth," "The Knowability of Truth," "Answering Postmodernism," "Answering Skepticism," and "Is History Knowable?"

being out of reach and perhaps out of reach for everyone. (Huxley, AAC, 1450–51) To the theist, these agnostic assumptions that seem to call for neutrality are not enough to rule out the possibility of miracles.

Those in Huxley's camp have chosen to defer judgment, taking an epistemologically neutral position that goes beyond the methodological neutrality that historian Ronald J. Sider says modern historiography requires of historians. He separates the personal beliefs of a historian from his or her professional role's requirement to maintain a neutral position toward God's existence or nonexistence.

Now the historian, *qua* historian, cannot assume that traditional theism has been either finally proven or finally disproven. To do either would be to include a significant metaphysical presupposition in one's historical methodology. The historian must remain methodologically neutral. Personally, the historian may be a theist or a non-theist, but *qua* historian he ought—according to the morality of historical knowledge—to be an agnostic. As a methodological agnostic, he knows that the God of traditional theism just may happen to exist and that miracles would therefore be a real possibility. Hence he must decide the historicity of alleged miracles on the basis of the evidence that can be adduced for each individual case. (Sider, HMAM, 28)

D. The Objection That Miracles Are Unscientific

Nowell-Smith claims that miracles are unscientific because they lack predictive value. Nowell-Smith draws again upon the trust in uniformity that Hume had said prevents the occurrence of miracles. Of anyone trusting in the possibility of miracles, Nowell-Smith says, "Let him consider the meaning of the word 'explanation' and let him ask himself whether this notion does not involve that of a law or hypothesis capable of predictive expansion. And then let him ask himself whether such an explanation would not be natural, in whatever terms it was couched, and how the notion of 'the supernatural' could play any part in it." (Nowell-Smith, "Miracles," 253)

1. Predictability and Explanation

However, contrary to Nowell-Smith's assertion, there are several natural events that lack predictive value, yet are still suitable as good explanations. As Geisler explains:

Nowell-Smith demands that all explanations have predictive value to qualify as true explanations. And yet there are many events he would call natural that no one can predict. We cannot predict if or when a bachelor will marry. But when he does say, "I do," do we not claim that he was simply "doing what comes naturally"? If naturalists reply, as indeed they must, that they cannot always predict in practice (but only in principle) when natural events occur, then supernaturalists can do likewise. In principle we know that a miracle will occur whenever God deems one necessary. If we knew all the facts (which include the mind of God), then we could predict in practice precisely when this would be. Furthermore, biblical miracles are past singularities that like the origin of the universe or of life are not presently being repeated. But predictions cannot be made from singularities. They can only be projected from patterns. The past is not known by empirical science, but by forensic science. Therefore, it is misdirected to ask for predictions (forward); rather, one is attempting to make a retroduction (backward). (Geisler, MMM, 46–47)

2. Replication of a Miracle Is Not Necessary

Some have further argued that miracles are unscientific because they are not replicable in controlled settings. However, this provides no reason to presume miracles do not happen. As Keener says,

> Events in history are not repeatable in controlled studies; yet should we draw from that observation the inference that they are therefore not *true*? One is compelled to ask what kind of narrow epistemology would require us to rule out virtually any reliable information in history. When one employs a method of verifying miracles that insists that they be replicable in controlled settings, yet regards as natural and nonmiraculous any event that is so replicable, one has framed the method so as to secure the expected antisupernatural outcome. (Keener, MCNTA, 667)

Keener goes on to explain the inadequacy of empirical science to lead us to conclusions about the metaphysical: "Pure science is inductive and thus does not rule on metaphysical possibilities. It may extrapolate from known cases or work deductively from mathematical principles, but neither excludes the possibility of specific divine action." Neither, in fact, can pose metaphysical questions: the metaphysical is not within their domain. Furthermore, "Since science works inductively from details to larger patterns, it looks for larger patterns and cannot address single anomalies like miracles." (Keener, MCNTA, 126)

3. Science Is Not the Only Mode of Knowledge

We must venture outside the realm of science to describe some aspects of human history, including the narrations of events that are described as miracles. Science alone cannot describe everything that exists in reality. Keener asserts:

Human experience necessitates metaphysical as well as scientific language; the languages describe different aspects of existence and are not intrinsically contradictory. Human history, therefore, is not subject to pure scientific description. "The so-called conflict between science and miracles," Ian Ramsey observes, "is a pseudo-conflict which only arises when complete adequacy is claimed for the language of science." (Keener, MCNTA, 184–185)

The objection, then, that miracles are not scientific should not lead us to conclude miracles are not possible or credible as explanations of our evidence. Science is not equipped to lead us to this conclusion. Keener notes: "Many scientifically inclined persons who rule out supernatural explanations *a priori* may do so not because the data in their specialties demand this approach but because their initial plausibility structures reflect philosophic assumptions borrowed from outside their discipline." (Keener, MCNTA, 692)

E. The Objection That Supposed Miracles Are Natural, Not Supernatural

Recall that we characterized miracles as supernatural. Some deny this classification and claim they are unnatural (as previously discussed). Others deny the supernatural character of miracles claiming they are in fact natural, thus, miracles will eventually be explained by natural means.

1. The Faith of Naturalism

Patrick Nowell-Smith claims "miracles" are simply "strange" natural events that either have or will have a strict scientific explanation. An explanation like this reflects the outlook of naturalism, which became widespread during the last third of the nineteenth century. Naturalism sees man as only matter, temporarily alive in a cosmos without

God. But this view does look to empirical science and reason to continue discovering the complex natural processes that explain the causes of events. According to Nowell-Smith, "No matter how strange an event someone reports, the statement that it must have been due to a supernatural agent cannot be a part of that report." (Nowell-Smith, *Miracles*, 246) He continues, "No scientist can at present explain certain phenomena. It does not follow that the phenomena are inexplicable by scientific methods, still less that they must be attributed to supernatural agents." (Nowell-Smith, *Miracles*, 247) To further his argument he states, "There is still the possibility that science may be able, in the future, to offer an explanation which, though couched in quite new terms, remains strictly scientific." (Nowell-Smith, *Miracles*, 248)

2. Naturalism Limits Knowledge

Nowell-Smith's objection to miracles is rooted in a kind of naturalistic faith, not scientific evidence. Norman Geisler exposes the flaws in Nowell-Smith's assertion as follows:

> While Nowell-Smith claims that the scientist should keep an open mind and not reject evidence that ruins his preconceived theories, it is clear that he has closed his mind to the possibility of any supernatural explanations. He arbitrarily insists that all explanations must be natural ones or they do not really count. He makes the grand assumption that all events will ultimately have a natural explanation, but doesn't offer any proof for that assumption. The only way he can know this is to know beforehand that miracles cannot occur. It is a leap of naturalistic faith! (Geisler and Brooks, WSA, 81)

According to Lewis, no amount of time will be sufficient to naturalize a legitimate

miracle: "When a thing professes from the very outset to be a unique invasion of Nature by something from outside, increasing knowledge of nature can never make it either more or less credible than it was at the beginning. In this sense it is mere confusion of thought to suppose that advancing science has made it harder for us to accept miracles." (Lewis, *Miracles*, 48)

Furthermore, scientific naturalism does not seem to distinguish between observable operations of nature and the unobservable sources of those operations' very existence. As Geisler notes,

> One of the problems behind this kind of scientific naturalism is the confusion of naturalistic origin and natural function. Motors function in accordance with physical laws but physical laws do not produce motors; minds do. In like manner, the origin of a miracle is not the physical and chemical laws of the universe, even though the resulting event will operate in accordance with these natural laws. In other words, a miraculous conception will produce a nine-month pregnancy (in accordance with natural law). So, while natural laws regulate the operation of things, they do not account for the origin of all things. (Geisler, MMM, 47)

3. Naturalism's Reductionist Assumptions about Medical Miracles

Many miracle claims involve an individual who has experienced physical healing. Some physicians reject that these claims are truly miraculous. It is important to discern what kind of authority should be heeded in these instances. As Keener writes:

> When a doctor reports that a condition is not genuinely cured or that it often resolves on its own, she speaks within her expertise and we should give heed. When a doctor denies that

a cure is miraculous based on a philosophic paradigm that excludes miracles, however, he speaks not as a doctor but as an amateur philosopher. In the latter case, the opinion merits no greater weight than that assigned to that of any other amateur philosopher. (Keener, MCNTA, 656)

A patient's psychological disposition can play a significant role in his or her recovery. Keener summarizes Rex Gardner's argument (Gardner, HM, 29–31): "Clearly natural factors are at work in much healing, but some observers contend that attributing *all* medically unexplained recovery claims to exclusively psychological causes, when other proposed factors may be at work, is reductionist." (Keener, MCNTA, 646) Psychological factors are not always sufficient for explaining remarkable instances of healing. As David Robertson notes,

No one will ever know how much of the cure depends on the patient's desire and expectation that he be healed. But most physicians do recognize that motivation is a powerful force aiding recovery. In spite of this, there are surely few in the field who have not, on some rare occasion at least, witnessed a recovery so contrary to the usual prognosis, and so apparently complete, that the word "miracle" seemed the only appropriate description of it. (Robertson, EL, 188–189)

Keener explains further what is meant by the argument that the exclusion of supernatural explanations for remarkable healings is reductionist: "Although one cannot prove special divine action where natural factors can account for a healing, to assume by contrast that the presence of natural factors must exclude supernatural ones is reductionist. Some critics carry the reductionism so far

that they attribute even healings without any currently explainable natural causes to natural causation that may someday be explained." (Keener, MCNTA, 711)

Some who concede that divine activity is possible still argue that it should serve as a credible explanation only when all other explanations have been ruled out. This reasoning embraces future scientific discoveries as more credible explanations than divine action. However, problems exist with accepting unknown laws of nature as a better explanation than divine healing: one ends up profoundly skeptical. The person arguing in this way has reduced the potential answer to the single one that has no existence yet and ambiguous evidence for its potential. According to Keener,

The burden of proof seems stacked impossibly against divine healing: any recovery that could be explained otherwise excludes divine healing, yet nearly any restoration noted in Scripture or today could potentially be explained on such terms. This criterion does not require the antisupernaturalist to offer a *plausible* explanation—just *any* explanation. Among viable explanations in the skeptic's arsenal is now that apparent miracles could reflect *unknown* laws of nature—a criterion that effectively excludes any appeal to evidence. (Keener, MCNTA, 653, emphasis in original)

We argue reasonably that divine activity is not necessarily the least likely explanation in every circumstance. It serves as a stronger explanation than the appeal to coincidence or undiscovered scientific laws. Keener concludes: "Granted that a supernatural interpretation presupposes the existence of something supernatural, the ruling out of such an interpretation presupposes the nonexistence of anything supernatural, and in some cases a supernatural explanation (such as theism) provides a more plausible explanation than coincidence would." (Keener, MCNTA, 703)

VI. Conclusion

James Burke began his 1985 PBS series *The Day the Universe Changed* with the anecdote of someone remarking to the philosopher Ludwig Wittgenstein about the foolishness of those who lived before Copernicus and thought that the sun went around the earth. According to the story, Wittgenstein's response was, "Yes. But what would it have looked like if the sun did so?" Our interpretations, clearly, come from presuppositions that govern what we expect to perceive. We began with my (Sean's) conversation with the physicist who presumed that normality governed all possible natural events. We have seen Hume's classic argument that also trusted in uniformity but at the same time questioned causality and reports that were not directly perceived, and we have noticed how he was situated between a refusal of his Scots Calvinist upbringing and the heady new deist proclamations of the Enlightenment. Our own postmodern world remembers and still holds traces of these earlier suppositions, along with modern confidence in reason and postmodern suspicion—especially when

traditional faith is involved. C. S. Lewis begins his book *Miracles* by saying,

> In all my life I have met only one person who has seen a ghost. And the interesting thing about the story is that the person disbelieved in the immortal soul before she saw the ghost and still disbelieves after seeing it. She says that what she saw must have been an illusion or a trick of the nerves. . . . For this reason, the question whether miracles occur can never be answered simply by experience. . . . If anything extraordinary seems to have happened, we can always say that we have been the victim of an illusion. If we hold a philosophy which excludes the supernatural, this is what we shall always say. What we learn from experience depends on the kind of philosophy we bring to experience. It is therefore useless to appeal to experience before we have settled, as well as we can, the philosophical question. (Lewis, *Miracles*, 7)

Serious thinkers are always invited to reflect on the expectations they bring to an experience or concept or conversation or project—or to the reading of a text. We usually begin to discover these presuppositions when something seems not to fit in the way that we expect. If the topic involves questions of whether an eternal, personal God cares about the world and the individual—and in fact intervenes within the world or an individual life—all the more so.

CHAPTER 32

IS HISTORY KNOWABLE?

OVERVIEW

I. Introduction

Christianity is a historical faith, meaning that it rests finally on the historical life, death, and resurrection of Jesus. If these events are not true, then the Christian faith is false, and its teachings are groundless (1 Cor. 15:14, 17). Yet if these claims can be established through normal historical methods, then we have a compelling reason to believe that Christianity is true. Rather than exploring particular events from the past, such as the exodus or resurrection, this section explores the task of historiography and answers objections that claim history, miraculous or otherwise, is not knowable.

Christian apologist Norman Geisler notes, "In order to verify these truth claims one must first establish the objectivity of historical fact. This leads the discussion naturally into the whole question of . . . whether history is really knowable." (Geisler, CA, 285)

A. Definition of History

Historian Louis Gottschalk provides a definition of history: "By its most common definition, the word *history* now means 'the past of mankind.' Compare the German word for *history—Geschichte*, which is derived from *geschehen*, meaning to happen. *Geschichte* is *that which has happened*." (Gottschalk, UH, 41)

Philosopher-historian Robin G. Collingwood notes, "Every historian would agree,

I think, that history is a kind of research or inquiry. . . . The point is that generically it belongs to what we call the sciences: that is, the forms of thought whereby we ask questions and try to answer them." (Collingwood, EPH, 9)

Richard Evans explains,

It [history] is not a science in the strong sense that it can frame general laws or predict the future. But there are sciences, such as geology, which cannot predict the future either. The fact seems to be that the differences between what in English are known as the sciences [branches of knowledge, as the term has been used since Aristotle] are at least as great as the differences between these disciplines taken together and a humane discipline such as history. (Evans, DH, 62)

John Warwick Montgomery presents a more detailed definition of history:

History . . . will here be defined as: An inquiry focusing on past human experience, both individual and societal, with a view towards the production of significant and comprehensive narratives, embracing men's actions and reactions in respect to the whole range of natural, rational, and spiritual powers. (Montgomery, SP, 13)

B. Historical Method

Regarding general historical methodology and historiography, Gottschalk states, "The process of critically examining and analyzing the records and survivals of the past is here called *historical method*. The imaginative reconstruction of the past from the data derived by that process is called historiography (the writing of history)." (Gottschalk, UH, 48)

Though historians take various approaches to uncovering the past, they tend to follow general methodological rules and principles that can be delineated, and the academic community at large generally holds historians accountable to these rules and principles.

II. Historical Process

A. Nature of Historical Thought

David Fischer, in his book *Historians' Fallacies*, describes the nature of historical thought as "a process of *abductive* reasoning in the simple sense of adducing answers to specific questions, so that a satisfactory explanatory 'fit' is obtained. The answers may be general or particular, as the question may require. History is, in short, a problem-solving discipline." He adds, "A historian is someone (anyone) who asks an open-ended question about past events and answers it with selected facts which are arranged in the form of an explanatory paradigm." (Fischer, HF, xv)

Noting further complexity, Fischer acknowledges that "historians are likely to agree in principle, but not in practice. Specific canons [tests] of historical proof are neither widely observed nor generally agreed upon." Nevertheless, Fischer has identified at least seven simple rules of thumb concerning the historian's methodology:

1. Historical evidence must be a direct answer to the question asked and not some other question.
2. A historian must not merely provide good relevant evidence but the best relevant evidence. And the best relevant evidence, all things being equal, is evidence which is most nearly immediate to the event itself.
3. Evidence must always be affirmative. Negative evidence is a contradiction in terms—it is no evidence at all.
4. The burden of proof, for any historical assertion, always rests upon its author.
5. All inferences from empirical evidence are probabilistic. . . . A historian must determine, as best he can, the probability *of A* in relation to the probability of alternatives.
6. The meaning of any empirical statement depends upon the context from which it is taken.
7. An empirical statement must not be more precise than its evidence warrants. (Fischer, HF, 62–63)

B. Historical Approach

According to C. Behan McCullagh, historians rely upon *inference to the best explanation*:

This is used when there is no evidence to provide strong direct support for a particular hypothesis about the kind of information an historian wants to discover, and so the historian has to draw upon very general knowledge to arrive at plausible hypotheses about its origin. As the name of this form of inference suggests, it proceeds by judging which of the plausible hypotheses provides the best explanation of what is known about the creation of the evidence in question. Strictly speaking, the best explanation is only likely to be true if the historian has considered all the plausible hypotheses, and not left the best explanation out of the list. (McCullagh, LH, 42)

McCullagh explains that inference to the best explanation is similar to how a detective approaches a crime scene:

He [R. G. Collingwood] illustrated it with a detective story in which a detective has to consider various hypotheses about who committed a murder, and settles upon one which fits quite a lot of the evidence and is inconsistent with no known facts. The range of suspects is limited to those known to have been near the place of the murder at the time. (McCullagh, LH, 42)

According to McCullagh, a credible hypothesis must "fit" five criteria. A credible hypothesis must:

1. "be as plausible as possible" (the data must imply something like the hypothesis).
2. "have great explanatory scope" (the hypothesis must explain great quantity and variety of the data).
3. "have great explanatory power" (the hypothesis must explain the data with a strong degree of probability).
4. "not [be] disconfirmed by other reasonable belief" (there must not be data that implies the hypothesis is improbable).
5. "not include additional ad hoc components" (the data must not be twisted to fit the theory). (McCullagh, LH, 51–52)

III. Historical Reliability, Knowability, and Facthood

A. Historical Fact vs. Self-Evident Truths

Philosopher Mortimer J. Adler notes the difference between self-evident truths and historical knowledge:

On the one hand, we have self-evident truths that have certitude and incorrigibility; and we also have truths that are still subject to doubt but that are supported by evidence and reason to a degree that puts them beyond reasonable doubt or at least gives them predominance over contrary views. All else is mere opinion—with no claim to being knowledge or having any hold on truth.

There is no question that the findings and conclusions of historical research are knowledge in this sense; no question that the findings and conclusions of the experimental or empirical sciences, both natural and social, are knowledge in this sense. (Adler, TPM, 100–101)

B. History Is a Discipline Based on Probability

McCullagh similarly indicates what in history should be accepted as reliably true:

If [historical descriptions] had not been based upon a careful and fairly exhaustive study of relevant evidence, if they had not been based upon well-established particular and general beliefs about the world, and had not been arrived at by sound inductive arguments, then they would not deserve to be believed. But those conditions generally do yield reliable beliefs about the world, and the conclusions drawn in accordance with them are generally true. (TH, 57)

In my (Sean's) historical research on the fate of the apostles, I set up a calculus to evaluate the probability that each apostle died as a martyr. The evidence varies substantially for each apostle, so I had to analyze carefully the quality and quantity of available evidence, and then make an assessment of the likelihood of his martyrdom. I set up a nine-point scale from "not possibly true" to "the highest possible probability." The purpose, of course, was to be as careful and precise with the evidence as possible. The critical point here is that history deals with probability and appropriate confidence, rather than mathematical certainty. Here is my historical probability scale (McDowell, FA, 4):

- *Not possibly true*—certainly not historical
- *Very probably not true*—doubtfully historical
- *Improbable*—unlikely
- *Less plausible than not*—slightly less possible than not
- *As plausible as not*—plausible
- *More plausible than not*—slightly more possible than not
- *More probable than not*—likely
- *Very probably true*—somewhat certain
- *The highest possible probability*—nearly historically certain

Historian Richard Evans notes, "No historians really believe in the *absolute* truth of what they are writing, simply in its *probable* truth, which they have done their utmost to establish by following the usual rules of evidence." (Evans, DH, 219; emphasis in original)

Apologist and historian Michael Licona concludes, "Accordingly it is especially true that historians interested in antiquity are never epistemically justified in having absolute certainty that an event occurred, the premises of all historical inferences are

*Accordingly it is especially true that historians interested in antiquity are never
epistemically justified in having absolute certainty that an event occurred,
the premises of all historical inferences are fallible. . . . Notwithstanding, the
inability to obtain absolute certainty does not prohibit historians from having
adequate certainty. Carefully examined inferences are generally reliable.*

Michael Licona

fallible. . . . Notwithstanding, the inability to obtain *absolute* certainty does not prohibit historians from having *adequate* certainty. Carefully examined inferences are generally reliable, and it is reasonable to believe that they correctly describe what actually occurred when the historian's horizon [worldview] is mature, he has been deliberate in serious attempts to minimize the negative impact of his horizon, and he has followed proper methodology." (Licona, RJ, 69; emphasis in original)

C. Objectivity in Historical Study
1. What Is Meant by "Objective"

Geisler explains what must be meant by the use of the term *objective*, and notes a potential equivocation: "If by 'objective' one means absolute knowledge, then of course no human historian can be objective. This we will grant. On the other hand, if 'objective' means a *fair but revisable* presentation that reasonable men should accept, then the door is still open to the possibility of objectivity." (Geisler, CA, 290; emphasis in original)

2. Minimizing Bias

In order to minimize the bias of one's horizon, or worldview, and guide the historian to arrive at the most accurate judgment possible, Licona suggests six important guidelines for the historian; the italicized six points are stated exactly as Licona does in his book *The Resurrection of Jesus*, but the descriptions are summary statements based on his work, which we have added for clarity:

- *Method.* Paying close attention to historical methodology can help avoid too much subjectivity. This involves many parts, such as how competing hypotheses are compared, testing the adequacy of hypotheses, and the manner in which data is collected, analyzed, and contextualized.
- *The historian's horizon and method should be public.* Historians should be clear about their guiding assumptions.
- *Peer pressure.* Peer critique and analysis can help minimize worldview and act as a check on bias.
- *Submitting ideas to unsympathetic experts.* Having critical experts review work and provide feedback is necessary for ensuring that conclusions are as accurate as possible.
- *Account for the relevant historical bedrock.* Some facts are so firmly established that any reputable theory must incorporate them or be built upon them.
- *Detachment from bias.* Historians must willingly confront data and arguments that are contrary to their preferred hypothesis. Historians must aim for sympathy to those

with different perspectives. (Licona, RJ, 52–61)

IV. Objections to the Knowability of History

Many of the following objections to the knowability of history are taken from Charles A. Beard's essay, "That Noble Dream." His doubts regarding the knowability of history have influenced many prominent historians through the last century and into the present. We consider a few prominent challenges to the knowability of history (mostly from Beard), and then provide a brief response to each claim.

A. History Is Not Directly Observable

1. Claim

Charles Beard contends, "The historian is not an observer of the past that lies beyond his own time. He cannot see it *objectively* as the chemist sees his test tubes and compounds. The historian must 'see' the actuality of history through the medium of documentation. That is his sole recourse." (Beard, TND, 323; emphasis in original)

2. Response

In response to the relativist claim that the historian is disadvantaged in comparison to the scientist, philosopher and apologist William Lane Craig poses two responses:

First, it is naïve to think that the scientist always has direct access to his objects of study. Not only is the scientist largely dependent on the reports of others' research (which, interestingly, constitute for him historical documents) for his own work, but furthermore, the objects of the scientist's research are often only indirectly accessible, especially in the highly theoretical fields like physics. (Craig, RF, 176)

He continues,

Secondly, while the historian does not have direct access to the past, the residue of the past, things that have really existed, is directly accessible to him. . . . For example, archaeological data furnish direct access to the objects of the historian's investigation. (Craig, RF, 176)

Geisler concludes, "The historian, no less than the scientist, has the tools for determining what really happened in the past. The lack of direct access to the original facts or events does not hinder the one more than the other." (Geisler, CA, 291)

B. The Fragmentary Nature of Historical Accounts

1. Claim

Charles Beard argues, "The documentation (including monuments and other relics) with which the historian must work covers only a part of the events and personalities that make up the actuality of history. In other words multitudinous events and personalities escape the recording of documentation." (Beard, TND, 323)

2. Response

Licona responds to this challenge by first readdressing our notions of historical knowledge:

If we think of history as an exhaustive description of the past, then history is certainly unknowable. However, if we regard history as an adequate description of a subject during a specific period, we are in a position to think that history is knowable to a degree. Although incomplete, adequate descriptions provide enough data for answering the questions being asked. (Licona, RJ, 33)

Noting the historical fallacy inherent in the assumption that complete knowledge is necessary for the establishment of truth, Fischer writes that such a fallacy "would prevent the historian from knowing anything until he knows everything, which is absurd and impossible." (Fischer, HF, 65)

Geisler replies to this claim as well:

> The fact that accounts of history are fragmentary does not destroy its objectivity. . . . History need be no less objective than geology simply because it depends on fragmentary accounts. Scientific knowledge is also partial and depends on assumptions and an overall framework which may prove to be inadequate upon the discovery of more facts. (Geisler, CA, 292–293)

C. The Selective Nature of Historical Methodology and of the Interpretive Structuring of the Facts of History

1. Claim

Charles Beard says: "Not only is the documentation partial, in very few cases can the historian be reasonably sure that he has assembled all the documents of a given period, region, or segment. In most cases he makes a partial selection or a partial reading of the partial record of the multitudinous events and personalities involved in the actuality with which he is dealing." (Beard, TND, 324)

2. Response

Contending against the claim that the element of selectivity in historical methodology renders history nonobjective, Geisler replies, "The fact that the historian must select his materials does not automatically make history purely subjective. Jurors make judgments 'beyond reasonable doubt' without having all the evidence. If the historian has the relevant and crucial evidence, it will be sufficient to attain objectivity." And as others above have noted, "One need not know everything in order to know something." (Geisler, CA, 293).

Philosopher Ronald Nash has also noted how selectivity is not necessarily antithetical to objective or reasonable historical judgment "since some selections can be more plausible, have more support, and be more reasonable than others." (Nash, CFHU, 86)

D. The Historian Cannot Avoid Value Judgments

1. Claim

Charles Beard writes, "The events and personalities of history in their very nature involve ethical and aesthetic considerations. They are not mere events in physics and chemistry inviting neutrality on the part of the 'observer.'" (Beard, TND, 324) Georg Iggers writes, "Historical scholarship is never value-free and historians not only hold political ideas that color their writing, but also work within the framework of institutions that affect the ways in which they write history." (Iggers, HTC, 475)

2. Response

Philosopher J. P. Moreland argues for *attentive influence*, which claims that "situatedness may influence and even distort knowledge by acquaintance or propositional knowledge of an object, but direct access is still possible and available for subsequent adjustment of conceptual or propositional judgments." (Moreland, TARD, 310) He provides an example:

> One day a missionary spoke in the seminary chapel, and without telling us where they were taken, he showed a set of slides from a culture he had just visited. He asked us to list on paper

everything we saw. After we were finished, he spoke a while, and then put the slides up again and asked us to start with a fresh sheet of paper and list everything we saw this time. Interestingly, people's second list was virtually identical with their first one. Why? Because people tend to look to confirm what they already see and believe rather than adopt a fresh perspective and launch out from scratch. Over time, people fall into ruts and adopt ways of seeing things according to which certain features are noticed and others are neglected.

I am not claiming this is a good or bad thing. I am simply noting that it happens. I suggest that situatedness functions as a set of habit forming [sic] background beliefs and concepts that direct our acts of noticing or failing to notice various features of reality. Depending on various factors, such situatedness may yield accurate or inaccurate experiences and beliefs. It is not that we cannot see reality itself. In fact, through effort we can look at things from a different perspective and further confirm or disconfirm our previous viewpoint. Habit-forming beliefs do not stand between a person and reality as do glasses. Rather, they habitualize ways of seeing and thinking which, through effort, can be changed or retained, hopefully on the basis of comparing them with reality itself. (Moreland, TARD, 311)

Adler describes the ways that the "subsequent adjustment" Moreland speaks of might take place, so that "through effort," as Moreland says, we gain "a different perspective." Adler says that with a new discovery or new thinking (TPM, 164), one's original view may come to be seen as false when one encounters any of these three:

experience, which produces evidence contrary to the evidence that has been employed to

support the opinion that claims to be true and to have the status of knowledge ... by rational argument, which advances reasons that correct and replace the reasons advanced to support the opinion ... [or by] a combination ... new and better evidence, together with new and better reasons for holding a view contrary to the one that has been refuted. (Adler, TPM, 104–5)

Adler describes how this careful thought can provide a working foundation of established knowledge to guide historical study:

Research amasses evidence about which historians think and, in the light of their thinking, advance conclusions that they regard as supported by a preponderance of the evidence and by good reasons. When they are reached in that way, historical conclusions can be regarded as established knowledge even though further research may change our view of the matter. (Adler, AE 166)

E. Every Historian Is a Product of His Time and Worldview

1. Claim

Beard claims, "The historian seeking to know the past, or about it, does not bring to the partial documentation with which he works a perfect and polished neutral mind. . . . Whatever acts of purification the historian may perform he yet remains human, a creature of time, place, circumstance, interests, predilections, culture." (Beard, TND, 324) Robert Anchor observes, "[H]istorians, like everyone else, are historically situated, and ... their reconstructions of the past are inevitably informed by their various existential interests and purposes. . . . [O]ur subjectivity is in large part itself a product of the historically evolved communities to which we belong." (Anchor, QBHP, 114, 117)

2. Response

While it may be true that every historian is a product of his time, Geisler notes, "It does not follow that because the *historian* is a product of his time that his *history* is also a product of the time.... The criticism confuses the *content* of knowledge and the *process* of attaining it. It confuses *the formation* of the view with its *verification*. Where one derives a hypothesis is not essentially related to how he can establish its truth." (Geisler, CA, 296–297, emphasis in original) Just because we are situated (to use J. P. Moreland's term above) does not mean we cannot access past reality with confidence. This objection also commits the genetic fallacy, which is when a claim is discounted because of some perceived fault in its origin. Fischer observes that there can also be

> confusion between the way knowledge is acquired and the validity of that knowledge. An American historian may chauvinistically assert that the United States declared its independence from England in 1776. That statement is true, *no matter what the motives of its maker may have been*. On the other hand, an English historian may patriotically insist that England declared its independence from the United States in 1776. That assertion is false, and always will be. (Fischer, HF, 42, emphasis in original)

F. The Selection and Arrangement of Materials Is Subjective to the Historian

1. Claim

Beard argues, "Into the selection of topics, the choice and arrangement of materials, the specific historian's 'me' will enter." And so, concludes Beard, "The historian's powers are limited. He may search for, but he cannot find, the 'objective truth' of history, or write it, 'as it actually was.'" (Beard, TND, 325)

2. Response

N. T. Wright notes, "The fact that *somebody*, standing *somewhere*, with a particular *point of view*, is knowing something does not mean that the knowledge is less valuable: merely that it is precisely *knowledge*.... [I]t must be asserted most strongly that to discover that a particular writer has a 'bias' tells us nothing whatever about the value of the information he or she presents. It merely bids us be aware of the bias (and our own, for that matter), and to assess the material according to as many sources as we can." (Wright, NTPG, 89)

Philosopher of history W. H. Walsh reinforces Wright's bidding to become aware of our own bias and to hold historians to that self-scrutiny:

> It is doubtful, all the same, whether we should regard bias of this kind as a serious obstacle to the attainment of objective truth in history.

The fact that somebody, *standing* somewhere, *with a particular* point of view, *is knowing something does not mean that the knowledge is less valuable: merely that it is precisely* knowledge. . . . *[I]t must be asserted most strongly that to discover that a particular writer has a 'bias' tells us nothing whatever about the value of the information he or she presents.*

N. T. Wright

It is doubtful for the simple reason that we all know from our own experience that this kind of bias can be corrected or at any rate allowed for. . . . And we do hold that historians ought to be free from personal prejudice and condemn those historians who are not. (Walsh, IPH, 101)

G. Weaving Events into Larger Historical Narratives Makes for an Artificial "Storytelling" Treatment
1. Claim

Postmodern writer Hayden White, while admitting to the existence of historical events, charges historians with artificially construing and connecting those events into larger narratives. This sort of "storytelling," he argues, reflects mental realities or constructs that are imposed upon past events. He does not deny that individual historical events can be known to a degree, but rejects historical narratives that are constructed to provide meaning. (White, CF, 1–6)

2. Response

David Carr argues that there is "continuity" between "historical reality" and "historical narrative." He writes, "It cannot then be said that [historical narratives] impose an alien structure on the realities they deal with, systematically distorting them in the process. Far from differing in structure from historical reality, historical narrative shares the form of its object, and can be seen as an extension and refinement by other means of the very reality it is about." He continues, "Just as the individual exists through the implicit life-story, so the community exists through a 'story' that draws together the shared memory and expectation or projection. Here too the social present derives its sense from the past and future."

(Carr, RH, 124) Nevertheless, Carr warns, "Our story-telling must come to grips with the world as it is, not as we wish it were." And so, he concludes, "'Making sense' cannot be separated from 'being true.'" (Carr, RH, 135)

V. Objections to the Knowability of Miraculous History

We have no good reason to doubt that we can have knowledge of the past. But what about *miraculous* claims from the past? In this section, we consider common objections against the knowability of miracles in history.

A. Philosophical Objections of David Hume

David Hume presents a historical-criteria argument against miraculous history by identifying problems with any alleged proof of a miracle from history.

1. The Problem of the Trustworthiness of the Recorders
a. Claim

Hume states,

For *first*, there is not to be found, in all history, any miracle attested by a sufficient number of men, of such unquestioned good-sense, education, and learning, as to secure us against all delusion in themselves; of such undoubted integrity, as to place them beyond all suspicion of any design to deceive others; of such credit and reputation in the eyes of mankind, as to have a great deal to lose in case of their being detected in any falsehood; and at the same time, attesting facts, performed in such a public manner, and in so celebrated a part of the world, as to render the detection unavoidable: All which circumstances are requisite to give us a full assurance in the testimony of men. (Hume, ECHU, 10.15)

b. Response

Philosopher Francis Beckwith recognizes that "in many respects this is certainly not an entirely unreasonable criterion to put forth by Hume. One would expect when examining any alleged eyewitness testimony that the eyewitnesses be of sufficient number and character. However, Hume's criterion demands much more than this." (Beckwith, DHAAM, 49)

Beckwith explains what that criterion demands by citing Colin Brown: "The qualifications [Hume] demands of such witnesses are such as would preclude the testimony of anyone without a Western university education, who lived outside a major cultural center in Western Europe prior to the sixteenth century, and who was not a public figure." (quoted in Beckwith, DHAAM, 50) As Beckwith notes, even this criterion does not work, for "if one succeeds in educating a liar, one only succeeds in making him a better liar." (Beckwith, DHAAM, 50)

"Furthermore," as Beckwith explains, "some of the latest scholarship lends support to the contention that the crowning miracle of Christian theism, the Resurrection of Jesus, seems to fulfill Hume's first criterion." (Beckwith, DHAAM, 50; see also section V.B in this chapter and chapter 10.)

2. The Suspiciousness of Historical Miraculous Records
a. Claim

Hume states,

The many instances of forged miracles, and prophecies, and supernatural events, which, in all ages, have either been detected by contrary evidence, or which detect themselves by their absurdity, prove sufficiently the strong propensity of mankind to the extraordinary and the marvelous, and ought reasonably to beget a suspicion against all relations of this kind. This is our natural way of thinking, even with regard to the most common and most credible events. (Hume, ECHU, 10.19)

b. Response

Beckwith indicates the fallacy of Hume's second point as follows: "Few doubt the fact that some allegedly miraculous events are the product of human imagination and the desire to believe the wonderful, but one cannot deduce from this that *all* alleged miracles did not take place. For to do so would be to commit *the fallacy of false analogy* [an argument that makes an erroneous conclusion]." (Beckwith, DHAAM, 51)

Further, as Beckwith notes, this contention also begs the question for naturalism: "After all, you cannot assume that all miracle-claims are involved in exaggeration unless you already know that miracles never occur." (Beckwith, DHAAM, 52)

3. The Problem of the Historical Quality of the Recorders
a. Claim

Hume states,

It forms a strong presumption against all supernatural and miraculous relations, that they are observed chiefly to abound among ignorant and barbarous nations; or if a civilized people has ever given admission to any of them, that people will be found to have received them from ignorant and barbarous ancestors, who transmitted them with that inviolable sanction and authority, which always attend received opinions. (Hume, ECHU, 10.20)

b. Response

Beckwith notes three problems with Hume's third criterion: "(1) Hume does not adequately define what he means by an uneducated and ignorant people; (2) this criterion does not apply to the miracles of Christian theism; and (3) Hume commits the informal fallacy of *argumentum ad hominem* [attacks against the person instead of his or her argument]." (Beckwith, DHAAM, 53)

Furthermore, there are massive numbers of educated people from all over the world who believe in the reality of miracles. Hume is simply mistaken that belief in miracles comes from barbarous people. In his massive two-volume study of ancient and modern miracles, New Testament scholar Craig Keener concludes that hundreds of millions of people alive today believe they have seen or personally experienced a miracle. He concludes:

> Regardless of how we interpret miracle reports and other supernatural claims, their frequency in various sectors of today's world indicates that large numbers of intelligent, sincere people believe that such cures are occurring today, including through their own prayers. This is true even in the modern West; how much more likely would this be the case in a generally less skeptical culture like the world of the first Christians? (Keener, MCNT, 219)*

4. The Problem of the Principle of Analogy
a. Claim
Hume writes,

> The maxim, by which we commonly conduct ourselves in our reasonings, is, that the objects, of which we have no experience, resemble those, of which we have; that what we have found to be most usual is always most probable; and that where there is an opposition of arguments, we ought to give the preference to such

as are founded on the greatest number of past observations. But though, in proceeding by this rule, we readily reject any fact which is unusual and incredible in an ordinary degree; yet in advancing farther, the mind observes not always the same rule; but when any thing [*sic*] is affirmed utterly absurd and miraculous, it rather the more readily admits of such a fact, upon account of that very circumstance, which ought to destroy all its authority. (Hume, ECHU, 10.16)

In a manner similar to Hume's reasoning, German theologian and historiographer Ernst Troeltsch argues,

> On the analogy of the events known to us we seek by conjecture and sympathetic understanding to explain and reconstruct the past ... since we discern the same process of phenomena in operation in the past as in the present, and see, there as here, the various historical cycles of human life influencing and intersecting one another. (Troeltsch, "Historiography," 718)

b. Response
Geisler first notes,

> It [the principle of analogy] begs the question in favor of a naturalistic interpretation of *all* historical events. It is a methodological exclusion of the possibility of accepting the miraculous in history. The testimony for regularity in *general* is in no way testimony against an unusual event in *particular*. (Geisler, CA, 302)

Similarly, Licona notes that if the principle of analogy were used without qualification,

---

* As noted in the chapter "Are Miracles Possible?", this in no way undermines the notion that miracles are unusual occurrences, and *relatively* rare. Most events and most experiences, even in cultures that recognize a fairly steady stream of miraculous events, still qualify as occurring through the normal, expected operation of natural laws.

"numerous established modern beliefs would fail." He continues,

> For example, we could not conclude that dinosaurs existed in the past. After all, historians and scientists do not experience them today. One may object that we can still establish dinosaurs scientifically, since their fossils remain. But the historian may reply that this is in spite of the principle of analogy and that we may likewise be able to establish miracles historically, because we have credible testimony that remains. (Licona, RJ, 140–141)

Beckwith notes,

> This argument confuses analogy as a *basis* for studying the past with the *object* of the past that is studied. That is to say, we assume consistency and continuity when studying the past, but it does not follow that what we discover about the past (that is, the object of our inquiry) cannot be a unique singularity. (Beckwith, HM, 97; emphasis in original)

Craig Keener states,

> To argue that a supernaturally caused event can have no analogies, one must presuppose that no other supernaturally caused events have occurred, and this constitutes a circular argument. Still more important, at least from the standpoint of what appear to be miracles, this appeal to analogy and experience today is more apt to cut the other way than when it was formulated, since supernatural claims belong to the widespread experience of much of humanity today. Thus some philosophers of religion today are appealing to contemporary miracle reports to reinforce the plausibility of miracles in principle. (Keener, MCNT, 188–189)

B. Theological Objections

In this section, we consider theological objections against the knowability of the historical truth concerning miracles.

1. Problem: Miracle Reports Are Theological, not Historical
a. Claim

In a debate with William Lane Craig, influential biblical scholar and agnostic-atheist Bart Ehrman claimed that the hypothesis that God raised Jesus from the dead is theological rather than historical. In his opening speech, Ehrman argued:

> But even if these [Gospel resurrection] stories were the best sources in the world, there would still be a major obstacle that we simply cannot overcome if we want to approach the question of the resurrection historically rather than theologically. I'm fine if Bill [Craig] wants to argue that theologically God raised Jesus from the dead or even if he wants to argue theologically that Jesus was raised from the dead. But this cannot be a historical claim.*

b. Response

According to Licona,

> Ehrman confuses historical conclusions with their theological implications. Most would admit that if Jesus rose from the dead, God is probably the best candidate for the cause. Thus, for Ehrman, since God is a subject for theologians rather than historians, the entire exercise of investigating the historicity of Jesus' resurrection is illegitimate. But this is to do history backward. Historians should approach the data neither presupposing nor *a priori* excluding the possibility of God's acting in raising Jesus. They should instead form and

---

* A transcript of this debate can be found at http://www.reasonablefaith.org/is-there-historical-evidence-for-the-resurrection-of-jesus-the-craig-ehrman.

weigh hypotheses for the best explanation. Probability ought to be determined in this manner rather than by forming a definition of *miracle* that excludes the serious consideration of a hypothesis prior to an examination of the data. (Licona, RJ, 177).

2. Problem: Tensions Between Faith and Historical Fact

a. Claim

Martin Kähler has been cited as declaring the role of historiography to be incompatible with faith. He writes,

> For historical facts which first have to be established by science cannot *as such* become experiences of faith. Therefore, Christian faith and a history of Jesus repel each other like oil and water. (Kähler, SCHJ, 74; emphasis in original)

Similarly, Paul Tillich firmly separates faith and history by an acceptance of the Biblical accounts as "stories and legends": "The truth of faith cannot be made dependent on the historical truth of the stories and legends in which faith has expressed itself. It is a disastrous distortion of the meaning of faith to identify it with the belief in the historical validity of the Biblical stories." (Tillich, DF, 100)

b. Response

Professor Millard J. Erickson offers a compelling response, declaring that historical accounts can contribute to faith:

> The theories we are considering do not fit the biblical picture of the relationship between faith and reason, including historical considerations. We could offer several examples. One is the response when the disciples of John the Baptist asked Jesus whether he was the one they had been looking for, or whether they should be looking for someone else (Luke 7:18–23). Jesus called attention to what he was doing: healing the blind, the lame, lepers, and the deaf; raising the dead; and preaching the good news to the poor (v. 22). There certainly was no separation here of the facts of history from faith. A second example is Paul's emphasis on the reality of Jesus' resurrection (1 Cor. 15). The validity of the Christian experience and message rests upon the genuineness of Christ's resurrection (vv. 12–19). A third consideration is Luke's obvious concern to attain correct information for his writing (Luke 1:1–4; Acts 1:1–5). While our first example might be affected by critical study of the passage, the second and especially the third confirm that the split between faith and historical reason is not a part of the biblical picture. (Erickson, WBF, 130–131)

VI. Conclusion

Despite the many objections we have considered concerning the knowability of history, the above analysis shows there are very good reasons to conclude that careful historians can make accurate assessments of the past, including miraculous events in the past.

As we pointed out at the beginning of this chapter: "Christianity is a historical faith, meaning that it rests finally on the historical life, death, and resurrection of Jesus. If these events are not true, then the Christian faith is false, and its teachings are groundless." (see 1 Cor. 15:14, 17) But the apostle Paul, after writing this startling declaration, immediately followed it up with these words: "But in fact Christ has been raised from the dead." (v. 20) Paul backs this up with eyewitness evidence by listing those to whom Jesus had appeared, mentioning numerous appearances—with at least one to a very large number of witnesses. He even names specific people whose character he could vouch for because he knew them personally. He concludes this list with the reminder that he had encountered Jesus himself (1 Cor. 15:1–11). Erickson has named this chapter as one of the examples of how the Bible presents the relationship between faith and reason, including the consideration of history. The entire chapter of 1 Corinthians 15 stunningly exhibits many of the definitions and criteria discussed in our examination of the knowability of history. After Paul lists the witnesses, even discussing his own change of mind, he tells the Corinthians that this verifiable evidence is the reasonable basis for their belief (v. 11) and ends the chapter by declaring the scope of this history-grounded outlook in its relevance for practical living and for thinking Christianly about history: He concludes, "Thanks be to God," encouraging them to live steadfastly in the confidence of knowing both what God has done in this past history and what he will accomplish in the end of history (1 Cor. 15:26–28, 57, 58).

In this chapter we have examined definitions of history as an inquiry into "that which happened" in human experience; as a method of examining records of events; as a problem-solving discipline that seeks direct answers from relevant evidence even while knowing that the process must be fair and conscious of how an initial bias may require revision when new discoveries or new experience (or both together) call for rethinking. We have explored many arguments that assert that we cannot know anything of certainty from the past, that is, from historical records—and we have seen how counter-arguments answer these objections to the knowability of history.

Paul's central argument in 1 Corinthians 15 beautifully illustrates the way that historians also use evidence and reason, and he presents a conclusion that establishes a community of people who can be grounded in remembering God's powerful love-in-action in history, knowing his presence as they carry out his work, and expecting his sovereignty over the future.

What we can say with certainty is that there is no question that the Christian faith is bound up with history. The evidence that certain events took place in specific places in real time in history is convincing and more than plausible. But beyond the academic and philosophical discussion and debate about history, there is the reality of the testimony of tens of millions of people who have claimed that because God has reached out to them in the person of Jesus Christ and invited them to respond to his love and forgiveness, they have grown to love God in ways that are unquestionably real.

I (Josh) am one of those who did not know God earlier in my life, but that changed. Let me explain. It was not all the surprising historical evidence that brought me to faith. Yes, it is true that God got my attention with the evidence. Once I was convinced that the Bible was true, then and only then did I consider its message. What brought me to Christ was the realization that if I were the only person alive, Christ still would have died for me. One might say, "When I was slamming the door on God, he stuck his foot (the evidence) in the door and got my attention." I had to let that door swing back open. He changed my life dramatically.

We invite you to read the epilogue (immediately following this chapter). Your life too could be forever changed.

FINAL THOUGHTS

Much of the material you've read in these pages has been pretty heady stuff. And that's good. God gave us minds to use to evaluate the evidence of his revelation of himself to us. In Isaiah 1:18, God invites us, "Come now, and let us reason together." Jesus indicated the importance of reason when he commanded, "You shall love the LORD your God with all your heart, with all your soul, and with all your mind" (Matt. 22:37).

But much more often in the Bible, God speaks to the heart, which in the Bible means the core of a person's being and ability to respond. Again and again God speaks of the importance of humility of the heart. He warns of the danger of developing a hardened heart. Though the Scriptures speak often about the mind, there are approximately five times that number that refer to the heart. God also wants to speak to us on a heart-to-heart level, not just on an intellectual level, so that we may respond to him as a whole person.

And that's our attitude as we close this book. How should we be responding to God? Are you at the point of realizing that God really loves you? Do you want to respond?

Perhaps you or someone you know may be struggling with some of the issues mentioned in this book. You may be saying, "I've never seen a miracle; how can I put my faith in a message that speaks of the miraculous?" We believe the only way to get to the truth is to throw out all preconceived ideas. What if there really is a God who is observing the pride in the hearts of those in high positions; the ego focus of those climbing the ladders of fame, power, and possessions; the insistence upon self-control of everything and everyone in order to be happy; the interior dislocation and general malaise or suffering from injuries inflicted by others; and the general selfishness of man? What if this God chose to reveal himself to certain people? What if he decided that he would reveal himself, not to the haughty, or the proud, or the arrogant; but to the humble, the downtrodden, and the poor in spirit? What if God really did become a man in the person of Jesus Christ in order to do this?

In fact, this is exactly the case because the Bible *is* true. (We have already seen that the evidence for the reliability of the Bible is staggering.) Though many people from all different philosophical and religious backgrounds like to talk about experiences they have had with "God," one of the truths revealed to the prophet Isaiah is that God really is not out to win any popularity contests. Though his desire, as stated in 2 Peter

3:9, is that he is passionately "not willing that any should perish but that all should come to repentance," at the same time, he's not out trying to reveal himself to everyone who comes along. As Isaiah records, "Truly You are a God, who hide yourself, O God of Israel, the Savior!" (Isa. 45:15).

Isn't that odd? Can you imagine God in hiding? Why would he do that? The answer is: he's waiting. He's waiting for those times in the lives of all people when they will be humble enough in their hearts to hear his voice and respond by opening the door of their lives to allow a personal relationship with him to begin. As Jesus says in Revelation 3:20, "Behold, I stand at the door and knock. If anyone hears My voice and opens the door, I will come in to him and dine with him, and he with Me."

Three times in the Bible it is explicitly stated (and many more times intimated) that God is opposed to the proud, but gives grace to the humble (Prov. 3:34; James 4:6; 1 Pet. 5:5). I believe God wants us to bring our questions to him, but there comes a time when he says, *It's time to act on the answers I have given you. Don't wait any longer.*

And if we respond to him at that point, that's when we open ourselves up for the possibility of observing the miraculous discovery of his presence in our lives as well as in all of history. At the beginning of this book, I (Josh) told you about the changed life of my father, the town drunk, who came to know Christ late in life and was so dramatically changed that many people came to know Christ because of what they saw in the remaining fourteen months of his life. After what I'd seen and been through, that was a miracle. Nothing but a truly powerful God could make that kind of change in a person's life. And as I look at my own life, I would have to say that nothing except a supernatural God who made himself known as Jesus Christ could make the kinds of changes I've seen him make in my life.

If you have never made the decision of trusting Christ, we invite you now to turn to the final pages of this book and read "How Can I Know God Personally?" It is a very simple explanation of the basic understanding and the next steps for those with a heart that seeks to know Christ. If your heart and mind have been moved by God's love for you, then we invite you to act upon it.

God bless you in your search.

Josh D. McDowell
Sean McDowell, PhD

RESPONDING TO THE CHALLENGES OF BART EHRMAN

I. Why Bart Ehrman?

In our conversations and interactions with Muslims, Mormons, atheists, and many others, both of us have confronted the ideas of Bart Ehrman. Given his widespread influence, we decided it was important to provide an appendix in this updated and expanded version of *Evidence That Demands a Verdict* to respond to some of his more popular claims.

Who Is Bart Ehrman?

Bart Ehrman is a New Testament scholar at the University of North Carolina, at Chapel Hill. He is most famous for his five *New York Times* bestselling books. In a book specifically responding to one of Ehrman's books, author Michael Bird summarizes why Ehrman's writings and story are important to understand:

Ehrman is something of a celebrity skeptic. The media attraction is easy to understand. Ehrman has a famous deconversion story from being a fundamentalist Christian to becoming a "happy agnostic." He's a *New York Times* bestselling author, having written several

books about the Bible, Jesus, and God with a view to debunking widely held religious beliefs as based on a mixture of bad history, deception, and myth. He's a publicist's dream since in talk shows and in live debates he knows how to stir a crowd through hefty criticism, dry wit, on the spot recall of historical facts, and rhetorical hyperbole. He also has a global audience. In fact, if I can offer a personal anecdote, on two occasions I've received emails from Christians in the Middle East asking how to respond to local Muslims who have been reading Ehrman's writings and are quoting them at Christians as evidence that the Christian Bible has been corrupted, and that Islam is the only religion with a pure set of sacred writings. So there is more at stake here than being the resident religious skeptic on the Colbert Report—much more! (Bird, HGBJ, 7)

How Influential Is Ehrman?

When I (Josh) first wrote *Evidence* in 1972, Ehrman was unheard of (he was only a teenager, after all!). But today he is one of the most influential living critics of Christianity. The works of Ehrman are widely read by skeptics, but also by people of various faiths including Islam and Mormonism. Many

Christians have read his works; in fact many young believers have told us his arguments significantly challenged their beliefs. Ehrman even appeared on *The Colbert Report* to promote his book *Jesus Interrupted.* (Ehrman, BE, website)

In the introduction to their book, *Truth in a Culture of Doubt,* authors Andreas Köstenberger, Darrell Bock, and Joshua Chatraw briefly describe his story and influence:

Perhaps you've seen one of Bart Ehrman's debate performances against a variety of opponents. Maybe you've read one of his many best-selling books. You may even have taken a class with Professor Ehrman. Or perhaps you've never even heard of him. No matter what your level of acquaintance with Bart Ehrman and his writings, the issues he raises are important for the faith. . . . Over the years Ehrman has attacked the Bible from what may seem like every conceivable angle. His story is well known. He started out at Moody Bible Institute before attending Wheaton College and later Princeton University, where one of his professors helped him conclude there might be errors in the Bible. What followed was a journey from faith to ever-increasing skepticism and eventual agnosticism. In his efforts to discredit historic Christianity, Ehrman has methodically sought to dismantle virtually every major plank in the Christian religion. In his earlier writings he strenuously argued that at the root the gospel was not based on the authoritative, commonly agreed-upon teaching of Jesus and his disciples but only gradually emerged as the result of various power struggles in the first few centuries of the Christian era. More recently Ehrman has contended that many of the New Testament writings were fabricated and not written by the authors to whom

they are ascribed. Ehrman's primary area of expertise is the study of early copies of the New Testament, and thus he has focused his energies on arguing that these early copies, on which our current translations are based, are likely corrupt. He expresses strong skepticism regarding the reliable handing down of the original text. He claims that most scholars in the field have all but abandoned the quest for the original wording of the biblical texts. In addition, Ehrman has also ventured into the area of biblical theology, alleging that there are numerous contradictions in Scripture. In his quest to demonstrate such incongruities, Ehrman has recycled many critical arguments made by liberal biblical scholars in the past, virtually all of which have been answered by conservative scholars. This includes supposed discrepancies among the Gospels, matters of chronology, and other historical or theological differences. Most recently he has claimed that the New Testament itself has contradicting and evolving views on the divinity of Jesus. (Köstenberger, Bock, and Chatraw, TCD, ix–x)

In this appendix, we examine a few of Ehrman's most important and influential claims. Our goal is to represent them as fairly as possible and then respond accordingly. The issues we address fall into three categories:

1. Did Jesus really claim to be God? Did his first followers misunderstand him? Did Paul think he was an incarnate angel? Ehrman claims that Jesus did not personally believe he was God, but was made out to be "divine" in different "senses" by his disciples post-crucifixion, and Christians ultimately made him "fully God" at Nicea. We respond to several aspects of this narrative.

2. Is the Bible full of contradictions? Does this undermine its reliability? We consider

some principles for approaching alleged contradictions and provide plausible harmonizations for some of Ehrman's specific claims.

3. Is the New Testament a forgery? Are the names attributed to the New Testament books misleading? We consider these questions and provide responses to common objections such as the claim that the disciples were illiterate and could not have been the authors of their respective gospels.

II. Preliminary Critiques

Concern #1: Selective Scholarship

Ehrman often appeals to the consensus of scholarship in his debates and books. Specifically, he claims that he was guided by religious presuppositions prior to his conversion to agnosticism, but once he began objectively examining the evidence, he discovered the truth. This can be seen in the introduction of his book *How Jesus Became God* in which he writes, "Now in middle age I am no longer a believer. Instead, I am a historian of early Christianity, who for nearly three decades has studied the New Testament and the rise of the Christian religion from a historical perspective." (Ehrman, HJBG, 2) Notice the contrast between "believer" and "historian." These appeals (whether intentional or not) create a dichotomy between "scholarship" and "faith." Whether he is willing to admit it or not, *all* historians are guided by presuppositions and some element of faith.

Köstenberger, Bock, and Chatraw explain how Ehrman selectively defines "scholarship":

Bart Ehrman is smart enough to know that if he can show that the Bible is full of contradictions, this will significantly weaken its appeal

and authority. Throughout Ehrman's writings, he regularly cites the "modern scholarly consensus" in support of his claims. According to Ehrman, his views are "standard fare," held by "all my closest friends," are "widely accepted among New Testament scholars," and are "widely taught in seminaries and divinity schools." [Ehrman, JI, 17–18] However, it is only by defining scholarship on his own terms and by excluding scholars who disagree with him that Ehrman is able to imply that he is supported by all other scholarship. (Köstenberger, Bock, and Chatraw, TCD, 33–34)

New Testament Christian scholar Michael Kruger echoes the above sentiment about Ehrman:

He fails to mention that of all the ATS-accredited seminaries in the United States, the top ten largest seminaries are all evangelical. These seminaries represent thousands and thousands of students, and hundreds and hundreds of professors. If virtually all seminary professors agree with Ehrman, then who are these professors teaching at the ten largest US seminaries? (Kruger, RJI, website)

There are some places where Ehrman does use more accurate phrases such as, "Scholars today, outside the ranks of fundamentalists and conservative evangelicals, are virtually unified." (Ehrman, DJE, 47) However, Köstenberger, Bock, and Chatraw demonstrate the logical problem with this:

The problem with this type of argument is that it is kind of like saying, "Everyone in the government, except for conservatives or Republicans, wants to raise taxes." Technically, the statement may be accurate, but the problem is that once you qualify "everyone" with "except for conservatives and Republicans," you are down to about half of America's elected officials. In other words, saying that all scholarship agrees with him on a particular point means very little since he gets to define what he means by "scholarship." (Köstenberger, Bock, and Chatraw, TCD, 35)

We don't fault Ehrman for having presuppositions. Clearly, we have them as well. And we don't criticize him for citing experts, or even the weight of scholarship, when it is appropriate and accurate. But we do think his claims to "scholarship" are often misrepresentative and selective.

Concern #2: Ignoring Leading Critics

Several scholars have noted that Ehrman fails to engage with the best scholars who disagree with him. Readers of Ehrman may not be familiar with scholars like Richard Bauckham, Larry Hurtado, James Dunn, and N. T. Wright, but Ehrman certainly is. Even though he had previously addressed many of Ehrman's claims, Bauckham is largely ignored in Ehrman's work. New Testamant scholar Chris Tilling writes, "Incidentally, I find it *astonishing* that Ehrman has not referred to Bauckham's important work at all in his book. Bauckham is the most creative and brilliant scholar working in early Christology, and Ehrman hasn't shown any evidence of having read him!" (quoted in Bird, HGBJ, 127–128)*

Köstenberger and colleagues make a similar observation here:

Paradigms are frequently proposed in scholarship, and Ehrman certainly has every right to try his hand at a model for understanding early

Christology. However when proposals are offered, the expectation is that the author will engage with the best of those who went before him. However, in this case, Ehrman rarely engages with the best of "high Christology" scholarship. Two of the most distinguished scholars on the subject of Christology in the early church are Richard Bauckham (University of St. Andrews) and Larry Hurtado (University of Edinburgh). In *How Jesus Became God* Ehrman never even mentions the work of Richard Bauckham, who has done some of the most penetrating and careful research on early Christology. Bauckham's work is a prominent force to be reckoned with if one is going to throw his own Christological proposal on the table, yet Ehrman does not engage with him at all. Not even a footnote! And while he does mention Larry Hurtado twice, he not only fails to offer any substantial responses, but takes him out of context and uses him in support of a position Hurtado actually denies holding! (Köstenberger, Bock, and Chatraw, TCD, 62)

Concern #3: Biased Hermeneutic
1. Defining Ehrman's Hermeneutic:

In his own journey away from the Christian faith, Ehrman recalls, "At about the time I started to doubt that God had inspired the words of the Bible, I began to be influenced by Bible courses taught from a historical-critical perspective. I started seeing discrepancies in the text. I saw that some of the books of the Bible were at odds with one another." (Ehrman, JI, 16) Ehrman summarizes his own hermeneutic:

The Historical-Critical method maintains that we are in danger of misreading a book

---

* Subsequently, in a debate with Justin Bass, when asked if he had read Bauckham's recent book, Ehrman did not answer the question. He did suggest a possible general critique to one of Bauckham's theories later in the debate, which may suggest familiarity with it. You may find the video of this debate here: https://www.youtube.com/watch?v=CTgig9F782s.

if we fail to let its author speak for himself, if we force his message to be exactly the same as another author's message, if we insist on reading all the books of the New Testament as one book instead of as twenty-seven books. These books were written in different times and places, under different circumstances, to address different issues; they were written by different authors with different perspectives, beliefs, assumptions, traditions, and sources. And they sometimes present different points of view on major issues. (Ehrman, JI, 64)

Ehrman's warning about the need to acknowledge diverse perspectives among the biblical authors touches upon a point that in fact applies more broadly to all communication. Hans-Georg Gadamer warns that a danger of misreading or mishearing occurs in *any* dialogue in which we do not let the author speak for himself, recognizing that our own expectations will differ from the writer and that we must engage with the possibilities of his or her potential meanings. At that point, an interpreter determines which possibility is reasonable. (Gadamer, TM, 269–270) When we read Scripture and determine its meaning, we must always allow the whole of Scripture itself to inform and transform our initial assumptions about what is reasonable or acceptable. We must guard against the modern habit of taking hold of a text and placing it under our judgment. C. S. Lewis spoke of such an attitude as putting "God in the dock," reversing the age-old assumption that we as human approach him as our judge. Lewis considered this reversal to be one of the new difficulties for apologetics, adding, "The trial may even end in God's acquittal. But the important thing is that Man is on the Bench and God in the Dock,"

(Lewis, GITD, 244) Instead, we must allow ourselves to taken hold of and judged by the Word of God. The problem here is not Ehrman's method but his assumption that diversity among the authors is incompatible with their overarching theological unity. We see, instead, the rich texture and multifaceted beauty of God's truth.

2. The Hermeneutic of Craig Blomberg

New Testament scholar Craig Blomberg suggests another view of how Christians should read the New Testament:

In the midst of Scripture's unity, we must not lose sight of its diversity. This takes several forms. The books of the Bible are written by different authors, in different times and places, to different audiences in distinct circumstances, using various literary genres. Each book thus displays unique purposes and themes. In some instances, different portions of Scripture are so closely parallel that we can postulate a literary relationship between them and assume that their differences are intentional: sometimes theologically motivated; sometimes merely for stylistic variation. (Blomberg, UD, 69–70)*

3. Different Hermeneutics, Different Conclusions

These hermeneutics obviously sound the same! Köstenberger et al. comment on this comparison:

Both Ehrman and Blomberg appear to be saying similar things, yet their tone and ultimate conclusions are in stark contrast. The difference between Ehrman and Blomberg seems bound up more in the presuppositions that they bring to the interpretive process rather than in the refusal, on the part of either

---

* For a more accessible book on a similar subject, please see, Craig L. Blomberg, *Can We Still Believe the Bible? An Evangelical Engagement with Contemporary Question* (Grand Rapids: Brazos, 2014).

scholar, to recognize diversity. Both argue that the different writers have diverse theological emphases and should be allowed to speak for themselves. However, based on their witness to the same core truths, Blomberg sees the New Testament documents as expressing different yet compatible theologies. Ehrman, maintaining a thorough-going skepticism, fails to see any unifying core beliefs and views these differences as contradictions. . . . Again, to reduce all (or even most) diversity to contradiction is more characteristic of the type of monochrome, black-and-white fundamentalism Ehrman professes to have left behind than of the kind of judicious, nuanced scholarship to which he professes allegiance. . . . Unfortunately, Ehrman regularly fails to award the New Testament documents the fair and balanced treatment they deserve. (Köstenberger, Bock, and Chatraw, TCD, 39–40)

While both Ehrman and Blomberg are accomplished New Testament scholars, they apply different hermeneutics, and thus have vastly different conclusions about the text. In truth, we all come to the New Testament with certain biases and backgrounds. New Testament scholar Dan Wallace concludes:

But from where I sit, it seems that Bart's black-and-white mentality as a fundamentalist has hardly been affected as he slogged through the years and trails of life and learning, even when he came out on the other side of the theological spectrum. He still sees things without sufficient nuancing, he overstates his case, and he is entrenched in the security that his own views are right. Bart Ehrman is one of the most brilliant and creative textual critics I have ever known, and yet his biases are so strong that, at times, he cannot even acknowledge them. (Wallace, GAB, 333)

III. The Claims of Bart Ehrman

Claim #1: The followers of Jesus invented his deity after his death.

This is the crucial question for Ehrman:

Jesus was a lower-class Jewish preacher from the backwaters of rural Galilee who was condemned for illegal activities and crucified for crimes against the state. Yet not long after his death, his followers were claiming that he was a divine being. Eventually they went even further, declaring that he was none other than God, Lord of heaven and earth. And so the question: How did a crucified peasant come to be thought of as the Lord who created all things? How did Jesus become God? (Ehrman, HJBG, 1)

According to Ehrman, the question is not how God became man, but how the followers of Jesus came to view him as God. In *How Jesus Became God*, Ehrman claims that for ancient monotheists, there was not always an unqualified divide between humanity and divinity. Rather, human figures could become divinized and divine figures could become humanized. There were many mythical figures, claims Ehrman, who crossed the divide between the realms:

It may not have come as a huge surprise to learn that pagans who held to a range of polytheistic religions sometimes imagined that humans could be divine in some sense. It is more surprising, for most people, to learn that the same is true within Judaism. It is absolutely the case that by the time of Jesus and his followers most Jews were almost certainly monotheists. But even as they believed that there was only one God Almighty, it was widely held that there were other divine beings—angels, cherubim, seraphim, principalities, powers, hypostases. Moreover, there was some sense of continuity—not only discontinuity—between the divine and human realms. And there was a kind of spectrum of divinity: the Angel of the Lord, already in scripture, could be both an angel and God. Angels were divine, and could be worshiped, but they could also come in human guise. Humans could become angels. Humans could be called the Son of God or even God. This did not mean that they were the One God who created heaven and earth; but it did mean that they could share some of the authority, status, and power of that One God. Thus, even within a strict monotheism, there could be other divine beings and the possibility of a graduation of divinity. And even among Jews at the time of Jesus there was not a sense of an absolute break, a complete divide, an unbridgeable chasm between the divine and human. (Ehrman, HJBG, 83)

Furthermore, according to Ehrman, Jesus did not consider himself divine during his lifetime, and neither did any of his core followers. After his death, his disciples had visionary experiences of Jesus still living, and *only then* did they begin to speak of him in exalted terms. Michael Bird explains what Ehrman means by "exalted":

Ehrman identifies two primary ways in which Jesus was divinized by the early church. First, and the earliest version, was "exaltation Christology," whereby Jesus was a man who was made divine at his resurrection or baptism. Second was "incarnation Christology," whereby Jesus was a preexistent being who became human. Applying this paradigm

to the New Testament, the gospel of Mark understands Jesus in terms of an exaltation Christology, while the gospel of John reflects an "incarnational Christology." In the case of Paul, Ehrman believes that Paul thought of Jesus as an angel who became human and was then exalted to a position besides God. (Bird, HGBJ, 17–18)

Ehrman claims that "exaltation Christology," the first view allegedly held by the church, was deemed heretical in the second century, climaxing in the fourth century with the development of the Nicene Creed. At this stage, other views became heretical.

1. Was Ancient Monotheism Inclusive or Exclusive?

Essentially, Ehrman claims the first views of Jesus contradict later Trinitarian views at Nicea. The key question, then, is what is meant by the divinity of Jesus at different stages of church history. And specifically, was there flexibility in ancient monotheism between the human and divine realms. Was monotheism inclusive or exclusive?

Richard Bauckham addresses this question directly:

If it is supposed that "rigorous" or "exclusive" monotheism must deny the existence of any supernatural or heavenly beings besides God, then it is clear that such monotheism never existed until the modern period. Traditional monotheism in the Jewish, Christian and Islamic traditions has always accepted the existence of vast numbers of supernatural beings: angels who serve and worship God, demons who oppose God within an overall sovereignty of God over all. But such beings have been considered creatures, created by and subject to God, no more a qualification of monotheism than the existence of earthly creatures is. (Bauckham, JGI, 108)*

And Chris Tilling explains:

All Ehrman has done is deploy this problematic notion of monotheism in the garb of an imprecise wordplay with terms "divine" "God," and so on. The game has worked to put all exalted language about Jesus in the New Testament in the "divine" box, all the while separating Jesus from "God Almighty." But the effect is a misleading rhetorical trick, not a position that sheds light on the data. (Tilling, PEIC, 128)

Commenting on the status of intermediary figures, and whether they should be worshiped, Michael Bird notes:

There is a reason why angels like Metatron or Michael could never level up and become the object of devotion equal to God. There was a strong Jewish prohibition about the worship of angels (e.g., Tob 12:16–22; 3 En. 16.1–5), which carries over into the New Testament (Col. 2:18; Rev. 19:10; 22:9). Ehrman infers from this: "We know that some Jews thought it was right to worship angels in no small part because a number of our surviving texts insist that it *not* be done." [Ehrman, HJBG, 54–55, emphasis in original] Well, okay, maybe some Jews were a bit too enthusiastic in their devotion to angels (much like teenage girls I've heard about in the American Bible Belt!). That

said, the worship of angels was not necessarily the same as worship of God. In our ancient sources angels could be venerated or invoked in any number of ways: (1) by prayers and even by magical manipulation for assistance, protection, good health, and vengeance; (2) their heavenly worship could be seen as mysterious and worthy of mimicking; (3) angels could be objects of thanksgiving in relation to various functions or activities that they performed on God's behalf. (Bird, GAM, 33)

Bird provides a helpful summary of ancient Jewish monotheism:

I am convinced by the study of several scholars that Jewish monotheism was, generally, strict. There is one Creator God, who stands above all other reality, and this is the God who covenants with Israel. God's unique identity is bound up with his sacred name, YHWH, revealed to Israel. Monotheism entails monolatry, the worship of the one true God to exclusion of all others. These elements of one creator, divine name, and exclusive worship make up the substance of Jewish Monotheism. (Bird, GAM, 29)

2. In What "Sense" Did Early Christians Think Jesus to Be "Divine"?

Using a paradigm of inclusive monotheism, Ehrman argues that when the early Christians called Jesus "divine," they did not call him "God Almighty"; instead, they used "divine" in the "sense" of an exalted

---

* Charles Taylor's *A Secular Age* helps us understand a strict monotheism that recognizes a large supernatural realm full of spirits without falling into polytheism. He argues for a huge shift from AD 1500 to the present in how we perceive ourselves—no longer as "porous," but as "buffered." By "porous," Taylor means the sense that we humans exist "in a field of spirits, some of whom were malign." In this older view (older to the West, but widely global to this day), we are always vulnerable, always standing open to the interventions or even attacks of all sorts of invisible powers. In contrast, we modern folk think of ourselves as "buffered" selves, serenely (or uneasily!) telling ourselves that we are in rational and moral control of our lives, much too modern to have such superstitions. So we hardly imagine that even traditional orthodox monotheism could have accepted the existence of supernatural beings without worshiping them as some gradient of divinity. As Bauckham reminds us, "'rigorous' or 'exclusive' monotheism" need not deny" multiple supernatural beings. In fact, it has not, as both Taylor and Bauckham point out. Why? Because monotheism does not see angels or other spirits as existing on a spectrum that a human could rise into or through by becoming "divine" like them. They are instead seen as creatures (as we are), and subject to God.

intermediary figure. This is specifically called an "adoption" or "exaltation" Christology, where "a human being (say, a great ruler or warrior or holy person) could be *made* divine by an act of God or a god, by being elevated to a level of divinity that she or he did not previously have." (Ehrman, HJBG, 5, emphasis in original) Upon having visionary experiences of Christ's resurrection, Ehrman says, the earliest Christians thought "God had showered his special favor upon Jesus and made him in a unique sense the Son of God. . . . Just as the emperors were both sons of God (since their adopted fathers were 'God') and gods, so too Jesus as the Son of God, was in that sense God." (Ehrman, HJBG, 209) This view, he argues, was the view held by the earliest disciples. This view is that Jesus was exalted "highly" to be an intermediary figure in the pyramid of "divine" power, but was not considered to be "divine" prior to his resurrection; neither was he preexistent or equal to the one Creator God of Israel. (Ehrman, HJBG, 246)

According to Ehrman, the Synoptic Gospels hold to the "exaltation Christology" view, which develops into the belief that God had "exalted" or "adopted" Jesus prior to his resurrection, which is why Mark's gospel has Jesus being "exalted" at his baptism, and Matthew and Luke's gospels have this beginning at Jesus' birth. (Ehrman, HJBG, 239–244)

In response to this claim, prominent New Testament scholar Simon Gathercole argues that the Synoptic Gospels do argue for the "preexistence" of Jesus. He observes the many "I have come" statements by Jesus, which indicate his preexistence. Here are some of the verses Gathercole references in order to show the weakness in Ehrman's argument for a biblical exaltation Christology (all references in this chart are to the ESV):

And when Jesus heard it, he said to them, "Those who are well have no need of a physician, but those who are sick. I came not to call the righteous, but sinners." — Mark 2:17 (See also Matt. 9:13 and Luke 5:32; Luke adds "to repentance.")

"Do not think that I have come to abolish the Law or the Prophets; I have not come to abolish them but to fulfill them." — Matthew 5:17

"I came to cast fire on the earth, and would that it were already kindled!" — Luke 12:49

"Do not think that I have come to bring peace to the earth. I have not come to bring peace, but a sword." — Matthew 10:34 (see also Luke 12:51)

"For I have come to set a man against his father, and a daughter against her mother, and a daughter-in-law against her mother-in-law." — Matthew 10:35

"For the Son of Man came to seek and to save the lost." — Luke 19:10

Gathercole explains the significance of these passages:

I would suggest that the natural sense of these sayings is that they imply that Jesus has come from somewhere to accomplish his mission. (Jesus is not talking in each case about how he has arrived in a particular town, having "come," for example, from Nazareth to Capernaum.) When one examines these sayings of Jesus, the closest matches with them in the Old Testament and Jewish tradition are statements that angels make about their earthly missions (within the Old Testament, see, e.g., Dan 9:22–23; 10:14; 11:2). I found twenty-four examples in the Old Testament and Jewish tradition of angels saying, "I have come in order to . . ." as a way of summing up their earthly missions. A prophet or a messiah in the Old Testament or Jewish tradition never sums up his life's work in this way. I am not for a moment suggesting that Jesus is viewed as an angel in the Gospels, but rather that he is seen as having come *from* somewhere to carry out his life's work, namely, from heaven. Ehrman insists that if you read Matthew and Luke carefully, "you will see that they have nothing to do with the idea that Christ existed before he was conceived." But I think if you read Matthew and Luke carefully in the light of their Jewish background, you can see that they have everything to do with Christ existing before he was conceived, before he "came" to embark on his earthly mission. (Gathercole, WDFCTJ, 96–98, emphasis in original)

Gathercole also responds to Ehrman's claim about the gospel of Mark:

Ehrman's view here is based on the words of the voice from heaven at Jesus' baptism. . . . What is striking is that voice from heaven comes later on in Mark's gospel and says something similar. At the transfiguration . . . presumably God is not adopting Jesus again. But it is hard to see how the voice at the baptism could refer to God's adoption of Jesus and the similar-sounding voice at the transfiguration could mean something different. (Gathercole, WDFCTJ, 98–99)

3. Did Paul Believe Christ Was an Incarnated Angel?

Since Ehrman believes that in the Markan tradition, God exalted Jesus at his baptism, he raises the following question: "How could Paul embrace 'higher' views of Christ than those found in the later writings such as Matthew, Mark, and Luke?" (Ehrman, HJBG, 251)

His solution is that Paul's "incarnational Christology" is not necessarily "higher" than the Gospels' Christology, simply "different." (Ehrman, HJBG, 252) It is "different" because for Paul, Jesus is a kind of "Angel," not God Almighty. One of his key arguments is his novel interpretation of Philippians 2. Ehrman believes the "poem" is an early, pre-Pauline text. He further claims that for "the author of that poem, as for Paul himself, Christ was some kind of angelic being before becoming a human—probably the 'chief angel' or the 'Angel of the Lord.' And as a result of his obedience to God unto death, he was given an even more exalted state of being." (Ehrman, HJBG, 278) The question, then, is whether Paul really believes Christ to be a kind of divine angel.

Interestingly, Ehrman cites the work of Hurtado to justify his arguments. (Ehrman, HJBG, 61, 135) Nevertheless, Hurtado argues that the early Christians, including Paul, did not think of Jesus as an intermediary divine figure (such as an angel). Hurtado says of Philippians 2:5–11:

This is commonly regarded as a hymn deriving from a Jewish-Christian setting. Here, as with Rom. 1:3–4, in this document from the middle of the first century C.E. we have a "window" opening upon the faith and devotion of Jewish Christians from still earlier years. Of the many interesting features of the passage, the description of the divine exaltation of Christ in vv. 9–11 is the most relevant for our inquiry. In apparent reference to Jesus' resurrection, we are told that God has "highly exalted" him and has bestowed upon him "the name which is above every name," with the intention that "every knee" in all spheres of creation is to bow and "every tongue confess that Jesus Christ is Lord, to the glory of God the Father." This passage is particularly important for my argument precisely because it combines an amazing description of the exalted status of the risen Christ together with a clear commitment to the uniqueness of God. Consider the following observations. First, there is the unusual and intensified Greek verb form to describe God's exaltation of Christ (*huperyposen*, v. 9), which seems intended to set off this exalted figure from all others. Then, the heavenly Christ is described in terms that liken him to God. That Christ has a name "above every name" (v. 9) suggests that the divine name itself (*Yahweh*) is meant. And of course the acclamation, "Jesus Christ is Lord," gives him the title that was also a Greek translation of *Yahweh*. Also, in vv. 10–11 the language of a classic monotheistic passage in the Old Testament (Isa. 45:23) is used to describe the eschatological acknowledgement to be given to Jesus. . . . To be sure, the status of the risen Christ is unsurpassed in any of the ancient Jewish references to God's chief agents. Further, if this passage was originally a hymn sung in early Jewish Christian gatherings, then it provides evidence that Christ was an object of cultic veneration, something unparalleled in the Jewish treatment of chief agents. (Hurtado, OGOL, 96–97)*

4. Where Does Nicea Fit In?

According to Ehrman, multiple theologies competed for orthodoxy within the early church. The views that the orthodox deemed "heretical" in the later centuries, according to Ehrman, existed side by side with the orthodox view, which eventually "won" allegiance at Nicea. Ehrman explains:

There were numerous views of Christ throughout the second and third Christian centuries. Some of Jesus' followers thought he was a human but not (by nature) divine; others thought he was divine but not a human; others thought he was two different beings, one human and one divine; yet others—the side that "won" these debates—maintained that he was a human and divine at one and the same time and yet was one being, not two. These debates, however need to be placed in their broader context. . . . Some Christians maintained that there was only one God. Others argued that there were two Gods—that the God of the Old Testament was not the same as the God of Jesus. Yet others argued that there were twelve gods, or thirty-six gods, or even 365 gods. How could someone with those views even be Christian? Why didn't they simply read their New Testament and see that they were wrong? The answer, of course, is that the New Testament did not yet exist. To be sure, all of the books that were later collected and placed in the New Testament and deemed, then, to be holy scripture were in existence. But so were lots of other books—other Gospels, epistles, and apocalypses, for example—all of them claiming to be written by the apostles of Jesus and claiming to represent the "true" view of the faith. What we think of as the twenty-seven books of "the" New Testament emerged out of these conflicts, and it was the side that won the debates over what to believe that decided which books were to be included in the canon of scripture. (Ehrman, HJBG, 286)

While there was certainly a diversity of views among groups labeled "Christian" in the second, third, and fourth centuries, the key question is whether there was such divergence in the *first* century when Christianity came into existence.

Ehrman recognizes this problem, which is why his narrative paints the earliest disciples

---

as having adopted exaltation Christologies, which were held by later "heretics." (Ehrman, HJBG, 289)

However, as Darrell Bock observes, evidence is lacking that these "heretical" groups go back to the first century:

> Evidence from the first century does not exist for a few of the four diverse groups in the opening chapters of Ehrman's *The New Testament: A Historical Introduction to Early Christian Writings,* 5th ed. (Oxford/New York: Oxford University Press, 2011). The only first-century evidence we have is for some Jewish groups that embraced Jesus but who questioned the deity of Jesus (the Ebionites). All the other groups noted such as the Gnostics and Marcionites lack first-century sources. So this makes his key opening claim for diversity in that textbook exaggerated. We also must note that early disputes about practice (circumcision or not as required for Gentiles) which the New Testament notes and about which there was vigorous debate does not touch on the core Christological orthodoxy to which these first-century "proto-orthodox" works also attest. (Köstenberger, Bock, and Chatraw, TCD, 113–114)

Köstenberger et al. summarize the Christian narrative of the first four hundred years of Christianity:

> It is inconceivable to believe that the early church fathers, who took great care to emphasize their roles as "handing down" the tradition, would have scrapped its core tenets in favor of their own novel teachings. . . . Yet Ehrman's argument implicitly forces one of the two options on the listener: either (1) the fourth-century creeds spoke in the same way as the New Testament, or (2) the creeds are in contradiction with Jesus and the apostles.

These fourth-century creeds were formulated in part to deal with then-current controversies that were especially philosophical in nature. This led to fresh expression being given to old teachings to deal with new issues. So maintaining that the Fathers preserved orthodoxy and conveyed it to those who articulated the creeds does not mean the New Testament authors would have conceived their theology in the same constructs as the formulations for the creeds. The creeds are an organic continuation of the theology of the New Testament without any transmutation of the DNA of the New Testament gospel message, which in turn is rooted in the Old Testament. . . . To recap, the orthodox creeds of the fourth and fifth centuries were not imposed onto the early church but were instead logical continuations of New Testament orthodoxy. As a way to see the bigger picture, the following serves as an approximate outline of the relationship between orthodox and divergent forms of heresy in the first 300 years of Christianity. (Köstenberger, Bock, and Chatraw, TCD, 122–125)

Here is the timeline of true Orthodoxy given by these authors (adapted from Köstenberger, Bock, and Chatraw, TCD, 125–126):

AD 33: Jesus dies and rises from the dead.

AD 40s–60s: Paul writes letters to various churches; orthodoxy is pervasive and mainstream; churches are organized around a central message; undeveloped heresies begin to emerge; Scripture, schooling, singing, and sacraments teach core theology along with emerging early orthodox writings circulating in the churches.

AD 60s–90s: The Gospels and the rest of the New Testament are written and continue to propagate the orthodoxy that preceded them; orthodoxy continues to be pervasive and mainstream; heresies are still undeveloped.

- AD 90s–130s: The New Testament writers pass from the scene; the apostolic fathers emerge and continue to propagate the orthodoxy that preceded them; orthodoxy is still pervasive and mainstream; heresies begin to organize but remain relatively undeveloped.
- AD 130s–200s: The apostolic fathers die out; subsequent Christian writers continue to propagate orthodoxy that preceded them; orthodoxy is still pervasive and mainstream, but various forms of heresy emerge; these heresies, however, remain subsidiary to orthodoxy and remain variegated.
- AD 200s–300s: Orthodoxy is solidified in the creeds, but various forms of heresy continue to rear their heads; orthodoxy, however, remains pervasive and mainstream.

We should also note that even if Ehrman's chronology for the rise of orthodoxy *were* correct, his argument does not actually pose a substantive threat to Christian orthodoxy. In short, his critique rests on the assumption that either *antiquity* or *plurality* are necessary for normativity. Ehrman implies that the validity of orthodoxy hinges on how mainstream or widespread it was in the early years of Christian history. To challenge this assumption, we might ask, "What does it really matter if within the first fifty years of Christian history, *most* people who considered themselves Christians in *most* places held beliefs that would qualify as heterodox when viewed through the lens

of later orthodoxy?" Christian truth, and the normativity of what we now recognize as Christian orthodoxy, does not depend on how many people believed it and when. Whether "orthodoxy" was a tenuous minority until the fourth century or the vast majority from the very beginning is not a fundamental consideration—because Christian truth doesn't depend on people's beliefs!

This is especially vital given a high view of Scripture. Even if the earliest Christian writers and interpreters of Scripture had a variety of fragmented understandings of Christian doctrines, God as the ultimate Author ensured that the text itself communicates the truth—and consequently we can expect that faithful Christian interpreters are bound to converge on orthodoxy, whether immediately or over the course of dozens or even hundreds of years. Ehrman's history may be poor, but even if it weren't, Christian truth remains utterly unthreatened by this particular critique. Though we can meet Ehrman on his (and Bauer's) playing field, as demonstrated by Köstenberger, Bock, and Chatraw above, we also know that the normativity of orthodox doctrine has never depended on its antiquity or popularity.

Claim #2: The New Testament Contains "Contradictions"

One of Ehrman's primary critiques of Christianity involves the claim that the Bible has contradictions. His book *Jesus, Interrupted* is devoted to this argument. He says, "This book is not, then, about my loss of faith. It is, however, about how certain kinds of faith—particularly the faith in the Bible as the historically inerrant and inspired Word of God—cannot be sustained in light of what we as historians know about the Bible." (Ehrman, JI, 18) Why can it not be sustained? Simple: the many contradictions in the New Testament. Here are two general considerations.

1. "Contradiction" or Difference?

Ehrman often categorizes any kind of difference between two accounts in the Bible as a contradiction. Köstenberger, Bock, and Chatraw counter Ehrman's tendency to confuse differences and contradictions:

> To give just one more example, according to Ehrman the accounts of Jesus' trial before Pontius Pilate as recorded in Mark and John are contradictory because Mark's account is "short and straightforward," with Jesus not saying much and Pilate not declaring Jesus innocent, while John's account is longer, Jesus having a lot more to say, and Pilate declaring Jesus to be innocent. We can agree that there are some differences here, but why Ehrman insists that differences must be discrepancies is difficult to understand. What we have, instead, is differing perspectives by different authors on the same event. John includes details absent from Mark, but only unwarranted skepticism forces these two perspectives into contradiction. (Köstenberger, Bock, and Chatraw, TCD, 55)

2. Can These Contradictions Be Harmonized?

Ehrman is very critical of attempts to harmonize different gospel accounts because he thinks it hides the differences in each account; in short, harmonizations hide contradictions in the Bible. For example, of the crucifixion accounts in Mark and Luke, Ehrman says, "Mark is trying to say something by this portrayal. . . . [Jesus] dies in agony, unsure of the reason he must die." (Ehrman, JI, 66) In Luke's gospel, on the other hand, Ehrman explains, "Jesus is not silent while being nailed to the cross, as in Mark. Instead he prays, 'Father forgive them, for they don't know what they are doing' (Luke 23:34)."

(Ehrman, JI, 67) Ehrman concludes, "It is hard to stress enough the differences between these two portrayals of Jesus' death. . . . The problem comes when readers take these two accounts and combine them into one over-arching account, in which Jesus says, does, and experiences everything narrated in both Gospels. When that is done, the messages of both Mark and Luke get completely lost and glossed over." (Ehrman, JI, 69)

Yet New Testament scholar N. T. Wright observes that harmonization attempts are common when dealing with ancient sources:

> I am after all, suggesting no more than that Jesus be studied like any other figure of the ancient past. Nobody grumbles at a book on Alexander the Great if, in telling the story, the author "harmonizes" two or three sources; that is his or her job, to advance hypotheses which draw together the data into a coherent framework rather than leaving it scattered. Of course, sources on Alexander, like sources on Jesus, Tiberius, Beethoven, Gandhi, or anybody else, have their own point of view, which must be taken carefully into account. (Wright, JVG, 88)

Köstenberger, Bock, and Chatraw also offer a penetrating response:

> Many scholars acknowledge that Mark and Luke offer different perspectives on Jesus' life and, as Ehrman has pointed out, also his death. The central questions appear to be whether it is illegitimate for two authors to highlight different aspects of Jesus' death and whether these different aspects are incompatible. . . . It is reasonable to assume that Jesus experienced a series of diverse emotions as he died on the cross. A closer look at Luke's version shows something interesting in relationship to Mark. Mark tells us that Jesus cried out a second time

while on the cross; however Mark does not tell us what Jesus said then. Luke has the text from Psalm 31:5 at the very spot Mark has a second but unspecified cry from Jesus. Now most scholars see Luke as using and knowing Mark. So it is not at all unreasonable to see Luke supplying a detail Mark lacked. (Köstenberger, Bock, and Chatraw, TCD, 40–41)

Clearly, differences exist between the Mark and Luke accounts, but these do not necessarily add up to contradictions.

Claim #3: The New Testament Books Are Forgeries

Ehrman claims the New Testament books were not really written by their accepted authors, but were forgeries. Ehrman states his view:

Many early Christian writings are "pseudonymous," going under a "false name." The more common word for this kind of writing is "forgery". . . . In the ancient world forgery was a bit different from today in that it was not, technically speaking, against the law. But even though it was not an illegal activity, it was a deceitful one that involved conscious lying, as the ancients themselves said. The crucial question is this: Is it possible that any of the early Christian forgeries made it into the New Testament? . . . That Peter's letters were not written by Peter? . . . Or—a somewhat different case, as we will see—that the Gospels of Matthew, Mark, Luke, and John were not actually written by Matthew, Mark, Luke, and John? Scholars for over a hundred years have realized that in fact this is the case. The authors of some of the books of the New Testament were not what they claimed to be or who they have been supposed to be. . . . Matthew probably did not write Matthew, for example, or John, John . . . on the other hand, neither

book actually claims to be written by a person named Matthew or John. In other instances it is because an author lied about who he was, claiming to be someone he was not. (Ehrman, FWNG, 9–10)

Ehrman's argument is twofold: first, he asserts that the earliest disciples were illiterate, so they could not have written the parts of the New Testament attributed to them. And second, our uncertainty about the identity of the New Testament authors undermines the historical reliability of the New Testament.

1. Were the disciples illiterate?

Ehrman argues, "Jesus' disciples were lower-class, illiterate peasants from remote rural areas of Galilee, where very few people could read, let alone write, and let alone create full-scale compositions." (Ehrman, HJBG, 244)

In response to the claim that the first disciples could not have written the books attributed to them, New Testament scholar Ben Witherington notes:

First of all, fishermen are not peasants. They often made a good living from the Sea of Galilee, as can be seen from the famous and large fisherman's house excavated in Bethsaida. Secondly, fishermen were businessmen and they had to either have a scribe or be able to read and write a bit to deal with tax collectors, toll collectors, and other business persons. Thirdly, if indeed Jesus had a Matthew/Levi and others who were tax collectors as disciples, they were indeed literate, and again were not peasants. As the story of Zacchaeus makes perfectly clear, they could indeed have considerable wealth, sometimes from bilking people out of their money. In other words, it is a caricature to suggest that all Jesus' disciples were illiterate peasants. (Witherington, BI, website)

In addition, the first disciples were not the only New Testament writers. Luke, who wrote both the gospel and the Acts—a quarter of the New Testament—traveled with Paul and became a first-hand witness to some of the events of Acts. Luke also describes his research for writing the gospel (Luke 1:1–4). Paul mentions that Luke was a physician (Col. 4:14), and Luke's language reflects precision and a wide vocabulary, about government and travel, for instance.

2. What about Peter?

Ehrman specifically claims that Peter was "a back-woods illiterate peasant." (Ehrman, FWNG, 75) In response, Köstenberger, Bock, and Chatraw note the significant role Peter played in the origin of the Christian faith:

> Ehrman has ignored certain things we know about Peter and his context. Apparently, Peter was literate enough to lead and help launch a religious movement that spanned continents by the time of his death. Peter led this movement in Greco-Roman contexts outside of Israel, as well as in the land. In the Greco-Roman settings, Greek would have been the main language. This means he must have been a solid oral communicator at the least, making him potentially capable of expressing himself in letters. Some of this communication took place in a context where Greek would have been important. In an *oral* culture he need only be able to *dictate* in order to compose his letters. Ehrman's argument seems trapped in a *literary* model of communication, not the predominantly oral world of the first century. Even if Ehrman were right about literacy and Peter (a point we are about to challenge), his conclusion regarding Peter's linguistic ability does not hold in an oral context. (Köstenberger, Bock, and Chatraw, TCD, 143, emphasis in original)

Specifically, Ehrman claims that in Acts 4:13, the Sanhedrin describe Peter and John as "illiterate," which is Ehrman's translation of the word *agrammatoi*. However, commentator Richard Longenecker notes that this is an inaccurate translation and that *agrammatoi* refers to being "uneducated" or "unschooled" in rabbinic training:

> Ἀγράμματοι (*agrammatoi*) appears in the Gr. nonliterary papyri in the sense of "illiterate," though here it undoubtedly means "uneducated" or "unschooled" in rabbinic training. The word ἰδιῶται (*idiōtai*), while at times signifying "ignorant" (cf. 1 Cor 14:23–24), is here used in its ordinary Gr. sense of "commoner," "layman," or "ordinary person." (Longenecker, AA, 307)

In his book *The Life and Witness of Peter*, Larry Helyer notes,

> The fact that he [Peter] had both an Aramaic and a Greek name is significant; he was bilingual and lived in an environment that was heavily influenced by Hellenism. The disparaging view of the Jerusalem religious leaders that Jesus' disciples were "uneducated and ordinary men" (Acts 4:13) probably means "no more than that they were ignorant of the finer points of the rabbinical interpretation of the Jewish Torah." (Helyer, LWP, 19)

3. Does the issue of authorship matter for the historical reliability of the Gospels?

In a debate with noted philosopher and apologist William Lane Craig, Ehrman raised the question of authorship, and tried to show that uncertainty about their identity undermines our confidence in the Gospels. After the debate, in a podcast that was transcribed to his website, Craig explained why he left this challenge unanswered at the time:

The reason why I didn't address it is because it doesn't matter. The names of the authors of Matthew, Mark and Luke doesn't [sic] matter. If they were named Horace and Susanna and Joakim, what difference would it make? It doesn't make any difference what their names are. What's critical is that Mark is an extremely early Gospel that embodies traditions in it like the passion story of Jesus that go right back to the first years of the early Jerusalem church, and is therefore a valuable source of historical information. Luke was written by a traveling companion of the apostle Paul as we know from the use of first person plural pronouns in the books of Acts from the sixteenth chapter on. And as such he traveled with Paul on his missionary journey back to Cesarea [sic] in Palestine and then to Jerusalem which means that the author of Luke/Acts was—just as he says in the prologue to the Gospel—able to interview eyewitnesses to the life of Jesus. So it doesn't matter what this man's name was. What counts is that we have here a traveling companion of Paul who was in contact with eye witnesses [sic] to the life and ministry of Jesus, and able to interview them in writing his Gospel. So the authorship of the Gospels is simply not the key to their historical credibility. (Craig, SBQ, website)

Nevertheless, there is good reason to think that traditional views of New Testament authorship are valid. Köstenberger, Bock, and Chatraw explain:

Ehrman's argument has several problems. First, he fails to explain why, if the church wanted to use early church figures to gain widespread acceptance for these documents, they chose Matthew, Mark, and Luke, three rather obscure figures in early Christianity. . . . This point can be illustrated rather vividly using Mark's Gospel as the example.

In the Ehrman model, one picks an author to enhance the stature of a work whose real author is unknown. So you can pick anyone to fill in the knowledge gap. In the case of Mark, early in the church Mark was understood to be the author who drew on Peter's preaching. Now let's consider Mark's credentials according to Acts. (1) He failed to make it successfully through the first missionary journey and went home. . . . (2) He caused a rift between Paul and Barnabas before the second missionary journey. These are hardly credentials to enhance a work's credibility. On the other side is Peter, a well-known and highly regarded early apostle. Now you have a choice to select between Mark and Peter an author to enhance the credibility of the work. Whom would you choose? (Köstenberger, Bock, and Chatraw, TCD, 136)

4. How can we trust "Mark" if he was not a disciple of Jesus?

Ehrman paints a picture of the disciples as illiterate and portrays the Gospels as lacking a meaningful connection to eyewitnesses of Jesus, relying instead on traditions from unreliable sources. (Ehrman, HJBG, 244) In contrast, Richard Bauckham argues Peter (along with other eyewitnesses) was a primary source for the gospel of Mark. He concludes that Mark's use of Peter "enables the reader to share the *eyewitness* perspective on the events that Peter's testimony embodied." (Bauckham, JE, 164, emphasis in original) Bauckham explains:

Mark's Gospel not only, by its use of the *inclusio* of eyewitness testimony, claims Peter as its main eyewitness source; it also tells the story predominantly (though by no means exclusively) from Peter's perspective. This Petrine perspective is deliberately, carefully, and subtly constructed. Mark's Gospel is no mere transcript of Peter's teaching, nor is the Petrine perspective merely an undesigned survival of the way Peter told his stories. While it does correspond to features of Peter's oral narration, Mark has deliberately designed the Gospel in such a way that it incorporates and conveys this Petrine perspective. Several literary features combine to give readers/hearers Peter's "point of view" (internal focalization), usually spatial and visual or auditory, sometimes also psychological. It is this literary construction of the Petrine perspective that has so far gone almost unnoticed in Markan scholarship. Not only has Mark carefully constructed the Petrine perspective; he has also integrated it into his overall concerns and aims in the Gospel so that it serves Mark's dominant focus on the identity of Jesus and the nature of discipleship. Thus, in deliberately preserving the perspective of his main eyewitness sources through much of the Gospel, Mark is no less a real author creating his own Gospel out of the traditions he had from Peter (as well as, probably, some others). (Bauckham, JE, 179, emphasis in original)

IV. Conclusion

Bart Ehrman is a brilliant scholar who has been influential in the lives of many people. He is witty, smart, and articulate. And even though he is a self-proclaimed agnostic, much of his research has actually helped to confirm the historical value of the Scriptures. However, our analysis shows that his arguments that attempt to undermine the deity of Christ and the value of the New Testament texts can and should be challenged because of their significant weaknesses. Taken as a whole, his arguments do not in any way undermine the accuracy of the New Testament and the traditional claims of Christianity.

BIBLIOGRAPHY

103 Torah Scrolls From Hungary Found By Jewish Leaders in Russia," Associated Press, February 18, 2014, http://www.huffingtonpost.com/2014/02/18/torah-scrolls-hungary-jewish-leaders_n_4810979.html?utm_hp_ref=tw.

Achtemeier, Elizabeth. "Isaiah of Jerusalem: Themes and Preaching Possibilities," in *Reading and Preaching the Book of Isaiah*, edited by Christopher R. Seitz, 23–38. Philadelphia, PA: Fortress Press, 1988.

Ackroyd, Peter R. and Christopher F. Evans. *The Cambridge History of the Bible*. Cambridge: Cambridge University Press, 2008.

Acosta, Ana M. "Conjectures and Speculations: Jean Astruc, Obstetrics, and Biblical Criticism in Eighteenth-Century France." *Eighteenth-Century Studies* 35, no. 2 (2002): 256–66.

Adams, Matthew J., Sivan Einhorn, and Israel Finkelstein. *Megiddo V: The 2004–2008 Seasons*. Winona Lake, IN: Eisenbrauns, 2013.

Adler, Mortimer. *Aristotle for Everybody: Difficult Thought Made Easy*. New York: Macmillan, 1978.

———. *Six Great Ideas*. New York: Macmillan, 1981.

———. *Ten Philosophical Mistakes*. New York: Macmillan, 1985.

———. *Truth in Religion: The Plurality of Religions and the Unity of Truth*. New York: Macmillan, 1990.

Ådna, Jostein. "The Encounter of Jesus with the Gerasene Demoniac," in *Authenticating the Activities of Jesus*, eds. Bruce Chilton and Craig A. Evans. Leiden: Brill, 2002.

Adalian, Rouben Paul. *Historical Dictionary of Armenia*, 2nd ed. Plymouth, U.K.: Scarecrow Press, 2010.

Aharoni, Yohanan. *The Land of the Bible: A Historical Geography*. Translated by Anson F. Rainey. 2nd ed. Louisville, KY: Westminster/Knox, 1981.

Ahlström, G. W. and D. Edelman. "Merneptah's Israel." *Journal of Near Eastern Studies* 44, no. 1 (January, 1985): 59–61. doi:10.2307/544372.

Albright, W. F. *The Archaeology of Palestine*, rev. ed. Baltimore: Penguin Books, 1960.

———. *The Archaeology of Palestine and the Bible*. 3rd ed. New York: Fleming H. Revell, 1935.

———. *The Archaeology and Religion of Israel*. 5th ed. Baltimore, MD: Johns Hopkins Press, 1968.

———. *The Biblical Period from Abraham to Ezra: An Historical Survey*. New York: Harper & Row, 1963.

———. "The Israelite Conquest of Canaan in the Light of Archaeology." *Bulletin of the American Journal of Oriental Research* 74 (April, 1939): 11–23.

———. *Recent Discoveries in Bible Lands*. New York: Funk and Wagnalls, 1955

Aleman, André and Frank Larøi. *Hallucinations: The Science of Idiosyncratic Perception.* Washington, DC: American Psychological Association, 2008.

Alexander, Denis R. *Creation or Evolution: Do We Have to Choose?* 2nd ed. Grand Rapids, MI: Monarch Books, 2014.

Alexander, L. C. A. "Chronology of Paul," in *Dictionary of Paul and His Letters*, eds. Gerald F. Hawthorne, Ralph P. Martin, and Daniel G. Reid. Downers Grove, IL: InterVarsity Press, 1993), 116, 120–23.

Alexander, T. D. "Authorship of the Pentateuch," in *Dictionary of the Old Testament: Pentateuch*, edited by T. D. Alexander and David W. Baker, 64–72. IVP Bible Dictionary Series. Downers Grove: InterVarsity Press, 2003.

Alexeev, Anatolij. "The Last but Probably Not the Least: The Slavonic Version As a Witness of the Greek NT Text," in *Methodios und Kyrillos in Ihrer Europaischen Dimension*, ed. Evangelos Konstantinou. Frankfurt: Peter Lang, 2005.

Allen, Isaac. *Is Slavery Sanctioned by the Bible? A Premium Tract.* (Amazon Digital Services), Kindle edition.

Allis, Oswald T. *The Unity of Isaiah: A Study in Prophecy.* Eugene, OR: Wipf and Stock Publishers, 2000.

Alt, Albrecht. *Essays on Old Testament History and Religion.* Translated by R. A. Wilson. Oxford: Basil Blackwell, 1966.

Alter, Robert. *The Five Books of Moses: A Translation with Commentary.* New York: W. W. Norton & Company, 2008. Kindle edition.

Alter, Robert. *The World of Biblical Literature.* New York: BasicBooks, 1992.

Anchor, R. "The Quarrel Between Historians and Postmodernists." *History and Theory* 38, no. 1 (1999): 111–21.

Anderson, C. Anthony. "Identity and Existence in Logic," in *The Continuum Companion to Philosophical Logic*, edited by Leon Horsten and Richard Pettigrew, 54–76. London: Continuum, 2011.

Anderson, Gary A. "What About the Canaanites?" In *Divine Evil? The Moral Character of the God of Abraham*, edited by Michael Bergmann, Michael J. Murray, and Michael C. Rea, 269–91. Oxford University Press, 2011.

Anderson, J. *The Bible, the Word of God.* Brighton: n.p., 1905.

Anderson, J. N. D. *Christianity: The Witness of History.* London: Tyndale Press, 1970.

Anderson, Walter Truett, ed. *The Truth About Truth: De-confusing and Re-constructing the Postmodern World.* New York: G. P. Putnam's Sons, 1995.

Andrews, Carol A. R. "Rosetta Stone," in *The Oxford Companion to Archaeology*, edited by Brian M. Fagan. Oxford University Press, 1996.

Angus, Joseph. *The Bible Handbook.* Religious Tract Society, 1910, orig. pub. 1856.

Angus, Samuel. *The Mystery-Religions: A Study in the Religious Background of Early Christianity.* NY: Dover Publications, 1975.

Ansberry, Christopher and Jerry Hwang. "No Covenant Before the Exile? The Deuteronomic Torah and Israel's Covenant Theology," in *Evangelical Faith and the Challenge of Historical Criticism*, edited by Christopher M. Hays, 74–94. Grand Rapids, MI: Baker Academic, 2013.

The Ante-Nicene Fathers: Translations of the Writings of the Fathers down to A.D. 325. Edited by Alexander, Roberts, James Donaldson, and A. Cleveland Coxe. 1885. Reprint, Grand Rapids, MI: Eerdmans, 1965 and 1967.

Aphrahat. "Demonstration XXI: Of Persecution," in *The Nicene and Post-Nicene Fathers of the Christian Church*, vol. 2, edited by Philip Schaff and Henry Wace. New York: The Christian Literature Company, 1898.

Archer, Gleason L., Jr., *Encyclopedia of Bible Difficulties.* Grand Rapids, MI: Zondervan, 1982.

Aristotle. *Categories*. Translated by E. M. Edgehill. Chicago, IL: William Benton, 1952.

———. *Metaphysics*. Translated by W. D. Ross. Chicago, IL: William Benton, 1952.

———. *The Complete Works of Aristotle: The Revised Oxford Translation*, vols. 1 and 2, 6th ed. Edited by Jonathan Barnes. Bollingen Series LXXI-2. Princeton, NJ: Princeton University Press, 1984.

Armacost, Barbara E. and Peter Enns. "Crying Out for Justice: Civil Law and the Prophets," in *Law and the Bible: Justice, Mercy and Legal Institutions*, edited by Robert F. Cochran Jr. and David VanDrunen, 121–50. Downers Grove, IL: InterVarsity Press, 2013.

Arnold, Bill T. "The Genesis Narratives," in *Ancient Israel's History: An Introduction to Issues and Sources*, edited by Bill T. Arnold and Richard S. Hess, 23–45. Grand Rapids, MI: Baker, 2014.

———. "History of Pentateuchal Criticism," in *Dictionary of the Old Testament: Pentateuch*, edited by T. Desmond Alexander and David W. Baker, 622–31. Downers Grove, IL: InterVarsity Press, 2003.

Arnold, Bill and Brian Beyer. "The Tale of Sinuhe," in *Readings from the Ancient Near East*, edited by Bill Arnold and Brian Beyer, 76–82. Grand Rapids, MI: Baker, 2002.

Arnold, Bill T. and Bryan E. Beyer, eds. *Readings from the Ancient Near East: Primary Sources for Old Testament Study*. Grand Rapids, MI: Baker, 2002.

Arnold, Clinton E. and Jeff Arnold, *Short Answers to Big Questions About God, the Bible & Christianity*. Grand Rapids, MI: Baker, 2015.

Ashley, Timothy R. *The Book of Numbers. The New International Commentary on the Old Testament*, edited by R. K. Harrison. Grand Rapids, MI: Eerdmans, 1993.

Askeland, Christian. "The Coptic Versions of the New Testament," in *The Text of the New Testament in Contemporary Research*, edited by.Bart D. Ehrman and Michael W. Holmes, 201–30. Leiden: Brill, 2013.

Athanasius. *Letters*, no. 39 (Easter 367), in *A Select Library of the Nicene and Post-Nicene Fathers of the Christian Church*, vol. 4. Edited by Philip Schaff. New York: The Christian Literature Company, 1888.

Athas, George. *The Tel Dan Inscription: A Reappraisal and a New Interpretation*. London: T&T Clark, 2003.

Audi, Robert. *Epistemology: A Contemporary Introduction to the Theory of Knowledge*, 3rd ed. New York: Routledge, 2011.

Auerbach, Erich. *Mimesis: The Representation of Reality in Western Literature*. Tranlated by W. R. Trask. Princeton University Press, 1953, orig. pub. 1946.

Augustine. "Appendix 7, Enchiridion 7.20," in *Against the Academicians and the Teacher*. Translated by Peter King. Indianapolis, IN: Hackett, 1995.

———. *The City of God: Books VIII–XVI*. Translated by Gerald G. Walsh and Grace Monahan. Washington DC: The Catholic University of America Press, 1952.

———. "On Christian Doctrine." Translated by J. F. Shaw, in Great Books of the Western World, edited by Robert Maynard Hutchens, vol. 18, 621–98. Chicago, IL: Encyclopaedia Britannica, 1952.

———. Reply to Faustus the Manichæan. Translated by Philip Schaff. *Nicene and Post-Nicene Fathers*, series 1, volume 4. Edinburgh: T&T Clark, and Grand Rapids, MI: Eerdmans, reprint 1993.

———. *The Works of Saint Augustine: A Translation for the 21st Century Part I, vol. 13*. Translated by Edmund Hill. Edited by John E. Rotelle. Hyde Park, NY: New City Press, 2002.

Averback, Richard E. "Pentateuchal Criticism and the Priestly Torah," in *Do Historical Matters Matter to Faith? A Critical Appraisal of Modern and Postmodern Approaches to*

Scripture, edited by James Karl Hoffmeier and Dennis Robert Magary, locations 3642–4308. Wheaton: Crossway, 2012. Kindle edition.

Ayala, Francisco. "The Myth of Eve: Molecular Biology and Human Origins." *Science* 270 (22 December 1995): 1930–36.

Aylesworth, Gary. "Postmodernism." *The Stanford Encyclopedia of Philosophy*. Last revised February 5, 2015. http://plato.stanford.edu/archives/spr2015/entries/postmodernism/.

Bacon, Francis. *The New Organon*, edited by Lisa Jardine. Cambridge, UK: Cambridge University Press, 2000.

Baden, Joel S. *The Composition of the Pentateuch: Renewing the Documentary Hypothesis*. New Haven: Yale University Press, 2012.

Baggett, David. *Did the Resurrection Happen? A Conversation with Gary Habermas and Antony Flew*. Downers Grove, IL: InterVarsity Press, 2009.

Balakirev, Evgeniy and Francisco Ayala. "Pseudogenes, Are They 'Junk' or Functional DNA?" *Annual Review of Genetics* 37 (2003): 123–51. doi: 10.1146/annurev.genet.37.040103.103949.

Ball, David A. "The Crucifixion and Death of a Man Called Jesus." *Journal of the Mississippi State Medical Association* 30, no. 3 (March 1989): 77–83.

Bandas, Rudolph. *Contemporary Philosophy and Thomistic Principles*. New York: Bruce Publishing, 1932.

Barclay, William J. *Barclay on the Lectionary: Matthew: Year A*. Edinburgh: St. Andrews Press, 2013.

Barker-Plummer, David, Jon Barwise, and John Etchemendy. *Language, Proof and Logic*. Stanford, CA: CSLI Publications, 1999.

Barnett, Paul. *Finding the Historical Christ*. Grand Rapids, MI: Eerdmans, 2009.

———. *Jesus and the Logic of History*. Leicester: Apollos, 1997.

Barr, Stephen. *Modern Physics and Ancient Faith*. Notre Dame: University of Notre Dame Press, 2003.

Barrett, Matthew and Ardel B. Caneday, eds. *Four Views on the Historical Adam*. Grand Rapids, MI: Zondervan, 2013.

Barrick, William D. "Exegetical Fallacies: Common Interpretive Mistakes Every Student Must Avoid." *The Master's Seminary Journal* 18, no. 1 (Spring 2008): 15–21.

———. "'Ur of the Chaldeans' (Gen 11:28–31): A Model for Dealing with Difficult Texts" *The Masters Seminary Journal* 20, no. 1 (Spring 2008): 7–18.

Battezzato, Luigi. "Renaissance Philology: Johannes Livineius (1546–1599) and the Birth of the Apparatus Criticus," in *History of Scholarship: A Selection of Papers from the Seminar on the History of Scholarship Held Annually at the Warburg Institute*, edited by Christopher Ligota and Jean-Louis Quantin. Oxford University Press, 2006.

Bauckham, Richard. *Gospel Women: Studies of the Named Women in the Gospels*. Grand Rapids, MI: Eerdmans, 2002.

———. *Jesus and the Eyewitnesses: The Gospels as Eyewitness Testimony*. Grand Rapids, MI: Eerdmans, 2006.

———. *Jesus and the God of Israel: God Crucified and Other Essays on the New Testament's Christology of Divine Identity*. Grand Rapids, MI: Eerdmans, 2008.

Beard, Charles A. "That Noble Dream," in *The Varieties of History: From Voltaire to the Present*, edited by Fritz Stern, 314–28. New York: Vintage Books, 1973.

Beasley-Murray, G. R. *Jesus and the Kingdom of God*. Grand Rapids, MI: Eerdmans, 1986.

Beaver, R. Pierce. *Eerdmans' Handbook to the World's Religions*. Grand Rapids, MI: Eerdmans, 1982.

Beckwith, Francis J. *David Hume's Argument Against Miracles: A Critical Analysis*. Lanham, MD: University Press of America, 1989.

———. "History & Miracles," in *In Defense of Miracles*, edited by R. Douglas Geivett and

Gary R. Habermas, 86–98. Downers Grove, IL: InterVarsity Press, 1997.

———. "Theism, Miracles, and the Modern Mind," in *The Rationality of Theism*, edited by Paul Copan and Paul K. Moser, 221–36. London: Routledge, 2003.

Beckwith, Francis J., William Lane Craig, and J. P. Moreland, eds. *To Everyone an Answer: A Case for the Christian Worldview.* Downers Grove, IL: InterVaristy Press, 2004.

Beckwith, Francis J. and Gregory Koukl. *Relativism: Feet Firmly Planted in Mid-Air.* Grand Rapids, MI: Baker Books, 1998.

Beckwith, Roger. *The Old Testament Canon of the New Testament Church and Its Background in Early Judaism.* Grand Rapids: Eerdmans, 1986. Reprint, Eugene, OR.: Wipf and Stock, 2008.

———. "Canon of the Hebrew Bible and the Old Testament," in *The Oxford Companion to the Bible*, edited by Bruce M. Metzger and Michael David Coogan, 100–102. Oxford University Press, 1993.

Beetham, Christopher A. *Knowing the Bible: Colossians and Philemon, A 12-Week Study.* Wheaton, IL: Crossway, 2015.

Beilby, James K. *Thinking About Christian Apologetics: What It Is and Why We Do It.* Downers Grove, IL: InterVarsity Press, 2011.

Benko, Stephen. "The Edict of Claudius of A.D. 49," *Theologische Zeitschrift* 25 (1969): 406–18.

Ben-Yosef, Erez, Ron Shaar, Lisa Tauxe, and Hagai Ron. "A New Chronological Framework for Iron Age Copper Production at Timna (Israel)." *Bulletin of the American Schools of Oriental Research* 367 (August, 2012): 31–71. doi:10.5615/bullamerschoorie.367.0031.

Berger, Lee R. et al. "Homo Naledi, a New Species of the Genus Homo from the Dinaledi Chamber, South Africa." *eLife* (2015): 4:e09560. doi:10.7554/eLife.09560.

Berkouwer, G. C. *The Person of Christ, Studies in Dogmatics.* Translated by John Vriend. Grand Rapids, MI: Eerdmans, 1954.

Berlinski, David. *The Devil's Delusion: Atheism and Its Scientific Pretensions.* New York: Crown Forum, 2008.

Biederwolf, W. E. "A Ringing Challenge to Unitarianism," *Moody Bible Institute Monthly* 21, no. 4 (Dec. 1920): 154.

Bird, Graeme D. *Multitextuality in the Homeric Iliad: The Witness of the Ptolemaic Papyri.* Washington, DC: Center for Hellenic Studies, 2010.

Bird, Michael F. "Birth of Jesus," in *The Routledge Encyclopedia of the Historical Jesus*, edited by Craig A. Evans, 71–75. New York: Routledge, 2010.

———. "Did Jesus Think He Was God?" in *How God Became Jesus – The Real Origins of Belief in Jesus' Divine Nature*, edited by Michael F. Bird, Craig A. Evans, Simon J. Gathercole, Charles E. Hill, and Chris Tilling. Grand Rapids, MI: Zondervan, 2014.

———. "Of Gods, Angels, and Men," in *How God Became Jesus: The Real Origins of Belief in Jesus' Divine Nature*, by Michael F. Bird, Craig A. Evans, Simon J. Gathercole, Charles E. Hill, and Chris Tilling. Grand Rapids, MI: Zondervan, 2014.

———. *The Gospel of the Lord: How the Early Church Wrote the Story of Jesus.* Grand Rapids, MI: Eerdmans, 2014.

Bird, Michael, Craig A. Evans, Simon Gathercole, Charles E. Hill, and Chris Tilling, eds. *How God Became Jesus: The Real Origins of Belief in Jesus' Divine Nature.* Grand Rapids, MI: Zondervan, 2014.

Blackburn, Barry L. "The Miracles of Jesus," in *Studying the Historical Jesus: Evaluations of the State of Current Research*, edited by Bruce Chilton and Craig A. Evans. Leiden: Brill, 1998.

Blackburn, Simon. *The Oxford Dictionary of Philosophy*, 2nd ed. Oxford University Press, 2008.

Blaiklock, Edward Musgrave. *The Acts of the Apostles.* Grand Rapids, MI: Eerdmans, 1959.

———. *Layman's Answer: An Examination of the New Theology*. London: Hodder and Stoughton, 1968.

Blaauw, Martijn and Duncan Pritchard. *Epistemology A–Z*. New York: Palgrave Macmillan, 2005.

Blenkinsopp, Joseph. *A History of Prophecy in Israel*. Louisville, KY: Westminster John Knox Press, 1996.

———. *The Pentateuch: An Introduction to the First Five Books of the Bible. The Anchor Bible Reference Library*. Yale University Press, 1992.

———. "The 'Servants of the Lord' in Third Isaiah: Profile of a Pietistic Group in the Persian Epoch," in *"The Place Is Too Small for Us": The Israelite Prophets in Recent Scholarship*, edited by Robert P. Gordon. Winona Lake, IN: Eisenbrauns, 1995.

Block, Daniel Isaac. *The Gods of the Nations: Studies in Ancient Near Eastern National Theology*. Jackson, MS: Evangelical Theological Society, 1988.

———. *Israel: Ancient Kingdom or Late Invention?* Nashville, TN: B&H Academic Group, 2008.

———. "Recovering the Voice of Moses: The Genesis of Deuteronomy." *Journal of the Evangelical Theological Society* 44, no. 3 (September 2001): 386–408.

Block, Daniel I., Peter Enns, Roy Gane, and John Walton. *NIVAC Bundle 1: Pentateuch*. HarperCollins Christian Publishing, 2015.

Blomberg, Craig L. *Can We Still Believe the Bible? An Evangelical Engagement with Contemporary Questions*. Grand Rapids, MI: Brazos Press, 2014.

———. *Contagious Holiness: Jesus' Meals with Sinners*. Downers Grove, IL: InterVarsity Press, 2005.

———. "Jesus of Nazareth: How Historians Can Know Him and Why It Matters," in *Christian Apologetics: A Comprehensive Case for Biblical Faith*, edited by Douglas Groothuis. Downers Grove: IVP Academic, 2011.

———. *Jesus and the Gospels*, 2nd ed. Nashville, TN: B&H, 2009.

———. *Matthew*. Vol. 22, The New American Commentary. Nashville, TN: B&H, 1992.

———. "Matthew," in *Commentary on the New Testament Use of the Old Testament*, eds. G. K. Beale and D. A Carson. Grand Rapids, MI: Baker Academic, 2007.

———. "Unity and Diversity," in *New Dictionary of Biblical Theology*, edited by T. Desmond Alexander and Brian S. Rosner. Downers Grove, IL: InterVarsity, 2000.

Bloom, John A. "On Human Origins: A Survey." *Christian Scholar's Review* 27, no. 2 (1997, updated 2014): 181–203.

Bloom, John A. and C. John Collins. "Creation Accounts and Ancient Near Eastern Religions." *Christian Research Journal* 35 (2012): 20–24.

Blum, Erhard. "Solomon and the United Monarchy: Some Textual Evidence," in *One God, One Cult, One Nation: Archaeological and Biblical Perspectives*, edited by Reinhard Gregor Kratz, Björn Corzilius, Hermann Spieckermann, and Tanja Pilger. Berlin: Walter De Gruyter, 2010.

Bock, Darrell L. "The Historical Jesus: An Evangelical View," in *The Historical Jesus: Five Views*, edited by James Beilby and Paul Rhodes Eddy. Downers Grove: IVP Academic, 2009.

———. "Jesus As Blasphemer," in *Who Do My Opponents Say That I Am? – An Investigation of the Accusations Against the Historical Jesus*, edited by Scot McKnight and Joseph B. Modica. New York: T&T Clark International, 2008.

———. *Luke 1:1–9:50, Baker Exegetical Commentary on the New Testament*. Grand Rapids, MI: Baker, 1996.

———. *The Missing Gospels: Unearthing the Truth behind Alternative Christianities*. Nashville, TN: Nelson Books, 2006.

———. *Studying the Historical Jesus*. Grand Rapids, MI: Baker Academic, 2002.

———. "A Theology of Luke and Acts," in *Biblical Theology of the New Testament*, edited by

Andreas J. Köstenberger. Grand Rapids, MI: Zondervan, 2012.

BonJour, Laurence. *Epistemology: Classic Problems and Contemporary Responses*, 2nd ed. Lanham, MD: Rowman & Littlefield Publishers, 2010.

——. "Foundationalism and the External World." *Philosophical Perspectives* 13 (1999): 229–49. http://www.jstor.org/stable/2676104.

——. *The Structure of Empirical Knowledge*. Cambridge, MA: Harvard University Press, 1985.

Borenstein, Seth. "Fossils Paint Messy Picture of Human Origins." MSNBC. August 8, 2007. http://www.msnbc.msn.com/id/20178936/ ns/technology_and_science-science/t/fossils -paint-messy-picture-human-origins/.

Borg, Marcus. *Evolution of the Word: The New Testament in the Order the Books Were Written*. New York: Harper Collins Publishers, 2012.

Bowman, Robert M., Jr. "How Jesus Became God – Or How God Became Jesus? A Review of Bart Ehrman's New Book and a Concurrent Response," March 24, 2014, http://credohouse. org/blog/how-jesus-became-god-or-how-god -became-jesus-a-review-of-bart-ehrmans-new -book-and-a-concurrent-response.

Bowman, Robert M., Jr. and J. Ed Komoszewski, *Putting Jesus in His Place: The Case for the Deity of Christ*. Grand Rapids, MI: Kregel Publications, 2007.

Boyd, Gregory A. and Paul Rhodes Eddy. *The Jesus Legend: A Case for the Historical Reliability of the Synoptic Jesus Tradition*. Grand Rapids, MI: Baker Academic, 2007.

Breisach, Ernst. *Historiography: Ancient Medieval and Modern*, 2nd ed. Chicago, IL: University of Chicago Press, 1994.

Brettler, Marc Zvi. "Compilation and Redaction of the Torah," in *The Jewish Study Bible*. *Oxford Biblical Studies Online*, http://www. oxfordbiblicalstudies.com/article/book/obso -9780195297515/obso-9780195297515-div1-13.

Briggs, Peter. "Testing the Factuality of the Conquest of Ai Narrative in the Book of Joshua." 2005. http://www.phc.edu/journalfiles/ factuality.pdf.

Briggs, Richard. "The Theological Function of Repetition in the Old Testament Canon." *Horizons in Biblical Theology* 28, no. 2 (November 2006): 95–112. http://dx.doi.org/ 10.1163/187122006X152726.

Bright, John. *A History of Israel*. 4th ed. Louisville: Westminster John Knox, 2000.

Britannica, The New Encyclopædia. 15th ed. Chicago, IL: Encyclopædia Britannica, 2010.

Brodie, Thomas L. *Genesis As Dialogue: A Literary, Historical, and Theological Commentary*. Oxford University Press, 2001. Oxford Scholarship Online. Last modified November 2003. http://dx.doi.org/10.1093/0195138368.001 .0001.

Brooks, Ronald M. and Norman L. Geisler. *When Skeptics Ask: A Handbook On Christian Evidences*. Grand Rapids, MI: Baker Books, 1990.

Brown, Dan. *The Da Vinci Code*. New York: Anchor Books, 2013.

Brown, Michael L. *Answering Jewish Objections to Jesus: Messianic Prophecy Objections*. Vols. 1–3. Grand Rapids, MI: Baker Books, 2003.

Brown, Raymond, trans. "The Gospel of Peter." Early Christian Writings, edited by Peter Kirby. Last accessed March 4, 2016, http:// www.earlychristianwritings.com/text/gospel peter-brown.html.

Brown, Raymond E. *The Birth of the Messiah: A Commentary on the Infancy Narratives in Matthew and Luke*, rev. ed. Garden City, NY: Doubleday, 1993.

——. *The Death of the Messiah: From Gethsemane to the Grave: A Commentary on the Passion Narratives in the Four Gospels: Volume 2*. New York: Doubleday, 1994.

——. *The Gospel According to John (i-xii)*. Anchor Bible Commentary, vol. 29. New York: Doubleday, 1966.

Brown, Virginia. "Latin Manuscripts of Caesar's Gallic War," in *Palaeographia Diplomatica et Archivestica: Studi in Onore di Giulio Battelli*. Rome: University of Rome, 1979.

Bruce, F. F. "Archaeological Confirmation of the New Testament," in *Revelation and the Bible*, edited Carl Henry. Grand Rapids, MI: Baker Book House, 1969.

———. "The Background to the Son of Man Sayings," in *Christ the Lord: Studies in Christology Presented to Donald Guthrie*, edited by H. H. Rowdon. Leicester: InterVarsity Press, 1982.

———. *The Books and the Parchments: How We Got Our English Bible*, rev. ed. Old Tappan, NJ: F. H. Revell, 1984.

———. *The Canon of Scripture*. Downers Grove, IL: InterVarsity Press, 1988.

———. *Epistle to the Hebrews*, rev. ed. New International Commentary on the New Testament, edited by Gordon D. Fee. Grand Rapids, MI: Eerdmans, 1990.

———. "Jesus, Lord & Savior," in *The Jesus Library*, edited by Michael Green. Downers Grove, IL: InterVarsity Press, 1986.

———. *The New Testament Documents: Are They Reliable?* Downers Grove, IL: InterVarsity Press, 1964.

———. *Philippians*. Understanding the Bible Commentary Series. Grand Rapids, MI: Baker Books, 2011.

Brumbaugh, Robert S. "Plato Manuscripts: Toward a Completed Inventory" *Manuscripta* 34, no. 2 (1990).

Bultmann, Rudolf. *Jesus and the Word*. Translated by Louise Pettibone Smith and Erminie Huntress. New York: Charles Scribner's Sons, 1958, orig. pub. 1934.

———. "New Testament and Mythology: The Problem of Demythologizing the New Testament Proclamation," in *New Testament Mythology and Other Basic Writings*, ed. and trans. Schubert M. Ogden. Philadelphia, PA: Fortress Press, 1984.

Bunson, Margaret. "Admonitions of Ipuwer," in *Encyclopedia of Ancient Egypt*. 3rd ed. New York: Facts on File, 2012.

Burian, Peter and Alan Shapiro, eds., *The Complete Sophocles*. Oxford University Press, 2010.

Burridge, Richard A. and Graham Gould, *Jesus Then and Now*. Grand Rapids, MI: Eerdmans, 2004.

Buttenwieser, Hilda. "Popular Authors of the Middle Ages: The Testimony of the Manuscripts," *Speculum* 17, no.1 (1942): 50–55.

Byrne, Máire. *The Names of God in Judaism, Christianity, and Islam: A Basis for Interfaith Dialogue*. London: Continuum, 2011.

Cairns, Alan. *Dictionary of Theological Terms: A Ready Reference of Over 800 Theological and Doctrinal Terms*, 3rd ed. Greenville, SC: Ambassador Emerald International, 2002.

Calloway, Joseph A. "New Evidence on the Conquest of Ai." *Journal of Biblical Literature* 87 (September, 1968): 312–20.

Calvin, John. "Calvin's Commentary on the Bible: Joshua 11." StudyLight.org. http://www.studylight.org/commentaries/cal/view.cgi?bk=5&ch=11.

Cann, Rebecca L., Mark Stoneking, and Allan C. Wilson. "Mitochondrial DNA and Human Evolution." *Nature* 325 (1 January 1987): 31–36.

Capes, David B. *Old Testament Yahweh Texts in Paul's Christology*. Tübingen, Germany: Mohr Siebeck, 1992.

Caramelli, David et al. "Evidence for a Genetic Discontinuity between Neanderthals and 24,000-Year-Old Anatomically Modern Europeans." *Proceedings of the National Academy of Sciences*, USA 100 (May 27, 2003): 6593–6597. doi: 10.1073/pnas.1130343100.

Carlson, Stephen C. *The Gospel Hoax: Morton Smith's Invention of Secret Mark*. Waco, TX: Baylor University Press, 2005.

Carnell, Edward J. *Introduction to Christian Apologetics*. Grand Rapids MI: Eerdmans, 1948.

Carr, David. "What Is Required to Identify Pre-priestly Narrative Connections Between Genesis and Exodus? Some General Reflections and Specific Cases," in *A Farewell to the Yahwist? The Composition of the Pentateuch in Recent European Interpretation*, edited by Thomas B. Dozeman and Konrad Schmid, Society of Biblical Literature Symposium Series, vol. 34, 159–80. Atlanta: Society of Biblical Literature, 2006.

Carrier, Richard C. "The Burial of Jesus in Light of Jewish Law," in *The Empty Tomb: Jesus Beyond the Grave*, eds. Robert M. Price and Jeffery Jay Lowder. Amherst: NY, Prometheus Books, 2005.

———. "The Plausibility of the Theft," in *The Empty Tomb: Jesus Beyond the Grave*, eds. Robert M. Price and Jeffery Jay Lowder. Amherst: NY, Prometheus Books, 2005.

———. "The Spiritual Body of Christ and the Legend of the Empty Tomb," in *The Empty Tomb: Jesus Beyond the Grave*, eds. Robert M. Price and Jeffery Jay Lowder. Amherst: NY, Prometheus Books, 2005.

Carroll, Robert Todd. "Occam's Razor," in *The Skeptics Dictionary*. Accessed November 8, 2015, http://skepdic.com/occam.html.

Carroll, Scott. Lecture at Discover the Evidence, Dallas, TX, December 3–4, 2013.

Carson, D. A. "Editorial." *Themelios* 34, no.2 (2009): 155–57.

Carson, D.A., ed. *NIV Zondervan Study Bible*. Grand Rapids, MI: Zondervan, 2015.

Carson, D. A. and Douglas J. Moo, *An Introduction to the New Testament*, 2nd ed. Grand Rapids, MI: Zondervan, 2005.

Casey, Maurice. *Jesus: Evidence and Argument or Mythicist Myths?* London: Bloomsbury Academic, 2014.

———. *Jesus of Nazareth: An Independent Historian's Account of His Life and Teaching*. London: T&T Clark International, 2010.

Cassuto, Umberto Moshe David. *The Documentary Hypothesis*. Jerusalem: Central Press,

1941. Prepared as an e-Book by Varda Graphics Inc, 2005, 2011. Kindle edition.

Charles, J. Daryl, ed. *Reading Genesis 1–2: An Evangelical Conversation*. Peabody, MA: Hendrickson, 2013.

Charles, Larry, director. *Religulous*. Santa Monica, CA: Lionsgate, 2008.

Charlesworth, James. *The Historical Jesus: An Essential Guide*. Nashville, TN: Abingdon, 2008.

———. "The Historical Jesus and Biblical Archaeology: Reflections on New Methodologies and Perspectives," in *Jesus and Archaeology*, edited by James H. Charlesworth, 690–93. Grand Rapids, MI: Eerdmans, 2006.

Chase, Mary Ellen. *The Bible and the Common Reader*. New York: MacMillan, 1945.

Chesterton, G. K. *Orthodoxy*. Chicago, IL: Moody Publishers, 2009.

Childers, Jeff W. "The Georgian Version of the New Testament," in *The Text of the New Testament in Contemporary Research: Essays on the Status Quaestionis*, 2nd ed., edited by Bart D. Ehrman and Michael W. Holmes, 329–50. Leiden: Brill, 2013.

Childs, Brevard S. *Introduction to the Old Testament As Scripture*. Philadelphia, PA: Fortress Press, 1979.

Chisholm, Roderick M. *The Foundations of Knowing*. Minneapolis, MN: University of Minnesota Press, 1982.

———. *Theory of Knowledge*, 3rd ed. Englewood Cliffs, NJ: Prentice Hall, 1989.

Chrysostom, John. "Homilies on the Gospel of St. Matthew." Christian Classics Ethereal Library. Last accessed on November 6, 2015, http://www.ccel.org/ccel/schaff/npnf110.iii.LXXXVI.html.

Churchill, Winston. 1939 quote on Russia's Foreign Policy. *Life Magazine*. October 18, 1943.

Churchland, Patricia. "Epistemology in the Age of Neuroscience," *Journal of Philosophy* 84, no. 10 (1987): 548.

Cicero, Marcus Tullius. *De Natura Deorum; Academica.* Translated by Harris Rackham. Cambridge, MA. Harvard University Press, 1979.

Cilliers, L., and F. P. Retief. "The History and Pathology of Crucifixion." *South African Medical Journal (Suid-Afrikannse tydskrif via geneeskunde)* 93, no. 12 (December 2003): 938–41.

Clark, Mary T. *An Aquinas Reader*, rev. ed. New York: Fordham University Press, 2000.

Clement of Rome. *Epistle to the Corinthians.* http://www.ewtn.com/library/patristc/anf1-1.htm.

Clements, Ronald E. "Beyond Tradition-History: Deutero-Isaianic Development of First Isaiah's Themes." *Journal for the Study of the Old Testament* 31 (February 1985): 95–113.

———. "The Unity of the Book of Isaiah." *Interpretation* 36, no. 2 (April 1982): 117–29.

———. "Who Is Blind but My Servant? (Isaiah 42:19): How Shall We Then Read Isaiah?" in *God in the Fray: A Tribute to Walter Brueggemann*, edited by Tod Linafelt and Timothy K. Beal. Minneapolis: Fortress Press: 1998.

Clifford, Ross and Philip Johnson. *The Cross Is Not Enough: Living as Witnesses to the Resurrection.* Grand Rapids, MI: Baker Books, 2012.

Clines, David J. A. "New Direction in Pooh Studies: Überlieferungs-Und Religionsgeschichtliche Studien Zum Pu-Buch," in *On the Way to the Postmodern: Old Testament Essays, 1967–1998*, 830–39. Sheffield: Sheffield Academic Press, 1998.

Cogan, Mordechai, trans. "Cyrus Cylinder," in *The Context of Scripture: Canonical Compositions, Monumental Inscriptions and Archival Documents from the Biblical World*, vol. 2, edited by William Hallo and K. Lawson Younger, 314–16. Leiden: Brill, 2000.

Cogan, Mordechai. "Literary-Critical Issues in the Hebrew Bible from an Assyriological Perspective: Literary-Ideological Alterations," in *Homeland and Exile: Biblical and Ancient Near Eastern Studies in Honour of Bustenay Oded Supplements to Vetus Testamentum*, edited by Gershon Galil, Markham J. Geller, and A R. Millard, 13–28. Leiden: Brill, 2009.

Cohen, A. *The Teachings of Maimonides.* London: George Routledge & Sons, Ltd., 1927.

Cohen, Jonathan. *The Origins and Evolution of the Moses Nativity Story.* New York: E. J. Brill, 1993.

Cohn, Norman. *Noah's Flood: The Genesis Story in Western Thought.* New Haven: Yale University Press, 1996.

Cole, Diane. "Carbon Dating Confirms World's Oldest Torah Scroll," *National Geographic*, May 30, 2013, http://news.nationalgeographic.com/news/2013/05/130530-worlds-oldest-torah-scroll-bible-bologna-carbon-dating/.

Cole, Graham A. *He Who Gives Life: The Doctrine of the Holy Spirit.* Wheaton, IL: Crossway Books, 2007.

Colbert, Stephen. Interview with Bart Ehrman. The Colbert Report, Comedy Central, April 9, 2009, http://www.cc.com/video-clips/lywaay/the-colbert-report-bart-ehrman.

Collingwood, Robin G. *Essays in the Philosophy of History.* Austin, TX: University of Texas Press, 1965.

Collins, Francis S. *The Language of God: A Scientist Presents Evidence for Belief.* New York: Free Press, 2006.

Collins, John C. *Introduction to the Hebrew Bible*, 2nd ed. Minneapolis, MN: Fortress Press, 2014.

———. *Did Adam and Eve Really Exist? Who They Were and Why You Should Care.* Wheaton, IL: Crossway, 2011.

———. *Genesis 1–4: A Linguistic, Literary, and Theological Commentary.* Phillipsburg, NJ: P&R Publishing, 2005.

Collins, John J. *Daniel: A Commentary on the Book of Daniel.* Minneapolis, MN: Augsburg Fortress, 1993.

Collins, Robin C. "A Scientific Argument for the Existence of God," in *Reason for the Hope*

Within, edited Michael J. Murray. Grand Rapids, MI: Eerdmans, 1999.

Collins, Steven. *The Defendable Faith: Lessons in Christian Apologetics*. Albuquerque, NM: TSU Press, 2012.

———. "Has Archaeology Gone Overboard in Throwing Out the Bible?" in *The Ancient Near East Today*. American Schools of Oriental Research (October 10, 2013). http://asor blog.org/2013/10/10/has-archaeology-gone -overboard-in-throwing-out-the-bible/.

Collins, Steven and J. W. Oller, Jr. "Is the Bible a True Narrative Representation?" in *Biblical Research Bulletin* I.3. 2001.

Colson, Charles W. "The Terrifying Truth: We Are Normal," *Jubilee* (July 1983), http://www.thepointradio.org/search-library/search?view=searchdetail&id=1395.

Colwell, Gary. "Miracles and History." *Sophia* 22, no. 2 (1983): 10. doi:10.1007/BF02891789.

Comfort, Philip Wesley, ed., *The Origin of the Bible*. Wheaton, IL: Tyndale House Publishers, 1992.

Cooper. Henry R. *Slavic Scriptures: The Formation of the Church Slavonic Version of the Holy Bible*. Madison, WI: Fairleigh Dickenson, 2003.

Copan, Paul. *How Do You Know You're Not Wrong?* Grand Rapids, MI: Baker, 2005.

———. *Is God a Moral Monster? Making Sense of the Old Testament God*. Grand Rapids, MI: Baker, 2011.

———. "Is Yahweh a Moral Monster? The New Atheists and Old Testament Ethics." *Philosophia Christi* 10, no. 1 (2008): 7–37.

———. "The Moral Argument for God's Existence," in *Evidence for God: 50 Arguments for Faith from the Bible, History, Philosophy, and Science*. Grand Rapids, MI: Baker 2010.

———. *True for You, But Not for Me*. Minneapolis, MN: Bethany House, 1998.

———. "Yahweh Wars and the Canaanites: Divinely-Mandated Genocide or Corporate Capital Punishment? Responses to Critics." *Philosophia Christi* 11, no. 1 (2009): 73–90.

Copan, Paul, and William Lane Craig. *Creation Out of Nothing: A Biblical, Philosophical, and Scientific Exploration*. Leicester, England: Apollos, 2004.

Copan, Paul and Matthew Flannagan. *Did God Really Command Genocide? Coming to Terms with the Justice of God*. Grand Rapids, MI: Baker Books, 2014.

Copan, Paul and Ronald K. Tacelli, eds. *Jesus' Resurrection: Fact or Figment? A Debate between William Lane Craig and Gerd Lüdemann*. Downers Grove, IL: InterVarsity Press, 2000.

Corduan, Winfried. *No Doubt About It: The Case for Christianity*. Nashville, TN: B&H, 1997.

Cowe, S. Peter. "The Armenian Version of the New Testament," in *The Text of the New Testament in Contemporary Research: Essays on the Status Quaestionis*, 2nd ed., edited by Bart D. Ehrman and Michael W. Holmes, 293–328. Leiden: Brill, 2013.

Cowan, Steven and James Spiegel. *The Love of Wisdom: A Christian Introduction to Philosophy*. Nashville, TN: B&H Academic, 2009.

Cowburn, John. *Scientism: A Word We Need*. Eugene: Wipf & Stock, 2013.

Craig, William Lane. *Apologetics: An Introduction*. Chicago, IL: Moody Press, 1984.

———. *Assessing the New Testament Evidence for the Historicity of the Resurrection of Jesus*. Lewiston: Edwin Mellen Press, 1989.

———. *Hard Questions, Real Answers*. Wheaton, IL: Crossway, 2003.

———. *Reasonable Faith: Christian Truth and Apologetics*, 3rd edition. Wheaton, IL: Crossway Books, 2008.

———. "The 'Slaughter' of the Canaanites Revisited." Reasonable Faith. Last revised August 8, 2011. http://www.reasonablefaith.org/the-slaughter-of-the-canaanites-re-visited.

———. "Some Bible Questions." Reasonable Faith, podcast audio, August 15, 2011, http://www

.reasonablefaith.org/some-bible-questions#ixzz3woOg1oaZ.

———. *The Son Rises: The Historical Evidence for the Resurrection of Jesus.* Eugene, OR: Wipf and Stock, 2000.

———. "What Price Biblical Errancy." Reasonable Faith. http://www.reasonablefaith.org/what-price-biblical-errancy.

Craig, William Lane and J. P. Moreland. *Philosophical Foundations for a Christian Worldview.* Downers Grove, IL: InterVarsity Press, 2003.

Craig, William Lane and James D. Sinclair. "The Kalam Cosmological Argument," in *The Blackwell Companion to Natural Theology,* edited by William Lane Craig and J. P. Moreland. West Sussex, UK: Wiley-Blackwell, 2009.

Cray, Dan. "God vs. Science." *Time Magazine.* November 5, 2006. http://www.time.com/time/printout/0,8816,1555132,00.html.

Creeds of Christendom. The Belgic Confession (1561). Accessed August 19, 2015, http://www.creeds.net/belgic/.

Cross, F. L., and E. A. Livingstone. *The Oxford Dictionary of the Christian Church,* 3rd ed. Oxford University Press, 2005.

Crossan, John Dominic. *The Historical Jesus: The Life of a Mediterranean Jewish Peasant.* New York: HarperSanFrancisco, 1992.

———. *Jesus: A Revolutionary Biography.* New York: HarperSanFrancisco, 1994.

———. *The Cross That Spoke: The Origins of the Passion Narrative.* San Francisco: Harper & Row, 1988.

———. *Four Other Gospels: Shadows on the Contours of Canon.* Minneapolis: Winston Press, 1985.

Currid, John D. *Against the Gods: The Polemical Theology of the Old Testament.* Wheaton, IL: Crossway, 2013.

———. *Ancient Egypt and the Old Testament.* Grand Rapids, MI: Baker, 1997.

———. *Doing Archaeology in the Land of the Bible: A Basic Guide.* Grand Rapids, MI: Baker, 1999.

Dalley, Stephanie, trans. *Myths from Mesopotamia: Creation, the Flood, Gilgamesh and Others.* Oxford University Press, 1989.

Dante Alighieri. "Letter to Can Grande Della Scala," in *Critical Theory Since Plato,* rev. ed., edited by Hazard Adams, 121–22. New York: Harcourt Brace Jovanovich, 1992.

Davies, G. I. "Introduction to the Pentateuch," in *The Oxford Bible Commentary.* Oxford Biblical Studies Online, http://www.oxfordbiblicalcstudies.com/article/book/obso-9780198755005/obso-9780198755005-div1-18.

Davies, Paul. *The Accidental Universe.* Cambridge: Cambridge University Press, 1982.

———. *Cosmic Jackpot.* New York: Houghton Mifflin, 2007.

Davies, Philip R. *In Search of "Ancient Israel."* JSOTSup 148. Sheffield, 1992.

Davis, C. T. "The Crucifixion of Jesus: The Passion of Christ from a Medical Point of View." *Arizona Medicine* 22 (1965): 183–187.

Davis, Stephen T. *Risen Indeed.* Grand Rapids, MI: Eerdmans, 1993.

Dawkins, Richard. *The God Delusion.* New York: Houghton Mifflin, 2008.

———. *River Out of Eden: A Darwinian View of Life.* New York: Basic Books, 1995.

———. *The Selfish Gene.* Oxford University Press, 1976.

Day, E. Hermitage. *On the Evidence for the Resurrection.* London: SPCK, 1906.

Day, John. *In Search of Preexilic Israel: Proceedings of the Oxford Old Testament Seminar.* London: Bloomsbury Publishing, 2004.

D'Costa, Gavin, ed. *Resurrection Reconsidered.* Rockport, MA: Oneworld Publications, 1996.

DeBoer, Scott L, and Charles L Maddow. "Emergency Care of the Crucifixion Victim." *Accident and Emergency Nursing* 10, no. 4 (October 2002): 235–39.

deClaissé-Walford, Nancy, Rolf A. Jacobson, and Beth LaNeel Tanner. *The Book of Psalms. The New International Commentary on the*

Old Testament, edited by Robert L. Hubbard. Grand Rapids, MI: Eerdmans, 2014.

De Montaigne, Michel. *An Apology for Raymond Sebond*. Translated by Roger Ariew and Marjorie Grene. Indianapolis, IN: Hackett, 2003.

Derrida, Jacques. *Dissemination*. Translated by Barbara Johnson. London: Continuum, 2004.

———. *Of Grammatology*. Translated by Gayatri C. Spivak. Baltimore, MD: Johns Hopkins University Press, 1976.

Descartes, René. *Discourse on Method, and Meditations*. Translated by Laurence J. Lafleur. New York: Macmillan, 1960.

———. *Meditations on First Philosophy*. Edited by Stanley Tweyman. Translated by Elizabeth S. Haldane and G. R. T. Ross. London, UK: Routledge, 1993.

Delitzsch, Friedrich. *Babel and Bible: Two Lectures on the Significance of Assyriological Research for Religion, Embodying the Most Important Criticisms and the Author's Replies*. Translated by Thomas J. McCormack and William Herbert Carruth. Chicago, IL: Open Court, 1903.

Dennett, Daniel. *Breaking the Spell: Religion as a Natural Phenomenon*. New York: Viking, 2006.

Denny, James. *Jesus and the Gospel: Christianity Justified in the Mind of Christ*, 2nd edition. London: Hodder and Stoughton, 1908.

Denton, Michael. *Evolution: Still a Theory in Crisis*. Seattle, WA: Discovery Institute Press, 2016.

Dever, William. "How to Tell a Canaanite from an Israelite," in *The Rise of Ancient Israel: Lectures Presented at a Symposium Sponsored by the Resident Associate Program, Smithsonian Institution*, edited by Hershel Shanks et al., 26–61. Washington, DC: Biblical Archaeology Society, 2013.

———. *What Did the Biblical Writers Know, and When Did They Know It? What Archaeology Can Tell Us about the Reality of Ancient Israel*. Grand Rapids, MI: Eerdmans, 2001. Kindle edition.

———. *Who Were the Early Israelites and Where Did They Come From?* Grand Rapids, MI: Eerdmans, 2003.

Dew, James K., Jr., and Mark W. Forman. *How Do We Know? An Introduction to Epistemology*. Downers Grove, IL: InterVarsity Press, 2014.

Dockery, David S., Kenneth A. Mathews, and Robert B. Sloan, *Foundations for Biblical Interpretation*. Nashville, TN: B&H, 1994.

Dillon, James. "Discernment," in *The Encyclopedia of Religious and Spiritual Development*, edited by W. George Scarlett and Elizabeth M. Dowling, 122–24. Thousand Oaks, CA: Sage Publications, 2006.

Dozeman, Thomas B. *Commentary on Exodus*. *The Eerdmans Critical Commentary*. Grand Rapids, MI: W. B. Eerdmans Pub. Co., 2009.

Dozeman, Thomas B., Konrad Schmid, and Baruch J. Schwartz, eds. *The Pentateuch: International Perspectives On Current Research*. Vol. 78 of Forschungen Sum Alten Testament. Tübingen: Mohr Siebeck, 2011.

Dozeman, Thomas B., Thomas Römer, and Konrad Schmid, eds. *Pentateuch, Hexateuch, or Enneateuch? Identifying Literary Works in Genesis through Kings*. Atlanta: Society of Biblical Literature, 2011.

Driver, S. R. *An Introduction to the Literature of the Old Testament*. New York: Meridian, 1956.

———. *Isaiah: His Life and Times and the Writings Which Bear His Name*. New York: Anson D. F. Randolph & Company, 1888.

Dunn, James D. G. *Jesus Remembered: Christianity in the Making*, vol. 1. Grand Rapids, MI: Eerdmans, 2003.

Durbin, Bill. "A Scientist Caught Between Two Faiths," *Christianity Today* 26, no. 13 (August 6, 1982): 14–18.

Earle, Ralph. *How We Got Our Bible*. Grand Rapids, MI: Baker Book House, 1971.

Easton, M. G., ed. "Seal," *Easton's Bible Dictionary*, 3rd ed. Nashville, TN: Thomas Nelson,

1897, n.p. version 3.3. Accordance Bible Software, version 11.4.1.

Eddy, Paul R. and Gregory A. Boyd, *The Jesus Legend: A Case for the Historical Reliability of the Synoptic Jesus Tradition*. Grand Rapids, MI: Baker Academic, 2007.

Edwards, James R. *The Gospel according According to Luke. Pillar New Testament Commentary*. Grand Rapids, MI: Eerdmans, 2015.

Edwards, Paul, ed. *The Encyclopedia of Philosophy*. New York: The Macmillan Co. & The Free Press, 1967.

Edwards, William, D., Wesley J. Gabel, and Floyd E. Hosmer. "On the Physical Death of Jesus." *The Journal of the American Medical Association* 255, no. 11 (March, 1986): 1455–63.

Ehrman, Bart D., ed. and trans. *The Apostolic Fathers*, vol. 1. Cambridge, MA: Harvard University Press, 2003.

Ehrman, Bart D. *The Bible: A Historical and Literary Introduction*. Oxford University Press, 2014.

———. *Did Jesus Exist? The Historical Argument for Jesus of Nazareth*. New York: HarperOne, 2012.

———. *Forged: Writing in the Name of God—Why the Bible's Authors Are Not Who We Think They Are*. San Francisco: HarperOne, 2011.

———. *How Jesus Became God – The Exaltation of a Jewish Preacher from Galilee*. San Francisco: HarperOne, 2014.

———. *Jesus, Interrupted: Revealing the Hidden Contradictions in the Bible (and Why We Don't Know About Them)*. New York: HarperCollins, 2010.

———. *Lost Christianities: The Battles for Scripture and the Faiths We Never Knew*. Oxford University Press, 2003.

———. *The Lost Gospel of Judas Iscariot: A New Look at Betrayer and Betrayed*. Oxford University Press, 2006.

———. *Peter, Paul, & Mary Magdalene: The Followers of Jesus in History and Legend*. Oxford University Press, 2006.

———. *Truth and Fiction in The Da Vinci Code: A Historian Reveals What We Really Know About Jesus, Mary Magdalene, and Constantine*. Oxford University Press, 2004.

———. "Why Was Jesus Killed?" The Bart Ehrman Blog: The History & Literature of Early Christianity (blog). October 16, 2012, http://ehrmanblog.org/why-was-jesus-killed/.

Elder, John. *Prophets, Idols, and Diggers*. New York: Bobbs Merrill Co., 1960

Elhassan, Nuha et al. "The Episode of Genetic Drift Defining the Migration of Humans out of Africa is Derived from a Large East African Population Size." PLoS ONE 9 (May 2014): e97674. doi:10.1371/journal.pone.0097674.

Ellegren, Hans. "Is Genetic Diversity Really Higher in Large Populations?" *Journal of Biology* 8 (21 April 2009): 41. doi: 10.1186/jbiol135.

Ellens, J. Harold. "Biblical Miracles and Psychological Process: Jesus As Psychotherapist," in *Miracles: God, Science, and Psychology in the Paranormal*, vol. 1, edited by J. Harold Ellens. Westport, CT: Praeger, 2008.

Elledge, Casey. "Josephus, Tacitus, and Suetonius: Seeing Jesus through the Eyes of Classical Historians," in *Jesus Research: New Methodologies and Perceptions*, edited by James H. Charlesworth. Grand Rapids, MI: Eerdmans, 2014.

Elliott, J. K. "Manuscripts, the Codex and the Canon." *Journal for the Study of the New Testament* 63 (1996): 105–123.

Elwell, Walter A. and Philip W. Comfort, eds., *Tyndale Bible Dictionary*. Carol Stream, IL: Tyndale House Publishers, 2001.

Enmarch, Roland. "The Reception of a Middle Egyptian Poem: The Dialogue of Ipuwer and the Lord of All in the Ramesside Period and Beyond," in *Ramesside Studies in Honour of K. A. Kitchen*, edited by Mark Collier and Steven Snape, 169–76. Bolton, England: Rutherford Press, 2011.

Emmel, Stephen. "The Christian Book in Egypt: Innovation and the Coptic Tradition," in *The*

Bible as Book: The Manuscript Tradition, eds. John L. Sharpe III and Kimberly van Kampen. Newcastle, DE: The British Library & Oak Knoll, 1998)

ENCODE Project Consortium, The. "An Integrated Encyclopedia of DNA Elements in the Human Genome." *Nature* 489 (6 September 2012): 57–74. doi:10.1038/nature11247.

Endo, Masanobu. *Creation and Christology: A Study on the Johannine Prologue in Light of Early Jewish Creation Accounts.* Tübingen, Germany: Mohr Siebeck, 2002), 232, 233.

Enns, Peter. *The Bible Tells Me So . . . Why Defending Scripture Has Made Us Unable to Read It.* New York: HarperCollins, 2015.

———. "Inerrancy, However Defined, Does Not Describe What the Bible Does," in *Five Views on Biblical Inerrancy*, edited by J. Merrick, Stephen M. Garrett, and Stanley N. Gundry, 83–116. Grand Rapids, MI: Zondervan, 2013.

———. *Inspiration and Incarnation: Evangelicals and the Problem of the Old Testament.* Grand Rapids, MI: Baker Academic, 2005.

Erickson, Millard J. *Postmodernizing the Faith: Evangelical Responses to the Challenge of Postmodernism.* Grand Rapids, MI: Baker Books, 1998.

———. *The Word Became Flesh: A Contemporary Incarnational Christology.* Grand Rapids, MI: Baker Book House, 1991.

The ESV Study Bible. Wheaton: Crossway, 2008.

Eusebius. *Ecclesiastical History.* Translated by Christian Frederick Cruse. New York: Stanford & Swords, 1850.

Evans, C. Stephen. *Why Believe?: Reason and Mystery As Pointers to God*, rev. ed. Grand Rapids, MI: Eerdmans, 1996.

Evans, Craig A. *Fabricating Jesus: How Modern Scholars Distort the Gospels.* Downers Grove, IL: IVP Books, 2006.

———. "Getting the Burial Traditions and Evidences Right" in *How God Became Jesus: A Response to Bart Ehrman.* Grand Rapids, MI: Zondervan, 2014.

———. *Jesus and His Contemporaries: Comparative Studies.* Leiden: Brill, 2001.

———. *Jesus and His World: The Archaeological Evidence.* Louisville, KY: Westminster John Knox Press, 2012.

———. "Jesus in Non-Christian Sources," in *Studying the Historical Jesus: Evaluations of the State of Current Research*, edited by Bruce Chilton and Craig Evans. New York: Brill, 1994.

———. "The Scriptures of Jesus and His Earliest Followers," in *The Canon Debate*, ed. Lee Martin McDonald and James A. Sanders, 185-195. Peabody, MA: Hendrickson Publishers, 2002.

———. "The Tomb of Jesus and Family? Second Thoughts." n.d., http://www.craigaevans.com/tombofjesus.htm.

Evans, Richard J. *In Defense of History.* London: Granta Publications, 1997.

Eve, Eric. *The Jewish Context of Jesus' Miracles, Journal for the Study of the New Testament Supplement* 231. London: Sheffield Academic Press, 2002.

Ewert, David. *From Ancient Tablets to Modern Translations: A General Introduction to the Bible.* Grand Rapids, MI: Zondervan, 1983.

Fairbairn, A. M. *Studies in the Life of Christ.* London: Hodder & Stoughton, 1896.

Falluomini, Carla. "The Gothic Version of the New Testament," in *The Text of the New Testament in Contemporary Research: Essays on the Status Quaestionis*, 2nd ed., edited by Bart D. Ehrman and Michael W. Holmes, 329–50. Leiden: Brill, 2013.

Fan, Yuxin et al. "Genomic Structure and Evolution of the Ancestral Chromosome Fusion Site in 2q13-2q14.1 and Paralogous Regions on Other Human Chromosomes." *Genome Research* 12 (2002): 1651–62. doi: 10.1101/gr.337602.

Faulkner, D. R. "A Proposal for a New Solution to the Light Travel Time Problem." *Answers Research Journal* 6 (2013): 279–84.

https://answersingenesis.org/astronomy/starlight/a-proposal-for-a-new-solution-to-the-light-travel-time-problem/.

Fausset, A. R. A. *Commentary Critical, Experimental and Practical on the Old and New Testament*, vol. 3. Grand Rapids, MI: Eerdmans, 1961.

Faust, Avraham. "Did Eilat Mazar Find David's Palace?" *Biblical Archaeology Review* 38, no. 5 (2012): 47.

Feldman, Richard. *Epistemology*. Upper Saddle River, NJ: Prentice Hall, 2003.

Ferry, Luc. *A Brief History of Thought: A Philosophical Guide to Living*. New York: Harper Perennial, 2011.

Fincher, Jonalyn. "Why Jesus Is Good News for Women," in *Apologetics for a New Generation*, edited by Sean McDowell. Eugene, OR: Harvest House, 2009.

Finkelstein, Israel. "A Low Chronology Update: Archaeology, History and Bible," in *The Bible and Radiocarbon Dating: Archaeology, Text and Science*, edited by Thomas Levy and Thomas Higham. London: Equinox Pub., 2005.

Finkelstein, Israel and Eli Piasetzky. "The Iron Age Chronology Debate: Is the Gap Narrowing?" *Near Eastern Archaeology* 74, no. 1 (March, 2011): 50–54. doi:10.5615/neareastarch.74.1.0050.

Finkelstein, Israel, and Neil Asher Silberman. *The Bible Unearthed: Archaeology's New Vision of Ancient Israel and the Origin of Its Sacred Texts*. New York: Simon and Schuster, 2001.

Firestein, Stuart. *Ignorance: How It Drives Science*. Oxford University Press, 2012. Kindle edition.

Fischer, David Hackett. *Historian's Fallacies: Toward a Logic of Historical Thought*. New York: Harper and Row, 1970.

Fisher, J. T. and L. S. Hawley. *A Few Buttons Missing*. Philadelphia, PA: Lippincott, 1951.

Fitzmyer, Joseph A. *The Gospel According to Luke I-IX*, Anchor Bible 28. New York: Doubleday, 1981.

Fleming, Daniel E. "Genesis in History and Tradition: The Syrian Background of Israel's Ancestors, Reprise," in *The Future of Biblical Archaeology: Reassessing Methodologies and Assumptions*, edited by James K. Hoffmeier and Alan Millard, 193–232. Grand Rapids, MI: Eerdmans, 2004.

Flew, Antony. *A Dictionary of Philosophy*, rev. 2nd ed. New York: St. Martin's Press, 1984.

Flew, Antony and Roy Abraham Varghese. *There Is a God: How the World's Most Notorious Atheist Changed His Mind*. New York: HarperOne, 2007.

Flint, Peter W. *The Dead Sea Scrolls*. Core Biblical Studies. Nashville, TN: Abingdon, 2013.

Folger, Tim. "Science's Alternative to an Intelligent Creator: The Multiverse Theory," *Discover*, December, 2008, published online November 10, 2008, http://discovermagazine.com/2008/dec/10-sciences-alternative-to-an-intelligent-creator.

Foster, Paul. *The Gospel of Peter: Introduction, Critical Edition and Commentary*. Leiden: Brill, 2010.

Foucault, Michel. *The Essential Works of Foucault 1954–1984 Aesthetics, Method, and Epistemology*, vol. 2. Edited by James D. Faubion. New York: New Press, 1998.

Fouts, David. "A Defense of the Hyperbolic Interpretation of Large Numbers in the Old Testament." *Journal of the Evangelical Theological Society* 40, no. 3 (September 1997): 377–87.

Frame, John M. *Cornelius Van Til: An Analysis of His Thought*. Phillipsburg: P&R Publishing, 1995.

——. *The Doctrine of the Word of God*. Phillipsburg, NJ: P&R Publishing, 2010.

France, R. T. *The Evidence for Jesus*. Downers Grove, MI: Intervarsity Press, 1996.

——. *The Gospel of Matthew*. New International Commentary on the New Testament. Grand Rapids, MI: Eerdmans, 2007.

Fredriksen, Paula. *Jesus of Nazareth, King of the Jews: A Jewish Life and the Emergence of Christianity*. New York: Alfred A. Knopf, 1999.

Free, Joseph P. *Archaeology and Bible History*. Wheaton: Scripture Press, 1950, 1969.

Freed, Edwin D. *The Stories of Jesus' Birth: A Critical Introduction*. St. Louis, MO: Chalice Press, 2001.

Frendo, Anthony. "Back to Basics: A Holistic Approach to the Problem of the Emergence of Ancient Israel," in *In Search of Pre-Exilic Israel*, edited by John Day, 41–64. London: T&T Clark, 2004.

———. "Two Long-lost Phoenician Inscriptions and the Emergence of Ancient Israel." *Palestine Exploration Quarterly* 134 (January, 2002): 37–43.

Freund, Richard. *Digging Through the Bible: Understanding Biblical People, Places, and Controversies Through Archaeology*. Lanham, MD: Rowman & Littlefield, 2009.

Fritz, Volkmar. "Israelites," in *The Oxford Encyclopedia of Archaeology in the Near East*. Oxford University Press, 1997.

Fu, Qiaomei et al. "Genome Sequence of a 45,000-year-old Modern Human from Western Siberia." *Nature* 514 (23 October 2014): 445–49. doi:10.1038/nature13810.

Fumerton, Richard. "Foundationalist Theories of Epistemic Justification." *The Stanford Encyclopedia of Philosophy*. Last revised June 14, 2010. http://plato.stanford.edu/archives/sum2010/entries/justep-foundational.

Funk, Robert W. and the Jesus Seminar. *The Acts of Jesus: What Did Jesus Really Do?: The Search for the Authentic Deeds of Jesus*. New York: HarperSanFrancisco, 1998.

Gadamer, Hans-Georg. *Truth and Method*. London: Continuum, 1989.

Galil, Gerson. "'*yyn ḥlq*' the Oldest Hebrew Inscription from Jerusalem." *STRATA: Bulletin of the Anglo-Israel Archaeological Society* 31 (January 2013): 11–26.

Gardeil, Henri-Dominique. *Introduction to the Philosophy of St. Thomas Aquinas*. Edited and translated by John A. Otto. Eugene, OR: Wipf & Stock, 2012.

Gardner, R. F. R. *Healing Miracles: A Doctor Investigates*. London: Darton, Longman and Todd, 1986.

Garfinkel, Yosef and Hoo-Goo Kang. "The Relative and Absolute Chronology of Khirbet Qeiyafa: Very Late Iron Age I or Very Early Iron Age IIA?" *Israel Exploration Journal* 61, no. 2 (January, 2011): 171–83. doi:10.2307/23214239.

Garfinkel, Yosef and Saar Ganor. "Khirbet Qeiyafa: Sha'arayim." *The Journal of Hebrew Scriptures* 8 (2008).

Garfinkel, Yosef, Mitka R. Golub, Haggai Misgav, and Saar Ganor. "The 'Išbaʿal Inscription from Khirbet Qeiyafa." *Bulletin of the American Schools of Oriental Research*, no. 373 (May, 2015): 217–33. doi:10.5615/bullamerschoorie.373.0217.

Garrett, Duane A. *Rethinking Genesis: The Sources and Authorship of the First Book of the Pentateuch*. Fearn, Great Britain: Christian Focus Publications, 2000.

———. "Traditio-Historical Criticism," in *Dictionary of the Old Testament: Pentateuch*, edited by T. D. Alexander and David W. Baker. Downers Grove, MI: InterVarsity Press, 2003.

Garrigou-Lagrange, Reginald. *Reality: A Synthesis of Thomistic Thought*. St. Louis and London: B. Herder, 1950.

Garstang, J. and J. B. E. Garstang. *The Story of Jericho*. London: Hodder & Stoughton 1940.

Gaster, Theodor H. *Myth, Legend, and Custom in the Old Testament*. New York: Harper & Row, 1969.

Gates, Bill. *The Road Ahead*. Boulder, CO: Blue Penguin, 1996.

Gathercole, Simon. *The Composition of the Gospel of Thomas: Original Language and Influences*. New York: Cambridge University Press, 2012.

————. "What Did the First Christians Think about Jesus?" in *How God Became Jesus*, edited by Michael F. Bird et al. Grand Rapids, MI: Zondervan, 2014.

Gauger, Ann, Douglas Axe, and Casey Luskin. *Science and Human Origins*. Seattle, WA: Discovery Institute Press, 2012.

Gaynor, William Jay. "Arrest and Trial of Jesus Viewed from a Legal Standpoint," *The American Lawyer* 5 (1897): 533.

Geisler, Norman L. "Resurrection, Evidence for," in *Baker Encyclopedia of Christian Apologetics*. Grand Rapids, MI: Baker Academic, 2006.

————. *The Battle for the Resurrection*. Nashville, TN: Thomas Nelson, 1989.

————. *Christian Apologetics*. Grand Rapids, MI: Baker, 1976.

————. "The Concept of Truth in the Inerrancy Debate," in *Bibliotheca Sacra*, vol. 137, edited by John F. Walvoord. Dallas, TX: Dallas Theological Seminary, 1980.

————. "Miracles and the Modern Mind," in *In Defense of Miracles*, edited by R. Douglas Geivett and Gary R. Habermas. Downers Grove, IL: InterVarsity Press, 1997.

————. "The Missing Premise in the Ontological Argument," in *Religious Studies*, vol. 8–9, edited by H. D. Lewis. London: Cambridge University Press, 1972.

————. *Signs and Wonders*. Eugene, OR: Wipf and Stock, 1988.

————. *Systematic Theology, Volume 4: Church, Last Things*. Bloomington: Bethany House, 2005.

————. *Thomas Aquinas: An Evangelical Appraisal*. Grand Rapids, MI: Baker Book House, 1991.

Geisler, Norman L. and Ronald M. Brooks. *When Skeptics Ask: A Handbook on Christian Evidences*, revised and updated ed. Grand Rapids, MI: Baker Books, 2013.

Geisler, Norman L. and Thomas Howe. *The Big Book of Bible Difficulties: Clear and Concise Answers from Genesis to Revelation*. Grand Rapids, MI: Baker Books, 2008.

Geisler, Norman L. and William E. Nix. *The Bible: From God to Us*. Walnut Creek, CA: ICBI Press, 1987.

————. *A General Introduction to the Bible*, revised and expanded edition. Chicago, IL: Moody Press, 1986.

Geivett, R. Douglas. "Is God a Story? Postmodernity and the Task of Theology," in *Christianity and the Postmodern Turn: Six Views*, edited by Myron B. Penner, 37–52. Grand Rapids, MI: Brazos, 2005.

Geller, Markham J. *Ancient Babylonian Medicine: Theory and Practice*. Chichester, West Sussex, U.K.: Wiley-Blackwell, 2010.

Ghose, Tia. "Minds Everywhere: 'Panpsychism' Takes Hold in Science," *Live Science*. February 22, 2016, http://www.livescience.com/53791-what-is-consciousness.html.

Ghosh, Pallab. "Cave Paintings Change Ideas about the Origin of Art." BBC News. October 8, 2014. http://www.bbc.com/news/science-environment-29415716.

Gibbons, Ann. "Out of Africa–at Last?" *Science* 267 (3 March 1995): 1272–73.

————. "Y Chromosome Shows That Adam Was an African." Science 278 (31 October 1997): 804–805.

————. "Who Was Homo habilis—And Was It Really Homo?" *Science* 332 (17 June 2011): 1370–71. doi: 10.1126/science.332.6036.1370.

Giberson, Karl. *Saving Darwin: How to Be a Christian and Believe in Evolution*. New York: HarperOne, 2008.

Gignilliant, Mark S. *A Brief History of Old Testament Criticism: From Benedict Spinoza to Brevard Childs*. Grand Rapids, MI: Zondervan, 2012.

Gilmour, Garth. *Gezer VI: The Objects from Phases I and II*. Winona Lake, IN: Eisenbrauns, 2014.

Glenny, W. Edward. "The Preservation of Scripture," in *The Bible Version Debate*. Minneapolis: Central Baptist Theological Seminary, 1977.

Gnuse, R. K. "The Elohist: A 7th-Century BCE Theological Tradition." *Biblical Theology Bulletin: Journal of Bible and Culture* 42, no. 2 (April 2012): 59–69. http://dx.doi.org/10.1177/0146107912441303.

Goldingay, John. "The Patriarchs in Scripture and History," in *Essays on the Patriarchal Narratives*, edited by A. R. Millard and D. J. Wiseman. Leciester, England: IVP, 1980.

——. *Word Biblical Commentary: Daniel.* Grand Rapids, MI: Zondervan, 1996.

Goldman, Alvin I. *Knowledge in a Social World.* Oxford University Press, 1999.

Goodacre, Mark. *Thomas and the Gospels: The Case for Thomas's Familiarity with the Synoptics.* Grand Rapids, MI: Eerdmans, 2012.

Gordon-Reed, Annette. *Thomas Jefferson and Sally Hemmings: An American Controversy.* Charlottesville: University of Virginia Press, 1998.

Gonzalez, Guillermo and Jay W. Richards. *The Privileged Planet: How Our Place In The Cosmos Is Designed For Discovery.* Washington, DC: Regnery, 2004.

Gordon, Cyrus H. and Gary Rendsburg. *The Bible and the Ancient Near East*, 4th ed. Lodon, NY: W. W. Norton, 1997.

Gottschalk, Louis Reichenthal. *Understanding History: A Primer of Historical Method*, 2nd ed. New York: Knopf, 1969.

Goulder, Michael. "The Baseless Fabric of Vision," in *Resurrection Reconsidered*, edited by Gavin D'Costa. Rockport, MA: Oneworld Publications, 1996.

Grabbe, Lester L. "Another Look at the Gestalt of 'Darius the Mede'." *The Catholic Biblical Quarterly* 50, no. 2 (April 1988): 198–213.

Grant, Bob. "What's Old Is New Again." *The Scientist* (June 1, 2015). Accessed October 30, 2015. http://www.the-scientist.com/?articles.view/articleNo/43069/title/What-s-Old-Is-New-Again/.

Graves, David E. *Biblical Archaeology: An Introduction with Recent Discoveries That Support the Reliability of the Bible.* Moncton, New Brunswick, Canada: Electronic Christian Media, 2014.

——. The Inspiration and Interpretation of Scripture: What the Early Church Can Teach Us. Grand Rapids, MI: Eerdmans, 2014.

Grayson, A. Kirk. *Assyrian and Babylonian Chronicles.* Winona Lake, IN: Eisenbrauns, 2000.

——. *Assyrian Rulers of the Early First Millennium BC II (858–745 BC), RIMA 3.* Toronto: University of Toronto Press, 1996.

Grayson, A. Kirk and Jamie Novotny. *The Royal Inscriptions of Sennacherib, King of Assyria (704–681 BC), Part 1*, RINAP 3/1 .Winona Lake, IN: Eisenbrauns, 2012.

Grayson, A. Kirk and Jamie Novotny. *The Royal Inscriptions of Sennacherib, King of Assyria (704–681 BC), Part 2*, RINAP 3/2. Winona Lake, IN: Eisenbrauns, 2014.

Grazer, Kevin R. "Jupiter: Cosmic Jekyll and Hyde," *Astrobiology* 16 (January 2016): 23–38.

Green, Joel B. "Death of Christ," in *Dictionary of Paul and His Letters*, eds. Gerald F. Hawthorne, Ralph P. Martin, and Daniel G. Reid. Downers Grove, IL: InterVarsity Press, 1993.

——. *The Gospel of Luke. The New International Commentary on the New Testament.* Grand Rapids, MI: Eerdmans, 1997.

Green, Michael. *Man Alive.* Downers Grove, IL: InterVarsity Press, 1968.

——. *Runaway World: Is Christian Belief Escapism?* Downers Grove, IL: InterVarsity Press, 1968.

Greenlee, J. H. *Introduction to New Testament Textual Criticism.* Grand Rapids, MI: Eerdmans, 1964, 1977.

Greenslade, Stanley Lawrence, ed. *Cambridge History of the Bible.* New York: Cambridge University Press, 1963.

Greenspahn, Fredrick. "Biblical Scholars, Medieval and Modern," in *Judaic Perspectives on Ancient Israel*, edited by Jacob Neusner et al., 245–59. Eugene: Wipf & Stock, 2004.

Gregory, Andrew F. and Christopher M. Tuckett, eds. *The New Testament and the Apostolic Fathers, Volume 1: The Reception of the New Testament in the Apostolic Fathers.* Oxford: Oxford University Press, 2005.

Grenz, Stanley J. *A Primer on Postmodernism.* Grand Rapids, MI: Eerdmans, 1996.

Grisanti, Michael A. "Inspiration, Inerrancy and the OT Canon: The Place of Textual Updating in an Inerrant View of Scripture." *Journal of the Evangelical Theology Society* 44, no. 4 (December 2001): 577–98.

———. "Recent Archaeological Discoveries That Lend Credence to the Historicity of the Scriptures." *Journal of the Evangelical Theological Society* 56, no. 3 (September 2013): 475–97.

Groothuis, Douglas. *Christian Apologetics: A Comprehensive Case for Biblical Faith.* Downers Grove, IL: IVP Academic, 2011.

———. "Jesus: Philosopher and Apologist," *Christian Research Journal* 25, no. 2 (2002): http://www.equip.org/article/jesus-philosopher-and-apologist/.

———. *Truth Decay: Defending Christianity Against the Challenges of Postmodernism.* Downers Grove, IL: InterVarsity Press, 2000.

Grossman, Maxine "Josephus Flavius" in *The Oxford Dictionary of the Jewish Religion*, edited by Adele Berlin. Oxford University Press, 2011.

Grounds, Vernon C. *The Reason for Our Hope.* Chicago, IL: Moody Press, 1945.

Grudem, Wayne. *Systematic Theology: An Introduction to Biblical Doctrine.* Grand Rapids, MI: Zondervan, 1994.

Gryson, Roger. *Altlateinische Handschriften: Manuscrits Vieux Latins.* Germany, Freiburg: Herder, 1999.

Guinness, Os. *Fool's Talk: Recovering the Art of Christian Persuasion.* Downers Grove, IL: InterVarsity Press, 2015.

Gurval, Robert Alan. *Actium and Augustus: The Politics and Emotions of Civil War.* Ann Arbor, MI: University of Michigan Press, 1995.

Guthrie, George H. *2 Corinthians. Baker Exegetical Commentary on the New Testament.* Grand Rapids, MI: Baker Academic, 2015.

Haarsma, Deborah B. and Loren D. Haarsma. *Origins: A Reformed Look at Creation, Design & Evolution.* Grand Rapids, MI: Faith Alive Christian Resources, 2007.

Habermas, Gary R. *The Historical Jesus: Ancient Evidence for the Life of Christ.* Joplin, MO: College Press Publishing Company, 2000.

———. *Philosophy of History, Miracles, and the Resurrection of Jesus.* Edgewood, MD: Academix Publishing Services, 2013.

———. "Recent Perspectives on the Reliability of the Gospels," *Christian Research Journal* 28, no. 1 (2005)

———. *The Resurrection of Jesus.* The Credo Courses [DVD], 2014.

———. *The Resurrection Volumes I: Heart of New Testament Doctrine.* Joplin, MO: College Press Publishing Company, 2000.

———. *The Resurrection Volumes II: Heart of the Christian Life.* Joplin, MO: College Press Publishing Company, 2000.

———. *The Risen Jesus & Future Hope.* Lanham, MD: Rowman & Littlefield, 2003.

———. *The Secret of the Talpiot Tomb: Unraveling the Mystery of the Jesus Family Tomb.* Nashville, TN: Holman Reference, 2007.

Habermas, Gary R. and Antony Flew. *Did Jesus Rise from the Dead? The Resurrection Debate*, ed. Terry L. Miethe. New York: Harper & Row, 1978.

Habermas, Gary R. and Michael R. Licona. *The Case for the Resurrection of Jesus.* Grand Rapids, MI: Kregel Publications, 2004.

Habermas, Gary R. and Kenneth E. Stevenson. *Verdict on the Shroud: Evidence for the Death and Resurrection of Jesus Christ.* Ann Arbor, MI: Servant Books, 1981.

Hagedorn, A. C. "Taking the Pentateuch to the Twenty-First Century." *The Expository Times* 119, no. 2 (November 2007): 53–58. http://dx.doi.org/10.1177/0014524607084083.

Hagner, Donald A. "The New Testament, History, and the Historical-Critical Method," in *New Testament Criticism and Interpretation*, eds. David Alan Black and David S. Dockery. Grand Rapids, MI: Zondervan, 1991.

———. *The New Testament: A Historical and Theological Introduction*. Baker Publishing Group, 2012.

Hagopian, David G., ed. *The Genesis Debate: Three Views on the Days of Creation*. Mission Viejo, CA: Crux Press, 2001.

Haleem, M. A. S. Abdel. *The Qur'an*. New York, NY: Oxford University Press, 2004.

Hall, Christopher A. *Reading Scripture with the Church Fathers*. Downers Grove, IL: InterVarsity Press, 1998.

Hallo, William and William Simpson. *The Ancient Near East: A History*. New York: Harcourt Brace Jovanovich, 1971.

Hallo, William and K. Lawson Younger, eds. *The Context of Scripture: Canonical Compositions, Monumental Inscriptions and Archival Documents from the Biblical World*. 3 volumes. Leiden: Brill, 1997–2003.

Halpern, Baruch. "The Exodus from Egypt: Myth or Reality?" in *The Rise of Ancient Israel: Lectures Presented at a Symposium Sponsored by the Resident Associate Program, Smithsonian Institution*, edited by Hershel Shanks et al., 86–117. Washington, DC: Biblical Archaeology Society, 2013.

Halton, Charles, James Karl Hoffmeier, Gordon J. Wenham, and Kenton L. Sparks. *Genesis: History, Fiction, or Neither? Three Views on the Bible's Earliest Chapters*. E-book edition. Grand Rapids, MI: Zondervan, 2015.

Hamilton, Floyd. *The Basis of Christian Faith*. New York: George H. Doran, 1927.

Hamilton, Victor P. *The Book of Genesis: Chapters 1–17. The New International Commentary on the Old Testament*, edited by Robert L. Hubbard. Grand Rapids, MI: Eerdmans, 1990.

———. *The Book of Genesis: Chapters 18–50. The New International Commentary on the Old Testament*, edited by Robert L. Hubbard. Grand Rapids, MI: Eerdmans, 1995.

Hammer, Michael F. "A Recent Common Ancestry for Human Y Chromosomes." *Nature* 378 (23 November 1995): 376–378.

Hardin, James W., Christopher A. Rollston, and Jeffrey A. Blakely. "Iron Age Bullae from Officialdom's Periphery: Khirbet Summeily in Broader Context." *Near Eastern Archaeology* 77, no. 4 (December, 2014): 299–301. doi:10.5615/neareastarch.77.4.0299.

Harris, Murray J. *Jesus As God: The New Testament Use of Theos in Reference to Jesus*. Grand Rapids, MI: Baker Book House, 1992.

———. *The Second Epistle to the Corinthians. New International Greek Testament Commentary*. Grand Rapids, MI: Eerdmans, 2005.

Harris, Sam. *Free Will*. New York: Free Press, 2012.

———. *Letter to a Christian Nation*. New York: Knopf, 2007)

Harrison, R. K. *Introduction to the Old Testament*. Grand Rapids, MI: Eerdmans, 1969.

Hartwig-Scherer, Sigrid and Robert D. Martin. "Was 'Lucy' More Human Than Her 'Child'? Observations on Early Hominid Postcranial Skeletons." *Journal of Human Evolution* 21 (1991): 439–49.

Harvey, A. E. *Jesus and the Constraints of History*. Philadelphia, PA: Westminster Press, 1982.

Hasel, Michael G. "Israel in the Merneptah Stela." *Bulletin of the American Schools of Oriental Research*, no. 296 (November, 1994): 45–61. doi:10.2307/1357179.

Hauser, Marc D. et al. "The Mystery of Language Evolution." *Frontiers in Psychology* 5 (7 May 2014). doi: 10.3389/fpsyg.2014.00401.

Hawkins, Ralph. *How Israel Became a People*. Nashville, TN: Abingdon Press, 2013.

Hawkins, Ralph K. and Shane Buchanan. "The Khirbet Qeiyafa Inscription and 11th–10th Century BCE Israel." *Stone-Campbell Journal* 14, no. 2 (September 2011): 219–34.

Hawking, Stephen and Leonard Mlodinow. *The Grand Design*. New York: Bantam Books, 2010.

Hayes, Christine Elizabeth. *Introduction to the Bible*. New Haven, CT: Yale University Press, 2012.

Hayward, Alan. *Creation and Evolution*. Minneapolis, MN: Bethany House, 1995.

Hazen, Craig. "Christianity in a World of Religions," in *Passionate Conviction: Contemporary Discourses On Christian Apologetics*, edited by Paul Copan and William Lane Craig, 140–153. Nashville, TN: B&H Academic, 2007.

Hedges, S. Blair. "Human Evolution: A Start for Population Genomics." *Nature* 408 (7 December 2000): 652–53.

Heidel, Alexander. *The Babylonian Genesis: The Story of Creation*. 2nd ed. Chicago, IL: University of Chicago, 1972.

———. *The Gilgamesh Epic and Old Testament Parallels*. Chicago, IL: University of Chicago, 1949.

Hemer, Colin J. *The Book of Acts in the Setting of Hellenistic History*. Winona Lake, IN: Eisenbrauns, 1990.

Hengel, Martin. *Crucifixion*. Philadelphia, PA: Fortress Press, 1977.

———. *The Son of God: The Origin of Christology and the History of Jewish Hellenistic Religion*. Eugene, OR: Wipf and Stock Publishers, 2007.

Hengstenberg, E. W. *Christology of the Old Testament and a Commentary of Messianic Predictions*. Grand Rapids, MI: Kregel, 1970.

Henn, T. R. *The Bible As Literature*. Oxford University Press, 1970.

Henry, Carl F. H. *God, Revelation And Authority*, vol. 4. Waco, TX: Word Books, 1979.

———. *The Identity of Jesus of Nazareth*. Nashville, TN: Broadman Press, 1992.

Henze, Matthias. *The Madness of King Nebuchadnezzar: The Ancient Near Eastern Origins and Early History of Interpretations of Daniel 4*. Boston: Brill, 1999.

Hess, Richard S. "The Jericho and Ai of the Book of Joshua," in *Critical Issues in Early Israelite History*, vol. 3. Winona Lake, IN: Eisenbranus, 2008.

Heuer, Mark H. "An Evaluation of John W. Burgon's Use of Patristic Evidence," *Journal of the Evangelical Theological Society* 38, no.4 (1995)

Helyer, Larry. *The Life and Witness of Peter*. Downers Grove, IL: InterVarsity Press, 2012.

Hess, R. S. "Joshua," in *New Dictionary of Biblical Theology: Exploring the Unity and Diversity of Scripture*, edited by T. Desmond Alexander, D. A. Carson, Graeme Goldsworthy, and Brian S. Rosner, 165–171. Downers Grove, IL: InterVarsity Press, 2000.

Hurtado, Larry. *One God and One Lord: Early Christian Devotion and Ancient Jewish Monotheism*. New York: Continuum, 1998.

Hill, Jonathan. *What Has Christianity Ever Done for Us?*. Downers Grove, IL: InterVarsity Press, 2005.

Hitchens, Christopher. *God Is Not Great: How Religion Poisons Everything*. New York: Hachette Book Group, 2007.

Hoehner, Harold. *Chronological Aspects of the Life of Christ*. Grand Rapids, MI: Zondervan, 1977.

Hoerth, Alfred J. *Archaeology & the Old Testament*. Grand Rapids, MI: Baker Academic, 1998.

Hoffmeier, James K. *Ancient Israel in Sinai: The Evidence for the Authenticity of the Wilderness Tradition*. Oxford University Press, 2005.

———. "Genesis 1–11 as History and Theology," in *Genesis: History, Fiction, or Neither? Three Views on the Bible's Earliest Chapters*, edited by Charles Halton. Grand Rapids, MI: Zondervan, 2015.

———. *Israel in Egypt: The Evidence for the Authenticity of the Exodus Tradition*. Oxford University Press, 1997.

———. *The Archaeology of the Bible*. Oxford: Lion Hudson, 2008.

———. "The Exodus and Wilderness Narratives," in *Ancient Israel's History: An Introduction to Issues and Sources*, edited by Bill Arnold and Richard Hess, 46–90. Grand Rapids, MI: Baker, 2014.

———. "Some Thoughts on Genesis 1 and 2 and Egyptian Cosmology." *Journal of the Ancient Near Eastern Society* 15 (1983): 39–49.

———. "The Memphis and Karnak Stelae of Amenhotep II," in *The Context of Scripture: Canonical Compositions, Monumental Inscriptions and Archival Documents from the Biblical World*, vol. 2, edited by William Hallo and K. Lawson Younger, 19–23. Leiden: Brill, 2000.

———. "These Things Happened: Why a Historical Exodus is Essential for Theology," in *Do Historical Matters Matter to Faith? A Critical Appraisal of Modern and Postmodern Approaches to Scripture*, edited by James Hoffmeier and Dennis Magary, 99–134. Wheaton: Crossway, 2012.

———. "What Is the Biblical Date for the Exodus? A Response to Bryant Wood." *Journal of the Evangelical Theological Society* 50, no. 2 (June 2007): 225–47.

Holden, Joseph M. and Norman L. Geisler. *The Popular Handbook of Archaeology and the Bible*. Eugene, OR: Harvest House, 2013.

Holmén, Tom. "Sinners," in *Routledge Encyclopedia of the Historical Jesus*, edited by Craig A. Evans. New York: Routledge, 2008.

Homer. *Homeri Ilias*. Edited by Thomas W. Allen. New York: Arno, 1979.

Horn, Robert M. *The Book That Speaks for Itself*. Downers Grove, IL: InterVarsity Press, 1970.

Horner, David A. *Mind Your Faith*. Downers Grove, IL: InterVarsity Press, 2011.

Hort, F. J. A. *The Way, the Truth, the Life*. New York: Macmillan, 1897.

Hort, F. J. A. and Brooke Foss Westcott. *The New Testament in the Original Greek*, vol. 1. New York: Macmillan, 1881.

Hössjer, Ola, Ann Gauger, and Colin Reeves. "Genetic Modeling of Human History Part 1: Comparison of Common Descent and Unique Origin Approaches," *BIO-Complexity* 2016 (3):1–15. doi:10.5048/BIO-C.2016.3.

Hoskyns, Edwyn. *The Fourth Gospel*. Edited by Francis Noel Davey, 2nd ed. London: Faber & Faber, 1961.

Hotz, Robert Lee. "Early Text Uncovered in Burned Scroll." *The Wall Street Journal*, Sept. 22, 2016: A3.

Houghton, H. A. G. *The Latin New Testament: A Guide to Its Early History, Texts, and Manuscripts*. Oxford University Press, 2016.

House, H. Wayne, ed. *Intelligent Design 101: Leading Experts Explain the Key Issues*. Grand Rapids, MI: Kregel, 2008.

Howard, Jeremy Royal, ed. *The Holman Apologetics Commentary on the Bible: The Gospels and Acts*. Nashville, TN: B&H Publishing Group, 2013.

Huddleston, Jonathon. "Recent Scholarship on the Pentateuch: Historical, Literary, and Theological Reflections." *Restoration Quarterly* 55, no. 4 (2013): 193–211.

Huggins, Ronald V. "Christopher Hitchens's Plagiarism," (blog), September 8, 2013, http://ronaldvhuggins.blogspot.com/2013/09/christopher-hitchenss-plagiarism.html.

———. "Krishna and Christ: Debunking the Parallels between Jesus and Krishna" (Grand Rapids, MI: Institute for Religious Research), http://bib.irr.org/krishna-and-christ-debunking-parallels-between-jesus-and-krishna.

Hume, David. *An Enquiry Concerning Human Understanding*. Edited by Peter Millican. Oxford University Press, 2007.

———. *A Treatise of Human Nature: Being an Attempt to Introduce the Experimental Method of Reasoning into Moral Subjects*. Kitchener, Ontario, CAN: Batoche Books, 1999.

Humphreys, D. Russell. *Starlight and Time: Solving the Puzzle of Distant Starlight in a Young Universe*. Green Forest, AR: Master Books, 1994.

Huxley, T. H. *The Works of T. H. Huxley*. New York: Appleton, 1896.

Iggers, Georg. "Historiography in the Twentieth Century." *History and Theory* 44 (2005): 469–76.

Ignatius. "The Epistle of Ignatius to the Smyrnaeans." New Advent. http://www.newadvent.org/fathers/0109.htm. The Institute for New Testament Textual Research, accessed January 9, 2012, http://www.uni-muenster.de/INTF/KgLSGII2010_02_04.pdf.

———. "Ignatius' Epistle to Trallians," in *Ante-Nicene Christian Library: Translations of the Writings of the Fathers*. Edited by Alexander Roberts and James Donaldson. Vol. 1. Edinburgh: T&T Clark, 1867.

"Introduction to the Torah," in *The Jewish Study Bible*. Oxford Biblical Studies Online. http://www.oxfordbiblicalstudies.com/article/book/obso-9780195297515/obso-9780195297515-sectionFrontMatter-1.

Irenaus, *Against Heresies*. Translated and annotated by Dominic J. Unger, with further revisions by John J. Dillon. New York: Paulist Press, 1992.

Isbell, Charles D. "The Limmûdîm in the Book of Isaiah." *Journal for the Study of the Old Testament* 34, no. 1 (September 2009): 99–109.

Jack, Alison M. *The Bible and Literature*. London: SCM Press, 2012.

Jaganay, Leo. *An Introduction to the Textual Criticism of the New Testament*. Translated by B. V. Miller. London: Sands and Company, 1937.

Jansen, John Frederick. *The Resurrection of Jesus Christ in New Testament Theology*. Philadelphia, PA: The Westminster Press, 1980.

Jeffery, Richard. *Formal Logic: Its Scope and Limits*. New York: McGraw-Hill, 1967.

Jeffery, Steve, Michael Ovey, and Andrew Sach. *Pierced for Our Transgressions: Rediscovering the Glory of Penal Substitution*. Wheaton, IL: Crossway Books, 2007.

Jenkins, Philip. *Hidden Gospels: How the Search for Jesus Lost Its Way*. Oxford University Press, 2001.

Jeremias, Joachim. *New Testament Theology: The Proclamation of Jesus*. New York: Scribner, 1971.

John of Salisbury. *The Metalogicon*. Translated by Daniel D. McGary. Philadelphia, PA: Paul Dry Books, Inc., 2009.

Jones, Clay. "The Bibliographical Test Updated," *Christian Research Journal* 35, no. 3 (2012). Available at www.equip.org/articles/the-bibliographical-test-updated/; Josh D. McDowell and Clay Jones, The Bibliographical Test Updated, revised 2/4/16 by Dr. Josh D. McDowell.

———. "Christians Don't Take Human Evil Seriously So We Don't Understand Why We Suffer." Paper presented at the annual meeting of the Evangelical Theological Society, New Orleans, LA, November, 2009.

———. "How Could It Be Fair to Kill Canaanite Children?" ClayJones.net. July 13, 2015. http://www.clayjones.net/2015/07/canaanite-children-2/.

———. "Killing the Canaanites: A Response to the New Atheism's 'Divine Genocide' Claims." *Christian Reseach Journal* 33, no. 4 (2010). http://www.equip.org/article/killing-the-canaanites/.

———. "We Don't Hate Sin So We Don't Understand What Happened to the Canaanites: An Addendum to 'Divine Genocide' Arguments." *Philosophia Christi* 11, no. 1 (2009): 53–72.

Josephus. *The Antiquities of the Jews*. New York: Ward, Lock, Bowden & Co., 1900.

———. "Flavius Josephus Against Apion," in *Josephus' Complete Works*. Translated by William Whiston. Grand Rapids, MI: Kregel Publications, 1960.

———. "Jewish Antiquities," in *Josephus, the Essential Writings: A Condensation of Jewish Antiquities and the Jewish War*. Grand Rapids, MI: Kregel Publications, 1988.

———. *The Works of Flavius Josephus*. Translated by William Whiston. Nashville TN: Thomas Nelson, 1987.

Jurgens, William A., ed. and trans. *The Faith of the Early Fathers*, Collegeville, MN: The Liturgical Press, 1970.

Kaeuffer, Renaud et al. "Unexpected Heterozygosity in an Island Mouflon Population Founded by a Single Pair of Individuals." *Proceedings of the Royal Society B: Biological Sciences* 274 (2007): 527–533. doi: 10.1098/rspb.2006.3743.

Kähler, Martin. *The So-Called Historical Jesus and the Historic, Biblical Christ*. Edited and translated by C. E. Baraaten. Philadelphia, PA: Fortress Press, 1988.

Kaiser, Walter. *Archaeological Study Bible*. Grand Rapids, MI: Zondervan, 2006.

———. *A History of Israel: From the Bronze Age Through the Jewish Wars*. Nashville, TN: Broadman & Holman, 1998.

———. *The Old Testament Documents: Are They Reliable and Relevant?* Downers Grove, IL: IVP, 2001.

Kaiser, Walter C. Jr., Peter H. Davids, F. F. Bruce, and Manfred T. Brauch. *Hard Sayings of the Bible*. Downers Grove, IL: IVP Academic, 1996.

Kaminsky, Joel S. et al. *The Abingdon Introduction to the Bible*. Nashville, TN: Abingdon Press, 2014.

Kant, Immanuel. *Critique of Pure Reason*. Edited and translated by Paul Guyer and Allen W. Wood. Cambridge: Cambridge University Press, 1998.

Kasser, Rodolphe, Marvin Meyer, and Gregor Wurst, eds. *The Gospel of Judas*. Washington, DC: National Geographic, 2006.

Kearns, Cleo McNelly. *T. S. Eliot and Indic Traditions: A Study in Poetry and Belief*. Cambridge University Press, 1987.

Keener, Craig S. *Acts: An Exegetical Commentary*, vol. 1. Grand Rapids, MI: Baker Academic, 2012.

———. *The Gospel of John: A Commentary*. Grand Rapids, MI: Baker Academic, 2003.

———. *The Gospel of Matthew: A Socio-Rhetorical Commentary*. Grand Rapids, MI: Eerdmans, 2009.

———. *The Historical Jesus of the Gospels*. Grand Rapids, MI: Eerdmans, 2009.

———. *Miracles: The Credibility of the New Testament Accounts*, vol. 1. Grand Rapids, MI: Baker Academic, 2011.

Keller, Timothy. "How Should Churches and Leaders Be Preparing to Address These Big Issues Facing the Church?" (blog), Redeemer City to City, February 24, 2010.

———. *The Reason for God: Belief in an Age of Skepticism*. New York: Dutton, 2008.

Kelly, Stewart. "Miracle, Method, and Metaphysics: Philosophy and the Quest for the Historical Jesus." *Trinity Journal* 29, no. 1 (2008): 55–56.

———. *Truth Considered and Applied: Examining Postmodernism, History, and Christian Faith*. Nashville, TN: B&H Publishing Group, 2011.

Kennedy, D. James and Jerry Newcombe, *What If Jesus Had Never Been Born?*. Nashville, TN: Thomas Nelson, 1994.

Kenyon, Frederic. *The Bible and Archaeology*. New York: Harper & Row, 1940.

———. *The Bible and Modern Scholarship*. London: John Murray, 1948.

———. *Handbook to the Textual Criticism of the New Testament*. London: Macmillan and Company, 1901.

———. *Our Bible and the Ancient Manuscripts*. New York and London: Harper & Brothers, 1939.

Kenyon, Kathleen M. *The Bible and Recent Archaeology*. London: British Museum Publications Ltd., 1978.

Kharche, Suresh Dinkar and Hemant Shankar Birade. "Parthenogenesis and Activation of Mammalian Oocytes for in vitro Embryo Production: A Review." *Advances in Bioscience and Biotechnology* 4, no. 2 (2013): 170–82.

Kierkegaard, Søren. *Concluding Unscientific Postscript to Philosophical Fragments*, vol. 1. Translated by Howard V. and Edna H. Hong. Princeton, NJ: Princeton University Press, 1985.

Kim, Jaegwon. *Mind in a Physical World*. Cambridge, MA: MIT Press, 2000.

Kimball, Dan. *They Like Jesus but Not the Church: Insights from Emerging Generations*. Grand Rapids, MI: Zondervan, 2007.

King, Karen L. *The Gospel of Mary of Magdala: Jesus and the First Woman Apostle*. Santa Rosa, CA: Polebridge, 2003.

Kinnaman, David. *You Lost Me: Why Young Christians Are Leaving Church . . . And Rethinking Faith*. Grand Rapids, MI: Baker Books, 2011.

Kitchen, K. A. *Ancient Orient and Old Testament*. Chicago, IL: InterVarsity Press, 1966.

———. *On the Reliability of the Old Testament*. Grand Rapids, MI: W. B. Eerdmans, 2003.

———. "The Aramaic of Daniel," in *Notes on Some Problems in the Book of Daniel*, edited by D. J. Wiseman. London: The Tyndale Press, 1965.

———. *On the Reliability of the Old Testament*. Grand Rapids, MI: W. B. Eerdmans, 2003.

———. "A Possible Mention of David in the Late Tenth Century BCE, and Deity Dod As Dead As the Dodo?" *Journal for the Study of the Old Testament* 22, no. 76 (December, 1997): 29–44. doi:10.1177/030908929702207602.

Kitchen, K. A. and Paul J. N. Lawrence. *Treaty, Law and Covenant in the Ancient Near East, vol. 1, The Texts*. Weisbaden, Germany: Harrossowitz-Verlag, 2012.

Kligerman, Aaron Judah. *Messianic Prophecy in the Old Testament*. Grand Rapids, MI: Zondervan, 1970.

Klingbeil, G. A. "Historical Criticism," in *Dictionary of the Old Testament: Pentateuch*, edited by T. Desmond Alexander and David W. Baker. Downers Grove, IL: IVP Academic, 2003.

Kloner, Amos. "Did a Rolling Stone Close Jesus' Tomb?" *Biblical Archaeology Review* 25, no.5 (Sep/Oct 1999): 22–25, 28–29, 76.

Knierim, Rolf P. *The Task of Old Testament Theology: Substance, Method, and Cases*. Grand Rapids, MI: Eerdmans, 1995.

Knoll, Andy. "How Did Life Begin?" Interview by Joe McMaster, *Nova*, PBS, July 1, 2004, http://www.pbs.org/wgbh/nova/evolution/how-did-life-begin.html.

Knoppers, Gary N. "Parallel Torahs and Inner-Scriptural Interpretation," in *The Pentateuch: International Perspectives on Current Research*, edited by Thomas B. Dozeman, Konrad Schmid, and Baruch J. Schwartz, Forschungen Sum Alten Testament, vol. 78. Tübingen, Germany: Mohr Siebeck, 2011.

———. "The Vanishing Solomon: The Disappearance of the United Monarchy from Recent Histories of Ancient Israel." *Journal of Biblical Literature* 116, no. 1 (1997): 19–44.

Koch, Peter O. *The Aztecs, the Conquistadors, and the Making of Mexican Culture*. Jefferson, NC: McFarland, 2006.

Koester, Helmut. *Ancient Christian Gospels: Their History and Development*. Philadelphia, PA: Trinity Press International, 1990.

———. *Introduction to the New Testament*. History and Literature of Early Christianity, vol. 2. New York: Walter de Gruyter, 1982.

Kofoed, Jens Bruun. "Epistemology, Historiographical Method and the 'Copenhagen School'," in *Windows into Old Testament History*, edited by V. Philips Long, David W. Baker, and Gordon J. Wenham, 23–40. Grand Rapids, MI: Eerdmans, 2002.

Komoszewski, J. Ed., M. James Sawyer, and Daniel B. Wallace. *Reinventing Jesus: How Contemporary Skeptics Miss the Real Jesus and Mislead Popular Culture*. Kregel, 2006.

Koskenniemi, Erkki. "Apollonius of Tyana: A Typical QEIOS ANHR [Theios Anēr, 'Divine Man']?" *Journal of Biblical Literature* 117 (1998): 461.

Köstenberger, Andreas J. "Review of Andrew T. Lincoln, *Born of a Virgin? Reconceiving Jesus in the Bible, Tradition, and Theology*." http://www.biblicalfoundations.org/wp-content/uploads/2014/02/Born-of-a-Virgin.pdf.

Köstenberger, Andreas J., Darrell L. Bock, and Josh D. Chatraw. *Truth in a Culture of Doubt: Engaging Skeptical Challenges of the Bible.* Nashville, TN: B&H Publishing Group, 2014.

Köstenberger, Andreas J. and Peter T. O'Brien. *Salvation to the Ends of the Earth: A Biblical Theology of Mission, New Studies in Biblical Theology.* Downers Grove, IL: InterVarsity Press, 2001.

Köstenberger, Andreas J. and Alexander E. Stewart. *The First Days of Jesus: The Story of the Incarnation.* Wheaton, IL: Crossway, 2015.

Krasovec, Joze, ed. *The Interpretation of the Bible: The International Symposium in Slovenia.* A&C Black, 1999.

Krauss, Lawrence. *A Universe from Nothing.* New York: Free Press, 2012.

Kreeft, Peter, and Ronald K. Tacelli. *Handbook of Christian Apologetics: Hundreds of Answers to Crucial Questions.* Downers Grove, IL: InterVarsity Press, 1994.

Kreeft, Peter. *Fundamentals of the Faith: Essays in Christian Apologetics.* San Francisco, CA: Ignatius Press, 1988.

Kruger, Michael J. *Canon Revisited: Establishing the Origins and Authority of the New Testament Books.* Wheaton, Illinois: Crossway, 2012.

——. "Origen's List of New Testament Books in *Homiliae Josuam 7.1*: A Fresh Look," in *Mark, Manuscripts, and Monotheism: Essays in Honor of Larry W. Hurtado,* ed. Chris Keith and Dieter T. Roth, 99–117. London: T&T Clark, 2014.

——. *The Question of Canon: Challenging the Status Quo in the New Testament Debate.* Downers Grove, Illinois: InterVarsity Press Academic, 2013.

——. "Review of *Jesus, Interrupted,* by Bart D. Ehrman." Reformation21, November 2009, http://www.reformation21.org/shelf-life/jesus-interrupted.php.

Kuhrt, Amelie. *The Ancient Near East c. 3000–330 BC,* vol. 1. New York: Routledge, 1995.

Kynes, William L. *A Christology of Solidarity: Jesus as the Representative of His People in Matthew.* Lanham, MD: University Press of America, 1991.

Ladd, George E. and Donald A. Hagner, *A Theology of the New Testament,* rev. ed. Grand Rapids, MI: Eerdmans, 1993.

Ladd, George Eldon. *I Believe in the Resurrection of Jesus.* Grand Rapids, MI: Eerdmans, 1984.

LaHaye, Tim. *Why Believe in Jesus?: Who He Is, What He Did, & His Message for You Today.* Eugene, OR: Harvest House Publishers, 2004.

Lamb, David. *God Behaving Badly: Is the God of the Old Testament Angry, Sexist, and Racist?* Downers Grove, IL: InterVarsity Press, 2011.

Lambert, W. G. "A New Look at the Babylonian Background Of Genesis 1." *The Journal of Theological Studies* 16, no. 2 (1965): 287–300.

Lamoureux, Denis O. *Evolutionary Creation: A Christian Approach to Evolution.* Eugene, OR: Wipf & Stock, 2008.

Laney, J. Carl. *John. Moody Gospel Commentary.* Chicago, IL: Moody Press, 1992.

Lapide, Pinchas. *The Resurrection of Jesus: A Jewish Perspective.* Eugene, OR: Wipf and Stock Publishers, 2002.

Larson, Mark. "Three Centuries of Objections to Biblical Miracles." *Bibliotheca Sacra* 160, no. 637 (2003): 89.

Latourette, Kenneth Scott. *A History of Christianity, Volume 1: Beginnings to 1500.* New York: Harper, 1953.

Lecky, William E. H. *History of European Morals from Augustus to Charlemagne,* 3rd ed., vol 2. London and New York: Longmans, Green, and Co., 1913, orig. pub. 1877.

Lemaire, André. "'House of David' Restored in Moabite Inscription." *Biblical Archaeology Review* 20, no. 3 (1994). http://www.onefaithonepeopleministries.com/uploads/1/6/1/8/16182720/house_of_david.pdf.

——. "The Mesha Stele and the Omri Dynasty." Compiled by Lester L. Grabbe. In *Ahab*

Agonistes: The Rise and Fall of the Omri Dynasty, 134–44. London: Bloomsbury Publishing, 2007.

———. "Tribute or Looting in Samaria and Jerusalem: Shoshenq in Jerusalem," in *Homeland and Exile: Biblical and Ancient Near Eastern Studies in Honour of Bustenay Oded*, edited by Markham J. Geller, A. R. Millard, Bustenay Oded, and Gershon Galil, 167. Leiden: Brill, 2009.

Lemann, Augustin. *Jesus Before the Sanhedrin.* Translated by Julius Magath. 1886.

Lennox, John C. *God's Undertaker: Has Science Buried God?* Oxford: Lion Hudson, 2007.

———. *Seven Days That Divide the World: The Beginning According to Genesis and Science.* Grand Rapids, MI: Zondervan, 2011.

Leon Levy Dead Sea Scrolls Digital Library, The. "Featured Scrolls." Israel Antiquities Authority. http://www.deadseascrolls.org.il/featured-scrolls?locale=en_US.

Lentricchia, Frank. *After the New Criticism.* Chicago, IL: University of Chicago Press, 1980.

Leslie, John. *Universes.* New York: Routledge, 1989.

Lessing, Gotthold. *Lessing's Theological Writings.* Stanford, CA: Stanford University Press, 1957.

Levine, Michael P. *Hume and the Problem of Miracles: A Solution.* Dordrecht, Netherlands: Kluwer Academic Publishers, 1989.

Levy, Thomas E., Thomas Higham, Christopher Bronk Ramsey, Neil G. Smith, Erez Ben-Yosef, Mark Robinson, Stefan Münger, Kyle Knabb, Jürgen P. Schulze, Mohammad Najjar, and Lisa Tauxe. "High-precision Radiocarbon Dating and Historical Biblical Archaeology in Southern Jordan." *Proceedings of the National Academy of Sciences* 105, no. 43 (October, 2008): 16460–6465. doi:10.1073/pnas.0804950105.

Lewis, C. S. *The Abolition of Man.* New York, MacMillan, 1960.

———. "Is Theology Poetry?" in *The Weight of Glory*, edited by Walter Hooper, 116–140. New York: HarperOne, 1980.

———. *Mere Christianity.* New York: Macmillan/Collier, 1952.

———. *Mere Christianity: A Revised and Amplified Edition, with a New Introduction, of the Three Books, Broadcast Talks, Christian Behaviour, and Beyond Personality.* San Francisco, CA: HarperSanFrancisco, 2001.

———. *Miracles: A Preliminary Study.* New York: Macmillan, 1947; 2nd ed., 1978.

———. *The Problem of Pain.* New York: HarperCollins, 1996, orig. pub. 1940.

Lewis, Peter. *The Glory of Christ.* London: Hodder & Stoughton, 1992.

Lichtheim, Miriam. *Ancient Egyptian Literature*, vol 1. Berkeley, CA: University of California Press, 1973.

Licona, Michael R. "A New Starting Point in Historical Jesus Research: The Easter Event," in *The Quest for the Real Jesus: Radboud Prestige Lectures by Prof. Dr. Michael Wolter*, edited by Jan van der Watt. Leiden: Brill, 2013.

———. *The Resurrection of Jesus: A New Historiographical Approach.* Downers Grove, IL: IVP Academic, 2010.

Lightfoot. *Evangelium Matthaei, horoe hebraicoe.* Cambridge, 1658.

Lightman, Alan. *The Accidental Universe.* New York: Vintage Books, 2014.

Lindberg, David C. and Ronald L. Numbers, eds. *When Science and Christianity Meet.* Chicago, IL: University of Chicago Press, 2003.

Linton, Irwin H. *The Sanhedrin Verdict.* New York: Loizeaux Brothers, 1943.

Liplady, Thomas. *The Influence of the Bible.* New York: Fleming H. Revell, 1924.

Lippi, Marta Mariotti et al. "Multistep Food Plant Processing at Grotta Paglicci (Southern Italy) around 32,600 Cal B.P." *Proceedings of the National Academy of Sciences*, USA 112 (September 8, 2015): 12075–80. doi:10.1073/pnas.1505213112.

Little, Paul E. *Know Why You Believe.* Downers Grove, IL: InterVarsity Press, 2000.

Lloyd Davies, Margaret and Trevor A. Lloyd Davies. "Resurrection or Resuscitation?" *Journal of the Royal College of Physicians of London* 25, no. 2 (1991): 167–70.

Lloyd-Jones, Hugh, ed. and trans. *Sophocles: Ajax. Electra. Oedipus Tyrannus*. Cambridge, MA: Harvard University Press, 1994.

Loader, James A. "Creating New Contexts: On the Possibilities of Biblical Studies in Contexts Generated by the Dead Sea Scrolls." In *The Dead Sea Scrolls in Context: Integrating the Dead Sea Scrolls in the Study of Ancient Texts, Languages, and Cultures*, Vol. 1, edited by Armin Lange, Emanuel Tov, and Matthias Weigold, 27–45. Leiden: Brill, 2011.

Long, V. Philips. "Introduction," in *Windows into Old Testament History*, edited by V. Philips Long, David W. Baker, and Gordon J. Wenham. Grand Rapids, MI: Eerdmans, 2002.

Longenecker, Richard. "The Acts of the Apostles," in *The Expositor's Bible Commentary: John and Acts*, vol. 9, edited by F. E. Gaebelein. Grand Rapids, MI: Zondervan, 1981.

Longman, Tremper III and Raymond B. Dillard. *An Introduction to the Old Testament*, 2nd ed. Grand Rapids, MI: Zondervan, 2006.

Longman, Tremper III. "Literary Approaches to Old Testament Study," in *The Face of Old Testament Studies: A Survey of Contemporary Approaches*, edited by David W. Baker and Bill T. Arnold. Grand Rapids, MI: Baker Academic, 2004.

———. *The NIV Application Commentary: Daniel*. Grand Rapids, MI: Zondervan, 1999.

Lowder, Jeffery Jay and Robert M. Price, eds. *The Empty Tomb: Jesus Beyond the Grave*. Amherst, NY: Prometheus Books, 2005.

Lubenow, Marvin L. *Bones of Contention: A Creationist Assessment of Human Fossils*. Grand Rapids, MI: Baker, 1992.

Lubetski, Meir and Society of Biblical Literature. *New Inscriptions and Seals Relating to the Biblical World*. Atlanta: SBL Press, 2012.

Lucas, Ernest. *Apollos Old Testament Commentary: Daniel*. Downers Grove, MI: InterVarsity Press, 2002.

Lucian of Samosata. *How to Write History*. Cambridge: Harvard University Press, 1959.

Lüdemann, Gerd. *The Resurrection of Christ: A Historical Inquiry*. Amherst, NY: Prometheus Books, 2004.

———. *Virgin Birth? The Real Story of Mary and Her Son Jesus*. Translated by John Bowden. Harrisburg, PA: Trinity Press International, 1998.

Luskin, Casey. "Francis Collins, Junk DNA, and Chromosomal Fusion," in *Science and Human Origins*, edited by Ann Gauger, Douglas Axe, and Casey Luskin. Discovery Institute Press, 2012.

———. "The ENCODE Embroilment: Part I: Why Are Biologists Lashing Out Against Empirically Verified Research Results?" *Salvo Magazine* Issue 31 (Winter 2014). http://www.salvomag.com/new/articles/salvo31/the-encode-embroilment-part-I.php

———. "The ENCODE Embroilment, Part II: Denying Data Won't Change the Emerging Facts of Biology." *Salvo Magazine* Issue 32 (Spring 2015). http://www.salvomag.com/new/articles/salvo32/the-encode-embroilment-part-II.php.

———. "The ENCODE Embroilment, Part III: Evolution Proves Our Genome Is Junky . . . Which Proves Evolution . . ." *Salvo Magazine* Issue 33 (Summer 2015). http://www.salvomag.com/new/articles/salvo33/the-encode-embroilment-part-III.php.

———. "The ENCODE Embroilment, Part IV: Rewriting History Won't Erase Bad Evolutionary Predictions." *Salvo Magazine* Issue 34 (Fall 2015). Republished at http://www.evolutionnews.org/2015/11/post-encode_pos100771.html.

Luskin, Casey and Logan Paul Gage. "A Reply to Francis Collins' Darwinian Arguments for

Common Ancestry of Apes and Humans," in *Intelligent Design 101: Leading Experts Explain the Key Issues*, edited by H. Wayne House. Grand Rapids, MI: Kregel, 2008.

Lutzer, Erwin W. *Christ Among Other Gods*. Chicago, IL: Moody Press, 1994.

Luz, Ulrich. *The Theology of the Gospel of Matthew, New Testament Theology*. Cambridge University Press, 1995.

Lyotard, Jean and Geoffrey Bennington. *The Postmodern Condition: A Report on Knowledge*. Minneapolis, MN: University of Minnesota Press, 1984.

MacDonald, Scott. "Theory of Knowledge," in *The Cambridge Companion to Aquinas*, edited by Norman Kretzmann and Eleonore Stump. Cambridge University Press, 1993.

Machen, John Grisham. *The Origin of Paul's Religion*. New York: The Macmillan Company, 1921.

Machinist, Peter. "The Man Moses," in *Who Was Moses? Was He More Than an Exodus Hero?* Biblical Archeology Society. http://www. biblicalarchaeology.org/daily/biblical-topics/ exodus/who-was-moses-was-he-more-than- an-exodus-hero/.

———. "The Road Not Taken: Wellhausen and Assyriology," in *Homeland and Exile: Biblical and Ancient Near Eastern Studies in Honour of Bustenay Oded*, edited by Gershon Galil, Markham J. Geller, and A R. Millard, 469–532. Leiden: Brill, 2009.

MacIntyre, Alasdair C. *First Principles, Final Ends, and Contemporary Philosophical Issues: The Aquinas Lecture*. Milwaukee, WI: Marquette University Press, 1990.

Mackie, J. L. *The Miracle of Theism*. Oxford: Clarendon, 1982.

Macksey, Richard. *The Structuralist Controversy: The Languages of Criticism and the Sciences of Man*. Baltimore, MD: Johns Hopkins University Press, 2007.

Madueme, Hans and Michael Reeves, eds. *Adam, the Fall, and Original Sin: Theological, Biblical, and Scientific Perspectives*. Grand Rapids, MI: Baker Academic, 2014.

Magness, Jodi. "Has the Tomb of Jesus Been Discovered?" *SBL Forum* 5, no.2 (2007). http:// sbl-site.org/Article.aspx?ArticleID=640.

———. *Stone and Dung, Oil and Spit: Jewish Daily Life in the Times of Jesus*. Grand Rapids, MI: Eerdmans, 2011

Maier, Gerhard. "Truth and Reality in the Historical Understanding of the Old Testament," in *Israel's Past in Present Research: Essays on Ancient Israelite Historiography*, edited by V. Philips Long. Winona Lake, IN: Eisenbrauns, 1999.

Maier, Paul L. *In the Fullness of Time: A Historian Looks at Christmas, Easter, and the Early Church*. Grand Rapids, MI: Kregel Publications, 1997.

Malloch, S. J. V. *The Annals of Tacitus: Book 11*. New York: Cambridge University Press, 2013.

Manning, Joseph G. *A History of Ancient Near Eastern Law*, vol. 2. Leiden: Brill, 2003.

Marcus, Joel. *Mark 8–16: A New Translation with Introduction and Commentary*. Binghamton: Yale University Press, 2009.

Martin, Ralph P. "Creed," in *Dictionary of Paul and His Letters*, edited by Gerald F. Hawthorne, Ralph P. Martin, and Daniel G. Reid. Downers Grove: Intervarsity Press, 1993.

Martyr, Justin. "Apology," in *Ante-Nicene Fathers*, ed. Alexander Roberts and James Donaldson. Grand Rapids, MI: Eerdmans, 1989.

———. *Dialogue with Trypho*. Translated by Thomas B. Falls. Washington, D.C.: The Catholic University of America Press, 2003.

———. *Letters to Trypho*. New Advent. http://www .newadvent.org/fathers/01287.htm.

———. *On the Resurrection*. New Advent. http:// www.newadvent.org/fathers/0131.htm.

Mason, Steve. *Josephus and the New Testament*, 2nd ed. Peabody, MA: Hendrickson, 2003.

Matera, Frank J. *New Testament Christology*. Louisville, KY: Westminster John Knox Press, 1999.

Matlock, Mark. "Apologetics and Emotional Development: Understanding Our Ways of Knowing and Finding Meaning," in *Apologetics for a New Generation*, edited by Sean McDowell. Eugene, OR: Harvest House, 2009.

Mathews, Kenneth A. *The New American Commentary. Vol. 1A*. Nashville, TN: Broadman & Holman, 1996.

Mathias, Ginny, Amihay Mazar, and England Institute of Jewish Studies. *Studies in the Archaeology of the Iron Age in Israel and Jordan. Journal for the Study of the Old Testament. Supplement Series*. Sheffield, UK: Continuum, 2001.

Matthews, Victor Harold and Don C. Benjamin. *Old Testament Parallels: Laws and Stories from the Ancient Near East*. New York: Paulist, 1991.

Matthews, Victor H. and Mark W. Chavalas. *The IVP Bible Background Commentary: Old Testament*. Downers Grove, IL: Intervarsity Press, 2000.

Mavrodes, George I. *Belief in God: A Study in the Epistemology of Religion*. New York: Random House, 1970.

May, Jordan Daniel. "The Virgin Birth in the Fourth Gospel? A Brief Note on the Triple-Negation in John 1:13," in *But These Are Written*, edited by Keener, Crenshaw, and May. Eugene, OR: Pickwick Publications, 2014.

Mayr, Ernst. *What Makes Biology Unique? Considerations on the Autonomy of a Scientific Discipline*. Cambridge University Press, 2004.

Mazar, Amihai. "The Divided Monarchy: Comments on Some Archaeological Issues," in *The Quest for the Historical Israel: Debating Archaeology and the History of Early Israel: Invited Lectures Delivered at the Sixth Biennial Colloquium of the International Institute for Secular Humanistic Judaism*. Atlanta, GA: Society of Biblical Literature, 2007.

——. "The Iron Age Chronology Debate: Is the Gap Narrowing? Another Viewpoint." *Near Eastern Archaeology* 74, no. 2 (June, 2011): 105–11. doi:10.5615/neareastarch.74.2.0105.

——. "The Search for David and Solomon: An Archaeological Perspective," in *The Quest for the Historical Israel: Debating Archaeology and the History of Early Israel: Invited Lectures Delivered at the Sixth Biennial Colloquium of the International Institute for Secular Humanistic Judaism*. Atlanta, GA: Society of Biblical Literature, 2007.

Mazar, Amihai, and Nava Panitz-Cohen. "It Is the Land of Honey: Beekeeping at Tel Reḥov." *Near Eastern Archaeology* 70, no. 4 (December, 2007): 202–19. doi:10.2307/20361335.

Mazar, Amihai and Shmuel Ahituv. "The Inscriptions from Tel Reh ' Ov and Their Contribution to the Study of Script and Writing during Iron Age IIA," in *"See, I Will Bring a Scroll Recounting What Befell Me" (Ps 40:8): Epigraphy and Daily Life from the Bible to the Talmud: Dedicated to the Memory of Professor Hanan Eshel*, edited by Esther Eshel, Yigal Levin, and Ḥanan Eshel, 69–88. Göttingen: Vandenhoeck & Ruprecht, 2014.

Mazar, Eilat. "Did I Find King David's Palace?" *Biblical Archaeology Review* 32, no. 1 (2006): 16–27.

McCarter, P. Kyle, trans. "The Royal Steward Inscription," in *The Context of Scripture: Canonical Compositions, Monumental Inscriptions and Archival Documents from the Biblical World*, vol. 2, edited by William Hallo and K. Lawson Younger, 54. Leiden: Brill, 2000.

McClain, Alva. *Daniel's Prophecy of the Seventy Weeks*. Grand Rapids, MI: Zondervan, 1972.

McCullagh, C. Behan. *Justifying Historical Descriptions*. Cambridge University Press, 1984.

——. *The Logic of History*. New York: Routledge, 2004.

——. *The Truth of History*. London: Routledge, 1998.

McDonald, Lee Martin. *The Biblical Canon: Its Origin, Transmission, and Authority*. Grand Rapids, MI: Baker Academic, 2007.

McDonald, Lee M. and James A. Sanders, eds. *The Canon Debate*. Peabody, MA: Hendrickson Press, 2002.

McDonald, Patricia M. "Resemblances between Matthew 1–2 and Luke 1–2," in *New Perspectives on the Nativity*, ed. Jeremy Corley. London: T&T Clark, 2009.

McDougall, Ian, Francis H. Brown, and John G. Fleagle. "Stratigraphic Placement and Age of Modern Humans from Kibish, Ethiopia." *Nature* 433 (17 February 2005): 733–736. doi:10.1038/nature03258.

McDowell, Josh and Bill Wilson. *He Walked Among Us: Evidence for the Historical Jesus*. Nashville, TN: Thomas Nelson, 1993.

McDowell, Josh and Sean McDowell. *Evidence for the Resurrection: What it Means for Your Relationship with God*. Grand Rapids, MI: Baker Books, 2009.

McDowell, Sean. "Former French Atheist Becomes a Christian: An Interview," (blog), December 2, 2015, http://seanmcdowell.org/blog/former-french -atheist-becomes-a-christian-an-interview.

———. *A New Kind of Apologist*. Eugene, OR: Harvest House, 2016.

———. *Ethix: Being Bold in a Whatever World*. Nashville, TN: B&H Publishing Group, 2006.

———. "Why Apologetics Has a Bad Name," *Christian Research Journal* 35, no. 3 (2012), http:// www.equip.org/article/why-apologetics-has- a-bad-name/.

———. *The Fate of the Apostles: Examining the Martyrdom Accounts of the Closest Followers of Jesus*. Farnham, England: Ashgate, 2015.

———. "Did the Apostles Really Die as Martyrs for Their Faith?" *Christian Research Journal* vol 39, no. 2 (2016): 10–16.

McDowell, Sean and James Corbett. "Is God the Best Explanation for Moral Values?" Debate at Saddleback College, uploaded November 3, 2010, https://vimeo.com/16483272.

McDowell, Sean and Jonathan Morrow. *Is God Just a Human Invention?* Grand Rapids, MI: Kregel, 2010.

McGinn, Colin. *The Mysterious Flame*. New York: Basic Books, 1999.

McGrath, Alister. *Christian Theology: An Introduction*, 5th ed. Oxford: Wiley-Blackwell, 2011.

———. *Understanding Jesus: Who Jesus Christ Is and Why He Matters*. Grand Rapids, MI: Zondervan, 1987.

———. "Augustine's Origin of Species," Christianity Today (May, 2009): 39–41.

McGrew, Lydia. *Hidden in Plain View: Undesigned Coincidences in the Gospels and Acts*. DeWard, 2017.

McGrew, Timothy. "Miracles." *The Stanford Encyclopedia of Philosophy*. Edited by Edward Zalta. Last revised December 3, 2014. http:// plato.stanford.edu/archives/win2015/entries/ miracles/.

McIlhaney Joe S. and Freda McKissic Bush. *Hooked: New Science on How Casual Sex Is Affecting Our Children*. Chicago, IL: Northfield Publishing, 2008.

McInnes, Jim. "A Methodological Reflection on Unified Readings of Isaiah." *Colloquium* 42, no. 1 (May 2010): 67–84.

McKenzie, Steven L. *King David : A Biography*. Oxford University Press, 2000. E-book.

Meacham, Jon. "The Birth of Jesus," *Newsweek*, December 12, 2004. http://www.newsweek .com/birth-jesus-123591

Meier, John P. *A Marginal Jew: Rethinking the Historical Jesus*, vol. 1. Anchor Yale Bible Reference Library. New York: Doubleday, 1991.

Mellars, Paul. "Neanderthals and the Modern Human Colonization of Europe." *Nature* 432 (25 November 2004): 461–65.

Mellor, Ronald. *Tacitus*. New York: Routledge, 1993.

Mendelsohn, Isaac. *Slavery in the Ancient Near East*. Westport, CT: Greenwood Press, 1978.

Mendenhall, George E. "The Hebrew Conquest of Palestine." *The Biblical Archaeologist* 25, no. 4 (September, 1962): 76–77.

Merrill, Eugene H. *Deuteronomy.*The New American Commentary, vol. 4. Edited by E. Ray Clendenen. Nashville, TN: B&H Publishing Group, 1994.

——. *Kingdom of Priests: A History of Old Testament Israel.* Grand Rapids, MI: Baker Academic, 1998.

Mettinger, Tryggve N. D. *The Riddle of Resurrection: Dying and Rising Gods in the Ancient Near East.* Winona Lake, IN: Eisenbrauns, 2013.

Metzger, Bruce M. *The Early Versions of the New Testament.* Clarendon Press, 1977.

——. *The Text of the New Testament.* New York: Oxford University Press, 1968.

Metzger, Bruce M. and Bart D. Ehrman. *The Text of the New Testament: Its Transmission, Corruption, and Restoration,* 4th ed. Oxford University Press, 2005, orig. pub. 1992.

Meyer, Stephen C. *Signature in The Cell: DNA and the Evidence for Intelligent Design.* New York: HarperOne, 2009.

Meyers, Carol. *Exodus: The New Cambridge Bible Commentary.* Cambridge University Press, 2005.

Mill, John Stuart. *Three Essays on Religion: Nature, the Utility of Religion, and Theism,* 3rd ed. London: Longmans, Green, Beader, and Dyer, 1874.

Millard, Alan R., trans. "Babylonian King Lists," in *The Context of Scripture: Canonical Compositions, Monumental Inscriptions and Archival Documents from the Biblical World,* vol. 1, edited by William Hallo and K. Lawson Younger, 134. Leiden: Brill, 1997.

Millard, Alan R. "Daniel in Babylon: An Accurate Record?" in *Do Historical Matters Matter to the Faith? A Critical Appraisal of Modern and Postmodern Approaches to Scripture,* edited by James K. Hoffmeier and Dennis R. Magary. Wheaton: Crossway, 2012.

——. "Exodus," in Dictionary of the Ancient Near East, edited by Piotr Bienkoswki and Alan Millard, 111–12. Philadelphia, PA: University of Pennsylvania Press, 2000.

——. "Israelite and Aramean History in the Light of Inscriptions." *Tyndale Bulletin* 41 (1990): 261–75.

——. "Were the Israelites Really Canaanites?" in *Israel: Ancient Kingdom or Late Invention?* edited by Daniel I. Block. Nashville, TN: B&H Publishing Group, 2008.

Miller, Johnny V. and John M. Soden. *In the Beginning—We Misunderstood: Interpreting Genesis 1 in Its Original Context.* Grand Rapids, MI: Kregel Publications, 2012.

Miller, Robert J. *Born Divine: The Births of Jesus & Other Sons of God.* Santa Rosa, CA: Polebridge Press, 2003.

Mineo, Bernard, ed. *A Companion to Livy.* Malden, MA: John Wiley & Sons, Inc., 2015.

Mittelberg, Mark. *The Questions Christians Hope No One Will Ask.* Carol Stream, IL: Tyndale, 2010.

"Modern Source Theories," in *The Jewish Study Bible.* Oxford Biblical Studies Online, http://www.oxfordbiblicalstudies.com/article/book/obso-9780195297515/obso-9780195297515-div1-12.

Möller, Karl. *A Prophet in Debate: The Rhetoric of Persuasion in the Book of Amos.* London: Sheffield Academic Press, 2003.

Momigliano, Arnaldo. *The Classical Foundations of Modern Historiography.* Berkeley, CA: University of California Press, 1990.

Monette, Greg. *The Wrong Jesus: Fact, Belief, Legend, Truth . . . Making Sense of What You've Heard.* Carol Stream, IL: NavPress, 2014.

Monson, John M. "Enter Joshua: The 'Mother of Current Debates' in Biblical Archaeology," in *Do Historical Matters Matter To Faith? A Critical Appraisal of Modern and Postmodern Approaches to Scripture,* edited by James K. Hoffmeier and Dennis R. Magary. Wheaton, IL: Crossway, 2012.

——. "The Role and Context and the Promise of Archaeology in Biblical Interpretation," in

The Future of Biblical Archaeology: Reassessing Methodologies and Assumptions, edited by James Karl Hoffmeier and Alan R. Millard, The Proceedings of a Symposium, August 12–14, 2001 at Trinity International University. Grand Rapids, MI: Eerdmans, 2004.

Montgomery, John W. "Evangelicals and Archaeology," *Christianity Today*, August 16, 1968.

———. *History and Christianity*. Downers Grove, IL: InterVarsity Press, 1971.

———. *Human Rights and Human Dignity*. Grand Rapids, MI: Zondervan, 1986.

Montgomery, John Warwick. *The Shape of the Past: A Christian Response to Secular Philosophies of History*, 2nd ed. Minneapolis: Bethany Fellowship, 1975.

Moo, Douglas. "The Law of Christ As the Fulfillment of the Law of Moses: A Modified Lutheran View," in *Five Views on Law and Gospel*, edited by Wayne G. Strickland. Grand Rapids, MI: Zondervan, 1996.

Moore, G. E. "Four Forms of Skepticism" in *Philosophical Papers*, 196–226. London: Unwin Brothers Limited, 1959.

———. "Proof of an External World" in *Philosophical Papers*, 127–150. London: Unwin Brothers Limited, 1959.

———. *Some Main Problems of Philosophy*. New York: Routledge: Taylor and Francis Group, 2014.

Moore, Megan Bishop and Brad E. Kelle. *Biblical History and Israel's Past: The Changing Study of the Bible and History*. Grand Rapids, MI: Eerdmans, 2011.

Moreland, J. P. "The Argument from Consciousness," in *The Blackwell Companion to Natural Theology*, edited by William Lane Craig and J. P. Moreland. West Sussex, U.K.: Wiley-Blackwell, 2009.

———. "The Historicity of the New Testament," Bethinking.org, 21 August 2005. Accessed May 19, 2016, http://www.bethinking.org/is-the-bible-reliable/the-historicity-of-the-new-testament.

———. *Love Your God with All Your Mind*. Carol Stream, IL: NavPress, 1997.

———. "Postmodernism and Truth," in *Reasons for Faith: Making a Case for the Christian Faith*, edited by Norman L. Geisler and Chad V. Meister, 113–126. Wheaton, IL: Crossway Books, 2007.

———. *Scaling the Secular City: A Defense of Christianity*. Grand Rapids, MI: Baker Books, 2005.

———. "Two Areas of Reflection and Dialogue with John Franke." *Philosophia Christi* 8, no. 2 (2006): 305–312.

Moreland J. P. and William Lane Craig. *Philosophical Foundations for a Christian Worldview*. Downers Grove, IL: InterVarsity Press, 2009.

Morgan, Donald. "Bible Inconsistencies: Bible Contradictions?" Secular Web. Accessed October 30, 2015, http://www.infidels.org/library/modern/donald_morgan/inconsistencies.html.

Morris, Leon. *The Gospel According to John. New International Commentary on the New Testament*. Grand Rapids, MI: Eerdmans, 1971.

Morriston, Wesley. "Did God Command Genocide? A Challenge to the Biblical Inerrantist." *Philosophia Christi* 11, no. 1 (2009): 7–26.

Mortenson, Terry and Thane H. Ury, eds. *Coming to Grips with Genesis: Biblical Authority and the Age of the Earth*. Green Forest, AR: Master Books, 2008.

Moser, Paul K. "Two Roads to Skepticism," in *Doubting: Contemporary Perspectives on Skepticism*, edited by Michael D. Roth and Glenn Ross, 127–39. Dordrecht: Kluwer Academic Publishers, 1990.

Moss, Candida R. *The Myth of Persecution: How Early Christians Invented a Story of Martyrdom*. New York: HarperCollins, 2013.

Moyer, Elgin S. *Who Was Who in Church History*, rev. ed. Chicago, IL: Moody Press, 1968.

Moyise, Steve. *Jesus and Scripture*. London: SPCK, 2010.

Muhlestein, Kerry. "Levantine Thinking in Egypt," in *Egypt, Canaan, and Israel: History,*

Imperialism, Ideology, and Literature, edited by Shay Bar, Dan'el Kahn, and J. J. Shirley, 190–235. Leiden: Brill, 2011.

Murray, John. "The Attestation of Scripture," in *The Infallible Word*, ed. N. B. Stonehouse and Paul Woolley, 1–52. Philadelphia, PA: Presbyterian and Reformed, 1946.

Murray, Michael J. "Reasons for Hope (in the Postmodern World)," in *Reasons for the Hope Within*, edited by Michael J. Murray. Grand Rapids, MI: Eerdmans, 1999.

Mykytiuk, Lawrence J. "Corrections and Updates to 'Identifying Biblical Persons in Northwest Semitic Inscriptions of 1200–539 B.C.E.'" Purdue E-Pubs. Paper 129. Libraries Research Publications, 2009. Accessed September 5, 2015. http://docs.lib.purdue.edu/lib_research/129/.

Na'aman, Nadav. "The 'Conquest of Canaan' in the Book of Joshua and in History," in *Canaan in the Second Millennium B.C.E: Collected Essays Volume 2*, edited by Israel Finkelstein and Nadav Na'aman, 325–28. Winona Lake, IN: Eisenbrauns, 2005.

———. "The Contribution of the Amarna Letters to the Debate on Jerusalem's Political Position in the Tenth Century BCE," in *Ancient Israel's History and Historiography: The First Temple Period*. Winona Lake, IN: Eisenbrauns, 2006.

———. "Does Archaeology Really Deserve the Status of a 'High Court' in Biblical Historical Research?" in *Between Evidence and Ideology: Essays on the History of Ancient Israel Read at the Joint Meeting of the Society for Old Testament Study and the Oud Testamentisch Werkgezelschap*, edited by Lester L. Grabbe and Bob Becking, 165–83. Leiden: Brill, 2011.

———. "In Search of the Ancient Name of Khirbet Qeiyafa." *The Journal of Hebrew Scriptures* 8 (2008): 1–8.

———. "The Trowel vs. the Text." *Biblical Archaeology Review* 35, no. 1 (2009): 52.

Nagel, Thomas. *The Last Word*. Oxford University Press, 1997.

———. *Mind and Cosmos: Why the Materialist Neo-Darwinian Conception of Nature Is Almost Certainly False*. Oxford University Press, 2012).

———. *The View from Nowhere*. Oxford University Press, 1986.

Nash, Ronald H. *Christian Faith & Historical Understanding*. Grand Rapids, MI: Zondervan, 1984.

———. *Faith & Reason: Searching for a Rational Faith*. Grand Rapids, MI: Academie Books, 1988.

———. *The Gospel and the Greeks: Did the New Testament Borrow from Pagan Thought?* Phillipsburg, NY: P&R Publishing, 2003.

———. *Life's Ultimate Questions*. Grand Rapids, MI: Zondervan, 1999.

———. *Worldviews in Conflict: Choosing Christianity in a World of Ideas*. Grand Rapids, MI: Zondervan, 1992.

Nash, Walter L. *Transactions of the Society of Biblical Archæology*. London: Longmans, Green, Reader, and Dyer, 1872.

National Geographic Genographic Project. "The Human Story: Migration Routes." National Geographic. Accessed October 2, 2015. https://genographic.nationalgeographic.com/human-journey/.

National Human Genome Research Institute. "All About the Human Genome Project (HGP)." Last updated October 1, 2015. Accessed October 19, 2015. http://www.genome.gov/10001772.

Neill, Stephen. *A History of Christian Missions*. Baltimore, MD: Penguin, 1964.

Nelson, Byron C. The Deluge Story in Stone: A History of the Flood Theory of Geology. Minneapolis, MN: Bethany Fellowship, 1968.

Neumann, Hans. "Slavery in Private Households Toward the End of the Third Millennium B.C," in *Slaves and Households in the Near East*, edited by Laura Culbertson, 21–32. Chicago, IL: University of Chicago, 2011. https://oi

.uchicago.edu/sites/oi.uchicago.edu/files/uploads/shared/docs/ois7.pdf.

Neusner, Jacob, trans. *The Mishna: A New Translation*. New Haven, CT: Yale University, 1988, version 2.2. Accordance Bible Software, version 11.4.1.

———. *A Rabbi Talks with Jesus*, rev. ed. Montreal: McGill-Queen's University Press, 2000.

Newman, Robert C., Perry G. Phillips, and Herman J. Eckelmann, Jr. *Genesis One and the Origin of the Earth*, 2nd ed. Interdisciplinary Biblical Research Institute, 2007. Kindle edition.

Newton, Isaac. *Isaac Newton: Philosophical Writings*. Edited by Andrew Janiak. New York: Cambridge University Press, 2014.

Nezikin, Seder, trans. *The Babylonian Talmud*. London: The Soncino Press, 1935.

Nicene and Post-Nicene Fathers, series 1, 14 vols. Edited by Philip Schaff. Edinburgh: T&T Clark, and Grand Rapids, MI: Eerdmans, reprint 1993.

Nicene and Post-Nicene Fathers, series 2, 14 vols. Edited by Philip Schaff and Henry Wace. Edinburgh: T&T Clark, and Grand Rapids, MI: Eerdmans, reprint 1991.

Nicholas of Autrecourt. *Nicholas of Autrecourt: His Correspondence with Master Giles and Bernard of Arezzo*. Edited and translated by L. M. De Rijk. Leiden: Brill, 1994.

Nichols, Terence L. "Miracles in Science and Theology." *Zygon* 37, no. 3 (2002): 704–705.

Nicholson, Ernest "Current 'Revisionism' and the Literature of the Old Testament," in *In Search of Pre-Exilic Israel: Proceedings of the Oxford Old Testament Seminar*, edited by John Day, 1–22. London: T&T Clark, 2004.

———. "The Theory Under Attack: Rolf Rendtorff's New Paradigm of the Origin of the Pentateuch," in *The Pentateuch in the Twentieth Century: The Legacy of Julius Wellhausen*. Oxford University Press, 2002. Oxford Scholarship Online. Last modified October 2011. DOI: 10.1093/acprof:oso/9780199257836.003.0004.

Nida, Eugene A. *Bible Translating: An Analysis of Principles and Procedures, with Special Reference to Aboriginal Languages*. New York: American Bible Society, 1947.

Niessen, Richard. "The Virginity of the ʿalmāh in Isaiah 7:14," *Bibliotheca Sacra* 137 (1980): 133–47.

Nietzsche, Friedrich. *The Portable Nietzsche*. Edited and translated by Walter Arnold Kaufmann. New York: Penguin Books, 1976.

———. *The Will to Power*. Translated by Walter Kaufmann and R. J. Hollingdale. New York: Vintage Books, 1968.

Nihan, Christophe Laurent. "The Emergence of the Pentateuch as 'Torah'." *Religion Compass* 4, no. 6 (June 2010): 353–64. http://dx.doi.org/10.1111/reco.2010.4.issue-6.

"Nine Unopened Dead Sea Scrolls Found," Fox News, March 13, 2014, http://www.foxnews.com/science/2014/03/13/nine-unopened-dead-sea-scrolls-found.html.

Nizkor Project. "The Trial of Adolf Eichmann – Session 68." The Nizkor Project. Accessed October 2, 2015. http://www.nizkor.org/hweb/people/e/eichmann-adolf/transcripts/Sessions/Session-068-01.html.

Noonan, Benjamin. "Egyptian Loanwords as Evidence for the Authenticity of the Exodus and Wilderness Traditions," in *"Did I Not Bring Israel Out of Egypt?": Biblical, Archaeological, and Egyptological Perspectives on the Exodus Narratives*, edited by James K. Hoffmeier, Alan R. Millard, and Gary A. Rendsburg. Winona Lake: Eisenbrauns, 2016.

North, J. Lionel. "The Use of the Latin Fathers for New Testament Textual Criticism," in *The Text of the New Testament in Contemporary Research: Essays on the Status Quaestionis*, edited by Bart D. Ehrman and Michael W. Holmes. Grand Rapids, MI: Eerdmans, 1994.

Nowell, April. "From A Paleolithic Art to Pleistocene Visual Cultures (Introduction to two Special Issues on 'Advances in the Study of Pleistocene Imagery and Symbol Use')."

Journal of Archaeological Method and Theory 13 (December 2006): 239–49. doi: 10.1007/s10816-006-9020-2.

Nowell-Smith, Patrick. "Miracles," in *New Essays in Philosophical Theology*, edited by Anthony Flew and Alasdair MacIntyre. New York: Macmillan, 1955.

Oden, Thomas C. *The Word of Life: Systematic Theology: Volume 2*. Peabody, MA: Prince Press, 1998.

Oller, J. W., Jr. and Steven Collins. "The Logic of True Narrative Representations." *Biblical Research Bulletin* I.2. 2001.

Opher, Avi. "The Monarchic Period in the Judaean Highland: A Spatial Overview," in *Studies in the Archaeology of the Iron Age in Israel and Jordan*, edited by Ginny Mathias, Amihay Mazar, and England Institute of Jewish Studies. Sheffield, England: Continuum International Publishing Group, 2001.

Oppenheim, A. Leo, trans. "The Babylonian King List A," in *Ancient Near Eastern Texts Relating to the Old Testament*, edited by J. B. Pritchard. Princeton, Princeton University Press, 1955.

Oppenheim, A. Leo, trans. "Nebuchadnezzar II," in *Ancient Near Eastern Texts Relating to the Old Testament*, edited by J. B. Pritchard. Princeton, Princeton University Press, 1955.

Origins of Life Initiative, Harvard University, http://origins.harvard.edu/.

Ortiz, Steven M. "Rewriting Philistine History: Recent Trends in Philistine Archaeology and Biblical Studies," in *Critical Issues in Early Israelite History*, edited by Paul J. Ray, Gerald A. Klingbeil, and Richard S. Hess, 191–204. Winona Lake, IN: Eisenbrauns, 2008.

Ortlund, Eric. "Reversed (Chrono-) Logical Sequences in Isaiah 1–39: Some Implications for Theories of Redaction." *Journal for the Study of the Old Testament* 35, no. 2 (December 2010): 209–24.

Ortlund, Raymond C., Jr. "The Deity of Christ and the Old Testament," in *The Deity of Christ*, edited by Christopher W. Morgan and Robert A. Peterson, 39–60. Wheaton, IL: Crossway, 2011.

Oswalt, John N. *The Bible Among the Myths: Unique Revelation or Just Ancient Literature?* Grand Rapids, MI: Zondervan, 2009.

Owens, Joseph. *An Elementary Christian Metaphysics*. Houston, TX: Center for Thomistic Studies, 1985.

Owens, Virginia Stem. "Colorizing Jacob," *Christianity Today* (Sept. 13, 1993): 48.

Pagan, Victoria Emma, ed. *A Companion to Tacitus*. Malden, MA: Blackwell, 2012.

Parker, Andrew. *The Genesis Enigma: Why the Bible Is Scientifically Accurate*. New York: Dutton, 2009.

Pascal, Blaise. *Pensees*. Translated by A. J. Krailsheimer. London: Penguin, 1995.

Payne, J. Barton. *Encyclopedia of Biblical Prophecy*. London: Hodder and Stoughton, 1973.

PCA Historical Center. Report of the Creation Study Committee. June, 2000, http://www.pcahistory.org/creation/report.html.

Pearcey, Nancy. *Total Truth: Liberating Christianity from Its Cultural Captivity*. Study guide edition. Wheaton, IL: Crossway Books, 2005.

Pearcey, Nancy and Charles Thaxton. *The Soul of Science*. Wheaton, IL: Crossway, 1994.

Pelikan, Jaroslav. *Jesus Through the Centuries: His Place in the History of Culture*. New Haven, CT: Yale University Press, 1999.

Perrin, Nicholas. *Thomas and Tatian: The Relationship Between the Gospel of Thomas and the Diatessaron*. Atlanta, GA: Society of Biblical Literature, 2002.

Peters, F. E. *The Harvest of Hellenism*. New York: Simon and Schuster, 1971.

Pfeiffer, Robert H. *Introduction to the Old Testament*. New York: Harper and Brothers Publishers, 1948.

Philo of Alexandria. "Vita Mosis [Life of Moses]," in *Philo: With an English Translation*, edited by F. H. Colson. Loeb Classical Library, vol.

VI. Cambridge, MA: Harvard University Press, 1959.

———. *The Works of Philo: Complete and Unabridged*. New updated ed. Peabody: Hendrickson, 1993.

Pinnock, Clark. "Apologetics," in *New Dictionary of Theology*, edited by Sinclair B. Ferguson, David F. Wright, and J. I. Packer. Downers Grove, IL: InterVarsity Press, 2000.

———. *Set Forth Your Case*. Nutley, NJ: The Craig Press, 1967.

Plantinga, Alvin. *God, Freedom, and Evil*. Grand Rapids, MI: Eerdmans, 1977.

———. *Where the Conflict Really Lies: Science, Religion & Naturalism*. Oxford University Press, 2011.

Plutarch. "Life of Alexander," in *Lives*, translated by Bernadotte Perrin, *Loeb Classical Library* 99. Cambridge; Harvard University Press, 1919.

Polkinghorne, John. *Quarks, Chaos and Christianity: Questions to Science and Religion*. New York: Crossroad, 2005.

Polycarp. *Epistle of Polycarp to the Philippians*. New Advent. http://www.newadvent.org/fathers/0136.htm.

Popkin, Richard H. *The High Road to Pyrrhonism*. San Diego, CA: Austin Hill Press, Inc., 1980.

Porteous, Norman W. *Daniel: A Commentary*. Philadelphia, PA: The Westminster Press, 1965.

Porter, Stanley E. and Andrew W. Pitts. *Fundamentals of New Testament Textual Criticism*. Grand Rapids, MI: Eerdmans, 2015.

Post, Stephen G., Lynn G. Underwood, Jeffrey P. Schloss, and William B. Hurlbut, eds. *Altruism and Altruistic Love: Science, Philosophy, & Religion in Dialogue*. Oxford University Press, 2002.

Potter, David. *Literary Tests and the Roman Historian*. Oxford: Routledge, 1999.

Powell, Mark Allan. *Jesus as a Figure in History*. Louisville, KY: Westminster John Knox, 2013.

Poznik, G. David et al. "Sequencing Y Chromosomes Resolves Discrepancy in Time to Common Ancestor of Males versus Females." *Science* 341 (2 August 2013): 562–565. doi:10.1126/science.1237619.

Price, Robert M. "Jesus at the Vanishing Point," in *The Historical Jesus: Five Views*, edited by James Beilby and Paul Rhodes Eddy. Downers Grove: IVP Academic, 2009.

———. "A Rejoinder to Josh McDowell's *Evidence That Demands a Verdict*: 'Jesus – God's Son' (1997)," accessed August 31, 2015, http://infidels.org/library/modern/robert_price/son.html, Sec. 1B.

Priestley, Jessica and Vasiliki Zali, eds. Brill's *Companion to the Reception of Herodotus in Antiquity and Beyond*. Leiden: Brill, 2016.

Pritchard, Duncan. "Contemporary Skepticism." *The Internet Encyclopedia of Philosophy*. http://www.iep.utm.edu/skepcont/.

Pritchard, J. B. *The Ancient Near East, Volume I—An Anthology of Texts and Pictures*. Princeton, NJ: Princeton University Press, 1958.

———. *Ancient Near Eastern Texts Relating to the Old Testament*. Princeton, NJ: Princeton University Press, 1955.

Provan, Ian, V. Phillips Long, and Tremper Longman, III. *A Biblical History of Israel*. Louisville, KY: Westminster John Knox Press, 2003, 2nd ed. 2015.

Purtill, Richard. "Defining Miracles," in *In Defense of Miracles*, edited by Douglas Geivett and Gary Habermas. Downers Grove, IL: InterVarsity Press, 1997.

Putnam, Hilary. "Brains in a Vat," in *Skepticism, a Contemporary Reader*, edited by Keith DeRose and Ernest Sosa. Oxford University Press, 1999.

Pudaite, Rochunga and James C. Hefley. *The Greatest Book Ever Written*. Hannibal, MO: Hannibal Books, 1989.

Qiaomei Fu et al. "Genome sequence of a 45,000-year-old modern human from Western

Siberia." *Nature* 514 (23 October 2014): 445–49. doi:10.1038/nature13810.

Quarles, Charles, ed. *Buried Hope or Risen Savior: The Search for the Jesus Tomb.* Nashville, TN: B&H Publishing Group, 2008.

Quinton, Anthony. *The Nature of Things.* London: Routledge, 1973.

Rainey, Anson F. "Whence Came the Israelites and Their Language?" *Israel Exploration Journal* 57, no. 1 (2007): 41–64.

Rajak, Tessa. *Josephus: The Historian and His Society.* Philadelphia, PA: Fortress, 1983.

Ramm, Bernard. *Protestant Christian Evidences: A Textbook of the Evidences of the Truthfulness of the Christian Faith for Conservative Protestants.* Chicago, IL: Moody Press, 1959.

Ramsay, W. M. *The Bearing of Recent Discovery on the Trustworthiness of the New Testament.* London: Hodder and Stoughton, 1915.

———. *St. Paul the Traveler and the Roman Citizen.* Grand Rapids, MI: Baker Book House, 1962.

Rana, Fazale. *The Cell's Design: How Chemistry Reveal's the Creator's Artistry.* Grand Rapids, MI: Baker Book House, 2008.

Rana, Fazale with Hugh Ross. *Who Was Adam? A Creation Model Approach to the Origin of Man,* 2nd ed. Covina, CA: Reasons to Believe, 2015.

Read, Kay Almere and Jason J. González. *Mesoamerican Mythology: A Guide to the Gods, Heroes, Rituals, and Beliefs of Mexico and Central America.* Oxford University Press, 2002.

Reader, John. "Whatever Happened to Zinjanthropus?" *New Scientist* (26 March 1981): 802.

Regis, L. M. *Epistemology.* Translated by Imelda Choquette Byrne. New York: Macmillan, 1959.

Reich, Ronny, Eli Shukron, and Omri Lernau. "Recent Discoveries in the City of David, Jerusalem." *Israel Exploration Journal* 57, no. 2 (January, 2007): 153–69. doi:10.2307/27927171.

Reid, Garnett H. "Minimalism and Biblical History." *Bibliotheca Sacra* 155, no. 620 (October 1998): 394–410.

Rendtorff, Rolf. "The Paradigm Is Changing: Hopes and Fears." *Biblical Interpretation* 1, no. 1 (1993): 34–53.

Reymond, Robert L. *A New Systematic Theology of the Christian Faith,* 2nd ed. Nashville, TN: Thomas Nelson, 1998.

Reynolds, John Mark. "Christianity and Culture: Defending Our Fathers and Mothers," in *Apologetics for a New Generation,* edited by Sean McDowell. Eugene, OR: Harvest House, 2009.

Richter, Sandra. "Eighth-Century Issues: The World of Jeroboam II, the Fall of Samaria, and the Reign of Hezekiah," in *Ancient Israel's History: An Introduction to Issues and Sources,* edited by Bill T. Arnold and Richard S. Hess, 319–49. Grand Rapids, MI: Baker, 2014.

Roberts, Hill and Mark Whorton. *Holman QuickSource Guide to Understanding Creation.* Nashville, TN: B&H Publishing Group, 2008.

Roberts, Mark D. "The Birth of Jesus: Hype or History?" Institute for Religious Research, last modified 2011, http://bib.irr.org/birth-of-jesus-hype-or-history.

Robertson, A. T. *Word Picture in the New Testament.* Nashville, TN: Broadman & Holman, 1930.

Robertson, David. "From Epidauros to Lourdes: A History of Healing by Faith," in *Faith Healing: Finger of God? Or, Scientific Curiosity?* compiled by Claude A. Frazier. New York: Thomas Nelson, 1973.

Robertson, Morgan. *The Wreck of the Titan: or Futility.* http://www.gutenberg.org/files/24880/24880-h/24880-h.htm.

Robinson, Bernard P. "Matthew's Nativity Stories: Historical and Theological Questions for Today's Readers," in *New Perspectives on the Nativity,* edited by Jeremy Corley. London: T&T Clark, 2009.

Rogerson, J. W. "Historical Criticism and the Authority of the Bible," in *The Oxford Handbook of Biblical Studies.* Oxford Biblical Studies Online. http://www.oxfordbiblicalstudies

.com/article/book/obso-9780199254255/
obso-9780199254255-chapter-45.

Rohl, David. *Exodus: Myth or History?* St. Louis
Park, MN: Thinking Man Media, 2015.

Römer, Thomas. "Extra-Pentateuchal Biblical
Evidence for the Existence of a Pentateuch?"
in *The Pentateuch: International Perspectives
on Current Research*, edited by Thomas B.
Dozeman, Konrad Schmid, and Baruch J.
Schwartz, Forschungen zum Alten Testament,
vol. 78, 487–88. Tübingen, Germany: Mohr
Siebeck, 2011.

Roper, Albert L. *Did Jesus Rise from the Dead?: A
Lawyer Looks at the Evidence.* Grand Rapids,
MI: Zondervan, 1965.

Rorty, Richard. *Consequences of Pragmatism:
Essays, 1972–1980.* Minneapolis, MN: University of Minnesota Press, 1982.

———. *Contingency, Irony, and Solidarity.* Cambridge: Cambridge University Press, 1989.

———. "Deconstructionist Theory," in *The Cam-
bridge History of Literary Criticism: From
Formalism to Poststructuralism*, edited by Peter
Brooks, H. B. Nisbet, and Claude Rawson.
Cambridge: Cambridge University Press,1995.

———. *Objectivity, Relativism, and Truth.* Cambridge: Cambridge University Press, 1991.

———. *Philosophy and the Mirror of Nature.*
Princeton, NJ: Princeton University Press,
1979.

Rosenau, Pauline Marie. *Post-Modernism and the
Social Sciences: Insights, Inroads, Intrusions.*
Princeton, NJ: Princeton University Press,
1992.

Ross, Allen P. "Genesis," in *The Bible Knowledge
Commentary: Old Testament*, edited by John F.
Walvoord and Roy B. Zuck, 15–101. Colorado
Springs, CO: ChariotVictory Publishing, 1985.

Ross, Hugh. *The Creator and the Cosmos.* Colorado Springs, CO: NavPress, 1995.

———. *A Matter of Days: Resolving a Creation
Controversy*, 2nd ed. Covina, CA: Reasons
to Believe, 2015.

———. *More Than a Theory: Revealing a Testable
Model for Creation.* Grand Rapids, MI: Baker,
2009.

Roth, Martha T. *Law Collections from Mesopotamia and Asia Minor.* Atlanta, GA: Scholars
Press, 1995.

Rowley, H. H. *The Growth of the Old Testament.*
London: Hutchinson House, 1950.

Runkle, Gerald. *Good Thinking: An Introduction to Logic.* New York: Holt, Rinehart and
Winston, 1978.

_____. *Navigating Genesis: A Scientist's
Journey through Genesis 1–11.* Covina, CA:
Reasons to Believe, 2014.

Russell, Bertrand. *An Inquiry into Meaning and
Truth: The William James Lectures for 1940
Delivered at Harvard University*, rev. ed.
London: Routledge, 1995.

———. *The Problems of Philosophy.* Amherst, NY:
Prometheus Books, 1988.

———. *Russell on Metaphysics: Selections from
the Writings of Bertrand Russell.* Edited by
Stephen Mumford. New York: Routledge:
Taylor and Francis Group, 2015.

Sailhamer, John H. *Biblical Archaeology.* Grand
Rapids, MI: Zondervan, 1998.

———. *Genesis Unbound: A Provocative New Look
at the Creation Account.* 2nd ed. Colorado
Springs, CO: Dawson Media, 2011.

———. *The Meaning of the Pentateuch: Revelation,
Composition, and Interpretation.* Downers
Grove, IL: IVP Academic, 2009.

Samples, Kenneth R. *7 Truths That Changed the
World: Discovering Christianity's Most Dangerous Ideas.* Grand Rapids, MI: Baker Books, 2012.

———. *Without a Doubt: Answering the 20 Tough-
est Faith Questions.* Grand Rapids, MI: Baker,
2004.

Sanders, C. *Introduction to Research in English
Literary History.* New York: Macmillan, 1952.

Sanders, E. P. *The Historical Figure of Jesus.* New
York: Penguin, 1993. Jesus and Judaism. London: SCM, 1985.

Sanders, Seth L. "Writing and Early Iron Age Israel: Before National Scripts, Beyond Nations and States," in *Literate Culture and Tenth-century Canaan: The Tel Zayit Abecedary in Context*, edited by P. Kyle McCarter and Ron E. Tappy, 97–112. Winona Lake, IN: Eisenbrauns, 2008.

Sandy, D. Brent, and Ronald L. Giese. *Cracking Old Testament Codes: A Guide to Interpreting Literary Genres of the Old Testament*. Nashville, TN: Broadman & Holman, 1995.

Sasson, Jack M. *Civilizations of the Ancient Near East*, vol. 3. NY: Charles Scribner's Sons, 1995.

Schaberg, Jane. *The Illegitimacy of Jesus: A Feminist Theological Interpretation of the Infancy Narratives*. Sheffield: Sheffield Academic Press, 1995.

Schaeffer, Francis A. *How Should We Then Live? The Rise and Decline of Western Thought and Culture*. Wheaton, IL: Crossway Books, 2005.

Schaff, Philip. *History of the Christian Church*, 3rd ed. New York: Charles Scribner's Sons, 1910.

———. *The Person of Christ: The Perfection of His Humanity Viewed as a Proof of His Divinity*. New York: Charles Scribner's Sons, © American Tract Society, 1881.

Schiffman, Lawrence H. *From Text to Tradition: A History of Second Temple and Rabbinic Judaism*. Hoboken, NJ: Ktav, 1991.

Schmid, Konrad. "Has European Scholarship Abandoned the Documentary Hypothesis? Some Reminders on Its History and Remarks on Its Current Status," in *The Pentateuch: International Perspectives on Current Research*, edited by Thomas B. Dozeman, Konrad Schmid, and Baruch J. Schwartz, Forschungen Zum Alten Testament, vol.78, 17–30. Tübingen, Germany: Mohr Siebeck, 2011.

Schnackenburg, Rudolf A. *The Johannine Epistles: A Commentary*. New York: Crossroad Publishing Company, 1992.

Schniedewind, William M. *How the Bible Became a Book: The Textualization of Ancient Israel*. Cambridge University Press, 2004.

Schroeder, Gerald L. *The Science of God: The Convergence of Scientific and Biblical Wisdom*. New York: Free Press, 1997.

Schultz, Richard L. "Isaiah, Isaiahs, and Current Scholarship," in *Do Historical Matters Matter to Faith? A Critical Appraisal of Modern and Postmodern Approaches to Scripture*, edited by James K. Hoffmeier and Dennis R. Magary, 243–61. Wheaton: Crossway, 2012.

Schüssler, Karlheinz. *Biblia Coptica: Die Koptischen Bibeltexte*, Band 3, Wiesbaden: Harrasowitz, 2004.

Schwartz, Baruch. "Does Recent Scholarship's Critique of the Documentary Hypothesis Constitute Grounds for Its Rejection," in *The Pentateuch: International Perspectives on Current Research*, edited by Thomas B. Dozeman, Konrad Schmid, and Baruch J. Schwartz, Forschungen Zum Alten Testament, vol.78, 3–11. Tübingen, Germany: Mohr Siebeck, 2011.

Scofield, C. I. *The Scofield Reference Bible*. Oxford University Press, 1945.

Scott, Walter. *The Monastery*. Boston: Houghton Mifflin, 1913.

Scotus, John Duns. *Philosophical Writings: A Selection*. Translated by Allan B. Wolter. Indianapolis, IN: Hackett Publishing, 1987.

"Scripture & Language Statistics 2014," Wycliffe Global Alliance Scripture Access Statistics, last modified November 2014, accessed August, 17, 2015, http://www.wycliffe.net/statistics.

"Scripture Distribution Increases in Persecution Hotspots," United Bible Societies, last modified November 22, 2013, http://www.unitedbiblesocieties.org/news/scripture-distribution-increases-in-persecution-hotspots/.

Sealey, Raphael. *Demosthenes & His Time: A Study in Defeat*. Oxford University Press, 1993.

Searle, John R. *The Construction of Social Reality*. New York: The Free Press, 1995.

———. *Mind, Language, and Society: Philosophy in the Real World.* New York: Basic Books, 1999.

Seitz, Christopher R. "The One Isaiah // The Three Isaiahs," in *Reading and Preaching the Book of Isaiah*, edited by Christopher R. Seitz, 13–22. Philadelphia, PA: Fortress Press, 1988.

———. *Prophecy and Hermeneutics: Towards a New Introduction to the Prophets.* Grand Rapids, MI: Baker Academic, 2007.

Seow, C. L. *Daniel.* Louisville, KY: Westminster John Knox Press, 2003.

Serrelli, Emanuele and Nathalie Gontier, eds. *Macroevolution: Explanation, Interpretation and Evidence.* Heidelberg: Springer-Verlag, 2015.

Seven Bridges. "Gibbon Genome Reveals New Insights Into Mechanisms of Primate Chromosomal Evolution." September 10, 2014. https://blog.sbgenomics.com/gibbon-genome/.

Sextus Empiricus. *Outlines of Scepticism.* Translated by Julia Annas and Jonathan Barnes. Cambridge, UK: Cambridge University Press, 1994.

Shanks. Monte A. *Papias and the New Testament.* Eugene, OR: Pickwick Publications, 2013.

"Sharing Our Story," Faith Comes By Hearing, accessed September 11, 2015, https://www.faithcomesbyhearing.com/about/our-story.

Shea, John J. and Daniel E. Lieberman, eds. *Transitions in Prehistory: Essays in Honor of Ofer Bar-Yosef.* Oxford, Oxbow, 2009.

Shea, William H. "Darius the Mede: An Update." *Andrews University Seminary Studies* 20, no. 3 (1982): 229–47.

———. "Darius the Mede in His Persian-Babylonian Setting." *Andrews University Seminary Studies* 29, no. 3 (Autumn 1991): 235–57.

Shedd, William G. T. *Dogmatic Theology.* 3rd ed. Edited by Alan W. Gomes. Phillipsburg, NJ: P & R Publishing, 2003.

Shelley, Bruce. *Church History in Plain Language.* Nashville, Tennessee: Thomas Nelson, 2013.

Shermer, Michael. *The Science of Good and Evil: Why People Cheat, Gossip, Care, Share, and Follow the Golden Rule.* New York: Owl Books, 2005.

Sherwin-White, A. N. *Roman Society and Roma Law in the New Testament.* Oxford: Clarendon Press, 1963.

Shupak, Nili. "The Prophecies of Neferti," in *The Context of Scripture: Canonical Compositions, Monumental Inscriptions and Archival Documents from the Biblical World*, vol. 1, edited by William Hallo and K. Lawson Younger, 106–10. Leiden: Brill, 1997.

Sider, Ronald J. "An Evangelical Vision for American Democracy: An Anabaptist Perspective," in *The Bible, Politics, and Democracy*, edited by Richard John Neuhaus, 32–54. Grand Rapids, MI: Eerdmans Publishing, 1987.

———. "Historical Methodology and Alleged Miracles: A Reply to Van Harvey." *Fides et Historia* 3, no. 1 (September 1970): 22–40.

Sigal, Gerald. "Jews for Judaism." http://jews-forjudaism.org/knowledge/articles/answers/jewish-polemics/texts/daniel/daniel-925-translation/.

Siger of Brabant. "Impossibilia," partially translated in *Medieval Skepticism and the Claim to Metaphysical Knowledge*, edited by Gyula Klima and Alexander W. Hall. Newcastle, UK: Cambridge Scholars Publishing, 2011.

Silberman, Lou H. "Wellhausen and Judaism." *Semeia* 25 (1982): 75–82.

Siker, Jeffrey S. "The Canonical Status of the Catholic Epistles in the Syriac New Testament." *Journal of Theological Studies* 38 (1987) 311–33.

Ska, Jean-Louis. "The Limits of Interpretation," in *The Pentateuch: International Perspectives on Current Research*, edited by Thomas B. Dozeman, Konrad Schmid, and Baruch J. Schwartz, Forschungen Zum Alten Testament, vol. 78. Tübingen, Germany: Mohr Siebeck, 2011.

Skell, Philip S. "Why Do We Invoke Darwin?" *The Scientist* 19 (August 29, 2005): 10.

Smelik, K. A. D., trans. "The Inscription of King Mesha," in *The Context of Scripture: Canonical Compositions, Monumental Inscriptions and Archival Documents from the Biblical World*, vol. 2, edited by William Hallo and K. Lawson Younger. Leiden: Brill, 2000.

Smith, Gary V. "Isaiah 40–55: Which Audience Was Addressed?" *Journal of the Evangelical Theological Society* 54, no. 4 (December 2011): 701–13.

Smith, James K. A. "Who's Afraid of Postmodernism? A Response to the 'Biola School,'" in *Christianity and the Postmodern Turn: Six Views*, edited by Myron B. Penner, 215–28. Grand Rapids, MI: Brazos, 2005.

Smith, R. Scott. *In Search of Moral Knowledge, Overcoming the Fact-Value Dichotomy.* Downers Grove, IL: InterVarsity Press, 2014.

———. "Post-Conservatives, Foundationalism, and Theological Truth: A Critical Evaluation." *Journal of the Evangelical Theological Society* 48 (2005): 351–63.

Smolin, Lee. *The Life of the Cosmos.* Oxford University Press, 1997.

Snir, Ainit, et al. "The Origin of Cultivation and Proto-Weeds, Long before Neolithic Farming." PLoS ONE (July 22, 2015). doi:10.1371/journal.pone.0131422.

Sokal, Alan D. "A Physicist Experiments with Cultural Studies." NYU.edu. Accessed October 22, 2015. http://www.physics.nyu.edu/faculty/sokal/lingua_franca_v4/lingua_franca_v4.html.

Sollamo, Raija. "The Significance of Septuagint Studies." In Supplements to Vetus Testamentum, vol. 94, *Emanuel: Studies in Hebrew Bible, Septuagint, and Dead Sea Scrolls in Honor of Emanuel Tov*, edited by Shalom M. Paul, Robert A. Kraft, Lawrence H. Schiffman, and Weston W. Fields, 497–512. Leiden: Brill, 2003.

Sparks, Kenton L. *God's Word in Human Words: An Evangelical Appropriation of Critical Biblical Scholarship.* Grand Rapids, MI: Baker Academic, 2008.

———. *The Pentateuch: An Annotated Bibliography*, vol. 1. Grand Rapids, MI: Baker Books, 2002.

Spoor, Fred et al. "Implications of New Early Homo Fossils from Ileret, East of Lake Turkana, Kenya." *Nature* 448 (9 August 2007): 688–91. doi: 10.1038/nature 05986.

Spoor, Fred, Bernard Wood, and Frans Zonneveld. "Implications of Early Hominid Labyrinthine Morphology for Evolution of Human Bipedal Locomotion." *Nature* 369 (23 June 1994): 645–48.

Sproul, R. C. *Essential Truths of the Christian Faith.* Carol Stream, IL: Tyndale House Publishers, 1992.

Sproul, R. C., John H. Gerstner, and Arthur W. Lindsley. *Classical Apologetics: A Rational Defense of the Christian Faith and a Critique of Presuppositional Apologetics.* Grand Rapids, MI: Zondervan, 1984.

Stager, Lawrence E. "Forging an Identity: The Emergence of Ancient Israel," in *The Oxford Dictionary of the Biblical World*, edited by Michael D. Coogan, 123–75. Oxford University Press, 1998.

Stanton, Graham. *The Gospels and Jesus*, 2nd ed. Oxford University Press, 2002.

Stark, Rodney. *For the Glory of God: How Monotheism Led to Reformations, Science, Witch-Hunts, and the End of Slavery.* Princeton, NJ: Princeton University Press, 2003.

———. *The Rise of Christianity: How the Obscure, Marginal Jesus Movement Became the Dominant Religious Force in the Western World in a Few Centuries.* New York: Harper Collins, 1996.

Steinmann, Andrew E. *Concordia Commentary: Daniel.* Saint Louis, MO: Concordia Publishing House, 2008.

Stenning, J. F., ed. *The Targum of Isaiah*. London: Clarendon Press, 1949.

Stern, David. "Recent Trends in Biblical Source Criticism." *Jewish Bible Quarterly* 36, no. 3 (2008): 182–86.

Stern, Fritz, ed. *The Varieties of History: From Voltaire to the Present*. New York: Vintage Books, 1973.

Steup, Matthias. "Epistemology." *The Stanford Encyclopedia of Philosophy*. December 14, 2005. Edward N. Zalta, ed. http://plato.stanford.edu/archives/spr2014/entries/epistemology/.

Stille, Alexander. "The World's Oldest Papyrus and What It Can Tell Us About the Great Pyramids." *Smithsonian Magazine*. October 2015. https://www.smithsonianmag.com/history/ancient-egypt-shipping-mining-farming-economy-pyramids-180956619/.

Stone, Lawson G. "Early Israel and Its Appearance in Canaan," in *Ancient Israel's History: An Introduction to Issues and Sources*, edited by Bill T. Arnold and Richard S. Hess, 127–64. Grand Rapids, MI: Baker Academic, 2014.

Stone, Nira and Michael Stone, *The Armenians: Art, Culture and Religion*. Dublin: Giles, 2007.

Stonehouse, Ned B. "The Authority of the New Testament," in *The Infallible Word*, ed. N. B. Stonehouse and Paul Woolley, 88–136. Philadelphia, PA: Presbyterian and Reformed, 1946.

Stott, John. *Basic Christianity*. Downers Grove, IL: IVP Books, 2008.

———. *Romans: God's Good News for the World*. Downers Grove, IL: IVP, 1994.

Strauss, David Friedrich. *A New Life of Jesus: Volumes 1 & 2*. 2nd edition. Charleston, SC: Forgotten Books, 2012.

Stringer, Christopher and Robin McKie. *African Exodus: The Origins of Modern Humanity*. New York: Henry Holt, 1996.

Strobel, Lee. *The Case for Christ: A Journalist's Personal Investigation of the Evidence for Jesus*. Grand Rapids, MI: Zondervan, 1998.

———. *The Case for a Creator*. Grand Rapids, MI: Zondervan, 2004.

Studevent-Hickman, Benjamin and Christopher Morgan. "Old Akkadian Period Texts," in *The Ancient Near East: Historical Sources in Translation*, edited by Mark Chavalas, 17–44. Malden, MA: Blackwell, 2006.

Stuhlmacher, Peter. "The Messianic Son of Man: Jesus' Claim to Deity," in *The Historical Jesus in Recent Research*, eds. James D. G. Dunn and Scot McKnight. Winona Lake, IN: Eisenbrauns, 2005.

Suetonius, *Lives of the Caesars*. Loeb Classical Library, rev. ed., vol. 31. Translated by John Carew Rolfe and K. R. Bradley. Cambridge, Massachusetts: Harvard University Press, 1998.

Sullivan, James Bacon. *An Examination of First Principles in Thought and Being in the Light of Aristotle and Aquinas*. Washington, DC, Catholic University Press, 1939.

Sweeney, Marvin A. "Resignifying a Prophetic Tradition: Redaction Criticism and the Book of Isaiah." *The Reconstructionist* 50, no. 2 (October 1984): 19–22.

Swinburne, Richard. "Evidence for the Resurrection," in *The Resurrection: An Interdisciplinary Symposium on the Resurrection of Jesus*, edited by Stephen T. Davis, Daniel Kendall, and Gerald O'Collins, 191–212. Oxford University Press, 1997.

———. *The Existence of God*, rev. ed. Oxford University Press, 1991.

———. *The Resurrection of God Incarnate*. Oxford University Press, 2006.

Tabor, James D. *The Jesus Dynasty: The Hidden History of Jesus, His Royal Family, and the Birth of Christianity*. New York: Simon & Schuster Paperbacks, 2007.

Tacitus. *The Annals and the Histories*, in Great Books of the Western World, vol. 15, ed. Robert Maynard Hutchins. Chicago, IL: William Benton, 1952.

Tadmor, Hayim and Shigeo Yamada. "The Royal Inscriptions of Tiglath-Pileser III (744–727 BC) and Shalmaneser V (726–722 BC), Kings of Assyria," in *Royal Inscriptions of the Neo-Assyrian Period 1.* Winona Lake: Eisenbrauns, 2011.

Tanner, Kathryn E. "Creation and Salvation in the Image of an Incomprehensible God," in *God of Salvation: Soteriology in Theological Perspective*, eds. Murray A. Rae and Ivor J. Davidson,. Burlington, VT: Ashgate, 2011.

Tappy, Ron E., P. Kyle McCarter, Marilyn J. Lundberg, and Bruce Zuckerman. "An Abecedary of the Mid-Tenth Century B.C.E. from the Judaean Shephelah." *Bulletin of the American Schools of Oriental Research* 344 (November, 2006): 5–46. doi:10.2307/25066976.

Tarnas, Richard. *The Passion of the Western Mind: Understanding the Ideas That Have Shaped Our World View.* New York: Ballantine Books, 1993.

Taylor, Charles. *A Secular Age.* Cambridge, MA: Harvard University Press, 2007.

Tegmark, Max. "On the Dimensionality of Spacetime." *Classical and Quantum Gravity* 14 (1997): L69–75.

Tenney, Merrill C. *John: The Gospel of Belief.* Grand Rapids, MI: Eerdmans, 1976.

"The Tenth Persecution, Under Diocletian, A.D. 303," Bible Study Tools, accessed May 20, 2016, http://www.biblestudytools.com/history/foxs-book-of-martyrs/the-tenth-persecution-under-diocletian-a-d-303.html/.

Tertullian. "De Spectaculis." *Early Christian Writings*, Peter Kirby ed. http://www.early-christianwritings.com/text/tertullian03.html.

Theissen, Gerd. *The Bible and Contemporary Culture.* Minneapolis, MN: Fortress Press, 2007.

Theodore of Mopsuestia. *Commentary on the Gospel of John.* Translated by Marco Conti, edited by Joel C. Elowsky, *Ancient Christian Texts*, series eds. Thomas C. Oden and Gerald

L. Bray. Downers Grove, IL: Intervarsity Press, 2010.

Thielman, Frank. *Theology of the New Testament: A Canonical and Synthetic Approach.* Grand Rapids, MI: Zondervan, 2005.

Thiering, Barbara. *Jesus & the Riddle of the Dead Sea Scrolls: Unlocking the Secrets of His Life Story.* New York: Harper, 1992.

Thomas Aquinas. *Summa Contra Gentiles.* Translated by Anton C. Pegis. Notre Dame, IN: University of Notre Dame Press, 1975.

———. *Summa Theologica.* Complete English edition. Allen, TX: Christian Classics, 1981.

———. *Summa Theologica.* Edited by Robert Maynard Hutchins. Translated by Fathers of the English Dominican Province. Chicago, IL: William Benton, 1952.

———. "The Meanings of Truth," in *Thomas Aquinas: Selected Writings.* Edited and translated by Ralph McInerny. New York: Penguin Group, 1998.

Thompson, Thomas L. *The Historicity of the Patriarchal Narratives: The Quest for the Historical Abraham.* Berlin: de Gruyter, 1974.

———. *The Mythic Past: Biblical Archaeology and the Myth of Israel.* New York: Perseus Books Group, 1999.

Thong, Chan Kei. *Faith of Our Fathers: God in Ancient China.* Shanghai: China Publishing Group, 2006.

Thorburn, Thomas James. *The Resurrection Narratives and Modern Criticism.* London: Kegan, Paul, Trench & Trubner, 1910.

Thorsrud, Harald. "Ancient Greek Skepticism." *Internet Encyclopedia of Philosophy.* http://www.iep.utm.edu/skepanci/.

Thucydides. *The Peloponnesian War.* Translated by Martin Hammond. Oxford University Press, 2009.

Tigay, Jeffry H. "Israelite Religion: The Onomastic and Epigraphic Evidence," in *Ancient Israelite Religion: Essays in Honor of Frank Moore Cross*, edited by Patrick D. Miller, Paul D. Hanson, and S. Dean McBride, 157–81. Minneapolis: Augsburg Fortress Publishers, 2009.

———. "The Documentary Hypothesis, Empirical Models and Holistic Interpretation," in *Modernity and Interpretations of Ancient Texts: The Collapse and Remaking of Traditions*, edited by Jun Ikeda et al. International Institute of Advanced Studies: Kizugawa-City, Kyoto, Japan, IIAS Reports, 2012.

Tillich, Paul. *Dynamics of Faith*. New York: HarperCollins, 2001.

Tilling, Chris. "Problems with Ehrman's Interpretative Categories," in *How God Became Jesus: The Real Origins of Belief in Jesus' Divine Nature*, 117–33. Grand Rapids, MI: Zondervan, 2014.

Toon, Peter. *Our Triune God*. Wheaton, IL: Bridgepoint Books, 1996.

Torrance, Thomas F. *The Doctrine of Jesus Christ, The Auburn Lectures 1938/39*. Eugene, OR: Wipf and Stock, 2002.

Torrey, Charles Cutler. *The Second Isaiah: A New Interpretation*. New York: Charles Scribner's Sons, 1928.

Tov, Emmanuel. *Scribal Practices and Approaches Reflected in the Texts Found in the Judean Desert*. Studies On the Texts of the Desert of Judah, vol. 54. Leiden: Brill, 2004.

———. *The Text-Critical Use of the Septuagint in Biblical Research*. Jerusalem: Simor, 1997.

———. *Textual Criticism of the Hebrew Bible*, 3rd ed. Minneapolis, MN: Fortress, 2012.

Toynbee, Arnold. *Study of History, vol. 6: The Disintegrations of Civilizations, Part 2*. London: Oxford University Press, 1939.

Trebolle Barrera, Julio C. "Origins of a Tripartite Old Testament Canon," in *The Canon Debate*, ed. Lee Martin McDonald and James A. Sanders, 128–45. Peabody, MA: Hendrickson Publishers, 2002.

Trimm, Charlie. *"YHWH Fights for Them!": The Divine Warrior in the Exodus Narrative*. Piscataway, NJ: Gorgias, 2014.

Troeltsch, Ernst. "Historiography," in *Encyclopedia of Religion and Ethics*, vol. 6, edited by James Hastings. New York: Charles Scribner's Sons, 1955.

Tucker, T. G. *Life in the Roman World of Nero and St. Paul*. NY: Macmillan, 1910.

Tuckett, C. M. *The Gospel of Mary*. Oxford University Press, 2007.

Turek, Frank. *Stealing from God*. Colorado Springs, CO: NavPress, 2014.

Turner, Ken and Brian Eisenback. "Discordant Views on Concordism." BioLogos Website. February 23, 2015, http://biologos.org/blogs/archive/discordant-views-on-concordism.

Turner, Kenneth J. "Teaching Genesis 1 at a Christian College", in *Reading Genesis 1–2: An Evangelical Conversation*, ed. J. Daryl Charles. Peabody, MA: Hendrickson, 2013.

Turyn, Alexander. *Studies in the Manuscript Tradition of the Tragedies of Sophocles*. Rome: L'erma di Bretschneider, 1970.

Twelftree, Graham F. "Jesus in Jewish Traditions," in *Gospel Perspectives: The Jesus Tradition Outside the Gospels*, ed. David Wenham. Sheffield: JSOT Press, 1984.

———. *Jesus the Exorcist*. WUNT 2/54. Tübingen: Mohr Siebeck, 1993.

———. *Jesus the Miracle Worker: A Historical & Theological* Study. Downers Grove, IL: InterVarsity Press, 1999.

Ulrich, Eugene C. "The Qumran Scrolls – The Scriptures of Late Second Temple Judaism." In *The Dead Sea Scrolls in Their Historical Context*, edited by Timothy H. Lim, 67–87. Edinburgh: T&T Clark, 2000.

Unger, Merrill F. *Archaeology and the Old Testament*. Grand Rapids, MI: Zondervan, 1954.

———. *The New Unger's Bible Dictionary*. Revised edition, edited by R. K. Harrison. Chicago: Moody Press, 1988.

Unger, Peter. *Ignorance: A Case for Scepticism*. Oxford, UK: Clarendon Press, 1975.

———. *Philosophical Relativity*. Oxford University Press, 2002.

"U.S. and World Population Clock," United States Census Bureau, accessed August 17, 2015, http://www.census.gov/popclock/.

Vaganay, Lion and Christain-Bernard Amphoux, *An Introduction to New Testament Criticism*, rev. ed. Cambridge University Press, 1991.

Van Daalen, D. H. *The Real Resurrection*. London: HarperCollins, 1972.

Van der Kooi, Casper J. and Tanja Schwander. "Parthenogenesis: Birth of a New Lineage or Reproductive Accident?" *Current Biology* 25, no. 15 (2015): R659–61, doi: 10.1016/j.cub.2015.06.055.

VanderKam, James C. *The Dead Sea Scrolls and the Bible*. Grand Rapids, MI: Eerdmans, 2012.

VanDoodewaard, William. *The Quest for the Historical Adam: Genetics, Hermeneutics, and Human Origins*. Grand Rapids, MI: Reformation Heritage Books, 2015.

Van Fraassen, Bas C. *Laws and Symmetry*. Oxford University Press, 1989.

Van Seters, John. *Abraham in History and Tradition*. Battleboro, VT: Echo Point Books, 1975.
———. "The Plagues of Egypt: Ancient Tradition or Literary Invention?" ZAW 98 (1986): 31–39.

Van Voorst, Robert E. *Jesus Outside the New Testament: An Introduction to the Ancient Evidence*. Grand Rapids, MI: Eerdmans, 2000.
———. "Sources, Extra-New Testamental," in *Routledge Encyclopedia of the Historical Jesus*, edited by Craig A. Evans. New York: Routledge, 2008.

Venema, Dennis. "William Lane Craig, Mouflon Sheep, and Heterozygosity." The BioLogos Forum, October 28, 2015. http://biologos.org/blogs/dennis-venema-letters-to-the-duchess/william-lane-craig-mouflon-sheep-and-heterozygosity.

Venema, Dennis and Darrel Falk. "Does Genetics Point to a Single Primal Couple?" The Biologos Forum, April 5, 2010. https://biologos.org/blogs/dennis-venema-letters-to-the-duchess/does-genetics-point-to-a-single-primal-couple/.

Vermes, Geza. *The Nativity: History & Legend*. New York: Doubleday, 2006.
———. *The Resurrection: History & Myth*. NY: Doubleday, 2008.

Vitz, Paul. "The Psychology of Atheism," in *A Place for Truth: Leading Thinkers Explore Life's Hardest Questions*, ed. Dallas Willard, 136–53. Downers Grove, IL: InterVarsity Press, 2010.

Vogt, Katja. "Ancient Skepticism." *Stanford Encyclopedia of Philosophy*. Last revised May 31, 2014. http://plato.stanford.edu/entries/skepticism-ancient/.

Von Salomé, Jenny, Ulf Gyllensten, and Tomas F. Bergström. "Full-length Sequence Analysis of the HLA-DRB1 Locus Suggests a Recent Origin of Alleles." *Immunogenetics* 59 (April 2007): 261–71. doi:10.1007/s00251-007-0196-8.

Vos, Howard F., ed. *Can I Trust the Bible?* Chicago, IL: Moody Press, 1963.

Wachowski, Andy and Lana Wachowski, directors. *The Matrix*. Burbank, CA: Warner Home Video, 2007. DVD.

Wade, Nicholas. "An Evolutionary Theory of Right and Wrong." *The New York Times*. October 31, 2006. http://www.nytimes.com/2006/10/31/health/psychology/31book.html.

Walker, Larry. "Biblical Languages," in *The Origin of the Bible*, edited by Philip W. Comfort, 217–38. Carol Stream, IL: Tyndale, 2012.

Wallace, Daniel B. *Granville Sharp's Canon and Its Kin: Semantics and Significance*. New York: Peter Lang, 2009.
———. *Greek Grammar Beyond the Basics: An Exegetical Syntax of the New Testament*. Grand Rapids, MI: Zondervan, 1996.
———. "How Badly Did the Scribes Corrupt the New Testament Text?" in *Revisiting the Corruption of the New Testament*, ed. Daniel B. Wallace. Grand Rapids, MI: Kregel, 2011.
———. Lecture at Discover the Evidence, Dallas, TX, December 3–4, 2013.

Wallace, J. Warner. "Are Young People Really Leaving Christianity?" Cold Case Christianity,

February 18, 2015, http://coldcasechristianity. com/2015/are-young-people-really-leaving-christianity/.

——. *Cold-Case Christianity: A Homicide Detective Investigates the Claims of the Gospels.* Colorado Springs, CO: David C. Cook, 2013.

——. *God's Crime Scene.* Colorado Springs, CO: David C. Cook, 2015.

Walsh, W. H. *An Introduction to Philosophy of History.* Bristol, England: Thoemmes Press, 1992.

Waltke, Bruce K. *The Book of Proverbs: Chapters 15–31. The New International Commentary on the Old Testament,* edited by Robert L. Hubbard. Grand Rapids, MI: Eerdmans, 2005.

Waltke, Bruce K. and Charles Yu. *An Old Testament Theology: An Exegetical, Canonical, and Thematic Approach.* Grand Rapids, MI: Zondervan, 2007.

Walton, John H. and D Brent Sandy. *The Lost World of Scripture: Ancient Literary Culture and Biblical Authority.* Downers Grove, IL: IVP Academic, 2013.

Walton, John H. *Ancient Israelite Literature in Its Cultural Context: A Survey of Parallels between Biblical and Ancient Near Eastern Texts.* Grand Rapids, MI: Regency Reference Library, 1989.

——. *Ancient Near Eastern Thought and the Old Testament: Introducing the Conceptual World of the Hebrew Bible.* Grand Rapids, MI: Baker Academic, 2006.

——. *Covenant: God's Purpose, God's Plan.* Grand Rapids, MI: Zondervan Publishing House, 1994.

——. *Genesis.* NIVAC. Grand Rapids, MI: HarperCollins, 2001.

——. *Genesis: From Biblical Text . . . to Contemporary Life.* Grand Rapids, MI: Zondervan, 2001.

——. *Genesis 1 As Ancient Cosmology.* Winona Lake, IN: Eisenbrauns, 2011.

——. *The Lost World of Genesis One: Ancient Cosmology and the Origins Debate.* Downers Grove, IL: IVP Academic, 2009.

Walvoord, John F., and Roy B. Zuck, eds. *The Bible Knowledge Commentary: Old Testament.* Wheaton, IL: Victor Books, 1985.

Ward, Keith. "Miracles and Testimony." *Religious Studies* 21, no. 2 (1985): 131–45.

Ward, William. "Summary and Conclusions," in *Exodus: The Egyptian Evidence,* edited by Ernest Frerichs and Leonard Lesko, 105–12. Winona Lake, IN: Eisenbrauns, 1997.

Warfield, Benjamin. "Introductory Note," *Apologetics, vol. 1: Fundamental Apologetics.* Richmond, VA: Presbyterian Committee of Publication, 1903.

Warner, Marina. *Alone of All Her Sex: The Myth and the Cult of the Virgin Mary.* London: Weidenfeld and Nicolson, 1976; with new preface, Oxford University Press, 2013.

Warnock, Adrian. *Raised with Christ: How the Resurrection Changes Everything.* Wheaton, IL: Crossway, 2010.

Watt, W. Montgomery. *Islam: A Short History.* Oxford, England: Oneworld, 1999, 1996.

Watzinger, C. "Zur Chronologie der Schichten von Jericho." *ZDGM* 80 (1926): 131–36.

Webb, William J. *Slaves, Women and Homosexuals: Exploring the Hermeneutics of Cultural Analysis.* Downers Grove, IL: InterVarsity Press, 2001. Kindle edition.

Wegner, Paul D. *A Student's Guide to Textual Criticism of the Bible: Its History, Methods and Results.* Downers Grove, IL: IVP Academic, 2006.

Weissenberg, Hanne Von. *4QMMT: Reevaluating the Text, the Function, and the Meaning of the Epilogue.* Leiden and Boston: Brill, 2009.

Wellhausen, Julius. *Prolegomena to the History of Ancient Israel.* Santa Cruz, CA: Evinity Publishing Inc., 2009. Kindle edition.

Wellum, Stephen J. "The Deity of Christ in the Synoptic Gospels," in *The Deity of Christ,* edited by Christopher W. Morgan and Robert A. Peterson. Wheaton, IL: Crossway, 2011.

——. "The Deity of Christ in the Apostolic Witness," in *The Deity of Christ,* edited by

Christopher W. Morgan and Robert A. Peterson. Wheaton, IL: Crossway, 2011.

Wen, Yan-Zi et al. "Pseudogenes Are Not Pseudo Any More." *RNA Biology* 9, no. 1 (January 2012): 27–32. doi: 10.4161/rna.9.1.18277.

Wenham, Gordon J. *Exploring the Old Testament: A Guide to the Pentateuch*, vol. 1. London: SPCK, 2003.

———. "Pentateuchal Studies Today." *Themelios* 22, no. 1 (October 1996): 3–13.

Wenham, John. *Easter Enigma: Are the Resurrection Accounts in Conflict?* Grand Rapids, MI: Academie Books, 1984.

West, Martin L. *Studies in the Text and Transmission of the Iliad*. München: K. G. Saur Verlag, 2001.

Westbrook, Raymond. "Slave and Master in the Ancient Near Eastern Law." *Chicago-Kent Law Review* 70, no. 4 (June 1995): 1631–76. http://scholarship.kentlaw.iit.edu/cklawreview/vol70/iss4/12.

Wevers, John William, Michael Weigl, Paul-Eugène Dion, and P. M. Michèle Daviau. *The World of the Aramaeans*. Sheffield: Continuum, 2001.

Whitcomb, John C. *Darius the Mede: The Historical Chronology of Daniel*. Phillipsburg, NJ: Presbyterian and Reformed Publishing Co., 1959.

Whitcomb, John C. and Henry M. Morris. *The Genesis Flood: The Biblical Record and Its Scientific Implications*. Philadelphia, PA: Presbyterian and Reformed Publishing, 1961.

White, Hayden. *The Content of Form: Narrative Discourse and Historical Representation*. Baltimore: Johns Hopkins University Press, 1987.

White, Randall. *Prehistoric Art: The Symbolic Journey of Humankind*. New York: Harry N. Abrams, 2003.

White, W., Jr. "Talmud," in *The Zondervan Pictorial Encyclopedia of the Bible*, edited by Merrill C. Tenney. Vol. 5. Grand Rapids: Zondervan, 1976.

Whybray, R. N. *Introduction to the Pentateuch*. Grand Rapids, MI: Eerdmans, 1995.

———. *The Making of the Pentateuch: A Methodological Study*. Journal for the Study of the Old Testament Supplement Series, vol. 53. Sheffield: JSOT, 1987.

Wilford, John Noble. "Finds in Egypt Date Alphabet in Earlier Era." *New York Times*, November 14, 1999. http://www.nytimes.com/1999/11/14/world/finds-in-egypt-date-alphabet-in-earlier-era.html?pagewanted=all.

Willard, Dallas. *The Allure of Gentleness: Defending the Faith in the Manner of Jesus*. New York: HarperCollins, 2015.

———. *The Divine Conspiracy: Rediscovering our Hidden Life in God*. New York: HarperCollins, 1998.

Williams, P. J. "The Syriac Versions of the New Testament," in *The Text of the New Testament in Contemporary Research: Essays on the Status Quaestionis*, 2nd ed., edited by Bart D. Ehrman and Michael W. Holmes, 143–66. Leiden: Brill, 2013.

———. "Textual Criticism," in *Dictionary of the Old Testament: Pentateuch*, edited by T. Desmond Alexander and David W. Baker. Downers Grove, IL: IVP Academic, 2003.

Wilkins, Michael J. *Matthew*. Grand Rapids, MI: Zondervan, 2002.

Wilson, J. D. *Did Daniel Write Daniel?* New York: Charles C. Cook, 1906.

Wilson, John. "Saving the Original Sinner: A Conversation with Karl Giberson." *Symposium on the Historical Adam*. Books & Culture (June 2015). http://www.booksandculture.com/articles/webexclusives/2015/june/saving-original-sinner.html?paging=off.

Wilson, Nigel G. *Herodotea: Studies on the Text of Herodotus*. Oxford University Press, 2015.

———. "A List of Plato Manuscripts," *Scriptorium* 16, no. 2 (1962): 386–95.

Winterbottom, M. "Tacitus," in *Texts and Transmission: A Survey of the Latin Classics*, ed. R. D. Reynolds. Oxford: Clarendon, 1983.

Wise, Kurt P. *Faith, Form and Time: What the Bible Teaches and Science Confirms about Creation and the Age of the Universe*. Nashville, TN: Broadman & Holman, 2002.

Wise-Bauer, Susan. *The History of the Ancient World: From the Earliest Accounts to the Fall of Rome*. New York: W. W. Norton, 2007.

Wiseman, D. J. "Some Historical Problems in the Book of Daniel," in *Notes on Some Historical Problems in the Book of Daniel*, edited by D. J. Wiseman, 9–18. London: Tyndale Press, 1965.

Wiseman, P. J. *Ancient Records and the Structure of Genesis: A Case for Literary Unity*. Nashville, TN: Thomas Nelson, 1985.

———. *Creation Revealed in Six Days: The Evidence of Scripture Confirmed in Archaeology*, 2nd ed. London: Marshall, Morgan and Scott, 1949.

Witherington, Ben. "Bart Interrupted." http://www.beliefnet.com/columnists/bibleandculture/?s=bart+interrupted.

———. *The Jesus Quest: The Third Search for the Jew of Nazareth*, new expanded ed. Downers Grove, IL: InterVarsity Press, 1997.

———. "The Martyrdom of the Zebedee Brothers," *Biblical Archaeological Review* 33 (May/June 2007): 26–27.

Witsius, Hermann. *Was Moses the Author of the Pentateuch? Answered in the Affirmative*. Translated by John Donaldson. Edinburgh: Maclaren & Macniven, 1877.

Wittgenstein, Ludwig. *Philosophical Investigations: The English Text of the Third Edition*. Translated by G. E. M. Anscombe. New York: Macmillan Publishing, 1968.

Wolf, Herbert. *An Introduction to the Old Testament Pentateuch*. Chicago, IL: Moody, 1991.

Wolters, Al. "The Text of the Old Testament," in *The Face of Old Testament Studies: A Survey of Contemporary Approaches*, edited by David W. Baker and Bill T. Arnold, 19–37. Grand Rapids, MI: Baker Academic, 1999.

Wolterstorff, Nicholas. "Reading Joshua," in *Divine Evil? The Moral Character of the God of Abraham*, edited by Michael Bergmann, Michael J. Murray, and Michael C. Rea, 236–65. Oxford University Press, 2011.

Wood, Bernard and Mark Collard. "The Human Genus." *Science* 284 (2 April 1999): 65–71. doi: 10.1126/science.284.5411.65.

Wood, Bryant G. "Carbon 14 Dating at Jericho." Associates for Biblical Research (blog). August 7, 2008, www.biblearchaeology.org/post/2008/08/Carbon-14-Dating-at-Jericho.aspx.

———. "Did the Israelites Conquer Jericho? A New Look at the Archaeological Evidence." *Biblical Archaeology Review* 16, no.2 (Mar/Apr 1990): 44–59.

"World Watch List," Open Doors, last modified 2015, accessed August 17, 2015, https://www.opendoorsusa.org/christian-persecution/world-watch-list/.

Wright, Christopher J. H. *Old Testament Ethics for the People of God*. Downers Grove, IL: IVP Academic, 2004.

Wright, Jacob L. *David*. New York: Cambridge University Press, 2014.

Wright, N. T. *The Challenge of Jesus*. Downers Grove, IL: InterVarsity Press, 1999.

———. "Christian Origins and the Resurrection of Jesus: The Resurrection of Jesus as a Historical Problem." *Sewanee Theological Review* 41, no. 2 (1998).

———. *The Climax of the Covenant: Christ and the Law in Pauline Theology*. London: T&T Clark, 1991.

———. *Jesus and the Victory of God*. Minneapolis: Fortress, 1996.

———. *The New Testament and the People of God*. Minneapolis: Augsburg, 1992.

———. *Paul and the Faithfulness of God*. Minneapolis: Fortress, 2013.

———. *The Resurrection of the Son of God*. Minneapolis, MN: Fortress Press, 2003.

Wurthwein, E. *The Text of the Old Testament: An Introduction to the Biblia Hebraica*. Translated by Erroll F. Rhodes. Grand Rapids, MI: Eerdmans, 1979.

Wynn-Williams, Damian J. *The State of the Pentateuch: A Comparison of the Approaches of M. Noth and E. Blum.* Berlin, Germany: Walter de Gruyter, 1997.

Yamauchi, Edwin. "Life, Death and the Afterlife in the Ancient Near East," in *Life in the Face of Death*, edited by Richard N. Longenecker, 21–50. Grand Rapids, MI: Eerdmans, 1998.

Yan-Zi Wen et al. "Pseudogenes are not pseudo any more." *RNA Biology* 9 (January, 2012): 27–32. doi: 10.4161/rna.9.1.18277.

Yarbrough, Robert W. *1–3 John: Baker Exegetical Commentary on the New Testament.* Grand Rapids, MI: Baker Academic, 2008.

Young, Edward J. "The Authority of the Old Testament," in *The Infallible Word*, ed. N. B. Stonehouse and Paul Woolley, 53–87. Philadelphia, PA: Presbyterian and Reformed, 1946.

Younger, K. Lawson, trans. "Nimrud Prisms D & E," in *The Context of Scripture: Canonical Compositions, Monumental Inscriptions and Archival Documents from the Biblical World*, vol. 2, edited by William Hallo and K. Lawson Younger. Leiden: Brill, 2000.

Younger, K. Lawson, trans. "Sargon II," in *The Context of Scripture: Canonical Compositions, Monumental Inscriptions and Archival Documents from the Biblical World*, vol. 2, edited by William Hallo and K. Lawson Younger, 293–300. Leiden: Brill, 2000.

Younger, K. Lawson, trans. "Shalmaneser III," in *The Context of Scripture: Canonical Compositions, Monumental Inscriptions and Archival Documents from the Biblical World*, vol. 2, edited by William Hallo and K. Lawson Younger, 261–71. Leiden: Brill, 2000.

Younger, K. Lawson, trans. "The Siloam Tunnel Inscription," in *The Context of Scripture: Canonical Compositions, Monumental Inscriptions and Archival Documents from the Biblical World*, vol. 2, edited by William Hallo and K. Lawson Younger, 145–46. Leiden: Brill, 2000.

Yuxin, Fan et al. "Genomic Structure and Evolution of the Ancestral Chromosome Fusion Site in 2q13-2q14.1 and Paralogous Regions on Other Human Chromosomes." *Genome Research* 12 (2002): 1651–62. doi: 10.1101/gr.337602.

Zacharias, Ravi. "An Apologetic for Apologetics," in *Beyond Opinion: Living the Faith We Defend*, edited by Ravi Zacharias, xi–xx. Nashville, TN: Thomas Nelson, 2007.

———. *Can Man Live Without God?* Nashville, TN: Thomas Nelson, 1994.

———. "Clarifying Truth-Claims," in *The Portable Seminary: A Master's Level Overview in One Volume*, edited by David Horton, 339–40. Bloomington, MN: Bethany House Publishers, 2006.

Zimmer, Carl. "Is Most of Our DNA Garbage?" *New York Times.* March 5, 2015. http://www.nytimes.com/2015/03/08/magazine/is-most-of-our-dna-garbage.html.

Zimmerman, Erin. "Did David, Solomon Exist? Dig Refutes Naysayers." Christian Broadcasting Network. June 7, 2013. http://www.cbn.com/cbnnews/insideisrael/2013/June/Did-David-Solomon-Exist-Dig-Refutes-Naysayers/.

Zukovskaja, Lidija P. et al., eds., *Svodnyj Katalog Slavjano-Russkix Rukopisnyx Knig, Xranjaščixsja [Preliminary List of Slavic Russian Manuscripts].* Moscow: Nauka, 1984.

Zuurmond, Rochus, revised by Curt Niccum. "The Ethiopic Version of the New Testament," in *The Text of the New Testament in Contemporary Research: Essays on the Status Quaestionis*, 2nd ed., edited by Bart D. Ehrman and Michael W. Holmes, 231–52. Leiden: Brill, 2013.

Zweerink, Jeffrey A. *Who's Afraid of the Multiverse?* Covina, CA: Reasons To Believe, 2008.

AUTHOR INDEX

SUBJECT INDEX

HOW TO KNOW GOD PERSONALLY

What does it take to begin a relationship with God? Devote yourself to unselfish religious deeds? Become a better person so that God will accept you?

You may be surprised that none of those things will work. But God has made it very clear in the Bible how we can know him.

The following principles will explain how you can personally begin a relationship with God, right now, through Jesus Christ.

Principle 1:
God loves you and offers a wonderful plan for your life.

God's Love

"For God so loved the world that He gave His only begotten Son, that whoever believes in Him should not perish but have everlasting life." — John 3:16

God's Plan

"I [Christ] have come that they may have life, and may have it abundantly" [*that it might be full and meaningful*]. — John 10:10

Why is it that most people are not experiencing the abundant life? Because . . .

Principle 2:
All of us sin and our sin has separated us from God.

We Are Sinful

"All have sinned and fall short of the glory of God." — Romans 3:23

We were created to have fellowship with God; but, because of our stubborn self-will, we chose to go our own independent way, and fellowship with God was broken. This self-will,

Adapted from *Have You Heard of the Four Spiritual Laws* and *Would You Like to Know God Personally,* by Bill Bright, co-founder of Campus Crusade for Christ. © Campus Crusade for Christ. All rights reserved.

characterized by an attitude of active rebellion or passive indifference, is evidence of what the Bible calls sin.

We Are Separated

"The wages of sin is death [spiritual separation from God]." — Romans 6:23

The above diagram illustrates that God is holy and people are sinful. A great gulf separates us. The arrows illustrate that we are continually trying to reach God and the abundant life through our own efforts, such as a good life, philosophy, or religion—but we inevitably fail.

The third principle explains the only way to bridge this gulf.

Principle 3:
Jesus Christ is God's only provision for our sin.
Through him we can know and experience
God's love and plan for our life.

He Died in Our Place

"God demonstrates His own love toward us, in that while we were yet sinners, Christ died for us." — Romans 5:8

He Rose From the Dead

"Christ died for our sins. . . . He was buried. . . . He was raised on the third day according to the Scriptures. . . . He was seen by Cephas, then by the twelve. After that He was seen by over five hundred." — 1 Corinthians 15:3–6

He Is the Only Way to God

"Jesus said to him, 'I am the way, and the truth, and the life; no one comes to the Father, but through Me.'" — John 14:6

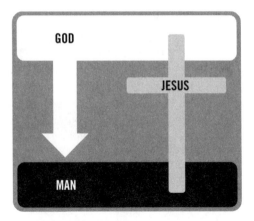

This diagram illustrates that God has bridged the gulf that separates us from him by sending his Son, Jesus Christ, to die on the cross in our place to pay the penalty for our sins. It is not enough just to know these three principles . . .

Principle 4:
We must individually receive Jesus Christ as Savior and Lord; then we can know and experience God's love and plan for our lives.

We Must Receive Christ

"As many as received Him, to them He gave the right to become children of God, even to those who believe in His name." — John 1:12

We Receive Christ Through Faith

"For by grace you have been saved through faith, and that not of yourselves; it is the gift of God, not of works, lest anyone should boast." — Ephesians 2:8, 9

When We Receive Christ, We Experience a New Birth

We Receive Christ by Personal Invitation

"Behold, I [Christ] stand at the door and knock. If any one hears My voice and opens the door, I will come in to him." — Revelation 3:20

Receiving Christ involves turning to God from self (repentance) and trusting Christ to come into our lives to forgive our sins and to make us what he wants us to be. Just to agree intellectually that Jesus Christ is the Son of God and that he died on the cross for your sins is not enough. Nor is it enough to have an emotional experience. You receive Jesus Christ by faith, as an act of the will.

These two circles represent two kinds of lives:

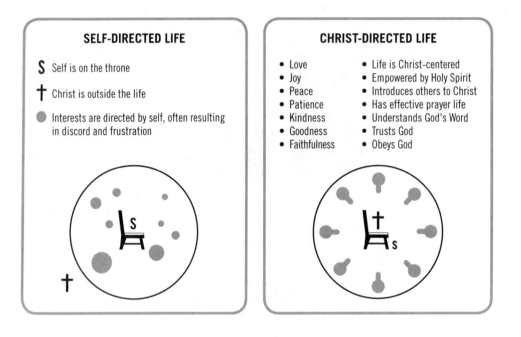

SELF-DIRECTED LIFE

S Self is on the throne

✝ Christ is outside the life

● Interests are directed by self, often resulting in discord and frustration

CHRIST-DIRECTED LIFE

- Love
- Joy
- Peace
- Patience
- Kindness
- Goodness
- Faithfulness

- Life is Christ-centered
- Empowered by Holy Spirit
- Introduces others to Christ
- Has effective prayer life
- Understands God's Word
- Trusts God
- Obeys God

Which circle best describes your life?

Which circle would you like to have represent your life?

The following explains how you can receive Christ:

You can receive Christ right now by faith through prayer.

Prayer is talking to God. God knows your heart and is not so concerned with your words as he is with the attitude of your heart. The following is a suggested prayer:

"Lord Jesus, I need you. Thank you for dying on the cross for my sins. I open the door of my life and receive you as my Savior and Lord. Thank you for forgiving my sins and giving me eternal life. Take control of the throne of my life. Make me the kind of person you want me to be."

If this prayer expresses the desire of your heart, then you can pray this prayer right now, and Christ will come into your life, as he promised.